Business Statistics
of the United States

Ninth Edition, 2004

Editor
Cornelia J. Strawser

Associate Editors
Mary Meghan Ryan
Mark Siegal
Katherine A. DeBrandt

BERNAN PRESS

© 2004 Bernan Press, an imprint of Bernan Associates, a division of the Kraus Organization Limited.

ISBN: 0-89059-858-4

ISSN: 1086-8488

Printed by Automated Graphic Systems, Inc., White Plains, MD, on acid-free paper that meets the American National Standards Institute Z39-48 standard.

2005 2004   4 3 2 1

BERNAN PRESS
4611-F Assembly Drive
Lanham, MD 20706
800-274-4447
email: info@bernan.com
www.bernanpress.com

Business Statistics
of the United States
Ninth Edition, 2004

CONTENTS

PART C: HISTORICAL DATA

CHAPTER 18: SELECTED ANNUAL DATA, 1939–1947

CHAPTER 19: SELECTED HISTORICAL DATA FOR QUARTERLY SERIES

CHAPTER 20: SELECTED HISTORICAL DATA FOR MONTHLY SERIES

PART D: STATE AND REGIONAL DATA

CHAPTER 21: STATE AND REGIONAL DATA

ACKNOWLEDGEMENTS

This volume would not have been possible without the knowledge, experience, judgment, and computer and organizational skills of Mary Meghan Ryan, Mark Siegal, and Katherine DeBrandt, all of whom assisted the editor with researching and compiling the data.

Bernan's editorial and production departments, under the direction of Tamera Wells-Lee, did the copy editing, layout, and graphics preparation. Kara Prezocki prepared the layout and graphics, assisted by Christopher Jorgenson. Jacalyn Houston served as the lead copy editor. Jacalyn, Kara, and Christopher capably handled all editorial and production aspects of this edition.

Finally, special thanks are due to the many federal agency personnel who, as always, responded generously to our frequent need for assistance in obtaining data and background information.

PREFACE

Business Statistics of the United States: Patterns of Economic Change, Ninth Edition, 2004 is a basic desk reference for everyone requiring historical information about the U.S. economy since World War II, or needing background information for the interpretation of new economic data as they are reported. It contains some 3,000 economic time series, predominantly from federal government sources, presenting a rich selection of the data most needed for analysis of economic trends and patterns. Of equal importance with the data themselves are the extensive background notes that enable the user to understand the data, use them appropriately, and, if desired, seek additional information from the source agencies.

THE 2004 EDITION

Business Statistics: 2004 retains the features of previous editions of Business Statistics but has been revamped to provide a richer, deeper, and more comprehensive picture of the American economy. Its new subtitle—*Patterns of Economic Change*—indicates the increased resources that it makes available for analyzing the economic history of the past half-century, for observing past trends, and for providing the basis for projecting such trends into the future.

- Whereas earlier editions typically presented data for only the latest 30 years, *Business Statistics* now presents data for the entire half-century since the end of World War II, with summary data covering the war years 1939–1947 as well, enabling the user to refer to earlier periods of war, recession, recovery, and cycles of inflation and disinflation.

- New data using the new North American Industry Classification System give a much clearer picture of the most dynamic sectors of the "new economy."

As always, each table in the 2004 edition has been updated through the latest full year for which data were available (usually 2002) and, in general, all historical revisions to the data available as of November 2003 have been incorporated. In some cases that occurred late in the production process, even later revised data are incorporated; this applies to energy, corporate profits by industry, and some monetary data.

THE PLAN OF THE BOOK

The history of the U.S. economy in the period since World War II is told in the major U.S. government sets of statistical data: the National Income and Product Accounts compiled by the Bureau of Economic Analysis (BEA); the data on labor force, employment, hours, earnings, and productivity compiled by the Bureau of Labor Statistics (BLS); the price indexes also collected by BLS; and financial market data compiled mainly by the Board of Governors of the Federal Reserve System (FRB). All of these sets exist in both annual and either monthly or quarterly form dating from shortly after the end of World War II—beginning in 1946, 1947, or 1948.

In Part A, *Business Statistics* presents all annual values for major indicators and their significant components back to the earliest postwar year available, along with recent quarterly or monthly data. This enables easy calculation of growth rates for periods or subperiods and more flexible comparisons of recent values with historical data.

For many purposes, however, historical data at a higher frequency than annual are required: comparison of activity before and after business cycle turning points, for example, or observation of the effects of the outbreak or the end of war. For the main series presented in Part A, historical quarterly or monthly data are presented in Part C, all the way back to the beginning of the postwar period where available.

In both Part A and Part C, the presentation begins with the National Income and Product Accounts, or NIPAs. The NIPAs comprise a comprehensive, thorough, and internally consistent data set. They measure the value of the output of the U.S. economy (the Gross Domestic Product, or GDP); they factor that value into its quantity, or "real", and price components; and they show how the value of output is distributed between the labor and capital that produce it.

Production estimates for the "industrial" sectors of the economy—manufacturing, mining, and utilities—follow the presentation of the overall accounts.

Then, more detail is presented for the final demand components of production. GDP by definition consists of the sum of consumption expenditures, business investment, government purchases of goods and services, and exports minus imports—the elementary economics blackboard equation "GDP =C + I + G + X – M." Chapters on each of those demand components are presented in Part A.

Following those, there is a chapter on prices; two that are concerned with the amount and compensation of labor and capital inputs into production; one on energy inputs into production; and one on money and financial markets.

While we initially define and measure Gross Domestic Product by adding up its final demand categories, this output is produced in industries—some in the old-line heavy industries such as manufacturing, mining, and utilities, but an increasing share in the huge and heterogeneous group known as "service-producing" industries. Part A gives a number of summary measures of activity classified by industry or industrial sector—industrial production, profits, and employment-related data.

Industry data are presented in more detail in Part B. The user will not, however, find the same degree of historical continuity as in Part A. The pace of technological and organizational change that the American economy has experienced over the past half-century has been so rapid that the statistical industry definitions have had difficulty keeping up with it. It has proved impossible in many cases to produce historical data series that cover the entire postwar period and also reflect in a meaningful way the detailed industrial structure of the economy as it exists today.

The industries that were used to categorize data during most of the postwar period were originally defined in the 1930s and modified only modestly since then. They do not provide an adequate framework for analyzing economic activity in the twenty-first century. An up-to-date system called the North American Industry Classification System (NAICS) has been put into effect beginning in 1997. Most of the government's statistical series have been converted to this system, and the remainder will be coming on line in the next 2 years. However, this system required breaks with the past at many disaggregated reporting levels, and data collected on the earlier Standard Industrial Classification system (SIC) are, in many areas, not easily convertible to the new system.

Different statistical agencies have dealt with this problem in different ways, and *Business Statistics* provides both detailed information for recent data and as much historical comparability as possible. For industrial production, the Federal Reserve Board has been able to carry estimates on the NAICS basis back to at least 1972 (1967 for some higher-level aggregates); these are shown in Chapters 2 and 20. The Bureau of Labor Statistics has calculated employment and related data back to 1939 for NAICS "supersectors," and these are shown in Chapters 10 and 18. On the other hand, the Census Bureau's capital expenditures survey gives data by NAICS industries beginning only in 1998 (Chapter 5).

In Part B, *Business Statistics* first presents a general description of NAICS and its differences from SIC, followed by a table summarizing the structure of the U.S.

economy as specified in NAICS. This table indicates how the NAICS statistical system is organized and shows— very roughly in some cases–how each NAICS industry relates to the earlier SIC industries. In the chapters that follow, *Business Statistics* presents detailed industry data on the NAICS basis as far back as it is available. For the BLS employment and related data, this means data for 1990 through 2002. For the Census Bureau data on manufacturers' shipments, orders, and inventories, and wholesale and retail sales and stocks, this means data beginning in 1992. For these Census data, *Business Statistics* shows roughly comparable data for earlier years, with an overlap shown in the year 1992, so that comparisons at a broad level can be observed. For selected service industries, NAICS data are available only from 1998 forward. NIPA data on gross product by industry have not yet been converted to NAICS, so they are presented on the SIC basis only. Profits by industry are presented on the SIC basis through 2000 and on the NAICS basis from 1998 through 2002.

Part C, Historical Data, begins with a table summarizing annual values for important economic aggregates for the years 1939–1947, giving some suggestion of the enormous changes the economy went through as it mobilized for World War II and subsequently demobilized. In the subsequent two chapters, quarterly or monthly data for NIPA data and other major indicators provide the opportunity to observe changes associated with all of the 10 business cycles that have been identified in the postwar period.

Part D, State and Regional Data, now includes not only data by state and region on personal income and employment back to 1972, but also values and quantity indexes for Gross Domestic Product by state and region back to 1977.

Notes and Definitions. Productive use of economic data requires accurate knowledge about the sources and meaning of the data. The Notes and Definitions for each chapter, shown immediately after that chapter's tables, contain definitions, descriptions of recent data revisions, and references to sources of additional technical information. They also include information about data availability and revision and release schedules, so that the user may readily access the latest current values if he or she needs to keep up with the data month by month or quarter by quarter.

THE HISTORY OF *BUSINESS STATISTICS*

The history of *Business Statistics* began with the publication, many years ago, by the U.S. Commerce

Department's Bureau of Economic Analysis (BEA) of the first edition of a volume of the same name and general purpose. After 27 periodic editions, the last of which appeared in 1992, the BEA found it necessary, for budgetary and other reasons, to discontinue not only that publication but also maintenance of the database from which the publication was derived.

The individual statistical series gathered together here are publicly available. However, the task of gathering them from a number of sources within the government, plus a few private sources, and assembling them into one coherent database is impractical for most data users. Even when current data are more-or-less readily available, obtaining the full historical time series often is time-consuming and difficult. Definitions and other documentation can be inconvenient to find as well. Believing that a *Business Statistics* compilation was too valuable to be lost to the public, Bernan Press published the first edition of the present publication in 1995, edited by Dr. Courtenay M. Slater. The first edition received a warm welcome among users of economic data. Dr. Slater, formerly Chief Economist of the Department of Commerce, continued to edit and improve *Business Statistics* through four subsequent annual editions. The current editor worked with Dr. Slater on the fourth and fifth editions, and in subsequent editions has continued in the tradition established by Dr. Slater of ensuring high-quality data while revising and expanding the book's scope to include significant new aspects of the U.S. economy.

Most of the statistical data in this book are from federal government sources and are in the public domain. A few series are from private sources and further use may be subject to copyright restrictions. Sources and restrictions, if any, are given in the Notes and Definitions.

The data in this volume meet the publication standards of the federal statistical agencies from which they were obtained. Every effort has been made to select data that are accurate, meaningful, and useful. All statistical data are subject to error arising from sampling variability, reporting errors, incomplete coverage, imputation, and other causes. The responsibility of the editor and publisher of this volume is limited to reasonable care in the reproduction and presentation of data obtained from established sources.

The 2004 edition has been edited by Cornelia J. Strawser, in association with Katherine DeBrandt, Mary Meghan Ryan, and Mark Siegal.

Dr. Strawser is Senior Economic Consultant to Bernan Press. She edited the seventh and eighth edition and was the co-editor on two previous editions of *Business Statistics*. She was co-editor of *Foreign Trade of the United States, 2001*, and also worked on the *Handbook of U.S. Labor Statistics*. She was formerly Senior Economist at the U.S. House of Representatives Budget Committee and has also served at the Senate Budget Committee, the Congressional Budget Office, and the Federal Reserve Board. Her fields of special concentration included analysis of current business conditions, including issues of economic measurement; monetary and fiscal policy; and income distribution and poverty.

Assistant editor Mary Meghan Ryan, a Bernan Press data analyst, is a former economist with the American Economics Group. Mary Meghan assisted with data collection and research as well as prepared data tables for this edition of *Business Statistics*. Mary Meghan, also an assistant editor of Bernan Press' *Handbook of U.S. Labor Statistics*, received her bachelor's degree in economics from the University of Maryland.

Mark Siegal, a research editor with Bernan Press, served as an assistant editor on this edition of *Business Statistics*. Mark previously worked as a staff assistant with the USDA Human Nutrition Research Center on Aging at Tufts University, and has a background in researching government data; statistics and data management; technical writing; and editing. Mark, also an assistant editor on *Vital Statistics of the United States*, has a B.S. in communication (with distinction in research) from Cornell University and a certificate in epidemiology from Tufts University.

Katherine DeBrandt is a senior data analyst with Bernan Press and has worked on *Business Statistics* for 4 years. As an assistant editor on this edition, Katherine provided Mary Meghan and Mark with guidance on data research matters. Katherine received her B.A. in political science from Colgate University. She is also co-editor of the *County and City Extra series*; *The Almanac of American Education*; and *Social Change in America: The Historical Handbook*, all published by Bernan Press.

The editor assumes full responsibility for the interpretations presented in this volume.

EXPANDED HISTORICAL STATISTICS GIVE PERSPECTIVE ON GROWTH, WAR, INFLATION, AND UNEMPLOYMENT

The ninth edition of *Business Statistics of the United States* provides deeper perspectives on the United States economy than previous editions. *Business Statistics* now includes a summary economic record of the Second World War and extensive detail describing the entire, remarkable half-century that has followed the end of that war. For the first time, *Business Statistics* enables its users to look at the entire postwar period as a whole; to compare the performance of the U.S. economy in different wars, large and small; to compare economic performance in each of the 10 postwar business cycles; and to examine the entire history of the cycle of inflation and disinflation that occurred from the 1960s through the 1990s.

Analytical techniques

In assessing the performance of an economy over longer periods of time, it is important to use analytical techniques that best allow underlying economic relationships to reveal themselves. In this article, and in the graphs and text that precede each *Business Statistics* data chapter, the editor will frequently make use of three such tools: the ratio-scale graph; the calculation of compound annual growth rates; and the use of cyclically comparable years to calculate longer-term trends.

Ratio-scale graphs. At the beginning of Chapter 1 is a time series graph of output per capita from 1946 through 2002, drawn on a ratio scale. Output per capita is the constant-dollar value of each year's U.S. Gross Domestic Product (GDP) divided by the size of that year's U.S. population. The reader will quickly see that equal distances on the vertical scale of this graph do not represent equal 1996-dollar differences in values. However, equal vertical distances do represent equal percent changes. Any upward-sloping straight line plotted on this scale would represent a constant rate of growth over the period, and any downward-sloping straight line would represent a constant percentage rate of decline.

This ratio-scale graph was produced by the following three steps: (1) Convert the values to be graphed into natural (base e) logarithms. (2) Graph the natural logarithms. (3) For ease in interpretation, relabel ("by hand," not using the computer graphing program) the vertical scale on the graph, replacing the actual numerical value of the logarithm that was plotted with the numerical value of its antilog, that is, the original value.

This technique is only valid, of course, for aggregate values that do not include zeroes or negative numbers, for which natural logs do not exist. Since percentage values such as the unemployment rate and percentage changes such as the inflation rate are already in percentage terms, and may include zero and/or negative values, they are not graphed in this fashion.

Compound annual growth rates. In the text of this article and in the highlights pages that precede many of the chapters, the editor has used compound annual growth rates to summarize the long-term history of important economic processes such as economic and demographic growth and inflation.

The compound annual growth rate is the percentage rate which, compounded annually, would cause a quantity "X(t)" observed in a period "t" to grow (or decline) to a quantity "X(t+i)" over a period of "i" years. Using this procedure, growth percentages for different periods spanning different numbers of years can be reduced to a common scale for comparison. The formula for calculating such a growth rate, "r," is as follows:

$$ r = \left(\sqrt[i]{X(t+i)\big/X(t)} - 1 \right) x100. $$

When growth rates are related to each other, such as the growth rates for output, hours worked, and output per hour worked (productivity), those rates will be arithmetically consistent as in the following formula, where "o" is the percentage growth rate for output, "h" the rate for hours worked, and "p" the growth rate for output per hour worked:

$$ p = [(100 + o \,/\, 100 + \ h)\text{-}1]x100 $$

Where the percentage growth rates are not very far from zero, the relationships can be approximated or verified by simple subtraction, for example, the productivity growth rate of 2.4 percent is approximately the difference between the output growth rate of 3.6 percent and the hours growth rate of 1.2 percent.

Using cyclically comparable end points. For economic processes that have significant business-cycle components, such as output and employment, it is important to use comparable points in the business cycle for estimating underlying growth rates. One commonly used method is simply to calculate growth rates between years with similar, high rates of resource utilization. The broadest readily available measure of resource utilization is the unemployment rate, which was 3.8 percent in 1948 and 4.0 percent in 2000. Hence, in the analysis that follows, postwar long-term growth rates are typically calculated as the rates for the 52-year period from 1948 to 2000.

For comparisons using monthly or quarterly data, an alternative is to use the dates of business cycle peaks, which are shown in the Notes and Definitions to Table 1-11, as beginning and end points.

A half-century of economic growth and change

Real gross domestic product (GDP), the broadest measure of the output of the U.S. economy, grew at an average 3.5 percent per year from 1948 to 2000. Year by year, growth varied from +8.7 percent in 1950—when a cyclical recovery coincided with the outbreak of the Korean War—to –2.0 percent in the 1982 recession. (Tables 1-2 and 1-3) Although there were 10 recessions in the postwar period—periods when output, employment, and other aggregate indicators all declined—they were outnumbered and outweighed by periods of expansion. (Table 1-11 and its Notes and Definitions)

GDP, by definition, is the sum of personal consumption spending, business investment, government consumption and investment, and exports, minus imports. In the standard blackboard equation, "$GDP = C + I + G + X - M$." This definition takes only final demands into account, eliminating any double-counting of intermediate stages of production. (See the Notes and Definitions to Chapter 15 for further explanation.) The measurement of GDP is based on summing these final demands, thereby not only providing the measure of output but also illuminating the sources of demand.

The composition of GDP has changed between 1948 and 2000. Personal consumption expenditures (PCE) rose from 65.1 percent to 68.0 percent of the total; private investment was almost unchanged at 17.8 percent to 17.9 percent; and government consumption and investment spending (federal, state, and local combined) rose from 15.1 percent to 17.8 percent. How could all three shares rise? The answer lies in the other two terms of the equation. Imports increased from 3.8 percent to 14.9 percent, while exports only rose from 5.8 percent to 11.2 percent. Recall that imports are a subtraction from final demands in the calculation of GDP: they represent demands that have been satisfied by foreign instead of domestic production. Thus, the United States is now consuming and investing more than it produces, reflected in an international balance on goods and services that is a negative 3.7 percent of GDP, compared with a positive balance of 2.0 percent in 1948. (See Chapters 1 and 7.)

The increase in the volume of both export and import trade and the change in the net international balance from surplus to deficit are perhaps the most dramatic shifts that have taken place over the postwar period. At the end of World War II, the United States had what amounted to the world's only fully functioning economy among all the industrialized nations. War-devastated countries needed U.S. consumption and investment goods to survive and rebuild, and were not yet able to generate enough exports to pay for them; the U.S. positive export balance had to be financed by U.S. government grants and loans.

Today, industries all over the world can compete with ours, and many countries generate balance of payments surpluses. These surpluses represent saving within these countries, evidently in excess of their own investment needs or opportunities, which they can invest in the United States, thus financing the U.S. trade deficit. (See Chapter 7 for data on foreign trade and finance.) One of the principal debates about today's economy concerns the sustainability of the U.S. trade deficit and the associated capital inflow.

While the shares of total consumption and investment in GDP seem to have changed relatively little, large and striking changes can be seen within each category.

Consumers in the aggregate were able to spend a smaller share of their total consumption on food, tobacco, clothing, and personal care, a greater share on transportation and miscellaneous categories, and a much larger share on medical care. This includes medical care paid for by private and government insurance, including Medicare and Medicaid. (Table 4-5)

Within investment spending, the share of information processing equipment was up sharply over the half-century. (Table 5-2)

The federal government's consumption and investment spending as a share of GDP fell from 9.0 percent to 6.0 percent. This does not, however, give a complete picture of the role of federal spending in the economy. Total federal spending includes not only the categories classified as consumption and investment in the National Income and Product Accounts but also federal transfer payments, of which more than half are Social Security and Medicare; federal interest payments; and federal grants to state and local governments. (See Chapter 6.) The role of these latter three categories in final demand is represented by the consumption, investment, and state and local government spending that they support. Furthermore, the receipts side of the federal accounts also affects final demands through tax rates and flows.

Federal transfer payments grew from 4.9 percent of personal income in 1948 to 12.7 percent in 2000. One particularly significant factor was the growth in Medicare and Medicaid, neither of which existed in 1948. (Table 4-1)

Total personal interest income grew from 3.9 percent to 12.8 percent of total personal income. (Table 4-1) It is difficult to trace federal (and other) interest payments through the economy because of the duplicative payments and receipts generated by financial intermediation. Given that the federal share of total domestic nonfinancial debt plummeted from 59.2 percent in 1948 to 18.6 percent in 2000 (Table 12-5), it can be surmised that the growth in personal interest income did not arise principally from federal interest payments.

On the receipts side of the federal government accounts, total tax receipts rose from 15.7 percent of GDP in 1948 to 20.7 percent in 2000. The latter percent is not representative of subsequent years, however, as it included unusually high receipts from the stock market boom and preceded the substantial tax cuts that began in 2001. By 2002, federal receipts had fallen to 17.9 percent of GDP. (Tables 6-1 and 1-1)

Finishing the accounting for GDP by final demands, the state and local government spending share of GDP jumped from 6.1 percent in 1948 to 11.8 percent in 2000. Federal grants-in-aid rose from 10.5 percent to 20.4 percent of total state receipts. On the receipts side, receipts other than federal grants, that is, state and local taxes and social insurance contributions, rose from 5.4 percent to 9.8 percent of GDP (Tables 6-2 and 1-1).

Labor force, employment, and productivity growth

The total U.S. population grew at a 1.3 percent annual rate from 1948 to 2000, while the growth in GDP was more than double that rate, leading to a significant rate of increase in the average real standard of living as measured by per capita GDP. (Table 1-10 and Chapter 1 graph) This happened because more and more Americans went to work, and their productivity grew even faster than their work input.

Labor force and employment. The civilian labor force—the number of persons either working or seeking work—rose 1.7 percent per year, as the labor force participation rate rose from 58.8 percent to 67.1 percent of the working-age civilian noninstitutional population. In addition, there was a shift of employment out of agriculture and into more-productive nonagricultural industries—a continuation of a trend that started at the dawn of the Industrial Revolution. Agricultural employment declined over the half-century and the total number of persons employed outside farms rose at a 1.9 percent rate. A separate count of nonfarm payroll jobs rose even faster, 2.1 percent. The payroll count is a count of jobs, so a person with two jobs is counted twice, whereas that person is counted only once as a "person employed." There are other important differences as well. (See Chapter 10, its Notes and Definitions, and the Special Notes.)

Unemployment, like economic growth, varied from year to year, with postwar unemployment rates ranging from a low of 2.9 percent in 1953, in the period of the Korean War, to 9.7 percent in 1982. At the height of World War II, even lower unemployment rates were achieved. (Tables 10-3 and 18-1)

Unemployment is, of course, directly related to economic growth over the business cycle—yet the relationship (known as "Okun's Law") is not always regular or predictable. Changes in productivity and the workweek affect the relationship of employment change to output change, and changes in labor force participation affect the relationship of the change in the unemployment rate to employment change.

Looking at the longer-term trend, output grew faster than employment during the past half-century because of increases in labor productivity, that is, output per hour worked. In Chapter 9, measures of productivity are presented for the total business sector, which was 77 percent of the value of GDP in 1996, and three important subsectors—nonfarm business, nonfinancial corporations, and manufacturing.

Hours worked and productivity. Business sector output per hour grew at a 2.4 percent annual rate from 1948 to 2000. This is the arithmetic result of business sector output growing 3.6 percent—only slightly faster than total GDP—while aggregate hours worked (the number of jobs times the average workweek per job) rose only 1.2 percent on average.

Factoring the change in hours worked into its employment and average hours components reveals another salient fact about the last half-century—the decline in the average job's workweek. The number of jobs in the business sector increased from 1948 to 2000 at a 1.5 percent rate, while the average workweek—the number of hours worked *per job*—declined at a rate of 0.3 percent. (Table 9-3)

Does this mean that the average American worker is working shorter hours, or that the average American family can be supported by less paid work effort? Not necessarily, because the precise meaning of "hours worked per job" must be understood. In the productivity accounts, as in the BLS payroll employment survey that provides much of the basic data for employment and hours worked, the employment concept is the number of jobs, not persons. If more workers take second, part-time jobs, these measures show higher "employment," even though no more persons are employed, and a shorter average workweek. If a spouse or other previously non-working family member takes a part-time job, employment increases and the "average workweek" declines, even while that family as a family unit is putting more time into paid employment.

Readers will note that Table 10-7 shows *increases* over the years in the average workweek in the old-line, relatively well-paid sectors—manufacturing, construction, utilities, natural resources, and mining. In these sectors, employers often prefer paying overtime to taking on more workers. The cost of health and other fringe benefits is often a consideration here. In the sectors where pay and benefits are lower, jobs, particularly part-time jobs, grow faster and average workweeks decline. (See Chapters 10 and 16.)

Interpretation and sources of labor productivity. As the Bureau of Labor Statistics points out, these measures of labor productivity "do not measure the specific contribution of labor, capital, or any other factor of production. Rather, they reflect the joint effects of many influences, including changes in technology; capital investment; level of output; utilization of capacity, energy, and materials; the organization of production; managerial skill; and the characteristics and effort of the work force." In measures of "total factor productivity," BLS undertakes further analysis of the sources of growth in output per hour. These can be found, along with extensive data on the composition and education of the work force, in *Handbook of U.S. Labor Statistics*, Bernan Press.

Measures of the capital stock are shown in *Business Statistics*. Tables 5-5 and 1-1 indicate that the current-cost value of total fixed assets was 2.95 times the value of GDP in 1948 and 2.75 times GDP in 2000. The ratio of private assets to GDP was unchanged at 2.16, while the ratio of government assets declined from 0.79 to 0.59. The quantity indexes in Table 5-6 indicate that the quantity (that is, the constant-dollar value) of fixed assets rose somewhat more slowly than real GDP—from 1948 to 2000, private fixed assets grew at a 3.2 percent annual rate and government assets 2.5 percent.

In Chapter 11, *Business Statistics* provides measures of energy consumption, indicating a decline in overall energy use per real dollar of GDP.

In Chapter 2, measures of capacity utilization are shown for the manufacturing, mining, and utility sectors.

Implications of productivity growth. Productivity growth interacts in important ways with labor compensation and inflation. In the business sector, the current-dollar value of compensation per hour worked (including wages, salaries, and employer-paid benefits) rose at a 5.7 percent annual rate from 1948 to 2000. However, the 2.4 percent increase in productivity meant that the labor cost of a unit of *output* only rose at a 3.2 percent annual rate. Since labor compensation makes up about 2/3 of national income (Table 1-8), unit labor costs are often considered to be a major determinant of inflation. Indeed, the two measures track each other closely over longer periods: the 1948–2000 rate of increase in the average price (implicit deflator) of the business sector was also 3.2 percent.

Productivity growth, since it allows increases in compensation without increases in labor cost, is also considered to be a major determinant of the real wage. The productivity accounts show that in the business sector, real hourly compensation rose at a 2.0 percent annual rate from 1948 to 2000, falling short of the 2.4 percent increase in productivity. However, the apparent difference between these two trends reflects not a decline in the share of the value of output going to employees as a group but a difference between the "market baskets" used to determine the real value of the two aggregates. The deflator for real compensation in this set of data is a variation of the consumer price index, while the gross product deflator that determines productivity is based on goods and services *produced* by the business sector rather than those *consumed* by U.S. consumers. Business sector output includes a substantial proportion of high-tech products, which have had dramatic price declines. Workers, on the other hand, buy proportionately fewer computers and other high-tech products and proportionately more commodity-based products, including imports. In other words, the average price of what workers buy went up more than the average price of what they produced. (Table 9-3)

A more complete accounting for the costs of production, taking capital as well as labor costs into account, can be observed in the productivity and cost data for nonfinancial corporations. These are only available back to 1958. To demonstrate some of the implications of these data, growth rates will be calculated here using 1960 as the earlier cyclical high—even though the 1960 unemployment rate, at 5.5 percent, was markedly higher than the 4.0 percent registered in 2000.

In that 40-year span, compensation per hour at nonfinancial corporations rose 5.4 percent and productivity 1.9 percent, for a unit labor cost increase of 3.4 percent. Unit non-labor costs (capital consumption, interest, and indirect taxes) rose 3.9 percent and unit profits rose 2.0

percent. The total price of a unit of output—which is the sum of the unit cost and unit profits growth rates, weighted by their shares—rose at a 3.4 percent rate—once again, the same as the rise in unit labor cost. The relative decline in profits echoes the rise in interest and fall in profits indicated in the national income accounts, which in turn reflects the rise in corporate indebtedness shown in Table 12-5. (Tables 9-3, 1-8, and 12-5.)

Whose standard of living?

In everything written so far, this article has been concerned with averages—average GDP per capita, average output and real compensation per hour worked, and so forth. It is important to note that an average, or "mean," is only one way of describing the "central tendency" of any set of statistical data, and not necessarily the one that produces the most representative data.

If we are interested in the economic well-being of a typical American family, we would probably judge that the best single number to characterize that well-being would be the standard of living of a family situated at the middle of the income distribution. Half of all families would have higher income and half would have lower incomes. This is the measure known as the "median," and data on median incomes are presented in Chapter 3. Medians are not the same as averages or means, and in the case of income distributions they are invariably lower.

This difference is sometimes illustrated by the image of a millionaire walking into a working-class bar. The "average income" of each person in the bar would jump, as a million dollars was added to the numerator of the average and just one unit to the denominator. However, the median would be little if at all changed, and this would accord with an accurate perception that the "typical" person in that bar had not experienced any increase in his income. The consequence of this difference is that means are higher than medians, and if the incomes of people at the upper end of the distribution increase faster than those at the middle and bottom, then the means will also *increase* more than the medians.

In Chapter 3, it can be seen that real median family cash income increased 1.9 percent from 1948 to 2000 (again using years of comparable low unemployment). This is less than the 2.2 percent increase in real per capita GDP (a mean) during that period and also less than the 2.1 percent increase in real mean income that can be derived from the census data. Had the median income increased as fast as the census mean—implying no change in the income distribution—the median family would have had over $6,000 more income in 2000, in that year's dollars.

The increasing inequality in the income distribution can also be seen by comparing the 1948 and 2000 income shares shown in Chapter 3. The top 20 percent of families received 47.7 percent of all income in 2000, compared with 42.4 percent in 1948. The shares of each of the lower four quintiles declined.

Of course, it can be argued that the postwar growth in real income and productivity required increasing rewards for the successful, so that the hypothetical potential increase just calculated for the median family could never actually occur. This is not a question that can be definitively answered, at least based on the kind of data available here; but it can be noted that productivity increases were quite rapid during the earlier postwar years, *before* the trend toward a more unequal income distribution began. (See Chapters 3 and 9.)

Inflation and unemployment

A number of important price indicators are presented in *Business Statistics*, both in Chapter 8: Prices and also in Table 1-4 which shows chain-type price indexes for GDP and various subsectors. Users should note that price indexes measure the average level of prices, relative to some base year, while "inflation" is the annual percent *rate of change* in a price index.

Biases in the most popular indicator—the CPI-U—are not retroactively corrected, although some alternative indexes are available and presented in *Business Statistics* showing estimated CPIs with better methodology for some periods overlapping the official CPI. See Table 8-1 and the associated Notes and Definitions. For this and other reasons the monetary authorities at the Federal Reserve pay particular attention to the chain-type price indexes for personal consumption expenditures, total and excluding food and energy, derived from the National Income and Product Accounts, which use the same basic price data as the CPIs but process those data in a more consistent fashion. (See Table 1-4 and the Notes and Definitions to Chapter 1.) But all of these indexes tell a similar story about the inflation rate—the rate of change in prices—for the broad sweep of the postwar period.

As the graph in Chapter 8 shows, inflation was high in 1946 and 1947, as wartime price controls were dismantled and pent-up purchasing power from the war period was released. Prices declined in the 1949 recession but rose sharply in 1950 and 1951 with recovery and the outbreak of the Korean War. Inflation was negative again in 1955 in the aftermath of the war's end and the 1954 recession. It rose during two recoveries in 1956–1957 and 1960, but fell back to about 1 percent—generally judged to represent price stability because of remaining and irremediable biases in the price indexes—in the slack years of 1961 and 1962.

As the 1960s progressed, however, the federal government embarked on a stimulative fiscal policy, with the intent of attaining an unemployment rate lower than those observed in the 1950s and early 1960s. (See Table 10-3.) Then fiscal policy became even more stimulative as the buildup in military spending for the Vietnam War progressed, without any attempt to raise taxes or cut back on other spending until late in the decade. (See Chapter 6.) An attempt was made to hold wages and prices down using voluntary "guidelines" in the early 1960s, but it collapsed in 1966, and inflation continued to accelerate during the sustained period of high employment through 1969.

The 1970 recession failed to bring inflation down and yet the 1971 recovery was weak. New expansionary moves to accelerate the recovery, including monetary stimulus and depreciation of the dollar, were undertaken in 1972, along with new price controls. But the 1972 decline in inflation was short-lived, followed by new peacetime highs as the controls collapsed and commodity prices soared. The 1975–1976 recession again gave only a temporary and incomplete respite, and inflation soared to double digits with recovery and new commodity price shocks.

Finally, under the impact of the most severe recession in the postwar period in 1981–1982, inflation began to unwind. A subsequent recession in 1990 ushered in even lower inflation rates throughout the rest of the 1990s, despite the achievement of the lowest unemployment rates since 1969.

As the above narrative indicates, the 1950s and 1960s were characterized by an apparent inverse relationship, often interpreted as a "trade-off," between inflation and high employment, with inflation falling as an apparent consequence of unemployment rising. By the 1970s, however, inflation became more stubborn, and failed to respond proportionately and negatively to increases in unemployment—indeed, at times the two indicators rose together. This was often ascribed, at the time, to "supply shocks"—for example, bad harvests, oil embargoes, and OPEC price increases—which, unlike changes in aggregate demand, tend to increase inflation even while depressing output. But in retrospect, many "supply shocks" should perhaps be considered as delayed reactions to demand shocks, since oil prices tend to increase when the dollar has declined, and tend to fall during worldwide recession as in 1986. (See price data in

Chapter 8 and data on the international value of the dollar in Table 13-7.)

Economists now take account of the role of expectations in maintaining the momentum of a given inflation rate, which is believed to explain the worsening of the tradeoff in the 1970s. They were again surprised, however, by the combination of low unemployment and low inflation in the late 1990s. The surprise was greater among those economists who looked at the unemployment rate as the sole measure of resource utilization. In fact, capacity utilization also plays a role in determining to what extent changes in aggregate demand affect prices and to what extent they lead to expanded volume of production instead. Federal Reserve Board measures (Table 2-3) indicate that average utilization of manufacturing capacity declined between the last three major business cycle peaks—from 1979 to 1989 and again from 1989 to 2000. This indicated less pressure on prices, helping to offset the effect of lower unemployment rates over the same intervals.

The issues involved in the relationships between inflation, economic growth, and unemployment cannot be said to be settled; debate continues about the relative roles of monetary policy, tax rates and other aspects of fiscal policy, global competition, other supply considerations, labor market institutions, and expectations.

With respect to monetary policy, *Business Statistics* provides data on the monetary and reserve aggregates in Tables 12-1 through 12-3. Rates of change in money and reserves have provided increasingly inaccurate forecasts of inflation and are not widely considered to be valid indicators of the state of monetary policy any more. The data on interest rates provided in Table 12-9, especially the federal funds rate which is directly controlled by the Federal Reserve, are currently the subject of more attention in assessing the monetary policy stance. However, they need to be converted to "real" interest rates—subtracting the inflation rate (actual or anticipated) from the nominal interest rate—to shed light on the size of the stimulative and inflationary effects of Federal Reserve policy.

War and the economy

The graph at the beginning of Chapter 6 makes clear how little impact federal spending on the wars against Afghanistan and Iraq could have had on the U.S. economy, at least as of Fiscal Year 2002. Relative to the value of GDP, defense spending had increased slightly but was not much higher than at the *low* point of the post-World-War-II demobilization. It was lower than Korean War levels (1950–1953), Vietnam War levels (1964–1975), and the 1980s defense buildup. (The 1990–1991 Gulf war was largely financed by U.S. allies, which actually led to a slight *decline* in the defense/GDP ratio.) However, analysts will continue to monitor defense spending, taking note of the tendency toward delayed recognition of war costs; recall the early administration underestimates of Vietnam spending and the failure of the administration to submit any early estimates at all of Iraq War spending.

Business cycle comparisons

Business Statistics now also provides expanded data on earlier cyclical recoveries that users may compare with current data. The reference dates for all of the postwar business cycles are shown in the Notes and Definitions to Table 1-11, and monthly and quarterly data for major indicators such as output, employment, and unemployment for the entire postwar period are shown in Chapters 19 and 20. A few statistical pitfalls need to be avoided; see the Special Notes.

...and more

This article has attempted to provide examples of the kinds of data analysis newly possible with this expanded version of *Business Statistics*. Regional and industrial details are also available, along with information on business and consumer balance sheets. The editor anticipates that users will find this volume even more useful than previous editions, and welcomes input on ways to make it even more useful.

SPECIAL NOTES:
CURRENT STATISTICAL ISSUES AND PITFALLS

Almost every day, some new set of information on the economy is released—a new estimate of the latest quarter's Gross Domestic Product, new figures on employment and unemployment, or a new month's inflation rate. Politicians, pundits, and stock market gurus give instant opinions on the significance of the new numbers. One of the purposes of *Business Statistics* is to provide background information to supplement and give perspective to this daily stream of new and updated economic data, and enable the users of this book to make their own informed judgments.

Sometimes the very richness of U.S. economic data makes comparisons and analysis more difficult for people who are not already immersed in the intricacies of the system. For example, one government agency issues two different estimates of what at first glance would seem to be the same thing, "employment." More generally, the constant labors of statistical agencies to incorporate new information and new understanding of the economy lead to frequent revisions of data.

To help users understand these difficulties, the Notes and Definitions at the end of each chapter in *Business Statistics* explain concepts, definitions, measurement methods, and revision procedures. In these Special Notes, the editor calls special attention to a few problems of particular concern this year: comprehensive revision of the National Income and Product Accounts, the measurement of employment, and the measurement of employee compensation per hour.

Revision of the National Income and Product Accounts

In the typical year, the National Income and Product Accounts (NIPAs)—the major source for data in Chapters 1, 4, 5, 6, 7, and 19—are revised for the latest few years in July, and *Business Statistics* is able to incorporate all the new data. In 2003, however, the usual July revision was made part of a comprehensive revision that was not completed until too late to incorporate in this volume's data tables. As this article is being written, late in the process of publication, many of the detailed tables of revised data were still not available, although enough information had been released to allow a few summary comparisons.

Because this was a comprehensive revision—involving changes in definitions and classifications and a shift in the base period for quantity and price indexes and for constant-dollar data—data issued in 2004 on the *levels* of the income and product aggregates and their quantity and price indexes are not continuous with those shown in this volume. The new current-dollar value of GDP for 2000, for example, is $9,817.0 billion, compared with $9,824.6 billion shown in Chapter 1. This surprisingly small difference, the effect of upward "statistical" revision offset by downward "definitional" revision, is less than 0.1 percent of GDP. Differences involving the separate measurement of the quantity and price components of GDP are much larger. The new "real" value of GDP in 2000 is also $9,817.0 billion, because the constant-dollar measures have all been restated from 1996 to 2000 dollars; this is 6.8 percent higher than the old "real" value, almost entirely because of the increase in prices between 1996 and 2000, and clearly cannot be consistent with the figures in this volume. The quantity and price indexes have been restated with the year 2000 equal to 100 and also cannot be directly compared with those in this volume.

The good news is that those aspects of the NIPAs that are most important—not their *levels* but their internal relationships and their *rates of change*, which depict growth, change, and inflation—have been generally little affected by this revision. For example, the real GDP growth rates from 1948 to 2000 and the changes in shares of GDP that are chronicled in the article that precedes these Special Notes are trivially changed if at all. Comparisons of this sort, along with observations of cyclical behavior in the expansions and contractions *preceding* the contraction that began in March 2001, that are based on the data in this volume should still be valid.

Even for the most recent period, the revisions in economic growth are small. It now appears that there was a slight decrease in real GDP in the third quarter of 2000, but the decline in real GDP in the latest recession, from the fourth quarter of 2000 to the third quarter of 2001, is now 0.5 percent instead of 0.6 percent. On the other hand, the recovery from the third quarter of 2001 to the second quarter of 2003 is now 2.6 percent instead of 2.7 percent.

There are more striking changes on the income side. There is a large upward revision of corporate profits for 2002, based on new IRS data and a new adjustment for the exercise of stock options. (As a result of a later production deadline, *Business Statistics 2004* incorporates these data in Tables 9-4 and 9-5, Corporate Profits with Inventory Valuation Adjustment by Industry Group.) Because of downward revisions to personal income and upward revisions to personal consumption spending, the personal saving rate beginning in 1987 has been revised downward, with the largest downward revision also in 2002.

This and other information on the revision can be found on the BEA Internet site, <http://www.bea.gov>.

Measures of employment

Each month, the Bureau of Labor Statistics updates two distinct measures of aggregate employment in the U.S. economy.

One measure, total civilian employment, is a count of the number of civilians holding jobs. It is derived from a large sample survey of households (Current Population Survey, or CPS) and periodically benchmarked to population levels or "controls" established by the decennial Census and other more comprehensive data.

The other measure is nonfarm payroll employment. It is derived from a very large sample of employers (Current Employment Statistics, or CES) and is benchmarked each year to a comprehensive count of employment from the records of the unemployment insurance system.

Recently, some analysts have suggested that the two different employment series imply very different judgments about how much (if at all) employment has recovered since the business cycle trough that has been identified in November 2001. To assess this issue, it is important to understand the differences between the two series. As outlined in the Notes and Definitions to Chapter 10, the differences are as follows:

- CPS employment is a count of persons employed. CES employment is a count of jobs. A person holding two nonfarm payroll jobs will appear as two persons employed in the CES but only one in the CPS.
- CPS employment includes farm employment.
- CPS employment also includes nonfarm self-employed workers, unpaid family workers, and private household workers (domestics). These are outside the scope of the CES.
- CPS employment is limited to those 16 years and older. There is no age limit on CES employment.
- CPS employment includes persons "with a job but not at work" who were temporarily absent from regular jobs because of vacation, illness, industrial dispute, bad weather, or similar reasons. The CES is based on payrolls, and persons in such situations are counted as employed only if they were paid for the absence.
- CPS employment can develop bias if the sample becomes unrepresentative of the population. On the other hand, because it is based on households, it is not necessarily biased by *firms* going out of business. CES employment, being based on a sample of firms, is subject to bias as firms in the sample go out of business

and disappear from the sample while new firms are not immediately incorporated into the sample but only appear at the time of the annual benchmark.

Differences between the methods of benchmark adjustment in the two series are particularly important.

- CPS population control adjustments are introduced in a "lump sum" in a single month, usually January. This makes for a discontinuity between the two adjoining months, and fails to spread the correction of the level over the months or years during which the misstatement gradually emerged.
- CES benchmark adjustments, on the other hand, are "wedged" back to the previous benchmark month, resulting in a smoother and more realistic pattern of revision.

Over time, increasingly sophisticated methods have been used to carry the CES benchmark adjustments forward in the current period and compensate for the reporting bias caused by the birth of new firms, but there is no getting around the fact that the latest year's data include an element of estimate and possible bias. For this reason, analysts will continue to compare the two series and attempt to make sense of the differences.

One such attempt can be found in an article by economist Alan B. Krueger in *The New York Times*, September 18, 2003 (page C2). For the period August 2002 to August 2003, it makes adjustments for the conceptual and data differences. Where the household survey showed an apparent increase of 842,000 in employment between those months, the establishment survey showed a job loss of 560,000. However, the adjustments resulted in a household survey change in payroll jobs of –425,000, very similar to the decline in the establishment survey.

These adjustments are difficult to make on a month-to-month basis because much of the required data is not published by BLS. However, two elements of the adjustments are responsible for most of the difference.

- Most important is the adjustment to new population controls that was introduced into the household survey in January 2003. This increased employment by 576,000—and created a discontinuity of that size between December 2002 and January 2003.
- The other large part of the adjustment is removing the self-employed from the household survey. From August 2002 to August 2003, self-employment had increased by 558,000. Self-employment is a volatile component of total employment. Some interpret it to represent enterprising entrepreneurs on their way to success, but

reported self-employment has some tendency to increase in slack job markets and decrease when the market is strong, suggesting that it is at least in part a disguised form of unemployment or underemployment.

Preliminary information on the next benchmark revision in the CES has just become available, indicating that "the March 2003 total nonfarm payroll employment estimate will be revised downward by approximately 145,000...." (Bureau of Labor Statistics Internet site, "CES Benchmark Update," October 3, 2003, http://www.bls.gov/CES.) This means that as of March 2003 the CES still had a small downward, not upward, bias, and will tend to increase rather than decrease the discrepancy between the series.

Past history gives conflicting evidence on which series is more reliable. The CES is said to have shown some downward bias in the early 1990s, but in the growing economy of the late 1990s it was the CPS that developed a downward bias because the sample became unrepresentative of immigration, resulting in eventual large lump-sum upward revisions in 2000 and again in 2003 as Census 2000 and other more recent data became available. (There will be another lump-sum adjustment in the CPS numbers for January 2004, the size and direction of which are unknown at this writing.)

The establishment survey, then, was apparently less subject to bias in the late 1990s arising from changes in immigration, despite its supposed problems in including new firms. However, because of the new-firm problem it is still possible that when the March 2004 benchmark becomes available—this will happen on a preliminary basis in late 2004, with the actual benchmarking taking place in early 2005—the establishment data will show more increase between March 2003 and March 2004 than before that benchmarking.

As is evident every month when the new month's employment data are released, financial market participants and other close observers of the current state of the economy pay attention mainly to the CES payroll employment series.

These differences have been discussed in a paper by Elise Gould, "Measuring Employment Since the Recovery: A comparison of the household and payroll surveys," available from the Economic Policy Institute, <http://epinet.org>.

Measures of employee compensation

Hourly earnings, wages, salaries, compensation—each of these terms is used to describe at least one data series in the U.S. statistical system, and each appears in at least one of three different data sets presented in *Business Statistics*. (Additional, more detailed data on labor compensation are presented in *Handbook of U.S. Labor Statistics*, Bernan Press.) It is important for the user to understand the characteristics of each of these series in order to select the one most suited for his or her purpose.

Wages typically mean gross amounts per hour paid to hourly workers. They are gross of withheld income and payroll taxes, dues, and other withholdings—in other words, they do not exclude those amounts—but they do exclude the employer share of payroll taxes and the cost of employer-provided benefits such as pensions and health insurance. Measures of wages and salaries together are presented in Chapter 9 and measures of hourly earnings are presented in Chapter 10, with precise definitions of each in the Notes and Definitions to those chapters.

Salaries represent gross amounts paid to those who are paid by the week, month, or year rather than by the hour. Measures of wages and salaries together are presented in Chapter 9, and salaried production or nonsupervisory workers are included in the hourly earnings measures in Chapter 10. As with wages, salaries do not exclude personal and payroll taxes on the individual or other withholdings, but do exclude the cost of employer-paid benefits and payroll taxes.

Compensation includes wages and salaries as defined above together with the employer-paid payroll taxes and benefit costs.

Compensation, then, represents the total cost of labor to the employer. Wages and salaries represent the gross taxable income to the employees. Only one measure in this book represents net spendable income after all income and payroll taxes—Personal Disposable Income, in Chapter 4—and this includes not only labor income but also all forms of capital income. There are no currently reported measures of the concept of "worker take-home pay," but the rate of change in worker paychecks can usually be inferred from the rate of change in a relevant measure of wages and salaries or hourly earnings.

Probably the principal use for *compensation* series, the use emphasized by the Federal Reserve System, is as an indicator of inflationary pressure. Labor costs represent about two/thirds of the cost of production on average. If labor costs rise faster than productivity, either because of the effects of a tight labor market or because of some autonomous source, there can be upward pressure on prices.

In evaluating trends in compensation, the differences between the two series presented in Chapter 9 are important. The Notes and Definitions for that chapter explain each one in a General Note and in the specific notes for each table. Briefly, the compensation component of the Productivity and Costs measures (Table 9-3) is simply an average of all compensation divided by all labor input, and will increase if there is a shift in the composition of output toward industries that pay their employees more, even if no individual worker experiences any increase in his or her hourly or weekly earnings. However, high-pay industries are typically high-productivity industries, and a shift toward those industries will also register as an increase in productivity even if productivity is unchanged in each individual industry. Thus, such a shift in the composition of output will not increase labor cost per unit of output or inflationary pressure.

The Employment Cost Index holds constant the composition of employment in order to isolate trends in hourly wages, salary rates, and compensation rates for individual occupations. One appropriate use of ECI measures would be to test the effect of changes in the unemployment rate or other measures of labor market tightness and other relevant variables on the rate of change in wages per unit of labor—the "Phillips Curve" relationship.

The Employment Cost Index includes sales commissions in its measures of wages and salaries. Since these are subject to temporary fluctuations that may not reflect underlying trends, ECIs excluding the sales occupations are also calculated and published.

Currently, the cost of stock options issued to employees is not included in the Employment Cost Index and is included in the compensation component of the productivity measures only with a lag. As illustrated in the Notes and Definitions, this led to large revisions in compensation per hour in some recent periods. Whether this is a significant failing in the Employment Cost Index depends on the extent to which employees accepted stock options as a substitute for demanding higher salaries and/or benefits. This substitution hypothesis has been suggested by anecdote and could be tested by comparing stock price data and relevant components of the Employment Cost Index.

Hourly earnings, as presented in Chapter 10, are a major source for the aggregate compensation measures in Productivity and Costs. They are reported monthly at the beginning of the following month, far more promptly than the quarterly measures, and represent the production or nonsupervisory workers that make up about four-fifths of the labor force, based on a very large sample survey of employers. Hourly earnings are described in the Notes and Definitions to Chapter 10; they exclude stock options and fluctuate as the composition of output and employment fluctuates between high- and low-pay industries. Weekly earnings, based on these hourly earnings data, are an important component of personal income and thus a major determinant of consumer income and purchasing power.

Hourly earnings give an early, if imperfect, indicator of inflationary wage pressures, subject to refinement and reinterpretation as the ECI data become available, while weekly earnings give an early look at recent income developments.

These notes provide general information about the data in Tables 1-1 through 21-2. Specific Notes and Definitions providing information about data sources, definitions, methodology, revisions, and sources of additional information follow the tables in each chapter.

Main Divisions of the Book

The tables are divided into four main parts.

Part A (Tables 1-1 through 13-7) pertains to the U.S. economy as a whole. Generally, each table presents annual averages for the full period since World War II, or as far back as available, and quarterly or monthly values for the most recent year or years. (Full quarterly or monthly histories for major series are shown in Part C.) Some chapters present data for the United States only in aggregate, while others—such as industrial production, capital expenditures, and employment, hours and earnings—also have detail for major industry groups. Data by industry on industrial production (Chapter 2), capital expenditures (Table 5-11), profits (Table 9-5), and payroll employment, hours, and earnings (Tables 10-5 through 10-10) are classified using the new North American Industry Classification System (NAICS), as far back as such data are made available by the source agencies.

Part B focuses on the individual industries that together produce the Gross Domestic Product (GDP). Chapter 14 provides an overview of the NAICS, presenting the overall structure of the classification system, the definition of each major industry group, and the approximate relationships of each group to the industries in the old Standard Industrial Classification (SIC). Chapter 15 contains data on GDP by industry, using the old SIC because this data set has not yet been converted to NAICS. Chapter 16 provides further detail on payroll employment, hours, and earnings classified according to NAICS. Chapter 17 presents various data sets for key economic sectors. Some of the tables are based on definitions of products, rather than producing establishments, and are valid for either classification system. This is the case for Tables 17-1, Petroleum and Petroleum Products; 17-2, New Construction; 17-3, Housing Starts and Building Permits, Home Sales and Prices; and 17-8, Motor Vehicle Sales and Inventories. Tables 17-4 through 17-7 and 17-9 through 17-11, covering manufacturing and retail and wholesale trade, show overlapping data for the year 1992 using the old and new classification systems, preserving the old-basis historical record for the years prior to 1992. Tables 17-14 and 17-15 for services firms also present data on the NAICS basis, while 17-12 and 17-13 show overlapping data for earlier years on SIC.

The 1987 SIC is published in *Standard Industrial Classification Manual, 1987*, Executive Office of the President, Office of Management and Budget (Washington, DC: U.S. Government Printing Office, 1988). The NAICS is fully described in U.S. Office of Management and Budget, *North American Industry Classification System: United States, 2002*, published by Bernan Press. Additional information is available on the Census Bureau Internet site <http://www.census.gov>.

Part C presents further historical detail. Chapter 18 shows selected data for the World War II years 1939–1947. These are shown on an annual basis only, as many of the series are not available quarterly or monthly. Chapters 19 and 20 present quarterly or monthly data back to the earliest postwar year available for major series; the corresponding annual values are shown in Part A.

Part D presents data by state and region, calculated by the Bureau of Economic Analysis consistent with the National Income and Product Accounts presented in Part A, but available on an annual basis only. Table 21-1 contains data on Gross Domestic Product originating by state, and Table 21-2 shows personal income, population, and employment.

Characteristics of the Tables and the Data

The table subtitles or column headings for the data tables normally indicate that the data are "seasonally adjusted" or "not seasonally adjusted" or "at a seasonally adjusted annual rate." These headings refer to the monthly or quarterly, rather than the annual, data. Annual data by definition require no seasonal adjustment. Annual values are normally calculated as totals or averages of unadjusted data, and such values are used in either adjusted or unadjusted data columns, or both.

Seasonal adjustment removes from the time series the average impact of variations that normally occur at about the same time each year due to, for example, weather, holidays, and tax payment dates.

A simplified example of the process of seasonal adjustment, or deseasonalizing, can indicate why it is so important for the interpretation of economic time series. Statisticians compare actual monthly data for a number of years with "moving average" trends of the monthly data for the 12 months centered on each month's data. For example, they may find that in November, sales values are usually about 95 percent of the moving average, while in December, usual sales values are 110 percent of the average. Suppose that actual November sales in the current year are $100 and December sales are $105. The seasonally adjusted value for November will be $105 ($100/0.95) while the value for December will be $95 ($105/1.10). Thus, an apparent increase in the unadjusted data turns out to be a decrease when adjusted for the usual seasonal pattern.

The statistical method used to achieve the seasonal adjustment may vary from one data set to another. Many of the data are adjusted by a computer method known as X-12-ARIMA, developed by the Bureau of the Census. A description of the method is found in "New Capabilities and Methods of the X-12-ARIMA Seasonal Adjustment Program," David F. Findley, Brian C. Monsell, William R. Bell, Mark C. Otto and Bor-Chung Chen, *Journal of Business and Economic Statistics*, April 1998. A preprint version of this article can be downloaded from the Bureau of the Census Web site.

Data that are presented at *annual rates* show values at their annual equivalents—the values that would be registered if the rate of activity measured during a particular month or quarter were maintained for a full year. In other words, seasonally adjusted monthly values have been multiplied by 12 and quarterly values by four to yield annual rates.

Detail may not add to totals due to rounding. Annual data are typically calculated by source agencies as the annual totals or averages of not-seasonally-adjusted data. Seasonal adjustment procedures are typically multiplicative rather than additive, and for this reason, seasonally adjusted data may not add or average to the annual figure.

Most of the data in this volume are from federal government sources and may be reproduced freely. A few series are from private sources and are used with permission; further use may be subject to copyright restrictions. A list of data sources is shown below.

The tables in this volume incorporate data revisions and corrections released by the source agencies through November 2003, with the exception of profits by industry, some monetary series, and energy per dollar of GDP, where later revisions could be incorporated.

Data Sources

Most of the data in this volume are from the government agencies and private sources listed below. The specific source(s) for each individual data set is identified at the beginning of the Notes and Definitions for the relevant data pages.

Board of Governors of the Federal Reserve System
Washington, DC 20551

Data Inquiries and Publication Sales:
  Publications Services
  Mail Stop 127
  Board of Governors of the
  Federal Reserve System
  Washington, DC 20551
  Telephone: (202) 452-3244 or 3245

Monthly Publication:
  Federal Reserve Bulletin

Internet Address:
  http://www.federalreserve.gov/

Bureau of the Census
U.S. Department of Commerce
Washington, DC 20233

Internet Address:
  http://www.census.gov

Ordering data products:
  Call Center: 301-763-INFO (4636)
E-mail questions:
  webmaster@census.gov
E-sales: <ProductCatalog>

Bureau of Economic Analysis
U.S. Department of Commerce
Washington, DC 20230

Data Inquiries:
  Public Information Office:
  (202) 606-9900

Monthly Publication:
  Survey of Current Business
  Available by subscription. Call 202-512-1800 or go to
  <bookstore.gpo.gov>.

Internet Address:
  http://www.bea.gov

Bureau of Labor Statistics
U.S. Department of Labor
2 Massachusetts Ave., NE
Washington, DC 20212-0001
(202) 691-5200

Internet Address:
  http://www.bls.gov

Data Inquiries:
  Blsdata_staff@bls.gov

Monthly Publications:
  Monthly Labor Review
  Employment and Earnings
  Compensation and Working Conditions
  Producer Price Indexes
  CPI Detailed Report
  Available by subscription from the Superintendent of
  Documents (see address below)

Conference Board, The
845 Third Avenue
New York, NY 10022

Internet Address:
  http://www.tcb-indicators.org

Monthly Publication:
  Business Cycle Indicators Report

Employment and Training Administration
U.S. Department of Labor
200 Constitution Ave., NW
Washington, DC 20210
1-877-US-2JOBS

Internet Address:
  http://www.doleta.gov
  http://www.itsc.state.md.us

Energy Information Administration
U.S. Department of Energy
1000 Independence Ave., SW
Washington, DC 20585

Data Inquiries and Publications:
National Energy Information Center
Phone: (202) 586-8800
Email: infoctr@eia.doe.gov

Monthly Publication:
  Monthly Energy Review

Internet Address:
  http://www.eia.doe.gov

National Agricultural Statistics Service
U.S. Department of Agriculture
14th St. & Independence Ave., SW
Washington, DC 20250

Data Inquiries:
  Information Hotline: (800) 727-9540 or 202-720-3878

Publication Sales:
  Telephone: (800) 999-6779
  Fax: (703) 834-0110

Internet Address:
  http://www.usda.gov/nass/

To order government publications:
Superintendent of Documents
Government Printing Office
Washington, DC 20402
(202) 512-1800

PART A

THE U.S. ECONOMY

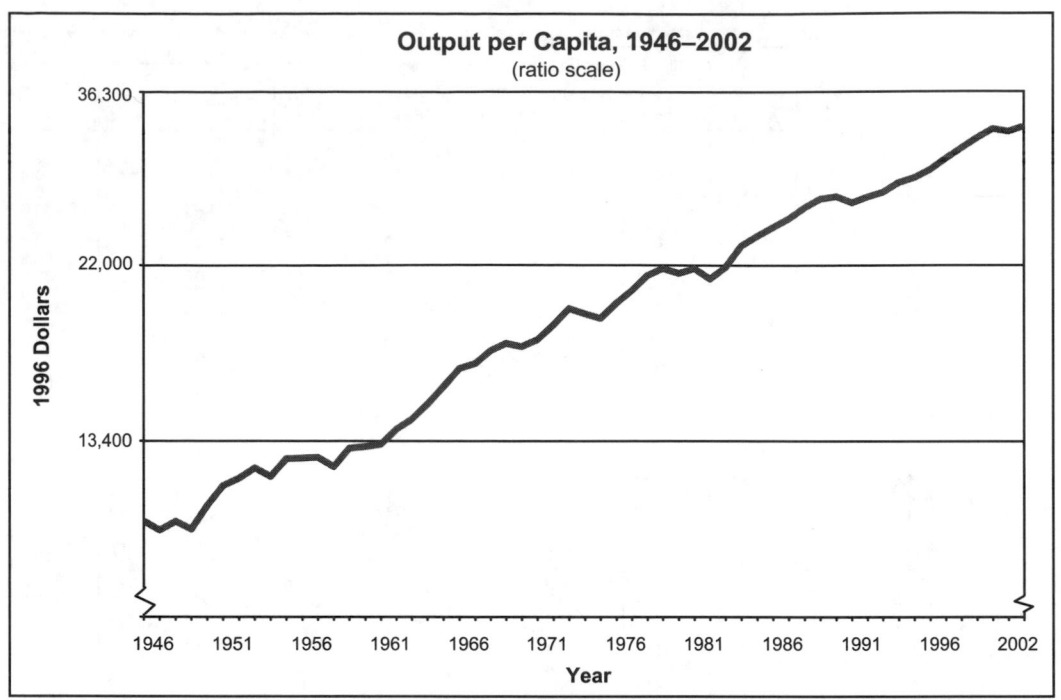

Output per Capita, 1946–2002
(ratio scale)

- Output of goods and services in the United States, expressed in constant 1996-value dollars to remove the effect of inflation (real Gross Domestic Product, or GDP), rose from $1.56 trillion in 1948 to $9.19 trillion in 2000—those two years being comparable high points in the business cycle. (Table 1-2) This nearly sixfold increase in real value over the 52-year period results from an average growth rate of 3.5 percent per year.

- Over the same period population nearly doubled, growing at a rate of 1.3 percent per year. As a result, real GDP per capita—the average value of production for each man, woman, and child in the population—rose at a rate of 2.2 percent per year, from $10,639 (1996 dollars) in 1948 to $32,579 in 2000. (Table 1-10) This value is charted in the graph above. It is graphed on a "ratio scale" so that equal vertical distances signify equal percent changes.

- As the graph indicates, growth is not always smooth or uninterrupted. There are periods of leveling-off or decline, marking the periods identified as recessions in economic activity. (Table 1-11 and the associated Notes and Definitions)

- Measured in current dollars, the value of GDP rose even faster, reflecting increases in the average price level. Current-dollar GDP rose from $270 billion in 1948 to nearly $10 trillion in 2000 (Table 1-1). The price level in 2000 was more than six times that in 1948, reflecting an average inflation rate of 3.6 percent per year. (Table 1-4) Annual rates of increase in the chain-type price index for GDP ranged from 9 percent or more in 1947, 1974–1975, and 1980–1981 to changes of no more than 1.1 percent in 1949–1950, 1954, 1959, 1961, 1963, and 2002. Over the latest 10 years, inflation averaged only 1.9 percent.

- Income shares have changed markedly over the postwar period. Farm proprietors' share of national income dropped from 7.8 percent in 1948—a year when American food was still providing relief for war-ravaged economies—to less than 1 percent in 2000. The share of capital income, other than rental, rose from 14.9 percent to 17.6 percent, with the interest portion rising sharply while the profits portion declined. "Rental" income of persons declined slightly, despite the increase in rent imputed to homeowners that is included in this item of national income. Labor compensation rose from 63.6 percent of national income in 1948 to 71.7 percent in 2000. (Table 1-8)

Table 1-1. Gross Domestic Product

(Billions of dollars, quarterly data are at seasonally adjusted annual rates.)

Year and quarter	Gross domestic product	Personal consumption expenditures	Gross private domestic investment					Exports and imports of goods and services			Government consumption expenditures and gross investment		
			Total	Fixed investment		Change in private inventories		Net exports	Exports	Imports	Total	Federal	State and local
				Nonresidential	Residential	Nonfarm	Farm						
1946	222.3	144.2	31.1	17.3	7.8	6.2	-0.2	7.1	14.1	7.0	39.8	29.0	10.8
1947	244.4	162.3	35.0	23.5	12.1	1.2	-1.8	10.8	18.7	7.9	36.4	22.6	13.9
1948	269.6	175.4	48.1	26.8	15.6	3.0	2.7	5.4	15.5	10.1	40.6	24.2	16.5
1949	267.7	178.8	36.9	24.9	14.6	-2.1	-0.6	5.2	14.4	9.2	46.8	27.6	19.2
1950	294.3	192.7	54.1	27.8	20.5	5.9	-0.1	0.7	12.3	11.6	46.9	26.0	20.9
1951	339.5	208.6	60.2	31.8	18.4	8.9	1.0	2.4	17.0	14.6	68.3	45.0	23.3
1952	358.6	219.7	54.0	31.9	18.6	2.1	1.4	1.0	16.3	15.3	83.9	59.2	24.7
1953	379.9	233.4	56.4	35.1	19.4	1.2	0.7	-0.8	15.2	16.0	90.8	64.4	26.4
1954	381.1	240.5	53.8	34.7	21.1	-2.1	0.2	0.3	15.7	15.4	86.5	57.3	29.2
1955	415.2	259.0	69.0	39.0	25.0	5.6	-0.6	0.4	17.6	17.2	86.8	54.9	31.9
1956	438.0	271.9	72.0	44.5	23.6	4.9	-1.0	2.3	21.2	18.9	91.8	56.7	35.1
1957	461.5	287.0	70.5	47.5	22.2	0.7	0.1	4.0	23.9	19.9	100.1	61.3	38.8
1958	467.9	296.6	64.5	42.5	22.3	-2.3	2.0	0.4	20.4	20.0	106.5	63.9	42.6
1959	507.4	318.1	78.5	46.5	28.1	5.5	-1.6	-1.7	20.6	22.3	112.5	67.4	45.1
1960	527.4	332.3	78.9	49.4	26.3	2.7	0.6	2.4	25.3	22.8	113.8	65.9	47.9
1961	545.7	342.7	78.2	48.8	26.4	2.1	0.9	3.4	26.0	22.7	121.5	69.5	52.0
1962	586.5	363.8	88.1	53.1	29.0	5.5	0.6	2.4	27.4	25.0	132.2	76.9	55.3
1963	618.7	383.1	93.8	56.0	32.1	5.1	0.5	3.3	29.4	26.1	138.5	78.5	59.9
1964	664.4	411.7	102.1	63.0	34.3	6.0	-1.2	5.5	33.6	28.1	145.1	79.8	65.3
1965	720.1	444.3	118.2	74.8	34.2	8.4	0.8	3.9	35.4	31.5	153.7	82.1	71.6
1966	780.3	481.8	131.3	85.4	32.3	14.1	-0.5	1.9	38.9	37.1	174.3	94.4	79.9
1967	834.1	508.7	128.6	86.4	32.4	9.0	0.9	1.4	41.4	39.9	195.3	106.8	88.6
1968	911.5	558.7	141.2	93.4	38.7	7.7	1.4	-1.3	45.3	46.6	212.8	114.0	98.8
1969	985.3	605.5	156.4	104.7	42.6	9.2	0.0	-1.2	49.3	50.5	224.6	116.1	108.5
1970	1 039.7	648.9	152.4	109.0	41.4	2.8	-0.8	1.2	57.0	55.8	237.1	116.4	120.7
1971	1 128.6	702.4	178.2	114.1	55.8	6.6	1.7	-3.0	59.3	62.3	251.0	117.6	133.5
1972	1 240.4	770.7	207.6	128.8	69.7	8.8	0.3	-8.0	66.2	74.2	270.1	125.6	144.4
1973	1 385.5	852.5	244.5	153.3	75.3	14.4	1.5	0.6	91.8	91.2	287.9	127.8	160.1
1974	1 501.0	932.4	249.4	169.5	66.0	16.8	-2.8	-3.1	124.3	127.5	322.4	138.2	184.2
1975	1 635.2	1 030.3	230.2	173.7	62.7	-9.6	3.4	13.6	136.3	122.7	361.1	152.1	209.0
1976	1 823.9	1 149.8	292.0	192.4	82.5	18.0	-0.8	-2.3	148.9	151.1	384.5	160.6	223.9
1977	2 031.4	1 278.4	361.3	228.7	110.3	17.8	4.5	-23.7	158.8	182.4	415.3	176.0	239.3
1978	2 295.9	1 430.4	436.0	278.6	131.6	24.4	1.4	-26.1	186.1	212.3	455.6	191.9	263.8
1979	2 566.4	1 596.3	490.6	331.6	141.0	14.4	3.6	-24.0	228.7	252.7	503.5	211.6	291.8
1980	2 795.6	1 762.9	477.9	360.9	123.2	-0.2	-6.1	-14.9	278.9	293.8	569.7	245.3	324.4
1981	3 131.3	1 944.2	570.8	418.4	122.6	21.0	8.8	-15.0	302.8	317.8	631.4	281.8	349.6
1982	3 259.2	2 079.3	516.1	425.3	105.7	-20.7	5.8	-20.5	282.6	303.2	684.4	312.8	371.6
1983	3 534.9	2 286.4	564.2	417.4	152.5	9.0	-15.4	-51.7	277.0	328.6	735.5	644.4	391.6
1984	3 932.7	2 498.4	735.5	490.3	179.8	59.7	5.7	-102.0	303.1	405.1	800.8	376.4	424.4
1985	4 213.0	2 712.6	736.3	527.6	186.9	16.1	5.8	-114.2	303.0	417.2	878.3	413.4	464.9
1986	4 452.9	2 895.2	747.2	522.5	218.1	8.0	-1.5	-131.9	320.3	452.2	942.3	438.7	503.6
1987	4 742.5	3 105.3	781.5	526.7	227.6	33.6	-6.4	-142.3	365.6	507.9	997.9	460.4	537.5
1988	5 108.3	3 356.6	821.1	568.4	234.2	30.4	-11.9	-106.3	446.9	553.2	1 036.9	462.6	574.3
1989	5 489.1	3 596.7	872.9	613.4	231.8	27.7	0.0	-80.7	509.0	589.7	1 100.2	482.6	617.7
1990	5 803.2	3 831.5	861.7	630.3	216.8	12.2	2.4	-71.4	557.2	628.6	1 181.4	508.4	673.0
1991	5 986.2	3 971.2	800.2	608.9	191.5	0.9	-1.1	-20.7	601.6	622.3	1 235.5	527.4	708.1
1992	6 318.9	4 209.7	866.6	626.1	225.5	10.1	5.0	-27.9	636.8	664.6	1 270.5	534.5	736.0
1993	6 642.3	4 454.7	955.1	682.2	251.8	27.0	-5.9	-60.5	658.0	718.5	1 293.0	527.3	765.7
1994	7 054.3	4 716.4	1 097.1	748.6	286.0	51.8	10.8	-87.1	725.1	812.1	1 327.9	521.1	806.8
1995	7 400.5	4 969.0	1 143.8	825.1	285.6	42.2	-9.2	-84.3	818.6	902.8	1 372.0	521.5	850.5
1996	7 813.2	5 237.5	1 242.7	899.4	313.3	22.1	7.9	-89.0	874.2	963.1	1 421.9	531.6	890.4
1997	8 318.4	5 529.3	1 390.5	999.4	328.2	59.9	2.9	-89.3	966.4	1 055.8	1 487.9	538.2	949.7
1998	8 781.5	5 856.0	1 538.7	1 101.2	364.4	72.3	0.9	-151.7	964.9	1 116.7	1 538.5	539.2	999.3
1999	9 274.3	6 246.5	1 636.7	1 173.5	403.7	61.1	-1.5	-249.9	989.3	1 239.2	1 641.0	565.0	1 076.0
2000	9 824.6	6 683.7	1 755.4	1 265.8	426.0	65.8	-2.2	-365.5	1 101.1	1 466.6	1 751.0	589.2	1 161.8
2001	10 082.2	6 987.0	1 586.0	1 201.6	444.8	-61.9	1.6	-348.9	1 034.1	1 383.0	1 858.0	628.1	1 229.9
2002	10 446.2	7 303.7	1 593.2	1 117.4	471.9	3.4	0.5	-423.6	1 014.9	1 438.5	1 972.9	693.7	1 279.2
2000													
1st quarter	9 649.5	6 552.2	1 711.4	1 236.6	428.0	58.7	-11.9	-330.6	1 055.9	1 386.5	1 716.5	575.7	1 140.8
2nd quarter	9 820.7	6 638.7	1 786.3	1 268.3	428.8	86.9	2.3	-353.2	1 098.0	1 451.1	1 748.8	598.5	1 150.3
3rd quarter	9 874.8	6 736.1	1 766.4	1 283.4	421.8	63.0	-1.9	-384.9	1 130.9	1 515.8	1 757.2	589.7	1 167.4
4th quarter	9 953.6	6 808.0	1 757.4	1 274.8	425.6	54.4	2.6	-393.2	1 119.8	1 513.0	1 781.4	592.9	1 188.5
2001													
1st quarter	10 028.1	6 904.7	1 671.1	1 258.3	440.0	-31.9	4.7	-372.7	1 100.0	1 472.8	1 825.0	613.3	1 211.7
2nd quarter	10 049.9	6 959.8	1 597.2	1 210.0	444.2	-54.1	-3.0	-365.7	1 059.7	1 425.3	1 858.5	624.8	1 233.7
3rd quarter	10 097.7	6 983.7	1 574.9	1 188.1	447.4	-62.3	1.8	-312.6	1 005.8	1 318.4	1 851.7	627.4	1 224.3
4th quarter	10 152.9	7 099.9	1 500.7	1 149.8	447.4	-99.5	3.0	-344.5	971.1	1 315.6	1 896.8	646.9	1 249.8
2002													
1st quarter	10 313.1	7 174.2	1 559.4	1 126.8	462.6	-35.3	5.3	-360.1	977.5	1 337.5	1 939.5	672.0	1 267.5
2nd quarter	10 376.9	7 254.7	1 588.0	1 115.8	468.7	3.0	0.4	-425.6	1 018.1	1 443.7	1 959.8	688.2	1 271.6
3rd quarter	10 506.2	7 360.7	1 597.3	1 109.8	469.9	19.8	-2.3	-432.9	1 038.6	1 471.5	1 981.1	697.7	1 283.3
4th quarter	10 588.8	7 425.4	1 628.1	1 117.1	486.5	26.0	-1.5	-476.0	1 025.4	1 501.4	2 011.3	716.9	1 294.4

Table 1-2. Real Gross Domestic Product

(Billions of chained [1996] dollars, quarterly data are at seasonally adjusted annual rates.)

Year and quarter	Gross domestic product	Personal consumption expenditures	Gross private domestic investment						Exports and imports of goods and services			Government consumption expenditures and gross investment		
			Total	Fixed investment		Change in private inventories			Net exports	Exports	Imports	Total	Federal	State and local
				Nonresidential	Residential	Nonfarm	Farm							
1946	1 505.5	956.9	175.0	...	...	29.1	-0.6	...	66.5	49.1	359.7	...	...
1947	1 495.1	976.4	168.6	...	...	4.0	-4.9	...	75.9	46.6	307.1	...	...
1948	1 560.0	998.1	215.3	...	...	11.4	6.9	...	59.8	54.4	328.9	...	...
1949	1 550.9	1 025.3	164.3	...	...	-7.9	-2.1	...	59.2	52.5	367.3	...	...
1950	1 686.6	1 090.9	232.5	...	...	20.9	-0.6	...	51.8	62.0	367.4	...	...
1951	1 815.1	1 107.1	233.2	...	...	26.0	1.5	...	63.5	64.5	500.0	...	...
1952	1 887.3	1 142.4	211.1	...	...	6.8	3.2	...	60.6	70.1	605.1	...	...
1953	1 973.9	1 197.2	221.0	...	...	4.1	2.0	...	56.5	76.7	647.5	...	...
1954	1 960.5	1 221.9	210.8	...	...	-6.9	0.3	...	59.3	72.9	602.9	...	...
1955	2 099.5	1 310.4	262.1	...	...	17.1	-1.9	...	65.6	81.7	580.4	...	...
1956	2 141.1	1 348.8	258.6	...	...	14.3	-3.2	...	76.5	88.4	580.8	...	...
1957	2 183.9	1 381.8	247.4	...	...	2.2	0.7	...	83.1	92.1	606.7	...	...
1958	2 162.8	1 393.0	226.5	...	...	-7.1	5.7	...	71.8	96.4	626.2	...	...
1959	2 319.0	1 470.7	272.9	...	...	18.1	-4.7	...	72.4	106.6	661.4	...	...
1960	2 376.7	1 510.8	272.8	...	...	8.8	1.8	...	87.5	108.0	661.3	...	...
1961	2 432.0	1 541.2	271.0	...	...	7.0	2.2	...	88.9	107.3	693.2	...	...
1962	2 578.9	1 617.3	305.3	...	...	18.4	1.3	...	93.7	119.5	735.0	...	...
1963	2 690.4	1 684.0	325.7	...	...	17.1	1.3	...	100.7	122.7	752.4	...	...
1964	2 846.5	1 784.8	352.6	...	...	20.0	-4.2	...	114.2	129.2	767.1	...	...
1965	3 028.5	1 897.6	402.0	...	...	27.7	2.7	...	116.5	142.9	791.1	...	...
1966	3 227.5	2 000.1	437.3	...	...	45.8	-1.6	...	124.3	164.2	862.1	...	...
1967	3 308.3	2 066.2	417.2	...	...	28.8	2.9	...	127.0	176.2	927.1	...	...
1968	3 466.1	2 184.2	441.3	...	...	24.1	3.9	...	136.3	202.4	956.6	...	...
1969	3 571.4	2 264.8	466.9	...	...	28.2	-0.1	...	143.7	213.9	952.5	...	...
1970	3 578.0	2 317.5	436.2	...	...	8.3	-3.0	...	159.3	223.1	931.1	...	...
1971	3 697.7	2 405.2	485.8	...	...	19.1	4.3	...	160.4	235.0	913.8	...	...
1972	3 898.4	2 550.5	543.0	...	...	24.7	0.2	...	173.5	261.3	914.9	...	...
1973	4 123.4	2 675.9	606.5	...	...	37.3	0.9	...	211.4	273.4	908.3	...	...
1974	4 099.0	2 653.7	561.7	...	...	35.4	-5.3	...	231.6	267.2	924.8	...	...
1975	4 084.4	2 710.9	462.2	...	...	-19.4	6.8	...	230.0	237.5	942.5	...	...
1976	4 311.7	2 868.9	555.5	...	...	34.6	-0.8	...	243.6	284.0	943.3	...	...
1977	4 511.8	2 992.1	639.4	...	...	32.5	7.6	...	249.7	315.0	952.7	...	...
1978	4 760.6	3 124.7	713.0	...	...	41.7	3.1	...	275.9	342.3	982.2	...	...
1979	4 912.1	3 203.2	735.4	...	...	21.7	4.0	...	302.4	347.9	1 001.1	...	...
1980	4 900.9	3 193.0	655.3	...	...	0.3	-8.2	...	334.8	324.8	1 020.9	...	...
1981	5 021.0	3 236.0	715.6	...	...	25.9	10.6	...	338.6	333.4	1 030.0	...	...
1982	4 919.3	3 275.5	615.2	...	...	-24.6	8.4	...	314.6	329.2	1 046.0	...	...
1983	5 132.3	3 454.3	673.7	...	...	11.1	-18.9	...	306.9	370.7	1 081.0	...	...
1984	5 505.2	3 640.6	871.5	...	...	68.7	7.5	...	332.6	461.0	1 118.4	...	...
1985	5 717.1	3 820.9	863.4	...	...	18.6	8.3	...	341.6	490.7	1 190.5	...	...
1986	5 912.4	3 981.2	857.7	...	...	10.8	-1.4	...	366.8	531.9	1 255.2	...	...
1987	6 113.3	4 113.4	879.3	572.5	290.7	38.7	-9.8	-156.2	408.0	564.2	1 292.5	597.8	695.6
1988	6 368.4	4 279.5	902.8	603.6	289.2	33.7	-14.2	-112.1	473.5	585.6	1 307.5	586.9	721.4
1989	6 591.8	4 393.7	936.5	637.0	277.3	29.9	0.1	-79.4	529.4	608.8	1 343.5	594.7	749.5
1990	6 707.9	4 474.5	907.3	641.7	253.5	13.8	2.6	-56.5	575.7	632.2	1 387.3	606.8	781.1
1991	6 676.4	4 466.6	829.5	610.1	221.1	1.4	-2.3	-15.8	613.2	629.0	1 403.4	604.9	798.9
1992	6 880.0	4 594.5	899.8	630.6	257.2	10.7	6.1	-19.8	651.0	670.8	1 410.0	595.1	815.3
1993	7 062.6	4 748.9	977.9	683.6	276.0	28.6	-7.9	-59.1	672.7	731.8	1 398.8	572.0	827.0
1994	7 347.7	4 928.1	1 107.0	744.6	302.7	53.6	13.0	-86.5	732.8	819.4	1 400.1	551.3	848.9
1995	7 543.8	5 075.6	1 140.6	817.5	291.7	42.6	-12.3	-78.4	808.2	886.6	1 406.4	536.5	869.9
1996	7 813.2	5 237.5	1 242.7	899.4	313.3	22.1	7.9	-89.0	874.2	963.1	1 421.9	531.6	890.4
1997	8 159.5	5 423.9	1 393.3	1 009.3	319.7	60.6	3.2	-113.3	981.5	1 094.8	1 455.4	529.6	925.8
1998	8 508.9	5 683.7	1 558.0	1 135.9	345.1	75.0	1.6	-221.1	1 002.4	1 223.5	1 483.3	525.4	957.7
1999	8 859.0	5 964.5	1 660.5	1 228.4	368.3	64.1	-2.0	-320.5	1 036.3	1 356.8	1 540.6	537.7	1 002.4
2000	9 191.4	6 223.9	1 762.9	1 324.2	372.4	67.2	-2.5	-398.8	1 137.2	1 536.0	1 582.5	544.4	1 037.4
2001	9 214.5	6 377.2	1 574.6	1 255.1	373.5	-63.2	2.0	-415.9	1 076.1	1 492.0	1 640.4	570.6	1 069.4
2002	9 439.9	6 576.0	1 589.6	1 183.4	388.2	4.1	1.1	-488.5	1 058.8	1 547.4	1 712.8	613.3	1 099.7
2000														
1st quarter	9 097.4	6 151.9	1 727.8	1 297.1	379.1	58.9	-14.0	-368.8	1 095.8	1 464.6	1 568.3	533.8	1 033.8
2nd quarter	9 205.7	6 198.2	1 798.1	1 329.1	376.2	88.6	2.8	-394.6	1 133.9	1 528.5	1 586.1	554.0	1 031.8
3rd quarter	9 218.7	6 256.8	1 770.3	1 340.7	367.2	64.6	-1.9	-413.1	1 165.5	1 578.6	1 582.2	543.7	1 037.8
4th quarter	9 243.8	6 288.8	1 755.2	1 329.9	367.2	56.8	3.0	-418.5	1 153.7	1 572.2	1 593.4	546.4	1 046.3
2001														
1st quarter	9 229.9	6 326.0	1 661.8	1 311.4	374.5	-32.6	5.8	-404.5	1 135.8	1 540.3	1 615.7	559.0	1 056.2
2nd quarter	9 193.1	6 348.0	1 583.5	1 261.0	374.0	-54.9	-3.3	-414.8	1 098.8	1 513.6	1 638.0	567.2	1 070.2
3rd quarter	9 186.4	6 370.9	1 562.7	1 241.7	374.3	-63.6	2.0	-419.0	1 048.0	1 467.0	1 633.3	568.9	1 064.1
4th quarter	9 248.8	6 464.0	1 490.3	1 206.4	371.0	-101.5	3.6	-425.3	1 021.8	1 447.2	1 674.5	587.2	1 087.1
2002														
1st quarter	9 363.2	6 513.8	1 554.0	1 188.4	383.6	-35.1	6.4	-446.6	1 030.6	1 477.1	1 697.3	597.8	1 099.3
2nd quarter	9 392.4	6 542.4	1 583.9	1 181.1	386.1	4.2	0.8	-487.4	1 065.5	1 552.9	1 703.3	608.7	1 094.7
3rd quarter	9 485.6	6 609.9	1 598.0	1 178.7	387.1	20.8	-2.2	-488.0	1 077.7	1 565.7	1 715.6	615.1	1 100.6
4th quarter	9 518.2	6 637.9	1 622.4	1 185.3	395.9	26.5	-0.8	-532.2	1 061.6	1 593.8	1 735.0	631.4	1 104.0

. . . = Not available.

Table 1-3. Chain-Type Quantity Indexes for Gross Domestic Product and Domestic Purchases

(Index numbers, 1996 = 100.)

Year and quarter	Gross domestic product	Personal consumption expenditures		Private fixed investment			Exports and imports of goods and services		Government consumption expenditures and gross investment			Gross domestic purchases
		Total	Excluding food and energy	Total	Nonresidential	Residential	Exports	Imports	Total	Federal	State and local	
1946	19.3	18.3	14.1	12.7	10.5	20.7	7.6	5.1	25.3	42.9	13.5	18.9
1947	19.1	18.6	14.7	15.2	12.2	26.7	8.7	4.8	21.6	31.9	15.4	18.5
1948	20.0	19.1	15.3	16.8	12.8	31.9	6.8	5.7	23.1	34.3	16.4	19.8
1949	19.9	19.6	15.8	15.3	11.7	29.5	6.8	5.5	25.8	37.5	18.9	19.7
1950	21.6	20.8	17.1	18.3	12.7	40.3	5.9	6.4	25.8	35.3	20.5	21.7
1951	23.2	21.1	17.2	17.5	13.3	33.8	7.3	6.7	35.2	58.4	20.6	23.2
1952	24.2	21.8	17.7	17.2	13.1	33.2	6.9	7.3	42.6	76.7	20.9	24.2
1953	25.3	22.9	18.7	18.4	14.2	34.3	6.5	8.0	45.5	82.7	22.0	25.5
1954	25.1	23.3	19.0	18.7	13.9	37.2	6.8	7.6	42.4	71.8	23.9	25.2
1955	26.9	25.0	20.6	21.2	15.5	43.2	7.5	8.5	40.8	65.1	25.6	27.1
1956	27.4	25.8	21.1	21.2	16.4	39.7	8.8	9.2	40.9	64.0	26.4	27.5
1957	28.0	26.4	21.7	21.0	16.6	37.3	9.5	9.6	42.7	66.3	28.0	28.0
1958	27.7	26.6	21.8	19.5	14.8	37.7	8.2	10.0	44.0	66.2	30.3	28.0
1959	29.7	28.1	23.2	22.2	15.9	47.3	8.3	11.1	46.5	70.9	31.4	30.1
1960	30.4	28.9	24.1	22.4	16.8	43.9	10.0	11.2	46.5	68.8	32.8	30.6
1961	31.1	29.4	24.6	22.3	16.7	44.0	10.2	11.1	48.8	71.5	34.8	31.3
1962	33.0	30.9	26.2	24.3	18.2	48.2	10.7	12.4	51.7	77.4	35.9	33.2
1963	34.4	32.2	27.5	26.2	19.2	53.9	11.5	12.7	52.9	77.2	38.0	34.6
1964	36.4	34.1	29.4	28.7	21.5	57.1	13.1	13.4	54.0	75.9	40.6	36.5
1965	38.8	36.2	31.4	31.7	25.2	55.4	13.3	14.8	55.6	76.0	43.3	39.0
1966	41.3	38.3	33.3	33.5	28.4	50.4	14.2	17.1	60.6	84.6	46.1	41.7
1967	42.3	39.5	34.5	32.8	28.0	48.8	14.5	18.3	65.2	92.8	48.4	42.8
1968	44.4	41.7	36.6	35.1	29.2	55.5	15.6	21.0	67.3	93.7	51.2	45.0
1969	45.7	43.2	38.0	37.3	31.4	57.1	16.4	22.2	67.0	90.6	52.7	46.4
1970	45.8	44.3	38.7	36.5	31.2	53.7	18.2	23.2	65.5	84.2	54.2	46.3
1971	47.3	45.9	40.6	39.3	31.2	68.5	18.4	24.4	64.3	78.2	56.0	48.0
1972	49.9	48.7	43.4	44.0	34.0	80.6	19.8	27.1	64.3	76.5	57.2	50.7
1973	52.8	51.1	46.1	48.0	39.0	80.1	24.2	28.4	63.9	72.8	58.8	53.1
1974	52.5	50.7	46.0	45.0	39.3	63.6	26.5	27.8	65.0	72.5	61.0	52.4
1975	52.3	51.8	46.9	40.1	35.4	55.3	26.3	24.7	66.3	72.5	63.0	51.7
1976	55.2	54.8	49.8	44.1	37.1	68.3	27.9	29.5	66.3	71.6	63.6	55.1
1977	57.8	57.1	52.3	50.4	41.3	83.0	28.6	32.7	67.0	72.9	63.9	58.0
1978	60.9	59.7	55.2	56.2	47.2	88.3	31.6	35.5	69.1	74.8	66.1	61.2
1979	62.9	61.2	56.9	59.4	51.9	85.0	34.6	36.1	70.4	76.6	67.1	62.7
1980	62.7	61.0	56.9	55.6	51.9	67.1	38.3	33.7	71.8	80.3	67.1	61.6
1981	64.3	61.8	58.1	56.8	54.8	61.7	38.7	34.6	72.4	84.1	65.8	63.2
1982	63.0	62.5	58.8	52.8	52.7	50.5	36.0	34.2	73.6	87.1	65.7	62.2
1983	65.7	66.0	62.6	56.8	52.2	71.2	35.1	38.5	76.0	92.6	66.2	65.7
1984	70.5	69.5	66.7	66.3	61.4	81.6	38.1	47.9	78.7	95.5	68.7	71.5
1985	73.2	73.0	70.6	69.8	65.5	82.7	39.1	51.0	83.7	102.8	72.4	74.5
1986	75.7	76.0	74.0	70.6	63.7	92.6	42.0	55.2	88.3	108.5	76.3	77.2
1987	78.2	78.5	76.8	70.6	63.7	92.8	46.7	58.6	90.9	112.5	78.1	79.6
1988	81.5	81.7	80.0	73.2	67.1	92.3	54.2	60.8	92.0	110.4	81.0	82.1
1989	84.4	83.9	82.3	75.1	70.8	88.5	60.6	63.2	94.5	111.9	84.2	84.5
1990	85.9	85.4	84.0	73.8	71.4	80.9	65.9	65.6	97.6	114.2	87.7	85.6
1991	85.5	85.3	83.8	68.7	67.8	70.6	70.2	65.3	98.7	113.8	89.7	84.6
1992	88.1	87.7	86.7	73.1	70.1	82.1	74.5	69.6	99.2	112.0	91.6	87.3
1993	90.4	90.7	89.7	79.0	76.0	88.1	77.0	76.0	98.4	107.6	92.9	90.1
1994	94.0	94.1	93.4	86.3	82.8	96.6	83.8	85.1	98.5	103.7	95.3	94.1
1995	96.6	96.9	96.5	91.5	90.9	93.1	92.5	92.1	98.9	100.9	97.7	96.5
1996	100.0	100.0	100.0	100.0	100.0	100.0	100.0	100.0	100.0	100.0	100.0	100.0
1997	104.4	103.6	104.2	109.6	112.2	102.0	112.3	113.7	102.4	99.6	104.0	104.7
1998	108.9	108.5	109.7	122.0	126.3	110.2	114.7	127.0	104.3	98.8	107.6	110.4
1999	113.4	113.9	115.6	131.5	136.6	117.6	118.6	140.9	108.3	101.2	112.6	115.9
2000	117.6	118.8	120.9	139.5	147.2	118.9	130.1	159.5	111.3	102.4	116.5	121.0
2001	117.9	121.8	124.4	134.2	139.6	119.2	123.1	154.9	115.4	107.3	120.1	121.5
2002	120.8	125.6	128.6	130.1	131.6	123.9	121.1	160.7	120.5	115.4	123.5	125.2
2000												
1st quarter	116.4	117.5	119.6	138.0	144.2	121.0	125.4	152.1	110.3	100.4	116.1	119.5
2nd quarter	117.8	118.3	120.2	140.3	147.8	120.1	129.7	158.7	111.6	104.2	115.9	121.1
3rd quarter	118.0	119.5	121.6	140.3	149.1	117.2	133.3	163.9	111.3	102.3	116.6	121.5
4th quarter	118.3	120.1	122.1	139.5	147.9	117.2	132.0	163.2	112.1	102.8	117.5	121.9
2001												
1st quarter	118.1	120.8	122.9	138.7	145.8	119.6	129.9	159.9	113.6	105.2	118.6	121.6
2nd quarter	117.7	121.2	123.8	134.7	140.2	119.4	125.7	157.2	115.2	106.7	120.2	121.2
3rd quarter	117.6	121.6	124.4	133.2	138.1	119.5	119.9	152.3	114.9	107.0	119.5	121.2
4th quarter	118.4	123.4	126.6	130.2	134.1	118.4	116.9	150.3	117.8	110.5	122.1	122.1
2002												
1st quarter	119.8	124.4	127.2	130.0	132.1	122.4	117.9	153.4	119.4	112.5	123.5	123.7
2nd quarter	120.2	124.9	128.0	129.7	131.3	123.3	121.9	161.2	119.8	114.5	123.0	124.5
3rd quarter	121.4	126.2	129.6	129.6	131.1	123.6	123.3	162.6	120.7	115.7	123.6	125.7
4th quarter	121.8	126.7	129.7	131.0	131.8	126.4	121.4	165.5	122.0	118.8	124.0	126.6

Table 1-4. Chain-Type Price Indexes for Gross Domestic Product and Domestic Purchases

(Index numbers, 1996 = 100.)

Year and quarter	Gross domestic product	Personal consumption expenditures		Private fixed investment			Exports and imports of goods and services		Government consumption expenditures and gross investment			Gross domestic purchases
	Gross domestic product	Total	Excluding food and energy	Total	Nonresidential	Residential	Exports	Imports	Total	Federal	State and local	Gross domestic purchases
1946	14.7	15.1	15.1	16.4	18.4	12.1	21.2	14.2	11.1	12.7	9.0	14.4
1947	16.3	16.6	16.4	19.2	21.4	14.4	24.6	17.0	11.9	13.3	10.1	15.9
1948	17.3	17.6	17.3	20.9	23.2	15.7	25.9	18.5	12.4	13.2	11.3	16.9
1949	17.3	17.4	17.4	21.3	23.8	15.9	24.3	17.6	12.7	13.8	11.4	16.9
1950	17.4	17.7	17.7	21.8	24.3	16.3	23.7	18.7	12.8	13.8	11.5	17.1
1951	18.6	18.9	18.7	23.6	26.6	17.4	26.8	22.6	13.7	14.5	12.7	18.3
1952	19.0	19.2	19.1	24.2	27.2	17.9	27.0	21.8	13.9	14.5	13.2	18.7
1953	19.2	19.5	19.6	24.4	27.4	18.0	26.9	20.9	14.0	14.6	13.5	18.9
1954	19.5	19.7	19.8	24.6	27.7	18.1	26.6	21.2	14.3	15.0	13.7	19.1
1955	19.7	19.8	20.0	25.0	28.0	18.5	26.8	21.1	15.0	15.8	14.0	19.4
1956	20.4	20.2	20.5	26.4	30.2	19.0	27.7	21.4	15.8	16.7	14.9	20.0
1957	21.1	20.8	21.1	27.4	31.8	19.0	28.8	21.7	16.5	17.4	15.6	20.7
1958	21.6	21.3	21.6	27.5	32.0	19.0	28.5	20.8	17.0	18.1	15.8	21.2
1959	21.9	21.6	22.1	27.7	32.4	19.0	28.5	21.0	17.0	17.9	16.1	21.4
1960	22.2	22.0	22.5	27.9	32.6	19.1	28.9	21.2	17.2	18.0	16.4	21.7
1961	22.4	22.2	22.7	27.8	32.4	19.2	29.3	21.2	17.5	18.3	16.8	21.9
1962	22.7	22.5	23.0	27.8	32.4	19.2	29.3	20.9	18.0	18.7	17.3	22.2
1963	23.0	22.8	23.3	27.7	32.4	19.0	29.2	21.3	18.4	19.1	17.7	22.5
1964	23.3	23.1	23.6	27.9	32.6	19.2	29.4	21.8	18.9	19.8	18.1	22.9
1965	23.8	23.4	23.9	28.4	33.0	19.7	30.4	22.1	19.4	20.3	18.6	23.3
1966	24.5	24.0	24.4	29.0	33.5	20.4	31.3	22.6	20.2	21.0	19.5	23.9
1967	25.2	24.6	25.1	29.8	34.4	21.2	32.6	22.7	21.1	21.6	20.6	24.6
1968	26.3	25.6	26.2	31.0	35.6	22.3	33.2	23.0	22.2	22.9	21.7	25.7
1969	27.6	26.7	27.4	32.6	37.1	23.8	34.3	23.6	23.6	24.1	23.1	26.9
1970	29.1	28.0	28.6	34.0	38.8	24.6	35.8	25.0	25.4	26.0	25.0	28.4
1971	30.5	29.2	30.0	35.7	40.7	26.0	37.0	26.5	27.4	28.2	26.8	29.8
1972	31.8	30.2	30.9	37.2	42.1	27.6	38.2	28.4	29.5	30.8	28.4	31.2
1973	33.6	31.9	32.1	39.3	43.7	30.0	43.4	33.3	31.7	33.0	30.6	33.0
1974	36.6	35.1	34.4	43.2	48.0	33.1	53.7	47.7	34.8	35.8	33.9	36.4
1975	40.0	38.0	37.2	48.6	54.6	36.2	59.2	51.7	38.3	39.4	37.3	39.7
1976	42.3	40.1	39.4	51.4	57.6	38.5	61.1	53.2	40.7	42.1	39.5	41.9
1977	45.0	42.7	42.0	55.5	61.5	42.4	63.6	57.9	43.6	45.3	42.1	44.8
1978	48.2	45.8	44.8	60.2	65.7	47.6	67.5	62.0	46.4	48.2	44.8	48.0
1979	52.2	49.8	48.0	65.7	71.1	53.0	75.6	72.6	50.3	51.9	48.8	52.3
1980	57.1	55.2	52.4	71.8	77.4	58.7	83.3	90.5	55.8	57.5	54.3	57.8
1981	62.4	60.1	56.9	78.6	84.9	63.5	89.4	95.3	61.3	63.1	59.7	63.1
1982	66.3	63.5	60.8	82.9	89.7	66.9	89.8	92.1	65.4	67.5	63.6	66.7
1983	68.9	66.2	63.9	82.8	88.9	68.4	90.2	88.7	68.1	70.0	66.4	69.1
1984	71.4	68.6	66.5	83.4	88.8	70.4	91.1	87.9	71.6	74.1	69.4	71.5
1985	73.7	71.0	69.2	84.5	89.6	72.2	88.7	85.0	73.8	75.7	72.1	73.6
1986	75.3	72.7	71.8	86.5	91.2	75.2	87.3	85.0	75.1	76.1	74.1	75.2
1987	77.6	75.5	74.8	88.1	92.0	78.3	89.6	90.0	77.2	77.0	77.3	77.7
1988	80.2	78.4	77.9	90.5	94.2	81.0	94.4	94.5	79.3	78.8	79.6	80.4
1989	83.3	81.9	81.2	92.8	96.3	83.6	96.2	96.9	81.9	81.1	82.4	83.5
1990	86.5	85.6	84.7	94.7	98.2	85.5	96.8	99.4	85.2	83.8	86.2	86.9
1991	89.7	88.9	88.2	96.1	99.8	86.6	98.1	98.9	88.0	87.2	88.6	89.8
1992	91.9	91.6	91.4	96.1	99.3	87.7	97.8	99.1	90.1	89.8	90.3	92.0
1993	94.1	93.8	93.8	97.5	99.8	91.2	97.8	98.2	92.4	92.2	92.6	94.1
1994	96.0	95.7	95.9	98.9	100.5	94.5	98.9	99.1	94.8	94.5	95.0	96.1
1995	98.1	97.9	98.2	100.1	100.9	97.9	101.3	101.8	97.6	97.2	97.8	98.2
1996	100.0	100.0	100.0	100.0	100.0	100.0	100.0	100.0	100.0	100.0	100.0	100.0
1997	102.0	101.9	101.9	99.9	99.0	102.7	98.5	96.4	102.2	101.6	102.6	101.6
1998	103.2	103.0	103.5	99.0	97.0	105.6	96.3	91.3	103.7	102.6	104.4	102.4
1999	104.7	104.7	105.0	98.9	95.5	109.6	95.5	91.3	106.5	105.1	107.3	104.0
2000	106.9	107.4	106.9	100.0	95.6	114.4	96.8	95.5	110.7	108.2	112.0	106.6
2001	109.4	109.6	108.8	101.2	95.7	119.1	96.1	92.7	113.3	110.1	115.0	108.7
2002	110.7	111.1	110.6	100.8	94.4	121.6	95.9	93.0	115.2	113.1	116.3	109.9
2000												
1st quarter	106.1	106.5	106.2	99.5	95.3	112.9	96.4	94.7	109.5	107.9	110.4	105.7
2nd quarter	106.7	107.1	106.7	99.8	95.4	114.0	96.8	95.0	110.3	108.1	111.5	106.3
3rd quarter	107.1	107.7	107.0	100.2	95.7	114.9	97.0	96.0	111.1	108.5	112.5	106.9
4th quarter	107.7	108.3	107.5	100.5	95.9	115.9	97.1	96.3	111.8	108.5	113.6	107.4
2001												
1st quarter	108.7	109.2	108.3	101.0	96.0	117.5	96.9	95.7	113.0	109.7	114.7	108.3
2nd quarter	109.3	109.6	108.6	101.3	96.0	118.8	96.5	94.2	113.5	110.2	115.3	108.8
3rd quarter	109.9	109.6	108.8	101.2	95.7	119.5	96.0	89.9	113.4	110.3	115.1	108.7
4th quarter	109.8	109.8	109.5	101.2	95.3	120.6	95.1	91.0	113.3	110.2	115.0	108.8
2002												
1st quarter	110.1	110.1	109.9	100.8	94.8	120.6	94.9	90.6	114.3	112.4	115.3	109.2
2nd quarter	110.5	110.9	110.4	100.8	94.5	121.4	95.6	93.0	115.1	113.1	116.2	109.8
3rd quarter	110.8	111.4	110.9	100.5	94.2	121.4	96.4	94.1	115.5	113.4	116.6	110.1
4th quarter	111.3	111.9	111.3	101.0	94.3	122.9	96.6	94.3	115.9	113.5	117.2	110.6

Table 1-5. Implicit Price Deflators for Gross Domestic Product

(Index numbers, 1996 = 100.)

Year and quarter	Gross domestic product	Personal consumption expenditures	Private fixed investment			Exports and imports of goods and services		Government consumption expenditures and gross investment		
			Total	Nonresidential	Residential	Exports	Imports	Total	Federal	State and local
1946	14.8	15.1	16.4	18.4	12.1	21.2	14.2	11.1	12.7	9.0
1947	16.4	16.6	19.2	21.4	14.4	24.6	17.0	11.9	13.3	10.1
1948	17.3	17.6	20.9	23.2	15.7	25.9	18.5	12.4	13.3	11.3
1949	17.3	17.4	21.3	23.8	15.9	24.3	17.6	12.7	13.9	11.4
1950	17.5	17.7	21.8	24.3	16.3	23.7	18.7	12.8	13.8	11.5
1951	18.7	18.9	23.6	26.6	17.4	26.8	22.6	13.7	14.5	12.7
1952	19.0	19.2	24.2	27.2	17.9	27.0	21.8	13.9	14.5	13.2
1953	19.3	19.5	24.4	27.4	18.0	26.9	20.9	14.0	14.7	13.5
1954	19.4	19.7	24.6	27.7	18.1	26.6	21.2	14.3	15.0	13.7
1955	19.8	19.8	25.0	28.0	18.5	26.8	21.1	15.0	15.9	14.0
1956	20.5	20.2	26.4	30.2	18.9	27.7	21.4	15.8	16.7	14.9
1957	21.1	20.8	27.4	31.8	19.0	28.8	21.7	16.5	17.4	15.6
1958	21.6	21.3	27.5	32.0	19.0	28.5	20.8	17.0	18.2	15.8
1959	21.9	21.6	27.7	32.4	19.0	28.5	21.0	17.0	17.9	16.1
1960	22.2	22.0	27.9	32.6	19.1	28.9	21.2	17.2	18.0	16.4
1961	22.4	22.2	27.8	32.4	19.2	29.3	21.2	17.5	18.3	16.8
1962	22.7	22.5	27.8	32.4	19.2	29.3	20.9	18.0	18.7	17.3
1963	23.0	22.8	27.7	32.4	19.0	29.2	21.3	18.4	19.2	17.7
1964	23.3	23.1	27.9	32.6	19.2	29.4	21.8	18.9	19.8	18.1
1965	23.8	23.4	28.4	33.0	19.7	30.4	22.1	19.4	20.3	18.6
1966	24.5	24.0	29.0	33.5	20.4	31.3	22.6	20.2	21.0	19.5
1967	25.2	24.6	29.8	34.4	21.2	32.6	22.7	21.1	21.6	20.6
1968	26.3	25.6	31.0	35.6	22.3	33.2	23.0	22.3	22.9	21.7
1969	27.6	26.7	32.6	37.1	23.8	34.3	23.6	23.6	24.1	23.1
1970	29.1	28.0	34.0	38.8	24.6	35.8	25.0	25.5	26.0	25.0
1971	30.5	29.2	35.7	40.7	26.0	37.0	26.5	27.5	28.3	26.8
1972	31.8	30.2	37.2	42.1	27.6	38.2	28.4	29.5	30.9	28.4
1973	33.6	31.9	39.3	43.7	30.0	43.4	33.3	31.7	33.0	30.6
1974	36.6	35.1	43.2	47.9	33.1	53.7	47.7	34.9	35.9	33.9
1975	40.0	38.0	48.6	54.6	36.2	59.2	51.7	38.3	39.5	37.3
1976	42.3	40.1	51.4	57.6	38.5	61.1	53.2	40.8	42.2	39.5
1977	45.0	42.7	55.5	61.5	42.4	63.6	57.9	43.6	45.4	42.1
1978	48.2	45.8	60.2	65.7	47.6	67.5	62.0	46.4	48.2	44.8
1979	52.3	49.8	65.7	71.1	53.0	75.6	72.6	50.3	52.0	48.8
1980	57.0	55.2	71.8	77.4	58.7	83.3	90.5	55.8	57.5	54.3
1981	62.4	60.1	78.6	84.9	63.5	89.4	95.3	61.3	63.1	59.7
1982	66.3	63.5	82.9	89.7	66.9	89.8	92.1	65.4	67.5	63.6
1983	68.9	66.2	82.8	88.9	68.4	90.2	88.7	68.1	70.0	66.4
1984	71.4	68.6	83.4	88.8	70.4	91.1	87.9	71.6	74.1	69.4
1985	73.7	71.0	84.5	89.6	72.2	88.7	85.0	73.8	75.7	72.1
1986	75.3	72.7	86.5	91.2	75.2	87.3	85.0	75.1	76.1	74.1
1987	77.6	75.5	88.1	92.0	78.3	89.6	90.0	77.2	77.0	77.3
1988	80.2	78.4	90.5	94.2	81.0	94.4	94.5	79.3	78.8	79.6
1989	83.3	81.9	92.8	96.3	83.6	96.2	96.9	81.9	81.1	82.4
1990	86.5	85.6	94.7	98.2	85.5	96.8	99.4	85.2	83.8	86.2
1991	89.7	88.9	96.1	99.8	86.6	98.1	98.9	88.0	87.2	88.6
1992	91.8	91.6	96.1	99.3	87.7	97.8	99.1	90.1	89.8	90.3
1993	94.1	93.8	97.5	99.8	91.2	97.8	98.2	92.4	92.2	92.6
1994	96.0	95.7	98.9	100.5	94.5	98.9	99.1	94.8	94.5	95.0
1995	98.1	97.9	100.1	100.9	97.9	101.3	101.8	97.6	97.2	97.8
1996	100.0	100.0	100.0	100.0	100.0	100.0	100.0	100.0	100.0	100.0
1997	102.0	101.9	99.9	99.0	102.7	98.5	96.4	102.2	101.6	102.6
1998	103.2	103.0	99.0	97.0	105.6	96.3	91.3	103.7	102.6	104.3
1999	104.7	104.7	98.9	95.5	109.6	95.5	91.3	106.5	105.1	107.3
2000	106.9	107.4	100.0	95.6	114.4	96.8	95.5	110.6	108.2	112.0
2001	109.4	109.6	101.2	95.7	119.1	96.1	92.7	113.3	110.1	115.0
2002	110.7	111.1	100.8	94.4	121.6	95.9	93.0	115.2	113.1	116.3
2000										
1st quarter	106.1	106.5	99.5	95.3	112.9	96.4	94.7	109.5	107.9	110.4
2nd quarter	106.7	107.1	99.8	95.4	114.0	96.8	94.9	110.3	108.0	111.5
3rd quarter	107.1	107.7	100.2	95.7	114.9	97.0	96.0	111.1	108.5	112.5
4th quarter	107.7	108.3	100.5	95.9	115.9	97.1	96.2	111.8	108.5	113.6
2001										
1st quarter	108.7	109.2	101.0	96.0	117.5	96.9	95.6	113.0	109.7	114.7
2nd quarter	109.3	109.6	101.3	96.0	118.8	96.4	94.2	113.5	110.2	115.3
3rd quarter	109.9	109.6	101.2	95.7	119.5	96.0	89.9	113.4	110.3	115.1
4th quarter	109.8	109.8	101.2	95.3	120.6	95.0	90.9	113.3	110.2	115.0
2002										
1st quarter	110.1	110.1	100.8	94.8	120.6	94.9	90.6	114.3	112.4	115.3
2nd quarter	110.5	110.9	100.8	94.5	121.4	95.6	93.0	115.1	113.1	116.2
3rd quarter	110.8	111.4	100.5	94.2	121.4	96.4	94.0	115.5	113.4	116.6
4th quarter	111.3	111.9	101.0	94.3	122.9	96.6	94.2	115.9	113.5	117.2

Table 1-6. Final Sales

(Billions of dollars, quarterly data are at seasonally adjusted annual rates.)

Year and quarter	Final sales of domestic product			Final sales to domestic purchasers		
	Billions of dollars	Billions of chained (1996) dollars	Chain-type price index, 1996 = 100	Billions of dollars	Billions of chained (1996) dollars	Chain-type price index, 1996 = 100
1946	216.3	1 483.3	14.6	209.2	1 469.8	14.2
1947	245.0	1 517.0	16.2	234.2	1 487.4	15.8
1948	263.9	1 544.8	17.1	258.5	1 549.5	16.7
1949	270.3	1 580.5	17.1	265.2	1 584.8	16.7
1950	288.5	1 672.4	17.3	287.9	1 699.4	16.9
1951	329.6	1 789.2	18.4	327.2	1 804.2	18.1
1952	355.1	1 887.0	18.8	354.1	1 914.9	18.5
1953	378.0	1 979.7	19.1	378.8	2 022.7	18.7
1954	383.0	1 984.3	19.3	382.7	2 019.3	19.0
1955	410.2	2 093.9	19.6	409.8	2 131.8	19.2
1956	434.0	2 141.9	20.3	431.7	2 172.7	19.9
1957	460.7	2 196.5	21.0	456.8	2 223.2	20.5
1958	468.3	2 179.3	21.5	467.9	2 225.7	21.0
1959	503.5	2 317.4	21.7	505.2	2 376.0	21.3
1960	524.1	2 378.5	22.0	521.7	2 419.7	21.6
1961	542.7	2 435.5	22.3	539.3	2 475.2	21.8
1962	580.4	2 569.5	22.6	578.0	2 617.6	22.1
1963	613.1	2 683.6	22.8	609.8	2 728.1	22.4
1964	659.6	2 844.1	23.2	654.1	2 880.8	22.7
1965	710.9	3 008.5	23.6	707.0	3 059.0	23.1
1966	775.7	3 191.1	24.3	773.8	3 255.6	23.8
1967	824.2	3 288.2	25.1	822.8	3 362.5	24.5
1968	902.4	3 450.0	26.2	903.7	3 540.2	25.5
1969	976.2	3 555.9	27.5	977.4	3 649.3	26.8
1970	1 037.7	3 588.6	28.9	1 036.5	3 671.1	28.2
1971	1 120.3	3 688.1	30.4	1 123.3	3 782.0	29.7
1972	1 231.3	3 887.7	31.7	1 239.3	3 993.5	31.0
1973	1 369.7	4 094.3	33.5	1 369.0	4 167.4	32.9
1974	1 487.0	4 080.7	36.4	1 490.2	4 118.2	36.2
1975	1 641.4	4 118.5	39.9	1 627.9	4 119.6	39.5
1976	1 806.8	4 288.8	42.1	1 809.1	4 331.1	41.8
1977	2 009.1	4 478.8	44.9	2 032.7	4 553.3	44.6
1978	2 270.1	4 722.9	48.1	2 296.2	4 797.0	47.9
1979	2 548.4	4 894.4	52.1	2 572.4	4 938.4	52.1
1980	2 801.9	4 928.1	56.9	2 816.8	4 890.3	57.6
1981	3 101.5	4 989.5	62.2	3 116.5	4 958.6	62.9
1982	3 274.1	4 954.9	66.1	3 294.7	4 951.7	66.5
1983	3 540.7	5 154.5	68.7	3 592.3	5 215.9	68.9
1984	3 867.3	5 427.9	71.3	3 969.3	5 569.5	71.3
1985	4 191.2	5 698.8	73.6	4 305.4	5 865.0	73.4
1986	4 446.3	5 912.6	75.2	4 578.2	6 096.6	75.1
1987	4 715.3	6 088.8	77.4	4 857.6	6 261.9	77.6
1988	5 089.8	6 352.6	80.1	5 196.1	6 474.0	80.3
1989	5 461.4	6 565.4	83.2	5 542.1	6 648.3	83.4
1990	5 788.7	6 695.6	86.5	5 860.1	6 752.6	86.8
1991	5 986.4	6 681.5	89.6	6 007.1	6 693.5	89.8
1992	6 303.9	6 867.7	91.8	6 331.7	6 884.1	92.0
1993	6 621.2	7 043.8	94.0	6 681.7	7 101.8	94.1
1994	6 991.8	7 285.8	96.0	7 078.9	7 372.2	96.0
1995	7 367.5	7 512.2	98.1	7 451.7	7 590.3	98.2
1996	7 783.2	7 783.2	100.0	7 872.1	7 872.1	100.0
1997	8 255.5	8 095.2	102.0	8 344.8	8 207.3	101.7
1998	8 708.4	8 431.8	103.3	8 860.1	8 644.0	102.5
1999	9 214.8	8 793.9	104.8	9 464.7	9 095.1	104.1
2000	9 761.1	9 121.1	107.0	10 126.6	9 490.7	106.7
2001	10 142.5	9 258.4	109.6	10 491.4	9 644.9	108.8
2002	10 442.4	9 424.4	110.8	10 866.0	9 874.1	110.0
2000						
1st quarter	9 602.6	9 042.9	106.2	9 933.3	9 386.3	105.8
2nd quarter	9 731.5	9 111.1	106.8	10 084.7	9 477.0	106.4
3rd quarter	9 813.6	9 150.4	107.3	10 198.5	9 532.5	107.0
4th quarter	9 896.6	9 179.8	107.8	10 289.8	9 566.8	107.6
2001						
1st quarter	10 055.3	9 243.8	108.8	10 428.0	9 618.7	108.4
2nd quarter	10 107.0	9 234.3	109.5	10 472.6	9 618.7	108.9
3rd quarter	10 158.3	9 230.5	110.1	10 470.9	9 620.3	108.8
4th quarter	10 249.4	9 324.9	109.9	10 593.9	9 722.3	109.0
2002						
1st quarter	10 343.0	9 379.4	110.3	10 703.1	9 794.4	109.3
2nd quarter	10 373.5	9 377.9	110.6	10 799.0	9 826.0	109.9
3rd quarter	10 488.7	9 457.2	110.9	10 921.5	9 906.1	110.3
4th quarter	10 564.3	9 483.1	111.4	11 040.3	9 970.1	110.7

Table 1-7. Gross Domestic Product, Gross and Net National Product, and National Income

(Billions of dollars, quarterly data are at seasonally adjusted annual rates.)

Year and quarter	Gross domestic product	Plus: Income receipts from rest of world	Less: Income payments to rest of world	Equals: Gross national product	Less: Consumption of fixed capital	Equals: Net national product	Less Indirect business taxes and nontaxes	Less Business transfer payments	Less Statistical discrepancy	Plus: Subsidies less current surplus of government enterprises	Equals: National income
1946	222.3	1.1	0.4	223.0	23.6	199.4	17.2	0.4	0.7	1.2	182.3
1947	244.4	1.6	0.4	245.6	26.2	219.4	18.6	0.4	2.1	0.2	198.6
1948	269.6	2.0	0.5	271.1	28.1	243.0	20.3	0.4	-0.7	0.3	223.3
1949	267.7	1.9	0.6	269.0	28.8	240.2	21.5	0.4	1.8	0.3	216.7
1950	294.3	2.2	0.7	295.8	29.7	266.1	23.5	0.5	1.7	0.6	241.0
1951	339.5	2.8	0.8	341.5	33.7	307.8	25.3	0.7	3.9	0.7	278.7
1952	358.6	2.9	0.8	360.7	36.2	324.5	27.8	0.8	3.1	0.4	293.3
1953	379.9	2.9	0.9	381.9	38.6	343.4	29.8	0.9	4.6	0.1	308.2
1954	381.1	3.1	0.9	383.3	40.5	342.8	29.7	0.8	3.9	-0.1	308.4
1955	415.2	3.5	1.0	417.8	42.8	375.0	32.3	0.9	3.1	-0.2	338.5
1956	438.0	4.0	1.1	440.8	47.3	393.6	35.1	1.0	-0.9	0.4	358.7
1957	461.5	4.3	1.2	464.7	51.1	413.6	37.6	1.1	0.6	0.7	375.0
1958	467.9	3.9	1.2	470.7	52.8	417.9	38.7	1.1	1.7	0.9	377.3
1959	507.4	4.3	1.5	510.3	54.8	455.5	41.9	1.4	0.8	0.1	411.5
1960	527.4	5.0	1.8	530.6	56.9	473.6	45.5	1.4	-0.6	0.2	427.5
1961	545.7	5.4	1.8	549.3	58.5	490.8	48.1	1.5	-0.2	1.2	442.5
1962	586.5	6.1	1.8	590.7	61.0	529.7	51.7	1.6	0.7	1.4	477.1
1963	618.7	6.6	2.1	623.2	63.6	559.6	54.7	1.8	-0.4	0.9	504.4
1964	664.4	7.4	2.4	669.4	66.6	602.8	58.8	2.0	1.2	1.4	542.1
1965	720.1	8.1	2.7	725.5	70.8	654.7	62.7	2.2	1.9	1.7	589.6
1966	789.3	8.3	3.1	794.5	76.5	717.9	65.4	2.3	6.4	3.0	646.7
1967	834.1	8.9	3.4	839.5	83.1	756.4	70.4	2.5	4.8	2.9	681.7
1968	911.5	10.3	4.1	917.6	90.9	826.7	79.0	2.8	4.3	3.0	743.6
1969	985.3	11.9	5.8	991.5	99.8	891.7	86.6	3.1	2.9	3.5	802.7
1970	1 039.7	13.0	6.6	1 046.1	109.1	937.0	94.3	3.2	6.9	4.8	837.5
1971	1 128.6	14.1	6.4	1 136.2	118.9	1 017.3	103.6	3.4	11.3	4.9	903.9
1972	1 240.4	16.4	7.7	1 249.1	130.9	1 118.2	111.4	3.9	8.7	6.1	1 000.4
1973	1 385.5	23.8	11.1	1 398.2	142.9	1 255.3	121.0	4.5	8.0	5.6	1 127.4
1974	1 501.0	30.3	14.6	1 516.7	164.8	1 351.9	129.3	5.0	10.0	4.2	1 211.9
1975	1 635.2	28.2	14.9	1 648.4	190.9	1 457.5	140.0	5.2	17.7	7.7	1 302.2
1976	1 823.9	32.9	15.7	1 841.0	209.0	1 632.1	151.6	6.5	24.5	6.9	1 456.4
1977	2 031.4	37.9	17.2	2 052.1	231.6	1 820.5	165.5	7.3	21.6	9.7	1 635.8
1978	2 295.9	47.4	25.3	2 318.0	261.5	2 056.5	177.8	8.2	21.0	10.6	1 860.2
1979	2 566.4	70.4	37.5	2 599.3	300.4	2 298.9	188.7	9.9	35.7	11.0	2 075.6
1980	2 795.6	81.8	46.5	2 830.8	345.2	2 485.6	212.0	11.2	33.9	14.5	2 243.0
1981	3 131.3	95.6	60.9	3 166.1	394.8	2 771.2	249.3	13.4	27.5	16.1	2 497.1
1982	3 259.2	102.4	65.9	3 295.7	436.5	2 859.2	256.7	15.2	2.5	18.1	2 603.0
1983	3 534.9	102.5	65.6	3 571.8	456.1	3 115.7	280.3	16.2	47.0	24.3	2 796.5
1984	3 932.7	122.9	87.6	3 968.1	482.4	3 485.7	309.1	18.6	18.6	22.9	3 162.3
1985	4 213.0	113.1	87.8	4 238.4	516.5	3 721.9	329.4	20.7	11.7	20.4	3 380.4
1986	4 452.9	111.1	95.6	4 468.3	551.6	3 916.8	346.8	23.8	43.9	23.6	3 525.8
1987	4 742.5	122.9	109.2	4 756.2	586.1	4 170.1	369.3	24.2	3.3	30.1	3 803.4
1988	5 108.3	151.8	133.4	5 126.8	627.4	4 499.4	392.6	25.3	-42.2	27.4	4 151.1
1989	5 489.1	177.2	156.8	5 509.4	677.2	4 832.2	420.7	25.8	16.3	22.6	4 392.1
1990	5 803.2	188.3	159.3	5 832.2	711.3	5 120.9	447.3	26.1	30.6	25.3	4 642.1
1991	5 986.2	167.7	143.0	6 010.9	748.0	5 262.8	482.3	25.9	19.6	21.5	4 756.6
1992	6 318.9	151.1	127.6	6 342.3	787.5	5 554.9	510.6	28.1	43.7	22.4	4 994.9
1993	6 642.3	154.4	130.1	6 666.7	812.8	5 853.9	540.1	27.8	63.8	29.6	5 251.9
1994	7 054.3	184.3	167.5	7 071.1	874.9	6 196.2	575.3	30.8	58.5	25.2	5 556.8
1995	7 400.5	232.3	211.9	7 420.9	911.7	6 509.1	594.6	33.5	26.5	22.2	5 876.7
1996	7 813.2	245.6	227.5	7 831.2	956.2	6 875.0	620.0	34.4	32.8	22.6	6 210.4
1997	8 318.4	281.3	274.2	8 325.4	1 013.3	7 312.1	646.2	36.8	29.7	19.1	6 618.4
1998	8 781.5	286.1	289.6	8 778.1	1 072.0	7 706.1	681.3	38.0	-31.0	23.5	7 041.4
1999	9 274.3	316.9	294.1	9 297.1	1 145.2	8 151.9	712.9	41.5	-38.8	32.5	7 468.7
2000	9 824.6	383.4	360.0	9 848.0	1 228.9	8 619.1	753.6	43.7	-128.5	34.1	7 984.4
2001	10 082.2	316.9	295.0	10 104.1	1 329.3	8 774.8	774.8	42.5	-117.3	47.3	8 122.0
2002	10 446.2	278.0	287.6	10 436.7	1 393.5	9 043.2	800.4	44.1	-108.8	32.5	8 340.1
2000											
1st quarter	9 649.5	365.2	344.2	9 670.5	1 194.7	8 475.8	745.1	43.4	-138.7	34.3	7 860.2
2nd quarter	9 820.7	390.5	364.7	9 846.4	1 218.2	8 628.2	750.3	44.1	-86.8	33.9	7 954.5
3rd quarter	9 874.8	383.5	365.8	9 892.5	1 240.8	8 651.7	757.9	43.5	-164.0	34.0	8 048.3
4th quarter	9 953.6	394.4	365.2	9 982.8	1 261.9	8 720.9	761.1	43.6	-124.5	34.2	8 074.8
2001											
1st quarter	10 028.1	364.2	354.3	10 038.0	1 281.7	8 756.4	770.6	42.1	-105.7	42.8	8 092.1
2nd quarter	10 049.9	332.5	301.4	10 081.0	1 315.0	8 766.0	775.9	42.5	-112.9	49.7	8 110.1
3rd quarter	10 097.7	302.0	290.5	10 109.3	1 381.8	8 727.5	772.7	42.6	-117.8	59.1	8 089.1
4th quarter	10 152.9	269.0	233.7	10 188.1	1 338.6	8 849.5	779.9	42.8	-132.6	37.5	8 196.8
2002											
1st quarter	10 313.1	264.7	262.8	10 314.9	1 363.5	8 951.5	786.2	43.8	-110.0	37.0	8 268.5
2nd quarter	10 376.9	276.0	296.1	10 356.8	1 389.8	8 967.0	795.1	43.9	-165.0	35.1	8 328.0
3rd quarter	10 506.2	287.3	298.2	10 495.3	1 405.3	9 090.0	806.9	44.4	-82.1	29.1	8 349.9
4th quarter	10 588.8	284.2	293.4	10 579.7	1 415.4	9 164.3	813.3	44.3	-78.2	29.0	8 413.9

Table 1-8. National Income by Type of Income

(Billions of dollars, quarterly data are at seasonally adjusted annual rates.)

Year and quarter	National income	Compensation of employees			Proprietors' income with IVA [1] and CCAdj [2]			Rental income of persons with CCAdj [2]	Corporate profits					Net interest
		Total	Wage and salary accruals	Supplements to wages and salaries	Total	Farm	Nonfarm		Total with IVA [1] and CCAdj [2]	Profits before tax	Profits after tax			
											Total	Dividends	Undistributed profits	
1946	182.3	119.6	112.0	7.6	36.5	14.8	21.7	7.0	17.4	24.9	15.8	5.6	10.3	1.8
1947	198.6	130.1	123.1	7.0	35.6	15.1	20.5	7.0	23.5	31.9	20.7	6.3	14.4	2.4
1948	223.3	142.0	135.5	6.5	40.4	17.5	22.9	7.6	30.8	35.9	23.5	7.0	16.4	2.4
1949	216.7	142.0	134.7	7.2	35.7	12.7	23.1	7.8	28.6	29.6	19.4	7.2	12.2	2.6
1950	241.0	155.4	147.2	8.1	38.6	13.5	25.1	8.7	35.4	43.2	25.3	8.8	16.5	3.0
1951	278.7	181.5	171.6	9.9	43.8	16.0	27.8	9.5	40.4	44.8	22.2	8.6	13.7	3.5
1952	293.3	196.3	185.6	10.7	44.3	15.1	29.2	10.5	38.4	40.2	20.8	8.6	12.3	3.8
1953	308.2	210.3	199.0	11.4	43.3	13.0	30.3	11.5	38.7	41.7	21.4	8.9	12.5	4.4
1954	308.4	209.3	197.2	12.0	43.5	12.5	31.0	12.5	37.9	39.3	21.7	9.3	12.4	5.3
1955	338.5	225.8	212.1	13.7	45.5	11.5	34.0	12.8	48.5	49.9	27.8	10.5	17.4	6.0
1956	358.7	244.6	229.0	15.6	47.0	11.3	35.7	13.1	47.4	50.5	28.5	11.3	17.2	6.6
1957	375.0	257.6	239.9	17.7	49.0	11.3	37.7	13.8	47.0	49.1	27.7	11.7	15.9	7.7
1958	377.3	259.6	241.3	18.3	51.4	13.1	38.3	14.5	42.4	43.0	24.0	11.6	12.4	9.4
1959	411.5	281.0	259.8	21.2	51.8	10.9	40.9	15.2	53.7	53.7	30.0	12.6	17.5	9.7
1960	427.5	296.4	272.8	23.6	51.9	11.4	40.4	16.2	52.3	51.5	28.8	13.4	15.5	10.7
1961	442.5	305.3	280.5	24.8	54.4	12.1	42.3	16.9	53.5	51.5	28.7	13.9	14.8	12.4
1962	477.1	327.2	299.3	27.9	56.5	12.1	44.4	17.8	61.6	56.9	32.9	15.0	17.9	14.1
1963	504.4	345.3	314.8	30.4	57.8	11.9	45.8	18.5	67.6	61.9	35.7	16.2	19.5	15.2
1964	542.1	370.7	337.7	33.0	60.6	10.8	49.9	18.6	74.8	68.9	40.9	18.2	22.7	17.3
1965	589.6	399.5	363.7	35.8	65.2	13.1	52.2	19.2	86.0	80.0	49.1	20.2	28.9	19.7
1966	646.7	442.6	400.3	42.4	69.6	14.1	55.5	19.9	92.0	86.5	52.8	20.7	32.1	22.6
1967	681.7	475.2	428.9	46.2	71.1	12.8	58.4	20.4	89.6	83.3	50.6	21.5	29.1	25.4
1968	743.6	524.3	471.9	52.4	75.4	12.8	62.6	20.2	96.5	92.2	52.8	23.5	29.3	27.2
1969	802.7	577.6	518.3	59.4	78.9	14.2	64.7	20.3	93.7	91.1	51.4	24.2	27.2	32.2
1970	837.5	617.2	551.5	65.7	79.8	14.3	65.5	20.3	81.6	80.6	46.2	24.3	21.9	38.4
1971	903.9	658.8	584.5	74.4	86.1	14.9	71.2	21.2	95.1	92.4	54.7	25.0	29.7	42.6
1972	1 000.4	725.1	638.7	86.5	97.7	18.8	78.9	21.6	109.8	107.3	65.5	26.8	38.6	46.2
1973	1 127.4	811.2	708.6	102.6	115.2	30.7	84.5	23.1	123.9	134.2	84.9	29.9	55.0	53.9
1974	1 211.9	890.2	772.2	118.0	115.5	25.2	90.3	23.0	114.5	146.8	95.0	33.2	61.8	68.8
1975	1 302.2	949.0	814.7	134.4	121.6	23.5	98.1	22.0	133.0	144.8	93.9	33.0	60.9	76.6
1976	1 456.4	1 059.3	899.6	159.7	134.3	18.7	115.6	21.5	160.6	178.6	114.4	39.0	75.4	80.8
1977	1 635.8	1 180.4	994.0	186.4	148.3	17.5	130.8	20.4	190.9	209.0	136.0	44.8	91.2	95.7
1978	1 860.2	1 336.0	1 121.0	215.0	170.1	21.5	148.5	22.4	217.2	244.9	161.4	50.8	110.6	114.5
1979	2 075.6	1 500.8	1 255.6	245.2	183.7	23.7	160.0	24.5	222.5	270.1	182.1	57.5	124.6	144.2
1980	2 243.0	1 651.7	1 377.4	274.3	177.6	13.1	164.5	31.3	198.5	251.4	166.6	64.1	102.6	183.9
1981	2 497.1	1 825.7	1 517.3	308.5	186.2	20.3	165.9	39.6	219.0	240.9	159.8	73.8	86.0	226.5
1982	2 603.0	1 926.0	1 593.4	332.6	179.9	14.4	165.4	39.6	201.2	195.5	132.4	76.2	56.2	256.3
1983	2 796.5	2 042.7	1 684.3	358.5	195.5	7.2	188.3	36.9	254.1	231.4	154.1	83.6	70.5	267.2
1984	3 162.3	2 255.9	1 854.8	401.1	247.5	21.6	225.9	39.5	309.8	266.0	172.0	91.0	81.0	309.6
1985	3 380.4	2 425.2	1 995.2	430.0	267.0	21.5	245.5	39.1	322.4	255.2	158.7	97.7	61.0	326.7
1986	3 525.8	2 570.7	2 114.4	456.3	278.6	23.0	255.6	32.2	300.7	243.4	136.9	106.3	30.6	343.6
1987	3 803.4	2 755.6	2 270.2	485.4	303.9	29.0	274.8	35.8	346.6	314.6	187.5	112.2	75.3	361.5
1988	4 151.1	2 973.8	2 452.7	521.1	338.8	26.0	312.7	44.1	405.0	381.9	241.8	129.6	115.2	389.4
1989	4 392.1	3 151.0	2 596.8	554.2	361.8	32.2	329.6	40.5	395.7	376.7	235.3	155.0	80.2	443.1
1990	4 642.1	3 351.0	2 754.6	596.4	381.0	31.1	349.9	49.1	408.6	401.5	260.9	165.6	95.3	452.4
1991	4 756.6	3 454.9	2 824.2	630.7	384.2	26.4	357.8	56.4	431.2	416.1	282.6	178.4	104.1	429.8
1992	4 994.9	3 644.8	2 966.8	677.9	434.3	32.7	401.7	63.3	453.1	451.6	308.4	185.5	122.9	399.5
1993	5 251.9	3 814.4	3 091.6	722.8	461.8	30.1	431.7	90.9	510.5	510.4	345.0	203.1	141.9	374.3
1994	5 556.8	4 016.2	3 254.3	761.9	476.6	31.9	444.6	110.3	573.2	573.4	386.7	234.9	151.8	380.5
1995	5 876.7	4 202.5	3 441.1	761.4	497.7	22.2	475.5	117.9	668.8	668.5	457.5	254.2	203.3	389.8
1996	6 210.4	4 395.6	3 630.1	765.4	544.7	34.3	510.5	129.7	754.0	726.3	502.7	297.7	205.0	386.3
1997	6 618.4	4 651.3	3 886.0	765.3	581.2	29.7	551.5	128.3	833.8	792.4	555.2	335.2	220.0	423.9
1998	7 041.4	4 989.6	4 192.1	797.5	623.8	25.6	598.2	138.6	777.4	721.1	482.3	348.7	133.6	511.9
1999	7 468.7	5 308.8	4 475.6	833.2	678.4	27.7	650.7	149.1	805.8	762.1	514.3	328.4	185.9	526.6
2000	7 984.4	5 723.4	4 836.3	887.1	714.8	22.6	692.2	146.6	788.1	782.3	522.9	376.1	146.8	611.5
2001	8 122.0	5 874.9	4 950.6	924.3	727.9	19.0	708.8	137.9	731.6	670.2	470.9	409.6	61.2	649.8
2002	8 340.1	5 969.5	4 996.4	973.1	756.5	12.9	743.7	142.4	787.4	665.2	451.9	434.3	17.6	684.2
2000														
1st quarter	7 860.2	5 627.3	4 757.4	869.9	702.5	22.3	680.2	151.4	807.6	796.9	526.1	351.1	174.9	571.3
2nd quarter	7 954.5	5 670.5	4 790.8	879.6	718.8	25.0	693.8	146.7	807.3	800.5	533.3	369.7	163.6	611.1
3rd quarter	8 048.3	5 773.1	4 879.3	893.8	718.6	21.7	696.9	144.9	787.7	780.6	523.2	386.1	137.1	624.0
4th quarter	8 074.8	5 822.7	4 917.8	904.9	719.3	21.2	698.1	143.5	749.7	751.1	509.2	397.6	111.6	639.6
2001														
1st quarter	8 092.1	5 878.9	4 960.4	918.5	721.2	19.3	701.9	137.0	706.5	707.0	489.7	402.9	86.8	648.5
2nd quarter	8 110.1	5 879.3	4 956.9	922.4	726.6	18.4	708.2	134.3	721.4	720.2	507.1	406.5	100.7	648.6
3rd quarter	8 089.1	5 880.4	4 953.7	926.7	732.4	19.3	713.1	140.8	687.2	654.3	458.1	411.4	46.7	648.3
4th quarter	8 196.8	5 860.9	4 931.4	929.4	731.3	19.2	712.1	139.3	811.4	599.1	428.5	417.7	10.8	653.9
2002														
1st quarter	8 268.5	5 908.4	4 957.8	950.7	748.4	21.7	726.7	141.3	797.6	639.4	437.0	424.2	12.8	672.8
2nd quarter	8 328.0	5 963.9	4 997.3	966.6	747.5	7.5	740.0	153.5	785.0	657.9	444.3	430.8	13.5	678.1
3rd quarter	8 349.9	5 988.4	5 007.4	981.0	758.7	10.7	748.0	144.1	771.0	668.5	453.8	437.7	16.1	687.6
4th quarter	8 413.9	6 017.4	5 023.1	994.3	771.6	11.7	759.9	130.6	796.1	694.9	472.5	444.3	28.2	698.3

[1] Inventory valuation adjustment.
[2] Capital consumption adjustment.

Table 1-9. Gross Product and Domestic Income of Nonfinancial Corporate Business

(Billions of dollars, quarterly data are at seasonally adjusted annual rates.)

Year and quarter	Gross product	Less: Consumption of fixed capital	Equals: Net product	Less: Indirect business taxes plus business transfer payments less subsidies	Equals: Domestic income	Compensation of employees	Corporate profits						Inventory valuation adjustment	Capital consumption adjustment	Net interest
							Total with IVA[1] and CCAdj[2]	Profits before tax	Profits tax liability	Profits after tax					
										Total	Dividends	Undistributed profits			
1946	99.9	7.3	92.6	10.1	82.5	67.2	14.6	22.1	8.6	13.5	4.8	8.7	-5.3	-2.3	0.7
1947	121.3	8.7	112.7	11.9	100.8	79.1	20.9	29.2	10.8	18.4	5.5	12.9	-5.9	-2.4	0.8
1948	138.9	10.2	128.7	13.1	115.6	87.7	27.0	31.9	11.8	20.1	6.0	14.2	-2.2	-2.8	0.9
1949	135.3	11.1	124.2	13.7	110.5	85.2	24.3	25.2	9.3	15.9	6.0	9.9	1.9	-2.8	1.0
1950	153.7	11.9	141.8	15.2	126.6	94.7	31.0	38.7	16.9	21.8	7.5	14.4	-5.0	-2.8	0.9
1951	176.5	13.7	162.7	16.4	146.4	110.1	35.2	39.4	21.2	18.2	7.1	11.1	-1.2	-3.1	1.1
1952	184.2	14.6	169.6	17.9	151.7	118.1	32.3	34.0	17.8	16.2	7.1	9.1	1.0	-2.7	1.2
1953	196.8	15.5	181.3	19.1	162.2	128.6	32.3	35.1	18.5	16.7	7.3	9.4	-1.0	-1.9	1.3
1954	193.7	16.2	177.5	18.5	159.0	126.4	31.1	32.4	15.6	16.7	7.4	9.3	-0.3	-1.0	1.6
1955	218.7	17.2	201.5	20.5	181.0	138.3	41.0	42.3	20.2	22.1	8.5	13.7	-1.7	0.4	1.6
1956	233.8	19.3	214.5	22.3	192.3	151.3	39.2	42.2	20.1	22.1	9.0	13.1	-2.7	-0.3	1.8
1957	244.3	21.3	223.0	23.6	199.4	158.9	38.3	40.2	19.1	21.1	9.3	11.8	-1.5	-0.4	2.2
1958	238.3	22.2	216.1	23.9	192.2	155.7	33.7	34.2	16.2	18.0	9.3	8.7	-0.3	-0.2	2.7
1959	267.3	23.1	244.2	26.1	218.2	171.3	43.7	43.6	20.7	22.9	10.0	12.9	-0.3	0.4	3.1
1960	278.0	24.0	254.0	28.4	225.6	181.0	41.1	40.3	19.2	21.1	10.6	10.5	-0.2	1.0	3.5
1961	285.5	24.6	260.9	29.6	231.3	185.2	42.1	40.1	19.5	20.6	10.6	10.1	0.3	1.8	4.0
1962	311.7	25.5	286.2	32.1	254.1	200.0	49.6	44.9	20.6	24.3	11.4	12.9	0.0	4.6	4.5
1963	331.8	26.5	305.4	34.1	271.2	210.9	55.5	49.8	22.8	27.1	12.6	14.4	0.1	5.6	4.8
1964	358.2	27.9	330.3	36.7	293.7	226.5	61.9	56.1	24.0	32.1	13.7	18.4	-0.5	6.2	5.3
1965	393.7	29.9	363.8	39.3	324.6	246.3	72.2	66.3	27.2	39.1	15.6	23.5	-1.2	7.1	6.1
1966	431.4	32.7	398.7	40.5	358.2	273.8	77.0	71.6	29.5	42.1	16.8	25.3	-2.1	7.5	7.4
1967	453.9	35.9	418.0	43.2	374.9	292.2	73.9	67.7	27.8	39.9	17.5	22.4	-1.6	7.8	8.8
1968	501.0	39.7	461.4	49.8	411.5	323.1	78.3	74.1	33.6	40.6	19.1	21.4	-3.7	7.8	10.1
1969	543.9	43.9	500.0	54.8	445.2	358.5	73.5	71.1	33.3	37.8	19.1	18.7	-5.9	8.2	13.2
1970	562.0	48.5	513.5	59.0	454.6	378.1	59.4	58.5	27.2	31.4	18.5	12.8	-6.6	7.4	17.1
1971	606.9	53.1	553.8	64.6	489.1	401.2	69.8	67.3	29.9	37.4	18.5	18.9	-4.6	7.1	18.1
1972	673.9	58.4	615.6	69.4	546.2	445.9	81.1	79.0	33.8	45.3	20.1	25.2	-6.6	8.7	19.2
1973	755.6	63.8	691.8	76.6	615.2	504.5	88.2	99.0	40.2	58.8	21.1	37.8	-19.6	8.8	22.5
1974	816.7	74.7	742.0	81.9	660.1	555.1	76.7	109.6	42.2	67.4	21.7	45.7	-38.2	5.3	28.3
1975	883.0	89.2	793.8	88.0	705.8	578.6	98.5	110.5	41.5	69.0	24.8	44.2	-10.5	-1.4	28.7
1976	997.1	98.9	898.2	95.9	802.4	655.0	119.9	137.9	53.0	84.9	28.0	56.9	-14.1	-3.8	27.5
1977	1 127.8	111.0	1 016.9	104.9	912.0	740.0	141.3	159.2	59.9	99.3	31.5	67.8	-15.7	-2.3	30.7
1978	1 285.0	126.8	1 158.2	114.4	1 043.8	851.0	156.5	184.4	67.1	117.3	36.4	80.9	-23.7	-4.2	36.3
1979	1 431.5	147.0	1 284.6	123.3	1 161.3	966.2	150.1	197.1	69.6	127.5	38.1	89.4	-40.1	-6.9	45.0
1980	1 556.6	169.4	1 387.2	139.5	1 247.8	1 056.9	132.7	183.6	67.0	116.6	45.3	71.3	-42.1	-8.8	58.1
1981	1 770.1	195.9	1 574.2	168.1	1 406.1	1 169.9	164.4	184.2	63.9	120.3	53.3	67.0	-24.6	4.8	71.8
1982	1 831.4	216.8	1 614.6	169.7	1 444.9	1 216.1	146.3	136.9	46.3	90.7	53.3	37.4	-7.5	16.9	82.5
1983	1 953.3	225.1	1 728.2	185.3	1 542.9	1 279.9	186.4	160.7	59.4	101.3	64.2	37.1	-7.4	33.1	76.6
1984	2 194.8	237.3	1 957.5	205.4	1 752.1	1 421.4	242.9	195.3	73.7	121.6	67.8	53.8	-4.0	51.7	87.7
1985	2 329.3	253.9	2 075.4	219.0	1 856.4	1 522.3	243.7	172.3	69.9	102.3	72.3	30.1	0.0	71.4	90.4
1986	2 414.4	270.3	2 144.1	231.2	1 912.9	1 603.8	210.7	147.9	75.6	72.3	73.9	-1.6	7.1	55.8	98.4
1987	2 595.3	283.8	2 311.6	241.9	2 069.7	1 716.3	248.3	209.5	93.5	116.0	75.9	40.1	-16.2	55.0	105.1
1988	2 814.5	302.0	2 512.5	256.3	2 256.2	1 844.1	288.6	257.3	101.9	155.5	79.8	75.7	-22.2	53.4	123.6
1989	2 961.4	322.8	2 638.6	275.9	2 362.7	1 946.6	264.2	235.6	98.9	136.7	104.2	32.6	-16.3	45.0	151.8
1990	3 096.2	338.4	2 757.9	290.6	2 467.3	2 052.7	258.5	237.2	95.8	141.4	119.2	22.2	-12.9	34.3	156.0
1991	3 150.6	354.9	2 795.7	313.1	2 482.6	2 086.9	252.8	221.6	85.5	136.1	125.8	10.3	4.9	26.3	143.0
1992	3 288.0	369.6	2 918.5	332.0	2 586.5	2 194.2	278.9	258.0	91.2	166.8	135.0	31.9	-2.8	23.7	113.3
1993	3 457.6	386.4	3 071.3	349.3	2 721.9	2 290.7	325.3	305.8	105.2	200.5	149.3	51.2	-4.0	23.6	105.9
1994	3 737.2	414.5	3 322.7	382.1	2 940.6	2 430.2	402.5	381.4	128.9	252.6	158.6	94.0	-12.4	33.5	107.9
1995	3 945.9	437.5	3 508.4	397.3	3 111.0	2 552.7	442.5	422.1	136.7	285.4	179.3	106.0	-18.3	38.7	115.8
1996	4 159.5	462.7	3 696.9	411.9	3 284.9	2 667.1	509.1	460.2	150.1	310.1	201.9	108.2	3.1	45.8	108.7
1997	4 435.1	493.0	3 942.1	431.4	3 510.7	2 835.1	555.6	496.1	158.3	337.7	218.1	119.6	8.4	51.1	120.0
1998	4 707.1	523.1	4 183.9	457.4	3 726.5	3 058.0	530.7	460.4	154.6	305.8	242.2	63.6	18.3	52.0	137.7
1999	4 981.0	556.2	4 424.9	478.4	3 946.5	3 272.0	518.5	460.1	166.9	293.2	239.2	54.0	-4.2	62.6	156.1
2000	5 295.0	599.4	4 695.6	508.9	4 186.6	3 542.1	461.8	437.9	172.4	265.5	259.6	5.9	-15.0	38.8	182.7
2001	5 354.2	652.8	4 701.4	523.7	4 177.7	3 573.5	407.4	328.8	123.5	205.3	278.5	-73.2	5.0	73.6	196.8
2002	5 493.1	686.6	4 806.5	549.1	4 257.5	3 605.0	458.4	328.6	131.5	197.0	285.8	-88.8	-6.9	136.7	194.1
2000															
1st quarter	5 228.7	581.2	4 647.5	503.2	4 144.3	3 482.9	490.9	463.6	183.8	279.8	252.3	27.6	-22.6	49.9	170.5
2nd quarter	5 275.1	593.7	4 681.4	506.3	4 175.1	3 503.6	490.1	466.0	183.6	282.5	250.4	32.1	-16.4	40.4	181.4
3rd quarter	5 335.5	605.8	4 729.7	510.5	4 219.2	3 575.3	456.2	430.7	169.1	261.6	266.3	-4.6	-8.3	33.9	187.7
4th quarter	5 340.7	617.1	4 723.6	515.8	4 207.8	3 606.4	410.0	391.3	153.2	238.1	269.7	-31.6	-12.5	31.3	191.3
2001															
1st quarter	5 318.6	627.6	4 691.0	523.3	4 167.7	3 589.0	384.3	362.8	134.3	228.4	276.7	-48.3	-10.1	31.7	194.4
2nd quarter	5 340.9	641.6	4 699.3	529.3	4 170.0	3 580.7	393.1	368.2	136.2	232.0	268.3	-36.3	-6.2	31.1	196.1
3rd quarter	5 365.7	684.9	4 680.8	508.0	4 172.8	3 572.5	403.0	349.8	129.4	220.4	283.8	-63.4	8.9	44.3	197.3
4th quarter	5 391.6	657.0	4 734.6	534.3	4 200.3	3 551.8	449.0	234.3	94.0	140.3	285.2	-144.9	27.2	187.4	199.5
2002															
1st quarter	5 423.8	670.7	4 753.1	539.3	4 213.9	3 570.1	452.4	289.2	119.8	169.5	293.1	-123.6	1.9	161.3	191.4
2nd quarter	5 489.0	685.1	4 803.8	545.6	4 258.2	3 604.4	459.3	324.4	130.8	193.6	280.2	-86.6	-5.7	140.6	194.6
3rd quarter	5 504.8	693.7	4 811.1	554.2	4 256.9	3 615.0	447.6	336.3	133.4	202.9	275.9	-73.0	-15.1	126.4	194.3
4th quarter	5 554.7	696.7	4 858.0	557.2	4 300.8	3 630.5	474.4	364.4	142.2	222.1	294.2	-72.1	-8.5	118.6	195.9

[1]Inventory valuation adjustment.
[2]Capital consumption adjustment.

Table 1-10. Per Capita Product and Income and U.S. Population

(Dollars, except as noted; quarterly data are at seasonally adjusted annual rates.)

Year and quarter	Current dollars							Chained (1996) dollars						Population (mid-period, thousands)
	Gross domestic product	Personal income	Disposable personal income	Personal consumption expenditures				Gross domestic product	Disposable personal income	Personal consumption expenditures				
				Total	Durable goods	Nondurable goods	Services			Total	Durable goods	Nondurable goods	Services	
1946	1 572	1 269	1 145	1 020	111	585	324	10 648	7 599	6 768	355	3 228	3 067	141 389
1947	1 696	1 333	1 194	1 126	142	631	354	10 374	7 183	6 775	414	3 081	3 158	144 126
1948	1 838	1 440	1 307	1 196	156	659	381	10 639	7 433	6 807	434	3 038	3 224	146 631
1949	1 794	1 396	1 281	1 199	168	636	395	10 396	7 343	6 872	461	3 032	3 249	149 188
1950	1 940	1 516	1 388	1 270	203	648	420	11 119	7 863	7 192	554	3 075	3 356	151 684
1951	2 201	1 677	1 499	1 352	194	708	451	11 764	7 953	7 176	496	3 103	3 457	154 287
1952	2 285	1 759	1 552	1 400	187	731	482	12 024	8 071	7 279	475	3 172	3 549	156 954
1953	2 381	1 834	1 622	1 463	205	738	520	12 371	8 319	7 503	525	3 218	3 643	159 565
1954	2 347	1 818	1 629	1 481	196	737	548	12 073	8 276	7 524	513	3 202	3 727	162 391
1955	2 512	1 917	1 715	1 567	235	755	577	12 703	8 675	7 928	616	3 299	3 849	165 275
1956	2 603	2 021	1 800	1 616	227	777	612	12 728	8 930	8 018	581	3 352	3 976	168 221
1957	2 694	2 098	1 867	1 675	233	800	642	12 751	8 988	8 068	576	3 353	4 054	171 274
1958	2 687	2 125	1 899	1 703	215	814	674	12 420	8 922	7 999	521	3 329	4 140	174 141
1959	2 865	2 224	1 983	1 796	241	838	717	13 092	9 167	8 303	574	3 408	4 284	177 130
1960	2 918	2 283	2 026	1 838	240	846	753	13 148	9 210	8 358	574	3 390	4 381	180 760
1961	2 970	2 342	2 081	1 865	227	852	785	13 236	9 361	8 388	543	3 396	4 485	183 742
1962	3 143	2 454	2 174	1 950	251	873	826	13 821	9 666	8 668	597	3 449	4 634	186 590
1963	3 268	2 541	2 249	2 024	273	888	863	14 212	9 886	8 896	646	3 472	4 775	189 300
1964	3 462	2 688	2 412	2 145	295	931	919	14 831	10 456	9 300	696	3 592	4 997	191 927
1965	3 705	2 868	2 567	2 286	325	986	975	15 583	10 965	9 764	774	3 735	5 198	194 347
1966	4 015	3 085	2 742	2 451	347	1 062	1 041	16 416	11 417	10 204	830	3 895	5 398	196 599
1967	4 197	3 272	2 899	2 559	354	1 092	1 113	16 646	11 776	10 396	834	3 914	5 602	198 752
1968	4 540	3 559	3 119	2 783	402	1 174	1 207	17 266	12 196	10 881	917	4 052	5 832	200 745
1969	4 860	3 851	3 329	2 987	424	1 249	1 314	17 616	12 451	11 171	940	4 118	6 048	202 736
1970	5 069	4 101	3 591	3 164	414	1 326	1 424	17 446	12 823	11 300	899	4 169	6 220	205 089
1971	5 434	4 358	3 860	3 382	467	1 375	1 541	17 804	13 218	11 581	977	4 191	6 376	207 692
1972	5 909	4 736	4 138	3 671	526	1 467	1 678	18 570	13 692	12 149	1 089	4 329	6 656	209 924
1973	6 537	5 254	4 619	4 022	583	1 619	1 821	19 456	14 496	12 626	1 190	4 428	6 904	211 939
1974	7 017	5 730	5 013	4 359	572	1 798	1 989	19 163	14 268	12 407	1 098	4 299	6 989	213 898
1975	7 571	6 166	5 470	4 771	618	1 948	2 205	18 911	14 393	12 551	1 087	4 320	7 157	215 981
1976	8 363	6 765	5 960	5 272	728	2 102	2 442	19 771	14 873	13 155	1 214	4 487	7 423	218 086
1977	9 221	7 432	6 519	5 803	823	2 257	2 724	20 481	15 256	13 583	1 314	4 550	7 674	220 289
1978	10 313	8 302	7 253	6 425	906	2 472	3 047	21 383	15 845	14 035	1 369	4 670	7 954	222 629
1979	11 401	9 247	8 033	7 091	952	2 774	3 365	21 821	16 120	14 230	1 349	4 742	8 121	225 106
1980	12 276	10 205	8 869	7 741	940	3 057	3 744	21 521	16 063	14 021	1 229	4 680	8 161	227 726
1981	13 614	11 301	9 773	8 453	1 006	3 299	4 148	21 830	16 265	14 069	1 232	4 688	8 200	230 008
1982	14 035	11 922	10 364	8 954	1 034	3 392	4 528	21 184	16 328	14 105	1 221	4 688	8 261	232 218
1983	15 085	12 576	11 036	9 757	1 200	3 547	5 010	21 902	16 673	14 741	1 389	4 801	8 589	234 332
1984	16 636	13 853	12 215	10 569	1 383	3 742	5 444	23 288	17 799	15 401	1 579	4 948	8 873	236 394
1985	17 664	14 738	12 941	11 373	1 523	3 894	5 956	23 970	18 229	16 020	1 719	5 038	9 254	238 506
1986	18 501	15 425	13 555	12 029	1 667	3 982	6 379	24 565	18 641	16 541	1 859	5 171	9 478	240 682
1987	19 529	16 317	14 246	12 787	1 728	4 181	6 878	25 174	18 870	16 938	1 874	5 248	9 798	242 842
1988	20 845	17 433	15 312	13 697	1 837	4 419	7 441	25 987	19 522	17 463	1 965	5 367	10 109	245 061
1989	22 188	18 593	16 235	14 539	1 891	4 711	7 937	26 646	19 833	17 760	1 987	5 461	10 291	247 387
1990	23 215	19 614	17 176	15 327	1 871	4 985	8 472	26 834	20 058	17 899	1 948	5 479	10 466	249 983
1991	23 637	20 080	17 669	15 681	1 749	5 050	8 882	26 363	19 873	17 637	1 796	5 386	10 471	253 253
1992	24 622	21 004	18 527	16 403	1 834	5 155	9 414	26 809	20 220	17 903	1 866	5 415	10 637	256 634
1993	25 546	21 576	18 981	17 133	1 975	5 289	9 869	27 163	20 235	18 264	1 993	5 501	10 778	260 011
1994	26 803	22 372	19 626	17 920	2 131	5 464	10 326	27 918	20 507	18 724	2 119	5 642	10 966	263 194
1995	27 787	23 283	20 361	18 657	2 214	5 622	10 821	28 325	20 798	19 058	2 191	5 741	11 127	266 327
1996	28 997	24 299	21 072	19 438	2 288	5 842	11 308	28 997	21 072	19 438	2 288	5 842	11 308	269 448
1997	30 505	25 439	21 887	20 277	2 356	6 020	11 901	29 922	21 470	19 891	2 411	5 940	11 541	272 687
1998	31 830	26 917	23 037	21 226	2 513	6 193	12 520	30 842	22 359	20 601	2 634	6 113	11 865	275 891
1999	33 234	27 902	23 749	22 384	2 709	6 558	13 117	31 746	22 678	21 373	2 912	6 325	12 167	279 062
2000	34 823	29 797	25 237	23 690	2 849	6 993	13 848	32 579	23 501	22 061	3 115	6 500	12 493	282 128
2001	35 398	30 494	25 957	24 531	2 935	7 167	14 430	32 352	23 692	22 390	3 272	6 565	12 622	284 822
2002	36 340	31 039	27 170	25 408	3 033	7 358	15 017	32 839	24 463	22 877	3 478	6 712	12 787	287 456
2000														
1st quarter	34 330	29 215	24 745	23 311	2 876	6 855	13 579	32 366	23 234	21 887	3 129	6 438	12 373	281 076
2nd quarter	34 855	29 636	25 118	23 562	2 837	6 974	13 751	32 672	23 451	21 998	3 093	6 501	12 451	281 758
3rd quarter	34 958	30 048	25 447	23 847	2 870	7 041	13 936	32 635	23 637	22 150	3 145	6 517	12 538	282 476
4th quarter	35 147	30 284	25 635	24 039	2 815	7 101	14 123	32 640	23 680	22 206	3 095	6 543	12 608	283 202
2001														
1st quarter	35 336	30 508	25 785	24 330	2 878	7 158	14 293	32 523	23 624	22 291	3 173	6 567	12 602	283 794
2nd quarter	35 332	30 502	25 805	24 468	2 884	7 189	14 396	32 320	23 537	22 317	3 208	6 547	12 619	284 442
3rd quarter	35 412	30 531	26 387	24 491	2 890	7 169	14 432	32 216	24 071	22 342	3 236	6 552	12 616	285 154
4th quarter	35 512	30 434	25 853	24 834	3 087	7 151	14 596	32 350	23 537	22 609	3 470	6 593	12 650	285 898
2002														
1st quarter	35 996	30 727	26 759	25 040	2 998	7 278	14 765	32 681	24 296	22 735	3 406	6 706	12 712	286 507
2nd quarter	36 147	31 052	27 144	25 271	2 985	7 344	14 942	32 718	24 479	22 790	3 416	6 691	12 771	287 072
3rd quarter	36 509	31 132	27 313	25 579	3 120	7 356	15 102	32 962	24 527	22 969	3 588	6 692	12 812	287 770
4th quarter	36 706	31 242	27 463	25 740	3 029	7 453	15 258	32 995	24 551	23 010	3 503	6 760	12 850	288 475

Table 1-11. Composite Indexes of Economic Activity and Selected Index Components

Year and month	Cyclical composite indexes, 1996 = 100				Selected components of leading index			Selected component of coincident index	Selected components of lagging index	
	Leading	Coincident	Lagging	Ratio, coincident to lagging	Vendor performance (slower deliveries diffusion index, percent)	Interest rate spread, 10-year Treasury bonds less federal funds [1]	Index of consumer expecta-tions [1,2]	Personal income less transfer payments (billions of 1996 dollars)	Change in manufac-turing labor cost per unit of output [3]	Consumer installment credit outstanding (percent of personal income)
1959	57.8	37.1	79.4	46.7	60.6	1.03	96.6	1 709.5	6.8	13.2
1960	56.8	37.8	81.8	46.2	35.7	0.90	98.3	1 759.5	2.8	14.1
1961	59.0	38.0	80.7	47.1	48.1	1.93	97.2	1 802.8	-7.6	14.1
1962	61.1	39.8	81.4	48.9	48.8	1.24	98.0	1 900.9	0.9	14.2
1963	63.5	41.2	82.8	49.7	51.1	0.82	97.1	1 973.6	-0.9	15.1
1964	66.3	43.0	84.5	50.9	62.8	0.69	99.2	2 092.2	0.5	15.9
1965	69.0	45.6	87.2	52.3	66.6	0.21	104.3	2 227.1	-1.0	16.5
1966	70.1	48.3	90.6	53.3	73.0	-0.19	94.6	2 359.9	3.9	16.4
1967	70.5	49.8	92.2	54.0	44.0	0.85	94.2	2 448.0	1.4	16.0
1968	72.9	51.9	93.0	55.7	52.6	-0.01	91.4	2 575.3	5.1	15.7
1969	73.5	53.9	95.7	56.3	65.2	-1.53	88.5	2 689.7	6.7	15.8
1970	70.6	54.0	96.2	56.1	50.3	0.17	73.7	2 738.2	0.4	15.4
1971	74.2	54.7	93.2	58.7	48.0	1.50	77.1	2 796.9	-2.0	15.5
1972	79.0	57.7	91.7	62.9	62.7	1.78	87.3	2 965.4	1.6	15.8
1973	79.9	61.0	95.2	64.0	88.0	-1.89	67.6	3 143.0	6.1	16.2
1974	74.6	61.4	99.3	61.8	65.8	-2.95	56.0	3 112.3	12.0	16.1
1975	73.1	59.3	95.8	62.0	30.2	2.16	65.5	3 062.5	2.9	15.0
1976	78.9	62.1	92.1	67.4	54.4	2.57	82.7	3 225.7	5.1	14.5
1977	81.4	65.1	92.5	70.5	55.7	1.88	81.3	3 375.2	4.9	14.9
1978	81.8	68.7	95.1	72.3	60.5	0.48	69.3	3 579.0	2.5	15.4
1979	79.9	71.0	99.0	71.7	57.9	-1.75	52.8	3 706.3	10.9	15.8
1980	77.3	70.7	100.2	70.6	40.6	-1.90	56.8	3 703.7	19.1	15.0
1981	78.0	71.6	99.2	72.2	46.3	-2.47	65.0	3 798.1	7.6	13.8
1982	77.7	70.0	97.5	71.8	43.5	0.74	62.7	3 803.3	3.3	13.6
1983	84.7	71.2	93.2	76.4	56.8	2.02	84.7	3 873.9	-3.4	13.7
1984	87.6	75.9	96.9	78.3	57.3	2.21	92.7	4 197.9	2.2	14.5
1985	89.4	78.2	99.5	78.5	48.0	2.52	86.5	4 357.9	2.2	15.9
1986	92.1	79.9	100.0	79.9	50.6	0.88	85.8	4 487.4	1.2	16.8
1987	94.5	82.5	99.5	82.9	57.4	1.73	81.3	4 627.4	-1.6	16.6
1988	95.2	85.6	100.4	85.2	57.7	1.28	85.2	4 812.5	3.0	16.4
1989	94.9	87.6	102.4	85.5	47.6	-0.72	85.3	4 958.8	2.3	16.5
1990	94.0	88.6	102.0	86.9	47.9	0.45	70.2	5 032.1	2.1	16.1
1991	93.7	87.6	99.2	88.3	47.3	2.17	70.3	4 966.2	1.1	15.4
1992	95.1	88.8	94.7	93.8	50.2	3.49	70.3	5 062.2	-0.5	14.4
1993	96.0	90.8	94.2	96.4	51.6	2.85	72.8	5 128.7	2.3	14.4
1994	97.7	94.2	95.1	99.0	60.1	2.88	83.8	5 280.6	-2.8	15.3
1995	97.6	97.2	99.1	98.1	52.8	0.74	83.2	5 428.9	-1.5	16.7
1996	100.0	100.0	100.0	100.0	50.5	1.14	85.7	5 618.2	-3.5	17.6
1997	103.1	103.9	100.4	103.4	53.9	0.89	97.7	5 860.6	-5.6	17.6
1998	105.3	108.3	102.2	106.0	51.1	-0.09	98.3	6 251.7	-2.4	17.3
1999	108.6	111.9	103.8	107.8	53.3	0.67	99.3	6 462.0	-1.8	17.6
2000	109.7	115.7	106.6	108.5	53.3	-0.21	102.7	6 831.0	-3.9	17.7
2001	108.6	115.2	105.3	109.5	48.0	1.13	82.3	6 859.1	0.0	18.7
2002	110.9	115.0	100.7	114.2	53.2	2.94	84.6	6 873.6	-1.9	19.1
2001										
January	108.3	116.1	107.4	108.1	49.7	-0.82	86.4	6 895.1	-1.4	18.2
February	108.1	116.0	106.9	108.5	50.6	-0.39	80.8	6 887.3	-1.4	18.3
March	107.8	115.9	106.7	108.6	48.2	-0.42	83.9	6 895.0	0.6	18.4
April	107.9	115.5	106.7	108.2	47.4	0.34	82.2	6 876.4	1.9	18.5
May	108.6	115.4	106.4	108.5	45.8	1.18	85.4	6 846.6	1.7	18.6
June	108.7	115.1	105.7	108.9	47.2	1.31	86.9	6 845.4	2.9	18.6
July	109.0	115.2	104.7	110.0	46.8	1.47	88.4	6 855.8	0.6	18.6
August	108.9	115.2	104.5	110.2	46.8	1.32	85.2	6 851.5	0.0	18.7
September	108.0	114.7	104.5	109.8	46.9	1.66	73.5	6 883.1	-0.4	18.8
October	108.4	114.7	103.7	110.6	49.1	2.08	75.5	6 809.4	-1.6	18.9
November	109.3	114.3	103.2	110.8	48.6	2.56	76.6	6 811.8	-1.4	19.1
December	110.5	114.4	102.9	111.2	48.9	3.27	82.3	6 852.0	-0.8	19.1
2002										
January	111.0	114.6	102.5	111.8	51.1	3.31	91.3	6 844.3	-2.6	19.1
February	111.0	114.4	102.1	112.0	51.9	3.17	87.2	6 857.5	-2.2	19.1
March	111.0	114.5	101.7	112.6	52.7	3.55	92.7	6 866.0	-2.0	19.1
April	110.8	114.7	101.1	113.5	53.4	3.46	89.1	6 846.9	-1.8	19.1
May	111.4	114.8	100.8	113.9	53.8	3.41	92.7	6 877.2	-1.2	19.1
June	111.2	115.1	100.4	114.6	54.5	3.18	87.9	6 922.4	-1.0	19.1
July	111.0	115.3	100.6	114.6	54.5	2.92	81.0	6 876.9	-2.1	19.2
August	110.9	115.3	100.4	114.8	53.7	2.52	80.6	6 879.2	-1.9	19.3
September	110.4	115.2	100.0	115.2	55.8	2.12	79.9	6 881.0	-1.9	19.2
October	110.4	115.2	99.9	115.3	53.0	2.19	73.1	6 863.9	-1.0	19.2
November	111.0	115.3	99.5	115.9	51.8	2.71	78.5	6 874.2	-2.1	19.2
December	111.2	115.2	99.3	116.0	52.6	2.79	80.8	6 893.8	-0.6	19.1

[1] Not seasonally adjusted.
[2] Copyright, University of Michigan, Survey Research Center, first quarter 1966 = 100.
[3] Monthly data are 6-month percent change at annual rate; annual data are for the 6-month period ending in September.

NOTES AND DEFINITIONS

TABLES 1-1 THROUGH 1-10 AND 19-1 THROUGH 19-8 NATIONAL INCOME AND PRODUCT

SOURCE: U.S. DEPARTMENT OF COMMERCE, BUREAU OF ECONOMIC ANALYSIS (BEA).

All data on these pages are from the national income and product accounts (NIPAs). The data are as published in the 1999 comprehensive NIPA revisions and as subsequently updated and revised through August 2003.

A new comprehensive revision of the accounts from 1929 forward is scheduled to be released in December 2003, too late for inclusion in this volume. This revision (like previous comprehensive revisions undertaken every 5 years) will affect the entire history of the accounts, including a change in the reference year for price and quantity measures from 1996 to 2000; this means that the data released after that date will not be directly comparable with the data in this volume. However, the editor of this volume expects that the revision will not lead to major differences in the trends, for example, the rates of change in output and prices and the movements of income, over the postwar period.

Definitions and notes on the data

The NIPAs show the composition of production and the distribution to labor and capital of the income resulting from production.

Gross domestic product (GDP), the featured measure of the value of U.S. output, is the market value of the goods and services produced by labor and property located in the United States. Market values include indirect business taxes, such as taxes on sales and property, and represent the values paid by the final customer. GDP is "gross" product in the sense that capital consumption allowances (economic depreciation) have not been deducted. GDP is the sum of personal consumption expenditures, gross private domestic investment (including change in private inventories and before deduction of charges for consumption of fixed capital), net exports of goods and services, and government consumption expenditures and gross investment. GDP represents a net rather than gross definition of "gross product," however, in that it excludes intermediate purchases of goods and services by business, because their value is already included in the value of the final products of business. In concept, it is equal to the sum of the economic value added by, or "gross product originating in," all industries in the United States.

GDP, rather than gross national product (GNP), has been the featured measure of U.S. production since the comprehensive NIPA revisions that were made in 1991. GDP refers to production taking place within the geographic boundaries of the United States, including production from capital and labor supplied by nonresidents; GNP refers to production by labor and property supplied by U.S. residents, whether located in the United States or abroad. GDP is consistent in coverage with other national economic indicators such as employment and productivity. It also is the measure used by almost all other countries and thus facilitates comparison of economic activity in the United States with that of other countries. GNP, however, provides a better comparison base for national saving.

Personal consumption expenditures (PCE) is goods and services purchased by persons residing in the United States. PCE consists mainly of purchases of new goods and services by individuals from business. It includes purchases that are financed by insurance, for example, by medical insurance. In addition, PCE includes purchases of new goods and services by nonprofit institutions, net purchases of used goods ("net" here meaning purchases of used goods from business less sales of used goods to business) by individuals and nonprofit institutions, and purchases abroad of goods and services by U.S. residents traveling or working in foreign countries. PCE also includes purchases for certain goods and services provided by government agencies. (See Notes and Definitions for Tables 4-1 through 4-5 for additional information.)

Gross private domestic investment consists of private fixed investment and change in private inventories.

Private fixed investment consists of both nonresidential and residential fixed investment. The term "residential" refers to the construction and equipping of living quarters for permanent occupancy; as will be seen below, hotels and motels are included in *nonresidential* fixed investment. Private fixed investment consists of purchases of fixed assets, which are commodities that will be used in a production process for more than 1 year, including replacements and additions to the capital stock, and it is measured "gross," before a deduction for consumption of existing fixed capital. It covers all investment by private businesses and nonprofit institutions in the United States, regardless of whether the investment is owned by U.S. residents. The residential component includes investment in owner-occupied housing; the homeowner is treated equivalently to a business in the investment accounts. Private fixed investment does not include purchases of the same types of equipment and structures by government agencies, which are included in government gross investment, nor does it include investment by U.S. residents in other countries.

Nonresidential fixed investment is the total of nonresidential structures and nonresidential equipment and software.

Nonresidential structures consists of new construction, brokers' commissions on sales of structures, and net purchases of used structures by private business and by nonprofit institutions from government agencies (that is, purchases of used structures from government minus sales of used structures to government). New construction also includes hotels, motels, and mining exploration, shafts, and wells.

Nonresidential equipment and software consists of private business purchases, on capital account, of new machinery, equipment, and vehicles; purchases and in-house production of software; dealers' margins on sales of used equipment; and net purchases of used equipment from government agencies, persons, and the rest of the world, that is, purchases of such equipment minus sales of such equipment. It does not, however, include the estimated personal-use portion of equipment purchased for both business and personal use, which is included in PCE.

Residential private fixed investment consists of both residential structures and residential producers' durable equipment, that is, equipment such as appliances owned by landlords and rented to tenants. Investment in structures consists of new units, improvements to existing units, manufactured homes, brokers' commissions on the sale of residential property, and net purchases of used residential structures from government agencies, that is, purchases of such structures from government minus sales of such structures to government. As noted above, it includes investment in owner-occupied housing.

Change in private inventories is the change in the physical volume of inventories held by businesses, valued at the average price of the period. It differs from the change in the book value of inventories reported by most businesses; an *inventory valuation adjustment* (IVA) converts book value change using historical cost valuations to the change in physical volume, valued at average replacement cost.

Net exports of goods and services is exports of goods and services less imports of goods and services. It does not include income payments or receipts or transfer payments to and from the rest of the world.

Government consumption expenditures is purchases by governments (federal, state, and local) of goods and services for current consumption. It includes compensation of general government employees and an allowance for consumption of general government fixed capital including software (depreciation). Receipts for certain services provided by government—primarily tuition payments for higher education and charges for medical care—are defined as government sales, which are treated as deductions from government purchases.

Gross government investment consists of general government and government enterprise expenditures for fixed

assets (structures and equipment and software). Government inventory investment is included in government consumption expenditures.

Real, or chained (1996) dollar, estimates are estimates from which the effect of price change has been removed. Prior to the 1996 comprehensive revision, constant-dollar measures were obtained by combining real output measures for different goods and services using the relative prices of a single year as weights for the entire time span of the series. In the recent environment of rapid technological change, which has caused the prices of computers and electronic components to decline dramatically relative to other prices, this method distorted the measurement of economic growth and caused excessive revisions of growth rates at each benchmark revision. The current, chained-dollar measure changes the relative price weights each year as relative prices shift over time.

Chained-dollar estimates, although expressed for continuity's sake as if they had occurred according to the prices of a single year (currently, 1996) are usually not additive; that is, because of the changes in price weights over the years, the 1996-dollar components in any given table usually do not add to the 1996-dollar total. In time periods close to the base year, the difference between the sum of components and the total is usually quite small. In earlier periods, the differences become much larger. For this reason, the BEA no longer publishes chained-dollar estimates prior to 1987, except for selected aggregate series. For the more detailed components, historical trends are represented by chain-type quantity indexes, which are presented in Tables 1-3, 4-4, 5-4, and 19-3.

Chain-weighting leads to complexity in estimating the contribution of economic sectors to an overall change in output: for example, answering the question "How much did the rise in defense spending contribute to the 3.3 percent annual rate of growth in GDP in the second quarter of 2003?" Using 1996-dollar estimates of total GDP and defense spending can only be done for recent years, when such estimates are published, and even so may give misleading answers if the period in question is not very close to the reference year (1996 in the current example). Users should refer to Table 2 in the monthly GDP release and Table 8.2 in the *Survey* tables for accurate calculations by BEA. To calculate contributions to growth for longer periods than those published by BEA, see Landefeld and Parker, "BEA's Chain Indexes, Time Series, and Measures of Long-Term Economic Growth," *Survey of Current Business*, May 1997, and "Preview of the Comprehensive Revision of the National Income and Product Accounts: BEA's New Featured Measures of Output and Prices," *Survey of Current Business*, July 1995.

GDP price indexes measure price changes between any 2 adjacent years for a fixed "market basket" of goods and services—the average quantities in those 2 years. The annual measures are chained together to form an index with prices in 1996 set to equal 100. This avoids the substitution bias, overstating price increase, that arises when the quantity weights are held constant over longer periods of time while the composition of output is changing.

Implicit price deflators are GDP price measures, 1996=100, consisting of the ratios of current-dollar to real GDP components (multiplied by 100). Because the price indexes now use the chain-type formula, they differ little from implicit price deflators and are now preferred for price measurement over the deflators.

Final sales of domestic product is GDP minus change in private inventories. Thus, it is the sum of personal consumption expenditures, gross private domestic fixed investment, government consumption expenditures and gross investment, and net exports of goods and services.

Gross domestic purchases is the market value of goods and services purchased by U.S. residents, regardless of where those goods and services were produced. It is GDP minus net exports (that is, minus exports plus imports) of goods and services; equivalently, it is the sum of personal consumption expenditures, gross private domestic investment, and government consumption expenditures and gross investment. The price index for gross domestic purchases is therefore a measure of price change for goods and services purchased by (rather than produced by) U.S. residents.

Final sales to domestic purchasers is gross domestic purchases minus change in private inventories.

Gross national product (GNP) refers to all goods and services produced by labor and property supplied by U.S. residents, whether located in the United States or abroad, expressed at market prices. It is equal to gross domestic product (GDP) plus income receipts from the rest of the world less income payments to the rest of the world. More information is given above under gross domestic product.

Net national product is the market value, net of depreciation, of goods and services attributable to the labor and property supplied by U.S. residents and is equal to GNP less the consumption of fixed capital. The measure of fixed capital consumption used relates only to fixed capital located in the United States. Investment in that capital is measured by private fixed investment and government gross investment.

National income is the income received by labor and capital as a result of their participation in the production process. It is expressed at factor cost—the remuneration paid to the labor and capital factors of production—rather than at market value. It consists of compensation

of employees; proprietors' income with inventory valuation and capital consumption adjustments; rental income of persons with capital consumption adjustment; corporate profits with inventory valuation and capital consumption adjustments; and net interest. By definition, national income and its components exclude all income from capital gains, which has no counterpart on the production side of the accounts.

Conceptually, national income can be derived from net national product by subtracting indirect business tax and nontax liability and business transfer payments and adding subsidies less current surplus of government enterprises. In practice, the product and income sides of the national accounts are estimated separately from different source data and there is always some *statistical discrepancy* between the two sides of the accounts.

Compensation of employees is the income accruing to employees as remuneration for their work. It is the sum of wage and salary accruals and supplements to wages and salaries.

Wage and salary accruals consists of the monetary remuneration of employees, including the compensation of corporate officers; corporate directors' fees paid to directors who are also employees of the corporation; commissions, tips, and bonuses; voluntary employee contributions to certain deferred compensation plans, such as 401(k) plans; and receipts in kind that represent income. In concept, it includes the value of the exercise by employees of "nonqualified stock options," in which an employee is allowed to buy stock for less than its current market price. (Actual measurement of these values involves a number of problems, particularly in the short run. Such stock options are not included in the Bureau of Labor Statistics wage data, which are the main source for current extrapolation of wages and salaries, and are not consistently reported in corporate financial statements. They are, however, generally included in the unemployment insurance wage data that are used to correct the preliminary wage and salary estimates.) Another form of stock option, the "incentive stock option," leads to a capital gain only and is not included in the definition of wages and salaries. *Wage and salary disbursements* is wages and salaries as just defined except that retroactive wage payments are recorded when paid, rather than when earned. In the NIPAs, wages accrued is the appropriate measure for national income, and wages disbursed is the appropriate measure for personal income.

Supplements to wages and salaries consists of employer contributions for social insurance and other labor income. Employer contributions for social insurance consists of employer payments under the following federal, state, and local government programs: Old-age, survivors, and disability insurance (Social Security); hospital

insurance (Medicare); unemployment insurance; railroad retirement; pension benefit guaranty; veterans life insurance; publicly administered workers' compensation; military medical insurance; and temporary disability insurance. Other labor income consists of employer payments (including payments in kind) to private pension and profit-sharing plans; private group health and life insurance plans; privately administered workers' compensation plans; government employee retirement plans; supplemental unemployment benefit plans; and several minor categories of employee compensation, including judicial fees to jurors and witnesses, compensation of prison inmates, and marriage fees to justices of the peace.

In the national accounts, all capital income—corporate profits, proprietors' income, and rental income—is converted from the basis usually shown in the books of business and reported to the Internal Revenue Service to a basis that more closely represents income from current production. In the source data, depreciation of structures and equipment will probably reflect a historical cost basis and a possibly arbitrary service life allowed by law to be used for tax purposes. These values are adjusted by BEA to reflect the average actual life of the capital good and the cost of replacing it in the current period's prices. This conversion is done for all three forms of capital income. In addition, the measurement of income from current production is defined to exclude any element of capital gains, so corporate and proprietors' income also require an adjustment for inventory valuation to exclude any profits or losses that might appear in the books if the cost of inventory acquisition is not valued in the current period's prices. These two adjustments are called the *capital consumption adjustment (CCAdj)* and the *inventory valuation adjustment (IVA)*. They will be described in more detail below.

Proprietors' income with inventory valuation and capital consumption adjustments is the current-production income (including income in kind) of sole proprietorships and partnerships and of tax-exempt cooperatives. The imputed net rental income of owner-occupants of farm dwellings is included, but the imputed net rental income of owner-occupants of nonfarm dwellings is included in rental income of persons. Fees paid to outside directors of corporations are included. Proprietors' income excludes dividends and monetary interest received by nonfinancial business and rental incomes received by persons not primarily engaged in the real estate business; these incomes are included in dividends, net interest, and rental income of persons.

Rental income of persons with capital consumption adjustment is the net current-production income of persons from the rental of real property (except for the income of persons primarily engaged in the real estate business); the imputed net rental income of owner-occupants of nonfarm dwellings; and the royalties received by persons

from patents, copyrights, and rights to natural resources. Consistent with the treatment of investment in owner-occupied housing as business investment, the homeowner is considered to receive as income the value of occupying the house and then to pay it to himself/herself as a component of consumer expenditures on services.

Corporate profits with inventory valuation and capital consumption adjustments (often referred to as "economic profits") is the current-production income, net of economic depreciation, of organizations treated as corporations in the NIPAs. These organizations consist of all entities required to file federal corporate tax returns, including mutual financial institutions and cooperatives subject to federal income tax; private noninsured pension funds; nonprofit institutions that primarily serve business; Federal Reserve Banks, which accrue the income stemming from the conduct of monetary policy; and federally sponsored credit agencies. With several differences, this income is measured as receipts less expenses as defined in federal tax law. Among these differences: receipts exclude capital gains and dividends received; expenses exclude depletion and capital losses and losses resulting from bad debts; inventory withdrawals are valued at replacement cost; and depreciation is on a consistent accounting basis and is valued at replacement cost. Because national income is defined as the income of U.S. residents, its profits component includes income earned abroad by U.S. corporations and excludes income earned in the United States by the rest of the world.

Profits before tax is also the net-of-depreciation income of organizations treated as corporations in the NIPAs, except that it reflects the inventory- and depreciation-accounting practices used for federal income tax returns. As a result, it includes gains or losses associated with price changes for inventory and fixed capital, rather than measuring profits from current production only. It comprises profits tax liability, dividends, and undistributed corporate profits.

Profits tax liability is the sum of federal, state, and local income taxes on all income subject to taxes; this income includes capital gains and other income excluded from profits before tax. The taxes are measured on an accrual basis, net of applicable tax credits.

Profits after tax is profits before tax less profits tax liability. It consists of dividends and undistributed corporate profits.

Dividends is payments in cash or other assets, excluding the corporations' own stock, that are made by corporations located in the United States and abroad to stockholders who are U.S. residents. The payments are measured net of dividends received by U.S. corporations. Dividends paid to state and local government social insurance funds and general government are included.

Undistributed profits is corporate profits after tax less dividends.

Inventory valuation adjustment (IVA) for corporations is the difference between the cost of inventory withdrawals as valued in the source data used to determine profits before tax and the cost of withdrawals valued at replacement cost. In the NIPAs, inventory profits or losses are shown as adjustments to business income (corporate profits and nonfarm proprietors' income); they are shown as the IVA with the sign reversed. No adjustment is needed to farm proprietors' income because farm inventories are measured on a current-market-cost basis.

Consumption of fixed capital is a charge for the using up of private and government fixed capital located in the United States. It is based not on depreciation schedules allowed in tax law but on studies of prices of used equipment and structures in resale markets. For general government and for nonprofit institutions that primarily serve individuals, it is recorded in government consumption expenditures and in personal consumption expenditures, respectively, as the value of the current services of the fixed capital assets owned and used by these entities.

Private capital consumption allowances consists of tax-return-based depreciation charges for corporations and nonfarm proprietorships and of historical-cost depreciation (calculated by BEA using a geometric pattern of price declines) for farm proprietorships, rental income of persons, and nonprofit institutions.

The *private capital consumption adjustment (CCAdj)* is the difference between private capital consumption allowances and private consumption of fixed capital, and therefore reflects the net effect of the two adjustments made to reported nonfarm business profits that convert historical to replacement costs and incorporate actual, rather than tax-based, service lives.

Net interest is the interest paid by private business less the interest received by private business, plus the interest received from the rest of the world less the interest paid to the rest of the world. Interest payments on mortgage and home improvement loans and on home equity loans are counted as interest paid by business because home ownership is treated as a business in the NIPAs. In addition to monetary interest, net interest includes imputed interest, which is paid by corporate financial business and is measured as the difference between the income received from the investment of depositors' or beneficiaries' funds and the amount of income paid out explicitly. The imputed interest paid by life insurance carriers and noninsured pension plans attributes their investment income to persons in the period it is earned. The remaining imputed interest payments have counter-entries on the product side of the accounts representing imputed service charges paid back to the financial institutions by persons and governments.

Gross product and domestic income of nonfinancial corporate business provide consistent information for the nonfinancial corporate sector of the economy on gross product, income, and the distribution of the total value of output among capital consumption, employee compensation, profits, and interest. Excluded from nonfinancial corporate business are households, institutions, general government, all noncorporate business, and financial business.

Per capita product and income estimates

In Table 1-10, annual and quarterly measures of product, income, and consumption spending are expressed in per capita terms—the aggregate dollar amount divided by the U.S. population. Population data from 1991 forward reflect the results of Census 2000.

National per capita totals as shown in Table 1-10 are based on definitions of income and population that differ slightly from the sum of the states shown in Table 21-2. See the Notes and Definitions to Chapter 21 for explanation.

Revisions

NIPA data normally undergo revision at the end of July each year. Typically these annual revisions cover annual and quarterly data for the previous 3 years, but may also include more limited revisions to data for earlier years. Approximately once every 5 years the NIPA data undergo "benchmark" revision, at which times definitional or other comprehensive changes may affect data back to 1929—the earliest year for which official national accounts data are available. Shown here are the results of the latest comprehensive revision of the NIPAs, which was released beginning in October 1999, concluding in April 2000. As indicated above, a new comprehensive revision is scheduled for December 2003. Because this revision was imminent, the usual July revision did not take place in July 2003.

In mid-2002, BEA inaugurated a new revision schedule for wages and salaries and related income-side components of the NIPAs. When "final" estimates of GDP are released each quarter, in June, September, December, and March following the end of that quarter, wages and salaries and related data will be revised for not only the "GDP" quarter but the previous quarter as well. Since these only affect income-side components, GDP itself will not be revised for that previous quarter. The purpose of this schedule change is to achieve a more timely incorporation of BLS quarterly tabulations of employees covered by state unemployment insurance. Previously, revisions based on these data were not incorporated until July of the following year. The same revision schedule will also be used in the monthly estimates of personal income.

Data availability

Annual data are available beginning with 1929; quarterly data begin with 1946 for current-dollar values and 1947 for quantity and price measures such as real GDP and the GDP price index. Not all data are available for all time periods.

New data normally are released toward the end of each month. The first estimates for each calendar quarter are released in the month after the quarter's end. Revisions for the most recent quarter are released in the second and third months after the quarter's end. As described above, wage and salary and related income-side components will be revised for previous quarters as well.

The most recent data are published each month in the *Survey of Current Business*; current and historical data may be obtained from the BEA Internet site at <http://www.bea.gov> and the STAT-USA subscription Internet site at <http://www.stat-usa.gov>.

References

The latest annual revision of the NIPAs is described in an article in the August 2002 *Survey of Current Business*. The previous year's annual revision is described in the August 2001 issue. The *Survey of Current Business* is available by mail subscription and on the BEA Web site.

For information about the 1999 comprehensive revisions, see articles in various issues of the *Survey of Current Business* on definitional and classificational changes (August 1999); new and redesigned tables (September 1999); statistical changes (October 1999); improved estimates of the NIPAs (December 1999); real inventories, sales, and inventory-sales ratios (January 2000); comparison of personal income and IRS adjusted gross income (February 2000); and improved NIPA estimates for 1929–99 (April 2000).

Description of various aspects of the upcoming 2003 comprehensive revision can be found in the following articles in indicated issues of the *Survey of Current Business*: "Preview of the 2003 Comprehensive Revision of the National Income and Product Accounts: Statistical Changes," September 2003; "Preview of the 2003 Comprehensive Revision of the National Income and Product Accounts: New and Redesigned Tables," August 2003; "Preview of the 2003 Comprehensive Revision of the National Income and Product Accounts: Changes in Definitions and Classifications," June 2003; "Income and Outlays of Households and of Nonprofit Institutions Serving Households," April 2003; "Preview of Revised NIPA Estimates for 1997: Effects of Incorporating the 1997 Benchmark I-O Accounts and Proposed Definitional and Statistical Changes," January 2003; "Note on the Upcoming Comprehensive Revision of the National Income and Product Accounts," November

2002; and "Selected Issues in the Measurement of U.S. International Services," June 2002.

General reference articles on NIPA concepts and methods in the *Survey of Current Business* are "Updated Summary NIPA Methodologies" (October 2002) and "A Guide to the NIPA's" (March 1998).

The treatment of employee stock options is discussed in Carol Moylan, "Treatment of Employee Stock Options in the U.S. National Economic Accounts," available on the BEA Web site.

TABLES 1-11 AND 20-9
COMPOSITE INDEXES OF ECONOMIC ACTIVITY

Source: The Conference Board.

The composite indexes of leading, coincident, and lagging indicators are intended to help predict and identify peaks and troughs in the business cycle. They are calculated from sets of component series selected for their utility as indicators of stages of the business cycle. The component series originate from a variety of sources, as indicated below. Several component series that are not published elsewhere in this volume appear on the page with the composites. For the other components, references to the appropriate tables in *Business Statistics* are given below.

The classification of indicators into leading, coincident, and lagging series grows out of an approach to the study of economic fluctuations pioneered by Wesley C. Mitchell and Arthur F. Burns early in the twentieth century, and carried on by other researchers affiliated with the National Bureau of Economic Research (NBER). It was observed that indicators of business activity tended to move up and down over periods that were longer than a year and therefore were not accounted for by seasonal variation. Although these periods of expansion and contraction were not uniform in length, their recurrent nature has caused them to be called "business cycles."

Furthermore, researchers found that some indicators that described the general state of business activity, such as different measures of production and income, tended to move together, with their peaks occurring within a few months of each other and their low points, or troughs, also tending to occur at about the same time. These are the *coincident indicators*. Other indicators also moved cyclically, but their peaks and troughs came noticeably before the peaks and troughs in the coincident indicators; these are the *leading indicators*, which of course are of great interest to anyone with a stake in the future performance of the economy. Finally, still other indicators had peaks and troughs noticeably later than those in the coincident indicators; these are the *lagging indicators*. Lagging indicators can be valuable in observing whether cyclical imbalances have been corrected and preconditions exist for a new cycle phase.

The dates of business cycles are currently established by the Business Cycle Dating Committee of the NBER; this committee was formed in 1978. (The first NBER-established business cycle dates were published in 1929.) Business cycle dates are based on monthly data, and the identification of a recession does not always follow the common definition of recession as two consecutive quarters of decline in real GDP. In all, the NBER has identified 31 cycles since December 1854.

The monthly and quarterly dates of the cycles from the trough marking the end of the Great Depression to the latest announced trough are shown in the table below. Quarterly turning points are identified by Roman numerals. NBER considers that the trough month is both the end of the decline and the beginning of the recovery, based on the concept that the actual turning point was some particular day within that month; thus, the latest recession ended in November 2001 and the recovery also began in November 2001. Similarly, the peak month of March 2001 was both the last month of expansion and the first month of recession.

BUSINESS CYCLE REFERENCE DATES
1933–2001

TROUGH	PEAK
March 1933 (I)	May 1937 (II)
June 1938(II)	February 1945 (I)
October 1945 (IV)	November 1948 (IV)
October 1949 (IV)	July 1953 (II)
May 1954 (II)	August 1957 (III)
April 1958 (II)	April 1960 (II)
February 1961 (I)	December 1969 (IV)
November 1970 (IV)	November 1973 (IV)
March 1975 (I)	January 1980 (I)
July 1980 (III)	July 1981 (III)
November 1982 (IV)	July 1990 (III)
March 1991 (I)	March 2001 (I)
November 2001 (IV)	

For additional information on NBER and its business cycle studies, see the NBER Internet site at <http://www.nber.org/cycles>.

The composite indexes were originally compiled and published by the Commerce Department, Bureau of Economic Analysis. In 1995, responsibility for compilation and publication was transferred to The Conference Board, a not-for-profit business research organization.

It is frequently said that the leading indicator index is designed to predict turning points in business activity 6 months in advance. However, the actual leads over the last six business cycles have varied between 3 and 15 months, and the index has sometimes turned down without a corresponding recession, so it is important not to rely mechanically on these composites.

Index components

The *index of leading economic indicators* consists of the following 10 components, with monthly data seasonally adjusted except as noted:

Average weekly hours are average hours worked per week by production workers in manufacturing. Source: Bureau of Labor Statistics. (Table 10-7)

Initial claims, unemployment insurance are average weekly claims for unemployment insurance under state programs. For inclusion in the leading index, the signs of the month-to-month changes are reversed, because claims increase when employment conditions worsen. Source: U.S. Department of Labor, Employment and Training Administration. (Table 10-4)

Manufacturers' new orders, consumer goods and materials are new orders, net of order cancellations, in billions of chained 1996 dollars. Source: Bureau of the Census, with inflation adjustment by The Conference Board. (Table 17-6 for current-dollar data.)

Vendor performance, slower deliveries diffusion index tracks the relative speed with which goods-producing companies receive deliveries from their suppliers. An increase in this series indicates a slowdown in deliveries and is generally caused by increased demand for manufacturing materials. The survey asks purchasing managers if their suppliers' deliveries were obtained faster, slower, or the same as the previous month's deliveries. The index records the percentage reporting slower deliveries plus one-half of the percentage reporting no change in delivery speed. Source: National Association of Purchasing Management.

Manufacturers' new orders, nondefense capital goods are in billions of chained 1996 dollars. Source: Bureau of the Census, with inflation adjustment by The Conference Board. (See Table 17-6 for new orders for nondefense capital goods in current dollars.)

Building permits, new private housing units is the number of new private housing units authorized by local building permits. Source: Bureau of the Census. (Table 17-3)

Stock prices: 500 common stocks is an index based on 1941–1943=10. Source: Standard and Poor's Corporation. (Table 12-10)

Money supply (M2) is in billions of chained 1996 dollars. Source: Federal Reserve Board of Governors, with inflation adjustment by The Conference Board. (See Table 12-1 for the M2 money supply in current dollars.)

Interest rate spread is equal to the rate on 10-year treasury bonds less the rate on federal funds. The interest rate series are not seasonally adjusted. Source: Federal Reserve Board of Governors.

Index of consumer expectations is based on the first quarter of 1966=100. The monthly data are not seasonally adjusted. Source: University of Michigan, Survey Research Center. This is a copyrighted series used by permission; it may not be reproduced without written permission from the source.

The ***index of coincident economic indicators*** consists of the following four components, with monthly data seasonally adjusted:

Employees on nonagricultural payrolls are total wage and salary employees, in thousands. Source: Bureau of Labor Statistics. (Table 10-5)

Personal income less transfer payments is in billions of chained 1996 dollars (seasonally adjusted annual rate). Source: Bureau of Economic Analysis, with inflation adjustment by The Conference Board, using the implicit deflator for personal consumption expenditures. (See Table 4-1 for total personal income and transfer payments in current dollars.)

Index of industrial production is an index of the output of the mining, manufacturing, and utility sectors of the U.S. economy. The index is based on 1992 = 100. Source: Federal Reserve Board of Governors. (Table 2-1)

Manufacturing and trade sales are in millions of chained 1996 dollars. Source: Bureau of Economic Analysis. (Table 5-9)

The ***index of lagging economic indicators*** consists of the following seven components, with monthly data seasonally adjusted except as noted.

Average duration of unemployment is in weeks. As with initial claims, the signs of the month-to-month changes are reversed. Source: Bureau of Labor Statistics. (Table 10-2)

Ratio: manufacturing and trade inventories to sales is calculated from sales and inventories in chained 1996 dollars. Source: Bureau of Economic Analysis. (Table 5-9)

Manufacturing labor cost per unit of output is the percent change over a 6-month span in this monthly index, which is constructed by The Conference Board. (For the Bureau of Labor Statistics quarterly index of manufacturing unit labor cost, see Table 9-3.)

Average prime interest rate is an average percentage rate per annum used by banks to price short-term business loans; not seasonally adjusted. Source: Federal Reserve Board of Governors. (Table 12-9)

Commercial and industrial loans outstanding is in billions of chained 1996 dollars. Sources: Federal Reserve Board of Governors, with inflation adjustment by The Conference Board. (See Table 12-4 for current-dollar data.)

Consumer credit outstanding is expressed as a percent of personal income. Sources: Bureau of Economic Analysis (Table 4-1) and Federal Reserve Board of Governors. (Table 12-8)

Consumer price index for services is the annual rate of change in the services component of the Consumer Price Index. Source: Bureau of Labor Statistics. (Table 8-1)

Notes on the data

Each composite index is scaled so that its average monthly value equals 100 in a base year, currently 1996. Changes in the components are calculated and standardized, using the standard deviation of each component, to equalize the volatility of each component in an index. Beginning with the January 2001 release, indicators that are not available at publication time are estimated using statistical imputation (an autoregressive model); in subsequent months the imputations are replaced by the actual reported data. This imputation procedure allows earlier release each month of preliminary values for the composite indexes.

Annual revisions to the indexes are normally made each January; the latest was made in January 2003. The most recent comprehensive revisions, which included addition and deletion of components, were introduced in 1996.

Data availability

Data are published each month by The Conference Board. The monthly report *Business Cycle Indicators* is available by subscription from The Conference Board, 845 Third Avenue, New York, NY 10022. A monthly press release from The Conference Board, with information about the indexes and their components, is available at <http://www.tcb-indicators.org>. The full historical database (with monthly data back to 1959) is available by subscription from the same Internet site.

References

In addition to The Conference Board's *Business Cycle Indicators* (referenced above), see the *Survey of Current Business*: "Business Cycle Indicators: Upcoming Revision of the Composite Indexes" (October 1993).

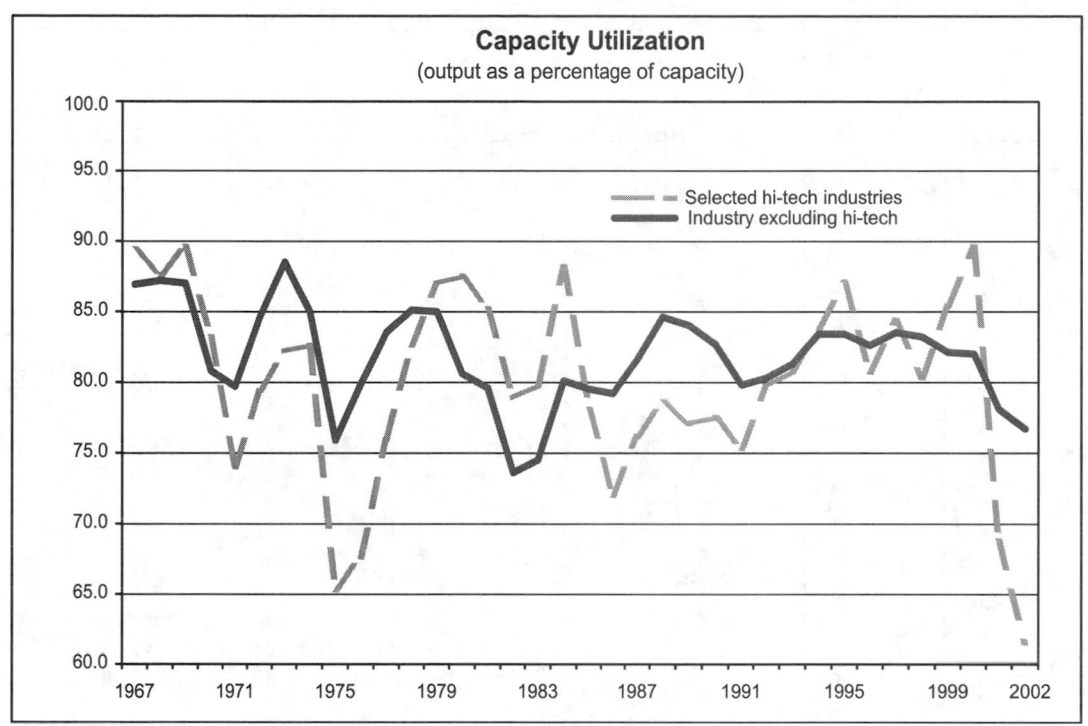

- Industrial production increased 154 percent from 1967 to 2002, which translates into an annual average growth rate of 2.7 percent. The most prominent high-tech industries—computers and office equipment, communications equipment, and semiconductors and related electronic components—grew at an annual rate of 18.6 percent, while the rest of manufacturing, mining, and utilities grew at a 1.7 percent rate. (Table 2-2)

- Capacity utilization in these high-tech industries was generally more volatile than in the rest of industry, as can be seen in the graph above. At their lowest levels, high-tech industries used 65.3 percent of capacity in 1975 and 61.5 percent in 2002—lower in both those recession years than the rest of industry. High-tech utilization soared to 89.6 percent of capacity in 2000, equaling its high in 1969. This was much higher than the rest of industry in 2000, but comparable to non-high-tech highs reached in the late 1960s and again in 1973. (Table 2-3)

- Of the major market groups in industrial production, consumer goods production grew at a 2.7 percent rate from 1967 to 2002; business equipment, 4.4 percent; defense and space equipment, 0.4 percent; construction supplies, 1.9 percent; energy materials, 1.1 percent; and non-energy materials, 2.9 percent. (Table 2-1)

- Output of defense and space equipment peaked in the late 1980s and then declined, only turning up again after 2000, while business equipment output grew throughout most of the period, only modestly interrupted by recession, to a peak in 2000. The plunge since then in business equipment production was 12.7 percent, comparable to the 11.6 percent decline from 1974 to 1975, and greater than the declines associated with the three other recessions in the 1967–2002 period. (Table 2-1)

Table 2-1. Industrial Production Indexes by Market Groups

(Seasonally adjusted, 1997=100)

| Year and month | Total industrial production | Final products and nonindustrial supplies | Consumer goods | Durable consumer goods | | | | | Nondurable consumer goods |
		Total	Total	Total	Automotive products	Home electronics	Appliances, furniture, and carpeting	Miscellaneous durable goods	Total
1967	43.7	42.6	48.7	36.3	37.0	2.0	48.6	48.4	54.4
1968	46.2	44.6	51.7	40.4	44.1	2.2	52.2	51.6	56.6
1969	48.3	46.3	53.6	42.1	44.3	2.3	55.0	55.8	58.5
1970	46.7	44.9	53.0	38.9	37.3	2.1	54.5	53.8	59.5
1971	47.4	45.5	56.0	44.0	47.5	2.3	57.5	56.8	61.2
1972	51.9	49.7	60.5	49.3	51.3	2.6	67.5	63.7	65.1
1973	56.1	53.4	63.3	52.9	55.5	3.0	72.9	66.6	67.1
1974	55.9	53.2	61.4	48.1	48.0	2.8	66.4	64.2	67.1
1975	50.9	49.4	59.0	43.7	46.1	2.4	56.8	57.1	66.0
1976	54.9	52.8	63.8	49.3	52.4	2.9	64.2	63.5	70.1
1977	59.1	57.2	67.7	55.3	59.1	3.4	72.1	70.3	72.6
1978	62.4	60.6	69.8	56.6	58.4	3.8	75.9	72.7	75.2
1979	64.2	62.6	68.8	54.5	52.6	3.8	76.1	73.2	74.8
1980	62.5	61.6	66.3	47.6	41.2	3.9	70.9	67.0	74.8
1981	63.4	62.9	66.8	48.3	42.5	4.0	69.9	68.0	75.2
1982	60.1	61.3	66.6	45.6	41.2	3.5	63.2	64.4	76.5
1983	61.7	62.9	69.0	50.5	47.3	5.2	69.8	66.2	77.3
1984	67.3	68.3	72.1	56.2	52.4	6.3	77.8	73.3	78.9
1985	68.1	70.0	72.7	56.2	52.2	6.5	77.2	73.3	79.9
1986	68.8	71.4	75.1	59.4	55.3	8.6	81.0	81.0	81.8
1987	72.3	74.8	78.1	62.7	58.5	8.4	85.3	85.3	84.7
1988	75.9	78.3	81.2	66.2	62.0	10.9	86.6	86.6	87.5
1989	76.6	79.0	81.4	67.5	64.1	11.4	87.6	87.6	87.2
1990	77.2	79.9	82.0	66.1	61.2	13.1	85.4	85.4	88.7
1991	76.1	78.6	82.0	63.6	57.9	15.6	79.5	79.5	90.0
1992	78.2	80.5	84.5	69.7	67.8	17.1	84.0	84.0	90.6
1993	80.8	83.1	87.4	76.6	75.3	26.9	88.8	88.8	91.9
1994	85.2	86.9	91.6	85.4	85.7	40.3	95.2	95.2	94.2
1995	89.3	90.4	94.5	89.7	89.1	61.0	94.7	94.7	96.5
1996	93.1	93.9	96.5	93.5	92.7	73.7	95.7	95.7	97.8
1997	100.0	100.0	100.0	100.0	100.0	100.0	100.0	100.0	100.0
1998	105.9	105.7	103.6	107.0	106.6	131.1	106.7	106.7	102.2
1999	110.6	108.7	105.3	113.5	116.5	145.5	109.9	109.9	102.1
2000	115.4	112.3	107.5	117.5	119.4	170.1	113.3	113.3	103.7
2001	111.5	109.3	105.9	110.4	113.9	132.7	109.1	109.1	104.0
2002	110.9	107.9	106.8	115.7	124.1	148.4	110.8	110.8	103.4
2000									
January	113.6	110.2	105.5	118.4	122.3	147.3	115.1	109.1	100.6
February	114.3	110.9	106.8	118.5	121.8	158.8	113.3	109.8	102.5
March	114.8	111.4	106.6	118.1	121.7	147.2	114.3	109.3	102.3
April	115.6	112.4	107.6	119.5	123.5	162.0	113.9	109.8	103.2
May	116.3	113.0	108.2	119.9	123.7	162.9	115.2	109.7	103.9
June	116.4	113.2	108.6	119.9	122.1	179.5	117.0	109.2	104.4
July	115.8	112.8	107.5	116.8	115.8	189.7	112.9	110.3	103.9
August	115.7	112.6	107.8	118.0	119.4	188.9	112.0	109.1	103.9
September	116.2	113.1	108.7	119.1	121.2	190.6	113.7	108.9	104.7
October	115.7	112.5	107.3	116.4	117.4	182.3	111.1	108.3	103.8
November	115.6	112.7	107.5	113.4	113.0	169.6	110.1	107.3	105.1
December	115.3	112.8	108.0	111.8	110.9	161.9	110.9	105.9	106.2
2001									
January	114.2	111.9	106.6	109.2	107.2	141.8	110.4	105.6	105.3
February	113.6	111.2	106.4	109.3	109.2	129.9	111.2	103.9	105.0
March	113.2	110.8	106.1	111.3	114.3	129.7	109.8	103.5	103.9
April	112.8	110.5	106.5	110.7	113.7	127.6	108.7	103.4	104.6
May	112.3	110.1	106.6	111.3	116.1	131.6	107.8	102.0	104.5
June	111.6	109.6	106.3	110.5	114.8	123.3	107.6	102.2	104.4
July	111.1	109.2	106.0	111.8	118.0	108.1	109.2	102.2	103.6
August	110.9	108.6	105.9	110.0	114.8	115.6	109.2	100.6	104.0
September	110.2	107.8	105.4	109.4	113.2	124.3	109.9	99.7	103.6
October	109.9	107.5	105.5	108.3	110.8	141.3	108.5	98.9	104.0
November	109.4	106.9	104.9	110.5	115.1	158.4	108.1	98.0	102.6
December	109.1	107.0	105.4	112.8	119.2	161.3	108.6	98.4	102.5
2002									
January	109.7	107.3	106.3	112.7	118.1	172.4	109.1	98.5	103.6
February	109.9	107.3	106.3	113.7	119.6	165.8	110.7	99.0	103.4
March	110.3	107.7	106.8	113.9	119.9	151.9	111.5	100.1	104.0
April	110.8	107.9	107.0	114.4	122.3	132.9	111.1	100.5	104.1
May	111.0	107.8	106.5	114.9	122.7	129.0	112.8	100.9	103.2
June	111.7	108.6	107.6	116.1	125.2	123.9	113.2	101.3	104.4
July	111.5	108.3	107.5	116.8	127.4	133.0	111.2	100.4	103.9
August	111.5	108.2	107.1	116.8	128.0	140.3	108.8	100.1	103.5
September	111.3	108.2	107.3	117.0	127.1	150.6	109.7	100.6	103.6
October	111.0	108.0	106.7	115.9	124.9	151.2	109.0	100.7	103.2
November	111.2	107.8	106.6	118.8	129.5	163.9	110.8	100.8	102.1
December	110.6	107.3	105.6	116.8	124.9	166.2	111.1	100.9	101.5

Table 2-1. Industrial Production Indexes by Market Groups—Continued

(Seasonally adjusted, 1997=100)

Year and month	Nondurable nonenergy consumer goods Total	Foods and tobacco	Clothing	Chemical products	Paper products	Consumer energy products	Business equipment Total	Transit	Information processing	Industrial and other	Defense and space equipment	Construction supplies	Business supplies
1967	55.4	57.8	96.9	30.7	54.4	48.2	24.4	70.7	2.8	50.7	90.9	52.6	37.0
1968	57.3	59.3	100.4	33.6	53.8	51.7	25.4	78.9	3.2	50.6	91.1	55.3	39.2
1969	59.0	60.9	101.9	35.2	55.8	55.3	27.1	77.8	3.5	53.9	86.7	57.7	41.7
1970	59.6	61.7	99.0	38.3	53.8	58.5	26.1	68.2	3.7	52.0	73.4	55.7	41.9
1971	61.1	63.6	98.4	40.5	54.9	61.2	24.8	66.0	3.4	49.7	66.0	57.5	43.2
1972	65.1	67.2	107.1	44.2	55.3	64.6	28.3	72.0	4.0	56.6	64.2	65.2	47.5
1973	67.3	69.0	109.2	47.6	57.2	65.7	32.7	86.7	4.6	64.4	69.9	70.7	50.4
1974	66.9	69.3	102.3	50.1	56.4	67.5	34.5	84.6	5.5	67.1	72.0	69.0	50.3
1975	65.2	68.2	99.4	48.3	53.2	68.9	30.5	74.0	5.0	58.9	73.2	58.5	46.4
1976	69.4	72.6	104.7	52.5	55.2	72.5	32.3	77.0	5.8	61.2	70.9	63.1	49.4
1977	71.9	74.1	109.9	54.7	60.4	75.3	37.4	92.1	7.6	66.8	63.4	68.7	53.5
1978	74.7	76.8	112.5	58.1	63.5	76.7	42.3	107.9	9.6	71.6	63.9	72.6	56.4
1979	73.7	76.3	106.3	58.2	64.1	78.6	47.6	124.9	12.1	75.9	68.7	74.4	58.4
1980	74.6	77.5	108.2	58.0	64.9	75.8	48.2	115.6	14.8	73.5	81.8	68.8	57.0
1981	75.1	77.9	108.1	58.8	66.4	75.3	49.5	108.0	17.4	73.3	88.7	67.6	58.4
1982	76.6	80.4	107.8	59.0	68.2	75.8	45.4	82.8	19.7	63.5	106.2	61.4	57.7
1983	77.6	80.5	110.8	59.6	71.1	76.3	45.3	82.3	22.1	58.8	107.0	65.7	60.4
1984	79.0	81.5	111.2	61.0	74.8	78.7	52.5	86.5	27.7	67.1	122.3	71.6	65.7
1985	80.2	83.9	106.3	61.6	78.6	78.7	54.6	89.6	30.0	68.0	136.9	73.4	67.4
1986	82.2	85.3	106.2	66.4	79.7	80.2	53.9	84.2	30.1	67.6	145.5	75.9	69.6
1987	85.0	87.3	107.0	71.5	84.2	83.1	57.3	87.0	33.7	70.0	148.3	80.5	73.8
1988	87.5	89.8	105.3	75.8	86.5	87.5	62.4	94.8	36.9	76.0	148.3	82.3	76.6
1989	87.0	89.1	100.4	77.3	86.9	88.0	64.4	99.3	37.7	78.5	148.3	81.9	77.7
1990	89.0	91.6	98.4	80.1	88.5	87.4	66.1	103.9	40.1	77.9	142.6	81.1	79.6
1991	89.9	92.1	98.0	83.0	89.1	90.1	64.6	106.4	39.9	73.9	131.6	76.6	78.5
1992	91.0	93.3	100.1	82.7	90.0	88.9	67.1	103.2	45.0	75.1	122.3	79.8	80.3
1993	91.7	92.6	102.0	85.0	92.1	92.8	69.7	95.3	48.1	80.2	115.6	83.4	82.9
1994	94.3	96.3	103.9	86.9	91.3	94.0	73.5	86.7	54.1	85.6	108.9	89.5	86.2
1995	96.4	98.8	103.3	90.4	92.0	96.5	79.4	81.8	64.4	90.9	106.0	91.4	89.9
1996	97.1	98.6	100.6	94.7	91.9	100.7	86.9	84.0	78.8	94.3	102.0	95.5	93.2
1997	100.0	100.0	100.0	100.0	100.0	100.0	100.0	100.0	100.0	100.0	100.0	100.0	100.0
1998	102.5	102.4	94.4	104.6	105.5	100.5	111.2	119.2	118.3	103.3	104.1	105.2	105.9
1999	101.8	100.4	90.6	106.2	107.9	104.1	117.1	118.1	141.9	101.0	101.4	107.9	110.7
2000	103.3	101.8	87.3	110.2	109.0	105.8	125.5	102.9	169.9	107.1	91.0	110.3	116.0
2001	103.5	101.8	78.2	115.8	106.7	106.5	117.6	97.7	165.3	97.1	102.6	105.2	111.6
2002	102.0	100.7	70.9	115.6	103.9	110.0	109.5	84.5	159.6	90.5	105.7	103.1	110.7
2000													
January	100.6	98.9	88.9	104.9	109.1	101.1	121.1	110.1	155.0	104.1	93.8	110.6	113.9
February	102.0	100.7	89.6	107.0	108.1	104.8	121.5	105.2	159.0	104.4	91.4	110.6	114.4
March	103.0	101.7	89.4	108.4	108.8	99.4	123.2	106.2	161.5	105.8	90.9	111.4	115.3
April	103.4	101.5	88.9	110.1	110.5	102.2	125.0	105.6	165.1	107.6	89.2	111.3	116.6
May	103.4	101.3	88.3	111.6	109.1	106.1	126.4	104.3	170.4	107.9	89.0	110.3	117.3
June	104.0	102.9	87.7	109.8	109.9	106.5	126.3	103.2	169.4	108.7	90.1	110.2	116.9
July	103.9	102.9	87.9	109.3	109.9	104.3	127.2	102.2	172.4	109.3	91.9	110.8	116.3
August	103.6	102.3	87.0	110.5	108.2	105.7	126.2	99.8	173.3	108.0	90.0	109.8	116.3
September	104.0	103.0	85.7	111.0	108.9	108.4	127.5	99.7	177.2	108.4	86.4	110.3	116.0
October	103.4	101.3	85.3	112.2	109.7	106.1	127.4	99.5	178.0	108.1	91.0	110.0	116.0
November	104.0	102.1	85.4	113.3	108.5	110.3	127.0	100.2	178.6	106.7	93.7	109.5	116.3
December	104.6	102.9	83.8	114.6	108.1	114.1	126.8	99.0	179.3	106.5	94.1	108.6	116.2
2001													
January	103.7	101.7	84.8	112.8	108.7	112.8	126.0	97.2	181.0	104.9	97.8	108.4	115.6
February	103.9	101.7	84.4	114.8	106.7	110.3	124.3	97.6	176.2	104.0	97.4	107.6	114.1
March	103.1	100.9	83.8	114.1	106.0	108.2	123.4	100.3	173.4	102.8	100.3	107.2	113.3
April	104.1	102.4	82.9	114.2	107.9	107.2	122.0	100.5	172.2	100.8	102.0	106.6	112.0
May	104.5	101.7	80.7	119.4	107.1	104.9	119.8	100.6	168.7	98.5	102.1	106.3	111.6
June	104.3	103.2	78.9	115.6	107.0	105.3	118.1	99.6	165.7	97.2	103.8	105.9	111.2
July	103.3	101.1	78.0	116.0	108.0	105.5	117.1	99.6	164.0	96.2	105.1	105.3	110.8
August	103.4	101.4	75.6	117.0	107.2	107.4	114.7	98.3	158.4	94.9	104.6	104.2	111.0
September	103.3	102.7	73.3	114.9	106.3	105.2	112.8	97.2	156.4	92.9	105.4	103.7	110.0
October	103.6	102.1	72.9	117.6	105.6	106.5	111.5	95.2	155.5	91.7	105.0	102.1	110.2
November	102.5	101.2	71.7	116.3	104.6	102.9	110.8	94.0	154.9	91.2	104.1	102.2	109.5
December	102.6	101.2	71.4	116.6	105.5	102.1	110.1	91.8	156.9	90.0	104.1	102.4	109.4
2002													
January	103.3	101.8	70.9	118.6	104.9	105.3	110.0	90.8	155.9	90.5	103.7	101.9	109.2
February	102.9	102.3	70.2	116.1	104.5	105.8	109.8	90.4	157.1	89.8	103.3	102.7	109.3
March	103.3	102.7	70.4	116.3	104.9	107.8	109.5	88.7	157.7	89.8	103.9	103.9	109.8
April	102.6	102.6	69.8	114.2	103.0	111.4	109.4	87.3	156.7	90.4	104.3	103.5	110.7
May	101.8	101.0	70.8	114.3	103.2	110.1	109.7	85.2	156.8	91.6	104.5	103.9	111.3
June	102.9	102.3	72.2	115.7	102.5	111.6	110.1	84.8	159.2	91.5	105.3	104.0	111.1
July	102.4	101.1	72.3	116.4	102.6	111.5	109.0	83.3	158.1	90.6	105.0	102.6	111.6
August	102.3	101.2	71.3	115.5	103.4	109.5	109.7	83.1	160.0	91.2	106.1	103.3	111.2
September	102.6	101.2	72.1	116.3	104.7	108.6	109.3	82.1	160.7	90.6	107.2	103.4	111.1
October	101.6	99.8	70.3	115.5	105.5	110.8	108.8	80.4	161.5	90.2	107.9	103.2	111.7
November	99.7	96.9	71.1	114.7	104.6	113.5	109.6	80.1	164.3	90.5	107.1	102.8	111.0
December	98.8	96.0	69.4	113.9	102.8	114.3	109.2	77.9	167.0	89.7	109.7	102.1	110.9

Table 2-1. Industrial Production Indexes by Market Groups—*Continued*
(Seasonally adjusted, 1997=100.)

Year and month	Total	Materials										Energy materials
		Non–energy materials										
		Total	Durable				Nondurable					
			Total	Consumer parts	Equipment parts	Other	Total	Textile	Paper	Chemical		
1967	44.2	37.6	32.9	50.3	13.8	57.1	46.8	66.0	46.9	34.0		68.9
1968	47.1	40.3	34.8	56.7	14.1	60.1	51.5	72.8	49.0	39.6		72.1
1969	49.9	42.8	36.6	57.1	15.0	64.0	55.7	74.8	53.2	43.9		75.7
1970	48.1	40.3	33.3	47.9	13.8	59.7	56.0	72.1	52.8	44.9		79.5
1971	48.9	41.0	33.4	53.0	13.8	57.5	58.4	75.5	55.1	47.6		80.2
1972	53.8	46.0	37.8	59.0	15.9	65.0	64.4	79.5	58.8	55.4		83.2
1973	58.7	50.9	43.1	68.5	18.7	72.0	67.6	77.3	63.4	61.1		85.2
1974	58.5	50.8	42.6	60.6	19.8	72.0	68.5	72.3	66.6	62.8		84.9
1975	52.1	43.7	35.7	48.9	17.0	60.2	61.4	70.8	57.9	52.6		84.0
1976	56.7	48.6	39.9	62.4	18.4	64.6	68.0	78.8	63.7	60.3		85.8
1977	60.7	52.7	43.6	68.4	20.9	68.5	72.9	84.0	66.6	67.0		88.5
1978	63.7	56.1	47.1	72.3	23.4	72.9	75.7	83.1	69.8	71.1		89.6
1979	65.4	57.7	48.6	68.3	25.8	74.7	77.1	82.4	72.6	74.0		92.0
1980	63.0	54.3	45.0	52.6	26.5	69.1	74.6	80.5	73.2	68.5		92.7
1981	63.3	54.5	45.1	50.1	27.2	69.3	75.2	78.7	74.6	69.1		93.6
1982	58.5	49.1	39.4	42.5	25.0	58.5	71.2	71.8	75.2	61.9		89.6
1983	60.0	52.4	42.0	51.7	25.5	61.2	76.3	80.6	80.0	68.5		86.8
1984	65.8	58.6	48.8	61.5	30.9	67.8	79.7	80.4	84.9	72.8		92.3
1985	65.7	58.6	49.2	63.9	31.0	67.3	79.0	76.1	84.4	71.4		91.7
1986	65.7	82.2	49.9	63.4	31.7	68.5	81.5	79.3	88.1	74.9		88.1
1987	69.2	85.0	53.4	65.1	34.7	73.3	86.3	89.0	92.4	81.3		90.2
1988	73.0	87.5	57.6	70.4	37.7	78.6	89.5	88.2	95.5	86.2		93.3
1989	73.5	87.0	57.8	66.8	38.9	78.9	90.4	90.1	95.4	87.4		94.2
1990	74.0	89.0	57.9	62.2	40.2	79.3	90.6	85.6	95.7	88.3		96.1
1991	72.9	89.9	56.3	58.9	40.3	75.9	89.6	85.5	93.7	87.1		96.2
1992	75.4	91.0	60.1	66.1	42.7	79.9	91.8	90.5	96.0	89.3		95.3
1993	77.9	91.7	64.1	75.1	45.4	83.0	92.8	94.2	96.0	89.7		95.5
1994	83.0	94.3	71.6	86.9	51.9	89.1	95.6	100.0	99.7	92.4		97.0
1995	87.9	96.4	79.4	90.5	64.1	92.4	96.5	98.3	102.2	93.1		98.5
1996	92.2	97.1	87.3	92.9	77.9	95.2	95.5	95.6	98.9	93.5		100.0
1997	100.0	100.0	100.0	100.0	100.0	100.0	100.0	100.0	100.0	100.0		100.0
1998	106.2	102.5	111.4	103.6	124.3	102.8	101.4	98.4	100.4	100.7		100.2
1999	113.1	101.8	124.6	113.3	154.4	104.4	103.0	96.4	102.2	103.9		100.2
2000	119.8	103.3	138.2	114.1	196.2	105.5	102.8	92.5	100.3	104.8		101.6
2001	114.6	103.5	131.2	101.1	196.6	98.1	96.7	81.8	94.5	98.2		100.4
2002	115.1	102.0	132.5	105.9	199.4	96.9	96.6	78.2	92.7	100.1		100.5
2000												
January	118.4	123.4	134.8	118.6	177.9	107.4	104.0	96.4	102.4	105.2		100.9
February	118.9	124.0	135.8	118.1	181.1	107.6	104.0	96.5	101.9	105.6		101.0
March	119.5	124.8	137.0	118.0	184.4	108.0	104.3	96.0	102.5	106.0		100.7
April	120.0	125.3	137.7	116.5	189.3	107.3	104.4	95.5	102.6	106.1		101.1
May	120.8	126.2	139.1	117.1	193.9	107.0	104.5	94.9	101.8	107.5		102.0
June	120.8	126.5	140.0	117.1	197.6	106.6	104.0	94.8	102.7	106.0		101.2
July	120.1	125.8	139.8	113.4	201.2	106.0	102.6	92.5	99.3	104.6		100.4
August	120.0	125.1	139.2	112.8	202.1	104.6	101.9	91.0	98.3	104.4		101.8
September	120.3	125.5	140.1	113.9	204.2	104.7	101.6	90.1	98.5	103.8		102.0
October	120.1	125.2	139.3	111.8	205.8	103.4	101.9	88.8	98.7	104.0		101.9
November	119.7	124.2	138.4	107.5	208.7	102.3	100.9	87.2	98.3	103.2		102.9
December	118.7	123.0	137.1	104.9	207.4	101.7	99.8	87.0	96.7	101.2		102.8
2001												
January	117.4	121.8	135.2	99.4	205.0	101.8	99.6	86.7	97.5	101.2		101.2
February	116.9	121.1	134.1	101.4	203.5	99.8	99.4	84.0	98.6	101.0		101.5
March	116.4	120.1	133.7	101.9	203.4	98.8	97.9	85.9	96.1	99.1		101.8
April	115.9	119.7	133.3	102.3	200.3	99.5	97.4	85.8	95.9	97.4		101.3
May	115.2	118.9	132.4	102.6	198.0	98.9	96.8	83.8	94.8	97.7		100.7
June	114.2	117.7	131.0	101.3	195.2	98.3	95.9	81.6	93.6	96.9		100.4
July	113.7	117.5	130.8	102.0	192.5	98.9	95.7	80.4	93.2	97.0		99.2
August	114.0	117.5	130.3	101.5	192.9	97.9	96.2	80.6	94.2	97.8		100.3
September	113.4	116.8	129.1	99.4	192.0	97.1	96.2	80.5	94.1	97.7		99.9
October	113.3	116.4	128.6	98.8	192.6	96.3	96.1	79.0	93.0	98.8		100.4
November	112.7	116.0	128.3	99.9	192.0	95.6	95.4	76.9	92.3	97.9		99.6
December	112.0	115.3	128.1	102.3	191.4	94.4	94.2	76.4	90.7	96.0		98.7
2002												
January	113.0	116.6	129.1	103.1	192.6	95.2	95.7	77.8	92.0	98.4		99.3
February	113.4	116.8	129.7	104.7	192.6	95.6	95.5	77.5	91.3	98.4		100.1
March	113.9	117.4	130.3	104.6	193.5	96.2	96.0	78.8	90.5	99.9		100.4
April	114.8	118.4	131.6	105.8	195.7	96.9	96.6	79.1	92.2	100.4		100.7
May	115.3	119.2	132.4	105.0	199.0	97.3	97.3	79.4	93.3	101.5		100.6
June	116.0	120.0	133.6	105.9	201.2	98.1	97.5	79.7	92.5	101.6		101.2
July	116.2	120.0	133.5	107.1	201.2	97.2	97.8	79.7	93.7	102.1		101.6
August	116.1	120.3	134.5	106.8	203.9	98.0	97.2	78.2	93.2	101.1		100.5
September	115.7	120.0	134.1	106.7	203.8	97.5	96.9	77.8	93.3	100.5		99.7
October	115.3	119.5	134.0	106.3	203.2	97.7	96.0	77.0	93.1	98.9		99.8
November	115.9	119.8	134.3	108.8	203.5	96.9	96.3	77.4	93.8	99.2		100.9
December	115.3	119.0	133.0	106.1	203.0	96.1	96.2	75.7	93.1	99.6		101.0

Table 2-1. Industrial Production Indexes by Market Groups—*Continued*

(Seasonally adjusted, 1997=100.)

Year and month	Energy						Non–energy					Total non–energy excluding hi-tech
									Selected hi–tech			
	Total	Consumer energy products	Commercial energy products	Oil and gas well drilling	Converted fuels	Primary energy	Total	Total	Computers and office equipment	Communications equipment	Semiconductors and related equipment	
1967	60.2	48.2	35.3	. . .	59.6	77.7	40.4	0.8	. . .	. . .	. . .	53.2
1968	63.5	51.7	38.3	. . .	63.8	79.9	42.6	0.8	. . .	. . .	. . .	56.1
1969	66.9	55.3	40.2	. . .	68.2	82.7	44.6	0.9	. . .	. . .	. . .	58.4
1970	70.1	58.5	43.3	. . .	71.8	86.6	42.6	0.9	. . .	. . .	. . .	55.7
1971	71.4	61.2	45.5	. . .	73.8	86.0	43.2	0.9	. . .	. . .	. . .	56.7
1972	74.7	64.6	48.0	88.3	78.3	87.4	47.7	1.0	0.2	14.1	0.7	62.3
1973	76.6	65.7	50.6	83.1	81.3	88.4	52.0	1.3	0.2	15.2	1.0	67.7
1974	76.9	67.5	50.7	96.5	80.2	88.8	51.7	1.5	0.3	15.5	1.1	66.9
1975	77.2	68.9	52.5	108.9	77.3	89.5	46.2	1.3	0.3	13.4	0.9	59.7
1976	79.6	72.5	55.1	122.7	81.3	89.5	50.3	1.6	0.5	13.7	1.2	64.7
1977	82.7	75.3	57.0	155.8	84.3	92.1	54.6	2.2	0.7	16.8	1.6	69.6
1978	84.1	76.7	58.7	173.6	83.6	94.3	58.0	2.7	1.1	18.3	1.9	73.4
1979	86.6	78.6	61.4	185.1	86.7	96.4	59.8	3.6	1.5	21.9	2.5	74.8
1980	86.9	75.8	60.4	218.8	85.0	98.4	57.7	4.3	2.2	24.0	2.8	71.3
1981	88.2	75.3	62.0	262.9	83.8	100.4	58.4	5.1	3.0	24.9	3.2	71.4
1982	85.0	75.8	62.8	231.4	77.1	97.5	55.1	5.9	3.6	26.4	3.7	66.6
1983	82.5	76.3	64.0	179.3	76.9	93.3	57.7	7.0	5.1	25.6	4.4	69.0
1984	87.4	78.7	67.4	195.2	81.8	99.2	63.5	9.3	7.3	28.9	6.0	75.0
1985	87.1	78.7	69.9	178.8	81.4	98.6	64.7	9.9	8.5	29.0	6.2	76.1
1986	84.1	80.2	71.8	87.1	78.5	94.5	66.2	10.2	9.1	27.3	6.6	77.8
1987	86.5	83.1	75.6	84.0	82.5	95.1	69.9	12.3	11.7	27.9	8.4	81.4
1988	89.9	87.5	78.2	100.9	86.3	97.7	73.5	14.2	14.4	29.4	9.7	85.0
1989	90.9	88.0	81.1	87.8	89.6	97.1	74.1	15.0	15.0	29.5	10.7	85.4
1990	92.3	87.4	83.3	92.9	90.4	99.7	74.6	16.8	16.2	32.7	12.4	85.4
1991	92.8	90.1	84.6	72.4	90.4	99.7	73.1	18.0	16.8	32.5	14.2	83.2
1992	91.6	88.9	84.1	50.5	92.1	97.3	75.9	21.8	21.1	37.4	17.2	85.4
1993	93.2	92.8	86.5	70.4	93.8	96.5	78.6	25.6	26.1	42.8	20.0	87.6
1994	95.1	94.0	90.0	83.5	95.3	98.1	83.4	33.2	33.1	53.0	26.9	91.5
1995	97.0	96.5	93.2	81.3	96.7	99.6	87.9	47.3	46.9	62.6	41.8	93.8
1996	99.4	100.7	96.1	87.2	98.4	100.9	92.0	66.7	68.1	76.0	62.2	95.3
1997	100.0	100.0	100.0	100.0	100.0	100.0	100.0	100.0	100.0	100.0	100.0	100.0
1998	100.5	100.5	102.0	98.3	101.3	99.5	106.9	140.2	140.5	114.2	154.3	103.6
1999	101.5	104.1	105.9	82.0	102.9	98.4	112.2	201.3	176.3	140.9	255.5	104.9
2000	103.8	105.8	110.0	110.3	105.2	99.3	117.5	286.7	202.6	188.0	412.1	106.0
2001	103.7	106.5	111.6	125.0	101.4	99.5	112.8	291.1	193.8	172.9	454.4	101.1
2002	104.1	110.0	112.6	91.0	103.6	98.5	111.9	311.4	226.5	146.2	539.7	99.7
2000												
January	101.7	101.1	107.3	96.2	104.1	98.9	115.7	244.6	181.9	166.3	337.8	106.1
February	102.7	104.8	107.4	96.5	105.2	98.6	116.3	252.9	186.0	172.6	349.9	106.3
March	101.4	99.4	108.5	97.9	102.9	99.2	117.2	260.2	190.0	176.0	362.8	106.8
April	102.4	102.2	108.7	99.6	102.9	99.9	117.9	270.9	194.1	181.4	382.8	107.1
May	104.3	106.1	112.0	105.3	105.6	99.9	118.4	283.3	198.8	190.7	402.2	107.0
June	103.7	106.5	110.4	108.5	104.4	99.2	118.6	287.0	204.2	186.2	413.8	107.1
July	102.6	104.3	108.3	121.6	100.6	99.7	118.2	295.2	209.5	190.5	427.0	106.4
August	104.2	105.7	111.2	123.3	105.6	99.5	117.7	299.8	213.8	192.2	434.3	105.7
September	104.8	108.4	110.2	115.1	106.3	99.5	118.2	307.2	215.8	200.1	442.7	105.8
October	104.2	106.1	109.8	119.4	106.3	99.3	117.7	309.9	215.5	199.6	451.5	105.3
November	106.2	110.3	112.6	120.2	109.2	99.4	117.2	314.5	213.1	198.8	468.4	104.6
December	107.1	114.1	114.1	120.2	109.6	99.1	116.6	315.6	208.8	201.1	471.7	104.0
2001												
January	105.9	112.8	112.5	132.7	102.9	100.0	115.6	311.1	204.0	203.8	457.2	103.2
February	105.4	110.3	112.4	131.6	103.8	99.9	114.9	306.4	200.6	194.5	460.1	102.7
March	105.2	108.2	112.1	135.6	103.8	100.4	114.4	304.1	199.2	188.2	464.3	102.3
April	104.6	107.2	111.2	139.8	103.9	99.5	114.1	297.4	198.2	182.9	451.5	102.3
May	103.7	104.9	111.8	136.5	102.6	99.4	113.7	292.3	195.1	178.3	445.6	101.9
June	103.7	105.3	112.9	133.3	100.1	100.1	112.8	286.6	188.4	173.3	442.5	101.3
July	102.7	105.5	111.4	129.8	99.3	98.7	112.5	281.0	181.1	170.2	437.2	101.1
August	103.8	107.4	112.6	122.6	102.0	99.0	111.9	277.0	177.4	162.3	443.5	100.7
September	102.9	105.2	111.4	118.4	99.5	99.7	111.3	277.0	180.3	158.3	448.0	100.1
October	103.4	106.5	111.5	111.7	100.9	99.7	110.9	282.9	188.7	156.8	461.9	99.5
November	101.8	102.9	109.6	109.0	99.5	99.3	110.5	286.7	200.2	153.5	468.3	99.1
December	100.9	102.1	110.0	99.9	99.1	98.2	110.4	291.3	212.1	152.4	472.4	98.8
2002												
January	101.8	105.3	108.6	98.5	100.0	98.5	111.0	291.3	221.3	145.3	476.2	99.3
February	102.6	105.8	110.4	94.1	101.9	98.7	111.0	294.1	224.2	147.2	479.1	99.3
March	103.3	107.8	111.4	92.0	103.7	98.2	111.4	295.8	219.7	147.8	489.1	99.6
April	104.6	111.4	113.9	87.0	103.8	98.8	111.7	298.9	211.9	148.8	507.7	99.8
May	104.2	110.1	113.3	86.1	103.5	98.8	112.0	302.3	207.0	147.5	528.4	100.0
June	104.9	111.6	113.1	89.2	104.2	99.3	112.7	308.3	209.3	150.0	541.9	100.5
July	105.3	111.5	114.2	90.2	106.4	98.7	112.4	311.2	217.2	144.0	554.6	100.2
August	103.8	109.5	111.8	90.6	103.8	98.4	112.7	318.9	227.0	144.4	569.4	100.2
September	103.2	108.6	112.5	91.6	105.6	96.2	112.6	323.2	235.6	142.6	578.4	100.0
October	104.2	110.8	115.8	92.1	104.0	97.2	112.0	325.8	242.6	140.8	582.6	99.4
November	105.2	113.5	113.3	89.0	103.3	99.2	112.0	332.5	248.7	146.7	587.0	99.2
December	105.6	114.3	113.5	92.1	103.2	99.5	111.2	334.7	253.8	149.8	582.0	98.5

. . . = Not available.

Table 2-2. Industrial Production Indexes by NAICS Industry Group

(Seasonally adjusted, 1997 = 100.)

Year and month	Total industrial production	Manu-facturing (SIC)	Manufacturing (NAICS)										
			Total	Durable goods manufacturing									
				Total	Wood products	Nonmetallic mineral products	Primary metals	Fabricated metal products	Machinery	Computer and electronic products	Electrical equipment, appliances, and components	Motor vehicles and parts	Aerospace and misc. transport equipment
1967	43.7	40.6	. . .	. . .	. . .	. . .	. . .	. . .	. . .	. . .	. . .	. . .	. . .
1968	46.2	42.9	. . .	. . .	. . .	. . .	. . .	. . .	. . .	. . .	. . .	. . .	. . .
1969	48.3	44.8	. . .	. . .	. . .	. . .	. . .	. . .	. . .	. . .	. . .	. . .	. . .
1970	46.7	42.8	. . .	. . .	. . .	. . .	. . .	. . .	. . .	. . .	. . .	. . .	. . .
1971	47.4	43.5	. . .	. . .	. . .	. . .	. . .	. . .	. . .	. . .	. . .	. . .	. . .
1972	51.9	48.0	47.1	38.8	76.1	75.7	108.3	67.4	60.7	3.2	66.1	51.6	72.7
1973	56.1	52.3	51.5	43.6	73.6	81.2	126.0	74.4	70.2	3.8	74.3	59.0	82.8
1974	55.9	52.1	51.3	43.3	66.9	80.3	129.1	73.1	73.6	4.1	72.6	50.7	84.2
1975	50.9	46.6	45.8	37.5	62.0	71.9	100.2	63.2	64.2	3.7	58.2	44.2	79.9
1976	54.9	50.8	50.0	41.0	69.8	76.0	106.3	67.7	67.0	4.3	65.7	56.4	74.8
1977	59.1	55.2	54.3	45.1	75.4	80.9	107.3	73.5	73.2	5.5	72.5	64.2	75.4
1978	62.4	58.6	57.6	48.6	76.3	86.3	114.1	77.1	78.9	6.8	76.9	66.9	83.2
1979	64.2	60.4	59.4	51.0	73.8	86.2	116.7	80.5	83.2	8.4	80.1	61.2	96.8
1980	62.5	58.2	57.1	48.7	68.4	77.6	102.3	75.9	79.2	10.1	75.3	45.0	104.2
1981	63.4	58.8	57.7	49.2	66.9	74.3	102.6	75.4	78.5	11.6	74.4	43.9	99.1
1982	60.1	55.6	54.4	45.1	59.9	65.8	72.7	67.6	65.7	13.1	67.0	39.6	92.8
1983	61.7	58.2	57.0	47.2	69.5	70.8	74.2	68.2	59.3	15.0	69.3	50.5	88.7
1984	67.3	64.0	62.8	54.0	74.4	76.4	81.5	74.3	69.3	18.7	78.0	60.6	94.6
1985	68.1	65.1	63.8	55.3	75.3	77.7	75.2	75.2	69.5	20.0	76.8	62.9	101.1
1986	68.8	66.5	65.3	56.2	81.8	81.0	73.4	74.7	68.4	20.8	78.2	62.8	106.4
1987	72.3	70.2	68.9	59.4	89.2	85.4	79.2	76.1	69.7	23.5	79.3	65.1	110.3
1988	75.9	73.8	72.6	63.6	89.1	87.2	88.6	80.1	76.8	25.8	83.1	69.6	114.9
1989	76.6	74.4	73.2	64.2	87.8	86.4	86.7	79.4	79.6	26.5	81.8	68.8	121.2
1990	77.2	74.9	73.8	64.4	86.8	85.1	85.5	78.3	77.6	28.7	79.7	64.7	121.6
1991	76.1	73.4	72.4	62.4	81.3	78.4	80.3	74.8	72.9	29.8	75.6	61.8	117.0
1992	78.2	76.1	75.3	65.6	85.7	81.9	82.2	77.1	72.6	33.6	80.2	70.4	108.3
1993	80.8	78.8	78.1	69.3	86.7	83.6	86.2	80.0	78.1	37.1	85.2	77.8	101.0
1994	85.2	83.6	83.1	75.4	91.8	88.3	92.6	87.0	85.5	44.2	91.4	89.4	90.7
1995	89.3	88.0	87.8	81.9	94.0	90.9	93.7	92.3	91.5	57.5	93.5	92.0	86.4
1996	93.1	92.1	92.1	89.0	97.1	96.7	95.9	95.8	94.9	73.8	96.4	92.7	89.6
1997	100.0	100.0	100.0	100.0	100.0	100.0	100.0	100.0	100.0	100.0	100.0	100.0	100.0
1998	105.9	106.8	106.8	110.7	105.0	104.7	102.3	103.0	102.6	129.1	104.1	105.2	115.9
1999	110.6	112.1	112.3	119.9	108.8	106.1	101.7	103.8	100.4	169.0	105.9	116.4	111.8
2000	115.4	117.4	117.7	129.5	107.2	106.0	98.5	107.9	105.8	224.0	111.6	116.2	98.3
2001	111.5	112.7	113.1	123.5	100.6	101.4	89.0	100.1	93.8	226.1	100.9	105.6	106.3
2002	110.9	111.8	112.5	122.9	100.6	99.9	86.5	97.4	86.8	234.7	96.4	114.5	97.5
2000													
January	113.6	115.6	115.8	126.5	111.5	105.5	103.4	107.3	104.8	197.1	110.1	121.5	101.9
February	114.3	116.2	116.4	127.1	111.1	105.7	102.0	108.7	104.7	202.8	109.9	120.6	98.2
March	114.8	117.0	117.3	128.1	111.5	107.2	104.0	108.8	105.5	206.9	111.5	120.1	98.3
April	115.6	117.8	118.0	129.3	111.0	106.5	100.1	109.5	105.9	214.1	112.0	121.2	96.3
May	116.3	118.2	118.5	130.5	109.1	106.6	100.0	109.4	106.4	221.9	111.4	120.7	96.2
June	116.4	118.4	118.8	130.9	107.0	106.2	99.1	109.4	107.3	225.1	113.6	118.9	97.3
July	115.8	118.1	118.4	130.7	106.6	107.3	97.3	109.1	108.2	230.8	112.8	112.8	98.4
August	115.7	117.6	118.0	130.3	104.6	106.4	96.4	107.7	105.9	232.3	111.9	115.2	96.6
September	116.2	118.1	118.5	131.1	105.9	106.0	97.1	107.7	106.7	236.6	113.1	116.5	94.8
October	115.7	117.6	118.0	130.5	104.0	106.3	94.4	106.6	105.9	238.3	111.4	113.3	98.7
November	115.6	117.1	117.5	129.7	103.5	104.2	93.6	106.5	104.3	240.9	111.0	108.1	101.1
December	115.3	116.5	116.9	128.9	100.8	104.3	94.2	104.7	104.0	240.9	110.3	105.0	101.5
2001													
January	114.2	115.4	115.8	127.4	98.9	104.2	93.3	104.9	102.5	238.4	109.0	99.4	103.9
February	113.6	114.8	115.3	126.5	98.5	104.1	90.6	103.0	102.0	234.9	105.7	102.4	103.9
March	113.2	114.3	114.9	126.6	100.0	103.4	88.8	102.3	99.9	233.9	104.1	106.8	106.1
April	112.8	114.1	114.5	125.8	100.0	102.6	91.1	101.8	98.3	230.8	102.5	106.3	107.4
May	112.3	113.5	114.0	124.8	101.2	102.1	90.8	101.0	95.1	227.4	101.6	108.3	107.6
June	111.6	112.7	113.1	123.6	102.0	101.8	90.8	100.0	93.9	224.4	100.2	106.8	107.5
July	111.1	112.4	112.7	123.4	100.8	101.1	91.5	100.0	92.2	221.3	98.9	109.3	107.2
August	110.9	111.8	112.1	122.1	102.0	100.2	89.7	99.2	91.4	218.3	99.7	106.6	107.6
September	110.2	111.2	111.5	120.9	102.7	100.3	89.0	97.6	89.6	217.9	98.4	104.0	108.5
October	109.9	110.8	111.2	120.1	100.0	98.2	86.2	97.7	87.5	220.1	97.6	101.9	107.6
November	109.4	110.5	110.9	120.3	100.2	100.3	85.9	96.5	87.2	221.5	96.3	105.7	105.6
December	109.1	110.4	110.7	120.4	101.3	98.6	80.1	96.8	85.9	224.1	96.4	109.8	102.7
2002													
January	109.7	111.0	111.4	120.8	102.3	97.9	84.8	96.5	86.8	224.3	97.4	108.8	102.4
February	109.9	111.0	111.5	121.1	101.2	99.0	85.2	96.8	86.9	225.1	98.0	110.8	100.7
March	110.3	111.4	111.9	121.4	102.5	99.2	86.7	96.8	87.0	226.1	96.9	110.7	100.3
April	110.8	111.6	112.3	122.0	101.5	99.4	85.7	97.4	87.0	226.9	97.1	113.4	99.0
May	111.0	111.9	112.6	122.7	101.1	100.0	86.6	98.2	87.6	229.2	98.6	113.5	97.5
June	111.7	112.6	113.3	123.5	101.9	99.3	87.3	98.3	87.8	233.0	98.7	115.8	96.9
July	111.5	112.4	113.1	123.3	100.4	98.8	85.7	98.1	86.4	233.9	97.6	117.8	95.3
August	111.5	112.6	113.4	124.1	100.5	100.3	88.6	98.0	87.5	238.3	94.8	117.9	96.3
September	111.3	112.5	113.1	123.8	99.5	101.4	86.7	97.4	86.8	241.2	93.8	117.0	96.4
October	111.0	111.9	112.4	123.5	100.1	101.1	87.9	97.7	86.1	242.4	94.1	115.1	95.7
November	111.2	111.9	112.6	124.5	98.4	100.9	88.8	96.5	86.5	246.5	94.8	118.9	94.6
December	110.6	111.3	111.9	123.6	97.5	101.2	84.3	96.6	85.6	248.9	94.8	114.6	94.8

. . . = Not available.

Table 2-2. Industrial Production Indexes by NAICS Industry Group—*Continued*

(Seasonally adjusted, 1997 = 100.)

Year and month	Durable goods manufacturing—*Continued*		Manufacturing (NAICS)—*Continued* Nondurable goods manufacturing									Other manufacturing (non-NAICS)
	Furniture and related products	Miscellaneous manufacturing	Total	Food, beverage, and tobacco products	Textile and product mills	Apparel and leather	Paper	Printing and support	Petroleum and coal products	Chemical	Plastics and rubber products	
1967	...	...	...	...	...	...	...	...	...	...	...	...
1968	...	...	...	...	...	...	...	...	...	...	...	...
1969	...	...	...	...	...	...	...	...	...	...	...	...
1970	...	...	...	...	...	...	...	...	...	...	...	...
1971	...	...	...	...	...	...	...	...	...	...	...	...
1972	60.6	49.7	61.3	66.8	74.4	109.0	62.6	46.8	77.7	53.1	37.5	66.9
1973	63.4	51.1	64.1	67.6	73.6	110.9	67.7	49.2	76.3	58.1	42.2	69.1
1974	58.4	49.9	64.4	68.5	67.7	104.2	70.6	47.7	82.4	60.3	41.0	69.6
1975	49.7	46.7	59.8	67.4	65.5	101.6	61.1	44.5	81.2	53.1	35.1	66.0
1976	55.5	50.8	65.2	72.0	72.9	106.8	67.5	47.8	90.0	59.4	38.8	68.1
1977	63.7	55.2	69.7	73.6	79.7	112.0	70.4	51.8	96.3	64.6	45.8	74.7
1978	68.7	56.3	72.1	76.2	79.5	114.5	73.6	54.8	97.3	67.9	47.3	77.4
1979	68.2	56.5	72.6	75.8	79.4	107.5	74.7	56.4	103.9	69.4	46.5	79.0
1980	65.8	53.4	70.3	77.0	76.1	109.6	74.5	56.8	92.1	65.6	41.4	81.8
1981	65.3	55.5	71.0	77.9	74.5	109.5	75.5	58.3	87.8	66.7	43.9	83.8
1982	61.5	56.2	69.9	80.1	69.0	108.9	74.2	62.7	83.9	62.4	43.1	84.7
1983	67.4	56.0	73.2	80.3	77.9	111.9	79.1	67.4	85.3	66.7	46.9	87.0
1984	75.6	60.7	76.6	81.4	79.9	111.8	83.1	73.4	87.2	70.6	54.2	91.1
1985	76.1	61.5	77.0	84.0	77.2	106.8	81.4	76.3	85.9	70.1	56.3	94.6
1986	79.6	63.0	79.2	85.1	80.4	106.3	84.8	80.2	85.4	73.2	58.6	96.7
1987	85.2	67.9	83.5	86.8	88.7	107.3	87.6	86.1	89.5	78.9	64.9	102.1
1988	84.1	74.4	86.3	89.2	87.9	105.4	91.1	88.8	92.3	83.4	67.9	101.7
1989	83.7	75.3	86.8	88.7	89.5	100.7	92.1	89.2	91.3	85.0	70.2	100.2
1990	82.0	79.1	88.2	91.2	85.9	98.4	92.0	92.5	91.4	87.0	72.0	99.0
1991	75.7	80.7	87.9	91.9	84.7	97.7	92.2	89.7	90.1	86.8	71.3	94.9
1992	81.7	84.1	90.1	93.1	89.3	100.3	94.5	94.6	89.7	88.0	76.7	92.8
1993	85.2	88.9	91.4	92.8	92.8	102.4	95.6	94.9	90.3	89.0	82.2	93.5
1994	88.1	89.5	94.6	96.0	97.9	103.6	99.7	95.9	92.8	91.3	89.0	92.8
1995	89.6	92.8	96.2	98.7	96.9	102.8	101.1	97.3	94.5	92.7	91.1	92.9
1996	90.3	97.5	96.5	98.0	94.7	100.4	98.0	98.0	96.7	94.6	94.3	92.1
1997	100.0	100.0	100.0	100.0	100.0	100.0	100.0	100.0	100.0	100.0	100.0	100.0
1998	107.1	106.0	101.5	102.8	98.8	94.6	101.1	101.0	99.9	101.8	103.4	106.5
1999	110.7	108.2	102.2	100.9	99.0	90.5	102.2	101.9	104.0	103.8	108.7	109.9
2000	113.0	114.8	102.8	102.2	97.2	87.3	99.9	102.3	101.9	105.5	110.5	112.2
2001	106.2	114.1	99.8	102.1	87.5	77.9	94.3	96.9	99.9	103.9	104.0	105.6
2002	103.4	116.0	99.2	101.3	83.9	70.8	93.5	93.7	100.6	105.3	104.3	102.0
2000												
January	112.2	110.2	102.1	99.6	100.5	88.9	102.6	101.8	100.9	103.8	112.3	112.5
February	110.3	112.5	102.8	101.3	100.0	89.5	102.1	101.1	100.9	104.8	112.4	112.0
March	112.3	112.1	103.4	102.2	99.8	89.4	102.2	102.8	103.9	105.4	111.3	112.7
April	114.0	113.9	103.6	102.0	100.4	88.7	102.3	103.6	101.4	106.2	112.5	114.1
May	116.8	114.7	103.5	101.8	98.8	88.2	100.5	104.1	102.5	106.9	111.5	113.0
June	116.4	115.5	103.5	103.1	98.7	87.7	101.9	103.5	101.9	105.5	111.2	113.0
July	113.8	115.4	102.9	103.3	98.2	87.9	98.6	102.5	101.2	104.8	111.2	113.3
August	112.8	117.2	102.5	102.7	95.3	87.1	97.4	102.1	101.8	105.3	100.9	111.6
September	112.7	115.7	102.7	103.3	95.4	85.8	97.3	102.2	103.0	105.3	110.1	111.6
October	111.9	116.2	102.3	101.8	94.3	85.3	98.9	101.4	101.9	105.9	109.2	111.8
November	111.2	116.7	102.2	102.4	92.8	85.4	97.7	101.5	102.3	106.1	107.9	110.9
December	111.9	116.9	101.8	103.0	92.7	83.8	96.8	100.8	101.2	105.4	106.5	110.0
2001												
January	110.1	117.8	101.1	101.9	91.8	84.5	96.7	100.7	100.7	104.2	107.1	109.5
February	109.3	116.1	101.2	102.0	90.4	84.1	97.8	100.6	100.7	104.9	105.8	106.0
March	109.5	116.4	100.3	101.2	91.0	83.4	94.4	100.8	100.1	103.8	105.1	104.9
April	107.3	115.5	100.3	102.5	90.4	82.5	96.1	97.4	99.9	103.0	105.5	106.2
May	107.1	113.5	100.3	101.8	88.3	80.3	94.7	97.6	100.6	105.1	104.5	105.5
June	105.5	112.1	99.8	103.3	87.6	78.5	93.3	96.4	101.4	102.8	104.1	105.4
July	106.9	113.7	99.1	101.5	86.6	77.7	93.5	95.4	100.5	102.9	104.5	106.7
August	104.7	113.1	99.3	101.8	86.3	75.4	94.0	96.2	98.9	103.9	103.5	105.9
September	104.1	111.1	99.3	102.9	86.9	72.9	94.8	94.2	98.8	103.3	103.0	105.1
October	104.0	114.3	99.4	102.4	84.3	72.6	93.2	94.3	100.1	105.2	102.5	104.4
November	103.4	112.2	98.7	101.8	83.2	71.4	91.8	95.2	99.6	104.5	101.1	103.5
December	102.7	113.3	98.2	101.8	83.6	71.1	90.8	93.8	98.1	103.7	101.5	104.0
2002												
January	103.1	113.8	99.2	102.4	83.1	70.7	91.5	95.3	100.2	105.7	101.7	103.2
February	102.7	112.8	99.0	102.8	83.0	70.1	91.6	94.2	101.6	104.6	102.0	102.9
March	102.7	113.7	99.5	103.1	84.7	70.3	90.8	93.7	100.9	105.4	103.8	103.1
April	103.1	115.9	99.6	103.0	84.8	69.8	92.6	94.0	101.5	104.9	104.6	101.6
May	104.0	117.3	99.5	101.6	85.3	70.8	94.0	94.4	100.0	105.6	105.2	101.6
June	104.9	116.5	100.2	102.8	86.2	72.1	94.0	93.5	100.3	106.2	106.1	101.2
July	104.7	117.6	100.0	101.6	84.7	72.4	94.3	94.3	101.2	106.8	105.6	101.1
August	103.0	116.9	99.7	101.8	83.9	71.3	94.4	93.8	100.9	105.9	105.4	101.4
September	104.1	115.9	99.5	101.7	83.2	71.9	94.7	92.9	99.3	105.9	105.1	102.5
October	103.1	116.0	98.5	100.4	82.3	70.3	94.2	92.6	97.1	104.7	104.7	102.8
November	103.8	116.8	97.8	97.7	83.2	71.1	95.3	92.7	101.3	104.3	103.9	101.6
December	102.0	119.0	97.4	97.1	82.3	69.4	94.2	93.0	103.0	104.0	103.4	100.5

. . . = Not available.

Table 2-2. Industrial Production Indexes by NAICS Industry Group—*Continued*

(Seasonally adjusted, 1997 = 100.)

Year and month	Mining	Utilities			Selected hi-tech industries	Excluding selected hi-tech industries	Stage-of-process groups		
		Total	Electric	Natural gas			Crude	Primary and semi-finished	Finished
1967	...	...	...	...	0.8	54.8	...	...	...
1968	...	...	...	...	0.8	57.8	...	...	...
1969	...	...	...	...	0.9	60.3	...	...	...
1970	...	...	...	...	0.9	58.2	...	...	...
1971	...	...	...	...	0.9	59.3	...	...	...
1972	98.7	56.5	46.4	110.4	1.0	64.7	...	...	...
1973	99.2	59.7	50.5	105.9	1.3	69.7	...	...	...
1974	97.8	59.4	50.8	102.4	1.5	69.0	...	...	...
1975	95.4	60.4	53.0	95.9	1.3	62.9	...	...	...
1976	96.1	63.1	56.4	95.0	1.6	67.6	...	...	...
1977	98.3	65.5	60.0	91.8	2.2	72.2	...	...	...
1978	101.4	67.3	61.9	92.5	2.7	75.6	...	...	...
1979	104.4	68.8	63.2	95.0	3.6	77.2	...	...	...
1980	106.4	69.3	64.3	93.0	4.3	74.4	...	...	...
1981	109.2	70.2	66.0	90.9	5.1	74.9	...	...	...
1982	103.8	68.0	64.4	85.4	5.9	70.4	...	...	...
1983	98.3	68.5	66.3	79.8	7.0	71.7	...	...	...
1984	104.6	72.5	70.1	84.9	9.3	77.4	...	...	...
1985	102.6	74.0	72.6	81.4	9.9	78.2	...	...	...
1986	95.2	74.6	74.2	77.4	10.2	78.9	92.0	64.3	69.3
1987	96.0	78.2	77.7	80.9	12.3	82.2	94.9	68.0	72.5
1988	98.4	82.6	82.0	85.9	14.2	85.8	98.2	71.6	76.2
1989	97.3	85.2	84.5	89.0	15.0	86.3	98.2	72.2	77.1
1990	98.8	86.8	86.9	86.0	16.8	86.6	99.7	72.3	78.4
1991	96.5	88.9	89.0	88.3	18.0	84.8	97.1	71.2	77.5
1992	94.4	88.9	88.5	90.8	21.8	86.4	96.3	74.1	79.3
1993	94.4	92.0	91.7	94.2	25.6	88.6	95.1	77.6	81.6
1994	96.6	93.9	93.7	94.9	33.2	92.1	97.1	83.0	85.1
1995	96.4	97.2	97.1	97.3	47.3	94.4	97.6	87.8	89.1
1996	98.1	100.0	99.7	102.0	66.7	96.0	97.3	92.6	92.7
1997	100.0	100.0	100.0	100.0	100.0	100.0	100.0	100.0	100.0
1998	98.2	102.5	104.1	93.4	140.2	103.1	98.2	106.8	106.7
1999	94.0	105.5	107.1	96.1	201.3	104.4	96.8	114.3	109.2
2000	96.3	108.6	110.2	99.1	286.7	105.7	96.7	121.0	113.1
2001	96.8	108.1	109.9	97.7	291.1	101.6	94.5	115.6	110.5
2002	93.0	111.3	113.3	99.9	311.4	100.5	92.6	116.3	108.6
2000									
January	95.7	105.6	107.4	95.1	244.6	105.4	97.5	119.4	110.4
February	95.8	107.4	108.7	99.6	252.9	105.7	97.2	120.0	111.3
March	96.3	104.2	107.3	87.0	260.2	105.9	97.4	120.3	112.1
April	96.2	106.4	108.4	95.4	270.9	106.3	97.2	121.1	113.1
May	95.7	110.4	112.6	97.9	283.3	106.6	96.7	122.2	113.8
June	96.2	109.0	111.0	98.0	287.0	106.5	96.8	122.2	114.0
July	96.7	106.1	107.7	96.7	295.2	105.7	96.6	121.3	113.8
August	96.7	108.8	110.1	101.1	299.8	105.4	96.5	121.1	113.7
September	96.5	109.6	110.8	102.1	307.2	105.7	96.3	121.6	114.3
October	97.2	108.2	109.9	98.0	309.9	105.1	96.7	120.9	113.8
November	96.5	112.0	112.6	107.1	314.5	104.9	96.4	121.0	113.6
December	95.6	115.2	115.6	111.4	315.6	104.6	95.2	120.7	113.5
2001									
January	96.8	112.3	113.3	106.0	311.1	103.7	95.6	119.4	112.4
February	97.5	110.8	112.0	103.5	306.4	103.2	96.0	118.2	112.2
March	98.0	109.6	110.8	102.2	304.1	102.9	95.6	117.4	112.1
April	98.1	108.5	110.5	97.8	297.4	102.7	95.4	116.8	112.0
May	97.8	107.4	109.5	95.8	292.3	102.3	94.5	116.0	111.9
June	97.1	107.9	110.1	96.2	286.6	101.8	93.7	115.5	111.0
July	96.6	106.6	108.0	97.9	281.0	101.5	93.6	115.0	110.5
August	96.4	109.1	110.8	99.0	277.0	101.3	93.9	115.2	109.6
September	96.8	106.7	108.1	98.3	277.0	100.6	94.8	114.1	108.9
October	96.1	108.0	109.4	99.0	282.9	100.2	94.3	113.9	108.6
November	95.8	105.2	108.7	86.8	286.7	99.6	93.9	113.1	108.3
December	94.5	104.8	107.4	90.3	291.3	99.2	92.3	112.7	108.6
2002									
January	93.5	106.6	109.2	92.5	291.3	99.8	92.4	113.7	108.9
February	93.7	107.7	110.2	94.1	294.1	99.9	92.5	114.3	108.6
March	93.0	109.9	111.9	98.5	295.8	100.3	92.0	115.2	108.7
April	92.8	112.3	114.3	101.5	298.9	100.7	92.6	116.2	108.6
May	93.1	111.4	113.0	102.8	302.3	100.7	93.4	116.6	108.3
June	93.6	112.5	114.4	101.9	308.3	101.3	93.5	117.2	109.4
July	92.8	113.4	115.7	100.3	311.2	101.1	93.4	117.3	108.9
August	93.0	110.9	113.2	97.9	318.9	100.9	92.8	117.1	109.2
September	91.3	111.6	114.3	96.3	323.2	100.7	91.5	117.0	109.2
October	91.8	113.4	115.5	101.5	325.8	100.3	91.4	117.2	108.3
November	93.8	112.8	113.8	106.5	332.5	100.3	92.7	117.3	108.1
December	94.2	112.8	114.0	105.2	334.7	99.8	93.2	116.4	107.7

. . . = Not available.

Table 2-3. Capacity Utilization by NAICS Industry Groups

(Output as a percentage of capacity, seasonally adjusted.)

Year and month	Total industry	Total manufac-turing (SIC)	Manufacturing (NAICS) Total	Durable goods manufacturing Total	Wood products	Nometallic mineral products	Primary metals	Fabricated metal products	Machinery	Computer and electronic products	Electrical equipment, appliances, and compo-nents	Motor vehicles and parts	Aircraft and miscella-neous transporta-tion equipment
1967	87.0	87.2	...	87.5	...	75.7	85.0	86.4	90.4	...	...	78.9	94.1
1968	87.3	87.0	...	87.3	...	78.4	84.8	87.3	85.0	...	...	90.0	89.4
1969	87.3	86.5	...	86.9	...	79.7	88.1	86.2	86.4	...	...	86.5	84.2
1970	81.0	79.2	...	77.4	...	73.8	79.1	78.5	79.3	...	...	66.0	72.3
1971	79.3	77.6	...	75.0	...	75.5	72.6	78.4	73.3	...	...	78.6	63.2
1972	84.4	83.2	83.1	81.7	92.1	79.9	82.6	84.9	82.3	80.7	89.5	83.8	64.9
1973	88.3	87.5	87.7	88.4	87.8	84.4	94.0	90.8	92.0	85.4	97.7	91.7	73.1
1974	84.9	84.1	84.2	84.2	77.9	82.0	95.4	85.9	90.9	83.3	90.9	76.5	73.5
1975	75.5	73.4	73.3	71.4	71.1	73.1	74.3	72.0	77.0	68.9	71.0	65.5	69.3
1976	79.5	78.0	78.0	75.9	80.4	77.2	79.0	75.2	79.7	71.1	79.8	81.8	63.5
1977	83.2	82.3	82.2	81.0	86.5	82.0	80.3	79.6	85.1	77.5	86.3	92.1	63.6
1978	85.0	84.5	84.5	84.2	85.2	86.3	85.2	80.7	88.7	84.1	88.4	92.2	69.7
1979	85.0	84.2	84.2	84.6	80.7	84.6	86.7	81.8	90.7	87.4	89.4	81.5	79.0
1980	80.9	78.8	78.5	77.8	73.0	75.5	76.5	75.6	84.2	86.8	82.1	60.0	83.2
1981	79.9	77.2	76.9	75.6	70.9	71.9	77.6	73.4	82.3	84.2	79.0	57.7	76.9
1982	73.8	71.1	70.6	66.7	63.3	63.5	55.6	65.4	67.6	80.9	69.5	51.4	70.5
1983	74.8	73.5	73.1	68.7	73.6	69.5	59.3	66.5	61.7	80.8	72.4	67.1	67.1
1984	80.5	79.5	79.1	76.9	78.8	74.8	69.1	72.7	72.6	86.9	82.0	80.3	71.0
1985	70.4	78.4	77.9	75.9	79.2	74.8	67.3	74.0	72.2	79.6	79.7	81.8	74.4
1986	78.8	78.5	78.1	75.4	83.6	77.3	69.9	73.9	71.2	76.0	79.8	77.5	76.6
1987	81.3	81.2	80.7	77.8	88.2	81.2	78.9	75.2	72.4	78.8	81.0	77.0	78.9
1988	84.3	84.1	83.9	82.1	86.6	83.2	89.9	78.9	80.1	80.4	85.4	83.1	82.4
1989	83.6	83.2	83.0	81.3	83.7	82.2	86.9	78.4	82.9	78.1	84.4	79.6	86.9
1990	82.4	81.6	81.5	79.1	81.9	80.3	84.6	76.7	79.8	78.9	81.7	70.4	87.6
1991	79.6	78.3	78.2	74.8	76.5	73.5	79.6	72.9	75.0	76.8	77.2	63.8	84.6
1992	80.3	79.4	79.4	76.8	80.2	76.4	82.4	74.8	74.2	79.0	81.4	72.0	78.1
1993	81.3	80.3	80.2	78.5	80.1	77.9	86.6	75.7	78.6	78.7	85.5	77.8	72.8
1994	83.4	82.6	82.6	81.5	83.3	81.5	91.9	80.2	84.1	80.7	91.1	86.2	65.2
1995	83.6	82.7	82.8	82.0	83.0	82.8	89.6	82.2	86.2	84.2	90.1	82.8	61.8
1996	82.4	81.1	81.3	80.7	83.0	86.2	88.7	82.2	85.8	79.5	87.9	79.6	63.9
1997	83.6	82.6	82.8	82.6	82.1	86.7	89.3	81.7	87.0	82.0	86.7	82.7	70.7
1998	83.0	82.0	82.0	81.9	83.6	88.3	88.5	80.2	85.4	78.5	86.7	81.0	80.5
1999	82.4	81.4	81.3	81.5	84.5	86.5	86.1	77.3	80.6	81.2	84.8	86.4	76.3
2000	82.6	81.1	80.9	81.5	81.2	83.8	02.7	79.4	82.2	84.5	86.4	85.4	66.7
2001	77.4	75.4	75.1	73.2	74.6	78.5	76.7	73.0	71.8	69.1	77.6	76.1	71.5
2002	75.6	73.9	73.6	70.6	74.5	76.9	76.5	70.1	67.0	63.0	75.1	80.7	65.8
2000													
January	82.8	81.7	81.5	82.7	85.3	84.4	86.8	78.8	82.5	84.8	86.3	89.7	69.3
February	83.0	81.8	81.6	82.5	84.8	84.4	85.6	79.8	82.2	85.3	85.9	89.0	66.8
March	83.0	82.0	81.8	82.6	84.9	85.3	87.2	79.9	82.6	85.0	86.9	88.6	66.8
April	83.3	82.2	82.0	82.8	84.4	84.5	83.9	80.4	82.7	85.8	87.1	89.3	65.4
May	83.5	82.2	82.0	83.0	82.8	84.4	83.9	80.4	82.9	86.8	86.4	89.0	65.3
June	83.3	82.0	81.8	82.7	81.1	84.0	83.1	80.5	83.3	85.9	87.9	87.6	66.1
July	82.7	81.4	81.2	81.9	80.6	84.6	81.6	80.4	83.9	86.0	87.1	83.0	66.8
August	82.3	80.8	80.6	81.2	79.0	83.8	80.9	79.4	81.9	84.6	86.3	84.7	65.5
September	82.4	80.8	80.6	81.2	79.8	83.2	81.6	79.4	82.3	84.2	87.1	85.6	64.2
October	81.8	80.2	80.0	80.3	78.2	83.4	79.5	78.6	81.6	83.0	85.6	83.0	66.8
November	81.5	79.6	79.4	79.3	77.7	81.6	78.9	78.5	80.2	82.2	85.3	79.1	68.4
December	81.0	79.0	78.7	78.4	75.6	81.5	79.7	77.2	79.9	80.6	84.6	76.7	68.6
2001													
January	80.1	78.0	77.8	77.1	73.9	81.3	79.1	77.3	78.6	78.3	83.6	72.5	70.1
February	79.5	77.4	77.2	76.1	73.5	81.1	77.0	75.8	78.1	75.9	81.1	74.5	70.0
March	79.0	76.9	76.8	75.8	74.4	80.4	75.8	75.1	76.5	74.4	79.9	77.5	71.5
April	78.6	76.6	76.3	75.0	74.3	79.6	77.9	74.7	75.2	72.3	78.7	77.0	72.3
May	78.1	76.1	75.9	74.2	75.1	79.1	77.9	73.9	72.7	70.4	78.0	78.2	72.4
June	77.5	75.4	75.1	73.2	75.5	78.8	78.2	73.0	71.8	68.6	77.0	77.0	72.3
July	77.0	75.1	74.7	72.8	74.6	78.1	79.1	72.9	70.5	66.9	76.1	78.6	72.0
August	76.7	74.6	74.3	71.9	75.3	77.4	77.8	72.1	69.9	65.3	76.7	76.5	72.3
September	76.1	74.1	73.8	71.0	75.8	77.4	77.4	70.8	68.5	64.5	75.8	74.5	72.9
October	75.8	73.8	73.4	70.3	73.8	75.7	75.2	70.8	67.0	64.5	75.3	72.8	72.4
November	75.3	73.5	73.2	70.3	73.9	77.3	75.1	69.8	66.7	64.3	74.4	75.4	71.0
December	75.1	73.4	73.0	70.2	74.7	76.0	70.2	69.9	65.8	64.3	74.6	78.2	69.1
2002													
January	75.4	73.7	73.4	70.3	75.4	75.4	74.5	69.6	66.5	63.8	75.5	77.3	69.0
February	75.4	73.7	73.4	70.3	74.6	76.2	75.0	69.7	66.7	63.3	76.0	78.6	67.8
March	75.6	73.8	73.5	70.3	75.7	76.4	76.4	69.7	66.8	62.9	75.3	78.4	67.6
April	75.8	73.9	73.7	70.5	75.0	76.5	75.7	70.1	66.9	62.5	75.5	80.2	66.8
May	75.8	74.1	73.8	70.8	74.7	77.0	76.5	70.7	67.5	62.5	76.8	80.2	65.8
June	76.2	74.4	74.2	71.1	75.4	76.5	77.3	70.7	67.7	62.9	76.9	81.7	65.4
July	76.0	74.3	74.0	70.8	74.4	76.1	75.9	70.6	66.7	62.5	76.1	83.0	64.4
August	75.9	74.3	74.1	71.1	74.5	77.3	78.5	70.5	67.6	63.0	74.0	82.9	65.1
September	75.7	74.2	73.9	70.8	73.9	78.2	76.9	70.1	67.2	63.1	73.3	82.1	65.2
October	75.4	73.7	73.3	70.5	74.5	77.9	77.9	70.3	66.7	62.8	73.7	80.6	64.7
November	75.4	73.6	73.3	70.9	73.2	77.8	78.7	69.4	67.1	63.2	74.2	83.2	64.0
December	74.9	73.1	72.8	70.2	72.6	78.0	74.8	69.5	66.4	63.2	74.3	80.0	64.1

. . . = Not available.

Table 2-3. Capacity Utilization by NAICS Industry Groups—*Continued*

(Output as a percentage of capacity, seasonally adjusted.)

Year and month	Durable goods manufacturing —Continued		Manufacturing (NAICS)—Continued Nondurable goods manufacturing									Other manufacturing (Non-NAICS)
	Furniture and related products	Miscellaneous manufacturing	Total	Food, beverage, and tobacco products	Textile and product mills	Apparel and leather	Paper	Printing and support	Petroleum and coal products	Chemical	Plastics and rubber products	
1967	91.9	...	86.3	85.0	...	...	89.7	...	94.9	78.9	88.3	...
1968	91.8	...	86.4	84.8	...	...	89.3	...	95.9	80.1	90.9	...
1969	93.7	...	86.0	85.0	...	...	90.9	...	96.6	78.9	89.8	...
1970	85.6	...	82.0	84.0	...	...	85.9	...	97.0	75.8	78.6	...
1971	87.1	...	81.6	83.9	...	...	86.5	...	96.1	75.0	78.9	...
1972	94.4	80.3	85.1	85.2	89.0	81.2	91.4	92.2	94.3	79.9	88.1	85.4
1973	94.0	79.3	86.6	84.7	86.1	81.9	95.2	93.8	90.6	83.8	92.4	84.6
1974	81.5	74.4	84.1	83.8	76.2	75.9	95.7	87.7	93.1	83.9	83.9	82.7
1975	67.5	67.9	76.0	80.3	72.6	74.5	81.0	79.2	83.9	71.5	69.9	77.2
1976	74.2	72.7	80.9	83.3	81.0	77.7	88.2	82.1	86.2	77.2	77.3	77.4
1977	82.6	78.1	84.0	82.8	88.8	81.3	90.6	85.9	87.9	80.5	88.0	83.3
1978	85.0	78.9	84.9	83.4	88.3	83.5	92.5	87.2	86.6	81.6	88.1	85.1
1979	80.8	77.8	83.6	81.4	87.9	78.6	91.3	85.8	90.2	81.4	83.1	85.5
1980	75.6	72.9	79.5	81.3	83.5	81.2	88.6	83.4	77.1	75.5	72.5	87.0
1981	72.9	75.5	78.8	80.9	80.4	80.8	87.2	81.0	74.0	75.2	75.6	87.3
1982	67.5	73.1	76.7	82.0	74.2	80.3	84.3	82.2	74.3	69.0	72.3	86.5
1983	73.4	70.8	79.8	81.6	82.8	83.0	88.3	84.6	78.8	73.0	79.5	86.9
1984	80.5	75.5	82.6	82.1	84.7	83.2	90.8	87.5	82.5	76.4	89.8	89.0
1985	78.8	73.1	81.1	83.1	81.2	79.7	87.2	85.8	82.3	74.4	86.3	90.8
1986	80.6	72.8	82.1	82.9	83.7	80.9	89.4	86.1	81.6	76.9	85.3	89.3
1987	84.5	76.3	85.1	83.4	91.1	82.8	90.9	89.3	84.1	81.6	90.3	90.1
1988	82.0	81.0	86.5	84.6	88.8	82.6	92.4	89.9	86.9	84.6	90.7	88.2
1989	80.3	79.3	85.3	83.2	88.7	80.5	91.1	88.2	86.8	84.5	87.1	86.1
1990	77.4	80.0	84.6	84.0	83.2	79.5	89.0	88.8	86.8	84.3	83.1	84.3
1991	71.6	78.6	82.6	83.2	81.2	80.6	86.9	83.9	84.3	81.9	79.0	80.0
1992	77.4	77.0	82.9	82.5	85.5	83.5	87.0	85.7	84.9	80.5	82.5	78.6
1993	80.1	79.2	82.5	80.8	87.3	85.5	86.3	84.7	86.9	79.4	86.2	80.8
1994	81.7	78.7	84.1	82.5	89.2	87.0	88.9	85.1	88.5	79.9	90.5	81.5
1995	81.3	79.4	83.9	83.2	86.1	85.9	90.0	84.7	89.3	79.5	88.4	80.8
1996	79.1	80.9	82.2	81.4	82.7	83.1	85.8	83.8	91.4	78.4	86.8	78.1
1997	82.0	80.5	83.0	81.5	85.6	82.3	86.6	82.9	93.5	80.3	87.5	79.9
1998	81.7	80.9	82.2	82.4	84.0	78.1	87.2	81.6	90.3	78.7	86.4	81.3
1999	81.2	77.8	80.9	79.5	84.2	76.0	88.1	80.3	92.4	77.3	85.9	83.1
2000	80.5	79.0	80.1	79.6	83.3	74.9	86.1	79.7	90.3	76.4	83.6	84.8
2001	74.0	75.7	77.8	79.5	76.7	68.9	82.1	76.9	88.1	74.0	78.6	80.4
2002	71.5	75.8	77.6	79.4	75.4	66.1	83.3	75.1	88.2	74.0	79.5	78.6
2000												
January	81.0	77.2	79.9	77.8	85.5	75.4	88.4	79.2	89.5	76.1	86.1	84.9
February	79.4	78.6	80.4	79.0	85.1	76.1	87.9	78.6	89.5	76.7	85.8	84.6
March	80.7	78.0	80.8	79.6	85.0	76.1	88.1	79.9	92.1	76.9	84.7	85.1
April	81.7	79.1	80.9	79.4	85.6	75.7	88.2	80.5	89.8	77.3	85.4	86.2
May	83.4	79.3	80.7	79.3	84.4	75.4	86.6	81.0	90.8	77.7	84.4	85.3
June	83.0	79.7	80.7	80.2	84.4	75.1	87.8	80.6	90.3	76.5	84.1	85.4
July	81.0	79.4	80.1	80.4	84.1	75.4	85.0	79.8	89.7	75.8	83.9	85.6
August	80.0	80.4	79.8	79.9	81.8	74.9	84.0	79.6	90.2	76.1	82.8	84.4
September	79.7	79.1	79.9	80.3	82.0	73.9	83.9	79.7	91.2	75.9	82.8	84.4
October	79.0	79.2	79.6	79.2	81.2	73.7	85.3	79.2	90.2	76.3	82.2	84.6
November	78.3	79.3	79.5	79.6	80.0	73.9	84.3	79.5	90.5	76.2	81.1	83.9
December	78.7	79.2	79.2	80.2	80.2	72.7	83.6	79.0	89.5	75.6	80.0	83.2
2001												
January	77.3	79.6	78.7	79.3	79.5	73.5	83.6	79.1	89.0	74.7	80.5	83.0
February	76.6	78.1	78.8	79.4	78.4	73.3	84.6	79.2	89.0	75.1	79.6	80.4
March	76.6	78.1	78.0	78.8	79.1	73.0	81.8	79.5	88.5	74.2	79.1	79.7
April	75.0	77.2	78.1	79.8	78.8	72.4	83.4	77.0	88.2	73.5	79.5	80.7
May	74.7	75.6	78.1	79.3	77.1	70.7	82.3	77.3	88.7	74.9	78.8	80.2
June	73.5	74.4	77.8	80.4	76.7	69.3	81.2	76.6	89.4	73.2	78.6	80.2
July	74.4	75.2	77.3	79.1	75.9	68.8	81.5	75.8	88.5	73.2	79.0	81.2
August	72.8	74.6	77.4	79.3	75.9	67.1	82.1	76.7	87.0	73.8	78.3	80.7
September	72.4	73.1	77.5	80.3	76.6	65.1	83.0	75.2	86.9	73.4	78.1	80.2
October	72.2	75.1	77.6	79.9	74.5	65.1	81.7	75.3	88.0	74.7	77.7	79.7
November	71.8	73.6	77.1	79.5	73.6	64.3	80.7	76.1	87.5	74.0	76.8	79.1
December	71.2	74.2	76.7	79.5	74.1	64.3	79.9	75.1	86.2	73.4	77.2	79.5
2002												
January	71.5	74.4	77.5	80.0	73.8	64.2	80.7	76.3	88.0	74.8	77.3	79.0
February	71.1	73.7	77.4	80.3	73.9	64.0	80.9	75.4	89.1	73.9	77.6	78.8
March	71.1	74.2	77.8	80.6	75.6	64.4	80.4	75.1	88.5	74.3	79.0	79.1
April	71.4	75.6	77.9	80.6	75.8	64.3	82.2	75.3	89.1	73.9	79.7	78.0
May	71.9	76.6	77.9	79.5	76.4	65.5	83.5	75.6	87.7	74.3	80.2	78.1
June	72.6	76.0	78.4	80.6	77.3	67.0	83.7	74.9	88.0	74.6	80.9	77.9
July	72.4	76.8	78.3	79.7	76.2	67.6	84.1	75.5	88.7	75.0	80.5	77.9
August	71.2	76.3	78.1	79.8	75.6	67.0	84.3	75.1	88.5	74.2	80.4	78.3
September	72.0	75.7	77.9	79.8	75.1	67.9	84.7	74.4	87.0	74.2	80.2	79.3
October	71.3	75.8	77.2	78.9	74.5	66.9	84.5	74.2	85.1	73.3	80.0	79.7
November	71.7	76.3	76.7	76.8	75.5	67.9	85.6	74.3	88.8	72.8	79.4	78.9
December	70.4	77.8	76.4	76.3	74.8	66.8	84.6	74.6	90.2	72.6	79.1	78.1

. . . = Not available.

Table 2-3. Capacity Utilization by NAICS Industry Groups—*Continued*

(Output as a percentage of capacity, seasonally adjusted.)

| Year and month | Mining | Utilities | Selected high-technology industries | | | | Measures excluding selected high-technology industries | | Stage-of-process groups | | |
			Total	Computers and office equipment	Communications equipment	Semiconductors and related electronic components	Total industry	Manufacturing	Crude	Primary and semi-finished	Finished
1967	81.2	94.5	89.4	. . .	. . .	. . .	86.9	86.8	81.1	85.0	88.2
1968	83.6	95.1	87.6	. . .	. . .	. . .	87.2	86.9	83.4	86.8	87.0
1969	86.8	96.6	89.6	. . .	. . .	. . .	87.0	86.2	85.6	87.9	85.4
1970	89.3	96.0	83.2	. . .	. . .	. . .	80.8	79.0	85.1	81.2	77.9
1971	87.9	94.4	74.0	. . .	. . .	. . .	79.7	77.9	84.3	81.3	75.4
1972	90.8	95.2	79.4	85.2	73.2	84.7	84.6	83.3	88.7	87.8	79.4
1973	91.9	94.1	82.2	82.5	76.0	92.1	88.5	87.8	90.8	92.0	83.1
1974	91.1	87.8	82.6	88.7	74.3	88.4	85.0	84.2	91.3	87.1	80.1
1975	89.2	84.3	65.3	69.8	62.5	64.2	75.9	73.8	84.1	74.8	73.5
1976	90.1	85.1	67.6	71.6	62.7	70.0	79.9	78.4	87.5	79.8	76.2
1977	90.4	84.8	76.0	73.6	74.6	80.5	83.5	82.6	89.7	84.4	79.3
1978	90.1	84.0	82.6	85.9	77.9	84.7	85.1	84.6	88.9	86.0	82.3
1979	91.1	85.5	87.0	83.5	87.8	91.0	85.0	84.1	89.5	85.9	82.0
1980	91.7	85.3	87.5	85.5	90.2	87.1	80.6	78.3	89.2	78.8	79.7
1981	91.6	84.1	85.2	86.7	87.5	81.8	79.6	76.8	89.5	77.1	78.3
1982	83.8	80.5	78.9	71.9	87.5	80.7	73.6	70.7	81.8	70.4	74.0
1983	78.4	79.5	79.8	77.2	80.8	82.0	74.5	73.2	78.5	74.2	73.7
1984	84.6	82.8	88.2	86.6	86.3	91.3	80.1	78.9	84.7	81.0	77.9
1985	83.4	82.4	78.1	77.5	82.9	75.4	79.5	78.5	83.3	79.9	77.3
1986	76.7	82.3	72.0	71.8	77.5	68.3	79.2	79.0	79.0	79.9	77.4
1987	79.5	84.0	76.2	73.9	78.0	77.5	81.6	81.5	83.0	82.8	79.0
1988	83.5	86.1	78.6	76.8	80.5	79.2	84.6	84.5	86.7	85.7	81.8
1989	84.3	86.7	77.1	74.9	78.8	78.1	84.0	83.7	87.5	84.5	81.3
1990	86.5	86.1	77.5	73.2	81.0	79.5	82.7	81.9	88.8	82.3	80.7
1991	84.8	86.8	75.3	68.1	74.7	81.3	79.8	78.5	86.0	79.4	77.9
1992	84.4	85.2	79.7	77.5	79.3	80.7	80.3	79.4	85.7	80.9	78.2
1993	85.7	87.7	80.8	80.8	79.1	81.4	81.3	80.2	85.5	83.0	78.2
1994	87.3	88.9	83.8	81.3	83.5	84.8	83.4	82.5	87.2	86.3	79.1
1995	87.1	90.0	87.1	83.2	84.3	89.9	83.4	82.3	87.9	86.4	79.2
1996	89.6	90.5	80.7	78.4	78.9	82.5	82.6	81.2	87.6	85.1	78.0
1997	90.8	89.1	84.4	81.8	79.3	88.7	83.5	82.4	89.0	85.7	79.8
1998	88.1	91.0	80.3	84.5	80.1	78.4	83.2	82.2	86.1	84.4	80.6
1999	85.7	92.5	85.4	85.2	84.5	86.0	82.1	80.9	85.9	84.8	78.8
2000	89.9	92.9	89.6	75.9	91.2	95.6	82.0	80.3	87.4	85.3	78.2
2001	89.0	89.8	68.8	65.9	70.6	69.2	78.1	76.1	85.1	78.6	74.3
2002	84.3	87.8	61.5	70.4	50.6	65.2	76.7	75.0	82.9	77.5	71.9
2000											
January	88.8	91.4	90.5	77.9	88.8	97.8	82.1	80.8	87.6	86.1	77.8
February	89.1	92.8	90.9	77.7	90.4	97.9	82.3	80.8	87.4	86.2	78.1
March	89.9	89.8	90.8	77.2	90.6	97.8	82.4	81.1	87.8	86.0	78.4
April	89.9	91.6	91.7	76.8	91.8	99.2	82.6	81.2	87.8	86.2	78.8
May	89.5	94.8	92.8	76.6	94.8	100.0	82.8	81.1	87.4	86.6	79.0
June	90.1	93.4	91.1	76.7	91.1	98.7	82.7	81.1	87.6	86.2	78.8
July	90.6	90.7	90.8	76.8	91.7	97.6	82.0	80.5	87.5	85.3	78.4
August	90.7	92.8	89.4	76.7	91.0	95.2	81.7	79.9	87.4	84.8	78.1
September	90.4	93.3	89.0	75.9	93.3	93.1	81.8	80.0	87.3	84.8	78.3
October	91.0	91.9	87.2	74.7	91.7	91.1	81.3	79.5	87.7	84.1	77.7
November	90.2	91.9	86.1	72.9	89.9	90.8	81.1	79.0	87.4	83.9	77.3
December	89.2	97.4	84.2	70.8	89.7	87.8	80.8	78.5	86.3	83.4	77.1
2001											
January	90.1	94.8	81.0	68.8	89.6	81.9	80.1	77.8	86.6	82.2	76.2
February	90.6	93.3	78.0	67.4	84.3	79.5	79.7	77.4	86.9	81.2	75.9
March	90.8	92.1	75.8	67.0	80.3	77.4	79.3	77.1	86.4	80.4	75.7
April	90.7	90.9	72.7	66.9	77.0	72.9	79.1	77.0	86.2	79.8	75.5
May	90.2	89.7	70.2	66.1	74.0	69.7	78.8	76.7	85.3	79.0	75.3
June	89.3	89.9	67.7	64.1	70.9	67.3	78.3	76.2	84.5	78.5	74.7
July	88.6	88.5	65.3	61.9	68.7	64.8	78.0	76.1	84.2	78.1	74.2
August	88.2	90.3	63.4	60.9	64.6	64.1	77.8	75.7	84.4	78.0	73.5
September	88.4	88.0	62.5	62.0	62.1	63.3	77.2	75.2	85.1	77.1	73.0
October	87.6	88.7	63.0	64.9	60.6	63.8	76.9	74.8	84.6	76.9	72.8
November	87.1	86.0	62.9	68.6	58.4	63.4	76.3	74.5	84.1	76.2	72.5
December	85.9	85.3	63.0	72.4	57.2	62.8	76.0	74.3	82.6	75.8	72.6
2002											
January	84.8	86.4	62.1	74.9	53.8	62.2	76.4	74.7	82.6	76.4	72.7
February	84.9	86.9	61.8	75.1	53.7	61.6	76.4	74.7	82.7	76.7	72.4
March	84.2	88.2	61.3	72.7	53.2	61.9	76.7	74.9	82.2	77.2	72.4
April	84.0	89.8	61.1	69.0	52.8	63.4	76.9	75.1	82.8	77.7	72.2
May	84.2	88.6	61.0	66.3	51.6	65.1	76.9	75.2	83.5	77.9	71.9
June	84.7	89.0	61.3	65.9	51.9	65.9	77.3	75.6	83.6	78.2	72.5
July	84.0	89.2	61.1	67.1	49.2	66.6	77.1	75.4	83.6	78.2	72.1
August	84.2	86.8	61.7	68.9	48.9	67.5	76.9	75.4	83.1	77.9	72.1
September	82.7	86.9	61.8	70.2	47.8	67.7	76.7	75.3	82.0	77.7	72.1
October	83.2	87.9	61.5	71.1	46.9	67.4	76.5	74.8	82.1	77.8	71.3
November	85.1	87.1	62.0	71.7	48.5	67.0	76.4	74.7	83.3	77.7	71.1
December	85.4	86.7	61.7	72.1	49.3	65.6	76.0	74.2	83.8	77.0	70.8

. . . = Not available.

NOTES AND DEFINITIONS

TABLES 2-1 THROUGH 2-3 AND 20-1
INDUSTRIAL PRODUCTION AND CAPACITY UTILIZATION

SOURCE: BOARD OF GOVERNORS OF THE FEDERAL RESERVE SYSTEM.

The industrial production index measures changes in the physical volume or quantity of output of manufacturing, mining, and electric and gas utilities. *Capacity utilization* is calculated by dividing a seasonally adjusted industrial production index for an industry or group of industries by a related index of productive capacity.

Around the 15th day of each month, the Federal Reserve issues estimates of industrial production and capacity utilization for the previous month. The production estimates are in the form of index numbers (currently 1997 = 100) reflecting the monthly levels of total output of the nation's factories, mines, and gas and electric utilities expressed as a percent of the monthly average in the 1997 base year. Capacity estimates are expressed as index numbers, 1997 *output* = 100 (not 1997 *capacity*), and capacity utilization is measured by the production index as a percent of the capacity index. Since for each industry the bases of those two indexes are the same, this procedure yields production as a percent of capacity. Monthly estimates are subject to revision in each of the three subsequent months, as well as annual and comprehensive revisions in subsequent years. Monthly series are seasonally adjusted using the Census X-12 ARIMA program.

Definitions and notes on the data

The index of industrial production measures a large portion of the goods output of the national economy on a monthly basis. That portion, together with construction, has also accounted for the bulk of the variation in output over the course of many historical business cycles. The substantial industrial detail included in the index illuminates structural developments in the economy.

The total industrial production index and indexes for its major components are constructed from individual industry series (295 series for data from 1997 forward) based on the 2002 North American Industry Classification System (NAICS). See Chapter 14 of this volume for a description of NAICS and a table outlining its structure.

The Federal Reserve has been able to provide a much longer continuous historical series on the NAICS basis than other government agencies. In a major research effort, the Federal Reserve and the Center for Economic

Studies of the Bureau of the Census re-coded data from seven Censuses of Manufactures, beginning in 1963, to establish benchmark NAICS data for output, value added, and capacity utilization. The resulting indexes are shown annually for the full 30 years (36 for aggregate levels) newly calculated by the Fed in Tables 2-1 through 2-3 and monthly in Table 20-1.

However, the Federal Reserve's featured indexes for total industry and total manufacturing do *not* observe the reclassifications under NAICS of the logging industry to agriculture and the publishing industry to the Information sector. (The reason cited by the Federal Reserve was to avoid "changing the scope or historical continuity of these statistics.") Totals without those industries are also published, however, for users who may prefer the new NAICS definitions.

The individual series are grouped in two ways: market groups and industry groups.

Market groups. For analyzing market trends and product flows, the individual series are grouped into final products, nonindustrial supplies, and industrial materials. Final products are those purchased by consumers, businesses, or government for final use. Nonindustrial supplies are expected to become inputs in nonindustrial sectors, such as construction, agriculture, and services. Materials comprise industrial output requiring further processing within the industrial sector.

Final products are divided into consumer goods and equipment, and equipment is divided into business equipment and defense and space equipment. Further subdivisions of each market group are based on type of product and the market destination for the product.

Industry groups typically are groupings by 3-digit NAICS industries and major aggregates of these industries—for example, durable and nondurable manufacturing, mining, and utilities. Indexes are also calculated for stage-of-processing industry groups—crude, primary and semifinished, and finished processing. The stage-of-processing grouping is a new feature in the 2002 revision, replacing the two narrower and less refined "primary processing manufacturing" and "advanced processing manufacturing" groups previously published. *Crude processing* consists of logging, much of mining, and certain basic manufacturing activities in the chemical, paper, and metals industries. *Primary and semifinished processing* represents industries producing materials and parts used as inputs by other industries. *Finished processing* includes industries producing goods in their finished form for use by consumers, business investment, and government.

The indexes of industrial production are constructed with data from a variety of sources. Current monthly estimates of production are based on measures of physical output where possible and appropriate. For a few high-tech industries, the estimated value of nominal output is deflated by a corresponding price index. For industries in which such direct measurement is not possible monthly, output is inferred from production-worker hours or the use of electric power, adjusted for trends in output relative to input derived from annual and benchmark revisions.

In annual and benchmark revisions, the individual indexes are revised using data from the quinquennial Censuses of Manufactures and Mineral Industries and the Annual Survey of Manufactures and Survey of Plant Capacity, prepared by the Bureau of the Census; deflators from the Producer Price Indexes and other sources; the Minerals Yearbook, prepared by the Department of the Interior; publications of the Department of Energy, and other sources.

The weights used in computing the indexes are based on Census value added—the difference between the value of production and the cost of materials and supplies consumed. (Census value added differs in some respects from the theoretical economic concept of industry value added. Industry value added is ideally measured by "gross product originating" but this is not available in sufficient detail for the industrial production indexes. See Chapter 15 for data and description of Gross Domestic Product by Industry.) Beginning with 1972, the index uses a version of the Fisher-ideal index formula, that is, a chain-weighting system similar to that in the National Income and Product Accounts. See Notes and Definitions to Chapter 1. Chain-weighting keeps the index from being distorted by the use of obsolete relative prices.

For the purpose of these value-added weights, value added per unit of output is based on data from the Censuses of Manufacturing and Mineral Industries, the Census Bureau's Annual Survey of Manufactures, and revenue and expense data reported by the Department of Energy and the American Gas Association, projected into recent years using changes in relevant producer price indexes.

To separate seasonal movements from cyclical patterns and underlying trends, each component of the index is seasonally adjusted by the Census X-12 ARIMA method.

The index does not cover production on farms, in the construction industry, in transportation, or in various trade and service industries. A number of groups and subgroups include data for individual series not published separately.

Capacity utilization is calculated for the manufacturing, mining, and electric and gas utilities industries. Output is measured by seasonally-adjusted indexes of industrial production. The capacity indexes attempt to capture the concept of sustainable maximum output, which is defined as the greatest level of output that a plant can maintain within the framework of a realistic work schedule, taking account of normal downtime, and assuming sufficient availability of inputs to operate the machinery and equipment in place. The 85 individual capacity indexes are based on a variety of data, including capacity data measured in physical units compiled by government agencies and trade associations, Census Bureau surveys of utilization rates and investment, and estimates of growth of the capital stock.

Revisions

Revisions to data for recent years normally occur annually, late in the year, taking into account additional source data that have become available. Late in 2002, a comprehensive historical revision was introduced, converting the index to the NAICS classification system, updating the base year from 1992 to 1997, and introducing newly available and more comprehensive data and improved methods for measuring the output of communications equipment, as well as the usual annual data updating. In November 2003, data for 2000 through 2002 were revised and these revisions are included in this volume.

A previous comprehensive revision in 1997 moved the reference year from 1987 to 1992 = 100 and introduced annual (instead of quinquennial) updating of the value-added weights for each industry. In the January 2001 revision, recalculation of the value-added weights each month was introduced.

Data availability

Data are available monthly in Federal Reserve release G.17. Selected data are subsequently published monthly in the *Federal Reserve Bulletin*. Historical data may be purchased on diskette from Publications Services, Board of Governors of the Federal Reserve System. Current and historical data and background information are available on the Federal Reserve Internet site at <http://www.federalreserve.gov>.

Chain-weighting makes it difficult for the user to analyze in detail the sources of aggregate output change. An Explanatory Note included in each month's index release provides some assistance for the user, including a reference to a Web site location representing the exact contribution of a monthly change in a component index to the monthly change in the total index.

References

The G.17 release each month contains extensive explanatory material, as well as references for further detail. The latest comprehensive revision is described in "Industrial Production and Capacity Utilization: The 2002 Historical and Annual Revision," *Federal Reserve Bulletin*, April 2003. The aggregation method is described in *Bulletin* articles in March 2001 and February 1997. *Bulletin* articles are also available on the FRB Internet site.

An earlier detailed description of the industrial production index, together with a history of the index, a glossary of terms, and a bibliography is presented in *Industrial Production—1986 Edition*, available from the Publication Services, Board of Governors of the Federal Reserve System.

CHAPTER 3: INCOME DISTRIBUTION AND POVERTY

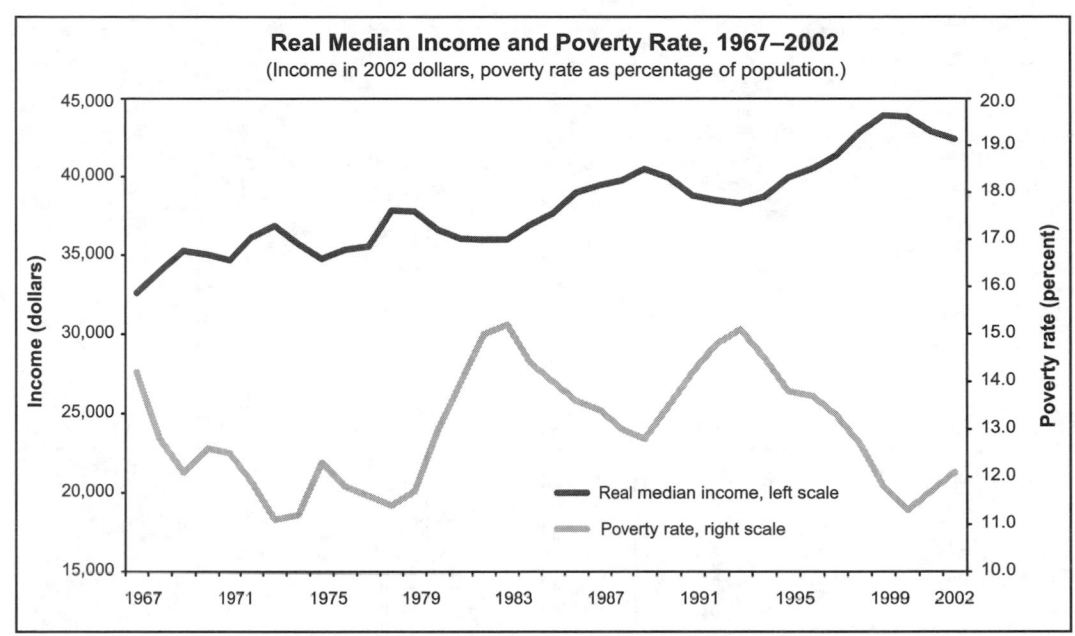

Real Median Income and Poverty Rate, 1967–2002
(Income in 2002 dollars, poverty rate as percentage of population.)

- Median household income in 2001 was $42,409, down 3.4 percent in constant (2002) dollars from the 1999 all-time high. Between 1967 and 1999, real median household income rose an average 0.9 percent per year. (Table 3-1)

- In earlier postwar years, the Census Bureau did not tabulate household income but did measure median family income. In constant dollars, median family income rose at a 2.8 percent annual rate from 1947 to 1967, then slowed to 1.2 percent from 1967 to 1999. Thus, family income growth in the more recent period was faster than the growth of household income, but still indicated a marked slowdown in the rate of increase in living standards. (Table 3-2)

- The ratio of women's to men's earnings for year-round, full-time workers rose from .607 in 1960 to .766 in 2002. In most years, this was because women's earnings rose faster than men's; however, in some years, such as 2001, it reflected an actual decline in men's earnings while women's continued to rise. (Table 3-2)

- The poverty rate has increased from 11.3 percent in 2000, which was near the all-time low reached in 1973, to 12.1 percent in 2002 (Table 3-6).

- The official income and poverty statistics just quoted are based on cash income before taxes. The Census Bureau also calculates alternative measures using the same poverty thresholds but defining income more broadly and including the effects of taxes and in-kind transfer payments such as Medicaid. In Table 3-10, it can be seen that they tell a similar story about poverty between 1979 and 2002. According to "Definition 14," poverty fell to below its 1979 low by 2000 but has increased since, just as in the official "Definition 1." Another measure that takes account of homeownership, Definition 15, also indicates an increase since 2000, and in addition indicates that the 2000 rate was still above the 1979 low. For median household income, these two alternative income definitions show less severe declines, as the effects of taxes and transfers help mitigate the effects of the declines in earned income; similarly, the increases in the poverty rate are somewhat smaller.

- Household income inequality as measured by the Gini coefficient declined slightly further in 2002 but remained near its 35-year high. Adjusted for taxes and transfer payments, inequality is lower than in the official definition but the upward trend since 1979 is quite similar. (Tables 3-2, 3-8)

Table 3-1. Median Household Income

(2002 dollars.)

Year	All races	White		Black	Asian, Native Hawaiian, and Other Pacific Islander	Hispanic (of any race)
		Total	Not Hispanic			
1967	32 591	33 988	. . .	19 734	. . .	. . .
1968	33 968	35 367	. . .	20 855	. . .	. . .
1969	35 266	36 805	. . .	22 247	. . .	. . .
1970	35 030	36 486	. . .	22 207	. . .	. . .
1971	34 669	36 263	. . .	21 421	. . .	. . .
1972	36 126	37 899	38 439	22 122	. . .	28 600
1973	36 855	38 626	38 966	22 737	. . .	28 553
1974	35 719	37 355	37 674	22 215	. . .	28 410
1975	34 763	36 354	36 628	21 824	. . .	26 116
1976	35 345	37 025	37 780	22 016	. . .	26 661
1977	35 545	37 378	38 120	22 057	. . .	27 884
1978	37 826	39 323	40 063	23 631	. . .	29 638
1979	37 784	39 616	40 173	23 259	. . .	29 936
1980	36 608	38 621	39 306	22 250	. . .	28 218
1981	36 042	38 081	38 631	21 370	. . .	28 911
1982	35 986	37 674	38 306	21 352	. . .	27 078
1983	36 001	37 743	. . .	21 365	. . .	27 053
1984	36 921	38 951	39 759	22 189	. . .	27 989
1985	37 648	39 704	40 597	23 622	. . .	27 840
1986	38 975	40 976	41 907	23 607	. . .	28 729
1987	39 453	41 568	42 711	23 725	. . .	29 272
1988	39 767	42 040	43 198	23 965	47 132	29 738
1989	40 484	42 585	43 501	25 326	50 562	30 701
1990	39 949	41 668	42 620	24 917	51 299	29 792
1991	38 791	40 649	41 619	24 216	46 932	29 217
1992	38 482	40 458	41 816	23 558	47 482	28 384
1993	38 287	40 394	41 881	23 939	46 996	28 048
1994	38 726	40 843	42 161	25 238	48 590	28 112
1995	39 931	41 911	43 566	26 240	47 592	26 788
1996	40 503	42 407	44 263	26 797	49 386	28 422
1997	41 346	43 544	45 338	27 989	50 558	29 752
1998	42 844	45 077	46 760	27 932	51 385	31 214
1999	43 915	45 673	47 650	30 118	54 991	33 178
2000	43 848	45 860	47 642	30 980	58 225	34 636
2001	42 900	45 225	47 041	29 939	54 488	34 099
2002	42 409	. . .	. . .	. . .	. . .	33 103
By Race:						
Race alone	. . .	45 086	46 900	29 026	52 291	. . .
Race alone or in combination	. . .	44 964	. . .	29 177	52 018	. . .

. . . = Not available.

Table 3-2. Median Family Income and Median Earnings by Sex

(2001 dollars, except where noted.)

Year	Median family income						Median earnings of year-round, full-time workers	
	All families	Married couples			Male householder [1]	Female householder [1]	Male workers	Female workers
		Total	Wife in workforce	Wife not in workforce				
1947	20 402	20 927	. . .	. . .	19 762	14 620	. . .	. . .
1948	19 846	20 375	. . .	. . .	20 518	12 853	. . .	. . .
1949	19 584	20 139	24 311	19 275	17 781	13 256	. . .	. . .
1950	20 668	21 458	24 927	20 643	19 397	11 968	. . .	. . .
1951	21 391	22 129	26 709	20 959	19 909	12 803	. . .	. . .
1952	22 040	23 009	27 763	21 599	20 482	12 663	. . .	. . .
1953	23 825	24 550	30 357	23 123	23 101	13 789	. . .	. . .
1954	23 252	24 179	29 775	22 605	22 398	12 801	. . .	. . .
1955	24 706	25 718	31 439	24 192	23 431	13 818	. . .	. . .
1956	26 387	27 453	32 885	25 642	23 003	15 203	. . .	. . .
1957	26 506	27 525	32 777	25 796	24 451	14 747	. . .	. . .
1958	26 387	27 570	32 233	25 847	22 097	14 218	. . .	. . .
1959	27 930	29 193	34 571	27 414	23 785	14 251	. . .	. . .
1960	28 464	29 746	34 947	27 958	24 615	15 032	27 188	16 496
1961	28 764	30 279	36 052	28 047	25 424	15 012	28 062	16 627
1962	29 585	31 110	37 061	28 631	28 368	15 552	28 582	16 948
1963	30 627	32 313	38 175	29 598	27 986	15 738	29 309	17 277
1964	31 773	33 529	39 516	30 655	28 015	16 726	30 003	17 746
1965	33 152	34 620	40 967	31 413	29 297	16 831	30 440	18 241
1966	34 861	36 277	42 794	32 991	29 770	18 560	31 732	18 264
1967	35 629	37 911	44 715	34 183	30 604	19 286	32 256	18 639
1968	37 275	39 486	46 145	35 474	31 614	19 333	33 095	19 246
1969	39 034	41 385	48 121	36 742	34 511	19 954	34 987	20 595
1970	38 954	41 516	48 465	36 732	35 579	20 107	35 397	21 015
1971	38 878	41 543	48 585	36 833	32 970	19 331	35 529	21 142
1972	40 764	43 650	50 962	38 710	37 790	19 590	37 412	21 647
1973	41 590	44 961	52 585	39 405	37 072	20 006	38 604	21 863
1974	40 513	43 719	50 935	38 406	36 607	20 373	37 251	21 886
1975	39 784	43 113	49 985	36 979	37 684	19 847	36 997	21 761
1976	41 023	44 438	51 371	38 207	35 269	19 777	36 901	22 212
1977	41 271	45 414	52 251	38 832	37 427	20 018	37 706	22 217
1978	43 601	47 803	54 647	39 933	39 463	21 101	38 880	23 111
1979	44 255	48 417	56 171	40 005	37 976	22 323	38 442	22 935
1980	42 776	47 086	54 691	38 603	35 646	21 177	37 870	22 783
1981	41 642	46 622	54 400	37 805	36 994	20 386	37 684	22 322
1982	41 151	45 693	53 285	37 404	35 368	20 167	37 014	22 854
1983	41 444	46 006	54 135	36 908	36 832	19 877	36 893	23 462
1984	42 858	48 012	56 210	38 235	37 819	20 759	37 645	23 964
1985	43 518	48 798	57 163	38 530	35 496	21 434	37 964	24 515
1986	45 393	50 551	59 089	39 761	38 465	21 029	38 918	25 013
1987	46 151	51 976	60 726	39 698	37 564	21 880	38 664	25 200
1988	46 285	52 321	61 408	39 137	38 572	22 065	38 326	25 314
1989	47 166	53 141	62 404	39 631	38 390	22 667	37 679	25 875
1990	46 429	52 394	61 432	39 747	38 146	22 237	36 349	26 032
1991	45 551	51 959	61 052	38 119	35 934	21 156	37 290	26 050
1992	45 221	51 795	61 544	37 309	34 096	21 051	37 337	26 429
1993	44 586	51 880	61 771	36 454	31 929	21 043	36 682	26 235
1994	45 820	53 118	62 984	36 834	32 787	21 546	36 454	26 235
1995	46 843	54 284	64 390	37 344	35 017	22 713	36 330	25 950
1996	47 516	55 836	65 580	37 910	35 497	22 366	36 108	26 634
1997	49 017	56 741	66 726	39 624	36 250	23 122	37 036	27 466
1998	50 689	58 761	69 142	40 303	38 698	24 037	38 334	28 049
1999	51 996	60 202	70 668	41 029	39 723	25 209	38 745	27 962
2000	52 148	60 748	71 167	41 098	38 780	26 434	38 292	28 228
2001	51 407	60 335	70 834	40 782	36 590	25 745	38 275	29 215
2002 Dollars								
2001	53 106	61 433	. . .	. . .	. . .	28 590	38 884	29 680
2002	52 704	61 254	. . .	. . .	. . .	29 001	39 429	30 203

[1]No spouse present.

. . . = Not available.

Table 3-3. Shares of Aggregate Income Received by Each Fifth and Top 5 Percent of Households

Year	Number (thousands)	Upper limit of each fifth (2002 dollars)				Lower limit of top 5 percent (2002 dollars)	Share of aggregate income (percent)						Mean income (2002 dollars)	Gini coefficient
		Lowest fifth	Second fifth	Third fifth	Fourth fifth		Lowest fifth	Second fifth	Third fifth	Fourth fifth	Highest fifth	Top 5 percent		
1967	60 813	13 688	26 692	37 898	54 027	86 692	4.0	10.8	17.3	24.2	43.8	17.5	36 452	0.399
1968	62 214	14 578	27 638	39 614	55 661	87 081	4.2	11.1	17.5	24.4	42.8	16.6	38 430	0.388
1969	63 401	15 025	28 838	41 702	58 434	91 644	4.1	10.9	17.5	24.5	43.0	16.6	40 122	0.391
1970	64 778	14 788	28 332	41 214	58 801	92 960	4.1	10.8	17.4	24.5	43.3	16.6	40 111	0.394
1971	66 676	14 593	27 818	40 936	58 371	92 694	4.1	10.6	17.3	24.5	43.5	16.7	39 873	0.396
1972	68 251	15 088	29 059	42 955	61 470	98 948	4.1	10.5	17.1	24.5	43.9	17.0	42 046	0.401
1973	69 859	15 490	29 426	43 650	63 056	99 953	4.2	10.5	17.1	24.6	43.6	16.6	42 623	0.397
1974	71 163	15 704	29 010	42 746	62 055	99 162	4.4	10.6	17.1	24.7	43.1	15.9	41 770	0.395
1975	72 867	14 804	27 840	41 969	60 381	96 278	4.4	10.5	17.1	24.8	43.2	15.9	40 593	0.397
1976	74 142	15 265	28 232	42 971	61 831	98 580	4.4	10.4	17.1	24.8	43.3	16.0	41 575	0.398
1977	76 030	15 224	28 547	43 295	63 118	102 039	4.4	10.3	17.0	24.8	43.6	16.1	42 166	0.402
1978	77 330	16 030	30 132	45 565	66 354	106 899	4.3	10.3	16.9	24.8	43.7	16.2	44 520	0.402
1979	80 776	16 088	29 920	45 964	66 788	108 949	4.2	10.3	16.9	24.7	44.0	16.4	44 883	0.404
1980	82 368	15 619	29 146	44 670	65 527	106 455	4.3	10.3	16.9	24.9	43.7	15.8	43 539	0.403
1981	83 527	15 419	28 408	44 209	65 381	106 385	4.2	10.2	16.8	25.0	43.8	15.6	43 059	0.406
1982	83 918	15 200	28 563	43 817	65 421	109 019	4.1	10.1	16.6	24.7	44.5	16.2	43 369	0.412
1983	85 290	15 416	28 730	44 052	66 628	110 652	4.1	10.0	16.5	24.7	44.7	16.4	43 865	0.414
1984	86 789	15 813	29 491	45 307	68 522	114 627	4.1	9.9	16.4	24.7	44.9	16.5	45 238	0.415
1985	88 458	15 940	30 051	46 262	69 833	116 784	4.0	9.7	16.3	24.6	45.3	17.0	46 332	0.419
1986	89 479	16 215	30 969	47 832	72 199	122 459	3.9	9.7	16.2	24.5	45.7	17.5	48 152	0.425
1987	91 124	16 350	31 034	48 444	73 215	122 515	3.8	9.6	16.1	24.3	46.2	18.2	49 065	0.426
1988	92 830	16 625	31 405	48 942	73 900	125 093	3.8	9.6	16.0	24.3	46.3	18.3	49 688	0.427
1989	93 347	16 941	32 212	49 509	75 223	128 499	3.8	9.5	15.8	24.0	46.8	18.9	51 148	0.431
1990	94 312	16 677	31 569	48 297	73 654	126 411	3.9	9.6	15.9	24.0	46.6	18.6	49 902	0.428
1991	95 669	16 208	30 903	47 732	73 085	124 126	3.8	9.6	15.9	24.2	46.5	18.1	48 829	0.428
1992	96 426	15 827	30 323	47 607	72 863	124 381	3.8	9.4	15.8	24.2	46.9	18.6	48 788	0.434
1993	97 107	15 892	30 245	47 543	73 901	128 240	3.6	9.0	15.1	23.5	48.9	21.0	50 772	0.454
1994	98 990	16 115	30 247	48 131	75 426	131 815	3.6	8.9	15.0	23.4	49.1	21.2	51 771	0.456
1995	99 627	16 874	31 538	49 218	76 313	132 415	3.7	9.1	15.2	23.3	48.7	21.0	52 659	0.450
1996	101 018	16 853	31 679	50 219	77 617	136 416	3.7	9.0	15.1	23.3	49.0	21.4	53 776	0.455
1997	102 528	17 207	32 626	51 397	79 888	141 397	3.6	8.9	15.0	23.2	49.4	21.7	55 522	0.459
1998	103 874	17 757	33 504	53 258	82 636	145 658	3.6	9.0	15.0	23.2	49.2	21.4	57 134	0.456
1999	106 434	18 492	34 445	54 370	85 500	153 234	3.6	8.9	14.9	23.2	49.4	21.5	59 067	0.458
2000	108 209	18 713	34 461	54 483	85 385	151 647	3.6	8.9	14.8	23.0	49.8	22.1	59 664	0.462
2001	109 297	18 256	33 844	53 843	84 828	152 893	3.5	8.7	14.6	23.0	50.1	22.4	59 134	0.466
2002	111 278	17 916	33 377	53 162	84 016	150 002	3.5	8.8	14.8	23.3	49.7	21.7	57 852	0.462

Table 3-4. Shares of Aggregate Income Received by Each Fifth and Top 5 Percent of Families

Year	Number of families (thousands)	Share of aggregate income (percent)						Mean family income (2001 dollars)						Gini coefficient
		Lowest fifth	Second fifth	Third fifth	Fourth fifth	Highest fifth	Top 5 percent	Lowest fifth	Second fifth	Third fifth	Fourth fifth	Highest fifth	Top 5 percent	
1947	37 237	5.0	11.9	17.0	23.1	43.0	17.5	. . .	. . .	. . .	. . .	. . .	. . .	0.376
1948	38 624	4.9	12.1	17.3	23.2	42.4	17.1	. . .	. . .	. . .	. . .	. . .	. . .	0.371
1949	39 303	4.5	11.9	17.3	23.5	42.7	16.9	. . .	. . .	. . .	. . .	. . .	. . .	0.378
1950	39 929	4.5	12.0	17.4	23.4	42.7	17.3	. . .	. . .	. . .	. . .	. . .	. . .	0.379
1951	40 578	5.0	12.4	17.6	23.4	41.6	16.8	. . .	. . .	. . .	. . .	. . .	. . .	0.363
1952	40 832	4.9	12.3	17.4	23.4	41.9	17.4	. . .	. . .	. . .	. . .	. . .	. . .	0.368
1953	41 202	4.7	12.5	18.0	23.9	40.9	15.7	. . .	. . .	. . .	. . .	. . .	. . .	0.359
1954	41 951	4.5	12.1	17.7	23.9	41.8	16.3	. . .	. . .	. . .	. . .	. . .	. . .	0.371
1955	42 889	4.8	12.3	17.8	23.7	41.3	16.4	. . .	. . .	. . .	. . .	. . .	. . .	0.363
1956	43 497	5.0	12.5	17.9	23.7	41.0	16.1	. . .	. . .	. . .	. . .	. . .	. . .	0.358
1957	43 696	5.1	12.7	18.1	23.8	40.4	15.6	. . .	. . .	. . .	. . .	. . .	. . .	0.351
1958	44 232	5.0	12.5	18.0	23.9	40.6	15.4	. . .	. . .	. . .	. . .	. . .	. . .	0.354
1959	45 111	4.9	12.3	17.9	23.8	41.1	15.9	. . .	. . .	. . .	. . .	. . .	. . .	0.361
1960	45 539	4.8	12.2	17.8	24.0	41.3	15.9	. . .	. . .	. . .	. . .	. . .	. . .	0.364
1961	46 418	4.7	11.9	17.5	23.8	42.2	16.6	. . .	. . .	. . .	. . .	. . .	. . .	0.374
1962	47 059	5.0	12.1	17.6	24.0	41.3	15.7	. . .	. . .	. . .	. . .	. . .	. . .	0.362
1963	47 540	5.0	12.1	17.7	24.0	41.2	15.8	. . .	. . .	. . .	. . .	. . .	. . .	0.362
1964	47 956	5.1	12.0	17.7	24.0	41.2	15.9	. . .	. . .	. . .	. . .	. . .	. . .	0.361
1965	48 509	5.2	12.2	17.8	23.9	40.9	15.5	. . .	. . .	. . .	. . .	. . .	. . .	0.356
1966	49 214	5.6	12.4	17.8	23.8	40.5	15.6	10 854	24 095	34 477	46 154	78 770	120 953	0.349
1967	50 111	5.4	12.2	17.5	23.5	41.4	16.4	11 031	24 666	35 454	47 549	83 960	132 839	0.358
1968	50 823	5.6	12.4	17.7	23.7	40.5	15.6	11 880	25 910	37 016	49 505	84 590	130 398	0.348
1969	51 586	5.6	12.4	17.7	23.7	40.6	15.6	12 269	27 096	38 773	51 941	88 955	136 630	0.349
1970	52 227	5.4	12.2	17.6	23.8	40.9	15.6	12 096	26 747	38 674	52 168	89 709	136 602	0.353
1971	53 296	5.5	12.0	17.6	23.8	41.1	15.7	12 100	26 339	38 538	52 191	89 894	137 065	0.355
1972	54 373	5.5	11.9	17.5	23.9	41.4	15.9	12 619	27 533	40 441	55 227	95 782	146 840	0.359
1973	55 053	5.5	11.9	17.5	24.0	41.1	15.5	12 949	28 047	41 210	56 319	96 628	145 828	0.356
1974	55 698	5.7	12.0	17.6	24.1	40.6	14.8	13 188	27 840	40 645	55 686	93 832	136 863	0.355
1975	56 245	5.6	11.9	17.7	24.2	40.7	14.9	12 664	26 772	39 807	54 503	91 848	134 735	0.357
1976	56 710	5.6	11.9	17.7	24.2	40.7	14.9	12 972	27 453	40 952	55 954	94 174	137 832	0.358
1977	57 215	5.5	11.7	17.6	24.3	40.9	14.9	12 908	27 592	41 498	57 244	96 438	140 591	0.363
1978	57 804	5.4	11.7	17.6	24.2	41.1	15.1	13 412	29 085	43 673	60 171	102 104	149 623	0.363
1979	59 550	5.4	11.6	17.5	24.1	41.4	15.3	13 552	29 300	44 188	60 835	104 345	154 454	0.365
1980	60 309	5.3	11.6	17.6	24.4	41.1	14.6	13 045	28 397	42 898	59 516	100 206	142 451	0.365
1981	61 019	5.3	11.4	17.5	24.6	41.2	14.4	12 654	27 517	42 087	59 089	99 145	138 539	0.369
1982	61 393	5.0	11.3	17.2	24.4	42.2	15.3	11 950	27 115	41 403	58 734	101 489	145 204	0.380
1983	62 015	4.9	11.2	17.2	24.5	42.4	15.3	11 781	27 105	41 703	59 436	103 056	148 587	0.382
1984	62 706	4.8	11.1	17.1	24.5	42.5	15.4	12 194	27 920	43 077	61 600	107 058	154 787	0.383
1985	63 558	4.8	11.0	16.9	24.3	43.1	16.1	12 347	28 333	43 744	62 704	111 435	166 528	0.389
1986	64 491	4.7	10.9	16.9	24.1	43.4	16.5	12 694	29 310	45 409	64 881	116 862	177 463	0.392
1987	65 204	4.6	10.7	16.8	24.0	43.8	17.2	12 677	29 671	46 073	65 940	120 507	188 647	0.393
1988	65 837	4.6	10.7	16.7	24.0	44.0	17.2	12 789	30 354	46 346	66 561	122 128	190 821	0.395
1989	66 090	4.6	10.6	16.5	23.7	44.6	17.9	13 047	30 354	47 157	67 846	127 746	204 638	0.401
1990	66 322	4.6	10.8	16.6	23.8	44.3	17.4	12 914	30 120	46 388	66 711	123 980	194 531	0.396
1991	67 173	4.5	10.7	16.6	24.1	44.2	17.1	12 337	29 285	45 439	65 904	121 080	187 351	0.397
1992	68 216	4.3	10.5	16.5	24.0	44.7	17.6	11 853	28 588	45 164	65 648	122 164	192 339	0.404
1993	68 506	4.1	9.9	15.7	23.3	47.0	20.3	11 749	28 217	44 715	66 285	133 927	231 154	0.429
1994	69 313	4.2	10.0	15.7	23.3	46.9	20.1	12 272	29 035	45 851	67 777	136 589	234 331	0.426
1995	69 597	4.4	10.1	15.8	23.2	46.5	20.0	12 994	29 938	46 873	68 582	137 785	236 303	0.421
1996	70 241	4.2	10.0	15.8	23.1	46.8	20.3	12 792	30 158	47 704	69 704	141 118	244 157	0.425
1997	70 884	4.2	9.9	15.7	23.0	47.2	20.7	13 261	31 072	49 025	71 888	147 691	258 483	0.429
1998	71 551	4.2	9.9	15.7	23.0	47.3	20.7	13 585	31 975	50 608	74 216	152 756	267 366	0.430
1999	72 031	4.3	9.9	15.6	23.0	47.2	20.3	14 149	32 924	51 977	76 642	156 973	270 695	0.428
2000	73 778	4.3	9.8	15.4	22.7	47.7	21.1	14 516	33 190	52 163	76 878	161 299	285 824	0.433
2001	74 340	4.2	9.7	15.4	22.9	47.7	21.0	14 021	32 466	51 538	76 646	159 644	280 312	0.435

. . . = Not available.

Table 3-5. Average Poverty Thresholds by Family Size

(Dollars.)

Year	Unrelated individuals			Families of 2 persons			Families, all ages								CPI-U, all items (1982–1984 = 100)
	All ages	Under 65 years	65 years and older	All ages	House-holder under 65 years	House-holder 65 years and over	3 persons	4 persons	5 persons	6 persons	7 persons or more (before 1980)	7 persons	8 persons	9 persons	
1959	1 467	1 503	1 397	1 894	1 952	1 761	2 324	2 973	3 506	3 944	4 849	...	...	...	29.2
1960	1 490	1 526	1 418	1 924	1 982	1 788	2 359	3 022	3 560	4 002	4 921	...	...	...	29.6
1961	1 506	1 545	1 433	1 942	2 005	1 808	2 383	3 054	3 597	4 041	4 967	...	...	...	29.9
1962	1 519	1 562	1 451	1 962	2 027	1 828	2 412	3 089	3 639	4 088	5 032	...	...	...	30.3
1963	1 539	1 581	1 470	1 988	2 052	1 850	2 442	3 128	3 685	4 135	5 092	...	...	...	30.6
1964	1 558	1 601	1 488	2 015	2 079	1 875	2 473	3 169	3 732	4 193	5 156	...	...	...	31.0
1965	1 582	1 626	1 512	2 048	2 114	1 906	2 514	3 223	3 797	4 264	5 248	...	...	...	31.5
1966	1 628	1 674	1 556	2 107	2 175	1 961	2 588	3 317	3 908	4 388	5 395	...	...	...	32.5
1967	1 675	1 722	1 600	2 168	2 238	2 017	2 661	3 410	4 019	4 516	5 550	...	...	...	33.4
1968	1 748	1 797	1 667	2 262	2 333	2 102	2 774	3 553	4 188	4 706	5 789	...	...	...	34.8
1969	1 840	1 893	1 757	2 383	2 458	2 215	2 924	3 743	4 415	4 958	6 101	...	...	...	36.7
1970	1 954	2 010	1 861	2 525	2 604	2 348	3 099	3 968	4 680	5 260	6 468	...	...	...	38.8
1971	2 040	2 098	1 940	2 633	2 716	2 448	3 229	4 137	4 880	5 489	6 751	...	...	...	40.5
1972	2 109	2 168	2 005	2 724	2 808	2 530	3 339	4 275	5 044	5 673	6 983	...	...	...	41.8
1973	2 247	2 307	2 130	2 895	2 984	2 688	3 548	4 540	5 358	6 028	7 435	...	...	...	44.4
1974	2 495	2 562	2 364	3 211	3 312	2 982	3 936	5 038	5 950	6 699	8 253	...	...	...	49.3
1975	2 724	2 797	2 581	3 506	3 617	3 257	4 293	5 500	6 499	7 316	9 022	...	...	...	53.8
1976	2 884	2 959	2 730	3 711	3 826	3 445	4 540	5 815	6 876	7 760	9 588	...	...	...	56.9
1977	3 075	3 152	2 906	3 951	4 072	3 666	4 833	6 191	7 320	8 261	10 216	...	...	...	60.6
1978	3 311	3 392	3 127	4 249	4 383	3 944	5 201	6 662	7 880	8 891	11 002	...	...	...	65.2
1979	3 689	3 778	3 479	4 725	4 878	4 390	5 784	7 412	8 775	9 914	12 280	...	...	...	72.6
1980	4 190	4 290	3 949	5 363	5 537	4 983	6 565	8 414	9 966	11 269	13 955	12 761	14 199	16 896	82.4
1981	4 620	4 729	4 359	5 917	6 111	5 498	7 250	9 287	11 007	12 449	...	14 110	15 655	18 572	90.9
1982	4 901	5 019	4 626	6 281	6 487	5 836	7 693	9 862	11 684	13 207	...	15 036	16 719	19 698	96.5
1983	5 061	5 180	4 775	6 483	6 697	6 023	7 938	10 178	12 049	13 630	...	15 500	17 170	20 310	99.6
1984	5 278	5 400	4 979	6 762	6 983	6 282	8 277	10 609	12 566	14 207	...	16 096	17 961	21 247	103.9
1985	5 469	5 593	5 156	6 998	7 231	6 503	8 573	10 989	13 007	14 696	...	16 656	18 512	22 083	107.6
1986	5 572	5 701	5 255	7 138	7 372	6 630	8 737	11 203	13 259	14 986	...	17 049	18 791	22 497	109.6
1987	5 778	5 909	5 447	7 397	7 641	6 872	9 056	11 611	13 737	15 509	...	17 649	19 515	23 105	113.6
1988	6 022	6 155	5 674	7 704	7 958	7 157	9 435	12 092	14 304	16 146	...	18 232	20 253	24 129	118.3
1989	6 310	6 451	5 947	8 076	8 343	7 501	9 885	12 674	14 990	16 921	...	19 162	21 328	25 480	124.0
1990	6 652	6 800	6 268	8 509	8 794	7 905	10 419	13 359	15 792	17 839	...	20 241	22 582	26 848	130.7
1991	6 932	7 086	6 532	8 865	9 165	8 241	10 860	13 924	16 456	18 587	...	21 058	23 582	27 942	136.2
1992	7 143	7 299	6 729	9 137	9 443	8 487	11 186	14 335	16 952	19 137	...	21 594	24 053	28 745	140.3
1993	7 363	7 518	6 930	9 414	9 728	8 740	11 522	14 763	17 449	19 718	...	22 383	24 838	29 529	144.5
1994	7 547	7 710	7 108	9 661	9 976	8 967	11 821	15 141	17 900	20 235	...	22 923	25 427	30 300	148.2
1995	7 763	7 929	7 309	9 933	10 259	9 219	12 158	15 569	18 408	20 804	...	23 552	26 237	31 280	152.4
1996	7 995	8 163	7 525	10 233	10 564	9 491	12 516	16 036	18 952	21 389	...	24 268	27 091	31 971	156.9
1997	8 183	8 350	7 698	10 473	10 805	9 712	12 802	16 400	19 380	21 886	...	24 802	27 593	32 566	160.5
1998	8 316	8 480	7 818	10 634	10 972	9 862	13 003	16 660	19 680	22 228	...	25 257	28 166	33 339	163.0
1999	9 035	9 214	8 494	11 549	11 920	10 710	14 126	18 103	21 396	24 163	...	27 551	30 796	36 606	166.6
2000	8 791	8 959	8 259	11 235	11 589	10 418	13 740	17 604	20 815	23 533	...	26 750	29 701	35 150	172.2
2001	9 039	9 214	8 494	11 569	11 920	10 715	14 128	18 104	21 405	24 195	...	27 517	30 627	36 286	177.1
2002	9 183	9 359	8 628	11 756	12 110	10 885	14 348	18 392	21 744	24 576	...	28 001	30 907	37 062	179.9

. . . = Not available.

Table 3-6. Poverty Status by Type of Family, Race and Hispanic Origin

(Thousands of persons or families, percent of population.)

Year, race and Hispanic origin	All persons			Married-couple families [1]			Female householder, no spouse present [1]			Unrelated individuals		
	Number of persons	Below poverty level		Number of families	Below poverty level		Number of families	Below poverty level		Number of persons	Below poverty level	
		Number	Percent		Number	Percent		Number	Percent		Number	Percent
All Races												
1959	176 557	39 490	22.4	39 335	...	...	4 493	1 916	42.6	10 699	4 928	46.1
1960	179 503	39 851	22.2	39 624	...	...	4 609	1 955	42.4	10 888	4 926	45.2
1961	181 277	39 628	21.9	40 405	...	...	4 643	1 954	42.1	11 146	5 119	45.9
1962	184 276	38 625	21.0	40 923	...	...	4 741	2 034	42.9	11 013	5 002	45.4
1963	187 258	36 436	19.5	41 311	...	...	4 882	1 972	40.4	11 182	4 938	44.2
1964	189 710	36 055	19.0	41 648	...	...	5 006	1 822	36.4	12 057	5 143	42.7
1965	191 413	33 185	17.3	42 107	...	...	4 992	1 916	38.4	12 132	4 827	39.8
1966	193 388	28 510	14.7	42 553	...	...	5 171	1 721	33.1	12 271	4 701	38.3
1967	195 672	27 769	14.2	43 292	...	...	5 333	1 774	33.3	13 114	4 998	38.1
1968	197 628	25 389	12.8	43 842	...	...	5 441	1 755	32.3	13 803	4 694	34.0
1969	199 517	24 147	12.1	44 436	...	...	5 591	1 827	32.7	14 626	4 972	34.0
1970	202 183	25 420	12.6	44 739	...	...	6 001	1 952	32.5	15 491	5 090	32.9
1971	204 554	25 559	12.5	45 752	...	...	6 191	2 100	33.9	16 311	5 154	31.6
1972	206 004	24 460	11.9	46 314	...	...	6 607	2 158	32.7	16 811	4 883	29.0
1973	207 621	22 973	11.1	46 812	2 482	5.3	6 804	2 193	32.2	18 260	4 674	25.6
1974	209 362	23 370	11.2	47 069	2 474	5.3	7 230	2 324	32.1	18 926	4 553	24.1
1975	210 864	25 877	12.3	47 318	2 904	6.1	7 482	2 430	32.5	20 234	5 088	25.1
1976	212 303	24 975	11.8	47 497	2 606	5.5	7 713	2 543	33.0	21 459	5 344	24.9
1977	213 867	24 720	11.6	47 385	2 524	5.3	8 236	2 610	31.7	23 110	5 216	22.6
1978	215 656	24 497	11.4	47 692	2 474	5.2	8 458	2 654	31.4	24 585	5 435	22.1
1979	222 903	26 072	11.7	49 112	2 640	5.4	8 705	2 645	30.4	26 170	5 743	21.9
1980	225 027	29 272	13.0	49 294	3 032	6.2	9 082	2 972	32.7	27 133	6 227	22.9
1981	227 157	31 822	14.0	49 630	3 394	6.8	9 403	3 252	34.6	27 714	6 490	23.4
1982	229 412	34 398	15.0	49 908	3 789	7.6	9 469	3 434	36.3	27 908	6 458	23.1
1983	233 816	33 700	14.4	50 350	3 488	6.9	10 129	3 498	34.5	30 268	6 609	21.8
1984	236 594	33 064	14.0	50 933	3 438	6.7	10 211	3 474	34.0	31 351	6 725	21.5
1985	231 700	35 303	15.2	50 081	3 815	7.6	9 896	3 564	36.0	29 158	6 740	23.1
1986	238 554	32 370	13.6	51 537	3 123	6.1	10 445	3 613	34.6	31 679	6 846	21.6
1987	240 982	32 221	13.4	51 675	3 011	5.8	10 696	3 654	34.2	32 992	6 857	20.8
1988	243 530	31 745	13.0	52 100	2 897	5.6	10 890	3 642	33.4	34 340	7 070	20.6
1989	245 992	31 528	12.8	52 137	2 931	5.6	10 890	3 504	32.2	35 185	6 760	19.2
1990	248 644	33 585	13.5	52 147	2 981	5.7	11 268	3 768	33.4	36 056	7 446	20.7
1991	251 192	35 708	14.2	52 457	3 158	6.0	11 693	4 161	35.6	36 845	7 773	21.1
1992	256 549	38 014	14.8	53 090	3 385	6.4	12 061	4 275	35.4	36 842	8 075	21.9
1993	259 278	39 265	15.1	53 181	3 481	6.5	12 411	4 424	35.6	38 038	8 388	22.1
1994	261 616	38 059	14.5	53 865	3 272	6.1	12 220	4 232	34.6	38 538	8 287	21.5
1995	263 733	36 425	13.8	53 570	2 982	5.6	12 514	4 057	32.4	39 484	8 247	20.9
1996	266 218	36 529	13.7	53 604	3 010	5.6	12 790	4 167	32.6	40 727	8 452	20.8
1997	268 480	35 574	13.3	54 321	2 821	5.2	12 652	3 995	31.6	41 672	8 687	20.8
1998	271 059	34 476	12.7	54 778	2 879	5.3	12 796	3 831	29.9	42 539	8 478	19.9
1999	276 208	32 791	11.9	56 290	2 748	4.9	12 818	3 559	27.8	43 977	8 400	19.1
2000	278 944	31 581	11.3	56 598	2 637	4.7	12 903	3 278	25.4	45 624	8 653	19.0
2001	281 475	32 907	11.7	56 755	2 760	4.9	13 146	3 470	26.4	46 392	9 226	19.9
2002	285 317	34 570	12.1	57 327	3 052	5.3	13 626	3 613	26.5	47 156	9 618	20.4
White												
1959	156 956	28 484	18.1	36 217	...	...	3 547	1 233	34.8	9 154	4 041	44.1
1960	158 863	28 309	17.8	36 400	...	...	3 673	1 252	34.0	9 405	4 047	43.0
1961	160 306	27 890	17.4	37 185	...	...	3 608	1 208	33.5	9 589	4 143	43.2
1962	162 842	26 672	16.4	37 657	...	...	3 627	1 230	33.9	9 494	4 059	42.7
1963	165 309	25 238	15.3	37 799	...	...	3 797	1 191	31.4	9 725	4 089	42.0
1964	167 313	24 957	14.9	38 171	...	...	3 882	1 125	29.0	10 415	4 241	40.7
1965	168 732	22 496	13.3	38 632	...	...	3 860	1 196	31.0	10 477	3 988	38.1
1966	170 247	19 290	11.3	39 007	...	...	4 010	1 036	25.7	10 686	3 860	36.1
1967	172 038	18 983	11.0	39 821	...	...	4 008	1 037	25.9	11 318	4 132	36.5
1968	173 732	17 395	10.0	40 355	...	...	4 053	1 021	25.2	11 955	3 849	32.2
1969	175 349	16 659	9.5	40 802	...	...	4 165	1 069	25.7	12 570	4 036	32.1
1970	177 376	17 484	9.9	41 092	...	...	4 408	1 102	25.0	13 500	4 161	30.8
1971	179 398	17 780	9.9	42 039	...	...	4 489	1 191	26.5	14 214	4 214	29.6
1972	180 125	16 203	9.0	42 585	...	...	4 672	1 135	24.3	14 495	3 935	27.1
1973	181 185	15 142	8.4	43 805	2 306	5.3	4 853	1 190	24.5	15 761	3 730	23.7
1974	182 376	15 736	8.6	43 049	1 977	4.6	5 208	1 289	24.8	16 295	3 555	21.8
1975	183 164	17 770	9.7	43 311	2 363	5.5	5 380	1 394	25.9	17 503	3 972	22.7
1976	184 165	16 713	9.1	43 397	2 071	4.8	5 467	1 379	25.2	18 594	4 213	22.7
1977	185 254	16 416	8.9	43 423	2 028	4.7	5 828	1 400	24.0	19 869	4 051	20.4
1978	186 450	16 259	8.7	43 636	2 033	4.7	5 918	1 391	23.5	21 257	4 209	19.8
1979	191 742	17 214	9.0	44 751	2 099	4.7	6 052	1 350	22.3	22 587	4 452	19.7

[1] These numbers and rates refer to families rather than persons.
. . . = Not available.

Table 3-6. Poverty Status by Type of Family, Race and Hispanic Origin—*Continued*

(Thousands of persons or families, percent of population.)

Year, race and Hispanic origin	All persons			Married-couple families [1]			Female householder, no spouse present [1]			Unrelated individuals		
	Number of persons	Below poverty level		Number of families	Below poverty level		Number of families	Below poverty level		Number of persons	Below poverty level	
		Number	Percent		Number	Percent		Number	Percent		Number	Percent
White—*Continued*												
1980	192 912	19 699	10.2	44 860	2 437	5.4	6 266	1 609	25.7	23 370	4 760	20.4
1981	194 504	21 553	11.1	45 007	2 712	6.0	6 620	1 814	27.4	23 913	5 061	21.2
1982	195 919	23 517	12.0	45 252	3 104	6.9	6 507	1 813	27.9	24 300	5 041	20.7
1983	198 941	22 955	11.5	45 643	2 858	6.3	6 941	1 878	27.1	26 094	5 181	19.9
1984	200 918	22 860	11.4	45 924	2 815	6.1	7 111	1 950	27.4	27 067	5 299	19.6
1985	197 496	23 984	12.1	45 470	3 125	6.9	6 796	1 926	28.3	25 206	5 189	20.6
1986	202 282	22 183	11.0	46 410	2 591	5.6	7 227	2 041	28.2	27 143	5 198	19.2
1987	203 605	21 195	10.4	46 510	2 382	5.1	7 297	1 961	26.9	28 290	5 174	18.3
1988	205 235	20 715	10.1	46 877	2 294	4.9	7 342	1 945	26.5	29 315	5 314	18.1
1989	206 853	20 785	10.0	46 981	2 329	5.0	7 306	1 858	25.4	29 993	5 063	16.9
1990	208 611	22 326	10.7	47 014	2 386	5.1	7 512	2 010	26.8	30 833	5 739	18.6
1991	210 133	23 747	11.3	47 124	2 573	5.5	7 727	2 192	28.4	31 207	5 872	18.8
1992	213 060	25 259	11.9	47 383	2 677	5.7	7 868	2 245	28.5	31 170	6 147	19.7
1993	214 899	26 226	12.2	47 452	2 757	5.8	8 131	2 376	29.2	32 112	6 443	20.1
1994	216 460	25 379	11.7	47 905	2 629	5.5	8 031	2 329	29.0	32 569	6 292	19.3
1995	218 028	24 423	11.2	47 877	2 443	5.1	8 284	2 200	26.6	33 399	6 336	19.0
1996	219 656	24 650	11.2	47 650	2 416	5.1	8 339	2 276	27.3	34 247	6 463	18.9
1997	221 200	24 396	11.0	48 070	2 312	4.8	8 308	2 305	27.7	34 858	6 593	18.9
1998	222 837	23 454	10.5	48 461	2 400	5.0	8 529	2 123	24.9	35 563	6 386	18.0
1999	225 361	22 169	9.8	49 493	2 207	4.5	8 462	1 901	22.5	36 441	6 411	17.6
2000	227 846	21 645	9.5	49 473	2 181	4.4	8 574	1 820	21.2	37 699	6 454	17.1
2001	229 675	22 739	9.9	49 612	2 242	4.5	8 641	1 939	22.4	38 294	6 996	18.3
White Alone												
2002	230 376	23 466	10.2	49 923	2 510	5.0	8 885	2 004	22.6	38 575	7 105	18.4
White, Not Hispanic												
1973	170 488	12 864	7.5	...	...	...	...	...	...	15 158	3 602	23.8
1974	171 463	13 217	7.7	41 155	1 700	4.1	4 676	1 005	21.5	15 699	3 364	21.4
1975	172 417	14 883	8.6	41 447	2 036	4.9	4 786	1 079	22.5	16 879	3 746	22.2
1976	173 235	14 025	8.1	41 437	1 759	4.2	4 849	1 059	21.8	17 912	3 959	22.1
1977	173 563	13 802	8.0	41 338	1 750	4.2	5 156	1 039	20.2	19 114	3 825	20.0
1978	174 731	13 755	7.9	41 574	1 790	4.3	5 236	1 047	20.0	20 410	3 957	19.4
1979	178 814	14 419	8.1	42 527	1 810	4.3	5 473	1 062	19.4	21 638	4 179	19.3
1980	179 798	16 365	9.1	42 564	2 083	4.9	5 593	1 264	22.6	22 455	4 474	19.9
1981	180 909	17 987	9.9	42 653	2 353	5.5	5 910	1 436	24.3	22 950	4 769	20.8
1982	181 903	19 362	10.6	42 847	2 648	6.2	5 778	1 413	24.5	23 329	4 701	20.2
1983	182 469	18 300	10.8	42 872	2 400	5.6	6 081	1 422	23.4	24 671	4 659	18.9
1984	183 455	17 839	10.0	43 036	2 316	5.4	6 180	1 460	23.6	25 544	4 789	18.7
1985	181 393	19 538	9.7	42 768	2 649	6.2	5 982	1 501	25.1	23 894	4 746	19.9
1986	184 119	17 244	9.4	43 370	2 081	4.8	6 255	1 542	24.7	25 525	4 668	18.3
1987	184 936	16 029	8.7	43 422	1 847	4.3	6 287	1 443	23.0	26 439	4 613	17.4
1988	185 961	15 565	8.4	43 591	1 763	4.0	6 287	1 426	22.7	27 552	4 746	17.2
1989	186 979	15 599	8.3	43 710	1 798	4.1	6 255	1 355	21.7	28 055	4 466	15.9
1990	188 129	16 622	8.8	43 682	1 799	4.1	6 408	1 480	23.1	28 688	5 002	17.4
1991	189 116	17 741	9.4	43 724	1 918	4.4	6 553	1 610	24.6	29 215	5 261	18.0
1992	189 001	18 202	9.6	43 661	1 978	4.5	6 629	1 637	24.7	28 775	5 350	18.6
1993	190 843	18 882	9.9	43 745	2 042	4.7	6 798	1 699	25.0	29 681	5 570	18.8
1994	192 543	18 110	9.4	44 178	1 915	4.3	6 764	1 678	24.8	30 157	5 500	18.2
1995	190 951	16 267	8.5	43 771	1 664	3.8	6 792	1 463	21.5	30 586	5 303	17.3
1996	191 459	16 462	8.6	43 276	1 628	3.8	6 875	1 538	22.4	31 410	5 455	17.4
1997	191 859	16 491	8.6	43 427	1 501	3.5	6 826	1 598	23.4	32 049	5 632	17.6
1998	192 754	15 799	8.2	43 669	1 639	3.8	6 909	1 428	20.7	32 573	5 352	16.4
1999	192 565	14 735	7.7	44 443	1 474	3.3	6 770	1 248	18.4	33 189	5 412	16.3
2000	193 691	14 366	7.4	44 278	1 435	3.2	6 891	1 226	17.8	33 943	5 356	15.8
2001	194 538	15 271	7.8	44 124	1 477	3.3	6 886	1 305	19.0	34 603	5 882	17.0
White Alone, Not Hispanic												
2002	194 144	15 567	8.0	44 109	1 628	3.7	7 072	1 374	19.4	34 614	5 947	17.2

[1]These numbers and rates refer to families rather than persons.
. . . = Not available.

Table 3-6. Poverty Status by Type of Family, Race and Hispanic Origin—*Continued*

(Thousands of persons or families, percent of population.)

Year, race and Hispanic origin	All persons			Married-couple families [1]			Female householder, no spouse present [1]			Unrelated individuals		
	Number of persons	Below poverty level		Number of families	Below poverty level		Number of families	Below poverty level		Number of persons	Below poverty level	
		Number	Percent		Number	Percent		Number	Percent		Number	Percent
Black												
1959	18 013	9 927	55.1	...	...	...	...	...	...	1 430	815	57.0
1966	21 206	8 867	41.8	...	...	...	...	...	...	...	777	54.4
1967	21 590	8 486	39.3	3 118	...	...	1 272	716	56.3	...	809	49.3
1968	21 944	7 616	34.7	3 141	...	...	1 327	706	53.2	...	777	46.3
1969	22 011	7 095	32.2	3 323	...	...	1 384	737	53.3	1 819	850	46.7
1970	22 515	7 548	33.5	3 301	...	...	1 535	834	54.3	1 791	865	48.3
1971	22 784	7 396	32.5	3 289	...	...	1 642	879	53.5	1 884	866	46.0
1972	23 144	7 710	33.3	3 233	...	...	1 822	972	53.3	2 028	870	42.9
1973	23 512	7 388	31.4	3 360	...	...	1 849	974	52.7	2 183	828	37.9
1974	23 699	7 182	30.3	3 357	435	13.0	1 934	1 010	52.2	2 359	927	39.3
1975	24 089	7 545	31.3	3 352	479	14.3	2 004	1 004	50.1	2 402	1 011	42.1
1976	24 399	7 595	31.1	3 406	450	13.2	2 151	1 122	52.2	2 559	1 019	39.8
1977	24 710	7 726	31.3	3 260	429	13.1	2 277	1 162	51.0	2 860	1 059	37.0
1978	24 956	7 625	30.6	3 244	366	11.3	2 390	1 208	50.6	2 929	1 132	38.6
1979	25 944	8 050	31.0	3 433	453	13.2	2 495	1 234	49.4	3 127	1 168	37.3
1980	26 408	8 579	32.5	3 392	474	14.0	2 634	1 301	49.4	3 208	1 314	41.0
1981	26 834	9 173	34.2	3 535	543	15.4	2 605	1 377	52.9	3 277	1 296	39.6
1982	27 216	9 697	35.6	3 486	543	15.6	2 734	1 535	56.2	3 051	1 229	40.3
1983	28 087	9 490	33.8	3 469	479	13.8	2 964	1 533	51.7	3 501	1 255	35.8
1984	28 485	8 926	31.3	3 680	447	12.2	2 874	1 452	50.5	3 641	1 264	34.7
1985	27 678	9 882	35.7	3 454	535	15.5	2 871	1 541	53.7	3 287	1 338	40.7
1986	28 871	8 983	31.1	3 742	403	10.8	2 967	1 488	50.1	3 714	1 431	38.5
1987	29 362	9 520	32.4	3 681	439	11.9	3 089	1 577	51.1	3 977	1 471	37.0
1988	29 849	9 356	31.3	3 722	421	11.3	3 223	1 579	49.0	4 095	1 509	36.8
1989	30 332	9 302	30.7	3 750	443	11.8	3 275	1 524	46.5	4 180	1 471	35.2
1990	30 806	9 837	31.9	3 569	448	12.6	3 430	1 648	48.1	4 244	1 491	35.1
1991	31 313	10 242	32.7	3 631	399	11.0	3 582	1 834	51.2	4 505	1 590	35.3
1992	32 411	10 827	33.4	3 777	490	13.0	3 738	1 878	50.2	4 410	1 569	35.6
1993	32 910	10 877	33.1	3 715	458	12.3	3 828	1 908	49.9	4 608	1 541	33.4
1994	33 353	10 196	30.6	3 842	336	8.7	3 716	1 715	46.2	4 649	1 617	34.8
1995	33 740	9 872	29.3	3 713	314	8.5	3 769	1 701	45.1	4 756	1 551	32.6
1996	34 110	9 694	28.4	3 851	352	9.1	3 947	1 724	43.7	4 989	1 606	32.2
1997	34 458	9 116	26.5	3 921	312	8.0	3 926	1 563	39.8	5 316	1 645	31.0
1998	34 877	9 091	26.1	3 979	290	7.3	3 813	1 557	40.8	5 390	1 752	32.5
1999	35 756	8 441	23.6	4 150	295	7.1	3 797	1 487	39.2	5 668	1 562	27.5
2000	35 425	7 982	22.5	4 214	266	6.3	3 785	1 300	34.3	5 885	1 702	28.9
2001	35 871	8 136	22.7	4 234	328	7.8	3 838	1 351	35.2	5 873	1 692	28.8
Black Alone												
2002	35 678	8 602	24.1	4 165	331	7.9	4 003	1 433	35.8	5 858	1 800	30.7
Black Alone or in Combination												
2002	37 207	8 884	23.9	4 268	340	8.0	4 072	1 454	35.7	6 034	1 851	30.7
Asian and Pacific Islander												
1987	6 322	1 021	16.1	...	...	...	...	...	...	516	138	26.8
1988	6 447	1 117	17.3	...	...	...	...	...	...	651	160	24.5
1989	6 673	939	14.1	...	...	...	...	...	...	712	144	20.2
1990	7 014	858	12.2	...	...	...	...	...	...	668	124	18.5
1991	7 192	996	13.8	...	...	...	...	...	...	785	209	26.6
1992	7 779	985	12.7	...	...	...	...	...	...	828	193	23.3
1993	7 434	1 134	15.3	...	...	...	...	...	...	791	228	28.8
1994	6 654	974	14.6	...	...	...	...	...	...	696	179	25.7
1995	9 644	1 411	14.6	...	...	...	...	...	...	1 013	260	25.6
1996	10 054	1 454	14.5	...	...	...	...	...	...	1 120	255	22.8
1997	10 482	1 468	14.0	...	...	...	...	...	...	1 134	327	28.9
1998	10 873	1 360	12.5	...	...	...	...	...	...	1 266	257	20.3
1999	11 955	1 285	10.7	...	...	...	...	...	...	1 415	270	19.1
2000	12 672	1 258	9.9	...	...	...	...	...	...	1 588	350	22.0
2001	12 465	1 275	10.2	...	...	...	...	...	...	1 682	393	23.4
Asian Alone												
2002	11 541	1 161	10.1	2 286	135	5.9	337	48	14.2	1 613	390	24.2
Asian Alone or in Combination												
2002	12 487	1 243	10.0	2 344	137	5.9	354	51	14.3	1 708	417	24.4

[1] These numbers and rates refer to families rather than persons.

. . . = Not available.

Table 3-6. Poverty Status by Type of Family, Race and Hispanic Origin—*Continued*

(Thousands of persons or families, percent of population.)

Year, race and Hispanic origin	All persons			Married-couple families [1]			Female householder, no spouse present [1]			Unrelated individuals		
	Number of persons	Below poverty level		Number of families	Below poverty level		Number of families	Below poverty level		Number of persons	Below poverty level	
		Number	Percent		Number	Percent		Number	Percent		Number	Percent
Hispanic (of Any Race)												
1972	10 588	2 414	22.8	...	...	...	...	...	...	488	162	33.2
1973	10 795	2 366	21.9	1 876	239	12.7	411	211	51.4	526	157	29.9
1974	11 201	2 575	23.0	1 926	278	14.4	462	229	49.6	617	201	32.6
1975	11 117	2 991	26.9	1 896	335	17.7	522	279	53.6	645	236	36.6
1976	11 269	2 783	24.7	1 978	312	15.8	517	275	53.1	716	266	37.2
1977	12 046	2 700	22.4	2 104	280	13.3	561	301	53.6	797	237	29.8
1978	12 079	2 607	21.6	2 089	248	11.9	542	288	53.1	886	264	29.8
1979	13 371	2 921	21.8	2 282	298	13.1	610	300	49.2	991	286	28.8
1980	13 600	3 491	25.7	2 365	363	15.3	706	362	51.3	970	312	32.2
1981	14 021	3 713	26.5	2 414	366	15.1	750	399	53.2	1 005	313	31.1
1982	14 385	4 301	29.9	2 448	465	19.0	767	425	55.4	1 018	358	35.1
1983	16 916	4 806	28.4	2 824	469	16.6	905	483	53.4	1 481	545	36.8
1984	18 075	5 236	29.0	2 962	505	17.0	980	521	53.1	1 602	532	33.2
1985	16 544	4 633	28.0	2 752	437	17.7	860	454	52.8	1 364	457	33.5
1986	18 758	5 117	27.3	3 118	518	16.6	1 032	528	51.2	1 685	553	32.8
1987	19 395	5 422	28.0	3 196	556	17.4	1 082	565	52.2	1 933	598	31.0
1988	20 064	5 357	26.7	3 398	547	16.1	1 112	546	49.1	1 864	597	32.0
1989	20 746	5 430	26.2	3 395	549	16.2	1 116	530	47.5	2 045	634	31.0
1990	21 405	6 006	28.1	3 454	605	17.5	1 186	573	48.3	2 254	774	34.3
1991	22 070	6 339	28.7	3 532	674	19.1	1 261	627	49.7	2 146	667	31.1
1992	25 646	7 592	29.6	3 940	743	18.8	1 348	664	49.3	2 577	881	34.2
1993	26 559	8 126	30.6	4 038	770	19.1	1 498	772	51.6	2 717	972	35.8
1994	27 442	8 416	30.7	4 236	827	19.5	1 485	773	52.1	2 798	926	33.1
1995	28 344	8 574	30.3	4 247	803	18.9	1 604	792	49.4	2 947	1 092	37.0
1996	29 614	8 697	29.4	4 520	815	18.0	1 617	823	50.9	2 985	1 066	35.7
1997	30 637	8 308	27.1	4 804	836	17.4	1 612	767	47.6	2 976	1 017	34.2
1998	31 515	8 070	25.6	4 945	775	15.7	1 728	756	43.7	3 218	1 097	34.1
1999	34 632	7 876	22.7	5 273	758	14.4	1 827	717	39.3	3 481	1 068	30.7
2000	35 955	7 747	21.5	5 426	772	14.2	1 826	664	36.4	3 978	1 163	29.2
2001	37 312	7 997	21.4	5 778	799	13.8	1 922	711	37.0	3 981	1 211	30.4
2002	39 216	8 555	21.8	6 189	927	15.0	2 033	717	35.3	4 364	1 255	28.8

[1] These numbers and rates refer to families rather than persons.
. . . = Not available.

Table 3-7. Poverty Status of Persons by Sex and Age

(Thousands of persons, percent of population.)

Year	Poverty status of persons by sex				Poverty status of persons by age					
	Males below poverty level		Females below poverty level		Children under 18 below poverty level		Persons 18 to 64 years old below poverty level		Persons 65 years and older below poverty level	
	Number (thousands)	Poverty rate	Number (thousands)	Poverty rate	Number (thousands)	Poverty rate	Number (thousands)	Poverty rate	Number (thousands)	Poverty rate
1959	. . .	. . .	. . .	. . .	17 552	27.3	16 457	17.0	5 481	35.2
1966	12 225	13.0	16 265	16.3	12 389	17.6	11 007	10.5	5 114	28.5
1967	11 813	12.5	15 951	15.8	11 656	16.6	10 725	10.0	5 388	29.5
1968	10 793	11.3	14 578	14.3	10 954	15.6	9 803	9.0	4 632	25.0
1969	10 292	10.6	13 978	13.6	9 691	14.0	9 669	8.7	4 787	25.3
1970	10 879	11.1	14 632	14.0	10 440	15.1	10 187	9.0	4 793	24.6
1971	10 708	10.8	14 841	14.1	10 551	15.3	10 735	9.3	4 273	21.6
1972	10 190	10.2	14 258	13.4	10 284	15.1	10 438	8.8	3 738	18.6
1973	9 642	9.6	13 316	12.5	9 642	14.4	9 977	8.3	3 354	16.3
1974	10 313	10.2	13 881	12.9	10 156	15.4	10 132	8.3	3 085	14.6
1975	10 908	10.7	14 970	13.8	11 104	17.1	11 456	9.2	3 317	15.3
1976	10 373	10.1	14 603	13.4	10 273	16.0	11 389	9.0	3 313	15.0
1977	10 340	10.0	14 381	13.0	10 288	16.2	11 316	8.8	3 177	14.1
1978	10 017	9.6	14 480	13.0	9 931	15.9	11 332	8.7	3 233	14.0
1979	10 535	10.0	14 810	13.2	10 377	16.4	12 014	8.9	3 682	15.2
1980	12 207	11.2	17 065	14.7	11 543	18.3	13 858	10.1	3 871	15.7
1981	13 360	12.1	18 462	15.8	12 505	20.0	15 464	11.1	3 853	15.3
1982	14 842	13.4	19 556	16.5	13 647	21.9	17 000	12.0	3 751	14.6
1983	15 182	13.5	20 084	16.8	13 911	22.3	17 767	12.4	3 625	13.8
1984	14 537	12.8	19 163	15.9	13 420	21.5	16 952	11 7	3 330	12.4
1985	14 140	12.3	18 923	15.6	13 010	20.7	16 598	11.3	3 456	12.6
1986	13 721	11.8	18 649	15.2	12 876	20.5	16 017	10.8	3 477	12.4
1987	14 029	12.0	18 518	15.0	12 843	20.3	15 815	10.6	3 563	12.5
1988	13 599	11.5	18 146	14.5	12 455	19.5	15 809	10.5	3 481	12.0
1989	13 366	11.2	18 162	14.4	12 590	19.6	15 575	10.2	3 363	11.4
1990	14 211	11.7	19 373	15.2	13 431	20.6	16 496	10.7	3 658	12.2
1991	15 082	12.3	20 626	16.0	14 341	21.8	17 586	11.4	3 781	12.4
1992	16 222	12.9	21 792	16.6	15 294	22.3	18 793	11.9	3 928	12.9
1993	16 900	13.3	22 365	16.9	15 727	22.7	19 781	12.4	3 755	12.2
1994	16 316	12.8	21 744	16.3	15 289	21.8	19 107	11.9	3 663	11.7
1995	15 683	12.2	20 742	15.4	14 665	20.8	18 442	11.4	3 318	10.5
1996	15 611	12.0	20 918	15.4	14 463	20.5	18 638	11.4	3 428	10.8
1997	15 187	11.6	20 387	14.9	14 113	19.9	18 085	10.9	3 376	10.5
1998	14 712	11.1	19 764	14.3	13 467	18.9	17 623	10.5	3 386	10.5
1999	14 079	10.4	18 712	13.2	12 280	17.1	17 289	10.1	3 222	9.7
2000	13 536	9.9	18 045	12.6	11 587	16.2	16 671	9.6	3 323	9.9
2001	14 327	10.4	18 580	12.9	11 733	16.3	17 760	10.1	3 414	10.1
2002	15 162	10.9	19 408	13.3	12 133	16.7	18 861	10.6	3 576	10.4

. . . = Not available.

Table 3-8. Poverty Status of Persons Inside and Outside Metropolitan Areas, and Persons In and Near Poverty

(Thousands of persons, percent of population.)

Year	Inside metropolitan areas						Outside metropolitan areas		Total in and near poverty (income below 1.25 times the poverty level)		Near-poor (income between 1 and 1.25 times poverty level)	
	Number (thousands)	Poverty rate	Central city		Outside central city		Number (thousands)	Poverty rate	Number (thousands)	Percent	Number (thousands)	Percent
			Number (thousands)	Poverty rate	Number (thousands)	Poverty rate						
1959	17 019	15.3	10 437	18.3	6 582	12.2	21 747	33.2	54 942	31.1	15 452	8.7
1960	...	...	...	...	...	...	...	...	54 560	30.4	14 709	8.2
1961	...	...	...	...	...	...	...	...	54 280	30.0	14 652	8.1
1962	...	...	...	...	...	...	...	...	53 119	28.8	14 494	7.9
1963	...	...	...	...	...	...	...	...	50 778	27.1	14 342	7.7
1964	...	...	...	...	...	...	...	...	49 819	26.3	13 764	7.3
1965	...	...	...	...	...	...	...	...	46 163	24.1	12 978	6.8
1966	...	...	...	...	...	...	...	...	41 267	21.3	12 757	6.6
1967	13 832	10.9	8 649	15.0	5 183	7.5	13 936	20.2	39 206	20.0	11 437	5.8
1968	12 871	10.0	7 754	13.4	5 117	7.3	12 518	18.0	35 905	18.2	10 516	5.3
1969	13 084	9.5	7 993	12.7	5 091	6.8	11 063	17.9	34 665	17.4	10 518	5.3
1970	13 317	10.2	8 118	14.2	5 199	7.1	12 103	16.9	35 624	17.6	10 204	5.0
1971	14 561	10.4	8 912	14.2	5 649	7.2	10 999	17.2	36 501	17.8	10 942	5.3
1972	14 508	10.3	9 179	14.7	5 329	6.8	9 952	15.3	34 653	16.8	10 193	4.9
1973	13 759	9.7	8 594	14.0	5 165	6.4	9 214	14.0	32 828	15.8	9 855	4.7
1974	13 851	9.7	8 373	13.7	5 477	6.7	9 519	14.2	33 666	16.1	10 296	4.9
1975	15 348	10.8	9 090	15.0	6 259	7.6	10 529	15.4	37 182	17.6	11 305	5.4
1976	15 229	10.7	9 482	15.8	5 747	6.9	9 746	14.0	35 509	16.7	10 534	5.0
1977	14 859	10.4	9 203	15.4	5 657	6.8	9 861	13.9	35 659	16.7	10 939	5.1
1978	15 090	10.4	9 285	15.4	5 805	6.8	9 407	13.5	34 155	15.8	9 658	4.5
1979	16 135	10.7	9 720	15.7	6 415	7.2	9 937	13.8	36 616	16.4	10 544	4.7
1980	18 021	11.9	10 644	17.2	7 377	8.2	11 251	15.4	40 658	18.1	11 386	5.1
1981	19 347	12.6	11 231	18.0	8 116	8.9	12 475	17.0	43 748	19.3	11 926	5.3
1982	21 247	13.7	12 696	19.9	8 551	9.3	13 152	17.8	46 520	20.3	12 122	5.3
1983	21 750	13.8	12 872	19.8	8 878	9.6	13 516	18.3	47 150	20.3	11 847	5.1
1984	...	...	...	...	...	...	...	...	45 288	19.4	11 588	5.0
1985	23 275	12.7	14 177	19.0	9 097	8.4	9 789	18.3	44 166	18.7	11 102	4.7
1986	22 657	12.3	13 295	18.0	9 362	8.4	9 712	18.1	43 486	18.2	11 116	4.7
1987	23 054	12.3	13 697	18.3	9 357	8.3	9 167	17.0	43 032	17.9	10 811	4.5
1988	23 059	12.2	13 615	18.1	9 444	8.3	8 686	16.0	42 551	17.5	10 806	4.4
1989	22 917	12.0	13 592	18.1	9 326	8.0	8 611	15.7	42 653	17.3	11 125	4.5
1990	24 510	12.7	14 254	19.0	10 255	8.7	9 075	16.3	44 837	18.0	11 252	4.5
1991	26 827	13.7	15 314	20.2	11 513	9.6	8 881	16.1	47 527	18.9	11 819	4.7
1992	28 380	14.2	16 346	20.9	12 034	9.9	9 634	16.9	50 592	19.7	12 578	4.9
1993	29 615	14.6	16 805	21.5	12 810	10.3	9 650	17.2	51 801	20.0	12 536	4.8
1994	29 610	14.2	16 098	20.9	13 511	10.3	8 449	16.0	50 401	19.3	12 342	4.7
1995	28 342	13.4	16 269	20.6	12 072	9.1	8 083	15.6	48 761	18.5	12 336	4.7
1996	28 211	13.2	15 645	19.6	12 566	9.4	8 318	15.9	49 310	18.5	12 781	4.8
1997	27 273	12.6	15 018	18.8	12 255	9.0	8 301	15.9	47 853	17.8	12 280	4.6
1998	26 997	12.3	14 921	18.5	12 076	8.7	7 479	14.4	46 036	17.0	11 560	4.3
1999	25 278	11.3	13 404	16.5	11 874	8.3	7 513	14.3	45 030	16.3	12 239	4.4
2000	24 603	10.8	13 257	16.3	11 346	7.8	6 978	13.4	43 612	15.6	12 030	4.3
2001	25 446	11.1	13 394	16.5	12 052	8.2	7 460	14.2	45 320	16.1	12 413	4.4
2002	27 096	11.6	13 784	16.7	13 311	8.9	7 474	14.2	47 084	16.5	12 514	4.4

. . . = Not available.

Table 3-9. Poor Persons 16 Years and Over by Work Experience

(Thousands of persons, percent of total poor persons.)

Year	Total number of poor persons, 16 years and over	Worked						Did not work	
		Number	Percent of total poor	Worked year-round, full-time		Worked less than year-round or full-time		Number	Percent of total poor
				Number	Percent of total poor	Number	Percent of total poor		
1978	16 914	6 599	39.0	1 309	7.7	5 290	31.3	10 315	61.0
1979	16 803	6 601	39.3	1 394	8.3	5 207	31.0	10 202	60.7
1980	18 892	7 674	40.6	1 644	8.7	6 030	31.9	11 218	59.4
1981	20 571	8 524	41.4	1 881	9.1	6 643	32.3	12 047	58.6
1982	22 100	9 013	40.8	1 999	9.0	7 014	31.7	13 087	59.2
1983	22 741	9 329	41.0	2 064	9.1	7 265	31.9	13 412	59.0
1984	21 541	8 999	41.8	2 076	9.6	6 923	32.1	12 542	58.2
1985	21 243	9 008	42.4	1 972	9.3	7 036	33.1	12 235	57.6
1986	20 688	8 743	42.3	2 007	9.7	6 736	32.6	11 945	57.7
1987	20 546	8 258	40.2	1 821	8.9	6 437	31.3	12 288	59.8
1988	20 323	8 363	41.2	1 929	9.5	6 434	31.7	11 960	58.8
1989	19 952	8 376	42.0	1 908	9.6	6 468	32.4	11 576	58.0
1990	21 242	8 716	41.0	2 076	9.8	6 640	31.3	12 526	59.0
1991	22 530	9 208	40.9	2 103	9.3	7 105	31.5	13 322	59.1
1992	23 951	9 739	40.6	2 211	9.2	7 528	31.4	14 212	59.3
1993	24 832	10 144	40.8	2 408	9.7	7 736	31.2	14 688	59.1
1994	24 108	9 829	40.8	2 520	10.5	7 309	30.3	14 279	59.2
1995	23 077	9 484	41.1	2 418	10.5	7 066	30.6	13 593	58.9
1996	23 472	9 586	40.8	2 263	9.6	7 323	31.2	13 886	59.2
1997	22 753	9 444	41.5	2 345	10.3	7 099	31.2	13 309	58.5
1998	22 256	9 133	41.0	2 804	12.6	6 329	28.4	13 123	59.0
1999	21 762	9 251	42.5	2 559	11.8	6 692	30.8	12 511	57.5
2000	21 080	8 511	40.4	2 439	11.6	6 072	28.8	12 569	59.6
2001	22 245	8 530	38.3	2 567	11.5	5 963	26.8	13 715	61.7
2002	23 601	8 954	37.9	2 635	11.2	6 319	26.8	14 647	62.1

Table 3-10. Median Household Income and Poverty Rates for Persons, Based on Alternative Definitions of Income

Year	Definition 1: Money income excluding capital gains (current official measure)				Definition 4: Money income before taxes and transfers, plus health insurance supplements			
	Median income (2001 dollars)	Poverty rate (percent) Official threshold	CPI-U-X1 threshold	Gini coefficient	Median income (2001 dollars)	Poverty rate (percent) Official threshold	CPI-U-X1 threshold	Gini coefficient
1979	37 192	11.7	10.6	0.403	36 659	18.8	17.8	0.460
1980	36 035	13.0	11.5	0.401	34 826	20.1	19.0	0.462
1981	35 478	14.0	12.2	0.404	34 057	21.1	19.8	0.466
1982	35 423	15.0	13.2	0.409	33 649	22.0	20.6	0.475
1983	35 438	15.2	13.7	0.412	34 082	21.8	20.6	0.478
1984	36 343	14.4	12.8	0.413	35 202	20.8	19.5	0.477
1985	37 059	14.0	12.5	0.418	35 853	20.4	19.1	0.486
1986	38 365	13.6	12.2	0.423	37 308	19.9	18.7	0.505
1987	38 835	13.4	12.0	0.424	37 549	19.7	18.7	0.488
1988	39 144	13.0	11.7	0.425	38 065	19.7	18.6	0.489
1989	39 850	12.8	11.4	0.429	38 773	19.4	18.3	0.492
1990	39 324	13.5	12.1	0.426	37 702	19.9	18.8	0.487
1991	38 183	14.2	12.7	0.425	36 493	21.1	20.0	0.490
1992	37 880	14.8	13.4	0.430	36 103	22.1	20.9	0.497
1993	37 688	15.1	13.7	0.448	35 983	22.6	21.4	0.514
1994	38 119	14.5	13.2	0.450	36 830	22.0	20.8	0.515
1995	39 306	13.8	12.3	0.444	37 856	21.1	19.9	0.509
1996	39 869	13.7	12.2	0.447	38 614	20.8	19.5	0.511
1997	40 699	13.3	11.8	0.448	39 567	20.3	19.1	0.513
1998	42 173	12.7	11.3	0.446	40 859	19.3	18.1	0.509
1999	43 355	11.9	10.6	0.445	42 267	18.7	17.4	0.508
2000	43 327	11.3	10.1	0.447	42 348	18.0	16.7	0.506
2001	42 228	11.7	10.4	0.450	41 346	18.5	17.4	0.510
2002	. . .	12.1	. . .	0.448	. . .	19.3	. . .	. . .
2002 Dollars								
2001	42 900	. . .	. . .	. . .	42 004	. . .	. . .	. . .
2002	42 409	. . .	. . .	. . .	41 294	. . .	. . .	. . .

Year	Definition 14: Income after all taxes and transfers				Definition 15: Income after all taxes and transfers, plus net imputed return on equity in own home			
	Median income (2001 dollars)	Poverty rate (percent) Official threshold	CPI-U-X1 threshold	Gini coefficient	Median income (2001 dollars)	Poverty rate (percent) Official threshold	CPI-U-X1 threshold	Gini coefficient
1979	34 099	8.9	7.9	0.359	36 352	7.5	6.7	0.352
1980	32 997	10.1	8.6	0.354	36 379	8.2	7.0	0.347
1981	32 242	11.5	9.8	0.358	37 721	8.7	7.3	0.350
1982	32 555	12.3	10.6	0.366	36 951	9.9	8.5	0.359
1983	33 064	12.7	11.0	0.374	36 763	10.4	9.0	0.368
1984	33 728	12.0	10.4	0.378	37 781	9.9	8.6	0.372
1985	34 363	11.7	10.1	0.385	37 925	9.9	8.6	0.381
1986	35 795	11.3	9.8	0.409	38 517	10.1	8.6	0.404
1987	36 275	11.0	9.5	0.382	39 516	9.7	8.3	0.380
1988	36 371	10.8	9.5	0.385	39 642	9.4	8.2	0.384
1989	37 103	10.4	8.9	0.389	40 091	9.1	7.7	0.387
1990	36 529	10.9	9.5	0.382	38 998	9.8	8.5	0.381
1991	36 031	11.4	9.9	0.380	38 705	10.3	8.9	0.379
1992	36 318	11.9	10.5	0.385	38 517	10.7	9.5	0.381
1993	36 667	12.1	10.7	0.398	38 713	11.2	9.8	0.395
1994	37 279	11.1	9.8	0.400	39 563	10.0	8.8	0.395
1995	38 417	10.3	9.0	0.394	40 670	9.4	8.1	0.388
1996	38 776	10.2	8.9	0.398	40 844	9.3	8.1	0.392
1997	39 440	10.0	8.8	0.403	41 379	9.2	8.0	0.397
1998	40 859	9.5	8.2	0.405	42 632	10.0	7.6	0.399
1999	41 707	8.9	7.6	0.408	43 657	8.2	6.9	0.402
2000	41 709	8.8	7.5	0.410	44 009	8.0	6.8	0.402
2001	41 533	9.0	7.8	0.412	43 237	8.3	7.2	0.407
2002	. . .	9.4	. . .	0.405	. . .	8.6	. . .	0.400
2002 Dollars								
2001	42 194	. . .	. . .	. . .	43 925	. . .	. . .	. . .
2002	42 061	. . .	. . .	. . .	43 760	. . .	. . .	. . .

Note: See Notes and Definitions for explanation of alternative definitions and thresholds, and of the Gini coefficient.
. . . = Not available.

Table 3-11. Median Income and Poverty Rates by State

State	Median household money income (2002 dollars)			Poverty rate (percent)		
	3-year-average median, 2000–2002	2-year average		3-year-average, 2000–2002	2-year average	
		2000–2001	2001–2002		2000–2001	2001–2002
United States	43 052	43 374	42 654	11.7	11.5	11.9
Alabama	36 771	36 355	36 661	14.6	14.6	15.2
Alaska	55 412	56 731	55 525	8.3	8.1	8.7
Arizona	41 554	42 463	41 559	13.3	13.2	14.1
Arkansas	32 423	32 440	33 128	18.0	17.1	18.8
California	48 113	48 451	47 725	12.8	12.6	12.8
Colorado	49 617	50 279	49 238	9.4	9.3	9.2
Connecticut	53 325	53 294	53 791	7.8	7.5	7.8
Delaware	50 878	51 492	50 020	8.1	7.6	7.9
District of Columbia	41 313	42 435	40 447	16.8	16.7	17.6
Florida	38 533	38 788	37 512	12.1	11.8	12.6
Georgia	43 316	43 504	43 096	12.1	12.5	12.1
Hawaii	49 775	51 010	47 748	10.6	10.2	11.4
Idaho	38 613	39 062	38 282	11.8	12.0	11.4
Illinois	45 906	47 504	44 808	11.2	10.4	11.5
Indiana	41 581	41 847	41 034	8.7	8.5	8.8
Iowa	41 827	42 216	41 338	8.3	7.8	8.3
Kansas	42 523	42 475	42 346	9.4	9.1	10.1
Kentucky	37 893	38 459	37 905	13.1	12.6	13.4
Louisiana	33 312	32 965	33 930	17.0	16.7	16.9
Maine	37 654	38 055	37 024	11.3	10.2	11.9
Maryland	55 912	55 665	55 394	7.3	7.3	7.3
Massachusetts	50 587	50 053	51 470	9.6	9.4	9.5
Michigan	45 335	46 645	44 239	10.3	9.6	10.5
Minnesota	54 931	55 085	54 070	6.5	6.5	6.9
Mississippi	32 447	33 229	30 761	17.6	17.1	18.9
Missouri	43 955	44 545	42 386	9.6	9.4	9.8
Montana	33 900	33 432	33 736	13.7	13.7	13.4
Nebraska	43 566	43 951	43 550	9.5	9.0	10.0
Nevada	46 289	46 954	45 542	8.3	8.0	8.0
New Hampshire	53 549	52 664	53 734	5.6	5.5	6.1
New Jersey	53 266	52 615	53 581	7.8	7.7	8.0
New Mexico	35 251	35 148	34 554	17.8	17.7	17.9
New York	42 432	42 666	42 375	14.0	14.0	14.1
North Carolina	38 432	39 391	37 642	13.1	12.5	13.4
North Dakota	36 717	36 976	36 281	11.9	12.1	12.7
Ohio	43 332	43 656	42 567	10.1	10.3	10.1
Oklahoma	35 500	35 021	36 317	14.7	15.0	14.6
Oregon	42 704	43 155	41 866	11.2	11.3	11.3
Pennsylvania	43 577	44 117	43 344	9.2	9.1	9.5
Rhode Island	44 311	45 257	44 434	10.3	9.9	10.3
South Carolina	38 460	38 784	38 074	13.5	13.1	14.7
South Dakota	38 755	39 196	39 087	10.2	9.6	10.0
Tennessee	36 329	35 979	36 691	14.2	13.8	14.5
Texas	40 659	40 914	40 829	15.3	15.2	15.3
Utah	48 537	48 875	47 978	9.3	9.1	10.2
Vermont	41 929	41 395	42 221	9.9	9.9	9.8
Virginia	49 974	50 145	50 336	8.7	8.1	8.9
Washington	44 252	43 786	44 174	10.8	10.8	10.8
West Virginia	30 072	30 429	29 752	16.0	15.6	16.6
Wisconsin	46 351	46 575	45 985	8.6	8.6	8.2
Wyoming	40 499	40 867	40 057	9.5	9.7	8.8

[1]See Notes and Definitions for an explanation of standard errors.

NOTES AND DEFINITIONS

TABLES 3-1 THROUGH 3-11
INCOME DISTRIBUTION AND POVERTY

SOURCE: U.S. DEPARTMENT OF COMMERCE, BUREAU OF THE CENSUS

All data in this chapter are derived from the Current Population Survey (CPS), which is also the source of data on labor force, employment, and unemployment. (See the Notes and Definitions for Tables 10-1 through 10-3.) Early in each year, the 60,000 households in this monthly survey are asked additional questions concerning earnings and other income in the previous year. This survey, informally known as the "March supplement," is now formally known as the Current Population Survey Annual Social and Economic Supplement, but was previously called the Annual Demographic Supplement.

The population represented by the survey is the civilian noninstitutional population of the United States and members of the Armed Forces in the United States living off post or with their families on post, but excluding all other members of the Armed Forces. Because it is a survey of households, homeless persons are not included.

Racial classification and Hispanic origin

In 2002 and all earlier years, the CPS allowed respondents to report identification with only one race group. Beginning in 2003, the CPS is now allowing respondents to choose more than one race. Since the income data for 2002 were collected in early 2003, the income data for the year 2002 incorporate for the first time data in which one individual could be reported in more than one race group. About 2.6 percent of people reported more than one race.

This means that the 2002 data classified by race are not strictly comparable with such data in 2001 and earlier years. As alternative approaches to dealing with this problem, the Census Bureau has, in a number of cases, tabulated two different race concepts for each racial category. In the case of Whites, for example, this means there is one income measure for "White alone," consisting of persons who report White and no other race, and one for "White alone or in combination" which includes all the "White alone" reporters *plus* those who report White in combination with any other race. The tables in this volume show both the "alone" and the "alone or in combination" values, where available.

The racial classifications used in the CPS are *White; Black; Asian, Native Hawaiian and Other Pacific Islander; and American Indians and Alaska Natives*. The Census Bureau does not publish data for the last group because it is too small to provide statistically reliable data.

Hispanic origin is not a racial classification, and Hispanics may be of any race. According to the Census Bureau, "Hispanic origin was reported by 11.4 percent of White householders who reported only one race; 3.5 percent for Black householders who reported only one race; 27.3 percent for American Indian or Alaska Native householders who reported only one race; 1.4 percent for Asian householders who reported only one race; and 19.0 percent for Native Hawaiian and Other Pacific Islander householders who reported only one race. Data users should exercise caution when interpreting aggregate results for the Hispanic population or for race groups because these populations consist of many distinct groups that differ in socio-economic characteristics, culture, and recency of immigration." ("Money Income in the United States: 2002", p. 3.) A subgroup of *White Non-Hispanic* is shown in some tables.

Definitions

Households consist of all persons who occupy a housing unit. A household includes the related family members and all the unrelated persons, if any, such as lodgers, foster children, wards, or employees who share the housing unit. A person living alone in a housing unit or a group of unrelated persons sharing a housing unit as partners is also counted as a household. The count of households excludes group quarters.

A *family* is a group of two or more persons related by birth, marriage, or adoption who reside together.

Unrelated individuals are persons 15 years and over who are not living with any relatives. The poverty status of unrelated individuals is determined independently of income of other persons with whom they may share a household.

Median income is the amount that divides the ranked income distribution into two equal groups, half having incomes above the median, half having incomes below the median. The medians for persons are based on persons 15 years old and over with income.

Where available, historical income figures are shown in constant *2002 dollars*. Some data for 2001 and earlier years are shown in *2001 dollars* as calculated in the previous year's report, because the Census Bureau has not made them available in 2002 dollars. However, overlap data for 2001 are provided, so that the user may if needed construct a continuous series using the ratio of the two measures in the overlap year.

In either case, the constant-dollar figures are Census Bureau estimates, converted from current-dollar values using the *CPI-U-RS*. This index measures changes in prices for past periods using the methodologies of the current CPI, and is similar in concept and behavior to the deflators used in the NIPAs for consumer income and spending. See the Notes and Definitions for Table 8-1 for further explanation of the CPI-U-RS.

Mean income is the amount obtained by dividing the total aggregate income of a group by the number of units in that group. Income means are larger than medians because of the skewed nature of the income distribution; see the section "Whose standard of living?" in the article at the beginning of this book.

Earnings include wages, salaries, armed forces pay, commissions, tips, piece-rate payments, and cash bonuses, before deductions such as taxes, bonds, pensions, and union dues; net income from nonfarm self-employment; and net income from farm self-employment.

Income, in the official definition used in the survey, is money income including earnings as defined above; unemployment compensation; workers' compensation; Social Security; Supplemental Security Income; cash public assistance (welfare payments); veterans' payments; survivor benefits; disability benefits; pension or retirement income; interest income; dividends (but not capital gains); rents, royalties, and payments from estates or trusts; educational assistance, such as scholarships or grants; child support; alimony; financial assistance from outside of the household; and other cash income regularly received, such as foster child payments, military family allotments, and foreign government pensions. Receipts not counted as income include capital gains or losses, withdrawals of bank deposits, money borrowed, tax refunds, gifts, and lump-sum inheritances or insurance payments.

The poverty population is the number of persons with family or individual incomes below a specified level intended to measure the cost of a minimum standard of living. These minimum levels vary by size and composition of family and are known as *poverty thresholds*. The poverty thresholds are based on a definition developed by Mollie Orshansky of the Social Security Administration in 1964 and are adjusted each year for price increase, using the percent change in the Consumer Price Index for all urban consumers (CPI-U). For more information, see Gordon Fisher, "The Development of the Orshansky Thresholds and Their Subsequent History as the Official U.S. Poverty Measure," available on the Census Bureau Internet site at <http://www.census.gov/hhes/poverty/povmeas/papers/orshansky.html>. The *poverty rate* for a demographic group is the number of poor persons or families in that group expressed as a percentage of the total number of persons or families in the group.

Average poverty thresholds. The actual poverty thresholds used to calculate poverty rates vary not only with the size of the family but with the number of children in the family; e.g., the threshold for a three-person family in 2002 was $14,072 if there were no children in the family but $14,494 if the family consisted of one adult and two children. To give a general sense of the "poverty line," the Census Bureau also publishes the *average* threshold for each size family, based on the actual mix of family types in that year. These are the values shown in Table 3-4 to represent the history of poverty thresholds. The average value for three-person families, as shown in Table 3-4, was $14,348, a weighted average of the values actually used for the three different possible family compositions.

A person with *work experience* is one who, during the preceding calendar year, did any work for pay or profit or worked without pay on a family-operated farm or business at any time during the year, on a part-time or full-time basis. A year-round worker is one who worked for 50 weeks or more during the preceding calendar year. A person is classified as having worked full time if he or she worked 35 hours or more per week during a majority of the weeks worked. A year-round, full-time worker is a person who worked 35 or more hours per week and 50 or more weeks during the previous calendar year.

Income distribution

Income distribution is portrayed by dividing the total ranked distribution of families or households into *fifths or quintiles*, and also tabulating separately the top 5 percent (which is also included in the highest fifth). The households or families are arrayed from those with the lowest income to those with the highest income, then divided into five groups each containing one-fifth of the total number of households. Within each quintile, incomes are summed and calculated as a share of total income for all quintiles, and averaged to show the average or mean income within that quintile.

A statistical measure that summarizes the dispersion of income across the entire income distribution is the *Gini coefficient* (also known as Gini ratio or index of income concentration), which can take values ranging from 0 to 1. A Gini value of 1 indicates "perfect" inequality: one household having all the income and the rest having none. A value of 0 indicates "perfect" equality: all households having equal shares of income. There are small differences between the Gini coefficients presented in the report's main tables and those presented in the tables comparing alternative definitions of income. In the latter, the coefficients were recalculated, for comparability with the other income definitions, using a slightly different method.

Alternative definitions of income

The Census Bureau calculates "alternative" income and poverty measures based on a number of different definitions of income, but the same concept of the poverty threshold, as the official measure. These measures in many cases require simulation—use of data from sources other than the CPS to estimate elements of family and individual income as reported in the CPS. *Business Statistics* shows median household income and poverty rates according to three of these alternative definitions, with the official definition also shown for comparison in the same table. (Table 3-10)

Definition 1 is the official Census definition of money income described above.

Definition 4 is Definition 1 income *minus* government cash transfers (Social Security, unemployment compensation, workers' compensation, veteran's payments, railroad retirement, Black Lung payments, government education assistance, Supplemental Security Income, and welfare payments), *plus* realized capital gains and employers' payments for health insurance coverage. Capital gains and health insurance are not collected in the CPS but are simulated using statistical data from the Internal Revenue Service and the National Medical Care Expenditure Survey. Definition 4 is, in effect, the income generated by the workings of the economy before government interventions in the form of taxes and transfer payments.

Definition 14 is income after all government income and earnings tax and transfer interventions. It consists of Definition 4 income *minus* payroll taxes and federal and state income taxes, plus the Earned Income Credit; all of the cash transfers listed above as being subtracted in Definition 4; the "fungible" value of Medicare and Medicaid (see below for definition); the value of regular-price school lunches provided by government; and the value of noncash transfers, including food stamps, rent subsidies, and free and reduced-price school lunches. The tax information is not collected in the CPS but is simulated using statistical data from the Internal Revenue Service, Social Security payroll tax formulas, and a model of each state's income tax regulations.

The "fungible" value approach to medical benefits counts such benefits as income only to the extent that they free up resources that could have been spent on medical care. Therefore, if family income is not sufficient to cover the family's basic food and housing requirements, Medicare and Medicaid are treated as having no income value. Data on average Medicare and Medicaid outlays per enrollee are used in the valuation process.

Food stamp values are reported in the March CPS. Estimates of other government subsidy payments use data from the Department of Agriculture (for school lunches) and the 1985 American Housing Survey.

Definition 15 is Definition 14 income plus the net imputed return on equity in owner-occupied housing—the calculated annual benefit of converting one's home equity into an annuity, net of property taxes. (It also can be thought of as measuring the extent to which equity in the

home relieves the owner of the need for rental or mortgage payments.) Information from the 1987 American Housing Survey is used to assign values of home equity and amounts of property taxes. Because disposable personal income in the NIPAs includes the imputed rent on owner-occupied housing plus most of the cash and in-kind transfers included in Definitions 14 and 15, Definition 15 is the Census income definition closest to the NIPA concept.

For each of these income definitions, poverty rates are also calculated and shown in this table for the years through 2001 using poverty thresholds that have been adjusted for price increase using the CPI-U-X1, instead of the CPI-U, which is used in the official thresholds. (See Notes and Definitions to Table 8-1.) The CPI-U-X1 is used with the intention of removing an upward bias that emerged in the CPI-U and CPI-W in the late 1970s and early 1980s due to a faulty method of measuring housing prices. Any upward bias in the price index used to inflate the poverty thresholds leads to an upward bias in the poverty rate as well *relative to the poverty rates estimated before the bias emerged*. (This is a bias in the behavior of the time series, not necessarily a bias in the level of poverty. As detailed below, there are other factors that can bias poverty thresholds and rates relative to some "real" definition of poverty.) After 1985, the rental equivalence method used in the CPI-U-X1 is also used to calculate the changes in the official CPI-U, and no further differences in *level* appear between the poverty rates using the CPI-U and using the CPI-U-X1.

Experimental poverty measures

While these alternative poverty rates, by using broader definitions of income and/or a less biased price index, seem to remedy *some* of the shortcomings of the official definition, they do not reflect improved data now available to be used to measure need. Experimental poverty measures which redefine both income and need are discussed in "Poverty in the United States: 2002" (see below for complete reference), including data on experimental measures for 2001 and 2002 using six different definitions. Each of these experimental measures yields a *higher* poverty rate than the official definition, due to the redefinition of the need thresholds (whereas the measures that redefine income and/or the price index cited above yield *lower* rates), but they show less change between 2001 and 2002 than the official rate and the changes are not statistically significant. Because of the relatively short time span for which these measures are available and the lack of consensus on a preferred definition, they are not shown in this volume. For more information, see "Poverty in the United States: 2002," pp. 14-17; Kathleen Short, U.S. Census Bureau, Current Population Reports, P60-216, *Experimental Poverty Measures: 1999*; and additional studies on the Web site <www.census.gov/hhes/poverty/povmeas.html>.

Notes on the data

The following are the principal changes that may affect year-to-year comparability of income and poverty data from the CPS.

Beginning in 1952, the estimates are based on 1950 census population controls. Earlier figures were based on the 1940 census.

Beginning in 1962, 1960 census sample design and population controls are fully implemented.

With 1971 and 1972 data, 1970 census sample design and population controls were introduced.

With 1984 data, 1980 census sample design was introduced; 1980 population controls were introduced, and were extended back to 1979 data.

With 1993 data, there was a major redesign of the CPS, including computer-assisted interviewing. The limits used to code income amounts were changed, resulting in reporting of higher income values for the highest income families and, consequently, an exaggerated year-to-year increase in income inequality. In addition, 1990 Census population controls were introduced, and were extended back to the 1992 data.

Data for 2001 implemented population controls based on Census 2000, which were also used to reestimate 2000 and for some data 1999 as well. Data from 2000 forward also incorporate results from a 28,000-household sample expansion.

For more information on these and other changes that could affect comparability, see "Current Population Survey Technical Paper 63RV: Design and Methodology" (March 2002) and footnotes to CPS historical income tables, both available at the Census Web site <http://www.census.gov/hhes/income>.

Data availability

Data are published annually, in September or October, by the Bureau of the Census, in a series with the general title *Current Population Reports: Consumer Income, P60*. Data in this report were derived from P60-221, "Money Income in the United States: 2002," and P60-222, "Poverty in the United States: 2002," issued in September 2003. These reports also contain extensive explanations and references to other relevant sources.

All reports and data are available on the Census Internet site at <http://www.census.gov>.

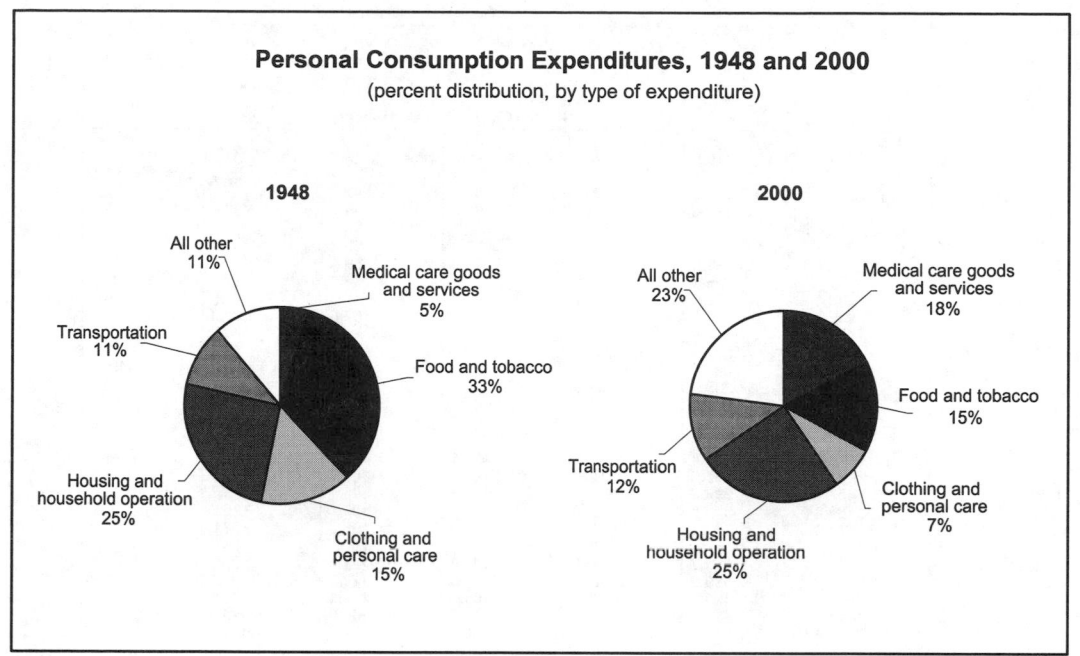

Personal Consumption Expenditures, 1948 and 2000
(percent distribution, by type of expenditure)

- Spending for medical care goods and services in 2000 made up 17.5 percent of personal consumption spending—more than 3-1/2 times the 1948 percentage. This includes medical care payments made by government and private insurance on behalf of individuals as well as consumer payments out of pocket. (Table 4-5)

- Much smaller shares were required for food and tobacco, clothing, and personal care, as can be seen on the graph. Housing held an unchanged share, transportation rose slightly, and the "all other" share doubled. It should be noted that the nonprofit sector is included in this tabulation, and its spending on education, research, religious, and welfare activities is included in the "all other" category. (Table 4-5)

- Labor compensation made up 64.0 percent of total personal income in 2000, down from 65.8 percent in 1948. Its composition was different, too. Wages and salaries accounted for 57.5 percent, down from 64.2 percent, while "other labor income" (the cost of fringe benefits) rose from 1.7 percent to 6.5 percent. Transfer payments accounted for a rising share of personal income; but it should be noted that just as consumption spending includes that financed by government health insurance programs such as Medicare and Medicaid, the transfer payment component of income includes the payments on behalf of persons by these same programs. Personal contributions for social insurance—that is, taxes for Social Security and Medicare withheld from wages—are a negative entry in the personal income calculation and increased as a share of total income. (Table 4-1)

- The shares of proprietors' and rental income declined from 1948 to 2000, while the share of dividends and especially of interest in personal income rose. (Table 4-1)

- Personal saving is defined as aggregate disposable, after-tax, personal income less aggregate personal outlays for consumption, interest, and payments overseas. As a percent of disposable personal income, saving has fluctuated from year to year, and recent personal saving rates of between 2 percent and 4 percent have been markedly lower than those registered earlier in the postwar period. (Table 4-2) It should be noted that personal income by definition does not include capital gains, while the taxes on realized capital gains are deducted to get after-tax income along with all other income taxes. Because of this definitional difference, individuals' understanding of their income and saving situations may differ from what these statistics portray.

Table 4-1. Personal Income by Source

(Billions of dollars, quarterly data are at seasonally adjusted annual rates.)

Year and quarter	Total	Wage and salary disbursements							Other labor income
		Total	Private industries					Government	
			Total	Goods-producing industries		Distributive industries	Service industries		
				Total	Manufacturing				
1946	179.5	112.0	91.3	46.0	36.5	31.0	14.3	20.7	2.5
1947	192.1	123.1	105.6	54.2	42.5	35.2	16.1	17.5	3.0
1948	211.1	135.5	116.5	61.1	47.1	37.5	17.9	19.0	3.5
1949	208.2	134.8	114.0	57.8	44.6	37.7	18.5	20.8	3.9
1950	229.9	147.2	124.6	64.8	50.3	39.9	19.9	22.6	4.8
1951	258.7	171.5	142.3	76.4	59.4	44.4	21.6	29.2	5.9
1952	276.1	185.6	152.3	82.1	64.2	47.0	23.2	33.3	6.5
1953	292.6	199.0	164.7	89.8	71.3	49.9	25.0	34.4	7.2
1954	295.2	197.2	162.4	85.8	67.6	50.3	26.2	34.9	7.4
1955	316.8	212.1	175.6	93.3	73.9	53.6	28.7	36.6	8.5
1956	340.0	229.0	190.2	100.8	79.5	58.0	31.5	38.8	10.0
1957	359.3	239.9	198.9	104.4	82.5	60.7	33.8	41.0	11.3
1958	370.0	241.3	197.2	100.3	78.7	61.1	35.9	44.1	12.0
1959	394.0	259.8	213.8	109.9	86.9	65.1	38.8	46.0	13.4
1960	412.7	272.8	223.7	113.4	89.8	68.6	41.7	49.2	14.4
1961	430.3	280.5	228.0	114.0	89.9	69.6	44.4	52.4	15.2
1962	457.9	299.3	243.0	122.2	96.8	73.3	47.6	56.3	16.7
1963	481.0	314.8	254.8	127.4	100.7	76.8	50.7	60.0	18.0
1964	515.8	337.7	272.9	136.0	107.3	82.0	54.9	64.9	20.3
1965	557.4	363.7	293.8	146.6	115.7	87.9	59.4	69.9	22.7
1966	606.4	400.3	321.9	161.6	128.2	95.1	65.3	78.3	25.5
1967	650.4	428.9	342.5	169.0	134.3	101.6	72.0	86.4	28.2
1968	714.5	471.9	375.3	184.1	146.0	110.8	80.4	96.6	32.5
1969	780.8	518.3	412.7	200.4	157.7	121.7	90.6	105.5	36.6
1970	841.1	551.5	434.3	203.7	158.4	131.2	99.4	117.1	41.9
1971	905.1	583.9	457.4	209.1	160.5	140.4	107.9	126.5	48.0
1972	994.3	638.7	501.2	228.2	175.6	153.3	119.7	137.4	55.3
1973	1 113.4	708.7	560.0	255.9	196.6	170.3	133.9	148.7	62.8
1974	1 225.6	772.6	611.8	276.5	211.8	186.8	148.6	160.9	73.3
1975	1 331.7	814.6	638.6	277.1	211.6	198.1	163.4	176.0	87.6
1976	1 475.4	899.5	710.8	309.7	238.0	219.5	181.6	188.6	105.3
1977	1 637.1	993.9	791.6	346.1	266.7	242.7	202.8	202.3	125.3
1978	1 848.3	1 120.7	901.2	392.6	300.1	274.9	233.7	219.6	143.4
1979	2 081.5	1 255.8	1 018.7	442.3	335.2	308.5	267.8	237.1	162.6
1980	2 323.9	1 377.5	1 116.2	472.3	356.2	336.7	307.2	261.3	185.4
1981	2 599.4	1 517.2	1 231.7	514.5	387.6	368.5	348.6	285.6	204.8
1982	2 768.4	1 593.4	1 286.1	514.6	385.7	385.9	385.6	307.3	222.8
1983	2 946.9	1 684.7	1 359.8	527.7	400.7	405.7	426.4	325.0	238.6
1984	3 274.8	1 854.6	1 507.0	586.1	445.4	445.2	475.6	347.6	262.1
1985	3 515.0	1 995.4	1 621.7	620.2	468.5	476.5	524.9	373.8	282.3
1986	3 712.4	2 114.4	1 717.8	636.8	480.7	501.6	579.3	396.6	298.4
1987	3 962.5	2 270.2	1 848.0	660.1	496.9	535.4	652.4	422.2	319.1
1988	4 272.1	2 452.7	2 001.8	706.7	529.9	575.1	720.1	450.9	336.5
1989	4 599.8	2 596.8	2 117.1	732.2	547.9	606.5	778.5	479.7	360.5
1990	4 903.2	2 754.6	2 237.9	754.4	561.4	633.6	849.9	516.7	390.0
1991	5 085.4	2 824.2	2 278.6	746.3	562.5	646.3	886.0	545.6	415.6
1992	5 390.4	2 982.6	2 414.9	765.7	583.5	680.2	969.0	567.7	449.5
1993	5 610.0	3 085.2	2 500.3	780.6	592.4	697.3	1 022.4	584.9	482.8
1994	5 888.0	3 236.7	2 632.8	824.0	620.3	738.4	1 070.4	603.9	507.5
1995	6 200.9	3 424.7	2 802.0	863.6	647.5	782.1	1 156.3	622.7	497.0
1996	6 547.4	3 626.5	2 985.5	908.2	673.7	822.4	1 254.9	641.0	490.0
1997	6 937.0	3 888.9	3 224.7	975.1	718.4	879.6	1 369.9	664.3	475.4
1998	7 426.0	4 192.8	3 500.1	1 038.5	756.6	948.9	1 512.7	692.7	490.6
1999	7 786.5	4 470.4	3 746.3	1 088.6	782.0	1 020.8	1 636.9	724.2	510.2
2000	8 406.6	4 836.3	4 067.4	1 163.7	829.4	1 094.8	1 808.9	768.9	544.2
2001	8 685.3	4 950.6	4 139.8	1 142.4	789.4	1 109.2	1 888.2	810.8	570.4
2002	8 922.2	4 996.4	4 143.6	1 115.7	758.7	1 114.4	1 913.5	852.8	610.6
2000									
1st quarter	8 211.6	4 757.4	4 001.2	1 166.9	839.0	1 076.8	1 757.4	756.2	530.5
2nd quarter	8 350.2	4 790.8	4 021.5	1 153.1	822.6	1 087.2	1 781.2	769.3	540.0
3rd quarter	8 487.8	4 879.3	4 106.9	1 171.8	835.8	1 105.2	1 829.9	772.4	548.7
4th quarter	8 576.6	4 917.8	4 139.9	1 163.0	820.3	1 109.8	1 867.0	777.9	557.4
2001									
1st quarter	8 658.1	4 960.4	4 165.2	1 156.3	807.2	1 115.0	1 893.9	795.2	564.7
2nd quarter	8 676.2	4 956.8	4 151.0	1 150.0	797.1	1 112.3	1 888.8	805.8	568.2
3rd quarter	8 706.2	4 953.7	4 136.6	1 140.0	783.4	1 110.8	1 885.8	817.1	572.4
4th quarter	8 700.9	4 931.4	4 106.2	1 123.3	769.9	1 098.6	1 884.3	825.2	576.3
2002									
1st quarter	8 803.4	4 957.8	4 117.4	1 116.9	759.4	1 110.1	1 890.4	840.4	590.8
2nd quarter	8 914.0	4 997.3	4 148.9	1 121.3	765.3	1 115.3	1 912.4	848.4	604.1
3rd quarter	8 958.9	5 007.4	4 150.3	1 115.2	757.9	1 117.8	1 917.3	857.1	617.5
4th quarter	9 012.5	5 023.1	4 157.7	1 109.3	752.0	1 114.6	1 933.9	865.4	630.2

Table 4-1. Personal Income by Source—*Continued*

(Billions of dollars, quarterly data are at seasonally adjusted annual rates.)

| Year and quarter | Proprietors' income [1] | | | Rental income of persons [2] | Personal dividend income | Personal interest income | Transfer payments to persons | | | | Less: Personal contributions for social insurance |
	Total	Farm	Nonfarm				Total	Social Security and Medicare	Government unemployment insurance benefits	Veterans and other transfers	
1946	36.5	14.8	21.7	7.0	5.6	6.8	10.5	0.4	1.1	9.0	1.6
1947	35.6	15.1	20.5	7.0	6.3	7.8	10.8	0.5	0.8	9.6	1.6
1948	40.4	17.5	22.9	7.6	7.0	8.3	10.3	0.6	0.9	8.9	1.6
1949	35.7	12.7	23.1	7.8	7.2	9.0	11.3	0.7	1.9	8.8	1.5
1950	38.6	13.5	25.1	8.7	8.8	10.0	13.9	1.0	1.5	11.5	2.1
1951	43.8	16.0	27.8	9.5	8.6	10.8	11.2	1.9	0.9	8.5	2.5
1952	44.3	15.1	29.2	10.5	8.6	11.5	11.8	2.2	1.1	8.5	2.8
1953	43.3	13.0	30.3	11.5	8.9	13.0	12.6	3.0	1.0	8.5	2.9
1954	43.5	12.5	31.0	12.5	9.3	14.3	14.5	3.6	2.2	8.7	3.5
1955	45.5	11.5	34.0	12.8	10.5	15.6	15.7	4.9	1.5	9.2	3.9
1956	47.0	11.3	35.7	13.1	11.3	17.4	16.6	5.7	1.5	9.4	4.3
1957	49.0	11.3	37.7	13.8	11.7	19.4	19.2	7.3	1.9	10.0	5.0
1958	51.4	13.1	38.3	14.5	11.6	21.0	23.3	8.5	4.1	10.7	5.0
1959	51.8	10.9	40.9	15.2	12.6	23.0	24.2	10.2	2.8	11.3	6.0
1960	51.9	11.4	40.4	16.2	13.4	25.6	25.7	11.1	3.0	11.6	7.2
1961	54.4	12.1	42.3	16.9	13.9	27.3	29.5	12.6	4.3	12.6	7.4
1962	56.5	12.1	44.4	17.8	15.0	30.2	30.3	14.3	3.1	13.0	7.9
1963	57.8	11.9	45.8	18.5	16.2	33.0	32.0	15.2	3.0	13.7	9.3
1964	60.6	10.8	49.9	18.6	18.2	36.9	33.2	16.0	2.7	14.4	9.8
1965	65.2	13.1	52.2	19.2	20.2	40.8	35.9	18.1	2.3	15.5	10.3
1966	69.6	14.1	55.5	19.9	20.7	45.3	39.6	20.8	1.9	17.0	14.5
1967	71.1	12.8	58.4	20.4	21.5	49.4	47.6	25.5	2.2	20.0	16.8
1968	75.4	12.8	62.6	20.2	23.5	54.1	55.6	30.2	2.1	23.2	18.7
1969	78.9	14.2	64.7	20.3	24.2	62.3	61.6	32.9	2.2	26.4	21.4
1970	79.8	14.3	65.5	20.3	24.3	71.5	74.3	38.5	4.0	31.9	22.5
1971	86.1	14.9	71.2	21.2	25.0	77.5	88.2	44.5	5.8	38.0	24.7
1972	97.7	18.8	78.9	21.6	26.8	84.2	98.0	49.6	5.7	42.7	28.0
1973	115.2	30.7	84.5	23.1	29.9	97.6	111.9	60.4	4.4	47.1	35.7
1974	115.5	25.2	90.3	23.0	33.2	116.1	132.3	70.1	6.8	55.4	40.5
1975	121.6	23.5	98.1	22.0	32.9	128.0	167.5	81.4	17.6	68.5	42.6
1976	134.3	18.7	115.6	21.5	39.0	140.5	182.3	92.9	15.8	73.7	46.9
1977	148.3	17.5	130.8	20.4	44.7	161.9	194.6	104.9	12.7	77.0	52.0
1978	170.1	21.5	148.5	22.4	50.7	191.3	209.3	116.2	9.7	83.4	59.7
1979	183.7	23.7	160.0	24.5	57.4	233.5	234.2	131.8	9.8	92.6	70.2
1980	177.6	13.1	164.5	31.3	64.0	286.4	279.0	154.2	16.1	108.8	77.2
1981	186.2	20.3	165.9	39.6	73.6	352.7	317.2	182.0	15.9	119.4	92.1
1982	179.9	14.4	165.4	39.6	76.1	401.6	354.2	204.5	25.2	124.5	99.1
1983	195.5	7.2	188.3	36.9	83.5	431.6	382.2	221.7	26.3	134.3	106.1
1984	247.5	21.6	225.9	39.5	90.8	505.3	393.4	235.7	15.9	141.9	118.4
1985	267.0	21.5	245.5	39.1	97.5	546.4	420.9	253.4	15.7	151.8	133.6
1986	278.6	23.0	255.6	32.2	106.1	579.2	449.0	269.2	16.3	163.5	145.6
1987	303.9	29.0	274.8	35.8	112.1	609.7	468.6	282.9	14.5	171.2	156.8
1988	338.8	26.0	312.7	44.1	129.4	650.5	496.9	300.5	13.2	183.3	176.8
1989	361.8	32.2	329.6	40.5	154.8	736.5	540.4	325.2	14.3	200.9	191.6
1990	381.0	31.1	349.9	49.1	165.4	772.4	594.4	352.1	18.0	224.3	203.7
1991	384.2	26.4	357.8	56.4	178.3	771.8	669.9	382.4	26.6	260.9	215.1
1992	434.3	32.7	401.7	63.3	185.3	750.1	751.7	414.0	38.9	298.8	226.6
1993	461.8	30.1	431.7	90.9	203.0	725.5	798.6	444.4	34.1	320.1	237.8
1994	476.6	31.9	444.6	110.3	234.7	742.4	833.9	473.0	23.6	337.2	254.1
1995	497.7	22.2	475.5	117.9	254.0	792.5	885.9	508.0	21.5	356.5	268.8
1996	544.7	34.3	510.5	129.7	297.4	810.6	928.8	537.6	22.1	369.1	280.4
1997	581.2	29.7	551.5	128.3	334.9	864.0	962.2	565.8	19.9	376.5	297.9
1998	623.8	25.6	598.2	138.6	348.3	964.4	983.7	578.1	19.5	386.2	316.3
1999	678.4	27.7	650.7	149.1	328.0	969.2	1 018.5	588.0	20.3	410.2	337.4
2000	714.8	22.6	692.2	146.6	375.7	1 077.0	1 070.3	617.2	20.5	432.5	358.4
2001	727.9	19.0	708.8	137.9	409.2	1 091.3	1 170.4	664.3	31.9	474.3	372.3
2002	756.5	12.9	743.7	142.4	433.8	1 078.5	1 288.0	699.8	62.9	525.4	384.0
2000											
1st quarter	702.5	22.3	680.2	151.4	350.8	1 028.7	1 044.8	602.3	20.1	422.5	354.5
2nd quarter	718.8	25.0	693.8	146.7	369.3	1 074.3	1 065.5	617.7	19.8	428.1	355.3
3rd quarter	718.6	21.7	696.9	144.9	385.7	1 094.6	1 076.6	621.2	20.3	435.1	360.6
4th quarter	719.3	21.2	698.1	143.5	397.2	1 110.3	1 094.2	627.7	22.0	444.5	363.1
2001											
1st quarter	721.2	19.3	701.9	137.0	402.5	1 108.4	1 135.0	652.9	24.2	457.9	371.1
2nd quarter	726.6	18.4	708.2	134.3	406.0	1 097.2	1 159.1	660.2	29.2	469.7	372.2
3rd quarter	732.4	19.3	713.1	140.8	411.0	1 086.4	1 182.5	670.1	33.1	479.3	373.1
4th quarter	731.3	19.2	712.1	139.3	417.3	1 072.9	1 205.0	674.0	41.0	490.1	372.7
2002											
1st quarter	748.4	21.7	726.7	141.3	423.7	1 069.9	1 252.0	690.2	52.3	509.5	380.5
2nd quarter	747.5	7.5	740.0	153.5	430.3	1 082.3	1 282.6	696.3	67.3	519.1	383.6
3rd quarter	758.7	10.7	748.0	144.1	437.3	1 080.7	1 298.4	701.9	67.6	528.9	385.3
4th quarter	771.6	11.7	759.9	130.6	443.8	1 080.9	1 319.1	710.8	64.2	544.1	386.8

[1]Includes inventory valuation and capital consumption adjustments.
[2]Includes capital consumption adjustment.

Table 4-2. Disposition of Personal Income

(Billions of dollars, except as noted; quarterly data are at seasonally adjusted annual rates.)

Year and quarter	Total personal income	Less: Personal tax and nontax payments	Equals: Disposable personal income	Less: Personal outlays — Total	Personal consumption expenditures	Interest paid by persons	Personal transfer payments to the rest of the world (net)	Equals: Personal saving — Billions of dollars	Percent of disposable personal income	Disposable personal income — Total, chained (1996) dollars	Per capita (dollars) — Current dollars	Per capita (dollars) — Chained (1996) dollars	Population (mid-period, thousands)
1946	179.5	17.5	162.0	145.6	144.2	0.7	0.7	16.3	10.1	1 074.4	1 145	7 599	141 400
1947	192.1	20.1	172.1	164.0	162.3	1.1	0.7	8.1	4.7	1 035.2	1 194	7 183	144 100
1948	211.1	19.6	191.6	177.5	175.4	1.4	0.7	14.1	7.3	1 090.0	1 307	7 433	146 600
1949	208.2	17.1	191.1	181.1	178.8	1.8	0.5	10.0	5.2	1 095.6	1 281	7 343	149 200
1950	229.9	19.3	210.6	195.4	192.7	2.3	0.4	15.2	7.2	1 192.7	1 388	7 863	151 700
1951	258.7	27.5	231.2	211.5	208.6	2.5	0.4	19.7	8.5	1 227.0	1 499	7 953	154 300
1952	276.1	32.5	243.6	223.0	219.7	2.9	0.4	20.6	8.5	1 266.8	1 552	8 071	157 000
1953	292.6	33.8	258.8	237.5	233.4	3.6	0.5	21.3	8.2	1 327.5	1 622	8 319	159 600
1954	295.2	30.7	264.5.	244.8	240.5	3.8	0.5	19.8	7.5	1 344.0	1 629	8 276	162 400
1955	316.8	33.4	283.4	263.8	259.0	4.4	0.4	19.5	6.9	1 433.8	1 715	8 675	165 300
1956	340.0	37.2	302.8	277.4	271.9	5.1	0.5	25.4	8.4	1 502.3	1 800	8 930	168 200
1957	359.3	39.6	319.7	292.9	287.0	5.5	0.5	26.8	8.4	1 539.5	1 867	8 988	171 300
1958	370.0	39.2	330.8	302.6	296.6	5.6	0.4	28.2	8.5	1 553.7	1 899	8 922	174 100
1959	394.0	42.8	351.2	324.7	318.1	6.1	0.5	26.5	7.6	1 623.8	1 983	9 167	177 100
1960	412.7	46.6	366.2	339.8	332.3	7.0	0.5	26.4	7.2	1 664.8	2 026	9 210	180 800
1961	430.3	47.9	382.4	350.5	342.7	7.3	0.5	31.9	8.3	1 720.0	2 081	9 361	183 700
1962	457.9	52.3	405.6	372.2	363.8	7.8	0.5	33.5	8.3	1 803.5	2 174	9 666	186 600
1963	481.0	55.3	425.8	392.7	383.1	8.9	0.7	33.1	7.8	1 871.5	2 249	9 886	189 300
1964	515.8	52.8	463.0	422.4	411.7	10.0	0.7	40.5	8.8	2 006.9	2 412	10 456	191 900
1965	557.4	58.4	498.9	456.2	444.3	11.1	0.8	42.7	8.6	2 131.0	2 567	10 965	194 300
1966	606.4	67.3	539.1	494.6	481.8	12.0	0.8	44.5	8.3	2 244.6	2 742	11 417	196 600
1967	650.4	74.2	576.2	522.3	508.7	12.5	1.0	54.0	9.4	2 340.5	2 899	11 776	198 800
1968	714.5	88.3	626.2	573.6	558.7	13.8	1.0	52.7	8.4	2 448.2	3 119	12 196	200 700
1969	780.8	105.9	675.0	622.3	605.5	15.7	1.1	52.6	7.8	2 524.3	3 329	12 451	202 700
1970	841.1	104.6	736.5	667.0	648.9	16.8	1.3	69.5	9.4	2 630.0	3 591	12 823	205 100
1971	905.1	103.4	801.7	721.6	702.4	17.8	1.3	80.1	10.0	2 745.3	3 860	13 218	207 700
1972	994.3	125.6	868.6	791.7	770.7	19.6	1.4	76.9	8.9	2 874.3	4 138	13 692	209 900
1973	1 113.4	134.5	979.0	876.5	852.5	22.4	1.5	102.5	10.5	3 072.3	4 619	14 496	211 900
1974	1 225.6	153.3	1 072.3	957.9	932.4	24.2	1.3	114.3	10.7	3 051.9	5 013	14 268	213 900
1975	1 331.7	150.3	1 181.4	1 056.2	1 030.3	24.5	1.3	125.2	10.6	3 108.5	5 470	14 393	216 000
1976	1 475.4	175.5	1 299.9	1 177.8	1 149.8	26.6	1.3	122.1	9.4	3 243.5	5 960	14 873	218 100
1977	1 637.1	201.2	1 436.0	1 310.4	1 278.4	30.7	1.3	125.6	8.7	3 360.7	6 519	15 256	220 300
1978	1 848.3	233.5	1 614.8	1 469.4	1 430.4	37.5	1.5	145.4	9.0	3 527.5	7 253	15 845	222 600
1979	2 081.5	273.3	1 808.2	1 642.4	1 596.3	44.5	1.6	165.8	9.2	3 628.6	8 033	16 120	225 100
1980	2 323.9	304.2	2 019.8	1 814.1	1 762.9	49.4	1.8	205.6	10.2	3 658.0	8 869	16 063	227 700
1981	2 599.4	351.5	2 247.9	2 004.2	1 944.2	54.6	5.5	243.7	10.8	3 741.1	9 773	16 265	230 000
1982	2 768.4	361.6	2 406.8	2 144.6	2 079.3	58.8	6.5	262.2	10.9	3 791.7	10 364	16 328	232 200
1983	2 946.9	360.9	2 586.0	2 358.2	2 286.4	65.0	6.8	227.8	8.8	3 906.9	11 036	16 673	234 300
1984	3 274.8	387.2	2 887.6	2 581.1	2 498.4	75.0	7.7	306.5	10.6	4 207.6	12 215	17 799	236 400
1985	3 515.0	428.5	3 086.5	2 803.9	2 712.6	83.2	8.1	282.6	9.2	4 347.8	12 941	18 229	238 500
1986	3 712.4	449.9	3 262.5	2 994.7	2 895.2	90.6	9.0	267.8	8.2	4 486.6	13 555	18 641	240 700
1987	3 962.5	503.0	3 459.5	3 206.7	3 105.3	91.5	9.9	252.8	7.3	4 582.5	14 246	18 870	242 800
1988	4 272.1	519.7	3 752.4	3 460.1	3 356.6	92.9	10.6	292.3	7.8	4 784.1	15 312	19 522	245 100
1989	4 599.8	583.5	4 016.3	3 714.4	3 596.7	106.4	11.4	301.8	7.5	4 906.5	16 235	19 833	247 400
1990	4 903.2	609.6	4 293.6	3 959.3	3 831.5	115.8	12.0	334.3	7.8	5 014.2	17 176	20 058	250 000
1991	5 085.4	610.5	4 474.8	4 103.2	3 971.2	118.9	13.0	371.7	8.3	5 033.0	17 669	19 873	253 300
1992	5 390.4	635.8	4 754.6	4 340.9	4 209.7	118.7	12.5	413.7	8.7	5 189.3	18 527	20 220	256 600
1993	5 610.0	674.6	4 935.3	4 584.5	4 454.7	115.4	14.4	350.8	7.1	5 261.3	18 981	20 235	260 000
1994	5 888.0	722.6	5 165.4	4 849.9	4 716.4	117.9	15.6	315.5	6.1	5 397.2	19 626	20 507	263 200
1995	6 200.9	778.3	5 422.6	5 120.2	4 969.0	134.7	16.5	302.4	5.6	5 539.1	20 361	20 798	266 300
1996	6 547.4	869.7	5 677.7	5 405.6	5 237.5	149.9	18.2	272.1	4.8	5 677.7	21 072	21 072	269 400
1997	6 937.0	968.8	5 968.2	5 715.3	5 529.3	164.8	21.2	252.9	4.2	5 854.5	21 887	21 470	272 700
1998	7 426.0	1 070.4	6 355.6	6 054.1	5 856.0	173.7	24.3	301.5	4.7	6 168.6	23 037	22 359	275 900
1999	7 786.5	1 159.1	6 627.4	6 453.3	6 246.5	179.5	27.3	174.0	2.6	6 328.4	23 749	22 678	279 100
2000	8 406.6	1 286.4	7 120.2	6 918.6	6 683.7	205.4	29.5	201.5	2.8	6 630.3	25 237	23 501	282 100
2001	8 685.3	1 292.1	7 393.2	7 223.5	6 987.0	205.4	31.1	169.7	2.3	6 748.0	25 957	23 692	284 800
2002	8 922.2	1 111.9	7 810.3	7 524.5	7 303.7	188.4	32.3	285.8	3.7	7 032.2	27 170	24 463	287 500
2000													
1st quarter	8 211.6	1 256.3	6 955.3	6 775.9	6 552.2	195.6	28.2	179.4	2.6	6 530.4	24 745	23 234	281 100
2nd quarter	8 350.2	1 273.0	7 077.2	6 869.8	6 638.7	202.0	29.0	207.5	2.9	6 607.6	25 118	23 451	281 800
3rd quarter	8 487.8	1 299.6	7 188.2	6 976.7	6 736.1	210.6	30.0	211.5	2.9	6 676.8	25 447	23 637	282 500
4th quarter	8 576.6	1 316.7	7 259.8	7 052.1	6 808.0	213.2	30.9	207.7	2.9	6 706.2	25 635	23 680	283 200
2001													
1st quarter	8 658.1	1 340.6	7 317.5	7 143.9	6 904.7	208.3	30.9	173.7	2.4	6 704.3	25 785	23 624	283 800
2nd quarter	8 676.2	1 336.1	7 340.0	7 198.5	6 959.8	207.7	30.9	141.6	1.9	6 694.8	25 805	23 537	284 400
3rd quarter	8 706.2	1 181.9	7 524.2	7 222.0	6 983.7	206.5	31.8	302.2	4.0	6 864.0	26 387	24 071	285 200
4th quarter	8 700.9	1 309.7	7 391.2	7 329.6	7 099.9	199.1	30.6	61.5	0.8	6 729.1	25 853	23 537	285 900
2002													
1st quarter	8 803.4	1 136.8	7 666.7	7 396.3	7 174.2	190.6	31.5	270.4	3.5	6 961.0	26 759	24 296	286 500
2nd quarter	8 914.0	1 121.8	7 792.2	7 477.9	7 254.7	191.3	31.9	314.3	4.0	7 027.2	27 144	24 479	287 100
3rd quarter	8 958.9	1 099.0	7 859.9	7 583.0	7 360.7	189.3	32.9	276.9	3.5	7 058.1	27 313	24 527	287 800
4th quarter	9 012.5	1 090.1	7 922.5	7 640.7	7 425.4	182.5	32.8	281.8	3.6	7 082.3	27 463	24 551	288 500

Table 4-2. Disposition of Personal Income—*Continued*

(Billions of dollars, except as noted; quarterly data are at seasonally adjusted annual rates.)

Year and quarter	Personal consumption expenditures											
	Current dollars				Chained (1996) dollars				Chain-type price indexes for personal consumption expenditures (1996 = 100)			
	Total	Durable goods	Nondurable goods	Services	Total	Durable goods	Nondurable goods	Services	Total	Durable goods	Nondurable goods	Services
1946	144.2	15.8	82.7	45.8	...	...	...	...	15.1	31.4	18.1	10.6
1947	162.3	20.4	90.9	51.0	...	...	...	...	16.6	34.2	20.5	11.2
1948	175.4	22.9	96.6	55.9	...	...	...	...	17.6	36.0	21.7	11.8
1949	178.8	25.1	94.9	58.9	...	...	...	...	17.4	36.4	21.0	12.2
1950	192.7	30.7	98.2	63.7	...	...	...	...	17.7	36.6	21.1	12.5
1951	208.6	29.9	109.2	69.6	...	...	...	...	18.9	39.0	22.8	13.1
1952	219.7	29.3	114.7	75.6	...	...	...	...	19.2	39.4	23.1	13.6
1953	233.4	32.7	117.8	82.9	...	...	...	...	19.5	39.1	22.9	14.3
1954	240.5	31.9	119.7	88.9	...	...	...	...	19.7	38.2	23.0	14.7
1955	259.0	38.8	124.7	95.4	...	...	...	...	19.8	38.1	22.9	15.0
1956	271.9	38.1	130.8	102.9	...	...	...	...	20.2	39.0	23.2	15.4
1957	287.0	40.0	137.1	109.9	...	...	...	...	20.8	40.5	23.9	15.8
1958	296.6	37.4	141.7	117.4	...	...	...	...	21.3	41.3	24.5	16.3
1959	318.1	42.7	148.5	127.0	...	...	...	...	21.6	42.0	24.6	16.7
1960	332.3	43.3	152.9	136.1	...	...	...	...	22.0	41.8	25.0	17.2
1961	342.7	41.8	156.6	144.3	...	...	...	...	22.2	41.9	25.1	17.5
1962	363.8	46.9	162.8	154.1	...	...	...	...	22.5	42.1	25.3	17.8
1963	383.1	51.6	168.2	163.4	...	...	...	...	22.8	42.2	25.6	18.1
1964	411.7	56.7	178.7	176.4	...	...	...	...	23.1	42.4	25.9	18.4
1965	444.3	63.3	191.6	189.5	...	...	...	...	23.4	42.0	26.4	18.8
1966	481.8	68.3	208.8	204.7	...	...	...	...	24.0	41.8	27.3	19.3
1967	508.7	70.4	217.1	221.2	...	...	...	...	24.6	42.5	27.9	19.9
1968	558.7	80.8	235.7	242.3	...	...	...	...	25.6	43.9	29.0	20.7
1969	605.5	85.9	253.2	266.4	...	...	...	...	26.7	45.1	30.3	21.7
1970	648.9	85.0	272.0	292.0	...	...	...	...	28.0	46.1	31.8	22.9
1971	702.4	96.9	285.5	320.0	...	...	...	...	29.2	47.8	32.8	24.2
1972	770.7	110.4	308.0	352.3	...	...	...	...	30.2	48.3	33.9	25.2
1973	852.5	123.5	343.1	385.9	...	...	...	...	31.9	49.0	36.6	26.4
1974	932.4	122.3	384.5	425.5	...	...	...	...	35.1	52.1	41.8	28.5
1975	1 030.3	133.5	420.7	476.1	...	...	...	...	38.0	56.8	45.1	30.8
1976	1 149.8	158.9	458.3	532.6	...	...	...	...	40.1	60.0	46.8	32.9
1977	1 278.4	181.2	497.2	600.0	...	...	...	...	42.7	62.6	49.6	35.5
1978	1 430.4	201.7	550.2	678.4	...	...	...	...	45.8	66.2	52.9	38.3
1979	1 596.3	214.4	624.4	757.4	...	...	...	...	49.8	70.6	58.5	41.4
1980	1 762.9	214.2	696.1	852.7	...	...	...	...	55.2	76.5	65.3	45.9
1981	1 944.2	231.3	758.9	954.0	...	...	...	...	60.1	81.6	70.4	50.6
1982	2 079.3	240.2	787.6	1 051.5	...	...	...	...	63.5	84.8	72.3	54.8
1983	2 286.1	281.2	831.2	1 174.0	...	...	...	...	66.2	86.4	73.9	58.3
1984	2 498.4	326.9	884.7	1 286.9	...	...	...	...	68.6	87.6	75.6	61.4
1985	2 712.6	363.3	928.8	1 420.6	...	...	...	...	71.0	88.6	77.3	64.4
1986	2 895.2	401.3	958.5	1 535.4	...	...	...	...	72.7	89.7	77.0	67.3
1987	3 105.3	419.7	1 015.3	1 670.3	4 113.4	455.2	1 274.5	2 379.3	75.5	92.2	79.7	70.2
1988	3 356.6	450.2	1 082.9	1 823.5	4 279.5	481.5	1 315.1	2 477.2	78.4	93.5	82.3	73.6
1989	3 596.7	467.8	1 165.4	1 963.5	4 393.7	491.7	1 351.0	2 546.0	81.9	95.1	86.3	77.1
1990	3 831.5	467.6	1 246.1	2 117.8	4 474.5	487.1	1 369.6	2 616.2	85.6	96.0	91.0	81.0
1991	3 971.2	443.0	1 278.8	2 249.4	4 466.6	454.9	1 364.0	2 651.8	88.9	97.4	93.8	84.8
1992	4 209.7	470.8	1 322.9	2 415.9	4 594.5	479.0	1 389.7	2 729.7	91.6	98.3	95.2	88.5
1993	4 454.7	513.4	1 375.2	2 566.1	4 748.9	518.3	1 430.3	2 802.5	93.8	99.1	96.2	91.6
1994	4 716.4	560.8	1 438.0	2 717.6	4 928.1	557.7	1 485.1	2 886.2	95.7	100.6	96.8	94.2
1995	4 969.0	589.7	1 497.3	2 882.0	5 075.6	583.5	1 529.0	2 963.4	97.9	101.1	97.9	97.3
1996	5 237.5	616.5	1 574.1	3 047.0	5 237.5	616.5	1 574.1	3 047.0	100.0	100.0	100.0	100.0
1997	5 529.3	642.5	1 641.6	3 245.2	5 423.9	657.3	1 619.9	3 147.0	101.9	97.8	101.3	103.1
1998	5 856.0	693.2	1 708.5	3 454.3	5 683.7	726.7	1 686.4	3 273.4	103.0	95.4	101.3	105.5
1999	6 246.5	755.9	1 830.1	3 660.5	5 964.5	812.5	1 765.1	3 395.4	104.7	93.0	103.7	107.8
2000	6 683.7	803.9	1 972.9	3 906.9	6 223.9	878.9	1 833.8	3 524.5	107.4	91.5	107.6	110.9
2001	6 987.0	835.9	2 041.3	4 109.9	6 377.2	931.9	1 869.8	3 594.9	109.6	89.7	109.2	114.3
2002	7 303.7	871.9	2 115.0	4 316.8	6 576.0	999.9	1 929.5	3 675.6	111.1	87.2	109.6	117.4
2000												
1st quarter	6 552.2	808.4	1 926.9	3 816.9	6 151.9	879.5	1 809.7	3 477.7	106.5	91.9	106.5	109.8
2nd quarter	6 638.7	799.3	1 964.9	3 874.5	6 198.2	871.3	1 831.6	3 508.2	107.1	91.7	107.3	110.5
3rd quarter	6 736.1	810.6	1 988.9	3 936.6	6 256.8	888.5	1 840.9	3 541.7	107.7	91.2	108.0	111.2
4th quarter	6 808.0	797.2	2 011.1	3 999.7	6 288.8	876.5	1 853.1	3 570.6	108.3	91.0	108.5	112.0
2001												
1st quarter	6 904.7	816.8	2 031.5	4 056.4	6 326.0	900.6	1 863.7	3 576.3	109.2	90.7	109.0	113.4
2nd quarter	6 959.8	820.3	2 044.8	4 094.7	6 348.0	912.4	1 862.3	3 589.3	109.6	89.9	109.8	114.1
3rd quarter	6 983.7	824.0	2 044.3	4 115.4	6 370.9	922.6	1 868.3	3 597.5	109.6	89.3	109.4	114.4
4th quarter	7 099.9	882.6	2 044.4	4 172.9	6 464.0	992.0	1 885.0	3 616.6	109.8	89.0	108.5	115.4
2002												
1st quarter	7 174.2	859.0	2 085.1	4 230.1	6 513.8	975.9	1 921.4	3 642.2	110.1	88.0	108.5	116.2
2nd quarter	7 254.7	856.9	2 108.2	4 289.5	6 542.4	980.7	1 920.9	3 666.2	110.9	87.4	109.8	117.0
3rd quarter	7 360.7	897.8	2 116.9	4 346.0	6 609.9	1 032.4	1 925.8	3 687.0	111.4	86.9	109.9	117.9
4th quarter	7 425.4	873.9	2 150.0	4 401.5	6 637.9	1 010.6	1 950.0	3 707.0	111.9	86.5	110.3	118.7

... = Not available.

Table 4-3. Personal Consumption Expenditures by Major Type of Product

(Billions of dollars, quarterly data are seasonally adjusted annual rates.)

Year and quarter	Total	Durable goods				Nondurable goods					
		Total	Motor vehicles and parts	Furniture and household equipment	Other	Total	Food	Clothing and shoes	Gasoline and oil	Fuel oil and coal	Other
1946	144.2	15.8	4.1	8.4	3.2	82.7	47.4	18.2	3.4	2.5	11.3
1947	162.3	20.4	6.6	10.6	3.3	90.9	52.3	18.8	4.0	3.0	12.8
1948	175.4	22.9	8.0	11.5	3.4	96.6	54.2	20.1	4.8	3.4	14.1
1949	178.8	25.1	10.6	11.3	3.2	94.9	52.5	19.3	5.3	3.1	14.7
1950	192.7	30.7	13.7	13.7	3.3	98.2	53.9	19.6	5.5	3.4	15.8
1951	208.6	29.9	12.2	14.1	3.6	109.2	60.7	21.3	6.1	3.5	17.6
1952	219.7	29.3	11.4	14.0	3.9	114.7	64.1	22.0	6.8	3.5	18.4
1953	233.4	32.7	13.9	14.7	4.1	117.8	65.4	22.2	7.4	3.4	19.4
1954	240.5	31.9	12.8	14.8	4.3	119.7	66.8	22.3	7.8	3.5	19.3
1955	259.0	38.8	17.7	16.4	4.6	124.7	68.6	23.3	8.6	3.8	20.4
1956	271.9	38.1	15.8	17.3	5.0	130.8	71.4	24.4	9.4	3.9	21.7
1957	287.0	40.0	17.6	17.2	5.2	137.1	75.1	24.5	10.2	4.1	23.2
1958	296.6	37.4	15.1	16.9	5.4	141.7	77.9	24.9	10.6	4.2	24.2
1959	318.1	42.7	18.9	18.1	5.7	148.5	80.7	26.4	11.3	4.0	26.1
1960	332.3	43.3	19.7	18.0	5.7	152.9	82.3	27.0	12.0	3.8	27.7
1961	342.7	41.8	17.8	18.3	5.7	156.6	84.0	27.6	12.0	3.8	29.2
1962	363.8	46.9	21.5	19.3	6.1	162.8	86.1	29.0	12.6	3.8	31.4
1963	383.1	51.6	24.4	20.7	6.6	168.2	88.3	29.8	13.0	4.0	33.1
1964	411.7	56.7	26.0	23.2	7.5	178.7	93.6	32.4	13.6	4.1	35.0
1965	444.3	63.3	29.9	25.1	8.2	191.6	100.7	34.1	14.8	4.4	37.6
1966	481.8	68.3	30.3	28.2	9.8	208.8	109.3	37.4	16.0	4.7	41.4
1967	508.7	70.4	30.0	30.0	10.4	217.1	112.5	39.2	17.1	4.8	43.5
1968	558.7	80.8	36.1	32.9	11.8	235.7	122.2	43.2	18.6	4.7	47.0
1969	605.5	85.9	38.4	34.7	12.9	253.2	131.5	46.5	20.5	4.6	50.2
1970	648.9	85.0	35.5	35.7	13.7	272.0	143.8	47.8	21.9	4.4	54.1
1971	702.4	96.9	44.5	37.8	14.6	285.5	149.7	51.7	23.2	4.6	56.4
1972	770.7	110.4	51.1	42.4	16.9	308.0	161.4	56.4	24.4	5.1	60.8
1973	852.5	123.5	56.1	47.9	19.5	343.1	179.6	62.5	28.1	6.3	66.6
1974	932.4	122.3	49.5	51.5	21.3	384.5	201.8	66.0	36.1	7.8	72.7
1975	1 030.3	133.5	54.8	54.5	24.2	420.7	223.2	70.8	39.7	8.4	78.5
1976	1 149.8	158.9	71.3	60.2	27.4	458.3	242.5	76.6	43.0	10.1	86.0
1977	1 278.4	181.2	83.5	67.2	30.5	497.2	262.7	84.1	46.9	11.1	92.4
1978	1 430.4	201.7	93.1	74.3	34.3	550.2	289.6	94.3	50.1	11.5	104.7
1979	1 596.3	214.4	93.5	82.7	38.2	624.4	324.7	101.2	66.2	14.4	118.0
1980	1 762.9	214.2	87.0	86.7	40.5	696.1	356.0	107.3	86.7	15.4	130.6
1981	1 944.2	231.3	95.8	92.1	43.4	758.9	383.5	117.2	97.9	15.8	144.5
1982	2 079.3	240.2	102.9	93.4	43.9	787.6	403.4	120.5	94.1	14.5	155.2
1983	2 286.4	281.2	126.9	106.6	47.7	831.2	423.8	130.9	93.1	13.6	169.8
1984	2 498.4	326.9	152.5	119.0	55.4	884.7	447.4	142.5	94.6	13.9	186.3
1985	2 712.6	363.3	175.7	128.5	59.0	928.8	467.6	152.1	97.2	13.6	198.2
1986	2 895.2	401.3	192.4	143.0	66.0	958.5	492.0	163.1	80.1	11.3	211.9
1987	3 105.3	419.7	193.1	153.4	73.2	1 015.3	515.3	174.4	85.4	11.2	229.1
1988	3 356.6	450.2	206.1	163.6	80.5	1 082.9	553.5	185.5	87.7	11.7	244.5
1989	3 596.7	467.8	211.4	171.4	84.9	1 165.4	591.9	198.9	97.0	11.9	265.7
1990	3 831.5	467.6	206.4	171.4	89.8	1 246.1	636.9	204.1	107.3	12.9	285.0
1991	3 971.2	443.0	182.8	171.5	88.7	1 278.8	657.6	208.7	102.5	12.4	297.8
1992	4 209.7	470.8	200.2	178.7	91.9	1 322.9	669.3	221.9	104.9	12.2	314.7
1993	4 454.7	513.4	222.1	192.4	98.9	1 375.2	697.9	231.1	106.6	12.9	326.8
1994	4 716.4	560.8	242.3	211.2	107.2	1 438.0	728.2	240.7	109.0	13.5	346.6
1995	4 969.0	589.7	249.3	225.0	115.4	1 497.3	755.8	247.8	113.3	14.1	366.4
1996	5 237.5	616.5	256.3	236.9	123.3	1 574.1	786.0	258.6	124.2	15.6	389.8
1997	5 529.3	642.5	264.2	248.9	129.4	1 641.6	812.2	271.7	128.1	15.1	414.5
1998	5 856.0	693.2	288.8	265.2	139.3	1 708.5	852.6	284.8	114.8	13.1	443.3
1999	6 246.5	755.9	319.1	285.5	151.2	1 830.1	898.9	301.0	129.3	13.6	487.4
2000	6 683.7	803.9	336.6	304.8	162.4	1 972.9	955.0	313.7	164.4	18.1	521.8
2001	6 987.0	835.9	361.3	306.1	168.4	2 041.3	992.4	315.3	162.1	16.5	555.0
2002	7 303.7	871.9	376.1	318.7	177.1	2 115.0	1 029.4	324.3	158.5	15.0	587.8
2000											
1st quarter	6 552.2	808.4	344.4	303.0	161.0	1 926.9	937.5	308.7	156.2	16.8	507.7
2nd quarter	6 638.7	799.3	332.4	305.4	161.5	1 964.9	952.7	312.1	164.2	17.3	518.6
3rd quarter	6 736.1	810.6	341.7	306.0	162.9	1 988.9	961.2	315.1	167.6	18.1	526.9
4th quarter	6 808.0	797.2	328.1	304.9	164.3	2 011.1	968.8	318.7	169.5	20.2	533.9
2001											
1st quarter	6 904.7	816.8	345.8	304.3	166.7	2 031.5	984.2	317.9	167.0	19.6	542.8
2nd quarter	6 959.8	820.3	349.0	303.9	167.5	2 044.8	988.7	313.6	175.4	16.2	550.8
3rd quarter	6 983.7	824.0	351.0	304.9	168.1	2 044.3	993.8	312.1	163.6	15.7	559.2
4th quarter	7 099.9	882.6	399.5	311.5	171.5	2 044.4	1 002.8	317.4	142.2	14.5	567.5
2002											
1st quarter	7 174.2	859.0	365.8	317.1	176.1	2 085.1	1 025.0	325.8	142.3	13.9	578.0
2nd quarter	7 254.7	856.9	362.1	319.1	175.8	2 108.2	1 023.9	323.9	160.7	14.0	585.6
3rd quarter	7 360.7	897.8	400.7	319.2	177.9	2 116.9	1 024.8	321.0	163.5	14.7	592.9
4th quarter	7 425.4	873.9	375.9	319.4	178.6	2 150.0	1 043.9	326.6	167.4	17.3	594.8

Table 4-3. Personal Consumption Expenditures by Major Type of Product—*Continued*

(Billions of dollars, quarterly data are seasonally adjusted annual rates.)

Year and quarter	Services								
	Total	Housing	Household operation			Transportation	Medical care	Recreation	Other
			Total	Electricity and gas	Other household operation				
1946	45.8	14.2	6.8	2.1	4.7	5.0	4.7	3.7	11.4
1947	51.0	16.0	7.5	2.3	5.1	5.3	5.7	3.8	12.7
1948	55.9	17.9	8.1	2.6	5.5	5.8	6.6	3.8	13.8
1949	58.9	19.6	8.6	2.9	5.6	5.9	6.7	3.8	14.2
1950	63.7	21.7	9.5	3.3	6.2	6.2	7.2	3.9	15.2
1951	69.6	24.3	10.4	3.7	6.7	6.8	7.7	4.0	16.3
1952	75.6	27.0	11.2	4.1	7.1	7.3	8.6	4.3	17.3
1953	82.9	29.9	12.1	4.5	7.6	8.0	9.6	4.5	18.8
1954	88.9	32.3	12.7	5.0	7.7	8.2	10.6	4.8	20.3
1955	95.4	34.4	14.2	5.5	8.6	8.5	11.3	5.2	22.0
1956	102.9	36.7	15.4	6.1	9.3	8.9	12.2	5.6	24.1
1957	109.9	39.3	16.4	6.5	9.9	9.4	13.4	5.6	25.8
1958	117.4	42.0	17.5	7.1	10.4	9.7	14.8	5.8	27.6
1959	127.0	45.0	18.7	7.6	11.1	10.5	16.4	6.4	29.9
1960	136.1	48.2	20.3	8.3	12.0	11.2	17.6	6.9	32.0
1961	144.3	51.2	21.2	8.8	12.4	11.7	18.7	7.5	34.0
1962	154.1	54.7	22.4	9.4	13.0	12.2	20.8	8.0	35.9
1963	163.4	58.0	23.6	9.9	13.8	12.7	22.6	8.5	37.9
1964	176.4	61.4	25.0	10.4	14.6	13.4	25.8	9.1	41.6
1965	189.5	65.4	26.5	10.9	15.7	14.5	27.9	9.6	45.5
1966	204.7	69.5	28.2	11.5	16.7	15.9	30.7	10.4	50.0
1967	221.2	74.1	30.2	12.2	18.0	17.3	33.9	11.1	54.7
1968	242.3	79.7	32.4	13.0	19.4	18.9	39.2	12.5	59.6
1969	266.4	86.8	35.2	14.1	21.1	20.9	44.8	13.8	64.9
1970	292.0	94.0	37.9	15.3	22.6	23.7	50.4	15.1	70.9
1971	320.0	102.7	41.3	16.9	24.4	27.1	56.9	16.3	75.7
1972	352.3	112.1	45.7	18.8	26.9	29.8	63.9	17.6	83.3
1973	385.9	122.7	50.2	20.4	29.8	31.2	71.5	19.7	90.5
1974	425.5	134.1	56.0	24.0	32.0	33.3	80.4	22.5	99.1
1975	476.1	147.0	64.3	29.2	35.2	35.7	93.4	25.4	110.3
1976	532.6	161.5	73.1	33.2	40.0	41.3	106.5	28.4	121.7
1977	600.0	179.5	82.7	38.5	44.3	49.2	122.6	31.4	134.6
1978	678.4	201.7	92.1	43.0	49.1	53.5	140.0	34.5	156.7
1979	757.4	226.5	101.0	47.8	53.2	59.1	158.1	38.3	174.5
1980	852.7	255.1	114.2	57.5	56.7	64.7	181.2	42.8	194.6
1981	954.0	287.7	127.3	64.8	62.5	68.7	213.0	49.3	208.0
1982	1 051.5	313.0	143.0	74.2	68.8	70.9	239.3	54.9	230.4
1983	1 174.0	338.7	157.6	82.4	75.2	79.4	267.9	61.7	268.9
1984	1 286.9	370.3	169.8	86.5	83.3	90.0	294.6	67.9	294.4
1985	1 420.6	406.8	182.2	90.8	91.4	100.0	322.5	75.6	333.6
1986	1 535.4	442.0	188.9	89.2	99.7	107.3	346.8	81.5	368.9
1987	1 670.3	476.4	196.9	90.9	106.0	118.2	381.8	87.7	409.3
1988	1 823.5	511.9	208.4	96.3	112.2	129.9	429.9	99.0	444.4
1989	1 963.5	546.4	221.3	101.0	120.2	136.6	479.2	110.1	469.9
1990	2 117.8	585.6	227.6	101.0	126.5	141.8	540.6	120.8	501.5
1991	2 249.4	616.0	238.6	107.4	131.2	142.8	591.0	126.4	534.5
1992	2 415.9	641.3	248.3	108.9	139.4	155.0	652.6	139.1	579.5
1993	2 566.1	666.5	268.9	118.6	150.4	166.2	700.6	151.2	612.6
1994	2 717.6	704.7	284.0	119.8	164.2	180.9	737.3	160.0	650.7
1995	2 882.0	740.8	298.1	122.5	175.6	197.7	780.7	176.0	688.7
1996	3 047.0	772.5	317.3	128.7	188.5	214.2	814.4	191.1	737.5
1997	3 245.2	810.5	333.0	130.4	202.7	234.4	854.6	206.2	806.5
1998	3 454.3	859.7	345.6	128.9	216.7	246.3	899.0	221.0	882.6
1999	3 660.5	912.6	360.4	129.9	230.4	259.4	937.2	237.6	953.4
2000	3 906.9	960.0	386.2	142.4	243.9	267.8	991.8	255.5	1 045.5
2001	4 109.9	1 014.5	406.3	154.5	251.8	271.4	1 072.2	271.9	1 073.6
2002	4 316.8	1 071.5	405.2	148.2	257.0	275.8	1 148.5	285.1	1 130.7
2000									
1st quarter	3 816.9	941.2	366.6	127.1	239.5	264.8	965.9	249.3	1 029.1
2nd quarter	3 874.5	953.5	382.6	139.1	243.4	267.1	982.3	253.5	1 035.6
3rd quarter	3 936.6	965.9	390.3	144.5	245.8	268.4	1 000.1	257.7	1 054.3
4th quarter	3 999.7	979.3	405.5	158.7	246.8	271.0	1 019.1	261.8	1 063.1
2001									
1st quarter	4 056.4	993.4	416.8	167.2	249.6	273.3	1 042.6	268.1	1 062.2
2nd quarter	4 094.7	1 007.9	406.7	155.8	250.9	273.2	1 064.2	271.2	1 071.4
3rd quarter	4 115.4	1 021.1	404.8	151.8	253.0	270.1	1 079.0	271.7	1 068.8
4th quarter	4 172.9	1 035.5	396.9	143.1	253.8	269.0	1 103.1	276.6	1 091.8
2002									
1st quarter	4 230.1	1 051.7	399.2	143.9	255.4	273.3	1 119.0	279.0	1 107.8
2nd quarter	4 289.5	1 066.0	400.9	144.9	256.1	275.6	1 139.3	283.8	1 123.8
3rd quarter	4 346.0	1 078.0	406.3	147.4	258.9	276.1	1 158.8	285.9	1 140.9
4th quarter	4 401.5	1 090.1	414.2	156.5	257.7	278.3	1 176.9	291.8	1 150.2

Table 4-4. Chain-Type Quantity Indexes for Personal Consumption Expenditures by Major Type of Product

(Index numbers, 1996 = 100.)

Year and quarter	Total	Durable goods				Nondurable goods					
		Total	Motor vehicles and parts	Furniture and household equipment	Other	Total	Food	Clothing and shoes	Gasoline and oil	Fuel oil and coal	Other
1946	18.3	8.1	8.1	6.5	9.8	29.0	38.1	18.2	18.7	183.1	17.7
1947	18.6	9.7	11.5	7.5	9.3	28.2	36.7	17.3	19.9	192.9	17.6
1948	19.1	10.3	13.0	7.8	9.4	28.3	36.2	17.5	21.2	193.8	18.3
1949	19.6	11.2	16.7	7.7	8.9	28.7	36.5	17.6	23.1	171.0	19.6
1950	20.8	13.6	21.5	9.2	9.4	29.6	37.1	18.0	23.9	183.7	21.0
1951	21.1	12.4	18.2	8.8	9.6	30.4	38.2	17.9	26.0	183.3	21.9
1952	21.8	12.1	16.4	8.9	10.2	31.6	39.4	18.9	28.2	178.2	22.9
1953	22.9	13.6	20.3	9.4	10.7	32.6	40.9	19.1	29.7	172.2	23.8
1954	23.3	13.5	19.4	9.6	11.2	33.0	41.7	19.2	30.6	175.5	23.7
1955	25.0	16.5	26.5	10.8	12.3	34.6	43.5	20.1	33.3	186.5	24.9
1956	25.8	15.9	22.6	11.3	13.3	35.8	44.9	20.7	35.3	186.9	26.0
1957	26.4	16.0	23.7	10.9	13.5	36.5	45.8	20.5	36.7	185.3	26.9
1958	26.6	14.7	19.6	10.8	13.8	36.8	45.8	20.7	38.4	192.4	27.4
1959	28.1	16.5	23.3	11.6	14.5	38.4	47.4	21.8	40.4	183.8	29.1
1960	28.9	16.8	24.8	11.5	14.4	38.9	47.7	22.0	41.8	176.0	30.4
1961	29.4	16.2	22.3	11.7	14.3	39.6	48.3	22.4	42.2	167.6	32.0
1962	30.9	18.1	26.5	12.4	15.3	40.9	48.9	23.4	44.0	167.2	34.3
1963	32.2	19.8	29.8	13.3	16.2	41.8	49.4	23.8	45.4	175.4	35.8
1964	34.1	21.7	31.6	15.0	18.1	43.8	51.4	25.7	47.8	182.3	37.5
1965	36.2	24.4	36.6	16.5	20.0	46.1	54.3	26.7	50.1	190.9	39.7
1966	38.3	26.5	37.3	18.6	23.9	48.7	56.5	28.5	53.2	196.4	42.9
1967	39.5	26.9	36.4	19.4	24.9	49.4	57.2	28.7	55.0	196.5	44.1
1968	41.7	29.9	42.4	20.7	27.2	51.7	60.0	29.9	58.8	186.0	46.0
1969	43.2	30.9	44.1	21.2	28.4	53.1	61.6	30.4	62.7	176.3	47.3
1970	44.3	29.9	39.7	21.4	29.8	54.3	63.5	30.1	66.6	164.0	48.8
1971	45.9	32.9	47.4	22.3	30.3	55.3	64.1	31.5	69.9	158.4	49.1
1972	48.7	37.1	54.2	24.7	34.2	57.7	66.1	33.6	72.7	174.2	51.7
1973	51.1	40.9	59.1	27.4	38.4	59.6	66.3	36.0	76.5	189.1	55.2
1974	50.7	38.1	49.0	27.7	39.5	58.4	65.3	35.5	72.7	149.2	55.0
1975	51.8	38.1	49.3	27.1	41.1	59.3	66.9	36.7	74.9	146.5	53.2
1976	54.8	43.0	59.7	28.8	44.3	62.2	70.4	38.4	77.9	164.5	55.2
1977	57.1	47.0	66.0	31.3	47.5	63.7	71.7	40.5	80.3	159.2	56.0
1978	59.7	49.4	68.9	33.2	50.6	66.1	72.4	44.5	82.1	158.0	60.1
1979	61.2	49.3	64.3	35.0	52.6	67.8	73.9	46.9	81.0	146.8	63.6
1980	61.0	45.4	55.7	34.4	48.7	67.7	74.5	48.0	76.4	113.5	64.6
1981	61.8	46.0	57.0	34.5	49.3	68.5	74.6	50.9	77.5	95.2	66.0
1982	62.5	46.0	58.6	33.7	48.6	69.2	75.8	51.7	78.5	88.4	65.6
1983	66.0	52.8	70.2	38.3	51.4	71.5	78.0	55.5	80.3	88.5	67.1
1984	69.5	60.5	82.2	42.9	58.7	74.3	79.6	60.2	82.8	88.1	71.1
1985	73.0	66.5	92.4	46.7	61.6	76.3	81.6	63.0	84.4	89.2	72.8
1986	76.0	72.6	98.3	52.5	67.8	79.1	83.4	68.1	88.5	92.5	74.9
1987	78.5	73.8	94.6	56.3	72.1	81.0	84.6	70.5	90.9	91.3	77.8
1988	81.7	78.1	99.4	60.1	76.1	83.6	87.9	72.6	92.6	94.7	79.5
1989	83.9	79.8	99.0	63.3	77.6	85.8	89.5	76.8	93.7	92.4	82.1
1990	85.4	79.0	96.0	63.7	78.5	87.0	91.9	76.3	91.1	83.9	83.8
1991	85.3	73.8	82.6	64.5	75.1	86.7	91.8	76.5	88.1	83.1	83.4
1992	87.7	77.7	88.1	68.2	76.3	88.3	92.3	80.8	90.6	85.0	85.0
1993	90.7	84.1	94.5	74.9	81.7	90.9	94.8	84.5	93.0	90.0	86.9
1994	94.1	90.5	99.5	82.9	87.3	94.4	97.3	89.6	94.6	96.3	91.5
1995	96.9	94.7	98.9	90.9	93.3	97.1	98.9	94.5	96.8	101.0	95.4
1996	100.0	100.0	100.0	100.0	100.0	100.0	100.0	100.0	100.0	100.0	100.0
1997	103.6	106.6	103.3	110.6	106.1	102.9	101.1	105.1	103.2	96.2	105.4
1998	108.5	117.9	113.9	123.8	115.0	107.1	104.3	112.3	106.2	92.0	110.5
1999	113.9	131.8	125.7	141.5	127.0	112.1	107.8	120.7	109.9	94.1	116.9
2000	118.8	142.6	132.0	157.9	137.5	116.5	111.8	127.4	109.3	90.1	122.4
2001	121.8	151.2	141.2	168.0	142.2	118.8	112.9	130.6	111.8	81.2	127.1
2002	125.6	162.2	149.2	185.0	150.7	122.6	114.8	138.1	116.8	81.8	132.3
2000											
1st quarter	117.5	142.7	135.5	154.5	136.1	115.0	110.8	124.6	108.2	85.7	120.5
2nd quarter	118.3	141.3	130.2	157.2	136.7	116.4	112.0	126.8	109.5	91.3	121.6
3rd quarter	119.5	144.1	134.1	159.2	138.4	117.0	112.1	128.5	109.6	90.2	122.9
4th quarter	120.1	142.2	128.4	160.7	138.9	117.7	112.5	129.6	109.8	93.0	124.4
2001											
1st quarter	120.8	146.1	134.7	163.0	140.4	118.4	113.1	129.3	110.8	89.1	125.7
2nd quarter	121.2	148.0	136.3	165.8	141.3	118.3	112.9	129.4	109.7	78.8	126.6
3rd quarter	121.6	149.7	137.6	168.7	142.0	118.7	112.5	130.4	112.7	78.5	127.4
4th quarter	123.4	160.9	156.2	174.6	145.1	119.8	112.9	133.3	113.9	78.4	128.8
2002											
1st quarter	124.4	158.3	144.4	180.8	149.4	122.1	114.7	137.6	116.9	79.8	130.9
2nd quarter	124.9	159.1	144.0	183.7	149.3	122.0	114.4	137.3	116.5	77.8	131.6
3rd quarter	126.2	167.5	159.0	186.3	151.7	122.4	114.2	137.4	117.1	79.9	132.9
4th quarter	126.7	163.9	149.4	188.9	152.5	123.9	115.9	139.9	116.9	89.9	133.9

Table 4-4. Chain-Type Quantity Indexes for Personal Consumption Expenditures by Major Type of Product—*Continued*

(Index numbers, 1996 = 100.)

Year and quarter	Services					Transportation	Medical care	Recreation	Other
	Total	Housing	Household operation						
			Total	Electricity and gas	Other household operation				
1946	14.2	13.3	13.5	9.8	15.2	24.2	8.6	13.8	18.1
1947	14.9	14.5	14.4	11.1	15.9	24.0	9.6	13.1	18.5
1948	15.5	15.3	15.1	12.2	16.3	24.0	10.5	12.8	18.9
1949	15.9	16.2	15.7	13.3	16.6	23.0	10.9	12.5	19.0
1950	16.7	17.4	17.1	15.1	17.6	22.8	11.6	12.5	19.6
1951	17.5	18.7	18.2	16.9	18.2	23.9	12.2	12.6	19.8
1952	18.3	19.9	18.7	18.4	18.2	24.1	12.8	12.9	20.5
1953	19.1	21.0	19.6	19.8	18.7	24.9	13.5	13.0	21.2
1954	19.9	22.0	20.4	21.7	18.8	24.6	14.3	13.3	22.2
1955	20.9	23.1	22.4	23.4	20.9	25.4	14.9	13.9	23.1
1956	22.0	24.3	23.9	25.5	22.1	26.7	15.8	14.5	23.9
1957	22.8	25.5	24.9	27.1	22.6	27.2	16.7	14.1	24.6
1958	23.7	26.7	25.7	28.6	23.1	26.6	17.8	14.1	25.7
1959	24.9	28.2	26.8	30.3	23.8	27.7	19.1	15.0	27.0
1960	26.0	29.6	28.1	31.9	24.8	28.6	19.7	15.8	28.0
1961	27.0	31.0	29.1	33.6	25.4	28.9	20.4	16.6	29.2
1962	28.4	32.8	30.5	35.9	26.3	30.0	22.1	17.5	29.9
1963	29.7	34.3	31.8	37.6	27.3	31.2	23.4	18.2	31.1
1964	31.5	35.9	33.4	39.6	28.6	32.9	26.0	18.9	33.2
1965	33.2	37.9	35.1	41.5	30.1	34.3	27.2	19.4	35.4
1966	34.8	39.6	36.9	43.8	31.6	36.5	28.5	20.3	37.4
1967	36.5	41.3	38.8	46.3	33.1	38.8	29.5	20.9	39.7
1968	38.4	43.3	40.4	49.0	34.1	41.1	31.8	22.2	41.3
1969	40.2	45.7	42.5	51.9	35.7	43.5	34.2	23.4	41.9
1970	41.9	47.4	44.0	54.4	36.7	44.8	36.1	24.4	43.4
1971	43.5	49.5	44.8	56.1	37.0	46.4	38.7	25.3	44.3
1972	45.9	52.1	47.1	59.3	38.8	49.3	41.3	26.6	46.4
1973	48.0	54.7	49.5	61.0	41.4	50.5	44.3	28.8	47.5
1974	49.1	57.5	50.0	61.8	41.7	50.8	46.1	30.8	46.1
1975	50.7	59.2	52.5	65.2	43.5	51.7	48.5	32.5	46.9
1976	53.1	60.9	54.8	67.6	45.7	53.9	50.8	34.8	50.1
1977	55.5	62.4	57.8	70.9	48.5	57.6	53.3	36.9	52.5
1978	58.1	65.5	60.8	74.0	51.4	59.4	55.5	38.5	55.4
1979	60.0	68.1	62.5	74.5	53.8	61.3	57.8	40.1	56.3
1980	61.0	70.1	63.9	76.6	54.8	58.2	59.9	41.7	56.1
1981	61.9	71.7	63.4	75.3	54.7	56.4	62.9	45.1	55.4
1982	63.0	71.9	63.8	76.3	54.8	55.6	63.7	47.8	58.0
1983	66.1	73.4	65.9	78.5	56.7	59.3	66.2	51.6	63.5
1984	68.8	76.2	67.5	79.0	59.2	65.1	68.2	54.4	66.7
1985	72.4	79.0	70.2	81.1	62.4	71.2	70.8	58.2	71.8
1986	74.9	81.0	71.7	80.2	65.7	74.0	73.7	60.5	74.7
1987	78.1	83.5	75.0	83.1	69.4	76.9	77.5	62.9	78.5
1988	81.3	85.9	78.2	87.3	72.0	80.7	81.0	68.4	81.4
1989	83.6	88.0	81.1	89.1	75.5	81.5	83.3	72.8	83.4
1990	85.9	90.1	81.9	87.6	77.9	81.0	87.3	75.9	85.5
1991	87.0	91.9	82.9	90.4	77.7	76.9	90.2	75.6	86.3
1992	89.6	93.1	84.3	88.9	80.5	79.9	94.0	80.9	88.6
1993	92.0	94.3	89.0	94.9	84.9	82.5	95.2	85.3	91.9
1994	94.7	97.0	92.3	95.4	90.3	88.3	96.2	88.6	95.3
1995	97.3	98.9	95.8	97.3	94.8	93.9	98.0	95.1	97.0
1996	100.0	100.0	100.0	100.0	100.0	100.0	100.0	100.0	100.0
1997	103.3	101.9	103.2	99.1	106.0	105.7	102.6	104.7	104.5
1998	107.4	104.7	108.3	101.7	112.8	109.6	105.3	109.4	111.1
1999	111.4	108.1	113.1	102.8	120.0	115.0	107.5	114.3	116.7
2000	115.7	110.2	119.1	106.5	127.6	118.1	110.5	118.6	124.1
2001	118.0	112.1	120.6	104.5	131.7	117.2	115.2	122.1	125.1
2002	120.6	113.9	121.3	106.0	131.8	116.9	120.2	124.3	127.8
2000									
1st quarter	114.1	109.3	114.3	99.3	124.5	117.5	109.1	117.1	122.7
2nd quarter	115.1	110.0	118.9	106.6	127.3	118.1	110.0	118.3	122.8
3rd quarter	116.2	110.5	120.0	106.8	129.0	118.2	110.9	118.9	125.2
4th quarter	117.2	111.0	123.1	113.2	129.6	118.7	112.0	120.0	125.6
2001									
1st quarter	117.4	111.6	122.7	110.7	130.7	118.3	113.1	121.9	124.4
2nd quarter	117.8	112.0	120.3	103.3	132.0	117.9	114.5	122.0	125.2
3rd quarter	118.1	112.2	120.4	102.8	132.5	116.7	116.0	121.5	124.9
4th quarter	118.7	112.6	119.0	101.1	131.5	116.1	117.3	122.9	126.0
2002									
1st quarter	119.5	113.1	120.2	103.7	131.6	117.2	118.3	123.3	126.8
2nd quarter	120.3	113.7	120.7	103.8	132.3	116.9	119.7	124.1	127.6
3rd quarter	121.0	114.2	121.2	105.4	132.1	116.6	120.9	124.1	128.4
4th quarter	121.7	114.7	122.9	110.9	131.0	116.8	121.8	125.8	128.5

Table 4-5. Personal Consumption Expenditures by Type of Expenditure

(Billions of dollars.)

Year and quarter	Personal consumption expenditures	Food and tobacco	Clothing, accessories, and jewelry	Personal care	Housing	House-hold operation	Medical care	Personal business	Transportation	Recreation	Education and research	Religious and welfare activities	Foreign travel and other, net
1939	67.2	20.9	8.4	1.0	9.4	9.6	3.0	3.1	6.5	3.5	0.7	1.0	0.2
1940	71.2	22.0	8.9	1.0	9.7	10.4	3.2	3.2	7.2	3.8	0.8	1.0	0.1
1941	81.0	25.4	10.5	1.2	10.4	11.8	3.5	3.3	8.6	4.3	0.8	1.1	0.1
1942	88.9	30.7	13.1	1.4	11.2	12.7	3.9	3.4	5.5	4.7	0.9	1.2	0.2
1943	99.7	35.8	16.0	1.6	11.8	13.1	4.4	3.7	5.5	5.0	1.1	1.5	0.3
1944	108.5	39.3	17.5	1.8	12.3	14.0	4.9	3.9	5.8	5.4	1.1	1.7	0.6
1945	119.8	43.5	19.6	2.0	12.8	15.5	5.2	4.2	6.8	6.2	1.1	1.8	1.2
1946	144.2	50.7	22.0	2.1	14.2	19.9	6.4	4.8	12.5	8.6	1.2	2.0	-0.1
1947	162.3	56.1	22.8	2.2	16.0	23.7	7.4	5.3	15.9	9.3	1.5	2.1	0.0
1948	175.4	58.2	24.2	2.3	17.9	26.1	8.5	5.8	18.5	9.7	1.7	2.3	0.3
1949	178.8	56.6	23.3	2.3	19.6	25.6	8.8	6.0	21.8	10.0	1.8	2.3	0.6
1950	192.7	58.1	23.7	2.4	21.7	29.1	9.4	6.6	25.4	11.2	1.9	2.4	0.7
1951	208.6	65.2	25.6	2.7	24.3	31.1	10.2	7.2	25.1	11.7	2.1	2.6	0.9
1952	219.7	69.0	26.6	2.9	27.0	31.5	11.2	7.5	25.4	12.3	2.2	3.0	1.1
1953	233.4	70.5	27.0	3.1	29.9	33.0	12.4	8.4	29.3	13.1	2.3	3.1	1.5
1954	240.5	71.7	27.2	3.4	32.3	33.7	13.4	9.1	28.9	13.6	2.5	3.3	1.5
1955	259.0	73.6	28.4	3.7	34.4	37.3	14.2	10.1	34.8	14.6	2.7	3.5	1.6
1956	271.9	76.7	29.7	4.1	36.7	39.8	15.5	11.0	34.1	15.5	3.0	3.9	1.7
1957	287.0	80.7	30.0	4.6	39.3	41.2	17.1	11.8	37.1	15.9	3.4	4.1	1.7
1958	296.6	83.9	30.3	4.9	42.0	42.3	18.7	12.7	35.4	16.3	3.7	4.4	1.9
1959	318.1	87.2	32.0	5.2	45.0	45.0	20.6	13.6	40.7	17.7	4.0	5.0	2.0
1960	332.3	89.2	32.7	5.6	48.2	46.7	22.1	14.6	42.9	18.5	4.4	5.3	2.1
1961	342.7	91.1	33.5	6.1	51.2	48.2	23.6	15.8	41.5	19.3	4.7	5.6	2.0
1962	363.8	93.3	35.0	6.7	54.7	51.0	26.2	16.4	46.3	20.8	5.1	5.8	2.3
1963	383.1	95.8	36.0	7.0	58.0	54.0	28.2	17.2	50.0	22.5	5.6	6.2	2.5
1964	411.7	101.1	39.1	7.5	61.4	58.4	31.7	19.0	53.0	24.6	6.2	7.2	2.6
1965	444.3	108.8	41.4	8.1	65.4	62.1	34.1	20.7	59.1	26.9	7.0	7.8	2.9
1966	481.8	117.9	45.5	9.0	69.5	67.3	37.2	22.8	62.2	30.9	8.0	8.5	3.1
1967	508.7	121.4	47.8	9.8	74.1	71.0	40.6	24.4	64.4	33.1	8.9	9.5	3.8
1968	558.7	131.7	52.5	10.5	79.7	76.4	46.8	26.9	73.5	36.7	10.1	10.4	3.7
1969	605.5	141.3	56.2	10.9	86.8	81.3	53.1	29.7	79.8	40.0	11.3	11.1	4.0
1970	648.9	154.6	57.6	11.5	94.0	85.0	60.0	32.6	81.1	43.1	12.7	12.2	4.5
1971	702.4	161.0	61.8	11.7	102.7	90.3	67.0	34.8	94.8	46.0	13.9	13.7	4.8
1972	770.7	173.6	67.1	12.3	112.1	99.7	75.0	38.2	105.3	51.5	15.3	15.4	5.2
1973	852.5	192.9	74.7	13.6	122.7	111.7	83.5	42.3	115.4	57.6	16.9	16.5	4.7
1974	932.4	215.9	79.3	14.8	134.1	123.8	93.6	47.2	119.0	63.4	18.5	18.1	4.7
1975	1 030.3	238.3	85.6	16.1	147.0	136.0	107.7	54.0	130.2	70.5	20.6	19.8	4.4
1976	1 149.8	259.3	93.7	17.5	161.5	152.6	122.1	60.6	155.7	78.2	22.5	22.4	3.8
1977	1 278.4	279.6	102.8	19.9	179.5	171.4	139.5	67.4	179.6	85.5	24.2	24.7	4.3
1978	1 430.4	307.8	115.1	21.9	201.7	190.5	159.2	81.7	196.7	95.9	26.8	28.7	4.3
1979	1 596.3	343.8	123.4	23.8	226.5	212.7	180.4	92.1	218.8	108.4	29.8	32.5	4.1
1980	1 762.9	376.8	132.3	25.5	255.1	233.8	206.5	103.6	238.4	116.7	33.5	37.2	3.5
1981	1 944.2	406.3	143.8	27.1	287.7	255.0	241.5	110.7	262.4	129.5	37.6	41.9	0.4
1982	2 079.3	427.7	147.0	28.0	313.0	272.4	270.8	123.8	268.0	138.9	41.3	45.9	2.5
1983	2 286.4	451.3	161.1	31.8	338.7	297.3	303.7	147.7	299.4	155.0	45.3	50.0	5.2
1984	2 498.4	476.7	175.8	34.7	370.3	323.2	335.1	160.9	337.0	172.9	49.4	56.1	6.4
1985	2 712.6	498.5	188.3	37.6	406.8	344.0	367.4	188.1	372.8	187.6	53.8	60.4	7.5
1986	2 895.2	524.2	204.1	40.7	442.0	360.8	396.7	212.9	379.7	204.7	58.1	67.1	4.1
1987	3 105.3	549.8	218.9	44.5	476.4	377.8	437.1	238.1	396.7	224.5	63.2	71.7	6.7
1988	3 356.6	588.3	235.7	47.7	511.9	399.8	492.1	254.4	423.6	248.4	70.2	81.2	3.2
1989	3 596.7	630.5	252.6	51.0	546.4	423.4	548.6	268.2	445.0	268.2	77.6	88.1	-2.9
1990	3 831.5	677.9	261.7	53.7	585.6	433.6	619.7	284.7	455.4	284.9	83.7	97.1	-6.3
1991	3 971.2	700.0	263.7	54.9	616.0	444.3	675.0	316.7	428.1	295.3	89.2	101.8	-13.7
1992	4 209.7	717.3	280.9	58.0	641.3	463.6	741.5	342.6	460.1	313.8	96.0	112.4	-18.0
1993	4 454.7	742.8	294.0	60.1	666.5	497.2	794.6	365.9	494.9	340.1	101.2	116.6	-19.3
1994	4 716.4	773.6	307.2	63.3	704.7	528.2	838.1	381.6	532.1	368.7	107.2	127.9	-16.2
1995	4 969.0	802.5	317.3	67.4	740.8	555.0	888.6	406.8	560.3	401.6	114.5	134.9	-20.7
1996	5 237.5	834.1	333.3	71.6	772.5	589.2	932.3	435.1	594.6	429.6	122.3	146.8	-24.1
1997	5 529.3	862.0	348.0	76.1	810.5	617.8	984.4	489.0	626.7	456.6	130.5	149.5	-21.8
1998	5 856.0	906.9	367.2	79.9	859.7	642.9	1 041.7	529.8	649.9	489.1	140.2	163.9	-15.1
1999	6 246.5	964.7	391.2	84.0	912.6	677.7	1 097.9	575.2	707.8	526.5	152.1	172.9	-16.0
2000	6 683.7	1 027.2	409.8	87.8	960.0	723.9	1 171.1	632.5	768.9	564.7	164.0	190.1	-16.1
2001	6 987.0	1 068.7	412.6	89.1	1 014.5	747.3	1 270.2	634.3	794.8	593.9	174.9	199.6	-12.9

NOTES AND DEFINITIONS

SOURCE: U.S. DEPARTMENT OF COMMERCE, BUREAU OF ECONOMIC ANALYSIS.

All personal income and personal consumption expenditure series are from the national income and product accounts (NIPAs). All series are shown at a seasonally adjusted annual rate and, except for the per capita series and the saving rate, are in billions of dollars.

TABLES 4-1 THROUGH 4-4 AND 19-5
SOURCES AND DISPOSITION OF PERSONAL INCOME; PERSONAL CONSUMPTION EXPENDITURE BY MAJOR TYPE OF PRODUCT

Definitions

Personal income is the income received by persons from participation in production; from government and business transfer payments; and from government interest, which is treated like a transfer payment rather than income from participation in production. Persons refers to individuals, nonprofit institutions that primarily serve individuals, private noninsured welfare funds, and private trust funds. Proprietors' income is treated in its entirety as received by individuals. Life insurance carriers and private noninsured pension funds are not counted as persons, but their saving is credited to persons.

Personal income is the sum of wage and salary disbursements, other labor income, proprietors' income with inventory valuation and capital consumption adjustments, rental income of persons with capital consumption adjustment, personal dividend income, personal interest income, and transfer payments to persons, less personal contributions for social insurance.

Personal income differs from national income in that it includes transfer payments and interest received by persons, regardless of source, while it excludes both employee and employer contributions for social insurance, business interest paid (other than to persons), and undistributed corporate profits.

Wage and salary disbursements consists of the monetary remuneration of employees, including the compensation of corporate officers; corporate directors' fees paid to directors who are also employees; the value of the exercise by employees of "nonqualified stock options"; commissions, tips, and bonuses; voluntary employee contributions to certain deferred compensation plans such as 401(k) plans; and receipts in kind that represent income. For fuller explanation, see the Notes and Definitions to Tables 1-1 through 1-10. As explained there, wage and salary *disbursements* is the appropriate concept for personal income whereas wage and salary *accruals* is used in computing national income.

Commodity-producing industries consists of the following Standard Industrial Classification (SIC) divisions: Agriculture, forestry, and fishing; mining; construction; and manufacturing. *Distributive industries* consists of the following SIC divisions: Transportation (excluding the U.S. Postal Service); communications; electric, gas, and sanitary services; wholesale trade; and retail trade. *Service industries* consists of the rest-of world sector and the following SIC divisions: Finance, insurance, real estate, and services. *Government* consists of federal, state, and local general government and government enterprises. Conversion to the North American Industry Classification System (NAICS) is expected at the time of the December 2003 revision.

Other labor income consists of employer payments to private pension and profit-sharing plans, private group health and life insurance plans, privately administered workers' compensation plans, supplemental unemployment benefit plans, and government employee retirement plans, along with several minor categories of employee compensation, including judicial fees to jurors and witnesses, compensation of prison inmates, and marriage fees to justices of the peace.

Proprietors' income with inventory valuation and capital consumption adjustments is the current-production income (including income-in-kind) of sole proprietors and partnerships and of tax-exempt cooperatives. The imputed net rental income of owner-occupants of farm dwellings is included. Dividends and monetary interest received by proprietors of nonfinancial business and rental incomes received by persons not primarily engaged in the real estate business are excluded; these incomes are included in dividends, net interest, and rental income of persons. Fees paid to outside directors of corporations are included. The two valuation adjustments are designed to obtain income measures that exclude any element of capital gains: inventory withdrawals are valued at replacement, rather than historical, cost and charges for depreciation are on a consistent accounting basis and are valued at replacement cost.

Rental income of persons with capital consumption adjustment is the net current production income of persons from the rental of real property, except income of persons primarily engaged in the real estate business; the imputed net rental income of owner-occupants of non-farm dwellings; and the royalties received by persons from patents, copyrights, and rights to natural resources. The capital consumption adjustment converts charges for depreciation to a consistent accounting basis valued at replacement cost.

Personal dividend income is the dividend income of persons from all sources, excluding capital gains distributions. It equals net dividends paid by corporations (dividends paid by corporations less dividends received by corporations) less a small amount of corporate dividends received by general government. Dividends received by government employee retirement systems are included in personal dividend income.

Personal interest income is the interest income (monetary and imputed) of persons from all sources, including interest paid by government to government employee retirement plans.

Transfer payments to persons is income payments to persons for which no current services are performed. It consists of business transfer payments to persons and government transfer payments. Government transfer payments consists of benefits from the following social insurance funds: Old-age, survivors, and disability insurance (*Social Security*); hospital insurance and supplementary medical insurance benefits (*Medicare*); *unemployment insurance*; railroad retirement; pension benefit guaranty; veterans' life insurance; workers' compensation; military medical insurance; and temporary disability insurance. Government transfer payments also includes benefits from certain other programs, including the value of benefits received in-kind as well as cash transfers. Among the programs included are veterans' benefits, in addition to veterans' life insurance; food stamps; black lung; supplemental security income; public assistance (including Medicaid); and educational assistance. Government payments to nonprofit institutions, other than for work under research and development contracts, also are included. Payments from government employee retirement plans are not included.

*Personal contribution*s for social insurance, which is subtracted to arrive at personal income, includes payments by employees, self-employed, and other individuals who participate in the following programs: Old-age, survivors, and disability insurance (Social Security); hospital insurance and supplementary medical insurance (Medicare); unemployment insurance; railroad retirement; veterans' life insurance; and temporary disability insurance. Contributions to government employee retirement plans are not included.

Personal tax and nontax payments is tax payments (net of refunds) by persons residing in the United States that are not chargeable to business expense and certain other personal payments to government agencies (except government enterprises) that are treated like taxes. Personal taxes includes taxes on income, including taxes on realized net capital gains, and on personal property. Nontaxes includes donations and fees, fines, and forfeitures. Personal contributions for social insurance is not included. As of the 1999 revisions, estate and gift taxes are classified as capital transfers and are not included in personal tax and nontax payments.

Disposable personal income is personal income less personal tax and nontax payments. It is the income from current production that is available to persons for spending or saving. Disposable personal income in chained (1996) dollars represents the inflation-adjusted value of disposable personal income.

Personal outlays is the sum of personal consumption expenditures (defined below), interest paid by persons, and personal transfer payments to the rest of the world (net). The last item is personal remittances in cash and in kind to the rest of the world less such remittances from the rest of the world.

Personal saving is derived by subtracting personal outlays and personal tax and nontax payments from personal income. It is the current saving of individuals (including proprietors), nonprofit institutions that primarily serve individuals, life insurance carriers, retirement funds (now including those of government employees), private non-insured welfare funds, and private trust funds. Conceptually, personal saving may also be viewed as the sum of the net acquisition of financial assets and the change in physical assets less the sum of net borrowing and consumption of fixed capital. In either case, it is defined to exclude capital gains, whether realized or unrealized.

Note that in the context of national income accounting the term just defined is "*saving*," not "savings." "Saving" refers to a *flow* of income in a particular period (a year or a quarter, for example) that is not consumed and is therefore available to finance a commensurate *flow* of investment. "Savings" denotes an accumulated stock of monetary funds—possibly the cumulative effects of successive periods of *saving*—available to the owner in asset form, such as a bank savings account.

Personal consumption expenditures (PCE) is goods and services purchased by persons residing in the United States. Persons are defined as individuals and nonprofit institutions that primarily serve individuals. Most of PCE consists of purchases of new goods and services by individuals from business, including purchases financed by insurance (for example, by medical insurance). In addition, PCE includes purchases of new goods and services by nonprofit institutions, net purchases of used goods by individuals and nonprofit institutions, and purchases abroad of goods and services by U.S. residents traveling or working in foreign countries. PCE also includes purchases for certain goods and services provided by the government, primarily tuition payments for higher education, charges for medical care, and charges for water and sanitary services. Finally, PCE includes imputed purchases that keep PCE invariant to changes in the way that certain activities are carried out. For example, to take account of the value of the services provided by owner-occupied housing, PCE includes an imputation equal to the estimated rent homeowners would pay if they rented their houses from themselves. (Actual purchases of residential structures by individuals are classified as gross private domestic investment.)

Tables 4-3 and 4-4 present personal consumption expenditures classified by major type of product: *durable goods*, *nondurable goods*, and *services*. Each of these three major categories is then subdivided according to major type of expenditure. In general, *durable goods* are commodities that can be stored or inventoried and that have an average life of at least 3 years. *Nondurable goods* are all other commodities that can be stored or inventoried.

This classification system can be misleading with respect to the objective of spending; for example, the *medical care* component of services does not include drugs and medicines, which are included in nondurable goods. For a more precise classification of consumption spending by objective, available only on an annual basis, see Table 4-5 and its description below.

Per capita product and income estimates

In Table 4-2, annual and quarterly (annual-rate) values of disposable personal income are expressed in per capita terms—that is, the aggregate dollar amount divided by the U.S. population. Population is the total population of the United States, including the Armed Forces overseas and the institutionalized population. The monthly population estimate is the average of estimates for the first of the month and the first of the following month; the quarterly and the annual estimates are averages of the monthly estimates. Estimates for January 1991 through June 2000 are interpolations between Census Bureau population estimates for 1990 and for 2000; estimates for July 2000 forward are Bureau of Economic Analysis (BEA) extrapolations.

Revisions

Data in this book reflect revisions to the NIPAs available through August 2003.

See the Notes and Definitions to Chapter 1 for an explanation of a new revision schedule for wages and salaries and related components of the income side of the NIPAs. This will mean revisions once a quarter of as many as 7 months of previous data, affecting incomes and saving but not PCE or other components of GDP.

An important conceptual change was made in the 1999 comprehensive revision of the NIPAs affecting the concepts of personal income and saving, in that the retirement plans of federal, state, and local employees are now treated like private pensions; formerly they were treated as government social insurance programs. The most significant differences are that employer contributions to, and the dividends and interest received by, these retirement funds are now treated as a component of personal income; but benefits paid by the plans are treated as transactions within the personal sector rather than transfer payments. In other words, this conceptual revision raised "Other labor income" and dividends and interest, while reducing transfer payments received and personal contributions for social insurance. The effect was to move the accumulation of assets in these pension funds from the government surplus to the personal saving sector.

Data availability

Monthly data are released monthly in a BEA press release, normally the first business day following the monthly release of the latest national income and product account (NIPA) estimates. Monthly and quarterly data are subsequently published each month in the *Survey of Current Business*. Current and historical data are available on the BEA Internet site at <http://www.bea.gov>, and may also be obtained from the STAT-USA subscription Internet site at <http://www.stat-usa.gov>.

References

A discussion of monthly estimates of personal income and its disposition appears in the November 1979 *Survey of Current Business*. A more detailed description of concepts, sources, and methods used in estimating personal consumption expenditures appears in *Personal Consumption Expenditures* (NIPA Methodology Paper No. 6, 1990), available on the BEA Internet site from the National Technical Information Service (NTIS Accession No. PB 90-254244). Additional and more recent information can be found in the articles listed in the Notes and Definitions for Tables 1-1 through 1-10.

TABLE 4-5
PERSONAL CONSUMPTION EXPENDITURES BY TYPE OF EXPENDITURE

SOURCE: BUREAU OF ECONOMIC ANALYSIS

In this table, also derived from the NIPA accounts, annual estimates of the current-dollar value of PCE are presented by "type of expenditure" instead of "by type of product," the latter of which is the classification scheme used in Tables 4-3 and 4-4. The "type of expenditure" tabulations provide a more precise delineation of consumer spending by its ultimate objective, and cut across the categories of durable goods, nondurable goods, and services that are used in the quarterly estimates.

Definitions

Food and tobacco includes food, beverages including alcoholic, and tobacco products whether purchased for home consumption or on the premises of eating and drinking places. All the components are included in nondurable goods in the "major type of product" classification system.

Clothing, accessories, and jewelry includes clothing and shoes from the nondurable goods category, jewelry and watches from durables, and cleaning, storage, and repair of clothing and shoes from services.

Personal care includes toilet articles and preparations from nondurable goods and barbershops, beauty parlors, and health clubs from services.

Housing includes rents paid for rental housing, imputed rent of owner-occupied dwellings, and rent of hotels, motels, clubs, schools, and other group housing, all from the services group.

Household operation includes furniture, appliances, and other durable household goods from durable goods; "semidurable" furnishings (such as textile goods), household supplies, and stationery from nondurable goods; and utilities, communications, domestic service, maintenance, insurance, and miscellaneous services.

Medical care includes drug preparations and sundries from nondurable goods, ophthalmic and orthopedic products from durable goods, and the services of medical professionals, hospitals, nursing homes, and health insurance.

Personal business includes financial, legal, funeral, and miscellaneous services.

Transportation includes purchase of motor vehicles and parts from the durable goods category; gasoline and oil from nondurables; and tolls, insurance, transit, taxis, rail, bus, airline, and other transportation services.

Recreation includes books, "wheel goods" (other than those classified in transportation), photo equipment, boats, pleasure aircraft, video, audio, musical instruments, computers, and software from durable goods; toys, sports

supplies, flowers, seeds, and potted plants from nondurables; and a long list of recreational and cultural services, including gambling.

Education and research includes all education and research expenditures in the service category, including the research of nonprofit institutions.

Religious and welfare activities are all classified as services in the "major type of product" system. For nonprofits, equals current expenditures (including consumption of fixed capital) of religious, social welfare, foreign relief, and political organizations, museums, libraries, and foundations. The expenditures are net of receipts—such as those from meals, rooms, and entertainments—accounted for separately in consumer expenditures, and exclude relief payments within the United States and expenditures by foundations for education and research. For proprietary and government institutions, equals receipts from users.

Foreign travel and other, net consists of foreign travel spending (services) and other expenditures abroad (nondurables) by U.S. residents less expenditures in the United States by nonresidents (services) and personal remittances in kind to nonresidents (nondurables). Negative figures indicate that the sum of the first two terms is less than the sum of the second two terms—in practice, that spending in the United States by foreigners exceeds spending on foreign travel by U.S. residents. Beginning with 1981, foreign travel spending by U.S. residents includes U.S. students' expenditures abroad, and expenditures in the United States by nonresidents includes nonresidents' student and medical care expenditures in the United States.

Data availability and revisions

Data are published once a year in supplemental NIPA tables in the *Survey of Current Business*, most recently in September 2003, reflecting the most recent NIPA revisions. They are also available on the BEA Web site referenced above.

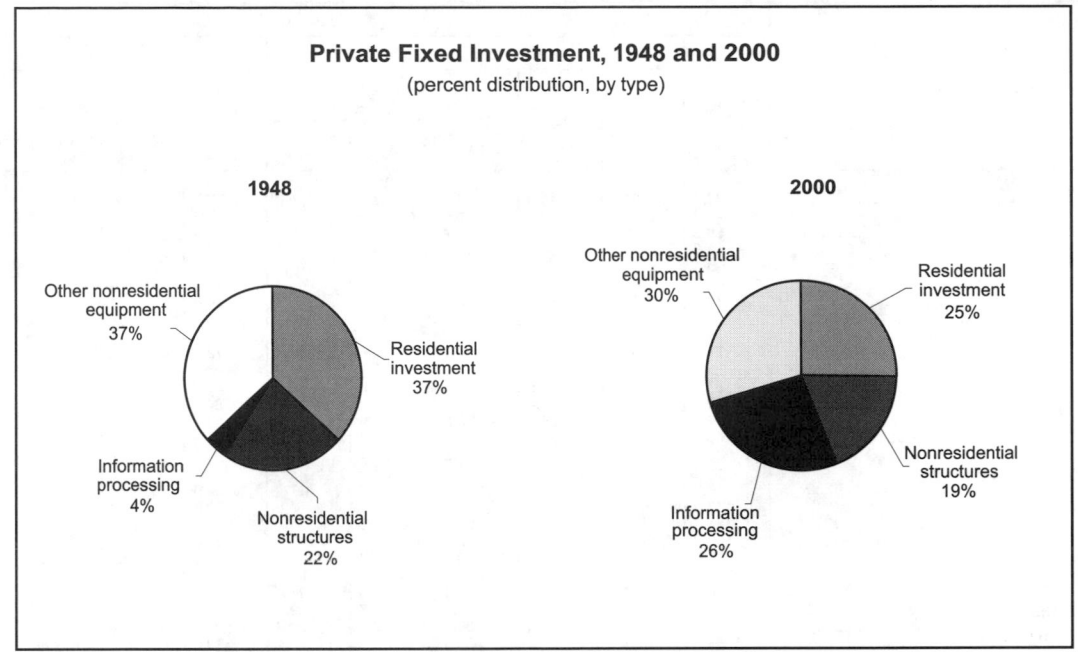

Private Fixed Investment, 1948 and 2000
(percent distribution, by type)

- Residential fixed investment accounted for a smaller percentage of the value of total private investment spending in 2000 than in 1948. As the graph shows, the share of nonresidential spending rose and its composition changed sharply, as investment in information processing equipment rose to over one-fourth of all private investment spending, while the shares of other kinds of equipment and of nonresidential structures declined. (Table 5-2)

- In terms of physical quantities, total fixed investment rose 756 percent from 1947 to 2002. Nonresidential investment rose 979 percent, with structures increasing 246 percent and total equipment and software up 1,678 percent. Residential investment rose 364 percent. (Table 5-4)

- The current-dollar amount of gross saving in the U.S. economy (including allowances for capital consumption) fell to a postwar low of 15.0 percent of Gross National Product (GNP) in 2002, reflecting a large swing to current federal government deficits and record state and local deficits as well, only partly offset by increases in private saving. More negative "net foreign investment"—increasing net inflows of foreign capital—outweighed nominal increases in the value of private and government investment. (Table 5-1)

- Aggregate capital-output ratios changed little over the postwar period. The ratio of the current-cost net stock of privately-owned fixed assets to the current-dollar value of GDP was 2.16 in both 1948 and 2000. The ratio of government fixed assets to GDP was down, from 0.79 in 1948 to 0.59 in 2000. Hence, the total capital-output ratio fell from 2.95 to 2.75. (Tables 5-5 and 1-1)

- In quantity terms, the net stock of private fixed assets rose 465 percent from 1946 to 2001, while the stock of government fixed assets rose 219 percent. (Table 5-6)

- Broad measures of the ratio of the value of inventories to the value of a month's sales are shown in Table 5-7. The broadest—all inventories to all sales—show a distinct downtrend over the postwar period, looking from the fourth quarter of 1947 to the fourth quarter of 1999. (Time periods just preceding the business cycle peak are chosen for this comparison.) Much of this decline, however, may reflect the shift in the composition of GDP toward services, which require relatively less inventory support. When nonfarm inventories are compared with final sales of goods and structures only, 1999 ratios are actually higher than those of 1947.

Table 5-1. Gross Saving and Investment

(Billions of dollars, quarterly data are at seasonally adjusted annual rates.)

Year and quarter	Total	Private Total [1]	Personal	Undistributed corporate profits [2]	Consumption of fixed capital Corporate	Noncorporate	Government Total	Consumption of fixed capital Federal	State and local	Current surplus or deficit (-) Federal	State and local
1946	38.9	31.6	16.3	2.7	7.5	5.2	7.3	9.4	1.5	-5.1	1.4
1947	46.8	29.5	8.1	5.9	8.9	6.7	17.3	8.8	1.8	5.2	1.4
1948	58.3	43.8	14.1	11.4	10.4	7.9	14.4	7.6	2.1	3.5	1.2
1949	45.6	41.1	10.0	11.1	11.4	8.7	4.5	6.6	2.1	-5.7	1.4
1950	60.3	45.6	15.2	8.6	12.2	9.5	14.7	5.9	2.1	5.5	1.3
1951	74.8	54.0	19.7	9.3	14.0	10.9	20.8	6.1	2.6	9.6	2.5
1952	73.8	57.6	20.6	10.4	14.9	11.7	16.2	6.9	2.7	3.7	2.9
1953	74.6	58.9	21.3	9.5	15.8	12.2	15.7	7.7	2.8	1.8	3.4
1954	72.7	60.0	19.8	11.0	16.6	12.7	12.7	8.3	2.9	-1.7	3.2
1955	87.4	66.5	19.5	16.0	17.6	13.4	20.9	8.7	3.1	5.7	3.4
1956	98.6	73.9	25.4	14.1	19.8	14.6	24.7	9.3	3.5	7.5	4.3
1957	99.0	78.0	26.8	13.8	21.9	15.4	21.1	9.9	3.9	3.2	4.1
1958	90.1	78.8	28.2	11.9	22.8	16.0	11.3	10.0	4.0	-5.5	2.8
1959	105.8	84.2	26.5	17.5	23.7	16.5	21.6	10.4	4.2	3.2	3.8
1960	110.9	84.4	26.4	16.3	24.7	17.1	26.5	10.7	4.4	7.1	4.3
1961	113.9	91.5	31.9	16.8	25.2	17.6	22.5	11.0	4.7	2.5	4.3
1962	124.6	100.4	33.5	22.6	26.2	18.1	24.2	11.6	5.0	2.4	5.2
1963	132.8	104.3	33.1	25.2	27.2	18.7	28.5	12.3	5.4	5.2	5.7
1964	143.0	117.6	40.5	28.6	28.7	19.7	25.5	12.5	5.7	0.8	6.4
1965	158.1	129.4	42.7	34.9	30.8	21.0	28.8	12.8	6.2	3.2	6.5
1966	169.1	138.5	44.5	37.6	33.7	22.6	30.7	13.3	6.9	2.7	7.7
1967	171.1	150.8	54.0	35.4	37.1	24.3	20.3	14.2	7.5	-8.3	7.0
1968	183.3	153.7	52.7	33.6	41.1	26.4	29.6	15.1	8.3	-1.3	7.5
1969	199.8	157.0	52.6	29.8	45.6	29.0	42.8	15.9	9.3	9.6	8.0
1970	194.3	174.3	69.5	23.0	50.5	31.4	20.0	16.7	10.6	-14.4	7.1
1971	211.4	202.6	80.1	32.4	55.4	34.4	8.8	17.4	11.8	-26.8	6.4
1972	241.6	217.0	76.9	41.1	60.9	38.5	24.6	18.7	12.9	-22.5	15.6
1973	294.6	256.4	102.5	44.8	66.8	42.3	38.2	19.5	14.3	-11.2	15.7
1974	304.0	270.7	114.3	29.5	78.5	48.4	33.3	20.2	17.7	-13.9	9.3
1975	298.4	323.5	125.2	49.1	94.0	55.2	-25.1	21.6	20.2	-69.3	2.4
1976	342.7	344.0	122.1	57.3	104.5	60.0	-1.3	23.2	21.3	-53.0	7.3
1977	398.2	383.1	125.6	73.1	117.5	66.9	15.1	24.6	22.6	-45.2	13.1
1978	481.6	439.1	145.4	82.9	134.5	76.2	42.5	26.3	24.4	-26.9	18.7
1979	544.9	487.8	165.8	77.0	156.4	88.5	57.1	28.0	27.4	-11.4	13.0
1980	555.5	537.8	205.6	49.6	181.1	101.5	17.7	30.9	31.7	-53.8	8.8
1981	656.5	631.7	243.7	64.1	210.1	113.7	24.8	34.7	36.3	-53.7	7.5
1982	625.7	681.6	262.2	61.9	233.4	124.0	-55.9	39.5	39.5	-132.6	-2.3
1983	608.0	693.8	227.8	93.2	244.4	128.3	-85.7	42.4	40.9	-173.9	4.8
1984	769.4	824.8	306.5	124.7	260.2	133.4	-55.4	46.4	42.4	-168.1	23.8
1985	772.5	833.4	282.6	128.3	280.9	141.7	-60.9	49.3	44.7	-177.1	22.3
1986	735.9	806.5	267.8	88.0	302.1	148.7	-70.5	52.9	47.9	-192.1	20.8
1987	810.4	838.3	252.8	107.3	320.8	157.4	-27.9	56.3	51.5	-147.9	12.2
1988	936.2	943.0	292.3	138.3	344.3	168.1	-6.7	60.2	54.9	-137.4	15.6
1989	967.6	955.1	301.8	99.2	370.6	183.4	12.5	64.4	58.8	-130.0	19.3
1990	977.7	1 016.2	334.3	102.4	391.1	188.4	-38.6	68.7	63.1	-173.0	2.6
1991	1 015.8	1 098.9	371.7	119.2	411.2	196.8	-83.2	73.0	66.9	-215.3	-7.8
1992	1 007.4	1 164.6	413.7	124.4	427.9	214.3	-157.2	75.4	69.9	-297.5	-4.9
1993	1 039.4	1 159.4	350.8	142.0	448.5	211.6	-120.0	78.7	73.9	-274.1	1.5
1994	1 155.9	1 199.3	315.5	151.6	482.7	231.9	-43.4	81.4	78.9	-212.3	8.6
1995	1 257.5	1 266.0	302.4	203.6	512.1	231.5	-8.5	84.0	84.1	-192.0	15.3
1996	1 349.3	1 290.4	272.1	232.7	543.5	238.5	58.9	85.3	88.9	-136.8	21.4
1997	1 502.3	1 343.7	252.9	261.3	581.5	250.9	158.6	86.8	94.2	-53.3	31.0
1998	1 647.2	1 375.0	301.5	189.9	620.2	264.2	272.2	88.2	99.5	43.8	40.7
1999	1 704.1	1 356.1	174.0	229.6	665.5	281.8	348.1	91.5	106.4	111.9	38.3
2000	1 807.9	1 372.1	201.5	152.6	721.1	296.8	435.8	95.9	115.0	206.9	18.0
2001	1 662.4	1 399.3	169.7	122.7	789.1	317.7	263.1	98.7	123.7	72.0	-31.3
2002	1 565.1	1 589.6	285.8	139.9	827.5	336.4	-24.5	101.9	127.7	-202.1	-52.0
2000											
1st quarter	1 815.7	1 353.7	179.4	185.7	698.6	290.0	462.0	94.5	111.5	223.2	32.7
2nd quarter	1 813.6	1 386.5	207.5	170.4	714.1	294.6	427.1	95.5	114.1	197.2	20.2
3rd quarter	1 828.9	1 383.7	211.5	144.2	728.9	299.1	445.2	96.5	116.3	213.2	19.2
4th quarter	1 773.4	1 364.4	207.7	110.2	742.8	303.7	409.0	97.2	118.1	193.8	-0.2
2001											
1st quarter	1 699.0	1 324.1	173.7	86.3	755.9	308.2	374.9	97.7	119.9	173.8	-16.5
2nd quarter	1 670.6	1 338.4	141.6	101.9	772.3	322.6	332.2	98.6	121.5	144.4	-32.3
3rd quarter	1 665.6	1 535.6	302.2	79.5	835.6	318.2	130.0	99.0	128.9	-51.7	-46.2
4th quarter	1 614.4	1 399.0	61.5	223.0	792.6	321.9	215.3	99.7	124.5	21.3	-30.2
2002											
1st quarter	1 603.2	1 578.3	270.4	171.0	808.3	328.6	24.9	100.6	125.9	-145.8	-55.8
2nd quarter	1 604.0	1 616.1	314.3	140.5	826.1	335.1	-12.1	101.3	127.3	-195.6	-45.1
3rd quarter	1 535.5	1 570.2	276.9	118.6	836.1	338.7	-34.7	102.2	128.3	-210.5	-54.7
4th quarter	1 517.5	1 593.8	281.8	129.4	839.3	343.3	-76.2	103.6	129.1	-256.6	-52.4

[1]Includes wage and salary accruals less disbursements, not shown separately.
[2]Includes inventory valuation and capital consumption adjustments.

Table 5-1. Gross Saving and Investment—*Continued*

(Billions of dollars, quarterly data are at seasonally adjusted annual rates.)

Year and quarter	Gross investment				Statistical discrepancy	Gross saving as a percent of GNP
	Total	Private domestic	Government	Net foreign		
1946	39.6	31.1	3.5	4.9	0.7	17.4
1947	48.8	35.0	4.6	9.3	2.1	19.0
1948	57.5	48.1	7.0	2.4	-0.7	21.5
1949	47.4	36.9	9.7	0.9	1.8	17.0
1950	62.0	54.1	9.8	-1.8	1.7	20.4
1951	78.7	60.2	17.6	0.9	3.9	21.9
1952	77.0	54.0	22.3	0.6	3.1	20.5
1953	79.2	56.4	24.0	-1.3	4.6	19.5
1954	76.6	53.8	22.5	0.2	3.9	19.0
1955	90.5	69.0	21.0	0.4	3.1	20.9
1956	97.7	72.0	22.9	2.8	-0.9	22.4
1957	99.6	70.5	24.4	4.8	0.6	21.3
1958	91.9	64.5	26.5	0.9	1.7	19.1
1959	106.7	78.5	29.3	-1.2	0.8	20.7
1960	110.4	78.9	28.3	3.2	-0.6	20.9
1961	113.8	78.2	31.3	4.3	-0.2	20.7
1962	125.3	88.1	33.3	3.9	0.7	21.1
1963	132.4	93.8	33.6	5.0	-0.4	21.3
1964	144.2	102.1	34.6	7.5	1.2	21.4
1965	160.0	118.2	35.6	6.2	1.9	21.8
1966	175.6	131.3	40.4	3.9	6.4	21.3
1967	175.9	128.6	43.8	3.5	4.8	20.4
1968	187.6	141.2	44.7	1.7	4.3	20.0
1969	202.7	156.4	44.4	1.8	2.9	20.1
1970	201.2	152.4	44.8	4.0	6.9	18.6
1971	222.7	178.2	44.0	0.6	11.3	18.6
1972	250.3	207.6	46.3	-3.6	8.7	19.3
1973	302.6	244.5	49.4	8.7	8.0	21.1
1974	314.0	249.4	57.4	7.1	10.0	20.0
1975	316.1	230.2	64.5	21.4	17.7	18.1
1976	367.2	292.0	66.4	8.9	24.5	18.6
1977	419.8	361.3	67.5	-9.0	21.6	19.4
1978	502.6	436.0	77.1	-10.4	21.0	20.8
1979	580.6	490.6	88.5	1.4	35.7	21.0
1980	589.5	477.9	100.3	11.4	33.9	19.6
1981	684.0	570.8	106.9	6.3	27.5	20.7
1982	628.2	516.1	112.3	-0.2	2.5	19.0
1983	655.0	564.2	122.8	-32.0	47.0	17.0
1984	787.9	735.5	139.4	-87.0	18.6	19.4
1985	784.2	736.3	158.8	-110.9	11.7	18.2
1986	779.8	747.2	173.2	-140.6	43.9	16.5
1987	813.8	781.5	184.3	-152.0	3.3	17.0
1988	894.0	821.1	186.2	-113.2	-42.2	18.3
1989	983.9	872.9	197.7	-86.7	16.3	17.6
1990	1 008.2	861.7	215.8	-69.2	30.6	16.8
1991	1 035.4	800.2	220.3	14.9	19.6	16.9
1992	1 051.1	866.6	223.1	-38.7	43.7	15.9
1993	1 103.2	955.1	220.9	-72.9	63.8	15.6
1994	1 214.4	1 097.1	225.6	-108.3	58.5	16.3
1995	1 284.0	1 143.8	238.2	-98.0	26.5	16.9
1996	1 382.1	1 242.7	250.1	-110.7	32.8	17.2
1997	1 532.1	1 390.5	264.6	-123.1	29.7	18.0
1998	1 616.2	1 538.7	277.1	-199.7	-31.0	18.8
1999	1 665.4	1 636.7	304.7	-276.0	-38.8	18.3
2000	1 679.4	1 755.4	319.8	-395.8	-128.5	18.4
2001	1 545.1	1 586.0	335.8	-376.7	-117.3	16.5
2002	1 456.2	1 593.2	351.9	-488.9	-108.8	15.0
2000						
1st quarter	1 677.0	1 711.4	322.5	-356.9	-138.7	18.8
2nd quarter	1 726.8	1 786.3	317.5	-377.1	-86.8	18.4
3rd quarter	1 664.9	1 766.4	317.7	-419.1	-164.0	18.5
4th quarter	1 648.9	1 757.4	321.5	-430.0	-124.5	17.8
2001						
1st quarter	1 593.2	1 671.1	331.6	-409.5	-105.7	16.9
2nd quarter	1 557.7	1 597.2	343.0	-382.5	-112.9	16.6
3rd quarter	1 547.8	1 574.9	323.7	-350.8	-117.8	16.5
4th quarter	1 481.8	1 500.7	345.0	-363.9	-132.6	15.8
2002						
1st quarter	1 493.2	1 559.4	355.5	-421.7	-110.0	15.5
2nd quarter	1 439.0	1 588.0	348.2	-497.2	-165.0	15.5
3rd quarter	1 453.4	1 597.3	351.7	-495.6	-82.1	14.6
4th quarter	1 439.3	1 628.1	352.2	-541.0	-78.2	14.3

Table 5-2. Gross Private Fixed Investment by Type

(Billions of dollars, quarterly data are at seasonally adjusted annual rates.)

Year and quarter	Total	Nonresidential										
		Total	Structures					Equipment and software				
			Total	Nonresidential buildings including farm	Utilities	Mining exploration, shafts, and wells	Other structures	Total	Information processing equipment and software			
									Computers and peripheral equipment [1]	Software [2]	Other	
1946	25.1	17.3	7.4	4.1	1.7	0.8	0.8	9.9	...	...	1.2	
1947	35.5	23.5	8.1	4.1	2.6	0.9	0.5	15.3	...	...	1.7	
1948	42.4	26.8	9.5	4.7	3.3	1.2	0.3	17.3	...	...	1.8	
1949	39.6	24.9	9.2	4.3	3.5	1.2	0.2	15.7	...	...	1.6	
1950	48.3	27.8	10.0	4.8	3.5	1.4	0.2	17.8	...	...	1.8	
1951	50.3	31.8	12.0	6.2	3.9	1.7	0.1	19.9	...	...	2.1	
1952	50.5	31.9	12.2	6.0	4.1	2.0	0.1	19.7	...	...	2.4	
1953	54.5	35.1	13.6	6.7	4.6	2.1	0.2	21.5	...	...	2.7	
1954	55.8	34.7	13.9	7.2	4.2	2.3	0.2	20.8	...	...	2.4	
1955	64.0	39.0	15.2	8.2	4.1	2.5	0.4	23.9	...	...	2.8	
1956	68.1	44.5	18.2	10.4	5.1	2.7	0.1	26.3	...	...	3.4	
1957	69.7	47.5	19.0	10.7	5.4	2.6	0.2	28.6	...	...	4.0	
1958	64.9	42.5	17.6	10.0	5.1	2.4	0.2	24.9	...	...	3.6	
1959	74.6	46.5	18.1	10.6	4.9	2.5	0.2	28.4	0.0	0.0	4.0	
1960	75.7	49.4	19.6	12.0	5.0	2.3	0.2	29.8	0.2	0.1	4.5	
1961	75.2	48.8	19.7	12.7	4.6	2.3	0.1	29.1	0.3	0.2	4.8	
1962	82.0	53.1	20.8	13.7	4.6	2.5	0.0	32.3	0.3	0.2	5.1	
1963	88.1	56.0	21.2	13.9	5.0	2.3	0.1	34.8	0.7	0.4	5.3	
1964	97.2	63.0	23.7	15.8	5.4	2.4	0.1	39.2	0.9	0.5	5.8	
1965	109.0	74.8	28.3	19.5	6.1	2.4	0.4	46.5	1.2	0.7	6.6	
1966	117.7	85.4	31.3	21.3	7.1	2.5	0.6	54.0	1.7	1.0	7.9	
1967	118.7	86.4	31.5	20.6	7.8	2.4	0.6	54.9	1.9	1.2	8.1	
1968	132.1	93.4	33.6	21.1	9.2	2.6	0.8	59.9	1.9	1.3	8.6	
1969	147.3	104.7	37.7	24.4	9.6	2.8	0.9	67.0	2.4	1.8	10.4	
1970	150.4	109.0	40.3	25.4	11.1	2.8	1.0	68.7	2.7	2.3	11.6	
1971	169.9	114.1	42.7	27.1	11.9	2.7	1.0	71.5	2.8	2.4	12.1	
1972	198.5	128.8	47.2	30.1	13.1	3.1	0.9	81.7	3.5	2.8	13.1	
1973	228.6	153.3	55.0	35.5	15.0	3.5	1.0	98.3	3.5	3.2	16.3	
1974	235.4	169.5	61.2	38.3	16.5	5.2	1.2	108.2	3.9	3.9	19.0	
1975	236.5	173.7	61.4	35.6	17.1	7.4	1.3	112.4	3.6	4.8	19.9	
1976	274.8	192.4	65.9	35.9	20.0	8.6	1.4	126.4	4.4	5.2	22.8	
1977	339.0	228.7	74.6	39.9	21.5	11.5	1.8	154.1	5.7	5.5	27.5	
1978	410.2	278.6	91.4	49.7	24.1	15.4	2.2	187.2	7.6	6.6	34.2	
1979	472.7	331.6	114.9	65.7	27.5	19.0	2.6	216.7	10.2	8.7	39.8	
1980	484.2	360.9	133.9	73.7	30.2	27.4	2.6	227.0	12.5	10.7	46.4	
1981	541.0	418.4	164.6	86.3	33.0	42.5	2.8	253.8	17.1	12.9	52.3	
1982	531.0	425.3	175.0	94.5	32.5	44.8	3.2	250.3	18.9	15.4	54.6	
1983	570.0	417.4	152.7	90.5	28.7	30.0	3.5	264.7	23.9	18.0	58.9	
1984	670.1	490.3	176.0	110.0	30.0	31.3	4.7	314.3	31.6	22.1	68.0	
1985	714.5	527.6	193.3	128.0	30.6	27.9	6.8	334.3	33.7	25.6	71.5	
1986	740.7	522.5	175.8	123.3	31.2	15.7	5.7	346.8	33.4	27.8	76.4	
1987	754.3	526.7	172.1	126.0	26.5	13.1	6.5	354.7	35.8	31.4	74.8	
1988	802.7	568.4	181.6	133.8	26.6	15.7	5.5	386.8	38.0	36.7	81.2	
1989	845.2	613.4	193.4	142.7	29.5	14.9	6.2	420.0	43.1	44.4	85.5	
1990	847.2	630.3	202.5	149.1	28.4	17.9	7.2	427.8	38.6	50.2	87.3	
1991	800.4	608.9	183.4	124.2	33.7	18.5	6.9	425.4	37.7	56.6	87.1	
1992	851.6	626.1	172.2	113.2	36.7	14.2	8.2	453.9	43.6	60.8	93.1	
1993	934.0	682.2	179.4	119.3	34.8	17.7	7.7	502.8	47.2	69.4	98.4	
1994	1 034.6	748.6	187.5	129.0	34.0	17.4	7.0	561.1	51.3	75.5	106.9	
1995	1 110.7	825.1	204.6	144.3	35.8	17.2	7.3	620.5	64.6	83.5	113.8	
1996	1 212.7	899.4	225.0	161.7	36.0	21.1	6.2	674.4	70.9	95.1	121.3	
1997	1 327.7	999.4	255.8	182.7	36.1	30.1	7.0	743.6	79.6	116.5	129.2	
1998	1 465.6	1 101.2	282.4	201.4	44.2	30.2	6.5	818.9	84.2	140.1	139.2	
1999	1 577.2	1 173.5	283.7	206.9	47.3	22.8	6.7	889.8	90.4	162.5	149.4	
2000	1 691.8	1 265.8	314.2	223.9	53.7	29.2	7.4	951.6	93.3	179.4	174.2	
2001	1 646.3	1 201.6	324.5	216.3	55.0	42.7	10.5	877.1	74.2	180.4	149.8	
2002	1 589.3	1 117.4	269.3	179.2	53.1	30.6	6.4	848.1	74.2	182.8	142.7	
2000												
1st quarter	1 664.6	1 236.6	299.5	216.2	50.8	25.6	7.0	937.1	90.1	174.5	168.6	
2nd quarter	1 697.1	1 268.3	308.5	222.8	52.5	26.2	7.0	959.8	95.7	178.2	175.2	
3rd quarter	1 705.2	1 283.4	320.9	227.4	54.7	31.1	7.7	962.5	95.7	182.2	175.4	
4th quarter	1 700.4	1 274.8	328.0	229.1	57.1	33.8	8.0	946.8	91.8	182.5	177.5	
2001												
1st quarter	1 698.3	1 258.3	333.7	231.9	54.9	39.7	7.1	924.6	84.0	183.4	165.8	
2nd quarter	1 654.3	1 210.0	329.9	221.3	56.2	45.5	6.9	880.2	75.8	180.7	151.5	
3rd quarter	1 635.5	1 188.1	332.0	211.5	54.6	45.1	20.7	856.1	67.6	178.7	144.5	
4th quarter	1 597.2	1 149.8	302.3	200.4	54.4	40.4	7.2	847.4	69.3	178.9	137.3	
2002												
1st quarter	1 589.4	1 126.8	288.3	192.4	56.3	32.3	7.3	838.5	71.9	177.2	139.6	
2nd quarter	1 584.6	1 115.8	275.2	182.3	53.9	31.7	7.3	840.7	72.8	181.0	143.3	
3rd quarter	1 579.7	1 109.8	259.4	171.1	51.5	31.0	5.8	850.4	76.8	186.3	143.8	
4th quarter	1 603.6	1 117.1	254.2	170.9	50.6	27.3	5.4	863.0	75.4	186.7	144.2	

[1] New computers and peripheral equipment only.
[2] Excludes software "embedded," or bundled, in computers and other equipment.
. . . = Not available.

Table 5-2. Gross Private Fixed Investment by Type—*Continued*

(Billions of dollars, quarterly data are at seasonally adjusted annual rates.)

Year and quarter	Nonresidential—*Continued* Equipment and software—*Continued*				Residential					
	Industrial equipment	Transportation equipment	Other equipment	Total	Structures					Equipment
					Total	New single family	New multifamily	Other structures		
1946	3.1	3.0	2.7	7.8	7.6	. . .	. . .	2.4	0.2
1947	4.6	4.9	4.1	12.1	11.8	. . .	. . .	3.5	0.3
1948	4.6	5.5	5.4	15.6	15.3	. . .	. . .	4.2	0.3
1949	3.7	5.7	4.7	14.6	14.3	. . .	. . .	3.7	0.3
1950	4.4	6.4	5.1	20.5	20.2	. . .	. . .	4.0	0.4
1951	5.6	6.6	5.5	18.4	18.1	. . .	. . .	4.3	0.4
1952	5.9	5.7	5.6	18.6	18.2	. . .	. . .	4.9	0.4
1953	6.7	6.6	5.6	19.4	19.0	. . .	. . .	5.1	0.4
1954	7.0	6.0	5.4	21.1	20.7	. . .	. . .	5.3	0.4
1955	7.2	7.5	6.4	25.0	24.6	. . .	. . .	6.0	0.4
1956	8.8	7.4	6.8	23.6	23.1	. . .	. . .	6.6	0.5
1957	9.6	8.3	6.7	22.2	21.7	. . .	. . .	6.6	0.5
1958	8.1	6.1	7.0	22.3	21.9	13.1	2.3	6.4	0.5
1959	8.4	8.3	7.6	28.1	27.5	16.7	3.0	7.9	0.6
1960	9.3	8.5	7.1	26.3	25.8	14.9	2.6	8.3	0.5
1961	8.7	8.0	7.1	26.4	25.9	14.1	3.3	8.5	0.5
1962	9.2	9.8	7.6	29.0	28.4	15.1	4.8	8.5	0.5
1963	10.0	9.4	8.9	32.1	31.5	16.0	6.4	9.1	0.6
1964	11.4	10.6	10.0	34.3	33.6	17.6	6.4	9.5	0.6
1965	13.6	13.2	11.2	34.2	33.5	17.8	6.0	9.7	0.7
1966	16.1	14.5	12.9	32.3	31.6	16.6	5.2	9.8	0.7
1967	16.8	14.3	12.6	32.4	31.6	16.8	4.7	10.1	0.7
1968	17.2	17.6	13.1	38.7	37.9	19.5	7.2	11.1	0.9
1969	18.9	18.9	14.5	42.6	41.6	19.7	9.5	12.4	1.0
1970	20.2	16.2	15.6	41.4	40.2	17.5	9.5	13.2	1.1
1971	19.4	18.4	16.4	55.8	54.5	25.8	12.9	15.8	1.3
1972	21.3	21.8	19.2	69.7	68.1	32.8	17.2	18.0	1.5
1973	25.9	26.6	22.8	75.3	73.6	35.2	19.4	19.0	1.7
1974	30.5	26.3	24.6	66.0	64.1	29.7	13.7	20.7	1.9
1975	31.1	25.2	27.9	62.7	60.8	29.6	6.7	24.5	1.9
1976	33.9	30.0	30.1	82.5	80.4	43.9	6.9	29.6	2.1
1977	39.2	39.3	37.1	110.3	107.9	62.2	10.0	35.7	2.4
1978	47.4	47.3	44.1	131.6	128.9	72.8	12.8	43.3	2.7
1979	55.9	53.6	48.6	141.0	137.9	72.3	17.0	48.6	3.2
1980	60.4	48.4	48.6	123.2	119.9	53.0	16.7	50.2	3.4
1981	65.2	50.6	55.6	122.6	119.0	52.0	17.5	49.5	0.0
1982	62.3	46.8	52.3	105.7	102.0	41.5	15.5	45.0	3.7
1983	58.4	53.7	51.8	152.5	148.3	72.2	22.4	53.7	4.2
1984	67.6	64.8	60.2	179.8	175.1	85.6	28.2	61.3	4.7
1985	71.9	69.7	61.8	186.9	181.9	86.1	28.5	67.2	5.1
1986	74.8	71.8	62.6	218.1	212.6	102.2	31.0	79.4	5.5
1987	76.1	70.4	66.2	227.6	221.8	114.5	25.5	81.9	5.8
1988	83.5	76.1	71.3	234.2	228.2	116.6	22.3	89.2	6.1
1989	92.7	71.4	83.0	231.8	225.7	116.9	22.3	86.5	6.1
1990	91.5	75.7	84.5	216.8	210.8	108.7	19.3	82.9	6.0
1991	88.7	79.5	75.8	191.5	185.8	95.4	15.1	75.2	5.7
1992	92.4	86.1	77.9	225.5	219.6	116.5	13.1	90.0	5.9
1993	101.8	98.1	87.9	251.8	245.4	133.3	10.8	101.3	6.4
1994	113.3	117.8	96.3	286.0	279.1	153.8	14.1	111.2	6.9
1995	128.7	126.1	103.7	285.6	278.3	145.0	17.9	115.4	7.3
1996	136.4	138.9	111.8	313.3	305.6	159.1	20.3	126.2	7.7
1997	141.0	151.4	126.0	328.2	320.4	163.2	22.9	134.3	7.9
1998	147.6	168.2	139.8	364.4	356.1	185.8	24.6	145.8	8.2
1999	150.4	194.7	142.4	403.7	394.8	208.6	27.4	158.8	8.8
2000	164.9	189.7	150.1	426.0	416.8	220.7	28.3	167.9	9.3
2001	159.0	165.8	148.0	444.8	435.4	232.1	30.7	172.7	9.3
2002	152.2	148.9	147.4	471.9	462.4	247.0	33.6	181.8	9.6
2000									
1st quarter	159.7	196.4	147.6	428.0	418.8	225.9	28.7	164.2	9.2
2nd quarter	163.2	195.5	152.0	428.8	419.5	223.1	29.1	167.3	9.3
3rd quarter	168.8	190.3	150.1	421.8	412.6	216.2	26.9	169.4	9.2
4th quarter	167.9	176.5	150.6	425.6	416.3	217.4	28.3	170.6	9.3
2001									
1st quarter	170.0	169.5	152.0	440.0	430.7	228.1	30.0	172.5	9.3
2nd quarter	161.8	162.7	147.7	444.2	435.0	231.6	30.4	173.0	9.2
3rd quarter	154.3	162.7	148.4	447.4	438.1	234.4	30.5	173.2	9.3
4th quarter	149.8	168.3	143.8	447.4	438.0	234.3	31.8	171.9	9.4
2002									
1st quarter	153.4	154.1	142.3	462.6	453.0	241.1	34.2	177.7	9.5
2nd quarter	150.5	145.2	148.0	468.7	459.2	244.3	34.2	180.7	9.6
3rd quarter	153.3	141.7	148.5	469.9	460.4	245.3	33.4	181.7	9.5
4th quarter	151.5	154.5	150.8	486.5	476.9	257.4	32.4	187.1	9.6

. . . = Not available.

Table 5-3. Real Gross Private Fixed Investment by Type

(Billions of chained [1996] dollars, quarterly data are at seasonally adjusted annual rates.)

Year and quarter	Total	Nonresidential									
		Total	Structures					Equipment and software			
			Total	Nonresidential buildings including farm	Utilities	Mining exploration, shafts, and wells	Other structures	Total	Information processing equipment and software		
									Computers and peripheral equipment [1]	Software [2]	Other
1987	856.0	572.5	224.3	162.6	34.9	18.6	8.2	360.0	10.3	27.9	78.0
1988	887.1	603.6	227.1	166.5	33.6	20.4	6.8	386.9	11.8	32.4	83.5
1989	911.2	637.0	232.7	171.4	35.4	18.4	7.5	414.0	14.4	40.1	86.8
1990	894.6	641.7	236.1	173.6	33.0	21.3	8.3	415.7	14.2	45.9	87.6
1991	832.5	610.1	210.1	142.7	38.9	20.8	7.8	407.2	15.4	51.4	86.4
1992	886.5	630.6	197.3	129.2	41.8	17.2	9.2	437.5	20.8	58.7	91.5
1993	958.4	683.6	198.9	131.7	38.4	20.5	8.5	487.1	26.4	66.8	96.4
1994	1 045.9	744.6	200.5	137.2	36.1	19.8	7.6	544.9	32.6	74.3	104.9
1995	1 109.2	817.5	210.1	147.6	36.8	18.2	7.5	607.6	49.2	82.0	113.1
1996	1 212.7	899.4	225.0	161.7	36.0	21.1	6.2	674.4	70.9	95.1	121.3
1997	1 328.6	1 009.3	245.4	177.0	35.3	26.2	6.8	764.2	102.9	119.0	129.8
1998	1 480.0	1 135.9	262.2	188.3	42.7	25.1	6.2	875.4	147.7	147.1	143.5
1999	1 595.2	1 228.4	258.6	185.5	45.7	21.6	6.4	975.9	207.4	169.3	157.5
2000	1 691.9	1 324.2	275.5	192.3	50.4	27.0	6.8	1 056.0	246.4	184.4	187.4
2001	1 627.4	1 255.1	270.9	178.7	50.3	34.0	9.3	988.2	239.9	182.0	163.9
2002	1 577.3	1 183.4	226.4	145.6	47.3	29.2	5.5	971.1	283.7	185.7	158.2
1991											
1st quarter	833.1	616.2	222.3	155.1	36.7	22.9	7.6	402.8	13.9	49.3	84.3
2nd quarter	829.5	611.9	216.6	148.1	38.4	22.6	7.5	403.4	14.4	50.8	86.3
3rd quarter	832.1	607.7	202.9	136.7	39.7	18.5	8.0	410.9	15.7	51.8	87.6
4th quarter	835.4	604.6	198.5	130.6	40.7	19.2	8.1	411.7	17.7	53.9	87.2
1992											
1st quarter	847.4	603.6	196.5	129.8	41.6	16.9	8.3	412.3	17.7	55.6	88.6
2nd quarter	881.4	626.1	196.2	128.6	42.0	16.2	9.3	434.1	20.5	57.8	89.7
3rd quarter	894.4	637.6	197.5	128.5	41.8	17.1	10.0	444.1	22.2	59.5	94.3
4th quarter	922.8	655.0	199.1	129.8	41.7	18.6	9.1	459.4	23.0	61.7	93.3
1993											
1st quarter	929.9	661.7	198.6	129.4	40.4	19.8	9.1	466.3	24.7	63.5	93.3
2nd quarter	944.3	676.6	197.6	131.0	38.3	19.5	8.9	481.4	25.3	65.5	94.3
3rd quarter	958.7	684.2	197.8	132.5	37.5	20.1	7.9	488.5	27.7	67.9	98.4
4th quarter	1 000.6	711.8	201.5	133.8	37.4	22.5	8.1	512.2	28.1	70.2	99.5
1994											
1st quarter	1 014.9	720.0	193.2	130.2	36.5	19.3	7.3	527.4	29.7	72.2	102.3
2nd quarter	1 039.9	734.1	202.9	140.7	35.7	19.2	7.4	532.6	31.2	73.7	103.4
3rd quarter	1 050.9	747.2	202.3	138.5	36.0	19.7	8.2	545.7	32.8	74.9	105.4
4th quarter	1 078.0	777.1	203.8	139.6	36.1	20.8	7.4	573.7	36.7	76.3	108.6
1995											
1st quarter	1 101.9	806.4	208.1	144.5	36.9	19.1	7.7	598.5	40.5	77.5	112.8
2nd quarter	1 095.0	811.4	211.0	148.3	37.3	17.6	7.8	600.7	47.0	80.1	113.9
3rd quarter	1 107.1	816.7	210.9	148.1	37.0	17.9	7.9	606.0	50.8	83.3	111.9
4th quarter	1 132.7	835.5	210.4	149.4	36.0	18.4	6.6	625.0	58.4	87.2	113.8
1996											
1st quarter	1 165.2	861.6	215.9	153.4	36.1	19.6	6.8	645.8	63.1	90.7	117.8
2nd quarter	1 203.7	885.6	221.3	158.3	35.7	21.0	6.4	664.3	67.9	93.6	119.7
3rd quarter	1 231.6	914.3	225.4	162.4	35.5	21.5	5.9	688.9	73.9	96.4	123.3
4th quarter	1 250.2	936.2	237.3	172.4	36.8	22.3	5.7	698.8	78.5	99.8	124.3
1997											
1st quarter	1 275.4	960.8	241.1	175.4	34.4	25.5	5.6	719.6	87.2	107.7	126.5
2nd quarter	1 311.1	992.7	239.3	172.8	34.4	26.1	5.7	753.7	98.1	115.3	127.4
3rd quarter	1 356.7	1 037.0	248.5	180.9	35.5	25.7	6.2	788.9	110.5	123.0	132.8
4th quarter	1 371.3	1 047.0	252.7	178.8	36.7	27.4	9.5	794.5	115.8	130.1	132.5
1998											
1st quarter	1 431.4	1 099.5	255.7	184.1	40.6	24.9	6.3	845.0	132.7	138.8	138.9
2nd quarter	1 471.4	1 132.3	264.8	189.6	43.0	26.0	6.5	868.6	142.4	144.6	143.0
3rd quarter	1 485.4	1 136.6	263.0	187.5	43.7	25.9	6.1	875.1	147.7	150.0	144.4
4th quarter	1 531.7	1 175.4	265.1	191.9	43.7	23.7	6.1	912.9	167.7	155.0	147.9
1999											
1st quarter	1 560.5	1 197.5	262.4	192.1	44.1	20.4	6.2	939.1	186.1	160.2	151.1
2nd quarter	1 587.6	1 220.4	258.9	186.0	44.3	21.9	7.1	967.1	209.2	167.8	157.1
3rd quarter	1 610.6	1 243.3	254.7	182.3	46.2	20.8	6.0	996.1	218.8	172.5	160.7
4th quarter	1 622.2	1 252.4	258.5	181.7	48.3	23.1	6.2	1 001.2	215.3	176.8	161.2
2000											
1st quarter	1 673.6	1 297.1	267.0	188.4	48.3	24.5	6.5	1 038.0	226.7	181.8	180.2
2nd quarter	1 700.9	1 329.1	272.3	192.4	49.3	25.0	6.4	1 065.3	249.2	184.3	188.2
3rd quarter	1 701.7	1 340.7	280.2	194.5	51.1	28.6	7.1	1 067.7	255.9	185.8	189.1
4th quarter	1 691.3	1 329.9	282.7	193.9	52.9	30.1	7.1	1 053.1	253.9	185.6	192.2
2001											
1st quarter	1 682.1	1 311.4	280.4	193.8	50.6	30.9	6.3	1 036.1	253.0	185.5	180.2
2nd quarter	1 633.5	1 261.0	274.4	183.2	51.5	34.6	6.1	989.9	239.0	181.7	165.7
3rd quarter	1 615.7	1 241.7	276.3	174.2	49.7	35.9	18.3	966.4	224.5	180.5	158.6
4th quarter	1 578.4	1 206.4	252.7	163.5	49.3	34.8	6.3	960.2	243.3	180.6	151.2
2002											
1st quarter	1 576.4	1 188.4	243.2	157.1	50.8	30.2	6.3	953.7	262.1	179.0	154.1
2nd quarter	1 572.6	1 181.1	231.7	148.2	48.4	30.3	6.3	961.4	271.6	184.3	158.5
3rd quarter	1 571.6	1 178.7	218.2	139.1	45.6	29.9	5.0	977.2	297.6	189.4	159.7
4th quarter	1 588.5	1 185.3	212.6	137.8	44.6	26.5	4.6	992.1	303.2	190.3	160.7

[1]New computers and peripheral equipment only.
[2]Excludes software "embedded," or bundled, in computers and other equipment.

Table 5-3. Real Gross Private Fixed Investment by Type—*Continued*

(Billions of chained [1996] dollars, quarterly data are at seasonally adjusted annual rates.)

| Year and quarter | Nonresidential—*Continued* | | | | Residential | | | | |
| | Equipment and software—*Continued* | | | | Structures | | | | Equipment |
	Industrial equipment	Transportation equipment	Other equipment	Total	Total	New single family	New multifamily	Other structures	
1987	99.9	88.0	83.8	290.7	284.7	149.5	29.3	104.9	6.1
1988	104.9	93.6	87.7	289.2	283.0	146.9	25.0	110.5	6.3
1989	112.4	84.9	98.1	277.3	271.0	142.0	24.9	103.4	6.4
1990	105.8	87.4	96.2	253.5	247.3	128.6	21.7	96.4	6.2
1991	99.0	87.7	83.6	221.1	215.1	112.3	16.8	85.6	5.9
1992	100.8	92.3	84.1	257.2	251.0	135.7	14.2	100.9	6.1
1993	109.6	103.4	93.3	276.0	269.4	148.0	11.5	109.9	6.5
1994	119.6	120.4	100.6	302.7	295.8	163.2	14.8	117.7	6.9
1995	131.3	128.2	106.2	291.7	284.4	147.7	18.4	118.3	7.4
1996	136.4	138.9	111.8	313.3	305.6	159.1	20.3	126.2	7.7
1997	140.0	150.5	124.7	319.7	311.8	158.6	21.9	131.3	7.9
1998	145.6	168.2	136.5	345.1	336.8	175.9	21.7	139.3	8.3
1999	147.5	193.2	137.7	368.3	359.4	189.0	23.4	147.0	9.0
2000	160.8	186.6	144.5	372.4	363.0	191.0	23.0	149.1	9.4
2001	153.8	163.6	140.7	373.5	364.0	192.6	24.4	146.9	9.5
2002	146.9	147.0	139.3	388.2	378.5	200.5	26.3	151.6	9.7
1991									
1st quarter	100.6	88.8	85.2	214.7	208.6	103.6	19.3	85.1	5.9
2nd quarter	99.3	86.2	84.1	215.6	209.4	105.9	16.9	86.1	6.1
3rd quarter	99.1	90.0	82.6	223.4	217.4	117.5	15.4	84.3	5.9
4th quarter	97.3	86.0	82.4	230.6	224.7	122.2	15.4	86.9	5.8
1992									
1st quarter	97.4	83.1	82.4	245.0	238.9	128.8	14.6	95.3	6.1
2nd quarter	99.0	96.0	82.1	256.6	250.5	135.8	16.4	98.1	6.1
3rd quarter	101.5	90.9	85.0	257.9	251.8	136.9	13.5	101.2	6.1
4th quarter	105.5	99.2	86.9	269.2	263.0	141.4	12.4	109.1	6.2
1993									
1st quarter	106.8	96.1	90.8	269.5	263.1	143.8	11.2	108.1	6.4
2nd quarter	107.2	106.3	92.4	268.6	262.1	143.9	11.0	107.2	6.5
3rd quarter	108.9	99.8	93.4	275.7	269.0	147.8	12.0	109.2	6.7
4th quarter	115.6	111.4	96.6	290.1	283.4	156.6	11.7	115.2	6.7
1994									
1st quarter	116.7	117.4	97.9	296.5	289.8	162.4	12.4	115.0	6.7
2nd quarter	117.1	115.0	99.9	307.5	300.6	168.3	14.1	118.2	6.9
3rd quarter	120.5	118.2	101.3	305.2	298.2	163.6	15.9	118.6	7.0
4th quarter	124.3	131.1	103.3	301.8	294.6	158.6	16.9	119.1	7.2
1995									
1st quarter	129.3	137.3	106.6	295.8	288.5	152.7	17.7	118.1	7.3
2nd quarter	131.8	124.7	105.9	283.5	276.3	143.0	17.6	115.7	7.2
3rd quarter	132.7	123.3	105.6	290.4	283.0	144.8	18.9	119.3	7.4
4th quarter	131.6	127.5	106.7	297.3	289.7	150.3	19.3	120.1	7.5
1996									
1st quarter	135.6	130.2	108.3	303.6	296.1	154.5	20.2	121.4	7.5
2nd quarter	138.0	134.7	110.2	318.1	310.4	161.5	21.9	127.1	7.7
3rd quarter	135.7	145.8	113.8	317.3	309.7	161.8	19.3	128.5	7.7
4th quarter	136.5	144.9	115.0	314.0	306.3	158.7	19.9	127.6	7.8
1997									
1st quarter	134.9	144.5	119.5	314.7	307.0	157.2	21.4	128.3	7.8
2nd quarter	140.2	150.8	123.7	318.7	310.8	158.7	22.2	130.0	7.8
3rd quarter	141.8	156.2	128.0	320.3	312.4	158.2	21.3	132.9	7.9
4th quarter	143.2	150.3	127.5	324.9	316.9	160.2	22.7	134.0	8.0
1998									
1st quarter	148.7	161.2	133.1	333.0	325.0	165.6	22.6	136.6	8.1
2nd quarter	145.6	166.4	137.7	340.5	332.2	172.5	21.2	138.6	8.3
3rd quarter	143.3	164.2	138.7	349.5	341.2	180.2	21.2	140.0	8.3
4th quarter	144.8	181.0	136.7	357.4	349.0	185.5	21.6	142.0	8.4
1999									
1st quarter	142.5	188.1	138.9	364.1	355.4	188.4	23.2	143.7	8.7
2nd quarter	146.9	188.6	136.0	368.4	359.5	187.3	23.1	149.2	9.0
3rd quarter	150.1	199.1	136.3	369.2	360.1	187.4	23.7	149.0	9.2
4th quarter	150.5	196.8	139.5	371.7	362.5	192.8	23.4	146.3	9.2
2000									
1st quarter	156.0	193.9	142.6	379.1	369.7	198.0	23.6	148.1	9.4
2nd quarter	159.3	192.5	146.5	376.2	366.8	193.8	23.7	149.3	9.4
3rd quarter	164.5	186.9	144.4	367.2	357.8	186.5	21.8	149.7	9.4
4th quarter	163.4	173.0	144.6	367.2	357.8	185.8	22.8	149.3	9.5
2001									
1st quarter	164.8	167.6	145.1	374.5	365.1	192.0	24.1	148.9	9.5
2nd quarter	156.4	161.6	140.6	374.0	364.6	193.1	24.3	147.2	9.4
3rd quarter	149.2	160.0	141.0	374.3	365.0	194.1	24.3	146.5	9.4
4th quarter	144.7	165.4	136.2	371.0	361.5	191.3	25.1	145.1	9.6
2002									
1st quarter	148.3	151.5	134.6	383.6	373.9	197.2	27.0	149.6	9.7
2nd quarter	145.6	143.4	140.1	386.1	376.4	198.4	26.8	151.0	9.7
3rd quarter	147.9	141.7	140.3	387.1	377.4	199.8	26.2	151.3	9.7
4th quarter	145.9	151.4	142.3	395.9	386.1	206.5	25.1	154.4	9.8

Table 5-4. Chain-Type Quantity Indexes for Private Fixed Investment by Type

(Index numbers, 1996 = 100)

Year and quarter	Total	Nonresidential										
		Total	Structures					Equipment and software				
			Total	Nonresidential buildings including farm	Utilities	Mining exploration, shafts, and wells	Other structures	Total	Information processing equipment and software			
									Computers and peripheral equipment [1]	Software [2]	Other	
1947	15.2	12.2	29.1	19.7	58.7	31.9	76.0	8.1	. . .	. . .	4.0	
1948	16.8	12.8	30.6	20.2	66.6	39.1	41.6	8.5	. . .	. . .	4.1	
1949	15.3	11.7	29.6	18.9	68.1	39.6	27.3	7.5	. . .	. . .	3.7	
1950	18.3	12.7	31.8	21.4	66.1	47.0	26.4	8.3	. . .	. . .	4.0	
1951	17.5	13.3	34.2	24.5	67.4	49.2	12.8	8.5	. . .	. . .	4.4	
1952	17.2	13.1	34.0	23.1	69.1	54.9	15.5	8.3	. . .	. . .	5.1	
1953	18.4	14.2	37.1	25.5	73.5	60.0	19.8	9.0	. . .	. . .	5.7	
1954	18.7	13.9	38.3	28.3	65.7	66.4	20.4	8.5	. . .	. . .	5.1	
1955	21.2	15.5	41.1	31.4	62.1	71.4	49.7	9.7	. . .	. . .	5.8	
1956	21.2	16.4	45.4	36.8	71.3	69.1	10.9	9.9	. . .	. . .	6.7	
1957	21.0	16.6	45.4	36.6	72.5	65.2	24.3	10.2	. . .	. . .	7.7	
1958	19.5	14.8	42.6	34.7	66.9	61.0	23.9	8.7	. . .	. . .	6.9	
1959	22.2	15.9	43.7	37.0	63.8	62.6	16.0	9.7	0.0	0.0	7.5	
1960	22.4	16.8	47.1	42.3	64.5	58.8	20.9	10.2	0.0	0.2	8.5	
1961	22.3	16.7	47.8	44.7	59.8	59.8	9.3	10.0	0.0	0.3	9.0	
1962	24.3	18.2	49.9	47.6	60.1	62.8	2.6	11.1	0.0	0.4	9.6	
1963	26.2	19.2	50.5	47.7	64.5	58.9	4.6	12.0	0.0	0.7	9.9	
1964	28.7	21.5	55.7	53.0	70.1	63.1	9.3	13.6	0.0	0.9	10.8	
1965	31.7	25.2	64.6	63.2	77.1	62.4	29.2	16.1	0.0	1.1	12.3	
1966	33.5	28.4	69.0	66.6	87.9	59.1	43.5	18.6	0.0	1.6	14.4	
1967	32.8	28.0	67.3	62.6	94.3	56.5	47.2	18.5	0.0	1.9	14.4	
1968	35.1	29.2	68.2	60.9	105.2	56.8	54.7	19.6	0.0	2.0	15.0	
1969	37.3	31.4	71.9	65.5	105.4	59.2	61.6	21.3	0.0	2.7	17.4	
1970	36.5	31.2	72.1	64.3	112.8	55.7	64.2	21.1	0.1	3.4	18.8	
1971	39.3	31.2	70.9	63.2	114.0	51.5	57.1	21.3	0.1	3.5	18.9	
1972	44.0	34.0	73.1	64.9	118.9	55.3	50.1	24.0	0.1	4.0	19.9	
1973	48.0	39.0	79.1	70.9	126.3	59.0	52.0	28.4	0.1	4.5	24.2	
1974	45.0	39.3	77.4	68.9	119.0	70.2	52.5	29.1	0.2	5.1	26.6	
1975	40.1	35.4	69.3	58.3	108.8	81.9	50.8	26.4	0.2	5.9	25.5	
1976	44.1	37.1	71.0	56.9	120.0	88.5	50.0	28.0	0.2	6.3	28.0	
1977	50.4	41.3	74.0	59.1	119.1	99.9	61.9	32.2	0.3	6.5	33.5	
1978	56.2	47.2	82.7	67.3	126.3	113.9	72.2	37.1	0.7	7.7	40.2	
1979	59.4	51.9	93.1	80.3	130.4	121.4	79.8	40.3	1.1	9.6	45.6	
1980	55.6	51.9	99.2	80.8	130.3	170.5	70.6	38.9	1.7	11.1	49.7	
1981	56.8	54.8	107.1	86.7	132.9	198.2	67.6	40.5	2.6	12.7	52.5	
1982	52.8	52.7	105.5	89.4	124.8	183.2	71.1	38.4	3.2	14.5	52.4	
1983	56.8	52.2	94.5	83.0	108.2	151.7	77.7	40.5	4.9	16.7	55.1	
1984	66.3	61.4	108.0	97.2	111.9	172.5	104.4	48.4	8.0	20.4	62.1	
1985	69.8	65.5	115.9	109.6	112.6	153.7	148.7	51.5	10.1	23.7	64.3	
1986	70.6	63.7	103.4	102.0	115.2	90.0	119.6	52.5	11.6	26.1	67.0	
1987	70.6	63.7	99.7	100.6	96.9	88.0	132.1	53.4	14.6	29.4	64.3	
1988	73.2	67.1	101.0	103.0	93.2	96.6	109.0	57.4	16.7	34.0	68.9	
1989	75.1	70.8	103.4	106.0	98.2	87.3	120.4	61.4	20.3	42.1	71.6	
1990	73.8	71.4	105.0	107.4	91.6	100.9	133.2	61.6	20.0	48.2	72.2	
1991	68.7	67.8	93.4	88.3	107.9	98.6	126.0	60.4	21.8	54.1	71.2	
1992	73.1	70.1	87.7	79.9	115.9	81.6	148.0	64.9	29.4	61.7	75.5	
1993	79.0	76.0	88.4	81.5	106.5	97.2	136.9	72.2	37.3	70.2	79.5	
1994	86.3	82.8	89.1	84.9	100.1	93.8	122.0	80.8	46.0	78.1	86.5	
1995	91.5	90.9	93.4	91.3	102.1	86.4	120.8	90.1	69.4	86.2	93.3	
1996	100.0	100.0	100.0	100.0	100.0	100.0	100.0	100.0	100.0	100.0	100.0	
1997	109.6	112.2	109.1	109.5	97.8	124.2	108.9	113.3	145.2	125.1	107.0	
1998	122.0	126.3	116.5	116.5	118.6	119.1	100.6	129.8	208.4	154.6	118.4	
1999	131.5	136.6	115.0	114.8	126.9	102.3	102.5	144.7	292.6	178.0	129.9	
2000	139.5	147.2	122.5	118.9	139.9	128.1	109.1	156.6	347.8	193.8	154.6	
2001	134.2	139.6	120.4	110.5	139.5	161.4	149.2	146.5	338.6	191.4	135.2	
2002	130.1	131.6	100.6	90.0	131.3	138.6	89.3	144.0	400.3	195.2	130.5	
2000												
1st quarter	138.0	144.2	118.7	116.6	134.0	116.0	104.9	153.9	320.0	191.1	148.6	
2nd quarter	140.3	147.8	121.0	119.0	136.9	118.3	102.7	158.0	351.8	193.7	155.2	
3rd quarter	140.3	149.1	124.5	120.3	141.9	135.5	113.8	158.3	361.1	195.3	156.0	
4th quarter	139.5	147.9	125.6	119.9	146.8	142.6	114.8	156.1	358.3	195.1	158.5	
2001												
1st quarter	138.7	145.8	124.6	119.9	140.5	146.6	101.9	153.6	357.0	194.9	148.6	
2nd quarter	134.7	140.2	122.0	113.3	142.9	163.9	98.8	146.8	337.3	190.9	136.6	
3rd quarter	133.2	138.1	122.8	107.7	137.8	170.2	294.7	143.3	316.9	189.7	130.8	
4th quarter	130.2	134.1	112.3	101.1	136.9	164.8	101.3	142.4	343.3	189.8	124.7	
2002												
1st quarter	130.0	132.1	108.1	97.2	141.0	143.2	101.8	141.4	369.9	188.1	127.0	
2nd quarter	129.7	131.3	103.0	91.7	134.2	143.6	101.0	142.6	383.4	193.7	130.7	
3rd quarter	129.6	131.1	97.0	86.1	126.5	142.0	80.0	144.9	420.1	199.1	131.7	
4th quarter	131.0	131.8	94.5	85.3	123.7	125.8	74.4	147.1	427.9	200.0	132.5	

[1]New computers and peripheral equipment only.
[2]Excludes software "embedded," or bundled, in computers and other equipment.
. . . = Not available.

Table 5-4. Chain-Type Quantity Indexes for Private Fixed Investment by Type—*Continued*

(Index numbers, 1996 = 100)

| Year and quarter | Nonresidential—*Continued* | | | | Residential | | | | | |
| | Equipment and software—*Continued* | | | Total | Structures | | | | | Equipment |
	Industrial equipment	Transportation equipment	Other equipment		Total	New single family	New multifamily	Other structures	
1947	30.2	18.6	25.7	26.7	27.5	. . .	. . .	. . .	6.9
1948	27.9	19.3	31.2	31.9	33.0	. . .	. . .	. . .	7.2
1949	21.5	19.2	26.2	29.5	30.5	. . .	. . .	. . .	6.8
1950	24.9	21.3	27.7	40.3	41.8	. . .	. . .	. . .	8.5
1951	28.0	20.4	27.9	33.8	34.9	. . .	. . .	. . .	7.9
1952	29.1	16.9	28.2	33.2	34.3	. . .	. . .	. . .	7.8
1953	32.1	20.1	27.4	34.3	35.5	. . .	. . .	. . .	8.2
1954	33.1	17.6	25.9	37.2	38.5	. . .	. . .	. . .	8.5
1955	32.9	22.4	30.5	43.2	44.7	. . .	. . .	. . .	9.6
1956	36.3	20.1	31.6	39.7	40.9	. . .	. . .	. . .	10.7
1957	36.7	21.5	29.8	37.3	38.4	. . .	. . .	. . .	10.7
1958	30.5	15.7	30.1	37.7	38.7	. . .	. . .	. . .	11.4
1959	31.0	20.7	32.4	47.3	48.7	56.6	75.3	33.0	13.6
1960	33.6	21.4	29.8	43.9	45.2	50.1	66.3	34.3	12.8
1961	31.8	20.2	29.5	44.0	45.3	47.4	83.5	35.0	12.8
1962	33.4	24.9	31.5	48.2	49.7	50.6	121.4	35.2	13.6
1963	36.1	24.1	36.7	53.9	55.6	54.0	163.0	38.0	15.2
1964	40.8	27.3	40.7	57.1	58.8	59.3	161.9	39.3	16.2
1965	48.1	34.2	45.1	55.4	56.9	57.9	145.5	39.3	18.2
1966	55.3	37.6	50.8	50.4	51.7	51.6	122.0	38.7	18.6
1967	55.6	36.3	48.2	48.8	50.0	50.6	106.0	38.6	19.0
1968	54.5	43.7	48.4	55.5	56.8	55.6	153.1	40.6	22.7
1969	58.1	45.4	51.6	57.1	58.3	52.8	190.5	41.5	25.9
1970	59.0	37.3	53.7	53.7	54.6	45.9	186.4	41.9	28.2
1971	54.2	40.3	53.7	68.5	69.8	63.6	237.3	47.7	31.6
1972	58.4	46.8	61.2	80.6	82.2	75.7	297.1	52.3	37.9
1973	69.0	56.2	71.2	80.1	81.4	74.0	305.4	51.1	42.6
1974	74.3	50.9	70.7	63.6	64.2	56.8	196.6	49.7	43.4
1975	62.9	43.9	65.8	55.3	55.7	51.9	87.7	53.9	40.4
1976	63.2	48.8	66.2	68.3	69.2	72.2	85.0	61.1	42.5
1977	67.0	59.3	75.0	83.0	84.2	92.8	112.6	66.8	46.6
1978	74.5	65.5	82.4	88.3	89.5	95.9	126.9	73.2	50.6
1979	79.9	68.4	83.2	85.0	86.0	85.0	155.0	73.9	55.5
1980	76.5	55.8	74.0	67.1	67.4	55.9	138.8	69.0	55.5
1981	75.3	54.3	76.0	61.7	61.9	50.9	133.4	62.8	55.5
1982	68.7	48.1	66.6	50.5	50.3	39.0	108.8	54.2	53.3
1983	63.1	54.3	64.4	71.2	71.5	67.3	148.9	62.9	59.5
1984	72.2	64.7	73.6	81.6	82.0	77.8	182.0	69.5	66.0
1985	75.5	67.6	74.1	82.7	83.0	76.7	177.3	74.0	71.2
1986	75.1	65.7	72.7	92.6	93.0	87.4	182.6	84.1	77.0
1987	73.2	63.4	74.9	92.8	93.2	94.0	144.0	83.2	80.1
1988	76.9	67.4	78.4	92.3	92.6	92.3	122.9	87.6	82.8
1989	82.4	61.1	87.7	88.5	88.7	89.2	122.6	82.0	83.3
1990	77.6	62.9	86.0	80.9	80.9	80.8	107.0	76.4	80.8
1991	72.6	63.2	74.8	70.6	70.4	70.6	82.4	67.8	77.6
1992	73.9	66.5	75.2	82.1	82.2	85.3	70.1	80.0	80.0
1993	80.3	74.4	83.4	88.1	88.2	93.0	56.5	87.1	85.5
1994	87.7	86.7	90.0	96.6	96.8	102.6	73.0	93.3	90.7
1995	96.3	92.3	95.0	93.1	93.1	92.8	90.5	93.8	96.3
1996	100.0	100.0	100.0	100.0	100.0	100.0	100.0	100.0	100.0
1997	102.6	108.3	111.5	102.0	102.0	99.7	107.7	104.1	102.9
1998	106.7	121.1	122.1	110.2	110.2	110.6	106.5	110.4	108.2
1999	108.1	139.1	123.1	117.6	117.6	118.8	115.0	116.6	117.5
2000	117.9	134.3	129.2	118.9	118.8	120.1	113.0	118.2	123.3
2001	112.7	117.8	125.8	119.2	119.1	121.1	120.2	116.5	123.7
2002	107.7	105.8	124.6	123.9	123.8	126.0	129.4	120.2	127.3
2000									
1st quarter	114.4	139.6	127.6	121.0	121.0	124.4	116.2	117.4	123.4
2nd quarter	116.8	138.6	131.0	120.1	120.0	121.8	116.5	118.4	123.3
3rd quarter	120.6	134.5	129.1	117.2	117.1	117.2	107.4	118.6	122.8
4th quarter	119.8	124.5	129.3	117.2	117.1	116.8	112.2	118.3	123.8
2001									
1st quarter	120.8	120.6	129.8	119.6	119.5	120.7	118.5	118.1	123.5
2nd quarter	114.6	116.3	125.7	119.4	119.3	121.3	119.5	116.7	123.0
3rd quarter	109.3	115.2	126.1	119.5	119.4	122.0	119.6	116.2	123.1
4th quarter	106.0	119.1	121.8	118.4	118.3	120.2	123.3	115.0	125.1
2002									
1st quarter	108.7	109.0	120.4	122.4	122.4	123.9	132.8	118.6	126.4
2nd quarter	106.7	103.2	125.3	123.3	123.2	124.7	132.0	119.7	127.3
3rd quarter	108.4	102.0	125.5	123.6	123.5	125.5	129.1	120.0	127.2
4th quarter	106.9	109.0	127.3	126.4	126.3	129.8	123.5	122.4	128.2

. . . = Not available.

Table 5-5. Current-Cost Net Stock of Fixed Assets

(Billions of dollars, year-end estimates.)

Year	Total	Private				Government				Private and government fixed assets				Government, by level	
		Total	Nonresidential		Residential	Total	Nonresidential		Residential	Total	Nonresidential		Residential	Federal	State and local
			Equipment and software	Structures			Equipment and software	Structures			Equipment and software	Structures			
1939	306.5	245.1	29.4	97.2	118.5	61.4	3.6	57.5	0.3	306.5	33.0	154.7	118.8	14.0	47.4
1940	329.6	262.2	31.7	102.2	128.3	67.4	4.0	62.9	0.6	329.6	35.6	165.1	128.9	15.7	51.7
1941	373.9	289.5	35.8	112.7	141.0	84.4	7.8	75.5	1.1	373.9	43.6	188.2	142.1	24.4	60.0
1942	428.4	310.4	36.7	121.8	152.0	118.0	22.3	94.1	1.7	428.4	58.9	215.8	153.7	50.9	67.1
1943	477.3	326.3	36.3	125.8	164.2	150.9	47.3	101.0	2.6	477.3	83.6	226.8	166.8	82.7	68.2
1944	517.6	344.1	37.4	129.9	176.7	173.5	69.2	101.3	3.0	517.6	106.6	231.2	179.7	106.8	66.7
1945	561.5	374.8	42.6	141.9	190.3	186.7	74.1	109.3	3.3	561.5	116.6	251.2	193.6	117.4	69.2
1946	639.9	445.7	52.1	169.0	224.7	194.2	64.6	125.4	4.2	639.9	116.7	294.3	228.9	116.6	77.6
1947	744.1	529.5	65.2	198.5	265.8	214.7	61.8	146.4	6.5	744.1	127.0	344.9	272.3	121.7	93.0
1948	796.5	582.2	77.2	214.2	290.8	214.2	52.1	157.1	5.0	796.5	129.4	371.3	295.8	113.0	101.2
1949	811.1	611.5	85.3	218.8	307.4	199.6	44.2	150.0	5.4	811.1	129.4	368.9	312.8	103.0	96.6
1950	883.2	671.5	96.9	235.1	339.5	211.7	40.5	164.5	6.7	883.2	137.4	399.6	346.2	102.7	109.0
1951	972.8	735.9	108.3	257.6	370.0	236.9	44.2	184.4	8.3	972.8	152.5	442.0	378.3	114.3	122.6
1952	1 030.4	776.3	115.5	270.9	390.0	254.1	50.7	195.8	7.6	1 030.4	166.2	466.7	397.5	124.2	129.9
1953	1 067.6	808.0	123.5	278.2	406.2	259.7	57.5	193.7	8.5	1 067.6	181.0	472.0	414.7	131.1	128.6
1954	1 117.6	842.2	129.6	285.5	427.2	275.4	64.0	200.4	11.0	1 117.6	193.6	485.9	438.2	141.2	134.3
1955	1 202.1	905.7	142.2	306.2	457.2	296.5	69.4	219.5	7.6	1 202.1	211.6	525.7	464.8	147.4	149.1
1956	1 305.0	976.1	158.8	335.7	481.6	328.9	74.0	245.8	9.1	1 305.0	232.8	581.5	490.7	159.8	169.1
1957	1 365.7	1 022.7	172.8	353.6	496.3	343.0	76.2	257.3	9.5	1 365.7	249.0	610.8	505.8	165.9	177.1
1958	1 416.8	1 055.2	179.7	363.5	512.0	361.6	77.9	273.3	10.4	1 416.8	257.6	636.8	522.4	172.3	189.3
1959	1 471.6	1 099.4	188.7	376.3	534.5	372.2	82.3	278.5	11.3	1 471.6	271.0	654.8	545.8	176.5	195.7
1960	1 516.9	1 131.4	194.8	381.0	555.6	385.5	85.2	288.4	12.0	1 516.9	280.0	669.4	567.5	180.5	205.0
1961	1 572.3	1 167.4	199.0	392.4	576.0	404.9	89.1	303.1	12.7	1 572.3	288.1	695.5	588.7	187.6	217.3
1962	1 640.3	1 209.0	206.5	405.1	597.5	431.3	96.4	321.2	13.6	1 640.3	302.9	726.3	611.1	198.7	232.6
1963	1 698.3	1 245.5	215.7	417.1	612.7	452.8	99.1	339.9	13.9	1 698.3	314.8	757.0	626.5	204.7	248.1
1964	1 804.9	1 330.3	228.5	439.9	661.9	474.7	102.0	357.9	14.8	1 804.9	330.5	797.8	676.6	210.0	264.7
1965	1 923.2	1 418.1	246.0	468.5	703.6	505.0	104.6	384.9	15.5	1 923.2	350.6	853.5	719.1	216.9	288.1
1966	2 085.0	1 538.7	273.8	504.2	760.7	546.3	110.0	419.8	16.5	2 085.0	383.8	923.9	777.2	228.1	318.2
1967	2 240.4	1 649.2	300.8	537.2	811.1	591.3	117.4	456.5	17.4	2 240.4	418.2	993.7	828.5	243.5	347.7
1968	2 458.0	1 815.7	332.5	586.1	897.1	642.3	122.9	499.8	19.6	2 458.0	455.5	1 085.8	916.7	256.2	386.1
1969	2 681.6	1 973.7	368.2	645.0	960.5	707.8	128.1	557.9	21.7	2 681.6	496.4	1 202.9	982.3	271.7	436.1
1970	2 918.1	2 129.6	404.6	709.3	1 015.7	788.6	135.1	630.2	23.2	2 918.1	539.7	1 339.6	1 038.9	290.9	497.6
1971	3 224.4	2 366.4	434.5	791.1	1 140.8	858.0	140.3	691.7	26.0	3 224.4	574.8	1 482.8	1 166.8	308.6	549.4
1972	3 553.9	2 613.5	468.4	866.2	1 278.9	940.3	150.7	760.5	29.2	3 553.9	619.0	1 626.7	1 308.1	338.2	602.1
1973	4 022.2	2 968.2	525.2	975.1	1 467.8	1 054.0	152.2	868.9	32.9	4 022.2	677.4	1 844.0	1 500.8	363.9	690.2
1974	4 776.0	3 489.4	648.8	1 172.9	1 667.7	1 286.5	160.7	1 089.1	36.8	4 776.0	809.4	2 262.0	1 704.5	411.4	875.2
1975	5 167.3	3 815.2	740.5	1 269.6	1 805.1	1 352.2	176.6	1 135.3	40.3	5 167.3	917.1	2 404.8	1 845.4	436.5	915.7
1976	5 633.5	4 207.5	818.9	1 385.1	2 003.4	1 426.0	189.8	1 191.3	45.0	5 633.5	1 008.7	2 576.4	2 048.4	470.4	955.6
1977	6 301.2	4 787.4	920.3	1 528.7	2 338.5	1 513.8	204.7	1 257.3	51.8	6 301.2	1 125.0	2 786.0	2 390.2	493.2	1 020.6
1978	7 123.3	5 473.0	1 048.0	1 724.8	2 700.2	1 650.4	215.2	1 375.4	59.7	7 123.3	1 263.2	3 100.2	2 760.0	528.4	1 122.0
1979	8 216.9	6 339.9	1 220.9	1 981.7	3 137.3	1 877.0	230.4	1 575.5	71.1	8 216.9	1 451.3	3 557.2	3 208.4	586.7	1 290.2
1980	9 363.4	7 212.7	1 420.1	2 255.8	3 536.8	2 150.7	256.5	1 816.2	78.0	9 363.4	1 676.6	4 072.0	3 614.7	652.7	1 497.9
1981	10 321.1	7 949.7	1 575.6	2 570.2	3 804.0	2 371.3	294.7	1 991.1	85.5	10 321.1	1 870.4	4 561.3	3 889.4	709.1	1 662.2
1982	10 884.6	8 376.1	1 665.7	2 737.0	3 973.4	2 508.5	324.5	2 093.4	90.7	10 884.6	1 990.2	4 830.4	4 064.0	752.5	1 756.0
1983	11 234.8	8 667.6	1 724.2	2 808.5	4 134.8	2 567.2	356.7	2 110.0	100.5	11 234.8	2 080.9	4 918.6	4 235.3	791.3	1 775.9
1984	11 832.0	9 163.5	1 814.4	2 980.2	4 368.9	2 668.6	376.5	2 187.0	105.1	11 832.0	2 190.9	5 167.2	4 473.9	826.5	1 842.1
1985	12 439.8	9 657.8	1 920.6	3 135.8	4 601.3	2 782.1	397.1	2 278.8	106.2	12 439.8	2 317.8	5 414.5	4 707.5	855.6	1 926.5
1986	13 215.2	10 266.6	2 035.1	3 263.7	4 967.8	2 948.6	422.1	2 416.5	110.1	13 215.2	2 457.2	5 680.1	5 077.9	895.5	2 053.1
1987	13 959.9	10 857.3	2 130.6	3 443.4	5 283.3	3 102.6	445.1	2 537.5	120.0	13 959.9	2 575.7	5 980.9	5 403.3	929.5	2 173.2
1988	14 803.1	11 540.9	2 264.9	3 669.9	5 606.1	3 262.2	479.3	2 647.2	135.7	14 803.1	2 744.2	6 317.1	5 741.8	985.9	2 276.3
1989	15 636.0	12 197.2	2 400.2	3 884.8	5 912.2	3 438.7	515.8	2 778.0	144.9	15 636.0	2 916.1	6 662.8	6 057.1	1 039.5	2 399.3
1990	16 371.9	12 760.3	2 541.9	4 080.7	6 137.7	3 611.6	558.8	2 903.1	149.7	16 371.9	3 100.7	6 983.8	6 287.4	1 087.1	2 524.5
1991	16 753.9	13 021.5	2 622.8	4 137.7	6 261.0	3 732.4	590.4	2 991.2	150.8	16 753.9	3 213.2	7 128.9	6 411.8	1 129.8	2 602.6
1992	17 477.3	13 582.6	2 708.2	4 278.6	6 595.8	3 894.6	619.1	3 116.0	159.6	17 477.3	3 327.2	7 394.6	6 755.5	1 176.0	2 718.6
1993	18 403.6	14 318.0	2 828.6	4 498.5	6 991.0	4 085.6	644.8	3 269.9	170.9	18 403.6	3 473.4	7 768.4	7 161.9	1 229.0	2 856.7
1994	19 526.1	15 203.7	2 992.4	4 739.1	7 472.2	4 322.4	672.0	3 468.2	182.3	19 526.1	3 664.4	8 207.2	7 654.5	1 279.2	3 043.2
1995	20 441.5	15 908.5	3 182.8	4 941.4	7 784.2	4 533.0	685.6	3 658.6	188.8	20 441.5	3 868.4	8 600.0	7 973.1	1 314.4	3 218.6
1996	21 447.3	16 722.5	3 352.2	5 175.0	8 195.3	4 724.8	691.9	3 836.7	196.2	21 447.3	4 044.1	9 011.7	8 391.5	1 343.2	3 381.5
1997	22 596.0	17 653.1	3 519.8	5 487.0	8 646.3	4 942.9	693.5	4 045.6	203.8	22 596.0	4 213.3	9 532.6	8 850.1	1 367.0	3 575.9
1998	23 791.3	18 649.6	3 711.6	5 746.2	9 191.8	5 141.7	697.7	4 230.7	213.3	23 791.3	4 409.2	9 976.9	9 405.1	1 381.4	3 760.3
1999	25 305.9	19 880.4	3 943.9	6 069.9	9 866.7	5 425.5	718.0	4 482.6	224.9	25 305.9	4 661.9	10 552.4	10 091.6	1 420.5	4 005.0
2000	26 973.9	21 215.2	4 215.5	6 480.0	10 519.8	5 758.7	731.0	4 792.3	235.4	26 973.9	4 946.4	11 272.3	10 755.2	1 454.1	4 304.6
2001	28 192.2	22 190.4	4 335.1	6 767.2	11 088.2	6 001.8	754.0	5 003.0	244.8	28 192.2	5 089.1	11 770.2	11 333.0	1 479.8	4 522.1

Table 5-6. Chain-Type Quantity Indexes for Net Stock of Fixed Assets

(Index numbers, 1996 = 100.)

Year	Total	Private				Government				Private and government fixed assets				Government, by level	
		Total	Nonresidential		Residential	Total	Nonresidential		Residential	Total	Nonresidential		Residential	Federal	State and local
			Equipment and software	Structures			Equipment and software	Structures			Equipment and software	Structures			
1939	18.24	19.50	7.12	29.12	20.26	15.53	3.19	21.53	2.52	18.24	5.68	25.77	19.88	10.79	18.38
1940	18.58	19.73	7.39	29.07	20.60	16.24	3.39	22.44	4.04	18.58	5.91	26.15	20.24	11.68	19.04
1941	19.30	20.09	7.83	29.21	20.97	18.17	6.26	23.97	7.05	19.30	6.78	26.91	20.67	17.04	19.40
1942	20.52	20.04	7.74	29.03	21.04	23.37	18.42	26.90	10.55	20.52	9.02	28.14	20.81	34.16	19.44
1943	21.94	19.89	7.61	28.73	20.99	29.80	42.23	28.06	15.02	21.94	13.23	28.50	20.86	56.57	19.27
1944	23.13	19.86	7.80	28.53	20.92	35.13	65.41	28.40	16.03	23.13	17.42	28.54	20.82	75.59	19.06
1945	23.64	19.99	8.41	28.49	20.86	37.00	73.85	28.57	16.25	23.64	19.35	28.59	20.76	82.61	18.90
1946	23.60	20.63	9.29	28.97	21.42	34.41	61.07	28.33	17.79	23.60	18.00	28.77	21.35	73.38	18.91
1947	23.80	21.46	10.63	29.37	22.23	32.21	49.11	28.36	18.27	23.80	17.14	29.00	22.14	64.95	19.14
1948	24.18	22.40	11.89	29.91	23.20	30.54	39.11	28.64	18.58	24.18	16.49	29.43	23.10	58.01	19.51
1949	24.67	23.15	12.67	30.41	24.07	30.02	33.90	29.21	19.67	24.67	16.27	29.96	23.97	54.49	20.16
1950	25.40	24.16	13.56	31.03	25.34	29.63	28.79	29.95	20.63	25.40	16.18	30.63	25.24	51.11	20.93
1951	26.34	25.04	14.39	31.71	26.33	30.81	30.84	30.87	22.09	26.34	17.22	31.42	26.24	53.23	21.73
1952	27.32	25.85	15.08	32.35	27.28	32.40	34.33	31.98	23.75	27.32	18.37	32.26	27.21	56.84	22.53
1953	28.37	26.73	15.87	33.10	28.26	34.12	38.19	33.17	25.22	28.37	19.67	33.19	28.20	60.64	23.43
1954	29.37	27.60	16.41	33.90	29.34	35.59	40.21	34.52	25.87	29.37	20.46	34.22	29.26	62.91	24.57
1955	30.48	28.66	17.21	34.80	30.62	36.82	41.05	35.89	26.40	30.48	21.27	35.31	30.53	64.06	25.83
1956	31.55	29.69	17.99	35.86	31.74	38.01	41.72	37.24	27.11	31.55	22.03	36.49	31.64	65.04	27.10
1957	32.56	30.65	18.76	36.88	32.75	39.22	42.17	38.64	28.38	32.56	22.75	37.67	32.66	65.84	28.47
1958	33.46	31.41	19.00	37.69	33.76	40.65	42.83	40.22	30.60	33.46	23.06	38.80	33.69	67.01	30.00
1959	34.61	32.42	19.49	38.57	35.12	42.32	44.69	41.79	33.12	34.61	23.78	39.97	35.08	69.03	31.55
1960	35.71	33.41	20.06	39.57	36.33	43.82	45.85	43.35	34.98	35.71	24.44	41.20	36.31	70.46	33.08
1961	36.84	34.36	20.51	40.57	37.53	45.57	47.57	45.06	37.24	36.84	25.11	42.49	37.53	72.41	34.75
1962	38.10	35.47	21.21	41.63	38.87	47.41	49.74	46.76	39.77	38.10	26.06	43.82	38.89	74.61	36.47
1963	39.46	36.71	22.06	42.68	40.42	49.18	51.13	48.65	41.07	39.46	27.00	45.21	40.43	76.11	38.36
1964	40.96	38.13	23.20	43.93	42.06	50.96	52.26	50.61	42.48	40.96	28.14	46.77	42.07	77.30	40.40
1965	42.63	39.76	24.88	45.54	43.60	52.75	52.89	52.71	43.99	42.63	29.65	48.58	43.61	78.13	42.59
1966	44.38	41.42	26.97	47.24	44.92	54.81	54.36	54.94	45.62	44.38	31.65	50.50	44.93	79.54	44.92
1967	46.03	42.94	28.76	48.85	46.14	56.98	56.31	57.17	47.47	46.03	33.47	52.38	46.17	80.97	47.41
1968	47.75	44.58	30.63	50.47	47.61	58.95	57.07	59.44	49.26	47.75	35.17	54.27	47.64	81.44	49.99
1969	49.48	46.32	32.72	52.20	49.12	60.63	57.23	61.46	51.54	49.48	36.94	56.12	49.17	81.43	52.35
1970	51.00	47.88	34.43	53.88	50.47	62.00	56.96	63.18	53.87	51.00	38.33	57.82	50.54	81.03	54.44
1971	52.58	49.60	35.93	55.47	52.36	63.07	55.35	64.83	56.13	52.58	39.30	59.43	52.44	79.90	56.37
1972	54.43	51.64	37.97	57.08	54.64	64.27	55.13	66.34	58.02	54.43	40.94	60.99	54.72	79.68	58.15
1973	56.43	53.93	40.88	58.90	56.89	65.28	53.94	67.81	59.80	56.43	43.10	62.66	56.96	78.87	59.89
1974	58.12	55.81	43.60	60.57	58.47	66.37	53.41	69.21	61.50	58.12	45.25	64.21	58.53	78.37	61.59
1975	59.42	57.16	45.23	61.87	59.69	67.50	53.33	70.54	63.53	59.42	46.60	65.52	59.77	78.18	63.22
1976	60.89	58.76	47.02	63.16	61.38	68.56	53.23	71.82	65.12	60.89	48.06	66.80	61.47	78.00	64.76
1977	62.70	60.82	49.60	64.52	63.61	69.47	53.12	72.93	66.62	62.70	50.18	68.05	63.68	77.89	66.10
1978	64.84	63.24	53.00	66.19	66.01	70.59	53.15	74.28	67.87	64.84	53.00	69.59	66.05	77.91	67.67
1979	67.08	65.74	56.64	68.22	68.24	71.87	54.00	75.65	69.08	67.08	56.17	71.35	68.26	78.24	69.34
1980	68.93	67.73	59.32	70.46	69.75	73.19	55.10	77.00	70.62	68.93	58.60	73.21	69.77	78.75	70.97
1981	70.70	69.67	61.84	73.00	71.03	74.34	56.35	78.10	72.44	70.70	60.90	75.14	71.06	79.53	72.27
1982	72.04	71.10	63.24	75.35	71.86	75.37	57.91	78.99	74.13	72.04	62.33	76.88	71.91	80.43	73.34
1983	73.58	72.75	64.80	77.12	73.47	76.53	60.36	79.82	76.16	73.58	64.05	78.25	73.53	81.82	74.41
1984	75.71	75.07	67.71	79.48	75.48	78.01	63.67	80.88	77.89	75.71	67.03	80.07	75.53	83.60	75.77
1985	78.00	77.48	70.54	82.23	77.47	79.85	68.15	82.14	80.00	78.00	70.16	82.19	77.53	86.01	77.38
1986	80.25	79.79	72.94	84.36	79.86	81.87	73.07	83.55	82.25	80.25	73.00	84.02	79.91	88.68	79.15
1987	82.38	81.94	74.71	86.42	82.22	83.95	78.11	85.03	84.60	82.38	75.33	85.83	82.27	91.52	80.93
1988	84.47	84.09	76.88	88.36	84.50	85.83	81.97	86.52	86.69	84.47	77.78	87.58	84.55	93.37	82.82
1989	86.54	86.21	79.24	90.28	86.62	87.72	86.19	87.98	88.52	86.54	80.45	89.30	86.67	95.05	84.79
1990	88.51	88.14	81.17	92.34	88.47	89.82	90.54	89.65	90.56	88.51	82.78	91.20	88.51	96.80	87.02
1991	90.02	89.52	82.58	93.75	89.82	91.77	93.68	91.39	92.31	90.02	84.48	92.75	89.87	98.05	89.25
1992	91.57	90.99	84.26	94.79	91.46	93.64	96.29	93.11	94.22	91.57	86.31	94.08	91.53	99.08	91.44
1993	93.39	92.88	86.91	95.94	93.47	95.22	97.64	94.73	95.86	93.39	88.74	95.43	93.53	99.47	93.51
1994	95.36	94.99	90.51	96.97	95.62	96.66	98.40	96.31	97.19	95.36	91.86	96.69	95.66	99.42	95.55
1995	97.50	97.30	94.90	98.31	97.66	98.23	98.97	98.06	98.81	97.50	95.60	98.20	97.68	99.40	97.76
1996	100.00	100.00	100.00	100.00	100.00	100.00	100.00	100.00	100.00	100.00	100.00	100.00	100.00	100.00	100.00
1997	102.69	102.96	105.98	102.04	102.32	101.75	100.68	101.97	101.21	102.69	105.07	102.01	102.30	99.63	102.59
1998	105.74	106.36	113.19	104.33	104.96	103.58	102.08	103.91	102.21	105.74	111.28	104.15	104.90	99.49	105.18
1999	108.96	109.89	120.59	106.70	107.79	105.67	104.14	106.08	102.92	108.96	117.76	106.43	107.69	99.55	108.06
2000	112.33	113.63	128.83	109.30	110.65	107.73	106.10	108.24	103.36	112.33	124.91	108.85	110.49	99.50	110.93
2001	115.11	116.62	133.57	111.56	113.48	109.81	108.22	110.39	103.95	115.11	129.19	111.06	113.27	99.50	113.79

Table 5-7. Inventories to Sales Ratios

(Seasonally adjusted, ratio of inventories at end of quarter to monthly rate of sales during the quarter, annual data are for fourth quarter.)

Year and quarter	Total private inventories to final sales of domestic business		Nonfarm inventories to			
			Final sales of domestic business		Final sales of goods and structures	
	Current dollars	Chained (1996) dollars	Current dollars	Chained (1996) dollars	Current dollars	Chained (1996) dollars
1946	4.55	. . .	2.59	. . .	3.41	. . .
1947	4.72	3.03	2.59	2.08	3.33	3.33
1948	4.51	3.17	2.72	2.14	3.55	3.46
1949	4.05	3.00	2.49	2.01	3.26	3.23
1950	4.47	2.97	2.74	2.08	3.59	3.34
1951	4.46	2.98	2.76	2.16	3.62	3.48
1952	3.97	2.92	2.62	2.11	3.47	3.40
1953	3.78	2.91	2.61	2.09	3.50	3.37
1954	3.62	2.79	2.49	1.99	3.33	3.19
1955	3.45	2.75	2.55	2.01	3.46	3.26
1956	3.49	2.76	2.63	2.06	3.60	3.39
1957	3.46	2.74	2.58	2.05	3.58	3.42
1958	3.49	2.72	2.47	1.99	3.46	3.32
1959	3.33	2.66	2.49	2.00	3.50	3.37
1960	3.31	2.68	2.48	2.02	3.53	3.42
1961	3.24	2.62	2.41	1.98	3.46	3.37
1962	3.23	2.62	2.40	2.00	3.46	3.41
1963	3.09	2.59	2.37	1.99	3.44	3.41
1964	3.01	2.54	2.36	2.00	3.43	3.43
1965	2.99	2.48	2.33	1.97	3.35	3.35
1966	3.12	2.62	2.48	2.14	3.60	3.66
1967	3.11	2.68	2.52	2.20	3.69	3.80
1968	3.03	2.67	2.45	2.19	3.57	3.77
1969	3.11	2.74	2.52	2.28	3.72	3.96
1970	3.05	2.73	2.51	2.29	3.76	4.03
1971	3.02	2.70	2.44	2.26	3.68	3.99
1972	3.01	2.60	2.37	2.19	3.53	3.82
1973	3.30	2.64	2.55	2.26	3.78	3.94
1974	3.61	2.81	3.01	2.45	4.56	4.43
1975	3.27	2.66	2.69	2.28	4.09	4.11
1976	3.22	2.65	2.72	2.30	4.17	4.15
1977	3.18	2.66	2.69	2.29	4.13	4.12
1978	3.25	2.61	2.68	2.27	4.07	4.02
1979	3.44	2.63	2.84	2.27	4.32	4.04
1980	3.45	2.59	2.91	2.27	4.50	4.09
1981	3.39	2.70	2.92	2.35	4.59	4.25
1982	3.21	2.65	2.74	2.27	4.46	4.18
1983	2.99	2.46	2.59	2.16	4.21	3.94
1984	3.03	2.53	2.64	2.23	4.31	4.02
1985	2.85	2.49	2.50	2.18	4.17	3.98
1986	2.64	2.42	2.34	2.12	3.94	3.86
1987	2.68	2.42	2.39	2.16	4.08	3.95
1988	2.65	2.35	2.37	2.13	4.07	3.90
1989	2.62	2.36	2.35	2.14	4.06	3.92
1990	2.60	2.38	2.34	2.16	4.11	4.00
1991	2.46	2.38	2.24	2.17	4.03	4.06
1992	2.36	2.30	2.13	2.09	3.85	3.89
1993	2.30	2.28	2.09	2.08	3.79	3.85
1994	2.34	2.33	2.13	2.11	3.86	3.89
1995	2.33	2.31	2.15	2.13	3.91	3.88
1996	2.25	2.26	2.06	2.08	3.76	3.77
1997	2.19	2.28	2.01	2.10	3.68	3.76
1998	2.11	2.29	1.97	2.12	3.57	3.74
1999	2.14	2.29	1.99	2.12	3.64	3.75
2000	2.19	2.33	2.04	2.17	3.77	3.86
2001	1.99	2.21	1.85	2.04	3.44	3.64
2002	1.98	2.18	1.84	2.02	3.51	3.64
2000						
1st quarter	2.15	2.28	2.00	2.12	3.63	3.73
2nd quarter	2.16	2.30	2.01	2.14	3.68	3.78
3rd quarter	2.17	2.31	2.03	2.15	3.72	3.81
4th quarter	2.19	2.33	2.04	2.17	3.77	3.86
2001						
1st quarter	2.16	2.30	2.01	2.14	3.70	3.79
2nd quarter	2.12	2.29	1.97	2.13	3.65	3.77
3rd quarter	2.07	2.27	1.93	2.11	3.60	3.75
4th quarter	1.99	2.21	1.85	2.04	3.44	3.64
2002						
1st quarter	1.97	2.18	1.83	2.02	3.42	3.60
2nd quarter	1.98	2.19	1.84	2.02	3.49	3.64
3rd quarter	1.98	2.17	1.84	2.01	3.48	3.61
4th quarter	1.98	2.18	1.84	2.02	3.51	3.64

. . . = Not available.

Table 5-8. Manufacturing and Trade Sales and Inventories

Classification basis, year and month	Sales, billions of dollars					Inventories, billions of dollars, end of period					Ratios, inventories to monthly sales, seasonally adjusted			
	Not seasonally adjusted, total	Seasonally adjusted				Not seasonally adjusted, total	Seasonally adjusted				Total	Manufacturing	Retail trade	Merchant wholesalers
		Total	Manufacturing	Retail trade	Merchant wholesalers		Total	Manufacturing	Retail trade	Merchant wholesalers				
SIC Basis														
1973	1 844.1	1 844.1	875.2	511.6	457.4	. . .	. . .	. . .	. . .	. . .	. . .	. . .	. . .	. . .
1974	2 134.9	2 134.9	1 017.5	541.7	575.8	. . .	. . .	. . .	. . .	. . .	. . .	. . .	. . .	. . .
1975	2 186.4	2 186.4	1 039.1	587.7	559.6	. . .	. . .	. . .	. . .	. . .	. . .	. . .	. . .	. . .
1976	2 449.8	2 449.8	1 185.6	655.9	608.4	. . .	. . .	. . .	. . .	. . .	. . .	. . .	. . .	. . .
1977	2 754.2	2 754.2	1 358.4	722.1	673.6	. . .	. . .	. . .	. . .	. . .	. . .	. . .	. . .	. . .
1978	3 123.8	3 123.8	1 522.9	804.0	797.0	. . .	. . .	. . .	. . .	. . .	. . .	. . .	. . .	. . .
1979	3 572.4	3 572.4	1 727.2	896.6	948.6	. . .	. . .	. . .	. . .	. . .	. . .	. . .	. . .	. . .
1980	3 926.8	3 926.8	1 852.7	956.9	1 117.2	. . .	. . .	. . .	121.1	122.6	. . .	. . .	. . .	. . .
1981	4 269.9	4 269.9	2 017.5	1 038.2	1 214.2	. . .	. . .	. . .	132.7	129.7	. . .	. . .	1.48	1.25
1982	4 171.5	4 171.5	1 960.2	1 068.7	1 142.5	566.5	573.9	311.9	134.6	127.4	1.67	1.95	1.49	1.36
1983	4 431.4	4 431.4	2 070.6	1 170.2	1 190.7	582.5	590.3	312.4	147.8	130.1	1.56	1.78	1.44	1.28
1984	4 921.5	4 921.5	2 288.2	1 286.9	1 346.4	640.5	649.8	339.5	167.8	142.5	1.53	1.73	1.49	1.23
1985	5 071.0	5 071.0	2 334.5	1 375.0	1 361.5	654.9	664.0	334.7	181.9	147.4	1.55	1.73	1.52	1.28
1986	5 165.0	5 165.0	2 335.9	1 449.6	1 379.5	653.3	662.7	322.7	186.5	153.6	1.55	1.68	1.56	1.32
1987	5 492.8	5 492.8	2 475.9	1 541.3	1 475.6	700.1	709.8	338.1	207.8	163.9	1.50	1.59	1.55	1.29
1988	5 965.9	5 965.9	2 695.4	1 656.2	1 614.2	758.0	767.2	369.4	219.0	178.8	1.49	1.57	1.54	1.30
1989	6 324.5	6 324.5	2 840.4	1 759.0	1 725.1	805.6	815.5	391.2	237.2	187.0	1.52	1.63	1.58	1.28
1990	6 550.9	6 550.9	2 912.2	1 844.6	1 794.1	830.9	840.7	405.1	239.8	195.8	1.52	1.65	1.56	1.29
1991	6 513.8	6 513.8	2 878.2	1 855.9	1 779.7	824.8	834.7	391.0	243.4	200.4	1.53	1.65	1.54	1.33
1992	6 806.1	6 806.1	3 004.7	1 951.6	1 849.8	832.8	842.9	382.5	252.2	208.2	1.48	1.54	1.52	1.32
NAICS Basis														
1992	6 494.7	6 494.7	2 904.0	1 859.1	1 731.6	827.6	840.8	379.2	267.9	193.7	1.53	1.57	1.67	1.31
1993	6 816.9	6 816.9	3 020.5	1 986.4	1 810.0	854.9	868.1	380.1	286.0	201.9	1.50	1.51	1.68	1.31
1994	7 328.0	7 328.0	3 238.1	2 156.3	1 933.6	917.5	931.4	400.3	312.2	218.9	1.47	1.44	1.66	1.30
1995	7 862.7	7 862.7	3 479.7	2 268.3	2 114.7	975.7	990.0	425.2	329.6	235.1	1.48	1.44	1.72	1.30
1996	8 249.7	8 249.7	3 597.2	2 412.7	2 239.8	994.4	1 009.2	430.8	340.6	237.8	1.46	1.43	1.67	1.28
1997	8 689.5	8 689.5	3 834.7	2 520.3	2 334.5	1 035.4	1 050.1	443.8	350.9	255.4	1.42	1.37	1.64	1.27
1998	8 924.6	8 924.6	3 899.8	2 645.0	2 379.8	1 067.7	1 082.7	449.2	365.1	268.4	1.44	1.39	1.62	1.32
1999	9 451.9	9 451.9	4 031.9	2 878.4	2 541.6	1 127.9	1 143.1	463.6	394.3	285.2	1.41	1.35	1.59	1.31
2000	10 022.9	10 022.9	4 208.6	3 071.7	2 742.6	1 186.1	1 201.7	481.4	417.8	302.5	1.41	1.35	1.59	1.30
2001	9 832.5	9 832.5	3 970.5	3 153.3	2 708.7	1 130.9	1 145.4	452.2	405.6	287.6	1.44	1.42	1.58	1.32
2002	9 888.2	9 888.2	3 891.8	3 245.4	2 751.0	1 155.6	1 169.4	444.2	436.3	288.8	1.40	1.37	1.56	1.25
1999														
January	675.7	757.6	327.9	229.9	199.8	1 076.1	1 082.1	446.8	366.6	268.7	1.43	1.36	1.59	1.34
February	715.0	767.7	332.8	232.2	202.8	1 088.0	1 087.4	446.9	369.6	270.9	1.42	1.34	1.59	1.34
March	809.6	768.5	330.1	233.3	205.0	1 095.5	1 095.2	449.1	374.4	271.7	1.43	1.36	1.60	1.33
April	769.5	771.8	331.5	234.4	205.9	1 103.6	1 097.8	448.5	377.4	271.9	1.42	1.35	1.61	1.32
May	784.0	781.8	333.9	237.9	210.1	1 099.9	1 100.8	450.3	378.2	272.3	1.41	1.35	1.59	1.30
June	825.4	783.5	334.0	238.1	211.4	1 091.7	1 103.6	449.7	381.3	272.7	1.41	1.35	1.60	1.29
July	753.8	787.8	335.1	240.4	212.4	1 096.3	1 108.8	451.6	381.7	275.5	1.41	1.35	1.59	1.30
August	808.5	796.7	340.1	242.6	214.0	1 099.1	1 111.1	451.8	382.9	276.4	1.39	1.33	1.58	1.29
September	821.1	798.1	338.0	244.2	215.9	1 112.6	1 117.3	454.3	384.9	278.1	1.40	1.34	1.58	1.29
October	809.8	803.3	340.6	244.2	218.5	1 147.0	1 121.1	455.6	384.6	280.8	1.40	1.34	1.58	1.29
November	810.4	812.3	344.4	246.9	221.0	1 165.2	1 133.5	459.5	389.8	284.2	1.40	1.33	1.58	1.29
December	869.2	818.6	343.7	252.0	222.9	1 127.9	1 143.1	463.6	394.3	285.2	1.40	1.35	1.56	1.28
2000														
January	737.9	828.5	352.9	251.1	224.4	1 140.1	1 145.7	463.7	394.1	287.9	1.38	1.31	1.57	1.28
February	789.9	821.1	343.7	254.3	223.2	1 152.4	1 151.9	466.6	395.6	289.6	1.40	1.36	1.56	1.30
March	878.8	834.5	350.4	257.6	226.5	1 156.6	1 156.6	467.3	397.6	291.7	1.39	1.33	1.54	1.29
April	807.7	834.0	353.5	253.3	227.3	1 168.5	1 163.3	470.2	399.1	294.0	1.39	1.33	1.58	1.29
May	859.6	831.9	351.0	253.7	227.2	1 168.5	1 169.5	470.2	403.5	295.8	1.41	1.34	1.59	1.30
June	887.3	840.4	355.3	254.6	230.5	1 167.7	1 179.9	474.0	407.9	297.9	1.40	1.33	1.60	1.29
July	787.2	836.4	351.2	255.8	229.4	1 167.8	1 181.2	476.0	406.7	298.5	1.41	1.36	1.59	1.30
August	860.7	832.4	348.2	255.5	228.8	1 176.2	1 188.7	477.2	412.1	299.3	1.43	1.37	1.61	1.31
September	858.6	843.6	353.3	259.5	230.8	1 183.9	1 188.9	477.4	411.8	299.7	1.41	1.35	1.59	1.30
October	851.2	838.5	348.5	258.0	232.0	1 222.3	1 195.2	479.5	414.4	301.2	1.43	1.38	1.61	1.30
November	833.6	835.2	346.7	257.3	231.2	1 235.2	1 202.1	481.8	417.3	303.0	1.44	1.39	1.62	1.31
December	870.4	839.3	347.7	258.0	233.6	1 186.1	1 201.7	481.4	417.8	302.5	1.43	1.38	1.62	1.29
2001														
January	762.8	830.2	337.9	259.9	232.5	1 198.6	1 204.5	484.3	418.2	302.0	1.45	1.43	1.61	1.30
February	775.0	837.9	346.7	259.7	231.5	1 201.8	1 201.4	483.4	415.9	302.1	1.43	1.39	1.60	1.30
March	862.0	827.8	341.6	257.9	228.3	1 197.6	1 198.0	479.9	416.2	301.9	1.45	1.40	1.61	1.32
April	804.2	820.2	332.0	260.7	227.5	1 203.1	1 198.5	479.6	416.5	302.4	1.46	1.44	1.60	1.33
May	860.2	828.9	339.3	262.6	226.9	1 196.0	1 197.1	477.2	416.9	303.0	1.44	1.41	1.59	1.34
June	851.7	817.1	332.0	261.3	223.7	1 177.9	1 190.1	473.2	416.1	300.8	1.46	1.43	1.59	1.35
July	780.2	817.2	330.8	261.5	224.9	1 171.0	1 185.0	470.3	416.9	297.7	1.45	1.42	1.59	1.32
August	851.0	818.6	330.1	262.6	225.9	1 170.9	1 183.9	466.8	420.2	296.9	1.45	1.41	1.60	1.31
September	797.7	803.5	320.4	258.4	224.7	1 173.2	1 178.0	462.3	419.4	295.8	1.47	1.44	1.62	1.32
October	843.3	818.6	321.9	275.6	221.1	1 189.0	1 161.4	460.3	407.9	293.1	1.42	1.43	1.48	1.33
November	808.7	808.6	320.1	267.2	221.3	1 183.7	1 151.1	456.4	404.8	289.9	1.42	1.43	1.52	1.31
December	835.5	808.7	321.9	265.7	221.2	1 130.9	1 145.4	452.2	405.6	287.6	1.42	1.40	1.53	1.30
2002														
January	746.2	810.7	323.8	264.8	222.1	1 138.6	1 144.1	448.9	408.3	286.9	1.41	1.39	1.54	1.29
February	746.9	810.4	320.1	266.1	224.2	1 141.8	1 141.5	446.4	410.7	284.5	1.41	1.39	1.54	1.27
March	829.0	808.0	318.5	265.9	223.5	1 140.9	1 140.5	445.4	410.4	284.6	1.41	1.40	1.54	1.27
April	818.7	823.1	325.9	270.0	227.2	1 143.2	1 139.1	444.6	411.7	282.8	1.38	1.36	1.52	1.24
May	853.4	819.7	326.0	266.2	227.4	1 140.5	1 142.4	442.9	416.6	282.9	1.39	1.36	1.56	1.24
June	838.6	821.5	322.8	270.1	228.6	1 132.9	1 145.0	442.4	418.7	283.9	1.39	1.37	1.55	1.24
July	810.5	831.0	328.4	272.9	229.7	1 137.1	1 152.0	442.6	423.4	286.1	1.39	1.35	1.55	1.25
August	860.4	833.1	326.2	274.6	232.4	1 138.4	1 153.1	442.8	423.6	286.7	1.38	1.36	1.54	1.23
September	830.2	828.9	326.2	270.4	232.3	1 153.9	1 158.4	443.6	427.9	286.9	1.40	1.36	1.58	1.24
October	860.4	833.5	329.3	271.7	232.5	1 187.1	1 160.2	443.5	431.0	285.7	1.39	1.35	1.59	1.23
November	825.6	835.4	326.5	273.6	235.3	1 195.9	1 163.6	442.5	434.7	286.4	1.39	1.36	1.59	1.22
December	868.3	834.2	323.4	277.1	233.7	1 155.6	1 169.4	444.2	436.3	288.8	1.40	1.37	1.57	1.24

. . . = Not available.

Table 5-9. Real Manufacturing and Trade Sales and Inventories

(Billions of chained [1996] dollars, ratios; seasonally adjusted; annual figures for sales are averages of seasonally adjusted monthly data.)

Classification basis, year and month	Sales, monthly average				Inventories, end of period				Ratios, end-of-period inventories to monthly average sales			
	Total	Manufac-turing	Retail trade	Merchant wholesalers	Total	Manufac-turing	Retail trade	Merchant wholesalers	Total	Manufac-turing	Retail trade	Merchant wholesalers
SIC Basis												
1973	408.3	203.8	114.8	90.6	531.4	281.6	144.4	98.7	1.30	1.38	1.26	1.09
1974	405.8	199.0	109.4	97.3	561.4	302.8	142.3	108.4	1.38	1.52	1.30	1.11
1975	376.2	179.0	110.1	87.5	540.7	295.2	135.3	102.1	1.44	1.65	1.23	1.17
1976	403.5	195.4	117.4	91.4	572.9	309.3	145.7	109.8	1.42	1.58	1.24	1.20
1977	431.8	211.2	123.2	98.0	601.1	317.9	153.9	121.5	1.39	1.51	1.25	1.24
1978	458.5	221.3	129.1	108.4	639.4	332.5	164.1	135.3	1.39	1.50	1.27	1.25
1979	469.5	224.2	131.3	114.0	660.1	345.3	164.1	142.5	1.41	1.54	1.25	1.25
1980	454.9	211.5	126.5	116.4	662.8	345.7	159.5	149.4	1.46	1.63	1.26	1.28
1981	457.7	213.1	127.0	117.1	679.3	350.3	168.4	153.1	1.48	1.64	1.33	1.31
1982	439.1	202.9	125.8	110.3	657.5	334.6	164.5	151.7	1.50	1.65	1.31	1.38
1983	460.7	212.4	135.1	113.5	670.0	334.2	177.9	152.6	1.45	1.57	1.32	1.35
1984	499.3	229.3	144.8	125.4	736.1	363.2	199.7	168.2	1.47	1.58	1.38	1.34
1985	513.8	233.5	151.2	129.4	751.5	356.9	215.1	176.9	1.46	1.53	1.42	1.37
1986	533.6	237.6	159.6	136.6	759.2	353.1	218.5	185.9	1.42	1.49	1.37	1.36
1987	553.2	248.0	164.2	141.3	796.5	361.6	239.7	194.5	1.44	1.46	1.46	1.38
1988	579.1	259.4	171.3	148.6	830.0	378.5	247.4	203.1	1.43	1.46	1.44	1.37
1989	590.5	261.9	175.6	153.1	862.4	392.7	261.9	207.0	1.46	1.50	1.49	1.35
1990	593.9	261.4	177.3	155.3	878.2	401.6	260.2	215.2	1.48	1.54	1.47	1.39
1991	586.4	257.1	174.0	155.3	876.7	394.9	260.8	220.4	1.50	1.54	1.50	1.42
1992	607.7	266.4	179.9	161.5	885.4	390.1	265.4	229.5	1.46	1.46	1.48	1.42
1993	632.7	274.5	188.7	169.4	911.1	393.7	280.8	236.3	1.44	1.43	1.49	1.39
1994	670.3	290.1	201.0	179.2	958.8	405.8	301.4	251.5	1.43	1.40	1.50	1.40
1995	699.5	301.1	208.2	190.2	996.4	419.9	313.6	262.9	1.42	1.39	1.51	1.38
1996	726.0	309.5	218.5	198.0	1 016.4	430.0	321.0	265.4	1.40	1.39	1.47	1.34
NAICS Basis												
1996	693.5	299.3	208.2	186.0	995.3	422.1	327.9	245.1	1.44	1.41	1.58	1.32
1997	736.3	320.9	218.4	199.1	1 043.8	436.8	339.9	266.9	1.42	1.36	1.56	1.34
1998	774.2	332.1	233.9	212.0	1 106.3	464.0	354.4	288.0	1.43	1.40	1.52	1.36
1999	820.9	344.4	254.6	227.5	1 163.5	478.3	380.0	305.0	1.42	1.39	1.49	1.34
2000	849.0	349.2	268.7	238.1	1 219.5	495.8	401.6	321.8	1.44	1.42	1.49	1.35
2001	842.2	329.5	281.6	237.9	1 149.5	459.6	381.3	308.5	1.36	1.39	1.35	1.30
2002	860.1	327.8	296.5	244.0	1 151.4	448.2	397.9	304.5	1.34	1.37	1.34	1.25
1999												
January	797.8	339.9	245.2	217.6	1 110.1	462.6	358.7	288.7	1.39	1.36	1.46	1.33
February	809.8	344.0	249.2	222.0	1 115.4	464.1	359.9	291.3	1.38	1.35	1.44	1.31
March	811.5	342.9	250.4	223.6	1 120.9	467.6	361.1	292.1	1.38	1.36	1.44	1.31
April	809.5	342.7	249.3	222.6	1 120.2	467.1	361.1	292.0	1.38	1.36	1.45	1.31
May	816.6	342.7	252.7	226.6	1 124.2	468.7	363.1	292.4	1.38	1.37	1.44	1.29
June	818.4	342.5	253.6	228.1	1 126.4	467.9	365.1	293.2	1.38	1.37	1.44	1.29
July	822.6	344.4	255.1	229.0	1 132.7	469.6	367.0	295.9	1.38	1.36	1.44	1.29
August	827.2	346.9	257.2	229.0	1 134.7	469.3	368.4	296.8	1.37	1.35	1.43	1.30
September	824.5	343.9	257.5	229.0	1 139.9	471.5	370.3	297.9	1.38	1.37	1.44	1.30
October	829.1	345.3	257.8	232.3	1 145.4	471.9	372.7	300.6	1.38	1.37	1.45	1.29
November	838.6	349.0	261.5	234.7	1 154.7	474.8	375.9	303.8	1.38	1.36	1.44	1.29
December	845.1	349.1	266.1	235.4	1 163.5	478.3	380.0	305.0	1.38	1.37	1.43	1.30
2000												
January	851.8	358.1	265.0	236.4	1 165.5	478.6	379.4	307.2	1.37	1.34	1.43	1.30
February	839.6	344.5	268.7	233.3	1 169.9	481.4	379.9	308.5	1.39	1.40	1.41	1.32
March	849.2	352.0	269.2	235.0	1 173.8	482.0	381.9	309.7	1.38	1.37	1.42	1.32
April	849.5	352.7	266.0	237.5	1 179.5	484.5	383.5	311.3	1.39	1.37	1.44	1.31
May	846.9	351.1	266.6	236.0	1 183.7	484.4	387.0	312.1	1.40	1.38	1.45	1.32
June	852.4	353.5	267.0	238.8	1 193.5	488.3	390.0	314.9	1.40	1.38	1.46	1.32
July	849.3	349.2	268.3	238.9	1 198.7	490.1	392.5	315.9	1.41	1.40	1.46	1.32
August	849.5	347.3	269.5	239.9	1 204.5	491.4	395.3	317.5	1.42	1.41	1.47	1.32
September	852.4	349.0	271.8	239.0	1 204.7	491.8	394.8	317.9	1.41	1.41	1.45	1.33
October	849.3	345.6	271.1	239.7	1 211.1	493.7	397.4	319.6	1.43	1.43	1.47	1.33
November	845.7	343.4	269.7	239.7	1 217.4	495.8	400.1	321.3	1.44	1.44	1.48	1.34
December	852.1	344.5	271.8	243.1	1 219.5	495.8	401.6	321.8	1.43	1.44	1.48	1.32
2001												
January	846.2	336.3	275.2	241.4	1 218.9	498.0	399.7	320.9	1.44	1.48	1.45	1.33
February	849.1	338.9	275.7	241.2	1 214.1	495.8	397.2	320.8	1.43	1.46	1.44	1.33
March	846.3	339.7	275.0	238.3	1 208.4	491.1	396.6	320.4	1.43	1.45	1.44	1.34
April	836.3	327.7	277.6	237.5	1 204.5	489.2	395.0	320.2	1.44	1.49	1.42	1.35
May	842.2	333.9	279.3	235.5	1 200.1	485.6	394.2	320.1	1.42	1.45	1.41	1.36
June	833.1	326.5	279.0	233.7	1 191.9	480.7	392.3	318.8	1.43	1.47	1.41	1.36
July	841.5	329.6	281.1	237.6	1 184.8	477.4	391.2	316.0	1.41	1.45	1.39	1.33
August	845.4	330.1	283.2	239.0	1 181.8	473.7	392.5	315.4	1.40	1.44	1.39	1.32
September	821.2	315.3	276.1	235.7	1 175.7	469.7	391.5	314.3	1.43	1.49	1.42	1.33
October	849.8	324.7	296.8	235.8	1 161.4	467.3	382.2	311.8	1.37	1.44	1.29	1.32
November	845.8	323.7	289.8	239.7	1 152.1	463.3	379.5	309.3	1.36	1.43	1.31	1.29
December	849.4	327.6	290.0	239.2	1 149.5	459.6	381.3	308.5	1.35	1.40	1.31	1.29
2002												
January	857.2	332.9	290.5	241.6	1 148.9	457.5	383.6	307.6	1.34	1.37	1.32	1.27
February	848.9	321.8	292.5	242.5	1 145.1	454.9	384.8	304.9	1.35	1.41	1.32	1.26
March	848.7	324.7	291.4	240.3	1 141.2	451.7	384.7	304.4	1.34	1.39	1.32	1.27
April	857.0	328.7	293.6	243.1	1 138.7	450.9	385.6	301.7	1.33	1.37	1.31	1.24
May	856.2	329.7	291.6	242.6	1 139.2	449.1	387.7	301.7	1.33	1.36	1.33	1.24
June	859.3	326.6	296.4	244.3	1 141.4	448.1	390.2	302.3	1.33	1.37	1.32	1.24
July	868.4	331.4	300.5	244.9	1 143.9	447.6	392.0	303.7	1.32	1.35	1.30	1.24
August	867.4	328.4	301.6	246.0	1 142.9	447.5	391.6	303.1	1.32	1.36	1.30	1.23
September	859.0	326.2	297.0	244.0	1 145.8	447.5	394.1	303.5	1.33	1.37	1.33	1.24
October	861.4	329.0	297.7	242.8	1 144.4	447.3	394.9	304.4	1.33	1.36	1.33	1.24
November	867.3	327.3	300.0	248.1	1 148.3	446.3	399.2	301.9	1.32	1.36	1.33	1.22
December	870.7	326.4	305.4	248.0	1 151.4	448.2	397.9	304.5	1.32	1.37	1.30	1.23

Table 5-10. Capital Expenditures, 1996–2001

(Millions of dollars.)

Capital expenditures	All companies					
	1996	1997	1998	1999	2000	2001
TOTAL	807 070	871 765	970 897	1 046 952	1 161 029	1 109 863
Structures	243 427	273 298	329 111	320 078	364 407	361 883
New	223 588	254 451	284 491	296 496	329 525	333 667
Used	19 839	18 849	44 620	23 583	34 882	28 216
Equipment	563 641	598 466	641 786	726 874	796 622	747 980
New	526 016	562 019	606 210	689 553	750 626	709 328
Used	37 625	36 447	35 577	37 321	45 996	38 652
Not distributed as structures or equipment	2	0	0	0	0	0
CAPITAL LEASE AND CAPITALIZED INTEREST EXPENSES [1]						
Capital leases	15 675	16 066	16 533	17 140	19 545	15 529
Capitalized interest	. . .	. . .	. . .	. . .	. . .	. . .

Capital expenditures	Companies with employees					
	1996	1997	1998	1999	2000	2001
TOTAL	707 110	772 343	896 452	974 631	1 089 862	1 053 203
Structures	204 345	236 166	300 283	293 787	338 120	344 356
New	191 867	225 107	260 008	276 094	309 541	322 000
Used	12 478	11 060	40 275	17 693	28 579	22 355
Equipment	502 762	536 177	596 169	680 843	751 742	708 847
New	481 785	515 965	570 397	656 344	718 227	681 801
Used	20 977	20 212	25 773	24 499	33 515	27 047
Not distributed as structures or equipment	2	0	0	0	0	0
CAPITAL LEASE AND CAPITALIZED INTEREST EXPENSES [1]						
Capital leases	13 023	14 549	15 631	16 594	19 184	15 500
Capitalized interest	6 827	7 273	9 799	9 591	11 423	11 969

Capital expenditures	Companies without employees					
	1996	1997	1998	1999	2000	2001
TOTAL	99 960	99 422	74 445	72 322	71 168	56 660
Structures	39 082	37 132	28 828	26 291	26 287	17 527
New	31 721	29 344	24 483	20 402	19 984	11 667
Used	7 361	7 789	4 345	5 889	6 303	5 860
Equipment	60 878	62 289	45 617	46 030	44 880	39 133
New	44 231	46 054	35 813	33 209	32 399	27 528
Used	16 648	16 235	9 804	12 821	12 481	11 605
Not distributed as structures or equipment	0	0	0	0	0	0
CAPITAL LEASE AND CAPITALIZED INTEREST EXPENSES [1]						
Capital leases	2 652	1 517	902	546	361	29
Capitalized interest	. . .	. . .	. . .	. . .	. . .	. . .

[1]Included in data shown above.
. . . = Not available.

Table 5-11. Capital Expenditures for Structures and Equipment for Companies With Employees by Major NAICS Industry Sector, 1998–2001

(Millions of dollars.)

NAICS code	Industry	Total expenditures	1998 Expenditures for structures			1998 Expenditures for equipment		
			Total	New	Used	Total	New	Used
	Total expenditures	896 452	300 283	260 008	40 275	596 169	570 397	25 773
113–115	Forestry, fishing, and agricultural services	854	206	158	49	648	603	46
21	Mining	40 424	26 503	24 714	1 789	13 921	12 625	1 296
22	Utilities	36 010	18 574	17 771	804	17 436	17 266	170
23	Construction	26 867	7 062	4 749	2 313	19 805	15 346	4 458
31–33	Manufacturing	203 587	39 028	37 122	1 906	164 559	159 363	5 196
321, 327, 33	Durable goods industries	117 901	19 406	18 449	957	98 496	95 571	2 925
31, 322–326	Nondurable goods industries	85 685	19 622	18 673	949	66 063	63 792	2 271
42	Wholesale trade	29 169	7 480	6 738	742	21 690	20 470	1 220
44–45	Retail trade	57 276	25 105	23 104	2 001	32 171	30 359	1 812
48–49	Transportation and warehousing	51 287	13 036	12 365	671	38 251	33 409	4 842
51	Information	96 487	24 721	24 218	503	71 766	70 827	939
52	Finance and insurance	118 173	27 221	16 858	10 362	90 952	90 058	894
53	Real estate and rental and leasing	85 184	36 775	24 109	12 666	48 409	46 877	1 532
54	Professional, scientific, and technical services	22 277	4 886	4 572	314	17 390	16 868	522
55	Management of companies and enterprises	1 821	753	502	251	1 068	1 030	38
56	Administrative and support and waste management	13 110	4 288	3 745	543	8 822	8 346	476
61	Educational services	12 983	9 109	8 734	374	3 874	3 825	49
62	Health care and social assistance	47 109	23 971	21 328	2 643	23 138	22 465	672
71	Arts, entertainment, and recreation	8 994	5 045	4 838	206	3 949	3 752	197
72	Accommodation and food services	20 822	12 045	10 402	1 643	8 777	8 005	772
81	Other services (except public administration)	20 627	13 737	13 280	457	6 890	6 296	594
	Structure and equipment expenditures serving multiple industry categories	3 392	738	699	39	2 654	2 609	46

NAICS code	Industry	Total expenditures	1999 Expenditures for structures			1999 Expenditures for equipment		
			Total	New	Used	Total	New	Used
	Total expenditures	974 631	293 787	276 094	17 693	680 843	656 344	24 499
113–115	Forestry, fishing, and agricultural services	1 716	344	331	13	1 371	1 190	182
21	Mining	30 586	17 626	17 039	587	12 960	12 167	793
22	Utilities	42 802	21 241	20 784	457	21 561	20 545	1 016
23	Construction	23 110	1 753	1 505	248	21 356	18 600	2 756
31–33	Manufacturing	196 399	33 985	32 814	1 171	162 414	157 715	4 699
321, 327, 33	Durable goods industries	117 005	17 320	16 581	739	99 685	96 434	3 251
31, 322–326	Nondurable goods industries	79 394	16 665	16 233	432	62 729	61 281	1 448
42	Wholesale trade	32 442	7 264	6 508	756	25 179	23 714	1 465
44–45	Retail trade	64 063	29 494	28 670	824	34 569	33 567	1 002
48–49	Transportation and warehousing	57 299	14 122	13 859	263	43 178	40 425	2 752
51	Information	122 827	34 924	33 733	1 191	87 903	85 310	2 593
52	Finance and insurance	130 101	20 080	17 918	2 162	110 021	109 577	444
53	Real estate and rental and leasing	100 629	33 903	30 295	3 608	66 726	63 555	3 171
54	Professional, scientific, and technical services	29 546	6 780	6 168	613	22 766	22 153	613
55	Management of companies and enterprises	6 065	1 668	1 509	159	4 397	4 319	78
56	Administrative and support and waste management	16 227	2 875	2 773	102	13 353	12 323	1 029
61	Educational services	13 532	9 767	9 140	627	3 766	3 668	97
62	Health care and social assistance	51 342	25 922	24 159	1 763	25 420	24 945	475
71	Arts, entertainment, and recreation	13 355	8 119	7 971	148	5 236	5 125	111
72	Accommodation and food services	23 328	13 431	11 391	2 040	9 897	9 324	573
81	Other services (except public administration)	16 902	9 975	9 033	941	6 928	6 370	558
	Structure and equipment expenditures serving multiple industry categories	2 359	516	495	21	1 843	1 752	91

Note: Detail may not add up to total because of rounding.

Table 5-11. Capital Expenditures for Structures and Equipment for Companies With Employees by Major NAICS Industry Sector, 1998–2001—*Continued*

(Millions of dollars.)

NAICS code	Industry	Total expenditures	Expenditures for structures			Expenditures for equipment		
			Total	New	Used	Total	New	Used
				2000				
	Total expenditures	1 089 862	338 120	309 541	28 579	751 742	718 227	33 515
113–115	Forestry, fishing, and agricultural services	1 488	139	134	5	1 350	1 086	264
21	Mining	42 522	28 620	25 500	3 120	13 902	12 854	1 048
22	Utilities	61 302	29 472	29 258	214	31 830	27 937	3 893
23	Construction	25 049	2 803	2 583	220	22 245	17 788	4 458
31–33	Manufacturing	214 827	39 434	36 643	2 791	175 393	169 454	5 939
321, 327, 33	Durable goods industries	133 786	21 228	19 748	1 480	112 558	108 703	3 856
31, 322–326	Nondurable goods industries	81 041	18 207	16 895	1 312	62 835	60 751	2 083
42	Wholesale trade	33 579	8 923	8 364	559	24 656	23 610	1 046
44–45	Retail trade	69 791	32 037	30 413	1 624	37 754	36 428	1 326
48–49	Transportation and warehousing	59 851	13 457	13 190	267	46 394	43 455	2 938
51	Information	160 177	41 502	40 062	1 440	118 675	117 835	841
52	Finance and insurance	133 684	23 010	20 298	2 712	110 675	109 678	997
53	Real estate and rental and leasing	92 456	24 815	17 793	7 022	67 641	62 175	5 466
54	Professional, scientific, and technical services	34 055	8 141	7 470	671	25 914	24 847	1 067
55	Management of companies and enterprises	5 054	1 570	955	615	3 484	3 403	81
56	Administrative and support and waste management	17 506	4 032	3 504	528	13 475	12 723	752
61	Educational services	18 223	13 699	12 965	735	4 523	4 338	186
62	Health care and social assistance	52 166	26 868	23 999	2 869	25 299	24 407	892
71	Arts, entertainment, and recreation	19 125	12 245	11 627	618	6 880	6 161	719
72	Accommodation and food services	26 307	13 873	12 879	993	12 434	11 501	933
81	Other services (except public administration)	21 125	13 274	11 705	1 569	7 852	7 192	659
	Structure and equipment expenditures serving multiple industry categories	1 572	206	200	6	1 366	1 357	10

NAICS code	Industry	Total expenditures	Expenditures for structures			Expenditures for equipment		
			Total	New	Used	Total	New	Used
				2001				
	Total expenditures	1 053 203	344 356	322 000	22 355	708 847	681 801	27 047
113–115	Forestry, fishing, and agricultural services	1 532	226	149	77	1 306	1 091	215
21	Mining	51 087	32 663	31 825	838	18 424	17 391	1 033
22	Utilities	82 823	38 093	36 504	1 588	44 731	42 939	1 792
23	Construction	24 802	3 859	3 389	470	20 943	17 432	3 511
31–33	Manufacturing	192 406	39 649	37 836	1 813	152 757	148 135	4 623
321, 327, 33	Durable goods industries	118 686	22 096	20 765	1 331	96 590	93 998	2 592
31, 322–326	Nondurable goods industries	73 720	17 553	17 071	482	56 167	54 137	2 030
42	Wholesale trade	29 717	7 172	5 597	1 575	22 545	20 252	2 292
44–45	Retail trade	66 803	29 905	29 012	892	36 898	35 066	1 833
48–49	Transportation and warehousing	57 478	16 316	14 201	2 116	41 161	38 521	2 640
51	Information	146 318	39 999	39 641	358	106 318	105 668	650
52	Finance and insurance	131 104	22 744	19 571	3 173	108 360	107 268	1 093
53	Real estate and rental and leasing	83 143	20 781	17 603	3 178	62 361	60 471	1 891
54	Professional, scientific, and technical services	30 481	7 063	6 598	465	23 418	22 542	876
55	Management of companies and enterprises	3 029	933	869	64	2 096	2 013	83
56	Administrative and support and waste management	15 950	3 642	3 475	167	12 308	11 691	617
61	Educational services	17 375	12 852	11 860	991	4 524	4 237	287
62	Health care and social assistance	52 932	27 030	25 241	1 789	25 902	24 573	1 329
71	Arts, entertainment, and recreation	14 974	8 998	8 157	841	5 976	5 590	386
72	Accommodation and food services	21 330	12 237	11 391	846	9 093	7 897	1 196
81	Other services (except public administration)	29 006	20 031	18 918	1 112	8 976	8 300	676
	Structure and equipment expenditures serving multiple industry categories	911	163	162	0	749	725	24

Note: Detail may not add up to total because of rounding.

NOTES AND DEFINITIONS

TABLES 5-1 THROUGH 5-4 AND 5-7
GROSS SAVING AND INVESTMENT ACCOUNTS; INVENTORIES TO SALES RATIOS

SOURCE: U.S. DEPARTMENT OF COMMERCE, BUREAU OF ECONOMIC ANALYSIS

Revisions

Data in this book reflect revisions to the national income and product accounts (NIPAs) available through August 2003.

Definitions

Personal saving is derived by subtracting personal outlays and personal tax and nontax payments from personal income. It is the current saving of individuals (including proprietors), nonprofit institutions that primarily serve individuals, life insurance carriers, retirement funds, private noninsured welfare funds, and private trust funds. Conceptually, personal saving may also be viewed as the sum for all persons (including institutions as just defined) of the net acquisition of financial assets and the change in physical assets less the sum of net borrowing and consumption of fixed capital. In either case, it is defined to exclude capital gains, that is, it excludes profits on the sale of homes, securities, and other property—whether realized or unrealized—and includes the noncorporate inventory valuation and capital consumption adjustments (IVA and CCAdj). (See Notes and Definitions to Tables 1-1 through 1-10.)

Undistributed profits is corporate profits after tax less dividends; in the saving and investment account table, it also excludes capital gain elements and hence includes the corporate IVA and corporate CCAdj. (See Notes and Definitions to Tables 1-1 through 1-10.)

Consumption of *fixed* capital is a charge for the using up of private and government fixed capital, including software, located in the United States. It is based on studies of prices of used equipment and structures in resale markets. For general government and for nonprofit institutions that primarily serve individuals, it is recorded in government consumption expenditures and in personal consumption expenditures, respectively, as the value of the current services of the fixed capital assets owned and used by these entities. *Private consumption of fixed capital* consists of tax-return-based depreciation charges for corporations and nonfarm proprietorships and of historical-cost depreciation (calculated by the Bureau of Economic Analysis (BEA) using a geometric pattern of price declines) for farm proprietorships, rental income of

persons, and nonprofit institutions, *minus* the capital consumption adjustments. (In other words, from the point of view of saving, the CCAdj is taken out of book depreciation and added to income and profits—it is a reallocation from one form of gross saving to another.)

Gross private domestic investment consists of gross private fixed investment and change in private inventories.

Private fixed investment comprises both nonresidential and residential fixed investment. It consists of purchases of fixed assets, which are commodities that will be used in a production process for more than 1 year, including replacements and additions to the capital stock. It is "gross" because it is measured before a deduction for consumption of fixed capital. It covers all investment by private businesses and nonprofit institutions in the United States, regardless of whether the investment is owned by U.S. residents. It does not include purchases of the same types of equipment and structures by government agencies, which are included in government gross investment, or investment by U.S. residents in other countries.

Gross nonresidential fixed investment consists of structures, equipment, and software not related to personal residences.

Nonresidential structures consists of new construction, brokers' commissions on sales of structures, and net purchases (purchases less sales) of used structures by private business and by nonprofit institutions from government agencies. New construction also includes hotels, motels, and mining exploration, shafts, and wells.

Nonresidential equipment and software consists of private business purchases, on capital account, of new machinery, equipment, and vehicles; purchases and in-house production of software; dealers' margins on sales of used equipment; and net purchases (purchases less sales) of used equipment from government agencies, persons, and the rest of the world. (It does not, however, include the personal-use portion of equipment purchased for both business and personal use, which is included in PCE.)

Residential private fixed investment consists of both structures and residential producers' durable equipment, that is, equipment owned by landlords and rented to tenants. Investment in structures consists of new units, improvements to existing units, manufactured homes, brokers' commissions on the sale of residential property, and net purchases (purchases less sales) of used structures from government agencies.

Change in private inventories is the change in the physical volume of inventories held by businesses, valued at the average price of the period. It differs from the change in the book value of inventories as reported by most businesses; the IVA converts historical cost valuations of inventories to replacement cost.

The *statistical discrepancy* is the difference between GDP estimated as the sum of the values of final and inventory purchases of goods and services and GDP estimated by summing the incomes and capital consumption incurred in the production of GDP (and also allowing for the differing price basis: GDP is at market prices, including indirect business taxes and excluding subsidies less the current surplus of government enterprises, whereas national income is at factor cost, excluding the former and including the latter). It reflects the fact that the product and income sides of the accounts use different source data. It is the amount that must be added to the income-side data to yield the product-side data, which are considered more reliable. Where it is negative, the income-side data exceed the product-side measurement, and this negative amount must be subtracted from—the absolute value must be added to—the product-side calculation to yield national income. (See Table 1-7 and the associated Notes and Definitions.) The statistical discrepancy similarly accounts for the difference between gross investment and gross saving, which by definition should be identical.

Inventories to sales ratios. The ratios shown in Table 5-7 are based on the inventory estimates underlying the measurement of inventory change in the NIPAs. They include data and estimates not only for the inventories held in manufacturing and trade (see the following Tables 5-8 and 5-9) but also for stocks held by all other businesses in the U.S. economy. For the current-dollar ratios, inventories at the end of each quarter are valued in the prices that prevailed at the end of that quarter. For the constant-dollar ratios, they are valued in chained (1996) dollars. In both cases, the inventory/sales ratio is the value of the inventories at the end of the quarter divided by quarterly total sales at *monthly* rates (that is, quarterly totals divided by 3). In other words, they represent how many months' supply businesses had on hand at the end of the period. Annual data are those for the fourth quarter.

Data availability

Current data for some of these series are included in the monthly release of the latest NIPA estimates; all of the series are subsequently published each month in the *Survey of Current Business*. Current and historical data may be obtained from the BEA Internet site (http://www.bea.gov) or the STAT-USA subscription Internet site (http://www.stat-usa.gov).

References

Sources of information about the NIPAs are listed in the notes for Tables 1-1 through 1-10.

TABLE 5-5 AND 5-6
CURRENT-COST NET STOCK OF FIXED ASSETS; CHAIN-TYPE QUANTITY INDEXES FOR NET STOCK OF FIXED ASSETS

Integrated with the NIPAs, BEA calculates measures of the level of the *stock* of fixed assets in the U.S. economy, or what is commonly called the "capital stock." (The fixed investment component of the GDP is a *flow*, the increment of new capital goods into the capital stock.) These two tables present two measures of the capital stock. The definitions of the capital stock categories are the same as used in the GDP investment categories (see Notes and Definitions to Tables 5-1 through 5-4, above).

The values of fixed capital and depreciation typically reported by businesses are inadequate for economic analysis and in general are not used in these measures. Such reported values are generally valued at historical costs—each year's capital acquisition in the prices of the year acquired—and therefore the totals represent a mixture of pricing bases.

Definitions and methods

The *net stock of fixed assets* is measured by a perpetual inventory method. That is, net stock at any given time is the cumulative value of past gross investment less the cumulative value of past depreciation, including damages from disasters and war losses that exceed normal depreciation, such as the attack on September 11, 2001.

Gross investment is the gross fixed investment component of GDP. Depreciation for privately-owned assets is the value of "consumption of fixed capital" in the NIPAs that is subtracted from gross domestic product in order to yield net domestic product. For government assets, the NIPA value of consumption of fixed capital does *not* include disaster and war loss damage, but the value of these damages is calculated by BEA and subtracted from the capital stock assets.

The initial calculations using this perpetual inventory method are performed in real terms for each type of asset. They are then aggregated to higher levels using an annual-weighted Fisher-type index; see the definition of *Real or chained-dollar estimates* in the Notes and Definitions to Chapter 1. This provides the *Chain-type quantity indexes* shown in Table 5-6. These values can be used to measure the real growth in the capital stock for the categories shown.

The real values are also converted to a *current-cost* basis to yield the values shown in Table 5-5. They are converted by multiplying the real values by the appropriate price index for the period under consideration. A major use of the current-cost net stock figures is comparison with the value of output in that year; for example, the current-cost net stock of fixed assets for the total economy divided by the current-dollar value of GDP yields a capital/output ratio for the entire economy. Growth rates calculated from current-cost values will reflect both the real growth measured by the quantity indexes and the increase in the value at current prices of the existing stock.

Data availability

The fixed asset values are revised and updated periodically in articles in the *Survey of Current Business*. The values shown here are from the September 2002 issue.

References

The fixed asset measures are described in *Fixed Reproducible Tangible Wealth in the United States, 1925-94*, available on the BEA Web site, and "Fixed Assets and Consumer Durable Goods," *Survey of Current Business*, April 2000, also available on the BEA Web site.

TABLES 5-8 AND 5-9
MANUFACTURING AND TRADE SALES AND INVENTORIES

SOURCES: *U.S. DEPARTMENT OF COMMERCE, BUREAU OF THE CENSUS (CURRENT DOLLAR SERIES) AND U.S. DEPARTMENT OF COMMERCE, BUREAU OF ECONOMIC ANALYSIS (CONSTANT DOLLAR SERIES)*

The current dollar data on these pages draw together summary data from the separate series on manufacturers' shipments, inventories, and orders; merchant wholesalers' sales and inventories; and retail sales and inventories included in Part B of this book. Generally, current-dollar inventories are collected on a current cost (or pre-LIFO) basis. See the notes to Tables 17-4, 17-5, and 17-9 through 17-11 for further information about these data.

Data for recent years are compiled using the new North American Industry Classification System (NAICS), replacing the old Standard Industrial Classification (SIC).

• The Census Bureau has restated the current-dollar historical data on the NAICS basis back to January 1992. To allow the user to observe the difference between the two systems, and to "link" the new data to older data if a longer time series is required, *Business Statistics* is republishing the previous SIC-based annual data up through 1992, providing an overlap with the new data in that year.

• The Bureau of Economic Analysis has restated the constant-dollar data on the NAICS basis back to 1996. *Business Statistics* is publishing the previous SIC-based annual data through 1996 to provide an overlap.

In the NAICS, a few major industries have been taken out of manufacturing and trade entirely. Publishing and aerospace research activities have been reclassified from manufacturing to the new information industry, and food services and drinking places have been reclassified from retail trade to a new services category, Accommodation and Food Services, which also includes hotels and the like. A number of other activities have been moved within the broad category of manufacturing and trade. Food items made in retail establishments have been reclassified into manufacturing. A significant number of businesses previously classified as wholesale have been shifted to retail. Finally, the retail trade data, and therefore total manufacturing and trade, are no longer subdivided into durable and nondurable goods.

Based on these current-dollar values and relevant price data, estimates of real sales, inventories, and inventory-sales ratios are made by the Bureau of Economic Analysis (BEA). Note, however, that annual figures for sales are shown as annual totals in Table 5-6 but as averages of the monthly data in Table 5-7.

Inventory values are as of the end of the month or year. In Table 5-6, annual values for monthly current-dollar inventory-sales ratios are averages of seasonally adjusted monthly data. However, for the real ratios in Table 5-7, annual figures for inventory/sales ratios are calculated by BEA as year-end (that is, December) inventories divided by the monthly average of sales for the entire year.

Data availability

Sales, inventories, and inventory-sales ratios for manufacturers, merchant wholesalers, and retailers are published monthly by the Census Bureau in a press release entitled "Manufacturing and Trade Inventories and Sales;" recent data are available on the Internet site (http://www.census.gov/mtis/www/mtis.html).

Sales and inventories in constant dollars are published regularly by the Bureau of Economic Analysis in the *Survey of Current Business*; recent data are available on the BEA Internet site (http://www.bea.gov) or from the STAT-USA subscription Internet site (http://www.stat-usa.gov).

References

Further information comparing NAICS and SIC industries can be found on the Census Internet site, http://www.census.gov.

For information about the 1996 historical revisions to sales and inventories in constant dollars, see "Real Inventories, Sales, and Inventory-Sales Ratios for Manufacturing and Trade, 1977–95," *Survey of Current Business*, May 1996.

TABLES 5-10 AND 5-11
ANNUAL CAPITAL EXPENDITURES

SOURCE: U.S. DEPARTMENT OF COMMERCE, CENSUS BUREAU

These data are from the Census Bureau's Annual Capital Expenditures Survey (ACES). The survey provides detailed information on capital investment in new and used structures and equipment by nonfarm businesses for the years 1996 through 2001.

The survey is based on a sample of approximately 46,000 companies with employees and 15,000 non-employer businesses (businesses with an owner but no employees). For companies with employees, Census reports data for the years 1998 through 2001 for 132 separate industry categories from the North American Industry Classification System (NAICS); Table 5-11 shows these data for the major NAICS sectors. Total capital expenditures, with no industry detail, are reported for the non-employer businesses and shown in Table 5-10, where they can be compared with the totals for companies with employees, for the years 1996 through 2001.

Capital expenditures include all capitalized costs during the year for both new and used structures and equipment, including software, chargeable to fixed asset

accounts for which depreciation or amortization accounts are ordinarily maintained. For projects lasting longer than 1 year, this definition includes gross additions to construction-in-progress accounts, even if the asset was not in use and not yet depreciated. For capital leases, the company using the asset (lessee) is asked to include the cost or present value of the leased assets in the year in which the lease was entered into. Also included in capital expenditures are capitalized leasehold improvements and capitalized interest charges on loans used to finance capital projects.

Data availability

The "Annual Capital Expenditure Survey: 2001" was published by the Census Bureau in January 2003 and contains data for 1999 and revised data for 2000. Previous surveys using NAICS, each containing the latest year's data and revisions for the preceding year, were issued in April 2002 and May 2001. The 1998 and 1997 surveys show data by industry using the 1987 Standard Industrial Classification (SIC). Current and past surveys are available on the Census Internet site, <http://www.census.gov/csd/ace>.

CHAPTER 6: GOVERNMENT

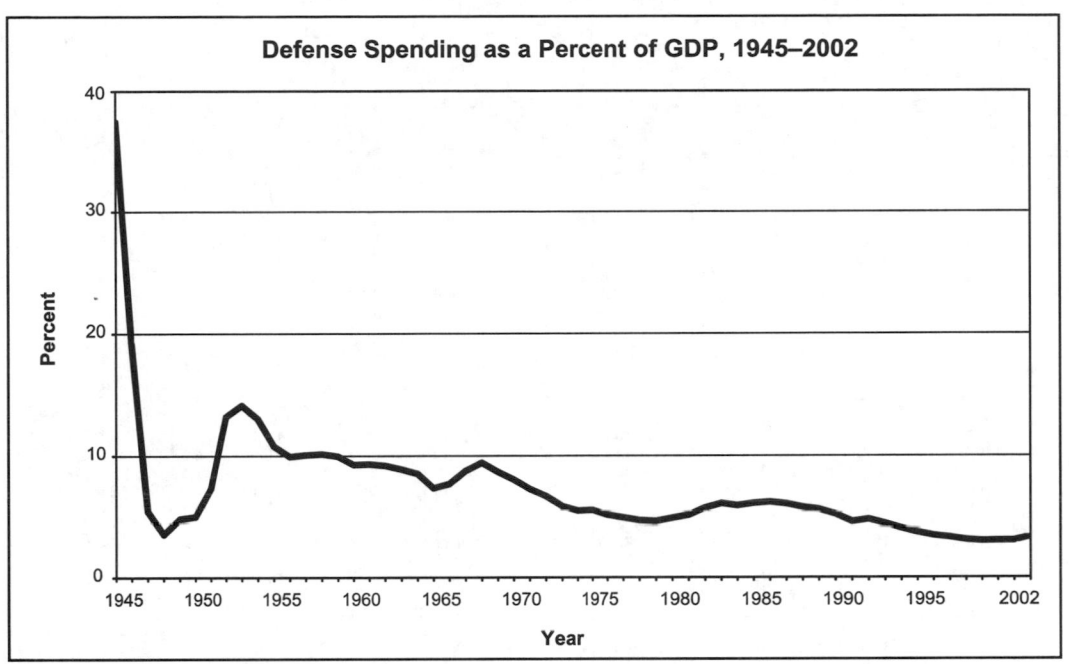

Defense Spending as a Percent of GDP, 1945–2002

- As of 2002, defense spending as a percent of GDP had increased slightly, but remained low by postwar standards, as the graph indicates. So far, the increase was less than those associated with the Korean and Vietnam wars, and similar to the increase at the beginning of the buildup of defense capability in 1980. (Table 6-7)

- Since 1955, total employment of civilians by all levels of government has increased 206 percent and risen from 13.8 percent to 16.5 percent of total payroll employment. Federal employment rose 21 percent; state government rose 329 percent, with half of the increase due to education; and local government rose 285 percent, with 58 percent of the rise due to education. (Tables 6-9 and 8-4)

- Defense investment spending (spending for assets with a life longer than one year) has seen long swings in the postwar period. Gross investment fell short of the depreciation of the existing stock in the immediate aftermath of World War II, the post-Vietnam 1970s, and the post-Cold-War 1990s: in all these periods, net defense investment was negative. It was positive in the 1950s, 1960s, and 1980s. (Table 6-3)

- In real (that is, quantity) terms, federal consumption and investment spending rose 169 percent from 1946 to 2002, while state and local spending rose 815 percent. (Table 6-4)

- Both state and local governments have been net borrowers of funds in most postwar years, financing new investment in excess of the using-up of old capital. (Tables 6-10 and 6-11)

- For both state and local governments, transportation spending dominates the economic affairs function. For states, transportation and higher education together made up 43 percent of all their spending in 2001. For local governments, transportation and elementary and secondary education accounted for 59 percent of their total spending. (Tables 6-12 and 6-13)

Table 6-1. Federal Government Current Receipts and Expenditures

(National Income and Product Accounts, calendar years, billions of dollars, quarterly data are at seasonally adjusted annual rates.)

Year and quarter	Current receipts					Current expenditures						Current surplus or deficit (-), national income and product accounts		
	Total	Personal tax and nontax receipts	Corporate profits tax accruals	Indirect business tax and nontax accruals	Contributions for social insurance	Total	Consumption expenditures	Transfer payments (net)	Grants-in-aid to state and local governments	Net interest paid	Subsidies less surplus of government enterprises	Total	Social insurance funds	Other
1946	39.5	16.4	8.6	7.9	6.5	44.6	27.1	10.9	1.0	4.1	1.6	-5.1	3.2	-8.4
1947	42.8	18.8	10.7	7.9	5.4	37.6	20.8	10.4	1.6	4.2	0.6	5.2	3.2	2.1
1948	42.4	18.1	11.8	8.1	4.4	38.9	21.2	11.0	1.7	4.3	0.6	3.5	2.4	1.1
1949	37.9	15.4	9.6	8.2	4.7	43.6	23.3	13.3	1.9	4.4	0.7	-5.7	1.5	-7.2
1950	48.8	17.5	17.2	8.9	5.3	43.3	22.0	13.8	1.9	4.5	1.0	5.5	-0.3	5.7
1951	62.9	25.4	21.7	9.4	6.4	53.3	34.4	11.0	2.0	4.6	1.2	9.6	2.6	7.0
1952	65.8	30.2	18.6	10.4	6.6	62.1	44.2	10.2	2.2	4.7	0.9	3.7	2.6	1.1
1953	68.6	31.4	19.5	11.0	6.8	66.8	48.3	10.7	2.3	4.8	0.7	1.8	2.1	-0.3
1954	62.5	28.1	16.9	9.8	7.8	64.2	44.0	12.5	2.3	4.9	0.6	-1.7	1.2	-2.9
1955	71.1	30.5	21.1	10.7	8.8	65.4	43.9	13.6	2.4	4.8	0.6	5.7	1.5	4.1
1956	75.8	34.0	20.9	11.3	9.6	68.3	45.1	14.2	2.5	5.3	1.2	7.5	1.7	5.8
1957	79.3	36.0	20.4	11.9	11.0	76.1	49.5	16.4	2.9	5.8	1.6	3.2	1.1	2.2
1958	76.0	35.5	18.0	11.6	11.0	81.5	50.9	20.0	3.3	5.4	1.8	-5.5	-2.7	-2.8
1959	87.0	38.5	22.5	12.6	13.4	83.8	52.0	20.4	3.8	6.4	1.2	3.2	-0.7	3.9
1960	92.8	41.9	21.4	13.5	16.0	85.8	51.5	21.7	4.0	7.1	1.5	7.1	0.6	6.5
1961	94.4	42.7	21.5	13.7	16.5	92.0	53.2	25.2	4.5	6.6	2.5	2.5	-2.1	4.6
1962	102.3	46.6	22.5	14.7	18.6	100.0	59.5	25.6	5.0	7.1	2.8	2.4	-0.3	2.7
1963	110.2	49.2	24.6	15.4	21.0	105.0	62.4	26.7	5.6	7.7	2.5	5.2	1.1	4.1
1964	110.2	46.0	26.1	16.3	21.7	109.3	64.2	27.2	6.5	8.4	3.0	0.8	1.5	-0.7
1965	119.3	51.1	28.9	16.6	22.7	116.1	67.4	29.3	7.2	8.9	3.3	3.2	0.8	2.4
1966	136.3	58.7	31.4	15.7	30.5	133.6	77.2	32.0	10.1	9.8	4.5	2.7	6.4	-3.6
1967	144.9	64.4	30.0	16.5	34.0	153.2	88.3	38.3	11.7	10.5	4.4	-8.3	4.9	-13.2
1968	168.5	76.5	36.1	18.2	37.8	169.8	97.0	43.5	12.7	12.1	4.5	-1.3	3.8	-5.1
1969	190.1	91.8	36.1	19.2	43.1	180.5	100.0	47.4	14.6	13.6	5.0	9.6	6.2	3.4
1970	184.3	88.9	30.6	19.5	45.3	198.6	100.4	57.4	19.3	15.3	6.2	-14.4	1.6	-16.0
1971	189.8	85.9	33.5	20.5	50.0	216.6	103.7	68.2	23.2	15.3	6.3	-26.8	-2.3	-24.5
1972	217.5	102.9	36.6	20.1	57.9	240.0	109.9	75.1	31.7	16.1	7.7	-22.5	0.1	-22.6
1973	248.5	109.7	43.3	21.5	74.0	259.7	111.6	86.4	34.8	19.9	7.0	-11.2	6.9	-18.1
1974	277.3	126.6	45.1	22.1	83.5	291.2	120.4	106.2	36.3	22.9	5.0	-13.9	4.0	-17.8
1975	276.1	120.9	43.6	24.2	87.5	345.4	131.2	135.6	45.1	25.6	7.9	-69.3	-15.4	-53.9
1976	318.9	141.4	54.6	23.8	99.1	371.9	138.0	146.3	50.7	29.9	7.1	-53.0	-14.4	-38.6
1977	359.9	162.3	61.6	25.6	110.3	405.0	151.3	155.0	56.6	32.5	9.8	-45.2	-12.6	-32.5
1978	417.3	189.1	71.4	28.9	127.9	444.2	164.3	165.3	65.5	38.5	10.7	-26.9	-3.0	-24.0
1979	478.3	224.8	74.4	30.1	148.9	489.6	180.0	185.9	66.3	47.0	10.3	-11.4	1.8	-13.2
1980	522.8	250.2	70.3	39.7	162.6	576.6	209.0	223.8	72.3	58.5	12.9	-53.8	-13.8	-40.0
1981	605.6	290.8	65.7	57.3	191.8	659.3	239.9	254.7	72.5	79.1	13.3	-53.7	-12.4	-41.3
1982	599.5	295.7	49.0	49.9	204.9	732.1	265.3	287.3	69.5	93.9	16.1	-132.6	-32.5	-100.1
1983	623.9	287.2	61.3	53.5	221.8	797.8	288.0	309.5	71.6	104.6	23.7	-173.9	-35.4	-138.5
1984	688.1	302.5	75.2	57.6	252.8	856.1	312.0	316.2	76.7	127.5	24.0	-168.1	-5.4	-162.7
1985	747.4	337.2	76.3	57.5	276.5	924.6	339.0	336.9	80.9	144.4	23.3	-177.1	2.6	-179.7
1986	786.4	351.4	83.8	53.7	297.5	978.5	358.3	356.0	87.6	150.5	26.1	-192.1	7.7	-199.9
1987	870.5	394.5	103.2	56.8	315.9	1 018.4	374.6	367.2	83.9	159.8	32.9	-147.9	16.4	-164.3
1988	928.9	405.7	111.1	58.9	353.1	1 066.2	382.8	387.9	91.6	172.1	31.9	-137.4	41.2	-178.6
1989	1 010.3	454.6	117.2	62.3	376.3	1 140.3	399.6	420.1	98.3	193.5	28.7	-130.0	45.6	-175.6
1990	1 055.7	473.6	118.1	63.9	400.1	1 228.7	419.9	455.3	111.4	210.5	31.6	-173.0	44.9	-217.9
1991	1 072.3	465.2	109.9	78.5	418.6	1 287.6	439.1	463.4	131.6	225.2	28.2	-215.3	27.4	-242.8
1992	1 121.3	479.4	118.8	81.3	441.8	1 418.9	445.8	565.2	149.1	229.2	29.6	-297.5	9.1	-306.7
1993	1 197.3	509.9	138.5	85.3	463.7	1 471.5	442.6	597.9	162.6	230.2	38.2	-274.1	6.9	-281.1
1994	1 293.7	547.8	156.7	95.2	493.9	1 506.0	439.7	618.6	174.5	239.6	33.6	-212.3	22.8	-235.1
1995	1 383.7	591.8	179.3	93.0	519.6	1 575.7	439.2	652.1	184.5	267.5	32.4	-192.0	19.9	-211.9
1996	1 499.1	670.0	190.6	95.1	543.3	1 635.9	445.3	691.6	190.4	273.6	35.1	-136.8	16.7	-153.5
1997	1 625.5	751.9	203.0	93.7	577.0	1 678.8	456.9	717.5	196.8	276.2	31.5	-53.3	30.5	-83.8
1998	1 749.7	834.9	204.2	97.4	613.1	1 705.9	453.1	730.6	210.3	278.5	33.4	43.8	58.0	-14.2
1999	1 867.2	903.3	213.0	100.2	650.7	1 755.3	471.6	745.8	231.0	263.8	43.0	111.9	95.9	16.0
2000	2 033.9	1 009.0	223.8	109.1	692.1	1 827.1	493.3	779.5	247.5	263.0	43.8	206.9	118.3	88.6
2001	2 008.4	1 010.9	170.2	110.3	716.9	1 936.4	528.4	842.2	277.4	238.1	50.3	72.0	93.3	-21.3
2002	1 873.3	845.8	179.8	110.6	737.1	2 075.5	586.5	931.7	305.7	207.8	43.7	-202.1	52.0	-254.1
2000														
1st quarter	2 009.6	984.5	233.7	107.0	684.5	1 786.4	480.0	758.5	239.4	264.2	44.2	223.2	122.4	100.8
2nd quarter	2 022.9	997.2	230.5	109.5	685.7	1 825.7	501.3	774.6	242.2	264.1	43.5	197.2	111.0	86.2
3rd quarter	2 049.1	1 020.5	222.1	109.8	696.6	1 835.9	494.2	781.3	253.8	263.0	43.6	213.2	120.2	93.0
4th quarter	2 054.1	1 033.6	208.9	110.1	701.5	1 860.3	497.7	803.5	254.6	260.5	44.0	193.8	119.4	74.4
2001														
1st quarter	2 072.9	1 057.9	186.9	112.3	715.8	1 899.1	517.3	816.3	266.8	254.1	44.6	173.8	108.6	65.3
2nd quarter	2 072.3	1 059.8	183.2	112.2	717.1	1 927.8	524.9	832.2	281.9	243.1	45.6	144.4	99.6	44.9
3rd quarter	1 896.0	900.4	168.0	109.5	718.1	1 947.7	527.9	849.3	271.4	233.6	65.5	-51.7	88.5	-140.2
4th quarter	1 992.3	1 025.5	142.9	107.3	716.6	1 971.0	543.6	870.9	289.4	221.6	45.5	21.3	76.4	-55.1
2002														
1st quarter	1 884.7	874.8	170.5	108.4	731.1	2 030.5	566.3	916.9	292.3	208.5	46.6	-145.8	64.1	-209.9
2nd quarter	1 883.7	856.6	180.2	110.2	736.7	2 079.3	581.0	927.6	309.6	214.9	46.3	-195.6	49.7	-245.3
3rd quarter	1 864.1	831.3	181.1	112.4	739.3	2 074.6	589.8	934.1	305.0	205.8	39.9	-210.5	48.1	-258.6
4th quarter	1 860.8	820.5	187.5	111.5	741.4	2 117.4	608.9	948.5	315.8	202.1	42.1	-256.6	46.0	-302.6

Table 6-2. State and Local Government Current Receipts and Expenditures

(National Income and Product Accounts, calendar years, billions of dollars, quarterly data are at seasonally adjusted annual rates.)

Year and quarter	Current receipts						Current expenditures						Current surplus or deficit (-), national income and product accounts		
	Total	Personal tax and nontax receipts	Corporate profits tax accruals	Indirect business tax and nontax accruals	Contributions for social insurance	Federal grants-in-aid	Total	Consumption expenditures	Transfer payments to persons	Net interest paid	Less: dividends received by government	Subsidies less surplus of government enterprises	Total	Social insurance funds	Other
1946	12.0	1.1	0.5	9.3	0.2	1.0	10.6	9.3	1.5	0.3	...	-0.4	1.4	0.1	1.4
1947	14.3	1.2	0.6	10.7	0.2	1.6	12.9	11.0	2.0	0.2	...	-0.4	1.4	0.1	1.3
1948	16.2	1.5	0.7	12.2	0.2	1.7	15.0	12.5	2.7	0.2	...	-0.3	1.2	0.1	1.1
1949	17.7	1.7	0.6	13.3	0.2	1.9	16.3	13.8	2.7	0.2	...	-0.4	1.4	0.1	1.4
1950	19.3	1.8	0.8	14.6	0.2	1.9	18.0	15.1	3.2	0.2	...	-0.4	1.3	0.1	1.2
1951	21.2	2.1	0.9	15.9	0.2	2.0	18.6	16.3	2.6	0.2	...	-0.5	2.5	0.1	2.4
1952	22.9	2.2	0.8	17.4	0.3	2.2	20.0	17.4	2.9	0.2	...	-0.5	2.9	0.1	2.8
1953	24.6	2.4	0.8	18.8	0.3	2.3	21.2	18.5	3.0	0.2	...	-0.6	3.4	0.1	3.3
1954	25.9	2.6	0.8	19.9	0.3	2.3	22.7	20.0	3.1	0.3	...	-0.7	3.2	0.1	3.1
1955	28.1	2.9	1.0	21.6	0.3	2.4	24.7	21.9	3.3	0.4	...	-0.8	3.4	0.1	3.3
1956	31.0	3.2	1.0	23.8	0.4	2.5	26.7	23.8	3.3	0.4	...	-0.9	4.3	0.1	4.2
1957	33.6	3.5	1.0	25.7	0.4	2.9	29.5	26.2	3.6	0.5	...	-0.9	4.1	0.1	4.0
1958	35.6	3.7	1.0	27.2	0.4	3.3	32.8	29.0	4.0	0.6	...	-0.9	2.8	0.0	2.7
1959	38.9	4.2	1.2	29.3	0.4	3.8	35.1	31.1	4.3	0.7	...	-1.1	3.8	0.0	3.7
1960	42.4	4.7	1.2	32.0	0.5	4.0	38.1	34.0	4.6	0.8	...	-1.2	4.3	0.0	4.3
1961	45.9	5.1	1.3	34.4	0.5	4.5	41.6	37.0	5.0	1.0	...	-1.3	4.3	0.0	4.3
1962	49.7	5.7	1.5	37.0	0.5	5.0	44.5	39.4	5.3	1.1	...	-1.4	5.2	0.0	5.2
1963	53.4	6.1	1.7	39.4	0.6	5.6	47.7	42.4	5.7	1.2	...	-1.6	5.7	0.0	5.7
1964	58.4	6.8	1.8	42.6	0.7	6.5	52.0	46.3	6.2	1.2	...	-1.6	6.4	0.0	6.3
1965	63.3	7.3	2.0	46.1	0.8	7.2	56.8	50.8	6.7	1.1	...	-1.7	6.5	0.1	6.4
1966	71.5	8.7	2.2	49.7	0.8	10.1	63.8	56.8	7.6	1.0	...	-1.6	7.7	0.1	7.6
1967	78.9	9.7	2.6	53.9	0.9	11.7	71.9	63.2	9.2	1.0	...	-1.5	7.0	0.1	6.8
1968	89.5	11.8	3.3	60.8	0.9	12.7	82.1	71.1	11.4	1.0	...	-1.5	7.5	0.1	7.3
1969	100.7	14.1	3.6	67.4	1.0	14.6	92.8	80.2	13.2	0.8	...	-1.4	8.0	0.2	7.8
1970	114.6	15.7	3.7	74.8	1.1	19.3	107.5	92.0	16.1	0.9	...	-1.5	7.1	0.2	6.9
1971	129.3	17.5	4.3	83.1	1.2	23.2	122.9	103.4	19.3	1.7	...	-1.3	6.4	0.2	6.2
1972	152.3	22.8	5.3	91.2	1.3	31.7	136.7	113.8	22.0	2.3	...	-1.5	15.6	0.3	15.3
1973	166.6	24.7	6.0	99.5	1.5	34.8	150.9	126.9	24.1	1.3	0.0	-1.4	15.7	0.3	15.4
1974	178.5	26.7	6.7	107.2	1.7	36.3	169.2	144.5	25.3	0.2	0.0	-0.8	9.3	0.4	8.9
1975	199.6	29.5	7.3	115.8	1.8	45.1	197.2	165.4	30.8	1.3	0.0	-0.2	2.4	0.5	1.9
1976	224.5	34.1	9.6	127.8	2.2	50.7	217.2	180.1	34.1	3.2	0.0	-0.2	7.3	0.6	6.7
1977	249.5	38.8	11.4	139.9	2.8	56.6	236.4	196.5	37.0	3.0	0.0	-0.1	13.1	1.0	12.1
1978	274.3	44.3	12.1	148.9	3.4	65.5	255.6	214.3	40.8	0.8	0.1	0.0	18.7	1.5	17.2
1979	290.8	48.4	13.6	158.6	3.9	66.3	277.8	235.0	44.3	-2.2	0.1	0.6	13.0	1.8	11.3
1980	316.6	53.9	14.5	172.3	3.6	72.3	307.8	260.5	51.2	-5.4	0.1	1.6	8.8	1.3	7.5
1981	344.4	60.6	15.4	192.0	3.9	72.5	336.9	284.6	57.1	-7.5	0.1	2.8	7.5	1.3	6.2
1982	360.3	65.9	14.0	206.8	4.0	69.5	362.5	306.8	61.2	-7.3	0.2	2.1	-2.3	1.2	-3.5
1983	392.1	73.7	15.9	226.8	4.1	71.6	387.3	325.1	66.9	-5.2	0.2	0.7	4.8	1.2	3.6
1984	436.4	84.8	18.8	251.5	4.7	76.7	412.6	349.5	71.2	-6.7	0.2	-1.1	23.8	1.4	22.4
1985	469.2	91.3	20.2	272.0	4.9	80.9	447.0	380.5	77.3	-7.9	0.2	-2.8	22.3	1.3	21.0
1986	507.9	98.6	22.7	293.1	6.0	87.6	487.2	410.8	84.4	-5.5	0.2	-2.5	20.8	1.9	18.9
1987	536.0	108.5	23.9	312.4	7.2	83.9	523.8	439.0	90.8	-3.1	0.2	-2.8	12.2	2.2	10.0
1988	573.7	114.0	26.0	333.7	8.4	91.6	558.1	467.9	98.6	-3.8	0.2	-4.5	15.6	2.5	13.1
1989	618.9	128.9	24.2	358.5	9.0	98.3	599.6	503.0	109.5	-6.6	0.2	-6.1	19.3	2.3	17.0
1990	663.4	136.0	22.5	383.4	10.0	111.4	660.8	545.8	127.8	-6.3	0.2	-6.3	2.6	2.0	0.7
1991	716.0	145.3	23.6	403.8	11.6	131.6	723.8	576.1	156.6	-2.1	0.2	-6.6	-7.8	2.4	-10.2
1992	772.2	156.4	24.4	429.2	13.1	149.1	777.2	601.6	180.1	2.8	0.2	-7.2	-4.9	3.1	-8.1
1993	823.2	164.7	26.9	454.8	14.1	162.6	821.7	629.5	195.4	5.6	0.2	-8.6	1.5	4.2	-2.7
1994	873.8	174.8	30.0	480.1	14.5	174.5	865.2	662.6	206.9	4.4	0.2	-8.5	8.6	4.6	4.0
1995	917.9	186.5	31.7	501.6	13.6	184.5	902.5	694.7	217.8	0.5	0.3	-10.2	15.3	4.0	11.4
1996	960.4	199.6	33.0	524.9	12.5	190.4	939.0	726.5	224.3	0.9	0.3	-12.5	21.4	2.7	18.7
1997	1 011.3	216.9	34.2	552.5	10.8	196.8	980.3	766.4	227.5	-0.9	0.3	-12.4	31.0	1.1	29.9
1998	1 074.4	235.5	34.6	583.9	10.1	210.3	1 033.7	808.3	235.3	0.4	0.4	-9.9	40.7	0.6	40.0
1999	1 144.1	255.8	34.8	612.7	9.7	231.0	1 105.8	864.7	252.7	-0.7	0.4	-10.5	38.3	0.9	37.4
2000	1 214.2	277.5	35.6	644.5	9.2	247.5	1 196.2	937.9	271.3	-2.8	0.4	-9.7	18.0	0.1	17.8
2001	1 261.3	281.2	29.1	664.4	9.2	277.4	1 292.6	993.7	304.4	-2.1	0.4	-3.1	-31.3	-0.1	-31.2
2002	1 304.5	266.1	33.5	689.8	9.4	305.7	1 356.4	1 034.5	335.6	-2.0	0.5	-11.2	-52.0	-0.1	-51.9
2000															
1st quarter	1 195.9	271.8	37.1	638.1	9.4	239.4	1 163.2	914.0	262.0	-2.4	0.4	-9.9	32.7	0.5	32.2
2nd quarter	1 204.7	275.7	36.8	640.8	9.2	242.2	1 184.5	930.0	267.4	-2.9	0.4	-9.6	20.2	0.2	20.0
3rd quarter	1 225.4	279.1	35.3	648.0	9.1	253.8	1 206.2	945.4	273.8	-3.0	0.4	-9.6	19.2	-0.1	19.2
4th quarter	1 230.8	283.2	33.0	650.9	9.2	254.6	1 231.0	962.2	282.1	-3.1	0.4	-9.8	-0.2	-0.1	-0.1
2001															
1st quarter	1 247.3	282.6	30.4	658.3	9.2	266.8	1 263.8	976.2	292.4	-2.4	0.4	-1.9	-16.5	-0.1	-16.4
2nd quarter	1 261.1	276.3	29.9	663.8	9.2	281.9	1 293.4	990.6	301.5	-2.2	0.4	4.1	-32.3	-0.1	-32.2
3rd quarter	1 253.6	281.6	28.2	663.2	9.3	271.4	1 299.8	1 000.1	308.5	-2.0	0.4	-6.4	-46.2	-0.1	-46.1
4th quarter	1 283.2	284.3	27.7	672.5	9.2	289.4	1 313.3	1 008.2	315.4	-1.8	0.4	-8.1	-30.2	-0.2	-30.0
2002															
1st quarter	1 273.3	262.0	32.0	677.8	9.3	292.3	1 329.1	1 017.7	323.4	-1.9	0.4	-9.6	-55.8	-0.2	-55.6
2nd quarter	1 302.5	265.3	33.5	684.9	9.4	309.6	1 347.6	1 030.6	330.7	-2.0	0.5	-11.2	-45.1	-0.1	-44.9
3rd quarter	1 310.3	267.7	33.7	694.5	9.4	305.0	1 365.0	1 039.6	338.7	-2.0	0.5	-10.8	-54.7	-0.1	-54.6
4th quarter	1 331.6	269.6	34.9	701.8	9.5	315.8	1 384.0	1 050.1	349.5	-1.9	0.5	-13.2	-52.4	-0.1	-52.3

. . . = Not available.

Table 6-3. Government Consumption Expenditures and Gross and Net Investment by Type [1]

(National Income and Product Accounts, calendar years, billions of dollars, quarterly data are at seasonally adjusted annual rates.)

Year and quarter	Total govern-ment	Federal Total	National defense Total	Consumption expenditures Total	Durable goods [2]	Nondura-ble goods	Services Compensa-tion of employees [3]	Services Consump-tion of fixed capital [4]	Services Other services	Gross investment Total	Structures	Equipment and software	Net investment
1946	39.8	29.0	25.3	23.8	-0.4	0.7	14.1	8.9	0.5	1.5	0.3	1.2	-7.4
1947	36.4	22.6	18.2	17.3	0.3	0.3	7.8	8.3	0.7	0.9	0.2	0.8	-7.4
1948	40.6	24.2	18.4	16.4	0.7	0.7	6.9	7.0	1.0	2.0	0.4	1.6	-5.0
1949	46.8	27.6	19.9	16.9	0.9	0.8	7.8	6.0	1.4	2.9	0.4	2.6	-3.1
1950	46.9	26.0	19.6	17.2	1.7	0.9	7.9	5.2	1.5	2.4	0.5	1.9	-2.8
1951	68.3	45.0	39.3	30.1	4.2	2.3	13.4	5.5	4.8	9.1	2.0	7.1	3.6
1952	83.9	59.2	52.4	38.9	8.0	2.7	16.0	6.2	6.1	13.4	3.3	10.1	7.2
1953	90.8	64.4	56.0	41.3	9.1	4.2	15.9	7.0	5.1	14.7	3.3	11.4	7.7
1954	86.5	57.3	49.3	37.1	6.8	3.2	15.3	7.6	4.2	12.1	2.7	9.4	4.5
1955	86.8	54.9	47.0	36.9	5.9	1.6	15.7	8.0	5.7	10.1	2.1	8.0	2.1
1956	91.8	56.7	49.3	38.8	6.0	1.7	16.0	8.6	6.5	10.5	2.1	8.4	1.9
1957	100.1	61.3	53.7	43.2	6.6	2.1	16.4	9.1	9.0	10.5	2.3	8.2	1.4
1958	106.5	63.9	55.5	44.2	6.9	2.1	16.9	9.2	9.1	11.3	2.6	8.7	2.1
1959	112.5	67.4	56.0	42.2	5.8	2.3	17.2	9.6	7.3	13.7	2.5	11.2	4.1
1960	113.8	65.9	55.2	42.8	4.8	2.5	17.6	9.9	8.1	12.3	2.2	10.1	2.4
1961	121.5	69.5	58.1	44.3	3.9	2.9	18.2	10.2	9.0	13.9	2.4	11.5	3.7
1962	132.2	76.9	62.8	48.3	4.9	3.6	19.3	10.7	9.7	14.5	2.0	12.5	3.8
1963	138.5	78.5	62.7	50.1	5.0	3.3	20.0	11.2	10.5	12.6	1.6	11.0	1.4
1964	145.1	79.8	61.8	50.3	4.1	3.6	21.5	11.3	9.8	11.5	1.3	10.2	0.2
1965	153.7	82.1	62.4	52.4	4.9	3.4	22.5	11.4	10.1	10.1	1.1	8.9	-1.3
1966	174.3	94.4	73.8	61.4	6.8	4.7	26.2	11.7	12.0	12.3	1.3	11.1	0.6
1967	195.3	106.8	85.8	71.5	7.2	7.3	29.3	12.3	15.4	14.3	1.2	13.1	2.0
1968	212.8	114.0	92.2	79.0	8.9	8.4	32.4	13.1	16.3	13.2	1.2	11.9	0.1
1969	224.6	116.1	92.6	80.1	7.8	7.6	34.7	13.7	16.4	12.5	1.5	11.0	-1.2
1970	237.1	116.4	90.9	78.7	7.5	5.3	36.6	14.2	15.0	12.3	1.3	10.9	-1.9
1971	251.0	117.6	89.0	79.3	5.8	4.4	38.2	14.6	16.2	9.7	1.8	7.9	-4.9
1972	270.1	125.6	93.5	82.3	5.9	4.8	40.5	15.8	15.4	11.2	1.8	9.4	-4.6
1973	287.9	127.8	93.9	82.6	5.3	4.4	41.4	16.4	15.3	11.3	2.1	9.2	-5.1
1974	322.4	138.2	99.7	87.5	4.6	5.3	44.0	16.7	16.8	12.3	2.2	10.1	-4.4
1975	361.1	152.1	107.9	93.4	6.5	5.1	47.8	17.5	16.5	14.5	2.3	12.1	-3.0
1976	384.5	160.6	113.2	97.9	5.9	4.5	50.2	18.8	18.5	15.3	2.1	13.2	-3.5
1977	415.3	176.0	122.6	105.8	7.9	4.6	53.5	19.9	20.0	16.7	2.4	14.4	-3.2
1978	455.6	191.9	132.0	114.2	9.6	4.9	57.4	21.2	21.1	17.8	2.5	15.3	-3.4
1979	503.5	211.6	146.7	125.3	11.5	6.3	61.5	22.3	23.6	21.4	2.5	18.9	-0.9
1980	569.7	245.3	169.6	145.3	12.8	10.1	68.4	24.4	29.6	24.3	3.2	21.1	-0.1
1981	631.4	281.8	197.8	168.9	16.1	12.0	78.6	27.2	35.1	28.9	3.2	25.7	1.7
1982	684.4	312.8	228.3	193.6	19.2	11.6	87.2	31.0	44.6	34.7	4.0	30.8	3.7
1983	735.9	344.4	252.5	210.6	25.0	11.3	92.2	33.4	48.6	41.9	4.8	37.1	8.5
1984	800.8	376.4	283.5	234.9	26.9	10.5	107.3	36.6	53.6	48.7	4.9	43.8	12.1
1985	878.3	413.4	312.4	254.9	29.2	10.0	115.0	38.6	62.0	57.5	6.2	51.3	18.9
1986	942.3	438.7	332.2	269.3	31.9	10.3	118.4	41.5	67.3	62.9	6.8	56.1	21.4
1987	997.9	460.4	351.2	284.8	33.6	10.3	123.2	44.1	73.6	66.4	7.7	58.8	22.3
1988	1 036.9	462.6	355.9	294.6	33.5	10.6	126.5	47.0	77.1	61.3	7.4	53.9	14.3
1989	1 100.2	482.6	363.2	300.5	32.0	10.8	131.2	50.1	76.4	62.7	6.4	56.3	12.6
1990	1 181.4	508.4	374.9	308.9	30.9	11.0	134.0	53.2	79.8	65.9	6.1	59.8	12.7
1991	1 235.5	527.4	384.5	321.1	31.2	10.7	141.3	56.3	81.6	63.4	4.6	58.8	7.1
1992	1 270.5	534.5	378.5	316.9	29.0	9.5	142.5	57.9	78.1	61.6	5.2	56.3	3.7
1993	1 293.0	527.3	364.9	309.2	27.1	8.4	138.1	60.2	75.3	55.7	5.1	50.7	-4.5
1994	1 327.9	521.1	355.1	301.1	23.3	7.6	134.2	61.8	74.2	54.0	5.7	48.3	-7.8
1995	1 372.0	521.5	350.6	297.5	21.0	6.3	130.4	63.0	76.8	53.1	6.3	46.9	-9.9
1996	1 421.9	531.6	357.0	302.4	21.0	7.7	133.1	63.0	77.7	54.6	6.7	47.9	-8.4
1997	1 487.9	538.2	352.6	304.2	21.1	7.5	132.5	62.8	80.2	48.4	5.7	42.7	-14.4
1998	1 538.5	539.2	349.1	299.7	21.1	6.9	131.2	62.3	78.2	49.4	5.4	44.0	-12.9
1999	1 641.0	565.0	364.3	312.0	22.4	8.1	133.1	62.5	85.9	52.3	5.3	47.0	-10.2
2000	1 751.0	589.2	374.9	321.4	22.5	10.4	138.3	63.6	86.7	53.5	5.3	48.2	-10.1
2001	1 858.0	628.1	399.9	344.5	24.2	10.5	143.7	63.5	102.5	55.5	5.4	50.0	-8.0
2002	1 972.9	693.7	447.4	386.6	25.3	11.5	154.4	64.2	131.3	60.8	5.3	55.5	-3.4
2000													
1st quarter	1 716.5	575.7	365.5	311.9	22.7	10.7	137.7	63.4	77.4	53.6	5.0	48.6	-9.8
2nd quarter	1 748.8	598.5	379.1	325.8	22.6	10.6	138.5	63.5	90.6	53.3	5.4	47.9	-10.2
3rd quarter	1 757.2	589.7	375.0	321.3	22.7	10.1	138.8	63.7	86.1	53.7	5.8	47.9	-10.0
4th quarter	1 781.4	592.9	380.0	326.5	22.1	10.0	138.1	63.7	92.5	53.5	5.2	48.3	-10.2
2001													
1st quarter	1 825.0	613.3	391.4	338.4	22.3	9.6	143.3	63.5	99.8	52.9	5.5	47.5	-10.6
2nd quarter	1 858.5	624.8	395.2	340.0	24.2	10.7	143.8	63.6	97.8	55.2	5.5	49.7	-8.4
3rd quarter	1 851.7	627.4	400.3	343.4	26.1	10.5	143.9	63.5	99.3	56.9	5.0	51.9	-6.6
4th quarter	1 896.8	646.9	412.8	356.0	24.0	11.3	143.9	63.6	113.2	56.8	5.7	51.1	-6.8
2002													
1st quarter	1 939.5	672.0	431.7	372.1	24.7	10.9	152.7	63.8	120.0	59.7	5.1	54.6	-4.1
2nd quarter	1 959.8	688.2	442.1	382.5	24.9	11.7	155.0	64.0	127.0	59.6	5.4	54.2	-4.4
3rd quarter	1 981.1	697.7	451.2	388.9	26.3	12.0	155.8	64.3	130.5	62.4	5.4	57.0	-1.9
4th quarter	2 011.3	716.9	464.7	403.2	25.2	11.4	153.9	64.9	147.7	61.5	5.3	56.3	-3.4

[1]Gross government investment consists of general government and government enterprise expenditures for fixed assets; inventory investment is included in government consumption expenditures.
[2]Consumption expenditures for durable goods excludes expenditures classified as investment, except for goods transferred to foreign countries by the federal government.
[3]Compensation of government employees engaged in new own-account investment and related expenditures for goods and services are classified as investment in structures and in software.
[4]Consumption of fixed capital, or depreciation, is included in government consumption expenditures as a partial measure of the value of the services of general government fixed assets; use of depreciation assumes a zero net return on these assets.

Table 6-3. Government Consumption Expenditures and Gross and Net Investment by Type [1]—Continued

(National Income and Product Accounts, calendar years, billions of dollars, quarterly data are at seasonally adjusted annual rates.)

Year and quarter	Federal—Continued												
	Nondefense												
		Consumption expenditures								Gross investment			
				Nondurable goods			Services						
	Total	Total	Durable goods [2]	Total	Commodity Credit Corporation inventory charge	Other nondurables	Compensation of employees [3]	Consumption of fixed capital [4]	Other services	Total	Structures	Equipment and software	Net investment
1946	3.6	3.2	-0.4	0.3	-0.5	0.8	2.1	0.5	0.8	0.4	0.0	0.4	-0.1
1947	4.3	3.5	-0.2	0.3	0.1	0.2	2.5	0.6	0.4	0.8	0.3	0.5	0.2
1948	5.8	4.8	-0.1	0.8	0.3	0.5	2.6	0.6	0.9	1.0	0.7	0.4	0.4
1949	7.8	6.3	0.0	2.1	1.5	0.6	2.9	0.6	0.8	1.4	1.1	0.3	0.8
1950	6.4	4.8	0.0	0.5	0.3	0.3	3.1	0.6	0.7	1.6	1.2	0.4	1.0
1951	5.8	4.2	0.0	0.1	-0.4	0.5	3.0	0.6	0.5	1.5	1.1	0.4	0.9
1952	6.8	5.2	0.0	0.4	0.2	0.3	3.1	0.6	1.1	1.6	1.1	0.5	1.0
1953	8.4	7.1	-0.1	2.3	2.0	0.3	3.0	0.6	1.2	1.4	1.1	0.3	0.8
1954	8.0	6.8	-0.1	2.2	1.9	0.3	2.8	0.6	1.3	1.2	0.9	0.3	0.6
1955	7.9	7.0	-0.1	2.4	2.0	0.4	3.1	0.6	1.0	0.9	0.6	0.2	0.3
1956	7.4	6.2	-0.1	0.7	0.2	0.6	3.4	0.6	1.5	1.2	0.9	0.3	0.6
1957	7.6	6.2	-0.1	0.7	-0.1	0.8	3.7	0.6	1.4	1.4	1.1	0.2	0.8
1958	8.4	6.8	-0.1	0.6	0.3	0.4	4.2	0.7	1.3	1.6	1.4	0.2	0.9
1959	11.4	9.8	-0.1	3.2	2.1	1.1	4.3	0.7	1.7	1.7	1.5	0.2	1.0
1960	10.7	8.7	-0.1	1.0	0.2	0.9	4.8	0.7	2.3	2.0	1.7	0.3	1.3
1961	11.3	8.9	-0.1	0.3	-0.8	1.1	5.2	0.7	2.7	2.4	1.9	0.6	1.7
1962	14.1	11.2	0.0	1.4	0.3	1.1	5.6	0.8	3.4	2.9	2.1	0.8	2.1
1963	15.8	12.3	0.1	1.1	-0.2	1.3	6.3	0.9	4.1	3.5	2.3	1.2	2.6
1964	18.0	13.9	0.2	1.0	-0.4	1.4	6.8	1.0	4.9	4.2	2.5	1.6	3.2
1965	19.7	15.0	0.2	1.1	-0.4	1.5	7.3	1.2	5.3	4.7	2.8	1.9	3.5
1966	20.7	15.8	0.2	0.3	-1.5	1.8	7.8	1.4	6.0	4.9	2.8	2.1	3.5
1967	21.0	16.9	0.1	1.1	-0.9	2.0	8.4	1.6	5.7	4.2	2.2	1.9	2.6
1968	21.8	18.0	-0.1	1.8	0.2	1.7	9.3	1.8	5.1	3.8	2.1	1.7	2.0
1969	23.5	19.9	-0.2	2.9	0.7	2.2	10.0	1.9	5.3	3.6	1.9	1.7	1.7
1970	25.5	21.7	-0.2	1.9	-0.4	2.3	11.5	2.1	6.3	3.8	2.1	1.7	1.7
1971	28.6	24.4	-0.2	2.0	-0.3	2.3	13.2	2.3	7.1	4.2	2.5	1.7	1.9
1972	32.2	27.6	-0.3	2.3	-0.4	2.7	14.6	2.4	8.6	4.5	2.7	1.8	2.1
1973	33.9	29.0	-0.5	1.8	-0.7	2.5	15.8	2.6	9.3	4.9	3.1	1.8	2.3
1974	38.5	32.9	-0.5	2.5	-0.5	3.0	17.8	2.9	10.3	5.6	3.4	2.2	2.7
1975	44.2	37.7	-0.4	2.7	0.3	2.4	20.3	3.3	11.9	6.5	4.1	2.4	3.2
1976	47.4	40.1	-0.6	3.3	0.2	3.1	22.9	3.5	11.0	7.3	4.6	2.7	3.8
1977	53.5	45.5	-0.7	3.8	0.4	3.4	26.1	3.7	12.5	8.0	5.0	3.0	4.3
1978	59.8	50.1	-0.8	3.9	0.0	3.8	28.1	4.0	14.9	9.8	6.1	3.7	5.8
1979	65.0	54.7	-1.0	3.9	0.0	4.0	29.9	4.6	17.4	10.2	6.3	4.0	5.6
1980	75.6	63.6	-0.4	5.6	1.5	4.1	33.7	5.2	19.5	12.0	7.1	4.9	6.8
1981	84.0	71.0	-0.2	9.4	0.9	8.5	36.0	6.1	19.8	13.0	7.7	5.3	6.9
1982	84.5	71.7	0.1	7.3	1.7	5.7	37.5	6.8	20.0	12.7	6.8	6.0	5.9
1983	92.0	77.4	0.1	8.8	2.5	6.3	39.5	7.3	21.7	14.5	6.7	7.8	7.2
1984	92.8	77.1	0.1	5.0	-1.8	6.8	41.4	8.0	22.6	15.7	7.0	8.7	7.7
1985	101.0	84.1	0.0	8.2	2.2	5.9	43.2	8.7	24.1	16.9	7.3	9.6	8.2
1986	106.5	89.0	-0.2	11.7	6.4	5.3	43.9	9.4	24.2	17.5	8.0	9.5	8.1
1987	109.3	89.9	-0.2	6.0	-0.2	6.2	46.3	10.1	27.7	19.4	9.0	10.4	9.3
1988	106.8	88.2	-0.5	-0.9	-7.1	6.2	50.5	10.9	28.1	18.6	6.8	11.7	7.7
1989	119.3	99.1	-0.4	4.8	-0.8	5.6	53.3	11.8	29.5	20.3	6.9	13.4	8.5
1990	133.6	111.0	-0.1	4.6	-1.5	6.1	58.6	12.7	35.1	22.6	8.0	14.6	9.9
1991	142.9	118.1	0.0	5.2	0.2	5.0	63.2	13.7	35.9	24.8	9.2	15.7	11.1
1992	156.0	128.8	0.3	6.1	-0.6	6.8	66.8	14.2	41.4	27.2	10.3	16.9	13.0
1993	162.4	133.4	0.5	6.6	-0.3	6.9	72.4	14.9	39.0	28.9	11.2	17.7	14.0
1994	165.9	138.6	1.0	6.6	-0.5	7.2	74.3	15.7	41.0	27.3	10.5	16.8	11.6
1995	170.9	141.8	0.9	6.5	-0.2	6.8	75.0	16.8	42.5	29.2	10.8	18.4	12.4
1996	174.6	142.9	1.1	6.1	-0.4	6.5	76.4	18.0	41.3	31.7	11.1	20.5	13.7
1997	185.6	152.7	1.2	7.9	-0.1	8.0	79.1	19.4	45.1	32.9	9.7	23.2	13.5
1998	190.1	153.4	-0.4	8.1	0.1	8.0	82.4	21.0	42.2	36.7	11.2	25.5	15.7
1999	200.7	159.6	1.0	6.3	0.2	6.1	86.9	23.6	41.9	41.1	11.6	29.4	17.5
2000	214.3	171.9	1.2	6.4	0.8	5.6	93.6	26.4	44.4	42.4	10.8	31.6	16.0
2001	228.2	184.0	1.3	8.7	0.8	7.9	95.2	28.7	50.1	44.2	10.4	33.8	15.5
2002	246.3	199.9	1.4	9.4	-0.2	9.6	104.3	30.8	54.0	46.4	12.3	34.1	15.6
2000													
1st quarter	210.2	168.1	1.2	6.8	0.5	6.3	93.4	25.3	41.4	42.1	11.6	30.6	16.8
2nd quarter	219.4	175.5	1.1	6.8	0.6	6.2	98.4	26.1	43.2	43.9	10.8	33.1	17.8
3rd quarter	214.7	172.8	1.2	7.5	0.8	6.6	92.2	26.7	45.3	41.9	10.3	31.5	15.2
4th quarter	213.0	171.3	1.4	4.4	1.1	3.2	90.3	27.4	47.9	41.7	10.5	31.2	14.3
2001													
1st quarter	221.9	178.8	1.3	8.2	0.7	7.5	94.3	27.9	47.1	43.1	10.7	32.4	15.2
2nd quarter	229.6	184.9	1.3	10.3	2.7	7.7	95.1	28.5	49.7	44.6	9.6	35.0	16.1
3rd quarter	227.2	184.5	1.3	8.0	0.0	8.0	95.7	29.0	50.6	42.6	9.8	32.8	13.6
4th quarter	234.1	187.5	1.4	8.2	0.0	8.3	95.6	29.5	52.8	46.6	11.6	35.0	17.1
2002													
1st quarter	240.3	194.2	1.4	8.6	-0.2	8.8	101.7	30.0	52.6	46.1	13.3	32.8	16.1
2nd quarter	246.1	198.6	1.4	10.1	0.3	9.8	102.7	30.5	53.9	47.5	12.1	35.4	17.0
3rd quarter	246.5	200.9	1.4	9.4	-0.2	9.6	104.6	31.0	54.5	45.5	11.3	34.3	14.5
4th quarter	252.2	205.8	1.6	9.4	-0.6	10.1	108.0	31.6	55.1	46.5	12.6	33.8	14.9

[1]Gross government investment consists of general government and government enterprise expenditures for fixed assets; inventory investment is included in government consumption expenditures.
[2]Consumption expenditures for durable goods excludes expenditures classified as investment, except for goods transferred to foreign countries by the federal government.
[3]Compensation of government employees engaged in new own-account investment and related expenditures for goods and services are classified as investment in structures and in software.
[4]Consumption of fixed capital, or depreciation, is included in government consumption expenditures as a partial measure of the value of the services of general government fixed assets; use of depreciation assumes a zero net return on these assets.

Table 6-3. Government Consumption Expenditures and Gross and Net Investment by Type [1]—Continued

(National Income and Product Accounts, calendar years, billions of dollars, quarterly data are at seasonally adjusted annual rates.)

Year and quarter		State and local										
		Consumption expenditures							Gross investment			
					Services							
	Total	Total	Durable goods [2]	Nondurable goods	Total	Compensation of employees [3]	Consumption of fixed capital [4]	Other services	Total	Structures	Equipment and software	Net investment
1946	10.8	9.3	0.1	1.0	8.2	6.2	1.2	0.9	1.6	1.4	0.2	0.4
1947	13.9	11.0	0.1	1.2	9.7	7.3	1.4	1.0	2.8	2.5	0.3	1.4
1948	16.5	12.5	0.1	1.2	11.1	8.4	1.7	1.0	4.0	3.6	0.4	2.3
1949	19.2	13.8	0.1	1.4	12.2	9.3	1.7	1.2	5.3	4.9	0.5	3.6
1950	20.9	15.1	0.2	1.7	13.2	10.0	1.7	1.6	5.9	5.4	0.5	4.2
1951	23.3	16.3	0.2	1.6	14.5	11.0	2.0	1.5	7.0	6.4	0.5	5.0
1952	24.7	17.4	0.2	1.5	15.6	12.1	2.2	1.4	7.3	6.7	0.6	5.1
1953	26.4	18.5	0.2	1.5	16.8	13.1	2.2	1.4	7.9	7.3	0.6	5.7
1954	29.2	20.0	0.2	1.6	18.2	14.5	2.2	1.5	9.2	8.5	0.7	7.0
1955	31.9	21.9	0.2	1.8	19.8	15.6	2.4	1.8	10.0	9.3	0.8	7.6
1956	35.1	23.8	0.3	1.7	21.8	17.4	2.8	1.7	11.3	10.4	0.9	8.5
1957	38.8	26.2	0.3	1.8	24.1	19.3	3.0	1.8	12.5	11.5	1.1	9.5
1958	42.6	29.0	0.3	2.2	26.5	21.3	3.1	2.1	13.5	12.5	1.1	10.4
1959	45.1	31.1	0.4	2.6	28.2	22.7	3.3	2.1	13.9	12.8	1.1	10.6
1960	47.9	34.0	0.4	2.8	30.8	25.1	3.5	2.3	13.9	12.7	1.2	10.4
1961	52.0	37.0	0.4	3.0	33.6	27.5	3.7	2.4	15.0	13.8	1.3	11.3
1962	55.3	39.4	0.5	3.0	36.0	29.8	3.9	2.2	15.9	14.5	1.3	12.0
1963	59.9	42.4	0.5	3.1	38.8	32.3	4.2	2.3	17.5	16.0	1.5	13.3
1964	65.3	46.3	0.6	3.3	42.4	35.4	4.5	2.5	19.0	17.2	1.8	14.5
1965	71.6	50.8	0.6	3.6	46.5	38.8	4.9	2.8	20.8	19.0	1.9	15.9
1966	79.9	56.8	0.7	3.9	52.1	43.5	5.5	3.2	23.1	21.0	2.1	17.6
1967	88.6	63.2	0.8	4.2	58.3	48.9	6.0	3.4	25.3	23.0	2.3	19.3
1968	98.8	71.1	0.9	4.7	65.5	55.2	6.6	3.7	27.7	25.2	2.4	21.1
1969	108.5	80.2	1.0	5.5	73.7	61.9	7.4	4.4	28.3	25.6	2.7	20.9
1970	120.7	92.0	1.1	6.5	84.3	70.3	8.4	5.6	28.7	25.8	3.0	20.3
1971	133.5	103.4	1.3	7.7	94.4	78.4	9.4	6.5	30.1	27.0	3.1	20.7
1972	144.4	113.8	1.5	8.4	104.0	86.9	10.2	6.9	30.6	27.1	3.5	20.4
1973	160.1	126.9	1.8	9.5	115.5	97.1	11.3	7.1	33.2	29.1	4.1	21.9
1974	184.2	144.5	2.2	12.3	130.0	106.7	14.1	9.2	39.6	34.7	4.9	25.5
1975	209.0	165.4	2.7	15.4	147.3	120.2	16.0	11.1	43.6	38.1	5.5	27.6
1976	223.9	180.1	3.1	17.6	159.3	132.1	16.6	10.6	43.8	38.1	5.7	27.2
1977	239.3	196.5	3.6	20.1	172.8	144.1	17.5	11.1	42.8	36.9	5.9	25.3
1978	263.8	214.3	3.9	21.8	188.6	157.9	18.8	11.9	49.5	42.8	6.6	30.7
1979	291.8	235.0	4.3	25.0	205.7	173.0	21.0	11.6	56.8	49.0	7.8	35.8
1980	324.4	260.5	4.7	28.3	227.5	191.5	24.3	11.7	64.0	55.1	8.9	39.7
1981	349.6	284.6	5.3	31.2	248.1	208.6	27.8	11.7	65.0	55.4	9.5	37.2
1982	371.6	306.8	5.9	32.0	268.9	225.9	30.3	12.7	64.8	54.2	10.6	34.5
1983	391.5	325.1	6.3	33.2	285.6	241.5	31.2	12.9	66.4	54.2	12.2	35.2
1984	424.4	349.5	6.9	35.5	307.1	259.4	32.0	15.7	75.0	60.5	14.4	43.0
1985	464.9	380.5	7.4	38.1	335.0	282.7	33.7	18.6	84.4	67.6	16.8	50.7
1986	503.6	410.8	8.2	37.6	365.0	305.2	36.2	23.6	92.8	74.2	18.6	56.6
1987	537.5	439.0	8.7	40.8	389.5	326.6	39.0	23.9	98.4	78.8	19.6	59.4
1988	574.3	467.9	9.2	42.8	415.9	351.3	41.6	23.0	106.3	84.8	21.5	64.7
1989	617.7	503.0	10.0	48.0	444.9	377.7	44.4	22.8	114.7	88.7	26.0	70.3
1990	673.0	545.8	10.6	53.6	481.5	411.2	48.1	22.2	127.2	98.5	28.7	79.1
1991	708.1	576.1	11.3	55.9	508.9	434.6	51.2	23.1	132.1	103.2	28.9	80.9
1992	736.0	601.6	11.9	59.0	530.8	456.3	53.4	21.0	134.3	104.2	30.1	80.9
1993	765.7	629.5	12.1	62.5	554.9	478.9	56.4	19.6	136.2	104.5	31.7	79.8
1994	806.8	662.6	12.2	66.7	583.7	501.7	60.0	22.1	144.2	108.7	35.5	84.2
1995	850.5	694.7	12.7	72.9	609.0	523.1	64.4	21.5	155.8	117.3	38.6	91.4
1996	890.4	726.5	13.1	79.9	633.6	542.3	68.2	23.0	163.8	122.5	41.3	95.6
1997	949.7	766.4	13.8	81.7	670.9	569.8	72.4	28.7	183.3	139.3	44.0	110.9
1998	999.3	808.3	14.8	83.4	710.1	597.0	76.8	36.2	191.0	142.4	48.6	114.2
1999	1 076.0	864.7	15.9	94.0	754.7	625.2	82.6	46.9	211.3	158.3	53.0	128.7
2000	1 161.8	937.9	17.1	114.0	806.8	660.8	89.5	56.5	223.9	167.4	56.5	134.4
2001	1 229.9	993.7	18.3	118.7	856.7	700.4	95.4	60.9	236.2	177.6	58.6	140.8
2002	1 279.2	1 034.5	19.4	121.1	894.0	733.8	100.0	60.3	244.7	188.2	56.5	144.7
2000												
1st quarter	1 140.8	914.0	16.7	109.1	788.2	647.8	86.8	53.5	226.8	172.2	54.6	140.0
2nd quarter	1 150.3	930.0	17.0	111.8	801.2	656.5	88.8	56.0	220.3	164.5	55.9	131.5
3rd quarter	1 167.4	945.4	17.3	115.5	812.6	665.0	90.5	57.1	222.1	164.8	57.3	131.6
4th quarter	1 188.5	962.2	17.5	119.4	825.3	673.9	92.1	59.4	226.3	168.0	58.4	134.2
2001												
1st quarter	1 211.7	976.2	17.8	120.0	838.4	682.4	93.6	62.4	235.6	177.8	57.7	142.0
2nd quarter	1 233.7	990.6	18.2	121.8	850.6	693.8	94.9	61.9	243.2	184.6	58.6	148.3
3rd quarter	1 224.3	1 000.1	18.4	119.1	862.5	707.3	95.9	59.4	224.2	164.8	59.4	128.3
4th quarter	1 249.8	1 008.2	18.8	113.9	875.5	718.1	97.3	60.1	241.7	183.1	58.6	144.4
2002												
1st quarter	1 267.5	1 017.7	19.1	115.3	883.3	723.9	98.6	60.8	249.7	192.5	57.2	151.1
2nd quarter	1 271.6	1 030.6	19.3	120.2	891.1	730.1	99.6	61.3	241.1	184.4	56.6	141.5
3rd quarter	1 283.3	1 039.6	19.5	122.6	897.5	737.1	100.4	59.9	243.8	187.4	56.4	143.4
4th quarter	1 294.4	1 050.1	19.7	126.3	904.1	744.0	101.1	59.0	244.2	188.6	55.6	143.1

[1]Gross government investment consists of general government and government enterprise expenditures for fixed assets; inventory investment is included in government consumption expenditures.
[2]Consumption expenditures for durable goods excludes expenditures classified as investment, except for goods transferred to foreign countries by the federal government.
[3]Compensation of government employees engaged in new own-account investment and related expenditures for goods and services are classified as investment in structures and in software.
[4]Consumption of fixed capital, or depreciation, is included in government consumption expenditures as a partial measure of the value of the services of general government fixed assets; use of depreciation assumes a zero net return on these assets.

Table 6-4. Chain-Type Quantity Indexes for Government Consumption Expenditures and Gross Investment by Type [1]

(Index numbers, 1996 = 100.)

Year and quarter	Total government	Federal										
		Total	National defense									
			Total	Consumption expenditures						Gross investment		
				Total	Durable goods [2]	Nondurable goods	Services			Total	Structures	Equipment and software
							Compensation of employees [3]	Consumption of fixed capital [4]	Other services			
1946	25.3	42.9	57.0	70.6	13.4	80.6	145.1	93.7	2.8	14.0	52.4	11.3
1947	21.6	31.9	38.4	48.1	8.4	28.8	79.0	76.1	4.7	7.7	24.3	6.4
1948	23.1	34.3	38.6	45.8	18.9	57.2	76.7	61.5	6.8	14.8	55.0	12.1
1949	25.8	37.5	40.3	45.7	23.8	67.9	81.1	51.6	9.0	21.5	53.8	18.8
1950	25.8	35.3	39.7	46.4	41.0	71.5	85.5	44.7	8.5	17.0	69.6	13.6
1951	35.2	58.4	76.0	78.5	95.6	189.2	148.2	43.4	23.0	60.1	264.0	47.0
1952	42.6	76.7	102.0	102.4	177.0	248.5	170.4	48.3	34.2	87.8	416.6	67.2
1953	45.5	82.7	108.3	106.9	198.2	400.3	166.9	54.0	27.4	97.7	423.8	76.8
1954	42.4	71.8	92.6	93.1	143.2	262.3	156.5	57.8	23.0	79.4	358.1	61.7
1955	40.8	65.1	83.5	86.7	119.0	119.3	148.6	58.8	28.8	64.1	275.2	50.5
1956	40.9	64.0	82.9	87.0	112.7	117.5	144.7	59.2	32.9	61.4	256.8	48.7
1957	42.7	66.3	86.4	92.9	117.5	142.7	142.6	59.4	44.3	58.2	262.6	45.3
1958	44.0	66.2	86.0	90.8	121.1	144.9	134.2	59.4	43.3	62.0	292.0	47.7
1959	46.5	70.9	88.2	88.9	100.4	162.4	130.8	60.8	45.5	74.6	281.8	60.8
1960	46.5	68.8	86.5	89.4	82.1	174.4	130.7	62.6	51.0	67.3	248.9	55.1
1961	48.8	71.5	90.0	91.1	67.4	206.0	133.3	64.0	54.9	75.2	264.8	62.1
1962	51.7	77.4	95.3	97.4	82.8	254.5	139.0	66.1	57.2	77.1	218.9	66.2
1963	52.9	77.2	92.9	98.4	82.1	241.4	136.6	67.6	61.9	66.0	178.7	57.1
1964	54.0	75.9	88.9	95.4	68.3	257.3	136.6	68.2	55.9	59.7	137.0	52.8
1965	55.6	76.0	87.3	96.0	78.9	244.7	136.8	68.1	55.0	52.3	122.1	46.2
1966	60.6	84.6	99.9	108.7	110.2	323.6	150.6	68.3	63.8	63.1	129.1	56.7
1967	65.2	92.8	112.6	122.6	114.1	501.4	164.3	70.0	76.2	71.2	119.0	65.2
1968	67.3	93.7	114.7	128.2	135.1	573.9	166.5	71.5	77.4	62.6	115.7	56.8
1969	67.0	90.6	109.2	123.1	114.9	509.0	166.7	71.8	72.9	56.8	124.2	50.5
1970	65.5	84.2	100.0	112.6	104.9	353.9	154.6	70.9	67.3	52.5	101.8	47.4
1971	64.3	78.2	89.9	103.7	77.3	288.6	142.8	68.7	67.3	39.2	128.1	32.4
1972	64.3	76.5	85.4	97.0	79.5	290.3	131.8	66.0	60.0	42.1	116.0	36.1
1973	63.9	72.8	79.9	90.3	68.9	216.6	125.0	63.5	56.2	40.9	114.7	34.9
1974	65.0	72.5	77.9	87.4	56.6	186.6	123.1	61.3	56.8	42.1	105.2	36.9
1975	66.3	72.5	77.0	84.9	71.8	153.0	121.3	60.0	50.9	46.5	101.8	41.8
1976	66.3	71.6	75.4	83.1	62.3	125.3	118.9	59.5	53.6	45.7	90.3	41.9
1977	67.0	72.9	75.9	83.6	78.5	116.9	117.8	58.9	53.7	46.4	91.4	42.6
1978	69.1	74.8	76.5	84.4	89.9	117.5	118.6	58.6	52.7	46.2	92.6	42.3
1979	70.4	76.6	78.7	85.3	95.1	121.9	117.6	58.8	54.8	52.9	78.3	50.5
1980	71.8	80.3	82.0	88.5	97.0	134.2	118.3	59.5	62.1	56.5	90.6	53.3
1981	72.4	84.1	87.0	93.4	110.4	142.9	122.0	60.7	68.2	62.1	86.2	59.8
1982	73.6	87.1	93.5	99.5	121.3	141.4	124.7	62.4	82.1	69.9	101.5	66.9
1983	76.0	92.6	99.8	104.4	145.9	146.1	126.6	64.9	86.9	81.8	120.7	78.2
1984	78.7	95.5	104.6	107.6	148.5	138.3	128.3	68.5	93.4	92.9	116.8	90.6
1985	83.7	102.8	113.3	114.0	160.7	136.8	130.7	73.5	106.0	111.7	142.9	108.6
1986	88.3	108.5	120.4	119.1	170.8	172.7	131.2	79.4	112.1	127.8	155.3	125.1
1987	90.9	112.5	126.1	123.4	180.3	169.9	132.4	85.4	118.9	139.7	167.5	137.0
1988	92.0	110.4	125.2	124.4	180.5	163.3	130.8	90.0	121.7	129.2	154.6	126.7
1989	94.5	111.9	124.2	123.2	170.1	157.9	130.7	93.8	117.8	129.6	124.2	130.6
1990	97.6	114.2	124.2	122.3	159.4	140.1	129.9	97.2	117.9	133.9	115.5	136.5
1991	98.7	113.8	122.8	122.2	157.0	141.7	129.5	99.8	116.7	126.0	85.3	131.3
1992	99.2	112.0	116.8	116.0	142.4	132.2	121.9	101.3	109.1	121.5	94.1	125.1
1993	98.4	107.6	110.6	111.2	131.3	121.0	116.5	101.8	103.5	107.3	85.4	110.2
1994	98.5	103.7	105.3	106.0	111.8	110.5	110.5	101.4	100.3	101.4	92.2	102.7
1995	98.9	100.9	101.4	102.1	100.4	89.4	104.4	100.6	101.0	97.5	96.5	97.6
1996	100.0	100.0	100.0	100.0	100.0	100.0	100.0	100.0	100.0	100.0	100.0	100.0
1997	102.4	99.6	97.4	98.7	101.0	100.5	96.4	99.5	101.3	90.0	82.6	91.0
1998	104.3	98.8	95.7	96.1	101.8	104.0	93.4	99.1	96.3	93.3	76.1	95.9
1999	108.3	101.2	97.7	97.7	108.2	115.8	90.9	99.1	104.0	98.3	72.2	102.2
2000	111.3	102.4	97.7	97.3	108.1	122.1	90.6	99.2	102.5	100.4	69.3	105.1
2001	115.4	107.3	102.5	102.2	116.0	129.0	91.1	99.0	118.1	104.9	68.0	110.6
2002	120.5	115.4	112.0	111.5	120.9	148.5	92.7	99.4	148.0	115.9	65.1	124.1
2000												
1st quarter	110.3	100.4	95.6	94.9	108.7	131.2	90.2	99.2	92.5	100.5	65.5	105.9
2nd quarter	111.6	104.2	99.0	98.9	108.7	130.3	90.7	99.2	107.4	100.1	70.6	104.5
3rd quarter	111.3	102.3	97.5	97.0	108.8	117.2	90.7	99.2	101.3	100.6	74.8	104.4
4th quarter	112.1	102.8	98.6	98.3	106.0	109.8	90.5	99.2	108.5	100.3	66.5	105.5
2001												
1st quarter	113.6	105.2	100.6	100.7	107.3	112.6	91.2	99.1	115.8	99.9	69.5	104.5
2nd quarter	115.2	106.7	101.2	100.8	115.9	128.0	91.1	99.0	113.1	104.0	69.1	109.4
3rd quarter	114.9	107.0	102.4	101.6	125.5	127.7	90.9	99.0	114.0	107.5	63.0	114.5
4th quarter	117.8	110.5	105.9	105.6	115.5	147.7	91.1	99.0	129.5	108.1	70.5	113.9
2002												
1st quarter	119.4	112.5	108.8	108.1	118.3	149.9	92.0	99.1	136.7	113.9	63.2	122.0
2nd quarter	119.8	114.5	110.9	110.4	118.9	152.0	93.0	99.2	143.7	113.8	66.5	121.3
3rd quarter	120.7	115.7	112.7	111.8	125.8	151.3	93.4	99.4	146.6	119.0	66.3	127.5
4th quarter	122.0	118.8	115.7	115.6	120.4	140.6	92.4	99.7	165.1	117.0	64.3	125.4

[1]Gross government investment consists of general government and government enterprise expenditures for fixed assets; inventory investment is included in government consumption expenditures.
[2]Consumption expenditures for durable goods excludes expenditures classified as investment, except for goods transferred to foreign countries by the federal government.
[3]Compensation of government employees engaged in new own-account investment and related expenditures for goods and services are classified as investment in structures and in software.
[4]Consumption of fixed capital, or depreciation, is included in government consumption expenditures as a partial measure of the value of the services of general government fixed assets; use of depreciation assumes a zero net return on these assets.

Table 6-4. Chain-Type Quantity Indexes for Government Consumption Expenditures and Gross Investment by Type [1]—*Continued*

(Index numbers, 1996 = 100.)

		Federal—Continued										
		Nondefense										
		Consumption expenditures								Gross investment		
				Nondurable goods			Services					
Year and quarter	Total	Total	Durable goods [2]	Total	Commodity Credit Corporation inventory charge	Other nondurables	Compensation of employees [3]	Consumption of fixed capital [4]	Other services	Total	Structures	Equipment and software
1946	15.8	18.9	...	...	...	64.4	44.1	12.9	15.6	6.1	0.0	6.4
1947	19.5	21.6	...	...	...	13.4	53.8	13.2	8.3	12.0	22.0	7.5
1948	26.8	30.6	...	...	...	34.0	60.7	13.5	15.3	14.6	42.1	5.5
1949	33.3	37.3	...	...	...	40.4	57.7	13.7	14.3	19.6	66.4	5.0
1950	28.0	28.9	...	...	...	17.3	64.1	14.0	10.8	22.3	75.0	5.8
1951	23.8	24.1	...	...	...	31.0	58.3	14.2	8.3	20.0	65.0	5.7
1952	26.7	28.3	...	...	...	17.4	56.4	14.2	16.1	19.5	60.7	6.2
1953	32.2	37.0	...	...	...	17.1	51.5	14.2	16.8	17.0	57.3	4.4
1954	30.7	35.5	...	...	...	16.8	49.0	14.2	18.1	15.4	49.8	4.4
1955	28.9	34.8	...	...	...	19.8	49.9	14.1	13.0	11.0	34.2	3.6
1956	26.6	30.6	...	...	...	32.9	51.2	13.9	20.0	14.1	46.4	3.8
1957	26.4	29.6	...	...	...	42.3	52.5	13.9	17.2	15.8	54.8	3.5
1958	27.2	29.5	...	...	...	18.3	54.1	13.9	15.9	18.7	68.9	3.0
1959	37.0	42.7	...	...	...	58.2	53.7	13.8	21.9	18.8	72.4	2.2
1960	34.1	37.4	...	...	...	45.3	58.3	13.7	28.0	22.2	81.6	3.5
1961	35.0	36.8	...	...	...	53.5	59.8	13.9	32.9	26.8	90.9	5.9
1962	42.2	44.8	...	...	...	53.1	63.1	14.8	38.6	31.3	101.2	8.0
1963	46.3	48.2	...	...	...	60.3	67.1	16.4	45.9	36.9	109.3	11.5
1964	50.3	51.6	...	...	...	65.0	68.8	18.5	54.1	42.4	117.8	14.7
1965	53.8	54.1	...	...	...	65.4	70.2	21.1	56.8	48.3	124.3	18.8
1966	54.5	54.6	...	...	...	76.9	73.0	24.2	62.7	49.6	123.6	20.3
1967	54.0	57.1	...	...	...	82.9	76.5	26.4	57.0	40.4	93.2	18.2
1968	52.6	57.0	...	...	...	65.9	78.6	28.0	49.0	35.3	83.7	15.4
1969	53.9	59.9	...	...	...	84.3	79.5	29.0	47.3	31.9	71.1	14.9
1970	53.1	59.4	...	...	...	86.2	80.6	29.7	54.0	30.1	71.6	13.1
1971	55.2	61.7	...	...	...	81.3	83.2	29.9	57.8	31.5	79.2	12.7
1972	58.9	66.2	...	...	...	91.3	85.5	30.0	66.9	32.7	81.8	13.3
1973	58.7	65.6	...	...	...	78.4	85.9	30.3	68.1	33.6	87.9	12.7
1974	61.8	69.4	...	...	...	87.3	90.4	30.6	69.3	34.4	85.7	14.1
1975	63.7	71.4	...	...	...	65.6	92.1	31.2	72.5	35.9	89.0	14.8
1976	64.5	71.6	...	...	...	82.6	96.8	31.8	63.9	38.2	95.0	15.7
1977	67.1	74.4	...	...	...	84.2	99.1	32.5	67.6	40.3	98.1	17.3
1978	71.8	78.1	...	...	...	93.8	101.6	34.7	75.6	47.7	113.4	21.2
1979	72.9	79.8	...	...	...	93.3	101.4	36.3	81.6	46.6	106.0	22.3
1980	77.4	84.5	...	...	...	90.2	104.1	38.7	82.3	50.3	107.2	26.6
1981	78.6	86.1	...	...	...	179.6	101.1	41.1	76.0	50.1	105.8	26.8
1982	74.4	81.7	...	...	...	116.3	99.1	43.2	71.2	46.6	86.6	29.4
1983	78.0	84.6	...	...	...	121.9	100.5	46.4	73.8	52.8	84.4	38.6
1984	76.8	81.8	...	...	...	134.4	100.5	50.4	74.4	56.8	86.9	43.0
1985	81.0	86.0	...	...	...	115.4	100.6	54.4	76.4	60.6	88.9	47.5
1986	83.5	88.8	...	...	...	101.4	99.2	58.2	74.7	62.0	94.8	47.1
1987	83.9	87.7	...	...	...	117.4	100.9	62.0	83.6	68.0	104.5	51.4
1988	79.6	83.4	...	...	...	115.3	103.4	65.8	82.5	63.6	76.8	57.0
1989	86.2	90.7	...	...	...	100.5	103.8	69.6	83.6	67.8	74.6	64.1
1990	93.4	98.0	...	...	...	108.9	108.9	73.7	96.5	74.2	83.6	69.1
1991	95.1	98.6	...	...	...	84.6	108.7	77.9	96.1	80.1	93.6	73.2
1992	101.9	105.0	...	...	...	113.3	110.6	81.3	108.1	88.5	104.1	80.5
1993	101.6	103.4	...	...	...	113.2	110.2	84.5	100.4	93.2	111.3	84.0
1994	100.5	103.6	...	...	...	113.2	107.1	88.3	103.7	87.1	100.4	80.2
1995	100.0	101.9	...	...	...	104.3	102.8	93.0	104.7	91.5	99.9	87.1
1996	100.0	100.0	...	...	...	100.0	100.0	100.0	100.0	100.0	100.0	100.0
1997	104.2	104.0	...	...	...	122.9	99.4	108.7	106.4	105.0	84.7	116.3
1998	105.3	102.5	...	...	...	124.1	100.5	118.9	97.8	118.4	95.1	131.5
1999	108.2	103.3	...	...	...	92.5	100.8	132.1	96.1	131.4	95.7	152.0
2000	112.1	107.6	...	...	...	79.8	104.0	145.1	99.7	133.6	85.5	161.9
2001	117.1	112.8	...	...	...	111.1	103.4	155.8	109.9	137.8	80.3	172.2
2002	122.2	117.4	...	...	...	132.7	105.6	167.0	116.1	144.8	93.2	175.2
2000												
1st quarter	110.1	105.2	...	...	...	90.1	103.2	140.6	93.7	133.8	92.8	157.6
2nd quarter	114.8	109.8	...	...	...	88.0	109.3	143.7	96.9	138.6	86.0	169.9
3rd quarter	112.0	108.0	...	...	...	93.0	102.5	146.6	101.5	131.4	81.3	161.2
4th quarter	111.3	107.3	...	...	...	48.1	101.0	149.4	106.9	130.4	81.9	159.1
2001												
1st quarter	114.5	110.2	...	...	...	104.6	103.1	151.9	104.1	134.6	82.8	165.5
2nd quarter	117.8	113.4	...	...	...	106.5	103.3	154.5	109.4	138.8	74.3	177.8
3rd quarter	116.4	112.9	...	...	...	113.3	103.8	157.1	110.8	132.8	75.3	167.4
4th quarter	119.8	114.6	...	...	...	119.9	103.4	159.9	115.1	144.9	88.9	178.2
2002												
1st quarter	119.9	115.0	...	...	...	127.2	104.0	162.6	113.6	143.4	101.1	167.6
2nd quarter	121.9	116.5	...	...	...	135.7	103.8	165.5	116.0	148.2	91.9	181.7
3rd quarter	121.8	117.5	...	...	...	129.4	105.3	168.5	116.9	142.3	84.9	176.6
4th quarter	125.1	120.7	...	...	...	138.4	109.5	171.6	117.8	145.3	94.8	174.8

[1]Gross government investment consists of general government and government enterprise expenditures for fixed assets; inventory investment is included in government consumption expenditures.
[2]Consumption expenditures for durable goods excludes expenditures classified as investment, except for goods transferred to foreign countries by the federal government.
[3]Compensation of government employees engaged in new own-account investment and related expenditures for goods and services are classified as investment in structures and in software.
[4]Consumption of fixed capital, or depreciation, is included in government consumption expenditures as a partial measure of the value of the services of general government fixed assets; use of depreciation assumes a zero net return on these assets.
. . . = Not available.

Table 6-4. Chain-Type Quantity Indexes for Government Consumption Expenditures and Gross Investment by Type [1]—Continued

(Index numbers, 1996 = 100.)

Year and quarter	Total	State and local									
		Consumption expenditures							Gross investment		
					Services						
		Total	Durable goods [2]	Nondurable goods	Total	Compensation of employees [3]	Consumption of fixed capital [4]	Other services	Total	Structures	Equipment and software
1946	13.5	16.2	3.0	6.9	18.0	20.0	12.6	5.5	7.3	9.7	1.8
1947	15.4	17.4	4.3	7.4	19.3	21.4	12.7	6.1	11.3	14.9	2.7
1948	16.4	17.6	5.6	7.0	19.6	22.0	13.0	5.8	14.3	18.9	3.5
1949	18.9	19.1	5.8	8.8	21.0	23.5	13.4	6.6	19.3	26.2	3.6
1950	20.5	20.3	5.9	9.9	22.2	24.3	14.0	8.3	21.9	30.1	3.7
1951	20.6	20.3	6.2	8.4	22.5	24.8	14.6	7.8	22.6	31.1	3.8
1952	20.9	20.5	6.7	8.4	22.8	25.6	15.2	6.8	23.1	31.7	4.2
1953	22.0	21.2	7.1	8.3	23.7	26.7	15.8	6.6	25.2	34.5	4.4
1954	23.9	22.1	7.9	8.5	24.7	27.9	16.6	6.7	30.0	41.5	4.9
1955	25.6	23.6	7.7	10.0	26.2	29.2	17.6	8.1	32.6	45.5	4.8
1956	26.4	24.4	8.5	9.2	27.3	31.0	18.5	7.0	33.4	46.2	5.4
1957	28.0	25.7	10.6	9.4	28.8	32.7	19.6	7.1	35.8	48.9	6.6
1958	30.3	27.7	10.5	11.5	30.7	34.7	20.8	8.3	39.3	54.2	6.6
1959	31.4	28.8	11.2	14.0	31.4	35.9	22.0	7.2	40.5	55.6	7.0
1960	32.8	30.4	12.0	14.6	33.3	37.9	23.3	7.9	41.0	55.8	7.9
1961	34.8	32.1	12.8	15.5	35.1	39.8	24.6	8.5	44.2	60.4	8.2
1962	35.9	33.0	13.6	15.7	36.1	41.2	25.9	7.9	45.8	62.4	8.7
1963	38.0	34.6	14.4	16.1	37.9	43.2	27.4	8.3	49.8	67.5	10.0
1964	40.6	36.9	15.6	17.2	40.4	45.9	29.1	9.5	53.4	72.0	11.3
1965	43.3	39.3	17.7	18.3	43.0	48.7	30.9	10.6	57.2	77.1	12.1
1966	46.1	41.8	19.2	19.3	45.7	51.6	32.9	11.7	61.0	82.0	13.4
1967	48.4	43.7	20.3	19.9	47.8	53.6	35.0	12.7	64.8	87.2	13.9
1968	51.2	46.5	21.8	21.8	50.8	56.9	37.1	13.9	67.7	91.1	14.5
1969	52.7	49.1	23.3	24.8	53.4	59.5	39.1	15.7	64.9	86.3	15.6
1970	54.2	52.1	25.0	28.7	56.2	62.1	40.9	18.8	60.8	79.9	16.4
1971	56.0	54.8	27.8	32.7	58.7	64.7	42.7	20.3	59.0	77.2	16.5
1972	57.2	56.8	29.9	34.6	60.8	67.0	44.2	21.0	57.1	73.3	18.4
1973	58.8	58.8	34.9	35.9	62.8	69.3	45.7	21.1	57.4	72.7	20.6
1974	61.0	61.4	39.0	37.1	65.5	71.8	47.4	24.3	57.9	72.6	22.5
1975	63.0	64.2	42.3	41.7	67.9	74.0	48.9	27.1	57.4	72.0	22.1
1976	63.6	65.3	46.2	45.4	68.5	75.0	50.3	25.2	56.4	70.8	21.7
1977	63.9	66.5	49.9	48.6	69.4	76.1	51.4	24.4	53.1	66.2	21.3
1978	66.1	67.9	51.1	50.0	70.7	77.9	52.6	23.9	58.1	72.8	22.5
1979	67.1	68.5	51.8	49.4	71.4	79.1	53.9	21.6	61.0	76.0	24.7
1980	67.1	68.3	50.8	46.6	71.8	80.0	55.2	19.0	61.3	75.6	26.3
1981	65.8	68.1	52.7	46.1	71.6	79.8	56.4	17.7	56.1	68.2	26.1
1982	65.7	68.9	54.9	47.2	72.3	80.2	57.4	19.5	52.6	62.5	27.7
1983	66.2	69.5	58.1	49.8	72.5	79.6	58.5	21.8	53.2	61.8	31.6
1984	68.7	70.9	61.7	52.7	73.6	79.9	60.0	27.1	59.7	68.6	37.1
1985	72.4	74.0	65.3	56.7	76.4	82.1	62.2	33.5	66.2	75.2	42.9
1986	76.3	77.7	71.4	62.5	79.8	84.3	64.6	44.1	70.7	79.8	47.0
1987	78.1	79.5	74.5	64.5	81.5	85.8	67.1	46.5	72.5	81.6	49.0
1988	81.0	82.1	76.8	66.5	84.3	88.6	69.9	48.0	76.3	85.2	53.0
1989	84.2	85.1	80.7	69.5	87.1	91.1	73.3	53.4	80.5	87.0	62.9
1990	87.7	87.9	83.6	72.4	90.0	93.5	77.2	58.9	86.8	93.5	68.7
1991	89.7	89.9	88.3	76.9	91.6	94.2	81.0	68.5	88.8	96.6	68.0
1992	91.6	91.9	92.5	81.4	93.2	95.2	84.5	74.3	90.0	96.9	71.2
1993	92.9	93.7	93.9	85.9	94.6	96.2	87.9	78.9	89.5	94.8	75.0
1994	95.3	96.0	94.7	91.1	96.6	97.4	91.6	94.8	92.4	95.5	83.8
1995	97.7	97.9	96.9	94.6	98.3	98.9	95.7	92.6	96.8	98.7	91.4
1996	100.0	100.0	100.0	100.0	100.0	100.0	100.0	100.0	100.0	100.0	100.0
1997	104.0	102.6	106.2	103.1	102.5	101.6	105.0	116.4	110.0	110.0	109.9
1998	107.6	106.3	114.5	110.7	105.6	103.3	111.0	143.4	113.4	109.4	126.6
1999	112.6	110.3	123.2	120.4	108.9	104.4	117.5	187.2	122.9	117.4	141.3
2000	116.5	114.4	131.6	128.9	112.4	106.5	124.0	216.7	126.1	118.5	151.6
2001	120.1	117.9	139.8	136.1	115.4	108.7	129.9	231.0	129.9	121.3	159.3
2002	123.5	121.3	147.5	141.4	118.5	111.0	135.7	246.7	133.4	126.5	156.2
2000											
1st quarter	116.1	113.1	128.8	126.0	111.4	105.9	121.6	209.4	129.5	124.3	146.4
2nd quarter	115.9	114.0	130.8	128.1	112.0	106.3	123.2	215.1	124.3	116.8	149.9
3rd quarter	116.6	114.8	132.9	129.8	112.7	106.7	124.8	219.2	124.4	116.0	153.3
4th quarter	117.5	115.6	134.2	131.7	113.4	107.2	126.3	223.1	126.0	117.1	156.7
2001											
1st quarter	118.6	116.1	136.5	133.5	113.7	107.2	127.7	224.4	130.1	122.4	156.3
2nd quarter	120.2	117.2	138.8	135.4	114.7	108.1	129.2	227.9	133.9	126.4	158.9
3rd quarter	119.5	118.6	140.9	136.8	116.1	109.4	130.7	231.6	123.3	112.6	161.4
4th quarter	122.1	119.8	143.1	138.6	117.2	110.2	132.2	240.2	132.2	123.9	160.6
2002											
1st quarter	123.5	120.6	145.1	139.9	117.8	110.5	133.9	245.1	136.6	130.1	157.3
2nd quarter	123.0	121.0	146.7	140.9	118.3	110.8	135.2	246.6	131.4	124.0	156.3
3rd quarter	123.6	121.5	148.3	141.9	118.7	111.1	136.3	247.4	132.8	125.7	156.5
4th quarter	124.0	122.0	150.0	142.9	119.0	111.4	137.3	247.9	132.9	126.2	154.8

[1]Gross government investment consists of general government and government enterprise expenditures for fixed assets; inventory investment is included in government consumption expenditures.

[2]Consumption expenditures for durable goods excludes expenditures classified as investment, except for goods transferred to foreign countries by the federal government.

[3]Compensation of government employees engaged in new own-account investment and related expenditures for goods and services are classified as investment in structures and in software.

[4]Consumption of fixed capital, or depreciation, is included in government consumption expenditures as a partial measure of the value of the services of general government fixed assets; use of depreciation assumes a zero net return on these assets.

Table 6-5. National Defense Consumption Expenditures and Gross and Net Investment [1]

(National Income and Product Accounts, calendar years, billions of dollars, quarterly data are at seasonally adjusted annual rates.)

Year and quarter	Defense consumption expenditures and gross investment, total	Defense consumption expenditures											
		Total	Durable goods [2]							Nondurable goods			
			Total	Aircraft	Missiles	Ships	Vehicles	Electronics	Other durable goods	Total	Petroleum products	Ammunition	Other nondurable goods
1972	93.5	82.3	5.9	3.0	1.2	0.2	0.4	0.8	0.2	4.8	1.8	2.0	0.9
1973	93.9	82.6	5.3	2.8	1.2	0.2	0.4	0.8	-0.1	4.4	1.7	1.7	0.9
1974	99.7	87.5	4.6	2.2	1.4	0.2	0.5	0.8	-0.5	5.3	2.8	1.4	1.1
1975	107.9	93.4	6.5	2.3	1.6	0.3	0.8	0.9	0.6	5.1	2.9	1.1	1.1
1976	113.2	97.9	5.9	2.2	1.3	0.3	0.6	0.7	0.9	4.5	2.5	0.6	1.4
1977	122.6	105.8	7.9	3.3	1.5	0.5	0.8	0.8	0.9	4.6	2.4	0.8	1.3
1978	132.0	114.2	9.6	3.6	2.3	0.7	1.1	1.0	1.0	4.9	2.5	1.0	1.3
1979	146.7	125.3	11.5	4.9	2.2	0.9	1.2	1.1	1.3	6.3	3.6	1.2	1.5
1980	169.6	145.3	12.8	5.6	2.3	0.7	1.5	1.4	1.3	10.1	6.8	1.4	1.9
1981	197.8	168.9	16.1	7.8	2.7	0.6	1.7	1.7	1.5	12.0	7.7	1.6	2.6
1982	228.3	193.6	19.2	10.3	3.0	0.4	1.7	2.0	1.7	11.6	6.8	2.1	2.7
1983	252.5	210.6	25.0	13.6	3.7	1.2	2.3	2.4	1.9	11.3	6.4	2.5	2.5
1984	283.5	234.9	26.9	14.0	4.0	1.0	2.8	2.7	2.4	10.5	5.9	2.2	2.3
1985	312.4	254.9	29.2	15.4	3.9	0.8	2.9	3.2	3.0	10.0	5.8	1.3	2.9
1986	332.2	269.3	31.9	17.2	4.6	0.8	3.2	3.3	2.7	10.3	3.6	3.6	3.1
1987	351.2	284.8	33.6	18.2	4.7	1.0	3.1	3.7	3.0	10.3	3.9	2.8	3.6
1988	355.9	294.6	33.5	17.9	5.0	1.1	2.5	3.7	3.3	10.6	3.5	3.5	3.6
1989	363.2	300.5	32.0	16.4	5.0	1.0	1.9	3.8	3.9	10.8	4.2	3.1	3.6
1990	374.9	308.9	30.9	14.8	5.2	1.7	1.7	3.8	3.6	11.0	5.3	2.8	2.9
1991	384.5	321.1	31.2	13.8	5.3	1.9	1.9	3.5	4.8	10.7	4.7	2.7	3.4
1992	378.5	316.9	29.0	12.6	4.7	2.2	1.5	3.3	4.7	9.5	3.5	2.6	3.4
1993	364.9	309.2	27.1	11.3	4.3	2.3	1.3	3.5	4.5	8.4	3.2	2.4	2.8
1994	355.1	301.1	23.3	9.5	3.5	1.6	0.9	3.0	4.6	7.6	3.0	1.8	2.8
1995	350.6	297.5	21.0	9.0	2.8	1.2	1.1	2.5	4.5	6.3	2.8	1.1	2.4
1996	357.0	302.4	21.0	9.0	2.6	0.9	0.9	2.5	5.0	7.7	3.4	1.4	2.9
1997	352.6	304.2	21.1	9.7	2.3	1.0	1.1	2.5	4.6	7.5	2.9	1.6	3.0
1998	349.1	299.7	21.1	10.0	2.3	0.9	1.0	2.3	4.6	6.9	2.1	1.8	3.1
1999	364.3	312.0	22.4	10.6	2.2	1.2	0.8	2.7	5.0	8.1	2.6	1.8	3.7
2000	374.9	321.4	22.5	10.2	2.3	1.3	0.8	2.9	5.0	10.4	4.1	1.7	4.6
2001	399.9	344.5	24.2	11.2	2.5	1.2	1.0	3.0	5.3	10.5	4.0	2.1	4.4
2002	447.4	386.6	25.3	11.3	2.8	1.3	1.1	3.1	5.6	11.5	4.2	2.5	4.8
2000													
1st quarter	365.5	311.9	22.7	10.6	2.1	1.3	0.6	3.0	5.0	10.7	3.8	1.6	5.4
2nd quarter	379.1	325.8	22.6	9.8	2.4	1.4	0.9	3.0	5.1	10.6	3.6	1.5	5.5
3rd quarter	375.0	321.3	22.7	10.5	2.3	1.3	0.8	2.7	5.0	10.1	4.5	2.0	3.6
4th quarter	380.0	326.5	22.1	9.8	2.5	1.2	0.9	3.0	4.7	10.0	4.3	1.9	3.9
2001													
1st quarter	391.4	338.4	22.3	10.0	2.7	1.2	0.9	2.9	4.6	9.6	4.0	1.9	3.6
2nd quarter	395.2	340.0	24.2	10.8	2.6	1.3	1.0	2.9	5.5	10.7	4.1	2.1	4.5
3rd quarter	400.3	343.4	26.1	12.5	2.5	1.3	1.1	3.1	5.6	10.5	4.3	2.2	4.0
4th quarter	412.8	356.0	24.0	11.4	2.1	1.1	1.0	3.1	5.3	11.3	3.6	2.1	5.6
2002													
1st quarter	431.7	372.1	24.7	11.1	2.6	1.3	1.0	3.1	5.6	10.9	3.8	2.4	4.7
2nd quarter	442.1	382.5	24.9	11.3	2.5	1.3	1.1	3.2	5.5	11.7	4.3	2.6	4.8
3rd quarter	451.2	388.9	26.3	11.6	3.0	1.5	1.0	3.3	5.8	12.0	4.7	2.7	4.6
4th quarter	464.7	403.2	25.2	11.4	3.1	1.2	1.2	2.8	5.5	11.4	4.0	2.4	5.0

[1]Gross government investment consists of general government and government enterprise expenditures for fixed assets; inventory investment is included in government consumption expenditures.
[2]Consumption expenditures for durable goods excludes expenditures classified as investment, except for goods transferred to foreign countries by the federal government.

Table 6-5. National Defense Consumption Expenditures and Gross and Net Investment [1]—Continued

(National Income and Product Accounts, calendar years, billions of dollars, quarterly data are at seasonally adjusted annual rates.)

Year and quarter	Defense consumption expenditures—Continued												
	Services												
	Total	Compensation of employees [3]			Consump-tion of fixed capital [4]	Other services							
		Total	Military	Civilian		Total	Research and develop-ment	Installation support	Weapons support	Personnel support	Transpor-tation of material	Travel of persons	Other
1972	71.7	40.5	27.0	13.5	15.8	15.4	5.1	4.3	1.6	1.9	1.8	0.9	-0.2
1973	73.0	41.4	27.6	13.7	16.4	15.3	5.3	4.3	1.6	1.7	1.6	1.0	-0.1
1974	77.5	44.0	29.1	14.9	16.7	16.8	5.7	4.6	1.8	2.0	1.7	1.1	-0.2
1975	81.9	47.8	31.1	16.8	17.5	16.5	5.9	4.8	1.7	2.1	1.8	1.0	-0.8
1976	87.5	50.2	32.4	17.7	18.8	18.5	6.4	5.3	1.9	2.3	1.8	1.0	-0.2
1977	93.4	53.5	34.0	19.6	19.9	20.0	6.8	6.1	2.1	2.3	1.9	1.2	-0.4
1978	99.7	57.4	36.2	21.2	21.2	21.1	7.1	6.2	2.4	2.6	1.9	1.4	-0.5
1979	107.5	61.5	38.7	22.8	22.3	23.6	7.7	7.1	2.9	2.9	2.2	1.3	-0.5
1980	122.4	68.4	43.5	25.0	24.4	29.6	10.2	8.4	4.4	3.2	2.6	1.6	-0.7
1981	140.9	78.6	50.5	28.1	27.2	35.1	12.4	9.2	5.2	4.3	2.8	2.1	-0.8
1982	162.9	87.2	56.6	30.6	31.0	44.6	14.1	13.4	6.0	6.0	3.1	2.6	-0.7
1983	174.2	92.2	59.8	32.4	33.4	48.6	14.5	15.1	7.3	6.5	3.4	2.4	-0.5
1984	197.5	107.3	72.8	34.5	36.6	53.6	16.2	16.5	8.6	6.8	3.3	2.9	-0.7
1985	215.7	115.0	78.2	36.8	38.6	62.0	21.7	16.5	9.8	8.5	3.1	3.1	-0.7
1986	227.2	118.4	80.6	37.8	41.5	67.3	23.8	17.8	10.4	9.4	3.4	3.3	-0.8
1987	240.8	123.2	83.7	39.5	44.1	73.6	27.0	18.4	11.0	10.9	3.5	3.7	-0.8
1988	250.6	126.5	85.2	41.3	47.0	77.1	31.5	18.2	9.8	11.4	3.6	3.7	-1.1
1989	257.7	131.2	87.4	43.8	50.1	76.4	28.6	18.1	10.3	12.4	4.0	4.0	-1.0
1990	267.0	134.0	89.1	44.9	53.2	79.8	26.1	21.2	11.7	13.1	4.8	4.0	-1.1
1991	279.2	141.3	93.8	47.5	56.3	81.6	21.9	22.7	10.2	12.8	8.8	6.9	-1.7
1992	278.5	142.5	93.2	49.3	57.9	78.1	23.7	22.2	8.5	14.6	5.9	5.5	-2.3
1993	273.6	138.1	88.0	50.1	60.2	75.3	23.1	23.8	7.2	14.4	4.5	4.8	-2.6
1994	270.2	134.2	84.4	49.9	61.8	74.2	22.3	24.4	8.5	15.1	3.8	4.4	-4.4
1995	270.4	130.4	81.5	48.9	63.0	76.8	20.3	24.3	9.1	16.9	4.2	4.2	-2.2
1996	273.7	133.1	84.2	48.8	63.0	77.7	22.3	24.5	7.3	17.3	4.9	3.9	-2.5
1997	275.6	132.5	84.0	48.5	62.8	80.2	23.2	23.7	8.4	18.6	4.6	3.7	-2.0
1998	271.7	131.2	83.5	47.7	62.3	78.2	20.2	23.1	8.7	19.6	4.6	3.7	-1.7
1999	281.5	133.1	85.2	47.9	62.5	85.9	23.0	23.4	9.4	22.9	4.8	4.1	-1.7
2000	288.5	138.3	89.3	48.9	63.6	86.7	22.5	23.4	10.0	23.6	4.8	4.2	-1.9
2001	309.8	143.7	94.1	49.6	63.5	102.5	29.6	25.5	12.2	28.0	4.9	4.2	-2.0
2002	349.9	154.4	102.1	52.3	64.2	131.3	42.0	28.5	18.3	35.5	5.0	4.0	-1.9
2000													
1st quarter	278.5	137.7	88.3	49.4	63.4	77.4	20.5	22.3	7.5	21.3	4.8	4.1	-3.1
2nd quarter	292.6	138.5	88.3	50.2	63.5	90.6	23.5	24.1	10.2	25.1	4.8	4.2	-1.3
3rd quarter	288.6	138.8	90.2	48.6	63.7	86.1	19.5	24.2	10.8	24.7	4.9	4.2	-2.1
4th quarter	294.3	138.1	90.6	47.5	63.7	92.5	26.6	23.2	11.3	23.4	4.8	4.3	-1.0
2001													
1st quarter	306.5	143.3	94.0	49.3	63.5	99.8	28.5	25.0	12.1	28.0	4.8	4.3	-3.0
2nd quarter	305.2	143.8	93.8	50.0	63.6	97.8	28.0	24.4	11.6	26.1	4.8	4.2	-1.4
3rd quarter	306.7	143.9	93.8	50.1	63.5	99.3	27.4	25.6	11.0	27.8	5.0	4.3	-1.7
4th quarter	320.7	143.9	94.8	49.1	63.6	113.2	34.6	27.0	14.0	30.2	5.1	4.3	-1.9
2002													
1st quarter	336.5	152.7	101.2	51.4	63.8	120.0	37.5	27.2	16.0	32.2	4.8	4.0	-1.7
2nd quarter	345.9	155.0	102.4	52.5	64.0	127.0	40.9	27.1	17.2	34.2	4.9	4.0	-1.3
3rd quarter	350.6	155.8	103.0	52.8	64.3	130.5	40.0	29.6	19.2	36.6	5.0	4.0	-3.9
4th quarter	366.6	153.9	101.5	52.4	64.9	147.7	49.5	30.2	20.7	39.0	5.2	4.1	-0.9

[1]Gross government investment consists of general government and government enterprise expenditures for fixed assets; inventory investment is included in government consumption expenditures.
[3]Compensation of government employees engaged in new own-account investment and related expenditures for goods and services are classified as investment in structures and in software. The compensation of all general government employees is shown in the addenda.
[4]Consumption of fixed capital, or depreciation, is included in government consumption expenditures as a partial measure of the value of the services of general government fixed assets; use of depreciation assumes a zero net return on these assets.

Table 6-5. National Defense Consumption Expenditures and Gross and Net Investment [1]—*Continued*

(National Income and Product Accounts, calendar years, billions of dollars, quarterly data are at seasonally adjusted annual rates.)

Year and quarter	Total	Structures	Defense gross investment Equipment and software Total	Aircraft	Missiles	Ships	Vehicles	Electronics and software	Other durable goods	Defense net investment
1972	11.2	1.8	9.4	2.6	1.5	1.8	0.4	0.8	2.2	-4.6
1973	11.3	2.1	9.2	2.3	1.5	1.6	0.3	0.9	2.5	-5.1
1974	12.3	2.2	10.1	2.3	1.7	2.2	0.3	1.0	2.6	-4.4
1975	14.5	2.3	12.1	3.6	1.3	2.2	0.3	1.2	3.6	-3.0
1976	15.3	2.1	13.2	3.4	1.4	2.4	0.5	1.3	4.2	-3.5
1977	16.7	2.4	14.4	3.7	1.2	3.1	0.6	1.5	4.2	-3.2
1978	17.8	2.5	15.3	3.7	1.1	3.9	0.8	1.8	4.0	-3.4
1979	21.4	2.5	18.9	4.8	1.8	4.3	0.9	2.1	5.0	-0.9
1980	24.3	3.2	21.1	6.1	2.3	4.1	1.2	2.6	4.8	-0.1
1981	28.9	3.2	25.7	7.5	2.8	5.1	1.1	3.2	6.1	1.7
1982	34.7	4.0	30.8	8.4	3.4	6.2	2.1	3.8	6.8	3.7
1983	41.9	4.8	37.1	10.1	4.6	7.1	3.4	4.6	7.3	8.5
1984	48.7	4.9	43.8	10.9	5.7	8.0	4.2	5.6	9.3	12.1
1985	57.5	6.2	51.3	13.4	6.6	9.0	3.7	7.0	11.5	18.9
1986	62.9	6.8	56.1	17.9	7.9	8.9	3.8	7.8	9.9	21.4
1987	66.4	7.7	58.8	17.6	8.7	8.8	4.3	8.7	10.6	22.3
1988	61.3	7.4	53.9	13.5	7.8	8.6	3.7	9.2	11.1	14.3
1989	62.7	6.4	56.3	12.2	8.8	10.0	3.1	9.6	12.6	12.6
1990	65.9	6.1	59.8	12.0	11.2	10.8	3.2	9.9	12.8	12.7
1991	63.4	4.6	58.8	9.2	10.8	10.2	3.4	9.7	15.4	7.1
1992	61.6	5.2	56.3	8.3	10.6	10.1	2.8	9.8	14.8	3.7
1993	55.7	5.1	50.7	9.3	7.9	8.7	1.9	10.4	12.5	-4.5
1994	54.0	5.7	48.3	10.5	5.7	8.1	1.0	10.3	12.7	-7.8
1995	53.1	6.3	46.9	9.0	4.7	8.0	1.1	10.5	13.6	-9.9
1996	54.6	6.7	47.9	9.2	4.1	6.8	1.2	11.6	15.2	-8.4
1997	48.4	5.7	42.7	5.9	2.9	6.1	1.4	12.4	14.0	-14.4
1998	49.4	5.4	44.0	5.6	3.3	6.4	1.5	13.4	13.8	-12.9
1999	52.3	5.3	47.0	6.9	2.7	6.8	1.7	14.2	14.7	-10.2
2000	53.5	5.3	48.2	7.7	2.5	6.6	1.8	14.9	14.7	-10.1
2001	55.5	5.4	50.0	8.3	3.3	7.2	1.8	13.7	15.7	-8.0
2002	60.8	5.3	55.5	9.3	3.1	8.7	2.6	15.0	16.8	-3.4
2000										
1st quarter	53.6	5.0	48.6	9.1	2.1	6.1	1.8	14.7	14.8	-9.8
2nd quarter	53.3	5.4	47.9	6.7	2.2	6.8	2.0	15.0	15.3	-10.2
3rd quarter	53.7	5.8	47.9	7.8	1.9	6.7	1.8	14.6	15.0	-10.0
4th quarter	53.5	5.2	48.3	7.2	3.7	6.8	1.7	15.3	13.7	-10.2
2001										
1st quarter	52.9	5.5	47.5	7.5	3.6	7.2	1.7	13.7	13.7	-10.6
2nd quarter	55.2	5.5	49.7	8.0	3.5	7.4	1.9	13.0	15.9	-8.4
3rd quarter	56.9	5.0	51.9	9.8	3.0	6.9	1.7	13.7	16.8	-6.6
4th quarter	56.8	5.7	51.1	8.0	3.0	7.3	2.0	14.3	16.4	-6.8
2002										
1st quarter	59.7	5.1	54.6	8.6	3.6	8.1	2.1	14.9	17.2	-4.1
2nd quarter	59.6	5.4	54.2	9.0	3.1	8.5	2.8	14.7	16.2	-4.4
3rd quarter	62.4	5.4	57.0	9.9	2.6	8.9	3.0	15.3	17.1	-1.9
4th quarter	61.5	5.3	56.3	9.9	3.1	9.0	2.7	14.9	16.7	-3.4

[1]Gross government investment consists of general government and government enterprise expenditures for fixed assets; inventory investment is included in government consumption expenditures.

Table 6-6. Real National Defense Consumption Expenditures and Gross Investment by Type [1]

(Index numbers, 1996 = 100; billions of chained [1996] dollars; quarterly data are at seasonally adjusted annual rates.)

Year, quarter, and series definition	Defense consumption expenditures and gross investment, total	Defense consumption expenditures Total	Durable goods [2] Total	Aircraft	Missiles	Ships	Vehicles	Electronics	Other durable goods	Nondurable goods Total	Petroleum products	Ammunition	Other nondurable goods
Index numbers, 1996 = 100													
1972	85.4	97.0	79.5	102.2	139.8	57.6	156.6	65.4	21.0	290.3	372.3	453.2	96.2
1973	79.9	90.3	68.9	88.4	140.2	64.6	136.2	61.2	8.5	216.6	235.7	353.4	89.9
1974	77.9	87.4	56.6	67.5	140.2	57.1	161.5	55.6	25.7	186.6	214.2	241.7	96.9
1975	77.0	84.9	71.8	62.8	149.7	57.7	252.7	53.6	28.4	153.0	180.4	168.0	88.5
1976	75.4	83.1	62.3	53.4	121.5	59.2	190.3	40.6	37.4	125.3	149.4	84.4	96.4
1977	75.9	83.6	78.5	78.0	129.9	112.3	227.6	45.4	37.5	116.9	127.0	115.5	87.1
1978	76.5	84.4	89.9	81.6	166.4	144.0	304.4	54.1	36.8	117.5	126.4	133.4	81.1
1979	78.7	85.3	95.1	99.5	143.3	164.4	257.1	52.7	44.6	121.9	128.6	148.4	82.9
1980	82.0	88.5	97.0	105.8	145.4	115.7	266.0	62.8	41.4	134.2	142.3	148.6	96.6
1981	87.0	93.4	110.4	131.0	161.0	94.9	258.0	74.5	44.3	142.9	139.7	168.0	128.3
1982	93.5	99.5	121.3	156.2	172.2	57.1	242.5	83.1	45.6	141.4	131.6	207.0	125.0
1983	99.8	104.4	145.9	188.7	177.5	168.7	313.0	97.2	47.7	146.1	140.9	242.7	105.5
1984	104.6	107.6	148.4	181.2	171.0	143.8	383.9	109.2	61.1	138.3	140.5	205.2	97.8
1985	113.3	114.0	160.7	198.0	158.5	106.6	439.5	131.7	75.0	136.8	143.0	122.3	126.4
1986	120.4	119.1	170.8	214.9	188.0	101.0	443.8	137.7	66.9	172.6	142.8	329.7	129.8
1987	126.1	123.4	180.3	232.1	187.2	126.2	401.0	151.0	72.8	169.9	146.6	250.1	155.9
1988	125.2	124.4	180.5	231.5	201.8	132.9	343.1	148.3	76.7	163.3	123.6	288.6	146.6
1989	124.2	123.2	170.1	208.6	201.3	125.4	260.5	151.5	86.8	157.9	135.6	241.7	141.2
1990	124.2	122.3	159.4	181.1	210.6	196.5	235.5	147.7	78.0	140.1	134.5	217.9	105.1
1991	122.8	122.2	157.0	163.8	206.6	221.4	239.0	133.5	104.1	141.7	132.8	205.6	117.3
1992	116.8	116.0	142.4	144.2	177.2	244.1	186.7	128.8	100.7	132.2	111.2	195.4	122.6
1993	110.6	111.2	131.3	128.6	153.7	257.2	155.6	137.6	93.5	121.0	106.7	188.3	102.2
1994	105.3	106.0	111.8	107.0	130.7	175.7	110.0	118.1	95.4	110.5	109.8	132.4	99.4
1995	101.4	102.1	100.4	100.1	106.6	128.8	118.0	95.9	91.7	89.4	99.8	80.7	82.6
1996	100.0	100.0	100.0	100.0	100.0	100.0	100.0	100.0	100.0	100.0	100.0	100.0	100.0
1997	97.4	98.7	101.0	108.6	89.2	104.7	109.6	101.1	91.2	100.5	90.9	117.8	103.2
1998	95.7	96.1	101.8	113.3	88.0	96.4	92.4	100.2	92.3	104.0	89.2	134.4	105.5
1999	97.7	97.7	108.2	119.6	83.5	133.8	74.3	117.0	99.3	115.8	96.7	137.1	125.6
2000	97.7	97.3	108.0	114.0	89.8	147.5	65.4	130.4	99.1	122.1	89.8	130.1	153.3
2001	102.5	102.2	116.0	125.0	96.2	135.5	81.1	137.4	104.5	129.0	100.6	154.7	146.4
Billions of chained (1996) dollars													
1987	450.2	373.2	37.8	20.9	4.9	1.1	3.8	3.8	3.7	13.0	5.0	3.4	4.5
1988	446.8	376.1	37.8	20.8	5.3	1.2	3.2	3.7	3.9	12.5	4.2	4.0	4.2
1989	443.3	372.4	35.7	18.8	5.3	1.1	2.4	3.8	4.4	12.1	4.6	3.3	4.1
1990	443.2	369.7	33.4	16.3	5.5	1.8	2.2	3.7	3.8	10.7	4.6	3.0	3.0
1991	438.4	369.5	32.9	14.7	5.4	2.0	2.2	3.3	5.2	10.9	4.5	2.8	3.4
1992	417.1	350.6	29.8	13.0	4.6	2.2	1.8	3.2	5.0	10.1	3.8	2.7	3.5
1993	394.7	336.1	27.5	11.6	4.0	2.3	1.5	3.5	4.7	9.3	3.6	2.6	3.0
1994	375.9	320.5	23.4	9.6	3.4	1.6	1.0	3.0	4.8	8.5	3.7	1.8	2.9
1995	361.9	308.7	21.1	9.0	2.8	1.2	1.1	2.4	4.6	6.9	3.4	1.1	2.4
1996	357.0	302.4	21.0	9.0	2.6	0.9	0.9	2.5	5.0	7.7	3.4	1.4	2.9
1997	347.7	298.5	21.2	9.8	2.3	1.0	1.0	2.5	4.6	7.7	3.1	1.6	3.0
1998	341.6	290.8	21.3	10.2	2.3	0.9	0.9	2.5	4.6	8.0	3.0	1.9	3.0
1999	348.8	295.3	22.7	10.8	2.2	1.2	0.7	2.9	5.0	8.9	3.3	1.9	3.6
2000	348.7	294.1	22.7	10.2	2.4	1.3	0.6	3.3	5.0	9.4	3.1	1.8	4.4
2001	366.0	308.9	24.3	11.2	2.5	1.2	0.8	3.4	5.2	9.9	3.4	2.1	4.2
2002	400.0	337.0	25.3	11.3	2.8	1.3	0.8	3.6	5.6	11.4	4.3	2.6	4.5
2000													
1st quarter	341.3	286.8	22.8	10.7	2.1	1.4	0.5	3.3	5.0	10.1	3.1	1.6	5.2
2nd quarter	353.4	299.0	22.8	9.9	2.4	1.4	0.7	3.4	5.1	10.0	3.1	1.6	5.3
3rd quarter	347.9	293.3	22.8	10.5	2.3	1.4	0.6	3.0	5.0	9.0	3.3	2.1	3.5
4th quarter	351.9	297.4	22.2	9.8	2.6	1.2	0.7	3.4	4.7	8.4	2.8	1.9	3.7
2001													
1st quarter	359.0	304.5	22.5	10.1	2.8	1.2	0.7	3.3	4.6	8.6	3.1	1.9	3.5
2nd quarter	361.4	304.9	24.3	10.9	2.7	1.3	0.7	3.3	5.5	9.8	3.3	2.2	4.3
3rd quarter	365.5	307.2	26.3	12.6	2.5	1.3	0.8	3.6	5.6	9.8	3.6	2.2	3.9
4th quarter	378.0	319.1	24.2	11.5	2.1	1.1	0.8	3.6	5.3	11.3	3.7	2.2	5.3
2002													
1st quarter	388.5	326.7	24.8	11.1	2.6	1.3	0.8	3.6	5.6	11.5	4.6	2.5	4.4
2nd quarter	395.8	333.9	24.9	11.2	2.6	1.3	0.8	3.7	5.5	11.7	4.4	2.7	4.5
3rd quarter	402.5	338.0	26.4	11.6	3.0	1.5	0.8	3.9	5.8	11.6	4.5	2.8	4.3
4th quarter	413.2	349.4	25.2	11.3	3.1	1.2	0.9	3.3	5.5	10.8	3.6	2.5	4.6

[1]Gross government investment consists of general government and government enterprise expenditures for fixed assets; inventory investment is included in government consumption expenditures.

[2]Consumption expenditures for durable goods excludes expenditures classified as investment, except for goods transferred to foreign countries by the federal government.

Table 6-6. Real National Defense Consumption Expenditures and Gross Investment by Type [1]—*Continued*

(Index numbers, 1996 = 100; billions of chained [1996] dollars; quarterly data are at seasonally adjusted annual rates.)

| Year, quarter, and series definition | Total | Compensation of employees [3] | | | Consumption of fixed capital [4] | Other services | | | | | | | |
		Total	Military	Civilian		Total	Research and develop- ment	Installa- tion support	Weapons support	Personnel support	Transpor- tation of material	Travel of persons	Other
Index numbers, 1996 = 100													
1972	93.2	131.8	139.3	118.9	66.0	60.0	49.2	59.2	75.4	54.0	92.7	82.1	30.1
1973	88.4	125.0	131.4	114.0	63.5	56.2	49.2	53.7	70.5	43.7	81.6	87.1	19.5
1974	87.2	123.1	126.8	116.9	61.3	56.8	48.9	54.1	75.4	48.5	73.7	93.2	22.8
1975	84.1	121.3	124.0	116.8	60.0	50.9	46.8	51.0	64.6	45.7	66.2	78.2	95.3
1976	83.8	118.9	121.0	115.4	59.5	53.6	48.6	52.4	67.6	45.8	64.9	72.2	25.1
1977	83.3	117.8	120.0	114.3	58.9	53.7	50.2	54.9	67.4	40.4	65.0	74.4	46.3
1978	83.2	118.6	118.8	118.4	58.6	52.6	49.5	51.1	73.1	41.9	60.4	80.5	57.4
1979	83.5	117.6	116.9	118.8	58.8	54.8	51.2	54.2	80.6	41.1	62.2	75.8	52.5
1980	86.5	118.3	118.1	118.7	59.5	62.1	63.2	58.5	108.2	41.8	61.0	70.9	61.6
1981	90.3	122.0	122.0	122.0	60.7	68.2	73.2	59.8	115.7	50.3	62.0	76.8	64.3
1982	96.5	124.7	124.1	125.9	62.4	82.1	78.9	82.1	125.9	66.9	67.5	96.1	53.8
1983	99.6	126.6	126.2	127.3	64.9	86.9	77.9	88.9	146.5	70.1	77.2	86.3	37.4
1984	103.3	128.3	127.8	129.4	68.5	93.4	84.1	94.5	166.7	71.8	77.3	103.0	44.1
1985	109.5	130.6	129.7	132.7	73.5	106.0	111.0	92.1	184.4	87.0	77.0	110.1	47.8
1986	113.2	131.2	130.9	131.9	79.4	112.1	119.2	94.4	193.5	92.5	87.5	114.6	47.6
1987	117.2	132.4	132.5	132.2	85.4	118.9	134.1	93.6	200.4	100.5	83.2	123.5	49.5
1988	118.5	130.8	131.5	129.4	90.0	121.7	157.9	89.8	174.9	93.9	91.0	119.1	65.1
1989	118.2	130.7	130.8	130.4	93.8	117.8	140.8	88.4	176.7	95.9	101.1	127.2	53.4
1990	118.7	129.9	131.1	127.4	97.2	117.9	126.0	98.7	193.7	93.3	114.0	122.0	54.5
1991	118.8	129.5	132.6	123.4	99.8	116.7	103.9	104.1	161.3	86.1	196.1	199.2	81.5
1992	113.4	121.9	121.3	122.8	101.3	109.1	109.6	99.5	128.9	93.4	136.0	158.2	102.7
1993	109.3	116.5	115.0	118.9	101.8	103.5	105.8	105.0	105.7	90.8	102.7	132.3	110.4
1994	105.4	110.5	109.5	112.1	101.4	100.3	100.7	104.9	122.6	96.1	84.3	119.0	190.0
1995	102.6	104.4	103.8	105.5	100.6	101.0	91.2	100.6	128.1	102.8	93.2	108.9	95.8
1996	100.0	100.0	100.0	100.0	100.0	100.0	100.0	100.0	100.0	100.0	100.0	100.0	100.0
1997	98.5	96.4	97.3	94.8	99.5	101.3	101.6	95.7	111.3	104.3	95.4	93.3	75.1
1998	95.5	93.4	95.1	90.4	99.1	96.3	86.5	91.3	113.0	105.0	94.2	93.0	61.1
1999	96.4	90.9	93.4	86.6	99.1	104.0	97.3	91.0	119.7	119.5	98.3	102.0	60.0
2000	95.9	90.6	94.2	84.4	99.2	102.4	93.2	90.2	123.1	118.5	94.7	105.0	66.3
2001	100.5	91.1	95.8	83.3	99.0	118.1	120.5	95.6	146.9	135.4	93.6	105.6	66.4
Billions of chained (1996) dollars													
1987	320.9	176.2	111.6	64.6	53.8	92.3	29.9	23.0	14.7	17.3	4.1	4.8	-1.2
1988	324.5	174.1	110.8	63.2	56.7	94.5	35.2	22.0	12.8	16.2	4.4	4.6	-1.6
1989	323.6	174.0	110.2	63.7	59.1	91.5	31.4	21.7	12.9	16.5	4.9	4.9	-1.3
1990	325.0	172.9	110.5	62.2	61.2	91.6	28.1	24.2	14.2	16.1	5.6	4.7	-1.4
1991	325.2	172.3	111.7	60.3	62.9	90.6	23.2	25.5	11.8	14.9	9.6	7.7	-2.0
1992	310.3	162.2	102.2	59.9	63.8	84.8	24.5	24.4	9.4	16.1	6.6	6.1	-2.6
1993	299.1	155.0	96.9	58.1	64.1	80.4	23.6	25.7	7.7	15.7	5.0	5.1	-2.8
1994	288.5	147.0	92.2	54.7	63.9	77.9	22.5	25.7	9.0	16.6	4.1	4.6	-4.8
1995	280.7	139.0	87.4	51.5	63.4	78.5	20.4	24.7	9.4	17.7	4.5	4.2	-2.4
1996	273.7	133.1	84.2	48.8	63.0	77.7	22.3	24.5	7.3	17.3	4.9	3.9	-2.5
1997	269.6	128.3	82.0	46.3	62.7	78.7	22.7	23.5	8.1	18.0	4.7	3.6	-1.9
1998	261.4	124.3	80.1	44.2	62.4	74.8	19.3	22.4	8.3	18.1	4.6	3.6	-1.5
1999	264.0	120.9	78.7	42.3	62.4	80.8	21.7	22.3	8.8	20.6	4.8	4.0	-1.5
2000	262.4	120.5	79.4	41.2	62.5	79.6	20.8	22.1	9.0	20.5	4.6	4.1	-1.7
2001	275.1	121.2	80.7	40.7	62.4	91.7	26.9	23.4	10.7	23.4	4.6	4.1	-1.7
2002	300.6	123.4	83.7	39.9	62.6	114.9	37.5	25.6	15.8	28.6	4.6	3.9	-1.6
2000													
1st quarter	254.4	120.1	78.7	41.5	62.5	71.8	19.1	21.2	6.9	18.7	4.7	4.0	-2.8
2nd quarter	266.5	120.7	78.7	42.1	62.5	83.4	21.8	22.8	9.3	21.8	4.6	4.0	-1.2
3rd quarter	261.8	120.7	79.8	41.0	62.5	78.7	18.0	22.8	9.7	21.3	4.6	4.1	-1.9
4th quarter	267.0	120.4	80.2	40.3	62.5	84.3	24.4	21.8	10.1	20.0	4.5	4.2	-0.9
2001													
1st quarter	273.5	121.4	80.8	40.7	62.4	89.9	26.0	23.1	10.8	23.6	4.5	4.1	-2.5
2nd quarter	271.1	121.2	80.4	40.9	62.4	87.8	25.5	22.5	10.3	21.9	4.5	4.0	-1.2
3rd quarter	271.7	121.0	80.2	41.0	62.4	88.5	24.8	23.4	9.7	23.1	4.6	4.1	-1.4
4th quarter	284.0	121.3	81.4	40.0	62.4	100.6	31.2	24.7	12.2	24.8	4.7	4.2	-1.5
2002													
1st quarter	290.7	122.4	83.0	39.6	62.4	106.2	33.7	24.8	13.9	26.3	4.5	3.8	-1.4
2nd quarter	297.6	123.8	84.0	40.0	62.5	111.6	36.7	24.5	14.9	27.6	4.5	3.8	-1.1
3rd quarter	300.5	124.3	84.5	40.1	62.6	113.8	35.6	26.4	16.6	29.4	4.5	3.9	-3.2
4th quarter	313.4	123.0	83.3	39.9	62.8	128.2	43.9	26.7	17.9	31.2	4.7	4.0	-0.7

[1]Gross government investment consists of general government and government enterprise expenditures for fixed assets; inventory investment is included in government consumption expenditures.
[3]Compensation of government employees engaged in new own-account investment and related expenditures for goods and services are classified as investment in structures and in software.
[4]Consumption of fixed capital, or depreciation, is included in government consumption expenditures as a partial measure of the value of the services of general government fixed assets; use of depreciation assumes a zero net return on these assets.

Table 6-6. Real National Defense Consumption Expenditures and Gross Investment by Type [1]—*Continued*

(Index numbers, 1996 = 100; billions of chained [1996] dollars; quarterly data are at seasonally adjusted annual rates.)

Year, quarter, and series definition	Total	Structures	Defense gross investment						
			Equipment and software						
			Total	Aircraft	Missiles	Ships	Vehicles	Electronics and software	Other durable goods
Index numbers, 1996 = 100									
1972	42.1	116.0	36.0	43.6	35.5	94.4	109.1	7.7	41.0
1973	40.9	114.7	34.9	38.4	37.2	79.7	83.6	8.5	45.5
1974	42.1	105.2	36.9	39.0	41.1	98.3	84.2	8.8	44.0
1975	46.5	101.8	41.8	59.3	30.2	88.0	69.0	9.9	57.1
1976	45.7	90.3	41.8	55.5	25.5	90.1	100.0	10.1	61.9
1977	46.4	91.4	42.6	57.9	19.5	105.2	123.1	11.1	58.8
1978	46.2	92.6	42.2	54.7	16.0	118.4	151.3	14.0	51.0
1979	52.9	78.3	50.5	68.5	32.6	121.9	158.7	15.5	59.0
1980	56.5	90.6	53.3	81.4	46.8	107.2	176.0	19.0	51.5
1981	62.1	86.2	59.8	94.0	54.3	122.1	119.3	22.4	58.5
1982	69.8	101.5	66.9	94.6	70.1	142.4	187.3	26.0	60.9
1983	81.8	120.7	78.2	106.3	88.6	158.2	318.0	31.7	63.6
1984	92.9	116.8	90.6	111.2	106.5	167.7	423.2	39.9	79.2
1985	111.7	142.9	108.6	151.0	121.6	184.3	383.2	51.1	96.8
1986	127.8	155.3	125.1	229.8	154.2	178.0	418.9	58.2	81.8
1987	139.7	167.5	137.0	263.9	175.8	173.1	436.7	66.6	86.7
1988	129.2	154.6	126.7	216.8	160.0	164.1	373.0	70.2	87.2
1989	129.6	124.2	130.6	196.2	181.6	182.0	311.2	73.4	95.9
1990	133.9	115.5	136.5	180.8	239.9	192.0	312.0	76.3	94.9
1991	126.0	85.2	131.3	130.0	240.9	172.3	328.4	74.8	111.6
1992	121.5	94.1	125.1	113.7	240.0	166.4	257.1	79.2	104.4
1993	107.3	85.4	110.2	122.7	174.9	140.2	163.4	84.6	86.6
1994	101.4	92.2	102.7	123.1	131.1	126.9	88.1	85.5	86.5
1995	97.4	96.5	97.6	100.9	112.1	118.1	92.2	87.4	90.8
1996	100.0	100.0	100.0	100.0	100.0	100.0	100.0	100.0	100.0
1997	90.0	82.6	91.0	68.0	74.1	88.6	115.0	112.1	92.3
1998	93.3	76.1	95.8	68.0	84.2	95.1	125.8	126.1	90.7
1999	98.3	72.2	102.2	77.1	72.0	100.9	140.2	137.0	96.7
2000	100.4	69.3	105.1	90.4	63.9	95.9	156.9	143.6	96.1
2001	104.9	68.0	110.6	104.9	86.2	105.3	160.6	132.7	102.0
Billions of chained (1996) dollars									
1987	76.3	11.2	65.7	24.2	7.1	11.7	5.2	7.7	13.1
1988	70.6	10.4	60.7	19.9	6.5	11.1	4.5	8.1	13.2
1989	70.8	8.3	62.6	18.0	7.4	12.3	3.7	8.5	14.5
1990	73.2	7.7	65.4	16.6	9.8	13.0	3.7	8.8	14.4
1991	68.9	5.7	62.9	11.9	9.8	11.7	3.9	8.7	16.9
1992	66.4	6.3	60.0	10.4	9.8	11.3	3.1	9.2	15.8
1993	58.6	5.7	52.8	11.3	7.1	9.5	2.0	9.8	13.1
1994	55.4	6.2	49.2	11.3	5.3	8.6	1.1	9.9	13.1
1995	53.2	6.5	46.8	9.3	4.6	8.0	1.1	10.1	13.8
1996	54.6	6.7	47.9	9.2	4.1	6.8	1.2	11.6	15.2
1997	49.1	5.5	43.6	6.2	3.0	6.0	1.4	13.0	14.0
1998	51.0	5.1	45.9	6.2	3.4	6.4	1.5	14.6	13.8
1999	53.7	4.8	49.0	7.1	2.9	6.8	1.7	15.8	14.7
2000	54.8	4.6	50.4	8.3	2.6	6.5	1.9	16.6	14.6
2001	57.3	4.6	53.0	9.6	3.5	7.1	1.9	15.3	15.5
2002	63.3	4.4	59.5	11.2	3.4	8.5	2.8	17.1	16.5
2000									
1st quarter	54.9	4.4	50.8	9.6	2.2	6.0	1.8	16.5	14.8
2nd quarter	54.7	4.7	50.1	7.2	2.3	6.7	2.0	16.7	15.2
3rd quarter	55.0	5.0	50.1	8.5	2.0	6.6	1.9	16.3	14.8
4th quarter	54.8	4.5	50.6	7.9	3.9	6.7	1.7	17.0	13.5
2001									
1st quarter	54.6	4.7	50.1	8.5	3.8	7.1	1.8	15.3	13.5
2nd quarter	56.8	4.6	52.4	9.1	3.7	7.3	2.0	14.5	15.6
3rd quarter	58.7	4.2	54.9	11.3	3.2	6.8	1.8	15.4	16.5
4th quarter	59.0	4.7	54.6	9.6	3.2	7.3	2.1	16.1	16.1
2002									
1st quarter	62.2	4.2	58.5	10.4	3.9	8.1	2.2	16.9	17.0
2nd quarter	62.2	4.5	58.2	10.8	3.4	8.4	2.9	16.7	15.9
3rd quarter	65.0	4.4	61.1	11.9	2.9	8.7	3.2	17.5	16.8
4th quarter	63.9	4.3	60.1	11.7	3.4	8.8	2.7	17.2	16.4

[1]Gross government investment consists of general government and government enterprise expenditures for fixed assets; inventory investment is included in government consumption expenditures.

Table 6-7. Federal Government Receipts and Outlays by Fiscal Year [1]

(Budget Accounts, millions of dollars.)

| Year | Fiscal year GDP | Receipts, outlays, deficit, and financing | | | | | | | | Receipts by source | | | | |
| | | Total receipts (net) | Total outlays (net) | Budget surplus or deficit (-) | | | Sources of financing, total | | Individual income taxes | Corporate income taxes | Social insurance taxes and contributions | | |
				Total	On-budget	Off-budget	Borrowing from the public	Other financing			Employ-ment taxes and contri-butions	Unemploy-ment insurance	Other retirement contribu-tions
1939	89 000	6 295	9 141	-2 846	-3 362	516	...	...	1 029	1 127	1 593		
1940	96 700	6 548	9 468	-2 920	-3 484	564	...	...	892	1 197	725	1 015	45
1941	114 000	8 712	13 653	-4 941	-5 594	653	5 451	-510	1 314	2 124	827	1 056	57
1942	144 200	14 634	35 137	-20 503	-21 333	830	19 530	973	3 263	4 719	1 064	1 299	89
1943	180 100	24 001	78 555	-54 554	-55 595	1 041	60 013	-5 459	6 505	9 557	1 338	1 477	229
1944	209 000	43 747	91 304	-47 557	-48 735	1 178	57 030	-9 473	19 705	14 838	1 557	1 644	272
1945	221 300	45 159	92 712	-47 553	-48 720	1 167	50 386	-2 833	18 372	15 988	1 592	1 568	291
1946	222 700	39 296	55 232	-15 936	-16 964	1 028	6 679	9 257	16 098	11 883	1 517	1 316	282
1947	234 600	38 514	34 496	4 018	2 861	1 157	-17 522	13 504	17 935	8 615	1 835	1 329	259
1948	256 400	41 560	29 764	11 796	10 548	1 248	-8 069	-3 727	19 315	9 678	2 168	1 343	239
1949	271 500	39 415	38 835	580	-684	1 263	-1 948	1 368	15 552	11 192	2 246	1 205	330
1950	273 400	39 443	42 562	-3 119	-4 702	1 583	4 701	-1 582	15 755	10 449	2 648	1 332	358
1951	321 000	51 616	45 514	6 102	4 259	1 843	-4 697	-1 405	21 616	14 101	3 688	1 609	377
1952	348 800	66 167	67 686	-1 519	-3 383	1 864	432	1 087	27 934	21 226	4 315	1 712	418
1953	373 400	69 608	76 101	-6 493	-8 259	1 766	3 625	2 868	29 816	21 238	4 722	1 675	423
1954	378 000	69 701	70 855	-1 154	-2 831	1 677	6 116	-4 962	29 542	21 101	5 192	1 561	455
1955	395 200	65 451	68 444	-2 993	-4 091	1 098	2 117	876	28 747	17 861	5 981	1 449	431
1956	427 700	74 587	70 640	3 947	2 494	1 452	-4 460	513	32 188	20 880	7 059	1 690	571
1957	450 700	79 990	76 578	3 412	2 639	773	-2 836	-576	35 620	21 167	7 405	1 950	642
1958	461 100	79 636	82 405	-2 769	-3 315	546	7 016	-4 247	34 724	20 074	8 624	1 933	682
1959	492 100	79 249	92 098	-12 849	-12 149	-700	8 365	4 484	36 719	17 309	8 821	2 131	770
1960	518 900	92 492	92 191	301	510	-209	2 139	-2 440	40 715	21 494	11 248	2 667	768
1961	531 800	94 388	97 723	-3 335	-3 766	431	1 517	1 818	41 338	20 954	12 679	2 903	857
1962	568 500	99 676	106 821	-7 146	-5 881	-1 265	9 653	-2 507	45 571	20 523	12 835	3 337	875
1963	599 700	106 560	111 316	-4 756	-3 966	-789	5 968	-1 212	47 588	21 579	14 746	4 112	946
1964	641 300	112 613	118 528	-5 915	-6 546	632	2 871	3 044	48 697	23 493	16 959	3 997	1 007
1965	687 900	116 817	118 228	-1 411	-1 605	194	3 929	-2 518	48 792	25 461	17 358	3 803	1 081
1966	754 200	130 835	134 532	-3 698	-3 068	-630	2 936	762	55 446	30 073	20 662	3 755	1 129
1967	813 500	148 822	157 464	-8 643	-12 620	3 978	2 912	5 731	61 526	33 971	27 823	3 575	1 221
1968	868 400	152 973	178 134	-25 161	-27 742	2 581	22 919	2 242	68 726	28 665	29 224	3 346	1 354
1969	949 200	186 882	183 640	3 242	-507	3 749	-11 437	8 195	87 249	36 678	34 236	3 328	1 451
1970	1 013 200	192 807	195 649	-2 842	-8 694	5 852	5 090	-2 248	90 412	32 829	39 133	3 464	1 765
1971	1 081 400	187 139	210 172	-23 033	-26 052	3 019	19 839	3 194	86 230	26 785	41 699	3 674	1 952
1972	1 181 500	207 309	230 681	-23 373	-26 423	3 050	19 340	4 033	94 737	32 166	46 120	4 357	2 097
1973	1 308 100	230 799	245 707	-14 908	-15 403	495	18 533	-3 625	103 246	36 153	54 876	6 051	2 187
1974	1 442 100	263 224	269 359	-6 135	-7 971	1 836	2 789	3 346	118 952	38 620	65 888	6 837	2 347
1975	1 559 800	279 090	332 332	-53 242	-55 260	2 018	51 001	2 241	122 386	40 621	75 199	6 771	2 565
1976	1 736 700	298 060	371 792	-73 732	-70 512	-3 220	82 704	-8 972	131 603	41 409	79 901	8 054	2 814
TQ [1]	454 800	81 232	95 975	-14 744	-13 339	-1 405	18 105	-3 361	38 801	8 460	21 801	2 698	720
1977	1 971 300	355 559	409 218	-53 659	-49 760	-3 899	53 595	64	157 626	54 892	92 199	11 312	2 974
1978	2 218 600	399 561	458 746	-59 185	-54 919	-4 266	58 022	1 163	180 988	59 952	103 881	13 850	3 237
1979	2 503 800	463 302	504 028	-40 726	-38 742	-1 984	33 180	7 546	217 841	65 677	120 058	15 387	3 494
1980	2 732 100	517 112	590 941	-73 830	-72 710	-1 120	71 617	2 213	244 069	64 600	138 748	15 336	3 719
1981	3 061 600	599 272	678 241	-78 968	-73 948	-5 020	77 487	1 481	285 917	61 137	162 973	15 763	3 984
1982	3 228 600	617 766	745 743	-127 977	-120 040	-7 937	135 165	-7 188	297 744	49 207	180 686	16 600	4 212
1983	3 440 500	600 562	808 364	-207 802	-208 014	212	212 693	-4 891	288 938	37 022	185 766	18 799	4 429
1984	3 839 400	666 486	851 853	-185 367	-185 629	262	169 707	15 660	298 415	56 893	209 658	25 138	4 580
1985	4 136 600	734 088	946 396	-212 308	-221 671	9 363	200 285	12 023	334 531	61 331	234 646	25 758	4 759
1986	4 401 400	769 215	990 430	-221 215	-237 946	16 731	233 363	-12 148	348 959	63 143	255 062	24 098	4 742
1987	4 647 000	854 353	1 004 082	-149 728	-169 298	19 570	149 130	598	392 557	83 926	273 028	25 575	4 715
1988	5 014 700	909 303	1 064 455	-155 152	-193 951	38 800	161 863	-6 711	401 181	94 508	305 093	24 584	4 658
1989	5 405 500	991 190	1 143 646	-152 456	-205 210	52 754	139 100	13 356	445 690	103 291	332 859	22 011	4 546
1990	5 735 600	1 031 969	1 253 165	-221 195	-277 786	56 590	220 842	353	466 884	93 507	353 891	21 635	4 522
1991	5 930 400	1 055 041	1 324 369	-269 328	-321 525	52 198	277 441	-8 113	467 827	98 086	370 526	20 922	4 568
1992	6 218 600	1 091 279	1 381 655	-290 376	-340 463	50 087	310 738	-20 362	475 964	100 270	385 491	23 410	4 788
1993	6 558 400	1 154 401	1 409 489	-255 087	-300 434	45 347	248 659	6 428	509 680	117 520	396 939	26 556	4 805
1994	6 944 600	1 258 627	1 461 877	-203 250	-258 904	55 654	184 669	18 581	543 055	140 385	428 810	28 004	4 661
1995	7 324 000	1 351 830	1 515 802	-163 972	-226 387	62 415	171 313	-7 341	590 244	157 004	451 045	28 878	4 550
1996	7 694 600	1 453 062	1 560 535	-107 473	-174 061	66 588	129 695	-22 222	656 417	171 824	476 361	28 584	4 469
1997	8 185 200	1 579 292	1 601 250	-21 958	-103 322	81 364	38 271	-16 313	737 466	182 293	506 751	28 202	4 418
1998	8 663 900	1 721 798	1 652 585	69 213	-29 982	99 195	-51 245	-17 968	828 586	188 677	540 014	27 484	4 333
1999	9 137 700	1 827 454	1 701 891	125 563	1 873	123 690	-88 736	-36 827	879 480	184 680	580 880	26 480	4 473
2000	9 718 800	2 025 218	1 788 773	236 445	86 626	149 819	-222 559	-13 886	1 004 462	207 289	620 451	27 640	4 761
2001	10 021 500	1 991 194	1 863 895	127 299	-33 382	160 681	-90 189	-37 110	994 339	151 075	661 442	27 812	4 713
2002	10 336 600	1 853 173	2 010 975	-157 802	-317 461	159 659	220 812	-63 010	858 345	148 044	668 547	27 619	4 594

[1]Fiscal years through 1976 are from July 1 through June 30. Beginning with October 1976 (fiscal year 1977), fiscal years are from October 1 through September 30. The period from July 1 through September 30, 1976 is a separate fiscal period known as the transition quarter (TQ) and not included in any fiscal year.
. . . = Not available.

Table 6-7. Federal Government Receipts and Outlays by Fiscal Year [1]—Continued

(Budget Accounts, millions of dollars.)

Year	Receipts by sources—Continued				Outlays by function						
	Excise taxes	Estate and gift taxes	Customs deposits	Miscellaneous receipts	National defense	International affairs	General science, space, and technology	Energy	Natural resources and environment	Agriculture	Commerce and housing credit
1939	1 871	675			...	...	...	...	...	...	...
1940	1 977	353	331	14	1 660	51	...	88	997	369	550
1941	2 552	403	365	14	6 435	145	...	91	817	339	398
1942	3 399	420	369	11	25 658	968	4	156	819	344	1 521
1943	4 096	441	308	50	66 699	1 286	1	116	726	343	2 151
1944	4 759	507	417	48	79 143	1 449	48	65	642	1 275	624
1945	6 265	637	341	105	82 965	1 913	111	25	455	1 635	-2 630
1946	6 998	668	424	109	42 681	1 935	34	41	482	610	-1 857
1947	7 211	771	477	84	12 808	5 791	5	18	700	814	-923
1948	7 356	890	403	168	9 105	4 566	1	292	780	69	306
1949	7 502	780	367	241	13 150	6 052	48	341	1 080	1 924	800
1950	7 550	698	407	247	13 724	4 673	55	327	1 308	2 049	1 035
1951	8 648	708	609	261	23 566	3 647	51	383	1 310	-323	1 228
1952	8 852	818	533	359	46 089	2 691	49	474	1 233	176	1 278
1953	9 877	881	596	379	52 802	2 119	49	425	1 289	2 253	910
1954	9 945	934	542	429	49 266	1 596	46	432	1 007	1 817	-184
1955	9 131	924	585	341	42 729	2 223	74	325	940	3 514	92
1956	9 929	1 161	682	427	42 523	2 414	79	174	870	3 486	506
1957	10 534	1 365	735	573	45 430	3 147	122	240	1 098	2 288	1 424
1958	10 638	1 393	782	787	46 815	3 364	141	348	1 407	2 411	930
1959	10 578	1 333	925	662	49 015	3 144	294	382	1 632	4 509	1 933
1960	11 676	1 606	1 105	1 212	48 130	2 988	599	464	1 559	2 623	1 618
1961	11 860	1 896	982	918	49 601	3 184	1 042	510	1 779	2 641	1 203
1962	12 534	2 016	1 142	843	52 345	5 639	1 723	604	2 044	3 562	1 424
1963	13 194	2 167	1 205	1 022	53 400	5 308	3 051	530	2 251	4 384	62
1964	13 731	2 394	1 252	1 086	54 757	4 945	4 897	572	2 364	4 609	418
1965	14 570	2 716	1 442	1 594	50 620	5 273	5 823	699	2 531	3 955	1 157
1966	13 062	3 066	1 767	1 876	58 111	5 580	6 717	612	2 719	2 447	3 245
1967	13 719	2 978	1 901	2 107	71 417	5 566	6 233	782	2 869	2 990	3 979
1968	14 079	3 051	2 038	2 491	81 926	5 301	5 524	1 037	2 988	4 545	4 280
1969	15 222	3 491	2 319	2 000	82 497	4 600	5 020	1 010	2 900	5 826	-119
1970	15 705	3 644	2 430	3 424	81 692	4 330	4 511	997	3 065	5 166	2 112
1971	16 614	3 735	2 591	3 858	78 872	4 159	4 182	1 035	3 915	4 290	2 366
1972	15 477	5 436	3 287	3 632	79 174	4 781	4 175	1 296	4 241	5 259	2 222
1973	16 260	4 917	3 188	3 920	76 681	4 149	4 032	1 237	4 775	4 854	931
1974	16 844	5 035	3 334	5 368	79 347	5 710	3 980	1 303	5 697	2 230	4 705
1975	16 551	4 611	3 676	6 712	86 509	7 097	3 991	2 916	7 346	3 036	9 947
1976	16 963	5 216	4 074	8 027	89 619	6 433	4 373	4 204	8 184	3 170	7 619
TQ [1]	4 473	1 455	1 212	1 611	22 269	2 458	1 162	1 129	2 524	983	931
1977	17 548	7 327	5 150	6 531	97 241	6 353	4 736	5 770	10 032	6 787	3 093
1978	18 376	5 285	6 573	7 419	104 495	7 482	4 926	7 992	10 983	11 357	6 254
1979	18 745	5 411	7 439	9 252	116 342	7 459	5 235	9 180	12 135	11 236	4 686
1980	24 329	6 389	7 174	12 748	133 995	12 714	5 832	10 156	13 858	8 839	9 390
1981	40 839	6 787	8 083	13 790	157 513	13 104	6 469	15 166	13 568	11 323	8 206
1982	36 311	7 991	8 854	16 161	185 309	12 300	7 200	13 527	12 998	15 944	6 256
1983	35 300	6 053	8 655	15 600	209 903	11 848	7 935	9 353	12 672	22 901	6 681
1984	37 361	6 010	11 370	17 060	227 413	15 876	8 317	7 073	12 593	13 613	6 959
1985	35 992	6 422	12 079	18 571	252 748	16 176	8 627	5 609	13 357	25 565	4 337
1986	32 919	6 958	13 327	20 008	273 375	14 152	8 976	4 690	13 639	31 449	5 059
1987	32 457	7 493	15 085	19 518	281 999	11 649	9 216	4 072	13 363	26 606	6 435
1988	35 227	7 594	16 198	20 259	290 361	10 471	10 841	2 297	14 606	17 210	19 164
1989	34 386	8 745	16 334	23 328	303 559	9 585	12 838	2 706	16 182	16 919	29 710
1990	35 345	11 500	16 707	27 978	299 331	13 764	14 444	3 341	17 080	11 958	67 600
1991	42 402	11 138	15 949	23 623	273 292	15 851	16 111	2 436	18 559	15 183	76 271
1992	45 569	11 143	17 359	27 284	298 350	16 107	16 409	4 500	20 025	15 205	10 919
1993	48 057	12 577	18 802	19 465	291 086	17 248	17 030	4 319	20 239	20 363	-21 853
1994	55 225	15 225	20 099	23 164	281 642	17 083	16 227	5 219	21 026	15 046	-4 228
1995	57 484	14 763	19 301	28 561	272 066	16 434	16 724	4 936	21 915	9 778	-17 808
1996	54 014	17 189	18 670	25 534	265 753	13 496	16 709	2 839	21 524	9 159	-10 472
1997	56 924	19 845	17 928	25 465	270 505	15 228	17 174	1 475	21 227	9 032	-14 624
1998	57 673	24 076	18 297	32 658	268 456	13 109	18 219	1 270	22 300	12 206	1 014
1999	70 414	27 782	18 336	34 929	274 873	15 243	18 125	912	23 968	23 011	2 647
2000	68 865	29 010	19 914	42 826	294 495	17 216	18 637	-1 060	25 031	36 641	3 211
2001	66 232	28 400	19 369	37 812	305 500	16 493	19 789	39	25 623	26 397	5 883
2002	66 989	26 507	18 602	33 926	348 555	22 357	20 772	483	29 454	22 188	-385

[1]Fiscal years through 1976 are from July 1 through June 30. Beginning with October 1976 (fiscal year 1977), fiscal years are from October 1 through September 30. The period from July 1 through September 30, 1976 is a separate fiscal period known as the transition quarter (TQ) and not included in any fiscal year.
. . . = Not available.

Table 6-7. Federal Government Receipts and Outlays by Fiscal Year [1]—Continued

(Budget Accounts, millions of dollars.)

Year	Transportation	Community and regional development	Education, employment, and social services	Health	Medicare	Income security	Social Security	Veterans benefits and services	Administration of justice	General government	Net interest
						Outlays by function—Continued					
1939	...	...	...	...	...	...	...	...	...	...	...
1940	392	285	1 972	55	...	1 514	28	570	81	274	899
1941	353	123	1 592	60	...	1 855	91	560	92	306	943
1942	1 283	113	1 062	71	...	1 828	137	501	117	397	1 052
1943	3 220	219	375	92	...	1 739	177	276	154	673	1 529
1944	3 901	238	160	174	...	1 503	217	-126	192	900	2 219
1945	3 654	243	134	211	...	1 137	267	110	178	581	3 112
1946	1 970	200	85	201	...	2 384	358	2 465	176	825	4 111
1947	1 130	302	102	177	...	2 820	466	6 344	176	1 114	4 204
1948	787	78	191	162	...	2 499	558	6 457	170	1 045	4 341
1949	916	-33	178	197	...	3 174	657	6 599	184	824	4 523
1950	967	30	241	268	...	4 097	781	8 834	193	986	4 812
1951	956	47	235	323	...	3 352	1 565	5 526	218	1 097	4 665
1952	1 124	73	339	347	...	3 655	2 063	5 341	267	1 163	4 701
1953	1 264	117	441	336	...	3 823	2 717	4 519	243	1 209	5 156
1954	1 229	100	370	307	...	4 434	3 352	4 613	257	799	4 811
1955	1 246	129	445	291	...	5 071	4 427	4 675	256	651	4 850
1956	1 450	92	591	359	...	4 734	5 478	4 891	302	1 201	5 079
1957	1 662	135	590	479	...	5 427	6 661	5 005	303	1 360	5 354
1958	2 334	169	643	541	...	7 535	8 219	5 350	325	655	5 604
1959	3 655	211	789	685	...	8 239	9 737	5 443	356	926	5 762
1960	4 126	224	968	795	...	7 378	11 602	5 441	366	1 184	6 947
1961	3 987	275	1 063	913	...	9 683	12 474	5 705	400	1 354	6 716
1962	4 290	469	1 241	1 198	...	9 207	14 365	5 619	429	1 049	6 889
1963	4 596	574	1 458	1 451	...	9 311	15 788	5 514	465	1 230	7 740
1964	5 242	933	1 555	1 788	...	9 657	16 620	5 675	489	1 518	8 199
1965	5 763	1 114	2 140	1 791	...	9 469	17 460	5 716	535	1 499	8 591
1966	5 730	1 105	4 363	2 543	64	9 678	20 694	5 916	563	1 603	9 386
1967	5 936	1 108	6 453	3 351	2 748	10 261	21 725	6 735	618	1 719	10 268
1968	6 316	1 382	7 634	4 390	4 649	11 816	23 854	7 032	659	1 757	11 090
1969	6 526	1 552	7 548	5 162	5 695	13 076	27 298	7 631	766	1 939	12 699
1970	7 008	2 392	8 634	5 907	6 213	15 655	30 270	8 669	959	2 320	14 380
1971	8 052	2 917	9 849	6 843	6 622	22 946	35 872	9 768	1 306	2 442	14 841
1972	8 392	3 423	12 529	8 674	7 479	27 650	40 157	10 720	1 653	2 960	15 478
1973	9 066	4 605	12 745	9 356	8 052	28 276	49 090	12 003	2 141	9 774	17 349
1974	9 172	4 229	12 457	10 733	9 639	33 713	55 867	13 374	2 470	10 032	21 449
1975	10 918	4 322	16 022	12 930	12 875	50 176	64 658	16 584	2 955	10 408	23 244
1976	13 739	5 442	18 910	15 734	15 834	60 799	73 899	18 419	3 328	9 747	26 727
TQ [1]	3 358	1 569	5 169	3 924	4 264	14 985	19 763	3 960	891	3 895	6 949
1977	14 829	7 021	21 104	17 302	19 345	61 060	85 061	18 022	3 605	12 833	29 901
1978	15 521	11 841	26 710	18 524	22 768	61 505	93 861	18 961	3 813	12 015	35 458
1979	18 079	10 480	30 223	20 494	26 495	66 376	104 073	19 914	4 173	12 293	42 633
1980	21 329	11 252	31 843	23 169	32 090	86 557	118 547	21 169	4 584	13 028	52 533
1981	23 379	10 568	33 151	26 866	39 149	100 299	139 584	22 973	4 769	11 429	68 766
1982	20 625	8 347	26 611	27 445	46 567	108 155	155 964	23 938	4 712	10 914	85 032
1983	21 334	7 564	26 196	28 641	52 588	123 031	170 724	24 824	5 105	11 235	89 808
1984	23 669	7 673	26 921	30 417	57 540	113 352	178 223	25 588	5 663	11 817	111 102
1985	25 838	7 680	28 593	33 542	65 822	128 979	188 623	26 262	6 270	11 588	129 478
1986	28 117	7 233	29 777	35 936	70 164	120 633	198 757	26 327	6 572	12 564	136 017
1987	26 222	5 051	28 922	39 967	75 120	124 088	207 353	26 750	7 553	7 560	138 611
1988	27 272	5 294	30 933	44 487	78 878	130 377	219 341	29 386	9 236	9 465	151 803
1989	27 608	5 362	35 330	48 390	84 964	137 426	232 542	30 031	9 474	9 249	168 981
1990	29 485	8 532	37 176	57 716	98 102	148 655	248 623	29 058	9 993	10 575	184 347
1991	31 099	6 813	41 234	71 183	104 489	172 441	269 015	31 305	12 276	11 719	194 448
1992	33 332	6 841	42 743	89 497	119 024	199 527	287 585	34 064	14 426	13 039	199 344
1993	35 004	9 149	47 376	99 415	130 552	209 934	304 585	35 671	14 955	13 086	198 713
1994	38 066	10 625	43 277	107 122	144 747	217 114	319 565	37 584	15 268	11 333	202 932
1995	39 350	10 749	51 020	115 418	159 855	223 736	335 846	37 890	16 247	13 967	232 134
1996	39 565	10 745	48 310	119 378	174 225	229 663	349 671	36 985	17 596	11 956	241 053
1997	40 767	11 055	48 961	123 843	190 016	234 952	365 251	39 313	20 243	12 821	243 984
1998	40 343	9 776	50 503	131 442	192 822	237 663	379 215	41 781	22 938	15 603	241 119
1999	42 533	11 870	50 591	141 074	190 447	242 356	390 037	43 212	26 082	15 599	229 756
2000	46 854	10 629	53 754	154 533	197 113	253 575	409 423	47 083	27 995	13 273	222 951
2001	54 449	11 907	57 143	172 270	217 384	269 615	432 958	45 039	29 660	14 589	206 168
2002	61 862	12 991	70 544	196 545	230 855	312 511	456 413	50 984	34 316	17 385	170 951

[1]Fiscal years through 1976 are from July 1 through June 30. Beginning with October 1976 (fiscal year 1977), fiscal years are from October 1 through September 30. The period from July 1 through September 30, 1976 is a separate fiscal period known as the transition quarter (TQ) and not included in any fiscal year.
. . . = Not available.

Table 6-8. Federal Government Debt by Fiscal Year [1]

(Billions of dollars, except as noted.)

Year	Federal government debt held by the public at end of fiscal year		Gross public debt at end of fiscal year held by:						
	Debt held by the public (billions of dollars)	Debt/GDP ratio (percent)	Total	Social Security funds	Other U.S. government accounts	Federal Reserve Banks	Private investors		
							Total	Foreign and international investors	Domestic investors
1945	235	106.3	260	7	18	22	213	. . .	. . .
1946	242	108.6	271	8	21	24	218	. . .	. . .
1947	224	95.6	257	9	24	22	202	. . .	. . .
1948	216	84.3	252	10	26	21	195	. . .	. . .
1949	214	78.9	253	11	27	19	195	. . .	. . .
1950	219	80.1	257	13	25	18	201	. . .	. . .
1951	214	66.8	255	15	26	23	191	. . .	. . .
1952	215	61.6	259	17	28	23	192	. . .	. . .
1953	218	58.5	266	18	29	25	194	. . .	. . .
1954	224	59.4	271	20	26	25	199	. . .	. . .
1955	227	57.3	274	21	27	24	203	. . .	. . .
1956	222	51.9	273	23	28	24	198	. . .	. . .
1957	219	48.7	272	23	30	23	196	. . .	. . .
1958	226	49.1	280	24	29	25	201	. . .	. . .
1959	235	47.7	287	23	30	26	209	. . .	. . .
1960	237	45.6	291	23	31	27	210	. . .	. . .
1961	238	44.8	293	23	31	27	211	. . .	. . .
1962	248	43.6	303	22	33	30	218	. . .	. . .
1963	254	42.4	310	21	35	32	222	. . .	. . .
1964	257	40.1	316	22	37	35	222	. . .	. . .
1965	261	37.9	322	22	39	39	222	12	209
1966	264	35.0	328	22	43	42	222	12	210
1967	267	32.8	340	26	48	47	220	11	209
1968	290	33.3	369	28	51	52	237	11	227
1969	278	29.3	366	32	56	54	224	10	214
1970	283	28.0	381	38	60	58	225	14	211
1971	303	28.0	408	41	64	66	238	32	206
1972	322	27.3	436	44	70	71	251	49	202
1973	341	26.1	466	44	81	75	266	59	206
1974	344	23.8	484	46	94	81	263	57	206
1975	395	25.3	542	48	99	85	310	66	244
1976	477	27.5	629	45	107	95	383	70	313
TQ [1]	496	27.2	644	44	105	97	399	75	324
1977	549	27.9	706	40	118	105	444	96	349
1978	607	27.4	777	35	134	115	492	121	371
1979	640	25.6	829	33	156	116	525	120	404
1980	712	26.1	909	32	165	121	591	122	469
1981	789	25.8	995	27	178	124	665	131	534
1982	925	28.6	1 137	19	193	134	790	141	649
1983	1 137	33.1	1 372	32	202	156	982	160	822
1984	1 307	34.0	1 565	32	225	155	1 152	176	976
1985	1 507	36.4	1 817	40	270	170	1 337	223	1 115
1986	1 741	39.5	2 121	46	334	191	1 550	266	1 284
1987	1 890	40.7	2 346	65	391	212	1 678	280	1 398
1988	2 052	40.9	2 601	104	445	229	1 822	346	1 476
1989	2 191	40.5	2 868	157	520	220	1 971	395	1 576
1990	2 412	42.0	3 206	215	580	234	2 177	440	1 737
1991	2 689	45.3	3 598	268	641	250	2 430	477	1 953
1992	3 000	48.2	4 002	319	683	296	2 703	535	2 168
1993	3 248	49.5	4 351	366	737	326	2 923	591	2 331
1994	3 433	49.4	4 643	423	788	355	3 078	656	2 422
1995	3 604	49.2	4 921	483	833	374	3 230	800	2 430
1996	3 734	48.5	5 181	550	898	391	3 343	978	2 365
1997	3 772	46.1	5 369	631	966	425	3 348	1 218	2 130
1998	3 721	42.9	5 478	730	1 027	458	3 263	1 217	2 046
1999	3 632	39.8	5 606	855	1 118	497	3 136	1 281	1 854
2000	3 410	35.1	5 629	1 007	1 212	511	2 898	1 058	1 840
2001	3 320	33.1	5 770	1 170	1 280	534	2 785	1 006	1 780
2002	3 540	34.3	6 198	1 329	1 329	604	2 936	1 134	1 802

[1]Fiscal years through 1976 are from July 1 through June 30. Beginning with October 1976 (fiscal year 1977), fiscal years are from October 1 through September 30. The period from July 1 through September 30, 1976 is a separate fiscal period known as the transition quarter (TQ) and not included in any fiscal year.
. . . = Not available.

Table 6-9. Government Employment

(Calendar years; payroll employment, thousands, seasonally adjusted, except as noted.)

Year and month	Total government employment	Federal			State			Local		
		Total	Department of Defense (not seasonally adjusted)	Postal Service (not seasonally adjusted)	Total	Education	State government hospitals (not seasonally adjusted)	Total	Education	Local government hospitals (not seasonally adjusted)
1946	5 705	2 365	746	473	...	...	...	...	...	...
1947	5 567	1 985	499	471	...	...	...	...	...	...
1948	5 742	1 954	511	498	...	...	...	...	...	...
1949	5 950	2 001	531	527	...	...	...	...	...	...
1950	6 120	2 023	533	516	...	...	...	...	...	...
1951	6 502	2 415	797	521	...	...	...	...	...	...
1952	6 727	2 539	868	542	...	...	...	...	...	...
1953	6 758	2 418	818	530	...	...	...	...	...	...
1954	6 858	2 295	744	533	...	...	...	...	...	...
1955	7 021	2 295	744	534	1 168	308	...	3 558	1 751	...
1956	7 386	2 318	749	539	1 249	334	...	3 819	1 884	...
1957	7 724	2 326	729	555	1 328	363	...	4 071	2 026	...
1958	7 946	2 298	695	567	1 415	389	...	4 232	2 115	...
1959	8 192	2 342	699	578	1 484	420	...	4 366	2 198	...
1960	8 464	2 381	681	591	1 536	448	...	4 547	2 314	...
1961	8 706	2 391	683	601	1 607	474	...	4 708	2 411	...
1962	9 004	2 455	697	601	1 669	511	...	4 881	2 522	...
1963	9 341	2 473	687	603	1 747	557	...	5 121	2 674	...
1964	9 711	2 463	676	604	1 856	609	...	5 392	2 839	...
1965	10 191	2 495	679	619	1 996	679	...	5 700	3 031	...
1966	10 910	2 690	741	686	2 141	775	...	6 080	3 297	...
1967	11 525	2 852	802	719	2 302	873	...	6 371	3 490	...
1968	11 972	2 871	801	729	2 442	958	...	6 660	3 649	...
1969	12 330	2 893	815	737	2 533	1 042	...	6 904	3 785	...
1970	12 687	2 865	756	741	2 664	1 104	...	7 158	3 912	...
1971	13 012	2 828	731	731	2 747	1 149	...	7 437	4 091	...
1972	13 465	2 815	720	703	2 859	1 188	459	7 790	4 262	467
1973	13 862	2 794	696	698	2 923	1 205	472	8 146	4 433	477
1974	14 303	2 858	698	710	3 039	1 267	483	8 407	4 584	483
1975	14 820	2 882	704	699	3 179	1 323	503	8 758	4 722	489
1976	15 001	2 863	693	676	3 273	1 371	518	8 865	4 786	492
1977	15 258	2 859	676	657	3 377	1 385	538	9 023	4 859	494
1978	15 812	2 893	661	660	3 474	1 367	541	9 446	4 958	535
1979	16 068	2 894	649	673	3 541	1 378	538	9 633	4 989	571
1980	16 375	3 000	645	673	3 610	1 398	530	9 765	5 090	604
1981	16 180	2 922	655	675	3 640	1 420	515	9 619	5 095	622
1982	15 982	2 884	690	684	3 640	1 433	494	9 458	5 049	635
1983	16 011	2 915	699	685	3 662	1 450	471	9 434	5 020	644
1984	16 159	2 943	716	706	3 734	1 488	459	9 482	5 076	623
1985	16 533	3 014	738	750	3 832	1 540	449	9 687	5 221	608
1986	16 838	3 044	736	792	3 893	1 561	438	9 901	5 358	601
1987	17 156	3 089	736	815	3 967	1 586	439	10 100	5 469	606
1988	17 540	3 124	719	835	4 076	1 621	446	10 339	5 590	619
1989	17 927	3 136	735	838	4 182	1 668	442	10 609	5 740	632
1990	18 415	3 196	722	825	4 305	1 730	426	10 914	5 902	646
1991	18 545	3 110	702	813	4 355	1 768	417	11 081	5 994	653
1992	18 787	3 111	702	800	4 408	1 799	419	11 267	6 076	665
1993	18 989	3 063	670	793	4 488	1 834	414	11 438	6 206	673
1994	19 275	3 018	657	821	4 576	1 882	407	11 682	6 329	673
1995	19 432	2 949	627	850	4 635	1 919	395	11 849	6 453	669
1996	19 539	2 877	597	867	4 606	1 911	376	12 056	6 592	648
1997	19 664	2 806	588	866	4 582	1 904	360	12 276	6 759	632
1998	19 909	2 772	550	881	4 612	1 922	346	12 525	6 921	630
1999	20 307	2 769	525	890	4 709	1 983	344	12 829	7 120	626
2000	20 790	2 865	510	880	4 786	2 031	343	13 139	7 294	622
2001	21 118	2 764	504	873	4 905	2 113	345	13 449	7 479	628
2002	21 489	2 767	500	845	5 006	2 219	351	13 716	7 657	644
2002										
January	21 385	2 755	501	861	5 009	2 208	346	13 621	7 578	638
February	21 421	2 758	496	855	5 012	2 215	347	13 651	7 599	638
March	21 447	2 755	496	851	5 019	2 223	349	13 673	7 617	640
April	21 458	2 753	496	848	5 020	2 223	348	13 685	7 625	638
May	21 504	2 780	497	862	5 023	2 231	348	13 701	7 639	639
June	21 492	2 779	501	855	5 019	2 234	350	13 694	7 648	643
July	21 448	2 761	504	836	5 015	2 236	352	13 672	7 661	646
August	21 479	2 765	504	833	5 013	2 233	354	13 701	7 674	647
September	21 526	2 774	501	832	4 993	2 213	354	13 759	7 684	647
October	21 544	2 781	500	829	4 984	2 203	354	13 779	7 692	648
November	21 540	2 782	497	828	4 983	2 203	355	13 775	7 697	650
December	21 556	2 778	504	848	4 984	2 203	355	13 794	7 698	651

. . . = Not available.

Table 6-10. State Government Current Receipts and Expenditures

(National Income and Product Accounts, calendar years, billions of dollars.)

Year	Total	Personal tax and nontax receipts		Corporate profits tax accruals	Indirect business tax and nontax accruals			Contributions for social insurance	Grants-in-aid		Current expenditures	
		Total [1]	Income taxes		Total [1]	Sales taxes	Property taxes		Federal	Local	Total [1]	Consumption expenditures
1959	21.1	3.2	2.0	1.1	12.7	10.0	0.5	0.4	3.4	0.3	19.9	8.8
1960	22.8	3.6	2.3	1.2	13.7	10.8	0.5	0.5	3.5	0.3	21.5	9.5
1961	24.6	3.9	2.5	1.3	14.6	11.6	0.5	0.5	4.0	0.3	23.4	10.2
1962	26.7	4.3	2.8	1.5	15.7	12.6	0.6	0.5	4.4	0.3	25.4	10.9
1963	28.7	4.6	3.1	1.6	16.7	13.4	0.6	0.6	4.9	0.3	27.6	11.8
1964	31.4	5.2	3.6	1.8	18.0	14.5	0.6	0.7	5.4	0.3	30.1	12.8
1965	34.7	5.7	3.9	1.9	19.9	16.1	0.7	0.8	6.1	0.3	33.6	14.2
1966	41.0	6.7	4.8	2.2	22.0	18.0	0.7	0.8	8.9	0.4	38.6	15.9
1967	45.2	7.4	5.3	2.5	23.6	19.4	0.7	0.9	10.3	0.5	44.7	18.2
1968	52.6	9.2	6.9	3.1	27.2	22.8	0.8	0.9	11.6	0.6	51.0	20.5
1969	60.0	11.2	8.6	3.4	30.4	25.7	0.9	1.0	13.3	0.7	58.2	23.3
1970	67.2	12.4	9.6	3.5	33.2	28.2	0.9	1.1	16.2	0.8	67.8	26.9
1971	76.3	14.0	11.0	4.0	36.8	31.4	1.0	1.2	19.4	0.9	77.4	30.1
1972	93.0	18.5	15.2	5.0	41.3	35.2	1.1	1.3	25.8	1.1	86.3	32.8
1973	100.1	20.5	16.8	5.7	45.4	38.8	1.2	1.5	25.8	1.2	96.0	36.9
1974	108.1	22.0	18.0	6.3	49.2	42.0	1.1	1.7	27.6	1.3	108.0	44.0
1975	121.3	24.2	19.9	6.9	52.7	44.7	1.4	1.8	33.9	1.8	125.4	51.1
1976	137.5	28.2	23.4	9.1	58.6	49.9	1.5	2.2	37.1	2.3	138.7	55.9
1977	153.2	32.3	27.2	10.8	64.3	55.0	1.5	2.8	40.6	2.4	150.2	60.8
1978	171.0	37.1	31.6	11.5	71.3	60.8	1.9	3.4	45.2	2.5	164.7	67.3
1979	186.4	40.6	34.6	12.9	78.5	65.7	2.3	3.9	48.3	2.2	182.5	75.3
1980	205.9	45.6	39.1	13.7	85.9	70.0	2.6	3.6	54.7	2.4	205.9	85.2
1981	224.7	50.6	43.6	14.5	95.4	76.5	2.7	3.9	57.7	2.6	226.4	94.1
1982	230.5	54.7	47.0	13.1	99.6	80.3	2.8	4.0	56.0	3.1	241.4	101.4
1983	252.9	61.6	53.2	14.9	109.6	90.0	3.0	4.1	58.6	4.1	257.0	107.4
1984	284.7	71.4	61.9	17.4	122.9	100.9	3.4	4.7	63.3	5.0	277.5	115.7
1985	305.5	76.9	66.1	18.7	132.5	109.0	3.5	4.9	67.3	5.2	302.7	126.3
1986	329.9	82.7	70.7	20.8	140.6	115.8	3.6	6.0	74.5	5.3	327.0	135.5
1987	349.6	92.2	79.1	21.8	148.0	124.6	3.7	7.2	74.9	5.5	350.9	144.1
1988	373.4	95.5	81.2	23.8	158.0	134.2	4.0	8.4	82.1	5.6	376.5	153.5
1989	404.8	108.9	93.3	22.2	167.5	142.8	4.3	9.0	91.5	5.7	406.7	164.4
1990	434.2	114.9	97.9	20.4	178.0	151.5	4.6	10.0	104.7	6.2	447.2	178.2
1991	473.2	122.9	102.3	21.5	185.0	157.1	4.9	11.6	124.6	7.6	495.5	186.1
1992	515.9	132.1	108.7	22.1	197.8	167.6	5.2	13.1	141.8	9.0	537.8	193.1
1993	553.6	138.6	114.6	24.3	211.5	179.1	6.1	14.1	155.0	10.1	572.8	203.0
1994	590.7	146.5	121.4	27.3	226.2	191.4	6.9	14.5	165.2	11.0	606.1	213.7
1995	622.7	155.9	129.6	29.1	238.8	201.5	7.5	13.6	174.2	11.1	636.2	223.3
1996	649.7	166.4	139.1	30.0	250.8	210.9	7.8	12.5	178.0	12.0	661.6	230.5
1997	685.0	181.2	152.7	30.9	265.2	222.0	8.0	10.8	183.5	13.4	686.8	239.7
1998	726.0	196.5	166.6	31.3	280.9	233.5	8.6	10.1	193.8	13.4	723.1	249.5
1999	775.8	213.8	182.3	31.6	295.3	246.2	8.7	9.7	212.5	12.9	782.8	270.0
2000	828.9	232.6	199.5	32.3	311.7	255.7	8.2	9.2	229.5	13.6	846.6	296.1
2001	859.5	234.5	199.9	26.3	317.6	259.9	7.9	9.2	257.7	14.2	923.5	319.1

[1]Includes components not shown separately.

Table 6-10. State Government Current Receipts and Expenditures—*Continued*

(National Income and Product Accounts, calendar years, billions of dollars.)

| Year | Current expenditures—*Continued* | | | | Current surplus or deficit (-), national income and product accounts | | | Addenda | | | |
	Transfer payments to persons	Grants-in-aid to local governments	Net interest paid	Subsidies less current surplus of enterprises	Total	Social insurance funds	Other	Consump-tion of fixed capital	Capital transfers received, net	Gross investment	Net lending or net borrowing (-) [1]
1959	3.6	7.7	0.1	-0.3	1.2	0.0	1.2	1.8	2.3	6.4	-1.5
1960	3.8	8.5	0.1	-0.4	1.3	0.0	1.3	1.9	1.7	5.7	-1.3
1961	4.1	9.4	0.1	-0.4	1.2	0.0	1.2	2.0	2.0	6.6	-1.9
1962	4.4	10.3	0.2	-0.4	1.3	0.0	1.3	2.1	2.1	7.0	-2.0
1963	4.7	11.3	0.2	-0.4	1.1	0.0	1.1	2.3	2.6	8.0	-2.6
1964	5.1	12.4	0.2	-0.4	1.3	0.0	1.3	2.5	3.1	8.5	-2.2
1965	5.5	14.2	0.2	-0.5	1.1	0.1	1.0	2.7	3.1	9.1	-2.8
1966	6.4	16.7	0.1	-0.5	2.4	0.1	2.3	3.0	3.4	10.4	-2.3
1967	7.7	19.2	0.1	-0.5	0.5	0.1	0.4	3.3	3.1	11.1	-4.8
1968	9.5	22.0	-0.4	-0.6	1.6	0.1	1.5	3.6	4.0	11.6	-3.0
1969	10.8	25.3	-0.6	-0.6	1.8	0.2	1.6	4.1	3.7	12.4	-3.0
1970	12.9	29.2	-0.7	-0.5	-0.6	0.2	-0.8	4.7	3.3	13.4	-6.2
1971	15.3	33.0	-0.5	-0.5	-1.1	0.2	-1.3	5.2	3.6	14.1	-7.1
1972	17.5	36.8	-0.4	-0.4	6.7	0.3	6.4	5.6	3.6	14.6	0.6
1973	19.4	41.1	-1.0	-0.4	4.1	0.3	3.8	6.3	3.1	15.2	-2.4
1974	19.9	45.9	-1.6	-0.2	0.1	0.4	-0.3	8.1	3.5	16.6	-5.8
1975	24.2	51.4	-1.2	-0.1	-4.1	0.5	-4.6	9.0	4.5	17.0	-8.5
1976	26.9	56.2	-0.2	-0.1	-1.2	0.6	-1.8	9.2	4.7	16.8	-4.9
1977	29.1	60.7	-0.3	-0.1	3.0	1.0	2.0	9.5	4.8	16.0	0.7
1978	32.0	67.2	-1.6	-0.1	6.3	1.5	4.8	10.1	4.9	17.7	2.9
1979	35.4	75.3	-3.5	0.1	3.9	1.8	2.1	11.2	6.1	21.2	-0.8
1980	41.3	83.7	-4.6	0.4	0.0	1.3	-1.3	13.1	7.6	23.5	-3.6
1981	46.7	90.4	-5.4	0.7	-1.7	1.3	-3.0	15.2	6.7	23.8	-4.4
1982	51.0	94.4	-5.6	0.4	-10.9	1.2	-12.1	16.6	6.1	23.0	-12.0
1983	55.9	98.9	-5.0	0.0	-4.1	1.2	-5.3	17.0	7.2	24.0	-4.9
1984	59.8	108.7	-6.0	-0.5	7.2	1.4	5.8	17.2	8.7	28.6	3.5
1985	65.2	120.0	-7.3	-1.3	2.8	1.3	1.5	18.1	10.6	32.8	-2.4
1986	71.5	128.9	-7.2	-1.5	2.9	1.9	1.0	19.5	11.1	35.7	-3.5
1987	77.5	137.8	-7.0	-1.3	-1.3	2.2	-3.5	21.2	10.5	38.0	-9.2
1988	84.5	148.4	-8.0	-1.7	-3.1	2.5	-5.6	22.4	11.6	41.4	-12.1
1989	94.5	159.5	-9.3	-2.2	-1.9	2.3	-4.2	23.7	11.5	43.2	-11.5
1990	111.2	169.4	-9.3	-2.1	-13.0	2.0	-15.0	25.3	12.2	47.3	-24.6
1991	137.7	181.9	-7.8	-2.2	-22.3	2.4	-24.7	26.6	12.5	48.6	-33.7
1992	159.6	194.8	-6.7	-2.8	-21.9	3.1	-25.0	27.5	13.5	49.9	-32.7
1993	173.7	205.9	-6.2	-3.4	-19.2	4.2	-23.4	28.8	14.4	52.0	-29.8
1994	184.6	218.8	-7.1	-3.7	-15.4	4.6	-20.0	30.5	15.5	56.3	-27.4
1995	195.0	231.5	-9.3	-4.0	-13.5	4.0	-17.5	32.7	16.3	59.1	-25.3
1996	202.6	242.3	-9.6	-3.9	-11.9	2.7	-14.6	34.6	17.0	60.8	-23.1
1997	206.9	255.4	-11.3	-3.6	-1.8	1.1	-2.9	36.6	18.1	65.6	-14.8
1998	214.4	274.1	-11.3	-3.2	2.9	0.6	2.3	38.4	18.4	69.8	-12.5
1999	230.8	297.6	-12.5	-2.7	-7.0	0.9	-7.9	40.9	21.1	76.4	-24.2
2000	248.3	319.3	-14.3	-2.4	-17.7	0.1	-17.8	44.1	23.0	80.5	-34.0
2001	279.7	334.5	-14.3	4.9	-64.0	-0.1	-63.9	46.6	25.6	86.9	-81.8

[1]Includes components not shown separately.

Table 6-11. Local Government Current Receipts and Expenditures

(National Income and Product Accounts, calendar years, billions of dollars.)

Year	Current receipts Total	Personal tax and nontax receipts Total [1]	Income taxes	Corporate profits tax accruals	Indirect business tax and nontax accruals Total [1]	Sales taxes	Property taxes	Contributions for social insurance	Grants-in-aid Federal	State	Current expenditures Total [1]	Consumption expenditures
1959	25.7	1.0	0.2	0.0	16.6	1.2	14.3	0.0	0.4	7.7	23.2	22.3
1960	28.3	1.1	0.3	0.0	18.2	1.3	15.7	0.0	0.5	8.5	25.3	24.4
1961	31.0	1.2	0.3	0.0	19.8	1.4	17.0	0.0	0.6	9.4	27.9	26.8
1962	33.5	1.4	0.3	0.0	21.2	1.5	18.4	0.0	0.6	10.3	29.6	28.5
1963	36.3	1.5	0.4	0.0	22.7	1.6	19.7	0.0	0.8	11.3	31.6	30.6
1964	39.6	1.6	0.5	0.0	24.5	1.9	21.1	0.0	1.1	12.4	34.5	33.5
1965	43.1	1.6	0.5	0.0	26.2	2.1	22.5	0.0	1.1	14.2	37.7	36.6
1966	47.6	2.0	0.6	0.0	27.7	2.0	23.8	0.0	1.2	16.7	42.4	40.9
1967	53.6	2.4	0.8	0.2	30.3	1.9	26.2	0.0	1.5	19.2	47.1	45.1
1968	59.6	2.5	0.9	0.3	33.7	2.3	29.1	0.0	1.1	22.0	53.7	50.6
1969	66.7	2.9	1.1	0.2	37.0	2.9	31.9	0.0	1.3	25.3	60.6	56.9
1970	77.4	3.2	1.3	0.2	41.6	3.5	35.7	0.0	3.2	29.2	69.8	65.1
1971	87.0	3.6	1.5	0.3	46.3	4.0	39.5	0.0	3.8	33.0	79.5	73.3
1972	97.3	4.3	2.0	0.3	50.0	4.6	42.2	0.0	5.9	36.8	88.3	81.0
1973	108.7	4.2	2.0	0.3	54.1	5.2	45.2	0.0	9.0	41.1	97.1	89.9
1974	117.6	4.7	2.3	0.3	58.0	6.1	47.9	0.0	8.7	45.9	108.4	100.5
1975	131.4	5.3	2.6	0.4	63.1	7.0	52.0	0.0	11.2	51.4	125.0	114.3
1976	145.4	5.9	2.8	0.5	69.2	7.9	56.7	0.0	13.6	56.2	137.0	124.2
1977	159.4	6.5	3.2	0.6	75.6	9.0	61.7	0.0	16.0	60.7	149.4	135.7
1978	173.0	7.2	3.4	0.6	77.6	10.2	61.0	0.0	20.4	67.2	160.6	147.0
1979	182.0	7.9	3.6	0.6	80.1	11.5	62.1	0.0	18.1	75.3	172.9	159.8
1980	196.7	8.3	3.5	0.7	86.4	12.8	66.2	0.0	17.6	83.7	187.9	175.2
1981	212.7	10.0	4.3	0.9	96.6	14.2	74.4	0.0	14.8	90.4	203.5	190.5
1982	227.3	11.3	4.9	0.9	107.2	15.9	82.5	0.0	13.5	94.4	218.7	205.4
1983	242.2	12.1	5.1	1.0	117.2	17.7	88.9	0.0	13.0	98.9	233.2	217.6
1984	265.3	13.3	5.6	1.4	128.6	20.1	96.3	0.0	13.3	108.7	248.7	233.7
1985	288.9	14.3	6.0	1.5	139.5	22.1	104.0	0.0	13.6	120.0	269.4	254.2
1986	312.2	15.9	6.8	1.8	152.5	24.1	112.6	0.0	13.1	128.9	294.3	275.4
1987	329.7	16.4	6.9	2.1	164.4	25.7	122.7	0.0	9.0	137.8	316.2	295.0
1988	354.3	18.5	8.6	2.2	175.7	27.3	132.8	0.0	9.5	148.4	335.6	314.4
1989	379.4	20.0	9.3	2.1	191.0	29.9	144.4	0.0	6.8	159.5	358.1	338.6
1990	404.7	21.1	9.8	2.1	205.4	31.7	156.5	0.0	6.7	169.4	389.1	367.5
1991	432.3	22.4	10.4	2.2	210.8	33.0	167.9	0.0	7.0	181.9	417.7	390.0
1992	460.2	24.3	10.9	2.3	231.4	34.6	177.6	0.0	7.4	194.8	443.1	408.5
1993	485.5	26.1	11.4	2.6	243.3	36.9	185.0	0.0	7.6	205.9	464.8	426.5
1994	513.0	28.2	12.0	2.7	253.9	39.6	190.7	0.0	9.4	218.8	488.9	448.9
1995	537.7	30.6	12.9	2.6	262.8	42.1	196.1	0.0	10.2	231.5	508.9	471.4
1996	565.1	33.3	13.8	3.0	274.1	44.6	203.6	0.0	12.4	242.3	531.7	496.1
1997	595.2	35.8	14.9	3.3	287.4	47.3	212.3	0.0	13.3	255.4	562.5	526.8
1998	635.9	39.0	16.0	3.3	303.0	50.7	221.7	0.0	16.5	274.1	598.0	558.8
1999	678.8	42.0	17.4	3.2	317.4	54.4	230.6	0.0	18.6	297.6	633.5	594.6
2000	718.1	44.8	18.6	3.3	332.7	58.6	239.8	0.0	18.0	319.3	682.4	641.8
2001	750.4	46.7	18.7	2.7	346.8	61.4	249.5	0.0	19.7	334.5	717.8	674.6

[1]Includes components not shown separately.

Table 6-11. Local Government Current Receipts and Expenditures—*Continued*

(National Income and Product Accounts, calendar years, billions of dollars.)

Year	Current expenditures—*Continued*				Current surplus or deficit (-), national income and product accounts			Addenda			
	Transfer payments to persons	Grants-in-aid to state governments	Net interest paid	Subsidies less current surplus of enterprises	Total	Social insurance funds	Other	Consumption of fixed capital	Capital transfers received, net	Gross investment	Net lending or net borrowing (-) [1]
1959	0.7	0.3	0.7	-0.8	2.5	...	2.5	2.4	1.2	7.5	-1.8
1960	0.8	0.3	0.7	-0.9	3.0	...	3.0	2.6	1.3	8.2	-1.7
1961	0.9	0.3	0.9	-1.0	3.1	...	3.1	2.7	1.3	8.4	-1.8
1962	0.9	0.3	0.9	-1.0	3.9	...	3.9	2.9	1.4	8.8	-1.1
1963	1.0	0.3	0.9	-1.2	4.7	...	4.7	3.1	1.5	9.5	-0.8
1964	1.0	0.3	0.9	-1.2	5.1	...	5.1	3.3	1.6	10.5	-1.1
1965	1.1	0.3	0.9	-1.2	5.4	...	5.4	3.6	1.6	11.8	-1.9
1966	1.3	0.4	0.9	-1.1	5.2	...	5.2	3.9	1.8	12.7	-2.5
1967	1.6	0.5	0.9	-1.0	6.5	...	6.5	4.3	2.0	14.2	-2.2
1968	2.0	0.6	1.4	-0.9	5.9	...	5.9	4.7	2.9	16.1	-3.4
1969	2.4	0.7	1.5	-0.9	6.1	...	6.1	5.3	3.2	15.9	-2.1
1970	3.2	0.8	1.6	-0.9	7.6	...	7.6	5.9	2.9	15.4	0.1
1971	4.0	0.9	2.2	-0.8	7.5	...	7.5	6.6	3.4	16.0	0.6
1972	4.5	1.1	2.7	-1.1	9.0	...	9.0	7.2	3.7	16.0	2.9
1973	4.7	1.2	2.3	-1.0	11.6	...	11.6	8.0	4.2	18.0	4.8
1974	5.4	1.3	1.8	-0.6	9.2	...	9.2	9.6	5.7	23.1	0.4
1975	6.6	1.8	2.5	-0.2	6.4	...	6.4	11.2	6.5	26.6	-3.5
1976	7.3	2.3	3.3	-0.1	8.4	...	8.4	12.1	7.3	27.1	-0.2
1977	8.0	2.4	3.3	0.0	10.0	...	10.0	13.1	8.3	26.7	3.8
1978	8.8	2.5	2.4	0.1	12.4	...	12.4	14.3	8.8	31.7	2.8
1979	8.9	2.2	1.3	0.6	9.1	...	9.1	16.3	10.1	35.7	-1.4
1980	9.9	2.4	-0.8	1.2	8.8	...	8.8	18.7	11.0	40.5	-3.4
1981	10.4	2.6	-2.1	2.1	9.2	...	9.2	21.1	11.1	41.2	-1.3
1982	10.2	3.1	-1.7	1.7	8.6	...	8.6	22.9	10.9	41.8	-0.8
1983	11.0	4.1	-0.2	0.7	9.0	...	9.0	23.9	10.8	42.4	-0.1
1984	11.4	5.0	-0.8	-0.6	16.6	...	16.6	25.1	11.4	46.3	5.1
1985	12.1	5.2	-0.5	-1.6	19.5	...	19.5	26.6	11.4	51.6	3.9
1986	12.9	5.3	1.7	-1.0	17.9	...	17.9	28.4	11.9	57.2	-1.4
1987	13.3	5.5	3.9	-1.5	13.5	...	13.5	30.3	11.9	60.4	-7.3
1988	14.1	5.6	4.2	-2.7	18.7	...	18.7	32.5	11.6	64.9	-4.9
1989	15.0	5.7	2.7	-3.9	21.3	...	21.3	35.1	12.0	71.5	-6.4
1990	16.6	6.2	3.0	-4.2	15.6	...	15.6	37.8	12.8	79.9	-17.7
1991	18.9	7.6	5.7	-4.5	14.6	...	14.6	40.4	13.1	83.5	-19.4
1992	20.5	9.0	9.5	-4.4	17.1	...	17.1	42.4	13.5	84.5	-15.5
1993	21.7	10.1	11.7	-5.2	20.7	...	20.7	45.1	14.3	84.2	-8.3
1994	22.3	11.0	11.5	-4.8	24.1	...	24.1	48.4	14.2	88.0	-6.0
1995	22.8	11.1	9.8	-6.2	28.8	...	28.8	51.4	16.0	96.7	-5.6
1996	21.7	12.0	10.5	-8.6	33.4	...	33.4	54.3	16.8	103.0	-3.8
1997	20.7	13.4	10.4	-8.8	32.7	...	32.7	57.6	17.2	117.6	-15.2
1998	20.9	13.4	11.6	-6.7	37.9	...	37.9	61.0	17.6	121.2	-10.9
1999	21.9	12.9	11.8	-7.7	45.3	...	45.3	65.5	18.6	134.9	-12.4
2000	23.0	13.6	11.4	-7.4	35.7	...	35.7	70.9	20.8	143.4	-23.0
2001	24.8	14.2	12.2	-8.0	32.6	...	32.6	77.1	22.7	149.3	-24.1

[1]Includes components not shown separately.
... = Not available.

Table 6-12. State Government Consumption Expenditures and Gross Investment by Function

(National Income and Product Accounts, calendar years, billions of dollars.)

| Year | Consumption expenditures and gross investment | | | | | | | | | | | | |
| | Total [1] | General public service | Public order and safety | | Economic affairs | | Housing and community services | Health | Education | | | Income security | |
			Total [1]	Prisons	Total [1]	Transportation			Total [1]	Elementary and secondary	Higher	Total [1]	Welfare and social services
1959	15.4	1.2	0.8	0.5	8.7	7.2	0.0	1.8	2.6	0.2	2.1	0.4	0.3
1960	15.5	1.3	0.9	0.5	8.3	6.7	0.0	1.8	2.8	0.2	2.3	0.4	0.3
1961	17.0	1.4	0.9	0.5	9.2	7.4	0.0	2.0	3.2	0.2	2.6	0.3	0.3
1962	18.2	1.4	1.0	0.5	9.8	8.0	0.0	2.0	3.6	0.2	3.0	0.4	0.3
1963	20.1	1.5	1.1	0.6	10.7	8.9	0.0	2.2	4.2	0.2	3.6	0.4	0.3
1964	21.6	1.8	1.2	0.6	11.2	9.1	0.0	2.4	4.7	0.2	4.0	0.4	0.4
1965	23.6	2.0	1.3	0.7	11.9	9.7	0.0	2.5	5.3	0.2	4.4	0.5	0.4
1966	26.6	2.4	1.4	0.7	13.2	10.8	0.0	2.7	6.4	0.3	5.2	0.6	0.5
1967	29.7	2.6	1.6	0.8	14.1	11.3	0.0	3.0	7.6	0.4	6.2	0.7	0.6
1968	32.6	3.1	1.8	0.9	15.1	12.2	0.0	3.3	8.4	0.4	6.7	0.8	0.8
1969	36.2	3.9	2.1	1.0	16.0	12.8	0.0	3.8	9.4	0.4	7.5	1.0	0.9
1970	40.8	4.0	2.4	1.2	17.9	14.4	0.0	4.4	10.8	0.5	8.5	1.2	1.1
1971	44.9	4.4	2.7	1.3	19.3	15.4	0.0	5.0	11.9	0.5	9.3	1.5	1.4
1972	48.1	4.8	3.1	1.5	19.8	15.7	0.0	5.3	13.1	0.5	10.2	1.8	1.7
1973	52.8	5.8	3.5	1.7	20.7	16.3	0.0	5.5	14.7	0.5	11.7	2.4	2.2
1974	61.3	6.9	4.1	2.0	24.2	19.2	0.0	6.5	16.4	0.5	13.0	2.9	2.7
1975	68.9	7.9	4.7	2.3	26.4	20.8	0.3	7.4	18.2	0.7	14.1	3.5	3.3
1976	73.4	8.3	5.2	2.7	26.6	20.3	0.2	8.1	20.2	0.7	15.8	4.1	3.9
1077	77.0	9.0	5.8	3.1	27.1	20.5	0.2	9.0	21.3	0.7	16.7	4.7	4.4
1978	86.1	9.9	6.9	3.6	29.9	22.6	0.3	9.9	22.9	0.9	18.1	5.4	5.1
1979	97.6	11.6	8.2	4.2	34.4	26.3	0.3	11.0	25.3	1.0	20.1	6.0	5.7
1980	110.0	13.6	9.5	4.8	38.6	29.3	0.4	12.7	28.1	1.1	22.4	6.3	6.0
1981	119.1	14.4	10.6	5.5	41.3	31.1	0.3	13.6	31.0	1.2	25.1	7.0	6.6
1982	125.9	15.2	12.1	6.5	42.8	31.9	0.3	14.2	33.1	1.2	27.0	7.4	7.0
1983	133.1	16.9	13.5	7.4	44.7	33.6	0.2	13.9	34.5	1.1	28.4	8.5	8.1
1984	146.3	19.3	15.2	8.4	49.3	37.5	0.2	14.7	37.2	1.2	30.9	9.3	8.8
1985	161.5	21.4	17.5	10.0	53.8	41.2	0.2	16.0	41.2	1.3	34.3	10.1	9.6
1986	174.1	24.0	19.3	11.3	57.6	43.9	0.3	17.0	43.9	1.4	36.6	10.7	10.1
1987	185.4	25.8	21.5	12.7	60.7	46.2	0.5	18.3	45.7	1.5	37.7	11.4	10.7
1988	198.0	26.6	23.9	14.2	64.1	48.7	0.8	19.7	48.8	1.6	40.4	12.5	11.7
1989	210.8	28.6	26.6	16.1	65.4	48.9	1.1	20.7	52.7	1.8	43.4	13.7	12.8
1990	228.8	30.5	30.3	18.6	70.7	52.9	1.4	22.3	56.2	2.0	46.3	15.3	14.2
1991	238.4	31.8	32.5	20.1	72.9	54.4	1.7	22.4	57.9	2.2	47.9	16.9	15.6
1992	246.9	33.0	34.0	21.0	75.6	56.0	1.9	21.7	60.1	2.4	49.6	18.5	17.0
1993	258.9	34.2	36.2	22.6	78.9	58.4	2.0	21.8	63.5	2.4	52.6	20.2	18.5
1994	274.2	36.5	39.4	25.0	82.9	61.9	2.2	21.6	66.7	2.3	55.4	22.6	20.8
1995	287.1	37.4	42.8	27.2	85.9	64.1	2.5	22.0	69.6	2.7	57.3	24.4	22.2
1996	295.8	37.7	45.5	28.8	89.1	67.1	2.3	21.8	71.2	3.0	58.2	25.3	22.9
1997	310.3	40.9	48.5	30.4	93.6	71.1	2.2	20.5	74.5	3.2	61.1	27.1	24.4
1998	323.9	43.4	50.5	31.1	98.0	75.4	2.3	18.9	78.5	3.4	64.3	29.3	26.3
1999	351.4	47.4	55.1	33.7	106.6	82.3	2.6	21.2	83.6	3.6	68.5	31.7	28.8
2000	382.4	52.4	60.3	36.5	113.6	87.2	2.9	24.8	90.8	3.8	74.4	34.3	31.4
2001	410.4	57.0	64.5	38.8	121.5	94.5	2.8	27.0	97.5	4.0	80.1	36.3	33.3

[1]Includes components not shown separately.

Table 6-13. Local Government Consumption Expenditures and Gross Investment by Function

(National Income and Product Accounts, calendar years, billions of dollars.)

Year	Consumption expenditures and gross investment												
	Total¹	General public service	Public order and safety		Economic affairs		Housing and community services	Health	Education			Income security	
			Total¹	Prisons	Total¹	Transportation			Total¹	Elementary and secondary	Higher	Total	Welfare and social services
1959	29.7	2.3	3.3	0.2	4.6	3.9	2.7	1.3	14.5	14.0	0.3	0.3	0.3
1960	32.4	2.5	3.6	0.3	5.1	4.3	2.7	1.4	16.1	15.5	0.3	0.4	0.4
1961	35.0	2.8	3.8	0.3	5.2	4.4	2.9	1.5	17.6	17.0	0.3	0.4	0.4
1962	37.1	2.9	4.0	0.3	5.4	4.5	3.3	1.5	18.7	18.1	0.3	0.5	0.5
1963	39.8	3.1	4.2	0.3	6.0	4.9	3.0	1.6	20.5	19.7	0.4	0.5	0.5
1964	43.7	3.4	4.5	0.3	6.3	5.0	3.6	1.7	22.7	21.8	0.5	0.6	0.6
1965	48.1	3.8	4.8	0.4	7.1	5.4	3.8	1.8	25.1	24.0	0.6	0.7	0.7
1966	53.3	4.1	5.3	0.4	7.4	6.0	3.9	1.9	28.7	27.3	0.9	0.9	0.9
1967	58.8	4.6	5.8	0.4	8.2	6.5	4.1	2.1	31.7	30.1	1.1	1.0	1.0
1968	66.2	5.5	6.8	0.5	9.0	7.3	5.0	2.4	34.9	33.1	1.2	1.2	1.2
1969	72.2	6.0	7.5	0.5	9.4	7.6	4.9	2.7	38.6	36.5	1.4	1.5	1.5
1970	79.9	6.7	8.5	0.6	9.6	7.7	5.1	3.1	43.2	40.7	1.8	1.8	1.8
1971	88.6	7.6	9.7	0.8	10.0	8.0	5.5	3.7	47.9	45.0	2.1	2.1	2.1
1972	96.3	8.8	10.7	0.9	10.8	8.6	5.6	3.7	52.3	49.0	2.5	2.5	2.5
1973	107.3	10.3	11.9	1.0	11.9	9.5	6.3	4.2	57.6	53.9	2.8	2.7	2.7
1974	122.8	12.2	13.5	1.2	14.3	11.3	7.7	5.0	64.3	60.0	3.3	3.0	3.0
1975	140.1	14.7	15.5	1.4	15.8	12.7	8.6	5.3	73.6	68.6	3.8	3.3	3.3
1976	150.5	16.2	17.0	1.6	16.6	13.0	9.2	5.0	79.7	74.5	4.0	3.5	3.5
1977	161.5	18.1	18.5	1.8	17.7	13.7	9.0	5.5	85.4	79.7	4.4	3.9	3.9
1978	177.7	19.5	20.7	1.9	20.8	15.4	11.0	5.8	91.9	85.9	4.6	4.0	4.0
1979	194.3	20.5	22.6	2.1	23.4	17.3	12.3	5.7	101.1	94.7	4.9	4.4	4.4
1980	214.5	22.1	25.1	2.5	26.1	19.5	14.7	6.4	110.4	103.2	5.5	5.0	5.0
1981	230.5	23.9	28.3	2.8	28.8	21.1	14.5	6.5	117.9	110.1	6.0	5.5	5.5
1982	245.7	25.4	31.5	3.3	30.3	22.6	14.3	6.7	126.0	117.7	6.4	5.9	5.9
1983	258.4	26.9	33.9	3.8	31.3	23.6	13.8	6.4	133.5	125.2	6.1	6.7	6.7
1984	278.1	28.4	36.3	4.3	32.5	24.9	15.4	6.9	145.2	136.6	6.2	7.1	7.1
1985	303.3	31.0	40.1	4.9	35.5	26.4	16.7	7.4	157.7	148.4	6.6	7.8	7.8
1986	329.5	33.8	43.8	5.7	37.7	28.6	18.7	7.4	171.8	161.7	7.3	8.5	8.5
1987	352.1	35.3	47.4	6.6	38.1	30.1	20.7	8.4	184.8	173.9	7.8	9.0	9.0
1988	376.2	37.6	51.0	7.3	39.4	31.5	21.5	9.1	199.1	187.1	8.7	9.6	9.6
1989	406.9	41.0	56.3	8.5	41.6	33.7	22.2	9.9	215.6	202.4	9.5	10.7	10.7
1990	444.2	44.7	61.7	9.6	45.4	37.2	24.1	11.3	234.0	219.7	10.3	12.0	12.0
1991	469.8	47.7	66.3	10.4	47.1	38.8	24.9	11.6	247.8	232.7	10.8	12.9	12.9
1992	489.1	50.2	71.3	11.0	48.2	39.7	25.0	11.8	256.8	242.6	9.8	13.9	13.9
1993	506.8	52.8	74.6	11.4	50.8	42.3	23.6	10.8	267.5	252.4	10.5	14.7	14.7
1994	532.7	56.2	79.4	12.2	53.4	44.8	23.0	10.9	281.8	265.7	11.3	15.3	15.3
1995	563.4	59.3	84.2	12.9	54.8	45.7	24.0	9.7	302.2	285.5	11.6	15.6	15.6
1996	594.6	62.0	90.2	13.8	57.0	48.2	25.5	10.6	318.9	301.7	11.8	16.0	16.0
1997	639.4	70.6	95.7	14.3	63.6	52.5	27.0	10.1	340.5	321.8	12.6	16.5	16.5
1998	675.4	75.4	103.2	15.9	65.7	54.6	25.8	12.0	359.4	339.7	13.3	17.8	17.8
1999	724.6	82.3	109.5	17.0	70.8	58.4	25.4	14.4	385.6	364.8	14.0	19.1	19.1
2000	779.3	89.9	118.5	18.4	76.2	61.3	23.9	16.4	415.1	392.8	15.0	21.1	21.1
2001	819.5	90.5	127.9	19.6	77.4	64.9	25.4	16.9	439.8	416.5	15.6	22.5	22.5

¹Includes components not shown separately.

NOTES AND DEFINITIONS

TABLES 6-1 THROUGH 6-6, 19-7, AND 19-8 GOVERNMENT RECEIPTS AND EXPENDITURES

Source: U.S. Department of Commerce, Bureau of Economic Analysis

These data are from the national income and product accounts (NIPAs), as published in the 1999 comprehensive NIPA revisions and as subsequently revised and updated through August 2003. For more information, see the Notes and Definitions for Tables 1-1 through 1-10.

Government receipts and expenditures data are derived from the accounts of the U.S. government and from a Census Bureau survey of *Government Finances* covering state and local governments. However, BEA makes a number of adjustments to the data to convert them to calendar year and quarter bases and to agree with the concepts of national income accounting. See the *References*, below, for a reference to tables that display these adjustments.

Notes on the data

The data on government receipts and expenditures record transactions of governments (federal, state, and local) with other U.S. residents and foreigners. Each entry in the government receipts and expenditures account has a corresponding entry elsewhere in the NIPAs. Thus, for example, the sum of personal tax and nontax receipts by federal and state and local governments is equal to personal tax and nontax payments as shown in the personal income table.

The government receipts and expenditures estimates are derived primarily from financial statements for federal, state, and local governments. However, a number of adjustments are made to place the data on the basis required for the NIPAs. Annual data are placed on a calendar year basis. Data are converted from the cash basis usually found in financial statements to the timing bases required for the NIPAs. In the NIPAs, receipts from businesses generally are on an accrual basis, purchases of goods and services are recorded when delivered, and receipts from and transfer payments to persons are on a cash basis.

The federal receipts and expenditure data from the NIPAs in Tables 6-1 through 6-6 therefore differ from the federal receipts and outlay data in Table 6-7 in that, among other differences, the latter are by fiscal year and are on a modified cash basis.

Definitions

Personal tax and nontax receipts is personal tax payments that are not chargeable to business expense and certain

other personal payments to government agencies (except government enterprises) that are treated like taxes. Personal taxes includes taxes on income, including on realized net capital gains, and on personal property. Nontaxes includes donations and fees, fines, and forfeitures. Personal contributions for social insurance are not included. As of the 1999 revisions, estate and gift taxes are classified as capital transfers and are no longer included in personal tax and nontax payments. However, estate and gift taxes continue to be included in federal government receipts in Table 6-7.

Corporate profits tax accruals is the sum of federal or state and local income taxes on all corporate earnings, including realized net capital gains. These taxes are net of refunds and applicable tax credits.

Indirect business tax and nontax accruals is tax liabilities that are chargeable to business expense in the calculation of profit-type incomes and certain other business liabilities to government agencies (except government enterprises) that are treated like taxes. Examples are sales, excise, and property taxes and regulatory and inspection fees. Employer contributions for social insurance are not included.

Contributions for social insurance includes employer and personal contributions for Social Security, Medicare, unemployment insurance, and other government social insurance programs. As of the 1999 revisions, contributions to government employee retirement plans are no longer included in this category, as these plans are now treated the same as private pension plans.

Government consumption expenditures is purchases by governments (federal or state and local) of goods and services for current consumption. It includes compensation of general government employees (including employer contributions to retirement plans, as of the 1999 revision) and an allowance for consumption of general government fixed capital, including software (depreciation). Receipts for certain services provided by government—primarily tuition payments for higher education and charges for medical care—are defined as government sales, which are treated as deductions from government purchases.

Transfer payments includes payments to persons for which they do not render current services. Examples are Social Security benefits, Medicare, Medicaid, unemployment benefits, and public assistance. Retirement payments to retired government employees from their pension plans are no longer included. U.S. government nonmilitary grants to other countries are included.

Federal grants-in-aid are net payments from federal to state and local governments to help finance programs such as health (Medicaid), public assistance (for example, the old Aid to Families with Dependent Children and the new Temporary Assistance for Needy Families), and education. Investment grants to state and local governments for highways, transit, air transportation, and water treatment plants are now classified as capital transfers and no longer included in this category. However, such investment grants continue to be included as federal government outlays in Table 6-7.

Net interest paid is interest paid to U.S. and foreign persons and businesses and to foreign governments less interest received from business and from foreigners. Interest paid consists of monetary interest paid on public debt and other financial obligations. Interest received consists of monetary and imputed interest received on loans and investments; in the NIPAs it no longer includes interest received by government employee retirement plans, which is now credited to personal income. However, such interest received is still deducted from interest paid in Table 6-7.

Subsidies less current surplus of government enterprises. Subsidies are monetary grants paid by government to business, including to government enterprises at another level of government. Subsidies no longer include federal maritime construction subsidies, which are now classified as a capital transfer. The current surplus of government enterprises is their current operating revenue and subsidies received from other levels of government less their current expenses. No deduction is made for depreciation charges and net interest paid.

Surplus or deficit(-), national income and product accounts is the sum of government receipts less the sum of current government expenditures. As of the 1999 revisions, these surpluses—particularly those of state and local governments—are measured as being significantly smaller than they were before the revisions, because the net accumulations of government employee retirement plans are now classified as personal saving rather than in the government sector.

Gross government investment consists of general government and government enterprise expenditures for fixed assets (structures, equipment, and software). Government inventory investment is included in government consumption expenditures.

Capital consumption. Consumption of fixed capital, or depreciation, is included in government consumption expenditures as a partial measure of the value of the services of general government fixed assets, including structures, equipment, and software. Because this depreciation allowance is the only entry on the product side of the accounts measuring the output associated with such capital, a zero net return on these assets is implicitly assumed.

Net investment is calculated by the editor, defined as gross investment minus consumption of fixed capital.

Data availability

The most recent data are published each month in the *Survey of Current Business.* Current and historical data may be obtained from the BEA Internet site at <http://www.bea.gov> and the STAT-USA subscription Internet site at <http://www.stat-usa.gov>.

References

Tables showing the "Relation of Federal Government Current Receipts and Expenditures in the National Income and Product Accounts to the Budget, Fiscal Years and Quarters," "Relation of State and Local Government Current Receipts and Expenditures in the National Income and Product Accounts to Bureau of Census *Government Finances* Data, Fiscal Years" and "Relation of Commodity Credit Corporation Expenditures in the National Income and Product Accounts to Commodity Credit Corporation Outlays in the Budget" are published in the October 2002 *Survey of Current Business*, pp. 15-16.

For information on the classification of government expenditures into current consumption and gross investment, first undertaken in the 1996 comprehensive revisions, see the *Survey of Current Business* article "Preview of the Comprehensive Revision of the National Income and Product Accounts: Recognition of Government Investment and Incorporation of a New Methodology for Calculating Depreciation," September 1995. Other sources of information about the NIPAs are listed in the Notes and Definitions for Tables 1-1 through 1-10.

TABLE 6-7
FEDERAL GOVERNMENT RECEIPTS AND OUTLAYS BY FISCAL YEAR

SOURCE: U.S. OFFICE OF MANAGEMENT AND BUDGET

These data on federal government receipts and outlays are on a modified cash basis and are from the *Budget of the United States Government: Historical Tables.* The data are by federal fiscal years: July 1–June 30 through 1976 and October 1–September 30 for 1977 and subsequent years. The period July 1–September 30, 1976, is a separate fiscal period known as the transition quarter (TQ) and is not included in any fiscal year.

There are numerous differences in both timing and definition between these estimates and the NIPA estimates in Tables 6-1 and 6-3 through 6-6. See the Notes and Definitions for those tables, above, for definitional differences that were introduced with the 1999 comprehensive revision and references to tables displaying the differences between the two sets of accounts.

Definitions

The definitions in these tables are not affected by the 1999 changes in the government sectors of the National Income and Product Accounts.

Receipts are composed of taxes or other compulsory payments to the government and gifts. Other types of payments to government are netted against outlays.

Outlays occur when the federal government liquidates an obligation through a cash payment or when interest accrues on public debt issues. Beginning with the data for 1992, outlays include the subsidy cost of direct and guaranteed loans made. Before 1992, the costs and repayments associated with such loans are recorded on a cash basis. As noted above, various types of nontax receipts are netted against cash outlays. These accounts do not distinguish between investment outlays and current consumption, and do not include allowances for depreciation.

The *total surplus (deficit-)* is receipts minus outlays.

On-budget and off-budget. By law, two government programs that are included in the federal receipts and outlays totals are "off-budget"—old age, survivors, and disability insurance (Social Security) and the Postal Service. The former accounts for nearly all of the off-budget activity. The surplus (deficit-) not accounted for by these two programs is the on-budget surplus or deficit.

Sources of financing are the means by which the total deficit is financed or the surplus is distributed. By definition, sources of financing sum to the total deficit or surplus with the sign reversed. The principal source is *borrowing from the public,* shown as a positive number, that is, the increase in the debt held by the public. When there is a budget surplus, as in Fiscal Years 1998 to 2000, debt can be reduced, indicated by a minus sign in this column. Other *financing* includes drawdown (or buildup, shown here with a minus sign) in Treasury cash balances, seigniorage on coins, direct and guaranteed loan account cash transactions, and miscellaneous other transactions.

Outlays by function present outlays according to the major purpose of the spending. Functional classifications cut across departmental and agency lines. Most categories of offsetting receipts are netted against cash outlays in the appropriate function, but there is also a category of *undistributed offsetting receipts* (not shown) that includes proceeds from the sale or lease of assets and payments from federal agencies to federal retirement funds and the Social Security and Medicare trust funds.

In order to provide authoritative comparisons of these budget values with the overall size of the economy, a special calculation of gross domestic product by fiscal year (supplied to the Office of Management and Budget by the Bureau of Economic Analysis) is included in this table.

References

Definitions and budget concepts are discussed in *Budget of the United States: Historical Tables*, available from the Government Printing Office and on the Internet site listed below.

Data availability

The annual data are from the *Budget of the United States Government: Historical Tables* and are available on the Internet site at <http://www.gpo.gov/usbudget>.

Similarly classified data for the latest month, the year-ago month, and the current and year-ago fiscal year to date are published in the *Monthly Treasury Statement* prepared by the Financial Management Service, U.S. Department of the Treasury. For those who need up-to-date budget information, this publication is available on the Financial Management Service Internet site at <http://www.fms.treas.gov>. Because these monthly figures are never revised to agree with the final annual data, they are not published in this volume.

TABLE 6-8
FEDERAL GOVERNMENT DEBT BY FISCAL YEAR

Debt outstanding at the end of each fiscal year is from the *Budget of the United States Government*. Most securities at recorded at sales price plus amortized discount or less amortized premium.

Federal government debt held by the public consists of all federal debt held outside the federal government accounts—by individuals, financial institutions including the Federal Reserve Banks, and foreign individuals, businesses, and central banks. It does not include federal debt held by federal government trust funds such as the Social Security trust fund. The level and change of the ratio of this debt to the value of GDP provide proportional measures of the impact of federal borrowing on credit markets.

Gross public debt—total. This is the total debt owed by the U.S. Treasury. It includes a small amount of matured debt. (The "debt subject to statutory limitation," not shown here, corresponds closely to the gross debt in concept and size, but there are some relatively minor definitional differences specified by law. The debt limit can only be changed by an Act of Congress. For information on the debt subject to limit and other debt subjects, see the latest *Budget of the United States Government: Historical Statistics and Analytical Perspectives*.)

Debt held by Social Security funds. Shows the holdings of the Old-Age, Survivors and Disability Insurance funds (OASDI).

Debt held by other U.S. government accounts. Shows the holdings of all other trust fund accounts including the Medicare trust funds.

Debt held by Federal Reserve Banks. Shows the investments of Federal Reserve Banks, largely acquired in Federal Reserve System open market operations undertaken to implement monetary policy.

Debt held by private investors. All Treasury debt not held by U.S. government funds or the Federal Reserve System, with a breakdown between domestic holdings and foreign holdings. Foreign holdings include holdings of international institutions.

Data availability

For the end-of-fiscal-year data see *Historical Tables in the Budget of the United States Government*, available at Internet site at <http://www.gpo.gov/usbudget>.

Recent quarterly data, but measured on a somewhat different basis, are found in the *Treasury Bulletin* in the chapter on "Ownership of Federal Securities (OFS)," tables OFS-1 and OFS-2. The *Bulletin* can be accessed on the Internet at <http://www.fms.treas.gov/bulletin>. Holdings by Social Security funds are also available in the *Bulletin* in the chapter on "Federal Debt," table FD-3. The Disability Fund is listed separately from the Old-Age and Survivors Fund.

TABLE 6-9
GOVERNMENT EMPLOYMENT

Source: *U.S. Department of Labor, Bureau of Labor Statistics (see Notes and Definitions to Table 10-5).*

The government division includes federal, state, and local activities such as legislative, executive, and judicial functions, as well as all government-owned and government-operated business enterprises, establishments, and institutions (arsenals, navy yards, hospitals, etc.), and government force account construction. The figures relate to civilian employment only. BLS considers regular full-time teachers (private and governmental) to be employed during the summer vacation period whether or not they are specifically paid in those months.

Employment in federal government establishments reflects employee counts as of the pay period including the 12th of the month, consistent with other CES industry series. Federal government employment excludes employees of the Central Intelligence Agency and the National Security Agency.

TABLES 6-10 THROUGH 6-13
STATE GOVERNMENT CURRENT RECEIPTS AND EXPENDITURES; LOCAL GOVERNMENT CURRENT RECEIPTS AND EXPENDITURES; STATE GOVERNMENT CONSUMPTION EXPENDITURES AND GROSS INVESTMENT BY FUNCTION; LOCAL GOVERNMENT CONSUMPTION EXPENDITURES AND GROSS INVESTMENT BY FUNCTION

Source: *Bureau of Economic Analysis.*

In the standard presentation of the NIPAs, for example Table 6-2 above, state and local governments are combined. Annual measures for aggregate state governments and aggregate local governments separately are now available and are presented in these four tables.

Definitions

See the Notes and Definitions to Tables 6-1 through 6-6 for most of the definitions used in these tables.

Net lending or net borrowing is derived from the NIPA current surplus or deficit as follows: *consumption of fixed capital* and *capital transfers received (net)* are added, as additional sources of funds; and *gross investment* and *net purchases of nonproduced assets* (the latter is a small component not shown here) are subtracted (these are uses of funds not accounted for in the NIPA current surplus or deficit). The resulting figure on net lending or net borrowing (minus sign indicating net borrowing) represents the net contribution to or draw on the capital market by the level of government measured.

The functions as defined in Tables 6-12 and 6-13, which include consumption expenditures and gross investment combined, are roughly similar to the federal government spending concept and functions displayed in Table 6-7. Specifically:

General public service includes executive and legislative functions, tax collection and financial management, and other.

Public order and safety includes police, fire, law courts, and *prisons*.

Economic affairs includes general economic and labor affairs, agriculture, energy, natural resources, *transportation*, and other. *Transportation* includes highways, air transportation, water transportation, transit, and railroads.

Housing and community services includes water, sewerage, sanitation, and other.

Education includes *elementary and secondary* and *higher* education, libraries, and other.

Income security includes disability, *welfare and social services*, and other transfer payments to individuals.

Total consumption expenditures and gross investment includes the groups listed above, *health*, and recreation and culture.

Data availability and references

These data are described and published in "Receipts and Expenditures of State Government and of Local Governments, 1959–2001," *Survey of Current Business*, June 2003.

CHAPTER 7: U.S. FOREIGN TRADE AND FINANCE

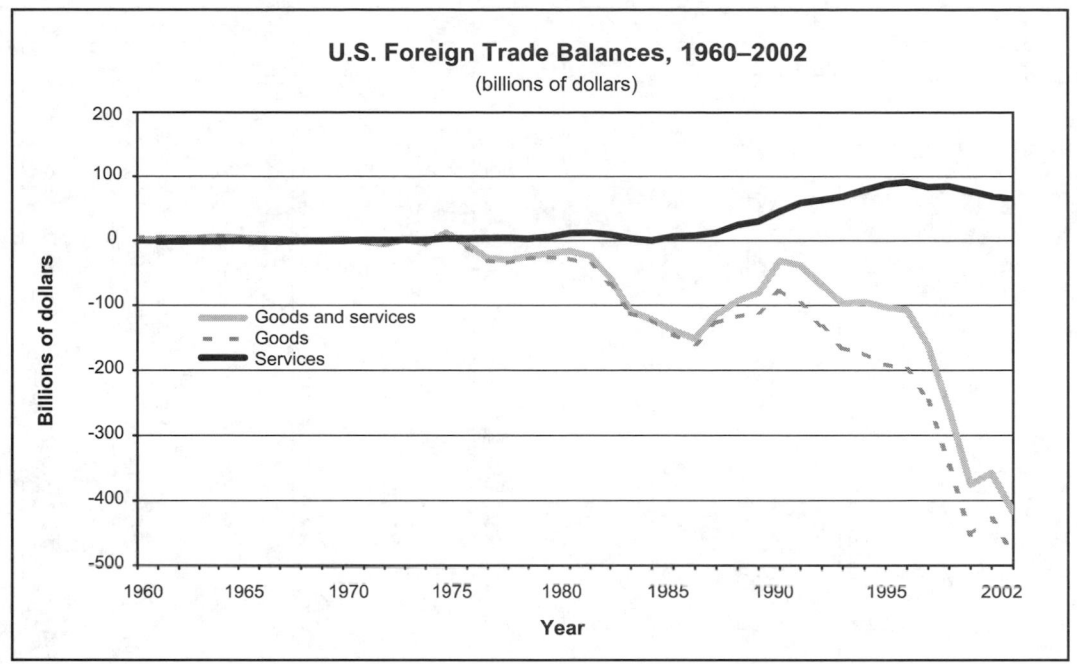

U.S. Foreign Trade Balances, 1960–2002
(billions of dollars)

- U.S. imports of goods and services exceeded exports by $418 billion in 2002, a new record. The record deficit in goods trade was only partly offset by the dwindling surplus in services trade. Goods imports rose in 2002, reflecting some improvement in the U.S. economy, while goods exports continued to fall. (Table 7-6)

- The "current-account balance" is a widely watched measure that is the sum of the goods and services balance, the income balance, and unilateral transfers. The U.S. balance on income—net income receipts from or income payments to foreigners—turned negative in 2002 for the first time on record, reflecting the erosion of the U.S. net international investment position (Table 7-7). Overall, the current-account deficit, which must be financed by equal financial inflows from abroad, was $481 billion in 2002, the highest on record. (Table 7-6)

- A similar concept is measured in the National Income and Product Accounts. "Net foreign investment" is the amount by which domestic investment exceeds domestic saving and is financed by foreigners. This too plunged to a new negative record. (Tables 7-1 and 5-1)

- All the major categories of goods and services in Table 7-5 show long-term growth in quantity of both exports and imports. Between 1967 and 2002, the slowest-growing category (imports of foods and feeds) tripled, and the fastest-growing, imports of capital goods, was over 100 times greater in real terms. The greatest growth has been in capital goods and in "other private services" (financial, professional, and computer-related). In both of those categories, the quantity of imports has grown even faster than the quantity of exports.

- Canada and Mexico are principal trading partners of the United States; goods exports to and imports from these two countries in 2001 were double those figures for the Euro area. Goods imports from those two countries also exceeded the sum of imports from Japan, China, and the newly industrialized countries of Asia. (Tables 7-12 and 7-13)

- For U.S. services trade, "other private services" is the largest single category. This includes such activities as education, financial services, and many types of business and professional services. The United States had a surplus of $53 billion on "other private services" in 2002, accounting for 82 percent of the total surplus in services. (Tables 7-14, 7-15, and 7-6)

Table 7-1. Foreign Transactions in the National Income and Product Accounts

(Billions of dollars, quarterly data are at seasonally adjusted annual rates.)

Year and quarter	Receipts from the rest of the world					Payments to the rest of the world						
	Total	Exports of goods and services			Income receipts	Total	Imports of goods and services			Income payments	Transfer payments (net)	Net foreign investment
		Goods[1]		Services[1]			Goods[1]		Services[1]			
		Durable	Nondurable				Durable	Nondurable				
1946	15.2	5.0	6.7	2.3	1.1	15.2	1.5	3.6	1.9	0.4	2.9	4.9
1947	20.3	8.5	7.6	2.6	1.6	20.3	1.8	4.2	2.0	0.4	2.6	9.3
1948	17.5	6.6	6.6	2.2	2.0	17.5	2.4	5.2	2.5	0.5	4.5	2.4
1949	16.4	6.1	6.1	2.2	1.9	16.4	2.1	4.8	2.4	0.6	5.6	0.9
1950	14.5	5.1	5.1	2.1	2.2	14.5	3.0	6.1	2.5	0.7	4.0	-1.8
1951	19.8	6.6	7.6	2.8	2.8	19.8	3.8	7.4	3.4	0.8	3.5	0.9
1952	19.2	6.9	6.5	2.9	2.9	19.2	4.1	6.7	4.5	0.8	2.5	0.6
1953	18.1	6.9	5.5	2.8	2.9	18.1	4.1	6.9	5.0	0.9	2.5	-1.3
1954	18.8	7.1	5.8	2.8	3.1	18.8	3.6	6.7	5.1	0.9	2.3	0.2
1955	21.1	8.2	6.2	3.2	3.5	21.1	4.5	7.1	5.7	1.0	2.5	0.4
1956	25.2	9.8	7.8	3.6	4.0	25.2	5.2	7.6	6.1	1.1	2.4	2.8
1957	28.2	10.9	8.6	4.3	4.3	28.2	5.3	8.0	6.7	1.2	2.3	4.8
1958	24.4	9.0	7.4	4.0	3.9	24.4	5.0	8.0	7.1	1.2	2.3	0.9
1959	25.0	8.9	7.5	4.2	4.3	25.0	6.6	8.7	7.0	1.5	2.4	-1.2
1960	30.2	11.3	9.2	4.8	5.0	30.2	6.4	8.9	7.6	1.8	2.4	3.2
1961	31.4	11.5	9.4	5.1	5.4	31.4	6.0	9.0	7.6	1.8	2.7	4.3
1962	33.5	12.0	9.7	5.7	6.1	33.5	6.9	9.9	8.1	1.8	2.8	3.9
1963	36.1	12.7	10.7	6.1	6.6	36.1	7.4	10.3	8.4	2.1	2.8	5.0
1964	41.0	14.7	12.0	6.9	7.4	41.0	8.4	11.0	8.7	2.4	3.0	7.5
1965	43.5	15.8	12.0	7.6	8.1	43.5	10.4	11.8	9.3	2.7	3.0	6.2
1966	47.2	17.5	13.2	8.2	8.3	47.2	13.3	13.1	10.7	3.1	3.2	3.9
1967	50.2	18.4	13.7	9.2	8.9	50.2	14.5	13.2	12.2	3.4	3.4	3.5
1968	55.6	21.0	14.3	10.0	10.3	55.6	18.8	15.1	12.6	4.1	3.2	1.7
1969	61.2	23.7	14.6	11.0	11.9	61.2	20.8	16.1	13.7	5.8	3.2	1.8
1970	69.9	27.1	17.4	12.4	13.0	69.9	22.8	18.1	14.9	6.6	3.6	4.0
1971	73.4	27.5	18.0	13.8	14.1	73.4	26.6	19.9	15.8	6.4	4.1	0.6
1972	82.6	31.0	20.8	14.4	16.4	82.6	33.3	23.6	17.3	7.7	4.3	-3.6
1973	115.6	41.4	32.6	17.8	23.8	115.6	40.8	31.0	19.3	11.1	4.6	8.7
1974	154.6	56.5	44.5	23.3	30.3	154.6	50.3	54.2	22.9	14.6	5.4	7.1
1975	164.4	63.8	45.8	26.7	28.2	164.4	45.6	53.4	23.7	14.9	5.4	21.4
1976	181.7	69.0	48.7	31.1	32.9	181.7	56.8	67.8	26.5	15.7	6.0	8.9
1977	196.6	72.0	51.6	35.1	37.9	196.6	69.2	83.4	29.8	17.2	6.0	-9.0
1978	233.5	85.3	60.1	40.7	47.4	233.5	89.0	88.4	34.8	25.3	6.4	-10.4
1979	299.1	108.0	76.0	44.7	70.4	299.1	100.4	112.3	39.9	37.5	7.5	1.4
1980	360.7	133.3	92.5	53.2	81.8	360.7	111.9	136.6	45.3	46.5	9.0	11.4
1981	398.4	140.1	99.0	63.7	95.6	398.4	126.0	141.8	49.9	60.9	13.4	6.3
1982	385.0	124.7	90.3	67.6	102.4	385.0	125.1	125.4	52.6	65.9	16.1	-0.2
1983	379.5	120.4	86.9	69.7	102.5	379.5	147.3	125.4	56.0	65.6	17.2	-32.0
1984	426.0	132.4	93.2	77.5	122.9	426.0	192.4	143.9	68.8	87.6	20.3	-87.0
1985	416.1	137.2	85.0	80.8	113.1	416.1	204.2	139.1	73.9	87.8	22.1	-110.9
1986	431.4	142.6	83.4	94.3	111.1	431.4	238.8	131.2	82.2	95.6	24.2	-140.6
1987	488.5	162.9	94.6	108.1	122.9	488.5	264.2	150.6	93.1	109.2	23.4	-152.0
1988	598.7	208.8	117.0	121.1	151.8	598.7	294.8	157.3	101.1	133.4	25.4	-113.2
1989	686.2	242.4	129.2	137.3	177.2	686.2	309.9	174.5	105.2	156.8	26.3	-86.7
1990	745.5	262.9	135.7	158.6	188.3	745.5	314.5	193.5	120.6	159.3	26.8	-69.2
1991	769.3	283.7	142.6	175.2	167.7	769.3	315.5	185.2	121.6	143.0	-11.0	14.9
1992	787.8	300.9	147.8	188.1	151.1	787.8	346.4	198.4	119.8	127.6	34.2	-38.7
1993	812.5	314.2	145.6	198.3	154.4	812.5	385.9	206.9	125.7	130.1	36.8	-72.9
1994	909.3	349.3	160.3	215.5	184.3	909.3	453.6	223.1	135.4	167.5	38.0	-108.3
1995	1 050.8	394.3	189.6	234.7	232.3	1 050.8	510.4	247.3	145.2	211.9	34.0	-98.0
1996	1 119.7	421.7	196.7	255.8	245.6	1 119.7	533.3	275.1	154.8	227.5	39.8	-110.7
1997	1 247.7	483.5	205.4	277.5	281.3	1 247.7	587.3	297.8	170.7	274.2	40.8	-123.1
1998	1 251.1	487.3	194.0	283.6	286.1	1 251.1	637.0	293.0	186.7	289.6	44.5	-199.7
1999	1 306.2	503.4	193.9	292.0	316.9	1 306.2	714.6	330.7	193.9	294.1	48.9	-276.0
2000	1 484.5	569.7	215.4	316.1	383.4	1 484.5	820.6	422.5	223.5	360.0	53.7	-395.8
2001	1 351.1	522.4	211.2	300.6	316.9	1 351.1	754.4	412.8	215.8	295.0	49.8	-376.7
2002	1 292.9	493.0	210.6	311.3	278.0	1 292.9	771.1	421.0	246.4	287.6	55.7	-488.9
2000												
1st quarter	1 421.1	540.6	206.4	308.9	365.2	1 421.1	785.2	387.1	214.1	344.2	47.2	-356.9
2nd quarter	1 488.5	567.9	210.5	319.6	390.5	1 488.5	818.4	413.3	219.5	364.7	49.6	-377.1
3rd quarter	1 514.4	591.2	223.4	316.4	383.5	1 514.4	843.0	442.7	230.1	365.8	52.0	-419.1
4th quarter	1 514.2	579.0	221.3	319.5	394.4	1 514.2	835.7	446.9	230.4	365.2	65.9	-430.0
2001												
1st quarter	1 464.3	568.4	218.9	312.7	364.2	1 464.3	801.0	439.1	232.7	354.3	46.7	-409.5
2nd quarter	1 392.2	536.4	214.2	309.1	332.5	1 392.2	761.5	428.3	235.5	301.4	48.0	-382.5
3rd quarter	1 307.8	502.8	205.7	297.3	302.0	1 307.8	734.2	406.3	177.8	290.5	49.7	-350.8
4th quarter	1 240.0	481.8	205.8	283.4	269.0	1 240.0	721.0	377.3	217.3	233.7	54.6	-363.9
2002												
1st quarter	1 242.2	477.2	202.6	297.7	264.7	1 242.2	732.4	369.9	235.2	262.8	63.5	-421.7
2nd quarter	1 294.1	499.3	210.0	308.8	276.0	1 294.1	781.6	421.3	240.8	296.1	51.5	-497.2
3rd quarter	1 325.9	509.5	213.1	316.0	287.3	1 325.9	783.8	437.2	250.6	298.2	51.8	-495.6
4th quarter	1 309.6	486.0	216.5	322.8	284.2	1 309.6	786.6	455.9	258.9	293.4	55.9	-541.0

[1] Exports and imports of certain goods, primarily military equipment purchased and sold by the federal government, are included in services. Beginning with 1986, repairs and alterations of equipment are reclassified from goods to services.

Table 7-2. Chain-Type Quantity Indexes for NIPA Foreign Transactions

(Index numbers, 1996 = 100.)

Year and quarter	Receipts from the rest of the world						Payments to the rest of the world					
	Exports of goods and services					Income receipts	Imports of goods and services					Income payments
	Total	Goods[1]			Services[1]		Total	Goods[1]			Services[1]	
		Total	Durable	Nondurable				Total	Durable	Nondurable		
1946	7.61	8.20	3.86	21.23	5.05	3.39	5.10	4.63	1.40	12.10	7.09	1.27
1947	8.69	9.43	5.85	21.43	5.55	4.42	4.84	4.45	1.41	11.43	6.52	1.37
1948	6.84	7.30	4.18	17.03	4.85	5.26	5.65	5.09	1.69	12.93	8.04	1.55
1949	6.78	7.26	4.14	16.89	4.71	5.09	5.45	4.89	1.60	12.63	7.85	1.78
1950	5.93	6.27	3.57	14.71	4.39	5.63	6.44	5.98	2.08	15.08	8.35	1.96
1951	7.27	7.64	4.06	18.98	5.57	6.78	6.69	5.86	2.13	14.56	10.62	2.14
1952	6.93	7.24	4.34	16.51	5.46	7.01	7.28	5.98	2.43	14.18	13.85	2.11
1953	6.47	6.75	4.42	14.32	5.12	6.83	7.97	6.32	2.55	15.13	16.36	2.28
1954	6.78	7.14	4.61	15.18	5.19	7.23	7.57	5.84	2.22	14.72	16.54	2.31
1955	7.50	7.89	5.20	15.99	5.77	8.10	8.49	6.52	2.78	15.68	18.67	2.53
1956	8.75	9.25	5.92	19.12	6.54	8.82	9.17	7.10	3.19	16.81	19.87	2.65
1957	9.51	9.98	6.40	20.57	7.35	9.30	9.56	7.31	3.25	17.61	21.24	2.73
1958	8.21	8.47	5.34	17.86	6.84	8.31	10.01	7.51	3.23	18.63	23.06	2.78
1959	8.28	8.41	5.23	17.86	7.35	8.89	11.07	8.82	4.27	20.06	22.61	3.32
1960	10.00	10.38	6.49	21.77	8.13	10.00	11.21	8.67	4.08	20.28	24.38	3.86
1961	10.17	10.43	6.53	21.93	8.67	10.76	11.14	8.66	3.93	20.96	23.96	3.88
1962	10.72	10.89	6.86	22.73	9.46	11.78	12.40	9.94	4.63	23.59	25.08	3.93
1963	11.52	11.75	7.24	25.00	10.06	12.75	12.74	10.34	4.87	24.19	25.06	4.38
1964	13.06	13.36	8.34	28.04	11.26	13.92	13.41	11.03	5.41	25.10	25.71	4.87
1965	13.33	13.43	8.69	27.26	12.15	14.80	14.84	12.59	6.69	26.88	26.47	5.33
1966	14.22	14.36	9.34	29.11	12.85	14.65	17.05	14.57	8.33	28.80	29.83	5.95
1967	14.53	14.43	10.79	24.20	13.97	15.25	18.29	15.34	8.92	29.60	33.47	6.35
1968	15.59	15.57	11.80	25.61	14.69	16.89	21.02	18.51	11.36	33.52	34.08	7.36
1969	16.44	16.39	12.76	25.86	15.59	18.67	22.21	19.52	12.14	34.78	36.22	9.72
1970	18.22	18.26	13.96	29.65	16.97	19.25	23.16	20.29	12.48	36.66	38.11	10.45
1971	18.35	18.18	13.86	29.68	17.77	19.84	24.40	21.99	13.74	38.94	37.03	9.82
1972	19.84	20.14	15.31	33.01	17.70	22.09	27.13	24.98	15.80	43.49	38.54	11.32
1973	24.19	24.77	19.08	39.84	20.85	30.10	28.39	26.74	16.82	46.91	37.24	15.29
1974	26.49	26.73	22.02	39.48	24.29	35.28	27.75	26.00	16.89	43.98	37.20	18.26
1975	26.32	26.11	21.56	38.43	25.91	30.04	24.66	22.72	13.80	40.80	35.59	17.20
1976	27.87	27.35	21.87	42.12	28.65	33.01	29.49	27.86	16.90	50.06	38.04	17.45
1977	28.57	27.71	21.82	43.60	30.67	35.66	32.70	31.25	19.12	55.75	39.94	17.95
1978	31.56	30.81	24.32	48.28	33.10	41.39	35.54	34.05	22.10	57.56	42.78	24.32
1979	34.59	34.45	27.69	52.63	33.64	56.61	36.13	34.64	22.61	58.23	43.37	33.09
1980	38.30	38.55	30.88	59.20	35.59	60.34	33.73	32.06	22.79	50.13	42.40	37.42
1981	38.74	38.14	29.78	60.75	39.32	64.17	34.61	32.72	24.68	48.63	44.85	44.72
1982	35.99	34.70	25.89	58.91	39.29	64.64	34.18	31.90	24.96	45.80	47.24	45.36
1983	35.11	33.70	25.36	56.55	38.86	62.30	38.49	36.24	30.09	48.77	51.06	43.57
1984	38.05	36.36	28.09	58.78	42.62	72.19	47.86	45.00	40.03	55.54	63.86	56.12
1985	39.08	37.58	30.37	56.76	43.01	64.34	50.95	47.80	44.03	56.20	68.71	54.33
1986	41.96	39.51	32.14	59.03	48.73	61.53	55.23	52.70	48.11	62.83	68.94	57.51
1987	46.67	43.89	36.69	62.55	54.38	65.81	58.58	55.15	50.24	65.99	77.64	63.29
1988	54.17	52.16	45.52	68.95	59.45	78.42	60.81	57.38	52.34	68.52	79.75	74.63
1989	60.56	58.74	52.47	74.37	65.18	87.83	63.21	59.80	54.61	71.24	81.98	84.40
1990	65.85	63.58	57.63	78.29	71.73	89.27	65.64	61.60	56.10	73.70	88.23	82.16
1991	70.15	68.09	62.03	83.02	75.40	76.71	65.31	61.56	56.42	72.90	86.18	70.82
1992	74.47	72.73	66.59	87.79	78.86	67.22	69.64	67.26	62.24	78.34	82.69	61.14
1993	76.95	74.93	70.00	86.71	82.07	67.03	75.98	74.03	69.54	83.92	86.60	61.17
1994	83.83	82.18	78.37	90.95	88.01	78.14	85.08	83.86	81.04	89.96	91.65	77.00
1995	92.45	91.97	89.65	97.09	93.65	96.29	92.05	91.43	90.33	93.72	95.40	95.05
1996	100.00	100.00	100.00	100.00	100.00	100.00	100.00	100.00	100.00	100.00	100.00	100.00
1997	112.27	114.51	118.17	106.66	106.98	112.71	113.67	114.20	116.22	110.33	110.94	117.79
1998	114.67	116.90	121.83	106.33	109.39	113.74	127.03	127.59	131.49	120.10	124.16	122.98
1999	118.55	121.29	127.47	107.97	112.13	123.97	140.88	143.19	150.32	129.49	129.42	122.89
2000	130.09	134.98	144.14	115.25	118.91	146.19	159.48	162.51	173.28	142.38	144.47	146.65
2001	123.10	126.97	132.39	115.23	114.18	118.90	154.91	157.18	162.31	146.27	143.71	118.35
2002	121.13	122.40	125.49	115.67	117.87	103.17	160.66	163.31	169.03	151.05	146.79	114.41
2000												
1st quarter	125.35	128.89	136.99	111.44	117.13	140.33	152.07	154.59	165.31	134.57	139.53	141.45
2nd quarter	129.71	133.80	143.81	112.28	120.28	149.32	158.70	161.91	172.39	142.23	142.76	148.94
3rd quarter	133.32	139.88	149.33	119.55	118.47	145.81	163.91	167.15	177.97	146.88	147.87	148.53
4th quarter	131.97	137.33	146.43	117.72	119.76	149.29	163.23	166.40	177.47	145.82	147.70	147.67
2001												
1st quarter	129.93	135.19	143.62	117.02	117.91	136.99	159.93	162.44	170.33	146.98	147.81	142.50
2nd quarter	125.70	129.39	135.65	115.81	117.17	124.63	157.15	158.49	163.11	148.35	150.84	120.78
3rd quarter	119.89	122.89	127.61	112.64	112.87	113.25	152.32	154.54	158.62	145.38	141.21	116.43
4th quarter	116.89	120.40	122.68	115.45	108.77	100.73	150.26	153.24	157.17	144.37	134.98	93.68
2002												
1st quarter	117.89	119.36	121.50	114.72	114.24	98.87	153.37	154.63	160.51	142.32	145.69	105.14
2nd quarter	121.89	123.84	127.18	116.56	117.18	102.55	161.24	164.44	171.12	150.62	144.92	117.90
3rd quarter	123.28	125.08	129.63	115.23	118.87	106.41	162.56	165.81	171.66	153.30	146.02	118.46
4th quarter	121.44	121.34	123.66	116.17	121.19	104.85	165.48	168.34	172.82	157.97	150.54	116.13

[1]Exports and imports of certain goods, primarily military equipment purchased and sold by the federal government, are included in services. Beginning with 1986, repairs and alterations of equipment are reclassified from goods to services.

Table 7-3. Chain-Type Price Indexes for NIPA Foreign Transactions

(Index numbers, 1996 = 100.)

Year and quarter	Receipts from the rest of the world						Payments to the rest of the world					
	Exports of goods and services					Income receipts	Imports of goods and services					Income payments
	Total	Goods[1]			Services[1]		Total	Goods[1]			Services[1]	
		Total	Durable	Nondurable				Total	Durable	Nondurable		
1946	21.17	23.19	30.84	16.16	17.89	13.14	14.21	13.54	19.66	10.82	17.39	12.40
1947	24.61	27.60	34.30	18.11	18.24	14.72	17.02	16.62	24.09	13.22	19.43	13.83
1948	25.91	29.38	37.58	19.81	17.98	15.72	18.50	18.36	26.53	14.54	20.11	14.80
1949	24.34	27.22	34.94	18.43	18.30	15.54	17.63	17.38	24.90	13.69	19.56	14.76
1950	23.70	26.31	33.65	17.75	18.47	15.82	18.73	18.80	26.90	14.69	19.60	15.09
1951	26.78	30.16	38.71	20.39	19.40	16.57	22.63	23.60	33.65	18.37	20.75	15.88
1952	26.98	30.03	37.97	20.04	20.71	16.73	21.81	22.43	31.68	17.25	20.80	16.16
1953	26.90	29.73	36.99	19.56	21.36	17.07	20.88	21.47	30.28	16.49	19.90	16.59
1954	26.56	29.30	36.72	19.41	21.23	17.24	21.16	21.93	30.59	16.62	19.85	16.71
1955	26.81	29.58	37.41	19.77	21.42	17.80	21.05	21.87	30.16	16.37	19.63	17.31
1956	27.71	30.70	39.16	20.68	21.73	18.35	21.42	22.30	30.45	16.51	19.90	17.99
1957	28.76	31.70	40.48	21.36	23.09	18.93	21.66	22.50	30.50	16.53	20.23	18.59
1958	28.50	31.36	39.95	21.10	23.05	19.29	20.76	21.33	28.79	15.58	19.81	18.91
1959	28.53	31.66	40.52	21.39	22.30	19.90	20.95	21.48	29.12	15.73	20.05	19.65
1960	28.88	31.87	41.21	21.43	23.11	20.24	21.15	21.71	29.29	15.87	20.20	20.08
1961	29.29	32.48	41.91	21.83	22.98	20.43	21.15	21.50	28.87	15.63	20.58	20.20
1962	29.27	32.23	41.38	21.78	23.59	20.92	20.90	20.99	28.16	15.29	20.85	20.66
1963	29.22	32.12	41.47	21.71	23.71	21.21	21.30	21.18	28.49	15.51	21.71	20.95
1964	29.42	32.34	41.75	21.81	23.87	21.58	21.75	21.76	29.14	15.92	21.89	21.37
1965	30.38	33.46	43.00	22.45	24.46	22.17	22.06	21.86	29.21	16.01	22.66	21.97
1966	31.32	34.61	44.45	23.09	24.93	22.95	22.57	22.36	29.89	16.48	23.23	22.80
1967	32.56	36.06	40.54	28.85	25.68	23.65	22.66	22.39	30.58	16.23	23.45	23.46
1968	33.23	36.62	42.17	28.32	26.69	24.79	23.00	22.69	31.07	16.40	23.91	24.65
1969	34.29	37.75	44.01	28.66	27.62	26.04	23.60	23.33	32.06	16.79	24.40	26.15
1970	35.77	39.46	46.06	29.88	28.64	27.43	25.00	24.91	34.23	17.93	25.27	27.57
1971	36.98	40.51	47.13	30.84	30.31	28.98	26.53	26.19	36.32	18.63	27.55	28.84
1972	38.17	41.59	48.08	31.97	31.88	30.28	28.40	28.20	39.51	19.77	28.97	30.05
1973	43.40	48.27	51.42	41.55	33.47	32.26	33.34	33.23	45.49	24.06	33.51	31.98
1974	53.68	61.08	60.81	57.33	37.57	34.92	47.70	49.73	55.88	44.81	39.85	35.02
1975	59.24	67.89	70.18	60.62	40.22	38.17	51.67	53.90	62.02	47.55	43.08	38.14
1976	61.11	69.63	74.88	58.80	42.44	40.53	53.22	55.34	63.02	49.25	45.03	39.64
1977	63.58	72.16	78.30	60.18	44.77	43.24	57.92	60.42	67.85	54.42	48.23	42.11
1978	67.48	76.32	83.13	63.32	48.12	46.65	62.01	64.45	75.53	55.82	52.61	45.74
1979	75.63	86.40	92.52	73.43	51.91	50.68	72.62	76.00	83.30	70.14	59.42	49.88
1980	83.32	94.71	102.38	79.40	58.40	55.21	90.45	95.90	92.11	99.09	68.95	54.67
1981	89.41	101.38	111.58	82.83	63.32	60.70	95.32	101.25	95.77	105.99	71.94	59.90
1982	89.83	100.21	114.21	77.95	67.31	64.49	92.10	97.16	94.00	99.56	71.99	63.89
1983	90.24	99.48	112.60	78.13	70.12	66.98	88.65	93.10	91.82	93.45	70.81	66.19
1984	91.13	100.34	111.74	80.65	71.06	69.34	87.89	92.46	90.14	94.18	69.60	68.60
1985	88.70	95.62	107.19	76.13	73.43	71.60	85.02	88.84	86.96	90.01	69.51	71.02
1986	87.33	92.49	105.24	71.81	75.66	73.50	85.01	86.85	93.07	75.93	77.02	73.05
1987	89.62	94.89	105.32	76.90	77.70	76.03	90.02	93.04	98.60	82.96	77.48	75.82
1988	94.39	101.00	108.78	86.27	79.67	78.83	94.46	97.47	105.61	83.49	81.89	78.56
1989	96.15	102.33	109.57	88.34	82.37	82.15	96.87	100.23	106.43	89.08	82.94	81.67
1990	96.79	101.36	108.17	88.09	86.47	85.90	99.43	102.02	105.12	95.44	88.31	85.26
1991	98.10	101.26	108.47	87.34	90.85	89.02	98.93	100.62	104.86	92.38	91.15	88.77
1992	97.82	99.75	107.15	85.58	93.26	91.52	99.09	100.21	104.38	92.08	93.58	91.78
1993	97.82	99.21	106.43	85.35	94.47	93.82	98.18	99.06	104.05	89.64	93.78	93.46
1994	98.94	100.27	105.72	89.58	95.72	96.04	99.12	99.83	104.97	90.16	95.47	95.60
1995	101.29	102.65	104.29	99.26	97.99	98.22	101.83	102.51	105.95	95.93	98.31	98.01
1996	100.00	100.00	100.00	100.00	100.00	100.00	100.00	100.00	100.00	100.00	100.00	100.00
1997	98.47	97.29	97.03	97.90	101.42	101.64	96.44	95.88	94.75	98.13	99.41	102.34
1998	96.26	94.25	94.86	92.75	101.37	102.46	91.27	90.17	90.84	88.69	97.14	103.51
1999	95.47	92.98	93.65	91.31	101.82	104.09	91.34	90.31	89.14	92.85	96.80	105.21
2000	96.83	94.05	93.72	95.00	103.94	106.80	95.49	94.63	88.80	107.89	99.97	107.92
2001	96.10	93.42	93.56	93.17	102.94	108.55	92.70	91.87	87.16	102.59	97.03	109.57
2002	95.87	92.98	93.19	92.54	103.27	109.74	92.99	90.32	85.57	101.23	108.47	110.47
2000												
1st quarter	96.36	93.71	93.58	94.15	103.13	105.98	94.69	93.85	89.06	104.70	99.17	107.00
2nd quarter	96.84	94.08	93.65	95.30	103.90	106.49	94.96	94.12	89.01	105.73	99.35	107.67
3rd quarter	97.04	94.17	93.89	94.99	104.42	107.11	96.03	95.17	88.82	109.65	100.54	108.26
4th quarter	97.08	94.25	93.78	95.58	104.32	107.58	96.26	95.37	88.30	111.49	100.80	108.72
2001												
1st quarter	96.87	94.19	93.86	95.12	103.71	108.28	95.66	94.48	88.20	108.67	101.74	109.28
2nd quarter	96.46	93.84	93.79	94.05	103.15	108.63	94.22	92.92	87.57	105.01	100.91	109.66
3rd quarter	96.00	93.26	93.45	92.86	102.99	108.60	89.93	91.36	86.83	101.65	81.38	109.67
4th quarter	95.06	92.39	93.16	90.64	101.89	108.73	90.97	88.71	86.05	95.04	104.08	109.66
2002												
1st quarter	94.88	92.14	93.17	89.78	101.90	109.02	90.61	88.24	85.60	94.52	104.37	109.86
2nd quarter	95.58	92.67	93.13	91.61	103.04	109.61	93.03	90.55	85.67	101.73	107.43	110.36
3rd quarter	96.41	93.45	93.23	94.02	103.97	109.95	94.05	91.15	85.65	103.71	110.92	110.64
4th quarter	96.62	93.67	93.22	94.76	104.18	110.39	94.27	91.36	85.38	104.96	111.16	111.03

[1]Exports and imports of certain goods, primarily military equipment purchased and sold by the federal government, are included in services. Beginning with 1986, repairs and alterations of equipment are reclassified from goods to services.

Table 7-4. Exports and Imports of Selected NIPA Types of Product

(Billions of dollars, quarterly data are at seasonally adjusted annual rates.)

Year and quarter	Exports Goods: Foods, feeds, and beverages	Industrial supplies and materials	Capital goods, except automotive	Automotive vehicles, engines, and parts	Consumer goods, except automotive	Exports Services: Travel	Other private services (financial, professional, etc.)	Imports Goods: Foods, feeds, and beverages	Industrial supplies and materials, except petroleum and products	Petroleum and products	Capital goods, except automotive	Automotive vehicles, engines, and parts	Consumer goods, except automotive	Imports Services: Travel	Other private services (financial, professional, etc.)
1967	5.0	10.0	9.9	2.8	2.1	1.6	0.7	4.6	9.9	2.1	2.5	2.4	4.2	3.2	0.4
1968	4.8	11.0	11.1	3.5	2.3	1.8	0.8	5.3	12.0	2.4	2.8	4.0	5.4	3.0	0.5
1969	4.7	11.7	12.4	3.9	2.6	2.0	0.9	5.2	11.7	2.6	3.4	5.1	6.5	3.4	0.6
1970	5.9	13.8	14.7	3.9	2.8	2.3	1.0	6.1	12.2	2.9	4.0	5.7	7.4	4.0	0.6
1971	6.1	12.6	15.4	4.7	2.9	2.5	1.3	6.4	13.6	3.7	4.3	7.6	8.4	4.4	0.7
1972	7.5	13.9	16.9	5.5	3.6	2.8	1.5	7.3	16.0	4.7	5.9	9.0	11.1	5.0	0.8
1973	15.2	19.7	22.0	7.0	4.8	3.4	1.7	9.1	19.2	8.4	8.3	10.7	12.9	5.5	0.9
1974	18.6	29.9	30.9	8.8	6.4	4.0	3.0	10.6	27.0	26.6	9.8	12.4	14.4	6.0	1.9
1975	19.2	29.3	36.6	10.8	6.6	4.7	3.7	9.6	23.6	27.0	10.2	12.1	13.2	6.4	2.3
1976	19.8	31.6	39.1	12.2	8.0	5.7	4.5	11.5	28.5	34.6	12.3	16.8	17.2	6.9	2.9
1977	19.7	33.2	39.8	13.5	8.9	6.2	4.9	14.0	33.4	45.0	14.0	19.4	21.8	7.5	3.2
1978	25.7	38.4	47.5	15.2	11.4	7.2	6.2	15.8	39.3	42.6	19.3	25.0	29.4	8.5	3.9
1979	30.5	53.3	60.2	17.9	14.0	8.4	7.3	18.0	45.0	60.4	24.6	26.6	31.3	9.4	4.6
1980	36.3	68.0	76.3	17.4	17.8	10.6	8.6	18.6	47.3	79.5	31.6	28.3	34.3	10.4	5.1
1981	38.8	65.7	84.2	19.7	17.7	12.9	13.2	18.6	52.0	78.4	37.1	31.0	38.4	11.5	6.3
1982	32.2	61.8	76.5	17.2	16.1	12.4	16.9	17.5	45.4	62.0	38.4	34.3	39.7	12.4	7.4
1983	32.1	57.1	71.7	18.5	14.9	10.9	17.6	18.8	51.1	55.1	43.7	43.0	47.3	13.2	7.3
1984	32.2	61.9	77.0	22.4	15.1	17.2	18.6	21.9	62.6	58.1	60.4	56.5	61.1	22.9	8.2
1985	24.6	59.4	79.3	24.9	14.6	17.8	19.4	21.8	59.2	51.4	61.3	64.9	66.3	24.6	9.4
1986	23.5	59.0	82.8	25.1	16.7	20.4	26.8	24.4	62.5	34.3	72.0	78.1	79.4	25.9	13.1
1987	25.2	67.4	92.7	27.6	20.3	23.6	28.2	24.8	66.1	42.9	85.1	85.2	88.8	29.3	16.5
1988	33.8	84.2	119.1	33.4	27.0	29.4	30.2	24.9	76.6	39.6	102.2	87.9	96.4	32.1	17.7
1989	37.5	96.9	138.9	34.9	37.3	36.2	35.9	24.9	78.6	50.9	112.2	87.4	103.6	33.4	18.9
1990	35.2	101.8	152.5	36.5	43.7	43.0	39.2	26.4	78.1	62.3	116.1	88.5	105.1	37.4	22.2
1991	35.8	106.3	166.5	40.0	46.9	48.4	46.5	26.2	75.6	51.7	120.8	85.7	107.8	35.3	25.6
1992	40.3	105.1	176.1	47.0	51.4	54.7	48.6	27.6	82.3	51.6	134.3	91.8	122.7	38.6	22.3
1993	40.7	102.7	182.1	52.5	54.7	57.9	52.5	27.9	88.9	51.5	152.3	102.4	134.1	40.7	26.3
1994	42.0	115.7	205.2	57.8	60.0	58.4	60.1	31.0	105.0	51.3	184.4	118.3	146.3	43.8	30.4
1995	50.5	141.3	233.8	61.8	64.4	63.4	63.5	33.2	119.9	56.2	221.4	123.8	160.0	44.9	35.2
1996	55.5	141.1	253.3	65.0	70.1	69.8	72.4	35.7	125.2	72.7	228.1	128.9	172.1	48.0	38.0
1997	51.5	152.5	295.7	74.0	77.4	73.4	84.5	39.7	135.4	71.8	253.3	139.8	193.9	52.1	43.3
1998	46.4	142.8	299.9	72.4	80.3	71.3	91.3	41.2	142.5	50.6	269.4	148.7	217.1	56.5	49.3
1999	46.0	142.4	311.2	75.3	80.9	74.7	98.2	43.6	147.9	67.8	295.7	179.0	242.0	58.9	46.3
2000	47.9	166.6	357.0	80.4	89.4	82.3	104.7	46.0	172.8	120.2	347.0	195.9	282.0	64.8	55.3
2001	49.4	155.3	321.7	75.4	88.3	73.1	108.1	46.6	164.8	103.6	298.0	189.8	284.5	60.1	54.6
2002	49.5	153.7	291.3	78.5	84.5	71.1	116.6	49.8	160.2	103.4	284.0	204.0	307.6	61.3	78.5
1995															
1st quarter	47.9	137.4	219.4	64.0	62.9	59.5	61.1	34.2	118.5	52.3	206.4	129.1	158.9	43.9	34.2
2nd quarter	48.6	141.7	228.4	59.9	64.2	60.2	62.3	32.6	122.6	59.4	219.4	126.6	161.8	45.2	35.0
3rd quarter	52.8	143.8	239.5	61.3	65.1	65.4	64.6	33.0	119.6	57.7	226.8	120.5	162.0	44.3	36.4
4th quarter	52.6	142.0	247.8	62.1	65.6	68.5	66.0	32.9	119.1	55.2	233.1	119.0	157.5	46.2	35.3
1996															
1st quarter	55.9	140.4	249.7	62.3	68.3	67.4	69.0	33.8	121.4	58.6	230.6	123.8	165.0	47.8	36.6
2nd quarter	57.4	137.6	249.6	63.6	69.0	70.6	71.3	35.7	122.9	74.2	225.3	129.8	167.5	47.1	37.4
3rd quarter	54.8	139.9	249.1	68.2	70.0	64.7	72.6	36.3	126.8	75.5	226.2	133.8	175.0	48.6	37.8
4th quarter	54.1	146.3	264.5	66.0	72.9	76.4	76.7	37.0	129.5	82.6	230.3	128.4	180.9	48.8	40.1
1997															
1st quarter	51.5	147.0	277.3	70.4	75.4	73.4	79.7	37.6	131.4	77.6	237.2	139.0	183.0	51.6	40.4
2nd quarter	51.2	153.4	295.3	73.3	77.9	73.1	83.9	39.5	133.6	70.8	250.5	138.6	191.6	51.4	41.9
3rd quarter	50.7	156.2	307.6	76.6	78.0	74.4	86.6	41.2	137.4	70.3	261.7	141.6	197.1	52.6	44.4
4th quarter	52.6	153.6	302.7	75.9	78.2	72.8	87.7	40.5	139.1	68.5	263.7	140.1	204.1	52.7	46.4
1998															
1st quarter	49.9	149.6	302.2	76.7	78.9	71.6	88.4	41.2	141.9	54.0	268.3	144.4	211.0	55.1	48.4
2nd quarter	46.1	143.7	293.0	71.6	80.7	72.7	91.7	41.3	144.8	53.2	269.0	145.7	217.3	56.4	50.6
3rd quarter	42.9	139.1	296.7	67.0	81.2	69.1	92.0	41.0	142.3	49.4	267.0	142.8	219.4	56.7	49.9
4th quarter	46.8	139.0	307.6	74.3	80.4	71.7	93.1	41.4	141.2	45.8	273.5	161.9	220.9	57.9	48.3
1999															
1st quarter	43.8	134.0	302.0	73.2	78.8	72.4	94.5	42.3	138.6	42.1	278.9	170.3	230.1	57.3	45.2
2nd quarter	45.8	138.0	301.2	74.7	79.4	73.4	96.6	43.9	143.2	63.7	291.6	175.2	234.6	58.2	46.2
3rd quarter	47.9	143.3	315.4	75.9	81.0	75.2	99.2	43.7	150.5	79.6	300.8	183.5	246.6	59.1	46.4
4th quarter	46.4	154.3	326.5	77.2	84.4	77.9	102.2	44.5	159.1	85.7	311.5	186.9	257.0	60.9	47.4
2000															
1st quarter	46.6	159.7	328.1	82.8	87.3	81.8	102.7	45.0	164.4	107.8	320.8	197.0	265.6	65.6	51.0
2nd quarter	47.8	163.6	356.9	80.6	88.6	84.0	104.0	46.0	170.1	117.9	347.4	196.1	280.3	64.5	53.3
3rd quarter	49.5	171.8	376.2	80.0	92.0	81.2	105.4	46.6	177.0	127.9	361.6	198.1	287.4	64.3	56.9
4th quarter	47.6	171.4	366.8	78.0	89.6	82.0	106.8	46.2	179.7	127.1	358.4	192.3	294.7	64.8	59.8
2001															
1st quarter	49.9	164.7	362.7	73.2	92.2	82.9	107.0	45.9	185.6	116.7	338.5	188.3	290.2	64.0	64.6
2nd quarter	49.3	158.5	330.9	77.1	91.1	79.2	107.7	45.9	167.9	114.2	301.5	191.5	287.3	66.8	64.8
3rd quarter	48.8	150.8	304.6	77.1	85.5	71.4	107.5	47.7	156.7	102.5	279.7	191.8	281.9	57.9	19.5
4th quarter	49.7	147.2	288.7	74.3	84.5	58.9	110.2	47.1	149.0	81.0	272.3	187.5	278.6	51.8	69.5
2002															
1st quarter	49.7	144.9	284.4	73.8	82.2	68.7	110.5	47.5	149.5	76.7	277.4	190.4	285.4	58.8	74.9
2nd quarter	48.6	155.6	294.1	80.4	84.2	69.3	115.9	49.4	159.0	108.1	288.4	207.5	307.2	59.2	76.4
3rd quarter	49.5	156.3	301.7	82.5	86.0	70.9	119.6	50.4	163.5	110.7	285.3	210.0	315.0	61.4	80.4
4th quarter	50.3	158.0	285.0	77.4	85.6	75.7	120.3	52.0	168.7	117.9	284.9	208.1	322.9	65.8	82.5

Table 7-5. Chain-Type Quantity Indexes for Exports and Imports of Selected NIPA Types of Product

(Index numbers, 1996 = 100.)

Year and quarter	Exports							Imports							
	Goods					Services		Goods						Services	
	Foods, feeds, and beverages	Industrial supplies and materials	Capital goods, except automotive	Automotive vehicles, engines, and parts	Consumer goods, except automotive	Travel	Other private services (financial, professional, etc.)	Foods, feeds, and beverages	Industrial supplies and materials, except petroleum and products	Petroleum and products	Capital goods, except automotive	Automotive vehicles, engines, and parts	Consumer goods, except automotive	Travel	Other private services (financial, professional, etc.)
1967	29.28	27.71	6.33	20.81	9.88	10.53	3.86	48.94	32.47	24.23	1.54	12.54	10.12	23.90	2.92
1968	28.81	31.52	6.53	25.65	10.74	10.88	4.00	55.53	38.65	27.90	1.77	19.50	12.77	21.66	3.31
1969	28.21	32.97	6.91	27.73	11.50	11.88	4.39	52.63	36.57	31.13	2.06	23.82	15.07	23.50	3.68
1970	34.04	36.91	7.73	27.09	12.19	12.81	4.71	56.21	36.95	33.63	2.15	24.36	16.20	27.11	3.86
1971	33.15	33.37	8.07	30.71	12.23	13.37	5.46	58.03	40.28	38.46	2.13	29.71	17.05	27.08	4.26
1972	39.12	35.54	8.84	34.46	14.30	14.36	6.09	61.77	44.19	46.97	2.72	32.19	20.78	29.29	4.39
1973	50.65	43.73	11.22	40.46	17.43	16.50	6.64	63.35	44.48	66.72	3.36	33.22	21.33	27.63	4.91
1974	45.39	45.00	14.01	45.13	21.69	17.95	10.84	58.61	43.33	64.23	3.58	35.28	19.19	24.81	9.88
1975	48.02	39.36	14.23	47.52	19.98	19.41	12.58	51.84	36.50	63.17	3.40	28.00	14.88	23.93	11.17
1976	54.49	42.51	14.04	49.68	22.54	22.12	14.55	59.00	44.45	76.17	4.12	37.10	19.20	25.45	13.42
1977	54.44	42.87	13.81	50.05	24.38	22.16	14.99	58.41	47.83	91.64	4.39	39.30	23.19	26.23	14.05
1978	67.26	47.38	15.76	51.38	28.15	23.81	17.75	65.58	52.37	86.64	5.67	42.53	28.49	27.09	16.42
1979	71.35	54.25	18.93	51.70	29.60	25.52	19.79	67.31	50.31	87.64	6.94	41.12	28.70	26.43	18.60
1980	80.43	61.58	22.09	43.54	35.87	28.51	21.15	58.59	43.91	70.78	8.18	40.74	28.92	26.40	18.99
1981	82.12	57.43	22.18	43.10	34.39	31.47	30.44	60.96	47.67	62.02	9.63	39.42	31.66	27.92	22.38
1982	77.15	55.69	19.62	35.32	30.96	28.06	36.71	62.14	43.21	53.34	10.48	42.19	33.10	33.10	25.37
1983	73.75	52.99	18.92	36.54	28.31	23.69	36.28	67.44	51.32	52.79	12.68	51.65	39.83	37.50	23.77
1984	71.76	55.70	20.96	43.12	28.17	35.33	36.78	76.40	63.64	55.76	18.95	66.36	50.28	68.54	26.64
1985	61.05	55.80	23.03	46.92	27.34	34.98	36.71	79.59	63.92	52.36	21.36	74.35	54.89	75.65	29.68
1986	62.99	58.29	25.13	46.14	30.24	39.03	49.09	81.47	67.32	64.73	24.25	80.49	60.82	70.33	40.25
1987	67.42	59.75	29.01	49.74	35.57	43.07	49.87	83.51	66.65	67.61	27.69	82.59	62.79	83.39	48.17
1988	74.08	67.36	36.88	59.04	45.44	51.96	51.54	80.19	67.38	74.78	31.92	80.52	63.72	85.69	49.62
1989	79.66	76.09	43.35	60.23	60.61	62.10	58.80	81.80	65.74	80.65	36.07	78.44	66.68	88.29	52.03
1990	79.86	79.19	49.27	61.23	68.68	70.05	61.82	85.21	66.78	81.74	38.92	78.83	65.56	94.33	59.71
1991	81.40	84.78	54.04	65.35	71.24	74.22	71.03	81.27	65.58	77.69	41.87	73.47	66.71	85.42	67.86
1992	92.14	86.23	58.99	75.39	76.54	82.34	72.21	85.76	72.10	80.52	48.34	77.31	73.71	87.95	59.08
1993	91.75	83.89	62.73	83.50	80.40	86.37	76.44	86.78	78.48	88.85	56.25	84.96	79.91	92.25	69.53
1994	91.58	88.66	72.46	90.96	87.93	86.80	86.02	88.96	89.99	94.37	69.08	95.04	86.55	95.53	80.38
1995	101.54	95.52	86.31	96.12	93.18	93.06	89.10	90.88	94.47	92.91	85.05	96.63	93.29	96.28	92.63
1996	100.00	100.00	100.00	100.00	100.00	100.00	100.00	100.00	100.00	100.00	100.00	100.00	100.00	100.00	100.00
1997	100.13	108.61	122.84	112.94	109.62	102.95	115.92	110.14	108.28	104.58	125.42	108.21	114.06	108.69	115.09
1998	99.14	107.45	128.03	110.31	113.76	98.84	126.21	118.20	119.91	111.35	143.85	114.93	129.44	122.92	134.53
1999	102.97	108.71	135.07	113.98	115.05	100.98	141.46	129.22	125.06	111.96	165.02	137.39	145.30	125.04	145.87
2000	109.03	119.61	155.85	120.70	126.55	106.07	153.94	138.38	133.52	118.52	198.28	149.33	170.79	139.48	164.83
2001	112.18	114.96	140.47	112.92	125.52	93.87	164.44	144.74	128.51	122.65	175.36	144.79	173.70	132.22	183.69
2002	109.72	115.43	128.25	117.01	120.78	92.39	175.07	152.98	133.19	119.13	172.40	155.17	189.78	128.88	185.49
1995															
1st quarter	103.65	93.41	79.40	99.92	91.59	88.27	86.44	92.74	95.27	88.46	78.12	102.07	93.33	97.83	90.78
2nd quarter	101.60	93.54	83.64	93.51	92.81	88.23	87.69	89.46	96.70	91.68	82.72	98.74	94.18	95.46	92.55
3rd quarter	102.97	96.82	88.94	95.35	93.83	95.75	90.20	89.96	93.16	98.16	87.06	93.60	94.11	93.27	94.21
4th quarter	97.96	98.30	93.27	95.72	94.48	99.99	92.07	91.38	92.75	93.36	92.29	92.10	91.56	98.56	92.99
1996															
1st quarter	101.71	98.42	95.50	96.07	97.80	97.43	95.65	96.01	95.86	90.94	94.38	96.01	95.60	101.24	95.84
2nd quarter	97.60	97.57	97.54	97.83	98.55	101.46	98.65	98.01	98.23	103.57	96.69	100.76	97.23	98.58	98.16
3rd quarter	96.72	99.81	99.21	104.76	99.86	92.36	100.21	102.39	102.14	104.83	101.25	103.71	101.74	100.14	100.05
4th quarter	103.98	104.20	107.75	101.34	103.79	108.75	105.49	103.59	103.77	100.66	107.68	99.52	105.43	100.04	105.95
1997															
1st quarter	98.70	104.45	114.04	107.57	107.04	103.93	109.29	104.86	104.01	98.72	114.41	107.79	107.17	106.75	107.07
2nd quarter	97.59	109.10	122.30	111.70	110.57	102.69	114.97	108.40	107.58	106.76	122.92	107.61	112.53	105.71	110.50
3rd quarter	99.12	110.89	128.10	116.72	110.32	104.07	118.97	114.12	109.97	108.25	130.24	109.51	116.05	110.06	118.70
4th quarter	105.13	109.99	126.94	115.75	110.56	101.09	120.44	113.20	111.56	104.59	134.10	107.94	120.47	112.24	124.08
1998															
1st quarter	104.04	109.67	127.67	116.92	111.43	99.84	121.59	117.11	116.78	105.51	139.90	111.30	125.04	121.44	131.01
2nd quarter	97.74	106.91	124.57	109.20	114.28	101.14	126.40	117.51	120.56	115.35	142.93	112.51	129.47	122.52	137.41
3rd quarter	92.50	105.79	127.39	102.20	115.17	95.73	127.29	118.71	120.80	115.67	144.11	110.75	131.29	124.06	136.68
4th quarter	102.29	107.44	132.51	112.93	114.17	98.64	129.57	119.49	121.51	108.85	148.45	125.15	131.98	123.67	133.03
1999															
1st quarter	96.65	104.53	130.38	111.21	112.10	99.65	134.10	124.34	119.63	109.89	152.18	131.14	137.48	121.95	137.15
2nd quarter	102.05	107.08	130.44	113.30	113.03	99.36	138.17	129.34	123.02	117.29	162.11	134.53	140.95	124.08	143.89
3rd quarter	107.87	108.62	137.41	115.01	115.27	101.11	143.84	130.71	126.20	115.55	169.69	140.73	148.33	125.73	148.73
4th quarter	105.32	114.59	142.03	116.41	119.80	103.80	149.73	132.51	131.39	105.12	176.11	143.16	154.46	128.38	153.73
2000															
1st quarter	105.83	116.28	143.35	124.67	123.63	107.17	149.68	133.79	132.63	111.95	181.80	150.67	160.13	138.33	157.56
2nd quarter	107.11	117.38	156.12	121.12	125.33	108.32	152.52	137.76	133.35	121.87	197.72	149.49	169.76	138.06	160.94
3rd quarter	115.05	122.53	163.97	120.04	130.13	104.14	154.83	140.99	135.05	121.15	206.79	150.78	174.19	138.79	166.40
4th quarter	108.11	122.24	159.96	116.99	127.11	104.64	158.73	140.98	133.06	119.13	206.81	146.37	179.10	142.72	174.44
2001															
1st quarter	113.10	118.41	157.81	109.80	130.99	105.89	160.76	139.44	133.23	125.54	196.22	143.43	176.42	140.67	184.06
2nd quarter	112.84	115.47	144.04	115.33	129.71	100.54	164.09	142.22	127.05	127.74	176.66	146.23	175.21	147.55	188.29
3rd quarter	109.12	112.66	133.34	115.39	121.55	91.80	163.96	149.98	127.11	118.10	165.67	146.62	172.24	126.87	186.88
4th quarter	113.67	113.29	126.71	111.16	119.81	77.24	168.96	147.33	126.66	119.23	162.89	142.87	170.94	113.80	175.52
2002															
1st quarter	114.08	112.39	124.79	110.26	117.51	90.11	168.24	149.04	128.49	113.11	167.52	145.23	175.71	131.42	181.81
2nd quarter	110.45	117.52	129.40	120.04	120.66	89.85	174.52	152.82	131.91	121.82	174.57	158.09	189.68	126.80	180.22
3rd quarter	106.97	115.60	132.98	122.83	122.79	91.99	178.52	154.14	135.07	117.54	173.17	159.66	194.30	124.92	187.59
4th quarter	107.39	116.21	125.82	114.90	122.17	97.59	179.02	155.91	137.29	124.05	174.33	157.72	199.42	132.40	192.35

Table 7-6. U.S. International Transactions

(Millions of dollars, seasonally adjusted.)

Year and quarter	Current account									Compensation of employees
	Exports of goods and services and income receipts									
	Total	Exports of goods and services	Exports of goods	Exports of services	Income receipts					
					Total	Income receipts on U.S. assets abroad				
						Total	Direct investment receipts	Other private receipts	U.S. government receipts	
1960	30 556	25 940	19 650	6 290	4 616	4 616	3 621	646	349	. . .
1961	31 402	26 403	20 108	6 295	4 999	4 999	3 823	793	383	. . .
1962	33 340	27 722	20 781	6 941	5 618	5 618	4 241	904	473	. . .
1963	35 776	29 620	22 272	7 348	6 157	6 157	4 636	1 022	499	. . .
1964	40 165	33 341	25 501	7 840	6 824	6 824	5 106	1 256	462	. . .
1965	42 722	35 285	26 461	8 824	7 437	7 437	5 506	1 421	510	. . .
1966	46 454	38 926	29 310	9 616	7 528	7 528	5 260	1 669	599	. . .
1967	49 353	41 333	30 666	10 667	8 021	8 021	5 603	1 781	636	. . .
1968	54 911	45 543	33 626	11 917	9 367	9 367	6 591	2 021	756	. . .
1969	60 132	49 220	36 414	12 806	10 913	10 913	7 649	2 338	925	. . .
1970	68 387	56 640	42 469	14 171	11 748	11 748	8 169	2 671	907	. . .
1971	72 384	59 677	43 319	16 358	12 707	12 707	9 160	2 641	906	. . .
1972	81 986	67 222	49 381	17 841	14 765	14 765	10 949	2 949	866	. . .
1973	113 050	91 242	71 410	19 832	21 808	21 808	16 542	4 330	936	. . .
1974	148 484	120 897	98 306	22 591	27 587	27 587	19 157	7 356	1 074	. . .
1975	157 936	132 585	107 088	25 497	25 351	25 351	16 595	7 644	1 112	. . .
1976	172 090	142 716	114 745	27 971	29 375	29 375	18 999	9 043	1 332	. . .
1977	184 655	152 301	120 816	31 485	32 354	32 354	19 673	11 057	1 625	. . .
1978	220 516	178 428	142 075	36 353	42 088	42 088	25 458	14 788	1 843	. . .
1979	287 965	224 131	184 439	39 692	63 834	63 834	38 183	23 356	2 295	. . .
1980	344 440	271 834	224 250	47 584	72 606	72 606	37 146	32 898	2 562	. . .
1981	380 928	294 398	237 044	57 354	86 529	86 529	32 549	50 300	3 680	. . .
1982	366 983	275 236	211 157	64 079	91 747	91 747	29 469	58 160	4 118	. . .
1983	356 106	266 106	201 799	64 307	90 000	90 000	31 750	53 418	4 832	. . .
1984	399 913	291 094	219 926	71 168	108 819	108 819	35 325	68 267	5 227	. . .
1985	387 612	289 070	215 915	73 155	98 542	98 542	35 410	57 633	5 499	. . .
1986	407 098	310 033	223 344	86 689	97 064	96 156	36 938	52 806	6 413	908
1987	457 053	348 869	250 208	98 661	108 184	107 190	46 288	55 592	5 311	994
1988	567 862	431 149	320 230	110 919	136 713	135 718	58 445	70 571	6 703	995
1989	648 290	487 003	359 916	127 087	161 287	160 270	61 981	92 638	5 651	1 017
1990	706 975	535 233	387 401	147 832	171 742	170 570	65 973	94 072	10 525	1 172
1991	727 557	578 344	414 083	164 261	149 214	147 924	58 718	81 186	8 019	1 290
1992	748 881	616 455	439 631	176 824	132 427	130 631	57 538	65 977	7 115	1 796
1993	776 921	642 376	456 943	185 433	134 545	132 725	67 246	60 353	5 126	1 820
1994	868 460	702 622	502 859	199 763	165 838	163 895	77 344	82 423	4 128	1 943
1995	1 005 645	793 725	575 204	218 521	211 920	209 741	95 260	109 768	4 713	2 179
1996	1 077 148	850 877	612 113	238 764	226 271	224 090	102 505	116 994	4 591	2 181
1997	1 194 899	933 873	678 366	255 507	261 026	258 756	115 323	139 874	3 559	2 270
1998	1 191 206	932 558	670 416	262 142	258 648	256 211	103 963	148 647	3 601	2 437
1999	1 255 671	965 473	683 965	281 508	290 198	287 450	131 626	152 627	3 197	2 748
2000	1 416 915	1 070 054	771 994	298 060	346 861	343 928	151 839	188 243	3 846	2 933
2001	1 284 942	1 007 580	718 712	288 868	277 362	274 272	124 333	146 378	3 561	3 090
2002	1 229 649	974 107	681 874	292 233	255 542	252 379	142 933	106 143	3 303	3 163
1997										
1st quarter	287 175	224 978	162 626	62 352	62 197	61 630	28 426	32 342	862	567
2nd quarter	300 275	234 336	170 171	64 165	65 939	65 373	29 801	34 606	966	566
3rd quarter	304 962	237 873	173 161	64 712	67 089	66 520	30 187	35 452	881	569
4th quarter	302 490	236 688	172 408	64 280	65 802	65 234	26 910	37 474	850	568
1998										
1st quarter	301 310	235 503	170 998	64 505	65 807	65 217	27 423	36 940	854	590
2nd quarter	297 869	231 506	165 511	65 995	66 363	65 763	27 396	37 446	921	600
3rd quarter	292 139	228 712	164 081	64 631	63 427	62 811	23 361	38 562	888	616
4th quarter	299 886	236 835	169 826	67 009	63 051	62 420	25 784	35 699	937	631
1999										
1st quarter	299 118	232 831	164 235	68 596	66 287	65 592	29 201	35 480	911	695
2nd quarter	306 214	236 123	166 084	70 039	70 091	69 394	31 630	36 953	811	697
3rd quarter	318 820	244 024	173 003	71 021	74 796	74 122	33 981	39 395	746	674
4th quarter	331 524	252 496	180 643	71 853	79 028	78 346	36 816	40 799	731	682
2000										
1st quarter	340 457	258 166	185 168	72 998	82 291	81 569	37 085	43 418	1 066	722
2nd quarter	354 103	266 323	191 175	75 148	87 780	87 050	38 140	47 771	1 139	730
3rd quarter	359 157	273 366	198 821	74 545	85 791	85 054	36 306	47 903	845	737
4th quarter	363 198	272 198	196 830	75 368	91 000	90 256	40 309	49 151	796	744
2001										
1st quarter	348 355	269 268	194 145	75 123	79 087	78 283	32 603	44 787	893	804
2nd quarter	331 765	259 158	184 457	74 701	72 607	71 847	31 489	39 581	777	760
3rd quarter	309 601	243 900	172 526	71 374	65 701	64 930	30 336	33 744	850	771
4th quarter	295 222	235 255	167 584	67 671	59 967	59 212	29 904	28 266	1 042	755
2002										
1st quarter	297 074	236 442	165 298	71 144	60 632	59 821	32 058	26 950	813	811
2nd quarter	307 616	243 696	171 421	72 275	63 920	63 140	34 874	27 560	706	780
3rd quarter	313 939	247 815	174 315	73 500	66 124	65 339	37 264	27 225	850	785
4th quarter	311 015	246 151	170 840	75 311	64 864	64 077	38 735	24 408	934	787

. . . = Not available.

Table 7-6. U.S. International Transactions—*Continued*

(Millions of dollars, seasonally adjusted.)

Year and quarter	Current account—*Continued*									
	Imports of goods and services and income payments [1]									
					Income payments					
						Income payments on foreign-owned assets in the U.S.				
	Total	Imports of goods and services	Imports of goods	Imports of services	Total	Total	Direct investment payments	Other private payments	U.S. government payments	Compensation of employees
1960	-23 670	-22 432	-14 758	-7 674	-1 238	-1 238	-394	-511	-332	. . .
1961	-23 453	-22 208	-14 537	-7 671	-1 245	-1 245	-432	-535	-278	. . .
1962	-25 676	-24 352	-16 260	-8 092	-1 324	-1 324	-399	-586	-339	. . .
1963	-26 970	-25 410	-17 048	-8 362	-1 560	-1 560	-459	-701	-401	. . .
1964	-29 102	-27 319	-18 700	-8 619	-1 783	-1 783	-529	-802	-453	. . .
1965	-32 708	-30 621	-21 510	-9 111	-2 088	-2 088	-657	-942	-489	. . .
1966	-38 468	-35 987	-25 493	-10 494	-2 481	-2 481	-711	-1 221	-549	. . .
1967	-41 476	-38 729	-26 866	-11 863	-2 747	-2 747	-821	-1 328	-598	. . .
1968	-48 671	-45 293	-32 991	-12 302	-3 378	-3 378	-876	-1 800	-702	. . .
1969	-53 998	-49 129	-35 807	-13 322	-4 869	-4 869	-848	-3 244	-777	. . .
1970	-59 901	-54 386	-39 866	-14 520	-5 515	-5 515	-875	-3 617	-1 024	. . .
1971	-66 414	-60 979	-45 579	-15 400	-5 435	-5 435	-1 164	-2 428	-1 844	. . .
1972	-79 237	-72 665	-55 797	-16 868	-6 572	-6 572	-1 284	-2 604	-2 684	. . .
1973	-98 997	-89 342	-70 499	-18 843	-9 655	-9 655	-1 610	-4 209	-3 836	. . .
1974	-137 274	-125 190	-103 811	-21 379	-12 084	-12 084	-1 331	-6 491	-4 262	. . .
1975	-132 745	-120 181	-98 185	-21 996	-12 564	-12 564	-2 234	-5 788	-4 542	. . .
1976	-162 109	-148 798	-124 228	-24 570	-13 311	-13 311	-3 110	-5 681	-4 520	. . .
1977	-193 764	-179 547	-151 907	-27 640	-14 217	-14 217	-2 834	-5 841	-5 542	. . .
1978	-229 870	-208 191	-176 002	-32 189	-21 680	-21 680	-4 211	-8 795	-8 674	. . .
1979	-281 657	-248 696	-212 007	-36 689	-32 961	-32 961	-6 357	-15 481	-11 122	. . .
1980	-333 774	-291 241	-249 750	-41 491	-42 532	-42 532	-8 635	-21 214	-12 684	. . .
1981	-364 196	-310 570	-265 067	-45 503	-53 626	-53 626	-6 898	-29 415	-17 313	. . .
1982	-355 975	-299 391	-247 642	-51 749	-56 583	-56 583	-2 114	-35 187	-19 282	. . .
1983	-377 488	-323 874	-268 901	-54 973	-53 614	-53 614	-4 120	-30 501	-18 993	. . .
1984	-473 923	-400 166	-332 418	-67 748	-73 756	-73 756	-8 443	-44 158	-21 155	. . .
1985	-483 769	-410 950	-338 088	-72 862	-72 819	-72 819	-6 945	-42 745	-23 129	. . .
1986	-530 142	-448 572	-368 425	-80 147	-81 571	-78 893	-6 856	-47 412	-24 625	-2 678
1987	-594 443	-500 552	-409 765	-90 787	-93 891	-91 553	-7 676	-57 659	-26 218	-2 338
1988	-663 741	-545 715	-447 189	-98 526	-118 026	-116 179	-12 150	-72 314	-31 715	-1 847
1989	-721 607	-580 144	-477 665	-102 479	-141 463	-139 177	-7 045	-93 768	-38 364	-2 286
1990	-759 287	-616 094	-498 435	-117 659	-143 192	-139 728	-3 450	-95 508	-40 770	-3 464
1991	-734 563	-609 479	-491 020	-118 459	-125 084	-121 058	2 266	-82 452	-40 872	-4 026
1992	-763 741	-654 639	-536 528	-118 111	-109 101	-104 349	-2 189	-63 079	-39 081	-4 752
1993	-821 797	-711 542	-589 394	-122 148	-110 255	-105 123	-7 943	-57 804	-39 376	-5 132
1994	-948 555	-799 811	-668 690	-131 121	-148 744	-142 792	-22 150	-76 450	-44 192	-5 952
1995	-1 075 674	-888 794	-749 374	-139 420	-186 880	-180 617	-30 318	-96 490	-53 809	-6 263
1996	-1 155 489	-953 746	-803 113	-150 633	-201 743	-195 443	-33 093	-97 079	-65 271	-6 300
1997	-1 281 291	-1 040 920	-876 485	-164 435	-240 371	-233 705	-42 950	-112 117	-78 638	-6 666
1998	-1 347 462	-1 095 711	-917 112	-178 599	-251 751	-244 757	-38 418	-127 052	-79 287	-6 994
1999	-1 499 762	-1 226 674	-1 029 987	-196 687	-273 088	-265 133	-53 437	-137 149	-74 547	-7 955
2000	-1 772 694	-1 445 438	-1 224 417	-221 021	-327 256	-319 737	-56 910	-179 854	-82 973	-7 519
2001	-1 632 072	-1 365 399	-1 145 927	-219 472	-266 673	-258 571	-17 848	-160 042	-80 681	-8 102
2002	-1 651 657	-1 392 145	-1 164 746	-227 399	-259 512	-251 108	-49 458	-127 735	-73 915	-8 404
1997										
1st quarter	-310 602	-252 806	-212 725	-40 081	-57 796	-56 190	-11 105	-26 496	-18 589	-1 606
2nd quarter	-317 518	-258 520	-218 027	-40 493	-58 998	-57 348	-10 604	-27 315	-19 429	-1 650
3rd quarter	-325 106	-263 379	-221 656	-41 723	-61 727	-60 045	-11 584	-28 278	-20 183	-1 682
4th quarter	-328 068	-266 218	-224 077	-42 141	-61 850	-60 123	-9 658	-30 028	-20 437	-1 727
1998										
1st quarter	-331 242	-269 144	-226 372	-42 772	-62 098	-60 411	-9 117	-30 964	-20 330	-1 687
2nd quarter	-336 183	-272 814	-228 721	-44 093	-63 369	-61 661	-10 189	-31 178	-20 294	-1 708
3rd quarter	-337 144	-273 307	-228 010	-45 297	-63 837	-62 071	-9 088	-33 187	-19 796	-1 766
4th quarter	-342 895	-280 449	-234 009	-46 440	-62 446	-60 613	-10 023	-31 723	-18 867	-1 833
1999										
1st quarter	-347 512	-284 913	-237 825	-47 088	-62 599	-60 645	-10 667	-31 536	-18 442	-1 954
2nd quarter	-364 498	-299 262	-250 654	-48 608	-65 236	-63 252	-13 174	-31 849	-18 229	-1 984
3rd quarter	-386 995	-315 454	-265 292	-50 162	-71 541	-69 537	-15 508	-35 290	-18 739	-2 004
4th quarter	-400 756	-327 045	-276 216	-50 829	-73 711	-71 698	-14 087	-38 474	-19 137	-2 013
2000										
1st quarter	-423 355	-344 884	-291 359	-53 525	-78 471	-76 592	-15 972	-40 727	-19 893	-1 879
2nd quarter	-440 583	-357 457	-302 905	-54 552	-83 126	-81 248	-15 912	-44 779	-20 557	-1 878
3rd quarter	-454 244	-371 306	-314 622	-56 684	-82 938	-81 098	-13 333	-46 784	-20 981	-1 840
4th quarter	-454 517	-371 796	-315 531	-56 265	-82 721	-80 799	-11 693	-47 564	-21 542	-1 922
2001										
1st quarter	-440 865	-362 708	-306 871	-55 837	-78 157	-76 145	-8 974	-45 821	-21 350	-2 012
2nd quarter	-420 408	-348 614	-291 627	-56 987	-71 794	-69 785	-7 323	-41 865	-20 597	-2 009
3rd quarter	-401 981	-332 943	-278 847	-54 096	-69 038	-67 015	-7 523	-39 730	-19 762	-2 023
4th quarter	-368 820	-321 137	-268 582	-52 555	-47 683	-45 625	5 973	-32 626	-18 972	-2 058
2002										
1st quarter	-387 864	-326 499	-271 331	-55 168	-61 365	-59 271	-8 134	-32 512	-18 625	-2 094
2nd quarter	-416 962	-348 584	-292 707	-55 877	-68 378	-66 246	-13 464	-33 773	-19 009	-2 132
3rd quarter	-422 666	-354 795	-297 627	-57 168	-67 871	-65 820	-15 350	-31 802	-18 668	-2 051
4th quarter	-424 165	-362 267	-303 081	-59 186	-61 898	-59 771	-12 510	-29 648	-17 613	-2 127

[1]A minus sign indicates imports of goods and services, or payments of incomes.
. . . = Not available.

Table 7-6. U.S. International Transactions—*Continued*

(Millions of dollars, seasonally adjusted.)

Year and quarter	Current account—*Continued*				Capital account transactions, net [2]	Financial account					
	Unilateral current transfers, net [2]					U.S.-owned assets abroad, net [2]					
	Total	U.S. government		Private remittances and other transfers		Total	U.S. official reserve assets, net				
		Grants	Pensions and other transfers				Total	Gold	Special drawing rights	Reserve position in the IMF	Foreign currencies
1960	-4 062	-3 367	-273	-423	. . .	-4 099	2 145	1 703	0	442	0
1961	-4 127	-3 320	-373	-434	. . .	-5 538	607	857	0	-135	-115
1962	-4 277	-3 453	-347	-477	. . .	-4 174	1 535	890	0	626	19
1963	-4 392	-3 479	-339	-575	. . .	-7 270	378	461	0	29	-112
1964	-4 240	-3 227	-399	-614	. . .	-9 560	171	125	0	266	-220
1965	-4 583	-3 444	-463	-677	. . .	-5 716	1 225	1 665	0	-94	-346
1966	-4 955	-3 802	-499	-655	. . .	-7 321	570	571	0	537	-538
1967	-5 294	-3 844	-571	-879	. . .	-9 757	53	1 170	0	-94	-1 023
1968	-5 629	-4 256	-537	-836	. . .	-10 977	-870	1 173	0	-870	-1 173
1969	-5 735	-4 259	-537	-939	. . .	-11 585	-1 179	-967	0	-1 034	822
1970	-6 156	-4 449	-611	-1 096	. . .	-8 470	3 348	787	16	389	2 156
1971	-7 402	-5 589	-696	-1 117	. . .	-11 758	3 066	866	468	1 350	382
1972	-8 544	-6 665	-770	-1 109	. . .	-13 787	706	547	7	153	-1
1973	-6 913	-4 748	-915	-1 250	. . .	-22 874	158	0	9	-33	182
1974	-9 249	-7 293	-939	-1 017	. . .	-34 745	-1 467	0	-172	-1 265	-30
1975	-7 075	-5 101	-1 068	-906	. . .	-39 703	-849	0	-66	-466	-317
1976	-5 686	-3 519	-1 250	-917	. . .	-51 269	-2 558	0	-78	-2 212	-268
1977	-5 226	-2 990	-1 378	-859	. . .	-34 785	-375	-118	-121	-294	158
1978	-5 788	-3 412	-1 532	-844	. . .	-61 130	732	-65	1 249	4 231	-4 683
1979	-6 593	-4 015	-1 658	-920	. . .	-64 915	6	-65	3	-189	257
1980	-8 349	-5 486	-1 818	-1 044	. . .	-85 815	-7 003	0	1 136	1 667	-6 472
1981	-11 702	-5 145	-2 041	-4 516	. . .	-113 054	-4 082	*	-730	-2 491	-861
1982	-16 544	-6 087	-2 251	-8 207	199	-127 882	-4 965	0	-1 371	-2 552	-1 041
1983	-17 310	-6 469	-2 207	-8 635	209	-66 373	-1 196	0	-66	-4 434	3 304
1984	-20 335	-8 696	-2 159	-9 479	235	-40 376	-3 131	0	-979	-995	-1 156
1985	-21 998	-11 268	-2 138	-8 593	315	-44 752	-3 858	0	-897	908	-3 869
1986	-24 132	-11 883	-2 372	-9 877	301	-111 723	312	0	-246	1 501	-942
1987	-23 265	-10 309	-2 409	-10 548	365	-79 296	9 149	0	-509	2 070	7 588
1988	-25 274	-10 537	-2 709	-12 028	493	-106 573	-3 912	0	127	1 025	-5 064
1989	-26 169	-10 860	-2 775	-12 534	336	-175 383	-25 293	0	-535	471	-25 229
1990	-26 654	-10 359	-3 224	-13 070	-6 579	-81 234	-2 158	0	-192	731	-2 697
1991	10 752	29 193	-3 775	-14 665	-4 479	-64 388	5 763	0	-177	-367	6 307
1992	-33 154	-16 320	-4 043	-12 791	-557	-74 410	3 901	0	2 316	-2 692	4 277
1993	-37 113	-17 036	-4 104	-15 973	-1 299	-200 552	-1 379	0	-537	-44	-797
1994	-37 583	-14 978	-4 556	-18 049	-1 723	-176 056	5 346	0	-441	494	5 293
1995	-35 188	-11 190	-3 451	-20 547	-927	-352 376	-9 742	0	-808	-2 466	-6 468
1996	-38 862	-15 401	-4 466	-18 995	-654	-413 923	6 668	0	370	-1 280	7 578
1997	-41 292	-12 472	-4 191	-24 629	-1 044	-487 599	-1 010	0	-350	-3 575	2 915
1998	-48 435	-13 270	-4 305	-30 860	-740	-347 829	-6 783	0	-147	-5 119	-1 517
1999	-46 755	-13 774	-4 406	-28 575	-4 843	-503 640	8 747	0	10	5 484	3 253
2000	-55 679	-16 714	-4 705	-34 260	-799	-569 798	-290	0	-722	2 308	-1 876
2001	-46 615	-11 517	-5 798	-29 300	-1 062	-349 939	-4 911	0	-630	-3 600	-681
2002	-58 853	-17 097	-5 125	-36 631	-1 285	-178 985	-3 681	0	-475	-2 632	-574
1997											
1st quarter	-8 899	-2 281	-1 027	-5 591	-206	-152 213	4 480	0	72	1 055	3 353
2nd quarter	-9 285	-2 308	-1 071	-5 906	-273	-93 616	-236	0	-133	54	-157
3rd quarter	-9 772	-2 476	-1 024	-6 272	-322	-119 283	-730	0	-139	-463	-128
4th quarter	-13 336	-5 407	-1 069	-6 860	-243	-122 489	-4 524	0	-150	-4 221	153
1998											
1st quarter	-10 868	-2 365	-1 080	-7 423	-191	-72 938	-444	0	-182	-85	-177
2nd quarter	-11 171	-2 209	-1 094	-7 868	-180	-137 128	-1 945	0	73	-1 032	-986
3rd quarter	-11 954	-2 882	-1 055	-8 017	-203	-57 020	-2 025	0	189	-2 078	-136
4th quarter	-14 441	-5 814	-1 075	-7 552	-166	-80 745	-2 369	0	-227	-1 924	-218
1999											
1st quarter	-10 899	-2 574	-1 066	-7 259	-188	-84 290	4 068	0	562	3	3 503
2nd quarter	-11 316	-3 097	-1 074	-7 145	-169	-180 642	1 159	0	-190	1 413	-64
3rd quarter	-11 092	-2 847	-1 085	-7 160	-175	-125 226	1 951	0	-184	2 268	-133
4th quarter	-13 449	-5 256	-1 181	-7 012	-4 311	-113 483	1 569	0	-178	1 800	-53
2000											
1st quarter	-12 123	-2 884	-1 168	-8 071	-194	-214 667	-554	0	-180	-237	-137
2nd quarter	-12 646	-3 173	-1 179	-8 294	-195	-108 046	2 020	0	-180	2 328	-128
3rd quarter	-13 480	-3 637	-1 183	-8 660	-218	-86 485	-346	0	-182	1 300	-1 464
4th quarter	-17 435	-7 020	-1 177	-9 238	-192	-160 602	-1 410	0	-180	-1 083	-147
2001											
1st quarter	-11 494	-2 426	-1 316	-7 752	-267	-192 224	190	0	-189	574	-195
2nd quarter	-11 321	-2 479	-1 291	-7 551	-260	-92 213	-1 343	0	-156	-1 015	-172
3rd quarter	-11 256	-2 867	-1 305	-7 084	-286	37 353	-3 559	0	-145	-3 242	-172
4th quarter	-12 542	-3 745	-1 886	-6 911	-249	-102 853	-199	0	-140	83	-142
2002											
1st quarter	-15 938	-6 397	-1 271	-8 270	-277	-35 227	390	0	-109	652	-153
2nd quarter	-13 481	-3 287	-1 279	-8 915	-286	-128 567	-1 843	0	-107	-1 607	-129
3rd quarter	-13 997	-3 075	-1 282	-9 640	-364	29 712	-1 416	0	-132	-1 136	-148
4th quarter	-15 436	-4 338	-1 292	-9 806	-358	-44 902	-812	0	-127	-541	-144

[2]A minus sign indicates net unilateral transfers to foreigners, net capital or financial outflows, or increases in U.S. official assets.
. . . = Not available.
* = Less than $500,000 (+/-).

Table 7-6. U.S. International Transactions—*Continued*

(Millions of dollars, seasonally adjusted.)

Year and quarter	Financial account—*Continued*								
	U.S.-owned assets abroad, net [3]—*Continued*								
	U.S. government assets other than official reserve assets, net				U.S. private assets, net				
								U.S. claims	
	Total	U.S. credits and other long-term assets	Repayments on U.S. credits and other long-term assets	U.S. foreign currency holdings and short-term assets	Total	Direct investment	Foreign securities	On unaffiliated foreigners reported by U.S. nonbanking concerns	Reported by U.S. banks, not included elsewhere
1960	-1 100	-1 214	642	-528	-5 144	-2 940	-663	-394	-1 148
1961	-910	-1 928	1 279	-261	-5 235	-2 653	-762	-558	-1 261
1962	-1 085	-2 128	1 288	-245	-4 623	-2 851	-969	-354	-450
1963	-1 662	-2 204	988	-447	-5 986	-3 483	-1 105	157	-1 556
1964	-1 680	-2 382	720	-19	-8 050	-3 760	-677	-1 108	-2 505
1965	-1 605	-2 463	874	-16	-5 336	-5 011	-759	341	93
1966	-1 543	-2 513	1 235	-265	-6 347	-5 418	-720	-442	233
1967	-2 423	-3 638	1 005	209	-7 386	-4 805	-1 308	-779	-495
1968	-2 274	-3 722	1 386	62	-7 833	-5 295	-1 569	-1 203	233
1969	-2 200	-3 489	1 200	89	-8 206	-5 960	-1 549	-126	-570
1970	-1 589	-3 293	1 721	-16	-10 229	-7 590	-1 076	-596	-967
1971	-1 884	-4 181	2 115	182	-12 940	-7 618	-1 113	-1 229	-2 980
1972	-1 568	-3 819	2 086	165	-12 925	-7 747	-618	-1 054	-3 506
1973	-2 644	-4 638	2 596	-602	-20 388	-11 353	-671	-2 383	-5 980
1974	366	-5 001	4 826	541	-33 643	-9 052	-1 854	-3 221	-19 516
1975	-3 474	-5 941	2 475	-9	-35 380	-14 244	-6 247	-1 357	-13 532
1976	-4 214	-6 943	2 596	133	-44 498	-11 949	-8 885	-2 296	-21 368
1977	-3 693	-6 445	2 719	33	-30 717	-11 890	-5 460	-1 940	-11 427
1978	-4 660	-7 470	2 941	-131	-57 202	-16 056	-3 626	-3 853	-33 667
1979	-3 746	-7 697	3 926	25	-61 176	-25 222	-4 726	-5 014	-26 213
1980	-5 162	-9 860	4 456	242	-73 651	-19 222	-3 568	-4 023	-46 838
1981	-5 097	-9 674	4 413	164	-103 875	-9 624	-5 699	-4 377	-84 175
1982	-6 131	-10 063	4 292	-360	-116 786	-4 556	-7 983	6 823	-111 070
1983	-5 006	-9 967	5 012	-51	-60 172	-12 528	-6 762	-10 954	-29 928
1984	-5 489	-9 599	4 490	-379	-31 757	-16 407	-4 756	533	-11 127
1985	-2 821	-7 657	4 719	117	-38 074	-18 927	-7 481	-10 342	-1 323
1986	-2 022	-9 084	6 089	973	-110 014	-23 995	-4 271	-21 773	-59 975
1987	1 006	-6 506	7 625	-113	-89 450	-35 034	-5 251	-7 046	-42 119
1988	2 967	-7 680	10 370	277	-105 628	-22 528	-7 980	-21 193	-53 927
1989	1 233	-5 608	6 725	115	-151 323	-43 447	-22 070	-27 646	-58 160
1990	2 317	-8 410	10 856	-130	-81 393	-37 183	-28 765	-27 824	12 379
1991	2 924	-12 879	16 776	-974	-73 075	-37 889	-45 673	11 097	-610
1992	-1 667	-7 408	5 807	-66	-76 644	-48 266	-49 166	-387	21 175
1993	-351	-6 311	6 270	-310	-198 822	-83 950	-146 253	766	30 615
1994	-390	-5 383	5 088	-95	-181 012	-80 167	-60 309	-36 336	-4 200
1995	-984	-4 859	4 125	-250	-341 650	-98 750	-122 506	-45 286	-75 108
1996	-989	-5 025	3 930	106	-419 602	-91 885	-149 829	-86 333	-91 555
1997	68	-5 417	5 438	47	-486 657	-104 803	-118 976	-121 760	-141 118
1998	-422	-4 678	4 111	145	-340 624	-142 644	-124 204	-38 204	-35 572
1999	2 750	-6 175	9 559	-634	-515 137	-224 934	-116 236	-97 704	-76 263
2000	-941	-5 182	4 265	-24	-568 567	-159 212	-121 908	-138 790	-148 657
2001	-486	-4 431	3 873	72	-344 542	-119 963	-84 637	-4 997	-134 945
2002	-32	-5 611	5 684	-105	-175 272	-137 836	15 801	-31 880	-21 357
1997									
1st quarter	-76	-1 170	1 119	-25	-156 617	-29 544	-23 836	-38 112	-65 125
2nd quarter	-298	-1 616	1 329	-11	-93 082	-24 883	-31 739	-9 885	-26 575
3rd quarter	377	-1 426	1 832	-29	-118 930	-21 217	-51 297	-22 173	-24 243
4th quarter	65	-1 205	1 158	112	-118 030	-29 161	-12 104	-51 590	-25 175
1998									
1st quarter	-80	-1 192	1 134	-22	-72 414	-41 844	-17 951	-7 822	-4 797
2nd quarter	-483	-1 156	699	-26	-134 700	-44 689	-41 461	-20 363	-28 187
3rd quarter	188	-1 286	1 336	138	-55 183	-20 479	9 283	-15 658	-28 329
4th quarter	-47	-1 044	942	55	-78 329	-35 634	-74 075	5 639	25 741
1999									
1st quarter	118	-1 314	1 554	-122	-88 476	-68 498	4 196	-47 211	23 037
2nd quarter	-392	-2 167	1 887	-112	-181 409	-50 190	-68 182	-27 021	-36 016
3rd quarter	-686	-1 595	1 026	-117	-126 491	-64 062	-38 290	-13 663	-10 476
4th quarter	3 710	-1 099	5 092	-283	-118 762	-42 185	-13 960	-9 809	-52 808
2000									
1st quarter	-127	-1 750	1 329	294	-213 986	-34 934	-31 042	-79 800	-68 210
2nd quarter	-570	-1 371	860	-59	-109 496	-52 029	-36 671	-25 287	4 491
3rd quarter	114	-1 051	1 266	-101	-86 253	-39 618	-30 863	-14 121	-1 651
4th quarter	-358	-1 010	810	-158	-158 834	-32 633	-23 332	-19 582	-83 287
2001									
1st quarter	77	-1 094	1 071	100	-192 491	-14 147	-23 849	-43 929	-110 566
2nd quarter	-783	-1 330	573	-26	-90 087	-30 809	-48 701	-7 404	-3 173
3rd quarter	77	-1 011	1 118	-30	40 835	-41 781	13 140	-101	69 577
4th quarter	143	-996	1 111	28	-102 797	-33 224	-25 227	46 437	-90 783
2002									
1st quarter	133	-853	994	-8	-35 750	-39 083	5 367	-1 886	-148
2nd quarter	42	-565	566	41	-126 766	-35 459	-5 843	-16 210	-69 254
3rd quarter	-27	-1 375	1 452	-104	31 155	-31 623	21 641	-11 862	52 999
4th quarter	-180	-2 818	2 672	-34	-43 910	-31 670	-5 364	-1 922	-4 954

[3]A minus sign indicates financial outflows.

Table 7-6. U.S. International Transactions—*Continued*

(Millions of dollars, seasonally adjusted.)

	Financial account—*Continued*												
	Foreign-owned assets in the United States, net [4]												
	Foreign official assets in the United States, net								Other foreign assets in the United States, net				
			U.S. government securities				U.S. liabilities reported by U.S. banks, not included elsewhere					U.S. securities other than Treasury securities	
Year and quarter	Total	Total	Total	U.S. Treasury securities	Other	Other U.S. government liabilities		Other foreign official assets	Total	Direct investment	U.S. Treasury securities		U.S. currency
1960	2 294	1 473	655	655	0	215	603	. . .	821	315	-364	282	. . .
1961	2 705	765	233	233	0	25	508	. . .	1 939	311	151	324	. . .
1962	1 911	1 270	1 409	1 410	-1	152	-291	. . .	641	346	-66	134	. . .
1963	3 217	1 986	816	803	12	429	742	. . .	1 231	231	-149	287	. . .
1964	3 643	1 660	432	434	-2	298	930	. . .	1 983	322	-146	-85	. . .
1965	742	134	-141	-134	-7	65	210	. . .	607	415	-131	-358	. . .
1966	3 661	-672	-1 527	-1 548	21	113	742	. . .	4 333	425	-356	906	. . .
1967	7 379	3 451	2 261	2 222	39	83	1 106	. . .	3 928	698	-135	1 016	. . .
1968	9 928	-774	-769	-798	29	-15	10	. . .	10 703	807	136	4 414	. . .
1969	12 702	-1 301	-2 343	-2 269	-74	251	792	. . .	14 002	1 263	-68	3 130	. . .
1970	6 359	6 908	9 439	9 411	28	-456	-2 075	. . .	-550	1 464	81	2 189	. . .
1971	22 970	26 879	26 570	26 578	-8	-510	819	. . .	-3 909	367	-24	2 289	. . .
1972	21 461	10 475	8 470	8 213	257	182	1 638	185	10 986	949	-39	4 507	. . .
1973	18 388	6 026	641	59	582	936	4 126	323	12 362	2 800	-216	4 041	. . .
1974	35 341	10 546	4 172	3 270	902	301	5 818	254	24 796	4 760	697	378	1 100
1975	17 170	7 027	5 563	4 658	905	1 517	-2 158	2 104	10 143	2 603	2 590	2 503	1 500
1976	38 018	17 693	9 892	9 319	573	4 027	969	2 205	20 326	4 347	2 783	1 284	1 500
1977	53 219	36 816	32 538	30 230	2 308	1 400	773	2 105	16 403	3 728	534	2 437	1 900
1978	67 036	33 678	24 221	23 555	666	2 476	5 551	1 430	33 358	7 897	2 178	2 254	3 000
1979	40 852	-13 665	-21 972	-22 435	463	-40	7 213	1 135	54 516	11 877	4 060	1 351	3 000
1980	62 612	15 497	11 895	9 708	2 187	615	-159	3 145	47 115	16 918	2 645	5 457	4 500
1981	86 232	4 960	6 322	5 019	1 303	-338	-3 670	2 646	81 272	25 195	2 927	6 905	3 200
1982	96 589	3 593	5 085	5 779	-694	605	-1 747	-350	92 997	12 635	7 027	6 085	4 000
1983	88 694	5 845	6 496	6 972	-476	602	545	-1 798	82 849	10 372	8 689	8 164	5 400
1984	117 752	3 140	4 703	4 690	13	739	555	-2 857	114 612	24 468	23 001	12 568	4 100
1985	146 115	-1 119	-1 139	-838	-301	844	645	-1 469	147 233	19 742	20 433	50 962	5 200
1986	230 009	35 648	33 150	34 364	-1 214	2 195	1 187	-884	194 360	35 420	3 809	70 969	4 100
1987	248 634	45 387	44 802	43 238	1 564	-2 326	3 918	-1 007	203 247	58 470	-7 643	42 120	5 400
1988	246 522	39 758	43 050	41 741	1 309	-467	-319	-2 506	206 764	57 735	20 239	26 353	5 800
1989	224 928	8 503	1 532	149	1 383	160	4 976	1 835	216 425	68 274	29 618	38 767	5 900
1990	141 571	33 910	30 243	29 576	667	1 868	3 385	-1 586	107 661	48 494	2 534	1 592	18 800
1991	110 808	17 389	16 147	14 846	1 301	1 367	-1 484	1 359	93 420	23 171	18 826	35 144	15 400
1992	170 663	40 477	22 403	18 454	3 949	2 191	16 571	-688	130 186	19 823	37 131	30 043	13 400
1993	282 040	71 753	53 014	48 952	4 062	1 313	14 841	2 585	210 287	51 362	24 381	80 092	18 900
1994	305 989	39 583	36 827	30 750	6 077	1 564	3 665	-2 473	266 406	46 121	34 274	56 971	23 400
1995	438 562	109 880	72 712	68 977	3 735	-105	34 008	3 265	328 682	57 776	77 249	77 249	12 300
1996	551 096	126 724	120 679	115 671	5 008	-982	5 704	1 323	424 372	86 502	147 022	103 272	17 362
1997	706 809	19 036	-2 161	-6 690	4 529	-881	22 286	-208	687 773	105 603	130 435	161 409	24 782
1998	423 569	-19 903	-3 589	-9 921	6 332	-3 326	-9 501	-3 487	443 472	179 045	28 581	156 315	16 622
1999	740 210	43 543	32 527	12 177	20 350	-2 863	12 964	915	696 667	289 444	-44 497	298 834	22 407
2000	1 026 139	37 724	30 676	-10 233	40 909	-1 825	5 746	3 127	988 415	321 274	-76 949	455 318	1 129
2001	765 531	5 104	31 665	10 745	20 920	-2 309	-29 978	5 726	760 427	151 581	-7 438	406 633	23 783
2002	706 983	94 860	73 521	43 144	30 377	137	17 594	3 608	612 123	39 633	96 217	291 492	21 513
1997													
1st quarter	173 005	27 763	23 105	22 351	754	-155	8 123	-3 310	145 242	28 626	29 053	38 490	3 484
2nd quarter	140 719	-6 019	-11 411	-12 373	962	-286	4 643	1 035	146 738	23 150	33 928	45 651	4 822
3rd quarter	167 223	23 474	10 316	7 604	2 712	-562	12 817	903	143 749	17 865	36 133	52 544	6 576
4th quarter	225 860	-26 182	-24 171	-24 272	101	122	-3 297	1 164	252 042	35 960	31 321	24 724	9 900
1998													
1st quarter	79 170	11 072	13 946	11 336	2 610	-954	-964	-956	68 098	19 759	-6 535	63 237	746
2nd quarter	155 055	-10 235	-20 051	-20 305	254	-760	9 744	832	165 290	20 391	21 814	56 146	2 349
3rd quarter	75 963	-46 640	-30 917	-32 823	1 906	-281	-12 948	-2 494	122 603	23 490	-5 082	6 628	7 277
4th quarter	113 381	25 900	33 433	31 871	1 562	-1 331	-5 333	-869	87 481	115 405	18 384	30 304	6 250
1999													
1st quarter	109 283	4 381	6 793	800	5 993	-1 244	-1 273	105	104 902	28 759	-13 327	49 157	2 440
2nd quarter	247 860	-757	-916	-6 708	5 792	-1 085	1 761	-517	248 617	140 759	-11 412	70 205	3 057
3rd quarter	156 858	12 625	14 798	12 963	1 835	-767	-1 617	211	144 233	50 758	3 685	86 202	4 697
4th quarter	226 210	27 294	11 852	5 122	6 730	233	14 093	1 116	198 916	69 169	-23 443	93 270	12 213
2000													
1st quarter	244 512	22 542	24 311	16 204	8 107	-430	-2 270	931	221 970	52 094	-15 199	129 306	-6 847
2nd quarter	242 481	6 548	6 334	-4 000	10 334	-899	209	904	235 933	91 669	-26 480	87 112	989
3rd quarter	240 954	12 952	5 271	-9 001	14 272	-185	7 554	312	228 002	79 979	-19 010	120 906	757
4th quarter	298 194	-4 318	-5 240	-13 436	8 196	-311	253	980	302 512	97 534	-16 260	117 994	6 230
2001													
1st quarter	313 923	4 290	2 547	-1 027	3 574	-601	1 341	1 003	309 633	44 924	-4 620	129 999	2 311
2nd quarter	213 471	-21 197	-10 866	-20 798	9 932	-1 154	-10 205	1 028	234 668	63 011	-14 688	113 548	2 772
3rd quarter	24 084	16 702	15 594	15 810	-216	-205	-675	1 988	7 382	14 962	-13 050	64 172	8 203
4th quarter	214 051	5 309	24 390	16 760	7 630	-349	-20 439	1 707	208 742	28 682	24 920	98 914	10 497
2002													
1st quarter	146 813	6 106	6 257	-1 039	7 296	-597	-280	726	140 707	10 607	11 789	74 461	4 525
2nd quarter	221 242	47 552	21 706	15 138	6 568	365	24 575	906	173 690	-456	14 218	104 187	7 183
3rd quarter	141 478	8 992	12 300	1 415	10 885	464	-4 607	835	132 486	14 199	57 505	45 880	2 556
4th quarter	197 448	32 210	33 258	27 630	5 628	-95	-2 094	1 141	165 238	15 281	12 705	66 964	7 249

[4]A minus sign indicates financial outflows or decrease in foreign official assets in the United States.
. . . = Not available.

Table 7-6. U.S. International Transactions—Continued

(Millions of dollars, seasonally adjusted.)

Year and quarter	Financial account—Continued				Balance on						
	Foreign-owned assets in the United States, net 4—Cont.		Statistical discrepancy 5								
	Other foreign assets in the United States, net—Cont.										
	U.S. liabilities		Total	Seasonal adjustment discrepancy	Goods	Services	Goods and services	Income	Goods, services, and income	Unilateral current transfers	Current account
	To unaffiliated foreigners reported by U.S. nonbanking concerns	Reported by U.S. banks not included elsewhere									
1960	-90	678	-1 019	0	4 892	-1 385	3 508	3 379	6 887	-4 062	2 824
1961	226	928	-989	0	5 571	-1 376	4 195	3 755	7 950	-4 127	3 822
1962	-110	336	-1 124	0	4 521	-1 151	3 370	4 294	7 664	-4 277	3 387
1963	-37	898	-360	0	5 224	-1 014	4 210	4 596	8 806	-4 392	4 414
1964	75	1 818	-907	0	6 801	-779	6 022	5 041	11 063	-4 240	6 823
1965	178	503	-457	0	4 951	-287	4 664	5 350	10 014	-4 583	5 431
1966	476	2 882	629	0	3 817	-877	2 940	5 047	7 987	-4 955	3 031
1967	584	1 765	-205	0	3 800	-1 196	2 604	5 274	7 878	-5 294	2 583
1968	1 475	3 871	438	0	635	-385	250	5 990	6 240	-5 629	611
1969	792	8 886	-1 516	0	607	-516	91	6 044	6 135	-5 735	399
1970	2 014	-6 298	-219	0	2 603	-349	2 254	6 233	8 487	-6 156	2 331
1971	369	-6 911	-9 779	0	-2 260	957	-1 303	7 272	5 969	-7 402	-1 433
1972	815	4 754	-1 879	0	-6 416	973	-5 443	8 192	2 749	-8 544	-5 795
1973	1 035	4 702	-2 654	0	911	989	1 900	12 153	14 053	-6 913	7 140
1974	1 844	16 017	-2 558	0	-5 505	1 213	-4 292	15 503	11 211	-9 249	1 962
1975	319	628	4 417	0	8 903	3 501	12 404	12 787	25 191	-7 075	18 116
1976	-578	10 990	8 955	0	-9 483	3 401	-6 082	16 063	9 981	-5 686	4 295
1977	1 086	6 719	-4 099	0	-31 091	3 845	-27 246	18 137	-9 109	-5 226	-14 335
1978	1 889	16 141	9 236	0	-33 927	4 164	-29 763	20 408	-9 355	-5 788	-15 143
1979	1 621	32 607	24 349	0	-27 568	3 003	-24 565	30 873	6 308	-6 593	-285
1980	6 852	10 743	20 886	0	-25 500	6 093	-19 407	30 073	10 666	-8 349	2 317
1981	917	42 128	21 792	0	-28 023	11 852	-16 172	32 903	16 731	-11 702	5 030
1982	-2 383	65 633	36 630	0	-36 485	12 329	-24 156	35 164	11 008	-16 544	-5 536
1983	-118	50 342	16 162	0	-67 102	9 335	-57 767	36 386	-21 381	-17 310	-38 691
1984	16 626	33 849	16 733	0	-112 492	3 419	-109 073	35 063	-74 010	-20 335	-94 344
1985	9 851	41 045	16 478	0	-122 173	294	-121 880	25 723	-96 157	-21 998	-118 155
1986	3 325	76 737	28 590	0	-145 081	6 543	-138 538	15 494	-123 044	-24 132	-147 177
1987	18 363	86 537	-9 048	0	-159 557	7 874	-151 684	14 293	-137 391	-23 265	-160 655
1988	32 893	63 744	-19 289	0	-126 959	12 393	-114 566	18 687	-95 879	-25 274	-121 153
1989	22 086	51 780	49 605	0	-117 749	24 607	-93 142	19 824	-73 318	-26 169	-99 486
1990	45 133	-3 824	25 208	0	-111 034	30 173	-80 861	28 550	-52 311	-26 654	-78 965
1991	-3 115	3 994	-45 688	0	-76 937	45 802	-31 135	24 130	-7 005	10 752	3 747
1992	13 573	16 216	-47 683	0	-96 897	58 712	-38 185	23 325	-14 860	-33 154	-48 013
1993	10 489	25 063	1 799	0	-132 451	63 285	-69 166	24 290	-44 876	-37 113	-81 989
1994	1 302	104 338	-10 532	0	-165 831	68 642	-97 189	17 094	-80 095	-37 583	-117 678
1995	59 637	30 176	19 958	0	-174 170	79 101	-95 069	25 040	-70 029	-35 188	-105 217
1996	53 736	16 478	-19 316	0	-191 000	88 131	-102 869	24 528	-78 341	-38 862	-117 203
1997	116 518	149 026	-90 482	0	-198 119	91 072	-107 047	20 655	-86 392	-41 292	-127 684
1998	23 140	39 769	129 691	0	-246 696	83 543	-163 153	6 897	-156 256	-48 435	-204 691
1999	76 247	54 232	59 119	0	-346 022	84 821	-261 201	17 110	-244 091	-46 755	-290 846
2000	170 672	116 971	-44 084	0	-452 423	77 039	-375 384	19 605	-355 779	-55 679	-411 458
2001	67 489	118 379	-20 785	0	-427 215	69 396	-357 819	10 689	-347 130	-46 615	-393 745
2002	72 142	91 126	-45 852	0	-482 872	64 834	-418 038	-3 970	-422 008	-58 853	-480 861
1997											
1st quarter	25 055	20 534	11 740	5 971	-50 099	22 271	-27 828	4 401	-23 427	-8 899	-32 326
2nd quarter	6 461	32 726	-20 302	-1 598	-47 856	23 672	-24 184	6 941	-17 243	-9 285	-26 528
3rd quarter	25 550	5 081	-17 702	-11 412	-48 495	22 989	-25 506	5 362	-20 144	-9 772	-29 916
4th quarter	59 452	90 685	-64 214	7 043	-51 669	22 139	-29 530	3 952	-25 578	-13 336	-38 914
1998											
1st quarter	39 833	-48 942	34 759	6 094	-55 374	21 733	-33 641	3 709	-29 932	-10 868	-40 800
2nd quarter	30 722	33 868	31 738	-1 381	-63 210	21 902	-41 308	2 994	-38 314	-11 171	-49 485
3rd quarter	14 976	75 314	38 219	-11 203	-63 929	19 334	-44 595	-410	-45 005	-11 954	-56 959
4th quarter	-62 391	-20 471	24 980	6 495	-64 183	20 569	-43 614	605	-43 009	-14 441	-57 450
1999											
1st quarter	51 307	-13 434	34 488	3 899	-73 590	21 508	-52 082	3 688	-48 394	-10 899	-59 293
2nd quarter	16 928	29 080	2 551	1 316	-84 570	21 431	-63 139	4 855	-58 284	-11 316	-69 600
3rd quarter	-8 777	7 668	47 810	-10 629	-92 289	20 859	-71 430	3 255	-68 175	-11 092	-79 267
4th quarter	16 789	30 918	-25 735	5 409	-95 573	21 024	-74 549	5 317	-69 232	-13 449	-82 681
2000											
1st quarter	72 433	-9 817	65 370	5 005	-106 191	19 473	-86 718	3 820	-82 898	-12 123	-95 021
2nd quarter	28 796	53 847	-35 114	187	-111 730	20 596	-91 134	4 654	-86 480	-12 646	-99 126
3rd quarter	16 914	28 456	-45 684	-8 423	-115 801	17 861	-97 940	2 853	-95 087	-13 480	-108 567
4th quarter	52 529	44 485	-28 646	3 241	-118 701	19 103	-99 598	8 279	-91 319	-17 435	-108 754
2001											
1st quarter	111 565	25 454	-17 428	6 244	-112 726	19 286	-93 440	930	-92 510	-11 494	-104 004
2nd quarter	752	69 273	-21 034	799	-107 170	17 714	-89 456	813	-88 643	-11 321	-99 964
3rd quarter	-22 623	-44 282	42 485	-8 244	-106 321	17 278	-89 043	-3 337	-92 380	-11 256	-103 636
4th quarter	-22 205	67 934	-24 809	1 200	-100 998	15 116	-85 882	12 284	-73 598	-12 542	-86 140
2002											
1st quarter	46 771	-7 446	-4 581	8 579	-106 033	15 976	-90 057	-733	-90 790	-15 938	-106 728
2nd quarter	24 610	23 948	30 438	2 091	-121 286	16 398	-104 888	-4 458	-109 346	-13 481	-122 827
3rd quarter	-8 102	20 448	-48 102	-12 409	-123 312	16 332	-106 980	-1 747	-108 727	-13 997	-122 724
4th quarter	8 863	54 176	-23 602	1 744	-132 241	16 125	-116 116	2 966	-113 150	-15 436	-128 586

4A minus sign indicates financial outflows or decrease in foreign official assets in the United States.
5Sum of credits and debits with the sign reversed.

Table 7-7. International Investment Position of the United States at Year-End

(Millions of dollars.)

Year	U.S. net international investment position — Direct investment at current cost	Direct investment at market value	Total, direct investment at current cost	Total, direct investment at market value	Official reserve assets	Other U.S. government assets	Direct investment — Current cost	Market value	Foreign bonds	Foreign corporate stocks	U.S. nonbank claims	U.S. bank claims
1976	164 832	...	456 964	...	44 094	44 978	222 283	...	34 704	9 453	20 317	81 135
1977	171 440	...	512 278	...	53 376	48 567	246 078	...	39 329	10 110	22 256	92 562
1978	206 423	...	621 227	...	69 450	53 187	285 005	...	42 148	11 236	29 385	130 816
1979	316 926	...	786 701	...	143 260	58 851	336 301	...	41 966	14 803	34 491	157 029
1980	360 838	...	929 806	...	171 412	65 573	388 072	...	43 524	18 930	38 429	203 866
1981	339 767	...	1 001 667	...	124 568	70 893	407 804	...	45 675	16 467	42 752	293 508
1982	328 954	235 947	1 108 436	961 015	143 445	76 903	374 059	226 638	56 604	17 442	35 405	404 578
1983	298 304	257 393	1 210 974	1 129 673	123 110	81 664	355 643	274 342	58 569	26 154	131 329	434 505
1984	160 695	134 088	1 204 900	1 127 132	105 040	86 945	348 342	270 574	62 810	25 994	130 138	445 631
1985	54 343	96 886	1 287 396	1 302 712	117 930	89 792	371 036	386 352	75 020	44 383	141 872	447 363
1986	-36 209	100 782	1 469 396	1 594 652	139 875	91 850	404 818	530 074	85 724	72 399	167 392	507 338
1987	-80 007	50 529	1 646 527	1 758 711	162 370	90 681	478 062	590 246	93 889	94 700	177 368	549 457
1988	-178 470	10 466	1 829 665	2 008 365	144 179	87 892	513 761	692 461	104 187	128 662	197 757	653 227
1989	-259 506	-46 987	2 070 868	2 350 235	168 714	86 643	553 093	832 460	116 949	197 345	234 307	713 817
1990	-245 347	-164 495	2 178 978	2 294 085	174 664	84 344	616 655	731 762	144 717	197 596	265 315	695 687
1991	-309 259	-260 819	2 286 456	2 470 629	159 223	81 422	643 364	827 537	176 774	278 976	256 295	690 402
1992	-431 198	-452 305	2 331 696	2 466 496	147 435	83 022	663 830	798 630	200 817	314 266	254 303	668 023
1993	-306 956	-144 268	2 753 648	3 091 421	164 945	83 382	723 526	1 061 299	309 666	543 862	242 022	686 245
1994	-311 882	-123 736	2 998 633	3 326 650	163 394	83 908	786 565	1 114 582	321 208	627 460	322 980	693 118
1995	-495 966	-343 340	3 451 983	3 930 269	176 061	85 064	885 506	1 363 792	392 827	776 809	367 567	768 149
1996	-521 545	-386 514	4 012 746	4 631 276	160 739	86 123	989 810	1 608 340	465 057	1 002 928	450 578	857 511
1997	-833 158	-835 208	4 567 906	5 379 128	134 836	86 198	1 068 063	1 879 285	543 396	1 207 787	545 524	982 102
1998	-918 679	-1 094 090	5 080 606	6 174 518	146 006	86 768	1 196 021	2 279 601	578 009	1 474 986	588 322	1 020 826
1999	-797 559	-1 068 759	5 965 148	7 390 432	136 418	84 227	1 414 355	2 839 639	521 620	2 003 726	704 517	1 100 285
2000	-1 387 741	-1 588 164	6 229 361	7 393 650	128 400	85 168	1 529 725	2 694 014	532 504	1 852 856	836 559	1 264 149
2001	-1 979 906	-2 314 271	6 187 410	6 891 251	129 961	85 654	1 598 072	2 301 913	502 061	1 612 673	835 780	1 423 209
2002	-2 387 211	-2 605 155	6 189 191	6 473 562	158 602	85 686	1 751 852	2 036 223	501 784	1 345 192	890 961	1 455 114

Year	Foreign-owned assets in the United States — Total, direct investment at current cost	Total, direct investment at market value	Foreign official assets	Direct investment in the United States — Current cost	Market value	U.S. Treasury securities	U.S. currency	Corporate and other bonds	Corporate stocks	U.S. nonbank liabilities	U.S. bank liabilities
1976	292 132	...	104 445	47 528	...	7 028	11 792	11 964	42 949	12 961	53 465
1977	340 838	...	140 867	55 413	...	7 562	13 656	11 456	39 779	11 921	60 184
1978	414 804	...	173 057	68 976	...	8 910	16 569	11 457	42 097	16 019	77 719
1979	469 775	...	159 852	88 579	...	14 210	19 552	10 269	48 318	18 669	110 326
1980	568 968	...	176 062	127 105	...	16 113	24 079	9 545	64 569	30 426	121 069
1981	661 000	...	180 425	164 623	...	18 505	27 295	10 694	64 391	30 606	165 361
1982	779 482	725 068	189 109	184 842	130 428	25 758	31 265	16 709	76 279	27 532	227 988
1983	912 670	872 280	194 468	193 708	153 318	33 846	36 776	17 454	96 357	61 731	278 330
1984	1 044 205	993 044	199 678	223 538	172 377	62 121	40 797	32 421	96 056	77 415	312 179
1985	1 233 053	1 205 826	202 482	247 223	219 996	87 954	46 036	82 290	125 578	86 993	354 497
1986	1 505 605	1 493 870	241 226	284 701	272 966	96 078	50 122	140 863	168 940	90 703	432 972
1987	1 726 534	1 708 182	283 058	334 552	316 200	82 588	55 584	166 089	175 643	110 187	518 833
1988	2 008 135	1 997 899	322 036	401 766	391 530	100 877	61 261	191 314	200 978	144 548	585 355
1989	2 330 374	2 397 222	341 746	467 886	534 734	166 541	67 118	231 673	251 191	167 093	637 126
1990	2 424 325	2 458 580	373 293	505 346	539 601	152 452	85 933	238 903	221 741	213 406	633 251
1991	2 595 715	2 731 448	398 538	533 404	669 137	170 295	101 317	274 136	271 872	208 908	637 245
1992	2 762 894	2 918 801	437 263	540 270	696 177	197 739	114 804	299 287	300 160	220 666	652 705
1993	3 060 604	3 235 689	509 422	593 313	768 398	221 501	133 734	355 822	340 627	229 038	677 147
1994	3 310 515	3 450 386	535 227	617 982	757 853	235 684	157 185	368 077	371 618	239 817	784 925
1995	3 947 949	4 273 609	682 873	680 066	1 005 726	330 210	169 484	459 080	510 769	300 424	815 043
1996	4 534 291	5 017 790	820 823	745 619	1 229 118	440 832	186 846	539 308	625 805	346 810	828 248
1997	5 401 064	6 214 336	873 716	824 136	1 637 408	550 613	211 628	618 837	893 888	459 407	968 839
1998	6 009 617	7 268 608	896 174	920 044	2 179 035	562 036	228 250	724 619	1 178 824	485 675	1 013 995
1999	6 762 707	8 459 191	951 088	1 101 709	2 798 193	462 761	250 657	825 175	1 526 116	578 046	1 067 155
2000	7 617 102	8 981 814	1 014 467	1 418 523	2 783 235	400 983	251 786	1 076 002	1 547 701	738 904	1 168 736
2001	8 167 316	9 205 522	1 027 194	1 514 374	2 552 580	389 000	275 569	1 391 616	1 464 089	799 120	1 306 354
2002	8 576 402	9 078 717	1 132 530	1 504 428	2 006 743	503 630	297 082	1 690 296	1 170 819	870 259	1 407 358

. . . = Not available.

Table 7-8. U.S. Exports and Imports of Goods and Services

(Balance of payments basis; millions of dollars, seasonally adjusted.)

Year and month	Goods and services			Goods			Services		
	Exports	Imports	Balance	Exports	Imports	Balance	Exports	Imports	Balance
1960	25 940	22 432	3 508	19 650	14 758	4 892	6 290	7 674	-1 384
1961	26 403	22 208	4 195	20 108	14 537	5 571	6 295	7 671	-1 376
1962	27 722	24 352	3 370	20 781	16 260	4 521	6 941	8 092	-1 151
1963	29 620	25 410	4 210	22 272	17 048	5 224	7 348	8 362	-1 014
1964	33 341	27 319	6 022	25 501	18 700	6 801	7 840	8 619	-779
1965	35 285	30 621	4 664	26 461	21 510	4 951	8 824	9 111	-287
1966	38 926	35 987	2 939	29 310	25 493	3 817	9 616	10 494	-878
1967	41 333	38 729	2 604	30 666	26 866	3 800	10 667	11 863	-1 196
1968	45 543	45 293	250	33 626	32 991	635	11 917	12 302	-385
1969	49 220	49 129	91	36 414	35 807	607	12 806	13 322	-516
1970	56 640	54 386	2 254	42 469	39 866	2 603	14 171	14 520	-349
1971	59 677	60 979	-1 302	43 319	45 579	-2 260	16 358	15 400	958
1972	67 222	72 665	-5 443	49 381	55 797	-6 416	17 841	16 868	973
1973	91 242	89 342	1 900	71 410	70 499	911	19 832	18 843	989
1974	120 897	125 190	-4 293	98 306	103 811	-5 505	22 591	21 379	1 212
1975	132 585	120 181	12 404	107 088	98 185	8 903	25 497	21 996	3 501
1976	142 716	148 798	-6 082	114 745	124 228	-9 483	27 971	24 570	3 401
1977	152 301	179 547	-27 246	120 816	151 907	-31 091	31 485	27 640	3 845
1978	178 428	208 191	-29 763	142 075	176 002	-33 927	36 353	32 189	4 164
1979	224 131	248 696	-24 565	184 439	212 007	-27 568	39 692	36 689	3 003
1980	271 834	291 241	-19 407	224 250	249 750	-25 500	47 584	41 491	6 093
1981	294 398	310 570	-16 172	237 044	265 067	-28 023	57 354	45 503	11 851
1982	275 236	299 391	-24 156	211 157	247 642	-36 485	64 079	51 749	12 329
1983	266 106	323 874	-57 767	201 799	268 901	-67 102	64 307	54 973	9 335
1984	291 094	400 166	-109 072	219 926	332 418	-112 492	71 168	67 748	3 420
1985	289 070	410 950	-121 880	215 915	338 088	-122 173	73 155	72 862	294
1986	310 033	448 572	-138 538	223 344	368 425	-145 081	86 689	80 147	6 543
1987	348 869	500 552	-151 684	250 208	409 765	-159 557	98 661	90 787	7 874
1988	431 149	545 715	-114 566	320 230	447 189	-126 959	110 919	98 526	12 393
1989	487 003	580 144	-93 141	359 916	477 665	-117 749	127 087	102 479	24 607
1990	535 233	616 093	-80 860	387 401	498 434	-111 033	147 832	117 659	30 173
1991	578 344	609 479	-31 135	414 083	491 020	-76 937	164 261	118 459	45 802
1992	616 455	654 639	-38 186	439 631	536 528	-96 898	176 824	118 111	58 712
1993	642 376	711 542	-69 166	456 943	589 394	-132 451	185 433	122 148	63 285
1994	702 622	799 811	-97 188	502 859	668 690	-165 830	199 763	131 121	68 642
1995	793 725	888 794	-95 069	575 204	749 374	-174 170	218 521	139 420	79 101
1996	850 877	953 746	-102 869	612 113	803 113	-191 000	238 764	150 633	88 131
1997	933 873	1 040 920	-107 048	678 366	876 485	-198 120	255 507	164 435	91 072
1998	932 558	1 095 711	-163 153	670 416	917 112	-246 696	262 142	178 599	83 543
1999	957 146	1 219 383	-261 202	683 965	1 029 987	-346 023	281 508	196 687	84 821
2000	1 070 054	1 445 438	-375 384	771 994	1 224 417	-452 423	298 060	221 021	77 039
2001	1 007 580	1 365 399	-357 819	718 712	1 145 927	-427 215	288 868	219 472	69 396
2002	974 107	1 392 145	-418 038	681 874	1 164 746	-482 872	292 233	227 399	64 834
2000									
January	85 362	111 965	-26 604	61 412	94 622	-33 211	23 950	17 343	6 607
February	85 745	114 798	-29 054	61 315	96 840	-35 526	24 430	17 958	6 472
March	87 059	118 121	-31 062	62 442	99 896	-37 454	24 617	18 225	6 392
April	88 484	117 507	-29 023	63 128	99 523	-36 395	25 356	17 984	7 372
May	87 541	118 107	-30 566	62 847	99 936	-37 089	24 694	18 171	6 523
June	90 298	121 844	-31 547	65 200	103 446	-38 247	25 098	18 398	6 700
July	89 776	122 135	-32 359	64 987	103 567	-38 580	24 789	18 568	6 221
August	91 872	122 684	-30 812	66 987	104 029	-37 042	24 885	18 655	6 230
September	91 719	126 487	-34 768	66 847	107 027	-40 180	24 872	19 460	5 412
October	91 118	125 415	-34 298	66 008	106 665	-40 658	25 110	18 750	6 360
November	90 934	123 509	-32 575	65 796	104 645	-38 849	25 138	18 864	6 274
December	90 147	122 872	-32 725	65 026	104 220	-39 194	25 121	18 652	6 469
2001									
January	90 206	123 942	-33 736	65 132	104 935	-39 803	25 074	19 007	6 067
February	90 277	118 141	-27 865	65 401	99 779	-34 379	24 876	18 362	6 514
March	88 785	120 625	-31 840	63 612	102 156	-38 544	25 173	18 469	6 704
April	86 822	118 174	-31 351	61 966	98 967	-37 000	24 856	19 207	5 649
May	87 089	115 730	-28 641	62 371	96 710	-34 339	24 718	19 020	5 698
June	85 246	114 710	-29 464	60 119	95 950	-35 831	25 127	18 760	6 367
July	83 085	113 048	-29 963	58 399	94 335	-35 936	24 686	18 713	5 973
August	83 516	111 850	-28 334	58 663	93 003	-34 340	24 853	18 847	6 006
September	77 298	108 045	-30 747	55 464	91 509	-36 045	21 834	16 536	5 298
October	78 235	109 104	-30 869	56 263	92 088	-35 825	21 972	17 016	4 956
November	78 552	107 628	-29 076	55 999	90 031	-34 032	22 553	17 597	4 956
December	78 467	104 406	-25 939	55 322	86 463	-31 141	23 145	17 943	5 202
2002									
January	78 580	106 879	-28 299	55 228	88 723	-33 495	23 352	18 156	5 196
February	78 579	109 628	-31 049	54 988	90 864	-35 876	23 591	18 764	4 827
March	79 286	109 990	-30 704	55 083	91 744	-36 661	24 203	18 246	5 957
April	80 674	114 899	-34 225	56 871	96 644	-39 773	23 803	18 255	5 548
May	81 050	116 147	-35 097	56 848	97 678	-40 830	24 202	18 469	5 733
June	81 974	117 537	-35 563	57 702	98 385	-40 683	24 272	19 152	5 120
July	82 954	117 023	-34 069	58 638	97 942	-39 304	24 316	19 081	5 235
August	82 566	118 815	-36 249	57 870	99 940	-42 070	24 696	18 875	5 821
September	82 294	118 957	-36 663	57 807	99 745	-41 938	24 487	19 212	5 275
October	82 159	117 314	-35 154	57 301	97 949	-40 647	24 858	19 365	5 493
November	82 917	121 545	-38 629	57 765	101 911	-44 147	25 152	19 634	5 518
December	81 075	123 406	-42 332	55 774	103 220	-47 447	25 301	20 186	5 115

Table 7-9. U.S. Exports of Goods by End-Use and Advanced Technology Categories

(Census basis, except as noted; billions of dollars, seasonally adjusted, except where noted.)

| Year and month | Total exports of goods | | | Principal end-use category | | | | | | | Advanced technology products [1] |
| | Total: Balance of payments basis | Net adjustments | Total: Census basis | Foods, feeds, and beverages | Industrial supplies and materials | | Capital goods, except automotive | Automotive vehicles, engines, and parts | Consumer goods (nonfood) except automotive | Other goods | |
					Total	Petroleum and products					
1978	142.08	-1.59	143.66	25.68	39.59	1.95	47.50	15.16	11.38	. . .	. . .
1979	184.44	2.64	181.80	30.50	58.50	2.44	60.18	17.90	13.98	. . .	. . .
1980	224.25	3.55	220.70	36.28	72.09	3.57	76.28	17.44	17.75	. . .	. . .
1981	237.04	3.31	233.74	38.84	70.19	4.56	84.17	19.69	17.70	. . .	. . .
1982	211.16	-1.12	212.28	32.20	64.05	6.87	76.50	17.23	16.13	. . .	. . .
1983	201.80	0.09	201.71	32.09	58.94	5.59	71.66	18.46	14.93	. . .	. . .
1984	219.93	1.18	218.74	32.20	64.12	5.43	77.01	22.42	15.09	. . .	. . .
1985	215.92	3.29	212.62	24.57	61.16	5.71	79.32	24.95	14.59	. . .	. . .
1986	223.34	-3.13	226.47	23.52	64.72	4.43	82.82	25.10	16.73	. . .	. . .
1987	250.21	-3.70	253.90	25.23	70.05	4.63	92.71	27.58	20.31	. . .	. . .
1988	320.23	-3.11	323.34	33.77	90.02	4.48	119.10	33.40	26.98	. . .	. . .
1989	359.92	-3.08	363.00	36.34	98.36	6.46	136.94	35.05	36.01	. . .	. . .
1990	387.40	-5.57	392.97	35.18	105.55	8.36	153.07	36.07	43.60	20.73	. . .
1991	414.08	-7.77	421.85	35.79	109.69	8.40	166.72	39.72	46.65	23.66	. . .
1992	439.63	-8.54	448.17	40.34	109.59	7.62	176.50	46.71	51.31	24.39	. . .
1993	456.94	-7.92	464.86	40.59	111.89	7.49	182.85	51.35	54.56	23.89	. . .
1994	502.86	-9.77	512.63	41.96	121.55	6.97	205.82	57.31	59.86	26.50	. . .
1995	575.20	-9.54	584.74	50.47	146.37	8.10	234.46	61.26	64.31	28.72	. . .
1996	612.11	-12.96	625.08	55.53	147.98	9.63	253.99	64.24	70.11	33.85	. . .
1997	678.37	-10.82	689.18	51.51	158.32	10.42	295.87	73.30	77.96	33.51	. . .
1998	670.42	-11.72	682.14	46.40	148.31	8.08	299.87	72.39	80.29	35.44	. . .
1999	683.97	-11.83	695.80	45.98	147.52	8.62	310.79	75.26	80.92	35.32	. . .
2000	771.99	-9.92	781.92	47.87	172.62	12.01	356.93	80.36	89.38	34.77	227.39
2001	718.71	-10.39	729.10	49.41	160.10	10.64	321.71	75.44	88.33	34.11	199.63
2002	681.87	-11.23	693.10	49.62	156.84	10.34	290.50	78.94	84.36	32.85	178.57
1999											
January	55.17	-1.10	56.27	3.67	11.36	0.57	25.60	6.13	6.59	2.93	. . .
February	54.39	-1.13	55.52	3.66	11.36	0.49	24.71	6.19	6.60	3.02	. . .
March	54.67	-1.08	55.75	3.63	11.50	0.56	25.18	6.00	6.51	2.94	. . .
April	55.50	-1.05	56.55	3.77	11.71	0.67	25.24	6.36	6.72	2.77	. . .
May	55.31	-1.19	56.50	3.78	11.76	0.69	25.18	6.16	6.54	3.10	. . .
June	55.28	-1.15	56.42	3.92	11.83	0.69	24.84	6.16	6.61	3.07	. . .
July	56.31	-0.96	57.27	3.88	11.72	0.67	25.69	6.32	6.74	2.93	. . .
August	57.81	-0.90	58.71	3.97	12.46	0.77	26.60	6.39	6.55	2.73	. . .
September	58.88	-1.18	60.05	4.12	13.13	0.77	26.52	6.27	6.97	3.04	. . .
October	59.22	-0.81	60.04	3.97	13.18	0.89	26.81	6.29	6.89	2.90	. . .
November	59.79	-0.42	60.21	3.79	13.81	0.86	26.49	6.35	6.95	2.81	. . .
December	61.63	-0.88	62.51	3.83	13.73	1.01	27.95	6.65	7.27	3.08	. . .
2000											
January	61.41	-1.13	62.54	3.88	13.71	0.95	27.86	6.99	7.16	2.95	16.66
February	61.32	-1.10	62.41	3.77	14.02	0.78	27.11	6.93	7.37	3.21	16.44
March	62.44	-0.69	63.14	3.96	14.70	1.02	27.40	6.97	7.38	2.73	18.55
April	63.13	-0.69	63.81	3.93	13.87	0.96	29.40	6.60	7.33	2.68	18.12
May	62.85	-0.79	63.63	3.99	13.72	0.87	29.34	6.64	7.18	2.77	18.62
June	65.20	-0.80	66.00	4.06	14.15	0.81	30.31	6.81	7.69	2.98	20.18
July	64.99	-0.72	65.71	4.12	14.09	0.87	30.82	6.44	7.49	2.76	18.26
August	66.99	-0.78	67.76	4.23	14.68	1.07	31.53	6.77	7.68	2.87	19.76
September	66.85	-0.72	67.56	4.09	15.19	1.12	31.20	6.59	7.72	2.78	20.12
October	66.01	-0.84	66.85	4.01	14.96	1.42	30.82	6.66	7.36	3.03	20.26
November	65.80	-0.89	66.69	3.94	15.09	1.10	30.71	6.48	7.49	2.99	19.54
December	65.03	-0.79	65.82	3.90	14.45	1.06	30.44	6.48	7.53	3.02	20.91
2001											
January	65.13	-0.85	65.98	3.98	14.31	0.95	30.94	6.19	7.66	2.90	18.29
February	65.40	-0.75	66.15	4.14	14.41	0.82	31.02	6.09	7.78	2.71	18.06
March	63.61	-0.77	64.38	4.30	14.26	0.88	29.17	6.22	7.70	2.73	20.63
April	61.97	-0.69	62.66	4.26	14.02	0.95	27.76	6.24	7.68	2.71	16.54
May	62.37	-1.05	63.42	4.08	13.91	0.93	28.15	6.35	7.88	3.04	17.25
June	60.12	-0.91	61.03	4.01	13.40	0.88	26.61	6.57	7.28	3.15	17.72
July	58.40	-1.03	59.43	4.03	12.88	0.83	26.06	6.23	7.29	2.95	14.87
August	58.66	-0.77	59.43	4.20	13.14	1.00	25.56	6.44	7.08	3.01	15.75
September	55.46	-0.87	56.34	4.04	12.27	0.79	24.06	6.38	6.92	2.66	14.80
October	56.26	-0.94	57.20	4.13	12.65	0.82	24.33	6.29	6.99	2.82	15.68
November	56.00	-0.88	56.88	4.15	12.40	0.78	24.27	6.40	6.92	2.75	14.92
December	55.32	-0.88	56.21	4.07	12.47	1.01	23.79	6.04	7.16	2.68	15.11
2002											
January	55.23	-0.73	55.96	4.23	12.38	0.76	23.78	6.21	6.89	2.48	13.61
February	54.99	-0.88	55.87	4.21	12.26	0.74	23.54	6.36	6.93	2.57	12.96
March	55.08	-1.06	56.15	3.94	12.37	0.73	24.04	6.35	6.79	2.66	17.10
April	56.87	-0.82	57.69	3.95	13.04	0.83	24.17	6.67	7.09	2.77	14.40
May	56.85	-1.25	58.10	3.99	13.25	0.79	24.22	6.73	6.93	2.98	14.76
June	57.70	-0.88	58.58	4.27	13.26	0.75	24.71	6.67	7.09	2.59	16.41
July	58.64	-0.92	59.56	4.31	13.21	0.83	25.15	6.89	7.22	2.79	14.86
August	57.87	-1.01	58.88	4.11	13.36	0.96	24.73	6.77	7.05	2.86	15.13
September	57.81	-0.86	58.66	4.06	13.31	0.88	24.81	6.69	7.07	2.73	14.84
October	57.30	-0.99	58.29	3.89	13.23	0.95	24.51	6.65	7.15	2.85	15.73
November	57.77	-0.93	58.69	4.31	13.55	0.94	24.37	6.50	7.19	2.78	14.62
December	55.77	-0.91	56.68	4.36	13.63	1.19	22.46	6.48	6.97	2.78	14.15

[1]Not seasonally adjusted.
. . . = Not available.

Table 7-10. U.S. Imports of Goods by End-Use and Advanced Technology Categories

(Census basis, except as noted; billions of dollars, seasonally adjusted, except where noted.)

Year and month	Total exports of goods			Principal end-use category							Advanced technology products [1]
	Total: Balance of payments basis	Net adjustments	Total: Census basis	Foods, feeds, and beverages	Industrial supplies and materials		Capital goods, except automotive	Automotive vehicles, engines, and parts	Consumer goods (nonfood) except automotive	Other goods	
					Total	Petroleum and products					
1978	176.00	1.31	174.69	15.84	79.26	...	19.29	25.11	29.40	...	...
1979	212.01	2.60	209.41	18.01	102.67	...	24.49	26.51	31.22	...	...
1980	249.75	4.23	245.52	18.55	124.96	...	30.72	28.13	34.22	...	...
1981	265.07	3.76	261.31	18.53	131.10	...	36.86	30.80	38.30	...	...
1982	247.64	3.70	243.94	17.47	107.82	...	38.22	34.26	39.66	...	...
1983	268.90	7.18	261.72	18.56	105.63	...	42.61	42.04	46.59	...	...
1984	332.42	1.91	330.51	21.92	122.72	...	60.15	56.77	61.19	...	...
1985	338.09	1.71	336.38	21.89	112.48	...	60.81	65.21	66.43	...	...
1986	368.43	2.75	365.67	24.40	101.37	...	71.86	78.25	79.43	...	...
1987	409.77	3.48	406.28	24.81	110.67	...	84.77	85.17	88.82	...	...
1988	447.19	5.26	441.93	24.93	118.06	...	101.79	87.95	96.42	...	...
1989	477.37	3.72	473.65	25.08	132.40	...	112.45	87.38	102.26	...	...
1990	498.34	2.36	495.98	26.65	143.41	62.16	116.04	87.69	105.29	16.09	...
1991	490.98	2.53	488.45	26.21	131.38	51.78	120.80	84.94	107.78	15.94	...
1992	536.46	3.80	532.66	27.61	138.64	51.60	134.25	91.79	122.66	17.71	...
1993	589.44	8.78	580.66	27.87	145.61	51.50	152.37	102.42	134.02	18.39	...
1994	668.59	5.33	663.26	27.87	145.61	51.28	152.37	102.42	134.02	18.39	...
1995	749.57	6.03	743.54	33.18	181.85	56.16	221.43	123.80	159.91	23.39	...
1996	803.33	8.04	796.77	35.74	204.43	72.75	228.07	128.95	172.00	26.11	...
1997	876.37	6.66	869.70	39.69	213.77	71.77	253.28	139.81	193.81	29.34	...
1998	917.18	5.28	911.90	41.24	200.14	50.90	269.56	149.05	216.52	35.39	...
1999	1 029.99	5.37	1 024.62	43.60	221.39	67.81	295.72	178.96	241.91	43.04	...
2000	1 224.42	6.40	1 218.02	45.98	298.98	120.28	347.03	195.88	281.83	48.33	222.08
2001	1 145.93	4.93	1 141.00	46.64	273.87	103.59	297.99	189.78	284.29	48.42	195.18
2002	1 164.75	3.38	1 161.37	49.69	267.68	103.51	283.32	203.74	307.85	49.08	195.15
1999											
January	77.97	0.19	77.78	3.56	15.32	3.43	22.96	13.78	18.84	3.33	...
February	80.06	0.22	79.84	3.56	15.28	3.31	23.59	14.38	19.71	3.32	...
March	79.80	0.23	79.57	3.46	15.99	3.79	23.18	14.41	18.95	3.58	...
April	81.08	0.28	80.80	3.59	17.01	4.78	23.50	13.81	19.41	3.48	...
May	83.43	0.23	83.20	3.67	17.93	5.61	24.21	14.68	19.21	3.49	...
June	86.15	0.28	85.87	3.71	18.12	5.56	25.19	15.30	19.99	3.56	...
July	87.38	0.20	87.19	3.62	18.70	6.11	25.42	15.34	20.58	3.53	...
August	88.43	0.59	87.84	3.63	19.97	6.75	24.82	15.14	20.53	3.75	...
September	89.48	0.97	88.51	3.67	20.30	7.05	24.97	15.40	20.50	3.68	...
October	90.46	0.53	89.92	3.61	20.59	7.15	25.59	15.11	21.18	3.85	...
November	91.91	0.93	90.98	3.71	20.87	7.11	25.87	15.41	21.40	3.72	...
December	93.85	0.73	93.12	3.81	21.31	7.17	26.41	16.20	21.62	3.76	...
2000											
January	94.62	0.72	93.90	3.67	21.70	7.95	26.24	16.73	21.72	3.84	14.67
February	96.84	0.94	95.90	3.69	23.53	9.28	26.54	16.09	22.03	4.02	15.44
March	99.90	0.72	99.18	3.87	24.71	9.74	27.33	16.49	22.88	3.90	17.63
April	99.52	0.28	99.24	3.83	23.46	9.17	28.47	16.41	23.20	3.88	16.51
May	99.94	0.29	99.65	3.82	24.19	9.56	28.67	15.95	23.27	3.75	17.82
June	103.45	0.43	103.02	3.82	25.68	10.75	29.41	16.50	23.47	4.13	19.11
July	103.57	0.22	103.35	3.89	25.85	10.65	29.36	16.54	23.65	4.06	18.51
August	104.03	0.36	103.67	3.92	25.27	10.46	30.02	16.35	23.85	4.26	20.04
September	107.03	0.63	106.40	3.89	26.47	10.90	31.17	16.44	24.22	4.21	21.12
October	106.67	0.61	106.06	3.86	26.42	11.13	30.28	16.65	24.77	4.08	21.40
November	104.65	0.65	103.99	3.94	25.43	10.41	29.60	16.21	24.64	4.18	20.38
December	104.22	0.55	103.67	3.80	26.28	10.29	29.94	15.50	24.13	4.03	19.46
2001											
January	104.94	0.58	104.35	3.90	27.10	10.46	28.80	15.94	24.51	4.11	17.67
February	99.78	0.56	99.22	3.80	24.97	9.54	27.74	15.50	23.12	4.09	16.12
March	102.16	0.58	101.58	3.75	25.04	9.16	28.00	15.67	25.27	3.84	18.61
April	98.97	0.60	98.37	3.76	24.37	9.60	25.83	15.89	24.39	4.14	16.13
May	96.71	0.76	95.95	3.75	24.12	9.64	24.66	15.71	23.54	4.17	15.26
June	95.95	0.58	95.37	3.90	23.14	9.30	24.55	16.04	23.71	4.03	16.65
July	94.34	0.21	94.12	4.02	22.41	8.56	23.83	16.08	23.72	4.06	16.49
August	93.00	0.24	92.76	3.93	22.05	8.58	23.53	16.08	23.24	3.93	15.42
September	91.51	0.23	91.28	4.04	21.69	8.50	22.73	15.61	23.33	3.89	14.77
October	92.09	0.21	91.88	4.04	21.07	7.92	22.97	15.76	23.97	4.06	17.02
November	90.03	0.21	89.83	3.97	19.62	6.57	22.81	15.97	23.36	4.10	16.16
December	86.46	0.17	86.29	3.77	18.28	5.76	22.54	15.54	22.15	4.02	14.89
2002											
January	88.72	0.23	88.49	3.87	18.86	6.33	22.84	15.52	23.43	3.98	14.78
February	90.86	0.22	90.64	3.99	18.96	5.93	22.96	16.35	24.35	4.02	14.50
March	91.74	0.28	91.47	3.99	19.65	6.88	23.20	16.24	24.17	4.21	16.20
April	96.64	0.32	96.33	4.04	22.60	9.10	23.73	16.90	25.07	3.99	15.53
May	97.68	0.30	97.38	4.09	22.92	9.29	23.80	17.02	25.50	4.05	15.63
June	98.39	0.30	98.09	4.13	22.34	8.66	23.99	17.12	26.07	4.43	16.37
July	97.94	0.28	97.66	4.22	22.67	9.03	23.85	17.17	25.72	4.03	16.96
August	99.94	0.30	99.64	4.22	23.56	9.58	23.74	17.42	26.67	4.04	16.55
September	99.75	0.31	99.43	4.15	23.50	9.31	23.78	17.66	26.20	4.14	16.83
October	97.95	0.32	97.63	4.09	24.53	10.61	22.34	17.07	25.51	4.08	17.39
November	101.91	0.29	101.63	4.40	23.84	9.51	24.39	17.59	27.46	3.95	17.60
December	103.22	0.23	102.99	4.50	24.26	9.27	24.69	17.68	27.69	4.16	16.80

[1]Not seasonally adjusted.
. . . = Not available.

Table 7-11. U.S. Exports and Imports of Goods by Principal End-Use Category in Constant Dollars

(Census basis; billions of 2000 chain-weighted dollars, except where noted; seasonally adjusted.)

Year and month	Exports Total	Foods, feeds, and beverages	Industrial supplies and materials	Capital goods, except auto-motive	Auto-motive vehicles, engines, and parts	Consumer goods (nonfood) except automotive	Other goods	Imports Total	Foods, feeds, and beverages	Industrial supplies and materials	Capital goods, except auto-motive	Auto-motive vehicles, engines, and parts	Consumer goods (nonfood) except automotive	Other goods
1986 [1]	227.20	22.30	57.30	75.80	21.70	. . .	. . .	365.40	24.40	101.30	71.80	78.20	79.40	. . .
1987 [1]	254.10	24.30	66.70	86.20	24.60	. . .	. . .	406.20	24.80	111.00	84.50	85.00	88.70	. . .
1988 [1]	322.40	32.30	85.10	109.20	29.30	. . .	. . .	441.00	24.80	118.30	101.40	87.70	95.90	. . .
1989 [1]	363.80	37.20	99.30	138.80	34.80	. . .	. . .	473.20	25.10	132.30	113.30	86.10	102.90	. . .
1990 [1]	393.60	35.10	104.40	152.70	37.40	39.22	18.70	495.30	26.60	146.20	116.40	87.30	105.70	14.46
1991 [1]	421.70	35.70	109.70	166.70	40.00	40.42	21.11	488.50	26.50	131.60	120.70	85.70	108.00	14.15
1992 [1]	448.20	40.30	109.10	175.90	47.00	43.60	21.71	532.70	27.60	138.60	134.30	91.80	122.70	15.46
1993 [1]	471.17	40.19	111.08	190.02	51.93	54.03	23.91	591.45	28.03	151.26	160.16	100.73	132.92	18.35
1994 [1]	522.29	40.43	114.17	225.76	56.54	58.97	26.41	675.05	29.52	168.80	199.56	112.13	144.22	20.82
1994	482.34	41.41	127.50	165.92	60.49	62.41	28.03	628.41	29.53	216.50	120.69	124.86	143.41	21.80
1995	531.74	45.70	136.13	192.70	64.02	66.02	28.79	682.73	30.28	222.84	145.53	126.99	154.37	23.01
1996	588.10	44.24	144.48	228.74	66.63	70.86	33.61	753.96	33.53	236.42	175.55	131.33	165.33	25.69
1997	666.61	44.12	156.35	280.22	75.18	77.82	33.38	858.67	36.75	252.73	219.82	141.98	188.23	29.06
1998	682.35	43.84	155.76	292.61	73.38	80.86	36.15	959.84	39.54	277.01	252.14	150.86	213.38	35.81
1999	704.29	45.35	156.88	308.44	75.99	81.42	36.12	1 075.39	43.18	281.43	289.21	180.17	239.60	43.70
2000	781.92	47.87	172.62	356.93	80.36	89.38	34.77	1 218.02	45.98	298.98	347.03	195.88	281.83	48.33
2001	733.67	49.18	164.89	321.92	75.13	88.38	34.16	1 177.48	47.77	297.18	306.82	189.87	286.47	48.80
2002	698.22	48.06	162.45	292.10	78.30	84.67	32.72	1 220.11	50.96	299.80	299.84	203.24	313.02	50.25
1998														
January	57.41	3.76	13.58	24.33	6.50	6.70	2.58	76.13	3.13	22.21	19.85	11.93	17.09	2.71
February	56.72	3.98	12.94	24.19	6.39	6.50	2.73	76.57	3.37	22.26	20.34	12.05	16.65	2.64
March	57.26	3.72	13.08	24.25	6.55	6.61	3.08	79.44	3.31	22.68	21.11	12.56	17.78	2.67
April	55.63	3.59	12.82	23.38	6.37	6.71	2.81	79.68	3.21	23.54	20.66	12.45	17.82	2.91
May	55.66	3.56	12.90	23.61	6.00	6.73	2.90	80.02	3.27	23.35	21.26	12.59	17.71	2.63
June	56.08	3.65	12.69	24.17	5.78	6.90	2.89	78.88	3.35	23.30	20.71	11.90	17.83	2.66
July	55.54	3.48	12.63	24.51	5.14	6.89	2.89	79.06	3.29	23.31	21.00	11.01	18.11	3.19
August	55.48	3.49	12.83	23.36	5.70	6.80	3.34	80.66	3.34	23.73	20.90	12.36	18.02	3.20
September	57.02	3.30	12.92	25.03	6.15	6.77	2.87	81.09	3.29	23.10	21.25	12.95	17.98	3.20
October	58.87	3.89	13.31	25.60	6.14	6.72	3.22	82.73	3.28	23.33	21.76	13.44	18.27	3.28
November	59.08	3.66	13.26	25.33	6.44	6.81	3.61	83.04	3.33	23.33	21.86	13.63	18.16	3.34
December	57.61	3.76	12.80	24.86	6.23	6.72	3.25	82.53	3.38	22.89	21.44	13.99	17.95	3.40
1999														
January	56.98	3.49	12.33	25.27	6.21	6.64	3.01	83.45	3.42	22.71	21.84	13.93	18.56	3.38
February	56.32	3.56	12.33	24.41	6.25	6.66	3.11	85.75	3.54	22.55	22.48	14.52	19.42	3.37
March	56.67	3.61	12.51	24.87	6.07	6.57	3.03	85.43	3.44	23.09	22.33	14.55	18.71	3.65
April	57.42	3.71	12.70	24.95	6.44	6.77	2.84	86.04	3.53	23.37	22.79	13.94	19.22	3.55
May	57.32	3.70	12.69	24.93	6.22	6.59	3.18	87.80	3.58	23.57	23.56	14.76	19.06	3.55
June	57.24	3.83	12.74	24.68	6.22	6.64	3.14	90.85	3.68	23.84	24.63	15.40	19.83	3.62
July	58.18	3.90	12.51	25.60	6.38	6.77	3.00	91.71	3.62	23.55	25.13	15.42	20.43	3.59
August	59.50	3.92	13.21	26.51	6.46	6.59	2.79	91.70	3.64	24.23	24.56	15.22	20.40	3.81
September	60.75	4.07	13.85	26.39	6.33	7.02	3.10	91.66	3.67	23.85	24.71	15.51	20.30	3.74
October	60.40	3.93	13.60	26.69	6.32	6.91	2.94	92.71	3.65	23.63	25.35	15.18	21.02	3.90
November	60.58	3.79	14.26	26.33	6.39	6.98	2.85	93.47	3.70	23.72	25.62	15.48	21.19	3.76
December	62.94	3.86	14.14	27.84	6.70	7.29	3.12	94.82	3.71	23.32	26.21	16.28	21.46	3.79
2000														
January	62.89	3.89	14.05	27.80	7.01	7.17	2.98	95.61	3.61	23.77	25.96	16.78	21.58	3.88
February	62.60	3.75	14.19	27.13	6.95	7.36	3.22	96.67	3.64	24.63	26.30	16.14	21.92	4.05
March	63.18	3.93	14.74	27.43	6.97	7.38	2.73	99.39	3.84	25.09	27.17	16.54	22.83	3.91
April	63.86	3.87	13.90	29.48	6.61	7.33	2.68	100.10	3.77	24.54	28.27	16.45	23.15	3.89
May	63.53	3.90	13.66	29.40	6.64	7.17	2.77	100.59	3.82	25.29	28.56	15.93	23.24	3.76
June	65.87	4.02	14.07	30.30	6.82	7.69	2.98	102.94	3.86	25.56	29.38	16.47	23.54	4.13
July	65.65	4.17	14.04	30.78	6.44	7.47	2.75	102.81	3.92	25.33	29.35	16.51	23.64	4.05
August	67.84	4.42	14.62	31.51	6.76	7.67	2.87	103.34	3.93	24.97	30.02	16.33	23.85	4.24
September	67.41	4.12	15.04	31.17	6.57	7.72	2.78	105.41	3.91	25.34	31.26	16.44	24.27	4.21
October	66.72	4.04	14.84	30.82	6.65	7.36	3.02	105.26	3.88	25.25	30.59	16.63	24.85	4.07
November	66.60	3.93	15.02	30.70	6.47	7.50	2.98	103.15	4.03	24.21	29.87	16.19	24.73	4.17
December	65.77	3.86	14.45	30.42	6.47	7.56	3.01	102.77	3.79	25.01	30.28	15.48	24.24	3.98
2001														
January	65.89	3.92	14.36	30.87	6.17	7.68	2.89	103.80	3.90	26.18	29.14	15.91	24.61	4.03
February	66.08	4.15	14.41	30.94	6.08	7.78	2.70	99.25	3.84	24.47	28.16	15.49	23.22	4.03
March	64.38	4.28	14.36	29.10	6.20	7.71	2.72	102.98	3.73	25.96	28.42	15.66	25.35	3.82
April	62.69	4.28	14.14	27.66	6.21	7.70	2.70	100.31	3.82	25.45	26.43	15.91	24.52	4.13
May	63.58	4.12	14.10	28.09	6.32	7.92	3.03	97.64	3.84	24.87	25.29	15.75	23.69	4.17
June	61.32	4.02	13.73	26.58	6.53	7.30	3.15	97.67	4.04	24.32	25.21	16.07	23.91	4.05
July	59.86	3.97	13.38	26.06	6.20	7.29	2.96	97.69	4.19	24.69	24.61	16.13	23.90	4.12
August	60.01	4.11	13.71	25.68	6.40	7.08	3.01	96.50	4.10	24.40	24.38	16.13	23.44	4.00
September	56.82	3.95	12.78	24.16	6.36	6.90	2.67	94.72	4.17	23.69	23.67	15.62	23.54	3.96
October	57.94	4.11	13.32	24.44	6.26	6.97	2.84	97.24	4.17	24.91	24.01	15.73	24.24	4.15
November	57.83	4.19	13.20	24.38	6.37	6.91	2.78	96.28	4.05	24.51	23.87	15.96	23.63	4.20
December	57.27	4.08	13.41	23.95	6.02	7.13	2.71	93.41	3.91	23.73	23.64	15.52	22.43	4.14
2002														
January	56.84	4.18	13.26	23.84	6.17	6.90	2.50	95.40	3.96	24.07	23.97	15.52	23.71	4.09
February	56.90	4.29	13.15	23.57	6.31	6.97	2.60	98.00	4.21	24.22	24.17	16.33	24.71	4.15
March	56.99	3.97	13.20	24.01	6.30	6.83	2.68	97.68	4.14	23.61	24.46	16.24	24.59	4.34
April	58.37	3.96	13.66	24.22	6.62	7.13	2.78	101.12	4.16	25.27	24.99	16.88	25.52	4.08
May	58.75	4.00	13.80	24.31	6.67	6.98	2.99	101.85	4.18	25.19	25.11	17.03	25.95	4.15
June	59.12	4.22	13.70	24.87	6.62	7.13	2.58	102.77	4.28	24.74	25.30	17.09	26.54	4.54
July	59.77	4.14	13.49	25.29	6.84	7.24	2.77	102.09	4.34	24.87	25.22	17.13	26.14	4.13
August	58.99	3.90	13.66	24.84	6.71	7.06	2.83	103.80	4.36	25.51	25.08	17.36	27.08	4.13
September	58.60	3.73	13.53	24.96	6.64	7.08	2.69	103.13	4.21	24.96	25.17	17.61	26.66	4.22
October	58.33	3.65	13.38	24.77	6.58	7.16	2.82	100.97	4.14	25.60	23.89	16.96	25.94	4.16
November	58.72	3.96	13.76	24.63	6.43	7.20	2.74	106.00	4.45	25.66	26.07	17.51	27.99	4.03
December	56.85	4.04	13.86	22.79	6.41	6.98	2.75	107.30	4.53	26.10	26.40	17.58	28.18	4.23

[1]Data on the 2000 chain-weighted dollar basis are only available for 1994 to date. To provide more historical data, values in 1992 dollars are shown for the years 1986–1994.
. . . = Not available.

Table 7-12. U.S. Exports of Goods by Selected Regions and Countries

(Census f.a.s. basis; millions of dollars, not seasonally adjusted.)

Year and month	Total, all countries	Selected regions				Selected countries					
		European Union	Euro area	Asian NICS	OPEC	Brazil	Canada	China	France	Germany	Hong Kong
1972	...	...	...	...	...	1 243	13 070	...	1 609	2 808	...
1973	...	...	...	...	...	1 916	16 146	...	2 263	3 756	...
1974	...	28 268	...	...	6 723	3 088	21 281	807	2 942	4 985	882
1975	...	22 862	...	...	10 767	3 056	22 948	304	3 031	5 194	808
1976	...	25 406	...	...	12 566	2 809	25 677	135	3 446	5 731	1 115
1977	...	26 476	...	...	14 019	2 490	27 738	171	3 503	5 989	1 292
1978	...	32 051	...	...	16 655	2 981	30 540	824	4 166	6 957	1 625
1979	...	42 582	...	...	15 051	3 442	37 599	1 724	5 587	8 478	2 083
1980	...	53 679	...	...	17 759	4 344	40 331	3 755	7 485	10 960	2 686
1981	...	52 363	...	...	21 533	3 798	44 602	3 603	7 341	10 277	2 635
1982	...	47 932	...	...	22 863	3 423	37 887	2 912	7 110	9 291	2 453
1983	201 708	44 311	...	...	16 905	2 557	43 345	2 173	5 961	8 737	2 564
1984	218 743	46 976	...	...	14 387	2 640	51 777	3 004	6 037	9 084	3 062
1985	212 621	48 994	...	16 918	12 480	3 140	53 287	3 856	6 096	9 050	2 786
1986	226 471	53 154	...	18 289	10 844	3 885	55 512	3 106	7 216	10 561	3 030
1987	253 904	60 575	...	23 548	11 058	4 040	59 814	3 497	7 943	11 748	3 983
1988	323 335	75 755	...	34 816	13 994	4 267	71 622	5 021	9 970	14 348	5 687
1989	363 836	86 331	...	38 404	13 196	4 804	78 809	5 755	11 579	16 862	6 246
1990	392 924	98 027	...	40 741	13 679	5 062	83 866	4 807	13 652	18 693	6 841
1991	421 764	103 123	...	45 628	19 054	6 148	85 150	6 278	15 346	21 302	8 137
1992	448 161	102 958	...	48 592	21 960	5 751	90 594	7 418	14 593	21 249	9 077
1993	465 090	96 973	...	52 502	19 500	6 058	100 444	8 763	13 267	18 932	9 874
1994	512 626	102 818	...	59 595	17 868	8 102	114 439	9 282	13 619	19 229	11 441
1995	584 742	123 671	...	74 234	19 533	11 439	127 226	11 754	14 245	22 394	14 232
1996	625 075	127 710	...	75 768	22 275	12 718	134 210	11 993	14 455	23 495	13 966
1997	689 182	140 773	...	78 225	25 526	15 915	151 767	12 862	15 965	24 458	15 117
1998	682 138	149 035	...	63 269	25 154	15 142	156 603	14 241	17 729	26 657	12 925
1999	695 797	151 814	...	70 989	20 166	13 203	166 600	13 111	18 877	26 800	12 652
2000	781 918	165 065	116 212	84 624	19 078	15 321	178 941	16 185	20 362	29 448	14 582
2001	729 100	158 768	112 903	71 982	20 053	15 880	163 424	19 182	19 865	29 995	14 028
2002	693 103	143 691	105 838	69 770	18 812	12 376	160 923	22 128	19 016	26 630	12 594
1999											
January	52 436	12 302	...	5 352	1 534	1 107	12 134	781	1 709	1 989	889
February	53 279	12 643	...	4 623	1 786	916	13 048	924	1 605	2 171	889
March	60 889	14 119	...	5 906	2 112	980	14 984	1 076	1 768	2 793	1 218
April	57 283	12 806	...	5 787	1 423	1 072	14 127	1 035	1 530	2 337	978
May	56 489	12 692	...	5 661	1 534	1 084	14 151	1 114	1 678	2 192	1 000
June	57 825	12 163	...	5 880	1 359	1 068	14 567	1 442	1 614	2 079	1 039
July	52 998	11 214	...	5 891	1 767	1 091	11 519	1 074	1 275	1 966	1 058
August	57 439	12 014	...	6 594	1 328	1 134	13 815	1 151	1 298	2 163	1 050
September	59 431	12 185	...	6 218	1 306	1 134	14 423	1 325	1 457	2 009	1 176
October	62 973	13 446	...	6 369	1 458	1 342	14 824	1 069	1 651	2 535	1 104
November	60 948	12 822	...	5 680	1 480	1 217	15 099	1 026	1 373	2 209	1 057
December	63 808	13 410	...	7 028	3 080	1 059	13 908	1 094	1 920	2 357	1 193
2000											
January	57 679	12 031	8 352	5 981	1 484	1 008	13 605	863	1 571	2 103	915
February	61 179	13 254	8 965	5 853	1 705	1 058	14 969	973	1 553	2 235	1 011
March	68 948	14 496	10 335	7 301	1 418	1 141	17 086	1 331	1 830	2 832	1 246
April	63 302	13 591	9 777	6 845	1 438	1 055	14 794	1 228	1 702	2 784	1 170
May	64 673	14 010	9 821	6 773	1 366	1 184	15 834	1 526	1 639	2 498	1 135
June	68 002	13 982	9 797	7 687	1 373	1 435	16 054	1 336	1 677	2 314	1 262
July	60 029	12 005	8 633	7 557	1 375	1 361	12 153	1 643	1 485	2 182	1 181
August	68 255	13 588	9 652	7 699	1 732	1 442	15 325	1 429	1 669	2 470	1 333
September	67 391	14 214	10 085	7 501	1 901	1 443	14 847	1 333	1 633	2 471	1 311
October	69 635	14 282	10 007	7 584	2 071	1 453	15 725	1 487	1 706	2 464	1 288
November	67 614	14 313	10 120	6 811	1 630	1 332	15 159	1 450	1 787	2 451	1 305
December	65 211	15 302	10 669	7 032	1 585	1 410	13 390	1 587	2 110	2 645	1 426
2001											
January	62 162	13 645	9 827	6 443	1 705	1 265	13 667	1 188	1 642	2 546	1 046
February	62 743	14 531	10 463	6 508	1 483	1 169	13 357	1 290	1 972	2 928	1 170
March	70 358	15 346	11 032	6 988	2 287	1 412	15 524	1 856	2 042	2 892	1 379
April	62 015	13 632	9 476	5 841	1 688	1 295	14 403	1 399	1 610	2 508	1 317
May	64 931	14 163	9 676	5 786	1 670	1 486	15 108	1 596	1 687	2 605	1 112
June	63 334	13 715	9 487	5 895	1 653	1 514	15 051	1 786	1 749	2 432	1 295
July	54 611	11 325	7 896	5 866	1 653	1 434	11 700	1 487	1 233	2 443	1 145
August	60 111	12 627	8 974	5 641	1 530	1 476	13 764	1 930	1 404	2 389	1 162
September	55 232	12 035	8 506	6 120	1 577	1 249	12 423	1 428	1 613	2 255	1 217
October	60 701	13 056	9 489	5 727	1 624	1 134	13 895	1 648	1 700	2 371	1 064
November	57 900	12 143	8 850	5 771	1 597	1 344	13 214	1 675	1 644	2 173	1 024
December	55 003	12 551	9 227	5 395	1 586	1 100	11 319	1 901	1 570	2 453	1 098
2002											
January	52 667	11 408	8 249	5 216	1 238	1 016	12 062	1 569	1 543	2 022	900
February	53 061	12 153	8 983	4 619	1 348	1 004	12 368	1 530	1 872	2 183	911
March	60 728	13 298	9 842	6 289	1 431	1 076	13 954	1 621	1 801	2 530	1 134
April	58 146	12 079	8 758	5 819	1 591	1 059	14 114	1 545	1 578	2 133	1 043
May	59 884	11 948	8 829	5 817	2 043	969	14 586	1 774	1 570	2 084	1 054
June	59 920	11 908	8 578	6 408	1 431	1 017	14 214	2 206	1 532	2 197	1 135
July	55 032	10 537	7 722	6 313	1 569	970	11 607	1 848	1 249	1 990	1 035
August	59 491	11 752	8 460	6 246	1 492	1 134	13 913	1 840	1 287	2 147	1 113
September	57 277	11 571	8 521	5 813	1 924	1 053	13 334	2 024	1 503	2 328	1 117
October	61 975	13 015	9 748	6 078	1 646	1 159	14 702	1 963	1 993	2 402	1 009
November	59 671	12 470	9 470	5 614	1 641	1 037	13 908	2 161	1 704	2 419	1 089
December	55 249	11 553	8 679	5 539	1 459	882	12 161	2 049	1 384	2 194	1 055

Note: See Notes and Definitions for definitions of regional groupings.
. . . = Not available.

Table 7-12. U.S. Exports of Goods by Selected Regions and Countries—Continued

(Census f.a.s. basis; millions of dollars, not seasonally adjusted.)

Year and month	Indonesia	Italy	Japan	Malaysia	Mexico	Netherlands	Singapore	South Korea	Taiwan	United Kingdom	Venezuela
1972	...	1 434	4 963	...	1 982	...	...	...	...	2 658	924
1973	...	2 119	8 313	...	2 937	...	...	...	...	3 564	1 033
1974	...	2 752	10 679	...	4 855	3 979	988	...	1 427	4 574	1 768
1975	...	2 867	9 563	...	5 141	4 183	994	...	1 660	4 527	2 243
1976	...	3 071	10 145	...	4 990	4 645	965	...	1 635	4 801	2 628
1977	...	2 790	10 529	...	4 806	4 796	1 172	...	1 798	5 951	3 171
1978	...	3 361	12 885	...	6 680	5 683	1 462	...	2 340	7 116	3 728
1979	...	4 362	17 581	...	9 847	6 907	2 331	...	3 271	10 635	3 934
1980	1 545	5 511	20 790	...	15 145	8 669	3 033	...	4 337	12 694	4 573
1981	1 302	5 360	21 823	...	17 789	8 555	3 003	...	4 305	12 439	5 445
1982	2 025	4 616	20 966	...	11 817	8 604	3 214	...	4 367	10 645	5 206
1983	1 466	3 908	21 894	...	9 082	7 767	3 759	...	4 667	10 621	2 811
1984	1 216	4 375	23 575	...	11 992	7 554	3 675	...	5 003	12 210	3 377
1985	795	4 625	22 631	...	13 635	7 269	3 476	5 956	4 700	11 273	3 399
1986	946	4 838	26 882	...	12 392	7 848	3 380	6 355	5 524	11 418	3 141
1987	767	5 530	28 249	...	14 582	8 217	4 053	8 099	7 413	14 114	3 586
1988	1 059	6 775	37 725	...	20 628	10 117	5 768	11 232	12 129	18 364	4 612
1989	1 247	7 215	44 494	...	24 982	11 364	7 345	13 478	11 335	20 837	3 025
1990	1 897	7 987	48 585	...	28 375	13 016	8 019	14 399	11 482	23 484	3 107
1991	1 891	8 570	48 125	3 900	33 277	13 511	8 804	15 505	13 182	22 046	4 656
1992	2 779	8 721	47 813	4 363	40 592	13 752	9 626	14 639	15 250	22 800	5 444
1993	2 770	6 464	47 892	6 064	41 581	12 839	11 678	14 782	16 168	26 438	4 590
1994	2 809	7 183	53 488	6 969	50 844	13 582	13 020	18 025	17 109	26 900	4 039
1995	3 360	8 862	64 343	8 816	46 292	16 558	15 333	25 380	19 290	28 857	4 640
1996	3 977	8 797	67 607	8 546	56 792	16 662	16 720	26 621	18 460	30 962	4 750
1997	4 522	8 995	65 549	10 780	71 388	19 827	17 696	25 046	20 366	36 425	6 602
1998	2 299	8 991	57 831	8 957	78 773	18 978	15 694	16 486	18 165	39 058	6 516
1999	2 038	10 091	57 466	9 060	86 909	19 437	16 247	22 958	19 131	38 407	5 354
2000	2 402	11 060	64 924	10 938	111 349	21 836	17 806	27 830	24 406	41 570	5 550
2001	2 521	9 916	57 452	9 358	101 297	19 485	17 652	22 181	18 122	40 714	5 642
2002	2 556	10 057	51 449	10 344	97 470	18 311	16 218	22 576	18 382	33 205	4 430
1999											
January	126	739	4 624	651	6 021	1 505	1 475	1 544	1 444	3 268	436
February	114	734	4 836	636	6 017	1 647	1 102	1 416	1 216	3 312	489
March	166	819	5 294	676	6 910	1 673	1 321	1 910	1 457	3 352	524
April	164	1 063	4 785	686	6 648	1 545	1 219	2 089	1 502	3 216	411
May	163	762	4 271	736	6 659	1 534	1 222	1 819	1 620	3 295	460
June	215	766	4 536	854	7 069	1 618	1 311	1 963	1 567	3 110	414
July	161	882	4 444	862	7 121	1 356	1 303	1 863	1 667	3 077	642
August	175	691	4 696	733	7 475	1 687	1 639	2 251	1 654	3 270	385
September	172	771	4 650	763	7 805	1 651	1 495	2 021	1 527	2 999	356
October	202	1 063	5 086	812	8 461	1 661	1 372	1 973	1 920	3 297	439
November	183	816	5 185	823	8 202	1 761	1 280	1 810	1 534	3 168	384
December	198	985	5 059	828	8 523	1 800	1 509	2 301	2 025	3 043	414
2000											
January	169	827	4 772	697	7 965	1 558	1 239	1 986	1 841	3 045	363
February	201	820	4 992	742	8 464	1 795	1 195	2 053	1 595	3 689	420
March	237	930	5 899	826	9 641	1 897	1 621	2 433	2 001	3 516	492
April	201	883	4 968	854	9 044	1 675	1 325	2 425	1 925	3 193	531
May	177	822	5 109	830	9 144	1 786	1 274	2 384	1 981	3 533	437
June	177	907	5 758	1 113	9 408	1 833	1 499	2 576	2 349	3 561	453
July	229	861	5 094	1 011	9 084	1 627	1 504	2 288	2 584	2 903	407
August	206	876	5 677	1 040	10 449	1 858	1 669	2 442	2 255	3 325	499
September	211	1 369	5 526	1 043	9 756	1 831	1 754	2 378	2 058	3 494	479
October	227	946	5 546	985	10 332	2 057	1 662	2 476	2 158	3 636	451
November	177	849	5 760	933	9 927	1 959	1 516	2 243	1 748	3 683	426
December	190	969	5 824	863	8 137	1 960	1 548	2 147	1 911	3 994	593
2001											
January	234	918	5 253	899	8 648	1 809	1 434	2 150	1 813	3 374	461
February	203	889	5 222	778	8 768	1 821	1 541	2 025	1 772	3 486	411
March	218	968	5 897	1 011	9 272	1 912	1 689	2 217	1 703	3 700	517
April	217	792	5 033	887	8 198	1 756	1 233	1 627	1 664	3 719	451
May	239	841	4 878	679	8 649	1 594	1 550	1 692	1 433	4 036	494
June	201	808	4 986	682	8 405	1 627	1 453	1 783	1 365	3 824	524
July	185	720	4 308	689	7 675	1 290	1 434	1 774	1 513	3 087	477
August	198	735	4 604	700	9 023	1 530	1 370	1 747	1 362	3 252	511
September	173	724	4 336	678	7 700	1 363	1 523	2 000	1 380	3 157	416
October	212	961	4 352	715	9 273	1 501	1 766	1 532	1 365	3 190	499
November	198	770	4 287	720	8 346	1 614	1 475	1 858	1 414	2 936	481
December	243	790	4 296	920	7 337	1 668	1 183	1 776	1 339	2 952	400
2002											
January	136	714	3 945	726	7 734	1 460	1 386	1 706	1 224	2 764	374
February	198	797	3 862	688	7 250	1 480	1 069	1 487	1 152	2 771	379
March	201	885	4 744	1 253	7 624	1 710	1 705	1 877	1 573	2 985	365
April	195	824	3 901	960	8 258	1 714	1 329	1 931	1 516	2 957	320
May	222	933	4 262	856	8 530	1 593	1 235	1 991	1 538	2 702	677
June	195	775	4 670	1 003	8 088	1 531	1 538	1 975	1 760	2 966	272
July	198	836	4 493	828	7 963	1 353	1 323	1 890	2 066	2 456	304
August	282	823	4 791	907	8 559	1 514	1 600	1 919	1 614	2 914	329
September	187	679	4 138	798	8 283	1 505	1 133	1 974	1 588	2 643	400
October	212	977	4 151	874	9 221	1 476	1 583	1 982	1 504	2 904	374
November	268	914	4 412	723	8 606	1 490	1 302	1 800	1 423	2 619	470
December	262	901	4 082	728	7 354	1 484	1 015	2 044	1 425	2 524	165

. . . = Not available.

Table 7-13. U.S. Imports of Goods by Selected Regions and Countries

(Census Customs basis; millions of dollars, not seasonally adjusted.)

Year and month	Total, all countries	Selected regions				Selected countries					
		European Union	Euro area	Asian NICS	OPEC	Brazil	Canada	China	France	Germany	Hong Kong
1972	...	...	...	...	...	942	14 927	...	1 369	4 250	...
1973	...	...	...	...	...	1 189	17 715	...	1 732	5 345	...
1974	...	19 035	...	...	...	1 700	21 924	...	2 257	6 324	...
1975	...	16 610	...	...	...	1 464	21 747	...	2 137	5 382	...
1976	...	17 848	...	...	...	1 737	26 237	...	2 509	5 592	...
1977	...	22 087	...	...	...	2 241	29 599	...	3 032	7 238	...
1978	...	29 009	...	...	...	2 826	33 525	...	4 051	9 962	...
1979	...	33 295	...	...	...	3 118	38 046	...	4 768	10 955	...
1980	...	35 958	...	...	...	3 715	41 455	...	5 247	11 681	...
1981	...	41 624	...	...	...	4 475	46 414	...	5 851	11 379	...
1982	...	42 509	...	...	...	4 285	46 477	...	5 545	11 975	...
1983	261 723	43 892	...	...	...	4 946	52 130	...	6 025	12 695	...
1984	330 510	57 360	...	...	...	7 621	66 478	...	8 113	16 996	...
1985	336 383	67 822	...	...	22 800	7 526	69 006	3 862	9 482	20 239	8 396
1986	365 672	75 736	...	...	19 750	6 813	68 253	4 771	10 129	25 124	8 891
1987	406 283	81 188	...	...	23 953	7 865	71 085	6 294	10 730	27 069	9 854
1988	441 926	84 939	...	...	22 962	9 294	81 398	8 511	12 509	26 362	10 238
1989	473 647	85 153	...	...	30 601	8 410	87 953	11 989	13 013	24 832	9 739
1990	495 980	91 868	...	...	38 017	7 976	91 372	15 224	13 124	28 109	9 488
1991	488 452	86 481	...	59 277	32 644	6 717	91 064	18 969	13 333	26 137	9 279
1992	532 663	93 993	...	62 384	33 200	7 609	98 630	25 728	14 797	28 820	9 793
1993	580 658	97 941	...	64 572	31 739	7 479	111 216	31 540	15 279	28 562	9 554
1994	663 256	110 875	...	71 388	31 685	8 683	128 406	38 787	16 699	31 744	9 696
1995	743 543	131 871	...	82 008	35 197	8 830	145 349	45 543	17 209	36 844	10 291
1996	795 289	142 947	...	82 770	44 285	8 773	155 893	51 513	18 646	38 945	9 865
1997	869 704	157 528	...	86 164	44 025	9 626	168 201	62 558	20 636	43 122	10 288
1998	911 896	176 380	...	85 961	33 925	10 102	173 256	71 169	24 016	49 842	10 538
1999	1 024 618	195 227	...	95 102	41 978	11 314	198 711	81 788	25 709	55 228	10 528
2000	1 218 022	220 019	163 520	111 438	67 090	13 853	230 838	100 018	29 800	58 513	11 449
2001	1 140 999	220 057	166 373	93 202	59 754	14 466	216 268	102 278	30 408	59 077	9 646
2002	1 161 366	225 771	172 573	91 850	53 245	15 781	209 088	125 193	28 240	62 506	9 328
1999											
January	71 766	13 403	...	6 938	2 543	768	14 550	5 654	1 872	3 551	805
February	73 849	14 492	...	6 451	2 214	756	15 295	5 563	1 932	4 053	727
March	84 072	16 739	...	7 441	2 771	860	17 100	5 204	2 178	4 852	701
April	79 980	15 777	...	7 210	3 075	895	16 121	5 819	2 069	4 471	699
May	80 965	15 670	...	7 584	3 277	933	16 344	6 363	2 114	4 548	744
June	87 880	16 778	...	8 274	3 341	1 053	17 132	7 117	2 096	4 756	918
July	86 775	17 443	...	8 375	3 704	963	14 632	7 406	2 229	4 987	992
August	89 749	16 150	...	8 332	4 213	1 066	17 237	8 022	2 338	4 569	1 042
September	90 244	15 658	...	8 376	4 184	1 042	17 325	8 198	2 031	4 315	1 054
October	94 460	17 630	...	8 518	4 191	1 000	17 787	8 208	2 254	4 853	1 038
November	93 581	18 083	...	8 743	4 183	980	18 176	7 544	5 379	5 085	924
December	91 296	17 405	...	8 861	4 282	1 000	17 012	6 690	2 216	5 189	883
2000											
January	87 188	15 345	11 530	8 375	4 382	1 099	17 579	6 902	2 329	4 207	961
February	91 688	16 772	12 192	7 971	4 826	1 091	18 092	6 585	2 092	4 474	842
March	103 244	19 988	14 651	8 555	5 414	1 053	20 762	6 424	2 636	5 410	796
April	95 141	17 801	13 324	8 223	5 000	1 024	18 638	7 071	2 442	5 018	731
May	101 067	18 762	13 839	8 992	5 452	1 101	19 836	7 850	2 625	4 829	916
June	104 527	17 992	13 307	9 665	6 085	1 421	20 391	8 542	2 362	4 644	1 016
July	101 986	18 415	13 728	9 772	5 884	1 224	16 889	9 246	2 368	4 940	1 063
August	108 166	18 362	13 845	10 303	6 193	1 414	19 815	10 054	2 248	5 295	1 151
September	106 355	17 834	13 514	10 340	6 158	1 178	19 379	10 062	2 317	4 710	1 231
October	113 812	20 399	15 133	10 417	6 520	1 070	20 500	10 612	2 821	5 162	1 043
November	106 395	19 939	14 767	9 846	5 653	1 043	19 969	9 067	2 775	4 961	898
December	98 453	18 410	13 690	8 979	5 524	1 135	18 990	7 605	2 785	4 866	802
2001											
January	101 869	18 896	14 082	9 064	5 793	1 360	20 442	8 428	2 525	4 875	982
February	91 639	17 861	13 275	7 286	4 781	1 050	18 263	6 376	2 344	4 846	617
March	103 536	20 172	15 379	8 416	5 642	1 202	19 976	7 590	3 309	5 345	751
April	96 265	19 218	14 508	7 669	5 439	1 077	18 733	7 687	2 734	5 378	662
May	96 605	19 039	14 431	7 578	5 790	1 261	19 603	7 758	2 612	5 219	759
June	95 663	17 843	13 484	7 733	5 224	1 188	18 915	8 398	2 303	4 783	868
July	94 625	19 522	14 876	7 784	5 300	1 211	15 793	8 975	2 629	5 423	930
August	96 728	17 466	13 495	7 694	4 933	1 428	18 001	10 043	2 364	5 055	910
September	89 484	15 292	11 553	7 323	4 872	1 209	16 698	9 928	1 873	4 147	915
October	101 177	20 147	15 071	8 261	4 717	1 175	17 542	10 808	2 714	5 037	922
November	91 705	18 015	13 524	7 595	3 778	1 183	17 170	8 879	2 469	4 582	712
December	81 703	16 587	12 694	6 800	3 487	1 123	15 132	7 409	2 533	4 387	619
2002											
January	85 111	16 057	12 180	7 275	3 733	1 093	16 335	8 415	2 284	4 195	836
February	83 473	16 651	12 876	6 478	3 298	1 024	16 180	8 021	2 184	4 636	603
March	91 415	18 829	14 445	7 185	3 898	1 104	17 481	7 259	2 465	5 255	589
April	96 891	18 997	14 189	7 635	4 512	1 250	18 186	9 098	2 576	5 185	674
May	97 649	18 932	14 229	7 753	4 586	1 261	18 794	9 847	2 043	4 900	738
June	96 415	18 236	13 848	7 437	4 153	1 384	17 436	10 727	2 311	4 620	787
July	100 472	20 953	16 084	7 988	4 714	1 400	15 911	11 213	2 687	5 796	934
August	102 277	18 168	14 043	8 027	5 139	1 581	17 943	12 671	2 201	5 108	867
September	99 429	17 705	13 475	7 935	4 880	1 350	17 862	12 292	2 166	4 914	861
October	106 251	20 897	16 032	7 862	5 130	1 649	19 044	11 455	2 526	5 993	896
November	102 564	19 711	15 057	8 349	4 591	1 296	17 685	12 570	2 275	5 750	818
December	99 418	20 635	16 116	7 927	4 611	1 390	16 232	11 625	2 523	6 156	725

Note: See Notes and Definitions for definitions of regional groupings.
. . . = Not available.

Table 7-13. U.S. Imports of Goods by Selected Regions and Countries—*Continued*

(Census Customs basis; millions of dollars, not seasonally adjusted.)

Year and month	Selected countries—*Continued*										
	Indonesia	Italy	Japan	Malaysia	Mexico	Netherlands	Singapore	South Korea	Taiwan	United Kingdom	Venezuela
1972	...	1 757	9 064	...	1 632	...	...	...	...	2 987	1 298
1973	...	2 002	9 676	...	2 306	...	...	...	...	3 657	1 787
1974	...	2 585	12 338	...	3 390	1 433	...	...	...	4 061	4 671
1975	...	2 397	11 268	...	3 059	1 083	...	...	...	3 784	3 624
1976	...	2 530	15 504	...	3 598	1 080	...	...	...	4 254	3 574
1977	...	3 037	18 550	...	4 694	1 477	...	...	...	5 141	4 084
1978	...	4 102	24 458	...	6 094	1 603	...	...	...	6 514	3 545
1979	...	4 918	26 248	...	8 800	1 852	...	...	...	8 028	5 166
1980	5 183	4 313	30 701	...	12 520	1 910	...	...	...	9 755	5 297
1981	6 022	5 189	37 612	...	13 765	2 366	...	...	...	12 835	5 566
1982	4 224	5 301	37 744	...	15 566	2 494	...	...	...	13 095	4 768
1983	5 285	5 455	41 183	...	16 776	2 970	...	...	...	12 470	4 938
1984	5 461	7 935	57 135	...	18 020	4 069	...	...	...	14 492	6 543
1985	4 569	9 674	68 783	...	19 132	4 081	4 260	10 031	16 396	14 937	6 537
1986	3 312	10 607	81 911	...	17 302	4 066	4 725	12 729	19 791	15 396	5 097
1987	3 394	11 040	84 575	...	20 271	3 964	6 201	16 987	24 622	17 341	5 579
1988	3 150	11 576	89 519	...	23 260	4 559	7 973	20 105	24 714	17 976	5 157
1989	3 529	11 933	93 586	...	27 162	4 810	8 950	19 742	24 326	18 319	6 771
1990	3 341	12 723	89 655	...	30 172	4 972	9 839	18 493	22 667	20 288	9 446
1991	3 241	11 764	91 511	6 102	31 130	4 811	9 957	17 019	23 023	18 413	8 179
1992	4 529	12 314	97 414	8 294	35 211	5 300	11 313	16 682	24 596	20 093	8 181
1993	5 435	13 216	107 246	10 563	39 917	5 443	12 798	17 118	25 102	21 730	8 140
1994	6 547	14 802	119 156	13 982	49 494	6 007	15 358	19 629	26 706	25 058	8 371
1995	7 435	16 348	123 479	17 455	61 684	6 405	18 560	24 184	28 972	26 930	9 721
1996	8 250	18 325	115 187	17 829	74 297	6 583	20 343	22 655	29 907	28 979	13 173
1997	9 188	19 408	121 663	18 027	85 938	7 293	20 075	23 173	32 629	32 659	13 477
1998	9 341	20 959	121 845	19 000	94 629	7 599	18 356	23 942	33 125	34 838	9 181
1999	9 525	22 357	130 864	21 424	109 721	8 475	18 191	31 179	35 204	39 237	11 335
2000	10 367	25 043	146 479	25 568	135 926	9 671	19 178	40 308	40 503	43 345	18 623
2001	10 104	23 790	126 473	22 340	131 338	9 515	15 000	35 181	33 375	41 369	15 251
2002	9 643	24 220	121 429	24 009	134 616	9 849	14 802	35 572	32 148	40 745	15 094
1999											
January	787	1 604	9 213	1 502	7 443	600	1 397	2 066	2 670	2 760	644
February	654	1 652	9 999	1 438	7 930	535	1 230	2 023	2 471	2 885	575
March	739	1 956	11 799	1 640	9 304	730	1 544	2 360	2 836	3 239	626
April	711	1 760	10 408	1 636	8 431	652	1 423	2 325	2 763	3 240	862
May	715	1 842	9 476	1 786	8 940	620	1 527	2 457	2 856	3 195	925
June	861	2 004	10 897	1 816	9 550	695	1 562	2 711	3 083	3 323	839
July	803	2 037	11 109	1 857	9 161	736	1 719	2 654	3 010	3 437	1 066
August	879	1 983	10 801	2 020	9 672	664	1 512	2 687	3 091	3 188	1 134
September	898	1 658	11 271	1 967	9 844	673	1 517	2 797	3 007	3 404	1 188
October	886	1 905	12 126	1 922	10 019	819	1 598	2 888	2 994	3 454	1 111
November	831	1 973	11 579	1 956	10 001	849	1 590	3 059	3 171	3 563	1 146
December	761	1 983	12 185	1 886	9 426	903	1 572	3 151	3 255	3 550	1 221
2000											
January	790	1 792	10 204	1 702	9 583	718	1 401	2 954	3 060	2 949	1 283
February	703	1 956	11 721	1 776	10 365	728	1 423	2 833	2 873	3 465	1 497
March	832	2 154	12 810	2 029	11 653	898	1 473	3 134	3 152	4 119	1 516
April	738	1 986	12 452	1 881	10 555	795	1 386	2 956	3 150	3 422	1 390
May	830	2 063	11 946	2 023	11 367	859	1 517	3 121	3 438	3 796	1 541
June	919	2 092	12 174	2 209	11 944	771	1 625	3 497	3 526	3 586	1 623
July	877	2 244	12 557	2 228	10 947	824	1 647	3 494	3 568	3 594	1 560
August	1 010	2 158	12 535	2 401	12 306	784	1 837	3 622	3 693	3 693	1 562
September	962	2 306	11 484	2 412	12 344	777	1 785	3 627	3 696	3 283	1 542
October	978	2 103	14 065	2 527	12 814	903	1 705	3 890	3 779	3 956	1 807
November	883	2 151	12 461	2 265	11 940	854	1 788	3 741	3 420	3 947	1 727
December	847	2 037	12 070	2 117	10 109	760	1 592	3 439	3 147	3 538	1 575
2001											
January	957	2 084	11 143	1 869	10 706	835	1 499	3 514	3 069	3 857	1 678
February	763	1 946	11 380	1 746	10 297	725	1 306	2 811	2 553	3 547	1 324
March	918	2 173	12 076	1 932	12 045	860	1 373	3 125	3 167	3 634	1 475
April	764	1 928	11 562	1 736	10 481	831	1 290	2 824	2 893	3 685	1 410
May	859	2 044	9 606	1 704	11 431	880	1 280	2 758	2 782	3 567	1 339
June	856	1 981	9 969	2 066	11 438	777	1 187	2 861	2 817	3 327	1 401
July	939	2 253	10 318	1 849	10 578	734	1 205	2 844	2 805	3 550	1 329
August	926	2 105	10 219	1 895	11 565	745	1 203	2 754	2 827	3 172	1 300
September	771	1 448	9 457	1 771	10 687	690	1 066	2 782	2 561	2 747	992
October	899	2 133	11 187	2 118	11 909	889	1 289	3 159	2 890	3 919	1 160
November	771	1 857	10 288	1 941	10 873	775	1 288	3 010	2 586	3 476	965
December	682	1 837	9 269	1 714	9 329	774	1 015	2 740	2 426	2 889	878
2002											
January	746	1 730	8 674	1 775	9 982	679	1 199	2 756	2 486	3 046	916
February	672	1 714	9 426	1 748	10 023	715	1 050	2 539	2 285	2 860	753
March	765	1 939	10 466	1 942	11 055	765	1 179	2 940	2 477	3 253	1 035
April	764	1 975	10 699	1 901	11 471	889	1 209	3 021	2 731	3 702	1 057
May	849	2 052	9 167	2 036	11 929	888	1 300	3 075	2 639	3 588	1 257
June	827	2 007	10 090	2 098	11 311	800	1 022	2 748	2 880	3 327	1 197
July	942	2 421	10 230	2 182	11 293	875	1 245	2 931	2 879	3 767	1 497
August	968	2 154	10 081	2 307	11 854	766	1 375	2 882	2 902	3 372	1 582
September	851	1 737	10 074	2 032	11 409	789	1 232	3 068	2 774	3 257	1 722
October	773	2 163	10 561	2 067	12 658	952	1 334	3 047	2 585	3 723	1 654
November	781	2 033	10 815	2 009	11 484	823	1 356	3 410	2 766	3 507	1 459
December	707	2 295	11 143	1 912	10 148	907	1 301	3 155	2 745	3 344	965

. . . = Not available.

Table 7-14. U.S. Exports of Services

(Balance of payments basis, millions of dollars, seasonally adjusted.)

Year and month	Total	Travel	Passenger fares	Other transportation	Royalties and license fees	Other private services (financial, professional, etc.)	Transfers under U.S. military sales contracts [1]	U.S. government miscellaneous services
1960	6 290	919	175	1 607	837	570	2 030	153
1961	6 295	947	183	1 620	906	607	1 867	164
1962	6 941	957	191	1 764	1 056	585	2 193	195
1963	7 348	1 015	205	1 898	1 162	613	2 219	236
1964	7 840	1 207	241	2 076	1 314	651	2 086	265
1965	8 824	1 380	271	2 175	1 534	714	2 465	285
1966	9 616	1 590	317	2 333	1 516	814	2 721	326
1967	10 667	1 646	371	2 426	1 747	951	3 191	336
1968	11 917	1 775	411	2 548	1 867	1 024	3 939	353
1969	12 806	2 043	450	2 652	2 019	1 160	4 138	343
1970	14 171	2 331	544	3 125	2 331	1 294	4 214	332
1971	16 358	2 534	615	3 299	2 545	1 546	5 472	347
1972	17 841	2 817	699	3 579	2 770	1 764	5 856	357
1973	19 832	3 412	975	4 465	3 225	1 985	5 369	401
1974	22 591	4 032	1 104	5 697	3 821	2 321	5 197	419
1975	25 497	4 697	1 039	5 840	4 300	2 920	6 256	446
1976	27 971	5 742	1 229	6 747	4 353	3 584	5 826	489
1977	31 485	6 150	1 366	7 090	4 920	3 848	7 554	557
1978	36 353	7 183	1 603	8 136	5 885	4 717	8 209	620
1979	39 692	8 441	2 156	9 971	6 184	5 439	6 981	520
1980	47 584	10 588	2 591	11 618	7 085	6 276	9 029	398
1981	57 354	12 913	3 111	12 560	7 284	10 250	10 720	517
1982	64 079	12 393	3 174	12 317	5 603	17 444	12 572	576
1983	64 307	10 947	3 610	12 590	5 778	18 192	12 524	666
1984	71 168	17 177	4 067	13 809	6 177	19 255	9 969	714
1985	73 155	17 762	4 411	14 674	6 678	20 035	8 718	878
1986	86 689	20 385	5 582	15 438	8 113	28 027	8 549	595
1987	98 661	23 563	7 003	17 027	10 174	29 263	11 106	526
1988	110 919	29 434	8 976	19 311	12 139	31 111	9 284	664
1989	127 087	36 205	10 657	20 526	13 818	36 729	8 564	587
1990	147 832	43 007	15 298	22 042	16 634	40 251	9 932	668
1991	164 261	48 385	15 854	22 631	17 819	47 748	11 135	690
1992	176 824	54 742	16 618	21 531	20 841	49 864	12 387	841
1993	185 433	57 875	16 528	21 958	21 695	53 023	13 471	883
1994	199 763	58 417	16 997	23 754	26 712	60 209	12 787	887
1995	218 521	63 395	18 909	26 081	30 289	64 386	14 643	818
1996	238 764	69 809	20 422	26 074	32 470	72 615	16 446	928
1997	255 507	73 426	20 868	27 006	33 228	83 349	16 675	955
1998	262 142	71 325	20 098	25 604	35 626	91 158	17 405	926
1999	281 508	74 801	19 785	26 916	39 670	103 523	15 928	885
2000	298 060	82 400	20 687	29 803	43 233	107 361	13 790	786
2001	288 868	71 893	17 926	28 442	41 098	116 139	12 539	831
2002	292 233	66 547	17 046	29 166	44 142	122 594	11 943	795
2000								
January	23 950	6 671	1 599	2 365	3 514	8 642	1 093	66
February	24 430	6 960	1 719	2 370	3 563	8 686	1 070	62
March	24 617	6 855	1 672	2 506	3 599	8 762	1 165	58
April	25 356	7 214	1 865	2 493	3 607	8 820	1 308	49
May	24 694	6 807	1 728	2 501	3 623	8 760	1 225	50
June	25 098	6 992	1 735	2 535	3 634	8 931	1 217	54
July	24 789	6 826	1 705	2 462	3 644	8 935	1 143	74
August	24 885	6 715	1 715	2 520	3 643	9 085	1 128	79
September	24 872	6 802	1 764	2 537	3 634	9 030	1 025	80
October	25 110	6 739	1 722	2 561	3 619	9 213	1 184	72
November	25 138	6 915	1 764	2 510	3 594	9 141	1 143	71
December	25 121	6 904	1 699	2 443	3 559	9 357	1 088	71
2001								
January	25 074	6 885	1 795	2 540	3 480	9 384	915	75
February	24 876	6 831	1 656	2 438	3 451	9 528	898	74
March	25 173	7 019	1 649	2 499	3 439	9 566	928	73
April	24 856	6 629	1 594	2 444	3 491	9 504	1 127	67
May	24 718	6 434	1 626	2 372	3 475	9 597	1 147	67
June	25 127	6 556	1 645	2 418	3 440	9 727	1 274	67
July	24 686	6 502	1 667	2 388	3 313	9 606	1 139	71
August	24 853	6 491	1 756	2 470	3 296	9 665	1 103	72
September	21 834	4 381	1 084	2 192	3 313	9 701	1 092	71
October	21 972	4 239	1 100	2 294	3 438	9 904	931	66
November	22 553	4 787	1 137	2 200	3 474	9 976	915	64
December	23 145	5 139	1 217	2 187	3 489	9 979	1 070	64
2002								
January	23 352	5 255	1 391	2 326	3 418	9 952	945	65
February	23 591	5 441	1 412	2 321	3 447	9 971	934	65
March	24 203	5 599	1 421	2 455	3 509	10 248	906	65
April	23 803	5 261	1 349	2 361	3 680	10 206	880	66
May	24 202	5 369	1 476	2 353	3 749	10 282	907	66
June	24 272	5 400	1 454	2 361	3 793	10 233	964	67
July	24 316	5 328	1 387	2 404	3 797	10 248	1 085	67
August	24 696	5 460	1 527	2 491	3 801	10 220	1 130	67
September	24 487	5 429	1 374	2 412	3 790	10 213	1 203	66
October	24 858	5 855	1 421	2 474	3 698	10 300	1 042	68
November	25 152	6 059	1 420	2 575	3 707	10 383	941	67
December	25 301	6 091	1 414	2 633	3 752	10 339	1 006	66

[1]Contains goods that cannot be separately identified.

Table 7-15. U.S. Imports of Services

(Balance of payments basis, millions of dollars, seasonally adjusted.)

Year and month	Total	Travel	Passenger fares	Other transportation	Royalties and license fees	Other private services (financial, professional, etc.)	Direct defense expenditures [1]	U.S. government miscellaneous services
1960	7 674	1 750	513	1 402	74	593	3 087	254
1961	7 671	1 785	506	1 437	89	588	2 998	268
1962	8 092	1 939	567	1 558	100	528	3 105	296
1963	8 362	2 114	612	1 701	112	493	2 961	370
1964	8 619	2 211	642	1 817	127	527	2 880	415
1965	9 111	2 438	717	1 951	135	461	2 952	457
1966	10 494	2 657	753	2 161	140	506	3 764	513
1967	11 863	3 207	829	2 157	166	565	4 378	561
1968	12 302	3 030	885	2 367	186	668	4 535	631
1969	13 322	3 373	1 080	2 455	221	751	4 856	586
1970	14 520	3 980	1 215	2 843	224	827	4 855	576
1971	15 400	4 373	1 290	3 130	241	956	4 819	592
1972	16 868	5 042	1 596	3 520	294	1 043	4 784	589
1973	18 843	5 526	1 790	4 694	385	1 180	4 629	640
1974	21 379	5 980	2 095	5 942	346	1 262	5 032	722
1975	21 996	6 417	2 263	5 708	472	1 551	4 795	789
1976	24 570	6 856	2 568	6 852	482	2 006	4 895	911
1977	27 640	7 451	2 748	7 972	504	2 190	5 823	951
1978	32 189	8 475	2 896	9 124	671	2 573	7 352	1 099
1979	36 689	9 413	3 184	10 906	831	2 822	8 294	1 239
1980	41 491	10 397	3 607	11 790	724	2 909	10 851	1 214
1981	45 503	11 479	4 487	12 474	650	3 562	11 564	1 287
1982	51 749	12 394	4 772	11 710	795	8 159	12 460	1 460
1983	54 973	13 149	6 003	12 222	943	8 001	13 087	1 568
1984	67 748	22 913	5 735	14 843	1 168	9 040	12 516	1 534
1985	72 862	24 558	6 444	15 643	1 170	10 203	13 108	1 735
1986	80 147	25 913	6 505	17 766	1 401	13 146	13 730	1 686
1987	90 787	29 310	7 283	19 010	1 857	16 485	14 950	1 893
1988	98 526	32 114	7 729	20 891	2 601	17 667	15 604	1 921
1989	102 479	33 416	8 249	22 172	2 528	18 930	15 313	1 871
1990	117 659	37 349	10 531	24 966	3 135	22 229	17 531	1 919
1991	118 459	35 322	10 012	24 975	4 035	25 590	16 409	2 116
1992	118 111	38 552	10 603	23 767	5 161	23 931	13 835	2 263
1993	122 148	40 713	11 410	24 524	5 032	26 129	12 086	2 255
1994	131 121	43 782	13 062	26 019	5 852	29 629	10 217	2 560
1995	139 420	44 916	14 663	27 034	6 919	33 222	10 043	2 623
1996	150 633	48 078	15 809	27 403	7 837	37 758	11 061	2 687
1997	164 435	52 051	18 138	28 959	9 161	41 657	11 707	2 762
1998	178 599	56 483	19 971	30 363	11 235	45 513	12 185	2 849
1999	196 687	58 963	21 315	34 139	13 107	53 007	13 335	2 821
2000	221 021	64 705	24 274	41 425	16 468	57 793	13 473	2 883
2001	219 472	60 200	22 633	38 682	16 713	63 387	14 975	2 882
2002	227 399	58 044	19 969	38 527	19 258	69 436	19 245	2 920
2000								
January	17 343	5 194	1 826	3 137	1 231	4 636	1 084	235
February	17 958	5 498	1 957	3 254	1 255	4 672	1 085	237
March	18 225	5 580	2 021	3 333	1 272	4 688	1 093	238
April	17 984	5 356	2 023	3 310	1 261	4 683	1 113	238
May	18 171	5 330	2 029	3 421	1 278	4 747	1 127	239
June	18 398	5 453	2 084	3 436	1 301	4 741	1 142	241
July	18 568	5 412	2 064	3 491	1 350	4 827	1 176	248
August	18 655	5 289	2 062	3 615	1 374	4 889	1 178	248
September	19 460	5 382	2 116	3 690	1 906	4 952	1 167	247
October	18 750	5 353	2 016	3 677	1 431	4 927	1 107	239
November	18 864	5 404	2 059	3 641	1 406	5 020	1 097	237
December	18 652	5 454	2 017	3 423	1 403	5 015	1 104	236
2001								
January	19 007	5 340	1 971	3 845	1 384	5 065	1 162	240
February	18 362	5 248	1 907	3 296	1 377	5 119	1 174	241
March	18 469	5 297	1 920	3 306	1 371	5 156	1 177	242
April	19 207	5 784	2 031	3 444	1 362	5 204	1 140	242
May	19 020	5 601	2 006	3 363	1 361	5 302	1 145	242
June	18 760	5 340	2 099	3 207	1 364	5 346	1 162	242
July	18 713	5 314	2 197	3 128	1 368	5 272	1 191	243
August	18 847	5 363	2 235	3 111	1 380	5 283	1 233	242
September	16 536	3 934	1 463	2 905	1 397	5 310	1 286	241
October	17 016	3 965	1 588	3 001	1 446	5 387	1 394	235
November	17 597	4 398	1 581	3 030	1 454	5 458	1 441	235
December	17 943	4 616	1 635	3 049	1 449	5 487	1 470	237
2002								
January	18 156	4 780	1 652	2 982	1 379	5 672	1 446	245
February	18 764	4 848	1 635	2 961	1 930	5 680	1 462	248
March	18 246	4 825	1 587	2 948	1 419	5 733	1 486	248
April	18 255	4 599	1 574	3 203	1 504	5 608	1 524	243
May	18 469	4 694	1 595	3 204	1 553	5 627	1 555	241
June	19 152	4 959	1 705	3 173	1 845	5 640	1 589	241
July	19 081	4 806	1 652	3 296	1 678	5 774	1 633	242
August	18 875	4 567	1 597	3 287	1 689	5 828	1 665	242
September	19 212	4 941	1 580	3 204	1 669	5 885	1 692	241
October	19 365	4 823	1 889	3 242	1 539	5 927	1 701	244
November	19 634	4 979	1 698	3 456	1 520	6 009	1 729	243
December	20 186	5 223	1 805	3 573	1 533	6 047	1 763	242

[1]Contains goods that cannot be separately identified.

Table 7-16. U.S. Export and Import Price Indexes

(2000 = 100, not seasonally adjusted.)

Year and month	Exports			Imports		
	All commodities	Agricultural	Nonagricultural	All commodities	Petroleum [1]	Nonpetroleum
1989	94.7	110.5	92.7	91.1	61.2	96.0
1990	95.5	105.1	94.4	94.0	75.5	97.1
1991	96.3	103.4	95.4	94.2	67.3	98.7
1992	96.3	102.5	95.7	94.9	62.9	100.0
1993	96.9	104.4	96.2	94.6	57.7	100.6
1994	98.9	109.4	98.0	96.2	54.3	103.2
1995	103.9	119.0	102.5	100.6	59.8	107.2
1996	104.5	132.6	101.6	101.6	71.1	106.4
1997	103.1	120.6	101.3	99.1	66.0	104.1
1998	99.7	108.8	98.8	93.1	44.8	100.4
1999	98.4	101.1	98.2	93.9	60.1	99.0
2000	100.0	100.0	100.0	100.0	100.0	100.0
2001	99.2	101.2	99.0	96.5	82.8	98.5
2002	98.2	103.2	97.8	94.1	85.3	96.2
1998						
January	101.3	113.8	100.1	95.9	54.0	102.2
February	101.0	112.1	99.9	95.0	50.5	101.7
March	100.7	111.5	99.6	94.1	46.0	101.4
April	100.3	109.7	99.4	93.9	46.1	101.1
May	100.4	110.8	99.3	93.7	46.4	100.9
June	99.9	110.8	98.8	93.1	44.3	100.5
July	99.5	111.2	98.4	92.3	42.0	100.0
August	99.0	106.7	98.3	92.0	41.7	99.6
September	98.5	103.5	98.0	92.2	44.4	99.4
October	98.4	103.7	97.9	92.3	45.4	99.5
November	98.6	105.5	97.9	91.8	41.0	99.6
December	98.5	106.1	97.8	91.0	35.5	99.4
1999						
January	98.5	106.2	97.8	91.3	37.1	99.5
February	98.3	103.7	97.8	91.2	36.9	99.4
March	97.9	100.6	97.7	91.5	42.0	99.0
April	98.1	101.0	97.9	92.4	50.6	98.8
May	98.2	101.4	97.9	93.1	54.3	99.0
June	98.2	101.1	97.9	92.9	54.5	98.8
July	98.1	98.9	98.0	93.8	61.9	98.6
August	98.4	100.8	98.2	94.8	69.1	98.7
September	98.5	100.7	98.3	95.8	74.9	98.9
October	98.8	100.6	98.7	96.0	76.1	99.0
November	99.0	99.6	99.0	96.7	79.2	99.4
December	99.0	98.9	99.0	97.4	84.2	99.4
2000						
January	99.2	99.0	99.2	97.8	87.2	99.4
February	99.6	100.0	99.6	99.7	100.2	99.7
March	100.0	100.4	100.0	99.9	99.4	100.0
April	100.0	101.3	99.9	98.5	88.1	100.1
May	100.2	101.9	100.1	98.8	92.1	99.9
June	100.1	100.5	100.0	100.2	101.9	99.9
July	100.0	98.3	100.2	100.2	100.4	100.2
August	99.8	96.3	100.1	100.4	101.3	100.3
September	100.4	99.4	100.5	101.6	111.8	100.0
October	100.3	99.9	100.3	101.2	108.7	100.0
November	100.3	100.9	100.2	101.2	109.8	99.9
December	100.1	102.0	99.9	100.5	99.0	100.7
2001						
January	100.3	102.5	100.1	100.5	93.1	101.6
February	100.2	101.0	100.1	99.9	93.3	100.8
March	100.0	101.3	99.9	98.3	87.2	100.0
April	99.9	100.8	99.8	97.8	86.2	99.5
May	99.6	100.8	99.5	98.0	90.3	99.2
June	99.4	100.9	99.3	97.6	89.4	98.9
July	99.0	101.8	98.8	96.1	84.6	97.8
August	98.8	102.8	98.5	96.0	86.1	97.5
September	99.0	102.5	98.6	95.9	86.7	97.3
October	98.3	100.7	98.1	93.7	73.4	96.8
November	97.8	99.2	97.7	92.3	63.8	96.6
December	97.6	100.2	97.4	91.4	59.9	96.2
2002						
January	97.5	100.9	97.2	91.6	63.0	96.1
February	97.3	98.3	97.2	91.6	65.7	95.7
March	97.6	98.9	97.5	92.8	76.9	95.8
April	98.0	99.6	97.8	94.3	86.7	96.3
May	98.0	99.5	97.8	94.4	88.4	96.2
June	98.0	100.7	97.8	94.1	85.3	96.2
July	98.3	103.4	97.9	94.5	88.5	96.2
August	98.5	105.2	97.9	94.8	91.8	96.3
September	98.8	108.6	98.0	95.5	97.1	96.4
October	98.7	106.6	98.1	95.5	97.0	96.4
November	98.8	108.7	98.0	94.6	89.0	96.3
December	98.6	108.2	97.8	95.2	94.0	96.5

[1] Petroleum and petroleum products.

NOTES AND DEFINITIONS

This chapter presents data from two different data systems on international flows of goods, services, income payments, and financial transactions as they impact the U.S. economy. Tables 7-1 through 7-5 present data on the value, quantities, and prices of foreign transactions in the National Income and Product Accounts (NIPAs). Table 7-6 shows foreign transactions in the U.S. International Transactions accounts. Both sets of accounts are prepared by the Bureau of Economic Analysis, and draw on the same source data. The source data are presented in greater detail in Tables 7-8 through 7-15 and the Notes and Definitions thereto.

Because of certain differences in concept, scope, and definitions, the aggregate values of international transactions in the NIPAs (as shown in Tables 7-1 and 7-4) are not exactly equal to similar concepts in the U.S. International Transactions accounts, which are the source for the data in Tables 7-6 through 7-15. The principal sources of difference are as follows:

- The NIPAs cover only the 50 states and the District of Columbia. The international transactions accounts also include U.S. territories and Puerto Rico;
- Differences in the treatment of gold; and
- Differences in the treatment of services without payment by financial intermediaries except life insurance carriers (imputed interest).

A reconciliation of the two sets of international accounts is published regularly as part of the NIPAs, most recently in the October 2003 *Survey of Current Business*, p. D-74, Table 2.

There is an additional difference in the two data sets as presented in this volume. In July 2003, the annual revision of the International Transactions accounts featured a definitional change in the measurement of insurance services. This change is conceptually superior to the previous treatment, and avoids the anomalous treatment of the losses of September 11, 2001, that distorted the accounts for that month. See the Notes and Definitions to Tables 7-8 through 7-15 for further detail. (The previous treatment was described in *Business Statistics of the United States: 2002*, pp. xxiii–xxiv and 218–219.) This improvement will also be introduced in the December 2003 comprehensive revision of the NIPAs, but is not reflected in the NIPA data published in this volume.

TABLES 7-1 AND 7-4
FOREIGN TRANSACTIONS IN THE NATIONAL INCOME AND PRODUCT ACCOUNTS

SOURCE: U.S. DEPARTMENT OF COMMERCE, BUREAU OF ECONOMIC ANALYSIS

See the Notes and Definitions to Chapter 1 for an overview of the National Income and Product Accounts. Tables 7-1 and 7-4 present current-dollar values.

Definitions

Exports and imports of goods and services. Goods are products that can be stored or inventoried; services are products that cannot be stored and are consumed at the place and time of their purchase. Goods include expenditures abroad by U.S. residents except for travel. Services include foreign travel by U.S. residents, expenditures in the United States by foreign travelers, and exports and imports of certain goods, primarily military equipment purchased and sold by the federal government.

Table 7-4 shows values for selected components of total goods and services; the components shown will not add to the total. In the case of *goods*, a miscellaneous "other" category is not shown. In the case of *services*, only two components are shown: *travel*, which does not include passenger fares but does include all other spending abroad by tourists from the United States, and by foreign tourists in the United States; and a category called "Other private services," which includes the professional and financial services (for example, computer services) which have accounted for a large part of the long-term growth in the service category. (In the case of this category, BEA uses the description "other" to mean private services other than travel, transportation, royalties and license fees, and a miscellaneous "other" category.)

Income receipts and payments. Income receipts—receipt from abroad of factor (labor or capital) income by U.S. residents—are analogous to exports, and are combined with them to yield total *Receipts from the rest of the world. Income payments* by U.S. entities of factor income to entities abroad are analogous to imports.

Transfer payments (net) consist of payments between the United States and abroad that do not involve either payment for the services of the labor and capital factors of production or purchase of goods and services. Personal remittances from U.S. residents to the rest of the world, remittances from foreigners to U.S. residents, government grants, and transfer payments from businesses are included. Usually transfers from the United States to abroad exceed the reverse flow; only the net is shown here, as a net payment to the rest of the world. There was an exception in 1991 when U.S. allies in the Gulf War reimbursed the United States for the cost of the war. This resulted in net payments to the United States from the rest of the world and therefore appears as a negative entry in the net transfer payments column.

Payments to the rest of the world. By definition, these are equal to receipts from the rest of the world. The balancing item is *Net foreign investment.* This is U.S. exports of goods and services, receipts of factor income, and capital grants received by the United States (mainly the occasional allocation of Special Drawing Rights), less imports, payments of factor income, and transfer payments to the rest of the world (net). It may also be viewed as the acquisition of foreign assets by U.S. residents less the acquisition of U.S. assets by foreign residents. It includes the statistical discrepancy in the balance of payments accounts. A positive entry indicates a flow of net U.S. investment overseas; a negative entry indicates a flow of net foreign investment into the United States.

TABLES 7-2, 7-3 AND 7-5
CHAIN-TYPE QUANTITY AND PRICE INDEXES FOR NIPA FOREIGN TRANSACTIONS

These indexes represent the separation of the current-dollar values in Tables 7-1 and 7-4 into their real quantity and price trends components. See the Notes and Definitions to Chapter 1 for a general explanation of chained-dollar estimates of real output and prices. As explained there, quantity indexes are shown instead of constant-dollar estimates because BEA no longer published its real output estimates before 1987 in any detail in the constant-dollar form. Therefore, quantity indexes are the only source of information about long-term trends in real volumes.

TABLES 7-6 AND 19-9
U.S. INTERNATIONAL TRANSACTIONS

SOURCE: *U.S. DEPARTMENT OF COMMERCE, BUREAU OF ECONOMIC ANALYSIS.*

The U.S. international transactions accounts, or "balance of payments," provide a comprehensive view of economic and financial transactions between the United States and foreign countries, measured in current dollars only (unlike the NIPAs in which price and quantity trends are also estimated). They are subdivided into three sets of accounts, each comprising credit and debit items, which in concept provide a complete accounting for U.S. international transactions and should therefore sum to zero. In practice, there are substantial discrepancies due to measurement problems.

The balance on the "current account" is the most frequently quoted statistic from these accounts, and is frequently if imprecisely called the "trade balance." The current account includes estimates of exports and imports of goods and of travel, transportation, and other services; receipts and payments of income between U.S. and foreign residents; and foreign aid and other current transfers. The "financial account" covers most international flows of capital, private and official, including direct investment. A "capital account," which is small relative to the other two accounts, includes certain transactions in existing assets.

More detailed data on exports and imports of goods and services as they are measured in these accounts are shown in Tables 7-8 through 7-15.

Definitions

Credits (+): The following items are treated as credits in the international transactions accounts: Exports of goods and services and income receipts; unilateral current transfers to the United States; capital account transactions receipts; financial inflows, that is, increases in foreign-owned assets (U.S. liabilities) and decreases in U.S.-owned assets (U.S. claims).

Debits (-): The following items are treated as debits in the international transactions accounts, indicated by minus signs in the data cells: Imports of goods and services and income payments; unilateral current transfers to foreigners; capital accounts transactions payments; financial outflows, that is, decreases in foreign-owned assets (U.S. liabilities) and increases in U.S.-owned assets (U.S. claims).

The *balance on goods* is the excess of exports of goods over imports of goods. (A minus sign indicates an excess of imports over exports.)

The *balance on services* is the excess of service exports over service imports. (A minus sign indicates an excess of imports over exports.)

The *balance on goods and services* is the sum of the balance on goods and the balance on services.

The *balance on income* is the excess of income receipts from abroad over income payments to foreigners. (A minus sign indicates an excess of payments over receipts.)

The *balance on goods, services, and income* is the excess of exports of goods, services, and income over imports of goods, services, and income. It is equal to the sum of the balance on goods and services and the balance on income. (A minus sign indicates an excess of imports over exports.)

The *balance on unilateral transfers* is equal to unilateral transfers, net, that is, transfers to the United States minus transfers from the United States. This category includes U.S. government grants, pensions, and other transfers, and private remittances and other transfers. It includes an adjustment for the difference between actual and normal insured losses; see the entry below, in the Notes for Tables 7-8 through 7-15, concerning the measurement of insurance services.

The *balance on current account* is equal to the sum of the balance on goods, services, and income and the balance on unilateral transfers.

The *capital account* covers net capital transfers and the acquisition and disposal of nonproduced nonfinancial assets. The major types of *capital transfers* are debt forgiveness and assets that accompany immigrants. *Nonproduced nonfinancial assets* include rights to natural resources, patents, copyrights, trademarks, franchises, and leases.

The *financial account* includes all other inflows and outflows of capital, that is, changes in U.S.-owned assets abroad and foreign-owned assets in the United States, including official reserve assets, direct investment, securities, currency, and bank deposits.

In concept, the balance on current account is necessarily offset exactly by the net financial and capital inflow or outflow; for example, a U.S. current account deficit results in more dollars held by foreigners, which *must* be reflected in additional claims on the United States held by foreigners, whether in the form of U.S. currency, securities, loans, or other forms of ownership or obligation. But because of different and incomplete data sources, the financial and capital accounts do not exactly offset the current account. The statistical discrepancy in the U.S. international accounts—the sum of all credits and debits, with the sign reversed—measures the amount by which the measured net financial and capital flow would have to be augmented (or diminished, in the case of a negative entry) to offset the current account balance exactly. (In the quarterly accounts, a part of this discrepancy, the seasonal adjustment discrepancy, results from separate seasonal adjustments.) The statistical discrepancy in the international accounts is not the same as the statistical discrepancy in the national income and product accounts, which arises from measurement differences between domestic output and domestic income.

Notes on the data

Exports and imports of goods in the international transactions account exclude exports of goods under U.S. military agency sales contracts identified in Census Bureau export documents and imports of goods under direct defense expenditures identified in import documents.

They also reflect various other adjustments (for valuation, coverage, and timing) of Census Bureau statistics to a balance-of-payments basis. See Tables 7-9 and 7-10 and the associated Notes and Definitions for further information.

Services include some goods, mainly military equipment (included in transfers under military agency sales contracts); major equipment, other materials, supplies, and petroleum products purchased abroad by U.S. military agencies (included in direct defense expenditures abroad); and fuels purchased by airline and steamship operators (included in other transportation).

U.S. government grants include transfers of goods and services under U.S. military grant programs. The data for 1974 include extraordinary U.S. government transactions with India.

Beginning in 1982, *private remittances and other transfers* includes taxes paid by U.S. private residents to foreign governments and taxes paid by private nonresidents to the U.S. government.

At the present time, all U.S. Treasury-owned *gold* is held in the United States.

Beginning with the data for 1982, *direct investment income* and the reinvested earnings component of *direct investment* financial flows are measured on a current-cost (replacement-cost) basis after adjustment to reported depreciation, depletion, and expensed exploration and development costs. For prior years, depreciation is valued in terms of the historical cost of assets and reflects a mix of prices for the various years in which capital investments were made. See *Survey of Current Business*, July 1999, pp 65–67, and *Survey of Current Business*, June 1992, pages 72ff.

Repayments on U.S. credits and other long-term assets includes sales of foreign obligations to foreigners. The data for 1974 include extraordinary U.S. government transactions with India, described in "Special U.S. Government Transactions," *Survey of Current Business*, June 1974, page 27.

Foreign official assets in the United States. U.S. Treasury securities consists of bills, certificates, marketable bonds and notes, and nonmarketable convertible and nonconvertible bonds and notes; other *U.S. government securities* consists of U.S. Treasury and Export-Import Bank obligations, not included elsewhere, and of debt securities of U.S. government corporations and agencies; *other U.S. government liabilities* includes, primarily, U.S. government liabilities to foreign official authorities associated with military agency sales contracts and other transactions arranged with or through foreign official agencies; *other foreign official assets* consists of official investments in

U.S. corporate stocks and in debt securities of private corporations and state and local governments.

Estimates of *U.S. currency flows abroad* were introduced for the first time as part of the July 1997 revisions. Data for 1974 and subsequent years were affected (see *Survey of Current Business*, July 1997). Beginning with the 1998 revisions, currency flows are published separately from U.S. Treasury securities.

For 1978–1983, *U.S. Treasury securities* includes foreign-currency-denominated notes sold to private residents abroad.

Revisions

The international transactions accounts are revised annually in July. Changes in definitions and methodology, as well as the incorporation of newly available source data, may be introduced in these revisions.

Data availability

Quarterly and annual data are available. Data first are reported in a press release and subsequently published in an article in the *Survey of Current Business*, which can also be found on the BEA Internet site. Revisions to historical data are published annually. The most recent historical revisions also appear in the July 2003 issue of the *Survey*. Complete historical data may be purchased on diskette from BEA. Historical data also are available on the BEA Internet site at <http://www.bea.doc.gov>.

References

Discussions of the impact of changes in methodology and incorporation of new data sources are found in the July (June for 1995 and earlier) issues of the *Survey of Current Business* each year, the most recent being "Annual Revision of the U.S. International Accounts, 1992–2002" (July 2003).

The Balance of Payments of the United States: Concepts, Data Sources, and Estimating Procedures (May 1990), available on the BEA Internet site or from NTIS (Accession No. PB 90-268715) describes the methodology in detail and provides a list of data sources.

TABLE 7-7
INTERNATIONAL INVESTMENT POSITION OF THE UNITED STATES

SOURCE: U.S. DEPARTMENT OF COMMERCE, BUREAU OF ECONOMIC ANALYSIS

The data presented in Tables 7-1 through 7-6 all represent *flows* of goods, services, and money over the designated time periods. Table 7-7, in contrast, is a measure of *stocks*, that is, total holdings, of money and other claims. The data on the international investment position of the United States measure the extent to which the United States and its residents hold claims of ownership on foreigners, or are creditors of foreigners; the extent to which foreigners, including foreign governments, hold claims of ownership on assets located in the United States or are creditors of U.S. residents and entities; and the net difference between the two amounts. This difference measures the amount by which the United States is a net creditor of the rest of the world or a net debtor to the rest of the world. A position of net U.S. indebtedness is represented by a minus sign in the net international investment position.

Changes in the net investment position can arise in two principal ways. The first way is through inflows or outflows of capital. A net inflow of capital increases U.S. indebtedness to foreigners, while a net outflow increases foreigners' indebtedness to the United States. A deficit in the U.S. international current account requires an equivalent inflow of foreign capital, while a surplus would require an equivalent outflow of U.S. capital; see notes on Table 7-6. The second way is through valuation adjustments, which are of several kinds: market prices of assets can change; changes in exchange rates can cause revaluation of foreign-currency-denominated assets; and there can be miscellaneous other adjustments due to changes in coverage, statistical discrepancies, etc.

Definitions

Direct investment occurs when an individual or business in one country (the parent) obtains a lasting interest in, and a degree of influence over the management of, a business enterprise in another country (the affiliate). The U.S. data define this degree of interest to be ownership of at least 10 percent of the voting securities of an incorporated business enterprise or the equivalent interest in an unincorporated business enterprise.

When direct investment positions are valued at the historical costs carried on the books of the affiliated companies, much of the investment will reflect the price levels of earlier time periods. Therefore, before calculating the overall U.S. position, BEA estimates the aggregate direct investment totals using two alternative valuation bases. (Detailed direct investment data by country and industry are available only on a historical cost basis.)

At *current cost*, the portion of the direct investment position representing parents' shares of their affiliates' tangible assets (property, plant, equipment, and inventories) is revalued to replacement cost in today's money, using a perpetual inventory model, appropriate price indexes, and depreciation allowances. This is an adjustment made to the asset side of the balance sheet and reflects prices of tangible assets only.

The *market value* method revalues the owners' equity portion of the direct investment positions using general country indexes of stock market prices. This adjustment is made on the liability and owner's equity side of the balance sheet. Stock price changes reflect changes not only in the value of tangible assets but also in the value of intangible assets and in the outlook for a country or industry.

Market values are more volatile than current cost, reflecting the volatility of stock markets. Note, for example, that in some years the total market value of direct investment is significantly greater than the current replacement cost, while in other years, such as 1982 through 1984, it is less.

U.S. official reserve assets include gold, valued at the current market price; special drawing rights; the U.S. reserve position in the International Monetary Fund; and official holdings of foreign currencies.

Other U.S. government assets include other U.S. government claims on foreigners and holdings of foreign currency and short-term assets.

U.S. nonbank claims are U.S. claims on affiliated foreigners reported by U.S. nonbanking concerns.

U.S. bank claims are claims on foreigners, such as loans and commercial paper, held by U.S. banks and not reported elsewhere in the accounts.

Foreign official assets include foreign government holdings of claims on the United States, including U.S. government securities and other liabilities and deposits held by such governments in U.S. banks.

Foreign-owned assets in the United States, other than official assets, also include *U.S. Treasury securities, U.S. currency, corporate and other bonds, corporate stocks, U.S. liabilities (to foreigners) reported by U.S. nonbanking concerns*, and *U.S. bank liabilities* (such as deposits) *to foreigners*.

Data availability

The annual (year-end) data are presented each year, along with revisions for earlier years and a descriptive article, in the July issue of the *Survey of Current Business*. The articles and the data are available on the BEA Internet site at <http://www.bea.doc.gov>.

References

Relevant articles in the July 2003 *Survey of Current Business* are: "The International Investment Position of the United States at Yearend 2002" and "Direct Investment Positions for 2002: Country and Industry Detail." For background on the valuation of direct

investment and other components, see "Valuation of the U.S. Net International Investment Position," *Survey of Current Business*, May 1991. Also see the references for Table 7-6.

TABLES 7-8 THROUGH 7-15
EXPORTS AND IMPORTS OF GOODS AND SERVICES

SOURCES: U.S. DEPARTMENT OF COMMERCE, BUREAU OF THE CENSUS AND BUREAU OF ECONOMIC ANALYSIS (BEA)

These tables present the source data which are used to build up the aggregate measures of goods and services flows shown in Tables 7-1 through 7-6. These data are compiled and published monthly and so make trends evident before the publication of the quarterly aggregate estimates, and also provide more detail than the quarterly aggregates.

Monthly and annual data on exports and imports of goods are compiled by the Bureau of the Census from documents collected by the U.S. Customs Service. BEA makes certain adjustments to these data (described below) to place the estimates on a "balance of payments" basis—a basis consistent with the national and international accounts. Data on exports and imports of services are prepared by BEA from a variety of sources. Monthly data on services are available from the beginning of 1992. Annual and quarterly data for earlier years are available as part of the international transactions accounts. Current data on goods and services are available each month in a joint Census-BEA press release.

In the case of some of the detailed breakdowns of exports and imports, by end-use categories, monthly data may not sum exactly to annual totals. This is because of later revisions, made only to annual data and not allocated to monthly data. Also, the constant-dollar figures expressed in 2000 dollars are now calculated using chain weights, so that in general the 2000-dollar detail will not add to the 2000-dollar totals.

In addition, monthly and annual data on exports and imports of goods for individual countries and various country groupings do not reflect subsequent revisions of annual total data. These country data are compiled by the Census Bureau in much greater detail than can be shown here, which can be accessed on the Census Internet site at <http://www.census.gov>.

Definitions: *Goods*

Goods: Census Basis. The Census basis goods data are compiled from documents collected by the U.S. Customs Service and reflect the movement of goods between foreign countries and the 50 states, the District of Columbia, Puerto Rico, the U.S. Virgin Islands, and U.S. Foreign Trade Zones. They include government and nongovernment shipments of goods. They exclude shipments between the United States and its territories and possessions, transactions with U.S. military, diplomatic and consular installations abroad, U.S. goods returned to the United States by its Armed Forces, personal and household effects of travelers, and in-transit shipments. The general import values reflect the total arrival of merchandise from foreign countries that immediately enters consumption channels, warehouses, or Foreign Trade Zones.

For *imports*, the value reported is the U.S. Customs Service appraised value of merchandise (generally, the price paid for merchandise for export to the United States). Import duties, freight, insurance, and other charges incurred in bringing merchandise to the United States are excluded.

Exports are valued at the f.a.s. (free alongside ship) value of merchandise at the U.S. port of export, based on the transaction price including inland freight, insurance, and other charges incurred in placing the merchandise alongside the carrier at the U.S. port of exportation.

Goods: Balance of payments (BOP) basis. Goods on a Census basis are adjusted by the BEA to goods on a BOP basis to bring the data in line with the concepts and definitions used to prepare the international and national accounts. Broadly, the adjustments include changes in ownership that occur without goods passing into or out of the customs territory of the United States. These adjustments are necessary to supplement coverage of the Census basis data, to eliminate duplication of transactions recorded elsewhere in the international accounts, and to value transactions according to a standard definition.

The export adjustments include: (1) Deduction of *U.S. military sales contracts*, because the Census Bureau has included these contracts in the goods data, but BEA includes them in the service category "Transfers Under U.S. Military Sales Contracts." BEA's source material for these contracts is more comprehensive, but does not distinguish between goods and services. (2) Addition of *private gift parcels* mailed to foreigners by individuals through the U.S. Postal Service. (Only commercial shipments are covered in Census goods exports.) (3) Addition to *nonmonetary gold exports* of gold purchased by foreign official agencies from private dealers in the United States and held at the Federal Reserve Bank of New York. The Census data include only gold that leaves the customs territory. (4) *Smaller adjustments* include deductions for repairs of goods, exposed motion picture film, and military grant aid, and additions for sales of fish in U.S. territorial waters, exports of electricity to Mexico, and vessels and oil rigs that change ownership without export documents being filed.

The *import adjustments* include: (1) On *inland freight in Canada*, the customs value for imports for certain Canadian goods is the point of origin in Canada. The

BEA makes an addition for the inland freight charges of transporting these Canadian goods to the U.S. border. (2) An addition is made to *nonmonetary gold imports* for gold sold by foreign official agencies to private purchasers out of stock held at the Federal Reserve Bank of New York. The Census Bureau data include only gold that enters the customs territory. (3) A deduction is made for *imports by U.S. military agencies* because the Census Bureau has included these contracts in the goods data, but BEA includes them in the service category "Direct Defense Expenditures." BEA's source material is more comprehensive, but does not distinguish between goods and services. (4) *Smaller adjustments* include deductions for repairs of goods and for exposed motion picture film, and additions for imported electricity from Mexico, conversion of vessels for commercial use, and repairs to U.S. vessels abroad.

Definitions: *Services*

The statistics are estimates of service transactions between foreign countries and the 50 states, the District of Columbia, Puerto Rico, the U.S. Virgin Islands, and other U.S. territories and possessions. Transactions with U.S. military, diplomatic, and consular installations abroad are excluded because they are considered to be part of the U.S. economy. Services are shown in the broad categories described below. For six of these, the categories are the same for imports and exports. For the seventh, exports is "Transfers under U.S. Military Sales Contracts" while for imports the category is "Direct Defense Expenditures."

Travel—Purchases of services and goods by U.S. travelers abroad and by foreign visitors to the United States. A traveler is defined as a person who stays for a period of less than one year in a country of which the person is not a resident. Included are expenditures for food, lodging, recreation, gifts, and other items incidental to a foreign visit. Not included are the international costs of the travel itself, which are covered in *passenger fares* (see below).

Passenger fares—Fares paid by residents of one country to residents in other countries. Receipts consist of fares received by U.S. carriers from foreign residents for travel between the United States and foreign countries and between two foreign points. Payments consist of fares paid by U.S. residents to foreign carriers for travel between the United States and foreign countries.

Break in series: Travel and passenger fares—Beginning with data for 1984, these items incorporate results from a survey administered by the U.S. Travel and Tourism Administration. See *Survey of Current Business*, June 1989, pages 57ff.

Other transportation—Charges for the transportation of goods by ocean, air, waterway, pipeline, and rail carriers to and from the United States. Includes freight charges, operating expenses that transportation companies incur in foreign ports, and payments for vessel charter and aircraft and freight car rentals. (*Break in series*. Estimates of freight charges for the transportation of goods by truck between the United States and Canada are included in the data beginning with 1986. Reliable estimates for earlier years are not available. See *Survey of Current Business*, June 1994, pages 70ff.)

Royalties and license fees—Transactions with foreign residents involving intangible assets and proprietary rights, such as the use of patents, techniques, processes, formulas, designs, know-how, trademarks, copyrights, franchises, and manufacturing rights. The term "royalties" generally refers to payments for the utilization of copyrights or trademarks, and "license fees" generally refers to payments for the use of patents or industrial processes.

Other private services—Includes transactions with "affiliated" foreigners for which no identification by type is available and transactions with unaffiliated foreigners.

The term "affiliated" refers to a direct investment relationship, which exists when a U.S. person has ownership or control, directly or indirectly, of 10 percent or more of a foreign business enterprise, or when a foreign person has a similar interest in a U.S. enterprise.

Transactions with "unaffiliated" foreigners consist of education services; financial services; insurance premiums and losses; telecommunications services; and business, professional, and technical services. Included in the last group are advertising services; computer and data processing services; database and other information services; research, development, and testing services; management, consulting, and public relations services; legal services; construction, engineering, architectural, and mining services; industrial engineering services; installation, maintenance and repair of equipment; and other services, including medical services and film and tape rental.

The "insurance premiums and losses" component of "other private services" was previously measured as premiums less actual losses paid or recovered. Furthermore, catastrophic losses were entered immediately when the loss occurred rather than when the insurance claim was actually paid out. This led to sharp swings in any month where catastrophic losses occurred, such as a large hurricane or September 2001. In the accounts as revised in July 2003 and presented here, insurance services are now measured as premiums less "normal" losses. Normal losses consist of a measure of expected regularly occurring losses based on 6 years of past experience *plus* an additional allowance for catastrophic loss. Catastrophic losses when they occur are added in equal increments to the estimate of regularly occurring losses over the 20 years following their occurrence. Because adoption of

this methodology introduces a difference between actual and normal losses, an amount equal to the difference is entered in the international accounts as a current unilateral transfer.

BEA conducts surveys of international transactions in financial services and "selected services" (largely business, professional, and technical services). Beginning with data for 1986, *other private services* includes estimates of business, professional, and technical services from the BEA surveys of selected services. (See *Survey of Current Business*, June 1989, pages 57ff.)

Breaks in series: Royalties and license fees and other private services—These items are presented on a gross basis beginning in 1982. The definition of exports is revised to exclude U.S. parents' payments to foreign affiliates and to include U.S. affiliates' receipts from foreign parents. The definition of imports is revised to include U.S. parents' payments to foreign affiliates and to exclude U.S. affiliates' receipts from foreign parents.

Transfers under U.S. military sales contracts (exports only)—Exports of goods and services in which U.S. government military agencies participate. Includes both goods, such as equipment, and services, such as repair services and training, that cannot be separately identified. Transfers of goods and services under U.S. military grant programs are included.

Direct defense expenditures (imports only)— Expenditures incurred by U.S. military agencies abroad, including expenditures by U.S. personnel, payments of wages to foreign residents, construction expenditures, payments for foreign contractual services, and procurement of foreign goods. Included are both goods and services that cannot be separately identified.

U.S. government miscellaneous services—Transactions of U.S. Government nonmilitary agencies with foreign residents. Most of these transactions involve the provision of services to, or purchases of services from, foreigners; transfers of some goods are also included.

Services estimates are based on quarterly, annual, and benchmark surveys and partial information generated from monthly reports. Service transactions are estimated at market prices. Estimates are seasonally adjusted when statistically significant seasonal patterns are present.

Definitions: *Area groupings*

European Union—Austria, Belgium, Denmark, Finland, France, Germany, Greece, Ireland, Italy, Luxembourg, Netherlands, Portugal, Spain, Sweden, and United Kingdom.

Euro Area-Austria, Belgium, Finland, France, Germany, Greece, Ireland, Italy, Luxembourg, Netherlands, Portugal, and Spain. Greece entered the euro area beginning in January 2001, and is included in the 2001 and 2002 but not the 2000 data.

Asian Newly Industrialized Countries (NICS)—Hong Kong, South Korea, Singapore, and Taiwan.

Organization of Petroleum Exporting Countries (OPEC)—Algeria, Gabon, Indonesia, Iran, Iraq, Kuwait, Libya, Nigeria, Qatar, Saudi Arabia, United Arab Emirates, and Venezuela.

Notes on the data

U.S./Canada data exchange and substitution. The data for U.S. exports to Canada are derived from import data compiled by Canada. The use of Canada's import data to produce U.S. export data requires several alignments in order to compare the two series. *Coverage:* Canadian imports are based on country of origin. U.S. goods shipped from a third country are included. U.S. exports exclude these foreign shipments. U.S. export coverage also excludes certain Canadian postal shipments. *Valuation:* Canadian imports are valued at point of origin in the United States. However, U.S. exports are valued at the port of exit in the United States and include inland freight charges, making the U.S. export value slightly larger. Canada requires inland freight to be reported. *Reexports:* U.S. exports include reexports of foreign goods. Again, the aggregate U.S. export figure is slightly larger. *Exchange Rate:* Average monthly exchange rates are applied to convert the published data to U.S. currency.

End-use categories and seasonal adjustment of trade in goods. Goods are initially classified under the Harmonized System, which describes and measures the characteristics of goods traded. Combining trade into approximately 140 export and 140 import end-use categories makes it possible to examine goods according to their principal uses. These categories are used as the basis for computing the seasonal and working-day adjusted data. These adjusted data are then summed to the six end-use aggregates for publication.

The seasonal adjustment procedure is based on a model that estimates the monthly movements as percentages above or below the general level of each end-use commodity series (unlike other methods that redistribute the actual series values over the calendar year). Imports of petroleum and petroleum products are adjusted for the length of the month.

Data availability

Data are released in a monthly joint Census-BEA press release (FT-900) about six weeks after the end of the month to which the data pertain. The data on trade in goods by end-use category (BOP basis) and trade in services are subsequently published each month in the *Survey of Current Business*. Additional data and information on goods is obtainable from the Foreign Trade Division, Bureau of the Census, Washington, DC 20233. Additional data and information on services is obtainable from the Balance of Payments Division, Bureau of Economic Analysis, Washington, DC 20230. Current releases and some historical data are available on the Bureau of the Census Internet site at <http://www.census.gov/foreign-trade/www/>.

Revisions

Data for recent years normally are revised annually. In some cases, revisions to annual totals are not distributed to monthly data, which therefore may not sum to the revised total shown. Data on trade in services may be subject to extensive revision as part of BEA's annual revision of the international transactions accounts, usually released in July.

References

Discussion of the impact of changes in methodology and incorporation of new data sources are found in discussions of annual revisions of the international transactions accounts in the July issue of the BEA publication, *Survey of Current Business*, the most recent being "Annual Revision of the U.S. International Accounts, 1992–2002" (July 2002).

TABLE 11-16
EXPORT AND IMPORT PRICE INDEXES

SOURCE: U.S. DEPARTMENT OF LABOR, BUREAU OF LABOR STATISTICS (BLS)

The BLS International Price Program produces monthly and quarterly export and import price indexes for non-military goods traded between the United States and the rest of the world.

Definitions

The *export* price index provides a measure of price change for all products sold by U.S. residents (businesses and individuals located within the geographic boundaries of the United States, whether or not owned by U.S. citizens) to foreign buyers.

The *import* price index provides a measure of price change for goods purchased from other countries by U.S. residents.

Notes on the data

The product universe for both the import and export indexes includes raw materials, agricultural products, and manufactures. Price data are collected primarily by mail questionnaire, in all but a few cases directly from the exporter or importer.

To the extent possible, the data refer to prices at the U.S. border for exports and at either the foreign border or the U.S. border for imports. For nearly all products, the prices refer to transactions completed during the first week of the month and represent the actual price for which the product was bought or sold, including discounts, allowances, and rebates.

For the export price indexes, the preferred pricing basis is f.a.s. (free alongside ship) U.S. port of exportation. Where necessary, adjustments are made to reported prices to place them on this basis. An attempt is made to collect two prices for imports: f.o.b. (free on board) at the port of exportation and c.i.f. (cost, insurance, and freight) at the U.S. port of importation. Adjustments are made to account for changes in product characteristics in order to obtain a "pure" measure of price change.

The indexes are weighted indexes of the Laspeyres type. The values assigned to each weight category are based on trade value figures compiled by the Bureau of the Census, which are updated every five years. Values for calendar 2000 are being used in the calculation of indexes beginning in 2002. For previous years, values from 1990 and 1995 were used as they became available. The indexes have been rebased to 2000 = 100, using the latest weight year as the comparison base. Rebasing changes the level but not the percent changes recorded by the previous version of the index.

Data availability

Indexes are published monthly in a press release and a more detailed report. Selected data subsequently are published in the *Monthly Labor Review*. Indexes are published for detailed product categories, as well as for all commodities. Aggregate import indexes by country or region of origin also are available, as are indexes for selected categories of internationally traded services. Additional information is available from the Division of International Prices, Bureau of Labor Statistics. Complete historical data are available on the BLS Internet site at <http://www.bls.gov>.

References

"BLS to Produce Monthly Indexes of Export and Import Prices," Monthly Labor Review (December 1988) and Chapter 15 "International Price Indexes," *BLS Handbook of Methods* Bulletin 2490 (April 1997).

CHAPTER 8: PRICES

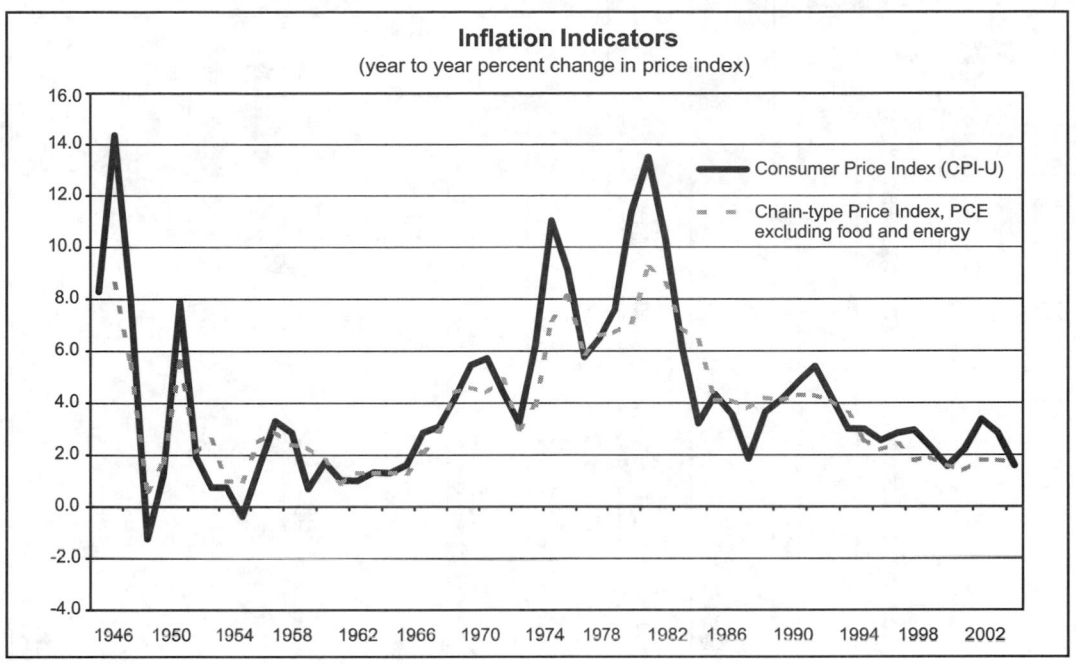

Inflation Indicators
(year to year percent change in price index)

- The Consumer Price Index for all urban consumers (CPI-U) is the most widely used measure of the general price level, and percent changes in the CPI-U are the most widely used measures of inflation. Economists also are interested in what can be called an "underlying rate of inflation," free of the volatile, short-term, and often supply-determined fluctuations of food and energy prices. In the graph, overall inflation as measured by the official CPI-U is shown along with one measure of the underlying rate, the chain-type price index for personal consumption expenditures excluding food and energy. (Tables 8-1 and 1-4)

- All the price indexes, however, tell the same basic story. Prices rose sharply as World War II controls were lifted and when the Korean War broke out. In the following periods of economic slack—1949, 1955, and 1959–1961—prices reverted to near-stability. In the 1960s and 1970s; each recession left inflation significantly higher than before. Only after the inflation of the late 1970s and early 1980s and the subsequent extended period of economic slack (see Table 10-3 for unemployment rates) has inflation subsided to levels comparable with the early postwar period. (Table 8-1)

- From 1946 to 2002, commodity prices in the CPI-U rose an average 3.4 percent per year, but service prices increased at a 4.9 percent annual rate. (Table 8-1)

- The Producer Price Index (PPI) measures prices at the point of production, rather than the consumer level, and only covers commodities, whereas the CPI covers both commodities and services. For these reasons, the PPI for finished goods—the most widely used component of the PPI—fluctuates more (both up and down) than the aggregate CPI-U, but has a less inflationary trend. (Table 8-2)

- The PPI data set also includes prices for intermediate materials, supplies, and components and crude materials for further processing. Intermediate materials prices fluctuate more than those of finished goods, and crude materials prices most of all. (Table 8-2)

Table 8-1. Consumer Price Indexes

(All urban consumers, 1982–1984 = 100, seasonally adjusted, except as noted.)

Year and month	All items Not seasonally adjusted	Seasonally adjusted Index	Seasonally adjusted Percent change	Total	Total food	Food at home Total	Cereals and bakery products	Meats, poultry, fish, and eggs	Dairy and related products	Fruits and vegetables	Non-alcoholic beverages	Other food at home	Food away from home	Alcoholic beverages
1946	19.5	19.5	8.3	...	19.8	...	16.4	...	26.0	20.4	...	...	...	...
1947	22.3	22.3	14.4	...	24.1	25.8	20.4	...	29.3	22.4	12.0	...	...	...
1948	24.1	24.1	8.1	...	26.1	28.0	22.4	...	32.2	23.0	13.1	...	...	...
1949	23.8	23.8	-1.2	...	25.0	26.9	22.3	...	29.4	23.3	14.2	...	...	...
1950	24.1	24.1	1.3	...	25.4	27.3	22.6	...	29.0	22.4	20.0	...	...	...
1951	26.0	26.0	7.9	...	28.2	30.3	24.7	...	32.4	24.4	22.1	...	...	...
1952	26.5	26.5	1.9	...	28.7	30.8	25.3	...	33.8	26.9	22.2	...	...	...
1953	26.7	26.7	0.8	...	28.3	30.3	25.8	...	33.2	26.0	22.8	...	21.5	39.6
1954	26.9	26.9	0.7	...	28.2	30.1	26.4	...	32.1	25.6	27.1	...	21.9	40.6
1955	26.8	26.8	-0.4	...	27.8	29.5	26.8	...	32.1	26.0	24.3	...	22.1	40.5
1956	27.2	27.2	1.5	...	28.0	29.6	27.2	...	32.9	27.3	25.4	...	22.6	41.0
1957	28.1	28.1	3.3	...	28.9	30.6	28.3	...	33.9	27.2	25.2	...	23.4	42.1
1958	28.9	28.9	2.8	...	30.2	32.0	28.8	...	34.4	29.1	23.4	...	24.1	42.0
1959	29.1	29.1	0.7	...	29.7	31.2	29.1	...	34.6	28.7	21.3	...	24.8	42.4
1960	29.6	29.6	1.7	...	30.0	31.5	29.7	...	35.4	29.4	21.1	...	25.4	43.1
1961	29.9	29.9	1.0	...	30.4	31.8	30.3	...	35.9	29.5	21.1	...	26.0	43.3
1962	30.2	30.2	1.0	...	30.6	32.0	30.9	...	35.7	29.8	20.8	...	26.7	43.4
1963	30.6	30.6	1.3	...	31.1	32.4	31.4	...	35.6	31.5	21.1	...	27.3	43.8
1964	31.0	31.0	1.3	...	31.5	32.7	31.5	...	35.9	32.7	23.6	...	27.8	44.2
1965	31.5	31.5	1.6	...	32.2	33.5	31.9	...	36.0	32.6	23.4	...	28.4	44.6
1966	32.4	32.4	2.9	...	33.8	35.2	33.3	...	38.3	33.3	23.3	...	29.7	45.4
1967	33.4	33.4	3.1	35.0	34.1	35.1	34.0	38.0	40.0	33.3	23.1	29.3	31.3	46.4
1968	34.8	34.8	4.2	36.2	35.3	36.3	34.2	39.1	41.3	35.9	23.5	29.8	32.9	48.0
1969	36.7	36.7	5.5	38.1	37.1	38.0	35.2	42.6	42.7	36.4	24.2	30.7	34.9	49.7
1970	38.8	38.8	5.7	40.1	39.2	39.9	37.1	44.6	44.7	37.8	27.1	32.9	37.5	52.1
1971	40.5	40.5	4.4	41.4	40.4	40.9	38.8	44.1	46.1	39.7	28.1	34.3	39.4	54.2
1972	41.8	41.8	3.2	43.1	42.1	42.7	39.0	48.0	46.8	41.6	28.0	34.6	41.0	55.4
1973	44.4	44.4	6.2	48.8	48.2	49.7	43.5	60.9	51.2	47.4	30.1	36.7	44.2	56.8
1974	49.3	49.3	11.0	55.5	55.1	57.1	56.5	62.2	60.7	55.2	35.9	47.8	49.8	61.1
1975	53.8	53.8	9.1	60.2	59.8	61.8	62.9	67.0	62.6	56.9	41.3	55.4	54.5	65.9
1976	56.9	56.9	5.8	62.1	61.6	63.1	61.5	68.0	67.7	58.4	49.4	56.4	58.2	68.1
1977	60.6	60.6	6.5	65.8	65.5	66.8	62.5	67.4	69.5	63.8	74.4	68.4	62.6	70.0
1978	65.2	65.2	7.6	72.2	72.0	73.8	68.1	77.6	74.2	70.9	78.7	73.6	68.3	74.1
1979	72.6	72.6	11.3	79.9	79.9	81.8	74.9	89.0	82.8	76.6	82.6	79.0	75.9	79.9
1980	82.4	82.4	13.5	86.7	86.8	88.4	83.9	92.0	90.9	82.1	91.4	88.4	83.4	86.4
1981	90.9	90.9	10.3	93.5	93.6	94.8	92.3	96.0	97.4	92.0	95.3	94.9	90.9	92.5
1982	96.5	96.5	6.2	97.3	97.4	98.1	96.5	99.6	98.8	97.0	97.9	97.3	95.8	96.7
1983	99.6	99.6	3.2	99.5	99.4	99.1	99.6	99.2	100.0	97.3	99.8	99.5	100.0	100.4
1984	103.9	103.9	4.3	103.2	103.2	102.8	103.9	101.3	101.3	105.7	102.3	103.1	104.2	103.0
1985	107.6	107.6	3.6	105.6	105.6	104.3	107.9	100.1	103.2	108.4	104.3	105.7	108.3	106.4
1986	109.6	109.6	1.9	109.1	109.0	107.3	110.9	104.5	103.3	109.4	110.4	109.4	112.5	111.1
1987	113.6	113.6	3.6	113.5	113.5	111.9	114.8	110.5	105.9	119.1	107.5	110.5	117.0	114.1
1988	118.3	118.3	4.1	118.2	118.2	116.6	122.1	114.3	108.4	128.1	107.5	113.1	121.8	118.6
1989	124.0	124.0	4.8	124.9	125.1	124.2	132.4	121.3	115.6	138.0	111.3	119.1	127.4	123.5
1990	130.7	130.7	5.4	132.1	132.4	132.3	140.0	130.0	126.5	149.0	113.5	123.4	133.4	129.3
1991	136.2	136.2	4.2	136.8	136.3	135.8	145.8	132.6	125.1	155.8	114.1	127.3	137.9	142.8
1992	140.3	140.3	3.0	138.7	137.9	136.8	151.5	130.9	128.5	155.4	114.3	128.8	140.7	147.3
1993	144.5	144.5	3.0	141.6	140.9	140.1	156.6	135.5	129.4	159.0	114.6	130.5	143.2	149.6
1994	148.2	148.2	2.6	144.9	144.3	144.1	163.0	137.2	131.7	165.0	123.2	135.6	145.7	151.5
1995	152.4	152.4	2.8	148.9	148.4	148.8	167.5	138.8	132.8	177.7	131.7	140.8	149.0	153.9
1996	156.9	156.9	3.0	153.7	153.3	154.3	174.0	144.8	142.1	183.9	128.6	142.9	152.7	158.5
1997	160.5	160.5	2.3	157.7	157.3	158.1	177.6	148.5	145.5	187.5	133.4	147.3	157.0	162.8
1998	163.0	163.0	1.6	161.1	160.7	161.1	181.1	147.3	150.8	198.2	133.0	150.8	161.1	165.7
1999	166.6	166.6	2.2	164.6	164.1	164.2	185.0	147.9	159.6	203.1	134.3	153.5	165.1	169.7
2000	172.2	172.2	3.4	168.4	167.8	167.9	188.3	154.5	160.7	204.6	137.8	155.6	169.0	174.7
2001	177.1	177.1	2.8	173.6	173.1	173.4	193.8	161.3	167.1	212.2	139.2	159.6	173.9	179.3
2002	179.9	179.9	1.6	176.8	176.2	175.6	198.0	162.1	168.1	220.9	139.2	160.8	178.3	183.6
2002														
January	177.1	177.6	0.2	175.8	175.3	175.4	197.0	162.2	169.9	218.3	138.9	161.1	176.4	181.8
February	177.8	177.9	0.2	176.3	175.8	175.8	197.6	162.1	170.1	222.2	138.8	160.6	177.0	182.3
March	178.8	178.5	0.3	176.5	176.0	176.1	197.5	163.0	169.4	224.7	139.1	159.7	177.1	182.5
April	179.8	179.3	0.4	176.6	176.1	176.2	197.9	163.2	168.7	221.5	139.8	161.2	177.2	182.9
May	179.8	179.5	0.1	176.4	175.9	175.6	198.1	163.3	169.0	218.6	138.7	160.1	177.6	183.3
June	179.9	179.8	0.2	176.5	175.9	175.2	198.0	162.2	168.0	218.9	138.2	160.5	178.2	183.5
July	180.1	180.1	0.2	176.7	176.1	175.4	197.9	162.2	167.6	220.1	138.9	160.6	178.5	183.7
August	180.7	180.5	0.2	176.6	176.0	174.9	197.8	161.6	167.2	220.5	137.4	160.2	178.8	184.1
September	181.0	180.9	0.2	177.0	176.4	175.4	198.5	161.1	166.3	220.8	140.5	160.7	179.2	184.1
October	181.3	181.2	0.2	177.2	176.6	175.3	199.0	160.8	166.5	219.9	140.3	161.2	179.6	184.7
November	181.3	181.4	0.1	177.6	177.0	175.9	199.2	161.8	167.1	222.2	139.3	161.4	179.8	185.1
December	180.9	181.6	0.1	178.0	177.3	176.3	198.1	162.3	167.3	223.3	140.7	161.7	180.1	185.3

. . . = Not available.

Table 8-1. Consumer Price Indexes—*Continued*

(All urban consumers; 1982–1984 = 100, except as noted; seasonally adjusted, except as noted.)

Year and month	Housing												
	Total	Shelter						Fuels and utilities				Household furnishings and operations	
		Total	Rent of shelter [1]	Rent of primary residence	Lodging away from home [2]	Owners' equivalent rent of primary residence [1]	Tenants' and household insurance [2,3]	Total	Fuels		Water and sewer and trash collection services [2]	Total	Household operations [2,3]
									Fuel oil and other fuels	Gas (piped) and electricity			
1946	...	...	...	...	...	...	...	...	7.9	18.3	...	...	...
1947	...	...	...	...	...	...	...	...	9.0	18.2	...	...	...
1948	...	...	...	...	...	...	...	...	10.6	18.7	...	...	...
1949	...	...	...	...	...	...	...	...	10.9	19.2	...	...	...
1950	...	...	...	...	...	...	...	...	11.3	19.2	...	...	...
1951	...	...	...	...	...	...	...	...	11.8	19.3	...	...	...
1952	...	...	...	...	...	...	...	...	12.1	19.5	...	...	...
1953	...	22.0	...	33.9	...	...	...	22.5	12.6	19.9	...	...	...
1954	...	22.5	...	35.1	...	...	...	22.6	12.6	20.2	...	...	...
1955	...	22.7	...	35.6	...	...	...	23.0	12.7	20.7	...	...	...
1956	...	23.1	...	36.3	...	...	...	23.6	13.3	20.9	...	...	...
1957	...	24.0	...	37.0	...	...	...	24.3	14.0	21.1	...	...	...
1958	...	24.5	...	37.6	...	...	...	24.8	13.7	21.9	...	...	...
1959	...	24.7	...	38.2	...	...	...	25.4	13.9	22.4	...	...	...
1960	...	25.2	...	38.7	...	...	...	26.0	13.8	23.3	...	...	...
1961	...	25.4	...	39.2	...	...	...	26.3	14.1	23.5	...	...	...
1962	...	25.8	...	39.7	...	...	...	26.3	14.2	23.5	...	...	...
1963	...	26.1	...	40.1	...	...	...	26.6	14.4	23.5	...	...	...
1964	...	26.5	...	40.5	...	...	...	26.6	14.4	23.5	...	...	...
1965	...	27.0	...	40.9	...	...	...	26.6	14.6	23.5	...	...	...
1966	...	27.8	...	41.5	...	...	...	26.7	15.0	23.6	...	...	...
1967	30.8	28.8	...	42.2	...	...	...	27.1	15.5	23.7	...	42.0	...
1968	32.0	30.1	...	43.3	...	...	...	27.4	16.0	23.9	...	43.6	...
1969	34.0	32.6	...	44.7	...	...	...	28.0	16.3	24.3	...	45.2	...
1970	36.4	35.5	...	46.5	...	...	...	29.1	17.0	25.4	...	46.8	...
1971	38.0	37.0	...	48.7	...	...	...	31.1	18.2	27.1	...	48.6	...
1972	39.4	38.7	...	50.4	...	...	...	32.5	18.3	28.5	...	49.7	...
1973	41.2	40.5	...	52.5	...	...	...	34.3	21.1	29.9	...	51.1	...
1974	45.8	44.4	...	55.2	...	...	...	40.7	33.2	34.5	...	56.8	...
1975	50.7	48.8	...	58.0	...	...	...	45.4	36.4	40.1	...	63.4	...
1976	53.8	51.5	...	61.1	...	...	...	49.4	38.8	44.7	...	67.3	...
1977	57.4	54.9	...	64.8	...	...	...	54.7	43.9	50.5	...	70.4	...
1978	62.4	60.5	...	69.3	...	...	...	58.5	46.2	55.0	...	74.7	...
1979	70.1	68.9	...	74.3	...	...	...	64.8	62.4	61.0	...	79.9	...
1980	81.1	81.0	...	80.9	...	...	...	75.4	86.1	71.4	...	86.3	...
1981	90.4	90.5	...	87.9	...	...	...	86.4	104.6	81.9	...	93.0	...
1982	96.9	96.9	...	94.6	...	...	...	94.9	103.4	93.2	...	98.0	...
1983	99.5	99.1	102.7	100.1	...	102.5	...	100.2	97.2	101.5	...	100.2	...
1984	103.6	104.0	107.7	105.3	...	107.3	...	104.8	99.4	105.4	...	101.9	...
1985	107.7	109.8	113.9	111.8	...	113.2	...	106.5	95.9	107.1	...	103.8	...
1986	110.9	115.8	120.2	118.3	...	119.4	...	104.1	77.6	105.7	...	105.2	...
1987	114.2	121.3	125.9	123.1	...	124.8	...	103.0	77.9	103.8	...	107.1	...
1988	118.5	127.1	132.0	127.8	...	131.1	...	104.4	78.1	104.6	...	109.4	...
1989	123.0	132.8	138.0	132.8	...	137.4	...	107.8	81.7	107.5	...	111.2	...
1990	128.5	140.0	145.5	138.4	...	144.8	...	111.6	99.3	109.3	...	113.3	...
1991	133.6	146.3	152.1	143.3	...	150.4	...	115.3	94.6	112.6	...	116.0	...
1992	137.5	151.2	157.3	146.9	...	155.5	...	117.8	90.7	114.8	...	118.0	...
1993	141.2	155.7	162.0	150.3	...	160.5	...	121.3	90.3	118.5	...	119.3	...
1994	144.8	160.5	167.0	154.0	...	165.8	...	122.8	88.8	119.2	...	121.0	...
1995	148.5	165.7	172.4	157.8	...	171.3	...	123.7	88.1	119.2	...	123.0	...
1996	152.8	171.0	178.0	162.0	...	176.8	...	127.5	99.2	122.1	...	124.7	...
1997	156.8	176.3	183.4	166.7	...	181.9	...	130.8	99.8	125.1	...	125.4	...
1998	160.4	182.1	189.6	172.1	109.0	187.8	99.8	128.5	90.0	121.2	101.6	126.6	101.5
1999	163.9	187.3	195.0	177.5	112.3	192.9	101.3	128.8	91.4	120.9	104.0	126.7	104.5
2000	169.6	193.4	201.3	183.9	117.5	198.7	103.7	137.9	129.7	128.0	106.5	128.2	110.5
2001	176.4	200.6	208.9	192.1	118.6	206.3	106.2	150.2	129.3	142.4	109.6	129.1	115.6
2002	180.3	208.1	216.7	199.7	118.3	214.7	108.7	143.6	115.5	134.4	113.0	128.3	119.0
2002													
January	178.3	205.1	213.4	196.8	117.7	211.4	106.4	142.9	108.9	134.5	111.6	128.9	117.8
February	178.6	205.9	214.5	197.5	118.6	212.1	106.8	142.1	108.1	133.5	111.8	128.7	117.9
March	179.0	206.3	214.9	198.0	117.6	212.8	106.8	142.5	109.4	133.7	112.1	128.7	118.9
April	179.4	207.0	215.6	198.5	118.8	213.4	107.2	142.6	112.5	133.6	112.5	128.6	118.4
May	179.9	207.5	216.1	199.0	119.0	213.9	107.6	143.3	113.9	134.4	112.6	128.8	118.4
June	180.1	207.8	216.5	199.5	118.0	214.5	107.8	143.5	114.9	134.5	112.8	128.6	118.8
July	180.4	208.2	216.9	200.0	117.2	215.1	108.6	143.4	116.4	134.2	113.0	128.4	119.0
August	180.8	208.9	217.6	200.4	118.5	215.6	109.6	143.8	117.9	134.4	113.4	128.1	119.2
September	181.1	209.4	218.1	200.8	118.4	216.2	110.0	144.1	119.2	134.6	113.6	127.9	119.7
October	181.6	209.9	218.6	201.3	118.3	216.8	110.0	144.6	120.9	135.0	114.0	128.1	119.7
November	181.8	210.3	219.0	201.9	118.9	217.1	111.4	144.7	121.8	134.9	114.4	127.8	119.9
December	182.2	210.8	219.4	202.3	118.9	217.7	112.3	145.3	123.0	135.6	114.7	127.4	119.9

[1] December 1982 = 100.
[2] December 1997 = 100.
[3] Not seasonally adjusted.
. . . = Not available.

Table 8-1. Consumer Price Indexes—*Continued*

(All urban consumers; 1982–1984 = 100, except as noted; seasonally adjusted.)

Year and month	Apparel					Transportation								
						Total	Private transportation							
							Total	New and used motor vehicles			Motor fuel		Motor vehicle parts and equipment	Motor vehicle maintenance and repair
	Total	Men's and boys' apparel	Women's and girls' apparel	Infants' and toddlers' apparel	Footwear			Total [2]	New vehicles	Used cars and trucks	Total	Gasoline (all types)		
1946	34.4	35.1	48.0	...	22.2	16.7	18.3	...	...	...	14.5	14.5	...	15.8
1947	39.9	41.6	55.6	43.8	27.7	18.5	20.8	...	34.1	...	16.4	16.4	...	17.1
1948	42.5	43.9	58.9	41.2	30.3	20.6	23.0	...	37.3	...	18.6	18.6	...	18.1
1949	40.8	42.7	55.7	38.4	30.1	22.1	24.4	...	40.9	...	19.1	19.1	...	18.6
1950	40.3	42.5	53.8	37.8	30.5	22.7	24.5	...	41.2	...	19.0	19.0	...	18.9
1951	43.9	46.0	57.9	41.5	34.5	24.1	25.6	...	43.1	...	19.5	19.5	...	20.4
1952	43.5	46.2	57.2	39.3	33.8	25.7	27.3	...	46.8	...	20.0	20.0	...	20.8
1953	43.1	45.9	56.6	39.2	33.8	26.5	27.8	...	47.3	26.7	21.2	21.2	...	22.0
1954	43.1	45.6	56.1	37.0	34.2	26.1	27.1	...	46.5	22.7	21.8	21.8	...	22.7
1955	42.9	45.1	55.6	37.6	34.5	25.8	26.7	...	44.9	21.5	22.1	22.1	...	23.2
1956	43.7	45.9	56.0	37.6	36.4	26.2	27.1	...	46.1	20.7	22.8	22.8	...	24.2
1957	44.5	46.6	56.3	37.7	37.5	27.7	28.6	...	48.6	23.2	23.8	23.8	...	25.0
1958	44.6	46.4	56.2	37.3	38.1	28.6	29.5	...	50.1	24.0	23.4	23.5	...	25.4
1959	45.0	46.3	56.5	36.9	39.7	29.8	30.8	...	52.3	26.8	23.7	23.7	...	26.0
1960	45.7	47.2	56.7	36.8	41.1	29.8	30.6	...	51.6	25.0	24.4	24.4	...	26.5
1961	46.1	47.7	56.9	35.5	41.4	30.1	30.8	...	51.6	26.0	24.1	24.1	...	27.1
1962	46.3	48.0	56.8	34.8	42.0	30.8	31.4	...	51.4	28.4	24.3	24.3	...	27.5
1963	46.9	48.6	57.3	34.8	42.5	30.9	31.6	...	51.1	28.7	24.2	24.2	...	27.8
1964	47.3	49.3	57.6	34.9	42.6	31.4	32.0	...	50.9	30.0	24.1	24.1	...	28.2
1965	47.8	49.9	58.1	35.1	43.4	31.9	32.5	...	49.8	29.8	25.1	25.1	...	28.7
1966	49.0	51.2	59.2	35.4	46.0	32.3	32.9	...	48.9	29.0	25.6	25.6	...	29.2
1967	51.0	53.1	61.9	35.8	48.2	33.3	33.8	...	49.3	29.9	26.4	26.4	...	30.4
1968	53.7	56.1	65.6	37.3	50.8	34.3	34.8	...	50.7	...	26.8	26.8	...	32.1
1969	56.8	59.7	69.2	38.4	53.9	35.7	36.0	...	51.5	30.9	27.6	27.7	...	34.1
1970	59.2	62.2	71.8	39.2	56.8	37.5	37.5	...	53.1	31.2	27.9	27.9	...	36.6
1971	61.1	63.9	74.4	40.0	58.6	39.5	39.4	...	55.3	33.0	28.1	28.1	...	39.3
1972	62.3	64.7	76.2	41.1	60.3	39.9	39.7	...	54.8	33.1	28.4	28.4	...	41.1
1973	64.6	67.1	78.8	42.5	62.8	41.2	41.0	...	54.8	35.2	31.2	31.2	...	43.2
1974	69.4	72.4	83.5	54.2	66.6	45.8	46.2	...	58.0	36.7	42.2	42.2	...	47.6
1975	72.5	75.5	85.5	64.5	69.6	50.1	50.6	...	63.0	43.8	45.1	45.1	...	53.7
1976	75.2	78.1	87.9	68.0	72.3	55.1	55.6	...	67.0	50.3	47.0	47.0	...	57.6
1977	78.6	81.7	90.6	74.6	75.7	59.0	59.7	...	70.5	54.7	49.7	49.7	...	61.9
1978	81.4	83.5	92.4	77.4	79.0	61.7	62.5	...	75.9	55.8	51.8	51.8	77.6	67.0
1979	84.9	85.4	94.0	79.0	85.3	70.5	71.7	...	81.9	60.2	70.1	70.2	85.1	73.7
1980	90.9	89.4	96.0	85.5	91.8	83.1	84.2	...	88.5	62.3	97.4	97.5	95.3	81.5
1981	95.3	94.2	97.5	92.9	96.7	93.2	93.8	...	93.9	76.9	108.5	108.5	101.0	89.2
1982	97.8	97.6	98.5	96.3	99.1	97.0	97.1	...	97.5	88.8	102.8	102.8	103.6	96.0
1983	100.2	100.3	100.2	101.1	99.8	99.3	99.3	...	99.9	98.7	99.4	99.4	100.7	100.3
1984	102.1	102.1	101.3	102.6	101.1	103.7	103.6	...	102.6	112.5	97.9	97.8	95.6	103.8
1985	105.0	105.0	104.9	107.2	102.3	106.4	106.2	...	106.1	113.7	98.7	98.6	95.9	106.8
1986	105.9	106.2	104.0	111.8	101.9	102.3	101.2	...	110.6	108.8	77.1	77.0	95.4	110.3
1987	110.6	109.1	110.4	112.1	105.1	105.4	104.2	...	114.4	113.1	80.2	80.1	96.1	114.8
1988	115.4	113.4	114.9	116.4	109.9	108.7	107.6	...	116.5	118.0	80.9	80.8	97.9	119.7
1989	118.6	117.0	116.4	119.1	114.4	114.1	112.9	...	119.2	120.4	88.5	88.5	100.2	124.9
1990	124.1	120.4	122.6	125.8	117.4	120.5	118.8	...	121.4	117.6	101.2	101.0	100.9	130.1
1991	128.7	124.2	127.6	128.9	120.9	123.8	121.9	...	126.0	118.1	99.4	99.2	102.2	136.0
1992	131.9	126.5	130.4	129.3	125.0	126.5	124.6	...	129.2	123.2	99.0	99.0	103.1	141.3
1993	133.7	127.5	132.6	127.1	125.9	130.4	127.5	91.8	132.7	133.9	98.0	97.7	101.6	145.9
1994	133.4	126.4	130.9	128.1	126.0	134.3	131.4	95.5	137.6	141.7	98.5	98.2	101.4	150.2
1995	132.0	126.2	126.9	127.2	125.4	139.1	136.3	99.4	141.0	156.5	100.0	99.8	102.1	154.0
1996	131.7	127.7	124.7	129.7	126.6	143.0	140.0	101.0	143.7	157.0	106.3	105.9	102.2	158.4
1997	132.9	130.1	126.1	129.0	127.6	144.3	141.0	100.5	144.3	151.1	106.2	105.8	101.9	162.7
1998	133.0	131.8	126.0	126.1	128.0	141.6	137.9	100.1	143.4	150.6	92.2	91.6	101.1	167.1
1999	131.3	131.1	123.3	129.0	125.7	144.4	140.5	100.1	142.9	152.0	100.7	100.1	100.5	171.9
2000	129.6	129.7	121.5	130.6	123.8	153.3	149.1	100.8	142.8	155.8	129.3	128.6	101.5	177.3
2001	127.3	125.7	119.3	129.2	123.0	154.3	150.0	101.3	142.1	158.7	124.7	124.0	104.8	183.5
2002	124.0	121.7	115.8	126.4	121.4	152.9	148.8	99.2	140.0	152.0	116.6	116.0	106.9	190.2
2002														
January	124.3	123.1	115.7	125.3	119.6	149.1	144.8	100.5	141.6	155.5	100.9	100.2	106.2	187.1
February	124.5	122.9	116.5	127.3	121.3	148.6	144.2	99.8	140.3	154.4	100.0	99.4	106.1	187.7
March	125.5	124.6	116.7	128.1	122.4	150.5	146.3	99.6	140.2	153.4	108.2	107.6	106.5	188.4
April	125.2	124.0	116.5	127.3	122.4	152.8	148.6	99.2	139.9	152.7	117.9	117.3	106.8	189.1
May	124.5	121.9	116.2	126.9	122.6	152.9	148.6	99.1	139.6	152.3	117.7	117.1	106.8	189.9
June	123.8	121.1	115.5	126.4	121.7	153.2	149.1	99.0	139.5	152.3	119.1	118.4	106.7	190.2
July	123.0	121.3	114.6	125.8	120.2	153.8	149.8	99.0	139.4	152.6	120.9	120.2	107.4	190.1
August	124.0	120.9	116.4	126.8	121.2	154.2	150.2	99.2	139.4	153.2	121.1	120.5	107.7	191.3
September	123.7	120.7	115.7	126.6	121.4	154.5	150.5	99.2	139.9	151.7	121.9	121.2	107.4	191.3
October	123.5	120.3	115.8	125.8	121.1	155.2	151.4	99.1	140.2	150.0	125.0	124.5	106.9	191.5
November	123.2	120.4	115.3	125.5	121.2	154.9	151.0	98.6	140.1	148.0	123.8	123.2	107.2	192.5
December	122.9	119.7	114.9	125.3	121.4	154.5	150.5	98.3	139.8	147.9	122.1	121.5	107.0	193.5

[2]December 1997 = 100.
. . . = Not available.

Table 8-1. Consumer Price Indexes—*Continued*

(All urban consumers; 1982–1984 = 100, except as noted; seasonally adjusted.)

Year and month	Transportation—Continued		Medical care		Medical care services			Recreation		Education and communication	Education		
	Public transportation	Transportation services	Medical care, total	Medical care commodities	Total	Professional services	Hospital and related services	Total[2]	Video and audio[2]	Total[2]	Total[2]	Educational books and supplies	Tuition, other school fees, and childcare
1946	9.4	12.7	12.5	34.2	10.4	...	...	...	...	...	...	...	...
1947	9.9	13.2	13.5	36.7	11.3	...	...	...	...	...	...	...	...
1948	11.2	14.7	14.4	38.6	12.1	...	...	...	...	...	...	...	...
1949	12.4	16.3	14.8	39.2	12.5	...	...	...	...	...	...	...	...
1950	13.4	17.4	15.1	39.7	12.8	...	...	...	...	...	...	...	...
1951	14.8	19.0	15.9	40.8	13.4	...	...	...	...	...	...	...	...
1952	15.8	20.4	16.7	41.2	14.3	...	...	...	...	...	...	...	...
1953	16.8	21.7	17.3	41.5	14.8	...	...	...	...	...	...	...	...
1954	18.0	22.6	17.8	42.0	15.3	...	...	...	...	...	...	...	...
1955	18.5	22.7	18.2	42.5	15.7	...	...	...	...	...	...	...	...
1956	19.2	23.0	18.9	43.4	16.3	...	...	...	...	...	...	...	...
1957	19.9	24.1	19.7	44.6	17.0	...	...	...	...	...	...	...	...
1958	20.9	25.6	20.6	46.1	17.9	...	...	...	...	...	...	...	...
1959	21.5	26.5	21.5	46.8	18.7	...	...	...	...	...	...	...	...
1960	22.2	27.2	22.3	46.9	19.5	...	...	...	...	...	...	...	...
1961	23.2	27.8	22.9	46.3	20.2	...	...	...	...	...	...	...	...
1962	24.0	28.3	23.5	45.6	20.9	...	...	...	...	...	...	...	...
1963	24.3	28.6	24.1	45.2	21.5	...	...	...	...	...	...	...	...
1964	24.7	29.2	24.6	45.1	22.0	...	...	...	...	...	...	...	...
1965	25.2	30.3	25.2	45.0	22.7	...	...	...	...	...	...	...	...
1966	26.1	31.6	26.3	45.1	23.9	...	...	...	...	...	...	...	...
1967	27.4	32.6	28.2	44.9	26.0	30.9	...	...	...	...	...	33.7	...
1968	28.7	33.9	29.9	45.0	27.9	32.5	...	...	...	...	...	35.4	...
1969	30.9	36.3	31.9	45.4	30.2	34.7	...	...	...	...	...	37.4	...
1970	35.2	40.2	34.0	46.5	32.3	37.0	...	...	...	...	...	38.8	...
1971	37.8	43.4	36.1	47.3	34.7	39.4	...	...	...	...	...	41.4	...
1972	39.3	44.4	37.3	47.4	35.9	40.8	...	...	...	...	...	44.2	...
1973	39.7	44.7	38.8	47.5	37.5	42.2	...	...	...	...	...	45.6	...
1974	40.6	46.3	42.4	49.2	41.4	45.8	...	...	...	...	...	47.2	...
1975	43.5	49.8	47.5	53.3	46.6	50.8	...	...	...	...	...	50.3	...
1976	47.8	56.9	52.0	56.5	51.3	55.5	...	...	...	...	...	53.7	...
1977	50.0	61.5	57.0	60.2	56.4	60.0	...	...	...	...	...	56.9	...
1978	51.5	64.4	61.8	64.4	61.2	64.5	55.1	...	...	...	...	61.6	59.8
1979	54.9	69.5	67.5	69.0	67.2	70.1	61.0	...	...	...	...	65.7	64.7
1980	69.0	79.2	74.9	75.4	74.8	77.9	69.2	...	...	...	...	71.4	71.2
1981	85.6	88.6	82.9	83.7	82.8	85.9	79.1	...	...	...	...	80.3	79.9
1982	94.9	96.1	92.5	92.3	92.6	93.2	90.3	...	...	...	...	91.0	90.5
1983	99.5	99.1	100.6	100.2	100.7	99.8	100.5	...	...	...	...	100.3	99.7
1984	105.7	104.8	106.8	107.5	106.7	107.0	109.2	...	...	...	...	108.7	109.8
1985	110.5	110.0	113.5	115.2	113.2	113.5	116.1	...	...	...	...	118.2	119.7
1986	117.0	116.3	122.0	122.8	121.9	120.8	123.1	...	...	...	...	128.1	129.6
1987	121.1	121.9	130.1	131.0	130.0	128.8	131.6	...	...	...	...	138.1	140.0
1988	123.3	128.0	138.6	139.9	138.3	137.5	143.9	...	...	...	...	148.1	151.0
1989	129.5	135.6	149.3	150.8	148.9	146.4	160.5	...	...	...	...	158.0	162.7
1990	142.6	144.2	162.8	163.4	162.7	156.1	178.0	...	...	...	...	171.3	175.7
1991	148.9	151.2	177.0	176.8	177.1	165.7	196.1	...	...	...	...	180.3	191.4
1992	151.4	155.7	190.1	188.1	190.5	175.8	214.0	...	...	...	...	190.3	208.5
1993	167.0	162.9	201.4	195.0	202.9	184.7	231.9	90.7	96.5	85.5	78.4	197.6	225.3
1994	172.0	168.6	211.0	200.7	213.4	192.5	245.6	92.7	95.4	88.8	83.3	205.5	239.8
1995	175.9	175.9	220.5	204.5	224.2	201.0	257.8	94.5	95.1	92.2	88.0	214.4	253.8
1996	181.9	180.5	228.2	210.4	232.4	208.3	269.5	97.4	96.6	95.3	92.7	226.9	267.1
1997	186.7	185.0	234.6	215.3	239.1	215.4	278.4	99.6	99.4	98.4	97.3	238.4	280.4
1998	190.3	187.9	242.1	221.8	246.8	222.2	287.5	101.1	101.1	100.3	102.1	250.8	294.2
1999	197.7	190.7	250.6	230.7	255.1	229.2	299.5	102.0	100.7	101.2	107.0	261.7	308.4
2000	209.6	196.1	260.8	238.1	266.0	237.7	317.3	103.3	101.0	102.5	112.5	279.9	324.0
2001	210.6	201.9	272.8	247.6	278.8	246.5	338.3	104.9	101.5	105.2	118.5	295.9	341.1
2002	207.4	209.1	285.6	256.4	292.9	253.9	367.8	106.2	102.8	107.9	126.0	317.6	362.1
2002													
January	209.0	205.6	279.6	252.9	286.1	250.8	352.6	105.7	102.1	107.0	122.2	301.4	352.1
February	208.2	206.3	280.4	253.6	286.9	250.9	355.1	105.9	102.5	107.2	123.1	311.9	353.8
March	207.4	206.8	281.5	254.0	288.2	251.4	358.2	106.0	102.5	106.8	123.7	313.1	355.4
April	208.6	207.6	282.7	254.6	289.6	251.9	361.9	106.3	102.6	106.5	124.2	314.8	356.9
May	210.5	208.6	283.9	255.3	291.0	252.6	364.7	106.3	102.8	107.1	124.7	317.2	358.3
June	208.9	208.8	284.6	255.9	291.7	252.9	366.0	106.1	102.8	107.4	125.6	318.8	360.9
July	206.1	209.2	286.4	257.0	293.7	254.8	368.3	106.1	102.5	108.2	126.3	320.4	363.0
August	206.8	210.1	287.1	257.4	294.5	254.8	370.8	106.2	102.3	108.9	127.1	321.0	365.2
September	205.7	210.7	288.0	258.0	295.5	255.1	373.6	106.3	102.7	108.8	127.8	321.4	367.6
October	204.6	211.3	289.7	258.7	297.6	256.4	377.2	106.5	103.1	108.8	128.3	321.9	369.0
November	205.7	212.1	291.2	259.7	299.2	257.2	381.0	106.5	103.4	108.8	128.9	324.1	370.6
December	206.5	212.4	292.3	260.0	300.6	258.0	383.9	106.7	103.8	109.0	129.4	324.8	372.0

[2]December 1997 = 100.
. . . = Not available.

Table 8-1. Consumer Price Indexes—Continued

(All urban consumers; 1982–1984 = 100, except as noted; seasonally adjusted, except as noted.)

Year and month	Education and communication—Continued					Other goods and services				
	Communication, not seasonally adjusted							Personal care		
		Information and Information processing				Total	Tobacco and smoking products			
				Information and information processing other than telephone services						
	Total [2]	Total [2]	Telephone services [2]	Total [4]	Personal computers and peripheral equipment [2]			Total	Personal care products	Personal care services
1946	...	...	...	...	...	...	18.2	22.7	27.6	...
1947	...	...	...	...	...	...	19.8	25.4	33.2	...
1948	...	...	...	...	...	...	20.7	26.3	34.2	...
1949	...	...	...	...	...	...	21.3	26.2	33.0	...
1950	...	...	...	...	...	...	21.7	26.2	32.2	...
1951	...	...	...	...	...	...	22.4	28.7	35.7	...
1952	...	...	...	...	...	...	23.5	29.0	35.0	...
1953	...	...	...	...	...	...	24.5	29.3	34.8	24.1
1954	...	...	...	...	...	...	24.9	29.4	34.6	24.4
1955	...	...	...	...	...	...	25.0	29.9	34.6	25.6
1956	...	...	...	...	...	...	25.5	31.2	35.4	27.2
1957	...	...	...	...	...	...	26.3	32.3	36.6	28.3
1958	...	...	...	...	...	...	27.1	33.4	37.9	29.0
1959	...	...	...	...	...	...	28.1	34.1	38.2	30.0
1960	...	...	...	...	...	...	29.1	34.6	38.2	31.0
1961	...	...	...	...	...	...	29.3	34.8	38.1	31.5
1962	...	...	...	...	...	...	29.5	35.4	38.5	32.2
1963	...	...	...	...	...	...	30.4	35.9	38.6	33.0
1964	...	...	...	...	...	...	31.2	36.3	38.6	33.9
1965	...	...	...	...	...	...	32.6	36.6	38.4	34.8
1966	...	...	...	...	...	...	34.2	37.3	38.0	36.4
1967	...	...	...	...	...	35.1	35.5	38.4	38.6	38.1
1968	...	...	...	...	...	36.9	37.8	40.0	39.8	40.1
1969	...	...	...	...	...	38.7	39.8	42.0	41.6	42.2
1970	...	...	...	...	...	40.9	43.1	43.5	42.7	44.2
1971	...	...	...	...	...	42.9	44.9	44.9	44.0	45.7
1972	...	...	...	...	...	44.7	47.4	46.0	45.2	46.8
1973	...	...	...	...	...	46.4	48.7	48.1	46.4	49.7
1974	...	...	...	...	...	49.8	51.1	52.8	51.5	53.9
1975	...	...	...	...	...	53.9	54.7	57.9	58.0	57.7
1976	...	...	...	...	...	57.0	57.0	61.7	61.3	61.9
1977	...	...	...	...	...	60.4	59.8	65.7	64.7	66.4
1978	...	...	...	...	...	64.3	63.0	69.9	68.2	71.3
1979	...	...	...	...	...	68.9	66.8	75.2	72.9	77.2
1980	...	...	...	...	...	75.2	72.0	81.9	79.6	83.7
1981	...	...	...	...	...	82.6	77.8	89.1	87.8	90.2
1982	...	...	...	...	...	91.1	86.5	95.4	95.1	95.7
1983	...	...	...	...	...	101.1	103.4	100.3	100.7	100.0
1984	...	...	...	...	...	107.9	110.1	104.3	104.2	104.4
1985	...	...	...	...	...	114.5	116.7	108.3	107.6	108.9
1986	...	...	...	...	...	121.4	124.7	111.9	111.3	112.5
1987	...	...	...	...	...	128.5	133.6	115.1	113.9	116.2
1988	...	...	...	...	...	137.0	145.8	119.4	118.1	120.7
1989	...	...	...	96.3	...	147.7	164.4	125.0	123.2	126.8
1990	...	...	...	93.5	...	159.0	181.5	130.4	128.2	132.8
1991	...	...	...	88.6	...	171.6	202.7	134.9	132.8	137.0
1992	...	...	...	83.7	...	183.3	219.8	138.3	136.5	140.0
1993	96.7	97.7	...	78.8	...	192.9	228.4	141.5	139.0	144.0
1994	97.6	98.6	...	72.0	...	198.5	220.0	144.6	141.5	147.9
1995	98.8	98.7	...	63.8	...	206.9	225.7	147.1	143.1	151.5
1996	99.6	99.5	...	57.2	...	215.4	232.8	150.1	144.3	156.6
1997	100.3	100.4	...	50.1	...	224.8	243.7	152.7	144.2	162.4
1998	98.7	98.5	100.7	39.9	78.2	237.7	274.8	156.7	148.3	166.0
1999	96.0	95.5	100.1	30.5	53.5	258.3	355.8	161.1	151.8	171.4
2000	93.6	92.8	98.5	25.9	41.1	271.1	394.9	165.6	153.7	178.1
2001	93.3	92.3	99.3	21.3	29.5	282.6	425.2	170.5	155.1	184.3
2002	92.3	90.8	99.7	18.3	22.2	293.2	461.5	174.7	154.7	188.4
2002										
January	93.4	92.2	100.3	19.4	24.6	287.2	432.8	173.2	155.2	186.3
February	93.1	92.0	100.3	19.0	23.8	290.2	449.3	173.7	155.5	186.4
March	92.0	90.8	99.1	18.8	23.1	288.5	433.4	174.1	155.1	187.3
April	91.2	90.0	98.2	18.6	22.9	292.9	461.4	174.4	155.4	187.9
May	91.9	90.7	99.3	18.5	23.0	291.5	449.0	174.7	154.8	188.3
June	91.8	90.6	99.2	18.4	22.6	294.4	467.4	174.9	155.4	188.3
July	92.6	90.8	99.5	18.4	22.3	294.5	467.2	175.0	154.6	188.7
August	93.2	91.5	100.6	18.3	22.0	295.9	478.2	174.9	154.3	189.1
September	92.5	90.7	100.1	17.8	21.1	297.0	485.8	174.9	154.4	189.2
October	92.2	90.4	99.9	17.7	20.7	295.4	470.6	175.3	154.6	189.3
November	91.8	90.0	99.8	17.3	20.0	295.6	470.4	175.5	154.2	189.9
December	91.8	90.0	99.9	17.2	19.7	295.8	472.5	175.4	153.4	189.9

[2]December 1997 = 100.
[4]December 1988 = 100.
. . . = Not available.

Table 8-1. Consumer Price Indexes—*Continued*

(All urban consumers, except as noted; 1982–1984 = 100, except as noted; seasonally adjusted, except as noted.)

| Year and month | Commodity and service groups of CPI-U | | Special indexes in CPI-U | | | | | Supplemental all items indexes based on CPI-U | | | Consumer Price Index, Urban wage earners and clerical workers (CPI-W)[5] |
	Commodities	Services	Energy	All items less Food	All items less Energy	All items less Food and energy Index	All items less Food and energy Percent change	CPI-U-X1[5]	CPI-U-RS[6]	C-CPI-U[7]	
1946	22.9	14.1	...	19.8	...	...	...	...	...	...	19.6
1947	27.6	14.7	...	21.7	...	...	...	24.2	...	...	22.5
1948	29.6	15.6	...	23.3	...	...	...	26.2	...	...	24.2
1949	28.8	16.4	...	23.5	...	...	...	25.9	...	...	24.0
1950	29.0	16.9	...	23.8	...	...	...	26.2	...	...	24.2
1951	31.6	17.8	...	25.3	...	...	...	28.3	...	...	26.1
1952	32.0	18.6	...	25.9	...	...	...	28.8	...	...	26.7
1953	31.9	19.4	...	26.4	...	...	...	29.0	...	...	26.9
1954	31.6	20.0	...	26.6	...	...	...	29.2	...	...	27.0
1955	31.3	20.4	...	26.6	...	...	...	29.1	...	...	26.9
1956	31.6	20.9	...	27.1	...	...	...	29.6	...	...	27.3
1957	32.6	21.8	21.5	28.0	28.9	28.9	...	30.5	...	...	28.3
1958	33.3	22.6	21.5	28.6	29.7	29.6	2.4	31.4	...	...	29.1
1959	33.3	23.3	21.9	29.2	29.9	30.2	2.0	31.6	...	...	29.3
1960	33.6	24.1	22.4	29.7	30.4	30.6	1.3	32.2	...	...	29.8
1961	33.8	24.5	22.5	30.0	30.7	31.0	1.3	32.5	...	...	30.1
1962	34.1	25.0	22.6	30.3	31.1	31.4	1.3	32.8	...	...	30.4
1963	34.4	25.5	22.6	30.7	31.5	31.8	1.3	33.3	...	...	30.8
1964	34.8	26.0	22.5	31.1	32.0	32.3	1.6	33.7	...	...	31.2
1965	35.2	26.6	22.9	31.6	32.5	32.7	1.2	34.2	...	...	31.7
1966	36.1	27.6	23.3	32.3	33.5	33.5	2.4	35.2	...	...	32.6
1967	36.8	28.8	23.8	33.4	34.4	34.7	3.6	36.3	...	...	33.6
1968	38.1	30.3	24.2	34.9	35.9	36.3	4.6	37.7	...	...	35.0
1969	39.9	32.4	24.8	36.8	38.0	38.4	5.8	39.4	...	...	36.9
1970	41.7	35.0	25.5	39.0	40.3	40.8	6.3	41.3	...	...	39.0
1971	43.2	37.0	26.5	40.8	42.0	42.7	4.7	43.1	...	...	40.7
1972	44.5	38.4	27.2	42.0	43.4	44.0	3.0	44.4	...	...	42.1
1973	47.8	40.1	29.4	43.7	46.1	45.6	3.6	47.2	...	...	44.7
1974	53.5	43.8	38.1	48.0	50.6	49.4	8.3	51.9	...	...	49.6
1975	58.2	48.0	42.1	52.5	55.1	53.9	9.1	56.2	...	...	54.1
1976	60.7	52.0	45.1	56.0	58.2	57.4	6.5	59.4	...	...	57.2
1977	64.2	56.0	49.4	59.6	61.9	61.0	6.3	63.2	...	...	60.9
1978	68.8	60.8	52.5	63.9	66.7	65.5	7.4	67.5	104.3	...	65.6
1979	76.6	67.5	65.7	71.2	73.4	71.9	9.8	74.0	114.1	...	73.1
1980	86.0	77.9	86.0	81.5	81.9	80.8	12.4	82.3	126.7	...	82.9
1981	93.2	88.1	97.7	90.4	90.1	89.2	10.4	90.1	138.6	...	91.4
1982	97.0	96.0	99.2	96.3	96.1	95.8	7.4	95.6	146.8	...	96.9
1983	99.8	99.4	99.9	99.7	99.6	99.6	4.0	99.6	152.9	...	99.8
1984	103.2	104.6	100.9	104.0	104.3	104.6	5.0	103.9	159.0	...	103.3
1985	105.4	109.9	101.6	108.0	108.4	109.1	4.3	107.6	164.3	...	106.9
1986	104.4	115.4	88.2	109.8	112.6	113.5	4.0	109.6	167.3	...	108.6
1987	107.7	120.2	88.6	113.6	117.2	118.2	4.1	113.6	173.0	...	112.5
1988	111.5	125.7	89.3	118.3	122.3	123.4	4.4	118.3	179.3	...	117.0
1989	116.7	131.9	94.3	123.7	128.1	129.0	4.5	124.0	187.0	...	122.6
1990	122.8	139.2	102.1	130.3	134.7	135.5	5.0	130.7	196.3	...	129.0
1991	126.6	146.3	102.5	136.1	140.9	142.1	4.9	136.2	203.4	...	134.3
1992	129.1	152.0	103.0	140.8	145.4	147.3	3.7	140.3	208.5	...	138.2
1993	131.5	157.9	104.2	145.1	150.0	152.2	3.3	144.5	213.7	...	142.1
1994	133.8	163.1	104.6	149.0	154.1	156.5	2.8	148.2	218.2	...	145.6
1995	136.4	168.7	105.2	153.1	158.7	161.2	3.0	152.4	223.5	...	149.8
1996	139.9	174.1	110.1	157.5	163.1	165.6	2.7	156.9	229.5	...	154.1
1997	141.8	179.4	111.5	161.1	167.1	169.5	2.4	160.5	234.4	...	157.6
1998	141.9	184.2	102.9	163.4	170.9	173.4	2.3	163.0	237.7	...	159.7
1999	144.4	188.8	106.6	167.0	174.4	177.0	2.1	166.6	242.7	...	163.2
2000	149.2	195.3	124.6	173.0	178.6	181.3	2.4	172.2	250.8	102.0	168.9
2001	150.7	203.4	129.3	177.8	183.5	186.1	2.6	177.1	257.8	104.3	173.5
2002	149.7	209.8	121.7	180.5	187.7	190.5	2.4	179.9	261.9	[8]105.6	175.9
2002											
January	146.6	206.8	114.0	178.1	186.0	188.7	0.2	177.6	257.9	[8]104.1	173.6
February	147.6	207.3	113.1	178.3	186.4	189.0	0.2	177.9	258.9	[8]104.5	173.9
March	149.0	207.8	117.2	178.9	186.6	189.2	0.1	178.5	260.3	[8]105.1	174.5
April	148.4	208.4	121.9	179.9	187.0	189.7	0.3	179.3	261.8	[8]105.7	175.4
May	148.5	209.1	122.1	180.2	187.2	190.0	0.2	179.5	261.7	[8]105.7	175.5
June	149.7	209.5	122.9	180.5	187.4	190.2	0.1	179.8	262.0	[8]105.7	175.8
July	149.9	210.0	123.7	180.8	187.7	190.5	0.2	180.1	262.3	[8]105.7	176.2
August	149.2	210.7	123.9	181.3	188.2	191.1	0.3	180.5	263.1	[8]106.0	176.6
September	150.4	211.2	124.4	181.6	188.4	191.4	0.2	180.9	263.5	[8]106.2	176.9
October	150.1	211.8	126.2	182.1	188.7	191.6	0.1	181.2	264.0	[8]106.4	177.2
November	150.3	212.3	125.6	182.2	188.9	191.8	0.1	181.4	264.0	[8]106.3	177.3
December	150.3	212.9	125.1	182.3	189.2	192.1	0.2	181.6	263.4	[8]106.0	177.5

[5]See Notes and Definitions; not seasonally adjusted.
[6]December 1977 = 100; not seasonally adjusted; see Notes and Definitions for more information.
[7]December 1999 = 100; not seasonally adjusted; see Notes and Definitions for more information.
[8]Interim values.
. . . = Not available.

Table 8-2. Producer Price Indexes and Purchasing Power of the Dollar

(1982 = 100, seasonally adjusted.)

Year and month	Finished goods Total	Finished goods Percent change from previous period	Finished consumer goods Total	Finished consumer foods Total	Finished consumer foods Crude	Finished consumer foods Processed	Finished consumer goods, except foods Total	Durable goods	Nondurable goods less foods	Capital equipment Total	Manufacturing industries	Nonmanufacturing industries
1947	26.4	. . .	28.6	31.9	39.3	31.1	27.4	32.9	24.2	19.8	17.5	21.9
1948	28.5	8.0	30.8	34.9	42.4	34.0	29.2	35.2	25.7	21.6	19.1	23.8
1949	27.7	-2.8	29.4	32.1	40.1	31.1	28.6	36.1	24.7	22.7	20.0	25.0
1950	28.2	1.8	29.9	32.7	36.5	32.4	29.0	36.5	25.1	23.2	20.6	25.5
1951	30.8	9.2	32.7	36.7	41.9	36.2	31.1	38.9	27.0	25.5	22.7	27.9
1952	30.6	-0.6	32.3	36.4	44.6	35.4	30.7	39.2	26.3	25.9	23.2	28.3
1953	30.3	-1.0	31.7	34.5	41.6	33.6	31.0	39.5	26.6	26.3	23.5	28.7
1954	30.4	0.3	31.7	34.2	37.5	34.0	31.1	39.8	26.7	26.7	23.9	29.0
1955	30.5	0.3	31.5	33.4	39.1	32.7	31.3	40.2	26.8	27.4	24.7	29.8
1956	31.3	2.6	32.0	33.3	39.1	32.7	32.1	41.6	27.3	29.5	26.8	31.8
1957	32.5	3.8	32.9	34.4	38.5	34.1	32.9	42.8	27.9	31.3	28.5	33.6
1958	33.2	2.2	33.6	36.5	41.0	36.1	32.9	43.4	27.8	32.1	29.3	34.5
1959	33.1	-0.3	33.3	34.8	37.3	34.7	33.3	43.9	28.2	32.7	29.8	35.1
1960	33.4	0.9	33.6	35.5	39.8	35.2	33.5	43.8	28.4	32.8	30.2	34.8
1961	33.4	0.0	33.6	35.4	38.0	35.3	33.4	43.6	28.4	32.9	30.3	34.8
1962	33.5	0.3	33.7	35.7	38.4	35.6	33.4	43.4	28.4	33.0	30.5	34.9
1963	33.4	-0.3	33.5	35.3	37.8	35.2	33.4	43.1	28.5	33.1	30.6	34.8
1964	33.5	0.3	33.6	35.4	38.9	35.2	33.3	43.3	28.4	33.4	31.0	35.1
1965	34.1	1.8	34.2	36.8	39.0	36.8	33.6	43.2	28.8	33.8	31.5	35.4
1966	35.2	3.2	35.4	39.2	41.5	39.2	34.1	43.4	29.3	34.6	32.5	36.0
1967	35.6	1.1	35.6	38.5	39.6	38.8	34.7	44.1	30.0	35.8	33.8	37.0
1968	36.6	2.8	36.5	40.0	42.5	40.0	35.5	45.1	30.6	37.0	35.0	38.2
1969	38.0	3.8	37.9	42.4	45.9	42.3	36.3	45.9	31.5	38.3	36.2	39.5
1970	39.3	3.4	39.1	43.8	46.0	43.9	37.4	47.2	32.5	40.1	38.1	41.3
1971	40.5	3.1	40.2	44.5	45.8	44.7	38.7	48.9	33.5	41.7	39.6	43.0
1972	41.8	3.2	41.5	46.9	48.0	47.2	39.4	50.0	34.1	42.8	40.5	44.2
1973	45.6	9.1	46.0	56.5	63.6	55.8	41.2	50.9	36.1	44.2	42.2	45.3
1974	52.6	15.4	53.1	64.4	71.6	63.9	48.2	55.5	44.0	50.5	48.8	51.2
1975	58.2	10.6	58.2	69.8	71.7	70.3	53.2	61.0	48.9	58.2	56.5	58.9
1976	60.8	4.5	60.4	69.6	76.7	69.0	56.5	63.7	52.4	62.1	60.3	62.9
1977	64.7	6.4	64.3	73.3	79.5	72.7	60.6	67.4	56.8	66.1	64.5	66.8
1978	69.8	7.9	69.4	79.9	85.8	79.4	64.9	73.6	60.0	71.3	70.1	71.8
1979	77.6	11.2	77.5	87.3	92.3	86.8	73.5	80.8	69.3	77.5	77.1	77.7
1980	88.0	13.4	88.6	92.4	93.9	92.3	87.1	91.0	85.1	85.8	86.0	85.7
1981	96.1	9.2	96.6	97.8	104.4	97.2	96.1	96.4	95.8	94.6	94.9	94.4
1982	100.0	4.1	100.0	100.0	100.0	100.0	100.0	100.0	100.0	100.0	100.0	100.0
1983	101.6	1.6	101.3	101.0	102.4	100.9	101.2	102.8	100.5	102.8	102.3	103.0
1984	103.7	2.1	103.3	105.4	111.4	104.9	102.2	104.5	101.1	105.2	104.9	105.4
1985	104.7	1.0	103.8	104.6	102.9	104.8	103.3	106.5	101.7	107.5	107.4	107.6
1986	103.2	-1.4	101.4	107.3	105.6	107.4	98.5	108.9	93.3	109.7	109.7	109.7
1987	105.4	2.1	103.6	109.5	107.1	109.6	100.7	111.5	94.9	111.7	111.8	111.6
1988	108.0	2.5	106.2	112.6	109.8	112.7	103.1	113.8	97.3	114.3	115.5	113.9
1989	113.6	5.2	112.1	118.7	119.6	118.6	108.9	117.6	103.8	118.8	120.3	118.2
1990	119.2	4.9	118.2	124.4	123.0	124.4	115.3	120.4	111.5	122.9	124.5	122.2
1991	121.7	2.1	120.5	124.1	119.3	124.4	118.7	123.9	115.0	126.7	127.8	126.3
1992	123.2	1.2	121.7	123.3	107.6	124.4	120.8	125.7	117.3	129.1	129.3	129.0
1993	124.7	1.2	123.0	125.7	114.4	126.5	121.7	128.0	117.6	131.4	131.2	131.4
1994	125.5	0.6	123.3	126.8	111.3	127.9	121.6	130.9	116.2	134.1	133.2	134.3
1995	127.9	1.9	125.6	129.0	118.8	129.8	124.0	132.7	118.8	136.7	135.8	137.0
1996	131.3	2.7	129.5	133.6	129.2	133.8	127.6	134.2	123.3	138.3	137.2	138.6
1997	131.8	0.4	130.2	134.5	126.6	135.1	128.2	133.7	124.3	138.2	137.7	138.4
1998	130.7	-0.8	128.9	134.3	127.2	134.8	126.4	132.9	122.2	137.6	137.9	137.4
1999	133.0	1.8	132.0	135.1	125.5	135.9	130.5	133.0	127.9	137.6	138.5	137.3
2000	138.0	3.8	138.2	137.2	123.5	138.3	138.4	133.9	138.7	138.8	139.5	138.6
2001	140.7	2.0	141.5	141.3	127.7	142.4	141.4	134.0	142.8	139.7	140.4	139.4
2002	138.9	-1.3	139.4	140.1	128.5	141.0	138.8	133.0	139.8	139.1	140.0	138.7
2002												
January	137.7	0.0	137.7	141.5	136.9	141.9	135.8	133.5	135.2	139.5	140.3	139.2
February	138.1	0.3	138.2	143.0	146.7	142.6	136.0	133.7	135.4	139.5	140.3	139.2
March	139.2	0.8	139.6	143.8	161.1	142.2	137.7	133.5	137.9	139.5	140.3	139.1
April	139.0	-0.1	139.6	139.6	116.8	141.5	139.2	133.3	140.3	139.2	140.0	138.8
May	138.4	-0.4	138.7	139.2	123.8	140.5	138.2	133.2	138.9	139.1	139.9	138.8
June	138.6	0.1	139.0	139.5	126.5	140.5	138.5	133.3	139.2	139.2	139.9	138.9
July	138.6	0.0	139.1	139.4	127.9	140.3	138.6	132.4	139.8	138.8	139.8	138.3
August	138.6	0.0	139.2	138.8	127.0	139.8	139.0	132.1	140.6	138.6	139.7	138.2
September	139.0	0.3	139.6	138.2	118.7	139.8	139.8	132.6	141.5	139.0	139.9	138.6
October	140.1	0.8	141.0	138.8	122.2	140.2	141.5	133.5	143.5	139.3	140.0	138.9
November	139.7	-0.3	140.5	139.3	120.7	140.8	140.7	132.7	142.7	139.1	140.0	138.6
December	139.3	-0.3	140.1	139.8	111.7	142.1	139.9	132.1	141.9	138.8	139.9	138.3

. . . = Not available.

Table 8-2. Producer Price Indexes and Purchasing Power of the Dollar—*Continued*

(1982 = 100, seasonally adjusted.)

| Year and month | Total | Intermediate materials, supplies, and components | | | | | Materials and components for construction | Processed fuels and lubricants | | | Containers, nonreturnable | Supplies | |
| | | Materials and components for manufacturing | | | | | | | | | | | |
		Total	Materials for food manufacturing	Materials for nondurable manufacturing	Materials for durable manufacturing	Components for manufacturing		Total	Manufacturing industries	Nonmanufacturing industries		Total	Manufacturing industries
1947	23.3	24.9	36.9	33.5	17.5	21.3	22.5	14.4	17.3	12.5	23.4	28.5	23.4
1948	25.2	26.8	38.0	35.4	19.8	23.0	24.9	16.4	19.3	14.5	24.4	29.8	24.7
1949	24.2	25.7	32.7	32.3	20.4	23.4	24.9	14.9	17.6	13.2	24.5	28.0	24.6
1950	25.3	26.9	34.0	33.9	21.5	24.3	26.2	15.2	17.9	13.6	25.2	29.0	26.3
1951	28.4	30.5	37.9	39.3	23.9	27.6	28.7	15.9	18.7	14.1	29.6	32.6	29.3
1952	27.5	29.3	36.4	35.4	24.0	27.6	28.5	15.7	18.5	13.9	28.0	32.6	28.5
1953	27.7	29.7	36.5	35.1	25.0	28.1	29.0	15.8	18.5	14.2	28.0	31.0	28.7
1954	27.9	29.8	36.1	34.5	25.6	28.3	29.1	15.8	18.5	14.1	28.5	31.7	29.1
1955	28.4	30.5	35.0	34.7	26.9	29.5	30.3	15.8	18.5	14.2	28.9	31.2	30.8
1956	29.6	32.0	35.2	35.2	28.5	32.2	31.8	16.3	19.1	14.6	31.0	32.0	32.2
1957	30.3	32.7	35.8	35.7	29.5	33.5	32.0	17.2	20.1	15.6	32.4	32.3	33.4
1958	30.4	32.8	36.6	35.3	29.7	33.8	32.0	16.2	19.1	14.5	33.2	33.1	33.9
1959	30.8	33.3	35.3	35.9	30.4	34.2	32.9	16.2	19.1	14.3	33.0	33.5	34.8
1960	30.8	33.3	35.7	35.9	30.4	34.0	32.7	16.6	19.7	14.6	33.4	33.3	36.2
1961	30.6	32.9	36.9	35.1	30.0	33.7	32.2	16.8	19.9	14.8	33.2	33.7	35.8
1962	30.6	32.7	36.1	34.9	30.0	33.4	32.1	16.7	19.9	14.7	33.6	34.5	36.0
1963	30.7	32.7	37.9	34.6	30.0	33.4	32.2	16.6	19.8	14.5	33.2	35.0	35.8
1964	30.8	33.1	37.3	34.8	30.6	33.7	32.5	16.2	19.4	14.1	32.9	34.7	35.9
1965	31.2	33.6	38.3	35.2	31.2	34.2	32.8	16.5	19.6	14.4	33.5	35.0	36.1
1966	32.0	34.3	40.0	35.4	31.8	35.4	33.6	16.8	19.9	14.7	34.5	36.5	37.1
1967	32.2	34.5	39.2	35.2	32.3	36.5	34.0	16.9	20.1	14.8	35.0	36.8	37.6
1968	33.0	35.3	39.8	35.6	33.4	37.3	35.7	16.5	19.8	14.2	35.9	37.1	38.7
1969	34.1	36.5	42.0	36.0	35.2	38.5	37.7	16.6	20.0	14.4	37.2	37.8	39.8
1970	35.4	38.0	44.3	36.5	37.0	40.6	38.3	17.7	21.5	15.2	39.0	39.7	41.4
1971	36.8	38.9	45.7	37.0	38.1	41.9	40.8	19.5	23.6	16.6	40.8	40.8	42.5
1972	38.2	40.4	47.0	38.5	39.9	42.9	43.0	20.1	24.5	16.9	42.7	42.5	43.3
1973	42.4	44.1	57.2	42.6	43.1	44.3	46.5	22.2	26.4	19.4	45.2	51.7	45.6
1974	52.5	56.0	82.0	54.6	55.4	51.1	55.0	33.6	35.5	32.7	53.3	56.8	53.3
1975	58.0	61.7	82.1	61.4	60.8	57.8	60.1	39.4	41.9	38.0	60.0	61.8	59.4
1976	60.9	64.0	70.6	64.8	64.8	60.8	64.1	42.3	44.8	41.1	63.1	65.8	62.6
1977	64.9	67.4	71.9	66.8	70.2	64.5	69.3	47.7	51.0	46.2	65.9	69.3	66.6
1978	69.5	72.0	81.0	69.2	76.2	69.2	76.5	49.9	53.7	48.1	71.0	72.9	71.2
1979	78.4	80.9	89.9	78.3	87.3	75.8	84.2	61.6	64.3	60.4	79.4	80.2	78.1
1980	90.3	91.7	103.7	91.2	97.1	84.6	91.3	85.0	85.5	84.7	89.1	89.9	87.2
1981	98.6	98.7	102.1	100.5	100.7	94.7	97.9	100.6	100.2	101.0	96.7	96.9	95.2
1982	100.0	100.0	100.0	100.0	100.0	100.0	100.0	100.0	100.0	100.0	100.0	100.0	100.0
1983	100.6	101.2	101.3	98.5	103.0	102.4	102.8	95.4	96.2	94.9	100.4	101.8	101.5
1984	103.1	104.1	106.3	102.1	104.9	105.0	105.6	95.7	97.1	94.6	105.9	104.1	105.0
1985	102.7	103.3	101.5	100.5	103.3	106.4	107.3	92.8	93.8	92.0	109.0	104.4	107.3
1986	99.1	102.2	98.4	98.1	101.2	107.5	108.1	72.7	75.1	71.2	110.3	105.6	108.3
1987	101.5	105.3	100.8	102.2	106.2	108.8	109.8	73.3	75.9	71.7	114.5	107.7	110.0
1988	107.1	113.2	106.0	112.9	118.7	112.3	116.1	71.2	73.3	69.9	120.1	113.7	114.8
1989	112.0	118.1	112.7	118.5	123.6	116.4	121.3	76.4	78.3	75.3	125.4	118.1	119.8
1990	114.5	118.7	117.9	118.0	120.7	119.0	122.9	85.9	87.3	85.0	127.7	119.4	122.1
1991	114.4	118.1	115.3	116.7	117.2	121.0	124.5	85.3	88.4	83.4	128.1	121.4	124.4
1992	114.7	117.9	113.9	115.4	117.2	122.0	126.5	84.5	87.5	82.6	127.7	122.7	125.9
1993	116.2	118.9	115.6	115.5	119.1	123.0	132.0	84.7	88.1	82.6	126.4	125.0	128.5
1994	118.5	122.1	118.5	119.2	125.2	124.3	136.6	83.1	86.1	81.1	129.7	127.0	130.7
1995	124.9	130.4	119.5	135.1	135.6	126.5	142.1	84.2	87.1	82.3	148.8	132.1	137.0
1996	125.7	128.6	125.3	130.5	131.3	126.9	143.6	90.0	92.4	88.4	141.1	135.9	138.7
1997	125.6	128.3	123.2	129.6	132.8	126.4	146.5	89.3	92.0	87.6	136.0	135.9	139.4
1998	123.0	126.1	123.2	126.7	128.0	125.9	146.8	81.1	85.8	78.1	140.8	134.8	140.6
1999	123.2	124.6	120.8	124.9	125.1	125.7	148.9	84.6	87.9	82.5	142.5	134.2	140.7
2000	129.2	128.1	119.2	132.6	129.0	126.2	150.7	102.0	100.9	102.3	151.6	136.9	143.5
2001	129.7	127.4	124.3	131.8	125.1	126.4	150.6	104.5	105.7	103.5	153.1	138.7	145.4
2002	127.8	126.1	123.2	129.2	124.7	126.1	151.3	96.3	98.7	94.8	152.1	138.9	144.7
2002													
January	125.6	124.6	122.7	125.4	122.7	126.2	150.6	90.0	93.5	87.9	152.6	138.2	144.7
February	125.5	124.7	123.3	125.4	122.9	126.3	150.5	89.7	93.2	87.5	151.9	138.1	144.6
March	126.4	125.1	123.3	126.4	123.6	126.3	150.7	92.9	95.5	91.3	151.7	138.3	144.3
April	127.5	125.4	122.1	127.8	123.6	126.2	150.9	97.1	99.3	95.7	151.2	138.5	144.5
May	127.1	125.5	121.1	128.0	123.9	126.2	151.0	95.0	97.3	93.6	151.0	138.4	144.7
June	127.4	125.8	121.8	128.7	124.6	126.2	151.2	95.3	97.9	93.6	151.3	138.7	144.7
July	127.7	126.2	122.2	129.6	125.1	126.1	151.4	95.7	97.9	94.3	151.4	139.1	144.7
August	128.2	126.4	122.4	130.3	125.1	126.0	151.8	97.2	99.5	95.7	151.5	139.3	144.7
September	128.9	126.9	122.3	131.5	125.7	125.9	152.0	98.8	101.4	97.2	152.5	139.6	144.7
October	129.8	127.4	123.9	133.0	125.9	125.9	151.8	102.0	103.0	101.4	153.3	139.5	144.8
November	129.7	127.7	125.4	133.0	126.5	126.0	151.6	101.0	103.5	99.4	153.4	139.6	144.9
December	129.6	127.3	127.2	131.6	126.5	125.9	151.5	101.2	102.7	100.2	153.2	139.6	144.9

Table 8-2. Producer Price Indexes and Purchasing Power of the Dollar—Continued

(1982 = 100, seasonally adjusted.)

Year and month	Intermediate materials, supplies, and components—Continued — Supplies—Continued — Nonmanufacturing industries			Total	Foodstuffs and feedstuffs	Crude materials for further processing — Nonfood materials						
	Total	Feeds	Other supplies			Total	Nonfood materials except fuel — Total	Manu-facturing	Construc-tion	Crude fuel — Total	Manu-facturing industries	Nonmanu-facturing industries
1947	31.8	60.8	26.5	31.7	45.1	...	24.0	24.0	23.5	7.5	6.5	8.5
1948	33.1	61.8	27.9	34.7	48.8	...	26.7	26.7	25.7	8.9	7.7	10.0
1949	30.4	52.5	26.7	30.1	40.5	...	24.3	24.1	26.6	8.8	7.6	9.9
1950	31.0	52.5	27.5	32.7	43.4	...	27.8	27.7	26.9	8.8	7.6	9.9
1951	35.1	58.5	31.3	37.6	50.2	...	32.0	32.1	28.5	9.0	7.7	10.1
1952	35.5	63.5	30.7	34.5	47.3	...	27.8	27.6	28.5	9.0	7.7	10.2
1953	32.8	51.9	30.1	31.9	42.3	...	26.6	26.3	29.6	9.3	8.0	10.6
1954	33.7	56.2	30.1	31.6	42.3	...	26.1	25.8	30.5	8.9	7.6	10.1
1955	31.8	44.7	30.7	30.4	38.4	...	27.5	27.3	31.5	8.9	7.6	10.1
1956	32.3	42.5	31.9	30.6	37.6	...	28.6	28.3	32.9	9.5	8.2	10.7
1957	32.1	39.4	32.6	31.2	39.2	...	28.2	27.8	34.3	10.1	8.7	11.4
1958	32.8	42.7	32.8	31.9	41.6	...	27.1	26.6	35.1	10.2	8.8	11.5
1959	33.1	43.6	32.8	31.1	38.8	...	28.1	27.6	35.4	10.4	8.9	11.7
1960	32.1	37.2	33.2	30.4	38.4	...	26.9	26.3	35.9	10.5	9.0	11.8
1961	32.9	40.9	32.9	30.2	37.9	...	27.2	26.6	35.9	10.5	9.0	11.8
1962	33.8	43.6	33.2	30.5	38.6	...	27.1	26.5	36.1	10.4	8.9	11.8
1963	34.6	45.9	33.2	29.9	37.5	...	26.7	26.1	36.0	10.5	9.0	11.9
1964	34.1	45.0	32.9	29.6	36.6	...	27.2	26.6	35.9	10.5	9.0	11.9
1965	34.5	45.9	33.0	31.1	39.2	...	27.7	27.2	36.1	10.6	9.0	11.9
1966	36.2	50.0	33.8	33.1	42.7	...	28.3	27.8	36.3	10.9	9.3	12.3
1967	36.3	48.3	34.5	31.3	40.3	21.1	26.5	25.8	37.0	11.3	9.7	12.8
1968	36.4	46.5	35.4	31.8	40.9	21.6	27.1	26.3	38.4	11.5	9.9	13.1
1969	36.9	46.4	36.0	33.9	44.1	22.5	28.4	27.6	39.8	12.0	10.2	13.8
1970	38.9	49.9	37.6	35.2	45.2	23.8	29.1	28.3	42.1	13.8	11.3	16.6
1971	39.9	50.4	38.9	36.0	46.1	24.7	29.4	28.4	44.1	15.7	12.6	19.3
1972	42.0	56.1	39.8	39.9	51.5	27.0	32.3	31.5	45.0	16.8	13.5	20.6
1973	54.7	97.3	42.7	54.5	72.6	34.3	42.9	42.7	46.2	18.6	14.8	22.9
1974	58.4	90.2	50.5	61.4	76.4	44.1	54.5	55.0	50.0	24.8	19.1	31.8
1975	62.9	84.0	58.9	61.6	77.4	43.7	50.0	49.7	55.9	30.6	24.4	38.0
1976	67.3	95.1	62.0	63.4	76.8	48.2	54.9	54.7	59.6	34.5	29.0	40.5
1977	70.7	99.3	65.2	65.5	77.5	51.7	56.3	56.0	63.1	42.0	37.2	47.4
1978	73.8	95.5	69.7	73.4	87.3	57.5	61.9	61.5	68.7	48.2	43.1	53.8
1979	81.2	106.9	76.3	85.9	100.0	69.6	75.5	75.6	76.6	57.3	53.1	62.0
1980	91.1	110.6	87.5	95.3	104.6	84.6	91.8	92.3	87.9	69.4	66.7	72.5
1981	97.8	111.3	95.4	103.0	103.9	101.8	109.8	110.9	96.8	84.8	83.6	86.2
1982	100.0	100.0	100.0	100.0	100.0	100.0	100.0	100.0	100.0	100.0	100.0	100.0
1983	102.0	109.1	101.0	101.3	101.8	100.7	98.8	98.6	100.1	105.1	105.8	104.4
1984	103.7	104.2	103.7	103.5	104.7	102.2	101.0	100.8	103.1	105.1	105.6	104.6
1985	103.0	86.6	105.3	95.8	94.8	96.9	94.3	93.1	105.7	102.7	102.7	102.5
1986	104.2	90.5	106.2	87.7	93.2	81.6	76.0	72.6	106.5	92.2	91.1	93.6
1987	106.6	94.6	108.3	93.7	96.2	87.9	88.5	84.7	114.8	84.1	82.1	86.3
1988	113.2	115.0	112.7	96.0	106.1	85.5	85.9	81.5	126.5	82.1	80.1	84.5
1989	117.2	114.4	117.5	103.1	111.2	93.4	95.8	91.0	136.9	85.3	83.9	87.0
1990	118.0	102.8	120.2	108.9	113.1	101.5	107.3	102.5	145.2	84.8	82.9	87.0
1991	119.9	101.3	122.5	101.2	105.5	94.6	97.5	92.2	147.5	82.9	82.3	84.1
1992	121.1	103.0	123.7	100.4	105.1	93.5	94.2	87.9	162.1	84.0	83.1	85.2
1993	123.2	105.4	125.8	102.4	108.4	94.7	94.1	85.6	193.6	87.1	85.9	88.6
1994	125.1	105.8	127.9	101.8	106.5	94.8	97.0	88.3	199.1	82.4	81.7	83.6
1995	129.5	103.4	133.2	102.7	105.8	96.8	105.8	97.3	201.7	72.1	72.5	72.9
1996	134.4	133.1	134.6	113.8	121.5	104.5	105.7	97.6	195.7	92.6	90.7	94.3
1997	134.1	129.1	134.8	111.1	112.2	106.4	103.5	95.0	201.4	101.3	98.4	103.3
1998	132.2	100.2	136.2	96.8	103.9	88.4	84.5	76.7	196.0	86.7	84.8	88.5
1999	131.4	89.2	136.5	98.2	98.7	94.3	91.1	83.0	195.7	91.2	90.0	92.9
2000	134.1	94.6	138.8	120.6	100.2	130.4	118.0	108.7	193.4	136.9	136.9	139.3
2001	135.8	96.8	140.5	121.0	106.1	126.8	101.5	93.2	181.7	151.4	150.2	154.2
2002	136.3	98.1	140.9	108.1	99.5	111.4	101.0	92.5	181.4	117.3	113.4	119.8
2002												
January	135.4	94.6	140.4	99.9	101.6	95.1	86.1	78.6	179.3	100.5	98.0	102.5
February	135.3	93.4	140.3	98.9	104.0	91.5	89.6	81.8	178.7	85.0	83.7	86.7
March	135.6	94.9	140.5	104.0	103.5	100.9	96.3	88.1	179.9	98.0	95.8	100.0
April	135.8	95.1	140.7	108.5	97.2	113.9	100.7	92.2	181.3	124.4	120.0	127.0
May	135.6	94.0	140.6	109.3	97.1	115.3	105.4	96.6	181.3	120.1	116.1	122.7
June	136.0	96.3	140.8	105.1	95.9	109.0	99.5	91.1	181.5	113.7	110.0	116.0
July	136.5	100.2	140.9	105.9	96.5	109.9	103.1	94.5	182.0	109.8	106.5	112.1
August	136.8	102.2	141.1	107.8	98.1	111.9	105.4	96.7	182.2	111.1	107.6	113.4
September	137.1	104.2	141.3	110.2	99.4	115.2	107.9	99.0	182.3	115.4	111.5	117.9
October	137.0	101.8	141.4	112.6	99.6	119.1	107.7	98.8	183.3	126.0	121.3	128.7
November	137.1	100.4	141.6	116.8	100.7	125.8	103.4	94.8	182.6	150.6	144.1	153.9
December	137.1	100.6	141.6	119.1	102.0	128.7	106.5	97.7	182.2	153.0	146.2	156.4

. . . = Not available.

Table 8-2. Producer Price Indexes and Purchasing Power of the Dollar—Continued

(1982 = 100, seasonally adjusted.)

Year and month	Finished energy goods	Finished goods excluding			Finished consumer goods excluding		Intermediate materials		Intermediate materials less			Crude materials		
		Foods	Energy	Foods and energy	Energy	Foods and energy	Foods and feeds	Energy goods	Foods and feeds	Energy	Foods and energy	Energy materials	Less energy	Nonfood materials less energy
1947	...	...	...	...	...	...	...	...	22.2	...	...	...	...	...
1948	...	...	...	...	...	...	...	...	24.1	...	...	...	...	...
1949	...	...	...	...	...	...	...	...	23.5	...	...	...	...	...
1950	...	...	...	...	...	...	...	...	24.6	...	...	...	...	...
1951	...	...	...	...	...	...	...	...	27.6	...	...	...	...	...
1952	...	...	...	...	...	...	...	...	26.7	...	...	...	...	...
1953	...	...	...	...	...	...	...	...	27.0	...	...	...	...	...
1954	...	...	...	...	...	...	...	...	27.2	...	...	...	...	...
1955	...	...	...	...	...	...	...	...	28.0	...	...	...	...	...
1956	...	...	...	...	...	...	...	...	29.3	...	...	...	...	...
1957	...	...	...	...	...	...	...	...	30.1	...	...	...	...	...
1958	...	...	...	...	...	...	...	...	30.1	...	...	...	...	...
1959	...	...	...	...	...	...	...	...	30.5	...	...	...	...	...
1960	...	...	...	...	...	...	...	...	30.7	...	...	...	...	...
1961	...	...	...	...	...	...	...	...	30.3	...	...	...	...	...
1962	...	...	...	...	...	...	...	...	30.2	...	...	...	...	...
1963	...	...	...	...	...	...	...	...	30.1	...	...	...	...	...
1964	...	...	...	...	...	...	...	...	30.3	...	...	...	...	...
1965	...	...	...	...	...	...	...	...	30.7	...	...	...	...	...
1966	...	...	...	...	...	...	...	...	31.3	...	...	...	...	...
1967	...	35.0	...	...	...	...	41.8	...	31.7	...	...	...	...	...
1968	...	35.9	...	...	...	...	41.5	...	32.5	...	...	...	...	...
1969	...	36.9	...	...	...	...	42.9	...	33.6	...	...	...	...	...
1970	...	38.2	...	...	...	...	45.6	...	34.8	...	...	...	...	...
1971	...	39.6	...	...	...	...	46.7	...	36.2	...	...	...	...	...
1972	...	40.4	...	...	...	...	49.5	...	37.7	...	...	...	...	...
1973	...	42.0	...	48.1	...	50.4	70.3	...	40.6	...	44.3	...	...	70.8
1974	26.2	46.8	...	53.6	58.7	55.5	83.6	33.1	50.5	56.2	54.0	27.8	78.4	83.3
1975	30.7	54.7	62.4	59.7	63.9	60.6	81.6	38.7	56.6	61.7	60.2	33.3	75.9	69.3
1976	34.3	58.1	64.8	63.1	65.7	63.7	77.4	41.5	60.0	64.7	63.8	35.3	77.6	80.2
1977	39.7	62.2	68.6	66.9	69.4	67.3	79.6	46.8	64.1	68.5	67.6	40.4	78.1	79.8
1978	42.3	66.7	74.0	71.9	74.9	72.2	84.8	49.1	68.6	73.4	72.5	45.2	87.5	87.8
1979	57.1	74.6	80.7	78.3	81.7	78.8	94.5	61.1	77.4	81.7	80.7	54.9	101.5	106.2
1980	85.2	86.7	88.4	87.1	89.3	87.8	105.5	84.9	89.4	91.4	90.3	73.1	106.5	113.1
1981	101.5	95.6	95.4	94.6	95.7	94.6	104.6	100.5	98.2	98.2	97.7	97.7	105.7	111.7
1982	100.0	100.0	100.0	100.0	100.0	100.0	100.0	100.0	100.0	100.0	100.0	100.0	100.0	100.0
1983	95.2	101.8	102.5	103.0	102.4	103.1	103.6	95.3	100.5	101.7	101.6	98.7	102.6	105.3
1984	91.2	103.2	105.5	105.5	105.6	105.7	105.7	95.5	103.0	104.6	104.7	98.0	106.3	111.7
1985	87.6	104.6	107.2	108.1	107.0	108.4	97.3	92.6	103.0	104.7	105.2	93.3	97.0	104.9
1986	63.0	101.9	109.7	110.6	109.7	111.1	96.2	72.6	99.3	104.5	104.9	71.8	95.4	103.1
1987	61.8	104.0	112.3	113.3	112.5	114.2	99.2	73.0	101.7	107.3	107.8	75.0	100.9	115.7
1988	59.8	106.5	115.8	117.0	116.3	118.5	109.5	70.9	106.9	114.6	115.2	67.7	112.6	133.0
1989	65.7	111.8	121.2	122.1	122.1	124.0	113.8	76.1	111.9	119.5	120.2	75.9	117.7	137.9
1990	75.0	117.4	126.0	126.6	127.2	128.8	113.3	85.5	114.5	120.4	120.9	85.9	118.6	136.3
1991	78.1	120.9	129.1	131.1	130.0	133.7	111.1	85.1	114.6	120.8	121.4	80.4	110.9	128.2
1992	77.8	123.1	131.1	134.2	131.8	137.3	110.7	84.3	114.9	121.3	122.0	78.8	110.7	128.4
1993	78.0	124.4	132.9	135.8	133.5	138.5	112.7	84.6	116.4	123.2	123.8	76.7	116.3	140.2
1994	77.0	125.1	134.2	137.1	134.2	130.0	114.8	83.0	118.7	126.3	127.1	72.1	119.3	156.2
1995	78.1	127.5	136.9	140.0	136.9	141.9	114.8	84.1	125.5	134.0	135.2	69.4	123.5	173.6
1996	83.2	130.5	139.6	142.0	140.1	144.3	128.1	89.8	125.6	133.6	134.0	85.0	130.0	155.8
1997	83.4	130.9	140.2	142.4	141.0	145.1	125.4	89.0	125.7	133.7	134.2	87.3	123.5	156.5
1998	75.1	129.5	141.1	143.7	142.5	147.7	116.2	80.8	123.4	132.4	133.5	68.6	113.6	142.1
1999	78.8	132.3	143.0	146.1	145.2	151.7	111.1	84.3	123.9	131.7	133.1	78.5	107.9	135.2
2000	94.1	138.1	144.9	148.0	147.4	154.0	111.7	101.7	130.1	135.0	136.6	122.1	111.7	145.2
2001	96.7	140.4	147.6	150.0	150.8	156.9	115.9	104.1	130.5	135.1	136.4	122.3	112.2	130.7
2002	88.8	138.3	147.3	150.2	150.8	157.6	115.5	95.9	128.5	134.5	135.8	102.0	108.7	135.7
2002														
January	82.6	136.5	147.7	150.2	151.1	157.4	114.1	89.7	126.2	133.4	134.7	82.8	107.7	126.5
February	83.1	136.6	148.0	150.2	151.6	157.3	114.1	89.3	126.1	133.4	134.7	76.9	110.0	128.2
March	86.9	137.7	148.2	150.1	152.0	157.3	114.6	92.5	127.1	133.8	135.0	89.9	109.8	128.9
April	89.6	138.7	147.3	150.3	150.7	157.8	113.8	96.7	128.3	134.0	135.3	107.3	105.8	131.4
May	87.5	138.0	147.2	150.3	150.5	157.8	112.8	94.8	127.8	133.9	135.3	108.3	106.4	133.9
June	87.6	138.2	147.3	150.4	150.8	158.0	114.0	95.1	128.1	134.3	135.6	97.8	106.6	137.7
July	88.6	138.1	147.0	150.0	150.5	157.6	115.5	95.1	128.4	134.7	135.9	98.1	107.6	140.0
August	89.8	138.4	146.7	149.8	150.1	157.4	116.3	96.5	128.9	135.0	136.2	101.2	108.6	139.5
September	90.9	139.0	146.9	150.2	150.2	157.8	117.6	98.6	129.6	135.3	136.4	105.9	109.5	139.2
October	94.0	140.2	147.4	150.7	150.8	158.4	117.2	102.0	130.5	135.5	136.7	111.3	109.8	139.6
November	92.5	139.6	147.3	150.5	150.8	158.2	117.8	100.8	130.4	135.6	136.8	120.0	111.1	141.5
December	92.7	139.0	146.8	149.6	150.1	156.8	119.0	100.3	130.2	135.6	136.7	124.0	112.1	141.8

. . . = Not available.

Table 8-2. Producer Price Indexes and Purchasing Power of the Dollar—*Continued*

(1982 = 100, except as noted; not seasonally adjusted.)

Year and month	Finished goods						Capital equipment	Inter-mediate materials, supplies, and components	Crude materials for further processing	Purchasing power of the dollar	
	Total	Finished consumer goods								Producer prices for finished goods (1982–1984 = $1.00)	Consumer prices (CPI-U, 1982–1984 = $1.00)
		Total	Foods	Consumer goods except foods							
				Total	Durable	Nondurable goods less foods					
1947	26.4	28.6	31.9	27.4	32.9	24.2	19.8	23.3	31.7	3.855	4.474
1948	28.5	30.8	34.9	29.2	35.2	25.7	21.6	25.2	34.7	3.571	4.151
1949	27.7	29.4	32.1	28.6	36.1	24.7	22.7	24.2	30.1	3.674	4.193
1950	28.2	29.9	32.7	29.0	36.5	25.1	23.2	25.3	32.7	3.609	4.151
1951	30.8	32.7	36.7	31.1	38.9	27.0	25.5	28.4	37.6	3.304	3.846
1952	30.6	32.3	36.4	30.7	39.2	26.3	25.9	27.5	34.5	3.326	3.765
1953	30.3	31.7	34.5	31.0	39.5	26.6	26.3	27.7	31.9	3.359	3.735
1954	30.4	31.7	34.2	31.1	39.8	26.7	26.7	27.9	31.6	3.348	3.717
1955	30.5	31.5	33.4	31.3	40.2	26.8	27.4	28.4	30.4	3.337	3.732
1956	31.3	32.0	33.3	32.1	41.6	27.3	29.5	29.6	30.6	3.251	3.678
1957	32.5	32.9	34.4	32.9	42.8	27.9	31.3	30.3	31.2	3.131	3.549
1958	33.2	33.6	36.5	32.9	43.4	27.8	32.1	30.4	31.9	3.065	3.457
1959	33.1	33.3	34.8	33.3	43.9	28.2	32.7	30.8	31.1	3.075	3.427
1960	33.4	33.6	35.5	33.5	43.8	28.4	32.8	30.8	30.4	3.047	3.373
1961	33.4	33.6	35.4	33.4	43.6	28.4	32.9	30.6	30.2	3.047	3.340
1962	33.5	33.7	35.7	33.4	43.4	28.4	33.0	30.6	30.5	3.038	3.304
1963	33.4	33.5	35.3	33.4	43.1	28.5	33.1	30.7	29.9	3.047	3.265
1964	33.5	33.6	35.4	33.3	43.3	28.4	33.4	30.8	29.6	3.038	3.220
1965	34.1	34.2	36.8	33.6	43.2	28.8	33.8	31.2	31.1	2.984	3.166
1966	35.2	35.4	39.2	34.1	43.4	29.3	34.6	32.0	33.1	2.891	3.080
1967	35.6	35.6	38.5	34.7	44.1	30.0	35.8	32.2	31.3	2.859	2.993
1968	36.6	36.5	40.0	35.5	45.1	30.6	37.0	33.0	31.8	2.781	2.873
1969	38.0	37.9	42.4	36.3	45.9	31.5	38.3	34.1	33.9	2.678	2.726
1970	39.3	39.1	43.8	37.4	47.2	32.5	40.1	35.4	35.2	2.589	2.574
1971	40.5	40.2	44.5	38.7	48.9	33.5	41.7	36.8	36.0	2.513	2.466
1972	41.8	41.5	46.9	39.4	50.0	34.1	42.8	38.2	39.9	2.435	2.391
1973	45.6	46.0	56.5	41.2	50.9	36.1	44.2	42.4	54.5	2.232	2.251
1974	52.6	53.1	64.4	48.2	55.5	44.0	50.5	52.5	61.4	1.935	2.029
1975	58.2	58.2	69.8	53.2	61.0	48.9	58.2	58.0	61.6	1.749	1.859
1976	60.8	60.4	69.6	56.5	63.7	52.4	62.1	60.9	63.4	1.674	1.757
1977	64.7	64.3	73.3	60.6	67.4	56.8	66.1	64.9	65.5	1.573	1.649
1978	69.8	69.4	79.9	64.9	73.6	60.0	71.3	69.5	73.4	1.458	1.532
1979	77.6	77.5	87.3	73.5	80.8	69.3	77.5	78.4	85.9	1.311	1.380
1980	88.0	88.6	92.4	87.1	91.0	85.1	85.8	90.3	95.3	1.156	1.215
1981	96.1	96.6	97.8	96.1	96.4	95.8	94.6	98.6	103.0	1.059	1.098
1982	100.0	100.0	100.0	100.0	100.0	100.0	100.0	100.0	100.0	1.018	1.035
1983	101.6	101.3	101.0	101.2	102.8	100.5	102.8	100.6	101.3	1.002	1.003
1984	103.7	103.3	105.4	102.2	104.5	101.1	105.2	103.1	103.5	0.981	0.961
1985	104.7	103.8	104.6	103.3	106.5	101.7	107.5	102.7	95.8	0.972	0.928
1986	103.2	101.4	107.3	98.5	108.9	93.3	109.7	99.1	87.7	0.986	0.913
1987	105.4	103.6	109.5	100.7	111.5	94.9	111.7	101.5	93.7	0.966	0.880
1988	108.0	106.2	112.6	103.1	113.8	97.3	114.3	107.1	96.0	0.942	0.846
1989	113.6	112.1	118.7	108.9	117.6	103.8	118.8	112.0	103.1	0.896	0.807
1990	119.2	118.2	124.4	115.3	120.4	111.5	122.9	114.5	108.9	0.854	0.766
1991	121.7	120.5	124.1	118.7	123.9	115.0	126.7	114.4	101.2	0.836	0.734
1992	123.2	121.7	123.3	120.8	125.7	117.3	129.1	114.7	100.4	0.826	0.713
1993	124.7	123.0	125.7	121.7	128.0	117.6	131.4	116.2	102.4	0.816	0.692
1994	125.5	123.3	126.8	121.6	130.9	116.2	134.1	118.5	101.8	0.811	0.675
1995	127.9	125.6	129.0	124.0	132.7	118.8	136.7	124.9	102.7	0.796	0.656
1996	131.3	129.5	133.6	127.6	134.2	123.3	138.3	125.7	113.8	0.775	0.638
1997	131.8	130.2	134.5	128.2	133.7	124.3	138.2	125.6	111.1	0.772	0.623
1998	130.7	128.9	134.3	126.4	132.9	122.2	137.6	123.0	96.8	0.779	0.614
1999	133.0	132.0	135.1	130.5	133.0	127.9	137.6	123.2	98.2	0.765	0.600
2000	138.0	138.2	137.2	138.4	133.9	138.7	138.8	129.2	120.6	0.737	0.581
2001	140.7	141.5	141.3	141.4	134.0	142.8	139.7	129.7	121.0	0.723	0.565
2002	138.9	139.4	140.1	138.8	133.0	139.8	139.1	127.8	108.1	0.733	0.556
2002											
January	137.4	137.2	141.1	135.4	133.9	134.4	139.7	125.5	98.9	0.729	0.565
February	137.7	137.5	142.3	135.4	134.1	134.3	139.8	125.2	98.0	0.739	0.562
March	138.7	138.9	143.4	136.9	133.6	136.7	139.5	126.1	103.7	0.734	0.559
April	138.8	139.2	139.2	138.9	133.5	139.8	139.3	127.2	108.3	0.733	0.556
May	138.6	139.1	139.4	138.6	133.0	139.5	139.1	127.1	109.9	0.734	0.556
June	139.0	139.6	139.8	139.3	132.8	140.6	139.0	127.7	105.7	0.732	0.556
July	138.8	139.6	139.8	139.1	131.5	141.0	138.4	128.1	106.8	0.733	0.555
August	138.8	139.6	139.3	139.3	131.0	141.5	138.2	128.4	107.7	0.733	0.554
September	139.1	140.0	138.7	140.2	131.1	142.8	138.3	129.3	110.9	0.732	0.553
October	140.7	141.6	139.2	142.2	134.8	143.8	139.9	129.7	112.6	0.724	0.552
November	139.7	140.4	139.2	140.5	133.6	142.0	139.5	129.7	116.1	0.729	0.552
December	139.0	139.6	139.5	139.3	132.8	140.6	139.1	129.4	118.1	0.732	0.553

Table 8-3. Producer Price Indexes by Commodity Groups

(1982 =100, Not seasonally adjusted.)

Year	All com- modities	Farm prod- ucts	Proces- sed foods and feeds	Industrial commodities													
				Total	Textile prod- ucts and apparel	Hides, leather, and related prod- ucts	Fuels and related prod- ucts and power	Chemi- cals and related prod- ucts	Rubber and plastics prod- ucts	Lumber and wood prod- ucts	Pulp, paper, and allied prod- ucts	Metals and metal prod- ucts	Machin- ery and equip- ment	Furni- ture and house- hold dura- bles	Nonme- tallic mineral prod- ucts	Trans- porta- tion equip- ment	Miscel- laneous prod- ucts
1947	25.6	45.1	33.0	22.7	50.6	31.7	11.1	32.1	29.2	25.8	25.1	18.2	19.3	37.2	20.7	. . .	26.6
1948	27.7	48.5	35.3	24.6	52.8	32.1	13.1	32.8	30.2	29.5	26.2	20.7	20.9	39.4	22.4	. . .	27.7
1949	26.3	41.9	32.1	24.1	48.3	30.4	12.4	30.0	29.2	27.3	25.1	20.9	21.9	40.1	23.0	. . .	28.2
1950	27.3	44.0	33.2	25.0	50.2	32.9	12.6	30.4	35.6	31.4	25.7	22.0	22.6	40.9	23.5	. . .	28.6
1951	30.4	51.2	36.9	27.6	56.0	37.7	13.0	34.8	43.7	34.1	30.5	24.5	25.3	44.4	25.0	. . .	30.3
1952	29.6	48.4	36.4	26.9	50.5	30.5	13.0	33.0	39.6	33.2	29.7	24.5	25.3	43.5	25.0	. . .	30.2
1953	29.2	43.8	34.8	27.2	49.3	31.0	13.4	33.4	36.9	33.1	29.6	25.3	25.9	44.4	26.0	. . .	31.0
1954	29.3	43.2	35.4	27.2	48.2	29.5	13.2	33.8	37.5	32.5	29.6	25.5	26.3	44.9	26.6	. . .	31.3
1955	29.3	40.5	33.8	27.8	48.2	29.4	13.2	33.7	42.4	34.1	30.4	27.2	27.2	45.1	27.3	. . .	31.3
1956	30.3	40.0	33.8	29.1	48.2	31.2	13.6	33.9	43.0	34.6	32.4	29.6	29.3	46.3	28.5	. . .	31.7
1957	31.2	41.1	34.8	29.9	48.3	31.2	14.3	34.6	42.8	32.8	33.0	30.2	31.4	47.5	29.6	. . .	32.6
1958	31.6	42.9	36.5	30.0	47.4	31.6	13.7	34.9	42.8	32.5	33.4	30.0	32.1	47.9	29.9	. . .	33.3
1959	31.7	40.2	35.6	30.5	48.1	35.9	13.7	34.8	42.6	34.7	33.7	30.6	32.8	48.0	30.3	. . .	33.4
1960	31.7	40.1	35.6	30.5	48.6	34.6	13.9	34.8	42.7	33.5	34.0	30.6	33.0	47.8	30.4	. . .	33.6
1961	31.6	39.7	36.2	30.4	47.8	34.9	14.0	34.5	41.1	32.0	33.0	30.5	33.0	47.5	30.5	. . .	33.7
1962	31.7	40.4	36.5	30.4	48.2	35.3	14.0	33.9	39.9	32.2	33.4	30.2	33.0	47.2	30.5	. . .	33.9
1963	31.6	39.6	36.8	30.3	48.2	34.3	13.9	33.5	40.1	32.8	33.1	30.3	33.1	46.9	30.3	. . .	34.2
1964	31.6	39.0	36.7	30.5	48.5	34.4	13.5	33.6	39.6	33.5	33.0	31.1	33.3	47.1	30.4	. . .	34.4
1965	32.3	40.7	38.0	30.9	48.8	35.9	13.8	33.9	39.7	33.7	33.3	32.0	33.7	46.8	30.4	. . .	34.7
1966	33.3	43.7	40.2	31.5	48.9	39.4	14.1	34.0	40.5	35.2	34.2	32.8	34.7	47.4	30.7	. . .	35.3
1967	33.4	41.3	39.8	32.0	48.9	38.1	14.4	34.2	41.4	35.1	34.6	33.2	35.9	48.3	31.2	. . .	36.2
1968	34.2	42.3	40.6	32.8	50.7	39.3	14.3	34.1	42.8	39.8	35.0	34.0	37.0	49.7	32.4	. . .	37.0
1969	35.6	45.0	42.7	33.9	51.8	41.5	14.6	34.2	43.6	44.0	36.0	36.0	38.2	50.7	33.6	40.4	38.1
1970	36.9	45.8	44.6	35.2	52.4	42.0	15.3	35.0	44.9	39.9	37.5	38.7	40.0	51.9	35.3	41.9	39.8
1971	38.1	46.6	45.5	36.5	53.3	43.4	16.6	35.6	45.2	44.7	38.1	39.4	41.4	53.1	38.2	44.2	40.8
1972	39.8	51.6	48.0	37.8	55.5	50.0	17.1	35.6	45.3	50.7	39.3	40.9	42.3	53.8	39.4	45.5	41.5
1973	45.0	72.7	58.9	40.3	60.5	54.5	19.4	37.6	46.6	62.2	42.3	44.0	43.7	55.7	40.7	46.1	43.3
1974	53.5	77.4	68.0	49.2	68.0	55.2	30.1	50.2	56.4	64.5	52.5	57.0	50.0	61.8	47.8	50.3	48.1
1975	58.4	77.0	72.6	54.9	67.4	56.5	35.4	62.0	62.2	62.1	59.0	61.5	57.9	67.5	54.4	56.7	53.4
1976	61.1	78.8	70.8	58.4	72.4	63.9	38.3	64.0	66.0	72.2	62.1	65.0	61.3	70.3	58.2	60.5	55.6
1977	64.9	79.4	74.0	62.5	75.3	68.3	43.6	65.9	69.4	83.0	64.6	69.3	65.2	73.2	62.6	64.6	59.4
1978	69.9	87.7	80.6	67.0	78.1	76.1	46.5	68.0	72.4	96.9	67.7	75.3	70.3	77.5	69.6	69.5	66.7
1979	78.7	99.6	88.5	75.7	82.5	96.1	58.9	76.0	80.5	105.5	75.9	86.0	76.7	82.8	77.6	75.3	75.5
1980	89.8	102.9	95.9	88.0	89.7	94.7	82.8	89.0	90.1	101.5	86.3	95.0	86.0	90.7	88.4	82.9	93.6
1981	98.0	105.2	98.9	97.4	97.6	99.3	100.2	98.4	96.4	102.8	94.8	99.6	94.4	95.9	96.7	94.3	96.1
1982	100.0	100.0	100.0	100.0	100.0	100.0	100.0	100.0	100.0	100.0	100.0	100.0	100.0	100.0	100.0	100.0	100.0
1983	101.3	102.4	101.8	101.1	100.3	103.2	95.9	100.3	100.8	107.9	103.3	101.8	102.7	103.4	101.6	102.8	104.8
1984	103.7	105.5	105.4	103.3	102.7	109.0	94.8	102.9	102.3	108.0	110.3	104.8	105.1	105.7	105.4	105.2	107.0
1985	103.2	95.1	103.5	103.7	102.9	108.9	91.4	103.7	101.9	106.6	113.3	104.4	107.2	107.1	108.6	107.9	109.4
1986	100.2	92.9	105.4	100.0	103.2	113.0	69.8	102.6	101.9	107.2	116.1	103.2	108.8	108.2	110.0	110.5	111.6
1987	102.8	95.5	107.9	102.6	105.1	120.4	70.2	106.4	103.0	112.8	121.8	107.1	110.4	109.9	110.0	112.5	114.9
1988	106.9	104.9	112.7	106.3	109.2	131.4	66.7	116.3	109.3	118.9	130.4	118.7	113.2	113.1	111.2	114.3	120.2
1989	112.2	110.9	117.8	111.6	112.3	136.3	72.9	123.0	112.6	126.7	137.8	124.1	117.4	116.9	112.6	117.7	126.5
1990	116.3	112.2	121.9	115.8	115.0	141.7	82.3	123.6	113.6	129.7	141.2	122.9	120.7	119.2	114.7	121.5	134.2
1991	116.5	105.7	121.9	116.5	116.3	138.9	81.2	125.6	115.1	132.1	142.9	120.2	123.0	121.2	117.2	126.4	140.8
1992	117.2	103.6	122.1	117.4	117.8	140.4	80.4	125.9	115.1	146.6	145.2	119.2	123.4	122.2	117.3	130.4	145.3
1993	118.9	107.1	124.0	119.0	118.0	143.7	80.0	128.2	116.0	174.0	147.3	119.2	124.0	123.7	120.0	133.7	145.4
1994	120.4	106.3	125.5	120.7	118.3	148.5	77.8	132.1	117.6	180.0	152.5	124.8	125.1	126.1	124.2	137.2	141.9
1995	124.7	107.4	127.0	125.5	120.8	153.7	78.0	142.5	124.3	178.1	172.2	134.5	126.6	128.2	129.0	139.7	145.4
1996	127.7	122.4	133.3	127.3	122.4	150.5	85.8	142.1	123.8	176.1	168.7	131.0	126.5	130.4	131.0	141.7	147.7
1997	127.6	112.9	134.0	127.7	122.6	154.2	86.1	143.6	123.2	183.8	167.9	131.8	125.9	130.8	133.2	141.6	150.9
1998	124.4	104.6	131.6	124.8	122.9	148.0	75.3	143.9	122.6	179.1	171.7	127.8	124.9	131.3	135.4	141.2	156.0
1999	125.5	98.4	131.1	126.5	121.1	146.0	80.5	144.2	122.5	183.6	174.1	124.6	124.3	131.7	138.9	141.8	166.6
2000	132.7	99.5	133.1	134.8	121.4	151.5	103.5	151.0	125.5	178.2	183.7	128.1	124.0	132.6	142.5	143.8	170.8
2001	134.2	103.8	137.3	135.7	121.3	158.4	105.3	151.8	127.2	174.4	184.8	125.4	123.7	133.2	144.3	145.2	181.3
2002	131.1	99.0	136.2	132.4	119.9	157.6	93.2	151.9	126.8	173.3	185.9	125.9	122.9	133.5	146.2	144.6	182.4
2002																	
January	128.5	99.9	135.7	129.4	120.3	152.4	84.0	147.1	126.4	171.7	184.7	123.7	123.3	133.5	145.7	145.4	182.0
February	128.4	101.8	136.5	129.1	119.9	152.5	82.5	147.3	125.8	173.0	184.4	124.0	123.3	133.4	145.3	145.8	181.8
March	129.8	104.4	136.4	130.5	120.0	154.3	87.4	148.8	126.0	175.3	184.4	124.5	123.4	133.2	145.1	145.3	181.4
April	130.8	94.3	135.8	132.4	119.8	154.4	93.7	150.5	126.2	175.6	184.9	125.0	123.2	133.2	145.7	145.1	183.0
May	130.8	96.6	135.3	132.3	119.8	156.5	93.4	150.6	126.6	174.4	184.9	125.6	123.0	133.1	146.4	144.9	182.9
June	130.9	96.2	135.6	132.4	119.9	158.0	92.9	151.3	127.1	173.3	185.6	126.4	122.9	133.4	146.5	144.4	183.0
July	131.2	97.9	136.2	132.6	119.9	158.5	93.5	152.9	126.7	173.3	186.2	126.8	122.7	133.8	146.4	143.0	183.0
August	131.5	99.7	136.0	132.8	119.8	160.4	94.5	153.6	127.1	173.8	186.6	126.6	122.7	133.7	146.6	142.5	182.9
September	132.3	99.8	136.3	133.7	119.8	161.0	97.5	154.1	127.8	173.0	186.8	127.1	122.7	133.8	146.7	142.5	183.2
October	133.2	99.1	136.4	134.8	119.7	160.9	99.7	155.3	127.8	172.3	187.2	127.0	122.5	133.9	146.7	146.4	183.2
November	133.1	99.1	136.5	134.7	119.8	160.9	99.5	155.6	127.3	171.8	187.5	127.3	122.5	133.9	146.5	145.5	183.1
December	132.9	99.1	137.5	134.4	120.0	161.0	99.4	155.1	127.3	171.8	187.4	127.2	122.3	133.5	146.3	144.8	179.1

. . . = Not available.

Table 8-4. Prices Received and Paid by Farmers

(1990–1992 = 100, not seasonally adjusted.)

Year and month	All farm prod-ucts	Prices received by farmers — Crops — Total	Food grains	Feed grains and hay	Cotton	Tobacco	Oil-bearing crops	Fruit and nuts	Com-mercial vege-tables	Pota-toes and dry beans	Livestock and products — Total	Meat animals	Dairy prod-ucts	Poultry and eggs	Food com-mod-ities	Prices paid by farmers — All items	Pro-duction items	Ratio of prices re-ceived to prices paid
1975	73	88	128	112	68	56	93	46	66	78	62	56	67	83	69	47	55	158
1976	75	87	105	105	99	63	97	45	67	75	64	57	74	83	71	50	59	150
1977	73	83	83	87	100	66	119	54	70	71	64	56	74	81	71	53	61	138
1978	83	89	102	88	91	72	110	72	74	73	78	75	81	87	83	58	67	144
1979	94	98	121	100	96	75	121	77	79	65	90	90	92	90	95	66	76	144
1980	98	107	136	115	114	80	118	73	80	93	89	84	100	91	96	75	85	131
1981	100	111	138	122	111	94	122	76	99	126	89	82	105	94	97	82	92	121
1982	94	98	119	103	92	99	103	78	92	88	90	86	104	89	93	86	94	109
1983	98	108	120	125	104	96	118	71	96	89	88	81	104	95	95	86	92	113
1984	101	111	117	127	108	98	125	85	97	111	91	83	103	109	98	89	94	114
1985	91	98	108	105	93	92	96	84	95	87	86	78	97	97	89	86	91	106
1986	87	87	89	84	91	82	89	83	92	81	88	80	96	105	87	85	86	103
1987	89	86	83	72	98	83	90	93	105	89	91	90	96	87	91	87	87	102
1988	99	104	113	102	95	86	126	96	104	88	93	91	93	98	99	91	90	108
1989	104	109	127	109	98	96	118	99	103	131	100	94	104	111	104	96	95	108
1990	104	103	100	105	107	97	105	97	102	133	105	105	105	105	104	99	99	105
1991	100	101	94	101	108	102	99	112	100	99	99	101	94	99	99	100	100	99
1992	98	101	113	98	88	101	100	99	111	88	97	96	100	97	99	101	101	97
1993	101	102	105	99	89	101	108	93	117	107	100	100	98	105	102	104	104	97
1994	100	105	119	106	109	102	110	90	109	110	95	90	99	106	98	106	106	94
1995	102	112	134	112	127	103	104	97	121	107	92	85	98	107	99	109	108	93
1996	112	127	157	146	122	105	128	118	111	114	99	87	114	120	108	115	115	98
1997	107	115	128	117	112	104	131	110	118	90	98	92	102	113	105	118	119	90
1998	101	107	103	100	107	104	107	111	123	99	97	79	119	117	101	115	113	89
1999	96	97	91	86	85	102	83	115	110	100	95	83	110	110	96	115	111	83
2000	96	96	85	86	82	107	85	98	121	93	97	94	94	106	97	120	116	80
2001	102	99	91	91	64	107	80	109	130	98	106	97	115	115	104	123	120	83
2002	98	105	104	100	55	108	88	105	142	129	90	87	93	94	97	124	119	79
1999																		
January	97	98	102	91	96	111	96	94	105	97	96	75	133	115	97	114	110	85
February	96	99	101	91	92	113	88	103	112	98	93	77	116	109	95	114	110	84
March	97	100	99	92	91	104	83	108	121	103	95	79	116	108	97	114	110	85
April	97	105	96	92	92	86	83	117	130	108	90	81	96	106	97	115	111	84
May	98	102	90	91	91	...	81	113	118	105	94	83	98	111	97	115	110	85
June	97	99	87	90	90	...	80	125	110	110	95	84	100	113	97	115	111	84
July	95	95	77	84	89	86	75	128	104	121	95	81	106	113	95	114	111	83
August	98	98	87	85	87	94	78	130	106	102	98	85	115	112	99	115	111	85
September	96	95	87	81	75	101	83	127	105	89	98	84	120	109	98	115	111	83
October	91	88	86	76	76	105	80	124	97	85	96	87	114	104	93	116	112	78
November	93	89	89	77	73	105	82	115	98	94	98	87	110	115	97	116	112	80
December	92	90	85	82	71	110	82	95	116	91	94	88	93	109	94	117	113	79
2000																		
January	90	88	85	84	71	111	82	86	98	94	93	90	92	100	90	118	114	76
February	92	91	85	88	77	113	86	88	86	98	93	92	90	97	91	118	114	78
March	95	95	85	90	79	109	88	88	107	103	94	95	90	98	94	119	115	80
April	100	102	85	91	75	90	89	97	135	108	98	99	91	106	101	119	115	84
May	100	103	86	96	79	...	93	87	131	105	97	98	92	102	100	119	115	84
June	98	98	84	90	74	...	88	105	117	101	98	97	94	106	98	120	116	82
July	97	94	78	82	81	97	81	108	119	110	99	96	96	106	98	120	116	81
August	96	96	81	78	85	106	79	109	129	92	96	92	96	105	98	119	115	81
September	97	97	82	78	83	107	85	113	143	80	98	90	99	114	99	120	116	81
October	93	91	88	80	92	112	81	111	125	76	97	92	96	111	94	121	117	77
November	98	97	92	85	96	114	85	100	144	76	99	92	96	119	100	121	118	81
December	98	96	94	90	95	107	88	81	115	78	101	95	100	113	98	122	119	80
2001																		
January	97	94	93	89	86	115	84	86	122	81	100	97	100	105	97	124	121	78
February	100	98	91	91	80	116	80	84	148	89	102	98	100	111	101	124	121	81
March	103	99	92	91	68	99	78	97	138	86	107	103	106	116	105	124	120	83
April	106	103	92	90	70	82	75	105	137	92	109	103	112	116	108	124	120	85
May	108	105	95	90	67	...	77	96	143	90	110	103	119	115	110	124	120	87
June	107	102	91	91	65	...	80	122	119	96	113	104	124	117	109	124	120	86
July	108	104	88	95	64	107	86	127	124	105	112	102	124	119	109	123	120	88
August	110	109	90	96	62	104	86	130	144	125	111	100	126	120	113	123	120	89
September	106	102	92	93	60	108	81	128	134	102	111	96	131	121	109	123	120	86
October	94	88	90	86	51	109	74	126	102	91	104	91	119	120	96	123	119	76
November	93	89	89	86	46	114	77	112	101	106	99	86	110	117	97	122	118	76
December	94	95	91	92	51	113	78	91	151	114	93	85	103	99	96	122	117	77
2002																		
January	95	93	89	90	45	116	76	83	158	123	96	90	104	101	96	122	117	78
February	98	101	85	91	46	113	77	83	190	128	96	93	100	96	99	122	117	80
March	105	117	85	91	47	98	79	94	270	142	94	92	96	96	107	123	118	85
April	94	100	84	92	45	107	80	90	121	138	89	87	96	87	93	123	118	76
May	96	104	86	95	44	...	83	104	120	148	89	85	93	92	95	123	118	78
June	97	104	95	98	56	...	88	114	111	158	90	85	88	100	95	123	118	79
July	99	109	105	103	58	103	96	117	117	169	88	87	85	94	97	123	119	80
August	100	113	114	110	54	104	99	124	120	135	87	84	87	93	97	124	120	81
September	98	109	129	112	58	106	88	125	118	104	85	81	89	92	95	125	121	78
October	95	101	128	106	64	113	90	123	106	93	87	84	93	86	95	125	121	76
November	97	103	122	103	69	115	97	110	116	105	89	86	91	96	96	125	121	78
December	100	107	124	106	69	108	98	95	154	108	91	88	91	96	99	125	121	80

[1]Includes commodities, services, interest, taxes, and wage rates.

. . . = Not available.

NOTES AND DEFINITIONS

TABLES 8-1 AND 20-4
CONSUMER PRICE INDEXES

SOURCE: U.S. DEPARTMENT OF LABOR, BUREAU OF LABOR STATISTICS (BLS)

The Consumer Price Index (CPI) is a statistical measure of the average change in the cost to consumers of a market basket of goods and services purchased by urban consumers. The reference base for the total index and most of its components currently is 1982–84 = 100; however, new products that have been introduced into the index since January 1982 are necessarily shown on later reference bases.

Except as noted, all of the consumer price indexes in this volume are components of the *CPI-U*, the index using the average market basket for all urban consumers, who comprised about 87 percent of the noninstitutional population in 1993–1995. Beginning with January 2002, the market basket represents expenditures in 1999–2000. Between January 1998 and December 2001, weights from 1993 to 1995 were used.

A slightly different index that is widely used for adjusting wages and government benefits is the *CPI-W*, which represents the buying habits only of urban wage earners and clerical workers—about 32 percent of the noninstitutional population in 1993–1995. The total CPI-W is displayed in the last column of the last page of Table 8-1.

The CPI was overhauled and updated in the latest major revision effective January 1998. In addition, new products and improved methods are regularly introduced into the index, usually in January. The latest such change was the introduction of a geometric mean formula for calculating many of the basic components of the index. Beginning with the index for January 1999, this formula is used for categories comprising approximately 61 percent of total consumer spending. The new formula allows for the possibility that some consumers may react to changing relative prices within a category by substituting items whose relative prices have declined for products whose relative prices have risen, while maintaining their overall level of satisfaction. The geometric mean formula is not being used for categories where demand elasticities are low and possibilities for substitution are limited, such as housing, utilities, and many health care services.

In the future, the consumption expenditure weights will be updated at 2-year intervals. With the index for January 2004, weights representing the market baskets of 2001–2002 will be introduced. Previously, new weights were introduced only at the time of a major revision, translating into a lag of a decade or more.

The CPI-U was introduced in 1978. Before that time, only CPI-W data were available. The movements of the CPI-U before 1978 are based on the changes in the CPI-W. The index levels are different, however, because the two indexes differed in the 1982–1984 base period.

There are several important differences between the CPI and measures of consumption spending and prices such as those in the National Income and Product Accounts. One of these has to do with the possibility of revision. Because the official CPI-U and CPI-W are so widely used in "escalation," that is, the calculation of cost-of-living adjustments for wages and for government payments and tax variables, these indexes are not retrospectively revised to incorporate new information and methods. (An exception is occasionally made for outright error, as happened in September 2000 with respect to the data for January through August of that year.) Instead, the new information and methods of calculation are introduced in the current index and affect future index changes only. See *Supplemental Indexes*, below, for information on certain special CPI indexes, published in this volume, that can be used to provide more consistent historical information.

Notes on the data

The CPI is based on prices of food, clothing, shelter, fuel, utilities, transportation, medical care, and other goods and services that people buy for day-to-day living. The quantity and quality of these items are kept essentially constant between major revisions so that only price changes will be measured. All taxes directly associated with the purchase and use of items, such as sales and property taxes, are included in the index; the effects of income and payroll tax changes are not.

As of 2003, data collected from about 23,000 retail establishments and about 37,000 housing units in 87 urban areas across the country are used to develop the U.S. city average.

Periodic major revisions of the indexes, in addition to updating the content and weights of the market basket of goods and services, update the statistical sample of urban areas, outlets, and unique items used in calculating the CPI and improve the statistical methods used. In addition, retail outlets and items are resampled on a rotating 5-year basis; adjustments for changing quality are made at times of major product changes, such as the annual auto model changeover; and other methodological changes are introduced from time to time.

CPI weights for 1964–1977 were derived from reported expenditures of a sample of wage-earner and clerical-worker families and individuals in 1960–1961 and adjusted for price changes between the survey dates and

1963. Weights for 1978–1986 were derived from a consumer expenditure survey (CES) undertaken over the 1972–1974 period and adjusted for price change between the survey dates and December 1977. For 1987 to 1997, the spending patterns reflected in the CPI were derived from a CES undertaken over the 1982–1984 period, and the reported expenditures were adjusted for price change between the survey dates and December 1986.

The CES is composed of two separate surveys: an interview survey and a diary survey, both conducted by the Bureau of the Census for BLS. Each expenditure reported in the two surveys is coded to detailed categories, which are then combined in expenditure classes and ultimately into major expenditure groups. Data as of 1998 are grouped into eight such groups: (1) food and beverages, (2) housing, (3) apparel, (4) transportation, (5) medical care, (6) recreation, (7) education and communication, and (8) other goods and services. Education and communication and recreation are new groups, and several subcategories have been rearranged as well.

The expenditure base of the CPI that is established by the CES encompasses only out-of-pocket consumer spending. Consumers also benefit from goods and services that are financed by government and private insurance, particularly in the medical care area. In the NIPAs, personal consumption expenditures (PCE) includes all spending whether purchased out of pocket or financed by government or employer-financed insurance, whereas the CES includes only out-of-pocket spending and payment of insurance premiums by individuals. For this reason, there is a large difference between the relatively small weight of medical care spending in the CPI and the markedly greater percentage of PCE accounted for by total medical care spending.

Seasonally adjusted national CPI indexes are published for selected series for which there is a significant seasonal pattern of price change. The factors currently in use were derived by the X-12-ARIMA seasonal adjustment method. Some series with extreme or sharp movements are seasonally adjusted using X-12-ARIMA Intervention Analysis Seasonal Adjustment. Seasonally adjusted indexes and seasonal factors for the preceding 5 years are updated annually based on data through the previous December. Because of these revisions, BLS advises against use of seasonally adjusted data for escalation. Detailed descriptions of BLS seasonal adjustment procedures are available upon request from the Bureau of Labor Statistics.

Definitions

Definitions of the major CPI groupings were modified beginning with the data for January 1998 and carried back to 1993. The definitions below are these current definitions.

The *food and beverage index* includes both food at home and food away from home (restaurant meals and other food bought and eaten away from home).

The *housing index* measures changes in rental costs and in expenses connected with the acquisition and operation of a home. The CPI-U, beginning with data for January 1983, and the CPI-W, beginning with data for January 1985, reflect a change in the methodology used to compute the homeownership component. A rental equivalence measure replaced the asset-price approach. The central purpose of the change was to separate shelter costs from the investment component of homeownership so that the index would reflect only the cost of shelter services provided by owner-occupied homes. In addition to these measures of the cost of shelter, the housing category includes insurance, fuel, utilities, and household furnishings and operations.

The *apparel index* includes the purchase of apparel and footwear.

The *private transportation index* includes prices paid by urban consumers on such items as new and used automobiles and other vehicles, gasoline, motor oil, tires, repairs and maintenance, insurance, registration fees, driver's licenses, parking fees, etc. Auto finance charges, like mortgage interest payments, are considered to be a cost of asset acquisition, not of current consumption, and therefore are no longer included in the CPI. City bus, streetcar, subway, taxicab, intercity bus, airplane, and railroad coach fares are some of the components of the *public transportation index*.

The *medical care index* includes prices for professional medical services; hospital and related services; prescription and nonprescription drugs; and other medical care commodities. The portion of health insurance premiums used to cover the costs of these medical goods and services is distributed among the items; the portion of health insurance costs attributable to administrative expenses and profits of insurance providers constitutes a separate health insurance item. Effective with the January 1997 data, the method of calculating the hospital cost component was changed from the pricing of individual commodities and services to a more comprehensive cost-of-treatment approach.

Recreation includes components formerly in housing, apparel, entertainment, and "other."

Education and communication is a new group including components formerly in housing and "other," such as telephone services and computers.

Other goods and services now includes tobacco, personal care, and miscellaneous.

Supplemental indexes

The *CPI-U-X1* is a special version of the CPI that has been used by many researchers to provide a more historically consistent series. As explained above, the official CPI-U treated homeownership on an asset price basis until January 1983 and then changed to a rental equivalence method. The CPI-U-X1 incorporates a rental equivalence approach to homeowners' costs for the years 1967–1982 as well. It is rebased to the December 1982 value of the CPI-U (1982–84 = 100); thus it is identical to the CPI-U in December 1982 and all subsequent periods, and for this reason is not updated or published in the CPI news release.

The *CPI-U-RS* is a "research series" CPI that retroactively incorporates estimates of the effects of most of the methodological changes that have been implemented since 1978, including the rental equivalence method, new or improved quality adjustments, and improvement of formulas to eliminate bias and allow for some consumer substitution within categories. This index is calculated from 1977 forward. Unlike the other CPI measures, its reference base is December 1977 = 100. Thus, although it generally shows less increase than the official index, its current levels are considerably higher. Unlike the official CPIs and the CPI-U-X1, its historical values will be revised each time that a significant change is made in the calculation of the current index. This index is not seasonally adjusted, and not included in the CPI news release; it is available on the BLS Internet site.

The *C-CPI-U* (Chained Consumer Price Index for All Urban Consumers) is a new, supplemental index that is published in the monthly CPI news release beginning in August 2002. It is available only from December 1999 to date and is calculated with the base December 1999 = 100; it is not seasonally adjusted. It is designed to be a closer approximation to a true cost-of-living index than the CPI-U and the CPI-W, which are based on a fixed market basket rather than the economic concept of a fixed basket of "consumer satisfaction."

The C-CPI-U is a "superlative" index, using a method known as the "Tornqvist" formula to incorporate the composition of consumer spending in the current period as well as in the earlier base period. Because it requires consumer expenditure data for the current as well as the earlier period, its final version can only be calculated after the expenditure data became available—about 2 years before the current period—and is approximated in more recent periods, making more extensive use of the "geometric mean" formula (see above). Of the data shown in this volume, the values for 2001 and earlier are "final" and the values for 2002 are "interim." At this writing, values announced each month for 2003 are "initial."

Data availability

The indexes are initially issued in a press release about 2 weeks following the month to which the data pertain. The *CPI Detailed Report* is issued about a month after the press release. Selected CPI data are published monthly in the *Monthly Labor Review*, which also contains periodic articles analyzing price developments. Complete historical data are available on the BLS Internet site at <http://www.bls.gov>.

References

Two special issues of the *Monthly Labor Review* cover the CPI in detail. The December 1996 issue describes the subsequently-implemented 1997 and 1998 revisions in a series of articles, and the December 1993 issue on "The Anatomy of Price Change" includes: "The Consumer Price Index: Underlying Concepts and Caveats"; "Basic Components of the CPI: Estimation of Price Changes"; "The Commodity Substitution Effect in CPI Data, 1982–1991"; and "Quality Adjustment of Price Indexes." The new formula for calculating basic components is described in "Incorporating a geometric mean formula into the CPI", *Monthly Labor Review*, October 1998. The CPI-U-RS is described in "Consumer Price Index research series using current methods, 1978-1998," *Monthly Labor Review*, June 1999. The C-CPI-U is discussed in the news release on the July 2002 CPI, available on the BLS Internet site.

For a detailed discussion of the treatment of homeownership, see "Changing the Homeownership Component of the Consumer Price Index to Rental Equivalence," *CPI Detailed Report* (January 1983).

BLS Handbook of Methods Bulletin 2490 (April 1997), Chapter 17 "Consumer Price Indexes" described the methodology used in computing the CPI.

For a comprehensive, up-to-date professional review of CPI concepts and methodology, see Charles Schultze and Christopher Mackie, ed., *At What Price? Conceptualizing and Measuring Cost-of-Living and Price Indexes*, Washington, DC: National Academy Press, 2001. Earlier discussions include: "Using Survey Data to Assess Bias in the Consumer Price Index," *Monthly Labor Review* (April 1998); Joel Popkin, "Improving the CPI: The Record and Suggested Next Steps," *Business Economics*, Vol. XXXII, No. 3 (July 1997), pages 42–47; *Measurement Issues in the Consumer Price Index*, Bureau of Labor Statistics, U.S. Department of Labor, June 1997; *Toward a More Accurate Measure of the Cost of Living*, Final Report to the Senate Finance Committee from the Advisory Commission to Study the Consumer Price Index, December 4, 1996 (the "Boskin Commission" report); and *Government Price Statistics*, U.S. Congress

Joint Economic Committee, 87th Congress, 1st Session, January 24, 1961 (the "Stigler Committee" report).

TABLES 8-2, 8-3, AND 20-4
PRODUCER PRICE INDEXES

SOURCE: U.S. DEPARTMENT OF LABOR, BUREAU OF LABOR STATISTICS

Producer Price Indexes (PPI) measure average changes in prices received by domestic producers. They are organized in three systems: by stage of processing, by commodity group, and by industry. Most of the indexes currently are published on a base of 1982 = 100, but there are a number of exceptions for products introduced since 1982, identified in this book in the column headings for the individual series.

Table 8-2 presents price indexes for commodities by stage of processing. Table 8-3 presents data by commodity groups; this is the grouping that has the longest continuous history. In current price analysis, the commodity groups—particularly the totals for all commodities and industrial commodities—have been de-emphasized because they aggregate successive stages of processing and thus often exaggerate price trends; it was to avoid this problem that the stage-of-processing groups were introduced. However, the individual commodity groups, For example, textile products and apparel, provide a longer perspective on individual industrial sectors than is available in the industry grouping, and are presented here for that reason.

The industry groupings will not be updated to the new North American Industry Classification System (NAICS) until the February 2004 release of January 2004 indexes. Since the classification system has not been updated and the historical values on the old SIC system are only available back to 1984, they are not shown here. Next year's edition will feature extensive coverage of PPIs by NAICS industry.

Definitions

The *stage-of-processing* PPI indexes organize commodities by class of buyer and degree of fabrication. These have been the featured measures since 1978. The three major indexes are (1) finished goods, commodities that will not undergo further processing and are ready for sale to the ultimate user (automobiles, meats, apparel, machine tools); (2) *intermediate materials, supplies, and components*, commodities that have been processed but require further processing before they become finished goods (steel mill products, cotton yarns, lumber, flour), as well as physically complete goods that are purchased by business firms as inputs for their operations (diesel fuel and paper boxes); and (3) *crude materials* for further processing, products entering the market for the first time

which have not been manufactured or fabricated but which will be processed before becoming finished goods (scrap metals, crude petroleum, raw cotton, livestock).

Notes on the data

The probability sample used for calculating the PPI provides more than 100,000 price quotations per month, selected to represent the movement of prices of all commodities produced in the manufacturing; agriculture, forestry, and fishing; mining; and gas and electricity and public utility sectors. In addition, new PPIs are gradually being introduced for the products of industries in the transportation, trade, finance, and services sectors.

To the extent possible, prices used in calculating the PPI represent prices received by domestic producers in the first important commercial transaction for each commodity. These indexes attempt to measure only price changes; that is, price changes not influenced by changes in quality, quantity, terms of sale, or level of distribution. Most quotations are the selling prices of selected manufacturers or other producers, although a few prices are those quoted on organized exchanges or markets. Transaction prices are sought instead of list or book prices.

Price data are generally collected monthly, primarily by mail questionnaire. Most prices are obtained directly from producing companies on a voluntary and confidential basis. Prices generally are reported for the Tuesday of the week containing the 13th day of the month.

The name "Producer Price Index" became effective with the release of March 1978 data, replacing the term "Wholesale Price Index." The change was made to reflect the coverage of the data more accurately. At the same time, there was a shift in analytical emphasis from the All Commodities Index and other traditional commodity grouping indexes to the Finished Goods Index and other stage-of-processing indexes.

The BLS revises the Producer Price Index weighting structure periodically when data from economic censuses become available. Beginning with data for January 1996, the weights used to construct the PPI reflect 1992 shipment values as measured by the 1992 Economic Censuses and other sources. Data for 1992 through 1995 reflect 1987 shipment values; 1987 through 1991 reflect 1982 values; 1976 through 1986 reflect 1972 values; and 1967 through 1975 reflect 1963 values.

BLS has been working for a number of years on a comprehensive overhaul of the theory, methods, and procedures use to construct the PPI. One aspect of this overhaul was the already mentioned shift in emphasis beginning in 1978 to the stage-of-processing measures. Other changes that have been phased in since 1978 include the replacement of judgment sampling with probability sampling techniques; expansion to systematic coverage of the net output of virtually all industries in the mining and manufacturing sectors; introduction of measures for selected services industries, including retail trade; a shift from a commodity to an industry orientation; the exclusion of imports from, and the inclusion of exports in, the survey universe.

Seasonal factors for the PPI are revised annually to take into account the most recent 12 months of data. Seasonally adjusted data for the previous 5 years are subject to these annual revisions.

Data availability

The indexes are initially issued in a press release about 2 weeks following the end of the month to which the data pertain and subsequently are published in greater detail in the monthly BLS publication, *PPI Detailed Report*. Selected PPI data also are published monthly in the *Monthly Labor Review*, which also contains periodic articles analyzing price developments. Historical data tables providing annual and monthly data for all available periods for all published series are available on request from BLS. Complete historical data are available on the BLS Internet site at <http://www.bls.gov>.

References

The following *Monthly Labor Review* articles and technical notes contain background information: "Comparing PPI Energy Indexes to Alternative Data Sources" (December 1998); "Are Producer Prices Good Proxies for Export Prices" (October 1997); "Effect of 1992 Weights on Producer Price Indexes" (July 1996); "Hospital Price Inflation: What Does the PPI Tell Us?" (July 1996); "Seasonal Adjustment of Producer Price Index for Passenger Cars" (June 1996); "Effect of Updated Weights on Producer Price Indexes" (March 1993); "Milestones in the Producer Price Index Methodology and Presentation" (August 1989); "New Stage of Process Price System Developed for the Producer Price Index" (April 1988); "Improving the Measurement of Producer Price Changes" (April 1977).

BLS Handbook of Methods Bulletin 2490 (April 1997), Chapter 14, "Producer Prices" describes the methodology used in computing the PPI.

TABLE 8-2
PURCHASING POWER OF THE DOLLAR

SOURCE: *U.S. DEPARTMENT OF LABOR, BUREAU OF LABOR STATISTICS; CALCULATIONS BY EDITORS*

The purchasing power of the dollar measures changes in the quantity of goods and services a dollar will buy at a particular date compared with a selected base date. It must be defined in terms of: (1) The specific commodities and services that are to be purchased with the dollar; (2) the market level (producer, retail, etc.) at which they are purchased; and (3) the dates for which the comparison is to be made. Thus, the purchasing power of the dollar for a selected period, compared with another period, may be measured in terms of a single commodity or a large group of commodities; for example, all goods and services purchased by consumers at retail, or all finished commodities sold in primary markets.

Broad prices indexes calculated by BLS that have been used to calculate the purchasing power of the dollar in the United States include: (1) The Producer Price Index (PPI) for Finished Goods, which relates to prices received by the producers of finished commodities at the primary market level, and (2) Two versions of the Consumer Price Index, which measures average changes in retail prices of goods and services   the CPI U and the CPI-W. These indexes are described above in the sections of the Notes and Definitions pertaining to the Producer Price Index and the Consumer Price Index, respectively.

The purchasing power of the dollar is computed by dividing the price index number for the base period by the price index number for the date to be compared, and expressing the result in dollars and cents. The base period is the period in which the price index equals 100, and the purchasing power is therefore $1.00. In this book, 1982 through 1984 is used as the base period for the two indexes shown so that they can be readily compared. Purchasing power estimates in terms of both the CPI-U and the CPI-W are calculated by BLS and published in the CPI press release. The CPI-U version is used here. The comparable purchasing power in terms of the PPI is calculated by the editors of *Business Statistics*, after rebasing the index from its published 1982 base to 1982-1984 = 100.

TABLE 8-4
PRICES RECEIVED AND PAID BY FARMERS

SOURCE: *U.S. DEPARTMENT OF AGRICULTURE, NATIONAL AGRICULTURAL STATISTICS SERVICE (NASS)*

The data on prices received and paid by farmers represent prices farmers received for commodities sold and prices paid for production input goods and services. Prices are weighted and aggregated into price indexes. These indexes provide measures of relative price changes for agricultural outputs and inputs. These price measures are based on voluntary reports from agribusiness firms, merchants, dealers, and farmers. Data are collected at regular intervals using mailed inquiries, telephone, and personal enumeration. In January 1995, these data were converted to a reference base of 1990–1992 = 100.

Prices-paid indexes were available only quarterly for several years but have been published monthly beginning with January 1996, with monthly indexes for 1995 constructed for historical comparison.

Definitions

Prices received by farmers represent sales from producers to first buyers. They include all grades and qualities. The average commodity price from the survey multiplied by the total quantity marketed theoretically should give the total cash receipts for the commodity.

Prices paid by farmers represent the average costs of inputs purchased by farmers and ranchers to produce agricultural commodities. Conceptually, the average price when multiplied by quantity purchased should equal total producer expenditures for the item.

Ratio of prices received to prices paid is the ratio of the index of prices received for all farm products to the index of prices paid for all commodities and services. (For some years, prices paid are available only for the first month of each quarter. Each month's ratio of prices received to prices paid is based on the latest data available.)

Notes on the data

In 1995, NASS reweighted and reconstructed the prices paid and received indexes. The indexes are now based on 5-year moving average weights compared with fixed weights previously. The changes in the construction of the indexes simplified updating component items and reference periods while maintaining appropriate weights. The overall changes to the weighting and construction of the indexes did not have a significant effect on the index levels and therefore had little effect on the level of parity prices. Indexes are now published on a 1990–1992 = 100 base. As required by law, the parity ratio (ratio of prices received to prices paid) also continues to be published on a base of 1910–1914 = 100.

Prices paid. Since 1995, the Prices Paid Survey of items purchased by farm establishments has been conducted annually in April. Surveys are conducted for feed, seed, fertilizer, agricultural chemicals, fuel, and farm machinery. About 135 selected items are priced to represent groups of similar items purchased which make up the major production expenditure categories. The number of input items consumed on farms is so extensive that it is not feasible to collect price data for all of the inputs. Items on the questionnaire are described in the simplest way consistent with definite identification. Firms are requested to report the prices for the most commonly sold item that meets the general specification on the questionnaire.

Reported data are summarized to regional estimates and then weighted to U.S. prices. Weights are based on available consumption or expenditure information. Average prices, including state and local taxes, are used in computing the indexes and are published in *Agricultural Prices* for the same month as the survey. Regional prices are published for feed, fuel, and fertilizer. U.S. prices are published for the remaining items surveyed.

Bureau of Labor Statistics (BLS) indexes are used to measure price change for the months when no survey data are collected. The BLS indexes measure price changes for farm supplies and repairs, autos and trucks, building materials, and marketing containers. Before 1995, quarterly prices-paid surveys were conducted by NASS. Quarterly feeder livestock surveys still are conducted.

Revisions: prices paid. Any revisions are published in the monthly and in annual issues of "Agricultural Prices." The basis for revision must be supported by additional data that directly affect the level of the estimate. More revisions are likely in April when separate prices paid surveys are conducted.

Survey procedures: prices received: Primary sales data used to determine grain prices are obtained from probability samples of mills and elevators. These procedures ensure that virtually all grain moving into commercial channels has a chance of being included in the survey. Livestock prices are obtained from packers, stockyards, auctions, dealers, and market check data. Inter-farm sales of grain and livestock are not included since they represent very small percentages of total marketings. Grain marketed for seed is also excluded. Fruit and vegetable prices are obtained from sample surveys and market check data.

Summary and estimation procedures: prices received: Survey quantities sold are expanded by strata to state levels and used to weight average strata prices to a state average. State prices are then weighted to a U.S. price.

Revisions: prices received: For most items, the current month's price represents a 3–5 day period around the mid-month. Previous month's prices represent actual dollars received for quantities sold during the entire month. Revisions are published in monthly issues of *Agricultural Prices* and in the annual summary published in July. A schedule of monthly revisions is published in the December issue of *Agricultural Prices* and in the July annual summary.

Reliability: prices received: U.S. price estimates generally have a sampling error of less than one-half percent for the major commodities such as corn, wheat, soybeans, cotton, and rice.

Data availability

Prices paid and received by farmers are available each month in a press release issued around the end of the month. Data are subsequently published monthly in *Agricultural Prices*. Data also are available on the NASS Internet site at <http://www.usda.gov/nass/>.

Reference

"Revised Prices Received and Paid Indexes, United States, 1975–1993 for Base Periods 1910–1914 = 100 and 1990–1992 = 100," Statistical Bulletin number 917 (National Agricultural Statistics Service, February 1995).

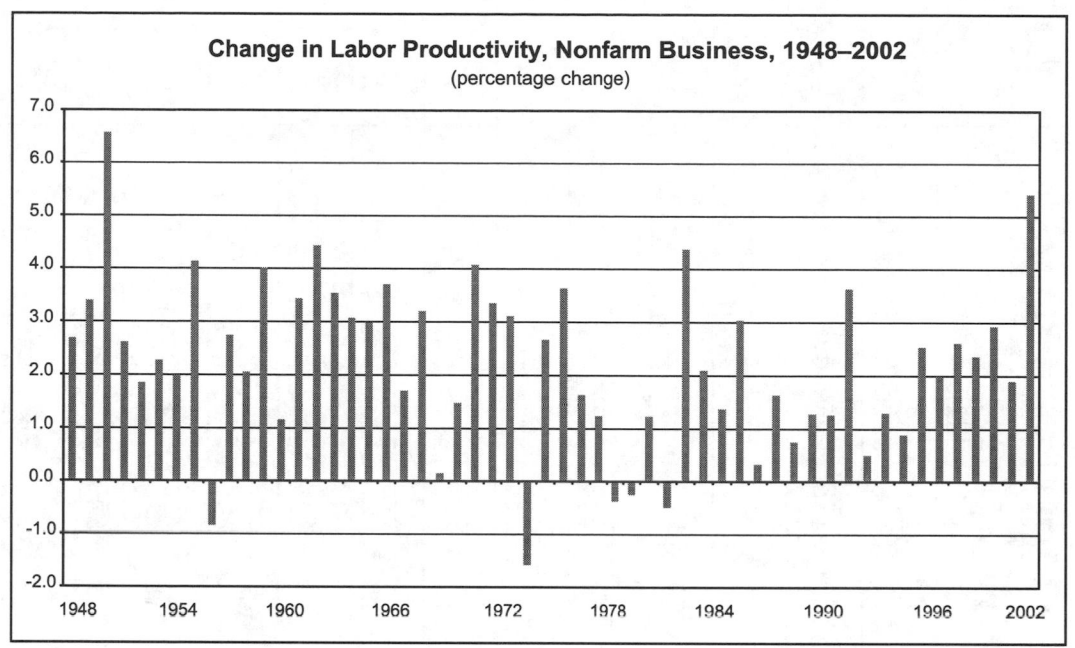

Change in Labor Productivity, Nonfarm Business, 1948–2002
(percentage change)

- Typically, for most of the postwar period, output per hour in nonfarm business declined in recession years. In 2001, however, productivity continued to increase. The recovery year 2002 saw the greatest annual increase in productivity since 1950, and large productivity increases continued into 2003. (Table 9-3)

- Unit labor costs declined by a record amount in 2002, signaling an absence of any inflationary pressures on the cost front. Very modest increases in compensation per hour— 2.8 percent on average—were more than offset by the productivity increase. (Table 9-3)

- For nonfinancial businesses, unit profits and "unit nonlabor costs" (for example, depreciation and interest) can be calculated separately. Unit nonlabor costs rose rapidly in 2001—which is typical of recession, since such costs cannot be reduced as fast as output declines—but slowed to a 1.0 percent rate of increase in 2002. Unit profits, which had been declining since 1997, rose in 2002, which is typical of recovery, as profits absorb a substantial share of the recovery productivity increase. (Table 9-3)

- Average hourly wages and salaries for all private industry workers as measured in the Employment Cost Index, measured in current dollars (not adjusted for inflation) and holding constant the mix of industries and occupations, rose 2.7 percent in 2002, slowing from increases of nearly 4 percent in both 2000 and 2001. Total compensation per hour rose by about half a percent more than wages and salaries in each year, driven by rising medical care costs. (Table 9-1)

- The decline in profits since 1997 was most pronounced in computer and motor vehicle manufacturing, transportation, and information, all of which suffered losses in both 2001 and 2002. Their losses were smaller in 2002, however, which contributed to an overall increase in profits in the recovery year, also driven by rising profits in financial industries. (Table 9-5)

Table 9-1. Employment Cost Indexes—Total Compensation

(June 1989 [not seasonally adjusted] =100; annual values are for December; quarterly values, seasonally adjusted, except as noted.)

Year and quarter	All civilian workers [1]	State and local government workers	Private industry workers														
			All private industry workers	Private industry workers excluding sales occupations [2]	By occupational group					By industry division						
									Goods-producing industries			Service-producing industries				
					Production and non supervisory occupations [2]	White-collar occupations	Blue-collar occupations	Service occupations	Total	Construction	Manufacturing	Total	Transportation and utilities	Wholesale trade	Retail trade	Finance, insurance, and real estate [2]	Services
1979	...	...	59.1	58.7	...	57.4	61.3	58.8	60.7	...	60.1	57.7	...	...	...	...	...
1980	...	...	64.8	64.8	...	62.9	67.5	64.4	66.7	...	66.0	63.3	...	...	...	...	...
1981	70.2	66.1	71.2	71.2	71.4	69.2	74.0	70.4	73.3	...	72.5	69.5	...	...	...	...	...
1982	74.8	70.8	75.8	75.9	76.1	73.7	78.4	76.3	77.8	...	76.9	74.1	...	...	...	...	...
1983	79.1	75.1	80.1	80.2	80.4	78.4	82.3	80.5	81.6	...	80.8	78.9	...	...	...	...	...
1984	83.2	80.1	84.0	84.3	84.2	82.4	85.8	85.8	85.4	...	85.0	82.9	...	...	...	...	...
1985	86.8	84.6	87.3	87.3	87.3	86.4	88.5	88.4	88.2	88.2	87.8	86.6	90.0	...	88.8	85.9	84.1
1986	89.9	89.0	90.1	90.2	89.8	89.4	90.9	91.1	91.0	90.7	90.7	89.3	92.0	88.7	90.8	88.6	87.7
1987	93.1	93.0	93.1	93.4	92.8	92.7	93.7	93.3	93.8	94.0	93.4	92.6	94.8	92.2	93.0	90.4	92.2
1988	97.7	98.2	97.6	97.7	97.5	97.3	97.9	98.2	97.9	98.0	97.6	97.3	97.5	96.1	98.4	96.2	97.5
1989	102.6	104.3	102.3	102.1	102.4	102.4	101.9	102.5	102.1	102.4	102.0	102.3	101.2	104.5	101.6	101.4	102.9
1990	107.6	110.4	107.0	107.1	106.9	107.4	106.4	107.3	107.0	105.6	107.2	107.0	105.1	106.5	106.0	105.5	109.3
1991	112.2	114.4	111.7	112.0	111.5	112.2	111.0	112.4	111.9	109.9	112.2	111.6	109.7	111.1	110.5	110.0	114.0
1992	116.1	118.6	115.6	115.9	115.5	115.9	115.0	115.9	116.1	113.8	116.5	115.2	113.5	114.4	113.4	111.3	118.9
1993	120.2	121.9	119.8	120.2	119.7	120.2	119.3	119.5	120.6	116.5	121.3	119.3	117.5	117.8	116.8	116.4	123.1
1994	123.8	125.6	123.5	123.9	123.1	124.1	122.6	122.9	124.3	120.8	125.1	122.8	122.1	121.5	120.1	118.9	126.6
1995	127.2	129.3	126.7	127.1	126.3	127.6	125.6	125.2	127.3	123.4	128.3	126.2	126.6	127.0	122.7	123.1	129.4
1996	130.9	132.7	130.6	130.8	130.0	131.7	129.0	128.9	130.9	126.4	132.1	130.2	130.4	130.9	127.4	126.0	133.4
1997	135.2	135.7	135.1	135.2	134.2	136.7	132.3	134.1	134.1	129.7	135.3	135.3	134.2	135.1	131.7	134.5	138.5
1998	139.8	139.8	139.8	139.4	139.0	142.0	135.9	138.0	137.8	134.3	138.9	140.5	139.3	142.8	135.6	142.5	142.7
1999	144.6	144.6	144.6	144.5	143.1	146.9	140.5	142.6	142.5	138.7	143.6	145.3	142.3	148.5	140.7	148.3	147.6
2000	150.6	148.9	150.9	150.9	149.5	153.6	146.4	148.1	148.8	146.7	149.3	151.7	148.3	154.4	146.6	155.7	154.1
2001	156.8	155.2	157.2	157.2	155.5	160.1	151.9	154.8	154.4	153.0	154.6	158.2	155.5	159.5	153.2	161.3	161.0
2002	162.2	161.5	162.3	162.4	160.5	165.2	157.3	159.8	160.1	157.9	160.5	163.1	161.7	166.7	155.8	168.5	165.4
1994																	
1st quarter	121.2	122.7	120.9	121.4	120.7	121.4	120.3	120.5	121.8	118.8	122.4	120.3	119.0	118.0	117.7	117.7	124.3
2nd quarter	122.3	123.6	121.9	122.3	121.6	122.4	121.1	121.0	123.0	120.0	123.4	121.2	119.8	119.4	119.0	117.7	125.0
3rd quarter	123.3	124.6	123.0	123.4	122.6	123.4	122.2	121.7	123.9	121.1	124.5	122.2	121.3	120.6	120.1	118.5	125.8
4th quarter	124.0	125.3	123.7	123.9	123.1	124.3	122.8	122.8	124.6	121.1	125.3	123.0	122.4	121.7	120.4	118.9	126.7
1995																	
1st quarter	124.9	126.4	124.5	125.0	124.1	125.2	123.5	123.3	125.5	121.3	126.0	124.0	123.8	123.3	121.0	120.2	127.4
2nd quarter	125.8	127.4	125.4	125.7	125.0	126.2	124.3	123.9	126.2	121.8	126.8	125.0	124.8	124.6	121.7	121.8	128.3
3rd quarter	126.5	128.3	126.2	126.5	126.3	126.9	125.0	124.5	126.9	122.8	127.3	125.8	125.9	126.1	122.3	122.7	128.8
4th quarter	127.3	129.1	126.9	127.1	126.3	127.8	125.8	125.0	127.8	123.7	128.4	126.5	126.8	127.2	123.0	123.1	129.5
1996																	
1st quarter	128.3	129.9	127.9	128.3	127.5	128.9	126.6	125.6	128.5	124.5	129.1	127.6	127.7	127.6	124.6	124.5	130.7
2nd quarter	129.2	130.8	128.9	129.2	128.6	129.9	127.5	126.3	129.6	125.1	130.3	128.6	128.5	129.1	124.7	126.3	131.8
3rd quarter	130.1	131.5	129.8	130.2	129.2	131.0	128.0	127.1	130.4	125.6	131.2	129.5	129.2	129.9	125.9	126.7	132.6
4th quarter	131.0	132.5	130.7	130.8	130.0	132.0	129.2	128.6	131.3	126.7	132.1	130.4	130.6	131.1	127.8	126.0	133.5
1997																	
1st quarter	131.9	133.2	131.6	131.9	131.1	133.0	129.7	129.5	131.6	127.4	132.5	131.5	131.1	133.0	128.6	128.6	134.6
2nd quarter	132.9	133.9	132.6	133.0	132.1	134.0	130.7	130.6	132.9	128.4	133.6	132.5	131.8	133.6	129.6	129.4	135.7
3rd quarter	133.9	134.6	133.7	134.1	133.2	135.1	131.6	132.7	133.8	129.4	134.5	133.6	132.8	134.6	130.8	130.5	136.9
4th quarter	135.2	135.4	135.2	135.2	134.2	137.0	132.5	133.8	134.4	130.0	135.4	135.6	134.3	135.2	132.1	134.5	138.6
1998																	
1st quarter	136.2	136.5	136.1	136.4	135.3	138.0	133.2	134.9	135.2	130.8	136.2	136.6	135.7	137.9	133.1	136.7	139.3
2nd quarter	137.3	137.5	137.3	137.5	136.6	139.3	134.1	135.7	136.3	132.4	137.0	137.7	137.1	138.3	134.3	138.4	140.3
3rd quarter	138.7	138.6	138.7	138.8	138.0	141.0	135.1	137.0	137.2	133.2	138.2	139.5	138.4	140.8	135.6	141.0	141.7
4th quarter	139.7	139.5	139.8	139.4	139.0	142.3	136.1	137.7	138.0	134.6	139.0	140.7	139.4	143.0	136.1	142.5	142.8
1999																	
1st quarter	140.2	140.4	140.2	140.5	139.3	142.3	137.0	139.1	138.9	135.8	139.7	140.8	139.7	142.9	136.8	141.5	143.5
2nd quarter	141.7	141.6	141.7	141.9	140.8	144.0	138.0	140.2	139.9	136.7	140.7	142.6	140.9	144.2	138.9	145.8	144.6
3rd quarter	143.0	142.6	143.0	143.2	141.9	145.5	139.3	140.6	141.2	137.8	142.0	144.0	141.7	146.3	139.7	147.6	145.9
4th quarter	144.6	144.2	144.7	144.5	143.1	147.2	140.7	142.2	142.7	138.9	143.8	145.6	142.5	148.7	141.2	148.3	147.7
2000																	
1st quarter	146.4	145.5	146.6	146.5	145.3	149.2	142.6	143.4	144.9	140.9	145.8	147.4	143.9	150.2	143.1	152.0	149.4
2nd quarter	147.9	146.6	148.2	148.2	146.9	150.9	143.9	145.0	146.7	143.0	147.3	148.9	145.6	151.4	144.6	153.1	151.2
3rd quarter	149.3	147.2	149.7	149.8	148.4	152.5	145.4	146.2	148.2	145.0	148.7	150.5	147.2	152.1	146.0	155.2	152.7
4th quarter	150.6	148.6	151.1	150.9	149.5	154.0	146.7	147.8	149.1	146.8	149.5	152.1	148.5	154.6	147.2	155.7	154.3
2001																	
1st quarter	152.3	150.2	152.8	153.0	151.4	155.6	148.2	149.6	150.7	148.3	151.1	153.8	150.5	155.3	148.5	157.9	156.5
2nd quarter	153.8	152.0	154.2	154.4	152.7	157.2	149.1	150.9	152.2	150.1	152.4	155.2	152.3	157.3	149.4	159.5	157.8
3rd quarter	155.4	153.7	155.7	156.0	154.3	158.6	150.9	152.3	153.4	151.7	153.3	156.8	153.3	158.6	150.7	160.9	159.8
4th quarter	156.9	154.8	157.4	157.2	155.5	160.5	152.2	154.5	154.8	153.1	154.8	158.6	155.8	159.7	153.8	161.3	161.2
2002																	
1st quarter	158.3	156.1	158.8	159.0	157.1	161.8	153.6	156.1	156.3	154.2	156.3	160.1	157.3	162.2	153.3	165.2	162.6
2nd quarter	159.9	157.5	160.5	160.5	158.7	163.5	154.9	157.2	157.8	155.1	157.8	161.8	158.8	165.7	155.3	167.3	163.7
3rd quarter	161.2	159.5	161.5	161.6	159.7	164.5	156.2	158.7	159.0	156.3	159.1	162.7	160.6	165.9	155.9	168.0	164.7
4th quarter	162.4	161.1	162.7	162.4	160.5	165.6	157.6	159.6	160.6	157.9	160.8	163.7	162.0	167.0	156.5	168.5	165.7

[1] Includes private industry and state and local government workers. Federal government workers are not included.
[2] Not seasonally adjusted.
. . . = Not available.

Table 9-2. Employment Cost Indexes—Wages and Salaries

(June 1989 [not seasonally adjusted] =100; annual values are for December; quarterly values, seasonally adjusted, except as noted.)

Year and quarter	All civilian workers [1]	State and local government workers	All private industry workers	Private industry workers excluding sales occupations [2]	Production and non-supervisory occupations [2]	White-collar occupations	Blue-collar occupations	Service occupations	Goods-producing Total	Construction	Manufacturing [2]	Service-producing Total	Transportation and utilities	Wholesale trade	Retail trade	Finance, insurance, and real estate [2]	Services
1975	...	...	45.9	45.8	45.7	44.9	47.0	46.6	46.9	...	46.3	45.1	45.5	...	...	...	43.5
1976	...	...	49.2	49.0	49.0	47.9	50.8	50.2	50.4	54.4	49.7	48.2	49.4	...	52.5	...	45.8
1977	...	...	52.6	52.4	52.5	51.1	54.7	53.4	54.3	58.0	53.6	51.4	54.0	50.4	55.5	...	48.2
1978	...	...	56.6	56.4	56.6	54.7	59.2	58.1	58.8	62.5	58.1	55.1	58.1	54.2	60.3	52.8	51.5
1979	...	...	61.5	61.4	61.7	59.5	64.5	62.2	63.7	67.0	63.0	60.0	63.6	58.5	65.0	59.7	55.8
1980	...	...	67.1	67.0	67.5	64.6	70.7	67.3	69.7	72.9	68.9	65.3	70.7	64.4	69.6	64.1	60.6
1981	72.2	68.3	73.0	73.0	73.6	70.5	76.7	72.9	75.7	79.3	74.9	71.1	76.6	69.4	74.8	70.5	67.0
1982	76.7	72.8	77.6	77.7	78.2	75.1	81.0	79.1	80.0	83.4	79.1	75.9	82.1	73.7	77.8	75.1	72.4
1983	80.6	76.6	81.4	81.5	82.0	79.6	84.1	82.7	83.2	85.8	82.5	80.2	86.3	78.2	81.1	80.5	77.2
1984	84.2	81.2	84.8	85.3	85.2	83.0	87.1	87.8	86.4	86.9	86.1	83.7	89.2	82.5	85.3	79.8	82.1
1985	87.8	85.7	88.3	88.4	88.6	87.1	90.1	89.9	89.4	89.6	89.2	87.7	92.5	86.1	89.4	87.1	85.0
1986	90.9	90.3	91.1	91.2	91.0	90.1	92.4	92.3	92.3	91.8	92.1	90.3	94.2	89.3	91.3	89.5	88.4
1987	94.1	94.1	94.1	94.5	93.9	93.4	95.2	94.5	95.2	94.8	95.2	93.4	96.2	93.0	93.7	90.6	93.2
1988	98.1	98.7	98.0	98.0	97.9	97.8	98.2	98.7	98.2	98.3	98.1	97.8	98.6	96.4	98.5	96.3	97.8
1989	102.4	103.9	102.0	101.9	102.2	102.4	101.6	102.3	102.0	101.7	101.9	102.2	101.2	105.2	101.6	101.3	102.5
1990	106.8	109.4	106.1	106.2	105.9	106.6	105.2	106.4	105.8	103.7	106.2	106.3	104.6	106.2	105.3	104.8	108.3
1991	110.6	113.2	110.0	110.2	109.6	110.7	108.8	110.6	109.7	106.8	110.3	110.2	108.4	110.3	109.2	108.4	112.2
1992	113.6	116.6	112.9	113.2	112.6	113.7	111.6	112.9	112.8	108.9	113.7	113.0	111.8	113.5	111.8	108.3	116.1
1993	117.1	119.7	116.4	116.6	115.9	117.5	114.8	115.3	116.1	111.1	117.3	116.6	115.4	116.4	115.0	112.9	119.6
1994	120.4	123.4	119.7	120.0	119.1	120.8	118.0	118.8	119.6	114.7	120.8	119.7	119.6	119.9	117.8	114.2	123.0
1995	123.9	127.3	123.1	123.4	122.4	124.3	121.4	121.4	122.9	117.4	124.3	123.2	123.7	125.5	120.6	118.4	126.0
1996	128.0	130.9	127.3	127.5	126.5	128.7	125.1	125.7	126.8	120.8	128.4	127.5	127.0	129.6	125.8	122.2	130.5
1997	132.8	134.4	132.3	132.4	131.2	134.2	129.1	131.1	130.6	124.9	132.2	133.1	131.3	133.6	130.6	130.6	136.2
1998	137.7	138.5	137.4	136.9	136.4	139.9	133.2	135.3	135.2	129.3	136.8	138.4	135.1	134.8	134.8	139.8	140.8
1999	142.5	143.5	142.2	142.0	140.4	144.8	137.7	139.6	139.7	133.6	141.5	143.3	137.9	146.5	139.6	145.2	146.0
2000	147.9	148.3	147.7	147.6	146.0	148.2	142.8	144.9	145.2	140.7	146.5	148.9	142.3	151.6	145.2	151.7	151.8
2001	153.4	153.7	153.3	153.3	151.5	156.1	148.3	150.6	150.5	146.3	151.7	154.5	149.2	154.8	150.7	156.0	158.2
2002	157.8	158.6	157.5	157.5	155.2	160.4	152.4	154.5	155.0	150.2	156.5	158.6	154.1	161.0	152.7	162.6	161.7
1994																	
1st quarter	117.7	120.4	117.1	117.5	116.6	118.3	115.6	116.3	116.9	112.4	118.0	117.3	116.3	116.5	115.4	113.7	120.7
2nd quarter	118.7	121.3	118.1	118.3	117.5	119.2	116.5	116.9	118.0	113.5	119.0	118.2	117.2	118.0	116.8	113.2	121.4
3rd quarter	119.6	122.3	119.0	119.4	118.5	120.1	117.5	117.5	118.9	114.4	120.0	119.1	118.9	119.0	117.7	113.8	122.1
4th quarter	120.4	123.2	119.7	120.0	119.1	121.0	118.0	118.7	119.6	114.9	120.8	119.8	119.7	119.9	118.1	114.2	123.1
1995																	
1st quarter	121.3	124.3	120.6	121.0	119.9	121.7	119.0	119.4	120.4	115.0	121.9	120.7	121.1	121.1	118.9	115.0	123.8
2nd quarter	122.2	125.3	121.5	121.8	121.0	122.7	120.1	120.0	121.4	115.5	122.9	121.6	122.1	122.4	119.4	117.0	124.5
3rd quarter	123.1	126.1	122.4	122.6	121.8	123.5	120.8	120.8	122.1	116.5	123.5	122.5	122.9	124.0	120.2	118.0	125.3
4th quarter	123.9	127.0	123.2	123.4	122.4	124.4	121.4	121.4	122.9	117.6	124.3	123.3	123.7	125.5	120.9	118.4	126.0
1996																	
1st quarter	125.1	127.8	124.4	124.7	123.7	125.8	122.5	122.2	123.9	118.5	125.4	124.7	124.5	126.3	122.9	119.8	127.5
2nd quarter	126.2	128.8	125.6	125.7	124.9	126.9	123.7	123.0	125.1	119.4	126.5	125.8	125.1	127.8	123.0	121.9	128.8
3rd quarter	127.0	129.7	126.4	126.8	125.6	127.9	124.3	124.1	126.1	120.1	127.7	126.6	125.9	128.5	124.1	122.2	129.6
4th quarter	128.0	130.6	127.4	127.5	126.5	128.8	125.1	125.7	126.8	121.1	128.4	127.7	127.0	129.6	126.2	122.2	130.6
1997																	
1st quarter	129.1	131.4	128.5	128.6	127.7	130.2	126.0	126.6	127.5	122.2	129.1	129.0	128.2	131.6	127.1	124.5	131.7
2nd quarter	130.2	132.2	129.7	129.9	128.8	131.2	127.3	127.6	128.9	123.4	130.3	130.1	128.9	132.1	128.3	125.3	133.1
3rd quarter	131.3	133.1	130.9	131.2	130.1	132.6	128.3	129.9	129.9	124.5	131.3	131.4	130.0	133.0	129.7	126.4	134.6
4th quarter	132.8	134.1	132.5	132.4	131.2	134.4	129.1	131.1	130.6	125.2	132.2	133.3	131.3	133.5	131.0	130.6	136.3
1998																	
1st quarter	133.9	135.2	133.7	133.7	132.3	135.7	130.2	132.1	132.0	126.1	133.7	134.4	132.1	136.4	131.9	132.6	137.2
2nd quarter	135.1	136.1	134.8	134.8	133.6	136.9	131.3	133.0	133.2	127.8	134.6	135.5	132.8	136.9	133.1	134.8	138.4
3rd quarter	136.6	137.1	136.5	136.3	135.2	138.9	132.4	134.4	134.3	128.3	136.0	137.5	134.3	139.3	135.0	138.1	139.9
4th quarter	137.7	138.2	137.6	136.9	136.4	140.1	133.2	135.3	135.2	129.6	136.8	138.6	135.1	141.2	135.2	139.8	140.9
1999																	
1st quarter	138.3	139.1	138.1	138.2	136.8	140.3	134.3	136.7	136.3	130.8	137.9	138.9	135.4	141.0	136.2	137.2	142.2
2nd quarter	139.8	140.4	139.7	139.6	138.2	142.0	135.6	137.8	137.3	131.7	139.0	140.7	136.8	142.0	138.1	142.4	143.3
3rd quarter	141.1	141.7	140.9	140.8	139.3	143.4	136.8	138.0	138.5	132.9	140.2	142.0	137.5	144.3	138.7	144.5	144.4
4th quarter	142.5	143.1	142.4	142.0	140.4	145.0	137.7	139.6	139.7	133.9	141.5	143.5	137.9	146.5	140.1	145.2	146.1
2000																	
1st quarter	144.0	144.4	143.9	143.5	142.1	146.6	139.1	141.0	141.3	136.1	142.9	145.0	138.5	147.8	142.0	148.7	147.4
2nd quarter	145.4	145.5	145.4	145.1	143.7	148.2	140.5	142.5	143.0	137.8	144.4	146.4	140.0	148.9	143.3	149.5	149.2
3rd quarter	146.7	146.6	146.7	146.5	145.0	149.6	141.9	143.5	144.3	139.3	145.7	147.8	141.3	149.7	144.6	151.7	150.4
4th quarter	147.9	147.9	147.9	147.6	146.0	150.8	142.8	144.9	145.2	140.9	146.5	149.1	142.3	151.7	145.7	151.7	151.9
2001																	
1st quarter	149.4	149.4	149.4	149.5	147.7	152.3	144.6	146.4	147.0	142.2	148.5	150.5	143.7	152.1	146.8	153.9	153.8
2nd quarter	150.8	150.9	150.8	150.8	149.0	153.6	145.9	147.5	148.6	143.7	150.0	151.8	145.7	153.8	147.5	154.6	155.1
3rd quarter	152.1	152.4	152.0	152.2	150.3	154.7	147.5	148.7	149.5	145.1	150.7	153.1	146.7	154.3	148.7	155.8	156.9
4th quarter	153.4	153.3	153.4	153.3	151.5	156.4	148.3	150.6	150.5	146.4	151.7	154.7	149.2	155.0	151.3	156.0	158.3
2002																	
1st quarter	154.7	154.5	154.8	154.9	152.7	157.7	149.6	152.0	151.7	147.1	153.1	156.1	150.5	157.7	150.7	160.3	159.5
2nd quarter	156.1	155.8	156.2	156.1	154.0	159.1	150.9	152.8	153.1	148.0	153.8	157.5	152.1	160.4	152.4	162.0	160.4
3rd quarter	157.0	157.1	156.9	157.0	154.7	159.9	151.7	153.9	153.9	149.0	155.4	158.3	153.4	160.6	152.8	162.4	161.3
4th quarter	157.8	158.2	157.7	157.5	155.2	160.7	152.4	154.5	155.0	150.3	156.5	158.9	154.1	161.3	153.3	162.6	161.9

[1] Includes private industry and state and local government workers. Federal government workers are not included.
[2] Not seasonally adjusted.
. . . = Not available.

Table 9-3. Productivity and Related Data

(1992 = 100, seasonally adjusted.)

Year and quarter	Business sector								Nonfarm business sector							
	Output per hour of all persons	Output	Hours of all persons	Compensation per hour	Real compensation per hour	Unit labor costs	Unit nonlabor payments	Implicit price deflator	Output per hour of all persons	Output	Hours of all persons	Compensation per hour	Real compensation per hour	Unit labor costs	Unit nonlabor payments	Implicit price deflator
1947	32.7	20.7	63.3	7.0	40.6	21.4	18.9	20.5	37.3	20.3	54.4	7.4	43.1	19.9	17.9	19.2
1948	34.2	21.8	63.8	7.6	40.7	22.2	20.9	21.7	38.3	21.2	55.3	8.1	43.4	21.1	19.5	20.5
1949	34.9	21.6	61.7	7.7	41.9	22.0	20.7	21.5	39.6	21.0	53.1	8.3	45.3	21.0	20.1	20.7
1950	37.8	23.7	62.6	8.2	44.2	21.8	21.8	21.8	42.2	23.1	54.8	8.8	47.3	20.9	21.0	20.9
1951	38.9	25.2	64.7	9.0	44.9	23.2	24.0	23.5	43.3	24.9	57.4	9.6	47.7	22.1	22.6	22.3
1952	40.1	26.0	64.8	9.6	46.8	23.9	23.4	23.7	44.1	25.6	58.0	10.1	49.3	22.9	22.4	22.7
1953	41.5	27.2	65.7	10.2	49.4	24.5	22.9	23.9	45.1	26.9	59.5	10.7	51.7	23.6	22.4	23.2
1954	42.4	26.9	63.4	10.5	50.6	24.8	22.8	24.1	46.0	26.4	57.4	11.0	53.0	23.9	22.5	23.4
1955	44.1	29.0	65.8	10.8	52.1	24.4	24.3	24.4	47.9	28.6	59.8	11.4	55.1	23.8	23.8	23.8
1956	44.1	29.5	66.8	11.5	54.7	26.0	23.7	25.2	47.5	29.1	61.2	12.1	57.7	25.5	23.2	24.7
1957	45.5	30.0	65.9	12.2	56.4	26.9	24.4	26.0	48.8	29.7	60.9	12.8	59.0	26.3	24.0	25.4
1958	46.8	29.4	62.9	12.8	57.3	27.3	25.0	26.5	49.8	29.1	58.3	13.3	59.7	26.7	24.3	25.9
1959	48.6	31.9	65.5	13.3	59.2	27.4	25.5	26.7	51.8	31.6	61.0	13.8	61.6	26.7	25.1	26.2
1960	49.5	32.5	65.6	13.9	60.7	28.0	25.1	27.0	52.4	32.1	61.3	14.5	63.2	27.6	24.5	26.5
1961	51.3	33.1	64.5	14.4	62.5	28.1	25.5	27.2	54.2	32.8	60.5	15.0	64.8	27.6	25.0	26.7
1962	53.6	35.2	65.7	15.1	64.6	28.1	26.3	27.4	56.6	35.0	61.9	15.6	66.7	27.5	25.9	26.9
1963	55.7	36.8	66.1	15.6	66.1	28.0	26.9	27.6	58.6	36.6	62.6	16.1	68.1	27.5	26.5	27.1
1964	57.6	39.2	68.0	16.2	67.7	28.1	27.5	27.9	60.4	39.1	64.8	16.6	69.4	27.5	27.3	27.5
1965	59.7	41.9	70.3	16.8	69.1	28.2	28.7	28.4	62.2	41.9	67.3	17.2	70.6	27.6	28.3	27.8
1966	62.1	44.8	72.1	17.9	71.7	28.9	29.4	29.1	64.5	44.9	69.6	18.2	72.6	28.2	29.0	28.5
1967	63.5	45.6	71.9	19.0	73.6	29.9	29.8	29.9	65.6	45.7	69.6	19.3	74.7	29.3	29.5	29.4
1968	65.5	47.9	73.2	20.4	76.0	31.2	30.7	31.0	67.7	48.1	71.1	20.7	76.9	30.5	30.4	30.5
1969	65.8	49.4	75.1	21.9	77.2	33.2	31.0	32.4	67.8	49.5	73.1	22.1	77.9	32.6	30.6	31.9
1970	67.1	49.4	73.6	23.6	78.6	35.1	31.7	33.9	68.8	49.5	71.9	23.7	79.0	34.4	31.3	33.3
1971	70.0	51.3	73.3	25.0	80.1	35.8	34.5	35.3	71.6	51.4	71.7	25.2	80.6	35.2	34.0	34.7
1972	72.2	54.7	75.7	26.6	82.3	36.8	35.9	36.5	74.0	54.9	74.2	26.8	82.9	36.2	35.0	35.8
1973	74.5	58.5	78.6	28.8	84.1	38.7	37.8	38.4	76.3	58.9	77.2	29.0	84.5	37.9	35.4	37.0
1974	73.2	57.6	78.7	31.6	83.1	43.2	40.1	42.1	75.1	58.0	77.2	31.8	83.5	42.3	38.1	40.8
1975	75.8	57.0	75.3	34.8	83.9	46.0	46.2	46.1	77.1	57.0	73.9	35.0	84.3	45.4	44.7	45.1
1976	78.4	60.9	77.7	37.9	86.2	48.3	48.7	48.5	79.9	61.1	76.5	38.0	86.5	47.5	47.6	47.6
1977	79.7	64.3	80.7	40.9	87.4	51.3	51.7	51.4	81.2	64.6	79.5	41.1	87.8	50.6	50.7	50.6
1978	80.6	68.3	84.8	44.5	88.9	55.2	55.0	55.1	82.2	68.8	83.6	44.7	89.4	54.4	53.5	54.1
1979	80.5	70.6	87.7	48.8	89.1	60.6	58.5	59.8	81.9	70.9	86.6	49.0	89.5	59.8	56.6	58.7
1980	80.3	69.8	86.9	54.1	88.9	67.3	61.7	65.2	81.7	70.2	85.9	54.3	89.3	66.4	60.6	64.3
1981	81.9	71.7	87.6	59.2	89.0	72.3	69.4	71.2	82.7	71.6	86.6	59.5	89.6	72.0	67.8	70.5
1982	81.6	69.6	85.2	63.7	90.5	78.1	70.5	75.3	82.3	69.4	84.3	64.0	91.0	77.8	69.6	74.8
1983	84.5	73.3	86.7	66.3	90.4	78.5	76.6	77.8	85.9	73.8	85.9	66.7	91.0	77.7	76.4	77.2
1984	86.8	79.7	91.8	69.2	90.7	79.7	80.6	80.0	87.7	80.0	91.1	69.5	91.2	79.3	79.6	79.4
1985	88.5	83.1	93.8	72.6	92.1	82.0	82.4	82.2	88.9	83.0	93.4	72.8	92.4	81.9	81.8	81.9
1986	91.2	86.1	94.4	76.4	95.2	83.8	83.0	83.5	91.6	86.2	94.1	76.6	95.5	83.6	82.6	83.2
1987	91.6	89.2	97.3	79.3	95.6	86.6	83.8	85.6	91.9	89.3	97.1	79.5	95.8	86.5	83.4	85.4
1988	93.0	92.9	99.9	83.4	97.0	89.7	85.8	88.3	93.4	93.3	99.9	83.4	97.0	89.3	85.6	87.9
1989	93.9	96.2	102.5	85.7	95.5	91.2	92.0	91.5	94.1	96.5	102.5	85.6	95.4	91.0	91.5	91.2
1990	95.3	97.6	102.5	90.7	96.3	95.2	94.0	94.8	95.3	97.8	102.6	90.5	96.1	94.9	93.7	94.5
1991	96.4	96.5	100.1	95.0	97.4	98.6	97.1	98.1	96.5	96.6	100.1	95.0	97.4	98.4	97.2	98.0
1992	100.0	100.0	100.0	100.0	100.0	100.0	100.0	100.0	100.0	100.0	100.0	100.0	100.0	100.0	100.0	100.0
1993	100.5	103.1	102.6	102.4	99.9	101.9	102.5	102.2	100.5	103.3	102.9	102.2	99.7	101.7	103.0	102.2
1994	101.7	108.1	106.3	104.4	99.7	102.6	106.4	104.0	101.8	108.2	106.3	104.3	99.6	102.5	106.9	104.1
1995	102.3	111.5	108.9	106.5	99.4	104.1	109.4	106.0	102.7	111.8	108.9	106.5	99.4	103.7	110.4	106.1
1996	105.1	116.4	110.7	109.9	99.8	104.6	113.2	107.7	105.3	116.7	110.8	109.8	99.7	104.3	113.4	107.6
1997	107.4	122.5	114.0	113.2	100.7	105.4	117.0	109.7	107.4	122.7	114.2	113.0	100.5	105.2	117.9	109.8
1998	110.2	128.5	116.6	119.4	104.8	108.4	114.3	110.6	110.2	128.8	116.9	119.1	104.5	108.1	115.5	110.8
1999	113.0	134.5	119.0	124.8	107.2	110.4	113.7	111.6	112.8	134.8	119.6	124.3	106.8	110.3	115.3	112.1
2000	116.5	140.0	120.1	133.5	111.0	114.6	111.8	113.5	116.1	140.2	120.7	133.0	110.6	114.6	113.3	114.1
2001	118.8	139.8	117.6	138.6	112.1	116.7	114.3	115.8	118.3	140.1	118.4	137.8	111.4	116.5	116.1	116.3
2002	125.1	143.5	114.7	142.5	113.5	113.9	120.4	116.3	124.7	143.9	115.4	141.7	112.8	113.6	122.5	116.9
1998																
1st quarter	109.6	126.7	115.6	117.3	103.5	107.0	115.9	110.3	109.5	127.0	116.0	117.0	103.2	106.8	117.1	110.5
2nd quarter	109.6	127.3	116.2	118.8	104.5	108.4	113.9	110.4	109.6	127.7	116.5	118.5	104.3	108.1	115.1	110.6
3rd quarter	110.2	128.7	116.8	120.2	105.2	109.0	113.5	110.7	110.2	129.0	117.1	119.9	105.0	108.8	114.7	111.0
4th quarter	111.5	131.3	117.8	121.4	105.9	108.9	114.1	110.8	111.4	131.6	118.2	121.1	105.6	108.7	115.3	111.1
1999																
1st quarter	112.3	132.4	117.9	123.9	107.6	110.3	112.7	111.2	112.0	132.7	118.4	123.3	107.1	110.0	114.1	111.5
2nd quarter	112.1	133.0	118.7	123.9	106.9	110.6	113.0	111.5	111.8	133.3	119.3	123.4	106.4	110.4	114.6	111.9
3rd quarter	113.1	134.9	119.4	125.0	107.0	110.6	113.9	111.8	112.7	135.3	120.0	124.4	106.5	110.4	115.5	112.3
4th quarter	114.7	137.7	120.1	126.5	107.5	110.3	115.2	112.1	114.5	138.0	120.6	126.2	107.2	110.2	116.9	112.6
2000																
1st quarter	114.8	138.4	120.6	131.1	110.3	114.1	110.4	112.8	114.6	138.7	121.0	130.8	110.1	114.2	112.0	113.4
2nd quarter	116.6	140.3	120.3	131.9	110.1	113.1	113.8	113.4	116.1	140.5	121.0	131.4	109.7	113.1	115.3	113.9
3rd quarter	116.8	140.4	120.2	134.6	111.4	115.3	111.0	113.7	116.4	140.6	120.8	134.2	111.0	115.3	112.6	114.3
4th quarter	117.5	140.7	119.7	135.9	111.7	115.6	111.9	114.3	117.0	141.0	120.5	135.3	111.2	115.6	113.3	114.8
2001																
1st quarter	117.4	140.4	119.6	137.4	111.9	117.1	112.0	115.2	116.9	140.7	120.3	136.7	111.3	117.0	113.5	115.7
2nd quarter	117.8	139.4	118.3	138.2	111.6	117.3	113.3	115.8	117.4	139.7	119.0	137.4	111.0	117.1	114.9	116.3
3rd quarter	118.8	139.1	117.1	139.1	112.1	117.1	115.1	116.4	118.3	139.4	117.8	138.2	111.4	116.8	116.8	116.8
4th quarter	121.3	140.3	115.6	139.8	112.8	115.2	117.0	115.9	120.7	140.4	116.3	138.9	112.1	115.1	119.0	116.5
2002																
1st quarter	123.9	142.3	114.9	141.0	113.4	113.8	119.7	116.0	123.4	142.5	115.5	140.2	112.8	113.6	121.5	116.4
2nd quarter	124.1	142.5	114.8	142.4	113.5	114.7	118.8	116.2	123.7	142.9	115.5	141.5	112.9	114.4	121.2	116.8
3rd quarter	125.9	144.4	114.6	143.1	113.5	113.6	120.9	116.3	125.5	144.7	115.3	142.2	112.8	113.3	123.1	116.9
4th quarter	126.4	145.0	114.7	143.7	113.4	113.7	122.1	116.8	126.0	145.3	115.3	142.8	112.7	113.3	124.3	117.3

Table 9-3. Productivity and Related Data—Continued

(1992 = 100, seasonally adjusted.)

Year and quarter	Nonfinancial corporations										Manufacturing					
	Output per hour of all employees	Output	Employee hours	Compensation per hour	Real compensation per hour	Unit costs Total	Labor costs	Non-labor costs	Unit profits	Implicit price deflator	Output per hour of all persons	Output	Hours of all persons	Compensation per hour	Real compensation per hour	Unit labor costs
1947	...	...	...	...	...	...	...	...	...	...	...	...	...	...	...	...
1948	...	...	...	...	...	...	...	...	...	...	...	...	...	...	...	...
1949	...	...	...	...	...	...	...	...	...	...	33.5	26.5	79.1	8.3	44.9	24.6
1950	...	...	...	...	...	...	...	...	...	...	34.0	29.1	85.5	8.7	46.6	25.5
1951	...	...	...	...	...	...	...	...	...	...	33.8	31.1	92.1	9.5	47.6	28.2
1952	...	...	...	...	...	...	...	...	...	...	35.2	32.9	93.3	10.2	49.8	28.9
1953	...	...	...	...	...	...	...	...	...	...	36.4	35.7	98.1	10.7	52.1	29.5
1954	...	...	...	...	...	...	...	...	...	...	37.3	33.4	89.6	11.2	54.1	30.1
1955	...	...	...	...	...	...	...	...	...	...	38.8	36.7	94.6	11.7	56.4	30.1
1956	...	...	...	...	...	...	...	...	...	...	38.6	37.1	96.0	12.4	59.1	32.1
1957	...	...	...	...	...	...	...	...	...	...	39.4	37.2	94.5	13.2	60.6	33.4
1958	51.8	25.5	49.3	14.4	64.5	26.6	27.8	23.5	47.3	28.4	40.0	34.7	86.6	13.8	61.7	34.4
1959	54.4	28.4	52.3	14.9	66.5	26.1	27.5	22.6	55.1	28.6	40.9	37.8	92.5	14.3	63.5	34.9
1960	55.4	29.4	53.0	15.6	68.1	26.8	28.1	23.3	50.2	28.8	41.8	38.5	92.1	14.9	65.0	35.6
1961	57.3	30.0	52.4	16.1	69.8	26.9	28.1	23.8	50.3	28.9	42.8	38.4	89.7	15.3	66.3	35.7
1962	59.7	32.5	54.5	16.7	71.7	26.8	28.0	23.4	54.6	29.1	44.2	41.3	93.4	15.9	68.1	36.0
1963	61.8	34.4	55.8	17.2	72.9	26.7	27.9	23.3	57.8	29.3	45.7	43.1	94.4	16.4	69.2	35.8
1964	64.1	36.9	57.5	18.0	75.0	26.7	28.0	23.3	60.2	29.6	47.4	45.7	96.4	17.0	71.2	36.0
1965	65.8	39.9	60.7	18.5	76.1	26.8	28.1	23.1	64.8	30.0	48.5	49.5	102.0	17.4	71.6	35.9
1966	66.7	42.7	64.0	19.5	77.9	27.6	29.2	23.2	64.7	30.7	49.1	53.3	108.6	18.2	72.8	37.1
1967	67.7	43.8	64.7	20.6	79.8	28.8	30.4	24.6	60.5	31.5	50.9	54.9	108.0	19.2	74.4	37.7
1968	70.0	46.6	66.5	22.1	82.4	30.2	31.6	26.2	60.3	32.7	52.7	57.7	109.6	20.7	76.9	39.2
1969	70.1	48.4	69.2	23.0	83.4	32.3	33.7	28.3	54.4	34.1	53.5	59.4	110.9	22.2	78.2	41.4
1970	70.4	48.0	68.1	25.3	84.4	34.8	35.9	31.9	44.4	35.6	54.2	56.5	104.4	23.7	79.2	43.8
1971	73.3	49.9	68.0	26.9	86.0	35.8	36.7	33.4	50.2	37.0	57.8	58.1	100.5	25.2	80.5	43.5
1972	75.3	53.8	71.5	28.4	88.1	36.6	37.8	33.5	54.1	38.1	60.3	63.3	105.1	26.5	82.0	43.9
1973	76.1	57.0	74.9	30.7	89.6	38.9	40.4	35.1	55.5	40.3	61.4	67.8	110.4	28.5	83.1	46.4
1974	74.5	56.0	75.2	33.7	88.4	43.9	45.2	40.5	49.2	44.4	61.2	66.1	107.9	31.6	83.1	51.7
1975	77.3	55.1	71.3	37.0	89.0	47.3	47.9	45.9	64.1	48.8	64.3	62.5	97.2	35.5	85.4	55.2
1976	79.8	59.5	74.6	40.0	91.1	49.0	50.2	45.9	72.3	51.0	67.0	68.2	101.9	38.4	87.5	57.4
1977	81.6	63.8	78.2	43.2	92.2	51.4	52.9	47.4	79.4	53.3	69.7	73.9	106.1	41.8	89.3	60.0
1978	82.1	68.1	82.9	46.8	93.6	55.1	57.0	50.0	82.5	57.4	70.4	77.8	110.6	45.2	90.3	64.2
1979	81.5	70.2	86.1	51.1	93.5	60.7	62.7	55.1	76.7	62.0	69.8	78.7	112.7	49.6	90.6	71.1
1980	81.1	69.2	85.3	56.5	92.9	68.4	69.6	65.1	68.8	68.4	70.1	75.3	107.5	55.6	91.4	79.3
1981	82.6	71.5	86.5	61.6	92.7	74.6	74.6	74.8	82.4	75.3	70.7	75.6	107.0	61.1	91.9	86.3
1982	83.4	70.0	83.9	66.1	93.8	80.0	79.2	82.3	75.0	79.6	74.2	72.7	97.9	67.0	95.1	90.2
1983	86.0	73.3	85.3	68.4	93.3	80.1	79.6	81.5	91.2	81.1	76.7	75.9	98.9	68.8	93.8	89.7
1984	88.2	80.2	90.9	71.2	93.4	80.9	80.7	81.1	108.6	83.2	79.5	83.7	105.3	71.2	93.4	89.6
1985	89.9	83.8	93.2	74.4	94.4	82.7	82.7	82.4	104.2	84.5	82.3	86.0	104.6	75.1	95.3	91.3
1986	91.7	85.9	93.7	78.0	97.2	85.3	85.1	85.7	88.0	85.5	85.9	88.5	103.0	78.5	97.8	91.3
1987	94.7	90.7	95.8	81.7	98.4	86.0	86.2	85.3	98.1	87.0	88.3	91.6	103.8	80.7	97.3	91.4
1988	96.0	95.8	99.8	84.2	97.9	87.6	87.7	87.4	108.0	89.4	90.2	96.1	106.6	84.0	97.7	93.1
1989	94.8	97.4	102.7	86.3	96.3	92.0	91.1	94.6	97.3	92.5	90.3	96.6	107.1	86.6	96.6	96.0
1990	95.5	98.3	103.0	90.9	96.5	95.9	95.2	98.0	94.3	95.8	92.9	97.3	104.8	90.8	96.4	97.8
1991	97.7	97.5	99.8	95.3	97.7	98.8	97.5	102.1	93.0	98.3	95.0	95.4	100.4	95.6	98.0	100.6
1992	100.0	100.0	100.0	100.0	100.0	100.0	100.0	100.0	100.0	100.0	100.0	100.0	100.0	100.0	100.0	100.0
1993	100.7	103.0	102.3	102.0	99.5	101.0	101.3	100.2	113.2	102.1	101.9	103.3	101.4	102.7	100.2	100.8
1994	103.1	109.6	106.3	104.2	99.5	101.1	101.0	101.3	131.7	103.7	105.0	108.7	103.6	105.6	101.0	100.7
1995	104.1	114.2	109.6	106.1	99.0	102.0	101.9	102.2	139.0	105.1	109.0	113.4	104.0	107.9	100.6	99.0
1996	107.5	119.9	111.6	108.9	98.9	101.2	101.4	100.6	152.2	105.5	112.8	117.0	103.6	109.4	99.4	96.9
1997	108.4	127.0	117.2	110.3	98.1	101.5	101.8	100.9	156.9	106.2	117.6	124.0	105.4	111.5	99.1	94.8
1998	111.7	134.3	120.3	115.9	101.6	103.8	103.8	103.8	141.7	106.6	123.3	128.8	105.2	117.4	103.0	95.2
1999	114.7	141.3	123.2	121.0	104.0	104.9	105.5	103.4	131.5	107.2	129.7	135.3	104.4	122.1	104.9	94.1
2000	118.7	148.4	125.1	129.1	107.3	108.2	108.8	106.7	111.6	108.5	134.9	138.7	102.8	131.1	109.0	97.2
2001	121.1	148.2	122.4	133.0	107.6	110.9	109.9	113.7	98.5	109.8	137.1	132.0	96.3	134.3	108.6	97.9
2002	128.1	152.9	119.3	137.7	109.6	109.4	107.5	114.8	107.5	109.3	145.5	130.5	89.7	140.6	112.0	96.7
1998																
1st quarter	109.8	131.2	119.5	113.7	100.3	103.1	103.6	101.7	143.8	106.5	121.3	128.3	105.8	115.5	101.9	95.2
2nd quarter	111.1	133.1	119.8	115.3	101.5	103.3	103.8	101.9	140.4	106.4	122.3	129.0	105.5	117.0	102.9	95.7
3rd quarter	112.6	135.6	120.4	116.6	102.1	103.1	103.6	101.8	144.9	106.7	124.3	130.0	104.5	118.2	103.5	95.1
4th quarter	113.1	137.3	121.4	117.7	102.6	103.9	104.1	103.3	137.7	106.7	125.5	131.8	105.0	119.0	103.8	94.8
1999																
1st quarter	114.2	139.3	122.0	120.1	104.3	104.2	105.1	101.6	137.1	107.0	128.0	133.4	104.3	120.6	104.8	94.3
2nd quarter	114.3	140.3	122.8	120.3	103.7	104.5	105.2	102.7	135.6	107.2	128.8	134.6	104.5	120.9	104.3	93.9
3rd quarter	114.7	141.7	123.6	121.1	103.6	105.3	105.6	104.5	127.7	107.2	129.8	135.8	104.7	122.6	104.9	94.4
4th quarter	115.6	144.0	124.5	122.6	104.2	105.7	106.0	104.6	126.0	107.4	132.1	137.3	103.9	124.2	105.5	94.0
2000																
1st quarter	117.7	147.3	125.2	126.8	106.7	106.9	107.8	104.5	119.5	108.0	133.6	138.3	103.5	131.4	110.6	98.4
2nd quarter	118.2	147.9	125.1	127.7	106.6	107.5	108.0	106.3	118.8	108.5	134.9	139.8	103.6	129.3	107.9	95.9
3rd quarter	119.4	149.4	125.1	130.3	107.8	108.6	109.1	107.1	109.5	108.6	135.4	139.3	102.9	132.2	109.4	97.7
4th quarter	119.4	149.2	124.9	131.6	108.1	109.8	110.2	108.9	98.6	108.9	135.9	137.6	101.3	131.5	108.0	96.8
2001																
1st quarter	118.7	147.9	124.7	131.2	106.8	110.8	110.6	111.6	93.1	109.3	135.1	134.8	99.8	132.0	107.5	97.7
2nd quarter	120.0	147.8	123.1	132.6	107.1	111.3	110.4	113.5	95.4	109.9	136.1	133.1	97.8	133.6	107.9	98.2
3rd quarter	121.3	147.7	121.7	133.8	107.8	111.7	110.3	115.5	97.9	110.5	137.9	131.2	95.1	135.0	108.8	97.9
4th quarter	124.5	149.6	120.2	134.7	108.7	109.8	108.2	114.1	107.6	109.6	140.6	129.7	92.3	136.7	110.3	97.2
2002																
1st quarter	126.0	150.8	119.7	135.9	109.4	109.5	107.9	114.0	107.6	109.4	144.0	130.4	90.6	138.3	111.3	96.1
2nd quarter	127.7	152.8	119.6	137.3	109.5	109.4	107.5	114.5	107.8	109.3	145.9	131.5	90.2	140.5	112.0	96.3
3rd quarter	128.7	153.4	119.2	138.2	109.7	109.6	107.4	115.4	104.6	109.1	147.7	132.0	89.4	141.3	112.1	95.7
4th quarter	129.9	154.5	118.9	139.2	109.9	109.3	107.1	115.2	110.1	109.4	147.9	131.1	88.6	142.4	112.4	96.3

. . . = Not available.

Table 9-4. Corporate Profits with Inventory Valuation Adjustment by Industry Group (SIC Basis)

(Billions of dollars.)

		Domestic industries										
		Financial			Nonfinancial							
						Manufacturing						
							Durable goods					
Classification basis, year and quarter	Total	Total	Federal Reserve banks	Other	Total	Total	Primary metal industries	Fabricated metal products	Industrial machinery and equipment	Electronic and other electric equipment	Motor vehicles and equipment	Other

1972 SIC BASIS												
1948	33.7	32.5	0.2	2.5	29.7	17.5	1.6	0.8	1.3	0.6	1.4	1.8
1949	31.5	30.3	0.2	3.1	27.0	16.2	1.5	0.7	1.3	0.8	2.1	1.7
1950	38.3	37.0	0.2	3.1	33.7	21.0	2.3	1.1	1.6	1.2	3.1	2.6
1951	43.6	41.8	0.3	3.4	38.1	24.7	3.1	1.3	2.3	1.3	2.4	2.8
1952	41.2	39.3	0.3	4.1	34.9	21.7	1.9	1.0	2.3	1.5	2.4	2.6
1953	40.7	38.9	0.4	4.4	34.0	22.0	2.5	1.0	1.9	1.4	2.6	2.6
1954	39.0	37.1	0.3	4.8	32.0	19.9	1.7	0.9	1.7	1.2	2.1	2.9
1955	48.1	45.8	0.3	5.0	40.5	26.1	2.9	1.1	1.7	1.1	4.1	3.5
1956	47.8	44.9	0.5	5.2	39.3	24.8	3.0	1.1	2.1	1.2	2.2	3.1
1957	47.5	44.4	0.6	5.4	38.5	24.1	3.1	1.1	2.0	1.5	2.6	3.1
1958	42.7	40.2	0.6	5.9	33.7	19.5	1.9	0.9	1.5	1.3	0.9	2.9
1959	53.5	50.8	0.7	6.9	43.2	26.5	2.3	1.1	2.2	1.7	3.0	3.5
1960	51.5	48.3	0.9	7.5	39.9	23.8	2.0	0.8	1.8	1.3	3.0	2.7
1961	51.8	48.5	0.8	7.6	40.2	23.4	1.6	1.0	1.9	1.3	2.5	2.9
1962	57.0	53.3	0.9	7.7	44.7	26.3	1.6	1.2	2.4	1.5	4.0	3.4
1963	62.1	58.1	1.0	7.3	49.8	29.7	2.0	1.3	2.6	1.6	4.9	4.0
1964	68.6	64.1	1.1	7.6	55.4	32.6	2.5	1.5	3.3	1.7	4.6	4.4
1965	78.9	74.2	1.3	8.0	64.9	39.8	3.1	2.1	4.0	2.7	6.2	5.2
1966	84.6	80.1	1.7	9.1	69.3	42.6	3.6	2.4	4.6	3.0	5.2	5.2
1967	82.0	77.2	2.0	9.2	66.0	39.2	2.7	2.5	4.2	3.0	4.0	4.9
1968	88.8	83.2	2.5	10.3	70.4	41.9	1.9	2.3	4.2	2.9	5.5	5.6
1969	85.5	78.9	3.1	10.5	65.3	37.3	1.4	2.0	3.8	2.3	4.8	4.9
1970	74.4	67.3	3.5	11.9	52.0	27.5	0.8	1.1	3.1	1.3	1.3	2.9
1971	88.3	80.4	3.3	14.3	62.8	35.1	0.8	1.5	3.1	2.0	5.2	4.1
1972	101.2	91.7	3.3	15.8	72.6	41.9	1.7	2.2	4.5	2.9	6.0	5.6
1973	115.3	100.4	4.5	16.0	79.9	47.2	2.3	2.7	4.9	3.2	5.9	6.2
1974	109.5	92.1	5.7	14.5	71.9	41.4	5.0	1.8	3.3	0.6	0.7	4.0
1975	135.0	120.4	5.6	14.6	100.2	55.2	2.8	3.3	5.1	2.6	2.3	4.7
1976	165.6	149.0	5.9	19.1	124.1	71.3	2.1	3.9	6.9	3.8	7.4	7.3
1977	194.7	175.6	6.1	25.8	143.7	79.3	1.0	4.5	8.6	5.9	9.4	8.5
1978	222.4	199.6	7.6	31.9	160.0	90.5	3.6	5.0	10.7	6.7	9.0	10.5
1979	231.8	197.2	9.4	30.9	156.8	89.6	3.5	5.3	9.5	5.6	4.7	8.5
1980	211.4	175.9	11.8	22.2	141.9	78.3	2.7	4.4	8.0	5.2	-4.3	2.7
1981	219.1	189.4	14.4	14.7	160.3	91.1	3.1	4.5	9.0	5.2	0.3	-2.6
1982	191.0	158.5	15.2	10.8	132.4	67.1	-4.7	2.7	3.1	1.7	0.0	2.1
1983	226.5	191.4	14.6	20.9	155.9	76.2	-4.9	3.1	4.0	3.5	5.3	8.4
1984	264.6	228.1	16.4	18.0	193.7	91.8	-0.4	4.7	6.0	5.1	9.2	14.6
1985	257.5	219.4	16.3	29.5	173.5	84.3	-0.9	4.9	5.7	2.6	7.4	10.1
1986	253.0	213.5	15.5	41.2	156.8	57.9	0.9	5.2	0.8	2.7	4.6	12.1
1987	301.4	253.4	15.7	44.1	193.5	86.3	2.6	5.5	5.4	5.9	3.7	17.6
1987 SIC BASIS												
1987	301.4	253.4	15.7	44.1	193.5	86.3	2.6	5.5	5.4	5.9	3.7	17.6
1988	363.9	306.9	17.6	51.1	238.2	121.2	6.0	6.5	11.1	7.7	6.2	16.5
1989	367.4	300.3	20.2	57.8	222.3	110.9	6.4	6.4	12.2	9.3	2.7	14.2
1990	396.6	320.5	21.4	73.0	226.1	113.1	3.5	6.0	11.8	8.5	-1.9	15.9
1991	427.9	351.4	20.3	103.9	227.3	98.0	1.5	5.3	5.7	10.0	-5.4	17.3
1992	458.3	385.2	17.8	111.9	255.4	99.5	0.0	6.2	7.5	10.4	-1.0	17.4
1993	513.1	436.1	16.2	120.6	299.3	115.6	0.4	7.4	7.5	15.2	6.0	19.4
1994	564.6	487.6	18.1	101.8	367.7	147.0	2.3	11.1	9.1	22.8	7.8	21.3
1995	656.0	563.2	22.5	139.7	401.0	173.7	7.1	11.8	14.8	21.5	0.0	25.8
1996	736.1	634.2	22.1	150.5	461.6	188.8	5.6	14.5	16.9	20.1	4.2	29.2
1997	812.3	701.4	23.8	169.2	508.4	209.0	6.3	17.0	16.7	25.3	4.8	33.0
1998	738.5	635.5	25.2	140.7	469.6	173.5	6.5	16.4	19.5	8.9	5.9	30.1
1999	776.8	655.3	26.3	170.1	458.9	175.2	2.4	16.2	12.4	5.3	7.3	35.3
2000	759.3	613.6	30.8	173.0	409.8	166.3	1.2	15.4	16.3	4.7	-1.5	28.8
1998												
1st quarter	752.0	643.1	25.0	147.9	470.2	178.5	6.9	14.9	14.4	12.2	6.4	28.8
2nd quarter	732.5	626.3	25.2	136.4	464.7	170.1	6.2	16.7	19.5	8.3	3.5	27.4
3rd quarter	743.5	647.3	25.4	136.9	485.0	176.6	6.1	18.5	20.4	6.6	4.5	31.3
4th quarter	725.9	625.3	25.1	141.8	458.4	168.8	6.8	15.7	23.7	8.3	9.3	32.9
1999												
1st quarter	771.3	657.3	24.9	163.0	469.5	175.0	3.8	15.9	9.8	4.3	8.9	33.9
2nd quarter	773.2	656.5	25.5	157.8	473.2	182.5	3.1	15.7	12.8	4.9	6.1	37.8
3rd quarter	766.8	648.3	26.2	175.3	446.8	174.2	1.5	16.2	12.3	6.9	7.3	34.3
4th quarter	796.1	659.1	28.6	184.5	446.0	169.1	1.2	17.1	14.7	4.9	6.7	35.3
2000												
1st quarter	766.8	635.7	30.0	179.5	426.2	172.6	2.1	18.8	12.6	2.5	1.2	33.3
2nd quarter	773.5	634.9	30.5	164.5	440.0	186.1	2.0	16.2	16.1	8.7	0.3	33.7
3rd quarter	756.3	611.7	31.1	171.1	409.5	164.9	0.5	15.2	18.1	3.4	-2.4	27.3
4th quarter	740.7	572.1	31.7	176.8	363.6	141.6	0.3	11.3	18.1	4.1	-5.2	21.0

Table 9-4. Corporate Profits with Inventory Valuation Adjustment by Industry Group (SIC Basis)—*Continued*

(Billions of dollars.)

Classification basis, year and quarter	Manufacturing—*Continued* Nondurable goods					Transportation and public utilities				Wholesale trade	Retail trade	Other	Rest of the world
	Total	Food and kindred products	Chemicals and allied products	Petroleum and coal products	Other	Total	Transportation	Communications	Electric, gas, and sanitary services				
1972 SIC BASIS													
1948	10.0	1.9	1.7	2.8	3.7	3.0	1.5	0.4	1.1	2.4	3.2	3.5	1.3
1949	8.1	1.6	1.8	1.9	2.8	3.0	1.2	0.5	1.4	1.9	2.8	3.1	1.1
1950	9.0	1.6	2.3	2.3	2.7	4.1	1.9	0.7	1.5	2.1	3.0	3.5	1.3
1951	11.4	1.4	2.8	2.8	4.4	4.7	1.9	1.0	1.8	2.6	2.6	3.6	1.7
1952	10.0	1.8	2.3	2.3	3.6	5.0	1.9	1.1	2.0	2.3	2.7	3.3	1.9
1953	10.0	1.8	2.2	2.7	3.3	5.0	1.6	1.2	2.2	1.8	2.3	3.0	1.8
1954	9.5	1.6	2.2	2.8	2.9	4.7	1.0	1.3	2.4	1.7	2.3	3.3	2.0
1955	11.8	2.2	3.0	3.0	3.6	5.7	1.5	1.7	2.5	2.4	2.9	3.5	2.4
1956	12.0	1.8	2.8	3.3	4.1	5.9	1.4	1.8	2.7	2.2	2.6	3.9	2.8
1957	10.8	1.8	2.8	2.6	3.6	5.9	1.1	2.0	2.7	2.2	2.6	3.8	3.1
1958	10.2	2.1	2.5	2.1	3.4	5.9	0.9	2.3	2.7	2.2	2.6	3.5	2.5
1959	12.9	2.5	3.5	2.6	4.3	7.1	1.1	2.8	3.1	2.9	3.3	3.4	2.7
1960	12.2	2.2	3.1	2.6	4.2	7.5	0.9	3.0	3.6	2.5	2.8	3.3	3.1
1961	12.1	2.4	3.3	2.3	4.2	7.9	1.0	3.2	3.7	2.5	3.0	3.4	3.3
1962	12.3	2.4	3.2	2.2	4.4	8.5	1.0	3.6	3.9	2.8	3.4	3.6	3.8
1963	13.3	2.7	3.7	2.2	4.7	9.5	1.4	3.9	4.2	2.0	3.6	4.1	4.1
1964	14.5	2.7	4.1	2.4	5.3	10.2	1.6	4.0	4.6	3.4	4.5	4.7	4.5
1965	16.5	2.9	4.6	2.9	6.1	11.0	2.1	4.3	4.6	3.8	4.9	5.4	4.7
1966	18.6	3.3	4.9	3.4	6.9	12.0	2.3	4.8	4.9	4.0	4.9	5.9	4.5
1967	18.0	3.3	4.3	4.0	6.4	10.9	1.3	4.8	4.8	4.1	5.7	6.1	4.8
1968	19.4	3.2	5.3	3.8	7.1	11.0	1.0	5.1	4.9	4.6	6.4	6.6	5.6
1969	18.1	3.1	4.6	3.4	7.0	10.7	0.7	5.4	4.6	4.9	6.4	6.1	6.6
1970	17.0	3.2	3.9	3.7	6.1	8.3	-0.1	4.8	3.6	4.4	6.0	5.8	7.1
1971	18.5	3.6	4.5	3.8	6.6	8.9	0.7	4.1	4.1	5.2	7.2	6.4	7.9
1972	19.2	3.0	5.3	3.3	7.6	9.5	1.5	3.9	4.0	6.9	7.4	7.0	9.5
1973	22.0	2.5	6.2	5.4	7.9	9.1	1.3	4.3	3.4	8.2	6.6	8.7	14.9
1974	26.1	2.6	5.3	10.9	7.3	7.6	2.0	4.1	1.5	11.5	2.3	9.1	17.5
1975	34.5	8.6	6.4	10.1	9.5	11.0	1.0	4.3	5.7	13.8	8.2	12.0	14.6
1976	39.9	7.1	8.2	13.5	11.1	15.3	3.0	5.7	6.5	12.9	10.5	14.0	16.5
1977	41.4	6.9	7.8	13.1	13.6	18.6	3.7	6.6	8.3	15.6	12.4	17.8	19.1
1978	45.1	6.2	8.3	15.8	14.8	21.8	4.1	8.6	9.1	15.6	12.3	19.8	22.9
1979	52.5	5.8	7.2	24.8	14.7	17.0	3.5	7.5	6.0	18.8	9.8	21.6	34.6
1980	59.5	6.1	5.7	34.7	13.1	18.4	2.7	7.7	8.0	17.2	6.2	21.8	35.5
1981	71.6	9.2	8.0	40.0	14.5	20.3	1.7	8.6	10.0	22.4	9.9	16.7	29.7
1982	62.1	7.3	5.1	34.7	15.0	23.1	-0.1	8.6	14.6	19.6	13.4	9.2	32.6
1983	56.7	6.3	7.4	23.9	19.1	29.5	3.2	9.9	16.4	21.0	18.7	10.4	35.1
1984	52.6	6.8	8.2	17.6	20.1	40.1	6.1	12.8	21.3	29.5	21.1	11.1	36.6
1985	54.6	8.8	6.6	18.7	20.5	33.8	1.8	14.2	17.8	23.9	22.2	9.2	38.1
1986	31.7	7.5	7.5	-4.7	21.3	35.8	3.4	17.6	14.7	24.1	23.5	15.5	39.5
1987	45.6	11.4	14.4	-1.5	21.3	41.9	3.4	19.4	19.1	18.6	23.4	23.4	48.0
1987 SIC BASIS													
1987	45.6	11.4	14.4	-1.5	21.3	41.9	3.4	19.4	19.1	18.6	23.4	23.4	48.0
1988	67.1	12.0	18.6	12.7	23.7	48.4	7.9	19.5	21.1	20.1	20.3	28.3	57.0
1989	59.7	11.1	18.2	6.5	23.9	43.3	1.3	18.2	23.9	21.8	20.8	25.5	67.1
1990	69.2	14.3	16.8	16.4	21.7	44.2	-0.4	20.1	24.5	19.2	20.7	29.0	76.1
1991	63.6	18.1	16.2	7.3	22.0	53.3	2.3	23.5	27.5	21.7	26.7	27.5	76.5
1992	59.0	18.2	16.0	-0.9	25.6	58.4	2.3	27.7	28.4	25.1	32.6	39.7	73.1
1993	59.7	16.4	15.9	2.7	24.7	69.5	7.0	32.9	29.6	26.3	39.1	48.9	76.9
1994	72.6	19.9	23.2	1.2	28.3	83.2	10.5	36.7	36.1	30.9	46.2	60.4	77.1
1995	92.8	27.1	27.9	7.1	30.6	85.8	11.5	33.6	40.8	27.3	43.1	71.2	92.8
1996	98.2	22.1	26.4	15.0	34.7	91.3	15.7	35.0	40.7	39.8	51.9	89.7	101.9
1997	105.9	24.6	32.3	17.3	31.7	84.2	19.0	25.5	39.7	47.6	64.2	103.4	110.9
1998	86.2	21.9	26.5	6.7	31.1	78.9	21.6	21.4	35.8	52.3	73.4	91.5	103.0
1999	96.4	28.1	25.2	4.3	38.9	56.8	15.8	4.6	36.3	52.6	74.6	99.7	121.5
2000	101.5	25.7	16.0	29.1	30.7	43.8	15.2	1.3	27.3	56.9	70.1	72.8	145.7
1998													
1st quarter	94.9	23.6	30.5	9.4	31.3	76.8	20.6	22.1	34.1	50.2	71.3	93.4	108.8
2nd quarter	88.5	24.6	22.9	8.9	32.1	81.0	21.5	24.0	35.5	52.6	72.5	88.6	106.2
3rd quarter	89.2	25.8	24.9	7.3	31.3	86.7	24.2	25.1	37.4	57.5	73.8	90.4	96.2
4th quarter	72.0	13.6	27.6	1.3	29.6	71.0	20.3	14.5	36.3	48.8	76.0	93.8	100.5
1999													
1st quarter	98.5	28.5	31.8	0.6	37.6	62.6	16.8	9.2	36.6	54.8	79.4	97.7	113.9
2nd quarter	102.1	28.6	31.8	4.0	37.7	52.1	16.0	3.4	32.8	53.1	79.0	106.6	116.6
3rd quarter	95.8	27.0	22.1	8.2	38.5	52.5	13.5	1.3	37.6	49.3	69.6	101.2	118.5
4th quarter	89.1	28.2	14.9	4.4	41.6	59.9	17.0	4.5	38.4	53.3	70.5	93.2	137.0
2000													
1st quarter	102.1	28.3	20.0	15.3	38.6	47.5	14.7	-0.3	33.0	52.4	75.5	78.3	131.1
2nd quarter	109.2	25.4	17.4	33.8	32.7	42.4	19.4	-3.4	26.4	63.2	70.8	77.4	138.5
3rd quarter	102.8	28.2	13.3	33.9	27.4	43.2	15.7	0.4	27.1	62.9	70.3	68.3	144.6
4th quarter	91.9	21.0	13.2	33.4	24.3	42.2	11.2	8.4	22.6	48.9	63.9	67.0	168.6

Table 9-5. Corporate Profits with Inventory Valuation Adjustment by Industry Group (NAICS Basis)

(Billions of dollars.)

Year and quarter	Total	Domestic industries					Manufacturing						
		Financial			Nonfinancial			Durable goods					
		Total	Federal Reserve banks	Other financial	Total	Utilities	Total	Fabricated metal products	Machinery	Computer and electronic products	Electrical equipment, appliances, and components	Motor vehicles, bodies and trailers, and parts	Other durable goods
1998	738.5	635.5	25.2	140.2	470.1	32.7	157.0	16.7	15.6	3.9	6.1	6.4	34.6
1999	776.8	655.3	26.3	168.0	461.1	33.1	150.6	16.5	12.4	-6.5	6.3	7.3	36.4
2000	759.3	613.6	30.8	169.4	413.4	24.4	144.3	15.5	8.2	4.0	5.6	-1.0	27.7
2001	705.9	544.4	28.3	197.3	318.8	24.1	54.0	9.7	3.2	-49.4	2.0	-7.2	16.7
2002	742.7	589.4	22.9	232.2	334.3	22.0	73.3	9.7	1.5	-18.4	1.7	-1.0	15.3
2001													
1st quarter	730.7	581.3	31.3	197.0	353.0	26.0	86.8	11.4	9.6	-19.3	3.0	-5.8	15.0
2nd quarter	731.4	578.6	29.2	190.6	358.8	27.1	79.3	10.5	5.8	-38.3	2.7	-8.2	22.9
3rd quarter	685.8	541.7	27.4	183.7	330.6	25.0	50.1	9.9	-5.2	-60.9	2.2	-4.0	20.4
4th quarter	675.7	476.0	25.2	218.0	232.7	18.4	-0.2	6.9	2.5	-79.0	0.3	-10.9	8.5
2002													
1st quarter	702.7	551.4	23.8	243.8	283.8	18.5	42.0	8.8	2.0	-40.1	3.1	-5.7	15.5
2nd quarter	738.9	594.8	23.9	236.7	334.2	25.3	69.2	9.3	2.6	-23.6	1.5	2.3	13.7
3rd quarter	745.1	594.0	22.6	226.4	345.0	21.5	87.2	8.4	2.6	-8.7	1.6	1.1	15.3
4th quarter	784.2	617.2	21.2	222.1	373.9	22.8	95.1	12.1	-1.3	-1.2	0.7	-1.7	16.6

Year and quarter	Domestic industries—Continued										Rest of the world
	Nonfinancial—Continued										
	Manufacturing—Continued										
	Nondurable goods					Wholesale trade	Retail trade	Transportation and warehousing	Information	Other nonfinancial	
	Total	Food and beverage and tobacco products	Petroleum and coal products	Chemical products	Other nondurable goods						
1998	73.6	21.8	4.9	25.1	21.8	53.2	66.4	21.0	20.1	119.8	103.0
1999	78.3	30.7	1.8	23.0	22.7	55.5	65.2	16.1	10.5	130.1	121.5
2000	84.3	25.4	26.9	14.2	17.8	59.7	59.6	14.9	-17.6	128.2	145.7
2001	78.9	27.5	29.9	13.8	7.7	51.6	71.1	-0.1	-27.2	145.3	161.5
2002	64.6	32.8	6.4	17.5	7.9	49.1	76.7	-2.3	-20.2	135.5	153.4
2001											
1st quarter	72.8	23.0	34.1	5.8	9.8	46.1	64.2	3.8	-23.0	149.2	149.3
2nd quarter	83.7	27.6	33.4	14.6	8.1	47.7	66.8	3.2	-21.5	156.2	152.8
3rd quarter	87.7	28.5	32.5	16.7	10.0	54.1	74.3	0.9	-26.3	152.4	144.1
4th quarter	71.4	31.0	19.6	18.1	2.7	58.5	79.1	-8.3	-38.0	123.3	199.7
2002											
1st quarter	58.3	31.4	4.1	16.2	6.6	48.8	75.8	-3.0	-25.9	127.5	151.3
2nd quarter	63.3	32.9	5.1	16.6	8.7	53.9	79.7	-5.2	-22.1	133.5	144.1
3rd quarter	66.8	34.4	7.7	17.7	7.0	45.7	77.5	-3.5	-20.1	136.7	151.1
4th quarter	69.9	32.4	8.7	19.4	9.4	47.9	73.9	2.4	-12.6	144.4	166.9

NOTES AND DEFINITIONS

General note on data on compensation per hour

Included in this chapter are two different data series with similar names but markedly different behavior. Both are compiled and published by the Bureau of Labor Statistics, but the sources and methods of compilation are different. Users should be aware of these differences and consequent differences in the uses and interpretations of the two series.

The *Employment Cost Index* measures changes in hourly compensation for all civilian workers (except federal government) and a number of industry and occupational subgroups including all nonfarm private industry. It is constructed by analogy with the Consumer Price Index, holding constant the composition of employment in order to isolate trends in hourly compensation that take place for individual occupations. It is based on a sample survey and is not subject to benchmark revision, although the seasonal adjustments for quarterly movements are subject to recalculation and revision. It is frequently and correctly used as the best available measure of the general trend of wages and the extent of inflationary pressure exerted on prices by labor costs. By design, it excludes any representation of employee stock options. Being based on a sample survey, it is measured "from the bottom up," starting with the individual reports and aggregating to higher levels.

The *Compensation per hour* component of the report on productivity and costs is calculated and published for total business, nonfarm business, nonfinancial corporations, and manufacturing. This is a "top-down" measure, starting with aggregate estimates of compensation and hours, then dividing the former by the latter. It is affected by changes in the composition of employment: if the composition of employment shifted toward higher-paid employees and/or industries, compensation per hour would rise even if there was no increase in hourly compensation for any individual worker.

In addition, *Compensation per hour* includes the value of exercised stock options as expensed by companies. Since these values are not reported currently but are incorporated at revisions to more comprehensive benchmark levels, this can lead to dramatic revisions. For example, the rise from a year ago for compensation per hour in nonfarm business for the third quarter of 2000 was initially reported at 5.1 percent; the latest estimate is 7.9 percent. The rise for the third quarter of 2001 was originally reported at 6.0 percent and is now shown at only 3.0 percent.

For both of these reasons, *Compensation per hour* should not be considered as an indicator of *wage* trends, especially for the great majority of workers. It is useful in conjunction with the productivity series, since aggregate productivity is also subject to composition shifts; thus, the measure of *unit labor costs* is not distorted when the composition of output shifts toward higher-productivity industries, since the shift affects equally the numerator and denominator of the ratio.

General note on profits data

Production deadlines made it impossible to include the December 2003 revision of the National Income and Profits Accounts in Chapters 1, 4, 5, 6, 7, and 19. (See the Special Notes at the front of this volume.) However, it was possible for Tables 9-4 and 9-5 in this chapter to include the revised data on corporate profits, which had a larger revision than other components of the accounts. These data in this chapter will not be exactly consistent with those in Tables 1-8 and 1-9, with the most significant differences in 2002.

TABLES 9-1 AND 9-2
EMPLOYMENT COST INDEXES

Source: U.S. Department of Labor, Bureau of Labor Statistics (BLS)

The Employment Cost Index (ECI) is a quarterly measure of the change in the cost of labor, free from the influence of employment shifts among occupations and industries. It uses a fixed market basket of labor, similar in concept to the Consumer Price Index's fixed market basket of goods and services, to measure changes over time in employer costs of employing labor. Data are quarterly in all cases; in most cases, index levels have a base period of June 1989 = 100.

Definitions

Total compensation includes wages, salaries, and the employer's costs for employee benefits. Excluded from wages and salaries and employee benefits are the value of stock option exercises and also such items as payment-in-kind, free room and board, and tips.

Wages and salaries consist of straight-time earnings per hour before payroll deductions, including production bonuses, incentive earnings, commissions, and cost-of-living adjustments. These wage rates exclude premium pay for overtime and for work on weekends and holidays, shift differentials, and nonproduction bonuses such as lump-sum payments provided in lieu of wage increases.

Benefits include the cost to employers for paid leave—vacations, holidays, sick leave, and other leave; supplemental pay—premium pay for work in addition to the regular work schedule (such as overtime, weekends, and holidays), shift differentials, and nonproduction bonuses (such as referral bonuses and lump-sum payments provided in lieu of wage increases); insurance benefits—life, health, short-term disability, and long-term disability;

retirement and savings benefits—defined benefit and defined contribution plans; legally required benefits— Social Security, Medicare, Federal and State unemployment insurance, and workers' compensation; and other benefits—severance pay and supplemental unemployment plans.

Private industry workers are workers in private nonfarm industry, not including proprietors, the self-employed, or private household workers.

Civilian workers includes private nonfarm industry workers and workers in state and local government. Federal workers are not included.

Notes on the data

Employee benefit costs are calculated as cents per hour worked for benefits ranging from employer payments for Social Security to paid time off for holidays.

The data are collected from probability samples of around 37,300 occupational observations in around 8,500 sample establishments in private industry, and around 3,650 occupations within around 800 establishments in state and local governments. Samples are rotated over approximately 5 years.

The sample establishments are classified in industry categories based on the 1987 Standard Industrial Classification (SIC). Within an establishment, specific job categories are selected and classified into about 500 occupational classifications according to the 1990 Census of Population. Data are collected each quarter for the pay period including the 12th day of March, June, September, and December.

Aggregate indexes are calculated using fixed employment weights. Beginning with March 1995, ECI weights are based on 1990 fixed employment counts, primarily from the BLS Occupational Employment Survey. From June 1986 through December 1994, ECI measures were based on 1980 census employment counts, while prior to June 1986, they were based on 1970 census employment counts. Use of fixed weights ensures that changes in the indexes reflect only changes in hourly compensation, not employment shifts among industries or occupations with different levels of wages and compensation. This feature distinguishes the ECI from other compensation series such as average hourly earnings (see Table 10-9 and its Notes and Definitions) and the compensation per hour component of the productivity series (see Table 9-3 and its Notes and Definitions, also the General Note above), each of which is affected by such employment shifts.

Data availability

Data for wages and salaries for the private nonfarm economy are available beginning with data for 1975; data

for compensation begin with 1980. The series for state and local government and the civilian nonfarm economy begin with 1981. All are available on the BLS Internet site at <http://www.bls.gov>.

Wage and salary change and compensation cost change data also are available from BLS by major occupational and industry groups, as well as by region and bargaining status. Wage and salary change information is available from 1975 to the present for most of these series. Compensation cost change data are available from 1980 to the present for most series. For 10 occupational and industry series, benefit cost change data are available from the early 1980s to the present. For state and local governments and the civilian economy (state and local governments plus private industry), wage and salary change and compensation cost change data are available for major occupational and industry series. BLS provides data for all these series from June 1981 to the present.

Updates are available about 4 weeks following the end of the reference quarter. Reference quarters end in March, June, September, and December.

References

Explanatory notes including references are included in each quarter's ECI news release, available on the BLS Internet site. References include: Chapter 8 "National Compensation Measures" *BLS Handbook of Methods* Bulletin 2490 (April 1997); *Employment Cost Indexes*, 1975–1999, BLS Bulletin 2532 (includes details on the sample design and seasonal adjustment methodology); and the following *Monthly Labor Review* articles: "Is the ECI Sensitive to the Method of Aggregation" (June 1997); "Employment Cost Index Rebased to June 1989" (April 1990); "Measuring the Precision of the Employment Cost Index" (March 1989); "Employment Cost Index to Replace Hourly Earnings Index" (July 1988); and "Estimation Procedures for the Employment Cost Index," May 1982.

TABLES 9-3 AND 19-10
PRODUCTIVITY AND RELATED DATA

SOURCE: U.S. DEPARTMENT OF LABOR, BUREAU OF LABOR STATISTICS (BLS)

Productivity measures relate real physical output to real input. As such, they encompass a family of measures that includes single-factor input measures, such as output per unit of labor input or output per unit of capital input, as well as measures of multifactor productivity (output per unit of combined labor and capital inputs). The indexes published in this book are indexes of labor productivity expressed in terms of output per hour. Data are provided for four sectors of the economy: Business, nonfarm business, the nonfinancial corporate sector, and manufacturing. All data are presented as indexes, 1992 = 100.

Definitions

Output per hour of all persons (labor productivity) is the value of goods and services in constant prices produced per hour of labor input. Because nonfinancial corporations by definition include no self-employed persons, productivity in this sector is expressed as *output per hour of all employees*.

Compensation per hour is the wages and salaries of employees plus employers' contributions for social insurance and private benefit plans, and the wages, salaries, and supplementary payments for the self-employed—the sum of these divided by hours at work. Included in compensation is the value of exercised stock options that companies report as a charge against earnings. These are not reported quarterly, so that recent values are estimated based on extrapolation. They are revised to actual values when the data become available.

Real compensation per hour is compensation per hour deflated by the CPI-U-RS for the period 1978 through 2002. (For explanation of the CPI-U-RS, see Notes and Definitions for Table 8-1.) Changes in the CPI-W are used for data before 1978.

Unit labor costs are the labor costs expended in the production of a unit of output and are derived by dividing compensation by output.

Unit nonlabor payments include profits, depreciation, interest, rental income of persons, and indirect taxes per unit of output. They are computed by subtracting compensation of all persons from current-dollar value of output and dividing by output.

Unit nonlabor costs is available for nonfinancial corporations only. It contains all the components of unit nonlabor payments except unit profits (and rental income of persons, which for nonfinancial corporations is zero by definition).

Hours of all persons are the total hours at work of payroll workers, self-employed persons, and unpaid family workers. In the case of the data for nonfinancial corporations, there are no self-employed persons and the data represent *employee hours*.

Notes on the data

The output for the business sector is equal to constant-dollar gross domestic product less the following: the rental value of owner-occupied dwellings; the output of nonprofit institutions; the output of paid employees of private households; and general government output. The measures are derived from NIPA data supplied by the U.S. Department of Commerce, Bureau of Economic Analysis (BEA). For manufacturing, annual estimates of sectoral output are produced by the BLS. Quarterly manufacturing output indexes derived from the Federal Reserve Board of Governors' monthly indexes of industrial production are adjusted to these annual measures by the BLS, and used to project the quarterly values in the current period.

Nonfinancial corporate output excludes unincorporated businesses and financial corporations from business sector output. It accounted for about 54 percent of the value of GDP in 1996. For this sector, it is possible to calculate unit profits and unit nonlabor costs separately.

Compensation and hours data are developed from BLS and BEA data. The primary source for hours and employment is the BLS Current Employment Statistics (CES) program (see Notes and Definitions for Tables 10-5 through 10-10). The CES provides data on hours paid for production or nonsupervisory workers. Paid hours of nonproduction and supervisory workers are estimated by the BLS Office of Productivity and Technology. Weekly paid hours are adjusted to hours at work using the annual BLS Hours at Work survey, conducted for this purpose. For paid employees, hours at work differs from hours paid in that it excludes paid vacation and holidays, paid sick leave, and other paid personal or administrative leave.

Although the labor productivity measures relate output to labor input, they do not measure the contribution of labor or any other specific factor of production. Rather, they reflect the joint effect of many influences, including changes in technology; capital investment; level of output; utilization of capacity, energy, and materials; the organization of production; managerial skill; and the characteristics and efforts of the work force.

Revisions

Data for recent years are revised frequently to take account of revisions in the output and labor input measures that underlie the estimates. Customarily, all revisions to source data are reflected in the release following the source data revision. Data in this volume do not reflect the December 2003 revision of the National Income and Product Accounts.

Data availability

Most of the series begin in 1959. Series are available quarterly and annually. Quarterly measures are based entirely on seasonally adjusted data. For some detailed manufacturing series (not shown here), only annual averages are available. Productivity indexes are published early in the second and third months of each quarter, reflecting new data for preceding quarters. Complete historical data are available on the BLS Internet site at <http://www.bls.gov>.

BLS also publishes productivity estimates for a number of individual industries. A listing is given in *Productivity Measures for Selected Industries and Government Services*, BLS Bulletin 2440.

References

Chapter 10 "Productivity Measures: Business Sector and Major Subsectors" *BLS Handbook of Methods* Bulletin 2490 (April 1997), and the following *Monthly Labor Review* articles: "Possible measurement bias in aggregate productivity growth" (February 1999); "Improvements to the Quarterly Productivity Measures" (October 1995); "Hours of Work: A New Base for BLS Productivity Statistics" (February 1990); and "New Sector Definitions for Productivity Series" (October 1976).

TABLE 9-4 AND 9-5
CORPORATE PROFITS WITH INVENTORY VALUATION ADJUSTMENT BY INDUSTRY GROUP

Source: U.S. Department of Commerce, Bureau of Economic Analysis

These profits measures are derived from the National Income and Product Accounts (NIPAs). See the Notes and Definitions to Tables 1-1 through 1-10 for definitions. Note that this industry breakdown of profits incorporates the inventory valuation adjustment, which eliminates any capital gain element in profits arising from changes in the prices at which stocks are valued, but does not incorporate the capital consumption adjustment, which adjusts historical costs to replacement costs and uses actual rather than tax-based service lives.

The data in these tables reflect the December 2003 revision of the National Income and Product Accounts, including the conversion to the new North American Industry Classification System (NAICS) beginning in 1998. Data for earlier years based on the December 2003 revision—including an overlap for the years 1998 through 2000—are still based on the older Standard Industrial Classification system (SIC) and are shown back to 1948 on that basis. See Chapter 14 for an outline and discussion of NAICS and its relation to SIC.

As noted in the General Note above, these data, because they include the December 2003 revision are not exactly consistent with the aggregate profits data in Tables 1-8 and 1-9, with the most significant differences occurring in 2000.

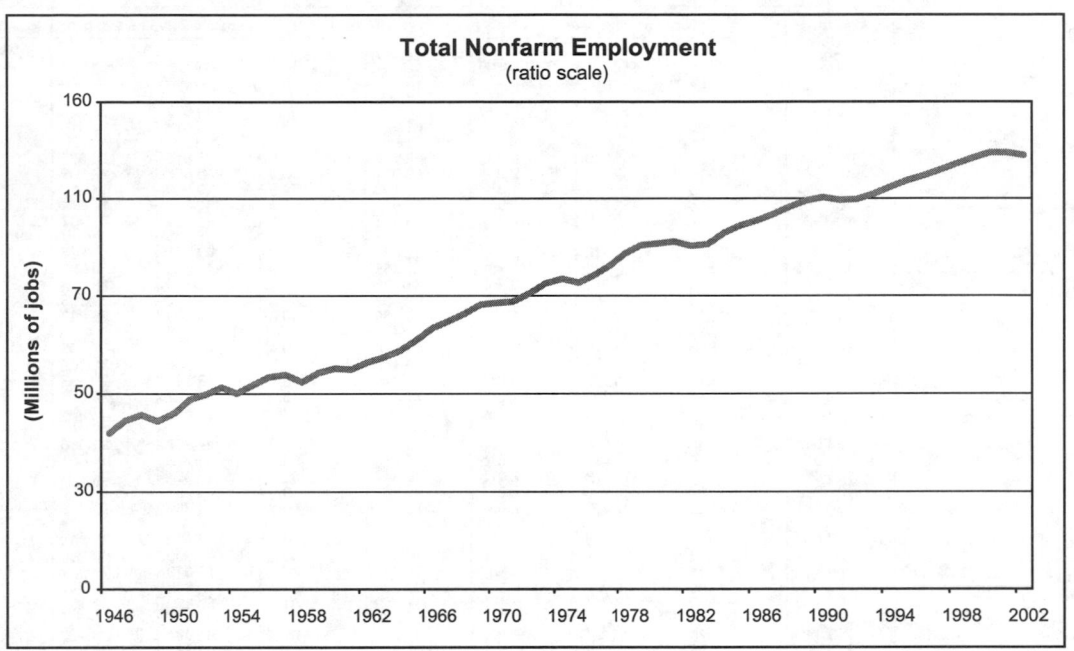

Total Nonfarm Employment
(ratio scale)

- Over the postwar period, the number of jobs on nonfarm payrolls in the United States has increased at an average 2.1 percent annual rate. As the graph shows, job growth has been interrupted by a number of recessions in which employment leveled off or declined. (Table 10-5)

- The total number of civilians employed in the United States, based on the Current Population Survey (CPS), shows somewhat less rapid growth from 1948 to 2000 than the payroll jobs series—1.65 percent, compared with 2.09 percent for payrolls in the same period. (Table 10-2) (The 1948–2000 period is cited because 1948 is the first year available for the CPS series and because the 2 years represent comparable high points in the business cycle.) The difference reflects the fact that the CPS includes persons whose only jobs are in agricultural employment and nonagricultural unpaid family work, both of which have declined, and self-employment, which has grown much more slowly. Also, the CPS includes household (domestic) service. The payroll survey counts multiple jobholders at each place of employment and may include employees younger than 16. See the Notes and Definitions and "Special Notes—Current Statistical Issues and Pitfalls."

- The civilian noninstitutional population of working age only grew 1.40 percent from 1948 to 2000. Therefore, the more rapid employment growth was possible only because of a rise in the labor force participation rate, from 58.8 percent in the earlier year to 67.1 percent in the latter. The entire increase in participation happened among women, as the participation rate of men declined. (Table 10-1)

- The unemployment rate was almost the same in 1948 and 2000—3.8 percent and 4.0 percent, respectively. In the intervening years, annual average unemployment fluctuated between 3.0 percent (at its low point during the Korean War) and 9.7 percent (at its high point in the 1982 recession). (Table 10-3)

- The average hours per week worked on a job by a production or nonsupervisory worker have fallen from 38.5 in 1964 to 34.3 in 2000. It should be noted that these are hours per job, not per person. In other words, a worker with two half-time jobs enters this average as 2 workers with 20 hours per week each, not one worker with 40 hours. The downtrend therefore reflects increases in the number of part-time jobs and the increasing role of retail trade and other service-producing industries where such jobs are frequently found. (Table 10-6)

Table 10-1. Civilian Population and Labor Force [1]

(Thousands of persons, 16 years of age and over.)

Year and month	Not seasonally adjusted				Civilian labor force (seasonally adjusted)					Not in labor force, want a job, seasonally adjusted
	Civilian noninstitutional population	Civilian labor force			Total		Persons 20 years and over		Both sexes, 16 to 19 years	
		Total	Employed	Unemployed	Thousands of persons	Participation rate [2]	Men	Women		
1948	103 068	60 621	58 343	2 276	60 621	58.8	40 687	15 500	4 435	...
1949	103 994	61 286	57 651	3 637	61 286	58.9	41 022	15 978	4 288	...
1950	104 995	62 208	58 918	3 288	62 208	59.2	41 316	16 678	4 216	...
1951	104 621	62 017	59 961	2 055	62 017	59.2	40 655	17 259	4 103	...
1952	105 231	62 138	60 250	1 883	62 138	59.0	40 558	17 517	4 064	...
1953	107 056	63 015	61 179	1 834	63 015	58.9	41 315	17 674	4 027	...
1954	108 321	63 643	60 109	3 532	63 643	58.8	41 669	17 997	3 976	...
1955	109 683	65 023	62 170	2 852	65 023	59.3	42 106	18 825	4 092	...
1956	110 954	66 552	63 799	2 750	66 552	60.0	42 658	19 599	4 296	...
1957	112 265	66 929	64 071	2 859	66 929	59.6	42 780	19 873	4 275	...
1958	113 727	67 639	63 036	4 602	67 639	59.5	43 092	20 285	4 260	...
1959	115 329	68 369	64 630	3 740	68 369	59.3	43 289	20 587	4 492	...
1960	117 245	69 628	65 778	3 852	69 628	59.4	43 603	21 185	4 841	...
1961	118 771	70 459	65 746	4 714	70 459	59.3	43 860	21 664	4 936	...
1962	120 153	70 614	66 702	3 911	70 614	58.8	43 831	21 868	4 916	...
1963	122 416	71 833	67 762	4 070	71 833	58.7	44 222	22 473	5 139	...
1964	124 485	73 091	69 305	3 786	73 091	58.7	44 604	23 098	5 388	...
1965	126 513	74 455	71 088	3 366	74 455	58.9	44 857	23 686	5 910	...
1966	128 058	75 770	72 895	2 875	75 770	59.2	44 788	24 431	6 558	...
1967	129 874	77 347	74 372	2 975	77 347	59.6	45 354	25 475	6 521	...
1968	132 028	78 737	75 920	2 817	78 737	59.6	45 852	26 266	6 619	...
1969	134 335	80 734	77 902	2 832	80 734	60.1	46 351	27 413	6 970	...
1970	137 085	82 771	78 678	4 093	82 771	60.4	47 220	28 301	7 249	3 907
1971	140 216	84 382	79 367	5 016	84 382	60.2	48 009	28 904	7 470	4 441
1972	144 126	87 034	82 153	4 882	87 034	60.4	49 079	29 901	8 054	4 476
1973	147 096	89 429	85 064	4 365	89 429	60.8	49 932	30 991	8 507	4 474
1974	150 120	91 949	86 794	5 156	91 949	61.3	50 879	32 201	8 871	4 541
1975	153 153	93 775	85 846	7 929	93 775	61.2	51 494	33 410	8 870	5 292
1976	156 150	96 158	88 752	7 406	96 158	61.6	52 288	34 814	9 056	5 217
1977	159 033	99 009	92 017	6 991	99 009	62.3	53 348	36 310	9 351	5 777
1978	161 910	102 251	96 048	6 202	102 251	63.2	54 471	38 128	9 652	5 459
1979	164 863	104 962	98 824	6 137	104 962	63.7	55 615	39 708	9 638	5 439
1980	167 745	106 940	99 303	7 637	106 940	63.8	56 455	41 106	9 378	5 682
1981	170 130	108 670	100 397	8 273	108 670	63.9	57 197	42 485	8 988	5 819
1982	172 271	110 204	99 526	10 678	110 204	64.0	57 980	43 699	8 526	6 563
1983	174 215	111 550	100 834	10 717	111 550	64.0	58 744	44 636	8 171	6 484
1984	176 383	113 544	105 005	8 539	113 544	64.4	59 701	45 900	7 943	6 054
1985	178 206	115 461	107 150	8 312	115 461	64.8	60 277	47 283	7 901	5 908
1986	180 587	117 834	109 597	8 237	117 834	65.3	61 320	48 589	7 926	5 848
1987	182 753	119 865	112 440	7 425	119 865	65.6	62 095	49 783	7 988	5 721
1988	184 613	121 669	114 968	6 701	121 669	65.9	62 768	50 870	8 031	5 370
1989	186 393	123 869	117 342	6 528	123 869	66.5	63 704	52 212	7 954	5 312
1990	189 164	125 840	118 793	7 047	125 840	66.5	64 916	53 131	7 792	5 481
1991	190 925	126 346	117 718	8 628	126 346	66.2	65 374	53 708	7 265	5 745
1992	192 805	128 105	118 492	9 613	128 105	66.4	66 213	54 796	7 096	6 172
1993	194 838	129 200	120 259	8 940	129 200	66.3	66 642	55 388	7 170	6 346
1994	196 814	131 056	123 060	7 996	131 056	66.6	66 921	56 655	7 481	6 218
1995	198 584	132 304	124 900	7 404	132 304	66.6	67 324	57 215	7 765	5 670
1996	200 591	133 943	126 708	7 236	133 943	66.8	68 044	58 094	7 806	5 451
1997	203 133	136 297	129 558	6 739	136 297	67.1	69 166	59 198	7 932	4 941
1998	205 220	137 673	131 463	6 210	137 673	67.1	69 715	59 702	8 256	4 812
1999	207 753	139 368	133 488	5 880	139 368	67.1	70 194	60 840	8 333	4 568
2000	212 577	142 583	136 891	5 692	142 583	67.1	72 010	62 301	8 271	4 413
2001	215 092	143 734	136 933	6 801	143 734	66.8	72 816	63 016	7 902	4 590
2002	217 570	144 863	136 485	8 378	144 863	66.6	73 630	63 648	7 585	4 677
2001										
January	213 888	142 828	136 181	6 647	143 797	67.2	72 665	62 893	8 239	4 425
February	214 110	143 100	136 577	6 523	143 638	67.1	72 589	62 900	8 149	4 500
March	214 305	143 664	137 155	6 509	143 871	67.1	72 616	63 183	8 072	4 347
April	214 525	143 026	137 022	6 004	143 624	66.9	72 760	62 897	7 966	4 492
May	214 732	143 023	137 121	5 901	143 280	66.7	72 635	62 894	7 751	4 508
June	214 950	144 553	137 737	6 816	143 395	66.7	72 616	62 847	7 932	4 614
July	215 180	145 097	138 239	6 858	143 616	66.7	72 751	62 950	7 915	4 531
August	215 420	143 826	136 809	7 017	143 331	66.5	72 763	62 984	7 583	4 904
September	215 665	143 601	136 835	6 766	144 042	66.8	73 125	63 073	7 844	4 589
October	215 903	144 060	136 885	7 175	144 128	66.8	73 124	63 133	7 870	4 745
November	216 117	143 987	136 370	7 617	144 296	66.8	73 196	63 223	7 877	4 705
December	216 315	144 042	136 269	7 773	144 379	66.7	73 283	63 381	7 715	4 725
2002										
January	216 506	143 228	134 177	9 051	143 826	66.4	73 111	63 093	7 623	4 836
February	216 663	144 266	135 443	8 823	144 510	66.7	73 269	63 603	7 637	4 455
March	216 823	144 334	135 558	8 776	144 367	66.6	73 307	63 314	7 746	4 658
April	217 006	144 158	135 903	8 255	144 763	66.7	73 525	63 616	7 622	4 581
May	217 198	144 527	136 559	7 969	144 911	66.7	73 766	63 551	7 594	4 795
June	217 407	145 940	137 181	8 758	144 852	66.6	73 689	63 556	7 607	4 713
July	217 630	146 189	137 495	8 693	144 786	66.5	73 670	63 534	7 581	4 900
August	217 866	145 565	137 295	8 271	145 123	66.6	73 802	63 760	7 561	4 628
September	218 107	145 167	137 377	7 790	145 634	66.8	74 108	63 858	7 667	4 702
October	218 340	145 320	137 551	7 769	145 393	66.6	73 883	63 975	7 535	4 542
November	218 548	144 854	136 684	8 170	145 180	66.4	73 770	63 921	7 489	4 727
December	218 741	144 807	136 599	8 209	145 150	66.4	73 744	64 036	7 369	4 546

[1]Changes in survey design, population estimates, and methodology in 1994 and several other years affect year-to-year comparisons. See Notes for more information.
[2]Labor force as a percent of population.
. . . = Not available.

Table 10-2. Civilian Employment and Unemployment [1]

(Thousands of persons, 16 years and over, except as noted; seasonally adjusted.)

Year and month	Employment						Unemployment						
	Total		By age and sex			By industry		Total	Long-term [3]	Persons 20 years and over		Both sexes, 16 to 19 years	Average (mean) weeks unemployed	Median weeks unemployed
	Thousands of persons	Ratio: employment to population [2]	Persons 20 years and over		Both sexes, 16 to 19 years	Agricultural	Nonagricultural			Men	Women			
			Men	Women										
1948	58 343	56.6	39 382	14 936	4 026	7 629	50 714	2 276	309	1 305	564	409	8.6	...
1949	57 651	55.4	38 803	15 137	3 712	7 658	49 993	3 637	684	2 219	841	576	10.0	...
1950	58 918	56.1	39 394	15 824	3 703	7 160	51 758	3 288	782	1 922	854	513	12.1	...
1951	59 961	57.3	39 626	16 570	3 767	6 726	53 235	2 055	303	1 029	689	336	9.7	...
1952	60 250	57.3	39 578	16 958	3 719	6 500	53 749	1 883	232	980	559	345	8.4	...
1953	61 179	57.1	40 296	17 164	3 720	6 260	54 919	1 834	210	1 019	510	307	8.0	...
1954	60 109	55.5	39 634	17 000	3 475	6 205	53 904	3 532	812	2 035	997	501	11.8	...
1955	62 170	56.7	40 526	18 002	3 642	6 450	55 722	2 852	702	1 580	823	450	13.0	...
1956	63 799	57.5	41 216	18 767	3 818	6 283	57 514	2 750	533	1 442	832	478	11.3	...
1957	64 071	57.1	41 239	19 052	3 778	5 947	58 123	2 859	560	1 541	821	497	10.5	...
1958	63 036	55.4	40 411	19 043	3 582	5 586	57 450	4 602	1 452	2 681	1 242	678	13.9	...
1959	64 630	56.0	41 267	19 524	3 838	5 565	59 065	3 740	1 040	2 022	1 063	654	14.4	...
1960	65 778	56.1	41 543	20 105	4 129	5 458	60 318	3 852	957	2 060	1 080	712	12.8	...
1961	65 746	55.4	41 342	20 296	4 108	5 200	60 546	4 714	1 532	2 518	1 368	828	15.6	...
1962	66 702	55.5	41 815	20 693	4 195	4 944	61 759	3 911	1 119	2 016	1 175	721	14.7	...
1963	67 762	55.4	42 251	21 257	4 255	4 687	63 076	4 070	1 088	1 971	1 216	884	14.0	...
1964	69 305	55.7	42 886	21 903	4 516	4 523	64 782	3 786	973	1 718	1 195	872	13.3	...
1965	71 088	56.2	43 422	22 630	5 036	4 361	66 726	3 366	755	1 435	1 056	874	11.8	...
1966	72 895	56.9	43 668	23 510	5 721	3 979	68 915	2 875	526	1 120	921	837	10.4	...
1967	74 372	57.3	44 294	24 397	5 682	3 844	70 527	2 975	448	1 060	1 078	839	8.7	2.3
1968	75 920	57.5	44 859	25 281	5 781	3 817	72 103	2 817	412	993	985	838	8.4	4.5
1969	77 902	58.0	45 388	26 397	6 117	3 606	74 296	2 832	375	963	1 015	853	7.8	4.4
1970	78 678	57.4	45 581	26 952	6 144	3 463	75 215	4 093	663	1 638	1 349	1 106	8.6	4.9
1971	79 367	56.6	45 912	27 246	6 208	3 394	75 972	5 016	1 187	2 097	1 658	1 262	11.3	6.3
1972	82 153	57.0	47 130	28 276	6 746	3 484	78 669	4 882	1 167	1 948	1 625	1 308	12.0	6.2
1973	85 064	57.8	48 310	29 484	7 271	3 470	81 594	4 365	826	1 624	1 507	1 235	10.0	5.2
1974	86 794	57.8	48 922	30 424	7 448	3 515	83 279	5 156	955	1 957	1 777	1 422	9.8	5.2
1975	85 846	56.1	48 018	30 726	7 104	3 408	82 438	7 929	2 505	3 476	2 684	1 767	14.2	8.4
1976	88 752	56.8	49 190	32 226	7 336	3 331	85 421	7 406	2 366	3 098	2 588	1 719	15.8	8.2
1977	92 017	57.9	50 555	33 775	7 688	3 283	88 734	6 991	1 942	2 794	2 535	1 663	14.3	7.0
1978	96 048	59.3	52 143	35 836	8 070	3 387	92 661	6 202	1 414	2 328	2 292	1 583	11.9	5.9
1979	98 824	59.9	53 308	37 434	8 083	3 347	95 477	6 137	1 241	2 308	2 276	1 555	10.8	5.4
1980	99 303	59.2	53 101	38 492	7 710	3 364	95 938	7 637	1 871	3 353	2 615	1 669	11.9	6.5
1981	100 397	59.0	53 582	39 590	7 225	3 368	97 030	8 273	2 285	3 615	2 895	1 763	13.7	6.9
1982	99 526	57.8	52 891	40 086	6 549	3 401	96 125	10 678	3 485	5 089	3 613	1 977	15.6	8.7
1983	100 834	57.9	53 487	41 004	6 342	3 383	97 450	10 717	4 210	5 257	3 632	1 829	20.0	10.1
1984	105 005	59.5	55 769	42 793	6 444	3 321	101 685	8 539	2 737	3 932	3 107	1 499	18.2	7.9
1985	107 150	60.1	56 562	44 154	6 434	3 179	103 971	8 312	2 305	3 715	3 129	1 468	15.6	6.8
1986	109 597	60.7	57 569	45 556	6 472	3 163	106 434	8 237	2 232	3 751	3 032	1 454	15.0	6.9
1987	112 440	61.5	58 726	47 074	6 640	3 208	109 232	7 425	1 983	3 369	2 709	1 347	14.5	6.5
1988	114 968	62.3	59 781	48 383	6 805	3 169	111 800	6 701	1 610	2 987	2 487	1 226	13.5	5.9
1989	117 342	63.0	60 837	49 745	6 759	3 199	114 142	6 528	1 375	2 867	2 467	1 194	11.9	4.8
1990	118 793	62.8	61 678	50 535	6 581	3 223	115 570	7 047	1 525	3 239	2 596	1 212	12.0	5.3
1991	117 718	61.7	61 178	50 634	5 906	3 269	114 449	8 628	2 357	4 195	3 074	1 359	13.7	6.8
1992	118 492	61.5	61 496	51 328	5 669	3 247	115 245	9 613	3 408	4 717	3 469	1 427	17.7	8.7
1993	120 259	61.7	62 355	52 099	5 805	3 115	117 144	8 940	3 094	4 287	3 288	1 365	18.0	8.3
1994	123 060	62.5	63 294	53 606	6 161	3 409	119 651	7 996	2 860	3 627	3 049	1 320	18.8	9.2
1995	124 900	62.9	64 085	54 396	6 419	3 440	121 460	7 404	2 363	3 239	2 819	1 346	16.6	8.3
1996	126 708	63.2	64 897	55 311	6 500	3 443	123 264	7 236	2 316	3 146	2 783	1 306	16.7	8.3
1997	129 558	63.8	66 284	56 613	6 661	3 399	126 159	6 739	2 062	2 882	2 585	1 271	15.8	8.0
1998	131 463	64.1	67 135	57 278	7 051	3 378	128 085	6 210	1 637	2 580	2 424	1 205	14.5	6.7
1999	133 488	64.3	67 761	58 555	7 172	3 281	130 207	5 880	1 480	2 433	2 285	1 162	13.4	6.4
2000	136 891	64.4	69 634	60 067	7 189	2 464	134 427	5 692	1 318	2 376	2 235	1 081	12.6	5.9
2001	136 933	63.7	69 776	60 417	6 740	2 299	134 635	6 801	1 752	3 040	2 599	1 162	13.1	6.8
2002	136 485	62.7	69 734	60 420	6 332	2 311	134 174	8 378	2 904	3 896	3 228	1 253	16.6	9.1
2001														
January	137 846	64.4	70 088	60 605	7 116	2 360	135 385	5 951	1 367	2 577	2 251	1 123	12.6	5.8
February	137 648	64.3	70 007	60 608	7 035	2 343	135 318	5 990	1 494	2 582	2 294	1 114	12.8	6.1
March	137 763	64.3	69 906	60 893	6 957	2 333	135 362	6 108	1 505	2 710	2 284	1 115	12.8	6.6
April	137 353	64.0	69 957	60 518	6 846	2 313	135 108	6 271	1 483	2 804	2 346	1 120	12.5	5.9
May	137 036	63.8	69 815	60 506	6 693	2 333	134 769	6 244	1 489	2 820	2 366	1 058	12.2	6.4
June	136 869	63.7	69 676	60 336	6 790	2 081	134 746	6 526	1 542	2 940	2 444	1 141	12.8	6.2
July	137 006	63.7	69 793	60 468	6 758	2 283	134 876	6 610	1 651	2 958	2 494	1 158	12.8	6.8
August	136 256	63.3	69 548	60 308	6 410	2 331	133 914	7 075	1 852	3 214	2 687	1 173	13.2	6.7
September	136 858	63.5	69 943	60 282	6 659	2 347	134 453	7 183	1 973	3 182	2 817	1 184	13.3	7.2
October	136 370	63.2	69 598	60 189	6 616	2 360	134 035	7 758	2 109	3 526	2 978	1 254	13.2	7.3
November	136 218	63.0	69 437	60 199	6 635	2 239	133 940	8 078	2 360	3 759	3 077	1 242	14.5	7.7
December	136 067	62.9	69 543	60 137	6 430	2 291	133 744	8 312	2 455	3 740	3 288	1 285	14.5	8.2
2002														
January	135 791	62.7	69 351	60 019	6 382	2 373	133 339	8 035	2 561	3 760	3 035	1 241	14.6	8.5
February	136 450	63.0	69 591	60 456	6 418	2 349	134 161	8 060	2 609	3 678	3 163	1 219	15.0	8.2
March	136 143	62.8	69 517	60 151	6 464	2 342	133 760	8 224	2 685	3 789	3 153	1 282	15.4	8.3
April	136 196	62.8	69 627	60 189	6 331	2 342	133 948	8 567	2 810	3 898	3 379	1 290	16.3	8.8
May	136 487	62.8	69 918	60 224	6 307	2 239	134 324	8 424	2 911	3 848	3 289	1 287	16.8	9.6
June	136 383	62.7	69 739	60 225	6 324	2 177	134 103	8 469	3 045	3 950	3 236	1 283	17.1	11.6
July	136 343	62.6	69 792	60 299	6 289	2 321	134 094	8 443	2 955	3 879	3 272	1 292	16.6	8.9
August	136 757	62.8	69 895	60 572	6 280	2 169	134 552	8 366	2 891	3 906	3 180	1 280	16.3	8.7
September	137 312	63.0	70 213	60 717	6 425	2 315	134 979	8 321	3 019	3 895	3 184	1 243	17.8	9.5
October	136 988	62.7	69 921	60 704	6 400	2 483	134 537	8 405	3 099	3 962	3 308	1 135	17.6	9.6
November	136 542	62.5	69 617	60 754	6 228	2 314	134 206	8 637	3 143	4 153	3 224	1 261	17.9	9.4
December	136 439	62.4	69 600	60 750	6 164	2 342	134 080	8 711	3 296	4 145	3 360	1 206	18.4	9.6

[1]Changes in survey design, population estimates, and methodology in 1994 and several other years affect year-to-year comparisons. See Notes and Definitions for more information.
[2]Civilian employment as a percent of the civilian noninstitutional population.
[3]Fifteen weeks and over.
... = Not available.

Table 10-3. Unemployment Rates [1]

(Percent of the civilian labor force in group, seasonally adjusted, except as noted.)

Year and month	All civilian workers	By age and sex 20 years and over Men	By age and sex 20 years and over Women	Both sexes, 16 to 19 years	By race White	By race Black	Persons of Hispanic origin	Married men, spouse present	Married women, spouse present	Women who maintain families	Private nonagri. Total	Construc-tion	Manufac-turing, total
1948	3.8	3.2	3.6	9.2	...	...	...	...	...	...	4.5	...	...
1949	5.9	5.4	5.3	13.4	...	...	...	...	...	...	7.3	...	...
1950	5.3	4.7	5.1	12.2	...	...	...	...	...	...	6.3	...	...
1951	3.3	2.5	4.0	8.2	...	...	...	...	...	...	3.9	...	...
1952	3.0	2.4	3.2	8.5	...	...	...	...	...	...	3.6	...	...
1953	2.9	2.5	2.9	7.6	...	...	...	...	...	...	3.4	...	...
1954	5.5	4.9	5.5	12.6	5.0	...	...	...	...	...	6.7	...	...
1955	4.4	3.8	4.4	11.0	3.9	...	...	2.6	3.7	...	5.1	...	...
1956	4.1	3.4	4.2	11.1	3.6	...	...	2.3	3.6	...	4.7	...	...
1957	4.3	3.6	4.1	11.6	3.8	...	...	2.8	4.3	...	4.9	...	...
1958	6.8	6.2	6.1	15.9	6.1	...	...	5.1	6.5	...	7.9	...	...
1959	5.5	4.7	5.2	14.6	4.8	...	...	3.6	5.2	...	6.1	...	...
1960	5.5	4.7	5.1	14.7	5.0	...	...	3.7	5.2	...	6.2	...	...
1961	6.7	5.7	6.3	16.8	6.0	...	...	4.6	6.4	...	7.5	...	...
1962	5.5	4.6	5.4	14.7	4.9	...	...	3.6	5.4	...	6.1	...	...
1963	5.7	4.5	5.4	17.2	5.0	...	...	3.4	5.4	...	6.1	...	...
1964	5.2	3.9	5.2	16.2	4.6	...	...	2.8	5.1	...	5.4	...	...
1965	4.5	3.2	4.5	14.8	4.1	...	...	2.4	4.5	...	4.6	...	...
1966	3.8	2.5	3.8	12.8	3.4	...	...	1.9	3.7	...	3.8	...	...
1967	3.8	2.3	4.2	12.9	3.4	...	...	1.8	4.5	4.9	3.9	...	...
1968	3.6	2.2	3.8	12.7	3.2	...	...	1.6	3.9	4.4	3.6	...	...
1969	3.5	2.1	3.7	12.2	3.1	...	...	1.5	3.9	4.4	3.5	...	...
1970	4.9	3.5	4.8	15.3	4.5	...	...	2.6	4.9	5.4	5.2	...	...
1971	5.9	4.4	5.7	16.9	5.4	...	...	3.2	5.7	7.3	6.2	...	...
1972	5.6	4.0	5.4	16.2	5.1	10.4	...	2.8	5.4	7.2	5.7	...	...
1973	4.9	3.3	4.9	14.5	4.3	9.4	7.5	2.3	4.7	7.1	4.9	...	...
1974	5.6	3.8	5.5	16.0	5.0	10.5	8.1	2.7	5.3	7.0	5.7	...	...
1975	8.5	6.8	8.0	19.9	7.8	14.8	12.2	5.1	7.9	10.0	9.1	...	...
1976	7.7	5.9	7.4	19.0	7.0	14.0	11.5	4.2	7.1	10.1	7.9	...	...
1977	7.1	5.2	7.0	17.8	6.2	14.0	10.1	3.6	6.5	9.4	7.1	...	...
1978	6.1	4.3	6.0	16.4	5.2	12.8	9.1	2.8	5.5	8.5	5.9	...	...
1979	5.8	4.2	5.7	16.1	5.1	12.3	8.3	2.8	5.1	8.3	5.8	...	...
1980	7.1	5.9	6.4	17.8	6.3	14.3	10.1	4.2	5.8	9.2	7.4	...	...
1981	7.6	6.3	6.8	19.6	6.7	15.6	10.4	4.3	6.0	10.4	7.7	...	...
1982	9.7	8.8	8.3	23.2	8.6	18.9	13.8	6.5	7.4	11.7	10.1	...	...
1983	9.6	8.9	8.1	22.4	8.4	19.5	13.7	6.5	7.0	12.2	9.9	...	...
1984	7.5	6.6	6.8	18.9	6.5	15.9	10.7	4.6	5.7	10.3	7.4	...	...
1985	7.2	6.2	6.6	18.6	6.2	15.1	10.5	4.3	5.6	10.4	7.2	...	...
1986	7.0	6.1	6.2	18.3	6.0	14.5	10.6	4.4	5.2	9.8	7.0	...	...
1987	6.2	5.4	5.4	16.9	5.3	13.0	8.8	3.9	4.3	9.2	6.2	...	...
1988	5.5	4.8	4.9	15.3	4.7	11.7	8.2	3.3	3.9	8.1	5.5	...	...
1989	5.3	4.5	4.7	15.0	4.5	11.4	8.0	3.0	3.7	8.1	5.3	...	...
1990	5.6	5.0	4.9	15.5	4.8	11.4	8.2	3.4	3.8	8.3	5.8	...	...
1991	6.8	6.4	5.7	18.7	6.1	12.5	10.0	4.4	4.5	9.3	7.1	...	...
1992	7.5	7.1	6.3	20.1	6.6	14.2	11.6	5.1	5.0	10.0	7.8	...	...
1993	6.9	6.4	5.9	19.0	6.1	13.0	10.8	4.4	4.6	9.7	7.1	...	...
1994	6.1	5.4	5.4	17.6	5.3	11.5	9.9	3.7	4.1	8.9	6.3	...	...
1995	5.6	4.8	4.9	17.3	4.9	10.4	9.3	3.3	3.9	8.0	5.8	...	...
1996	5.4	4.6	4.8	16.7	4.7	10.5	8.9	3.0	3.6	8.2	5.5	...	...
1997	4.9	4.2	4.4	16.0	4.2	10.0	7.7	2.7	3.1	8.1	5.0	...	...
1998	4.5	3.7	4.1	14.6	3.9	8.9	7.2	2.4	2.9	7.2	4.6	...	...
1999	4.2	3.5	3.8	13.9	3.7	8.0	6.4	2.2	2.7	6.4	4.3	...	...
2000	4.0	3.3	3.6	13.1	3.5	7.6	5.7	2.0	2.7	5.9	4.1	6.2	3.5
2001	4.7	4.2	4.1	14.7	4.2	8.6	6.6	2.7	3.1	6.6	5.0	7.1	5.2
2002	5.8	5.3	5.1	16.5	5.1	10.2	7.5	3.6	3.7	8.0	6.2	9.2	6.7
2002													
January	5.6	5.1	4.9	16.3	5.0	9.8	7.7	3.5	3.5	8.2	6.9	13.6	7.4
February	5.6	5.0	5.0	16.0	4.9	9.7	7.0	3.4	3.8	8.3	6.6	12.2	7.0
March	5.7	5.2	5.0	16.6	5.0	10.4	7.3	3.5	3.7	7.9	6.5	11.8	7.3
April	5.9	5.3	5.3	16.9	5.2	10.8	7.9	3.9	3.8	8.2	6.2	10.1	7.2
May	5.8	5.2	5.2	17.0	5.2	10.1	7.1	3.6	3.9	8.1	5.9	7.4	6.6
June	5.8	5.4	5.1	16.9	5.2	10.6	7.4	4.0	3.8	8.2	6.2	6.9	6.6
July	5.8	5.3	5.1	17.0	5.2	9.9	7.5	3.5	3.8	8.6	6.1	6.9	6.6
August	5.8	5.3	5.0	16.9	5.1	9.9	7.6	3.5	3.6	7.6	5.9	7.4	6.2
September	5.7	5.3	4.9	16.2	5.1	9.8	7.5	3.6	3.6	7.0	5.7	7.0	6.1
October	5.8	5.4	5.1	15.1	5.1	9.9	7.8	3.6	3.8	7.7	5.7	7.7	5.9
November	5.9	5.6	5.0	16.8	5.2	10.8	7.8	3.6	3.8	8.0	6.0	8.5	6.3
December	6.0	5.6	5.2	16.4	5.1	11.2	7.9	3.7	3.8	7.9	6.1	10.9	6.6

[1]Changes in survey design, population estimates, and methodology in 1994 and several other years affect year-to-year comparisons. See Notes and Definitions for more information.
[2]Not seasonally adjusted.
. . . = Not available.

Table 10-3. Unemployment Rates [1]—Continued

(Percent of the civilian labor force in group, seasonally adjusted, except as noted.)

Year and month	By industry of last job [2]—Continued								By occupation [2]						Augmented unemployment rate [3]
	Private nonagricultural wage and salary workers—Continued						Government workers	Agricultural wage and salary workers	Management, professional, and related occupations	Sales and office occupations	Natural resources, construction, and maintenance	Farming, forestry, and fishing	Production, transportation, and material moving occupations	Service occupations	
	Manufacturing		Transportation and utilities	Wholesale and retail trade	Financial activities	Professional and business services									
	Durable goods	Nondurable goods													
1948	...	...	...	...	...	...	...	...	...	...	...	...	...	...	...
1949	...	...	...	...	...	...	...	...	...	...	...	...	...	...	...
1950	...	...	...	...	...	...	...	...	...	...	...	...	...	...	...
1951	...	...	...	...	...	...	...	...	...	...	...	...	...	...	...
1952	...	...	...	...	...	...	...	...	...	...	...	...	...	...	...
1953	...	...	...	...	...	...	...	...	...	...	...	...	...	...	...
1954	...	...	...	...	...	...	...	...	...	...	...	...	...	...	...
1955	...	...	...	...	...	...	...	...	...	...	...	...	...	...	...
1956	...	...	...	...	...	...	...	...	...	...	...	...	...	...	...
1957	...	...	...	...	...	...	...	...	...	...	...	...	...	...	...
1958	...	...	...	...	...	...	...	...	...	...	...	...	...	...	...
1959	...	...	...	...	...	...	...	...	...	...	...	...	...	...	...
1960	...	...	...	...	...	...	...	...	...	...	...	...	...	...	...
1961	...	...	...	...	...	...	...	...	...	...	...	...	...	...	...
1962	...	...	...	...	...	...	...	...	...	...	...	...	...	...	...
1963	...	...	...	...	...	...	...	...	...	...	...	...	...	...	...
1964	...	...	...	...	...	...	...	...	...	...	...	...	...	...	...
1965	...	...	...	...	...	...	...	...	...	...	...	...	...	...	...
1966	...	...	...	...	...	...	...	...	...	...	...	...	...	...	...
1967	...	...	...	...	...	...	...	...	...	...	...	...	...	...	...
1968	...	...	...	...	...	...	...	...	...	...	...	...	...	...	...
1969	...	...	...	...	...	...	...	...	...	...	...	...	...	...	...
1970	...	...	...	...	...	...	...	...	...	...	...	...	...	...	9.2
1971	...	...	...	...	...	...	...	...	...	...	...	...	...	...	10.6
1972	...	...	...	...	...	...	...	...	...	...	...	...	...	...	10.2
1973	...	...	...	...	...	...	...	...	...	...	...	...	...	...	9.4
1974	...	...	...	...	...	...	...	...	...	...	...	...	...	...	10.0
1975	...	...	...	...	...	...	...	...	...	...	...	...	...	...	13.3
1976	...	...	...	...	...	...	4.4	...	...	...	...	...	...	...	12.5
1977	...	...	...	...	...	...	4.2	...	...	...	...	...	...	...	12.2
1978	...	...	...	...	...	...	4.0	...	...	...	...	...	...	...	10.8
1979	...	...	...	...	...	...	3.8	...	...	...	...	...	...	...	10.5
1980	...	...	...	...	...	...	4.1	...	...	...	...	...	...	...	11.8
1981	...	...	...	...	...	...	4.7	...	...	...	...	...	...	...	12.3
1982	...	...	...	...	...	...	4.9	...	...	...	...	...	...	...	14.8
1983	...	...	...	...	...	...	5.3	...	...	...	...	...	...	...	14.6
1984	...	...	...	...	...	...	4.5	...	...	...	...	...	...	...	12.2
1985	...	...	...	...	...	...	3.9	...	...	...	...	...	...	...	11.7
1986	...	...	...	...	...	...	3.6	...	...	...	...	...	...	...	11.4
1987	...	...	...	...	...	...	3.5	...	...	...	...	...	...	...	10.5
1988	...	...	...	...	...	...	2.8	...	...	...	...	...	...	...	9.5
1989	...	...	...	...	...	...	2.8	...	...	...	...	...	...	...	9.2
1990	...	...	...	...	...	...	2.7	...	...	...	...	...	...	...	9.5
1991	...	...	...	...	...	...	3.3	...	...	...	...	...	...	...	10.9
1992	...	...	...	...	...	...	3.6	...	...	...	...	...	...	...	11.8
1993	...	...	...	...	...	...	3.3	...	...	...	...	...	...	...	11.3
1994	...	...	...	...	...	...	3.4	...	...	...	...	...	...	...	10.4
1995	...	...	...	...	...	...	2.9	...	...	...	...	...	...	...	9.5
1996	...	...	...	...	...	...	2.9	...	...	...	...	...	...	...	9.1
1997	...	...	...	...	...	...	2.6	...	...	...	...	...	...	...	8.3
1998	...	...	...	...	...	...	2.3	...	...	...	...	...	...	...	7.7
1999	...	...	...	...	...	...	2.2	...	...	...	...	...	...	...	7.3
2000	3.2	4.0	3.4	4.3	2.4	4.8	2.1	9.0	1.8	1.8	5.3	10.2	5.1	5.2	6.9
2001	5.2	5.2	4.3	4.9	2.9	6.1	2.2	11.2	2.3	2.3	6.4	13.4	6.4	5.8	7.7
2002	6.9	6.2	4.9	6.1	3.5	7.9	2.5	10.1	3.0	3.0	7.8	12.0	7.6	6.6	8.7
2002															
January	7.9	6.7	6.6	6.3	3.0	8.9	2.4	14.8	3.1	5.6	10.7	17.2	9.2	7.3	8.7
February	7.6	6.0	5.7	6.6	3.5	7.7	2.5	14.8	2.8	6.0	9.8	17.5	8.2	7.3	8.4
March	7.4	7.1	5.6	6.6	3.2	7.5	2.4	19.6	2.8	5.9	10.0	23.1	8.4	6.7	8.6
April	7.5	6.8	5.0	6.4	3.3	7.3	2.2	10.8	2.7	5.9	8.3	12.1	8.0	6.3	8.8
May	6.4	6.8	4.5	5.8	3.8	7.7	2.3	6.8	3.1	5.5	6.7	7.9	7.1	6.3	8.8
June	7.0	6.0	4.9	6.2	4.1	8.2	2.8	6.3	3.3	5.9	6.6	8.4	7.4	6.8	8.8
July	7.0	6.0	4.9	5.6	3.8	8.2	3.2	7.3	3.5	5.5	6.5	8.7	7.8	6.7	8.9
August	6.5	5.8	3.9	5.8	3.8	7.2	3.0	9.0	3.4	5.6	6.8	10.8	6.9	6.0	8.7
September	6.2	6.1	4.2	5.9	3.3	7.8	2.6	6.3	3.3	5.4	6.5	7.7	6.2	6.2	8.7
October	5.9	6.0	4.7	6.1	3.5	7.5	2.5	6.6	2.8	5.6	6.6	7.5	6.7	6.3	8.6
November	6.7	5.6	4.2	6.2	3.7	8.2	2.3	11.1	2.9	5.6	7.2	13.9	7.4	6.6	8.9
December	7.0	5.9	4.6	5.7	3.6	8.3	2.2	9.8	2.8	5.0	8.7	10.7	8.1	6.9	8.9

[1]Changes in survey design, population estimates, and methodology in 1994 and several other years affect year-to-year comparisons. See Notes and Definitions for more information.
[2]Not seasonally adjusted.
[3]See Notes and Definitions.
. . . = Not available.

Table 10-4. Insured Unemployment

(Averages of weekly data; thousands of persons, except as noted.)

Year and month	State programs (seasonally adjusted)			Federal programs (not seasonally adjusted)					
				Initial claims		Persons claiming benefits			
	Initial claims	Insured unemployment	Insured unemployment rate (percent) [1]	Federal employees	Newly discharged veterans	Federal employees	Newly discharged veterans	Railroad retirement	Extended benefits
1967	227	1 205	...	...	...	...	...	...	...
1968	197	1 088	...	...	...	...	...	...	...
1969	197	1 093	...	...	...	...	...	...	...
1970	297	1 849	...	...	...	...	...	...	...
1971	296	2 152	4.1	...	...	...	...	...	...
1972	263	1 843	3.5	...	...	...	...	...	...
1973	244	1 628	2.7	...	...	...	...	...	...
1974	352	2 278	3.5	...	...	...	...	...	...
1975	473	3 958	6.0	...	...	...	...	...	...
1976	383	2 975	4.5	...	...	...	...	...	...
1977	374	2 645	3.9	...	...	...	...	...	...
1978	341	2 339	3.3	...	...	...	...	...	...
1979	383	2 427	3.0	...	...	...	...	...	...
1980	487	3 363	3.9	...	...	...	...	...	...
1981	452	3 034	3.5	...	...	...	...	...	...
1982	586	4 096	4.7	...	...	...	...	...	...
1983	441	3 341	3.9	...	...	...	...	...	...
1984	374	2 453	2.8	...	...	...	...	...	...
1985	392	2 585	2.9	...	...	...	...	...	...
1986	377	2 631	2.8	2.13	2.52	20.24	17.11	...	...
1987	325	2 273	2.4	2.19	2.57	21.29	17.71	...	9.51
1988	309	2 075	2.1	2.32	2.74	22.91	18.13	13.28	1.17
1989	329	2 172	2.1	2.14	2.31	22.17	15.09	10.37	0.61
1990	385	2 535	2.4	2.45	2.54	23.89	18.43	10.56	2.36
1991	447	3 336	3.1	2.55	2.93	30.50	22.12	10.73	32.16
1992	409	3 205	3.1	2.75	4.95	32.10	60.25	8.77	4.61
1993	343	2 767	2.6	2.55	3.94	32.06	54.90	7.40	7.59
1994	340	2 670	2.5	2.54	3.02	32.21	37.65	6.21	31.09
1995	358	2 589	2.4	4.57	2.51	31.68	29.78	5.48	14.27
1996	352	2 553	2.3	7.33	2.13	29.84	24.30	5.40	5.53
1997	322	2 301	2.0	2.01	1.75	23.58	19.66	4.00	5.35
1998	318	2 216	1.9	1.64	1.41	19.60	15.68	3.19	6.43
1999	297	2 187	1.8	1.48	1.18	16.85	14.25	3.24	3.05
2000	299	2 112	1.7	1.73	1.05	18.60	12.54	3.92	0.58
2001	406	3 015	2.4	1.47	1.15	18.57	13.98	...	0.57
2002	405	3 575	2.8	1.46	1.22	17.54	16.07	...	10.79
2000									
January	287	2 099	1.7	1.62	1.16	20.20	13.95	4.75	0.00
February	292	2 134	1.7	1.14	1.05	18.01	13.69	6.50	0.00
March	274	2 070	1.7	0.95	1.05	16.71	13.15	6.00	1.34
April	273	2 010	1.6	0.95	0.93	13.79	12.35	4.50	2.81
May	283	1 992	1.6	1.03	0.93	11.36	11.76	3.60	2.23
June	293	2 035	1.6	1.59	0.98	11.89	11.45	2.75	0.60
July	295	2 091	1.7	2.29	1.12	14.69	11.65	2.75	0.00
August	313	2 126	1.7	2.09	1.17	18.05	12.25	3.00	0.00
September	303	2 135	1.7	1.98	1.08	19.27	12.39	3.00	0.00
October	303	2 132	1.7	3.10	1.11	23.45	12.40	3.00	0.00
November	333	2 218	1.8	2.27	0.94	26.01	12.30	3.00	0.00
December	344	2 301	1.8	1.78	1.05	28.80	12.99	4.25	0.00
2001									
January	337	2 380	1.9	2.36	1.21	27.69	13.60	...	0.00
February	366	2 464	2.0	1.38	1.11	25.87	13.77	...	0.00
March	386	2 567	2.0	1.07	1.07	22.32	13.45	...	1.07
April	400	2 688	2.1	1.23	1.02	18.07	12.96	...	2.61
May	396	2 826	2.2	1.10	0.99	15.32	12.75	...	2.39
June	401	2 964	2.3	1.45	1.04	14.53	12.56	...	0.85
July	397	3 037	2.4	1.84	1.25	15.70	12.95	...	0.00
August	398	3 135	2.5	1.23	1.34	16.43	13.92	...	0.00
September	441	3 295	2.6	1.22	1.29	15.28	14.30	...	0.00
October	486	3 564	2.8	1.74	1.33	16.18	15.20	...	0.00
November	445	3 674	2.9	1.52	1.11	17.00	15.51	...	0.00
December	416	3 588	2.8	1.58	1.09	19.16	16.55	...	0.01
2002									
January	402	3 521	2.7	1.81	1.24	20.30	16.81	...	12.96
February	389	3 514	2.7	1.11	1.10	18.77	16.56	...	32.84
March	414	3 573	2.8	0.99	1.03	16.56	15.76	...	26.14
April	432	3 664	2.9	1.26	1.04	15.30	14.66	...	4.02
May	414	3 713	2.9	1.24	0.99	13.49	14.06	...	3.00
June	391	3 656	2.9	1.57	1.05	13.93	13.56	...	1.36
July	387	3 514	2.7	1.78	1.23	16.16	13.84	...	0.52
August	396	3 546	2.8	1.33	1.40	18.75	15.00	...	1.82
September	417	3 605	2.8	1.44	1.44	17.77	16.19	...	7.06
October	413	3 605	2.8	1.69	1.59	18.94	17.70	...	12.03
November	391	3 505	2.7	1.69	1.26	19.23	18.87	...	12.47
December	411	3 489	2.7	1.71	1.29	21.76	20.13	...	15.55

[1]Insured unemployed as a percent of employment covered by state programs.
. . . = Not available.

Table 10-5. Nonfarm Employment by NAICS Supersector

(Thousands of persons, seasonally adjusted.)

Year and month	Total	Private						
		Total	Goods-producing					
			Total	Natural resources and mining	Construction	Manufacturing		
						Total	Durable	Nondurable
1946	41 759	36 054	16 122	885	1 724	13 513	7 535	5 978
1947	43 945	38 379	17 314	976	2 051	14 287	8 079	6 208
1948	44 954	39 213	17 579	1 014	2 241	14 324	8 028	6 296
1949	43 843	37 893	16 464	948	2 236	13 281	7 240	6 041
1950	45 287	39 167	17 343	924	2 405	14 013	7 809	6 204
1951	47 930	41 427	18 703	956	2 678	15 070	8 738	6 332
1952	48 909	42 182	18 928	928	2 709	15 291	8 979	6 312
1953	50 310	43 552	19 733	902	2 700	16 131	9 690	6 441
1954	49 093	42 235	18 515	825	2 688	15 002	8 773	6 229
1955	50 744	43 722	19 234	828	2 881	15 524	9 161	6 363
1956	52 473	45 087	19 799	859	3 082	15 858	9 435	6 424
1957	52 959	45 235	19 669	864	3 007	15 798	9 452	6 346
1958	51 426	43 480	18 319	801	2 862	14 656	8 480	6 176
1959	53 374	45 182	19 163	789	3 050	15 325	8 988	6 337
1960	54 296	45 832	19 182	771	2 973	15 438	9 071	6 367
1961	54 105	45 399	18 647	728	2 908	15 011	8 711	6 300
1962	55 659	46 655	19 203	709	2 997	15 498	9 099	6 399
1963	56 764	47 423	19 385	694	3 060	15 631	9 226	6 405
1964	58 391	48 680	19 733	697	3 148	15 888	9 414	6 474
1965	60 874	50 683	20 595	694	3 284	16 617	9 973	6 644
1966	64 020	53 110	21 740	690	3 371	17 680	10 803	6 878
1967	65 931	54 406	21 882	679	3 305	17 897	10 952	6 945
1968	68 023	56 050	22 292	671	3 410	18 211	11 137	7 074
1969	70 512	58 181	22 893	683	3 637	18 573	11 396	7 177
1970	71 006	58 318	22 179	677	3 654	17 848	10 762	7 086
1971	71 335	58 323	21 602	658	3 770	17 174	10 229	6 944
1972	73 798	60 333	22 299	672	3 957	17 669	10 630	7 039
1973	76 912	63 050	23 450	693	4 167	18 589	11 414	7 176
1974	78 389	64 086	23 364	755	4 095	18 514	11 432	7 082
1975	77 069	62 250	21 318	802	3 608	16 909	10 266	6 643
1976	79 502	64 501	22 025	832	3 662	17 531	10 640	6 891
1977	82 593	67 334	22 972	865	3 940	18 167	11 132	7 035
1978	86 826	71 014	24 156	902	4 322	18 932	11 770	7 162
1979	89 932	73 864	24 997	1 008	4 562	19 426	12 220	7 206
1980	90 528	74 154	24 263	1 077	4 454	18 733	11 679	7 054
1981	91 289	75 109	24 118	1 180	4 304	18 634	11 611	7 023
1982	89 677	73 695	22 550	1 163	4 024	17 363	10 610	6 753
1983	90 280	74 269	22 110	997	4 065	17 048	10 326	6 722
1984	94 530	78 371	23 435	1 014	4 501	17 920	11 050	6 870
1985	97 511	80 978	23 585	974	4 793	17 819	11 034	6 784
1986	99 474	82 636	23 318	829	4 937	17 552	10 795	6 757
1987	102 088	84 932	23 470	771	5 090	17 609	10 767	6 842
1988	105 345	87 806	23 909	770	5 233	17 906	10 969	6 938
1989	108 014	90 087	24 045	750	5 309	17 985	11 004	6 981
1990	109 487	91 072	23 723	765	5 263	17 695	10 736	6 959
1991	108 374	89 829	22 588	739	4 780	17 068	10 219	6 849
1992	108 726	89 940	22 095	689	4 608	16 799	9 945	6 854
1993	110 844	91 855	22 219	666	4 779	16 774	9 900	6 873
1994	114 291	95 016	22 774	659	5 095	17 021	10 131	6 890
1995	117 298	97 866	23 156	641	5 274	17 241	10 372	6 869
1996	119 708	100 169	23 410	637	5 536	17 237	10 485	6 752
1997	122 776	103 113	23 886	654	5 813	17 419	10 704	6 716
1998	125 930	106 021	24 354	645	6 149	17 560	10 910	6 650
1999	128 993	108 686	24 465	598	6 545	17 322	10 830	6 492
2000	131 785	110 996	24 649	599	6 787	17 263	10 876	6 388
2001	131 826	110 707	23 873	606	6 826	16 441	10 335	6 107
2002	130 376	108 886	22 619	581	6 732	15 306	9 517	5 789
2002								
January	130 578	109 193	22 960	598	6 777	15 585	9 707	5 878
February	130 510	109 089	22 887	594	6 776	15 517	9 666	5 851
March	130 481	109 034	22 792	589	6 753	15 450	9 617	5 833
April	130 415	108 957	22 713	588	6 719	15 406	9 590	5 816
May	130 411	108 907	22 667	584	6 716	15 367	9 567	5 800
June	130 383	108 891	22 639	580	6 725	15 334	9 541	5 793
July	130 204	108 756	22 588	576	6 703	15 309	9 516	5 793
August	130 224	108 745	22 527	575	6 719	15 233	9 472	5 761
September	130 289	108 763	22 497	573	6 728	15 196	9 435	5 761
October	130 408	108 864	22 435	572	6 720	15 143	9 400	5 743
November	130 409	108 869	22 409	573	6 745	15 091	9 362	5 729
December	130 198	108 642	22 323	572	6 731	15 020	9 316	5 704

Table 10-5. Nonfarm Employment by NAICS Supersector—*Continued*

(Thousands of persons, seasonally adjusted.)

Year and month	Total	Service-providing									
			Private								
		Total	Trade, transportation, and utilities			Information	Financial activities	Professional and business services	Education and health services	Leisure and hospitality	Other services
			Total	Wholesale trade	Retail trade						
1946	25 637	19 932	8 945	1 962	4 118	1 594	1 619	2 666	1 885	2 485	737
1947	26 631	21 064	9 452	2 116	4 393	1 658	1 674	2 828	2 015	2 650	788
1948	27 376	21 634	9 716	2 230	4 524	1 669	1 742	2 893	2 077	2 726	812
1949	27 379	21 430	9 579	2 227	4 520	1 583	1 768	2 853	2 097	2 729	820
1950	27 945	21 824	9 694	2 255	4 580	1 625	1 825	2 928	2 144	2 769	839
1951	29 227	22 725	10 089	2 335	4 758	1 718	1 890	3 061	2 221	2 877	870
1952	29 981	23 254	10 302	2 408	4 880	1 736	1 964	3 128	2 281	2 950	894
1953	30 577	23 820	10 504	2 444	5 012	1 785	2 036	3 215	2 335	3 030	916
1954	30 578	23 720	10 357	2 454	4 998	1 693	2 118	3 197	2 385	3 034	936
1955	31 510	24 489	10 612	2 505	5 158	1 735	2 212	3 320	2 491	3 140	978
1956	32 674	25 288	10 921	2 583	5 315	1 778	2 299	3 437	2 593	3 242	1 018
1957	33 290	25 566	10 942	2 592	5 328	1 780	2 348	3 504	2 676	3 267	1 050
1958	33 107	25 161	10 656	2 550	5 266	1 674	2 386	3 449	2 695	3 243	1 058
1959	34 211	26 018	10 960	2 638	5 453	1 718	2 454	3 591	2 822	3 365	1 107
1960	35 114	26 650	11 147	2 690	5 589	1 728	2 532	3 694	2 937	3 460	1 152
1961	35 458	26 752	11 040	2 681	5 560	1 693	2 590	3 744	3 030	3 468	1 188
1962	36 455	27 451	11 215	2 737	5 672	1 723	2 656	3 885	3 172	3 557	1 243
1963	37 379	28 038	11 367	2 780	5 781	1 735	2 731	3 990	3 288	3 639	1 288
1964	38 658	28 947	11 677	2 856	5 977	1 766	2 811	4 137	3 438	3 772	1 346
1965	40 279	30 089	12 139	2 967	6 262	1 824	2 878	4 306	3 587	3 951	1 404
1966	42 280	31 370	12 611	3 080	6 530	1 908	2 961	4 517	3 770	4 127	1 475
1967	44 049	32 524	12 950	3 158	6 711	1 955	3 087	4 720	3 986	4 269	1 558
1968	45 731	33 759	13 334	3 236	6 977	1 991	3 234	4 918	4 191	4 453	1 638
1969	47 619	35 288	13 853	3 344	7 295	2 048	3 404	5 156	4 428	4 670	1 731
1970	48 827	36 139	14 144	3 418	7 463	2 041	3 532	5 267	4 577	4 789	1 789
1971	49 734	36 721	14 318	3 424	7 657	2 009	3 651	5 328	4 675	4 914	1 827
1972	51 499	38 034	14 788	3 547	8 038	2 056	3 784	5 523	4 863	5 121	1 900
1973	53 462	39 600	15 349	3 688	8 371	2 135	3 920	5 774	5 092	5 341	1 990
1974	55 025	40 721	15 693	3 823	8 536	2 160	4 023	5 974	5 322	5 471	2 078
1975	55 751	40 932	15 606	3 810	8 600	2 061	4 047	6 034	5 497	5 544	2 144
1976	57 477	42 476	16 128	3 920	8 966	2 111	4 155	6 287	5 756	5 794	2 244
1977	59 620	44 362	16 765	4 055	9 359	2 185	4 348	6 587	6 052	6 065	2 359
1978	62 670	46 858	17 658	4 280	9 879	2 287	4 599	6 972	6 427	6 411	2 505
1979	64 935	48 868	18 303	4 485	10 180	2 375	4 843	7 312	6 767	6 631	2 637
1980	66 265	49 891	18 413	4 557	10 244	2 361	5 025	7 544	7 072	6 721	2 755
1981	67 172	50 991	18 604	4 634	10 364	2 382	5 163	7 782	7 357	6 840	2 865
1982	67 127	51 145	18 457	4 574	10 372	2 317	5 209	7 848	7 515	6 874	2 924
1983	68 171	52 160	18 668	4 559	10 635	2 253	5 334	8 039	7 766	7 078	3 021
1984	71 095	54 936	19 653	4 788	11 223	2 398	5 553	8 464	8 193	7 489	3 186
1985	73 926	57 393	20 379	4 915	11 733	2 437	5 815	8 871	8 657	7 869	3 366
1986	76 156	59 318	20 795	4 935	12 078	2 445	6 128	9 211	9 061	8 156	3 523
1987	78 618	61 462	21 302	5 003	12 419	2 507	6 385	9 608	9 515	8 446	3 699
1988	81 436	63 897	21 974	5 153	12 808	2 585	6 500	10 090	10 063	8 778	3 907
1989	83 969	66 042	22 510	5 284	13 108	2 622	6 562	10 555	10 616	9 062	4 116
1990	85 764	67 349	22 666	5 268	13 182	2 688	6 614	10 848	10 984	9 288	4 261
1991	85 787	67 241	22 281	5 185	12 896	2 677	6 558	10 714	11 506	9 256	4 249
1992	86 631	67 845	22 125	5 110	12 828	2 641	6 540	10 970	11 891	9 437	4 240
1993	88 625	69 636	22 378	5 093	13 021	2 668	6 709	11 495	12 303	9 732	4 350
1994	91 517	72 242	23 128	5 247	13 491	2 738	6 867	12 174	12 807	10 100	4 428
1995	94 142	74 710	23 834	5 433	13 897	2 843	6 827	12 844	13 289	10 501	4 572
1996	96 299	76 759	24 239	5 522	14 143	2 940	6 969	13 462	13 683	10 777	4 690
1997	98 890	79 227	24 700	5 664	14 389	3 084	7 178	14 335	14 087	11 018	4 825
1998	101 576	81 667	25 186	5 795	14 609	3 218	7 462	15 147	14 446	11 232	4 976
1999	104 528	84 221	25 771	5 892	14 970	3 419	7 648	15 957	14 798	11 543	5 087
2000	107 136	86 346	26 225	5 933	15 280	3 631	7 687	16 666	15 109	11 862	5 168
2001	107 952	86 834	25 983	5 773	15 239	3 629	7 807	16 476	15 645	12 036	5 258
2002	107 757	86 267	25 493	5 641	15 047	3 420	7 843	16 010	16 184	11 969	5 348
2002											
January	107 618	86 233	25 564	5 687	15 050	3 492	7 836	16 030	15 968	12 002	5 341
February	107 623	86 202	25 570	5 672	15 069	3 470	7 826	15 995	16 017	11 969	5 355
March	107 689	86 242	25 565	5 664	15 081	3 454	7 823	16 013	16 057	11 966	5 364
April	107 702	86 244	25 560	5 656	15 087	3 443	7 828	16 023	16 100	11 929	5 361
May	107 744	86 240	25 536	5 651	15 069	3 434	7 825	16 035	16 130	11 922	5 358
June	107 744	86 252	25 530	5 650	15 065	3 424	7 830	16 026	16 183	11 904	5 355
July	107 616	86 168	25 513	5 642	15 062	3 410	7 830	15 973	16 194	11 918	5 330
August	107 697	86 218	25 458	5 624	15 033	3 401	7 830	16 008	16 241	11 940	5 340
September	107 792	86 266	25 430	5 625	15 016	3 383	7 851	16 008	16 273	11 975	5 346
October	107 973	86 429	25 439	5 619	15 025	3 392	7 872	16 036	16 315	12 032	5 343
November	108 000	86 460	25 406	5 605	15 014	3 382	7 880	16 014	16 357	12 069	5 352
December	107 875	86 319	25 378	5 604	15 006	3 353	7 889	15 972	16 373	12 019	5 335

Table 10-5. Nonfarm Employment by NAICS Supersector—*Continued*

(Thousands of persons, seasonally adjusted.)

Year and month	Total	Government						
		Federal			State		Local	
		Total	Department of Defense		Total	Education	Total	Education
1946	5 705	2 365	746		...	...	...	...
1947	5 567	1 985	499		...	...	...	...
1948	5 742	1 954	511		...	...	...	...
1949	5 950	2 001	531		...	...	...	...
1950	6 120	2 023	533		...	...	...	...
1951	6 502	2 415	797		...	...	...	...
1952	6 727	2 539	868		...	...	...	...
1953	6 758	2 418	818		...	...	...	...
1954	6 858	2 295	744		...	...	...	...
1955	7 021	2 295	744		1 168	308	3 558	1 751
1956	7 386	2 318	749		1 249	334	3 819	1 884
1957	7 724	2 326	729		1 328	363	4 071	2 026
1958	7 946	2 298	695		1 415	389	4 232	2 115
1959	8 192	2 342	699		1 484	420	4 366	2 198
1960	8 464	2 381	681		1 536	448	4 547	2 314
1961	8 706	2 391	683		1 607	474	4 708	2 411
1962	9 004	2 455	697		1 669	511	4 881	2 522
1963	9 341	2 473	687		1 747	557	5 121	2 674
1964	9 711	2 463	676		1 856	609	5 392	2 839
1965	10 191	2 495	679		1 996	679	5 700	3 031
1966	10 910	2 690	741		2 141	775	6 080	3 297
1967	11 525	2 852	802		2 302	873	6 371	3 490
1968	11 972	2 871	801		2 442	958	6 660	3 649
1969	12 330	2 893	815		2 533	1 042	6 904	3 785
1970	12 687	2 865	756		2 664	1 104	7 158	3 912
1971	13 012	2 828	730		2 747	1 149	7 437	4 091
1972	13 465	2 815	720		2 859	1 188	7 790	4 262
1973	13 862	2 794	696		2 923	1 205	8 146	4 433
1974	14 303	2 858	698		3 039	1 267	8 407	4 584
1975	14 820	2 882	704		3 179	1 323	8 758	4 722
1976	15 001	2 863	693		3 273	1 371	8 865	4 786
1977	15 258	2 859	676		3 377	1 385	9 023	4 859
1978	15 812	2 893	661		3 474	1 367	9 446	4 958
1979	16 068	2 894	649		3 541	1 378	9 633	4 989
1980	16 375	3 000	645		3 610	1 398	9 765	5 090
1981	16 180	2 922	655		3 640	1 420	9 619	5 095
1982	15 982	2 884	690		3 640	1 433	9 458	5 049
1983	16 011	2 915	699		3 662	1 450	9 434	5 020
1984	16 159	2 943	716		3 734	1 488	9 482	5 076
1985	16 533	3 014	738		3 832	1 540	9 687	5 220
1986	16 838	3 044	736		3 893	1 561	9 901	5 358
1987	17 156	3 089	736		3 967	1 586	10 100	5 469
1988	17 540	3 124	719		4 076	1 620	10 339	5 590
1989	17 927	3 136	734		4 182	1 668	10 609	5 740
1990	18 415	3 196	722		4 305	1 730	10 914	5 902
1991	18 545	3 110	702		4 355	1 768	11 081	5 994
1992	18 787	3 111	702		4 408	1 799	11 267	6 076
1993	18 989	3 063	670		4 488	1 834	11 438	6 206
1994	19 275	3 018	657		4 576	1 882	11 682	6 329
1995	19 432	2 949	627		4 635	1 919	11 849	6 453
1996	19 539	2 877	597		4 606	1 911	12 056	6 592
1997	19 664	2 806	588		4 582	1 904	12 276	6 758
1998	19 909	2 772	550		4 612	1 922	12 525	6 921
1999	20 307	2 769	525		4 709	1 983	12 829	7 120
2000	20 790	2 865	510		4 786	2 031	13 139	7 294
2001	21 118	2 764	504		4 905	2 113	13 449	7 479
2002	21 489	2 767	500		5 006	2 219	13 716	7 657
2002								
January	21 385	2 755	501		5 009	2 208	13 621	7 578
February	21 421	2 758	496		5 012	2 215	13 651	7 599
March	21 447	2 755	496		5 019	2 223	13 673	7 617
April	21 458	2 753	496		5 020	2 223	13 685	7 625
May	21 504	2 780	497		5 023	2 231	13 701	7 639
June	21 492	2 779	501		5 019	2 234	13 694	7 648
July	21 448	2 761	504		5 015	2 236	13 672	7 661
August	21 479	2 765	504		5 013	2 233	13 701	7 674
September	21 526	2 774	501		4 993	2 213	13 759	7 684
October	21 544	2 781	500		4 984	2 203	13 779	7 692
November	21 540	2 782	497		4 983	2 203	13 775	7 697
December	21 556	2 778	504		4 984	2 203	13 794	7 698

. . . = Not available.

Table 10-6. Production or Nonsupervisory Workers on Private Nonfarm Payrolls by NAICS Supersector

(Thousands of persons, seasonally adjusted.)

Year and month	Total private	Natural resources and mining	Construc-tion	Manu-facturing	Trade, transportation, and utilities Total	Wholesale trade	Retail trade	Information	Financial activities	Profes-sional and business services	Education and health services	Leisure and hospitality	Other services
1947	...	866	1 938	12 453	...	...	...	...	...	...	...	...	...
1948	...	898	2 106	12 383	...	...	...	...	...	...	...	...	...
1949	...	829	2 100	11 355	...	...	...	...	...	...	...	...	...
1950	...	811	2 251	12 032	...	...	...	...	...	...	...	...	...
1951	...	838	2 493	12 808	...	...	...	...	...	...	...	...	...
1952	...	801	2 510	12 797	...	...	...	...	...	...	...	...	...
1953	...	772	2 491	13 437	...	...	...	...	...	...	...	...	...
1954	...	691	2 467	12 300	...	...	...	...	...	...	...	...	...
1955	...	688	2 628	12 735	...	...	...	...	...	...	...	...	...
1956	...	709	2 804	12 869	...	...	...	...	...	...	...	...	...
1957	...	702	2 730	12 640	...	...	...	...	...	...	...	...	...
1958	...	630	2 573	11 532	...	...	...	...	...	...	...	...	...
1959	...	615	2 730	12 089	...	...	...	...	...	...	...	...	...
1960	...	596	2 651	12 074	...	...	...	...	...	...	...	...	...
1961	...	556	2 582	11 612	...	...	...	...	...	...	...	...	...
1962	...	538	2 656	11 986	...	...	...	...	...	...	...	...	...
1963	...	525	2 719	12 051	...	...	...	...	...	...	...	...	...
1964	40 575	526	2 794	12 298	10 303	...	...	1 217	2 390	3 360	3 303	3 278	1 107
1965	42 302	523	2 906	12 905	10 702	...	...	1 268	2 434	3 515	3 443	3 443	1 161
1966	44 292	517	2 977	13 703	11 095	...	...	1 334	2 492	3 715	3 623	3 607	1 230
1967	45 185	501	2 903	13 714	11 369	...	...	1 365	2 585	3 890	3 818	3 734	1 306
1968	46 519	491	2 986	13 908	11 688	...	...	1 394	2 700	4 067	4 008	3 898	1 379
1969	48 246	501	3 177	14 147	12 152	...	...	1 438	2 841	4 252	4 196	4 089	1 452
1970	48 180	496	3 158	13 490	12 388	...	...	1 422	2 922	4 321	4 305	4 185	1 494
1971	48 151	474	3 238	13 034	12 502	...	...	1 392	2 978	4 354	4 372	4 286	1 521
1972	49 971	494	3 425	13 497	12 954	2 920	7 257	1 437	3 066	4 518	4 531	4 467	1 583
1973	52 235	502	3 576	14 227	13 437	3 041	7 551	1 504	3 164	4 748	4 747	4 664	1 666
1974	52 846	550	3 469	14 040	13 700	3 148	7 673	1 516	3 217	4 907	4 941	4 766	1 740
1975	51 010	581	2 990	12 576	13 578	3 121	7 714	1 416	3 227	4 939	5 088	4 821	1 795
1976	52 916	606	2 999	13 127	14 038	3 212	8 048	1 459	3 300	5 153	5 309	5 046	1 880
1977	55 207	636	3 209	13 591	14 579	3 323	8 396	1 514	3 452	5 404	5 561	5 284	1 978
1978	58 188	658	3 544	14 150	15 329	3 509	8 861	1 586	3 645	5 717	5 874	5 588	2 099
1979	60 403	737	3 760	14 458	15 843	3 667	9 113	1 650	3 825	5 993	6 157	5 772	2 209
1980	60 372	785	3 623	13 667	15 907	3 708	9 158	1 626	3 957	6 197	6 442	5 850	2 318
1981	60 960	861	3 469	13 492	16 004	3 753	9 238	1 633	4 052	6 396	6 694	5 944	2 414
1982	59 465	834	3 208	12 315	15 821	3 662	9 254	1 564	4 055	6 421	6 812	5 976	2 458
1983	60 005	698	3 240	12 121	15 999	3 639	9 494	1 502	4 128	6 581	7 032	6 161	2 542
1984	63 316	714	3 614	12 821	16 797	3 821	9 964	1 631	4 289	6 918	7 368	6 491	2 672
1985	65 436	686	3 868	12 648	17 427	3 935	10 399	1 660	4 476	7 258	7 770	6 817	2 827
1986	66 802	577	3 984	12 449	17 769	3 941	10 704	1 663	4 698	7 532	8 107	7 066	2 957
1987	68 700	541	4 088	12 537	18 196	3 989	10 986	1 717	4 861	7 859	8 488	7 310	3 104
1988	71 029	545	4 199	12 765	18 771	4 132	11 306	1 775	4 894	8 256	8 956	7 587	3 280
1989	72 927	526	4 257	12 805	19 230	4 235	11 565	1 807	4 931	8 648	9 432	7 833	3 459
1990	73 684	538	4 115	12 669	19 032	4 198	11 308	1 866	4 973	8 889	9 748	8 299	3 555
1991	72 520	515	3 674	12 164	18 640	4 122	11 008	1 871	4 911	8 748	10 212	8 247	3 539
1992	72 786	478	3 546	12 020	18 506	4 071	10 931	1 871	4 908	8 971	10 555	8 406	3 526
1993	74 591	462	3 704	12 070	18 752	4 072	11 104	1 896	5 057	9 451	10 908	8 667	3 623
1994	77 382	461	3 973	12 361	19 392	4 196	11 502	1 928	5 183	10 078	11 338	8 979	3 689
1995	79 845	458	4 113	12 566	19 984	4 361	11 841	2 007	5 165	10 645	11 765	9 330	3 812
1996	81 773	461	4 325	12 532	20 325	4 423	12 057	2 096	5 279	11 161	12 123	9 565	3 907
1997	84 158	479	4 546	12 673	20 698	4 523	12 274	2 181	5 415	11 896	12 478	9 780	4 013
1998	86 316	473	4 807	12 729	21 059	4 605	12 440	2 217	5 605	12 566	12 791	9 947	4 124
1999	88 430	438	5 105	12 524	21 576	4 673	12 772	2 351	5 728	13 184	13 089	10 216	4 219
2000	90 336	446	5 295	12 428	21 965	4 686	13 040	2 502	5 737	13 790	13 362	10 516	4 296
2001	89 983	457	5 332	11 677	21 709	4 555	12 952	2 530	5 810	13 588	13 846	10 662	4 373
2002	88 419	435	5 208	10 799	21 333	4 465	12 791	2 416	5 866	13 075	14 297	10 561	4 429
2002													
January	88 839	453	5 288	11 001	21 409	4 511	12 805	2 465	5 846	13 169	14 135	10 631	4 442
February	88 795	451	5 282	10 952	21 434	4 506	12 827	2 450	5 848	13 138	14 181	10 606	4 453
March	88 724	446	5 244	10 901	21 436	4 502	12 839	2 440	5 851	13 144	14 206	10 601	4 455
April	88 624	445	5 220	10 866	21 434	4 491	12 848	2 428	5 855	13 138	14 234	10 549	4 455
May	88 521	439	5 202	10 836	21 396	4 482	12 825	2 423	5 856	13 130	14 263	10 533	4 443
June	88 430	433	5 200	10 818	21 377	4 474	12 814	2 415	5 856	13 086	14 316	10 497	4 432
July	88 279	427	5 172	10 804	21 348	4 462	12 803	2 404	5 856	13 030	14 329	10 495	4 414
August	88 208	427	5 183	10 740	21 300	4 445	12 775	2 395	5 857	13 038	14 348	10 505	4 415
September	88 204	425	5 184	10 715	21 271	4 450	12 756	2 387	5 882	13 020	14 367	10 539	4 414
October	88 278	426	5 173	10 685	21 252	4 436	12 752	2 404	5 899	13 047	14 390	10 590	4 412
November	88 204	425	5 177	10 648	21 209	4 420	12 738	2 397	5 899	13 019	14 411	10 601	4 418
December	88 017	422	5 163	10 595	21 174	4 414	12 728	2 377	5 904	12 963	14 421	10 600	4 398

. . . = Not available.

Table 10-7. Average Weekly Hours of Production or Nonsupervisory Workers on Private Nonfarm Payrolls by NAICS Supersector

(Hours per week, seasonally adjusted.)

Year and month	Total private	Natural resources and mining	Construction	Manufacturing		Trade, transportation, and utilities			Informa-tion	Financial activities	Profes-sional and business services	Education and health services	Leisure and hospitality	Other services
				Average weekly hours	Overtime hours	Total	Wholesale trade	Retail trade						
1947	...	42.3	38.7	40.5	...	...	...	...	...	...	...	...	...	...
1948	...	41.1	38.6	40.1	...	...	...	...	...	...	...	...	...	...
1949	...	38.2	38.2	39.2	...	...	...	...	...	...	...	...	...	...
1950	...	39.8	37.9	40.6	...	...	...	...	...	...	...	...	...	...
1951	...	40.2	38.6	40.7	...	...	...	...	...	...	...	...	...	...
1952	...	40.5	39.4	40.8	...	...	...	...	...	...	...	...	...	...
1953	...	40.7	38.4	40.6	...	...	...	...	...	...	...	...	...	...
1954	...	40.3	37.7	39.7	...	...	...	...	...	...	...	...	...	...
1955	...	42.3	37.6	40.8	...	...	...	...	...	...	...	...	...	...
1956	...	42.3	38.0	40.5	2.8	...	...	...	...	...	...	...	...	...
1957	...	41.7	37.5	39.9	2.3	...	...	...	...	...	...	...	...	...
1958	...	40.6	37.3	39.2	2.0	...	...	...	...	...	...	...	...	...
1959	...	42.1	37.5	40.3	2.7	...	...	...	...	...	...	...	...	...
1960	...	41.9	37.2	39.8	2.5	...	...	...	...	...	...	...	...	...
1961	...	42.1	37.4	39.9	2.4	...	...	...	...	...	...	...	...	...
1962	...	42.5	37.5	40.5	2.8	...	...	...	...	...	...	...	...	...
1963	...	43.0	37.8	40.6	2.8	...	...	...	...	...	...	...	...	...
1964	38.5	43.4	37.7	40.8	3.1	39.7	...	...	38.2	37.2	37.4	35.5	32.8	36.3
1965	38.6	43.7	37.9	41.2	3.6	39.6	...	...	38.3	37.1	37.3	35.2	32.5	36.1
1966	38.5	44.1	38.1	41.4	3.9	39.1	...	...	38.3	37.2	37.0	34.9	31.9	35.8
1967	37.9	43.9	38.1	40.6	3.3	38.5	...	...	37.6	36.9	36.6	34.5	31.3	35.4
1968	37.7	44.0	37.8	40.7	3.5	38.2	...	...	37.6	36.8	36.3	34.1	30.8	35.0
1969	37.5	44.3	38.4	40.6	3.6	37.9	...	...	37.6	36.9	36.3	34.1	30.4	35.0
1970	37.0	43.9	37.8	39.8	2.9	37.6	...	...	37.2	36.6	35.9	33.8	30.0	34.7
1971	36.8	43.7	37.6	39.9	2.9	37.4	...	...	37.0	36.4	35.5	33.3	29.9	34.2
1972	36.9	44.0	37.0	40.6	3.4	37.4	39.8	35.1	37.3	36.4	35.5	33.3	29.7	34.2
1973	36.9	43.8	37.2	40.7	3.8	37.2	39.6	34.8	37.3	36.4	35.5	33.3	29.4	34.1
1974	36.4	43.7	37.1	40.0	3.2	36.8	39.2	34.3	37.0	36.3	35.3	33.1	29.1	33.9
1975	36.0	43.7	36.9	39.5	2.6	36.4	39.1	34.0	36.6	36.2	35.1	33.0	28.8	33.8
1976	36.1	44.2	37.3	40.1	3.1	36.3	39.1	33.8	36.7	36.2	34.9	32.7	28.5	33.6
1977	35.9	44.7	37.0	40.3	3.4	36.0	39.2	33.3	36.8	36.2	34.7	32.5	28.1	33.4
1978	35.8	44.9	37.3	40.4	3.6	35.6	39.2	32.7	36.8	36.1	34.6	32.3	27.7	33.2
1979	35.6	44.7	37.5	40.2	3.3	35.4	39.2	32.4	36.6	35.9	34.4	32.2	27.4	33.0
1980	35.2	44.9	37.5	39.7	2.8	35.0	38.8	31.9	36.3	36.0	34.3	32.1	27.0	33.0
1981	35.2	45.1	37.4	39.8	2.8	34.9	38.9	31.9	36.3	36.0	34.3	32.1	26.9	33.0
1982	34.7	44.1	37.2	38.9	2.3	34.6	38.7	31.7	35.8	36.0	34.2	32.1	26.8	33.0
1983	34.9	43.9	37.6	40.1	2.9	34.6	38.8	31.6	36.2	35.9	34.4	32.1	26.8	33.0
1984	35.1	44.6	38.2	40.7	3.4	34.7	38.9	31.6	36.6	36.2	34.3	32.0	26.7	32.9
1985	34.9	44.6	38.2	40.5	3.3	34.4	38.8	31.2	36.5	36.1	34.2	31.9	26.4	32.8
1986	34.7	43.6	37.9	40.7	3.4	34.1	38.7	31.0	36.4	36.1	34.3	32.0	26.2	32.9
1987	34.7	43.5	38.2	40.9	3.7	34.1	38.5	31.0	36.5	36.0	34.3	32.0	26.3	32.8
1988	34.6	43.3	38.2	41.0	3.8	33.8	38.5	30.9	36.1	35.6	34.2	32.0	26.3	32.9
1989	34.5	44.1	38.3	40.9	3.8	33.8	38.4	30.7	36.1	35.6	34.2	32.0	26.1	32.9
1990	34.3	45.0	38.3	40.5	3.8	33.7	38.4	30.6	35.8	35.5	34.2	31.9	26.0	32.8
1991	34.1	45.3	38.1	40.4	3.8	33.7	38.4	30.4	35.6	35.5	34.0	31.9	25.6	32.7
1992	34.2	44.6	38.0	40.7	4.0	33.8	38.6	30.7	35.8	35.6	34.0	32.0	25.7	32.6
1993	34.3	44.9	38.4	41.1	4.4	34.1	38.5	30.7	36.0	35.5	34.0	32.0	25.9	32.6
1994	34.5	45.3	38.8	41.7	5.0	34.3	38.8	30.9	36.0	35.5	34.1	32.0	26.0	32.7
1995	34.3	45.3	38.8	41.3	4.7	34.1	38.6	30.8	36.0	35.5	34.0	32.0	25.9	32.6
1996	34.3	46.0	38.9	41.3	4.8	34.1	38.6	30.7	36.4	35.5	34.1	31.9	25.9	32.5
1997	34.5	46.2	38.9	41.7	5.1	34.3	38.8	30.9	36.3	35.7	34.3	32.2	26.0	32.7
1998	34.5	44.9	38.8	41.4	4.8	34.2	38.6	30.9	36.6	36.0	34.3	32.2	26.2	32.6
1999	34.3	44.2	39.0	41.4	4.8	33.9	38.6	30.8	36.7	35.8	34.4	32.1	26.1	32.5
2000	34.3	44.4	39.2	41.3	4.7	33.8	38.8	30.7	36.8	35.9	34.5	32.2	26.1	32.5
2001	34.0	44.6	38.7	40.3	4.0	33.5	38.4	30.7	36.9	35.8	34.2	32.3	25.8	32.3
2002	33.9	43.2	38.4	40.5	4.2	33.6	38.0	30.9	36.5	35.6	34.2	32.4	25.8	32.0
2002														
January	33.8	43.3	38.7	40.2	3.9	33.5	38.1	30.8	36.7	35.6	33.9	32.2	25.7	32.1
February	33.9	43.7	38.7	40.3	4.0	33.6	38.0	30.9	36.6	35.7	34.0	32.3	26.0	32.3
March	33.9	43.6	38.4	40.6	4.1	33.6	38.0	30.9	36.6	35.6	34.1	32.3	25.9	32.1
April	33.9	43.1	38.5	40.5	4.1	33.6	37.9	31.0	36.6	35.6	34.1	32.3	25.8	32.0
May	33.9	43.2	38.2	40.6	4.2	33.7	38.0	31.0	36.7	35.6	34.2	32.4	25.7	32.0
June	34.0	43.4	38.5	40.7	4.2	33.7	38.2	31.0	36.8	35.6	34.2	32.5	25.7	32.1
July	33.8	43.0	38.2	40.4	4.2	33.5	37.9	30.9	36.4	35.5	34.0	32.4	25.6	32.0
August	33.9	43.3	38.5	40.5	4.2	33.5	38.0	30.8	36.4	35.6	34.2	32.6	25.7	32.0
September	33.9	43.0	38.7	40.5	4.2	33.7	38.0	30.9	36.3	35.6	34.4	32.5	25.9	32.1
October	33.8	43.0	38.2	40.3	4.2	33.6	37.8	30.9	36.5	35.5	34.2	32.5	25.9	32.0
November	33.8	42.3	38.0	40.4	4.3	33.6	37.9	30.8	36.6	35.6	34.2	32.5	25.9	32.0
December	33.8	43.0	38.2	40.5	4.3	33.5	37.8	30.8	36.4	35.7	34.2	32.4	25.8	31.9

. . . = Not available.

Table 10-8. Indexes of Aggregate Weekly Hours of Production or Nonsupervisory Workers on Private Nonfarm Payrolls by NAICS Supersector

(2002 = 100, seasonally adjusted.)

Year and month	Total private	Natural resources and mining	Construc-tion	Manu-facturing	Trade, transportation, and utilities			Information	Financial activities	Profes-sional and business services	Education and health services	Leisure and hospitality	Other services
					Total	Wholesale trade	Retail trade						
1947	...	195.4	37.5	115.3	...	...	...	...	...	...	...	...	...
1948	...	196.7	40.6	113.6	...	...	...	...	...	...	...	...	...
1949	...	168.8	40.1	101.9	...	...	...	...	...	...	...	...	...
1950	...	172.2	42.6	111.6	...	...	...	...	...	...	...	...	...
1951	...	179.7	48.1	119.4	...	...	...	...	...	...	...	...	...
1952	...	172.8	49.4	119.4	...	...	...	...	...	...	...	...	...
1953	...	167.2	47.7	124.9	...	...	...	...	...	...	...	...	...
1954	...	148.5	46.4	111.8	...	...	...	...	...	...	...	...	...
1955	...	155.2	49.3	118.9	...	...	...	...	...	...	...	...	...
1956	...	159.9	53.2	119.3	...	...	...	...	...	...	...	...	...
1957	...	156.0	51.2	115.5	...	...	...	...	...	...	...	...	...
1958	...	136.2	47.9	103.5	...	...	...	...	...	...	...	...	...
1959	...	137.9	51.2	111.6	...	...	...	...	...	...	...	...	...
1960	...	133.3	49.3	109.8	...	...	...	...	...	...	...	...	...
1961	...	124.6	48.3	106.0	...	...	...	...	...	...	...	...	...
1962	...	121.9	49.7	111.0	...	...	...	...	...	...	...	...	...
1963	...	120.4	51.3	111.8	...	...	...	...	...	...	...	...	...
1964	52.2	121.7	52.6	114.7	57.0	...	...	52.6	42.5	28.2	25.3	39.5	28.4
1965	54.6	122.0	55.1	121.7	59.1	...	...	55.1	43.3	29.3	26.2	41.1	29.6
1966	56.9	121.5	56.7	129.7	60.5	...	...	57.9	44.4	30.8	27.3	42.2	31.1
1967	57.2	117.4	55.3	127.4	61.1	...	...	58.2	45.7	31.8	28.4	42.9	32.6
1968	58.5	115.3	56.4	129.6	62.3	...	...	59.4	47.6	33.0	29.5	44.1	34.0
1969	60.5	118.4	60.9	131.5	64.3	...	...	61.3	50.2	34.5	30.9	45.7	35.8
1970	59.5	116.1	59.6	122.9	64.9	...	...	59.9	51.2	34.7	31.4	46.1	36.5
1971	59.1	110.2	60.9	118.9	65.1	...	...	58.3	52.0	34.6	31.5	47.0	36.7
1972	61.5	116.0	63.3	125.3	67.5	68.5	64.4	60.6	53.5	35.9	32.6	48.6	38.1
1973	64.3	117.4	66.5	132.5	69.7	71.1	66.4	63.6	55.2	37.7	34.1	50.4	40.1
1974	64.3	128.1	64.3	128.5	70.3	72.8	66.6	63.5	55.9	38.7	35.3	50.9	41.6
1975	61.3	135.4	55.0	113.5	69.0	71.9	66.4	58.6	56.0	38.8	36.2	51.0	42.8
1976	63.8	142.9	55.8	120.4	71.0	74.0	68.7	60.7	57.2	40.3	37.5	52.8	44.5
1977	66.2	151.6	59.3	125.4	73.1	76.8	70.7	63.0	59.8	42.0	39.0	54.5	46.5
1978	69.5	157.4	66.0	130.8	76.2	81.1	73.4	66.1	63.1	44.2	40.9	56.7	49.0
1979	71.8	175.7	70.4	132.9	78.3	84.7	74.7	68.5	65.9	46.2	42.7	58.0	51.4
1980	71.0	187.8	67.8	124.0	77.7	84.9	74.0	66.9	68.1	47.6	44.6	57.9	53.9
1981	71.6	206.9	64.8	122.7	78.0	86.1	74.5	67.1	69.8	49.1	46.3	58.8	56.1
1982	69.0	196.2	59.6	109.6	76.4	83.6	74.2	63.5	69.8	49.2	47.2	58.8	57.1
1983	70.0	163.4	60.8	111.3	77.2	83.4	76.0	61.6	71.0	50.6	48.8	60.5	59.2
1984	74.3	169.8	68.9	119.2	81.3	87.7	79.7	67.5	74.3	53.1	50.9	63.7	62.0
1985	76.2	163.2	73.7	117.1	83.6	90.1	82.2	68.6	77.4	55.5	53.5	66.1	65.4
1986	77.4	134.0	75.3	115.9	84.5	90.0	83.8	68.6	81.3	57.7	55.9	68.0	68.5
1987	79.7	125.6	77.9	117.4	86.6	90.6	86.3	70.9	83.7	60.3	58.6	70.6	71.8
1988	82.1	126.0	80.2	119.9	88.6	93.7	88.5	72.5	83.5	63.2	61.9	73.1	76.0
1989	84.1	123.6	81.5	119.9	90.5	96.1	89.9	73.8	84.0	66.2	65.2	75.0	80.1
1990	84.4	129.0	78.6	117.3	89.6	95.1	87.5	75.6	84.6	68.0	67.2	79.0	82.2
1991	82.6	124.2	70.0	112.4	87.5	93.5	84.8	75.5	83.4	66.6	70.3	77.4	81.5
1992	83.1	113.6	67.4	112.0	87.4	92.6	85.0	75.9	83.6	68.3	73.0	79.3	81.0
1993	85.4	110.6	71.1	113.5	89.1	92.6	86.3	77.4	85.9	71.8	75.4	82.2	83.2
1994	89.2	111.3	77.1	118.0	92.7	95.9	89.8	78.6	88.1	76.9	78.4	85.7	84.9
1995	91.5	110.6	79.7	118.6	95.1	99.4	92.3	81.9	87.8	81.1	81.3	88.6	87.5
1996	93.7	113.1	84.1	118.4	96.6	100.9	93.7	86.3	89.8	85.1	83.5	90.9	89.5
1997	97.0	118.0	88.3	121.0	98.9	103.6	95.8	89.7	92.7	91.3	86.8	93.5	92.4
1998	99.4	113.2	93.2	120.6	100.3	105.0	97.2	91.9	96.6	96.6	89.0	95.6	94.8
1999	101.4	103.3	99.5	118.6	101.9	106.4	99.5	97.7	98.1	101.5	90.7	98.0	96.7
2000	103.5	105.5	103.8	117.3	103.6	107.3	101.3	104.1	98.6	106.4	92.9	100.7	98.3
2001	102.0	108.7	103.0	107.7	101.6	103.1	100.5	105.8	99.6	103.9	96.7	100.8	99.5
2002	100.0	100.0	100.0	100.0	100.0	100.0	100.0	100.0	100.0	100.0	100.0	100.0	100.0
2002													
January	100.3	104.6	102.2	101.2	100.0	101.4	99.8	102.5	99.7	99.9	98.3	100.2	100.5
February	100.5	105.1	102.1	101.0	100.4	101.0	100.3	101.6	100.0	100.0	98.9	101.2	101.4
March	100.5	103.7	100.6	101.3	100.5	100.9	100.4	101.1	99.8	100.3	99.1	100.7	100.8
April	100.3	102.3	100.4	100.7	100.4	100.4	100.8	100.6	99.8	100.3	99.3	99.9	100.5
May	100.2	101.1	99.3	100.7	100.6	100.5	100.6	100.7	99.8	100.5	99.8	99.3	100.2
June	100.4	100.2	100.0	100.7	100.5	100.9	100.5	100.7	99.8	100.2	100.4	99.0	100.3
July	99.7	97.9	98.7	99.9	99.7	99.8	100.1	99.1	99.6	99.1	100.2	98.6	99.6
August	99.9	98.6	99.7	99.5	99.5	99.7	99.6	98.7	99.9	99.8	101.0	99.1	99.6
September	99.9	97.4	100.2	99.3	100.0	99.8	99.7	98.1	100.3	100.2	100.8	100.2	99.9
October	99.7	97.7	98.7	98.5	99.6	98.9	99.7	99.4	100.3	99.9	101.0	100.6	99.5
November	99.6	95.8	98.3	98.4	99.4	98.8	99.3	99.4	100.6	99.6	101.1	100.7	99.7
December	99.4	96.7	98.5	98.2	98.9	98.4	99.2	98.0	100.9	99.2	100.9	100.3	98.9

. . . = Not available.

Table 10-9. Average Hourly Earnings of Production or Nonsupervisory Workers on Private Nonfarm Payrolls by NAICS Supersector

(Dollars, seasonally adjusted.)

Year and month	Total private	Natural resources and mining	Construction	Manu-facturing	Trade, transportation, and utilities			Information	Financial activities	Professional and business services	Education and health services	Leisure and hospitality	Other services
					Total	Wholesale trade	Retail trade						
1947	...	1.43	1.12	1.10	...	...	...	...	...	...	...	...	...
1948	...	1.61	1.29	1.20	...	...	...	...	...	...	...	...	...
1949	...	1.67	1.37	1.25	...	...	...	...	...	...	...	...	...
1950	...	1.72	1.44	1.32	...	...	...	...	...	...	...	...	...
1951	...	1.88	1.60	1.45	...	...	...	...	...	...	...	...	...
1952	...	1.95	1.71	1.53	...	...	...	...	...	...	...	...	...
1953	...	2.08	1.86	1.63	...	...	...	...	...	...	...	...	...
1954	...	2.09	1.96	1.66	...	...	...	...	...	...	...	...	...
1955	...	2.15	2.03	1.74	...	...	...	...	...	...	...	...	...
1956	...	2.27	2.15	1.84	...	...	...	...	...	...	...	...	...
1957	...	2.39	2.29	1.93	...	...	...	...	...	...	...	...	...
1958	...	2.42	2.40	1.99	...	...	...	...	...	...	...	...	...
1959	...	2.50	2.51	2.08	...	...	...	...	...	...	...	...	...
1960	...	2.55	2.65	2.15	...	...	...	...	...	...	...	...	...
1961	...	2.59	2.78	2.20	...	...	...	...	...	...	...	...	...
1962	...	2.65	2.89	2.27	...	...	...	...	...	...	...	...	...
1963	...	2.70	2.99	2.34	...	...	...	...	...	...	...	...	...
1964	2.53	2.76	3.08	2.41	2.85	...	...	4.35	2.29	3.17	2.01	1.06	1.14
1965	2.63	2.87	3.23	2.49	2.94	...	...	4.47	2.38	3.28	2.12	1.14	1.25
1966	2.73	3.00	3.41	2.60	3.04	...	...	4.56	2.47	3.39	2.23	1.23	1.37
1967	2.85	3.14	3.63	2.71	3.15	...	...	4.68	2.58	3.51	2.36	1.34	1.49
1968	3.02	3.30	3.92	2.89	3.32	...	...	4.85	2.75	3.65	2.49	1.49	1.62
1969	3.22	3.54	4.30	3.07	3.48	...	...	5.05	2.92	3.84	2.68	1.64	1.81
1970	3.40	3.77	4.74	3.23	3.65	...	...	5.25	3.07	4.04	2.88	1.78	2.01
1971	3.63	3.99	5.17	3.45	3.86	...	...	5.53	3.23	4.26	3.11	1.90	2.24
1972	3.90	4.28	5.55	3.70	4.23	4.58	3.52	5.87	3.37	4.50	3.33	2.03	2.46
1973	4.14	4.59	5.89	3.97	4.45	4.80	3.69	6.17	3.55	4.72	3.54	2.15	2.67
1974	4.43	5.09	6.29	4.31	4.74	5.11	3.92	6.52	3.80	5.01	3.82	2.34	2.95
1975	4.73	5.68	6.78	4.71	5.02	5.45	4.14	6.92	4.08	5.29	4.09	2.52	3.21
1976	5.06	6.19	7.17	5.09	5.31	5.75	4.36	7.37	4.30	5.60	4.39	2.71	3.51
1977	5.44	6.70	7.56	5.55	5.67	6.12	4.65	7.84	4.58	5.95	4.72	2.96	3.84
1978	5.87	7.44	8.11	6.05	6.10	6.61	5.00	8.34	4.93	6.32	5.07	3.25	4.19
1979	6.33	8.20	8.71	6.57	6.55	7.12	5.34	8.86	5.31	6.71	5.44	3.54	4.56
1980	6.84	8.97	9.37	7.15	7.04	7.68	5.71	9.47	5.82	7.22	5.93	3.89	5.05
1981	7.43	9.89	10.24	7.86	7.55	8.28	6.09	10.21	6.34	7.80	6.49	4.26	5.61
1982	7.86	10.64	11.04	8.36	7.91	8.81	6.34	10.76	6.82	8.30	7.00	4.52	6.11
1983	8.19	11.14	11.36	8.70	8.23	9.27	6.60	11.18	7.32	8.70	7.39	4.76	6.51
1984	8.48	11.54	11.56	9.05	8.45	9.61	6.73	11.50	7.65	8.98	7.67	4.87	6.79
1985	8.73	11.87	11.75	9.40	8.60	9.88	6.83	11.81	7.97	9.28	7.98	4.98	7.10
1986	8.92	12.14	11.92	9.59	8.74	10.07	6.93	12.08	8.37	9.55	8.25	5.07	7.38
1987	9.13	12.17	12.15	9.77	8.92	10.32	7.02	12.36	8.73	9.85	8.57	5.17	7.69
1988	9.43	12.45	12.52	10.05	9.15	10.71	7.23	12.63	9.07	10.22	8.96	5.37	8.08
1989	9.80	12.91	12.98	10.35	9.46	11.12	7.46	12.99	9.54	10.69	9.46	5.62	8.58
1990	10.19	13.40	13.42	10.78	9.83	11.58	7.71	13.40	9.99	11.14	10.00	5.88	9.08
1991	10.50	13.82	13.65	11.13	10.08	11.95	7.89	13.90	10.42	11.50	10.49	6.06	9.39
1992	10.76	14.09	13.81	11.40	10.30	12.21	8.12	14.29	10.86	11.78	10.87	6.20	9.66
1993	11.03	14.12	14.04	11.70	10.55	12.57	8.36	14.86	11.36	11.96	11.21	6.32	9.90
1994	11.32	14.41	14.38	12.04	10.80	12.93	8.61	15.32	11.82	12.15	11.50	6.46	10.18
1995	11.64	14.78	14.73	12.34	11.10	13.34	8.85	15.68	12.28	12.53	11.80	6.62	10.51
1996	12.03	15.10	15.11	12.75	11.46	13.80	9.21	16.30	12.71	13.00	12.17	6.82	10.85
1997	12.49	15.57	15.67	13.14	11.90	14.41	9.59	17.14	13.22	13.57	12.56	7.13	11.29
1998	13.00	16.20	16.23	13.45	12.39	15.07	10.05	17.67	13.93	14.27	13.00	7.48	11.79
1999	13.47	16.33	16.80	13.85	12.82	15.62	10.45	18.40	14.47	14.85	13.44	7.76	12.26
2000	14.00	16.55	17.48	14.32	13.31	16.28	10.86	19.07	14.98	15.52	13.95	8.11	12.73
2001	14.53	17.00	18.00	14.76	13.70	16.77	11.29	19.80	15.59	16.33	14.64	8.35	13.27
2002	14.95	17.22	18.51	15.29	14.02	16.97	11.67	20.23	16.17	16.81	15.22	8.57	13.72
2002													
January	14.74	17.08	18.25	15.05	13.88	16.81	11.53	19.93	15.81	16.63	14.90	8.48	13.53
February	14.77	17.09	18.28	15.12	13.86	16.82	11.52	19.91	15.83	16.65	15.01	8.47	13.57
March	14.80	17.16	18.34	15.15	13.93	16.88	11.59	19.92	15.86	16.64	15.06	8.49	13.68
April	14.81	17.18	18.41	15.17	13.91	16.86	11.60	20.00	15.92	16.67	14.99	8.50	13.58
May	14.86	17.17	18.42	15.23	13.96	16.94	11.61	20.11	15.99	16.67	15.09	8.54	13.62
June	14.93	17.17	18.45	15.27	14.01	16.94	11.66	20.32	16.10	16.78	15.15	8.56	13.69
July	14.97	17.16	18.55	15.27	14.01	16.95	11.67	20.20	16.21	16.88	15.23	8.59	13.75
August	15.02	17.27	18.57	15.34	14.06	17.02	11.71	20.13	16.34	16.96	15.33	8.60	13.80
September	15.05	17.29	18.65	15.38	14.10	17.05	11.75	20.43	16.40	16.89	15.36	8.61	13.81
October	15.10	17.21	18.66	15.45	14.13	17.09	11.77	20.49	16.51	16.99	15.42	8.62	13.86
November	15.14	17.48	18.69	15.48	14.17	17.14	11.79	20.55	16.51	17.04	15.45	8.66	13.89
December	15.20	17.37	18.81	15.55	14.19	17.13	11.83	20.74	16.56	17.09	15.52	8.73	13.94

. . . = Not available.

Table 10-10. Average Weekly Earnings of Production or Nonsupervisory Workers on Private Nonfarm Payrolls by NAICS Supersector

(Dollars, seasonally adjusted.)

Year and month	Total private	Natural resources and mining	Construc-tion	Manu-facturing	Trade, transportation, and utilities			Information	Financial activities	Profes-sional and business services	Education and health services	Leisure and hospitality	Other services
					Total	Wholesale trade	Retail trade						
1947	...	60.49	43.34	44.55	...	...	...	...	...	...	...	...	...
1948	...	66.17	49.79	48.12	...	...	...	...	...	...	...	...	...
1949	...	63.79	52.33	49.00	...	...	...	...	...	...	...	...	...
1950	...	68.46	54.58	53.59	...	...	...	...	...	...	...	...	...
1951	...	75.58	61.76	59.02	...	...	...	...	...	...	...	...	...
1952	...	78.98	67.37	62.42	...	...	...	...	...	...	...	...	...
1953	...	84.66	71.42	66.18	...	...	...	...	...	...	...	...	...
1954	...	84.23	73.89	65.90	...	...	...	...	...	...	...	...	...
1955	...	90.95	76.33	70.99	...	...	...	...	...	...	...	...	...
1956	...	96.02	81.70	74.52	...	...	...	...	...	...	...	...	...
1957	...	99.66	85.88	77.01	...	...	...	...	...	...	...	...	...
1958	...	98.25	89.52	78.01	...	...	...	...	...	...	...	...	...
1959	...	105.25	94.13	83.82	...	...	...	...	...	...	...	...	...
1960	...	106.85	98.58	85.57	...	...	...	...	...	...	...	...	...
1961	...	109.04	103.97	87.78	...	...	...	...	...	...	...	...	...
1962	...	112.63	108.38	91.94	...	...	...	...	...	...	...	...	...
1963	...	116.10	113.02	95.00	...	...	...	...	...	...	...	...	...
1964	97.41	119.78	116.12	98.33	113.15	...	...	166.17	85.19	118.56	71.36	34.77	41.38
1965	101.52	125.42	122.42	102.59	116.42	...	...	171.20	88.30	122.34	74.62	37.05	45.13
1966	105.11	132.30	129.92	107.64	118.86	...	...	174.65	91.88	125.43	77.83	39.24	49.05
1967	108.02	137.85	138.30	110.03	121.28	...	...	175.97	95.20	128.47	81.42	41.94	52.75
1968	113.85	145.20	148.18	117.62	126.82	...	...	182.36	101.20	132.50	84.91	45.89	56.70
1969	120.75	156.82	165.12	124.64	131.89	...	...	189.88	107.75	139.39	91.39	49.86	63.35
1970	125.80	165.50	179.17	128.55	137.24	...	...	195.30	112.36	145.04	97.34	53.40	69.75
1971	133.58	174.36	194.39	137.66	144.36	...	...	204.61	117.57	151.23	103.56	56.81	76.61
1972	143.91	188.32	205.35	150.22	158.20	182.28	123.55	218.95	122.67	159.75	110.89	60.29	84.13
1973	152.77	201.04	219.11	161.58	165.54	190.08	128.41	230.14	129.22	167.56	117.88	63.21	91.05
1974	161.25	222.43	233.36	172.40	174.43	200.31	134.46	241.24	137.94	176.85	126.44	68.09	100.01
1975	170.28	248.22	250.18	186.05	182.73	213.10	140.76	253.27	147.70	185.68	134.97	72.58	108.50
1976	182.67	273.60	267.44	204.11	192.75	224.83	147.37	270.48	155.66	195.44	143.55	77.24	117.94
1977	195.30	299.49	279.72	223.67	204.12	239.90	154.85	288.51	165.80	206.47	153.40	83.18	128.26
1978	210.15	334.06	302.50	244.42	217.16	259.11	163.50	306.91	177.97	218.67	163.76	90.03	139.11
1979	225.35	366.54	326.63	264.11	231.87	279.10	173.02	324.28	190.63	230.82	175.17	97.00	150.48
1980	240.77	402.75	351.38	283.86	246.40	297.98	182.15	343.76	209.52	247.65	190.35	105.03	166.65
1981	261.54	446.04	382.98	312.83	263.50	322.09	194.27	370.62	228.24	267.54	208.33	114.59	185.13
1982	272.74	469.22	410.69	325.20	273.69	340.95	200.98	385.21	245.52	283.86	224.70	121.14	201.63
1983	285.83	489.05	427.14	348.87	284.76	359.68	208.56	404.72	262.79	299.28	237.22	127.57	214.83
1984	297.65	514.68	441.59	368.34	293.22	373.83	212.67	420.90	276.93	308.01	245.44	130.03	223.39
1985	304.68	529.40	448.85	380.70	295.84	383.34	213.10	431.07	287.72	317.38	254.56	131.47	232.88
1986	309.52	529.30	451.77	390.31	298.03	389.71	214.83	439.71	302.16	327.57	264.00	132.83	242.80
1987	316.81	529.40	464.13	399.59	304.17	397.32	217.62	451.14	314.28	337.86	274.24	135.97	252.23
1988	326.28	539.09	478.26	412.05	309.27	412.34	223.41	455.94	322.89	349.52	286.72	141.23	265.83
1989	338.10	569.33	497.13	423.32	319.75	427.01	229.02	468.94	339.62	365.60	302.72	146.68	282.28
1990	349.29	602.54	513.43	436.16	331.55	444.48	235.62	479.50	354.65	380.61	319.27	152.47	297.91
1991	358.06	625.42	520.41	449.73	339.19	459.27	240.15	495.20	369.57	391.09	334.55	155.16	306.91
1992	367.83	629.02	525.13	464.43	348.68	470.51	249.63	512.01	386.01	400.64	348.29	159.54	315.08
1993	378.40	634.77	539.81	480.80	359.33	484.46	256.89	535.25	403.02	406.20	359.08	163.45	322.69
1994	390.73	653.14	558.53	502.12	370.38	501.17	265.77	551.28	419.20	414.16	368.14	168.00	332.44
1995	399.53	670.32	571.57	509.26	378.79	515.14	272.56	564.98	436.12	426.44	377.73	171.43	342.36
1996	412.74	695.07	588.48	526.55	390.64	533.29	282.76	592.68	451.49	442.81	388.27	176.48	352.62
1997	431.25	720.11	609.48	548.22	407.57	559.39	295.97	622.40	472.37	465.51	404.65	185.81	368.63
1998	448.04	727.28	629.75	557.12	423.30	582.21	310.34	646.52	500.95	490.00	418.82	195.82	384.25
1999	462.49	721.74	655.11	573.17	434.31	602.77	321.63	675.32	517.57	510.99	431.35	202.87	398.77
2000	480.41	734.92	685.78	590.65	449.88	631.40	333.38	700.89	537.37	535.07	449.29	211.79	413.41
2001	493.20	757.92	695.89	595.19	459.53	643.45	346.16	731.11	558.02	557.84	473.39	215.19	428.64
2002	506.22	743.11	711.61	618.87	471.09	643.99	360.53	739.41	575.43	574.59	493.02	221.15	439.65
2002													
January	498.21	739.56	706.28	605.01	464.98	640.46	355.12	731.43	562.84	563.76	479.78	217.94	434.31
February	500.70	746.83	707.44	609.34	465.70	639.16	355.97	728.71	565.13	566.10	484.82	220.22	438.31
March	501.72	748.18	704.26	615.09	468.05	641.44	358.13	729.07	564.62	567.42	486.44	219.89	439.13
April	502.06	740.46	708.79	614.39	467.38	638.99	359.60	732.00	566.75	568.45	484.18	219.30	434.56
May	503.75	741.74	703.64	618.34	470.45	643.72	359.91	738.04	569.24	570.11	488.92	219.48	435.84
June	507.62	745.18	710.33	621.49	472.14	647.11	361.46	747.78	573.16	573.88	492.38	219.99	439.45
July	505.99	737.88	708.61	616.91	469.34	642.41	360.60	735.28	575.46	573.92	493.45	219.90	440.00
August	509.18	747.79	714.95	621.27	471.01	646.76	360.67	732.73	581.70	576.61	499.76	221.02	441.60
September	510.20	743.47	721.76	622.89	475.17	647.90	363.08	741.61	583.84	581.02	499.20	223.00	443.30
October	510.38	740.03	712.81	622.64	474.77	646.00	363.69	747.89	586.11	581.06	501.15	223.26	443.52
November	511.73	739.40	710.22	625.39	476.11	649.61	363.13	752.13	587.76	582.77	502.13	224.29	444.48
December	513.76	746.91	718.54	629.78	475.37	647.51	364.36	754.94	591.19	584.48	502.85	225.23	444.69

. . . = Not available.

NOTES AND DEFINITIONS

General note on employment data

This chapter includes two different data sets measuring employment. Both are compiled and published by the Bureau of Labor Statistics, but the two sets differ in their sources and other characteristics. Users should be aware of these differences and consequent differences in the uses and interpretations of data from the two systems. This issue is discussed below and also in the "Special Notes" at the front of the book.

One set of employment estimates comes from a sample survey of households, the Current Population Survey. In their scope (that is, the universe that they are planned to measure), these are the most comprehensive estimates; their total is of all civilian workers, including farm, household, self-employed, and unpaid family workers that are excluded from the other set of estimates. However, CPS data are characterized by periodic discontinuities when new benchmarks for Census measures of the total population are introduced. These updates are made in one month, usually January, and data for previous months are not modified to provide a smooth transition. Therefore, shorter-term comparisons, for a year or two or for a business cycle phase, will be misleading if such a discontinuity is included in the period. Currently, this will be the case for data for 2003, which should not be directly compared with the data for 2002 and earlier years presented in this volume. It should also be noted that the CPS is a count of persons employed, not of jobs; a person appears in these data only once no matter how many jobs he or she may hold.

The second set of employment estimates comes from a large survey of employers. It is benchmarked annually to a survey of all employers. Benchmark data are introduced with a smooth adjustment back to the previous benchmark, thus preserving the continuity of the series and making it more appropriate for measurement of employment change over the business cycle. The scope of the survey is wage and salary workers on nonfarm payrolls, and it is a count of jobs: a person with more than one job is counted as employed in each job.

These and other conceptual and technical differences between the two sets of estimates are described in more detail in the Notes and Definitions below.

TABLES 10-1 THROUGH 10-3 AND 20-5 LABOR FORCE, EMPLOYMENT, AND UNEMPLOYMENT

SOURCE: U.S. DEPARTMENT OF LABOR, BUREAU OF LABOR STATISTICS (BLS)

The labor force, employment and unemployment data are derived from the Current Population Survey (CPS), a sample survey of households conducted each month by the Bureau of the Census for the Bureau of Labor Statistics. The data pertain to the U.S. civilian noninstitutional population (population not in institutions) 16 years of age and over.

Due to changes in questionnaire design and survey methodology, data for 1994 and subsequent years are not fully comparable with data for 1993 and earlier years. In addition, discontinuities in the reported numbers of persons in the population, employment, unemployment, and labor force are introduced whenever periodic updates are made to U.S. population estimates. Population controls based on Census 2000 have been introduced beginning with the data for January 2000, which therefore are not comparable with data for December 1999 and earlier. Data for 1990 through 1999 incorporate 1990 census-based population controls and are not comparable with earlier years. An additional large population adjustment was introduced in January 2003, making the data from that time forward not comparable with the 2000–2002 data shown in this volume. Other discontinuities have been introduced in various years, usually with January data. See "Notes on the Data" below for additional information.

For the most part, these adjustments distort comparisons involving the *numbers of persons* in the population and labor force; they have little if any effect on the *percentages* that comprise the most important features of the CPS, that is the unemployment rates, the labor force participation rates, and the employment/population ratios.

Beginning with the data for January 2000, data classified by industry and occupation use the 2002 NAICS (see Chapter 14) and the 2000 Standard Occupational Classification System. This creates breaks in the time series for occupational and industry data at all levels of aggregation. For this reason, nearly all of the unemployment rates by industry and occupation shown in Table 10-3 are shown only from 2000 forward.

Other changes affecting classification by race and Hispanic origin have been introduced beginning with the January 2003 data. Since these do not affect the data shown in this volume, they will not be discussed at this time. These changes are described in the February 2003 issue of *Employment and Earnings*.

Definitions

The *civilian noninstitutional population* comprises all civilians 16 years of age and older who are not inmates of penal or mental institutions, sanitariums, or homes for the aged, infirm, or needy.

Civilian employment includes those civilians who (1) worked for pay or profit at any time during the week that includes the 12th day of the month (the survey week) or who worked unpaid for 15 hours or more in a family-operated enterprise or (2) were temporarily absent from regular jobs because of vacation, illness, industrial dispute, bad weather, or similar reasons. Each employed person is counted only once; those who hold more than one job are counted in the job at which they worked the greatest number of hours during the survey week.

Unemployed persons are all civilians who were not employed (according to the above definition) during the survey week, but were available for work, except for temporary illness, and had made specific efforts to find employment sometime during the prior 4 weeks. Persons who did not look for work because they were on layoff are also counted as unemployed.

The *civilian labor force* comprises all civilians classified as employed or unemployed.

Civilians in the noninstitutional population, 16 years of age and over, who are not classified as employed or unemployed are defined as "not in the labor force." This group includes those engaged in own-home housework, in school, unable to work because of long-term illness, retired, too old, seasonal workers for whom the survey week fell in an "off" season (not reported as unemployed), persons who became discouraged and gave up the search for work, and the voluntarily idle. Also included are those doing only incidental work (less than 15 hours) in a family business during the survey week.

Not in the labor force, want a job consists of persons who are not employed; are not counted as unemployed under the criteria given above; but who did want a job at the time of the survey.

The civilian *labor force participation rate* represents the percent of the civilian noninstitutional population (age 16 and over) that is in the civilian labor force.

The *employment to population ratio* represents the percent of the civilian noninstitutional population (age 16 and over) that is employed.

The *long-term unemployed* are persons currently unemployed (searching or on layoff) who have been unemployed for 15 consecutive weeks or longer. If a person ceases to look for work for 2 weeks or more, or is temporarily employed, the continuity of long-term unemployment is broken. If he or she starts searching for work or is laid off again, the monthly CPS will record the length of his or her unemployment as the time since the search was recommenced or since the latest layoff.

Median and average weeks unemployed are summary measures of the length of time that persons classified as unemployed have been looking for work. For persons on layoff, the duration represents the number of full weeks they have been on layoff. Mean number of weeks is the

arithmetic average computed by aggregating all the weeks of unemployment experienced by all unemployed persons (during their current spell of unemployment) and dividing by the number of unemployed. Median number of weeks unemployed is the number of weeks of unemployment experienced by the person at the midpoint of the distribution of all unemployed persons, ranked by duration of unemployment.

The civilian *unemployment rate* is the number of unemployed as a percent of the civilian labor force. The unemployment rates for groups within the civilian population (such as, for example, males 20 years and over) are the number of unemployed in a group as a percent of the labor force in that group. The unemployment rates by industry and occupation refer to experienced wage and salary workers and are based on industry or occupation of the last job held, according to the NAICS or the 2000 Standard Occupational System.

The *augmented unemployment rate* is a broader measure of potential labor availability used by the Federal Reserve Board, based on BLS data. The numbers shown here, as percentages, are calculated by the editors of *Business Statistics* using the Federal Reserve definition: the numerator, augmented unemployment, is the number of unemployed plus those who are not in the labor force and want a job; the denominator, the augmented labor force, is the number in the civilian labor force plus the number of those who are not in the labor force and want a job.

Notes on the data

The CPS data are collected monthly by trained interviewers from sample households selected to represent the U.S. population 16 years of age and older. Sample size was about 60,000 households from mid-1989 to mid-1995 but was reduced in two stages to about 50,000 households beginning in January 1996, establishing the level maintained from 1996 through 2000. Beginning with the data for July 2001, the sample size has been increased back to 60,000 households, as part of a plan to meet the requirements of the State Children's Health Insurance Program legislation. The data collected are based on the activity or status reported for the calendar week, Sunday through Saturday, that includes the 12th day of the month. Households are interviewed on a rotating basis so that three-fourths of the sample is the same for any 2 consecutive months and one-half is common with the same month a year earlier.

Data relating to 1994 and subsequent years are not strictly comparable with data for 1993 and earlier years because of the introduction of a major redesign of the survey questionnaire and collection methodology. The redesign includes new and revised questions for the classification of individuals as employed or unemployed, the collection of new data on multiple job holding, a change in the definition of discouraged workers, and the implementation of more completely automated data collection.

The 1994 redesign of the CPS was the most extensive in many years. However, there are other significant periods of year-to-year noncomparability in the labor force data, which typically result from the introduction of new decennial census data into the CPS estimation procedures, expansions of the sample, and other improvements made to increase the reliability of the estimates. Each change introduces a discontinuity, usually between December of the previous year and January of the newly altered year. The discontinuities are usually minor or negligible with respect to figures expressed as percents (unemployment rate or labor force participation rate), but can be significant with respect to levels (labor force and employment in thousands of persons). A list of the major discontinuities follows. They occur in January unless otherwise indicated.

- 1953: 1950 census data introduced.
- 1960: Alaska and Hawaii included.
- 1962: 1960 census data introduced.
- 1972: 1970 census data introduced.
- March 1973: further 1970 census data introduced, affecting racial groups.
- July 1975: adjustment for refugee inflow.
- 1978: sample expansion and revised estimation procedures.
- 1982: change in estimation procedures.
- 1986, with revisions carried back to 1980: adjustment for better estimates of immigration.
- 1994: 1990 census data introduced and carried back to 1990.
- 1997: new estimates of immigration and emigration.
- 1998: new population estimates and estimation procedures.
- 1999: new information on immigration.
- 2000: Census 2000 data introduced, using the 2002 NAICS and the 2000 Standard Occupational Classification System.
- 2003: Further population estimates introduced but not carried back to 2000.

For further information on any of these changes, including the magnitude of the discontinuity introduced, see the BLS publication *Employment and Earnings*, February 2003.

Nonagricultural employment estimates from the CPS differ in level and trend from estimates compiled from establishment payrolls (as shown in Table 10-5). The differences are attributable in part to differences in definitions and coverage and in part to differences in sample design, collection methodology, and the sampling variability inherent in the surveys.

- The CPS data cover the total farm and nonfarm economy and include domestics and other private household workers, self-employed persons, and unpaid family workers who worked 15 hours or more in the survey week in family-operated enterprises. The payroll or establishment survey, on the other hand, covers only employees on payrolls of nonfarm establishments.
- Persons holding more than one job during the survey week are counted once in the household survey, but multiple jobholders are counted each time (on each payroll) in the establishment survey.
- Persons with a job but not at work (absent because of bad weather, work stoppages, personal reasons, etc.) are included in the household survey but are excluded from the payroll survey if on leave without pay for the entire payroll period.

See recent issues of *Employment and Earnings*.

The monthly labor force, employment, and unemployment data are seasonally adjusted by the X-12-ARIMA method. All seasonally adjusted civilian labor force and unemployment rate statistics, as well as the major employment and unemployment estimates, are computed by aggregating independently adjusted series. For example, the seasonally adjusted level of total unemployment is the sum of the seasonally adjusted levels of unemployment for the four sex-age groups (men and women 16 to 19, and men and women 20 years and over). Seasonally adjusted employment is the sum of the seasonally adjusted levels of employment for the same four groups. The seasonally adjusted civilian labor force is the sum of all eight components. Finally, the seasonally adjusted civilian worker unemployment rate is calculated by taking total seasonally adjusted unemployment as a percent of the total seasonally adjusted civilian labor force. Seasonal adjustment factors are revised at the end of each year to reflect recent experience, and the revisions affect the preceding 4 years as well. See *Employment and Earnings*, February 2003, for further information.

Data availability

Data for each month usually are released on the first Friday of the following month in a press release that also contains data from the establishment survey (Tables 10-5 through 10-10). Data are subsequently published in the BLS monthly periodical *Employment and Earnings*, which also contains detailed explanatory notes. Selected data are published each month in the *Monthly Labor Review*, which also contains frequent articles analyzing labor force, employment, and unemployment developments.

Monthly and annual data beginning with 1948 are available. Historical unadjusted data are published in *Labor*

Force Statistics Derived from the Current Population Survey, BLS Bulletin 2307. Historical seasonally-adjusted data are available from BLS upon request. Complete historical data are available on the BLS Internet site at <http://www.bls.gov>.

References

Historical background on the CPS, as well as a description of the 1994 redesign, are found in three articles in the September 1993 *Monthly Labor Review*: "Why Is It Necessary to Change"; "Redesigning the Questionnaire"; and "Evaluating Changes in the Estimates." The redesign also is described in the February 1994 issue of *Employment and Earnings*. See also Chapter 1, "Labor Force Data Derived from the Current Population Survey," *BLS Handbook of Methods*, Bulletin 2490 (April 1997).

TABLE 10-4
INSURED UNEMPLOYMENT

SOURCE: U.S. DEPARTMENT OF LABOR, EMPLOYMENT AND TRAINING ADMINISTRATION

State programs of unemployment insurance cover operations of regular programs under state unemployment insurance laws. In 1976, the law was amended to extend coverage (effective January 1, 1978) to include virtually all state and local government employees plus many agricultural and domestic workers.

The federal civilian employees unemployment insurance program (UCFE) provides unemployment insurance protection to civilian employees of the federal government or of wholly or partially owned instrumentalities, with the following exceptions: Elective officers in the executive and legislative branches of government, certain foreign service personnel, temporary emergency workers, and other small groups.

Unemployment compensation for ex-service members (UCX) provides unemployment insurance protection to veterans under the law of the state in which the claim for compensation is filed.

An *initial claim* is the first claim in a benefit year filed by a worker after losing his job, or the first claim filed at the beginning of a subsequent period of unemployment in the same benefit year. The initial claim establishes the starting date for any insured unemployment that may result if the claimant is unemployed for 1 week or longer. Transitional claims (filed by persons as they start a new benefit year in a continuing spell of unemployment) are excluded; therefore, the data more closely represent instances of new unemployment.

Monthly averages in this book are averages, calculated by the editors, of the weekly data published by the

Employment and Training Administration. Annual data are averages of the monthly data.

Data availability

Data are published in weekly press releases from the Employment and Training Administration. These releases are available on their Internet site at <http://www.doleta.gov>. Also, historical data on weekly claims are available at the Department of Labor's Information Technology Support Center at <http://www.itsc.state.md.us>.

TABLES 10-5, 10-6, 16-1, 16-2, AND 20-6
NONAGRICULTURAL EMPLOYMENT

SOURCE: U.S. DEPARTMENT OF LABOR, BUREAU OF LABOR STATISTICS (BLS)

The nonagricultural employment data, as well as the hours and earnings data in Tables 10-7 through 10-10, 16-3 through 16-7, and 20-6, are compiled from payroll records. Information is reported monthly on a voluntary basis to the BLS and its cooperating state agencies by a large sample of establishments representing all industries except agriculture.

The survey, originally based on a stratified quota sample, has been replaced on a phased-in basis by a stratified probability sample. The new sampling procedure went into effect for wholesale trade in June 2000; for mining, construction, and manufacturing in June 2001; and for retail trade, transportation and public utilities, finance, insurance, and real estate in June 2002. The phase-in was completed in June 2003 when it was extended to the service industries. The phase-in schedule was slightly different for the state and area series.

The sample has always been very large. Currently, it includes about 160,000 businesses and government agencies covering approximately 400,000 individual worksites, accounting for about one-third of total benchmark employment of payroll workers.

These data, formally known as the Current Employment Statistics (CES) survey, often are referred to as the "establishment data" or the "payroll data" and are also known as the BLS-790 survey. The data by industry conform to the definitions in the new North American Industry Classification System (NAICS) beginning in 2003. Historical time series have been reconstructed on NAICS and all published series have a NAICS-based history extending back to at least January 1990. For total nonfarm and other high-level aggregates, NAICS history extends back to January 1939. For more detailed series, the starting date for NAICS data varies depending on the scope of the definitional changes between the old Standard Industrial Classification (SIC) and NAICS.

Definitions

An *establishment* is an economic unit that produces goods or services (such as a factory or store) at a single location and is engaged in one type of economic activity.

Employment comprises all persons who received pay (including holiday and sick pay) for any part of the payroll period including the 12th day of the month. Included are all full-time and part-time workers in nonfarm establishments. Persons holding more than one job are counted in each establishment that reports them. Not covered are proprietors, the self-employed, unpaid volunteer or family workers, farm workers, domestic workers in households, and military personnel; salaried officers of corporations are included.

Persons on an establishment payroll who are on paid sick leave (when pay is received directly from the employer), on paid holiday or vacation, or who work during a portion of the pay period even though they are unemployed or on strike during the rest of the period are counted as employed. Not counted as employed are persons who are laid off, on leave without pay, or on strike for the entire period, or who are hired but have not been paid during the period.

Intermittent workers are counted if they performed any service during the month. BLS considers regular full-time teachers (private and governmental) to be employed during the summer vacation period whether or not they are specifically paid in those months.

The government division includes federal, state, and local activities such as legislative, executive, and judicial functions, as well as the Postal Service and all government-owned and government-operated business enterprises, establishments, and institutions (arsenals, navy yards, hospitals, state-owned utilities, etc.), and government force account construction. The definition and measurement of federal government employment has been changed somewhat. The previous national series was an end-of-month federal employee count produced by the Office of Personnel Management that excluded some workers, mostly employees who work in Department of Defense-owned establishments such as military base commissaries. The national series now includes these workers. Also, employment is now estimated from a sample of federal establishments, is benchmarked annually to counts from unemployment insurance tax records, and reflects employee counts as of the pay period including the 12th of the month, consistent with other CES industry series. As before, however, the CES excludes the military and employees of the Central Intelligence Agency, the National Security Agency, and the Defense Intelligence Agency.

Nonagricultural employment in these series differs from the measures in the household survey (Tables 10-1 through 10-3) in that, among other factors, it excludes domestics and other private household workers, self-employed persons, and unpaid family workers. Persons holding more than one job during the survey week are counted once in the household survey, but multiple jobholders are counted each time (on each payroll) in the establishment survey. Persons with a job but not at work (absent because of bad weather, work stoppages, personal reasons, etc.) are included in the household survey but are excluded from the payroll survey if on leave without pay for the entire payroll period. Finally, there is no age limit in the establishment survey, whereas the household survey is limited to persons 16 years and older.

The *diffusion index of employment change*, currently based on 278 nonagricultural industries, represents the percent of industries in which employment was rising over a 6-month span, plus one-half of the industries with unchanged employment. It is based on seasonally adjusted data and centered within the span; that is, the diffusion index reported for June represents the change from March to September. *Business Statistics* uses the June value to represent the year. Diffusion indexes measure the dispersion of economic gains and losses, with values below 50 percent associated with recessions.

Production or nonsupervisory workers. These data are collected for the private nonfarm sector and cover all production and related workers in mining and manufacturing; construction workers in construction; and nonsupervisory workers in transportation, communication, electric, gas, and sanitary services; wholesale and retail trade; finance, insurance, and real estate; and services. These groups account for about four-fifths of the total employment on private nonagricultural payrolls.

Production and related workers include working supervisors and all nonsupervisory workers (including group leaders and trainees) engaged in fabricating, processing, assembling, inspecting, receiving, storing, handling, packing, warehousing, shipping, trucking, hauling, maintenance, repair, janitorial, guard services, product development, auxiliary production for plant's own use (for example, power plant), record keeping, and other services closely associated with these production operations.

Construction workers include the following employees in the construction division of the SIC: Working supervisors, qualified craft workers, mechanics, apprentices, laborers, etc., engaged in new work, alterations, demolition, repair, maintenance, etc., whether working at the site of construction or working in shops or yards at jobs (such as precutting and preassembling) ordinarily performed by members of the construction trades.

Nonsupervisory employees include employees (not above the working supervisory level) such as office and clerical workers, repairers, salespersons, operators, drivers, physicians, lawyers, accountants, nurses, social workers, research aides, teachers, drafters, photographers, beauticians, musicians, restaurant workers, custodial workers, attendants, line installers and repairers, laborers, janitors, guards, and other employees at similar occupational levels whose services are closely associated with those of the employees listed.

Notes on the data

Benchmark adjustments. The establishment survey data are adjusted annually to comprehensive counts of employment (called "benchmarks"). Benchmark information on employment, by industry, is compiled by state agencies from reports of establishments covered under state unemployment insurance laws, in an annual compilation of administrative data known as the ES-202. These tabulations cover about 98 percent of all employees on nonfarm payrolls. Benchmark data for the residual are obtained from the records of the Social Security Administration and a number of other agencies in private industry or government. The latest benchmark adjustment (which is incorporated in the data in this volume) lowered the employment level in March 2002 by 203,000 below the previous estimate.

The estimates for the benchmark month are compared with new benchmark levels, industry by industry. If revisions are necessary, the monthly series of estimates between benchmark periods are adjusted by graduated amounts between the new benchmark and the preceding one, and the new benchmark level for each industry is then carried forward to the current month by use of the sample changes.

The probability sampling frame and sample are updated twice a year with new quarters of UI-based data which help keep the sample up to date by adding new firm births and deleting business deaths. Additional model-based procedures are used to estimate business births and deaths that occur after the latest quarterly report. A principal purpose of the new procedure is to better capture cyclical turning points.

Not-seasonally-adjusted data for all months since the last benchmark to which the series has been adjusted are subject to revision.

Seasonal adjustment. The seasonal movements that recur periodically (such as warm and cold weather, holidays, vacations, etc.) are generally the largest single component of month-to-month changes in employment. After adjusting the data to remove such seasonal variation, the basic trends are more evident. BLS now uses X-12 ARIMA software to produce the seasonal factors and is

using concurrent seasonal adjustment, developing new factors each month using the most current data. Seasonal adjustment factors are directly applied to the component levels. Seasonally adjusted totals for employment series are then obtained by aggregating seasonally adjusted components directly, while hours and earnings series represent weighted averages of the seasonally adjusted component series. Seasonally adjusted data are not published for a small number of series characterized by small seasonal components relative to their trend and/or irregular components. These series, however, are used in aggregating to broader seasonally adjusted levels.

Seasonal adjustment factors for federal government employment are derived from unadjusted data that include Christmas temporary workers employed by the Postal Service. The number of temporary census workers for the decennial census was removed, however, from the calculation of seasonal adjustment factors.

Revisions of the seasonally adjusted data, usually for the most recent 5-year period, are made once a year coincident with the benchmark revisions.

Data availability

Employment data by industry division are available beginning with 1919. Data for each month usually are released on the first Friday of the following month in a press release that also contains data from the household survey (Tables 10-1 through 10-3). Data are subsequently published in the BLS monthly periodical *Employment and Earnings*, which also contains detailed explanatory notes. Selected data are published each month in the *Monthly Labor Review*, which also contains frequent articles analyzing labor force, employment, and unemployment developments. Complete historical data are available on the BLS Internet site at <http://www.bls.gov>.

References

The changes incorporated in June 2003 are described in "Recent changes in the national Current Employment Statistics survey," *Monthly Labor Review*, June 2003, and in the June 2003 issue of *Employment and Earnings*. Descriptive material is also available on the BLS Internet site. Also see Chapter 2 "Employment, Hours, and Earnings from the Establishment Survey," *BLS Handbook of Methods*, Bulletin 2490 (April 1997).

TABLES 10-7, 10-8, 16-3, 16-6, AND 20-6 AVERAGE HOURS PER WEEK; AGGREGATE EMPLOYEE HOURS

Source: U.S. Department of Labor, Bureau of Labor Statistics (BLS)

See the Notes and Definitions to Tables 10-5 and 10-6,

just preceding, for an overall description of the "establishment" or "payroll" survey that is the source of hours data.

Definitions

Hours represent the average weekly hours for which production or nonsupervisory workers received pay. Average weekly hours are different from standard or scheduled hours. Such factors as unpaid absenteeism, labor turnover, part-time work, and work stoppages cause average weekly hours to be lower than scheduled hours of work for an establishment. These hours pertain to jobs, not to persons; thus, a person with two half-time jobs is represented as two jobs each with a 20-hour workweek in this series, not as one person with a 40-hour week.

Overtime hours represent the portion of average weekly hours which was in excess of regular hours and for which overtime premiums were paid. Weekend and holiday hours are included only if overtime premiums were paid. Hours for which only shift differential, hazard, incentive, or other similar types of premiums were paid are excluded.

Production or nonsupervisory workers. See the Notes and Definitions to Tables 10-5 and 10-6.

Aggregate hours. These provide a partial measure of labor input to the industry. Data pertain to production and nonsupervisory workers in nonfarm establishments. The indexes are obtained by multiplying seasonally adjusted production or nonsupervisory worker employment by seasonally adjusted average weekly hours and dividing by the monthly average for the 2002 period. For total private, goods-producing, service-producing, and major industry divisions, the indexes are obtained by summing the seasonally adjusted aggregate weekly employee hours for the component industries and dividing by the monthly average for the 2002 period.

Notes on the data

Benchmark adjustments. Independent benchmarks are not available for the hours and earnings series. At the time of the annual adjustment of the employment series to new benchmarks, the levels of hours and earnings may be affected by the revised employment weights (which are used in computing the industry averages for hours and earnings), as well as by the changes in seasonal adjustment factors also introduced with the benchmark revision.

Method of computing industry series. "Average weekly hours" for individual industries are computed by dividing production or nonsupervisory worker hours (reported by establishments classified in each industry) by the number of production or nonsupervisory workers reported for the same establishments. Estimates for divisions and major industry groups are averages (weighted by employment) of the figures for component industries.

Seasonal adjustment. Hours and earnings series are seasonally adjusted by applying factors directly to the corresponding unadjusted series. Data for some industries are not seasonally adjusted because the seasonal component is small relative to the trend-cycle and/or irregular components and consequently cannot be separated with sufficient precision.

Data availability

Data for each month usually are released on the first Friday of the following month in a press release that also contains employment data from the household and establishment surveys (Tables 10-1 through 10-3, 10-5, and 10-6). Data subsequently are published in the BLS monthly periodical *Employment and Earnings*, which also contains detailed explanatory notes. Selected data are published each month in the Monthly Labor Review. Complete historical data are available on the BLS Internet site at <http://www.bls.gov>.

References

See references for Tables 10-5 and 10-6, above.

TABLES 10-9, 10-10, 16-4, 16-5, AND 20-6 HOURLY AND WEEKLY EARNINGS

Source: U.S. Department of Labor, Bureau of Labor Statistics (BLS)

See the Notes and Definitions to Tables 10-5 and 10-6 for an overall description of the "establishment" or "payroll" survey that is the source of these earnings data.

Definitions

Earnings are the payments that production or nonsupervisory workers receive during the survey period (before deductions for taxes and other items), including premium pay for overtime or late-shift work but excluding irregular bonuses, tips, and other special payments.

Real earnings are earnings adjusted to reflect the effects of changes in consumer prices as measured by the Consumer Price Index for Urban Wage Earners and Clerical Workers (CPI-W).

Production or nonsupervisory workers. See the Notes and Definitions to Tables 10-5 and 10-6.

Notes on the data

The hours and earnings series are based on reports of gross payroll and corresponding paid hours for full- and part-time production and related workers, construction workers, or nonsupervisory workers who received pay for any part of the pay period that included the 12th of the month.

Total payrolls are before deductions; for the employee share of old-age and unemployment insurance, group insurance, withholding taxes, bonds, and union dues. The payroll figures also include pay for overtime, holidays, vacations, and sick leave (paid directly by the employer for the period reported). Excluded from the payroll figures are fringe benefits (health and other types of insurance, contributions to retirement, etc., paid by the employer, and the employer share of payroll taxes); bonuses (unless earned and paid regularly each pay period); other pay not earned in the pay period reported (retroactive pay); tips; and the value of free rent, fuel, meals, or other payment in kind. The exclusion of tips is particularly significant for hotels, motels, and eating and drinking places.

Average hourly earnings data are on a "gross" basis; that is, they reflect not only changes in basic hourly and incentive wage rates but also such variable factors as premium pay for overtime and late-shift work, and changes in output of workers paid on an incentive basis. Also, shifts in the volume of employment between relatively high-paid and low-paid work affect the general average of hourly earnings.

Averages of hourly earnings should not be confused with *wage rates*, which represent the rates stipulated for a given unit of work or time, while earnings refer to the actual return to the worker for a stated period of time. The earnings series do not represent total labor cost to the employer because of the exclusion of irregular bonuses, retroactive items, the cost of employer-provided benefits, payroll taxes paid by employers, and earnings for those employees not covered under the production-worker or nonsupervisory-worker definition. Additionally, average weekly earnings are not the amounts available to workers for spending, since they do not reflect such deductions as those for income and social security taxes, etc.

Method of computing industry series. Average hourly earnings are obtained by dividing the reported total production or nonsupervisory worker payroll by the total production or nonsupervisory worker hours. Estimates for both hours and hourly earnings for nonfarm divisions and major industry groups are employment-weighted averages of the figures for component industries.

Average weekly earnings are computed by multiplying average hourly earnings by average weekly hours. In addition to the factors mentioned above, which exert varying influences upon average hourly earnings, average weekly earnings are affected by changes in the length of the workweek, part-time work, work stoppages, labor turnover, and absenteeism. Persistent long-term increases in the proportion of part-time workers in retail trade and many of the service industries have reduced average workweeks and have affected the average weekly earnings series.

Average weekly earnings are per job, not per person; a person with two half-time jobs will be reflected as two jobs with low weekly earnings rather than one person with the total earnings from his or her two jobs.

Independent benchmarks are not available for the hours and earnings series. At the time of the annual adjustment of the employment series to new benchmarks, the levels of hours and earnings may be affected by the revised employment weights (which are used in computing the industry averages for hours and earnings), as well as by the changes in seasonal adjustment factors also introduced with the benchmark revision.

Seasonal adjustment. Hours and earnings series are seasonally adjusted by applying factors directly to the corresponding unadjusted series; seasonally adjusted average weekly earnings are the product of seasonally adjusted hourly earnings and weekly hours. Weekly earnings in constant dollars, seasonally adjusted, are obtained by dividing seasonally adjusted average weekly earnings by the seasonally adjusted Consumer Price Index for Urban Wage Earners and Clerical Workers (CPI-W).

Data availability

Data for each month usually are released on the first Friday of the following month in a press release that also contains employment and hours data from the household and establishment surveys (Tables 10-1 through 10-3 and 10-5 through 10-8). Data subsequently are published in the BLS monthly periodical *Employment and Earnings*, which also contains detailed explanatory notes. Selected data are published each month in the *Monthly Labor Review*. Complete historical data are available on the BLS Internet site at <http://www.bls.gov>.

References

See references for Tables 10-5 and 10-6 above.

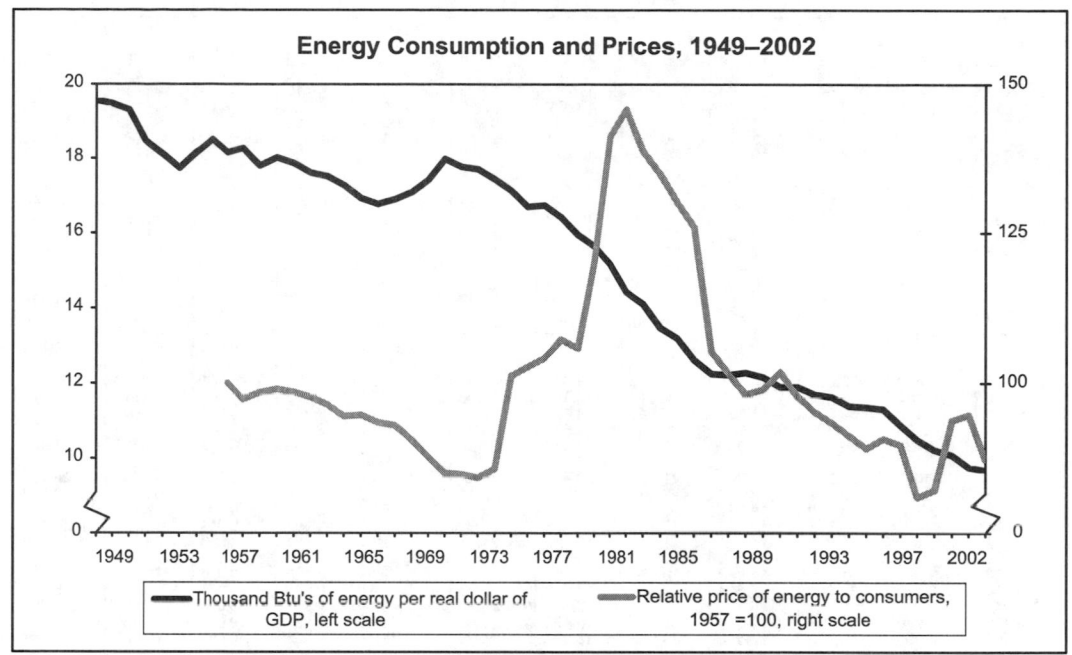

Energy Consumption and Prices, 1949–2002

Thousand Btu's of energy per real dollar of GDP, left scale

Relative price of energy to consumers, 1957 =100, right scale

- Throughout the postwar period, there appears to have been a long-term downtrend in the relationship of energy use to real gross domestic product (GDP). This may be because the relative share of services and high-tech goods in the composition of output is rising, with a correspondingly falling relative importance of energy-intensive production processes such as primary metals and chemicals manufacturing. Still, this trend is striking in light of the continued rise in motor vehicle use, air conditioning, air travel, and other consumer uses of energy. (Table 11-2)

- Changes in energy prices relative to other prices provide only a partial explanation, as the graph suggests. The decline in energy use accelerated as energy prices rose from 1973 through 1981. Since then, relative prices of energy (consumer energy prices divided by all other consumer prices) have declined, reaching below 1972 levels by 1998. Yet the energy efficiency of aggregate production continued to increase, although at a slower rate. (Tables 11-2 and 8-1)

- Comparing business cycle peak years 1973 and 2000, the greatest savings in energy relative to GDP were achieved in industrial use, which rose only 6 percent between those years while real GDP increased by 126 percent and industrial production rose 106 percent. But relative economies were also achieved in aggregate use of energy for residential and commercial purposes, which rose 54 percent, and for transportation, which rose 44 percent. (Table 11-1)

- Most of the decline in energy relative to GDP in recent years has been in the use of petroleum and natural gas. Before 1973, on the other hand, oil and gas use was rising relative to GDP while the use of other energy sources was declining. (Table 11-2)

- Imports supplied 30 percent of total energy consumption in 2002, compared with 19 percent in 1973 and only 5 percent in 1949. Domestic production of both crude oil and natural gas increased up until the early 1970s. Both have declined since then, with the greater decline in crude oil. Domestic coal production and nuclear energy generation have increased. (Table 11-1)

Table 11-1. Energy Supply and Consumption

(Quadrillion Btu.)

Year and month	Imports	Exports	Production, by source								Consumption, by end-use sector			
			Total[1]	Coal	Natural gas	Crude oil	Natural gas plant liquids	Nuclear electric power	Hydro-electric power	Geo-thermal energy	Total	Residential and commercial	Industrial	Transportation
1949	1.448	1.592	31.722	11.974	5.377	10.683	0.714	0.000	1.425	...	31.982	9.275	14.717	7.990
1950	1.913	1.465	35.540	14.060	6.233	11.447	0.823	0.000	1.415	...	34.616	9.890	16.233	8.493
1951	1.892	2.622	38.751	14.419	7.416	13.037	0.920	0.000	1.424	...	36.974	10.263	17.669	9.042
1952	2.146	2.365	37.917	12.734	7.964	13.281	0.998	0.000	1.466	...	36.748	10.443	17.302	9.003
1953	2.313	1.866	38.181	12.278	8.339	13.671	1.062	0.000	1.413	...	37.664	10.340	18.201	9.123
1954	2.348	1.696	36.518	10.542	8.682	13.427	1.113	0.000	1.360	...	36.639	10.590	17.146	8.903
1955	2.790	2.286	40.148	12.370	9.345	14.410	1.240	0.000	1.360	...	40.208	11.185	19.472	9.551
1956	3.207	2.945	42.622	13.306	10.002	15.180	1.283	0.000	1.435	...	41.754	11.698	20.196	9.860
1957	3.529	3.439	42.983	13.061	10.605	15.178	1.289	0.000	1.516	...	41.787	11.686	20.205	9.897
1958	3.884	2.050	40.133	10.783	10.942	14.204	1.287	0.002	1.592	...	41.645	12.333	19.307	10.005
1959	4.076	1.534	41.949	10.778	11.952	14.933	1.383	0.002	1.548	...	43.466	12.800	20.316	10.349
1960	4.188	1.477	42.804	10.817	12.656	14.935	1.461	0.006	1.608	0.001	45.087	13.667	20.823	10.597
1961	4.437	1.377	43.280	10.447	13.105	15.206	1.549	0.020	1.656	0.002	45.739	14.032	20.937	10.770
1962	4.994	1.473	44.877	10.901	13.717	15.522	1.593	0.026	1.816	0.002	47.828	14.839	21.768	11.221
1963	5.087	1.835	47.174	11.849	14.513	15.966	1.709	0.038	1.771	0.004	49.646	15.261	22.730	11.655
1964	5.447	1.815	49.056	12.524	15.298	16.164	1.803	0.040	1.886	0.005	51.817	15.730	24.090	11.998
1965	5.892	1.829	50.676	13.055	15.775	16.521	1.883	0.043	2.059	0.004	54.017	16.509	25.075	12.434
1966	6.146	1.829	53.534	13.468	17.011	17.561	1.996	0.064	2.062	0.004	57.017	17.517	26.397	13.102
1967	6.159	2.115	56.379	13.825	17.943	18.651	2.177	0.088	2.347	0.007	58.908	18.541	26.616	13.752
1968	6.905	1.998	58.225	13.609	19.068	19.308	2.321	0.142	2.349	0.009	62.419	19.665	27.888	14.866
1969	7.676	2.126	60.541	13.863	20.446	19.556	2.420	0.154	2.648	0.013	65.621	21.000	29.114	15.506
1970	8.342	2.632	63.501	14.607	21.666	20.401	2.512	0.239	2.634	0.011	67.844	22.105	29.641	16.098
1971	9.535	2.151	62.723	13.186	22.280	20.033	2.544	0.413	2.824	0.012	69.289	22.959	29.601	16.729
1972	11.387	2.118	63.920	14.092	22.208	20.041	2.598	0.584	2.864	0.031	72.704	24.036	30.953	17.716
1973	14.613	2.033	63.585	13.992	22.187	19.493	2.569	0.910	2.861	0.043	75.708	24.437	32.653	18.612
1974	14.304	2.203	62.372	14.074	21.210	18.575	2.471	1.272	3.177	0.053	73.991	24.046	31.819	18.119
1975	14.032	2.323	61.357	14.989	19.640	17.729	2.374	1.900	3.155	0.070	71.999	24.308	29.447	18.244
1976	16.760	2.172	61.602	15.654	19.480	17.262	2.327	2.111	2.976	0.078	76.012	25.476	31.429	19.099
1977	19.948	2.052	62.052	15.755	19.565	17.454	2.327	2.702	2.333	0.077	78.000	25.866	32.307	19.820
1978	19.106	1.920	63.137	14.910	19.485	18.434	2.245	3.024	2.937	0.064	79.986	26.637	32.733	20.615
1979	19.460	2.855	65.948	17.540	20.076	18.104	2.286	2.776	2.931	0.084	80.903	26.469	33.962	20.471
1980	15.796	3.695	67.241	18.598	19.908	18.249	2.254	2.739	2.900	0.110	78.289	26.442	32.152	19.696
1981	13.719	4.307	67.007	18.377	19.699	18.146	2.307	3.008	2.758	0.123	76.335	25.990	30.836	19.506
1982	11.861	4.608	66.574	18.639	18.319	18.309	2.191	3.131	3.266	0.105	73.234	26.457	27.704	19.069
1983	11.752	3.693	64.106	17.247	16.593	18.392	2.184	3.203	3.527	0.129	73.066	26.411	27.511	19.141
1984	12.471	3.786	68.832	19.719	18.008	18.848	2.274	3.553	3.386	0.165	76.693	27.239	29.643	19.808
1985	11.781	4.196	67.647	19.325	16.980	18.992	2.241	4.076	2.970	0.198	76.417	27.393	28.958	20.070
1986	14.151	4.021	67.087	19.509	16.541	18.376	2.149	4.380	3.071	0.219	76.722	27.527	28.375	20.817
1987	15.398	3.812	67.608	20.141	17.136	17.665	2.215	4.754	2.635	0.229	79.156	28.184	29.519	21.455
1988	17.296	4.366	68.951	20.738	17.599	17.279	2.260	5.587	2.334	0.217	82.774	29.640	30.818	22.312
1989	18.766	4.661	69.364	21.346	17.847	16.117	2.158	5.602	2.837	0.317	84.886	30.930	31.396	22.551
1990	18.817	4.752	70.729	22.456	18.326	15.571	2.175	6.104	3.046	0.336	84.605	30.181	31.918	22.526
1991	18.335	5.141	70.362	21.594	18.229	15.701	2.306	6.422	3.016	0.346	84.522	30.873	31.527	22.122
1992	19.372	4.937	69.933	21.629	18.375	15.223	2.363	6.479	2.617	0.349	85.866	30.734	32.673	22.459
1993	21.273	4.258	68.262	20.249	18.584	14.494	2.408	6.410	2.892	0.364	87.579	32.037	32.669	22.883
1994	22.390	4.061	70.676	22.111	19.348	14.103	2.391	6.694	2.683	0.338	89.248	32.194	33.557	23.503
1995	22.260	4.511	71.156	22.029	19.082	13.887	2.442	7.075	3.205	0.294	91.221	33.317	33.941	23.960
1996	23.702	4.633	72.472	22.684	19.344	13.723	2.530	7.087	3.590	0.316	94.224	34.803	34.905	24.511
1997	25.215	4.514	72.389	23.211	19.394	13.658	2.495	6.597	3.640	0.325	94.727	34.746	35.167	24.808
1998	26.581	4.299	72.787	23.935	19.613	13.235	2.420	7.068	3.297	0.328	95.146	35.016	34.777	25.357
1999	27.252	3.715	71.652	23.186	19.341	12.451	2.528	7.610	3.268	0.331	96.774	35.981	34.679	26.108
2000	28.974	4.006	71.218	22.623	19.662	12.358	2.611	7.862	2.811	0.317	98.942	37.619	34.616	26.705
2001	30.157	3.770	71.372	23.053	20.227	12.282	2.547	8.028	2.201	0.311	96.320	37.565	32.480	26.274
2002	29.401	3.661	70.803	22.564	19.561	12.163	2.559	8.145	2.668	0.304	97.625	38.397	32.568	26.657
2001														
January	2.697	0.346	6.280	2.169	1.732	1.043	0.162	0.717	0.191	0.028	9.250	4.301	2.814	2.136
February	2.285	0.285	5.422	1.695	1.557	0.939	0.181	0.640	0.177	0.024	8.093	3.511	2.622	1.965
March	2.624	0.289	6.079	1.937	1.762	1.057	0.212	0.649	0.208	0.027	8.500	3.458	2.829	2.217
April	2.605	0.313	5.764	1.852	1.672	1.020	0.205	0.585	0.183	0.025	7.657	2.805	2.694	2.162
May	2.663	0.356	6.033	1.952	1.728	1.048	0.221	0.642	0.195	0.024	7.630	2.643	2.725	2.264
June	2.441	0.303	5.964	1.908	1.670	1.003	0.214	0.710	0.210	0.025	7.650	2.831	2.609	2.209
July	2.588	0.278	5.950	1.837	1.697	1.034	0.220	0.722	0.183	0.027	8.150	3.141	2.660	2.345
August	2.541	0.338	6.173	2.044	1.708	1.029	0.226	0.714	0.192	0.026	8.311	3.241	2.755	2.310
September	2.460	0.291	5.767	1.837	1.646	0.993	0.228	0.662	0.155	0.026	7.428	2.715	2.578	2.135
October	2.461	0.314	6.108	2.068	1.721	1.033	0.234	0.631	0.155	0.026	7.750	2.700	2.824	2.227
November	2.408	0.328	5.896	1.947	1.644	1.023	0.224	0.651	0.156	0.026	7.583	2.765	2.696	2.122
December	2.384	0.329	5.936	1.807	1.691	1.059	0.219	0.704	0.196	0.027	8.317	3.453	2.678	2.184
2002														
January	2.413	0.292	6.260	2.104	1.664	1.051	0.211	0.741	0.219	0.027	8.830	3.934	2.778	2.120
February	2.148	0.290	5.587	1.862	1.486	0.954	0.198	0.644	0.204	0.024	7.905	3.380	2.591	1.938
March	2.427	0.267	5.937	1.860	1.669	1.058	0.220	0.658	0.213	0.026	8.419	3.441	2.784	2.197
April	2.434	0.292	5.805	1.853	1.600	1.019	0.215	0.610	0.248	0.024	7.755	2.904	2.663	2.191
May	2.510	0.294	6.042	1.886	1.671	1.065	0.224	0.658	0.274	0.026	7.804	2.772	2.751	2.282
June	2.442	0.308	5.868	1.760	1.629	1.029	0.209	0.693	0.287	0.024	7.886	2.944	2.675	2.263
July	2.528	0.270	5.978	1.780	1.685	1.037	0.213	0.735	0.257	0.026	8.421	3.292	2.776	2.346
August	2.588	0.344	6.052	1.901	1.668	1.045	0.224	0.739	0.210	0.026	8.314	3.188	2.773	2.347
September	2.349	0.301	5.715	1.905	1.554	0.942	0.212	0.673	0.168	0.025	7.646	2.834	2.627	2.182
October	2.565	0.333	5.798	1.951	1.596	0.964	0.217	0.632	0.171	0.026	7.802	2.810	2.758	2.237
November	2.549	0.313	5.758	1.822	1.651	0.974	0.212	0.642	0.198	0.025	8.014	3.080	2.729	2.208
December	2.448	0.359	6.004	1.880	1.689	1.025	0.203	0.720	0.218	0.026	8.828	3.816	2.666	2.348

[1]Includes categories not shown separately.
. . . = Not available.

Table 11-2. Energy Consumption per Dollar of Real Gross Domestic Product

Year	Consumption (quadrillion Btu)			Gross domestic product (billions of chained [2000] dollars)	Energy consumption per dollar of GDP (thousand Btu per chained [2000] dollar)		
	Total	Petroleum and natural gas	Other energy		Total	Petroleum and natural gas	Other energy
1949	31.982	17.028	14.954	1 634.6	19.57	10.42	9.15
1950	34.616	19.284	15.332	1 777.3	19.48	10.85	8.63
1951	36.974	21.477	15.497	1 915.0	19.31	11.21	8.09
1952	36.748	22.505	14.243	1 988.3	18.48	11.32	7.16
1953	37.664	23.462	14.202	2 079.5	18.11	11.28	6.83
1954	36.639	24.169	12.470	2 065.4	17.74	11.70	6.04
1955	40.208	26.253	13.955	2 212.8	18.17	11.86	6.31
1956	41.754	27.551	14.203	2 255.8	18.51	12.21	6.30
1957	41.787	28.122	13.665	2 301.1	18.16	12.22	5.94
1958	41.645	29.190	12.455	2 279.2	18.27	12.81	5.46
1959	43.466	31.040	12.426	2 441.3	17.80	12.71	5.09
1960	45.087	32.305	12.782	2 501.8	18.02	12.91	5.11
1961	45.739	33.143	12.596	2 560.0	17.87	12.95	4.92
1962	47.828	34.780	13.048	2 715.2	17.61	12.81	4.81
1963	49.646	36.104	13.542	2 834.0	17.52	12.74	4.78
1964	51.817	37.589	14.228	2 998.6	17.28	12.54	4.74
1965	54.017	39.014	15.003	3 191.1	16.93	12.23	4.70
1966	57.017	41.396	15.621	3 399.1	16.77	12.18	4.60
1967	58.908	43.228	15.680	3 484.6	16.91	12.41	4.50
1968	62.419	46.189	16.230	3 652.7	17.09	12.65	4.44
1969	65.621	49.016	16.605	3 765.4	17.43	13.02	4.41
1970	67.844	51.316	16.529	3 771.9	17.99	13.60	4.38
1971	69.289	53.030	16.259	3 898.6	17.77	13.60	4.17
1972	72.704	55.645	17.059	4 105.0	17.71	13.56	4.16
1973	75.708	57.352	18.356	4 341.5	17.44	13.21	4.23
1974	73.991	55.187	18.804	4 319.6	17.13	12.78	4.35
1975	71.999	52.678	19.321	4 311.2	16.70	12.22	4.48
1976	76.012	55.520	20.492	4 540.9	16.74	12.23	4.51
1977	78.000	57.053	20.947	4 750.5	16.42	12.01	4.41
1978	79.986	57.966	22.021	5 015.0	15.95	11.56	4.39
1979	80.903	57.789	23.114	5 173.4	15.64	11.17	4.47
1980	78.289	54.596	23.693	5 161.7	15.17	10.58	4.59
1981	76.335	51.859	24.476	5 291.7	14.43	9.80	4.63
1982	73.234	48.737	24.497	5 189.3	14.11	9.39	4.72
1983	73.066	47.411	25.655	5 423.8	13.47	8.74	4.73
1984	76.693	49.558	27.135	5 813.6	13.19	8.52	4.67
1985	76.417	48.756	27.661	6 053.7	12.62	8.05	4.57
1986	76.722	48.904	27.818	6 263.6	12.25	7.81	4.44
1987	79.156	50.609	28.547	6 475.1	12.22	7.82	4.41
1988	82.774	52.774	30.000	6 742.7	12.28	7.83	4.45
1989	84.886	53.923	30.963	6 981.4	12.16	7.72	4.44
1990	84.605	53.282	31.323	7 112.5	11.90	7.49	4.40
1991	84.522	52.994	31.528	7 100.5	11.90	7.46	4.44
1992	85.866	54.362	31.504	7 336.6	11.70	7.41	4.29
1993	87.579	55.193	32.386	7 532.7	11.63	7.33	4.30
1994	89.248	56.512	32.736	7 835.5	11.39	7.21	4.18
1995	91.221	57.338	33.884	8 031.7	11.36	7.14	4.22
1996	94.224	58.954	35.270	8 328.9	11.31	7.08	4.23
1997	94.727	59.594	35.133	8 703.5	10.88	6.85	4.04
1998	95.146	59.869	35.277	9 066.9	10.49	6.60	3.89
1999	96.774	60.970	35.804	9 470.3	10.22	6.44	3.78
2000	98.942	62.356	36.586	9 817.0	10.08	6.35	3.73
2001	96.320	61.202	35.117	9 866.6	9.76	6.20	3.56
2002	97.625	61.544	36.081	10 083.0	9.68	6.11	3.58

NOTES AND DEFINITIONS

TABLES 11-1 AND 11-2
ENERGY SUPPLY AND CONSUMPTION

SOURCES: U.S. DEPARTMENT OF ENERGY, ENERGY INFORMATION ADMINISTRATION; U.S. DEPARTMENT OF COMMERCE, BUREAU OF ECONOMIC ANALYSIS

Definitions

The *British thermal unit (Btu)* is a measure used to combine data for different energy sources into a consistent aggregate. It is the amount of energy required to raise the temperature of 1 pound of water 1 degree Fahrenheit when the water is near 39.2 degrees Fahrenheit. To illustrate one of the factors used to convert volumes to Btu, conventional motor gasoline has a heat content of 5.253 million Btu per barrel. For further information, see Appendix A, *Monthly Energy Review*.

Notes on the data

These data are published in the *Monthly Energy Review*, Tables 1.2, 1.3, 1.8, and 2.1. Consumption by end-use sector is based on total, not net, consumption. The gross domestic product (GDP) data used to calculate energy consumption per dollar of GDP are from the Bureau of Economic Analysis and include revisions through December 2003, which are more recent than the GDP data that were available in time to be shown elsewhere in the volume.

Energy Production: Crude oil includes lease condensates. Hydroelectric power includes electrical utility and industrial generation. Energy production components not shown here (the difference between total production and the sum of the categories shown) include energy generated for distribution from wood, waste, alcohol, solar, and wind sources and an allowance for net hydroelectric energy losses related to pumped storage.

The sum of domestic energy production and net imports of energy does not equal domestic energy consumption. The difference is attributed to inventory changes; losses and gains in conversion, transportation, and distribution; the addition of blending compounds; shipments of anthracite to U.S. Armed Forces in Europe; and adjustments to account for discrepancies between reporting systems.

References

Energy Information Administration, *Monthly Energy Review*. Current and historical data are available on the EIA Internet site at <http://www.eia.doe.gov>.

CHAPTER 12: MONEY AND FINANCIAL MARKETS

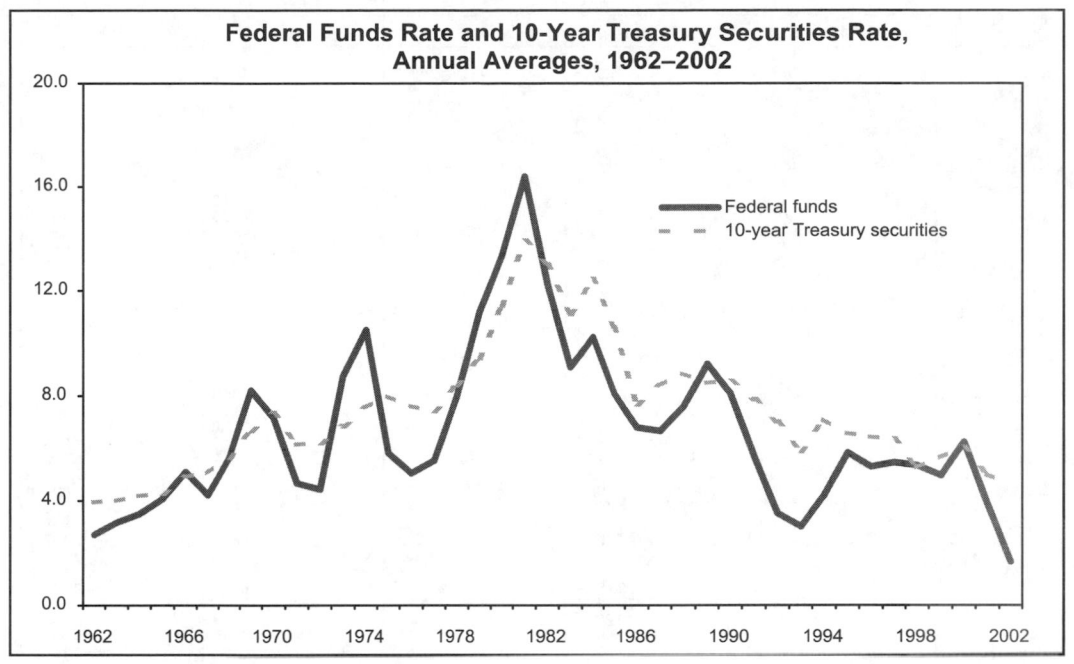

Federal Funds Rate and 10-Year Treasury Securities Rate, Annual Averages, 1962–2002

- Inflation has fallen back to the levels of the early postwar period (see Chapter 8), and as the graph shows, the same has happened with interest rates (Table 12-9).

- Comparisons of interest rates and other financial data over the half-century span are not always straightforward, because financial institutions and instruments have changed. In particular, interest rates were held low until 1952 because the Federal Reserve was pegging Treasury bill and bond rates. Rates before 1953 are therefore not shown (and for many series are not available). Since then, rates have been free to reflect changing degrees of monetary tightness as well as changing inflation expectations and fluctuating views of the productivity of capital.

- In the short-term markets, where Federal Reserve policy governs the price of overnight money, the effective Federal Funds rate was 1.24 percent at the end of 2002, even lower than in years such as 1958 when the economy was slack and inflation expectations were nonexistent. This rate had averaged 16 percent in 1981 because of high inflation and tight monetary policy. Similar comparisons can be made looking at the rate on the 3-month Treasury bill. (Table 12-9)

- In the longer-term market, the 10-year Treasury rate in late 2002 fell to levels last seen in the early 1960s. (Table 12-9)

- Treasury bonds are risk-free, and market rates on these bonds are usually taken as a pure representation of inflation expectations and the "real" (after-inflation) interest rate. Corporate bond rates on the other hand include a risk premium, and even the top-rated bonds (Aaa) commanded higher rates in 2002 than in the early postwar period, although far lower than the double-digit rates reached in the early 1980s. (Table 12-9)

- Even after declines in the stock market after 2000, stock valuations have remained high relative to earnings and dividends. The recent dividend-price and earnings-price ratios shown in Table 12-10 remain well below rates registered in the years before 1997.

- The Federal Reserve has published new measures of household debt service and financial obligations relative to personal disposable income for the period 1980 to date. These ratios have declined only slightly from the highs reached in late 2001 and remain high by historical standards. (Table 12-6)

Table 12-1. Money Stock Measures

(Billions of dollars, monthly data are averages of daily figures, annual data are for December.)

Year and month	Seasonally adjusted			Not seasonally adjusted		
	M1	M2	M3	M1	M2	M3
1959	140.0	297.8	299.7	143.6	300.6	302.4
1960	140.7	312.4	315.2	144.5	315.3	318.0
1961	145.2	335.5	340.8	149.2	338.5	343.7
1962	147.8	362.7	371.3	151.9	365.8	374.0
1963	153.3	393.2	405.9	157.5	396.4	408.7
1964	160.3	424.7	442.4	164.9	428.3	445.5
1965	167.8	459.2	482.1	172.6	463.1	485.5
1966	172.0	480.2	505.4	176.9	483.7	508.6
1967	183.3	524.8	557.9	188.4	528.0	560.9
1968	197.4	566.8	607.2	202.8	569.7	610.0
1969	203.9	587.9	615.9	209.4	590.1	618.2
1970	214.3	626.4	677.0	220.1	627.8	678.2
1971	228.2	710.1	775.9	234.5	711.2	776.6
1972	249.1	802.1	885.8	256.1	803.1	886.2
1973	262.7	855.3	984.9	270.2	856.5	985.2
1974	274.0	901.9	1 069.7	281.8	903.5	1 070.8
1975	286.8	1 016.0	1 169.9	295.3	1 017.8	1 173.3
1976	305.9	1 151.7	1 309.7	314.5	1 153.5	1 313.6
1977	330.5	1 269.9	1 470.1	340.0	1 273.0	1 476.2
1978	356.9	1 365.6	1 644.2	367.9	1 370.8	1 652.6
1979	381.4	1 473.3	1 808.3	393.2	1 479.0	1 815.2
1980	408.1	1 599.4	1 995.1	419.5	1 604.8	2 000.8
1981	436.2	1 754.9	2 254.0	447.0	1 760.3	2 259.0
1982	474.3	1 909.8	2 460.2	485.8	1 918.2	2 469.1
1983	520.8	2 125.9	2 697.0	533.3	2 137.0	2 708.5
1984	551.2	2 309.6	2 990.5	564.6	2 322.0	3 004.6
1985	619.1	2 494.9	3 207.6	633.3	2 507.7	3 221.6
1986	724.0	2 731.6	3 498.7	739.8	2 745.0	3 513.3
1987	749.4	2 830.6	3 685.9	765.4	2 843.4	3 698.7
1988	786.0	2 993.8	3 928.3	803.1	3 006.8	3 941.1
1989	792.1	3 157.4	4 076.0	810.6	3 171.3	4 089.3
1990	824.1	3 276.9	4 152.1	842.7	3 290.8	4 164.1
1991	896.3	3 376.5	4 204.8	915.6	3 391.8	4 219.0
1992	1 024.3	3 430.6	4 215.8	1 045.6	3 448.1	4 232.0
1993	1 129.3	3 483.2	4 277.6	1 153.3	3 503.8	4 297.0
1994	1 149.9	3 496.2	4 360.0	1 174.2	3 517.8	4 379.7
1995	1 126.7	3 640.1	4 625.2	1 152.1	3 663.5	4 647.8
1996	1 078.4	3 815.3	4 971.8	1 104.5	3 836.1	4 994.5
1997	1 071.4	4 031.4	5 446.2	1 096.9	4 052.6	5 473.6
1998	1 094.8	4 384.4	6 036.4	1 120.2	4 406.8	6 070.6
1999	1 121.4	4 649.7	6 534.9	1 147.8	4 676.8	6 577.5
2000	1 084.7	4 931.5	7 099.4	1 112.1	4 966.9	7 154.0
2001	1 172.9	5 444.6	8 004.5	1 202.9	5 487.6	8 076.3
2002	1 210.4	5 791.8	8 522.7	1 240.3	5 841.1	8 600.3
2000						
January	1 118.2	4 676.6	6 582.5	1 125.8	4 685.6	6 610.2
February	1 108.9	4 693.7	6 616.1	1 096.2	4 685.8	6 639.9
March	1 108.1	4 719.5	6 682.9	1 107.4	4 746.5	6 731.3
April	1 108.2	4 758.2	6 734.6	1 124.2	4 814.9	6 791.2
May	1 105.2	4 765.3	6 758.9	1 099.7	4 741.7	6 745.3
June	1 106.0	4 786.1	6 809.2	1 102.0	4 766.1	6 786.2
July	1 104.7	4 803.6	6 859.9	1 103.2	4 784.0	6 817.6
August	1 103.0	4 836.3	6 930.9	1 095.0	4 816.7	6 887.0
September	1 100.2	4 868.1	6 988.6	1 089.5	4 852.4	6 938.4
October	1 100.7	4 882.4	7 007.5	1 092.9	4 864.1	6 961.8
November	1 092.8	4 893.3	7 022.0	1 092.7	4 893.6	7 024.3
December	1 084.7	4 931.5	7 099.4	1 112.1	4 966.9	7 154.0
2001						
January	1 093.1	4 985.7	7 205.8	1 099.4	4 993.5	7 238.0
February	1 099.8	5 030.4	7 278.1	1 087.1	5 022.5	7 308.4
March	1 107.5	5 082.8	7 344.3	1 106.9	5 113.7	7 401.6
April	1 105.9	5 128.7	7 461.0	1 122.2	5 187.7	7 518.3
May	1 116.7	5 153.7	7 540.5	1 110.6	5 125.4	7 523.9
June	1 125.8	5 198.3	7 628.0	1 122.7	5 177.7	7 603.9
July	1 138.0	5 232.7	7 666.4	1 136.3	5 207.4	7 615.3
August	1 149.2	5 265.9	7 676.8	1 141.4	5 244.4	7 627.0
September	1 201.2	5 376.5	7 834.9	1 190.7	5 358.8	7 769.2
October	1 163.9	5 362.4	7 869.9	1 154.9	5 343.2	7 814.2
November	1 165.3	5 402.8	7 943.8	1 164.2	5 406.7	7 950.0
December	1 172.9	5 444.6	8 004.5	1 202.9	5 487.6	8 076.3
2002						
January	1 179.0	5 468.7	8 016.3	1 185.2	5 476.0	8 058.1
February	1 185.2	5 507.2	8 068.1	1 171.2	5 494.3	8 100.5
March	1 187.1	5 508.2	8 081.2	1 188.7	5 543.2	8 146.8
April	1 172.6	5 494.8	8 083.3	1 187.9	5 557.0	8 142.0
May	1 183.3	5 557.3	8 150.5	1 177.6	5 525.7	8 128.7
June	1 188.9	5 587.4	8 178.8	1 186.5	5 563.7	8 152.4
July	1 195.7	5 635.2	8 224.9	1 193.4	5 606.6	8 171.7
August	1 184.5	5 673.1	8 291.4	1 176.6	5 650.9	8 240.0
September	1 191.2	5 698.7	8 333.0	1 181.3	5 676.7	8 258.1
October	1 202.6	5 736.6	8 344.3	1 192.3	5 715.9	8 287.6
November	1 202.2	5 776.5	8 467.2	1 200.8	5 791.1	8 483.0
December	1 210.4	5 791.8	8 522.7	1 240.3	5 841.1	8 600.3

Table 12-2. Selected Components of the Money Stock

(Billions of dollars, monthly data are averages of daily figures, seasonally adjusted, annual data are for December.)

Year and month	Currency	Demand deposits	Other checkable deposits	Repurchase agreements	Eurodollars	Money market funds Retail	Money market funds Institutional	Savings deposits At banks	Savings deposits At thrifts	Small time deposits At banks	Small time deposits At thrifts	Large time deposits At banks	Large time deposits At thrifts
1959	28.8	110.8	0.0	0.0	0.7	0.0	0.0	54.8	91.7	8.9	2.5	1.2	0.0
1960	28.7	111.6	0.0	0.0	0.8	0.0	0.0	58.3	100.8	9.7	2.8	2.0	0.0
1961	29.3	115.5	0.0	0.0	1.5	0.0	0.0	64.2	111.3	11.1	3.7	3.9	0.0
1962	30.3	117.1	0.0	0.0	1.6	0.0	0.0	71.3	123.4	15.5	4.6	7.0	0.0
1963	32.2	120.6	0.1	0.0	1.9	0.0	0.0	76.8	137.6	19.9	5.7	10.8	0.0
1964	33.9	125.8	0.1	0.0	2.4	0.0	0.0	82.9	152.4	22.4	6.8	15.2	0.0
1965	36.0	131.3	0.1	0.0	1.8	0.0	0.0	92.4	164.5	26.7	7.8	21.2	0.0
1966	38.0	133.4	0.1	0.0	2.2	0.0	0.0	89.9	163.3	38.7	16.3	23.1	0.0
1967	40.0	142.5	0.1	0.0	2.2	0.0	0.0	94.1	169.6	50.7	27.1	30.9	0.0
1968	43.0	153.6	0.1	0.0	2.9	0.0	0.0	96.1	172.8	63.5	37.1	37.4	0.0
1969	45.7	157.3	0.2	4.9	2.7	0.0	0.0	93.8	169.8	71.6	48.8	20.4	0.0
1970	48.6	164.7	0.1	3.0	2.4	0.0	0.0	98.6	162.3	79.3	71.9	44.4	0.7
1971	52.0	175.1	0.2	5.2	2.9	0.0	0.0	112.8	179.4	94.7	95.1	56.1	1.5
1972	56.2	191.6	0.2	6.6	3.8	0.0	0.0	124.8	196.6	108.2	123.5	70.8	2.5
1973	60.8	200.3	0.3	12.8	5.8	0.1	0.0	128.0	198.7	116.8	149.0	107.4	3.6
1974	67.0	205.1	0.4	14.5	8.5	1.4	0.2	136.8	201.8	123.1	164.8	139.3	5.4
1975	72.8	211.3	0.9	13.8	10.0	2.4	0.5	161.2	227.6	142.3	195.5	123.3	6.4
1976	79.5	221.5	2.7	24.0	15.2	1.8	0.6	201.8	251.4	155.5	235.2	110.3	7.8
1977	87.4	236.4	4.2	32.2	21.7	1.8	1.0	218.8	273.4	167.5	278.0	135.0	10.2
1978	96.0	249.5	8.5	44.4	35.1	5.8	3.5	216.5	265.4	185.1	335.8	179.1	16.5
1979	104.8	256.6	16.8	48.8	52.7	33.9	10.4	195.0	228.8	235.5	398.7	190.9	32.2
1980	115.3	261.2	28.1	58.1	61.4	62.5	16.0	185.7	214.5	286.2	442.3	215.2	45.0
1981	122.5	231.4	78.7	67.8	88.8	151.7	38.2	159.0	184.9	347.7	475.4	250.5	53.8
1982	132.5	234.1	104.1	71.8	104.2	184.5	48.8	190.1	210.0	379.9	471.0	261.9	63.7
1983	146.2	238.5	132.1	97.5	116.6	136.1	40.9	363.2	321.7	350.9	433.1	219.4	96.7
1984	156.1	243.4	147.4	107.6	108.9	164.9	62.3	389.3	315.4	387.9	500.9	255.1	147.1
1985	167.7	266.7	179.8	121.5	104.2	174.9	65.3	456.6	358.6	386.4	499.3	269.9	151.8
1986	180.4	302.7	235.6	146.2	115.7	208.4	86.3	533.5	407.4	369.4	489.0	268.6	150.4
1987	196.7	287.5	259.5	178.3	121.5	222.8	93.7	534.8	402.6	391.7	529.3	299.1	162.7
1988	212.0	287.0	280.9	196.7	131.7	244.3	93.8	542.4	383.9	451.2	585.9	337.8	174.5
1989	222.2	278.6	285.1	169.0	109.4	320.3	112.3	541.1	352.6	533.8	617.6	366.4	161.5
1990	246.5	276.9	293.7	151.5	103.3	356.5	140.8	581.4	341.6	610.7	562.7	358.5	121.1
1991	267.1	289.7	332.4	131.2	92.3	370.8	190.0	664.5	379.4	602.3	463.3	331.3	83.5
1992	292.2	340.0	384.6	141.6	79.5	351.4	213.9	753.9	432.9	508.1	360.0	282.8	67.3
1993	321.6	385.5	414.8	172.6	72.8	352.5	217.2	785.3	434.0	467.9	314.1	270.2	61.6
1994	354.0	383.6	404.2	196.4	86.3	380.0	211.3	752.6	397.2	502.5	313.8	305.0	64.8
1995	372.1	389.3	356.8	198.5	94.0	447.8	264.5	774.6	359.5	574.8	356.6	353.9	74.2
1996	394.1	400.3	275.7	210.5	114.7	516.1	322.7	906.4	367.6	593.3	353.6	430.8	77.9
1997	424.6	393.1	245.7	254.0	147.5	591.4	395.6	1 023.1	377.5	625.3	342.7	532.6	85.1
1998	459.9	377.1	249.5	293.4	150.2	732.8	539.1	1 188.1	417.1	626.0	325.6	581.1	88.3
1999	517.7	352.1	243.4	335.7	170.5	833.4	634.8	1 288.6	452.0	634.6	319.5	652.2	91.9
2000	531.5	306.9	238.2	363.5	194.3	925.4	788.8	1 422.9	454.3	699.5	344.8	718.2	103.0
2001	581.9	326.1	257.2	375.0	208.6	991.5	1 190.3	1 734.6	572.4	634.2	339.1	670.9	114.9
2002	627.3	297.1	278.5	474.6	227.9	925.9	1 234.5	2 048.3	714.5	591.0	302.2	676.3	117.3
2000													
January	524.6	343.2	242.1	333.7	175.1	852.5	648.7	1 291.9	450.5	641.1	322.3	653.7	94.7
February	517.5	341.3	242.0	344.4	174.7	860.4	651.8	1 301.3	451.1	647.8	324.0	656.0	95.6
March	516.1	342.4	241.5	345.8	185.9	872.4	669.8	1 306.3	452.7	654.1	325.8	665.8	96.2
April	517.0	340.3	242.8	345.2	181.5	884.5	673.7	1 326.2	450.9	663.0	325.2	680.0	96.0
May	518.9	336.9	241.1	352.4	185.5	889.8	679.3	1 323.1	455.0	666.3	325.8	681.1	95.3
June	520.8	335.5	240.9	358.6	185.6	889.4	691.3	1 333.5	455.1	674.7	327.4	690.5	97.1
July	521.9	333.3	240.2	362.7	182.5	883.2	715.7	1 347.6	455.5	681.1	331.5	696.1	99.3
August	522.9	329.2	241.7	362.8	184.8	893.2	736.7	1 361.1	456.9	686.1	335.9	709.1	101.2
September	524.3	326.3	240.8	367.4	188.6	902.9	759.1	1 380.5	456.3	689.2	338.9	703.5	101.9
October	526.7	324.3	241.4	368.4	189.9	907.2	766.1	1 384.8	456.7	691.5	341.4	697.3	103.3
November	528.7	316.5	239.6	362.5	191.7	910.2	771.9	1 396.9	455.5	694.5	343.5	698.7	103.7
December	531.5	306.9	238.2	363.5	194.3	925.4	788.8	1 422.9	454.3	699.5	344.8	718.2	103.0
2001													
January	534.7	310.7	239.6	362.3	198.8	941.6	823.8	1 443.0	455.8	703.7	348.5	729.5	105.7
February	537.3	312.7	241.8	353.1	204.0	946.5	884.9	1 467.2	464.5	702.0	350.4	698.5	107.0
March	540.0	314.6	245.0	350.6	216.3	962.2	912.3	1 490.7	473.7	698.5	350.3	674.4	107.8
April	543.2	307.8	247.2	374.9	210.7	971.3	942.8	1 526.0	481.2	693.0	351.4	694.3	109.6
May	546.3	314.3	248.2	377.7	211.3	962.8	986.6	1 542.6	492.4	685.7	353.5	700.0	110.9
June	548.2	314.5	254.9	377.1	210.9	970.1	1 026.6	1 568.5	503.1	678.7	352.2	705.1	109.8
July	553.4	316.0	259.9	374.2	214.8	972.0	1 037.5	1 586.9	513.5	672.1	350.3	695.3	111.7
August	562.2	319.3	259.1	372.0	212.2	966.6	1 030.6	1 613.2	521.7	667.9	347.3	681.1	114.9
September	567.9	366.2	258.8	363.3	213.5	979.6	1 085.9	1 655.3	530.9	663.4	346.1	680.1	115.5
October	572.2	331.5	252.1	360.2	210.1	988.0	1 150.0	1 665.8	544.0	657.7	343.0	671.6	115.6
November	576.4	327.8	253.4	376.7	213.3	989.4	1 170.1	1 704.8	555.9	648.4	338.9	666.5	114.3
December	581.9	326.1	257.2	375.0	208.6	991.5	1 190.3	1 734.6	572.4	634.2	339.1	670.9	114.9
2002													
January	587.5	325.4	258.3	373.0	208.6	980.2	1 175.0	1 764.7	583.7	627.3	333.8	675.1	115.5
February	592.2	325.6	259.5	372.8	214.3	973.4	1 180.2	1 796.7	601.9	620.5	329.5	677.9	115.4
March	595.9	323.9	259.5	374.5	216.1	958.8	1 185.2	1 805.5	616.0	614.6	326.3	681.8	115.2
April	600.0	305.8	259.1	375.3	215.5	938.3	1 189.1	1 822.5	628.1	610.1	323.1	692.9	115.6
May	605.0	307.1	263.4	371.3	211.8	947.3	1 188.7	1 862.4	636.8	613.2	314.3	708.6	112.5
June	609.5	306.2	265.0	371.7	208.8	943.6	1 197.2	1 885.2	646.2	612.3	311.1	702.3	111.1
July	613.7	305.1	268.4	373.3	208.1	951.6	1 192.8	1 910.4	658.1	609.7	309.6	703.9	111.3
August	616.4	290.0	269.8	400.9	209.6	948.4	1 192.0	1 956.0	669.8	606.3	308.0	702.8	112.7
September	618.3	292.7	272.3	424.3	212.8	935.7	1 183.9	1 983.3	681.2	601.2	306.1	699.9	113.0
October	620.9	299.7	274.4	423.4	221.8	932.1	1 143.4	2 006.0	693.6	597.8	304.5	704.8	114.0
November	623.6	294.6	276.6	443.4	226.4	932.9	1 209.1	2 041.9	701.6	595.0	303.1	695.9	115.7
December	627.3	297.1	278.5	474.6	227.9	925.9	1 234.5	2 048.3	714.5	591.0	302.2	676.3	117.3

Table 12-3. Aggregate Reserves of Depository Institutions and Monetary Base

(Millions of dollars, monthly data are averages of daily figures, adjusted for seasonality and changes in reserve requirements, annual data are for December.)

Year and month	Reserves				Monetary base
	Total	Nonborrowed	Nonborrowed plus extended credit	Required	
1959	11 109	10 168	10 168	10 603	40 880
1960	11 247	11 172	11 172	10 503	40 977
1961	11 499	11 366	11 366	10 915	41 853
1962	11 604	11 344	11 344	11 033	42 957
1963	11 730	11 397	11 397	11 239	45 003
1964	12 011	11 747	11 747	11 605	47 161
1965	12 316	11 872	11 872	11 892	49 620
1966	12 223	11 690	11 690	11 884	51 565
1967	13 180	12 952	12 952	12 805	54 579
1968	13 767	13 021	13 021	13 341	58 357
1969	14 168	13 049	13 049	13 882	61 569
1970	14 558	14 225	14 225	14 309	65 013
1971	15 230	15 104	15 104	15 049	69 108
1972	16 645	15 595	15 595	16 361	75 167
1973	17 021	15 723	15 723	16 717	81 073
1974	17 550	16 823	16 970	17 292	87 535
1975	17 822	17 692	17 704	17 556	93 887
1976	18 388	18 335	18 335	18 115	101 515
1977	18 990	18 420	18 420	18 800	110 324
1978	19 753	18 885	18 885	19 521	120 445
1979	20 720	19 248	19 248	20 279	131 143
1980	22 015	20 325	20 328	21 501	142 004
1981	22 443	21 807	21 956	22 124	149 021
1982	23 600	22 966	23 152	23 100	160 127
1983	25 367	24 593	24 595	24 806	175 467
1984	26 896	23 710	26 314	26 061	187 241
1985	31 541	30 223	30 722	30 478	203 540
1986	38 841	38 015	38 317	37 668	223 430
1987	38 918	38 141	38 624	37 899	239 846
1988	40 428	38 712	39 956	39 366	256 866
1989	40 430	40 164	40 184	39 489	267 669
1990	41 699	41 374	41 397	40 035	293 267
1991	45 451	45 258	45 259	44 461	317 507
1992	54 332	54 208	54 209	53 178	350 754
1993	60 460	60 378	60 378	59 390	386 462
1994	59 369	59 160	59 160	58 209	418 194
1995	56 430	56 173	56 173	55 140	434 400
1996	50 149	49 994	49 994	48 733	451 921
1997	46 848	46 523	46 523	45 163	479 838
1998	45 141	45 024	45 024	43 627	513 708
1999	41 809	41 488	41 488	40 512	593 155
2000	38 537	38 327	38 327	37 110	584 765
2001	41 243	41 177	41 177	39 595	635 617
2002	40 217	40 138	40 138	38 208	681 900
2000					
January	42 215	41 842	41 842	40 196	590 750
February	40 961	40 854	40 854	39 849	573 522
March	40 346	40 167	40 167	39 137	571 987
April	40 527	40 223	40 223	39 369	572 675
May	40 630	40 268	40 268	39 658	574 036
June	40 412	39 932	39 932	39 295	575 580
July	40 317	39 747	39 747	39 173	576 412
August	39 762	39 183	39 183	38 743	577 337
September	39 722	39 244	39 244	38 603	578 037
October	39 413	38 995	38 995	38 264	580 271
November	39 440	39 157	39 157	38 132	582 281
December	38 537	38 327	38 327	37 110	584 765
2001					
January	37 836	37 763	37 763	36 452	588 195
February	38 285	38 234	38 234	36 778	590 140
March	38 247	38 189	38 189	36 847	592 670
April	38 467	38 416	38 416	37 190	595 877
May	38 551	38 338	38 338	37 532	599 003
June	39 233	39 003	39 003	37 871	601 580
July	39 791	39 508	39 508	38 383	606 823
August	40 019	39 836	39 836	38 811	615 202
September	58 186	54 801	54 801	39 169	639 481
October	45 489	45 362	45 362	44 163	630 484
November	40 965	40 881	40 881	39 513	630 301
December	41 243	41 177	41 177	39 595	635 617
2002					
January	41 576	41 526	41 526	40 181	641 597
February	41 335	41 305	41 305	39 964	646 583
March	40 768	40 689	40 689	39 347	649 991
April	40 635	40 565	40 565	39 424	654 077
May	39 406	39 294	39 294	38 145	657 784
June	39 469	39 327	39 327	38 231	662 317
July	39 679	39 487	39 487	38 301	666 838
August	39 961	39 628	39 628	38 353	669 833
September	39 209	38 980	38 980	37 722	671 399
October	39 171	39 028	39 028	37 636	674 250
November	39 760	39 489	39 489	38 122	677 612
December	40 217	40 138	40 138	38 208	681 900

Table 12-4. Commercial Banks: Bank Credit and Selected Liabilities

(All commercial banks in the United States, billions of dollars, seasonally adjusted, annual data are for December.)

| Year and month | Total | Securities in bank credit | | | Loans and leases in bank credit | | | | |
| | | Total | U.S. government securities | Other securities | Total | Commercial and industrial | Real estate | | |
							Total	Revolving home equity	Other
1947	111.0	77.0	72.1	4.8	34.0	14.4	8.9	...	...
1948	109.1	70.8	65.7	5.1	38.3	15.3	10.3	...	...
1949	115.7	76.3	70.5	5.9	39.4	13.8	11.0	...	...
1950	120.4	72.2	65.1	7.1	48.2	17.6	12.9	...	...
1951	126.5	72.4	64.5	8.0	54.1	21.3	14.1	...	...
1952	134.1	74.3	66.3	7.9	59.8	23.6	15.0	...	...
1953	139.7	77.0	67.7	9.4	62.7	23.6	16.1	...	...
1954	150.8	85.8	74.9	10.8	65.0	22.9	17.6	...	...
1955	152.2	76.5	65.6	10.9	75.7	27.2	19.9	...	...
1956	158.0	73.2	62.1	11.1	84.9	33.0	21.7	...	...
1957	162.7	73.5	61.0	12.4	89.2	34.7	22.3	...	...
1958	184.1	85.9	70.5	15.4	98.2	35.4	25.1	...	...
1959	189.5	77.4	61.9	15.5	112.1	39.5	28.1	...	...
1960	197.6	79.5	63.9	15.6	118.1	42.4	28.7	...	...
1961	213.1	88.2	70.4	17.9	124.8	44.1	30.2	...	...
1962	231.0	92.2	70.7	21.5	138.8	47.7	34.0	...	...
1963	250.7	92.6	67.4	25.2	158.1	52.5	38.9	...	...
1964	270.4	94.7	66.7	28.1	175.6	58.7	43.5	...	...
1965	297.1	96.1	64.3	31.9	201.0	69.5	48.9	...	...
1966	318.6	97.2	61.0	36.2	221.4	79.3	53.8	...	...
1967	350.5	111.4	70.7	40.6	239.2	86.5	58.2	...	...
1968	390.5	121.9	73.8	48.1	268.6	96.5	64.8	...	...
1969	401.6	112.4	64.2	40.2	289.2	100.9	69.9	...	...
1970	434.4	129.7	73.4	56.3	304.6	111.6	72.9	...	...
1971	485.2	147.5	79.8	67.7	337.6	118.0	81.7	...	...
1972	555.3	160.6	85.4	75.2	394.7	133.6	98.8	...	...
1973	638.6	168.4	89.7	78.7	470.1	162.8	119.4	0.0	119.4
1974	701.7	173.8	87.9	85.9	527.9	193.0	132.5	0.0	132.5
1975	732.9	206.7	117.9	88.9	526.2	184.3	137.2	0.0	137.2
1976	790.7	228.6	137.3	91.3	562.1	186.3	151.3	0.0	151.3
1977	876.0	236.3	137.4	98.9	639.7	205.8	178.0	0.0	178.0
1978	989.4	242.2	138.4	103.8	747.2	239.0	213.5	0.0	213.5
1979	1 111.4	260.7	147.2	113.4	850.7	282.2	245.0	0.0	245.0
1980	1 207.1	296.8	173.2	123.6	910.3	314.5	265.7	0.0	265.7
1981	1 302.7	311.1	181.8	129.3	991.6	353.3	287.5	0.0	287.5
1982	1 412.3	338.6	204.7	133.9	1 073.7	396.4	303.8	0.0	303.8
1983	1 566.7	403.8	263.4	140.4	1 163.0	419.1	334.8	0.0	334.8
1984	1 733.4	406.6	262.9	143.7	1 326.9	479.4	380.8	0.0	380.8
1985	1 922.2	455.9	273.8	182.2	1 466.3	506.5	431.0	0.0	431.0
1986	2 106.6	510.0	312.8	197.2	1 596.5	544.0	499.9	0.0	499.9
1987	2 255.3	535.0	338.9	196.1	1 720.2	575.0	595.7	32.2	563.5
1988	2 434.7	562.2	366.6	195.6	1 872.5	611.7	678.0	42.6	635.5
1989	2 604.2	585.1	400.0	185.1	2 019.1	642.6	771.0	53.5	717.5
1990	2 751.5	635.1	456.3	178.8	2 116.4	645.5	858.2	66.3	791.9
1991	2 857.7	747.0	566.8	180.3	2 110.7	623.3	884.3	74.3	810.1
1992	2 956.7	843.1	666.2	176.9	2 113.6	599.4	907.3	78.4	828.9
1993	3 116.0	917.9	733.1	184.8	2 198.1	590.3	948.3	78.0	870.3
1994	3 322.4	942.6	724.2	218.4	2 379.9	650.3	1 012.1	80.5	931.7
1995	3 605.1	986.7	703.7	283.0	2 618.4	723.8	1 091.0	84.4	1 006.5
1996	3 757.2	981.9	701.8	280.1	2 775.3	784.6	1 142.7	90.8	1 052.0
1997	4 101.6	1 096.6	755.2	341.4	3 004.9	854.1	1 245.8	104.9	1 140.9
1998	4 537.8	1 236.1	797.6	438.5	3 301.7	947.7	1 336.6	103.8	1 232.8
1999	4 769.5	1 281.4	814.6	466.8	3 488.0	999.4	1 475.8	101.5	1 374.4
2000	5 224.3	1 346.9	791.8	555.0	3 877.5	1 088.0	1 656.4	130.0	1 526.4
2001	5 433.5	1 491.6	852.3	639.3	3 942.0	1 028.5	1 783.8	155.5	1 628.3
2002	5 891.5	1 716.9	1 028.4	688.4	4 174.6	965.1	2 027.6	213.4	1 814.2
2001									
January	5 263.5	1 364.4	790.0	574.4	3 899.1	1 098.3	1 658.3	128.2	1 530.1
February	5 266.8	1 356.2	777.8	578.4	3 910.5	1 099.1	1 670.7	129.3	1 541.3
March	5 282.7	1 354.9	762.4	592.5	3 927.8	1 095.0	1 682.4	132.0	1 550.5
April	5 305.3	1 373.8	773.3	600.6	3 931.5	1 092.1	1 689.2	132.9	1 556.3
May	5 314.6	1 380.2	774.9	605.2	3 934.4	1 088.2	1 700.7	134.4	1 566.3
June	5 317.0	1 394.5	773.7	620.8	3 922.5	1 071.9	1 704.7	135.7	1 569.0
July	5 322.3	1 395.0	782.3	612.7	3 927.2	1 064.8	1 716.4	138.1	1 578.3
August	5 344.3	1 425.0	793.1	631.9	3 919.4	1 059.7	1 719.0	141.1	1 578.0
September	5 419.4	1 442.7	802.4	640.2	3 976.7	1 061.8	1 728.7	144.4	1 584.3
October	5 414.4	1 474.3	826.1	648.2	3 940.1	1 049.6	1 752.9	150.5	1 602.5
November	5 446.6	1 491.9	836.9	655.0	3 954.7	1 038.4	1 772.7	152.8	1 619.9
December	5 433.5	1 491.6	852.3	639.3	3 942.0	1 028.5	1 783.8	155.5	1 628.3
2002									
January	5 407.4	1 481.2	834.2	647.0	3 926.3	1 018.7	1 778.3	158.4	1 619.9
February	5 415.0	1 479.1	829.0	650.2	3 935.9	1 023.0	1 786.4	161.5	1 624.9
March	5 407.5	1 479.5	846.3	633.1	3 928.0	1 016.2	1 788.9	167.0	1 621.9
April	5 432.8	1 499.4	868.4	631.0	3 933.4	1 005.4	1 793.8	171.1	1 622.7
May	5 481.6	1 529.2	889.7	639.5	3 952.4	998.3	1 816.7	178.6	1 638.1
June	5 526.3	1 559.6	908.7	650.9	3 966.7	989.9	1 839.7	185.2	1 654.5
July	5 579.1	1 591.8	917.5	674.3	3 987.3	978.5	1 871.7	192.3	1 679.3
August	5 661.4	1 629.5	943.7	685.8	4 031.9	978.4	1 903.7	197.3	1 706.4
September	5 721.5	1 642.6	962.7	679.9	4 078.9	972.9	1 937.4	200.8	1 736.6
October	5 756.5	1 645.2	981.8	663.4	4 111.4	968.2	1 970.7	204.7	1 766.0
November	5 835.1	1 687.4	1 012.5	674.9	4 147.7	967.1	2 005.6	208.7	1 796.9
December	5 891.5	1 716.9	1 028.4	688.4	4 174.6	965.1	2 027.6	213.4	1 814.2

. . . = Not available.

Table 12-4. Commercial Banks: Bank Credit and Selected Liabilities—*Continued*

(All commercial banks in the United States, billions of dollars, seasonally adjusted, annual data are for December.)

Year and month	Bank credit—*Continued*			Deposits	Selected liabilities		
	Loans and leases in bank credit—*Continued*				Borrowings		
	Consumer	Security	Other		Total	From banks in the U.S.	From nonbanks in the U.S.
1947	5.7	2.3	2.8	...	...	...	...
1948	6.9	2.5	3.2	...	...	...	...
1949	8.1	2.9	3.5	...	...	...	...
1950	10.2	3.1	4.3	...	...	...	...
1951	10.7	2.7	5.2	...	...	...	...
1952	12.7	3.2	5.3	...	...	...	...
1953	14.7	3.6	4.8	...	...	...	...
1954	14.9	4.4	5.1	...	...	...	...
1955	17.3	5.1	6.1	...	...	...	...
1956	19.1	4.8	6.2	...	...	...	...
1957	20.0	4.6	7.6	...	...	...	...
1958	20.4	4.7	12.7	...	...	...	...
1959	24.1	5.0	15.4	...	...	...	...
1960	26.3	5.2	15.6	...	...	...	...
1961	27.6	6.1	16.8	...	...	...	...
1962	30.3	6.6	20.2	...	...	...	...
1963	34.2	7.9	24.6	...	...	...	...
1964	39.5	8.3	25.7	...	...	...	...
1965	45.0	8.0	29.7	...	...	...	...
1966	47.7	8.3	32.4	...	...	...	...
1967	51.2	9.6	33.8	...	...	...	...
1968	57.7	10.5	39.2	...	...	...	...
1969	62.6	10.0	39.8	...	...	...	...
1970	65.3	10.4	44.5	...	...	...	...
1971	73.3	10.9	53.9	...	...	...	...
1972	85.4	14.4	62.5	...	...	...	...
1973	98.3	11.2	78.4	651.6	70.5	44.1	26.4
1974	102.1	10.6	89.6	718.9	76.3	47.8	28.6
1975	104.6	12.7	87.5	759.3	72.1	45.1	27.0
1976	115.9	17.7	91.0	815.3	95.5	56.3	39.2
1977	138.1	20.7	97.2	899.4	111.7	61.8	49.9
1978	164.6	19.1	110.9	996.7	138.4	72.6	65.8
1979	184.5	17.4	121.6	1 069.3	176.6	97.4	79.2
1980	179.2	17.2	133.6	1 181.6	212.3	118.1	94.2
1981	182.7	20.2	148.0	1 247.4	256.0	142.3	113.7
1982	188.2	23.6	161.7	1 365.5	282.2	153.9	128.3
1983	213.2	26.5	169.4	1 478.8	282.8	149.1	133.7
1984	253.6	34.1	179.0	1 607.0	316.9	165.8	151.1
1985	294.5	42.9	191.4	1 752.1	372.6	192.4	180.1
1986	314.5	38.6	199.5	1 911.2	410.2	213.3	196.9
1987	327.7	34.8	187.0	1 971.7	427.2	222.2	204.9
1988	354.8	40.3	187.7	2 110.9	491.3	252.2	239.1
1989	375.4	40.9	189.3	2 237.3	552.7	283.1	269.6
1990	380.9	44.6	187.2	2 339.5	576.0	296.8	279.2
1991	364.1	53.9	185.0	2 468.2	497.0	222.9	274.2
1992	356.4	63.4	187.1	2 501.3	498.9	213.6	285.3
1993	387.6	86.5	185.3	2 535.3	535.6	214.5	321.1
1994	448.3	75.9	193.3	2 536.2	621.6	257.3	364.3
1995	491.5	83.3	228.7	2 668.9	696.0	288.7	407.4
1996	513.2	75.4	259.5	2 868.0	728.6	300.2	428.5
1997	503.0	94.6	307.4	3 118.2	852.8	307.9	544.9
1998	497.3	145.8	374.2	3 329.9	1 019.0	321.6	697.4
1999	491.2	150.4	371.1	3 529.8	1 122.8	347.6	775.3
2000	540.1	177.2	415.8	3 844.2	1 239.7	380.2	859.5
2001	557.4	145.5	426.7	4 225.4	1 245.6	402.2	843.3
2002	588.1	189.5	404.3	4 487.4	1 403.4	417.5	985.9
2001							
January	544.5	174.2	423.9	3 894.0	1 267.5	385.5	882.0
February	545.1	171.1	424.5	3 905.9	1 258.0	384.6	873.4
March	544.3	178.6	427.5	3 946.5	1 251.5	384.3	867.2
April	549.2	177.1	424.0	3 999.5	1 279.8	397.0	882.8
May	552.5	168.8	424.2	4 012.3	1 250.5	379.5	871.0
June	552.8	169.5	423.6	4 040.8	1 221.3	379.4	842.0
July	553.5	168.2	424.3	4 069.1	1 230.3	384.9	845.3
August	553.7	167.7	419.2	4 090.8	1 233.8	389.8	844.0
September	553.5	178.4	454.2	4 220.2	1 284.9	435.9	849.0
October	551.1	155.5	431.0	4 174.9	1 264.8	411.8	852.9
November	558.3	155.0	430.3	4 193.1	1 252.3	401.0	851.4
December	557.4	145.5	426.7	4 225.4	1 245.6	402.2	843.3
2002							
January	559.7	151.7	417.9	4 241.7	1 233.4	399.0	834.4
February	561.8	154.0	410.7	4 251.7	1 232.8	395.1	837.8
March	560.5	161.7	400.8	4 293.0	1 207.1	383.0	824.1
April	565.1	168.2	400.8	4 313.9	1 220.0	383.1	836.9
May	568.3	169.9	399.2	4 350.2	1 241.3	383.4	857.9
June	567.7	169.5	399.9	4 373.6	1 233.0	378.5	854.5
July	564.0	178.0	395.1	4 414.4	1 228.5	384.3	844.1
August	574.3	176.9	398.5	4 462.5	1 290.6	403.7	886.8
September	582.9	180.9	404.8	4 478.4	1 325.8	415.9	909.9
October	584.7	183.0	404.8	4 486.7	1 338.1	414.9	923.1
November	585.5	185.8	403.7	4 509.3	1 372.1	421.9	950.2
December	588.1	189.5	404.3	4 487.4	1 403.4	417.5	985.9

. . . = Not available.

Table 12-5. Credit Market Debt Outstanding, By Borrower and Lender

(Billions of dollars, except as noted; end of period; not seasonally adjusted.)

Year and quarter	Total	Credit market debt outstanding — Owed by: Domestic financial sectors			Domestic nonfinancial sectors Total		Federal government			Households		Nonfinancial business		
		Total	Federal govern-ment-related	Private	Billions of dollars	Percent of GDP	Total	Treasury securities	Budget agency securities and mortgages	Billions of dollars	Percent of DPI	Total	Corporate Total	Percent of sector GDP
1945	355	2	1	1	348	. . .	251	251	0	28	. . .	56	45	. . .
1946	351	3	1	2	340	153	228	228	0	35	22	64	50	50
1947	368	4	1	3	352	144	221	221	0	44	26	73	57	47
1948	382	5	2	4	363	135	215	214	1	52	27	80	63	45
1949	398	6	2	5	378	141	218	217	1	60	32	83	64	47
1950	425	9	2	7	403	137	217	216	0	73	35	92	70	46
1951	449	10	2	8	425	125	216	216	0	82	35	104	79	45
1952	485	11	2	9	458	128	221	221	1	94	37	113	85	46
1953	517	13	2	10	488	128	228	226	2	106	41	118	89	45
1954	542	12	2	10	513	135	231	228	2	117	44	124	93	48
1955	582	15	3	12	550	132	230	228	2	138	47	136	101	46
1956	611	18	4	14	576	132	224	223	1	153	49	149	111	47
1957	643	21	5	16	603	131	222	220	2	165	51	161	120	49
1958	682	21	5	16	640	137	231	229	2	176	52	172	128	54
1959	739	28	7	20	689	136	238	236	2	198	55	187	136	51
1960	780	33	8	24	724	137	236	234	2	215	58	201	145	52
1961	828	35	9	26	768	141	243	241	2	232	59	215	153	53
1962	888	39	10	29	821	140	250	247	3	253	62	233	163	52
1963	954	47	12	35	876	142	254	251	3	280	64	253	174	52
1964	1 028	53	13	40	940	141	260	256	4	309	65	275	188	52
1965	1 107	62	15	47	1 007	140	262	257	5	338	65	305	208	53
1966	1 187	73	20	53	1 075	136	265	259	6	360	65	339	232	54
1967	1 268	72	20	51	1 153	138	278	268	10	381	65	377	259	57
1968	1 373	84	24	60	1 243	136	291	278	13	412	64	414	285	57
1969	1 493	112	34	78	1 332	135	287	277	11	445	64	462	318	58
1970	1 602	128	44	84	1 423	137	299	290	10	460	61	513	361	64
1971	1 753	139	50	89	1 558	138	324	316	8	503	61	564	389	64
1972	1 938	163	58	105	1 714	138	339	330	9	560	61	634	428	63
1973	2 175	210	78	132	1 898	137	346	337	10	631	62	727	493	65
1974	2 413	258	99	160	2 073	138	358	349	9	686	62	821	549	67
1975	2 621	260	109	152	2 265	138	444	435	9	739	60	862	569	64
1976	2 908	284	123	161	2 508	138	513	504	9	824	61	934	610	61
1977	3 297	338	146	192	2 830	139	569	561	8	951	63	1 053	685	61
1978	3 785	413	183	230	3 214	140	622	615	7	1 111	66	1 187	760	59
1979	4 284	505	232	273	3 607	141	658	652	6	1 201	68	1 346	843	59
1980	4 733	578	277	301	3 958	142	735	730	5	1 402	66	1 477	909	58
1981	5 269	682	324	358	4 366	139	820	816	5	1 513	65	1 661	1 027	58
1982	5 779	778	389	389	4 788	147	982	978	4	1 582	64	1 811	1 117	61
1983	6 477	883	457	426	5 365	152	1 167	1 163	4	1 739	64	1 998	1 229	63
1984	7 442	1 052	531	521	6 151	156	1 364	1 361	3	1 950	65	2 324	1 437	65
1985	8 629	1 257	632	626	7 132	169	1 590	1 587	3	2 278	72	2 587	1 616	69
1986	9 810	1 594	810	783	7 975	179	1 806	1 802	4	2 536	76	2 882	1 839	76
1987	10 821	1 896	978	918	8 678	183	1 950	1 945	5	2 752	77	3 135	2 034	78
1988	11 862	2 146	1 098	1 047	9 462	185	2 105	2 082	23	3 040	79	3 422	2 234	79
1989	12 830	2 399	1 248	1 151	10 166	185	2 251	2 227	24	3 334	81	3 636	2 401	81
1990	13 755	2 616	1 418	1 197	10 850	187	2 498	2 466	32	3 598	83	3 762	2 533	82
1991	14 404	2 787	1 564	1 222	11 313	189	2 776	2 758	19	3 788	83	3 671	2 477	79
1992	15 197	3 046	1 720	1 326	11 832	187	3 080	3 062	19	3 990	82	3 667	2 503	76
1993	16 148	3 346	1 885	1 461	12 413	187	3 336	3 310	27	4 229	84	3 695	2 550	74
1994	17 190	3 822	2 173	1 649	12 993	184	3 492	3 466	27	4 554	86	3 841	2 683	72
1995	18 415	4 279	2 377	1 902	13 683	185	3 637	3 609	28	4 885	89	4 116	2 910	74
1996	19 783	4 829	2 608	2 221	14 413	184	3 782	3 755	27	5 230	90	4 371	3 092	74
1997	21 265	5 458	2 821	2 637	15 199	183	3 805	3 778	27	5 561	91	4 762	3 382	76
1998	23 244	6 543	3 292	3 251	16 241	185	3 752	3 724	29	6 012	92	5 338	3 790	81
1999	25 576	7 611	3 884	3 727	17 302	187	3 681	3 653	28	6 503	95	5 941	4 206	84
2000	27 319	8 430	4 317	4 113	18 166	185	3 385	3 358	27	7 080	97	6 508	4 578	86
2001	29 316	9 363	4 944	4 419	19 302	191	3 380	3 353	27	7 718	103	6 907	4 812	90
2002	31 615	10 274	5 498	4 776	20 677	197	3 637	3 610	27	8 489	107	7 108	4 873	89
1999														
1st quarter	24 009	6 833	3 434	3 399	16 532	182	3 760	3 732	28	6 090	92	5 525	3 938	80
2nd quarter	24 422	7 094	3 581	3 514	16 693	183	3 652	3 623	28	6 219	94	5 652	4 020	81
3rd quarter	25 026	7 369	3 746	3 623	17 005	183	3 633	3 605	28	6 380	95	5 821	4 136	82
4th quarter	25 566	7 611	3 884	3 727	17 302	183	3 681	3 653	28	6 503	95	5 941	4 206	82
2000														
1st quarter	25 957	7 749	3 940	3 809	17 526	182	3 653	3 626	28	6 575	93	6 118	4 338	83
2nd quarter	26 338	7 971	4 035	3 936	17 695	180	3 464	3 436	28	6 737	94	6 307	4 467	85
3rd quarter	26 756	8 168	4 164	4 004	17 891	181	3 410	3 382	28	6 909	95	6 392	4 509	85
4th quarter	27 306	8 430	4 317	4 113	18 166	182	3 385	3 358	27	7 080	97	6 508	4 578	86
2001														
1st quarter	27 756	8 630	4 423	4 207	18 422	184	3 409	3 382	27	7 165	97	6 629	4 658	88
2nd quarter	28 123	8 829	4 592	4 237	18 607	185	3 251	3 224	27	7 345	100	6 757	4 738	89
3rd quarter	28 684	9 093	4 796	4 297	18 931	188	3 320	3 293	27	7 516	99	6 835	4 779	89
4th quarter	29 325	9 363	4 944	4 419	19 302	190	3 380	3 353	27	7 718	103	6 907	4 812	89
2002														
1st quarter	29 777	9 554	5 117	4 437	19 546	190	3 430	3 404	26	7 832	101	6 964	4 842	89
2nd quarter	30 294	9 763	5 239	4 524	19 857	191	3 451	3 425	27	8 018	102	7 017	4 857	88
3rd quarter	30 831	9 965	5 344	4 621	20 200	192	3 541	3 514	27	8 223	104	7 042	4 848	88
4th quarter	31 617	10 274	5 498	4 776	20 677	195	3 637	3 610	27	8 489	107	7 108	4 873	88

. . . = Not available.

Table 12-5. Credit Market Debt Outstanding, By Borrower and Lender—*Continued*

(Billions of dollars, except as noted; end of period; not seasonally adjusted.)

Year and quarter	Credit market debt outstanding owed by:—*Continued*				Credit market assets held by:								
	Domestic nonfinancial sectors—*Continued*			Foreign credit market debt held in United States	Total	Government-related sectors						Selected domestic financial sectors	
	Nonfinancial business—*Continued*		State and local governments			Total	Federal government	Government-sponsored enterprises	Federally related mortgage pools	State and local governments	State and local retirement funds	Total, selected sectors	Monetary authority
	Nonfarm noncorporate	Farm											
1945	5	7	13	5	355	17	5	2	0	8	3	219	24
1946	7	7	13	8	351	20	8	2	0	7	3	219	24
1947	9	7	14	12	368	26	13	2	0	8	3	229	23
1948	9	8	16	14	382	28	14	3	0	8	4	236	24
1949	10	9	17	14	398	31	15	3	0	9	4	245	19
1950	12	10	21	14	425	33	16	3	0	9	5	262	21
1951	14	11	24	15	449	36	17	4	0	10	5	281	24
1952	16	12	31	15	485	41	19	4	0	12	6	303	24
1953	17	12	36	16	517	45	21	4	0	13	8	323	25
1954	19	12	41	17	542	47	20	4	0	13	9	346	25
1955	21	14	46	17	582	51	21	5	0	15	10	368	24
1956	24	15	50	17	611	56	22	6	0	16	12	390	25
1957	25	16	55	19	643	59	22	7	0	16	13	411	24
1958	28	17	61	21	682	63	24	8	0	16	15	444	26
1959	32	19	67	21	739	70	26	10	0	17	17	471	27
1960	36	20	72	23	780	76	27	11	0	19	19	502	27
1961	41	22	78	25	828	82	28	12	0	20	21	541	29
1962	46	24	84	28	888	89	30	14	0	22	23	587	31
1963	53	26	89	31	953	97	32	15	1	23	26	637	34
1964	59	29	96	35	1 028	105	35	16	1	25	28	694	37
1965	65	32	103	37	1 106	116	38	18	1	28	31	757	41
1966	71	36	110	39	1 187	130	43	23	1	27	35	804	44
1967	79	39	117	43	1 268	139	47	23	2	28	38	869	49
1968	87	42	126	46	1 373	154	52	27	3	31	42	942	53
1969	100	45	138	49	1 493	176	55	35	3	36	45	999	57
1970	104	48	150	52	1 602	192	58	44	5	35	50	1 072	62
1971	123	52	167	57	1 753	201	60	45	10	33	53	1 182	70
1972	149	57	181	61	1 938	223	62	49	14	40	57	1 326	71
1973	168	65	195	67	2 175	260	65	64	18	50	63	1 491	80
1974	198	73	208	81	2 413	305	72	85	21	56	69	1 631	85
1975	211	82	219	96	2 621	346	86	90	29	64	78	1 764	94
1976	231	92	238	116	2 908	399	94	95	41	82	88	1 960	100
1977	261	106	256	129	3 297	472	104	101	57	111	99	2 218	109
1978	305	122	296	158	3 785	583	121	128	70	148	116	2 513	117
1979	358	146	322	173	4 284	695	140	158	95	175	127	2 825	125
1980	406	161	344	197	4 733	803	164	184	114	193	147	3 092	128
1981	457	178	372	221	5 269	929	188	218	129	226	169	3 399	137
1982	510	184	414	213	5 779	1 059	206	234	179	250	191	3 640	145
1983	580	188	461	230	6 477	1 178	215	236	245	282	199	4 046	159
1984	699	188	514	238	7 442	1 340	233	266	289	319	233	4 603	168
1985	798	173	678	239	8 629	1 618	251	291	368	456	252	5 178	186
1986	886	156	752	241	9 810	1 920	258	308	532	526	297	5 880	205
1987	956	144	841	247	10 821	2 156	243	331	669	584	329	6 439	230
1988	1 054	134	895	255	11 862	2 296	217	364	745	619	351	6 971	241
1989	1 100	134	945	265	12 830	2 484	209	360	870	664	381	7 390	233
1990	1 093	135	992	289	13 755	2 742	243	374	1 020	703	402	7 755	241
1991	1 058	135	1 078	304	14 404	2 951	251	389	1 156	751	405	8 017	273
1992	1 028	135	1 095	319	15 197	3 163	239	458	1 272	752	442	8 402	300
1993	1 008	138	1 152	389	16 148	3 391	230	545	1 357	785	474	8 996	337
1994	1 016	142	1 106	375	17 190	3 574	215	666	1 472	730	491	9 502	368
1995	1 062	145	1 045	454	18 415	3 707	208	761	1 570	639	530	10 238	381
1996	1 129	150	1 029	542	19 783	3 920	207	832	1 711	605	565	10 846	393
1997	1 224	156	1 071	608	21 265	4 211	210	938	1 826	605	632	11 740	431
1998	1 384	164	1 138	639	23 423	4 936	222	1 252	2 018	739	705	12 907	452
1999	1 566	169	1 177	652	25 566	5 616	261	1 543	2 292	768	751	13 931	478
2000	1 750	180	1 192	709	27 306	6 141	273	1 804	2 492	767	806	14 932	512
2001	1 907	188	1 298	660	29 325	6 835	279	2 110	2 830	828	788	16 040	552
2002	2 039	196	1 444	666	31 617	7 427	289	2 324	3 158	853	802	17 284	629
1999													
1st quarter	1 425	163	1 157	644	24 009	5 121	225	1 300	2 112	760	725	13 154	466
2nd quarter	1 466	166	1 170	635	24 422	5 291	225	1 376	2 183	777	730	13 366	485
3rd quarter	1 516	169	1 171	652	25 026	5 490	264	1 471	2 246	769	740	13 628	489
4th quarter	1 566	169	1 177	652	25 566	5 616	261	1 543	2 292	768	751	13 925	478
2000													
1st quarter	1 610	170	1 180	681	25 957	5 700	264	1 582	2 322	765	767	14 175	502
2nd quarter	1 665	175	1 186	672	26 338	5 816	264	1 646	2 355	776	775	14 365	505
3rd quarter	1 706	177	1 180	697	26 756	5 948	271	1 711	2 414	766	785	14 636	512
4th quarter	1 750	180	1 192	709	27 306	6 141	273	1 804	2 492	767	806	14 923	512
2001													
1st quarter	1 791	180	1 220	704	27 756	6 257	275	1 874	2 534	785	788	15 174	524
2nd quarter	1 833	185	1 254	687	28 123	6 473	275	1 953	2 636	802	808	15 402	535
3rd quarter	1 871	186	1 260	660	28 684	6 666	279	2 022	2 759	817	789	15 694	534
4th quarter	1 907	188	1 298	660	29 325	6 835	279	2 110	2 830	828	788	16 033	552
2002													
1st quarter	1 935	187	1 320	676	29 777	7 030	281	2 159	2 955	828	806	16 228	575
2nd quarter	1 968	192	1 371	674	30 294	7 152	280	2 195	3 042	842	792	16 422	591
3rd quarter	1 999	195	1 394	666	30 831	7 255	288	2 248	3 085	845	790	16 789	604
4th quarter	2 039	196	1 444	666	31 617	7 427	289	2 324	3 158	853	802	17 264	629

Table 12-5. Credit Market Debt Outstanding, By Borrower and Lender—*Continued*

(Billions of dollars, except as noted; end of period; not seasonally adjusted.)

Year and quarter	Commercial banks	Savings institutions	Credit unions	Life insurance companies	Other insurance companies	Private pension funds	Money market mutual funds	Mutual funds	Asset-backed security issuers	Finance companies	Households	Foreign holdings in United States	All other financial and non-financial sectors
1945	118	24	0	41	4	4	0	0	0	4	91	3	25
1946	112	27	0	44	4	4	0	0	0	4	90	2	19
1947	115	29	0	47	5	4	0	0	0	5	92	3	19
1948	113	31	1	51	6	5	0	0	0	6	94	3	21
1949	119	34	1	54	6	5	0	0	0	7	95	3	24
1950	126	37	1	58	7	5	0	0	0	8	96	5	29
1951	133	40	1	62	8	6	0	1	0	8	97	5	30
1952	141	44	1	66	9	7	0	1	0	10	105	5	31
1953	145	50	1	71	10	8	0	1	0	12	110	6	33
1954	155	56	2	75	11	10	0	1	0	12	109	6	32
1955	159	63	2	80	12	11	0	1	0	16	118	7	38
1956	165	70	2	86	12	13	0	1	0	17	125	7	34
1957	170	77	3	90	13	14	0	1	0	18	132	7	33
1958	185	85	3	96	13	16	0	1	0	18	133	8	35
1959	190	95	4	101	15	18	0	2	0	21	143	12	43
1960	200	104	5	106	16	20	0	2	0	24	151	13	38
1961	216	115	5	111	17	21	0	2	0	25	155	13	37
1962	235	128	6	117	18	23	0	3	0	27	158	15	39
1963	253	145	6	123	19	25	0	3	0	30	160	16	44
1964	276	160	7	130	20	27	0	3	0	34	166	17	46
1965	305	174	8	138	21	29	0	4	0	38	170	17	47
1966	323	182	9	146	22	32	0	5	0	41	191	17	46
1967	360	195	10	153	23	33	0	4	0	41	196	19	45
1968	399	209	12	161	25	34	0	4	0	46	207	19	50
1969	418	221	14	168	27	35	0	5	0	53	217	19	83
1970	455	237	15	175	31	37	0	6	0	55	216	30	93
1971	507	272	17	183	35	35	0	6	0	59	204	57	110
1972	576	315	20	192	38	41	0	6	0	67	199	65	124
1973	662	348	24	205	42	47	0	7	0	77	221	66	137
1974	738	370	26	218	46	56	1	7	0	84	262	72	143
1975	769	415	32	235	54	71	1	8	0	86	278	81	152
1976	833	477	38	258	66	78	2	8	0	98	280	94	175
1977	925	548	46	286	84	88	2	12	0	118	290	142	175
1978	1 053	614	52	319	100	99	5	13	0	141	330	170	189
1979	1 182	672	54	352	114	121	25	15	0	167	401	161	204
1980	1 290	723	53	385	124	151	42	17	0	180	425	186	226
1981	1 398	749	55	420	132	179	107	20	0	202	444	217	281
1982	1 483	757	57	463	137	225	138	25	0	210	507	255	318
1983	1 626	879	69	514	139	267	120	35	3	235	590	281	382
1984	1 800	1 019	85	570	150	306	164	54	20	267	695	358	447
1985	1 989	1 098	98	647	176	329	178	130	35	311	849	432	552
1986	2 188	1 191	114	734	219	334	213	260	71	351	866	544	599
1987	2 323	1 310	131	823	259	347	215	291	113	396	1 028	596	603
1988	2 479	1 409	149	927	288	369	225	304	148	431	1 228	698	668
1989	2 647	1 316	156	1 028	318	421	294	327	201	449	1 316	816	823
1990	2 772	1 176	167	1 135	344	464	371	360	252	471	1 556	889	813
1991	2 853	1 013	179	1 219	377	490	404	440	317	453	1 635	905	895
1992	2 949	937	197	1 304	389	516	409	566	381	453	1 677	989	966
1993	3 091	914	219	1 415	423	552	429	726	463	428	1 648	1 109	1 004
1994	3 254	921	247	1 487	446	591	459	719	533	476	1 935	1 216	963
1995	3 520	913	263	1 587	469	608	546	771	653	526	1 940	1 493	1 036
1996	3 708	933	288	1 657	491	601	634	820	774	545	2 141	1 840	1 037
1997	4 032	929	305	1 751	515	647	722	901	938	568	2 142	2 098	1 074
1998	4 336	965	324	1 828	521	621	966	1 028	1 219	645	2 253	2 273	1 054
1999	4 648	1 032	352	1 886	518	635	1 148	1 077	1 414	743	2 558	2 307	1 154
2000	5 006	1 089	380	1 944	509	666	1 291	1 098	1 586	851	2 473	2 477	1 282
2001	5 210	1 131	421	2 075	518	673	1 537	1 224	1 852	846	2 438	2 724	1 288
2002	5 615	1 167	464	2 308	558	701	1 512	1 365	2 098	868	2 440	3 131	1 336
1999													
1st quarter	4 340	991	330	1 854	517	627	1 036	1 054	1 276	664	2 338	2 314	1 082
2nd quarter	4 384	1 012	341	1 870	524	632	1 002	1 087	1 345	686	2 400	2 300	1 066
3rd quarter	4 491	1 030	348	1 880	520	629	1 050	1 086	1 399	704	2 458	2 365	1 084
4th quarter	4 648	1 032	352	1 886	518	635	1 148	1 077	1 407	743	2 558	2 307	1 160
2000													
1st quarter	4 727	1 043	359	1 902	515	639	1 217	1 058	1 435	777	2 525	2 355	1 201
2nd quarter	4 850	1 060	370	1 914	511	646	1 159	1 072	1 465	813	2 530	2 376	1 251
3rd quarter	4 930	1 080	375	1 935	512	660	1 213	1 087	1 501	831	2 500	2 389	1 284
4th quarter	5 006	1 089	380	1 944	509	666	1 291	1 098	1 577	851	2 473	2 477	1 291
2001													
1st quarter	5 014	1 100	387	1 970	510	669	1 404	1 114	1 633	849	2 451	2 537	1 338
2nd quarter	5 041	1 116	392	2 005	510	674	1 414	1 160	1 674	880	2 399	2 591	1 257
3rd quarter	5 101	1 118	408	2 055	511	678	1 495	1 188	1 745	861	2 385	2 647	1 291
4th quarter	5 210	1 131	421	2 075	518	673	1 537	1 224	1 844	846	2 438	2 724	1 295
2002													
1st quarter	5 231	1 135	434	2 141	528	685	1 497	1 277	1 891	834	2 448	2 789	1 282
2nd quarter	5 328	1 131	453	2 192	536	690	1 420	1 292	1 941	848	2 485	2 901	1 334
3rd quarter	5 476	1 154	455	2 266	542	700	1 411	1 334	1 985	861	2 418	3 003	1 366
4th quarter	5 615	1 167	464	2 308	558	701	1 512	1 365	2 078	868	2 440	3 131	1 355

Table 12-6. Household Assets, Financial Obligations, and Delinquency Rates

(Billions of dollars, except as noted; end of period; not seasonally adjusted, except as noted.)

Year and quarter	Total	Foreign deposits	Checkable deposits and currency	Time and savings deposits	Money market fund shares	Open market paper	U.S. savings bonds	Other Treasury securities	Agency securities	Municipal securities	Corporate and foreign bonds	Corporate equities	Mutual fund shares	Mortgages
1945	563	0	54	50	0	0	43	24	0	4	8	110	1	12
1946	603	0	59	57	0	0	44	21	0	4	8	101	1	14
1947	643	0	59	60	0	0	46	19	0	5	7	99	1	15
1948	667	0	56	62	0	0	48	18	0	5	7	98	2	16
1949	688	0	54	65	0	0	49	18	0	4	6	105	3	17
1950	739	0	57	67	0	0	50	17	0	6	6	129	3	18
1951	805	0	61	72	0	1	49	16	0	6	6	151	4	19
1952	830	0	63	80	0	1	49	18	0	11	6	151	4	19
1953	849	0	64	88	0	1	49	19	0	14	6	146	4	20
1954	928	0	66	97	0	1	50	16	0	16	5	199	6	21
1955	1 016	0	67	105	0	1	50	19	1	19	5	248	8	23
1956	1 085	0	69	115	0	1	50	20	1	22	6	271	9	24
1957	1 096	0	68	127	0	2	48	23	1	24	7	244	9	26
1958	1 225	0	70	140	0	2	48	21	1	25	8	322	13	29
1959	1 301	0	72	151	0	2	46	26	2	28	8	357	16	31
1960	1 351	0	74	163	0	3	46	27	1	31	11	360	17	34
1961	1 497	0	73	182	0	2	46	26	1	33	11	443	23	37
1962	1 540	0	73	207	0	3	47	27	0	32	10	431	21	39
1963	1 639	0	77	233	0	4	48	25	0	32	10	470	25	40
1964	1 793	0	80	259	0	5	49	25	0	35	10	544	28	42
1965	1 961	0	87	287	0	6	50	25	1	37	9	616	34	43
1966	1 985	0	89	306	0	8	50	29	6	41	12	548	34	45
1967	2 236	0	99	340	0	10	51	28	6	38	16	682	43	46
1968	2 503	0	109	371	0	12	52	30	6	36	21	815	50	49
1969	2 470	0	105	378	0	15	52	36	7	36	21	587	41	49
1970	2 565	0	113	419	0	13	52	25	11	35	29	572	40	50
1971	2 856	0	126	483	0	9	54	15	11	32	37	651	48	47
1972	3 272	0	137	554	0	3	58	15	5	32	38	814	51	48
1973	3 279	0	145	615	0	8	60	22	4	39	41	598	39	47
1974	3 252	0	150	670	2	16	63	24	8	47	53	373	28	51
1975	3 717	0	151	748	4	12	67	34	1	50	63	499	34	50
1976	4 212	0	161	848	3	8	72	19	5	52	71	637	36	53
1977	4 481	0	175	950	3	23	77	18	0	56	61	543	36	55
1978	5 020	0	188	1 051	8	36	81	19	1	80	51	550	36	62
1979	5 765	0	206	1 121	38	43	80	65	0	96	45	675	39	72
1980	6 632	0	220	1 239	62	38	73	88	5	104	30	875	46	87
1981	7 029	0	262	1 307	148	27	68	84	1	131	31	780	47	101
1982	7 617	2	276	1 414	180	30	68	101	1	171	24	832	57	101
1983	8 383	7	284	1 614	149	25	71	143	0	212	27	936	88	111
1984	8 902	7	295	1 840	191	42	75	184	13	252	27	863	105	103
1985	10 034	8	313	1 970	193	35	80	183	7	348	77	1 058	198	120
1986	11 155	9	425	2 058	229	31	93	157	7	355	107	1 330	333	116
1987	11 833	10	428	2 177	250	33	101	180	12	454	124	1 306	382	124
1988	13 014	11	425	2 355	265	67	110	257	28	524	117	1 586	400	126
1989	14 416	12	424	2 434	342	57	118	247	49	548	163	1 947	463	135
1990	14 842	13	412	2 465	369	63	126	345	84	575	219	1 781	457	144
1991	16 380	15	462	2 394	383	33	138	365	67	614	273	2 549	570	145
1992	17 189	16	570	2 292	342	30	157	441	62	579	271	2 869	707	137
1993	18 384	16	615	2 183	342	46	172	468	7	535	294	3 232	969	126
1994	19 024	19	585	2 154	352	47	180	653	124	485	331	3 096	982	116
1995	21 617	23	544	2 281	450	48	185	598	143	431	425	4 141	1 153	109
1996	24 072	35	471	2 434	501	55	187	648	228	401	514	4 864	1 502	110
1997	27 546	37	437	2 566	582	56	187	550	249	420	571	6 242	1 961	110
1998	30 508	38	422	2 733	712	64	187	511	266	427	688	7 074	2 394	110
1999	34 971	44	346	2 811	822	68	186	620	385	450	738	9 052	3 115	110
2000	33 912	59	226	3 100	968	73	185	402	432	461	808	7 474	3 036	113
2001	32 568	54	300	3 337	1 116	42	190	301	354	513	926	6 184	2 870	113
2002	30 333	64	265	3 631	1 076	48	195	192	179	621	1 091	4 601	2 539	114
1999														
1st quarter	31 280	40	396	2 731	766	65	187	475	284	432	785	7 415	2 521	111
2nd quarter	32 395	42	355	2 739	732	66	186	455	316	448	818	7 867	2 733	111
3rd quarter	31 708	43	340	2 777	746	67	186	448	370	443	833	7 377	2 681	111
4th quarter	34 971	44	346	2 811	822	68	186	620	385	450	738	9 052	3 115	110
2000														
1st quarter	36 082	49	311	2 911	905	69	185	566	389	449	755	9 489	3 320	112
2nd quarter	35 336	49	264	2 967	871	70	185	456	421	470	816	8 841	3 241	112
3rd quarter	35 288	53	219	3 042	904	71	184	407	445	464	815	8 486	3 277	113
4th quarter	33 912	59	226	3 100	968	73	185	402	432	461	808	7 474	3 036	113
2001														
1st quarter	32 079	57	256	3 212	1 058	68	185	374	331	479	902	6 269	2 732	112
2nd quarter	32 944	56	253	3 250	1 006	59	185	271	341	511	919	6 658	2 935	113
3rd quarter	30 931	55	257	3 301	1 072	50	186	267	370	501	898	5 430	2 588	113
4th quarter	32 568	54	300	3 337	1 116	42	190	301	354	513	926	6 184	2 870	113
2002														
1st quarter	32 661	54	303	3 474	1 101	41	192	281	327	545	949	5 922	2 937	113
2nd quarter	31 075	55	252	3 525	1 039	39	193	240	306	592	1 002	5 049	2 744	114
3rd quarter	29 245	61	223	3 635	1 071	44	193	245	232	587	1 003	4 087	2 430	114
4th quarter	30 333	64	265	3 631	1 076	48	195	192	179	621	1 091	4 601	2 539	114

[1] Includes nonprofit organizations.

Table 12-6. Household Assets, Financial Obligations, and Delinquency Rates—*Continued*

(Billions of dollars, except as noted; end of period; not seasonally adjusted, except as noted.)

Year and quarter	Financial assets of the household sector [1]—*Continued*						Tangible assets of the household sector		Debt as a percent of total assets	Ratios to disposable personal income (percent, seasonally adjusted)				Household debt delinquency rate on credit card accounts held at banks (percent of loans serviced)
	Security credit	Life insurance reserves	Pension fund reserves	Equity in noncorporate business	Bank personal trusts	Miscellaneous assets	Total [1]	Household real estate [2]		Household debt service	Household financial obligations			
											Total	Homeowners	Renters	
1945	1	40	12	198	0	6	199	131	...	...	...	...	...	...
1946	1	43	14	230	0	7	231	150	...	...	...	...	...	...
1947	1	47	16	262	0	8	275	178	...	...	...	...	...	...
1948	1	49	18	279	0	8	309	200	...	...	...	...	...	...
1949	1	52	21	284	0	8	336	218	...	...	...	...	...	...
1950	1	55	24	297	0	9	382	244	...	...	...	...	...	...
1951	1	58	28	325	0	9	425	272	...	...	...	...	...	...
1952	1	61	33	323	0	10	458	296	7	...	...	...	...	...
1953	1	64	39	324	0	11	488	316	8	...	...	...	...	...
1954	1	66	44	328	0	11	516	338	8	...	...	...	...	...
1955	1	69	52	336	0	11	560	368	9	...	...	...	...	...
1956	1	73	58	353	0	12	603	395	9	...	...	...	...	...
1957	1	75	65	364	0	12	638	418	10	...	...	...	...	...
1958	1	79	75	379	0	12	664	439	9	...	...	...	...	...
1959	1	82	85	380	0	13	698	464	10	...	...	...	...	...
1960	1	85	94	392	0	13	730	488	10	...	...	...	...	...
1961	1	89	107	410	0	14	762	512	10	...	...	...	...	...
1962	1	92	114	428	0	14	795	534	11	...	...	...	...	...
1963	1	97	128	433	0	15	831	554	11	...	...	...	...	...
1964	2	101	145	452	0	16	876	580	12	...	...	...	...	...
1965	3	106	162	479	0	17	922	606	12	...	...	...	...	...
1966	3	111	172	514	0	18	995	650	12	...	...	...	...	...
1967	5	116	196	539	0	20	1 003	686	12	...	...	...	...	...
1968	7	120	219	584	0	22	1 188	769	11	...	...	...	...	...
1969	5	125	231	620	135	24	1 295	833	12	...	...	...	...	...
1970	4	131	254	650	138	26	1 375	875	12	...	...	...	...	...
1971	5	137	293	717	163	29	1 500	958	12	...	...	...	...	...
1972	5	144	349	800	187	31	1 695	1 099	11	...	...	...	...	...
1973	5	151	358	938	175	34	1 920	1 252	12	...	...	...	...	...
1974	4	158	368	1 052	147	37	2 035	1 262	13	...	...	...	...	...
1975	4	169	467	1 153	169	41	2 253	1 415	12	...	...	...	...	...
1976	6	178	535	1 286	196	46	2 504	1 591	12	...	...	...	...	...
1977	6	188	590	1 454	194	53	2 903	1 888	13	...	...	...	...	...
1978	9	199	691	1 691	207	60	3 357	2 212	13	...	...	...	...	...
1979	10	210	801	1 966	231	67	3 901	2 605	13	...	...	...	...	...
1980	16	221	970	2 219	265	74	4 378	2 945	13	10.60	15.36	11.20	23.61	...
1981	15	230	1 065	2 380	272	80	4 838	3 295	13	10.69	15.62	11.37	24.29	...
1982	18	238	1 292	2 424	289	87	5 063	3 449	12	10.77	15.80	11.55	24.15	...
1983	21	247	1 541	2 486	318	103	5 307	3 604	13	10.78	15.79	11.81	22.33	...
1984	22	253	1 711	2 486	331	104	5 934	4 112	13	11.16	16.18	12.15	23.35	...
1985	35	264	2 085	2 543	384	133	6 610	4 660	14	12.00	17.30	13.09	25.18	...
1986	44	283	2 325	2 674	429	150	7 205	5 091	14	12.47	17.89	13.62	26.09	...
1987	39	310	2 492	2 795	442	175	7 765	5 505	14	12.06	17.45	13.26	25.73	...
1988	41	336	2 748	2 958	470	191	8 415	5 982	14	11.82	17.04	13.02	25.02	...
1989	53	365	3 221	3 092	541	206	9 066	6 477	14	12.08	17.36	13.37	24.86	...
1990	62	392	3 376	3 182	552	224	9 260	6 579	15	11.96	17.26	13.28	24.59	...
1991	87	419	3 838	3 156	639	234	9 511	6 812	15	11.54	16.85	12.89	23.69	5.27
1992	76	448	4 151	3 131	661	251	9 836	7 121	15	10.78	16.00	12.20	22.15	4.66
1993	102	485	4 613	3 224	691	264	10 145	7 360	15	10.74	15.94	12.06	22.53	3.89
1994	109	520	4 882	3 413	699	277	10 458	7 527	15	11.15	16.45	12.41	24.04	3.26
1995	128	566	5 671	3 624	803	292	11 053	7 996	15	11.83	17.20	13.13	25.06	3.92
1996	163	611	6 325	3 852	872	301	11 504	8 325	15	12.17	17.52	13.51	25.49	4.58
1997	215	665	7 323	4 121	942	312	12 151	8 786	14	12.22	17.56	13.63	25.56	4.75
1998	277	718	8 210	4 356	1 001	321	13 131	9 545	14	12.23	17.45	13.53	25.81	4.70
1999	324	784	9 068	4 582	1 130	334	14 175	10 400	13	12.64	17.89	13.87	27.18	4.51
2000	412	819	9 071	4 841	1 096	339	15 477	11 430	14	12.99	18.03	14.05	27.93	4.59
2001	454	880	8 681	4 938	961	355	16 708	12 537	16	13.58	18.71	14.54	29.62	4.75
2002	413	921	8 003	5 155	841	384	18 171	13 772	17	13.29	18.15	14.13	29.03	4.94
1999														
1st quarter	262	736	8 316	4 418	1 017	324	13 335	9 703	14	12.30	17.55	13.59	26.12	1.88
2nd quarter	270	750	8 654	4 465	1 062	326	13 620	9 929	14	12.43	17.71	13.71	26.60	1.83
3rd quarter	285	756	8 375	4 518	1 018	333	13 934	10 194	14	12.58	17.88	13.85	26.97	1.57
4th quarter	324	784	9 068	4 582	1 130	334	14 175	10 400	13	12.64	17.89	13.87	27.18	1.46
2000														
1st quarter	371	801	9 264	4 623	1 178	336	14 489	10 662	13	12.56	17.70	13.76	26.94	1.51
2nd quarter	359	807	9 195	4 716	1 156	340	14 839	10 910	13	12.67	17.76	13.82	27.19	1.44
3rd quarter	373	819	9 336	4 769	1 169	342	15 185	11 188	14	12.81	17.86	13.91	27.48	1.48
4th quarter	412	819	9 071	4 841	1 096	339	15 477	11 430	14	12.99	18.03	14.05	27.93	1.53
2001														
1st quarter	412	823	8 582	4 887	1 000	340	15 878	11 766	15	13.13	18.18	14.16	28.29	1.59
2nd quarter	413	840	8 855	4 908	1 025	346	16 170	12 047	15	13.28	18.36	14.28	28.74	1.73
3rd quarter	495	844	8 274	4 958	916	356	16 457	12 319	16	13.13	18.13	14.07	28.73	1.92
4th quarter	454	880	8 681	4 938	961	355	16 708	12 537	16	13.58	18.71	14.54	29.62	1.93
2002														
1st quarter	428	894	8 813	4 964	963	360	17 009	12 802	16	13.31	18.29	14.21	29.18	1.78
2nd quarter	400	901	8 375	5 029	894	372	17 394	13 124	17	13.26	18.17	14.12	29.09	1.75
3rd quarter	401	903	7 719	5 106	812	381	17 825	13 482	17	13.28	18.16	14.12	29.09	1.69
4th quarter	413	921	8 003	5 155	841	384	18 171	13 772	18	13.29	18.15	14.13	29.03	1.62

[1]Includes nonprofit organizations.
[2]Excludes nonprofit organizations.
. . . = Not available.

Table 12-7. Mortgage Debt Outstanding

(Billions of dollars, except as noted; end of period; not seasonally adjusted.)

| Year and quarter | Total | By type of property | | | | | By type of holder | | | | | | | |
| | | Home | | Multi-family residences | Commercial | Farm | Commercial banks | Savings institutions | Life insurance companies | Federal and related agencies | Mortgage pools or trusts | | | Other |
		Billions of dollars	Percent of value of real estate								Total [1]	Federally related agencies	ABS issuers	
1945	36	19	14	5	8	5	5	10	7	2	0	0	0	10
1946	42	23	15	5	9	5	7	12	7	2	0	0	0	12
1947	49	28	16	6	10	5	9	14	9	2	0	0	0	15
1948	56	33	17	7	11	5	11	16	11	2	0	0	0	17
1949	63	37	17	8	12	6	12	18	13	2	0	0	0	18
1950	73	45	18	9	13	6	14	22	16	3	0	0	0	20
1951	82	51	19	11	14	7	15	25	19	3	0	0	0	21
1952	91	58	20	11	14	7	16	29	21	4	0	0	0	21
1953	101	66	21	12	16	8	17	34	23	5	0	0	0	22
1954	113	75	22	13	17	8	19	40	26	5	0	0	0	24
1955	129	88	24	13	19	9	21	48	29	5	0	0	0	26
1956	144	98	25	14	22	10	23	55	33	6	0	0	0	28
1957	156	107	26	15	24	10	23	60	35	7	0	0	0	30
1958	172	117	27	17	27	11	26	68	37	8	0	0	0	33
1959	191	130	28	19	30	12	28	77	39	10	0	0	0	36
1960	208	141	29	21	33	13	29	86	42	11	0	0	0	40
1961	228	153	30	24	37	14	30	96	44	12	0	0	0	45
1962	252	167	31	27	42	15	34	109	47	12	0	0	0	49
1963	278	184	33	30	47	17	39	125	51	11	1	1	0	52
1964	306	201	35	35	51	19	44	140	55	12	1	1	0	55
1965	334	219	36	38	56	21	50	153	60	13	1	1	0	58
1966	358	232	36	41	61	23	54	160	65	16	1	1	0	61
1967	381	245	36	45	66	25	59	170	68	19	2	2	0	64
1968	411	262	34	48	73	27	65	182	70	23	3	3	0	68
1969	442	280	34	53	79	29	71	194	72	28	3	3	0	74
1970	472	294	34	60	87	30	73	205	74	34	5	5	0	80
1971	520	321	33	70	97	32	83	231	75	37	10	10	0	85
1972	592	360	33	83	114	35	99	268	77	40	14	14	0	94
1973	669	402	32	93	134	40	119	300	81	47	18	18	0	104
1974	731	438	35	100	148	45	132	321	86	61	21	21	0	110
1975	788	477	34	101	161	50	136	351	89	73	29	29	0	111
1976	873	538	34	106	174	55	151	398	92	76	41	41	0	116
1977	1 002	631	33	114	193	64	179	459	97	84	57	57	0	126
1978	1 154	741	34	125	215	73	214	517	106	100	70	70	0	146
1979	1 321	859	33	135	239	87	245	565	118	121	95	95	0	176
1980	1 462	962	33	143	260	97	263	594	131	143	114	114	0	217
1981	1 584	1 035	31	142	300	107	284	612	138	160	129	129	0	261
1982	1 666	1 075	31	146	334	111	301	576	142	177	179	179	0	291
1983	1 856	1 192	33	161	389	114	331	627	151	188	245	245	0	314
1984	2 097	1 326	32	186	472	112	381	710	157	202	300	289	11	347
1985	2 377	1 524	33	206	542	106	431	766	172	213	393	368	25	403
1986	2 664	1 726	34	239	603	95	505	785	194	202	550	532	19	428
1987	2 965	1 924	35	259	694	88	595	824	212	189	702	669	32	443
1988	3 282	2 158	36	275	766	83	677	888	233	192	787	745	41	505
1989	3 553	2 383	37	288	801	80	771	873	254	198	923	870	53	534
1990	3 808	2 620	40	288	821	79	849	802	268	239	1 088	1 020	68	562
1991	3 960	2 789	41	285	807	79	881	705	260	266	1 275	1 156	118	573
1992	4 072	2 957	42	272	763	80	901	628	242	286	1 451	1 272	179	565
1993	4 209	3 119	42	269	740	81	948	598	224	326	1 580	1 357	224	532
1994	4 381	3 301	44	270	727	83	1 013	596	216	316	1 726	1 472	254	515
1995	4 577	3 478	44	276	739	84	1 090	597	213	308	1 849	1 570	279	519
1996	4 864	3 720	45	288	769	87	1 145	628	208	294	2 038	1 711	326	550
1997	5 201	3 978	45	300	833	90	1 245	632	207	285	2 232	1 826	407	600
1998	5 712	4 363	46	331	921	97	1 337	644	214	292	2 581	2 018	562	645
1999	6 315	4 787	46	368	1 057	102	1 495	668	231	320	2 947	2 292	654	654
2000	6 883	5 205	46	401	1 168	109	1 660	723	236	341	3 226	2 492	734	697
2001	7 582	5 739	46	445	1 281	116	1 790	758	243	373	3 701	2 830	870	717
2002	8 463	6 463	47	488	1 387	125	2 058	781	250	436	4 161	3 158	1 003	776
1999														
1st quarter	5 840	4 456	46	341	945	98	1 337	647	219	287	2 705	2 112	593	645
2nd quarter	5 979	4 565	46	347	967	100	1 361	657	225	287	2 801	2 183	618	649
3rd quarter	6 180	4 697	46	357	1 025	102	1 419	676	226	320	2 882	2 246	636	657
4th quarter	6 315	4 787	46	368	1 057	102	1 495	668	231	320	2 947	2 292	654	654
2000														
1st quarter	6 428	4 864	46	376	1 084	104	1 547	680	229	320	2 990	2 322	668	660
2nd quarter	6 592	4 987	46	385	1 114	106	1 614	701	233	330	3 040	2 355	685	673
3rd quarter	6 744	5 106	46	391	1 140	108	1 649	721	235	333	3 120	2 414	705	687
4th quarter	6 883	5 205	46	401	1 168	109	1 660	723	236	341	3 226	2 492	734	697
2001														
1st quarter	7 010	5 301	45	410	1 190	110	1 688	740	235	344	3 298	2 534	764	705
2nd quarter	7 210	5 461	45	421	1 216	113	1 722	752	237	353	3 426	2 636	791	719
3rd quarter	7 401	5 605	46	432	1 249	115	1 737	758	239	359	3 571	2 759	812	737
4th quarter	7 582	5 739	46	445	1 281	116	1 790	758	243	373	3 701	2 830	870	717
2002														
1st quarter	7 747	5 877	46	453	1 299	118	1 800	746	243	380	3 854	2 955	899	722
2nd quarter	7 962	6 050	46	464	1 329	120	1 873	743	245	391	3 971	3 042	930	739
3rd quarter	8 196	6 248	46	472	1 353	124	1 962	774	246	407	4 052	3 085	968	756
4th quarter	8 463	6 463	47	488	1 387	125	2 058	781	250	436	4 161	3 158	1 003	776

[1]Outstanding principal balances of mortgage-backed securities issued or guaranteed by the holder indicated.

Table 12-8. Consumer Credit

(Outstanding at end of period, billions of dollars.)

Year and month	Seasonally adjusted			Not seasonally adjusted							
	Total	By major credit type		Total	By major holder						
		Revolving	Non-revolving		Commercial banks	Finance companies	Credit unions	Federal government and Sallie Mae	Savings institutions	Nonfinancial businesses	Securitized pools [1]
1945	6.6	...	6.6	6.8	2.2	0.9	0.0	0.0	0.3	3.4	0.0
1946	9.4	...	9.4	9.8	3.8	1.5	0.0	0.0	0.4	4.0	0.0
1947	12.9	...	12.9	13.3	5.4	2.4	0.1	0.0	0.6	4.9	0.0
1948	15.8	...	15.8	16.3	6.6	3.2	0.1	0.0	0.7	5.8	0.0
1949	18.8	...	18.8	19.4	7.7	4.3	0.2	0.0	0.7	6.4	0.0
1950	23.2	...	23.2	23.9	9.7	5.3	0.3	0.0	0.9	7.7	0.0
1951	24.6	...	24.6	25.4	10.0	5.6	0.3	0.0	0.9	8.5	0.0
1952	29.7	...	29.7	30.5	12.3	7.1	0.6	0.0	0.9	9.7	0.0
1953	33.7	...	33.7	34.6	14.0	8.6	0.9	0.0	1.0	10.1	0.0
1954	35.0	...	35.0	36.0	14.3	9.1	1.1	0.0	1.1	10.5	0.0
1955	41.9	...	41.9	42.9	17.2	11.8	1.3	0.0	1.4	11.2	0.0
1956	45.4	...	45.4	46.6	18.9	12.7	1.7	0.0	1.5	11.8	0.0
1957	48.1	...	48.1	49.2	20.2	13.2	2.1	0.0	1.6	12.1	0.0
1958	48.4	...	48.4	49.5	20.7	12.3	2.3	0.0	1.8	12.3	0.0
1959	56.0	...	56.0	57.2	24.2	14.1	2.9	0.0	2.1	14.0	0.0
1960	60.0	...	60.0	61.2	26.4	15.4	3.4	0.0	2.4	13.5	0.0
1961	62.2	...	62.2	63.4	27.9	15.5	3.6	0.0	2.9	13.6	0.0
1962	68.1	...	68.1	69.3	30.6	17.3	4.1	0.0	3.0	14.3	0.0
1963	76.6	...	76.6	77.9	34.7	19.6	4.5	0.0	3.6	15.5	0.0
1964	86.0	...	86.0	87.4	39.8	21.6	5.4	0.0	3.7	16.8	0.0
1965	96.0	...	96.0	97.5	45.2	23.9	6.5	0.0	3.9	18.1	0.0
1966	101.8	...	101.8	103.4	48.2	24.8	7.5	0.0	4.0	19.0	0.0
1967	106.8	...	106.8	108.6	51.7	24.6	8.3	0.0	4.1	19.9	0.0
1968	117.4	2.0	115.4	119.3	58.5	26.1	9.7	0.0	4.3	20.8	0.0
1969	127.2	3.6	123.6	129.2	63.4	27.8	11.7	0.0	4.4	21.9	0.0
1970	131.6	5.0	126.6	133.7	65.6	27.6	13.0	0.0	4.4	23.0	0.0
1971	146.9	8.2	138.7	149.2	74.3	29.2	14.8	0.0	4.7	26.2	0.0
1972	166.2	9.4	156.8	168.8	87.0	31.9	17.0	0.0	5.1	27.8	0.0
1973	190.1	11.3	178.7	193.0	99.6	35.4	19.6	0.0	8.5	29.8	0.0
1974	198.9	13.2	185.7	201.9	103.0	36.1	21.9	0.0	9.1	31.8	0.0
1975	204.0	14.5	189.5	207.0	106.1	32.6	25.7	0.0	10.1	32.6	0.0
1976	225.7	16.5	209.2	229.0	118.0	33.7	31.2	0.0	10.8	35.2	0.0
1977	260.6	37.4	223.1	264.9	140.3	37.3	37.6	0.5	11.8	37.4	0.0
1978	306.1	45.7	260.4	311.3	166.5	44.4	45.2	0.9	13.1	41.2	0.0
1979	348.6	53.6	295.0	354.6	185.7	55.4	47.4	1.5	20.0	44.6	0.0
1980	351.9	55.0	297.0	358.0	180.2	62.2	44.1	2.6	22.7	46.2	0.0
1981	371.3	60.9	310.4	377.9	184.2	70.1	46.7	4.8	24.0	48.1	0.0
1982	389.8	66.3	323.5	396.7	190.9	75.3	48.8	6.4	26.6	48.7	0.0
1983	437.1	79.0	358.0	444.9	213.7	83.3	66.1	4.6	31.5	55.7	0.0
1984	517.3	100.4	416.9	526.6	258.8	89.9	67.9	5.6	44.2	60.2	0.0
1985	599.7	124.5	475.2	610.6	297.2	111.7	74.0	6.8	57.6	63.3	0.0
1986	654.8	141.1	513.7	666.4	320.2	134.0	77.1	8.2	62.9	64.0	0.0
1987	686.3	160.9	525.5	698.6	334.1	140.0	81.0	10.0	65.3	68.1	0.0
1988	731.9	184.6	547.3	745.2	360.8	144.7	88.3	13.2	66.8	71.4	0.0
1989	794.6	211.2	583.4	809.3	383.3	138.9	91.7	16.0	62.5	69.6	47.3
1990	808.2	238.6	569.6	824.4	382.0	133.4	91.6	19.2	49.6	71.9	76.7
1991	798.0	263.8	534.3	815.6	370.2	121.6	90.3	21.1	42.2	67.3	103.0
1992	806.1	278.4	527.7	824.8	362.9	118.1	91.7	24.2	37.4	70.3	120.3
1993	865.7	309.9	555.7	886.2	395.7	116.1	101.6	27.2	37.9	77.2	130.5
1994	997.1	365.6	631.6	1 021.0	458.8	134.4	119.6	37.1	38.5	86.6	146.1
1995	1 140.6	443.1	697.5	1 168.0	502.0	152.1	131.9	44.2	40.1	85.1	212.6
1996	1 242.2	498.9	743.2	1 271.7	526.8	154.9	144.1	51.3	44.7	77.7	272.1
1997	1 305.0	521.7	783.4	1 333.8	512.6	167.5	152.4	57.8	47.2	78.9	317.4
1998	1 400.3	562.8	837.5	1 430.6	508.9	183.3	155.4	65.7	51.6	76.2	389.4
1999	1 512.8	590.5	922.3	1 542.7	499.8	201.6	167.9	84.7	61.5	78.7	448.4
2000	1 686.2	658.9	1 027.4	1 719.0	541.5	220.5	184.4	104.0	64.6	82.7	521.3
2001	1 822.2	703.9	1 118.3	1 856.7	558.4	238.1	189.6	119.5	69.1	82.3	599.7
2002	1 902.7	716.7	1 186.0	1 938.1	587.2	237.8	195.7	129.6	68.5	82.2	637.1
2001											
January	1 702.9	664.2	1 038.7	1 718.0	539.5	214.1	184.1	107.3	64.9	79.4	528.8
February	1 720.8	678.4	1 042.4	1 719.5	534.6	214.8	183.4	108.0	65.2	78.2	535.3
March	1 732.3	684.1	1 048.2	1 721.7	532.7	213.8	182.8	108.8	65.5	79.1	539.1
April	1 746.1	689.4	1 056.6	1 734.5	540.6	218.5	184.1	110.0	65.5	78.7	537.2
May	1 754.0	693.1	1 060.9	1 742.1	542.7	218.8	185.7	110.7	65.4	78.5	540.4
June	1 760.9	694.8	1 066.1	1 750.6	540.2	215.4	186.4	111.6	65.3	77.7	554.0
July	1 768.4	697.4	1 071.0	1 755.7	535.4	216.8	185.6	111.6	66.4	76.5	563.4
August	1 774.6	696.4	1 078.2	1 772.0	537.7	224.4	187.4	112.8	67.5	76.8	565.5
September	1 780.3	699.4	1 080.9	1 781.3	536.2	222.3	187.3	118.1	68.5	75.3	573.5
October	1 795.0	699.5	1 095.5	1 796.7	540.6	225.7	187.7	118.8	68.7	75.4	579.8
November	1 817.7	706.7	1 111.0	1 825.7	550.3	240.4	188.7	119.0	68.9	78.1	580.3
December	1 822.2	703.9	1 118.3	1 856.7	558.4	238.1	189.6	119.5	69.1	82.3	599.7
2002											
January	1 828.4	705.9	1 122.5	1 845.4	557.1	231.8	188.5	122.4	68.9	78.0	598.6
February	1 838.3	705.6	1 132.8	1 837.9	551.9	235.0	187.4	123.1	68.8	75.1	596.5
March	1 850.8	708.5	1 142.3	1 839.5	550.7	234.3	187.7	124.1	68.6	74.6	599.5
April	1 859.0	710.8	1 148.2	1 847.2	556.0	233.2	188.9	124.3	69.2	74.0	601.5
May	1 867.7	712.7	1 155.0	1 856.0	557.5	234.5	190.7	124.9	68.8	74.2	605.4
June	1 876.6	716.2	1 160.4	1 865.5	554.9	238.3	191.6	125.1	68.5	73.7	613.5
July	1 886.1	718.5	1 167.7	1 872.2	557.3	245.0	194.0	125.7	67.4	72.9	609.9
August	1 892.9	722.2	1 170.7	1 888.9	572.4	243.1	195.5	128.2	66.3	73.8	609.6
September	1 896.4	721.4	1 175.0	1 897.2	575.7	249.7	195.9	134.3	65.2	72.6	603.8
October	1 901.4	721.8	1 179.6	1 903.2	577.4	242.8	197.1	132.9	66.3	72.7	614.0
November	1 902.6	721.7	1 180.8	1 911.4	580.3	233.1	196.8	131.2	67.4	74.6	628.1
December	1 902.7	716.7	1 186.0	1 938.1	587.2	237.8	195.7	129.6	68.5	82.2	637.1

[1]Outstanding balances of pools upon which securities have been issued; these balances are no longer carried on the balance sheets of the loan originators.
. . . = Not available.

Table 12-9. Selected Interest Rates and Bond Yields

(Percent per annum.)

Year and month	Short-term rates							
	Federal funds	Federal Reserve discount rate [1]	Eurodollar deposits, 1-month	U.S. Treasury bills, secondary market, 3-month	U.S. Treasury bills, secondary market, 6-month	Commercial paper, 3-month [2]	CDs (secondary market), 3-month	Bank prime rate
1954	...	...	...	0.94	...	...	...	...
1955	1.79	...	...	1.72	...	...	...	...
1956	2.73	2.77	...	2.62	...	...	...	3.77
1957	3.11	3.12	...	3.22	...	...	...	4.20
1958	1.57	2.15	...	1.77	3.01	...	...	3.83
1959	3.31	3.36	...	3.39	3.81	...	...	4.48
1960	3.21	3.53	...	2.87	3.20	...	...	4.82
1961	1.95	3.00	...	2.35	2.59	...	...	4.50
1962	2.71	3.00	...	2.77	2.90	...	...	4.50
1963	3.18	3.23	...	3.16	3.26	...	...	4.50
1964	3.50	3.55	...	3.55	3.68	...	3.92	4.50
1965	4.07	4.04	...	3.95	4.05	...	4.36	4.54
1966	5.11	4.50	...	4.86	5.06	...	5.45	5.63
1967	4.22	4.19	...	4.29	4.61	...	4.99	5.63
1968	5.66	5.17	...	5.34	5.47	...	5.82	6.31
1969	8.21	5.87	...	6.67	6.86	...	7.23	7.96
1970	7.17	5.95	...	6.39	6.51	...	7.55	7.91
1971	4.67	4.88	6.40	4.33	4.52	...	5.00	5.73
1972	4.44	4.50	5.00	4.06	4.47	4.67	4.66	5.25
1973	8.74	6.45	9.19	7.04	7.20	8.20	9.30	8.03
1974	10.51	7.83	10.79	7.85	7.95	10.02	10.29	10.81
1975	5.82	6.25	6.35	5.79	6.10	6.25	6.44	7.86
1976	5.05	5.50	5.26	4.98	5.26	5.24	5.27	6.84
1977	5.54	5.46	5.75	5.26	5.52	5.55	5.63	6.83
1978	7.94	7.46	8.33	7.18	7.58	7.94	8.21	9.06
1979	11.20	10.29	11.66	10.05	10.04	10.97	11.20	12.67
1980	13.35	11.77	13.77	11.39	11.32	12.66	13.02	15.26
1981	16.39	13.42	16.72	14.04	13.81	15.33	15.93	18.87
1982	12.24	11.01	12.74	10.60	11.06	11.89	12.27	14.85
1983	9.09	8.50	9.38	8.62	8.74	8.88	9.07	10.79
1984	10.23	8.80	10.45	9.54	9.78	10.10	10.39	12.04
1985	8.10	7.69	8.12	7.47	7.65	7.95	8.04	9.93
1986	6.80	6.32	6.78	5.97	6.02	9.40	6.51	8.33
1987	6.66	5.66	6.88	5.78	6.03	6.81	6.87	8.21
1988	7.57	6.20	7.69	6.67	6.91	7.66	7.73	9.32
1989	9.21	6.93	9.16	8.11	8.03	8.99	9.09	10.87
1990	8.10	6.98	8.15	7.50	7.46	8.06	8.15	10.01
1991	5.69	5.45	5.81	5.38	5.44	5.87	5.83	8.46
1992	3.52	3.25	3.62	3.43	3.54	3.75	3.68	6.25
1993	3.02	3.00	3.07	3.00	3.12	3.22	3.17	6.00
1994	4.21	3.60	4.34	4.25	4.64	4.66	4.63	7.15
1995	5.83	5.21	5.86	5.49	5.56	5.93	5.92	8.83
1996	5.30	5.02	5.32	5.01	5.08	5.41	5.39	8.27
1997	5.46	5.00	5.52	5.06	5.18	3.72	5.62	8.44
1998	5.35	4.92	5.45	4.78	4.83	25.37	5.47	8.35
1999	4.97	4.62	5.15	4.64	4.75	5.22	5.33	8.00
2000	6.24	5.73	6.33	5.82	5.90	6.33	6.46	9.23
2001	3.88	3.40	3.81	3.40	3.34	3.64	3.71	6.91
2002	1.67	1.17	1.71	1.61	1.68	1.70	1.73	4.67
2001								
January	5.98	5.52	5.79	5.15	4.95	5.51	5.62	9.05
February	5.49	5.00	5.44	4.88	4.71	5.19	5.26	8.50
March	5.31	4.81	5.06	4.42	4.28	4.81	4.89	8.32
April	4.80	4.28	4.76	3.87	3.85	4.47	4.53	7.80
May	4.21	3.73	4.08	3.62	3.62	3.96	4.02	7.24
June	3.97	3.47	3.83	3.49	3.45	3.69	3.74	6.98
July	3.77	3.25	3.74	3.51	3.45	3.62	3.66	6.75
August	3.65	3.16	3.55	3.36	3.29	3.44	3.48	6.67
September	3.07	2.77	2.94	2.64	2.63	2.84	2.87	6.28
October	2.49	2.02	2.41	2.16	2.12	2.29	2.31	5.53
November	2.09	1.58	2.06	1.87	1.88	2.00	2.03	5.10
December	1.82	1.33	1.88	1.69	1.78	1.81	1.83	4.84
2002								
January	1.73	1.25	1.74	1.65	1.73	1.72	1.74	4.75
February	1.74	1.25	1.78	1.73	1.82	1.80	1.82	4.75
March	1.73	1.25	1.83	1.79	2.01	1.87	1.91	4.75
April	1.75	1.25	1.79	1.72	1.93	1.83	1.87	4.75
May	1.75	1.25	1.78	1.73	1.86	1.80	1.82	4.75
June	1.75	1.25	1.78	1.70	1.79	1.78	1.81	4.75
July	1.73	1.25	1.77	1.68	1.70	1.76	1.79	4.75
August	1.74	1.25	1.74	1.62	1.60	1.71	1.73	4.75
September	1.75	1.25	1.77	1.63	1.60	1.74	1.76	4.75
October	1.75	1.25	1.75	1.58	1.56	1.71	1.73	4.75
November	1.34	0.83	1.37	1.23	1.27	1.37	1.39	4.35
December	1.24	0.75	1.35	1.19	1.24	1.32	1.34	4.25

[1] Federal Reserve Bank of New York.
[2] Prior to September 1997 this series represents both nonfinancial and financial commercial paper rates. Beginning September 1997, rates for financial companies only are shown. See Notes and Definitions.
... = Not available.

Table 12-9. Selected Interest Rates and Bond Yields—*Continued*

(Percent per annum.)

Year and month	U.S. Treasury securities, constant maturities					Bond yields			Fixed-rate first mortgages
	1-year	3-year	10-year	20-year	30-year	Domestic corporate (Moody's)		State and local bonds (Bond Buyer)	
						Aaa	Baa		
1954	...	...	...	...	...	...	...	2.39	...
1955	...	...	...	...	...	...	...	2.48	...
1956	...	...	...	...	...	...	...	2.76	...
1957	...	...	...	...	...	...	...	3.28	...
1958	...	...	...	...	...	...	...	2.73	...
1959	...	...	...	...	...	...	...	2.73	...
1960	...	...	...	...	...	...	...	2.73	...
1961	...	...	...	...	...	...	...	3.45	...
1962	3.10	3.47	3.95	...	...	...	...	3.15	...
1963	3.36	3.67	4.00	...	...	...	...	3.17	...
1964	3.85	4.03	4.19	...	...	...	...	3.21	...
1965	4.15	4.22	4.28	...	...	...	...	2.92	...
1966	5.20	5.23	4.93	...	...	...	...	2.92	...
1967	4.88	5.03	5.07	...	...	...	...	3.94	...
1968	5.69	5.68	5.64	...	...	...	...	4.45	...
1969	7.12	7.02	6.67	...	...	...	...	5.72	...
1970	6.90	7.29	7.35	...	...	...	...	6.33	...
1971	4.89	5.66	6.16	...	...	...	...	3.72	...
1972	4.95	5.72	6.21	...	...	...	...	3.81	7.38
1973	7.32	6.96	6.85	...	...	...	...	3.90	8.04
1974	8.20	7.84	7.56	...	...	...	...	3.93	9.19
1975	6.78	7.50	7.99	...	...	...	...	4.00	9.04
1976	5.88	6.77	7.61	...	...	8.43	9.75	6.64	8.86
1977	6.08	6.68	7.42	...	7.75	8.02	8.97	5.68	8.84
1978	8.34	8.29	8.41	...	8.49	8.73	9.49	6.02	9.63
1979	10.65	9.70	9.43	...	9.28	9.63	10.69	6.52	11.19
1980	12.00	11.51	11.43	...	11.27	11.94	13.67	8.59	13.77
1981	14.80	14.46	13.92	...	13.45	14.17	16.04	11.33	16.63
1982	12.27	12.93	13.01	...	12.76	13.79	16.11	11.66	16.08
1983	9.58	10.45	11.10	...	11.18	12.04	13.55	9.51	13.23
1984	10.91	11.92	12.46	...	12.41	12.71	14.19	10.10	13.87
1985	8.42	9.64	10.62	...	10.79	11.37	12.72	9.10	12.42
1986	6.45	7.06	7.67	...	7.78	9.02	10.39	7.32	10.18
1987	6.77	7.68	8.39	...	8.59	9.38	10.58	7.64	10.20
1988	7.65	8.26	8.85	...	8.96	9.71	10.83	7.68	10.34
1989	8.53	8.55	8.49	...	8.45	9.26	10.18	7.23	10.32
1990	7.89	8.26	8.55	...	8.61	9.32	10.36	7.27	10.13
1991	5.86	6.82	7.86	...	8.14	8.77	9.80	6.92	9.25
1992	3.89	5.30	7.01	...	7.67	8.14	8.98	6.44	8.40
1993	3.43	4.44	5.87	6.29	6.59	7.22	7.93	5.60	7.33
1994	5.32	6.27	7.09	7.49	7.37	7.97	8.63	6.18	8.35
1995	5.94	6.25	6.57	6.95	6.88	7.59	8.20	5.95	7.95
1996	5.52	5.99	6.44	6.83	6.71	7.37	8.05	5.76	7.80
1997	5.63	6.10	6.35	6.69	6.61	7.27	7.87	5.52	7.60
1998	5.05	5.14	5.26	5.72	5.58	6.53	7.22	5.09	6.94
1999	5.08	5.49	5.65	6.20	5.87	7.05	7.88	5.43	7.43
2000	6.11	6.22	6.03	6.23	5.94	7.62	8.37	5.71	8.06
2001	3.49	4.09	5.02	5.63	5.49	7.08	7.95	5.15	6.97
2002	2.00	3.10	4.61	5.43	5.43	6.49	7.80	5.04	6.54
2001									
January	4.81	4.77	5.16	5.65	5.54	7.15	7.93	5.10	7.03
February	4.68	4.71	5.10	5.62	5.45	7.10	7.87	5.18	7.05
March	4.30	4.43	4.89	5.49	5.34	6.98	7.84	5.13	6.95
April	3.98	4.42	5.14	5.78	5.65	7.20	8.07	5.27	7.08
May	3.78	4.51	5.39	5.92	5.78	7.29	8.07	5.29	7.15
June	3.58	4.35	5.28	5.82	5.67	7.18	7.97	5.20	7.16
July	3.62	4.31	5.24	5.75	5.61	7.13	7.97	5.20	7.13
August	3.47	4.04	4.97	5.58	5.48	7.02	7.85	5.03	6.95
September	2.82	3.45	4.73	5.53	5.48	7.17	8.03	5.09	6.82
October	2.33	3.14	4.57	5.34	5.32	7.03	7.91	5.05	6.62
November	2.18	3.22	4.65	5.33	5.12	6.97	7.81	5.04	6.66
December	2.22	3.62	5.09	5.76	5.48	6.77	8.05	5.25	7.07
2002									
January	2.16	3.56	5.04	5.69	5.45	6.55	7.87	5.16	7.00
February	2.23	3.55	4.91	5.61	5.40	6.51	7.89	5.11	6.89
March	2.57	4.14	5.28	5.93	...	6.81	8.11	5.29	7.01
April	2.48	4.01	5.21	5.85	...	6.76	8.03	5.22	6.99
May	2.35	3.80	5.16	5.81	...	6.75	8.09	5.19	6.81
June	2.20	3.49	4.93	5.65	...	6.63	7.95	5.09	6.65
July	1.96	3.01	4.65	5.51	...	6.53	7.90	5.02	6.49
August	1.76	2.52	4.26	5.19	...	6.37	7.58	4.95	6.29
September	1.72	2.32	3.87	4.87	...	6.15	7.40	4.74	6.09
October	1.65	2.25	3.94	5.00	...	6.32	7.73	4.88	6.11
November	1.49	2.32	4.05	5.04	...	6.31	7.62	4.95	6.07
December	1.45	2.23	4.03	5.01	...	6.21	7.45	4.85	6.05

1Federal Reserve Bank of New York.
2Prior to September 1997 this series represents both nonfinancial and financial commercial paper rates. Beginning September 1997, rates for financial companies only are shown. See Notes and Definitions.
. . . = Not available.

Table 12-10. Common Stock Prices and Yields

Year and month	Stock price indexes			Yields based on Standard and Poor's composite (percent)	
	Dow Jones industrials (30 stocks)	Standard and Poor's composite (500 stocks) (1941–1943 = 10)	Nasdaq composite (Feb. 5, 1971 = 100)	Dividend-price ratio	Earnings-price ratio
1955	442.72	40.49	...	4.08	7.95
1956	493.01	46.62	...	4.09	7.55
1957	475.71	44.38	...	4.35	7.89
1958	491.66	46.24	...	3.97	6.23
1959	632.12	57.38	...	3.23	5.78
1960	618.04	55.85	...	3.47	5.90
1961	691.55	66.27	...	2.98	4.62
1962	639.76	62.38	...	3.37	5.82
1963	714.81	69.87	...	3.17	5.50
1964	834.05	81.37	...	3.01	5.32
1965	910.88	88.17	...	3.00	5.59
1966	873.60	85.26	...	3.40	6.63
1967	879.12	91.93	...	3.20	5.73
1968	906.00	98.70	...	3.07	5.67
1969	876.72	97.84	...	3.24	6.08
1970	753.19	83.22	...	3.83	6.45
1971	884.76	98.29	107.44	3.14	5.41
1972	950.71	109.20	128.52	2.84	5.50
1973	923.88	107.43	109.90	3.06	7.12
1974	759.37	82.85	76.29	4.47	11.59
1975	802.49	86.16	77.20	4.31	9.15
1976	974.92	102.01	89.90	3.77	8.90
1977	894.63	98.20	98.71	4.62	10.79
1978	820.23	96.02	117.53	5.28	12.03
1979	844.40	103.01	136.57	5.47	13.46
1980	891.41	118.78	168.61	5.26	12.66
1981	932.92	128.05	203.18	5.20	11.96
1982	884.36	119.71	188.97	5.81	11.60
1983	1 190.34	160.41	285.43	4.40	8.03
1984	1 178.48	160.46	248.88	4.64	10.02
1985	1 328.23	186.84	290.19	4.25	8.12
1986	1 792.76	236.34	366.96	3.49	6.09
1987	2 275.99	286.83	402.57	3.08	5.48
1988	2 060.82	265.79	374.43	3.64	8.01
1989	2 508.91	322.84	437.81	3.45	7.42
1990	2 678.94	334.59	409.17	3.61	6.47
1991	2 929.33	376.18	491.69	3.24	4.79
1992	3 284.29	415.74	599.26	2.99	4.22
1993	3 522.06	451.41	715.16	2.78	4.46
1994	3 793.77	460.42	751.65	2.82	5.83
1995	4 493.76	541.72	925.19	2.56	6.09
1996	5 742.89	670.50	1 164.96	2.19	5.24
1997	7 441.15	873.43	1 469.49	1.77	4.57
1998	8 625.52	1 085.50	1 794.91	1.49	3.46
1999	10 464.88	1 327.33	2 728.15	1.25	3.17
2000	10 734.90	1 427.22	3 783.67	1.15	3.63
2001	10 189.13	1 194.18	2 035.00	1.32	2.95
2002	9 226.43	993.94	1 539.73	1.61	...
2001					
January	10 682.74	1 335.63	2 656.86	1.16	...
February	10 774.57	1 305.75	2 449.57	1.22	...
March	10 081.32	1 185.85	1 986.66	1.33	3.92
April	10 234.52	1 189.84	1 933.93	1.32	...
May	11 004.96	1 270.37	2 181.13	1.23	...
June	10 767.20	1 238.71	2 112.05	1.27	3.00
July	10 444.50	1 204.45	2 033.98	1.30	...
August	10 314.68	1 178.51	1 929.71	1.34	...
September	9 042.56	1 044.64	1 573.31	1.48	2.72
October	9 220.75	1 076.59	1 656.43	1.45	...
November	9 721.82	1 129.68	1 870.06	1.38	...
December	9 979.88	1 144.93	1 977.71	1.36	2.15
2002					
January	9 923.80	1 140.21	1 976.77	1.38	...
February	9 891.05	1 100.67	1 799.72	1.43	...
March	10 500.95	1 153.79	1 863.05	1.37	2.15
April	10 165.18	1 112.03	1 758.80	1.42	...
May	10 080.48	1 079.27	1 660.31	1.47	...
June	9 492.44	1 014.05	1 505.49	1.58	2.70
July	8 616.52	903.59	1 346.09	1.76	...
August	8 685.48	912.55	1 327.36	1.72	...
September	8 160.78	867.81	1 251.07	1.80	3.68
October	8 048.12	854.63	1 241.91	1.86	...
November	8 625.72	909.93	1 409.15	1.73	...
December	8 526.66	899.18	1 387.15	1.77	...

. . . = Not available.

NOTES AND DEFINITIONS

TABLES 12-1, 12-2, AND 20-5
MONEY STOCK MEASURES; SELECTED COMPONENTS OF THE MONEY STOCK

Source: Board of Governors of the Federal Reserve System

Estimates of three monetary aggregates (M1, M2, and M3) and the components of these measures are published weekly. The monthly data are averages of daily figures.

Definitions

M1 consists of (1) currency outside the U.S. Treasury, Federal Reserve Banks, and the vaults of depository institutions; (2) travelers checks of nonbank issuers; (3) demand deposits at all commercial banks other than those due to depository institutions, the U.S. government, and foreign banks and official institutions, less cash items in the process of collection and Federal Reserve float; and (4) other checkable deposits, consisting of negotiable order of withdrawal (NOW) and automatic transfer service (ATS) accounts at depository institutions, credit union share draft accounts, and demand deposits at thrift institutions.

M2 consists of M1 plus savings deposits (including money market deposit accounts), small-denomination time deposits (time deposits—including retail repurchase agreements [RPs]—in amounts of less than $100,000), and balances in retail money market mutual funds. It excludes individual retirement account (IRA) and Keogh balances at depository institutions and money market funds.

M3 consists of M2 plus large-denomination time deposits (in amounts of $100,000 or more), balances in institutional money funds, RP liabilities (overnight and term) issued by all depository institutions, and Eurodollars (overnight and term) held by U.S. residents at foreign branches of U.S. banks worldwide and at all banking offices in the United Kingdom and Canada. It excludes amounts held by depository institutions, the U.S. government, money funds, and foreign banks and official institutions.

Currency consists of currency outside the U.S. Treasury, the Federal Reserve Banks, and the vaults of depository institutions.

Demand deposits consists of demand deposits at commercial banks and foreign-related institutions other than those due to depository institutions, the U.S. government, and foreign banks and official institutions, less cash items in the process of collection and Federal Reserve float.

Other checkable deposits consists of NOW and ATS balances at all depository institutions; credit union share draft balances; and demand deposits at thrift institutions.

Repurchase agreements (RPs) are commitments by depository institutions to repurchase securities (often government securities) that a client has purchased from the institution. A repurchase agreement constitutes a ready source of liquidity for the client, similar in nature to other components of M2 and M3. Both overnight and longer-term repurchase agreements are included in the data.

Eurodollars are dollar-denominated deposits—both overnight and term—held by U.S. residents at foreign branches of U.S. banks worldwide and at all banking offices in the United Kingdom and Canada.

Savings deposits includes money market deposit accounts and other savings deposits at both commercial banks and thrift institutions.

Small time deposits are those issued at commercial banks and thrift institutions in amounts of less than $100,000. Retail RPs are included. All IRA and Keogh account balances at commercial banks and thrift institutions are subtracted from small time deposits.

Large time deposits are those issued in amounts of $100,000 or more at commercial banks and thrift institutions, excluding those booked at international banking facilities. Deposits held at commercial banks by money market mutual funds, depository institutions, the U.S. government, and foreign banks and official institutions also are excluded.

Notes on the data

Seasonal adjustment. Seasonally adjusted M1 is calculated by summing currency, travelers checks, demand deposits, and other checkable deposits, each seasonally adjusted separately. Seasonally adjusted M2 is computed by adjusting each of its non-M1 components and then adding this result to seasonally adjusted M1. Similarly, seasonally adjusted M3 is obtained by adjusting each of its non-M2 components and then adding this result to seasonally adjusted M2.

Revisions. Money stock measures are revised annually, usually in February, based on a benchmark and seasonal factor review. These revisions typically extend back a number of years. The monetary aggregates were redefined in major revisions in 1980.

Data availability

Estimates are released weekly in Federal Reserve Statistical Release H.6, "Money Stock, Liquid Assets, and

Debt Measures" and are subsequently published each month in the *Federal Reserve Bulletin*. Historical data beginning with 1959 are available from Publications Services, Board of Governors of the Federal Reserve System. Current and historical data are available on the Federal Reserve Internet site at <http://www.federalreserve.gov/releases/>.

References

An explanation of the 1980 redefinition of the monetary aggregates is found in the *Federal Reserve Bulletin* for February 1980.

TABLES 12-3 AND 20-5
AGGREGATE RESERVES OF DEPOSITORY INSTITUTIONS AND MONETARY BASE

SOURCE: BOARD OF GOVERNORS OF THE FEDERAL RESERVE SYSTEM

The data presented here are in millions of dollars, seasonally adjusted and adjusted for changes in reserve requirements ("break-adjusted") so as to provide a consistent gauge of the effect of Federal Reserve open-market operations. To illustrate, an observed increase in reserves will not represent an easing in monetary conditions if it is simply equal to an increase in reserves required by the Federal Reserve. Therefore, the mandated increases and decreases are deducted to provide the "break-adjusted" series. Monthly data are averages of daily figures. Annual data are for December.

Definitions

Total reserves consists of reserve balances with Federal Reserve Banks plus vault cash used to satisfy reserve requirements. Seasonally adjusted, break-adjusted total reserves equal seasonally adjusted, break-adjusted required reserves plus unadjusted excess reserves.

Seasonally adjusted, break-adjusted *nonborrowed reserves* equal seasonally adjusted, break-adjusted total reserves less unadjusted total borrowings of depository institutions from the Federal Reserve.

Extended credit consists of borrowing at the discount window under the terms and conditions established for the extended credit program to help depository institutions deal with sustained liquidity pressures. Because there is not the same need to repay such borrowing promptly as there is with traditional short-term adjustment credit, the money market impact of extended credit is similar to that of nonborrowed reserves. The extended credit program has not been used in recent years but was significant in the 1980s.

To adjust *required reserves* for discontinuities due to regulatory changes in reserve requirements, a multiplicative procedure is used to estimate what required reserves would have been in past periods had current reserve requirements been in effect. Break-adjusted required reserves include required reserves against transactions deposits and personal time and savings deposits (but not reservable nondeposit liabilities).

The seasonally adjusted, break-adjusted *monetary base* consists of (1) seasonally adjusted, break-adjusted total reserves plus (2) the seasonally adjusted currency component of the money stock plus (3) for all quarterly reporters on the "Report of Transaction Accounts, Other Deposits and Vault Cash" and for all those weekly reporters whose vault cash exceeds their required reserves, the seasonally adjusted, break-adjusted difference between current vault cash and the amount applied to satisfy current reserve requirements.

Data availability

Data are released weekly in Federal Reserve release H.3 and subsequently published in the *Federal Reserve Bulletin*. Historical data are available from the Money and Reserves Projections Section, Division of Monetary Affairs, Board of Governors of The Federal Reserve System, Washington, DC 20551. Current and historical data also are available on the Federal Reserve Internet site at <http://www.federalreserve.gov/releases/>.

TABLE 12-4
COMMERCIAL BANKS: BANK CREDIT AND SELECTED LIABILITIES

SOURCE: BOARD OF GOVERNORS OF THE FEDERAL RESERVE SYSTEM

These data on the assets and liabilities of commercial banks are published in the Federal Reserve's H.8 Release.

Definitions and notes on the data

The data are for all commercial banks in the United States. This category covers the following types of institutions in the 50 states and the District of Columbia: domestically chartered commercial banks that report weekly (large domestic); other domestically chartered commercial banks (small domestic); branches and agencies of foreign banks, and Edge Act and Agreement corporations (foreign related institutions). International Banking Facilities are excluded.

Data are collected weekly for Wednesday values; monthly data are pro rata averages of Wednesday values; annual data represent December figures.

Data are complete for large domestic banks. Data for others are estimated on the basis of weekly samples and end of quarter condition reports. Data are adjusted for breaks caused by reclassifications of assets and liabilities.

Data before 1988 are based on a previous version of the H.8, the G.7 release on Loans and Securities at Commercial Banks, and the G.10 on Major Nondeposit Funds of Commercial Banks.

Security loans—a component of *loans and leases in bank credit*—consist of loans to purchase and carry securities, and reverse repurchase agreements with brokers and dealers and others. In a reverse RP a bank has provided liquidity to a borrower by buying a security from him, which the borrower promises to repurchase at a certain date.

Interbank loans, cash assets, and other assets are not components of bank credit and are omitted from Table 12-4. Interbank loans include loans made to commercial banks, reverse repurchase agreements with commercial banks, and Federal funds sold to commercial banks.

Selected liabilities show *deposits* and *borrowings*. Two components of total liabilities, "net due to foreign offices" and "other liabilities," are omitted.

Revisions

Data are revised annually to reflect new benchmark information and revised seasonal factors.

Data availability

Assets and Liabilities of Commercial Banks, Federal Reserve release H.8, is issued each Friday around 4:30 p.m. eastern time. Selected data are subsequently published in the *Federal Reserve Bulletin*. Historical data may be purchased on diskette from Publications Services, Board of Governors of the Federal Reserve System. Current and historical data are available on the Federal Reserve Internet site at <http://www.federalreserve.gov/releases/>.

TABLE 12-5
CREDIT MARKET DEBT OUTSTANDING, BY BORROWER AND LENDER

Source: Board of Governors of the Federal Reserve System

The flow of funds accounts, compiled quarterly by the Federal Reserve Board, supplement the national income and product accounts by providing a comprehensive and detailed accounting of financial transactions, with a balance sheet for each financial and nonfinancial sector of the economy. Table 12-5 shows the credit market debt

that is owed by the major sectors in the economy and it also shows the major lending sectors in the credit markets. Aggregates of these data can include multiple layers of financial intermediation, such as banks making advances to finance companies that are lending to households. One purpose of these statistics is to show the comparative growth of the various sectors.

In macroeconomic analysis, the most widely used flow of funds measure is the total debt of domestic nonfinancial sectors. By eliminating the financial sectors, this measure has little duplication due to financial intermediation. It is used by the Federal Reserve along with the monetary aggregates as an indicator of monetary conditions.

Definitions and notes on the data

Quarterly data on debt outstanding are shown on an end-of-period basis, not adjusted for seasonal variation or for "breaks" or discontinuities in the series. Because of these discontinuities, caution should be used in interpreting changes in debt levels. Break-adjusted values of the changes or "flows" can be found in the quarterly Flow-of-Funds report, along with a suggested method for calculating percent changes. The data on credit market debt exclude corporate equities and mutual fund shares.

Data for the current and preceding years are revised each year to reflect revisions in source data.

Sectors owing debt:

Domestic financial sectors:

Federal government-related sectors include federally sponsored credit agencies, federally related mortgage pools, and the monetary authority (Federal Reserve). (However, the Federal Reserve usually has no credit market debt.)

The *private* sector includes commercial banks, thrift institutions, life insurance companies, asset-backed securities (ABS) issuers, finance and mortgage companies, REITs (real estate investment trusts), brokers and dealers, and funding corporations.

Domestic nonfinancial sectors:

Federal government consists of all federal government agencies and funds that are in the unified budget. The District of Columbia government, however, is included in the state and local sector.

Treasury securities as shown here exclude securities issued by the Treasury but held by agencies within the U.S. government (for example, in the Social Security trust funds). In this respect it corresponds to "Federal debt," shown in Table 6-8, except that the latter table uses a fiscal year rather than a calendar year basis. Federal government debt as shown here is smaller than the official total public debt and the "debt subject to limit," both of which also include the securities held by U.S. government agencies. The value shown here is considered a more accurate measure of the effect of government borrowing in relation to the economy and credit markets.

Budget agency securities and mortgages are those issued by government-owned corporations and agencies, such as the Export-Import Bank, that issue securities individually.

Households also include personal trusts and nonprofit organizations.

State and local governments represent operating funds only; retirement funds are included in the financial sector.

Foreign credit market debt held in the United States shows foreign credit market debt owed to U.S. residents. This debt is included along with the debt of domestic financial and nonfinancial sectors in total credit market debt outstanding.

Percentage measures

Table 12-5 includes three measures of relative debt burdens, calculated by the editor.

Domestic nonfinancial debt as a percent of GDP is the total debt owed by domestic nonfinancial sectors as a percent of the current-dollar value of Gross Domestic Product (Table 1-1).

Household debt as a percent of DPI is the value of debt owed by households as a percent of the current-dollar value of disposable personal income (Table 4-2).

Corporate nonfinancial business debt as a percent of sector GDP is the total debt owed by corporate nonfinancial business as a percent of the current-dollar gross product of nonfinancial corporate business (Table 1-9).

Credit market assets held by sector:

Government related sectors:

This grouping includes two nonfinancial and three financial sectors. The nonfinancial sectors are the *Federal government*, as reflected in the U.S. Budget accounts, and the operations of *state and local governments*, including the District of Columbia; *state and local employee retirement funds* are shown separately as a financial sector. Other government related financial sectors are the following:

Government-sponsored enterprises are financial institutions that provide credit to housing, agriculture and other

specific areas of the economy, such as Federal Home Loan Banks, Fannie Mae, Freddie Mac, and others.

Federally related mortgage pools are entities established for bookkeeping purposes that record the issuance of pooled securities representing an interest in mortgages originally held by federally related agencies such as Fannie Mae. Rather than being composed of a group of institutions, the sector is made up of a set of contractual arrangements in regard to pooled mortgages.

Selected domestic financial sectors:

This grouping includes major financial sectors, such as *commercial banks, savings institutions*, and *credit unions*. The monetary authority (the Federal Reserve) has also been put in this grouping because it is sometimes included in banking sector totals. Other financial sectors are *life insurance companies, other insurance companies*, and *private pension funds*. Additional sectors are *money market mutual funds*, which issue shares and invest in short-term liquid assets; *mutual funds*, whose investments are not restricted to the short-term area; *asset backed security (ABS) issuers*, which issue debt obligations that are backed by pooled assets, a financial procedure similar to that of federally related mortgage pools; and *finance companies* which provide credit to businesses and individuals.

Private domestic nonfinancial sectors:

Households are the dominant private nonfinancial lenders.

A number of small lending sectors, nonfinancial and financial, are included in the category *"Other"*. One of those is nonfinancial business, a sector that is important on the borrowing side, but not on the lending side.

Data availability

Debt estimates are released quarterly, about nine weeks following the end of a quarter, in Federal Reserve Statistical Release Z.1, "Flow of Funds of the United States," and are subsequently published in the *Federal Reserve Bulletin*. Releases and data on diskettes are available from Publications Services, Board of Governors of the Federal Reserve System. Current and historical data also are available on the Federal Reserve Internet site at<http://www.federalreserve.gov/releases>.

References

A *Guide to the Flow of Funds Accounts* can be purchased from Publications Services, Board of Governors of the Federal Reserve System. The *Federal Reserve Bulletin* for July 2001 includes an article on "The U.S. Flow of Funds Accounts and Their Uses."

TABLE 12-6
HOUSEHOLD ASSETS, FINANCIAL OBLIGATIONS,
AND DELINQUENCY RATES

Source: Board of Governors of the Federal Reserve System

The quarterly data on household sector assets are obtained from the Federal Reserve Board's Flow of Funds Accounts. These also are the source of the credit market data in Table 12-5; descriptions of the flow of funds accounts are provided in the Notes and Definitions to Table 12-5, above.

The household debt service ratio relates required debt service (interest and principal) payments to disposable personal income; it has been completely revised to incorporate improved data sources. The new financial obligations ratio includes not only required debt payments but also rental payments, automobile lease payments, homeowners' insurance, and property taxes and is also expressed as a percent of disposable personal income. Unlike the debt service ratio, the financial obligations ratio is not distorted by the trends toward debt-financed homeownership and toward auto leasing in preference to loan financing.

The delinquency rate shows delinquent household credit-card debt at banks as a percent of total debt.

Definitions and notes on the data

Quarterly data on holdings of *financial assets* are shown on an end-of-period basis, not adjusted for seasonal variations. Data for the current and preceding years are revised each year to reflect revisions in source data. For most categories, the values for the household sector are calculated as residuals. That is, starting with known totals, such as total Treasury securities, amounts held by other sectors are subtracted, and the remainders are assigned to the household sector.

Financial assets of the household sector include nonprofit organizations, which are difficult to estimate separately, but exclude holdings by unincorporated businesses.

The table shows several types of *deposit holdings*, as well as a number of types of *securities*. In contrast to the credit market data, which exclude equities, Table 12-6 includes *corporate equities, mutual fund shares*, and *equity in noncorporate business*. Other special assets that are estimated are *life insurance reserves, pension fund reserves*, and *bank personal trust funds*. *Pension fund reserves* include insurance and pension fund reserves of federal, state, and local government employee funds—but not the Social Security system—as well as private industry funds. *Miscellaneous assets* are mainly claims on insurance companies, such as unearned premium

reserves of other insurance companies and health insurance reserves of life insurance companies.

Tangible assets complete the asset side of the household balance sheet. Tangible assets comprise real estate, equipment and software owned by nonprofit organizations, and consumer durable goods. *Household real estate* is valued at market value, while equipment, software, and consumer durables are valued at replacement (current) cost.

Debt as a percent of total assets is calculated by the editor as household credit market debt outstanding, from Table 12-5, as a percent of the total of tangible and financial assets in this table. It covers both households and nonprofit organizations.

The *household debt-service and financial obligations ratios* are estimated on a quarterly basis by the Federal Reserve based on aggregate and consumer survey data and are seasonally adjusted, unlike the other data in Table 12-6. Fourth-quarter values are shown to represent the calendar year. The denominator for the aggregate ratio is personal disposable income from the National Income and Product Accounts (NIPAs) (see Chapter 4). The allocation of the NIPA data between *renters* and *homeowners* is estimated by the Federal Reserve based on data from the Federal Reserve's triennial Survey of Consumer Finances and the Current Population Survey (see Chapter 3).

Debt service payments are the minimum required monthly payments of principal and interest on mortgage debt (including home equity loans), revolving credit (credit-card debt), and auto, student, mobile-home, recreational vehicle, marine, and personal loans.

The *financial obligations ratios* include, in addition to debt service, rental payments on primary residences, property taxes, homeowners' insurance, and automobile lease payments.

Delinquency rates of credit card accounts held at banks are compiled from the quarterly FFIEC (Federal Financial Institutions Examination Council) Consolidated Reports of Condition and Income (FFIEC 031 through 034). Data for each calendar quarter become available approximately 60 days after the end of the quarter.

Data availability

Household asset estimates are released quarterly, about 9 weeks following the end of a quarter, in the Federal Reserve Statistical Release Z.1, "Flow of Funds Accounts of the United States." Further information on data availability is given in the Notes to Table 12-5, a table that is also based on the flow of funds accounts.

The revised debt service ratio and the new financial obligations ratios are described in "Recent Changes to a Measure of U.S. Household Debt Service," *Federal Reserve Bulletin*, October 2003. The data are estimated by the Federal Reserve about three months after the end of each quarter. Current and historical data are available on the Internet site at <http://www.federalreserve.gov/releases>.

Delinquency rates of credit card accounts held at banks are also available on the Federal Reserve Internet site, listed under Charge-off and Delinquency Rates on Loans at Commercial Banks.

TABLE 12-7
MORTGAGE DEBT OUTSTANDING

Source: Board of Governors of the Federal Reserve System

These data are published in the Federal Reserve's "Flow of Funds Accounts." They are based on reports from various Government and private organizations.

Definitions and notes on the data

Home mortgages include home equity loans; these are also shown separately in the Flow of Funds Accounts.

Multifamily residential refers to mortgages on structures of five or more units.

Mortgage pools or trusts show mortgages that were refinanced by their holders through the issuance of mortgage-backed securities. They are shown in two columns: refinancings by *Federally related agencies*—mainly the Federal National Mortgage Association, the Federal Home Loan Mortgage Corporation, and the Government National Mortgage Association—and refinancings by private conduits (these are referred to as ABS issuers in the Flow of Funds Accounts, which stands for issuers of asset-backed securities).

Other holders include a variety of groups including finance companies, individuals, state and local governments, credit unions, and others.

Home mortgage debt as a percentage of the value of real estate is calculated by the editor, using total home mortgage debt as a percentage of the value of household real estate shown in Table 12-6.

Data availability

Mortgage debt data are compiled quarterly, about 9 weeks following the end of the quarter, in Federal Reserve Statistical Release Z.1, "Flow of Funds Accounts of the United States." Similar data are also provided in Table 1.54 on Mortgage Debt Outstanding in the *Federal*

Reserve Bulletin. Releases and data on diskettes are available from Publications Services, Board of Governors of the Federal Reserve System. Current and historical data are available on the Federal Reserve Internet site at <http://www.federalreserve.gov/releases>.

TABLE 12-8
CONSUMER CREDIT

Source: Board of Governors of the Federal Reserve System

The consumer credit series cover most short- and intermediate-term credit extended to individuals through regular business channels, excluding loans secured by real estate (e.g., first and second mortgages and home equity credit). In October 2003 the scope of the statistics was extended to incorporate student loans extended by the federal government and by SLM Holding Corporation (SLM), the parent company of Sallie Mae. The historical data have been revised back to 1977 to reflect this inclusion. The household debt series presented in Table 12-5 is more comprehensive, comprising both mortgage and consumer debt. Consumer credit is categorized by major types of credit and by major holders.

Definitions and notes on the data

The major types of consumer credit are *revolving and nonrevolving*. *Revolving credit* includes credit arising from purchases on credit card plans of retail stores and banks, cash advances and check credit plans of banks, and some overdraft credit arrangements. *Non-revolving credit* includes automobile loans (new and passenger automobiles), mobile home loans, and all other loans not included in revolving credit, such as loans for education, boats, trailers, or vacations. These loans may be secured or unsecured.

Debt secured by real estate (including first liens, junior liens, and home equity loans) is excluded. Credit extended to governmental agencies and nonprofit or charitable organizations, as well as credit extended to business or to individuals exclusively for business purposes, is excluded.

Categories of holders include *commercial banks, finance companies, credit unions, federal government and Sallie Mae, savings institutions, nonfinancial businesses*, and *pools of securitized assets*. Retailers and gasoline companies are included in the nonfinancial businesses category. *Pools of securitized assets* comprises the outstanding balances of pools upon which securities have been issued; these balances are no longer carried on the balance sheets of the loan originators.

The consumer credit series are based on comprehensive benchmark data that become available periodically. Current monthly estimates are brought forward from the latest benchmarks in accordance with weighted changes indicated by sample data. Classifications are made on a "holder" basis. Thus, installment paper sold by retail outlets is included in figures for the banks and finance companies that purchased the paper.

The amount of outstanding credit represents the sum of the balances in the installment receivable accounts of financial institutions and retail outlets at the end of each month.

The estimates of the amount of credit outstanding include any finance and insurance charges included as part of the installment contract. Unearned income on loans is included in some cases where lenders cannot separate the components.

The seasonally adjusted data are adjusted for differences in the number of trading days and for seasonal influences. The seasonal factors used are derived by the X-11-ARIMA process.

Data availability

Current data are available monthly in the Federal Reserve statistical release G.19, Consumer Credit, and in the *Federal Reserve Bulletin*. The data for earlier years may be purchased on diskette from Publication Services, Board of Governors of the Federal Reserve System. Current and historical data are available on the Federal Reserve Internet site at <http://www.federalreserve.gov/releases/>.

TABLES 12-9, 12-10 AND 20-6
INTEREST RATES, BOND YIELDS, STOCK PRICES AND YIELDS

SOURCES: BOARD OF GOVERNORS OF THE FEDERAL RESERVE SYSTEM; MOODY'S INVESTORS SERVICE; THE BOND BUYER; DOW JONES, INC.; STANDARD AND POOR'S CORPORATION; NEW YORK STOCK EXCHANGE

Definitions and notes on the data

Interest rates and bond yields are percents per year and are averages of business day figures, except as noted.

The daily effective *federal funds rate* is a weighted average of rates on trades through New York brokers. Monthly figures include each calendar day in the month. Annualized figures use a 360-day year.

The *Federal Reserve discount rate* is the rate for discount window borrowing at the Federal Reserve Bank of New York. Monthly figures include each calendar day in the month. Annualized figures use a 360-day year.

The *Eurodollar rate* shown is the bid rate for Eurodollar deposits at about 9:30 a.m. Eastern time for 1-month deposits. Annualized figures use a 360-day year.

The *U.S. Treasury bills, 3-month rate and the U.S. Treasury bills, 6-month rate* shown are the yields on these securities based on their prices as traded in the secondary market. The rates are quoted on a discount basis, and annualized figures use a 360-day year.

Commercial paper, 3-month rates are interpolated from data on certain commercial paper trades settled by the Depository Trust Company. This company is a clearing house and custodian for nearly all domestic commercial paper activity. The trades, which are on a discount basis, represent sales of commercial paper by dealers or direct issuers. Annualized figures use a 360-day year. Prior to September 1997 the series represents both nonfinancial and financial commercial paper; beginning September 1997 only rates for financial companies are shown, introducing a slight discontinuity into the series.

CDs (secondary market), 3-month rates are averages of dealer offering rates on nationally traded certificates of deposit. Annualized figures use a 360-day year.

The *bank prime rate* is one of several base rates used by banks to price short-term business loans. It is the rate posted by a majority of the top 25 (by assets in domestic offices) insured U.S.-chartered commercial banks. Monthly figures include each calendar day in the month. Annualized figures use a 360-day year.

U.S. Treasury securities. The rates shown for 1-year, 3-year, 10-year, 20-year, and 30-year securities are yields on actively traded issues adjusted to constant maturities. Yields on Treasury securities at "constant maturity" are interpolated by the U.S. Treasury from the daily yield curve. This curve, which relates the yield on a security to its time to maturity, is based on the closing market bid yields on actively traded Treasury securities in the over-the-counter market. These market yields are calculated from composites of quotations reported by U.S. Government securities dealers to the Federal Reserve Bank of New York. The constant maturity yield values are read from the yield curve at fixed maturities. This method provides a yield for a 10-year maturity, for example, even if no outstanding security has exactly 10 years remaining to maturity. The 30-year series was discontinued as of February 2002, because the Treasury is no longer issuing such bonds. The current 20-year series begins in 1993 and is not comparable with an earlier 20-year series. For further information, see Table 1.35 in the *Federal Reserve Bulletin* and the historical data series on the Federal Reserve Internet site.

Domestic corporate bond yields. The rates shown are for general obligation bonds based on Thursday figures and are provided by Moody's Investors Service and republished by the Federal Reserve. The Aaa rates through December 6, 2001 are averages of Aaa utility and Aaa industrial bond rates. As of December 7, 2001, these rates are averages of Aaa industrial bonds only.

The state and local bond yields are the Bond Buyer index as republished by the Federal Reserve. The index is based on 20 state and local government general obligation bonds of mixed quality maturing in 20 years or less. Quotes are as of Thursday.

The *fixed rate mortgage* rates are contract interest rates on commitments for fixed-rate first mortgages. The rates are obtained by the Federal Reserve from the Federal Home Loan Mortgage Corporation (FHLMC).

Stock price indexes. The *Dow Jones industrial* average is an average of 30 stocks compiled by Dow Jones, Inc. The *Standard and Poor's composite* is an index of 500 stocks based on 1941–1943=10 compiled by Standard and Poor's Corporation. The *dividend-price ratio* is compiled by Standard and Poor's, covering the 500 stocks in the S&P index, and represents aggregate cash dividends (based on the latest known annual rate) divided by aggregate market value based on Wednesday closing prices. The *earnings/price ratio* measures earnings (after taxes) for 4 quarters ending with the indicated quarter as a ratio to the price index for the last day of that quarter. Monthly data are averages of weekly figures; annual data are averages of monthly or quarterly figures. The *Nasdaq composite index* is an average of over 4,000 stocks traded on the Nasdaq exchange.

Data availability

Interest rates and bond yields are published weekly in the Federal Reserve's H.15 release. Most are subsequently published in the *Federal Reserve Bulletin*. The starting dates for individual interest rate series vary; some date back to 1911, and many begin in the 1950s and 1960s. Historical data may be purchased on diskette from Publications Services, Board of Governors of the Federal Reserve System. Current and historical data are available on the Federal Reserve Internet site at <http://www.federalreserve.gov/releases/>. Stock market data are published monthly in *Economic Indicators*, available by subscription from the Superintendent of Documents, Government Printing Office, Washington, DC 20402-9328; and annually in *Economic Report of the President*, available from the same source.

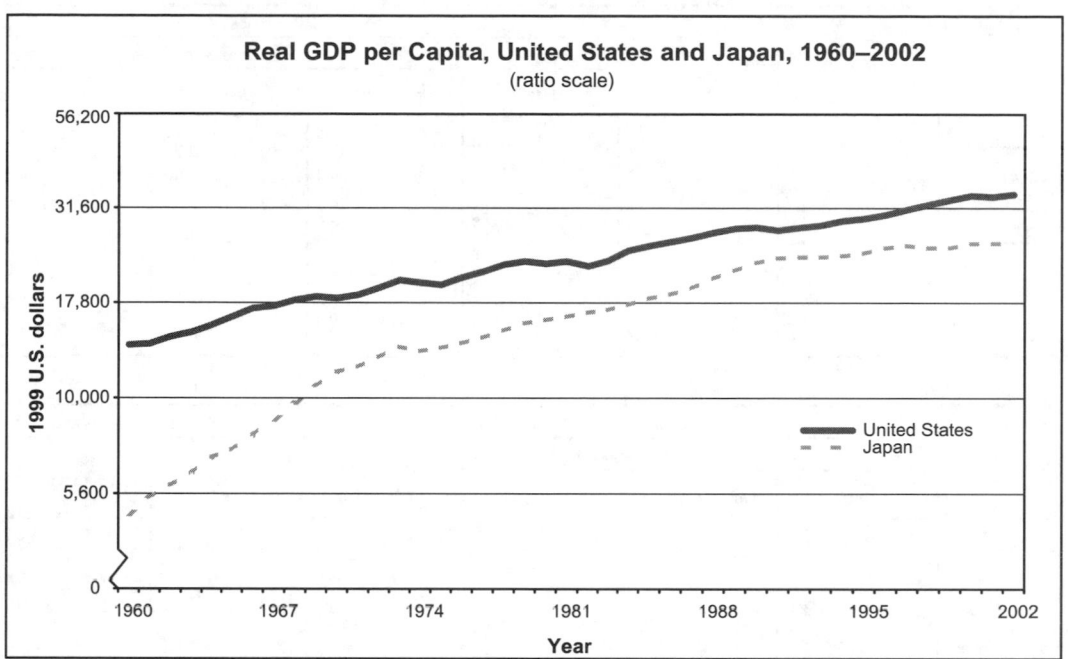

Real GDP per Capita, United States and Japan, 1960–2002
(ratio scale)

- In the United States, gross domestic product per capita grew at a 2.3 percent annual rate between 1960 and 2000. The major industrial nations that had the next-highest average levels of living in 1960—Germany, the United Kingdom, and Canada—grew at similar rates of 2.1 percent, 2.2 percent, and 2.4 percent respectively. (German growth would have been higher, perhaps 2.4 percent, but for the effect of unification of West Germany with the poorer East in 1991.) Industrial nations that were further behind in 1960—Japan, France, and Italy—grew faster: 4.2 percent, 2.6 percent, and 2.9 percent respectively. The growth paths of the United States and Japan are compared in the graph above. (Table 13-2)

- In Japan and the three European countries that are compared here, the growth in GDP per employed person—a measure of labor productivity—was similar to the growth in GDP per capita. In the United States and Canada, on the other hand, growth in GDP per employee was only 1.6 percent per year. In these two North American countries, productivity growth was less than per capita growth, meaning that a significant fraction of the growth in GDP per capita was obtained by putting a larger proportion of the population to work. (Table 13-3)

- Inflation in 2002, as measured by the consumer price index, was low in six of the seven industrial countries shown, while Japan suffered its fourth successive year of deflation. (Table 13-5)

- The rise in unemployment in 2002 in the other six countries was less sharp than in the United States. Japan and the United Kingdom had lower unemployment rates than the United States, while the rates in Germany, France, Italy, and Canada were higher. (Table 13-6)

- The value of the U.S. dollar against the new European currency, the euro, rose 36 percent between January 1999, when the euro was introduced, and June 2001. In that month the dollar bought 1.1724 euros, up from only 0.8627 euros in January 1999. (This exchange rate is frequently quoted as dollars to one euro; in those terms the euro was worth $1.159 in January 1999 but only $0.853 in June 2001. In this way of expressing the rate, it is high when the euro is strong. In the method used in *Business Statistics*, the rate is high when the dollar is strong, for consistency with the other measures shown in the table.) Since 2001, and continuing into 2003, the dollar has declined against major currencies—but not against "Other important trading partners" such as China. (Table 13-7)

Table 13-1. International Comparisons: Growth Rates in Real Gross Domestic Product

(Percent change at annual rate.)

Year	Total, world	Advanced economies					
		Total	Major advanced economies				
			Total	United States	Japan	Germany	France
1984–1993	3.3	3.2	3.0	3.2	3.7	2.8	2.0
1994	3.7	3.4	3.1	4.0	0.9	2.3	1.9
1995	3.7	2.7	2.4	2.7	1.7	1.7	1.8
1996	4.0	3.0	2.8	3.6	3.6	0.8	1.1
1997	4.2	3.4	3.2	4.4	1.8	1.4	1.9
1998	2.8	2.7	2.8	4.3	-1.2	2.0	3.5
1999	3.6	3.4	3.0	4.1	0.8	2.0	3.2
2000	4.7	3.8	3.4	3.8	2.4	2.9	4.2
2001	2.2	0.8	0.6	0.3	-0.3	0.6	1.8
2002 [1]	2.8	1.7	1.4	2.2	-0.5	0.5	1.2

Year	Advanced economies—Continued				Special groupings, advanced economies		
	Major advanced economies—Continued			Other advanced economies	European Union	Euro area	Newly industrialized Asian economies
	Italy	United Kingdom	Canada				
1984–1993	2.1	2.4	2.6	3.8	2.4	2.4	8.0
1994	2.2	4.7	4.8	4.6	2.8	2.4	7.7
1995	2.9	2.9	2.8	4.3	2.4	2.2	7.5
1996	1.1	2.6	1.6	3.8	1.7	1.4	6.3
1997	2.0	3.4	4.2	4.3	2.6	2.3	5.8
1998	1.8	2.9	4.1	2.2	2.9	2.9	-2.4
1999	1.6	2.4	5.4	5.0	2.8	2.8	8.0
2000	2.9	3.1	4.5	5.3	3.5	3.5	8.5
2001	1.8	1.9	1.5	1.6	1.6	1.5	0.8
2002 [1]	0.7	1.7	3.4	2.6	1.1	0.9	4.7

Year	Developing countries					Countries in transition			
	Total	Africa	Developing Asia	Middle East, Malta, and Turkey	Western Hemisphere	Total	Central and eastern Europe	Commonwealth of Independent States and Mongolia	Russia
1984–1993	5.1	2.0	7.6	3.5	2.9	-1.4	. . .	. . .	. . .
1994	6.7	2.3	9.7	0.5	5.0	-8.5	3.2	-14.5	-13.5
1995	6.2	3.0	9.0	4.4	1.8	-1.6	5.2	-5.5	-4.2
1996	6.5	5.6	8.3	4.7	3.6	-0.5	4.1	-3.3	-3.4
1997	5.9	3.1	6.6	6.2	5.2	1.6	2.6	1.1	0.9
1998	3.5	3.4	4.0	3.6	2.3	-0.7	2.4	-2.8	-4.9
1999	4.0	2.8	6.1	1.2	0.2	3.7	2.2	4.6	5.4
2000	5.7	3.0	6.7	6.1	4.0	6.6	3.8	8.4	9.0
2001	3.9	3.5	5.6	1.5	0.6	5.0	3.0	6.3	5.0
2002 [1]	4.2	3.1	6.1	3.6	-0.6	3.9	2.7	4.6	4.4

[1] IMF estimates, January 2003.
. . . = Not available.

Table 13-2. International Comparisons: Real GDP per Capita

(1999 U.S. dollars.)

Year	United States	Japan	Germany [1]	France	United Kingdom	Italy	Canada
1960	13 765	4 950	10 925	8 461	10 328	7 822	11 104
1961	13 857	5 485	11 280	8 834	10 500	8 431	11 225
1962	14 469	5 901	11 669	9 256	10 536	8 881	11 771
1963	14 879	6 354	11 881	9 577	10 990	9 309	12 144
1964	15 527	6 990	12 546	10 097	11 509	9 474	12 697
1965	16 314	7 305	13 071	10 490	11 703	9 706	13 275
1966	17 186	7 992	13 316	10 946	11 866	10 209	13 884
1967	17 426	8 775	13 244	11 370	12 066	10 850	14 044
1968	18 076	9 710	13 916	11 767	12 506	11 476	14 569
1969	18 442	10 743	14 813	12 489	12 699	12 098	15 127
1970	18 264	11 712	15 409	13 087	12 955	12 645	15 307
1971	18 639	12 060	15 717	13 585	13 154	12 829	15 638
1972	19 441	12 777	16 281	14 063	13 589	13 159	16 284
1973	20 368	13 613	16 974	14 709	14 541	13 926	17 242
1974	20 062	13 267	16 985	15 068	14 308	14 565	17 709
1975	19 798	13 510	16 834	14 958	14 231	14 182	17 840
1976	20 698	13 904	17 816	15 531	14 628	15 033	18 573
1977	21 442	14 378	18 362	15 959	14 970	15 322	18 992
1978	22 386	15 002	18 935	16 422	15 474	15 825	19 570
1979	22 844	15 693	19 724	16 893	15 860	16 652	20 192
1980	22 530	16 010	19 851	17 077	15 501	17 196	20 210
1981	22 853	16 336	19 833	17 188	15 267	17 307	20 575
1982	22 177	16 738	19 661	17 538	15 416	17 406	19 750
1983	22 929	17 014	20 076	17 707	16 145	17 614	20 087
1984	24 380	17 556	20 725	17 912	16 527	18 096	21 055
1985	25 094	18 244	21 198	18 083	17 079	18 629	21 861
1986	25 717	18 683	21 680	18 428	17 712	19 099	22 169
1987	26 354	19 410	21 997	18 793	18 471	19 667	22 807
1988	27 205	20 596	22 678	19 541	19 393	20 433	23 630
1989	27 895	21 595	23 267	20 236	19 755	21 004	23 816
1990	28 092	22 642	24 132	20 655	19 855	21 401	23 504
1991	27 599	23 288	22 608	20 756	19 512	21 687	22 742
1992	28 066	23 432	22 940	20 961	19 515	21 810	22 661
1993	28 436	23 432	22 527	20 689	19 963	21 545	22 927
1994	29 226	23 608	22 987	21 042	20 848	21 961	23 753
1995	29 653	24 004	23 316	21 318	21 404	22 565	24 156
1996	30 357	24 769	23 427	21 478	21 922	22 774	24 284
1997	31 326	25 163	23 708	21 812	22 628	23 188	25 044
1998	32 288	24 816	24 179	22 473	23 235	23 573	25 845
1999	33 234	24 801	24 656	23 099	23 723	23 941	27 042
2000	34 106	25 450	25 329	23 858	24 387	24 644	28 204
2001	33 869	25 480	25 427	24 230	24 819	25 017	28 451
2002	34 379	25 482	25 427	24 395	. . .	25 055	29 100

[1]Data prior to 1991 are for West Germany only. In 1991, real GDP per capita in West Germany alone was $25,025 (1999 U.S. dollars).

Table 13-3. International Comparisons: Real GDP per Employed Person

(1999 U.S. dollars.)

Year	United States	Japan	Germany [1]	France	United Kingdom	Italy	Canada
1960	36 434	10 610	23 237	19 937	22 425	18 668	31 514
1961	37 267	11 712	23 978	21 037	22 753	20 072	32 004
1962	38 830	12 573	25 010	22 446	22 928	21 380	33 280
1963	39 951	13 563	25 652	23 458	24 005	22 960	34 187
1964	41 364	14 859	27 337	24 714	24 986	23 685	35 194
1965	42 955	15 462	28 639	25 816	25 321	25 070	36 147
1966	44 448	16 687	29 528	26 961	25 750	27 012	36 986
1967	44 507	18 161	30 429	28 153	26 643	28 595	37 037
1968	45 669	19 945	32 061	29 439	27 876	30 482	38 328
1969	45 927	22 114	33 924	31 024	28 434	32 574	39 168
1970	45 755	24 112	35 188	32 363	29 178	34 146	39 782
1971	47 103	25 006	36 117	33 759	30 226	34 795	41 054
1972	48 240	27 052	37 503	35 047	31 128	35 986	42 039
1973	49 396	28 485	38 866	36 449	32 741	37 807	42 948
1974	48 203	28 239	39 420	37 259	32 145	39 193	42 964
1975	48 575	29 213	40 000	37 481	32 134	38 360	43 174
1976	49 660	30 089	42 355	38 767	33 292	40 455	44 653
1977	50 168	30 995	43 498	39 684	34 013	41 283	45 536
1978	50 770	32 234	44 440	40 813	34 869	42 648	46 022
1979	50 959	33 582	45 550	41 950	35 324	44 513	46 000
1980	50 596	34 175	45 298	42 516	34 941	45 405	45 330
1981	51 263	34 829	45 391	43 199	35 657	45 796	45 361
1982	50 636	35 576	45 506	44 283	36 747	45 991	45 407
1983	52 148	35 813	46 975	45 083	38 219	46 410	46 255
1984	53 750	36 982	48 220	45 930	38 428	47 693	47 782
1985	54 717	38 408	48 835	46 957	39 248	48 652	48 731
1986	55 343	39 203	49 298	47 907	40 501	49 540	48 451
1987	55 799	40 516	49 667	48 749	41 423	50 903	49 093
1988	56 889	42 452	51 118	50 539	42 177	52 351	49 983
1989	57 724	43 804	52 210	51 778	42 041	53 488	50 198
1990	58 056	45 179	53 595	52 618	42 028	53 688	49 929
1991	58 325	45 758	47 025	53 041	42 469	53 435	49 704
1992	59 793	45 708	48 809	54 248	43 506	54 105	50 442
1993	60 567	45 708	48 942	54 440	45 345	55 000	51 235
1994	61 648	46 136	50 172	55 491	47 124	57 059	52 648
1995	62 421	47 002	50 933	56 160	48 002	58 793	53 150
1996	63 772	48 379	51 477	56 540	48 808	59 065	53 598
1997	65 172	48 736	52 282	57 468	49 669	60 033	54 552
1998	67 000	48 522	52 726	58 555	50 530	60 476	55 336
1999	68 726	48 971	53 154	59 307	51 194	60 807	56 836
2000	69 564	50 447	53 720	60 140	52 175	61 546	58 346
2001	69 714	50 909	53 799	60 158	52 909	61 494	58 809
2002	71 638	51 636	54 213	. . .	. . .	60 893	59 438

[1]Data prior to 1991 are for West Germany only. In 1991, real GDP per capita in West Germany alone was $54,933 (1999 U.S. dollars).
. . . = Not available.

Table 13-4. International Comparisons: Industrial Production Indexes

(1990 = 100, seasonally adjusted.)

Year and month	United States	Japan	Germany (Federal Republic)	France	United Kingdom	Italy	Canada
1945	23.5	...	...	...	...	...	...
1946	20.3	...	...	...	...	...	...
1947	22.9	...	...	...	...	...	...
1948	23.8	1.8	8.6	...	36.0	11.8	...
1949	22.5	2.3	12.6	...	38.6	12.8	...
1950	26.0	2.9	15.3	...	41.5	14.1	...
1951	28.2	3.9	18.3	22.8	43.1	15.8	...
1952	29.3	4.2	19.5	22.8	41.7	16.2	...
1953	31.8	5.0	21.3	23.1	43.6	17.5	...
1954	30.0	5.4	24.2	25.3	47.3	19.1	...
1955	33.8	5.9	29.9	27.6	50.0	20.7	...
1956	35.3	7.3	32.5	31.3	50.5	22.2	...
1957	35.8	8.6	34.4	34.2	51.6	23.9	...
1958	33.5	8.5	34.4	35.5	51.4	24.7	...
1959	37.5	10.1	36.7	35.9	53.9	27.4	...
1960	38.3	12.7	40.7	39.1	57.8	31.7	...
1961	38.6	15.1	43.7	41.6	58.0	35.1	33.4
1962	41.8	16.3	45.5	43.9	58.6	38.5	36.8
1963	44.3	18.2	47.0	46.1	60.9	41.8	39.2
1964	47.3	21.1	50.8	49.0	65.2	42.3	43.1
1965	52.1	21.9	53.6	49.9	67.2	44.3	47.0
1966	56.7	24.8	54.0	52.8	68.0	49.5	50.0
1967	57.9	29.6	52.7	54.0	67.6	53.2	51.6
1968	61.1	34.2	57.8	56.1	70.7	56.4	55.2
1969	63.9	39.6	65.0	62.6	73.1	58.4	58.9
1970	61.8	45.0	69.0	66.1	73.5	62.2	58.0
1971	62.7	46.2	69.8	69.1	73.1	62.2	61.3
1972	68.6	49.6	72.1	74.2	74.4	64.9	66.7
1973	74.1	57.0	76.5	79.8	81.0	71.2	74.6
1974	73.7	54.8	75.2	81.8	79.4	74.4	76.0
1975	67.0	48.7	70.5	74.5	75.1	67.5	70.5
1976	72.1	54.1	75.8	81.5	77.6	76.0	75.2
1977	77.5	56.4	77.6	82.9	81.6	76.8	77.7
1978	81.8	59.9	78.8	84.8	83.9	78.2	80.4
1979	84.2	64.3	82.7	88.6	87.2	83.5	84.3
1980	81.8	67.3	82.9	87.6	81.5	88.1	81.5
1981	82.9	68.0	81.3	86.7	78.9	86.7	83.1
1982	78.6	68.3	78.7	86.0	80.4	84.0	75.0
1983	80.6	70.4	79.1	86.0	83.3	81.4	79.8
1984	87.8	77.0	81.4	87.5	83.4	84.1	89.5
1985	88.8	79.8	85.5	88.1	88.0	85.0	94.5
1986	89.6	79.7	87.2	89.1	90.1	88.1	93.8
1987	93.9	82.4	87.5	90.9	93.7	91.5	98.4
1988	98.4	90.7	90.6	94.6	98.2	97.0	103.6
1989	99.2	96.0	94.9	98.0	100.3	100.0	103.4
1990	100.0	100.0	99.9	100.0	100.0	100.0	100.0
1991	98.4	101.9	102.7	98.8	96.1	99.3	95.8
1992	101.0	96.1	100.3	97.6	95.6	99.1	96.9
1993	104.3	92.0	92.3	93.9	97.9	96.7	101.2
1994	109.8	92.5	95.2	97.5	103.1	101.6	108.3
1995	115.1	95.4	96.0	99.2	105.9	107.7	112.0
1996	120.1	98.5	96.7	99.0	106.3	102.9	113.3
1997	128.9	102.5	100.2	102.8	107.5	106.8	119.7
1998	136.2	95.6	104.4	108.1	108.5	108.3	123.9
1999	142.6	96.1	106.0	110.2	109.9	107.5	131.1
2000	148.8	101.0	112.6	114.1	111.9	112.0	141.8
2001	143.8	94.8	113.2	115.5	110.2	110.8	137.7
2002	143.0	93.7	111.8	114.3	107.2	109.3	140.4
2001							
January	147.3	99.8	115.9	116.3	112.4	113.7	140.9
February	146.4	100.7	115.9	116.0	112.1	113.2	139.7
March	145.9	99.0	114.5	115.6	111.8	113.1	139.0
April	145.4	98.3	113.5	115.3	111.2	111.5	139.6
May	144.8	96.3	114.0	115.8	110.3	112.1	140.1
June	143.9	95.2	113.7	115.8	110.3	111.4	138.6
July	143.3	93.9	112.1	116.2	109.6	110.6	137.1
August	143.0	92.7	113.9	117.6	110.6	109.7	137.5
September	142.0	90.8	112.8	115.8	109.9	109.4	134.8
October	141.7	90.8	111.2	114.2	108.5	108.8	135.3
November	141.0	89.4	109.7	113.7	107.9	107.4	135.7
December	140.7	90.4	110.8	113.7	107.7	108.4	134.5
2002							
January	141.5	89.8	111.3	113.8	107.5	108.3	136.5
February	141.7	91.0	110.7	113.5	107.2	109.3	138.4
March	142.2	91.4	111.3	114.6	107.7	109.3	138.6
April	142.9	91.2	111.6	114.9	108.1	108.2	140.9
May	143.0	94.9	110.2	115.0	109.8	110.3	139.8
June	144.0	93.9	112.5	114.7	104.4	109.6	140.4
July	143.8	94.6	112.1	114.5	107.0	110.3	141.8
August	143.8	95.0	113.3	114.8	107.1	108.9	141.6
September	143.5	95.7	112.2	114.6	107.2	109.6	141.6
October	143.1	95.8	112.1	113.5	106.7	108.9	141.9
November	143.4	95.6	113.8	114.6	106.6	109.4	141.4
December	142.6	95.3	110.8	113.3	106.9	108.9	141.6

. . . = Not available.

Table 13-5. International Comparisons: Consumer Price Indexes

(1982–1984 = 100, except as noted; not seasonally adjusted; percent changes are from previous year's average for annual data, from the same quarter of the previous year for quarterly data.)

Year and month	United States Index	United States Percent change	Japan Index	Japan Percent change	Germany [1] Index	Germany [1] Percent change	France Index	France Percent change	United Kingdom Index	United Kingdom Percent change	Italy Index	Italy Percent change	Canada Index	Canada Percent change
1950	24.1	...	14.8	...	34.5	...	11.1	...	9.8	...	...	...	21.6	...
1951	26.0	7.9	17.2	16.2	37.2	7.8	13.0	17.1	10.7	9.2	...	...	23.9	10.6
1952	26.5	1.9	18.0	4.7	38.0	2.2	14.6	12.3	11.7	9.3	...	...	24.5	2.5
1953	26.7	0.8	19.2	6.7	37.3	-1.8	14.4	-1.4	12.1	3.4	10.3	...	24.2	-1.2
1954	26.9	0.7	20.5	6.8	37.3	0.0	14.3	-0.7	12.3	1.7	10.6	2.9	24.4	0.8
1955	26.8	-0.4	20.2	-1.5	38.0	1.9	14.5	1.4	12.9	4.9	10.9	2.8	24.4	0.0
1956	27.2	1.5	20.3	0.5	39.0	2.6	14.8	2.1	13.5	4.7	11.2	2.8	24.8	1.6
1957	28.1	3.3	20.9	3.0	39.8	2.1	15.3	3.4	14.0	3.7	11.4	1.8	25.6	3.2
1958	28.9	2.8	20.8	-0.5	40.6	2.0	17.6	15.0	14.4	2.9	11.7	2.6	26.3	2.7
1959	29.1	0.7	21.1	1.4	41.0	1.0	18.7	6.2	14.5	0.7	11.7	0.0	26.6	1.1
1960	29.6	1.7	21.8	3.3	41.6	1.5	19.4	3.7	14.6	0.7	11.9	1.7	26.9	1.1
1961	29.9	1.0	23.0	5.5	42.6	2.4	20.0	3.1	15.1	3.4	12.2	2.5	27.1	0.7
1962	30.2	1.0	24.6	7.0	43.8	2.8	21.0	5.0	15.8	4.6	12.7	4.1	27.4	1.1
1963	30.6	1.3	26.4	7.3	45.1	3.0	22.0	4.8	16.1	1.9	13.7	7.9	27.9	1.8
1964	31.0	1.3	27.4	3.8	46.2	2.4	22.7	3.2	16.6	3.1	14.5	5.8	28.4	1.8
1965	31.5	1.6	29.5	7.7	47.8	3.5	23.3	2.6	17.4	4.8	15.2	4.8	29.1	2.5
1966	32.4	2.9	31.0	5.1	49.4	3.3	23.9	2.6	18.1	4.0	15.5	2.0	30.2	3.8
1967	33.4	3.1	32.3	4.2	50.1	1.4	24.6	2.9	18.5	2.2	16.1	3.9	31.3	3.6
1968	34.8	4.2	34.0	5.3	50.8	1.4	25.7	4.5	19.4	4.9	16.3	1.2	32.5	3.8
1969	36.7	5.5	35.8	5.3	51.8	2.0	27.3	6.2	20.5	5.7	16.7	2.5	34.0	4.6
1970	38.8	5.7	38.5	7.5	53.5	3.3	28.8	5.5	21.8	6.3	17.5	4.8	35.1	3.2
1971	40.5	4.4	40.9	6.2	56.2	5.0	30.3	5.2	23.8	9.2	18.4	5.1	36.2	3.1
1972	41.8	3.2	42.9	4.9	59.2	5.3	32.2	6.3	25.5	7.1	19.4	5.4	37.9	4.7
1973	44.4	6.2	47.9	11.7	63.2	6.8	34.6	7.5	27.9	9.4	21.6	11.3	40.7	7.4
1974	49.3	11.0	59.1	23.4	67.6	7.0	39.3	13.6	32.3	15.8	25.7	19.0	45.2	11.1
1975	53.8	9.1	66.0	11.7	71.7	6.1	43.9	11.7	40.1	24.1	30.0	16.7	50.1	10.8
1976	56.9	5.8	72.2	9.4	74.8	4.3	48.2	9.8	46.8	16.7	35.1	17.0	53.8	7.4
1977	60.6	6.5	78.1	8.2	77.4	3.5	52.7	9.3	54.2	15.8	41.0	16.8	58.1	8.0
1978	65.2	7.6	81.4	4.2	79.4	2.6	57.5	9.1	58.7	8.3	46.0	12.2	63.3	9.0
1979	72.6	11.3	84.4	3.7	82.4	3.8	63.6	10.6	66.6	13.5	52.8	14.8	69.1	9.2
1980	82.4	13.5	90.9	7.7	86.7	5.2	72.3	13.7	78.5	17.9	64.0	21.2	76.1	10.1
1981	90.9	10.3	95.4	5.0	92.2	6.3	82.0	13.4	87.9	12.0	75.4	17.8	85.6	12.5
1982	96.5	6.2	98.0	2.7	97.1	5.3	91.6	11.7	95.4	8.5	87.8	16.4	94.9	10.9
1983	99.6	3.2	99.8	1.8	100.2	3.2	100.5	9.7	99.8	4.6	100.7	14.7	100.4	5.8
1984	103.9	4.3	102.1	2.3	102.7	2.5	107.9	7.4	104.8	5.0	111.5	10.7	104.7	4.3
1985	107.6	3.6	104.2	2.1	104.7	1.9	114.2	5.8	111.1	6.0	121.8	9.2	108.9	4.0
1986	109.6	1.9	104.8	0.6	104.5	-0.2	117.2	2.6	114.9	3.4	129.0	5.9	113.4	4.1
1987	113.6	3.6	104.9	0.1	104.6	0.1	120.9	3.2	119.7	4.2	135.1	4.7	118.4	4.4
1988	118.3	4.1	105.7	0.8	105.7	1.1	124.2	2.7	125.6	4.9	141.9	5.0	123.2	4.1
1989	124.0	4.8	108.1	2.3	108.8	2.9	128.6	3.5	135.4	7.8	150.8	6.3	129.3	5.0
1990	130.7	5.4	111.4	3.1	111.7	2.7	133.0	3.4	148.2	9.5	160.5	6.5	135.5	4.8
1991	136.2	4.2	115.1	3.3	115.9	3.8	137.2	3.2	156.9	5.9	170.6	6.3	143.1	5.6
1992	140.3	3.0	117.0	1.7	86.1	5.1	140.6	2.5	162.7	3.7	179.4	5.2	145.3	1.5
1993	144.5	3.0	118.5	1.3	89.9	4.4	143.5	2.1	165.3	1.6	187.5	4.5	147.9	1.8
1994	148.2	2.6	119.3	0.7	92.3	2.7	145.9	1.7	169.3	2.4	195.0	4.0	148.2	0.2
1995	152.4	2.8	119.2	-0.1	93.9	1.7	148.4	1.7	175.2	3.5	205.1	5.2	151.4	2.1
1996	156.9	3.0	119.3	0.1	95.3	1.5	151.3	2.0	179.4	2.4	213.4	4.0	153.8	1.6
1997	160.5	2.3	121.5	1.8	97.1	1.9	153.2	1.3	185.1	3.2	217.7	2.0	156.2	1.6
1998	163.0	1.6	122.2	0.6	98.0	0.9	154.3	0.7	191.4	3.4	222.0	2.0	157.7	0.9
1999	166.6	2.2	121.8	-0.3	98.6	0.6	155.0	0.5	194.3	1.5	225.7	1.7	160.5	1.7
2000	172.2	3.4	121.0	-0.7	100.0	1.4	157.7	1.7	200.1	3.0	231.4	2.5	164.8	2.7
2001	177.1	2.8	120.1	-0.7	102.0	2.0	160.3	1.6	203.6	1.7	237.8	2.7	169.0	2.6
2002	179.9	1.6	119.1	-0.8	103.4	1.4	163.4	1.9	207.0	1.7	243.7	2.5	172.8	2.2
2000														
1st quarter	...	3.2	...	-0.7	...	1.6	...	1.5	...	2.3	...	2.4	...	2.7
2nd quarter	...	3.3	...	-0.7	...	1.2	...	1.5	...	3.1	...	2.5	...	2.4
3rd quarter	...	3.5	...	-0.7	...	1.4	...	1.9	...	3.2	...	2.6	...	2.7
4th quarter	...	3.4	...	-0.5	...	1.8	...	1.9	...	3.1	...	2.7	...	3.1
2001														
1st quarter	...	3.4	...	-0.4	...	1.7	...	1.3	...	2.5	...	2.9	...	2.8
2nd quarter	...	3.4	...	-0.7	...	2.5	...	2.0	...	1.9	...	3.1	...	3.6
3rd quarter	...	2.7	...	-0.8	...	2.1	...	1.8	...	1.8	...	2.8	...	2.7
4th quarter	...	1.9	...	-1.0	...	1.6	...	1.4	...	1.0	...	2.4	...	1.1
2002														
1st quarter	...	1.3	...	-1.4	...	1.9	...	2.1	...	1.2	...	2.4	...	1.5
2nd quarter	...	1.3	...	-0.9	...	1.2	...	1.6	...	1.2	...	2.3	...	1.3
3rd quarter	...	1.6	...	-0.8	...	1.1	...	1.8	...	1.5	...	2.4	...	2.3
4th quarter	...	2.2	...	-0.5	...	1.2	...	2.1	...	2.6	...	2.8	...	3.8

[1]Former West Germany only, 1950–1991. From 1992 forward, unified Germany, 2000 = 100. In 1991, the index for unified Germany, 2000 = 100, was 81.9.
. . . = Not available.

Table 13.6. International Comparisons: Unemployment Rates and Civilian Labor Forces [1]

(Quarterly data, seasonally adjusted.)

Year and quarter	United States Unemployment rate	United States Labor force (thousands)	Japan Unemployment rate	Japan Labor force (thousands)	Germany [2] Unemployment rate	Germany [2] Labor force (thousands)	France Unemployment rate	France Labor force (thousands)	United Kingdom Unemployment rate	United Kingdom Labor force (thousands)	Italy Unemployment rate	Italy Labor force (thousands)	Canada Unemployment rate	Canada Labor force (thousands)
1959	5.5	68 369	2.3	43 320	2.0	25 850	1.6	18 480	2.8	23 880	4.8	21 020	5.6	6 286
1960	5.5	69 628	1.7	44 120	1.1	25 990	1.5	18 520	2.2	24 130	3.7	20 820	6.5	6 462
1961	6.7	70 459	1.5	44 610	0.6	26 160	1.2	18 530	2.0	24 380	3.2	20 830	6.7	6 575
1962	5.5	70 614	1.3	45 040	0.6	26 210	1.4	18 720	2.7	24 720	2.8	20 680	5.5	6 670
1963	5.7	71 833	1.3	45 430	0.5	26 290	1.6	19 100	3.3	24 940	2.4	20 240	5.2	6 805
1964	5.2	73 091	1.2	46 040	0.4	26 270	1.2	19 430	2.5	25 070	2.7	20 220	4.4	6 994
1965	4.5	74 455	1.2	46 780	0.3	26 360	1.6	19 650	2.1	25 240	3.5	19 900	3.6	7 207
1966	3.8	75 770	1.4	47 850	0.3	26 290	1.6	19 850	2.3	25 320	3.7	19 620	3.4	7 493
1967	3.8	77 347	1.3	48 810	1.3	25 730	2.1	20 070	3.3	25 290	3.4	19 800	3.8	7 747
1968	3.6	78 737	1.2	49 690	1.1	25 690	2.7	20 190	3.2	25 180	3.5	19 780	4.5	7 951
1969	3.5	80 734	1.1	50 140	0.6	25 960	2.3	20 470	3.1	25 160	3.5	19 620	4.4	8 194
1970	4.9	82 771	1.2	50 730	0.5	26 240	2.5	20 800	3.1	25 110	3.2	19 720	5.7	8 395
1971	5.9	84 382	1.3	51 120	0.6	26 380	2.8	21 000	3.9	24 950	3.3	19 660	6.2	8 639
1972	5.6	87 034	1.4	51 320	0.7	26 470	2.9	21 150	4.2	25 190	3.8	19 450	6.2	8 897
1973	4.9	89 429	1.3	52 590	0.7	26 780	2.8	21 430	3.2	25 440	3.7	19 590	5.5	9 276
1974	5.6	91 949	1.4	52 440	1.6	26 660	2.9	21 660	3.1	25 470	3.1	19 900	5.3	9 639
1975	8.5	93 775	1.9	52 530	3.4	26 430	4.2	21 770	4.6	25 730	3.4	20 090	6.9	9 974
1976	7.7	96 158	2.0	53 100	3.4	26 290	4.6	22 050	5.9	25 900	3.9	20 290	6.8	10 391
1977	7.1	99 009	2.0	53 820	3.4	26 330	5.2	22 380	6.4	26 050	4.1	20 510	7.8	10 650
1978	6.1	102 251	2.3	54 610	3.3	26 520	5.4	22 540	6.3	26 260	4.1	20 570	8.1	11 006
1979	5.8	104 962	2.1	55 210	2.9	26 860	6.1	22 780	5.4	26 350	4.4	20 850	7.3	11 377
1980	7.1	106 940	2.0	55 740	2.8	27 260	6.5	22 930	7.0	26 520	4.4	21 120	7.3	11 707
1981	7.6	108 670	2.2	56 320	4.0	27 540	7.6	23 090	10.5	26 500	4.0	21 320	7.3	12 067
1982	9.7	110 204	2.4	56 980	5.6	27 710	8.3	23 320	11.3	26 560	5.4	21 410	10.6	12 139
1983	9.6	111 550	2.7	58 110	6.9	27 670	8.6	23 400	11.8	26 610	5.9	21 590	11.5	12 368
1984	7.5	113 544	2.8	58 480	7.1	27 800	10.0	23 560	11.7	27 110	5.9	21 670	10.9	12 579
1985	7.2	115 461	2.6	58 820	7.2	28 020	10.5	23 620	11.2	27 350	6.0	21 800	10.2	12 825
1986	7.0	117 834	2.8	59 410	6.6	28 240	10.6	23 760	11.2	27 550	7.5	22 290	9.2	13 075
1987	6.2	119 865	2.9	60 050	6.3	28 390	10.8	23 890	10.3	27 870	7.9	22 350	8.4	13 331
1988	5.5	121 669	2.5	60 860	6.3	28 610	10.3	23 980	8.6	28 270	7.9	22 660	7.3	13 589
1989	5.3	123 869	2.3	61 920	5.7	28 840	9.6	24 170	7.2	28 580	7.8	22 530	7.1	13 848
1990	5.6	125 840	2.1	63 050	5.0	29 410	9.1	24 290	6.9	28 730	7.0	22 670	7.7	14 044
1991	6.8	126 346	2.1	64 280	5.6	39 080	9.5	24 440	8.8	28 610	6.9	22 940	9.8	14 135
1992	7.5	128 105	2.2	65 040	6.7	39 010	9.9	24 440	10.1	28 410	7.3	22 910	10.6	14 177
1993	6.9	129 200	2.5	65 470	8.0	39 100	11.3	24 480	10.4	28 050	10.2	22 570	10.8	14 308
1994	6.1	131 056	2.9	65 780	8.5	39 070	11.8	24 670	9.5	27 990	11.2	22 450	9.5	14 400
1995	5.6	132 304	3.2	65 990	8.2	38 980	11.3	24 750	8.7	28 040	11.8	22 460	8.6	14 517
1996	5.4	133 943	3.4	66 450	9.0	39 140	11.9	25 000	8.1	28 140	11.7	22 570	8.8	14 669
1997	4.9	136 297	3.4	67 200	9.9	39 420	11.8	25 130	7.0	28 270	11.9	22 680	8.4	14 958
1998	4.5	137 673	4.1	67 240	9.3	39 750	11.3	25 440	6.3	28 380	12.0	22 960	7.7	15 237
1999	4.2	139 368	4.7	67 090	8.6	39 800	10.6	25 800	6.0	28 610	11.5	23 130	7.0	15 536
2000	4.0	142 583	4.8	66 990	8.1	39 750	9.1	26 050	5.5	28 780	10.7	23 340	6.1	15 789
2001	4.7	143 734	5.1	66 870	8.0	39 780	8.5	26 340	5.1	28 870	9.6	23 540	6.4	16 027
2002	5.8	144 863	5.4	66 240	8.4	. . .	8.8	. . .	5.2	. . .	9.1	23 750	7.0	16 475
1997														
1st quarter	5.2	. . .	3.3	. . .	9.6	. . .	11.9	. . .	7.4	. . .	11.9	. . .	8.6	. . .
2nd quarter	5.0	. . .	3.4	. . .	10.0	. . .	11.9	. . .	7.2	. . .	11.9	. . .	8.6	. . .
3rd quarter	4.9	. . .	3.4	. . .	10.0	. . .	11.8	. . .	6.9	. . .	11.7	. . .	8.1	. . .
4th quarter	4.7	. . .	3.5	. . .	10.0	. . .	11.6	. . .	6.6	. . .	11.9	. . .	8.1	. . .
1998														
1st quarter	4.6	. . .	3.7	. . .	9.8	. . .	11.5	. . .	6.4	. . .	11.9	. . .	8.0	. . .
2nd quarter	4.4	. . .	4.2	. . .	9.4	. . .	11.3	. . .	6.3	. . .	12.0	. . .	7.7	. . .
3rd quarter	4.5	. . .	4.3	. . .	9.1	. . .	11.2	. . .	6.3	. . .	12.0	. . .	7.6	. . .
4th quarter	4.4	. . .	4.5	. . .	8.9	. . .	11.1	. . .	6.2	. . .	12.0	. . .	7.4	. . .
1999														
1st quarter	4.3	. . .	4.7	. . .	8.8	. . .	11.0	. . .	6.2	. . .	11.8	. . .	7.3	. . .
2nd quarter	4.3	. . .	4.8	. . .	8.7	. . .	10.8	. . .	6.1	. . .	11.7	. . .	7.3	. . .
3rd quarter	4.3	. . .	4.8	. . .	8.6	. . .	10.5	. . .	5.9	. . .	11.5	. . .	6.9	. . .
4th quarter	4.1	. . .	4.7	. . .	8.5	. . .	10.1	. . .	5.9	. . .	11.3	. . .	6.3	. . .
2000														
1st quarter	4.0	. . .	4.8	. . .	8.3	. . .	9.6	. . .	5.8	. . .	11.2	. . .	6.1	. . .
2nd quarter	4.0	. . .	4.7	. . .	8.1	. . .	9.3	. . .	5.5	. . .	10.9	. . .	6.1	. . .
3rd quarter	4.0	. . .	4.7	. . .	8.0	. . .	9.0	. . .	5.4	. . .	10.5	. . .	6.1	. . .
4th quarter	3.9	. . .	4.8	. . .	7.8	. . .	8.7	. . .	5.2	. . .	10.1	. . .	6.1	. . .
2001														
1st quarter	4.2	. . .	4.8	. . .	7.9	. . .	8.5	. . .	5.1	. . .	10.0	. . .	6.2	. . .
2nd quarter	4.4	. . .	4.9	. . .	8.0	. . .	8.4	. . .	5.0	. . .	9.7	. . .	6.3	. . .
3rd quarter	4.8	. . .	5.2	. . .	8.0	. . .	8.5	. . .	5.1	. . .	9.5	. . .	6.5	. . .
4th quarter	5.6	. . .	5.5	. . .	8.1	. . .	8.6	. . .	5.2	. . .	9.4	. . .	6.8	. . .
2001														
1st quarter	5.6	. . .	5.3	. . .	8.2	. . .	8.7	. . .	5.1	. . .	9.2	. . .	7.1	. . .
2nd quarter	5.9	. . .	5.4	. . .	8.4	. . .	8.7	. . .	5.2	. . .	9.1	. . .	6.9	. . .
3rd quarter	5.8	. . .	5.5	. . .	8.5	. . .	8.9	. . .	5.3	. . .	9.1	. . .	7.0	. . .
4th quarter	5.9	. . .	5.5	. . .	8.6	. . .	8.9	. . .	5.1	. . .	9.0	. . .	6.9	. . .

[1]Data for other countries adjusted to approximate U.S. concepts.
[2]Data prior to 1991 are for West Germany only. In 1991, the unemployment rate for West Germany alone was 4.3 percent.
. . . = Not available.

Table 13-7. Exchange Rates

(Not seasonally adjusted.)

Year and month	Foreign currency per U.S. dollar						Trade-weighted exchange indexes of value of U.S. dollar					
							Nominal				Price-adjusted	
	European currency unit	Japanese yen	German mark	French franc	British pound	Canadian dollar	G-10 countries (March 1973 = 100)	Broad (January 1997 = 100)	Major currencies (March 1973 = 100)	Other important trading partners (January 1997 = 100)	Broad (March 1973 = 100)	Other important trading partners (March 1973 = 100)
1971	...	346.62	3.4673	5.4889	0.4092	1.0099	117.81	...	...	...	...	...
1972	...	303.11	3.1889	5.0448	0.4005	0.9908	109.07	...	...	...	...	...
1973	...	271.40	2.6719	4.4549	0.4084	1.0002	99.14	29.72	100.28	1.95	98.53	95.06
1974	...	291.94	2.5873	4.8104	0.4277	0.9781	101.41	30.55	102.06	2.06	96.12	88.71
1975	...	296.77	2.4614	4.2885	0.4521	1.0173	98.50	31.64	102.35	2.30	94.43	89.08
1976	...	296.48	2.5184	4.7805	0.5567	0.9861	105.63	33.58	105.95	2.60	94.31	87.81
1977	...	268.38	2.3225	4.9149	0.5733	1.0635	103.35	34.60	105.48	2.91	92.55	88.15
1978	...	210.46	2.0089	4.5101	0.5214	1.1408	92.39	32.95	96.33	3.05	86.83	86.92
1979	...	219.21	1.8331	4.2545	0.4720	1.1716	88.07	33.34	94.94	3.27	87.99	87.31
1980	...	226.58	1.8183	4.2269	0.4304	1.1694	87.39	34.41	94.85	3.61	89.57	86.63
1981	...	220.45	2.2606	5.4348	0.4978	1.1989	103.26	38.08	103.55	4.11	96.74	89.11
1982	...	249.05	2.4281	6.5761	0.5727	1.2339	116.50	44.22	114.21	5.28	106.09	99.61
1983	...	237.45	2.5545	7.6220	0.6601	1.2326	125.32	49.91	118.12	7.14	110.56	109.02
1984	...	237.59	2.8483	8.7439	0.7521	1.2952	138.34	57.02	125.85	9.44	117.79	115.53
1985	...	238.47	2.9443	8.9870	0.7792	1.3659	143.24	64.15	130.58	12.76	122.73	123.37
1986	...	168.50	2.1711	6.9258	0.6821	1.3898	112.27	59.89	107.26	16.00	107.19	127.47
1987	...	144.63	1.7976	6.0111	0.6117	1.3261	96.95	58.29	94.86	19.31	98.46	124.88
1988	...	128.14	1.7561	5.9565	0.5621	1.2309	92.75	59.00	88.17	23.37	91.85	114.20
1989	...	138.00	1.8792	6.3753	0.6111	1.1841	98.52	65.08	91.81	28.96	93.47	108.74
1990	...	144.82	1.6159	5.4449	0.5630	1.1670	89.05	70.22	87.82	39.47	91.74	111.69
1991	...	134.51	1.6585	5.6388	0.5667	1.1460	89.73	73.30	86.37	46.07	90.37	111.18
1992	...	126.75	1.5624	5.2956	0.5699	1.2088	86.64	76.10	84.89	52.60	88.45	107.51
1993	...	111.23	1.6537	5.6644	0.6662	1.2902	93.17	82.89	87.15	63.11	89.80	104.86
1994	...	102.19	1.6219	5.5467	0.6531	1.3659	91.32	90.40	85.63	80.61	89.65	105.06
1995	...	94.11	1.4331	4.9889	0.6337	1.3727	84.30	92.50	80.80	92.59	87.17	105.09
1996	...	108.81	1.5049	5.1158	0.6410	1.3637	87.34	97.40	84.60	98.26	89.19	101.98
1997	...	121.06	1.7339	5.8361	0.6106	1.3849	96.35	104.44	91.23	104.67	93.91	103.05
1998	...	130.99	1.7593	5.8979	0.6034	1.4836	98.82	116.48	95.75	126.03	101.81	116.53
1999	0.9387	113.73	1.8359	6.1575	0.6184	1.4858	...	116.87	94.02	129.94	101.13	115.20
2000	1.0832	107.80	2.1185	7.1053	0.6598	1.4855	...	119.44	101.57	129.80	104.99	115.38
2001	1.1171	121.57	2.1848	7.3275	0.6946	1.5487	...	125.91	107.66	135.86	111.02	120.02
2002	1.0578	125.22	2.0688	6.9384	0.6656	1.5704	...	126.75	105.98	140.55	111.18	122.66
2000												
January	0.9871	105.30	1.9305	6.4747	0.6096	1.4486	...	115.12	96.06	128.18	100.50	113.37
February	1.0169	109.39	1.9889	6.6706	0.6250	1.4512	...	116.56	98.26	128.08	101.79	112.91
March	1.0370	106.31	2.0282	6.8021	0.6330	1.4608	...	116.56	98.65	127.43	102.51	113.55
April	1.0583	105.63	2.0698	6.9419	0.6320	1.4689	...	117.22	99.34	127.93	103.12	114.07
May	1.0269	118.61	2.0084	6.7360	0.6595	1.5053	...	119.81	102.46	129.24	105.40	115.37
June	1.0521	106.13	2.0577	6.9013	0.6626	1.4770	...	118.59	99.86	130.50	104.63	116.92
July	1.0654	108.21	2.0837	6.9886	0.6633	1.4778	...	118.92	100.81	129.73	105.02	116.24
August	1.1056	108.08	2.1623	7.2521	0.6716	1.4828	...	119.71	102.36	129.14	105.52	115.29
September	1.1501	106.84	2.2494	7.5443	0.6976	1.4864	...	121.17	104.07	129.99	106.75	115.67
October	1.1730	108.44	2.2941	7.6942	0.6893	1.5125	...	122.89	105.68	131.62	108.25	116.82
November	1.1694	109.01	2.2871	7.6706	0.7014	1.5426	...	123.82	106.56	132.48	108.76	116.94
December	1.1132	112.21	2.1772	7.3021	0.6836	1.5219	...	122.85	104.63	133.23	107.68	117.38
2001												
January	1.0666	116.67	2.0860	6.9963	0.6768	1.5032	...	122.72	103.49	134.77	108.12	118.87
February	1.0863	116.23	2.1247	7.1259	0.6885	1.5216	...	123.41	104.80	134.31	108.92	118.64
March	1.1010	121.51	2.1533	7.2219	0.6923	1.5587	...	125.42	107.30	135.21	110.68	119.52
April	1.1204	123.77	2.1914	7.3495	0.6970	1.5578	...	126.39	108.45	135.71	111.47	120.11
May	1.1424	121.77	2.2344	7.4940	0.7010	1.5411	...	126.24	108.51	135.26	111.52	120.29
June	1.1724	122.35	2.2930	7.6904	0.7133	1.5245	...	127.08	109.53	135.67	112.47	120.89
July	1.1608	124.50	2.2703	7.6143	0.7068	1.5308	...	127.50	109.59	136.61	112.66	121.28
August	1.1094	121.37	2.1699	7.2774	0.6958	1.5399	...	125.41	107.15	135.42	110.68	119.99
September	1.0972	118.61	2.1459	7.1969	0.6831	1.5679	...	125.77	106.70	137.05	111.12	121.35
October	1.1050	121.45	2.1611	7.2481	0.6896	1.5717	...	126.61	107.64	137.60	111.37	120.88
November	1.1258	122.41	2.2019	7.3847	0.6966	1.5922	...	127.13	108.99	136.66	111.76	119.52
December	1.1221	127.59	2.1947	7.3606	0.6938	1.5788	...	127.20	109.50	136.02	111.43	118.90
2002												
January	1.1323	132.68	2.2146	7.4274	0.6982	1.5997	...	128.79	111.20	137.20	112.84	119.71
February	1.1211	128.20	2.1928	7.3542	0.6927	1.5802	...	129.54	111.97	137.79	113.38	119.65
March	1.1407	131.06	2.2311	7.4826	0.7027	1.5877	...	128.79	110.95	137.57	113.09	120.25
April	1.1287	130.77	2.2075	7.4036	0.6930	1.5815	...	128.42	110.14	137.93	113.00	121.00
May	1.0906	126.38	2.1330	7.1536	0.6850	1.5502	...	126.90	107.14	138.97	111.52	121.84
June	1.0459	123.29	2.0456	6.8605	0.6740	1.5318	...	125.51	104.32	140.11	110.26	122.80
July	1.0065	117.90	1.9686	6.6023	0.6425	1.5456	...	123.76	101.76	140.01	108.74	122.65
August	1.0224	118.99	1.9997	6.7067	0.6507	1.5694	...	125.20	103.21	141.18	110.13	123.82
September	1.0198	121.08	1.9945	6.6891	0.6425	1.5761	...	126.14	103.43	143.19	110.80	125.16
October	1.0192	123.91	1.9934	6.6856	0.6421	1.5780	...	127.06	103.90	144.73	111.42	126.10
November	0.9987	121.61	1.9533	6.5511	0.6365	1.5715	...	125.78	102.44	143.96	109.95	124.63
December	0.9810	121.89	1.9186	6.4347	0.6304	1.5592	...	125.13	101.47	144.00	109.07	124.30

. . . = Not available.

NOTES AND DEFINITIONS

TABLE 13-1
INTERNATIONAL COMPARISONS: GROWTH RATES IN REAL GROSS DOMESTIC PRODUCT

SOURCE: ECONOMIC REPORT OF THE PRESIDENT, ANNUAL REPORT OF THE COUNCIL OF ECONOMIC ADVISERS, FEBRUARY 2003

This table is reprinted from the 2003 *Annual Report* of the U.S. Council of Economic Advisers. It is based on data from the U.S. Department of Commerce, Bureau of Economic Analysis, and the International Monetary Fund. Because these data were compiled in late 2002, the data for recent years may differ somewhat from the latest available data, such as the U.S. GDP data shown in Chapter 1 of this volume.

TABLES 13-2 AND 13-3
INTERNATIONAL COMPARISONS: REAL GDP PER CAPITA, REAL GDP PER EMPLOYED PERSON

SOURCE: BUREAU OF LABOR STATISTICS

Real GDP per capita can be taken as a rough measure of potential economic welfare, that is, the potential standard of living available to a country's residents. Because income distributions are typically "skewed," it should not be taken as a representation of the standard of living actually enjoyed by a typical ("median") individual.

Real GDP per employee, on the other hand, is a rough measure of productivity (ignoring any differences in hours worked by employees).

The GDP, population, and employment measures for each country come from its own national accounts and population sources. Not all countries use annual chain-weighted methods such as those incorporated in U.S. GDP (see Notes and Definitions to Chapter 1). Some of the employment and population figures have been recalculated for greater comparability by BLS. GDP figures are converted from national currency values to U.S. dollar equivalents using Purchasing Power Parities (PPPs) published by the OECD in the OECD-Eurostat PPP Program.

PPPs are currency conversion rates that allow output in different currency units to be expressed in a common unit of value (U.S. dollars in this case). They are preferred to international market exchange rates for this purpose because, according to BLS, "At best, market exchange rates represent only the relative prices of goods and services that are traded internationally, not the relative value of total domestic output, which also consists of goods, and particularly services, that are not traded internationally, or which are isolated from the effects of foreign trade. Market exchange rates also are affected by...currency traders' views of the stability of governments in various countries, relative interest rates among

countries, and other incentives for holding financial assets in one currency rather than another."

Measuring PPPs is difficult and subject to error, and BLS points out that statistics using PPPs should be used with caution. "The per capita GDPs of most OECD countries fall within a relatively narrow range, and changes in rankings can occur as a result of relatively minor adjustments to PPP estimates."

References

U.S. Department of Labor, Bureau of Labor Statistics, Office of Productivity and Technology, "Comparative Real Gross Domestic Product Per Capita and Per Employed Person, Fourteen Countries, 1960–2002," July 29, 2003, available at <http://www.bls.gov/fls>.

TABLE 13-4
INTERNATIONAL COMPARISONS: INDUSTRIAL PRODUCTION INDEXES

SOURCE: THE CONFERENCE BOARD

These data have been collected by The Conference Board from national sources, such as the Federal Reserve Board which is the source for U.S. data (see Chapter 2), and placed on a common comparison base, 1990 = 100.

TABLE 13-5
INTERNATIONAL COMPARISONS: CONSUMER PRICE INDEXES

SOURCE: U.S. DEPARTMENT OF LABOR, BUREAU OF LABOR STATISTICS.

These data are prepared by the BLS Office of Productivity and Technology, based on national consumer price indexes as published by each country. The data have not been adjusted for comparability across countries. National differences exist with respect to population coverage, frequency of market basket weight changes, and treatment of homeowner costs. BLS links published indexes together to form historical series and rebases the foreign indexes to the U.S. base 1982–1984. The data for Germany are for West Germany only. For a description of the U.S. index, see the Notes and Definitions for Table 8-1.

TABLE 13-6
INTERNATIONAL COMPARISONS: UNEMPLOYMENT RATES AND CIVILIAN LABOR FORCES

SOURCE: U.S. BUREAU OF LABOR STATISTICS.

These data have been adjusted by BLS to approximate U.S. concepts and definitions. (See Notes and Definitions for Tables 10-1 through 10-3.) The German data are for West Germany only through 1990, and for unified Germany from 1991 to the present. Adding former East

Germany raised the 1991 unemployment rate from 4.3 percent, for West Germany alone, to 5.6 percent for unified Germany.

No adjustment is made to unemployment rates from Canada. Slight adjustments are made to those from Japan. Substantial adjustments were made to the Italian data prior to a 1992 definitional change. For France, Germany, and the United Kingdom before 1992, unemployment adjustment factors were based on annual household labor force surveys.

The concept of "layoff" differs from country to country. In the United States and Canada, persons who are laid off are classified as unemployed. The employees do not remain on the payroll, receive no payments from their firms, and are frequently not rehired. However, in Europe and Japan, these people are classified as employed. In general, employers reduce hours or days worked, rather than letting people go for weeks without work. The workers continue to receive pay, which is supplemented by a subsidy for time not worked. Because of these differences, the strict U.S. definition of unemployment is not applied on this point.

The adjusted statistics use the age at which compulsory schooling ends in each country instead of the U.S. standard of 16 years and older. This is 16 years in France and in the United Kingdom since 1973; 15 years in Canada, Japan, Germany, Italy since 1993, and the United Kingdom before 1973; and 14 years in Italy before 1993. Data pertain to the noninstitutional population except in Japan and Germany, where the institutionalized population of working age is included.

There are several breaks in the series due to changes in methods or definitions. Among the more important of these are ones for the United States (1994), France (1992), Germany (1983 and 1991), and Italy (1986, 1991, and 1993).

These data and more in-depth information on measurement procedures and standards are available from the Bureau of Labor Statistics Internet site at <http://www.bls.gov>.

TABLE 13-7
EXCHANGE RATES

SOURCE: BOARD OF GOVERNORS OF THE FEDERAL RESERVE SYSTEM.

Definitions and notes on the data

This table shows measures of the U.S. dollar relative to foreign currencies—both to the currencies of some important individual countries and to average values for major groups of countries. All measures are defined as the foreign currency price of the U.S. dollar, so that where the value is relatively high, the dollar is relatively "strong"—but less competitive—and the other currencies in question are relatively "weak" and more competitive.

For consistency, this is done in *Business Statistics* even in the case of currencies that are commonly quoted in the financial press, and elsewhere, in dollars per foreign currency unit instead of foreign currency units per dollar. Notably, this is the case for the new euro and for the British pound. Where *Business Statistics* shows the 2000 value of the dollar as 1.0832 euros, the more usual statement would be that during 2000 the euro on average was worth $0.9232 (one divided by 1.0832). Where *Business Statistics* shows the 2000 value of the dollar as 0.6598 British pounds, the more usual statement would be that the pound averaged $1.5156. The Canadian dollar is also sometimes quoted relative to the U.S. dollar, rather than as shown here.

Foreign exchange rates shown are averages of the daily noon buying rates in New York City for cable transfers payable in foreign currencies; annual figures are averages of monthly data.

The introduction in January 1999 of the euro as the common currency for 11 European countries—Austria, Belgium, Finland, France, Germany, Ireland, Italy, Luxembourg, Netherlands, Portugal, and Spain—marked a major change in the international currency system. (A 12th country, Greece, entered the European Monetary Union in January 2001.) The values of the currencies of these countries no longer fluctuate relative to each other, but the value of the euro still fluctuates relative to the dollar and to currencies for countries outside the European Monetary Union. The currency and coins of the individual countries continued to circulate from 1999 through the end of 2001; in January 2002, new euro currency and coins were introduced, replacing the currency and coins of the individual countries. Once a country has entered the monetary union, its value relative to the dollar continues to fluctuate—but due only to fluctuations in the value of the euro relative to the dollar.

To provide continuous series after 1998 for Germany and France, *Business Statistics* converts the euro to its equivalent in the former currencies for those countries, using the following fixed values for 1 euro: 1.95583 German marks and 6.55957 French francs.

There is no fully satisfactory historical equivalent to the euro. For comparisons over time, the Federal Reserve Board uses a "restated German mark," derived simply by dividing each historical value of the mark by the euro conversion factor, 1.95583. The same trends can be derived using the values for the mark shown in this table.

Trade-weighted indexes of the value of the dollar against groups of foreign currencies also appear in this table. In each case, weighted averages of the individual currency values of the dollar are set at 100 in a base period. The weights are based on goods trade only, excluding trade in services. Base periods differ for different indexes.

The first four columns show the more familiar type of foreign exchange indexes, which use nominal values of each currency. The last two columns are price-adjusted (they are indexes of "real" exchange rates), aggregating values of the dollar in terms of each currency that have been adjusted for inflation, using each country's consumer price index. Where any currency has had an episode of hyperinflation with the consequent huge depreciation in terms of the dollar, the nominal index will not reflect the actual competitiveness of the dollar in terms of that currency over the longer term. Because there have been hyperinflations in some of the countries making up the Broad Index and its Other Important Trading Partners component (see below), price-adjusted indexes are also shown for those two groupings in the final two columns.

G-10 Index (March 1973 = 100: This measure is an index of the exchange value of the U.S. dollar in terms of the weighted average currencies of the G-10 (other industrialized) countries, which are Belgium, Canada, France, Germany, Italy, Japan, the Netherlands, Sweden, Switzerland, and the United Kingdom. Unlike the three indexes that follow, the weights in this index, which represented "multilateral" (world market) trade shares, were fixed. The Federal Reserve ceased to calculate this index as of December 1998.

The three newer indexes use weights that focus more directly on U.S. competitiveness and that change as trade flows shift. Each country's weight is based on an average of the country's share of U.S. imports, the country's share of U.S. exports, and the country's share of exports that go to other countries that are large importers of U.S. goods.

The Broad Index (January 1997 = 100): The new overall index includes currencies of all countries that have a share of U.S. nonoil goods imports or nonagricultural goods exports of at least 0.5 percent. The list of currencies and the weights are updated each year. These countries are then classified as either Major Currencies or Other Important Trading Partners as outlined below.

Major Currency Index (March 1973 = 100): This index serves purposes similar to those of the discontinued G-10 index, and its level and movements are similar. It is a measure of the competitiveness of U.S. goods in the major industrial countries and a gauge of financial pressure on the dollar. The index includes countries whose currencies are traded in deep and relatively liquid financial markets and circulate widely outside the country of issue, and for which information on short and long-term interest rates is readily available. As of November 1999, this index includes the currencies of the following countries: Canada, the euro countries, Japan, United Kingdom, Switzerland, Australia, and Sweden.

Other Important Trading Partners (OITP) Index (January 1997 = 100): This index captures the competitiveness of U.S. goods in key emerging markets in Latin America, Asia, the Middle East, and Eastern Europe, whose currencies do not circulate widely outside the country of issue. Hyperinflations and large depreciations for some of these countries have led to a persistent upward trend in the nominal version of this index. Hence, the nominal OITP index is mainly useful for analysis of short-term developments, and the price-adjusted index is shown to give a more appropriate measure of longer-term competitiveness. The countries that make up this index include, as of November 1999, Mexico, China, Taiwan, South Korea, Singapore, Hong Kong, Malaysia, Brazil, Thailand, Indonesia, Philippines, Russia, India, Saudi Arabia, Israel, Argentina, Venezuela, Chile, and Colombia.

References and data availability

More information on the dollar value indexes can be found in the article "New Summary Measures of the Foreign Exchange Value of the Dollar," *Federal Reserve Bulletin*, vol. 84 (October 1998). This is available on the Federal Reserve Web site at <www.federalreserve.gov>, as are the exchange rate indexes and the H.10 and G.5 releases containing daily, weekly, and monthly data for bilateral exchange rates.

Additional information can be found on the Federal Reserve Bank of St. Louis Web site at <http://www.stls.frb.org/fred/data/exchange.html>.

PART B

INDUSTRY PROFILES

CHAPTER 14: INDUSTRY DEFINITION AND STRUCTURE

THE STRUCTURE OF U.S. INDUSTRY: AN INTRODUCTION TO THE NORTH AMERICAN INDUSTRY CLASSIFICATION SYSTEM (NAICS)

In 2003, the Labor Department's Current Employment Statistics Survey was converted to the new North American Industry Classification System (NAICS), and will be published on that basis from now on. There are now 141 different NAICS-defined industries and industry groups (sectors) for which seasonally adjusted employment data are published monthly by the Bureau of Labor Statistics (BLS), with historical information going back to 1990. For 37 less detailed groups, data on hours and earnings of production and nonsupervisory workers are also available monthly, seasonally adjusted, and back to 1990.

The conversion of the U.S. statistical system to NAICS is not yet complete, as the new system has not yet been incorporated into the Producer Price Indexes, Employment Cost Index, some of the National Income and Product Account (NIPA) series, or the BLS 10-year projections of employment. Nevertheless, the editor of *Business Statistics* judged that the data available warranted extensive coverage in the pages of this volume. Here, the emphasis has been placed on annual rather than monthly data, in order to focus on trend and medium-term changes.

Industry data collection is important because demand for goods and services is channeled into demand for labor through the industries in which the goods and services are produced. NAICS delineates industries that are better defined in relation to today's demands, and groups together industries that are more closely related to each other by technology. Notable examples of these new features of NAICS are the more detailed data available on service industries; the more rational grouping of the computer and electronic product manufacturing subsector; and the new "Information" sector. Because of these improved classifications, anyone interested in how employment, wages, and hours of work have reflected the technological and demand changes shaping the American economy over the period since 1990 will find new and pertinent material in the BLS data series in this part of *Business Statistics*.

As a guide to the contents of the new NAICS categories, the editor has prepared a table of "NAICS Industry Definitions," showing the NAICS 2-digit industry sectors and their component 3-digit subsectors. The table follows this introduction and precedes the chapters of statistical

tables. Where the short NAICS sector titles are not sufficiently self-explanatory, parenthetical listings are shown of the component activities.

For the user who needs information on the ways that the new classifications do–and do not–relate to the old Standard Industrial Classification System (SIC), a column has been added showing a rough match between the 2002 NAICS and the 1987 SIC. It must be emphasized that this match is approximate, not exact, and does not reflect every aspect of the change in classification systems. But even without providing exact equivalents, this column indicates just how thoroughly the SIC industries have been mixed and matched to comprise the new industries, and therefore explains why it has been so difficult for the statistical agencies to produce longer spans of historical data on the new basis.

As a further illustration, in this table the reader will note frequent references to parts of SIC industries that have been parceled out among different NAICS industries. In some cases the editor has included in parentheses the part of the old SIC industry that has been included in the new NAICS industry. For an example, see the entry for the new NAICS subsector 711, "Performing arts and spectator sports," demonstrating that this subsector includes dinner theaters, which used to be included in "Eating places" (which in turn were a subdivision of retail trade).

(For an idea of the orders of magnitude of noncomparability among roughly-matched industries, the reader may refer to Table 17-4, Manufacturers' Shipments. In this table–and in the three tables that follow, derived from the same survey–the editor has shown values for 1992 on both classification bases for roughly-matching industries such as Nonmetallic mineral products, Primary metals, Fabricated metal products, and Transportation equipment. Despite the basic similarities in general definition between these industries in the old and new systems, the tabulated values can be quite different, and it is evident that roughly-matched industries cannot be viewed as continuous series.)

NAICS industries are groupings of producing units—not of products as such—and are grouped according to similarity of production processes. This is done in order to collect consistent data on inputs and outputs, and thus measure important concepts such as productivity and input-output parameters. This emphasis on production process helps to explain a number of the ways in which NAICS differs from SIC.

Manufacturing activities at retail locations, such as bakeries, have been classified separately from the retail activity and put in the food manufacturing industry.

- Central administrative offices of companies have a new sector of their own; for example, the headquarters office of a food-producing corporation is no longer considered part of the food manufacturing industry but is part of sector 55, Management of companies and enterprises.

- Reproduction of packaged software, classified as a "business service" in the SIC, is now classified as a manufacturing process, in sector 334, Computer and electronic product manufacturing.

- "Electronic markets and agents and brokers," once undifferentiated components of wholesale trade industries, now have their own sector, 425.

- Retail trade in NAICS (sectors 44 and 45) now includes establishments such as office supply stores, computer and software stores, building materials dealers, plumbing supply stores, and electrical supply stores, that display merchandise and use mass-media advertising to sell to individuals as well as to businesses, and were formerly classified in wholesale trade.

References

The reader needing more precise information on NAICS definitions and differences from the SIC should refer to Executive Office of the President, Office of Management and Budget, *North American Industry Classification System: United States, 1997*, which contains matches between the 1997 NAICS and the 1987 SIC, and *North American Industry Classification System: United States, 2002*, which contains matches showing the relatively few changes from the 1997 NAICS to the 2002 NAICS. Both volumes are available from Bernan. These volumes describe fully the development and application of the new classification system, and are the sources for the material presented here. Information is also available on the NAICS Web site, <http://www.census.gov/naics>. Additional background information can also be found in Bernan, *Business Statistics of the United States: 2002*, pp. xxiv–xxviii.

Table 14-1. NAICS Industry Definitions: With Rough Derivation from SIC and Monthly Data Availability

NAICS Code	NAICS 2-digit industry sector and 3-digit industry subsector	Roughly corresponding major component SIC industry group or industry
11	AGRICULTURE, FORESTRY, FISHING AND HUNTING	Division A, Agriculture, forestry, and fishing; 241, Logging
111	Crop production	
112	Animal production	
113	Forestry and logging	
114	Fishing, hunting and trapping	
115	Agriculture and forestry support activities	
21	MINING	Division B, Mining
211	Oil and gas extraction	
212	Mining, except oil and gas (includes coal mining, mining for ores, and mining and quarrying of nonmetallic minerals)	
213	Support activities for mining (includes oil and gas well drilling and other support activities)	
22	UTILITIES	49, Electric, gas, and sanitary services (with some exclusions)
221	Utilities (includes electric power generation, transmission and distribution; natural gas distribution; water, sewage, irrigation, steam, and air-conditioning systems)	
23	CONSTRUCTION	Division C, Construction
236	Construction of buildings	
237	Heavy and civil engineering construction	
238	Specialty trade contractors	
31-33	MANUFACTURING	Division D, Manufacturing (excluding 241, Logging; 271, 272, 273, and 274, Publishing; and with other exclusions and inclusions)
311	Food manufacturing	20, Food and kindred products, excluding 208, Beverages
312	Beverage and tobacco product manufacturing	208, Beverages; 21, Tobacco products
313	Textile mills	221-4, 226, 228, Yarns, fabrics, and finishing

Table 14-1. NAICS Industry Definitions: With Rough Derivation from SIC and Monthly Data Availability—*Continued*

NAICS Code	NAICS 2-digit industry sector and 3-digit industry subsector	Roughly corresponding major component SIC industry group or industry
314	Textile product mills (including household and miscellaneous products)	227, Carpets and rugs; 229, Miscellaneous textile products
315	Apparel manufacturing	23, Apparel; 225, Knitting mills
316	Leather and allied product manufacturing	31, Leather and leather products
321	Wood product manufacturing	24, Lumber and wood products, excluding 241, Logging
322	Paper manufacturing	26, Paper and allied products
323	Printing and related support activities, including quick and instant	275-9, Commercial printing and miscellaneous printing and trade services
324	Petroleum and coal products manufacturing (includes refineries, asphalt, oil and grease, and coke manufacturing)	29, Petroleum and coal products
325	Chemical manufacturing (includes basic organic and inorganic chemicals; plastics materials; synthetic fibers and rubber; agricultural chemicals; pharmaceuticals and medicine; paint, adhesives, cleaning and toilet preparations, ink, explosives, and misc.)	28, Chemicals and allied products
326	Plastics and rubber products	30, Rubber and misc. plastics products
327	Nonmetallic mineral product manufacturing (includes pottery, plumbing fixtures, bricks and structural clay products, glass and products, cement and concrete, lime, gypsum, and stone products)	32, Stone, clay and glass products
331	Primary metal manufacturing (primary and secondary ferrous and nonferrous metals, rolling, drawing, and extruding, and foundries)	33, Primary metal industries
332	Fabricated metal product manufacturing (includes forging and stamping, cutlery, hardware, structural metal work, boilers, containers, machine shops, valves, fixtures, bearings, metal testing, small arms, ordnance, ammunition)	34, Fabricated metal products
333	Machinery manufacturing (includes machinery for agriculture, construction, mining, manufacturing, commercial, and service industries, metalworking machinery, turbine and power transmission, pumps and compressors, elevators and material handling, cranes and misc. general purpose machinery)	Parts of 35, Industrial machinery and equipment; 36, Electronic and other electric equipment; and 38, Instruments and related products
334	Computer and electronic product manufacturing (includes electronic computers and equipment, communications equipment, audio and video equipment, semiconductors and other electronic components, electromedical equipment, navigation, measuring, and controlling instruments, reproducing software and media)	Parts of 357, Computer and office equipment; 36, Electronic and other electric equipment; 38, Instruments and related products; 73, Business services; and 78, Motion picture services
335	Electrical equipment and appliance manufacturing (includes electrical lighting, household appliances, electrical equipment, batteries, wire and cable manufacturing)	Parts of 36, Electronic and other electric equipment and 335, Nonferrous wire drawing
336	Transportation equipment manufacturing (includes motor vehicles and parts, truck trailers, aerospace products and parts, railroad rolling stock, ship and boat building and repairing, motorcycles, bicycles, military armored vehicles, and parts)	37, Transportation equipment
337	Furniture and related product manufacturing	25, Furniture and fixtures; parts of other industries
339	Miscellaneous manufacturing (includes medical equipment and supplies, jewelry, silverware, sporting goods, toys, games, office supplies, art supplies, burial caskets, and other goods)	Parts of 38, Instruments; 39, Miscellaneous; 25, Furniture; and other industries

Table 14-1. NAICS Industry Definitions: With Rough Derivation from SIC and Monthly Data Availability—*Continued*

NAICS Code	NAICS 2-digit industry sector and 3-digit industry subsector	Roughly corresponding major component SIC industry group or industry
42	WHOLESALE TRADE	
423	Merchant wholesalers, durable goods	Parts of 50, Wholesale trade-durable goods, and other industries
424	Merchant wholesalers, nondurable goods	Parts of 51, Wholesale trade-nondurable goods, and other industries
425	Electronic markets and agents and brokers	Parts of 50 and 51, Wholesale trade
44-45	RETAIL TRADE	
441	Motor vehicle and parts dealers	Parts of 55, Automotive dealers and service stations, Wholesale trade, and other industries
442	Furniture and home furnishings stores	Parts of 57, Furniture and homefurnishing stores, Wholesale trade, and other industries
443	Electronics and appliance stores	5722, Household appliance stores; 5734, Computer and software stores; 5946, Camera and photo supply stores; and parts of wholesale trade and other industries
444	Building material and garden supply stores	52, Retail building materials and garden supplies, and parts of Wholesale trade
445	Food and beverage stores	54, Food stores, and 5921, Liquor stores
446	Health and personal care stores	5912, Drug stores and proprietary stores, and parts of Wholesale trade, Food stores and Miscellaneous stores
447	Gasoline stations (including stations with convenience stores)	Parts of 55, Automotive dealers and service stations, and 54, Food stores
448	Clothing and clothing accessories stores	56, Apparel and accessory stores; 5944, Jewelry stores; and 5948, Luggage and leather goods stores
451	Sporting goods, hobby, book and music stores	Parts of 59, Miscellaneous retail; 57, Furniture and homefurnishing stores; and other industries
452	General merchandise stores (includes department stores, warehouse clubs, superstores, and other general merchandise)	53, General merchandise, and parts of other retail
453	Miscellaneous store retailers (includes florists, office supply & stationery, gift, used merchandise, pet, manufactured and mobile home, tobacco, and misc. other store retailers)	Parts of 59, Misc. retail, and other industries
454	Nonstore retailers (includes electronic shopping and auctions, mail order, vending machines, and fuel and other direct selling)	Parts of 59, Misc. retail, and 517, Wholesale petroleum
48-49	TRANSPORTATION AND WAREHOUSING	
481	Air transportation	Parts of 45, Transportation by air
482	Rail transportation	Parts of 40, Railroad transportation
483	Water transportation	Parts of 44, Water transportation
484	Truck transportation	Parts of 42, Trucking and warehousing
485	Transit and ground passenger transportation	Parts of 41, Local and suburban transportation

Table 14-1. NAICS Industry Definitions: With Rough Derivation from SIC and Monthly Data Availability—*Continued*

NAICS Code	NAICS 2-digit industry sector and 3-digit industry subsector	Roughly corresponding major component SIC industry group or industry
486	Pipeline transportation	46, Pipelines except natural gas, and parts of 492, Gas production and distribution
487	Scenic and sightseeing transportation	Parts of 41, Local and suburban, 44, Water, 45, Air, 47, Transportation services, and 7999, Amusement and recreation n.e.c.
488	Support activities for transportation	Parts of 11 industries in transportation, communications, manufacturing, and services
491	Postal service	4311, U.S. Postal Service, and part of 7389, Business services n.e.c.
492	Couriers and messengers	4513, Air couriers, and 4215, Courier services except air
493	Warehousing and storage	Parts of 422, Public warehousing and storage
51	INFORMATION	
511	Publishing industries, except Internet	
5111	Newspaper, book, and directory publishers	Parts of 271, Newspapers, 272, Periodicals, 273, Books, 274, Misc. publishing, 277, Greeting cards, and 733, Mailing, reproduction, and stenographic services
5112	Software publishers	Part of 7372, Prepackaged software
512	Motion picture and sound recording industries (includes music books and sheet music)	781, Motion picture production and services; 783, Motion picture theaters; and parts of 782, Motion picture distribution and services, and other manufacturing and service industries
515	Broadcasting, except Internet	483, Radio and television broadcasting; part of 484, Cable and other pay TV services
516	Internet publishing and broadcasting	Parts of publishing and service industries
517	Telecommunications	Parts of 481, Telephone communications, 482, Telegraph and other communications, and 484, Cable and other pay TV services
518	ISPs, search portals, and data processing	7374, Data processing and preparation; 7375, Information retrieval services; and parts of other service industries
519	Other information services (includes news syndicates, libraries, archives, and other information services)	8231, Libraries, and parts of other service industries
52	FINANCE AND INSURANCE	
521	Monetary authorities-central bank	6011, Federal Reserve Banks
522	Credit intermediation and related activities (includes commercial banking, savings institutions, credit unions, credit card issuing, sales financing, consumer lending, real estate credit, trade financing, loan brokers, and processing and clearing)	Parts of 60, Depository institutions, and 61, Nondepository institutions
523	Securities, commodity contracts, investments	62, Security and commodity brokers, and parts of 60, Depository institutions, 61, Nondepository institutions, 63, Insurance carriers, and 67, Holding and other investment offices
524	Insurance carriers and related activities	64, Insurance agents, brokers, and service, and parts of 63, Insurance carriers
525	Funds, trusts, and other financial vehicles	672, Investment offices; 6798, Real estate investment trusts; parts of 63, Insurance carriers, and 673, Trusts

n.e.c. = Not elsewhere classified.

Table 14-1. NAICS Industry Definitions: With Rough Derivation from SIC and Monthly Data Availability—*Continued*

NAICS Code	NAICS 2-digit industry sector and 3-digit industry subsector	Roughly corresponding major component SIC industry group or industry
53	REAL ESTATE AND RENTAL AND LEASING	
531	Real estate	Parts of 65, Real estate, and 4225, General warehousing and storage (mini-warehouses and self-storage units)
532	Rental and leasing services	7352, Medical equipment rental; 7377, Computer rental and leasing; 751, Automotive rentals, no drivers; 7841, Video tape rental; and parts of 4499, Water transportation n.e.c., 4741, Rental of railroad cars, 7299, Misc. personal services n.e.c., 735, Misc. equipment rental, 7922, Theatrical producers and services, and 7999, Amusement and recreation n.e.c.
533	Lessors of nonfinancial intangible assets (except copyrighted)	6794, Patent owners and lessors, and part of 6792, Oil royalty traders
54	PROFESSIONAL AND TECHNICAL SERVICES (includes legal, accounting, bookkeeping, architectural, engineering, design, computer design and programming, management and other consulting, scientific research and development, advertising and public relations, market research, polling, and other services)	0741, Veterinary services; 6541, Title abstract offices; 731, Advertising; 7221, Photographic studios, portrait; 7921, Tax return preparation; 7336, Commercial art and graphic design; 7361, Employment agencies, 7371, Computer programming; 7373, Computer systems design; 7376, Computer facilities management; 8111, Legal services; 871, Engineering and architectural services; 873, Research and testing; and parts of mining, 37 (aircraft and guided missiles), 73, Business services, 87, Engineering and management services, and other industries
55	MANAGEMENT OF COMPANIES AND ENTERPRISES	671, Holding companies, and establishments classified as auxiliaries in producing industries
56	ADMINISTRATIVE AND WASTE SERVICES	
561	Administrative and support services (Includes office administrative, employment placement, temporary help, telephone call centers, collection agencies, credit bureaus, court reporting, travel arrangement, investigation and security, services to buildings, and other support services)	0782, Lawn and garden services, 0783 Ornamental shrub and tree services, 4724, Travel agencies, 4725, Tour operators, 7217, Carpet and upholstery cleaning, 732, credit reporting and collection, 7338, Secretarial and court reporting, 734, Services to buildings, 7363, Help supply services, 7381,Detective and armored car services, 7382, Security systems, 8744 Facilities support, and parts of 458, Airfields, 472, Passenger transportation arrangement, 495, Sanitary services, 729, Misc. personal services, 73, Business services, 769, Misc. repair shops, 7819, Services allied to motion pictures, 79, Amusement and recreation services, 86, Membership organizations, and 8741, Management services
562	Waste management and remediation services	4953, Refuse systems, and parts of 1799, Special trade contractors, 4212, Local trucking, 4959, Sanitary services, 735, Misc. equipment rental and leasing (portable toilet rental) and 769, Misc. repair shops
61	EDUCATIONAL SERVICES	82, Educational services, except 823, Libraries; and parts of 7231, Beauty shops, 7241, Barber shops, 7911, Dance studios, 7999, Amusement and recreation n.e.c. and 8748, Business consulting n.e.c. (educational testing services)
62	HEALTH CARE AND SOCIAL ASSISTANCE	
621	Ambulatory health care services	Offices and clinics for 801, Doctors, 802, Dentists, 803, Osteopaths, and 804, Other health practicioners; 8071, Medical laboratories; 8082, Home health care services; 4119, Ambulances; 4522, Air ambulances; and parts of 809, Health and allied services n.e.c.
622	Hospitals	806, Hospitals
623	Nursing and residential care facilities	805, Nursing and personal care facilities, and 836, Residential care
624	Social assistance	8322, Individual and family services, except parole and probation offices; 8331, Job training, and 8351, Child day care services

n.e.c. = Not elsewhere classified.

Table 14-1. NAICS Industry Definitions: With Rough Derivation from SIC and Monthly Data Availability—*Continued*

NAICS Code	NAICS 2-digit industry sector and 3-digit industry subsector	Roughly corresponding major component SIC industry group or industry
71	ARTS, ENTERTAINMENT, AND RECREATION	
711	Performing arts and spectator sports	7929, Bands and other entertainment groups; 7941, Professional sports clubs and promoters; 7948, Racing; parts of 5812, Eating places (dinner theaters) and 6512, Building operators (stadium and arena owners); and agents, artists, writers, performers, correspondents, taxidermists, and antique restorers, previously classified as part of 738, Misc. business services; 76, Misc. repair services; 7819, Motion picture services; 7999, Amusement and recreation n.e.c.; and 8999, Membership organizations, n.e.c.
712	Museums, historical sites, zoos, and parks	84, Museums, botanical, and zoological gardens, and part of 7999, Amusement and recreation n.e.c. (caverns and misc. commercial parks)
713	Amusements, gambling, and recreation	4493, Marinas; 793, Bowling centers; 7991, Physical fitness facilities; 7992, Public golf courses, 7995, Coin operated amusements; 7996, Amusement parks; 7997, Membership sports and recreation clubs; and parts of 7911, Dance studios, and 7999, Amusement and recreation n.e.c.
72	ACCOMMODATION AND FOOD SERVICES	
721	Accommodation (includes hotels, motels, bed-and-breakfast inns, RV parks, camps, and rooming and boarding houses)	70, Hotels and other lodging places
722	Food services and drinking places	5812, Eating places (other than dinner theaters), 5813, Drinking places, and parts of 4789, Transportation services n.e.c. (contract dining car operations), 5641, Retail bakeries, and 5963 Direct selling (mobile food wagons)
81	OTHER SERVICES, EXCEPT PUBLIC ADMINISTRATION	
811	Repair and maintenance	753, Automotive repair shops (other than tire retreading); 7542, carwashes; 7631, Watch, clock and jewelery repair; 7692, Welding repair; and parts of 3732 (boat repair), 7219 (clothing alteration and repair), 7251(shoe repair), 7378 (computer repair), 7549 (auto window tinting), 7622 (radio and tv repair), 7623 (refrigeration repair), 7629, Electrical repair n.e.c., 7641, Reupholstery and furniture repair, 7694, Armature, rewinding, and 7699, Repair services n.e.c.
812	Personal and laundry services	6553, Cemetery subdividers and developers; 7211, power laundries; 7212, Garment pressing and cleaners' agents; 7213, Linen supply; 7215, Coin operated laundries and cleaning; 7216, Drycleaning except rugs; 7218, Industrial launderers; 7261, Funeral service and crematories; 7384, photofinishing laboratories; 7521, Auto parking; and parts of 0752 (pet care), 6531, Real estate agents and managers (cemetery management), 7219 (diaper and misc. services), 7231 (beauty shops), 7241 (barber shops), 7251 (shoe shine parlors), and 7389 (apparel pressing for the trade, bail bonding)
813	Membership associations and organizations	6732, Educational, religious and charitable trusts; 8399, Social services n.e.c. (voluntary health organizations, human rights organizations, environment, conservation, and wildlife, and other grant making, giving, and social advocacy organizations); 8611, Business associations; 8621, Professional organizations; 8631, Labor organizations; 8651, Political organizations; 8661, Religious organizations; and parts of 6531, Real estate agents and managers (condominium associations), 8641, Civic and social organizations (all except tribal governments), and 8699, Membership organizations n.e.c. (all except motor travel clubs)
814	Private households	8811, Private households

n.e.c. = Not elsewhere classified.

Table 14-1. NAICS Industry Definitions: With Rough Derivation from SIC and Monthly Data Availability—*Continued*

NAICS Code	NAICS 2-digit industry sector and 3-digit industry subsector	Roughly corresponding major component SIC industry group or industry
92	PUBLIC ADMINISTRATION	
921	Executive, legislative, and general government	91, Executive, legislative, and general; 9311, Finance, taxation, and monetary policy; and part of 8641, Civic and social associations (tribal governments)
922	Justice, public order, and safety activities	92, Justice, public order, and safety, and part of 8322, Individual and family services (parole and probation)
923	Administration of human resource programs	94, Administration of human resources
924	Administration of environmental programs	951, Environmental quality
925	Community and housing program administration	953, Housing and urban development
926	Administration of economic programs	9611, Administration of general economic programs; 9631, Regulation and administration of utilities; 9641, Regulation of agricultural marketing; 9651, Misc. commercial regulation; and parts of 9621, Regulation and administration of transportation (all except air traffic control)
927	Space research and technology	9661, Space research and technology
928	National security and international affairs	97, National security and international affairs

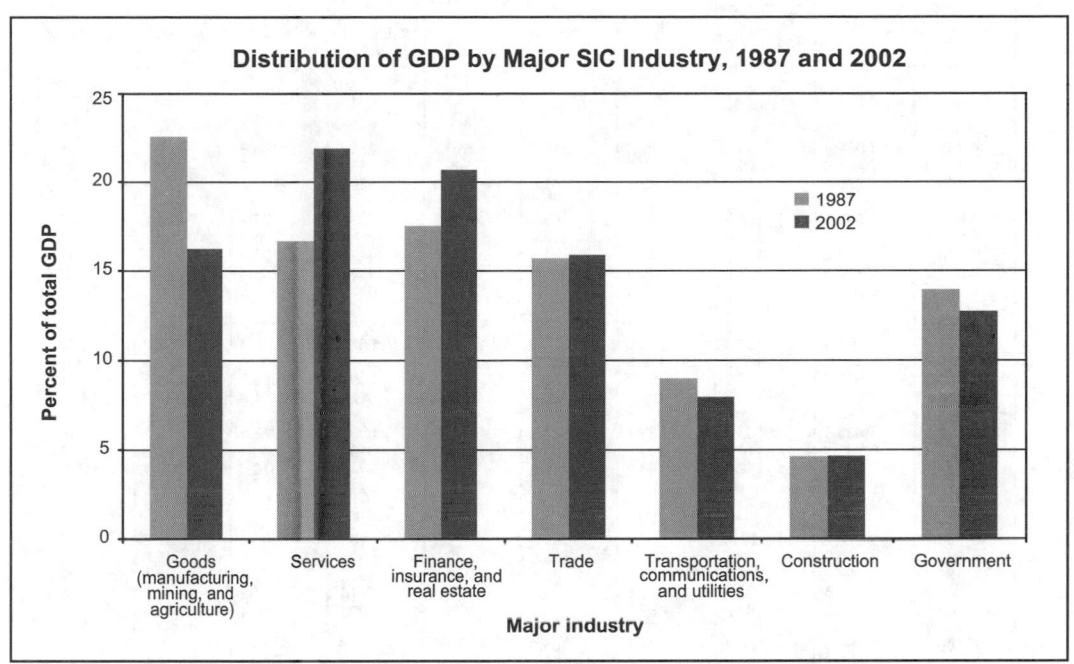

Distribution of GDP by Major SIC Industry, 1987 and 2002

- Of seven major industry groups based on the old Standard Industrial Classification (SIC), goods production broadly defined—manufacturing, mining, and agriculture—contributed 23 percent of the value of total gross domestic product in 1987, but only 16 percent in 2002.

- Services (health, business, and miscellaneous), on the other hand, rose from 17 percent to 22 percent.

- Finance, insurance, and real estate also contributed an increasing share, rising from 18 percent to 21 percent. Government and transportation, communications, and utilities had declining shares while the shares of trade and construction were about unchanged.

- Of 13 more detailed SIC industry groups, the greatest increases in real output (the quantity index) from 1987 to 2002 occurred in the communications and wholesale trade sectors (150 percent and 122 percent respectively) and the smallest rises in nondurable goods manufacturing and mining (6 percent and 10 percent respectively).

Table 15-1. Gross Domestic Product by Industry

(Billions of dollars; index numbers, 1996 = 100.)

Year and series definition	Gross domestic product	Private industries										
		Total	Agriculture, forestry, and fishing	Mining	Construc-tion	Manufacturing		Transpor-tation	Communi-cations	Electric, gas, and sanitary services	Wholesale trade	Retail trade
						Durable goods	Nondurable goods					
VALUE												
1987	4 742.5	4 081.4	88.9	92.2	219.3	516.8	371.8	158.8	125.5	141.9	308.9	434.5
1988	5 108.3	4 401.8	89.1	99.2	237.2	566.3	413.6	169.2	132.8	147.0	346.6	461.5
1989	5 489.1	4 735.5	102.0	97.1	245.8	582.7	434.9	172.2	137.4	159.0	364.7	492.7
1990	5 803.2	4 996.7	108.3	111.9	248.7	586.6	454.0	177.4	148.1	165.4	376.1	507.8
1991	5 986.2	5 129.1	102.9	96.7	232.7	575.5	468.0	186.1	155.7	176.5	395.6	523.7
1992	6 318.9	5 424.5	111.7	87.6	234.4	594.0	488.0	193.4	163.9	181.2	414.6	551.7
1993	6 642.3	5 717.5	108.3	88.4	248.9	632.8	498.6	206.0	178.6	188.7	432.5	578.0
1994	7 054.3	6 096.5	118.5	90.2	275.3	694.1	529.1	223.2	190.7	197.4	479.2	620.6
1995	7 400.5	6 411.1	109.8	95.7	290.3	729.8	559.2	233.4	202.3	206.9	500.6	646.8
1996	7 813.2	6 792.8	130.4	113.0	316.4	748.4	567.6	243.4	214.7	208.3	529.6	687.1
1997	8 318.4	7 253.6	130.0	118.9	338.2	791.2	588.4	261.8	220.8	205.9	566.8	740.5
1998	8 781.5	7 678.2	128.0	100.2	380.8	830.7	600.8	288.7	238.5	204.8	607.9	790.4
1999	9 274.3	8 123.0	127.7	104.1	425.4	853.8	627.5	301.9	257.2	211.0	645.3	831.7
2000	9 824.6	8 606.9	134.3	133.1	461.3	886.4	633.9	313.7	279.1	216.5	696.8	887.3
2001	10 082.2	8 800.8	140.7	139.0	480.0	812.8	610.2	306.1	291.5	221.9	680.7	931.8
2002	10 446.2	9 101.1	142.1	123.2	490.3	814.4	634.0	310.4	302.4	226.6	707.7	970.8
QUANTITY INDEX												
1987	78.2	76.7	84.6	87.2	88.0	72.3	90.2	66.7	61.8	79.6	66.8	74.5
1988	81.5	80.2	77.6	101.3	93.0	79.1	93.6	68.8	65.6	82.2	71.6	79.3
1989	84.4	83.2	85.4	91.0	93.6	78.8	92.5	70.9	68.1	87.7	75.4	81.9
1990	85.9	84.5	90.9	93.6	91.9	78.2	91.7	74.2	72.3	91.2	74.6	81.4
1991	85.5	84.0	93.0	89.5	84.9	74.7	90.0	76.4	75.5	94.1	78.7	80.7
1992	88.1	86.6	100.2	84.7	85.9	76.0	91.6	79.5	78.9	92.8	84.0	82.9
1993	90.4	89.0	94.0	89.4	88.2	80.2	92.6	82.7	84.8	92.8	85.4	84.7
1994	94.0	93.0	104.1	95.6	93.9	87.7	97.1	89.8	88.9	94.5	90.9	89.8
1995	96.6	95.8	94.4	99.9	94.7	95.5	100.5	92.5	94.3	99.5	91.2	93.4
1996	100.0	100.0	100.0	100.0	100.0	100.0	100.0	100.0	100.0	100.0	100.0	100.0
1997	104.4	105.3	110.1	103.5	102.6	108.6	101.3	102.3	101.4	97.0	110.3	108.5
1998	108.9	110.3	111.5	105.9	110.3	119.3	97.9	106.0	107.7	93.0	125.3	116.4
1999	113.4	115.6	118.5	101.5	116.2	126.8	100.6	110.4	118.9	100.3	133.8	123.2
2000	117.6	120.1	127.8	90.1	119.5	139.5	98.3	116.1	133.6	102.7	141.7	132.3
2001	117.9	120.6	125.6	94.4	117.5	132.3	91.3	111.1	150.0	93.3	141.4	138.5
2002	120.8	123.5	125.8	95.8	117.7	132.2	95.2	114.8	154.8	98.5	148.4	146.6

Table 15-1. Gross Domestic Product by Industry—*Continued*

(Billions of dollars; index numbers, 1996 = 100.)

Year and series definition	Private industries—*Continued*								Statistical discrepancy	Government		
	Finance, insurance and real estate [1]				Services [1]					Total	Federal	State and local
	Total	Depository institutions	Real estate		Total	Business services	Health services	Other services				
			Nonfarm housing services	Other real estate								
VALUE												
1987	829.7	143.9	391.9	139.5	789.9	145.0	230.6	103.3	3.3	661.0	258.9	402.1
1988	893.7	147.6	424.3	162.0	887.9	166.9	253.6	119.8	-42.2	706.5	273.3	433.2
1989	954.5	157.2	456.7	174.0	976.0	183.7	280.7	135.8	16.3	753.6	287.1	466.5
1990	1 010.3	171.3	488.3	177.3	1 071.5	203.9	314.4	149.2	30.6	806.6	300.2	506.4
1991	1 072.2	193.9	515.5	173.6	1 123.8	205.3	345.3	150.0	19.6	857.1	322.4	534.7
1992	1 140.9	205.3	543.4	181.8	1 219.4	229.4	377.8	161.1	43.7	894.4	333.9	560.5
1993	1 205.3	200.9	558.1	193.5	1 287.7	247.6	394.5	170.6	63.8	924.8	336.2	588.6
1994	1 254.8	200.7	593.9	197.5	1 365.0	273.2	413.9	178.6	58.5	957.6	339.6	618.0
1995	1 347.2	227.4	628.9	203.7	1 462.4	302.0	433.1	194.4	26.5	989.5	342.3	647.2
1996	1 436.8	241.0	654.6	217.0	1 564.2	342.3	459.1	208.9	32.8	1 020.4	346.9	673.5
1997	1 569.9	273.9	679.1	241.0	1 691.5	395.5	472.2	229.7	29.7	1 064.8	354.7	710.1
1998	1 708.5	300.0	718.7	262.9	1 829.9	439.8	491.1	254.5	-31.0	1 103.3	359.9	743.4
1999	1 798.8	330.3	766.9	283.5	1 977.2	501.0	515.4	276.0	-38.8	1 151.3	369.8	781.5
2000	1 976.7	361.1	811.4	312.3	2 116.4	534.4	548.5	300.3	-128.5	1 217.7	389.5	828.2
2001	2 076.9	359.8	845.1	326.6	2 226.6	544.1	589.8	320.7	-117.3	1 281.3	396.2	885.1
2002	2 183.8	. . .	. . .	. . .	2 312.2	. . .	. . .	. . .	-116.7	1 345.2	. . .	. . .
QUANTITY INDEX												
1987	81.4	91.5	81.4	71.2	75.5	54.7	85.5	73.2	. . .	91.9	106.5	84.5
1988	84.2	90.3	84.2	83.5	80.2	61.0	86.9	79.9	. . .	94.2	107.4	87.5
1989	85.9	95.8	87.0	84.8	84.0	66.0	88.9	87.9	. . .	96.5	108.8	90.2
1990	87.0	101.2	88.6	84.3	87.1	70.5	92.2	91.6	. . .	98.8	110.9	92.7
1991	88.4	102.3	90.9	80.2	86.5	68.9	94.3	87.4	. . .	99.2	111.0	93.2
1992	90.3	97.4	93.0	87.9	89.0	74.4	96.4	86.8	. . .	99.5	110.2	94.1
1993	92.5	97.1	93.1	90.2	90.7	78.8	95.3	90.5	. . .	99.3	107.7	95.1
1994	93.8	94.6	96.5	90.5	93.2	86.2	95.5	92.0	. . .	99.6	105.8	96.4
1995	97.0	100.6	99.0	94.4	96.6	91.7	96.8	95.7	. . .	99.7	102.1	98.4
1996	100.0	100.0	100.0	100.0	100.0	100.0	100.0	100.0	. . .	100.0	100.0	100.0
1997	105.9	102.1	101.0	111.9	104.4	112.2	100.1	105.9	. . .	101.5	100.1	102.2
1998	112.9	106.4	103.5	123.9	108.6	120.0	100.4	114.2	. . .	102.6	100.2	103.9
1999	117.5	114.1	107.6	128.7	113.1	131.3	102.5	119.7	. . .	104.0	99.9	106.1
2000	124.8	119.2	110.4	136.2	116.7	134.4	106.3	126.3	. . .	106.7	102.3	108.9
2001	128.3	120.5	110.9	137.4	117.8	134.2	109.2	127.9	. . .	108.5	101.2	112.3
2002	130.3	. . .	. . .	. . .	119.7	. . .	. . .	. . .	. . .	110.6	. . .	. . .

[1]Includes industries not shown separately.
. . . = Not available.

NOTES AND DEFINITIONS

TABLE 15-1
GROSS DOMESTIC PRODUCT BY INDUSTRY

Gross product, or gross product originating (GPO), by industry is the contribution of each private industry and government sector to the gross domestic product (GDP). For explanation of GDP, see the Notes and Definitions to Tables 1-1 through 1-10. GPO is equivalent to the economists' concept of "value added," but the latter term is not often used in the context of U.S. economic statistics, to avoid confusion with a somewhat different concept known as "Census value added" that is used in censuses and surveys of manufactures. GPO is calculated only on an annual basis.

Definitions and notes on the data

The value of an industry's GPO is equal to the market value of its gross output (which consists of sales or receipts and other operating income, commodity taxes, and inventory change) minus the value of its intermediate inputs (which consist of energy, raw materials, semi-finished goods, and services that are purchased from domestic industries or from foreign sources). In concept, this is equal to the sum of the factor incomes earned in that industry and the depreciation of capital goods incurred in the production of GDP plus the commodity taxes.

Because the gross output and particularly the intermediate input values are not available on a timely basis, BEA measures *current-dollar gross product by industry* as the sum of labor and property-type incomes originating in that industry plus indirect business taxes. Property-type income is the sum of corporate profits, proprietors' income, rental income of persons, net interest, capital consumption allowances, business transfer payments, and the current surplus of government enterprises less subsidies. (Indirect business taxes, business transfer payments, and subsidies less current surplus of government enterprises comprise the conceptual differences between net national product and national income. See Table 1-7 for the relation of gross product and net product to income.) In the GPO estimates, the *statistical discrepancy* (between total GDP and national income, after allowing for conceptual differences; see Notes and Definitions to Chapter 1) is added to the sum of the calculated GPOs for individual private industries to yield a total GPO for all private industries. This reflects BEA's judgments that the expenditure estimates are more accurate than the income estimates, and that most of the income measurement problems arise in private industries. Since this discrepancy cannot be allocated to individual industries, it should be noted as a source of some uncertainty about the accuracy of GPO for individual industries. Still, at its peak in 2000 the statistical discrepancy was only 1.5 percent of total GPO in private industries.

The *quantity indexes of gross product by industry* represent estimates of the real output of each industry, net of intermediate inputs, based on chained constant-dollar estimates, and expressed as index numbers, 1996 = 100.

The preferred method for measuring real gross product by industry is known as "double deflation." This means constructing constant-dollar measures of the gross output of the industry and subtracting from those values constant-dollar measures of the intermediate inputs to the industry. Values of gross output are found in Census Annual Surveys of major industries, which are available only with a lag; adequate data on the value of intermediate inputs are only available at 5-year intervals, when the economic censuses and the input/output accounts based on them become available. Therefore, implicit deflators using the double-deflation method are derived from interpolations and extrapolations of the gross output and intermediate inputs data, and then applied to the values of GPO described above to yield constant-dollar GPO estimates, which are then chained to yield the quantity indexes. As described in the Notes and Definitions to Chapter 1, the quantity weights used in calculating the deflators are changed each year as relative prices and quantities shift over time.

Beginning with data for 1987, the double-deflation method is used to calculate real output for 63 industry groups—all except general government and private households, for which GPO by definition is equivalent to measured gross output. Before 1987, double deflation is used for 51 industry groups.

Data for the most recent year are extrapolated using incomplete data.

Data availability and references

Accelerated GPO estimates for 2002 were published in the *Survey of Current Business* for May 2003, using limited source data and an abbreviated methodology. The full set of estimates for 1998–2001, along with definitions and references, was published in "Gross Domestic Product by Industry for 1999–2001," *Survey of Current Business*, November 2002. Values for 1997 through 2000 were published in "Gross Domestic Product by Industry for 1998–2000," Survey of Current Business, November 2001. Concepts and methodology were described in "Improved Estimates of Gross Product by Industry for 1947–1998," *Survey of Current Business*, June 2000. All *Survey* articles are available on the BEA Web site, <http://www.bea.gov>.

Revised estimates for 2002 reclassified to the North American Industry Classification System (NAICS) basis will be released in spring 2004 as part of a comprehensive revision, and at that time accelerated estimates for 2003 will also be released.

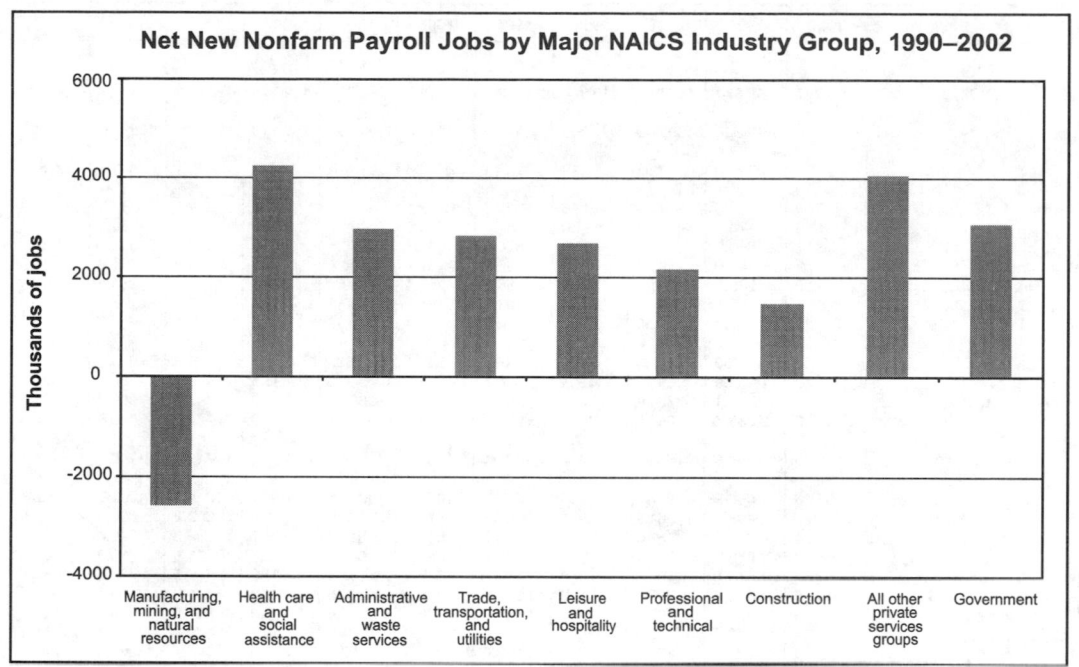

Net New Nonfarm Payroll Jobs by Major NAICS Industry Group, 1990–2002

- Statistics on employment, hours, and earnings based on the new North American Industry Classification System (NAICS) have been tabulated back to 1990. This enables users to assess job growth and other labor market issues based on industry groupings more closely attuned to today's conditions. Between 1990 and 2002, U.S. industries added nearly 21 million jobs. Labor market conditions in these 2 years were somewhat similar, with the unemployment rate 5.6 percent in the earlier year and 5.8 percent in the latest year. Therefore, looking at the industry composition of that job growth gives a good idea of underlying trends. (Graph and Table 16-1)

- Of the major sectors, health care and social assistance was the single biggest source of net new jobs, providing 4.2 million jobs of which 0.9 million were in social assistance and the rest in health care.

- Administrative and waste services provided 3.0 million net new jobs, of which 1.0 million were in the temporary help sector.

- Leisure and hospitality provided 2.7 million net new jobs, 1.9 million at food services and drinking places.

- Government provided 3.1 million net new jobs—2.8 million at local government and 0.7 million at state governments, partly offset by a loss at the federal level.

- Trade, transportation, and utilities added 2.8 million net new jobs, mostly at retail trade.

- Goods production at manufacturing and natural resource establishments lost 2.6 million jobs. Even the manufacturing of computer and electronic products lost jobs. (There were, however, gains in net new jobs at computer service industries and in the new information sector.)

- Long workweeks, averaging 40 hours or more, characterized most of the goods-producing industries, while retail trade and some service industries, noticeably leisure and hospitality, had short average workweeks indicating many part-time jobs. (Table 16-3)

- Showing a somewhat similar pattern, average hourly earnings were high in most goods-producing industries (with the conspicuous exception of apparel) and low in leisure and hospitality and retail trade. (Table 16-4)

Table 16-1. Nonfarm Employment by NAICS Sector and Industry

(Wage and salary workers on nonfarm payrolls, thousands.)

Industry	1990	1991	1992	1993	1994	1995	1996	1997	1998	1999	2000	2001	2002
Total nonfarm	109 487	108 374	108 726	110 844	114 291	117 298	119 708	122 776	125 930	128 993	131 785	131 826	130 376
Total private	91 072	89 829	89 940	91 855	95 016	97 866	100 169	103 113	106 021	108 686	110 996	110 707	108 886
Goods–producing	23 723	22 588	22 095	22 219	22 774	23 156	23 410	23 886	24 354	24 465	24 649	23 873	22 619
Natural resources and mining	765	739	689	666	659	641	637	654	645	598	599	606	581
Logging	84.6	78.7	78.7	81.0	82.0	82.5	80.7	82.1	80.0	80.8	79.0	73.5	69.1
Mining	680.1	660.5	609.8	584.9	576.5	558.1	556.4	571.3	564.7	517.4	520.2	532.5	511.9
Oil and gas extraction	190.2	191.0	182.2	170.9	162.4	151.7	146.9	144.1	140.8	131.2	124.9	123.7	122.5
Mining, except oil and gas [1]	302.2	285.1	271.8	250.9	255.2	252.4	249.4	249.5	243.1	234.5	224.8	218.7	212.1
Coal mining	136.0	125.6	117.5	100.2	103.5	96.7	90.5	89.4	85.3	78.6	72.2	74.3	74.9
Support activities for mining	188	184	156	163	159	154	160	178	181	152	171	190	177
Construction	5 263	4 780	4 608	4 779	5 095	5 274	5 536	5 813	6 149	6 545	6 787	6 826	6 732
Construction of buildings	1 413.0	1 252.9	1 187.3	1 227.4	1 300.8	1 325.4	1 380.2	1 435.4	1 508.8	1 586.3	1 632.5	1 588.9	1 583.9
Heavy and civil engineering	813.0	759.1	734.2	738.4	761.7	774.7	800.1	824.9	865.3	908.7	937.0	953.0	929.9
Specialty trade contractors	3 037.3	2 768.4	2 686.0	2 813.6	3 032.5	3 174.1	3 355.1	3 552.6	3 775.1	4 049.6	4 217.0	4 283.9	4 217.9
Manufacturing	17 695	17 068	16 799	16 774	17 021	17 241	17 237	17 419	17 560	17 322	17 263	16 441	15 306
Durable goods	10 736	10 219	9 945	9 900	10 131	10 372	10 485	10 704	10 910	10 830	10 876	10 335	9 517
Wood products	540.6	498.5	501.9	524.1	560.6	573.7	582.8	595.4	609.2	620.3	613.0	574.1	556.8
Nonmetallic mineral products	528.4	494.7	487.3	491.1	505.3	513.1	517.3	525.7	535.3	540.8	554.2	544.5	519.0
Primary metals	688.6	656.1	630.3	618.4	630.4	641.7	639.3	638.8	641.5	625.0	621.8	570.9	510.9
Fabricated metal products	1 610.0	1 541.3	1 497.2	1 509.5	1 565.3	1 623.4	1 647.5	1 695.8	1 739.5	1 728.4	1 752.6	1 676.4	1 547.8
Machinery	1 407.8	1 345.8	1 309.1	1 328.8	1 379.2	1 440.2	1 466.8	1 493.7	1 511.9	1 466.1	1 454.7	1 368.3	1 237.4
Computer and electronic products [1]	1 902.5	1 809.3	1 707.3	1 656.0	1 651.1	1 688.4	1 746.6	1 803.3	1 830.9	1 780.5	1 820.0	1 748.8	1 521.3
Computer and peripheral equipment	367.4	348.6	328.5	305.7	297.7	295.6	304.6	316.7	322.1	310.1	301.9	286.2	249.8
Communications equipment	231.5	220.6	209.7	210.3	218.0	232.8	237.6	243.9	246.4	237.4	247.7	233.9	190.9
Semiconductors and electronic components	574.0	546.6	519.4	519.4	535.4	571.0	606.6	639.8	649.8	630.5	676.3	645.4	531.4
Electronic instruments	626.3	590.0	548.5	517.6	493.4	482.0	489.1	493.9	500.2	489.6	478.6	475.1	450.6
Electrical equipment and appliances	633.1	597.7	579.4	575.8	588.5	592.8	591.0	586.3	591.6	588.0	590.9	556.9	498.9
Transportation equipment	2 133.3	2 028.2	1 976.9	1 913.7	1 936.1	1 977.2	1 973.7	2 026.2	2 077.0	2 087.3	2 055.8	1 937.9	1 828.5
Furniture and related products	601.4	561.0	562.8	575.4	600.2	606.7	603.8	615.1	641.2	664.8	679.7	642.4	604.6
Miscellaneous manufacturing	690.4	686.6	692.5	707.4	713.8	714.5	715.6	723.1	731.7	729.0	733.0	714.5	691.9
Nondurable goods	6 959	6 849	6 854	6 873	6 890	6 869	6 752	6 716	6 650	6 492	6 388	6 107	5 789
Food manufacturing	1 507.3	1 515.2	1 518.3	1 534.6	1 539.2	1 560.0	1 562.0	1 557.9	1 554.9	1 549.8	1 553.1	1 551.2	1 525.1
Beverages and tobacco products	217.7	214.7	208.5	207.1	204.6	202.6	204.4	206.3	208.9	208.3	207.0	209.0	205.4
Textile mills	491.8	479.9	479.0	478.7	477.6	468.5	443.2	436.2	424.5	397.1	378.2	332.9	293.2
Textile product mills	209.3	199.4	202.0	207.3	218.6	219.0	216.3	217.0	217.1	217.3	216.3	205.7	196.2
Apparel	929.1	902.6	905.2	882.5	856.3	814.1	743.1	700.2	639.0	555.6	496.8	426.5	357.6
Leather and allied products	133.2	124.4	120.8	118.1	113.9	104.9	94.2	89.5	82.9	74.9	68.8	58.0	49.9
Paper and paper products	647.2	638.5	639.6	639.7	639.4	639.5	631.4	630.6	624.9	615.6	604.7	577.6	549.8
Printing and related support activities	808.6	792.3	780.2	785.2	802.2	817.3	815.8	821.1	827.9	814.6	806.8	768.4	709.9
Petroleum and coal products	152.8	154.8	152.3	146.2	144.0	140.4	137.3	136.0	134.5	127.8	123.2	121.1	119.1
Chemicals	1 035.7	1 024.1	1 028.9	1 024.9	1 004.7	987.9	984.5	986.8	992.6	982.5	980.4	959.0	929.5
Plastics and rubber products	825.9	803.2	819.0	849.0	889.4	915.1	920.1	934.1	942.8	948.3	952.2	897.4	853.5
Service–providing	85 764	85 787	86 631	88 625	91 517	94 142	96 299	98 890	101 576	104 528	107 136	107 952	107 757
Private service–providing	67 349	67 241	67 845	69 636	72 242	74 710	76 759	79 227	81 667	84 221	86 346	86 834	86 267
Trade, transportation, and utilities	22 666	22 281	22 125	22 378	23 128	23 834	24 239	24 700	25 186	25 771	26 225	25 983	25 493
Wholesale trade	5 268.4	5 185.3	5 109.7	5 093.2	5 247.3	5 433.1	5 522.0	5 663.9	5 795.2	5 892.5	5 933.2	5 772.7	5 641.0
Durable goods	2 833.7	2 766.6	2 698.8	2 687.0	2 786.0	2 908.8	2 977.8	3 071.9	3 162.4	3 219.6	3 250.7	3 130.4	3 007.2
Nondurable goods	1 900.2	1 891.3	1 891.5	1 888.3	1 927.0	1 969.3	1 977.5	2 007.9	2 032.7	2 061.1	2 064.8	2 031.3	2 015.1
Electronic markets, agents, and brokers	534.5	527.4	519.4	517.9	534.4	555.0	566.7	584.1	600.1	611.8	617.7	611.1	618.8

[1] Includes other industries, not shown separately.

Table 16-1. Nonfarm Employment by NAICS Sector and Industry—*Continued*

(Wage and salary workers on nonfarm payrolls, thousands.)

Industry	1990	1991	1992	1993	1994	1995	1996	1997	1998	1999	2000	2001	2002
Retail trade	13 182.3	12 896.4	12 827.9	13 020.5	13 490.8	13 896.7	14 142.5	14 388.9	14 609.3	14 970.1	15 279.8	15 238.6	15 047.2
Motor vehicle and parts dealers [1]	1 494.4	1 435.1	1 428.1	1 475.3	1 564.7	1 627.1	1 685.6	1 723.4	1 740.9	1 796.6	1 846.9	1 854.6	1 879.2
Automobile dealers	983.3	938.3	934.8	970.4	1 031.8	1 071.6	1 113.0	1 134.5	1 142.0	1 179.7	1 216.5	1 225.1	1 250.4
Furniture and home furnishings stores	431.5	412.8	410.3	418.6	441.6	461.2	474.2	484.7	499.1	524.4	543.5	541.2	539.9
Electronics and appliance stores	382.3	381.1	378.1	386.9	417.0	448.7	470.2	494.0	510.2	542.2	564.4	554.5	528.8
Building material and garden supply stores	891	863	872	892	946	982	1 007	1 043	1 062	1 101	1 142	1 152	1 179
Food and beverage stores	2 778.8	2 767.9	2 743.9	2 774.8	2 825.0	2 879.8	2 927.8	2 956.9	2 965.7	2 984.5	2 993.0	2 950.5	2 871.6
Health and personal care stores	792.0	788.5	780.2	778.6	797.0	811.9	826.4	853.3	876.0	898.2	927.6	951.5	946.6
Gasoline stations	910.2	889.3	876.4	881.2	902.3	922.3	946.4	956.2	961.3	943.5	935.7	925.3	903.6
Clothing and clothing accessories stores	1 313.0	1 275.8	1 249.1	1 259.9	1 261.7	1 246.3	1 220.6	1 235.9	1 268.6	1 306.6	1 321.6	1 321.1	1 307.8
Sporting goods, hobby, book, and music stores	532.0	527.7	534.4	545.2	577.6	605.8	614.0	626.2	635.4	664.3	685.7	679.2	660.1
General merchandise stores [1]	2 499.8	2 416.7	2 414.2	2 450.2	2 541.0	2 635.4	2 657.3	2 657.6	2 686.5	2 751.8	2 819.8	2 842.2	2 820.7
Department stores	1 493.9	1 440.8	1 445.2	1 486.8	1 560.4	1 629.8	1 645.0	1 653.5	1 679.2	1 709.2	1 755.0	1 768.3	1 709.8
Miscellaneous store retailers	738.2	734.7	736.8	752.9	795.7	841.1	874.3	913.2	950.3	985.5	1 007.1	993.3	962.5
Nonstore retailers	419.2	403.7	404.5	404.9	421.2	435.4	438.5	444.5	453.0	471.6	492.4	473.5	447.3
Transportation and warehousing	3 475.6	3 462.8	3 461.8	3 553.8	3 701.0	3 837.8	3 935.3	4 026.5	4 168.0	4 300.3	4 410.3	4 372.0	4 205.3
Air transportation	529.2	525.4	519.6	516.6	511.2	510.9	525.7	542.0	562.7	586.3	614.4	615.3	559.3
Rail transportation	271.8	255.6	248.1	242.2	234.6	232.5	225.2	221.0	225.0	228.8	231.7	226.7	218.1
Water transportation	56.8	57.4	56.7	52.8	52.3	50.8	51.0	50.7	50.5	51.7	56.0	54.0	51.6
Truck transportation	1 122.4	1 104.6	1 107.4	1 154.8	1 206.2	1 249.1	1 282.4	1 308.2	1 354.4	1 391.5	1 405.8	1 386.8	1 339.1
Transit and ground passenger transportation	274.2	283.9	287.9	299.9	316.6	327.9	339.1	349.6	362.7	371.0	372.1	374.8	371.5
Pipeline transportation	59.8	60.7	60.1	58.7	57.0	53.6	51.4	49.7	48.1	46.9	46.0	45.4	41.5
Scenic and sightseeing transportation	15.7	16.5	17.7	19.3	21.3	22.0	23.2	24.5	25.4	26.1	27.5	29.1	25.9
Support activities for transportation	364.1	376.6	369.9	381.8	404.7	430.4	445.8	473.4	496.8	518.1	537.4	539.2	526.7
Couriers and messengers	375.0	378.9	388.8	414.3	466.2	516.8	539.9	546.0	568.2	585.9	605.0	587.0	558.0
Warehousing and storage	406.6	403.2	405.6	413.4	431.0	443.8	451.8	461.5	474.2	494.1	514.4	513.8	513.6
Utilities	740.0	736.1	726.0	710.7	689.3	666.2	639.6	620.9	613.4	608.5	601.3	599.4	599.8
Information	2 688	2 677	2 641	2 668	2 738	2 843	2 940	3 084	3 218	3 419	3 631	3 629	3 420
Publishing industries, except Internet	870.6	863.4	854.2	873.1	891.0	910.7	927.2	955.5	982.3	1 004.8	1 035.0	1 020.7	969.4
Motion picture and sound recording industries	254.6	258.9	254.3	259.6	278.4	311.1	334.7	353.0	369.5	384.4	382.6	376.8	387.1
Broadcasting, except Internet	283.8	281.2	279.7	284.0	290.1	298.1	309.1	313.0	321.2	329.4	343.5	344.6	333.8
Internet publishing and broadcasting	16.7	16.2	16.1	16.4	16.9	18.6	21.0	23.5	27.1	37.1	50.5	45.5	34.8
Telecommunications	980.3	973.1	946.0	942.2	961.1	975.7	997.0	1 059.5	1 107.8	1 179.7	1 262.6	1 302.1	1 200.9
ISPs, search portals, and data processing	252.2	251.7	258.5	263.1	268.0	291.2	311.6	338.8	369.1	439.3	510.1	493.6	447.4
Other information services	29.9	32.9	32.3	29.4	32.8	38.2	39.4	40.1	41.4	43.8	46.2	46.1	46.6
Financial activities	6 614	6 558	6 540	6 709	6 867	6 827	6 969	7 178	7 462	7 648	7 687	7 807	7 843
Finance and Insurance	4 978.6	4 937.3	4 914.7	5 035.5	5 135.2	5 071.7	5 154.2	5 305.1	5 532.0	5 668.4	5 680.4	5 773.1	5 814.9
Monetary authorities-central bank	24.0	24.2	23.7	23.4	23.4	23.0	22.8	22.1	21.7	22.6	22.8	23.0	23.1
Credit intermediation and related activities [1]	2 424.8	2 352.4	2 317.3	2 360.7	2 375.7	2 314.4	2 368.2	2 433.6	2 531.9	2 591.0	2 547.8	2 597.7	2 682.3
Depository credit intermediation [1]	1 908.5	1 830.7	1 769.0	1 760.5	1 736.7	1 700.2	1 691.4	1 696.6	1 708.9	1 709.7	1 681.2	1 701.2	1 738.2
Commercial banking	1 361.8	1 333.7	1 302.8	1 308.7	1 297.4	1 281.7	1 275.1	1 277.9	1 286.0	1 281.2	1 250.5	1 258.4	1 284.7
Securities, commodity contracts, investments	457.9	455.0	475.7	507.9	553.4	562.2	589.6	636.1	692.2	737.3	804.5	830.5	800.8
Insurance carriers and related activities	2 016.1	2 048.2	2 039.5	2 082.5	2 118.8	2 108.2	2 108.0	2 143.6	2 209.4	2 236.1	2 220.6	2 233.7	2 223.1
Funds, trusts, and other financial vehicles	55.7	57.5	58.5	61.0	63.9	63.9	65.6	69.8	76.9	81.5	84.8	88.3	85.6
Real estate and rental and leasing	1 634.0	1 620.8	1 625.5	1 673.8	1 731.5	1 755.4	1 814.3	1 872.8	1 930.3	1 979.0	2 006.8	2 034.5	2 027.8
Real estate	1 106.8	1 107.6	1 114.5	1 146.1	1 183.2	1 178.9	1 205.8	1 240.7	1 274.2	1 299.0	1 312.2	1 339.5	1 347.7
Rental and leasing services	514.2	499.4	496.4	511.0	529.9	557.4	587.7	609.5	630.8	653.1	666.8	666.3	652.3
Lessors of nonfinancial intangible assets	13.9	13.9	14.6	16.7	18.4	19.0	20.8	22.6	25.3	26.8	27.8	28.7	27.8

[1] Includes other industries, not shown separately.

Table 16-1. Nonfarm Employment by NAICS Sector and Industry—*Continued*

(Wage and salary workers on nonfarm payrolls, thousands.)

Industry	1990	1991	1992	1993	1994	1995	1996	1997	1998	1999	2000	2001	2002
Professional and business services	10 848	10 714	10 970	11 495	12 174	12 844	13 462	14 335	15 147	15 957	16 666	16 476	16 010
Professional and technical services [1]	4 556.7	4 526.5	4 593.5	4 708.2	4 843.6	5 101.3	5 337.1	5 655.5	6 021.0	6 375.4	6 733.9	6 902.2	6 715.0
Legal services	943.6	946.0	949.8	963.9	965.6	959.2	968.4	987.5	1 021.1	1 051.4	1 065.7	1 091.3	1 111.8
Accounting and bookkeeping services	664.1	655.4	657.8	654.2	670.1	706.3	729.8	761.2	802.0	837.6	866.4	872.2	867.1
Architectural and engineering services	941.5	906.2	901.8	922.7	952.0	997.1	1 024.5	1 063.4	1 114.8	1 168.1	1 237.9	1 274.7	1 251.1
Computer systems design and related services	409.7	419.9	444.9	484.8	531.4	611.2	701.4	826.7	974.9	1 132.9	1 254.3	1 297.8	1 162.7
Management and technical consulting services	323.6	331.6	358.1	385.4	416.8	474.8	517.1	568.4	619.2	649.0	704.9	746.2	731.8
Management of companies and enterprises	1 667.4	1 638.1	1 623.4	1 640.1	1 665.9	1 685.8	1 702.7	1 729.7	1 756.1	1 773.8	1 796.0	1 779.0	1 711.1
Administrative and waste services	4 624.3	4 549.3	4 752.6	5 146.5	5 664.1	6 056.8	6 422.1	6 949.9	7 369.3	7 807.4	8 136.0	7 794.9	7 583.8
Administrative and support services [1]	4 394.9	4 317.0	4 515.9	4 897.8	5 403.4	5 783.4	6 140.0	6 659.4	7 069.9	7 496.9	7 823.1	7 477.6	7 266.8
Employment services [1]	1 493.7	1 448.7	1 592.5	1 865.1	2 226.5	2 425.2	2 600.8	2 927.2	3 217.0	3 551.5	3 817.0	3 437.1	3 248.8
Temporary help services	1 155.8	1 123.3	1 212.5	1 388.8	1 632.2	1 743.8	1 849.0	2 059.7	2 245.2	2 469.6	2 635.6	2 337.7	2 185.7
Business support services	504.6	503.3	524.5	549.0	574.4	629.8	678.3	733.9	772.2	780.5	786.7	779.7	757.0
Services to buildings and dwellings	1 174.6	1 150.9	1 159.7	1 197.9	1 267.2	1 302.4	1 361.5	1 424.1	1 460.0	1 534.7	1 570.5	1 606.2	1 597.3
Waste management and remediation services	229.4	232.4	236.7	248.6	260.7	273.3	282.0	290.5	299.3	310.5	312.9	317.3	316.9
Education and health services	10 984	11 506	11 891	12 303	12 807	13 289	13 683	14 087	14 446	14 798	15 109	15 645	16 184
Educational services	1 688.0	1 736.6	1 713.1	1 755.4	1 894.9	2 010.2	2 077.6	2 155.0	2 232.9	2 320.4	2 390.4	2 510.6	2 650.6
Health care and social assistance	9 295.8	9 769.8	10 178.0	10 548.1	10 911.7	11 278.4	11 604.9	11 932.2	12 213.5	12 477.1	12 718.0	13 134.0	13 533.2
Ambulatory health care services [1]	2 842	3 028	3 200	3 386	3 579	3 768	3 940	4 093	4 161	4 227	4 320	4 462	4 633.4
Offices of physicians	1 278.0	1 345.2	1 401.1	1 442.0	1 480.9	1 540.4	1 603.8	1 660.5	1 723.6	1 786.6	1 839.9	1 911.2	1 982.6
Outpatient care centers	260.5	271.4	286.5	303.1	314.5	328.8	340.2	352.1	363.3	375.4	386.4	399.7	409.7
Home health care services	287.5	340.7	393.4	463.8	553.2	621.8	667.2	702.8	659.5	629.6	633.3	638.6	675.1
Hospitals	3 512.6	3 617.3	3 711.4	3 740.0	3 724.0	3 733.7	3 772.8	3 821.6	3 892.4	3 935.5	3 954.3	4 050.9	4 153.1
Nursing and residential care facilities [1]	1 856.4	1 972.0	2 043.5	2 128.1	2 227.0	2 307.7	2 379.9	2 443.4	2 487.3	2 528.8	2 583.2	2 675.8	2 743.2
Nursing care facilities	1 169.8	1 240.2	1 273.4	1 319.3	1 377.1	1 413.0	1 448.4	1 474.6	1 489.3	1 501.0	1 513.6	1 546.8	1 573.7
Social assistance [1]	1 085.1	1 152.2	1 223.3	1 294.4	1 381.9	1 469.5	1 512.3	1 574.2	1 672.6	1 786.2	1 860.2	1 945.9	2 003.5
Child day care services	387.8	413.2	446.5	468.9	510.0	557.1	559.2	570.4	615.1	673.7	695.8	714.6	734.2
Leisure and hospitality	9 288	9 256	9 437	9 732	10 100	10 501	10 777	11 018	11 232	11 543	11 862	12 036	11 969
Arts, entertainment, and recreation	1 132	1 177	1 236	1 302	1 376	1 459	1 522	1 600	1 645	1 709	1 788	1 824	1 778
Performing arts and spectator sports	272.7	282.7	289.5	286.8	296.1	307.7	328.6	349.6	350.0	361.1	381.8	382.3	357.9
Museums, historical sites, zoos, and parks	68.0	71.0	75.0	78.3	81.8	83.9	88.9	93.8	97.4	103.1	110.4	115.0	112.5
Amusements, gambling, and recreation	791.3	823.4	871.8	936.8	997.7	1 067.8	1 104.5	1 156.5	1 197.9	1 244.9	1 295.7	1 327.1	1 307.6
Accommodations and food service	8 155.6	8 078.9	8 200.5	8 430.4	8 724.1	9 041.6	9 254.3	9 417.9	9 586.2	9 833.7	10 073.5	10 211.3	10 191.2
Accommodations	1 616.0	1 574.3	1 561.5	1 580.5	1 615.3	1 652.5	1 698.9	1 729.5	1 773.5	1 831.7	1 884.4	1 852.2	1 779.4
Food services and drinking places	6 539.6	6 504.6	6 639.0	6 849.9	7 108.7	7 389.1	7 555.4	7 688.5	7 812.7	8 002.0	8 189.1	8 359.1	8 411.7
Other services	4 261	4 249	4 240	4 350	4 428	4 572	4 690	4 825	4 976	5 087	5 168	5 258	5 348
Repair and maintenance	1 009.0	960.0	964.0	998.0	1 023.5	1 078.9	1 135.5	1 169.3	1 189.2	1 222.0	1 241.5	1 256.5	1 240.6
Personal and laundry service	1 119.9	1 109.2	1 098.9	1 116.0	1 120.3	1 143.9	1 165.7	1 180.4	1 205.6	1 220.3	1 242.9	1 255.0	1 246.7
Membership associations and organizations	2 132.2	2 179.5	2 177.1	2 236.4	2 284.5	2 348.9	2 389.1	2 474.9	2 581.3	2 644.4	2 683.3	2 746.4	2 860.7
Government	18 415	18 545	18 787	18 989	19 275	19 432	19 539	19 664	19 909	20 307	20 790	21 118	21 489
Federal	3 196	3 110	3 111	3 063	3 018	2 949	2 877	2 806	2 772	2 769	2 865	2 764	2 767
Federal, except U.S. Postal Service	2 370.5	2 296.2	2 310.7	2 269.4	2 197.2	2 098.8	2 009.8	1 940.2	1 891.3	1 879.5	1 984.8	1 891.0	1 922.5
U.S. Postal Service	825.1	813.2	800.0	793.2	820.6	849.9	867.2	866.0	880.5	889.7	879.7	873.0	844.8
State government	4 305	4 355	4 408	4 488	4 576	4 635	4 606	4 582	4 612	4 709	4 786	4 905	5 006
State government education	1 729.9	1 767.6	1 798.6	1 834.1	1 881.9	1 919.0	1 910.7	1 904.0	1 922.2	1 983.2	2 030.6	2 112.9	2 218.8
State government, excluding education	2 574.6	2 587.3	2 609.7	2 653.8	2 693.6	2 715.5	2 695.1	2 677.9	2 690.2	2 725.6	2 755.9	2 791.8	2 787.4
Local government	10 914	11 081	11 267	11 438	11 682	11 849	12 056	12 276	12 525	12 829	13 139	13 449	13 716
Local government education	5 902.1	5 994.1	6 075.9	6 206.3	6 329.4	6 453.1	6 592.3	6 758.5	6 920.9	7 120.4	7 293.9	7 479.3	7 657.2
Local government, excluding education	5 012.4	5 086.9	5 191.6	5 231.9	5 352.2	5 396.0	5 464.1	5 516.9	5 603.9	5 708.6	5 844.6	5 970.0	6 058.5

[1]Includes other industries, not shown separately.

Table 16-2. Production or Nonsupervisory Workers on Private Nonfarm Payrolls by NAICS Industry

(Wage and salary workers on nonfarm payrolls, thousands.)

Industry	1990	1991	1992	1993	1994	1995	1996	1997	1998	1999	2000	2001	2002
Total private	73 684	72 520	72 786	74 591	77 382	79 845	81 773	84 158	86 316	88 430	90 336	89 983	88 419
Goods–producing	17 322	16 352	16 043	16 236	16 795	17 137	17 318	17 698	18 008	18 067	18 169	17 466	16 442
Natural resources and mining	538	515	478	462	461	458	461	479	473	438	446	457	435
Construction	4 115	3 674	3 546	3 704	3 973	4 113	4 325	4 546	4 807	5 105	5 295	5 332	5 208
Manufacturing	12 669	12 164	12 020	12 070	12 361	12 566	12 532	12 673	12 729	12 524	12 428	11 677	10 799
Durable goods	7 396	7 000	6 852	6 879	7 132	7 351	7 425	7 597	7 720	7 650	7 658	7 163	6 551
Wood products	449.9	412.8	417.0	436.8	468.7	477.5	484.9	496.6	507.9	514.4	505.6	468.3	450.2
Nonmetallic mineral products	413.2	384.1	378.4	380.7	392.3	399.7	404.8	412.5	420.6	426.0	439.5	427.1	401.1
Primary metals	525.1	496.9	478.7	473.3	487.4	500.3	500.3	501.6	505.3	491.9	490.0	446.9	397.4
Fabricated metal products	1 190.1	1 131.6	1 101.0	1 116.9	1 172.0	1 223.0	1 241.6	1 285.3	1 319.6	1 304.9	1 325.8	1 253.5	1 146.7
Machinery	937.6	883.6	856.3	874.1	921.1	968.5	983.2	1 005.5	1 014.7	977.0	959.9	889.1	790.2
Computer and electronic products	980.2	925.6	876.3	856.4	863.9	890.3	915.2	951.1	964.7	932.9	949.3	875.8	751.6
Electrical equipment and appliances	465.2	435.6	425.0	421.8	434.7	438.4	433.9	427.7	431.8	433.2	433.1	402.2	353.6
Transportation equipment	1 472.5	1 405.5	1 387.7	1 366.1	1 414.6	1 471.1	1 480.0	1 520.8	1 529.2	1 525.4	1 496.7	1 397.7	1 309.7
Furniture and related products	475.2	440.0	442.8	454.2	475.7	480.0	477.9	489.7	512.1	532.4	544.3	509.0	475.3
Miscellaneous manufacturing	487.2	484.2	489.1	498.2	502.1	502.2	503.3	506.6	514.3	512.2	513.2	493.1	474.9
Nondurable goods	5 273	5 164	5 168	5 192	5 229	5 215	5 107	5 076	5 009	4 873	4 770	4 514	4 249
Food manufacturing	1 165.0	1 174.2	1 182.0	1 195.3	1 200.4	1 221.0	1 227.7	1 227.7	1 227.6	1 228.7	1 227.9	1 221.3	1 201.9
Beverages and tobacco products	117.2	116.9	116.2	117.6	118.2	117.3	120.1	121.4	122.5	120.1	116.0	115.6	118.4
Textile mills	417.9	407.2	406.0	403.9	403.3	393.2	371.7	367.1	357.2	333.7	315.2	275.8	244.1
Textile products mills	170.1	160.9	163.0	167.2	176.0	176.3	173.4	174.7	173.9	173.4	171.8	163.9	155.0
Apparel	830.0	805.1	809.8	788.0	763.1	719.3	650.2	611.5	549.9	471.8	415.4	351.2	292.4
Leather and allied products	116.6	107.5	104.4	101.4	97.2	88.5	78.5	73.6	67.0	59.9	55.4	46.8	39.8
Paper and paper products	493.2	488.4	489.9	490.9	492.8	493.8	487.5	488.7	484.1	474.0	467.5	446.3	423.9
Printing and related support activities	597.6	581.7	573.6	579.7	591.4	599.1	594.0	597.0	598.4	585.1	575.7	544.4	494.9
Petroleum and coal products	97.5	97.4	96.8	93.0	90.9	88.8	87.2	87.8	87.1	84.6	83.1	80.9	78.7
Chemicals	620.3	599.7	586.2	590.1	595.6	598.4	595.1	593.3	600.6	595.2	587.7	562.2	532.4
Plastics and rubber products	647.7	624.8	639.8	664.7	699.6	719.8	721.3	732.7	740.4	747.0	753.6	705.3	667.2
Private service–providing	56 362	56 168	56 743	58 355	60 587	62 708	64 455	66 460	68 308	70 363	72 167	72 517	71 977
Trade, transportation, and utilities	19 032	18 640	18 506	18 752	19 392	19 984	20 325	20 698	21 059	21 576	21 965	21 709	21 333
Wholesale trade	4 198.3	4 122.2	4 070.7	4 072.2	4 196.4	4 360.8	4 423.2	4 523.2	4 605.0	4 673.1	4 686.4	4 555.1	4 465.0
Retail trade	11 308.4	11 007.9	10 931.4	11 104.0	11 502.1	11 841.0	12 056.7	12 273.6	12 439.8	12 771.5	13 039.8	12 952.3	12 791.4
Transportation and warehousing	2 940.8	2 928.4	2 934.3	3 019.4	3 152.8	3 260.2	3 339.3	3 406.8	3 521.6	3 641.9	3 753.2	3 718.2	3 595.7
Utilities	584.9	581.5	569.5	556.5	540.9	521.8	505.5	493.8	492.2	489.2	485.1	482.8	481.3
Information	1 866	1 871	1 871	1 896	1 928	2 007	2 096	2 181	2 217	2 351	2 502	2 530	2 416
Financial activities	4 973	4 911	4 908	5 057	5 183	5 165	5 279	5 415	5 605	5 728	5 737	5 810	5 866
Professional and business services	8 889	8 748	8 971	9 451	10 078	10 645	11 161	11 896	12 566	13 184	13 790	13 588	13 075
Education and health services	9 748	10 212	10 555	10 908	11 338	11 765	12 123	12 478	12 791	13 089	13 362	13 846	14 297
Leisure and hospitality	8 299	8 247	8 406	8 667	8 979	9 330	9 565	9 780	9 947	10 216	10 516	10 662	10 561
Other services	3 555	3 539	3 526	3 623	3 689	3 812	3 907	4 013	4 124	4 219	4 296	4 373	4 429

Table 16-3. Average Weekly Hours of Production or Nonsupervisory Workers on Private Nonfarm Payrolls by NAICS Industry

Industry	1990	1991	1992	1993	1994	1995	1996	1997	1998	1999	2000	2001	2002
Total private	34.3	34.1	34.2	34.3	34.5	34.3	34.3	34.5	34.5	34.3	34.3	34.0	33.9
Goods–producing	40.1	40.1	40.2	40.6	41.1	40.8	40.8	41.1	40.8	40.8	40.7	39.9	39.9
Natural resources and mining	45.0	45.3	44.6	44.9	45.3	45.3	46.0	46.2	44.9	44.2	44.4	44.6	43.2
Construction	38.3	38.1	38.0	38.4	38.8	38.8	38.9	38.9	38.8	39.0	39.2	38.7	38.4
Manufacturing	40.5	40.4	40.7	41.1	41.7	41.3	41.3	41.7	41.4	41.4	41.3	40.3	40.5
Durable goods	41.1	40.9	41.3	41.9	42.6	42.1	42.1	42.6	42.1	41.9	41.8	40.6	40.8
Wood products	40.4	40.2	40.9	41.2	41.7	41.0	41.2	41.4	41.4	41.3	41.0	40.2	39.9
Nonmetallic mineral products	40.9	40.5	41.0	41.5	42.2	41.8	42.0	41.9	42.2	42.1	41.6	41.6	42.0
Primary metals	42.0	41.5	42.4	43.1	44.1	43.4	43.6	44.3	43.5	43.8	44.2	42.4	42.4
Fabricated metal products	41.0	40.8	41.2	41.6	42.3	41.9	41.9	42.3	41.9	41.7	41.9	40.6	40.6
Machinery	42.1	41.9	42.4	43.2	43.9	43.5	43.3	44.0	43.1	42.3	42.3	40.9	40.5
Computer and electronic products	41.3	40.9	41.4	41.8	42.2	42.2	41.9	42.5	41.8	41.5	41.4	39.8	39.7
Electrical equipment and appliances	41.2	41.5	41.8	42.4	43.0	41.9	42.1	42.1	41.8	41.8	41.6	39.8	40.1
Transportation equipment	42.0	41.9	41.9	43.0	44.3	43.7	43.8	44.2	43.2	43.6	43.3	41.9	42.5
Furniture and related products	38.0	37.8	38.7	39.0	39.3	38.5	38.3	39.1	39.4	39.3	39.2	38.3	39.2
Miscellaneous manufacturing	39.0	39.1	39.3	39.2	39.4	39.2	39.1	39.7	39.2	39.3	39.0	38.8	38.6
Nondurable goods	39.6	39.7	40.0	40.1	40.5	40.1	40.1	40.5	40.5	40.4	40.3	39.9	40.1
Food manufacturing	39.3	39.2	39.2	39.3	39.8	39.6	39.5	39.8	40.1	40.2	40.1	39.6	39.6
Beverages and tobacco products	38.9	38.8	38.7	38.3	39.3	39.3	39.7	40.0	40.3	41.0	42.0	40.9	39.4
Textile mills	40.2	40.7	41.3	41.6	41.9	40.9	40.8	41.6	41.0	41.0	41.4	40.0	40.7
Textile products mills	39.0	39.1	39.2	39.8	39.9	39.1	39.2	39.6	39.5	39.4	39.0	38.6	39.2
Apparel	34.8	35.4	35.6	35.5	35.7	35.3	35.2	35.5	35.5	35.4	35.7	36.0	36.7
Leather and allied products	37.4	37.6	37.9	38.4	38.2	37.7	37.8	38.2	37.4	37.2	37.5	36.4	37.5
Paper and paper products	43.6	43.6	43.8	43.8	44.2	43.4	43.5	43.9	43.6	43.6	42.8	42.1	41.9
Printing and related support activities	38.7	38.6	39.0	39.2	39.6	39.1	39.1	39.5	39.3	39.1	39.2	38.7	38.4
Petroleum and coal products	44.4	43.9	43.6	44.0	44.3	43.7	43.7	43.1	43.6	42.6	42.7	43.8	43.0
Chemicals	42.8	43.1	43.3	43.2	43.4	43.3	43.3	43.4	43.2	42.7	42.2	41.9	42.3
Plastics and rubber products	40.6	40.5	41.2	41.4	41.8	41.1	41.0	41.4	41.3	41.3	40.8	40.0	40.6
Private service–providing	32.5	32.4	32.5	32.5	32.7	32.6	32.6	32.8	32.8	32.7	32.7	32.5	32.5
Trade, transportation, and utilities	33.7	33.7	33.8	34.1	34.3	34.1	34.1	34.3	34.2	33.9	33.8	33.5	33.6
Wholesale Trade	38.4	38.4	38.6	38.5	38.8	38.6	38.6	38.8	38.6	38.6	38.8	38.4	38.0
Retail Trade	30.6	30.4	30.7	30.7	30.9	30.8	30.7	30.9	30.9	30.8	30.7	30.7	30.9
Transportation and warehousing	37.7	37.4	37.4	38.9	39.5	38.9	39.1	39.4	38.7	37.6	37.4	36.7	36.8
Utilities	41.5	41.5	41.7	42.1	42.3	42.3	42.0	42.0	42.0	42.0	42.0	41.4	40.9
Information	35.8	35.6	35.8	36.0	36.0	36.0	36.4	36.3	36.6	36.7	36.8	36.9	36.5
Financial activities	35.5	35.5	35.6	35.5	35.5	35.5	35.5	35.7	36.0	35.8	35.9	35.8	35.6
Professional and business services	34.2	34.0	34.0	34.0	34.1	34.0	34.1	34.3	34.3	34.4	34.5	34.2	34.2
Education and health services	31.9	31.9	32.0	32.0	32.0	32.0	31.9	32.2	32.2	32.1	32.2	32.3	32.4
Leisure and hospitality	26.0	25.6	25.7	25.9	26.0	25.9	25.9	26.0	26.2	26.1	26.1	25.8	25.8
Other services	32.8	32.7	32.6	32.6	32.7	32.6	32.5	32.7	32.6	32.5	32.5	32.3	32.0

Table 16-4. Average Hourly Earnings of Production or Nonsupervisory Workers on Private Nonfarm Payrolls by NAICS Industry

(Dollars.)

Industry	1990	1991	1992	1993	1994	1995	1996	1997	1998	1999	2000	2001	2002
Total private	10.19	10.50	10.76	11.03	11.32	11.64	12.03	12.49	13.00	13.47	14.00	14.53	14.95
Goods–producing	11.46	11.76	11.99	12.28	12.63	12.96	13.38	13.82	14.23	14.71	15.27	15.78	16.33
Natural resources and mining	13.40	13.82	14.09	14.12	14.41	14.78	15.10	15.57	16.20	16.33	16.55	17.00	17.22
Construction	13.42	13.65	13.81	14.04	14.38	14.73	15.11	15.67	16.23	16.80	17.48	18.00	18.51
Manufacturing	10.78	11.13	11.40	11.70	12.04	12.34	12.75	13.14	13.45	13.85	14.32	14.76	15.29
Durable goods	11.40	11.81	12.09	12.41	12.78	13.05	13.45	13.83	14.07	14.46	14.93	15.38	16.01
Wood products	8.82	9.03	9.24	9.41	9.66	9.92	10.24	10.53	10.85	11.18	11.63	11.99	12.33
Nonmetallic mineral products	11.11	11.34	11.57	11.83	12.11	12.39	12.80	13.17	13.59	13.97	14.53	14.86	15.39
Primary metals	12.97	13.37	13.72	14.08	14.47	14.75	15.12	15.40	15.66	16.00	16.64	17.06	17.68
Fabricated metal products	10.64	10.97	11.16	11.40	11.64	11.91	12.26	12.64	12.97	13.34	13.77	14.19	14.68
Machinery	11.73	12.12	12.40	12.73	12.94	13.14	13.49	13.94	14.24	14.77	15.22	15.49	15.93
Computer and electronic products	10.89	11.35	11.64	11.95	12.19	12.29	12.75	13.24	13.85	14.37	14.73	15.42	16.19
Electrical equipment and appliances	10.00	10.30	10.50	10.65	10.94	11.25	11.80	12.24	12.51	12.90	13.23	13.78	13.97
Transportation equipment	14.44	15.12	15.59	16.22	16.94	17.21	17.67	18.00	17.92	18.24	18.89	19.48	20.64
Furniture and related products	8.52	8.74	9.00	9.24	9.51	9.75	10.08	10.50	10.88	11.27	11.72	12.14	12.62
Miscellaneous manufacturing	8.87	9.16	9.44	9.65	9.90	10.23	10.60	10.89	11.18	11.56	11.93	12.46	12.91
Nondurable goods	9.87	10.18	10.45	10.70	10.96	11.30	11.68	12.04	12.45	12.85	13.31	13.75	14.15
Food manufacturing	9.04	9.32	9.59	9.82	10.00	10.27	10.50	10.77	11.09	11.40	11.77	12.18	12.54
Beverages and tobacco products	13.24	13.65	14.07	14.30	14.97	15.40	15.73	16.00	16.03	16.54	17.40	17.67	17.68
Textile mills	8.17	8.49	8.82	9.12	9.35	9.63	9.88	10.22	10.58	10.90	11.23	11.40	11.73
Textile products mills	7.53	7.77	8.03	8.27	8.45	8.76	9.12	9.45	9.75	10.18	10.43	10.60	10.96
Apparel	6.22	6.43	6.60	6.74	6.95	7.22	7.45	7.76	8.05	8.35	8.60	8.82	9.10
Leather and allied products	7.18	7.43	7.68	7.88	8.23	8.50	8.94	9.31	9.68	9.93	10.35	10.69	11.01
Paper and paper products	12.06	12.45	12.78	13.13	13.49	13.94	14.38	14.76	15.20	15.58	15.91	16.38	16.89
Printing and related support activities	11.11	11.32	11.53	11.67	11.89	12.08	12.41	12.78	13.20	13.67	14.09	14.48	14.93
Petroleum and coal products	17.00	17.90	18.83	19.43	19.96	20.24	20.18	21.10	21.75	22.22	22.80	22.90	23.06
Chemicals	12.85	13.30	13.70	13.97	14.33	14.86	15.37	15.78	16.23	16.40	17.09	17.57	17.97
Plastics and rubber products	9.76	10.07	10.35	10.55	10.66	10.86	11.17	11.48	11.79	12.25	12.69	13.21	13.55
Private service–providing	9.71	10.05	10.33	10.60	10.87	11.19	11.57	12.05	12.59	13.07	13.60	14.16	14.56
Trade, transportation, and utilities	9.83	10.08	10.30	10.55	10.80	11.10	11.46	11.90	12.39	12.82	13.31	13.70	14.02
Wholesale trade	11.58	11.95	12.21	12.57	12.93	13.34	13.80	14.41	15.07	15.62	16.28	16.77	16.97
Retail trade	7.71	7.89	8.12	8.36	8.61	8.85	9.21	9.59	10.05	10.45	10.86	11.29	11.67
Transportation and warehousing	12.50	12.61	12.77	12.71	12.84	13.18	13.45	13.78	14.12	14.55	15.05	15.33	15.77
Utilities	16.14	16.70	17.17	17.95	18.66	19.19	19.78	20.59	21.48	22.03	22.75	23.58	23.94
Information	13.40	13.90	14.29	14.86	15.32	15.68	16.30	17.14	17.67	18.40	19.07	19.80	20.23
Financial activities	9.99	10.42	10.86	11.36	11.82	12.28	12.71	13.22	13.93	14.47	14.98	15.59	16.17
Professional and business services	11.14	11.50	11.78	11.96	12.15	12.53	13.00	13.57	14.27	14.85	15.52	16.33	16.81
Education and health services	10.00	10.49	10.87	11.21	11.50	11.80	12.17	12.56	13.00	13.44	13.95	14.64	15.22
Leisure and hospitality	5.88	6.06	6.20	6.32	6.46	6.62	6.82	7.13	7.48	7.76	8.11	8.35	8.57
Other services	9.08	9.39	9.66	9.90	10.18	10.51	10.85	11.29	11.79	12.26	12.73	13.27	13.72

Table 16-5. Average Weekly Earnings of Production or Nonsupervisory Workers on Private Nonfarm Payrolls

(Dollars.)

Industry	1990	1991	1992	1993	1994	1995	1996	1997	1998	1999	2000	2001	2002
Total private	349.29	358.06	367.83	378.40	390.73	399.53	412.74	431.25	448.04	462.49	480.41	493.20	506.22
Goods–producing	459.55	471.32	482.58	498.82	519.58	528.62	546.48	568.43	580.99	599.99	621.86	630.04	651.60
Natural resources and mining	602.54	625.42	629.02	634.77	653.14	670.32	695.07	720.11	727.28	721.74	734.92	757.92	743.11
Construction	513.43	520.41	525.13	539.81	558.53	571.57	588.48	609.48	629.75	655.11	685.78	695.89	711.61
Manufacturing	436.16	449.73	464.43	480.80	502.12	509.26	526.55	548.22	557.12	573.17	590.65	595.19	618.87
Durable goods	468.43	483.28	499.59	519.92	544.66	549.49	566.53	589.10	591.68	606.67	624.38	624.54	652.83
Wood products	356.38	362.69	377.76	387.38	402.86	406.51	422.32	435.78	449.78	461.61	477.23	481.36	491.98
Nonmetallic mineral products	453.98	459.20	474.55	490.54	510.92	517.68	537.81	552.02	572.96	587.53	604.88	618.79	646.74
Primary metals	545.22	555.37	581.34	606.37	637.69	639.70	658.68	681.47	681.64	700.76	734.62	723.95	749.08
Fabricated metal products	436.12	447.98	459.64	474.21	492.07	498.48	513.57	534.48	543.20	555.86	576.68	576.60	596.44
Machinery	493.39	507.96	525.53	549.98	568.12	571.25	584.69	613.49	613.87	625.40	643.92	632.77	645.81
Computer and electronic products	450.09	464.25	482.09	499.15	514.92	518.25	534.42	562.69	579.70	596.25	609.70	613.07	642.86
Electrical equipment and appliances	412.42	426.96	439.04	451.28	470.21	471.63	496.69	515.73	522.51	538.98	550.56	548.00	560.09
Transportation equipment	606.87	633.87	652.95	697.16	750.67	751.74	773.95	795.82	774.82	796.25	817.98	817.08	877.84
Furniture and related products	324.08	330.49	348.03	360.63	373.87	375.06	385.68	410.38	428.50	443.38	459.69	464.57	494.14
Miscellaneous manufacturing	346.02	358.56	370.75	378.28	389.79	400.85	414.13	431.89	437.99	454.56	465.02	483.44	499.09
Nondurable goods	390.65	404.17	417.95	429.15	443.82	452.83	467.88	487.04	503.99	519.91	536.82	548.41	567.11
Food manufacturing	355.61	364.90	375.69	386.04	398.54	406.66	414.74	428.58	444.81	458.63	472.09	481.67	496.78
Beverages and tobacco products	515.73	530.09	544.25	547.60	588.39	605.00	624.82	639.69	646.26	679.06	730.35	721.68	697.09
Textile mills	328.11	345.48	364.45	379.74	391.64	394.17	403.08	425.53	434.15	447.38	464.51	456.64	476.70
Textile products mills	293.77	303.81	314.47	329.26	336.96	342.17	356.90	373.95	385.13	401.01	406.24	408.56	429.49
Apparel	216.10	227.76	235.20	239.45	248.33	254.85	261.90	275.61	286.07	295.20	307.00	317.15	333.77
Leather and allied products	268.32	279.41	291.11	302.85	314.18	319.98	337.86	355.63	361.87	369.80	388.46	388.83	413.05
Paper and paper products	525.71	542.26	560.27	575.49	596.19	604.74	625.38	647.55	662.20	679.24	681.34	690.06	707.36
Printing and related support activities	429.93	437.00	450.02	457.91	470.74	472.37	484.99	504.46	518.32	534.15	552.15	560.89	573.42
Petroleum and coal products	754.13	786.05	821.72	855.36	883.81	883.68	881.24	908.50	949.28	947.60	973.53	1 003.34	992.05
Chemicals	550.25	573.27	593.17	603.71	622.46	644.30	666.00	685.26	700.53	700.45	721.90	735.54	759.57
Plastics and rubber products	396.07	408.22	426.56	436.96	445.87	445.91	458.15	474.87	487.00	505.31	517.74	528.69	549.57
Private service–providing	315.49	325.31	335.46	345.03	354.97	364.14	376.72	394.77	412.78	427.30	445.00	460.32	473.10
Trade, transportation, and utilities	331.55	339.19	348.68	359.33	370.38	378.79	390.64	407.57	423.30	434.31	449.88	459.53	471.09
Wholesale trade	444.48	459.27	470.51	484.46	501.17	515.14	533.29	559.39	582.21	602.77	631.40	643.45	643.99
Retail trade	235.62	240.15	249.63	256.89	265.77	272.56	282.76	295.97	310.34	321.63	333.38	346.16	360.53
Transportation and warehousing	471.72	471.12	478.02	494.36	507.27	513.37	525.60	542.55	546.86	547.97	562.31	562.70	580.68
Utilities	670.40	693.40	716.36	756.35	789.98	811.52	830.74	865.26	902.94	924.59	955.66	977.18	978.44
Information	479.50	495.20	512.01	535.25	551.28	564.98	592.68	622.40	646.52	675.32	700.89	731.11	739.41
Financial activities	354.65	369.57	386.01	403.02	419.20	436.12	451.49	472.37	500.95	517.57	537.37	558.02	575.43
Professional and business services	380.61	391.09	400.64	406.20	414.16	426.44	442.81	465.51	490.00	510.99	535.07	557.84	574.59
Education and health services	319.27	334.55	348.29	359.08	368.14	377.73	388.27	404.65	418.82	431.35	449.29	473.39	493.02
Leisure and hospitality	152.47	155.16	159.54	163.45	168.00	171.43	176.48	185.81	195.82	202.87	211.79	215.19	221.15
Other services	297.91	306.91	315.08	322.69	332.44	342.36	352.62	368.63	384.25	398.77	413.41	428.64	439.65

Table 16-6. Indexes of Aggregate Weekly Hours of Production or Nonsupervisory Workers on Private Nonfarm Payrolls by NAICS Industry

(2002 = 100.)

Industry	1990	1991	1992	1993	1994	1995	1996	1997	1998	1999	2000	2001	2002
Total private	84.4	82.6	83.1	85.4	89.2	91.5	93.7	97.0	99.4	101.4	103.5	102.0	100.0
Goods–producing	105.8	99.9	98.4	100.5	105.3	106.5	107.8	110.9	112.0	112.3	112.8	106.3	100.0
Natural resources and mining	129.0	124.2	113.6	110.6	111.3	110.6	113.1	118.0	113.2	103.3	105.5	108.7	100.0
Construction	78.6	70.0	67.4	71.1	77.1	79.7	84.1	88.3	93.2	99.5	103.8	103.0	100.0
Manufacturing	117.3	112.4	112.0	113.5	118.0	118.6	118.4	121.0	120.6	118.6	117.3	107.7	100.0
Durable goods	113.8	107.2	106.0	107.9	113.8	115.9	117.1	121.2	121.6	120.2	120.0	108.9	100.0
Wood products	101.2	92.3	94.9	100.1	108.8	108.9	111.3	114.4	117.1	118.2	115.4	104.7	100.0
Nonmetallic mineral products	100.2	92.3	92.1	93.7	98.2	99.1	100.9	102.6	105.3	106.3	108.5	105.5	100.0
Primary metals	131.1	122.5	120.4	121.1	127.6	128.8	129.4	131.9	130.6	128.0	128.5	112.6	100.0
Fabricated metal products	104.7	99.1	97.3	99.7	106.3	110.9	111.6	116.6	118.6	116.7	119.2	109.3	100.0
Machinery	123.1	115.6	113.2	117.9	126.2	131.5	133.0	138.1	136.6	129.1	126.8	113.4	100.0
Computer and electronic products	135.7	126.8	121.6	119.8	122.3	125.8	128.6	135.4	135.3	129.7	131.7	116.7	100.0
Electrical equipment and appliances	135.4	127.4	125.3	126.2	131.8	129.7	128.8	127.1	127.2	127.7	127.2	112.9	100.0
Transportation equipment	111.1	105.7	104.3	105.4	112.5	115.4	116.4	120.7	118.7	119.5	116.3	105.2	100.0
Furniture and related products	97.1	89.4	92.0	95.2	100.4	99.2	98.2	102.9	108.4	112.5	114.7	104.7	100.0
Miscellaneous manufacturing	103.5	103.3	104.7	106.4	107.7	107.2	107.1	109.5	109.8	109.7	108.9	104.2	100.0
Nondurable goods	122.6	120.4	121.4	122.3	124.4	122.8	120.2	120.6	119.1	115.8	113.0	105.7	100.0
Food manufacturing	96.2	96.6	97.3	98.7	100.5	101.6	101.8	102.6	103.4	103.8	103.5	101.5	100.0
Beverages and tobacco products	97.8	97.3	96.3	96.4	99.6	98.7	102.3	104.0	105.9	105.6	105.2	101.2	100.0
Textile mills	169.1	167.1	169.0	169.5	170.3	162.2	152.9	154.0	147.8	138.0	131.4	111.3	100.0
Textile products mills	109.3	103.6	105.1	109.6	115.5	113.4	111.8	113.8	113.1	112.5	110.2	104.1	100.0
Apparel	269.1	265.9	269.2	261.1	254.2	236.9	213.3	202.7	182.3	155.6	138.3	117.8	100.0
Leather and allied products	292.1	270.9	265.5	261.0	240.7	223.4	199.0	188.5	167.8	149.4	139.4	114.1	100.0
Paper and paper products	121.1	119.9	121.0	121.2	122.7	120.7	119.4	120.8	118.8	116.4	112.8	106.0	100.0
Printing and related support activities	121.7	118.1	117.8	119.7	123.2	123.3	122.2	124.0	123.7	120.3	118.8	111.0	100.0
Petroleum and coal products	127.8	126.4	124.9	121.0	119.0	114.5	112.5	111.7	112.4	106.6	104.8	104.7	100.0
Chemicals	118.0	114.9	112.8	113.3	115.0	115.3	114.6	114.5	115.2	113.0	110.3	104.6	100.0
Plastics and rubber products	97.1	93.6	97.4	101.7	108.1	109.2	109.3	112.0	113.0	113.9	113.6	104.3	100.0
Private service–providing	78.3	77.8	78.8	81.2	84.7	87.3	89.7	93.1	95.8	98.4	101.0	100.9	100.0
Trade, transportation, and utilities	89.6	87.5	87.4	89.1	92.7	95.1	96.6	98.9	100.3	101.9	103.6	101.6	100.0
Wholesale trade	95.1	93.5	92.6	92.6	95.9	99.4	100.9	103.6	105.0	106.4	107.3	103.1	100.0
Retail trade	87.5	84.8	85.0	86.3	89.8	92.3	93.7	95.8	97.2	99.5	101.3	100.5	100.0
Transportation and warehousing	83.8	82.7	83.0	88.7	94.1	95.9	98.6	101.3	103.0	103.6	106.0	103.1	100.0
Utilities	123.5	122.7	120.8	119.2	116.4	112.2	107.9	105.5	105.2	104.4	103.6	101.7	100.0
Information	75.6	75.5	75.9	77.4	78.6	81.9	86.3	89.7	91.9	97.7	104.1	105.8	100.0
Financial activities	84.6	83.4	83.6	85.9	88.1	87.8	89.8	92.7	96.6	98.1	98.6	99.6	100.0
Professional and business services	68.0	66.6	68.3	71.8	76.9	81.1	85.1	91.3	96.6	101.5	106.4	103.9	100.0
Education and health services	67.2	70.3	73.0	75.4	78.4	81.3	83.5	86.8	89.0	90.7	92.9	96.7	100.0
Leisure and hospitality	79.0	77.4	79.3	82.2	85.7	88.6	90.9	93.5	95.6	98.0	100.7	100.8	100.0
Other services	82.2	81.5	81.0	83.2	84.9	87.5	89.5	92.4	94.8	96.7	98.3	99.5	100.0

Table 16-7. Indexes of Aggregate Weekly Payrolls of Production or Nonsupervisory Workers on Private Nonfarm Payrolls by NAICS Industry

(2002 = 100.)

Industry	1990	1991	1992	1993	1994	1995	1996	1997	1998	1999	2000	2001	2002
Total private	57.5	58.0	59.8	63.1	67.6	71.3	75.4	81.1	86.4	91.4	97.0	99.2	100.0
Goods–producing	74.3	71.9	72.3	75.6	81.4	84.6	88.3	93.9	97.7	101.2	105.5	102.7	100.0
Natural resources and mining	100.4	99.6	93.0	90.7	93.1	94.9	99.1	106.7	106.4	97.9	101.4	107.3	100.0
Construction	57.0	51.6	50.2	53.9	59.9	63.4	68.7	74.8	81.7	90.2	98.0	100.1	100.0
Manufacturing	82.7	81.9	83.5	86.8	92.9	95.8	98.7	104.0	106.1	107.4	109.8	104.0	100.0
Durable goods	81.0	79.1	80.1	83.6	90.8	94.5	98.4	104.7	106.8	108.5	111.8	104.6	100.0
Nondurable goods	85.5	86.6	89.6	92.5	96.3	98.0	99.2	102.6	104.8	105.2	106.3	102.7	100.0
Private service–providing	52.2	53.7	55.9	59.1	63.2	67.1	71.3	77.0	82.8	88.3	94.3	98.0	100.0
Trade, transportation, and utilities	62.8	62.9	64.2	67.0	71.5	75.3	79.0	83.9	88.7	93.2	98.3	99.3	100.0
Wholesale trade	64.9	65.8	66.6	68.6	73.1	78.1	82.0	88.0	93.2	98.0	102.9	101.9	100.0
Retail trade	57.8	57.3	59.2	61.9	66.3	70.0	73.9	78.8	83.7	89.1	94.3	97.2	100.0
Transportation and warehousing	66.4	66.1	67.2	71.5	76.6	80.2	84.1	88.5	92.2	95.6	101.1	100.2	100.0
Utilities	83.3	85.6	86.6	89.4	90.7	89.9	89.2	90.7	94.4	96.0	98.4	100.2	100.0
Information	50.1	51.9	53.6	56.8	59.5	63.5	69.5	76.0	80.2	88.9	98.2	103.6	100.0
Financial activities	52.2	53.8	56.1	60.4	64.4	66.7	70.6	75.8	83.2	87.8	91.3	96.0	100.0
Professional and business services	45.0	45.5	47.8	51.1	55.6	60.4	65.8	73.7	82.0	89.7	98.2	100.9	100.0
Education and health services	44.2	48.5	52.2	55.6	59.2	63.0	66.8	71.6	76.0	80.1	85.2	93.0	100.0
Leisure and hospitality	54.2	54.8	57.4	60.7	64.6	68.5	72.3	77.8	83.4	88.7	95.4	98.2	100.0
Other services	54.4	55.8	57.1	60.0	63.0	67.0	70.7	76.0	81.4	86.4	91.2	96.3	100.0

NOTES AND DEFINITIONS

TABLES 16-1 THROUGH 16-7
EMPLOYMENT, HOURS, AND EARNINGS BY NAICS INDUSTRY

See the Notes and Definitions to Tables 10-5 through 10-10 for definitions of employment, production or nonsupervisory workers, average weekly hours, average hourly earnings, average weekly earnings, and the indexes of aggregate weekly hours.

Indexes of aggregate weekly payrolls for private nonfarm production or nonsupervisory workers are calculated at the basic industry level as the product of average hourly earnings and aggregate weekly hours. At higher levels, payroll aggregates are the sum of the component aggregates. Index levels are calculated by dividing the current month's aggregate by the average of the 12 monthly figures for 2002.

See Chapter 14 for information on the NAICS.

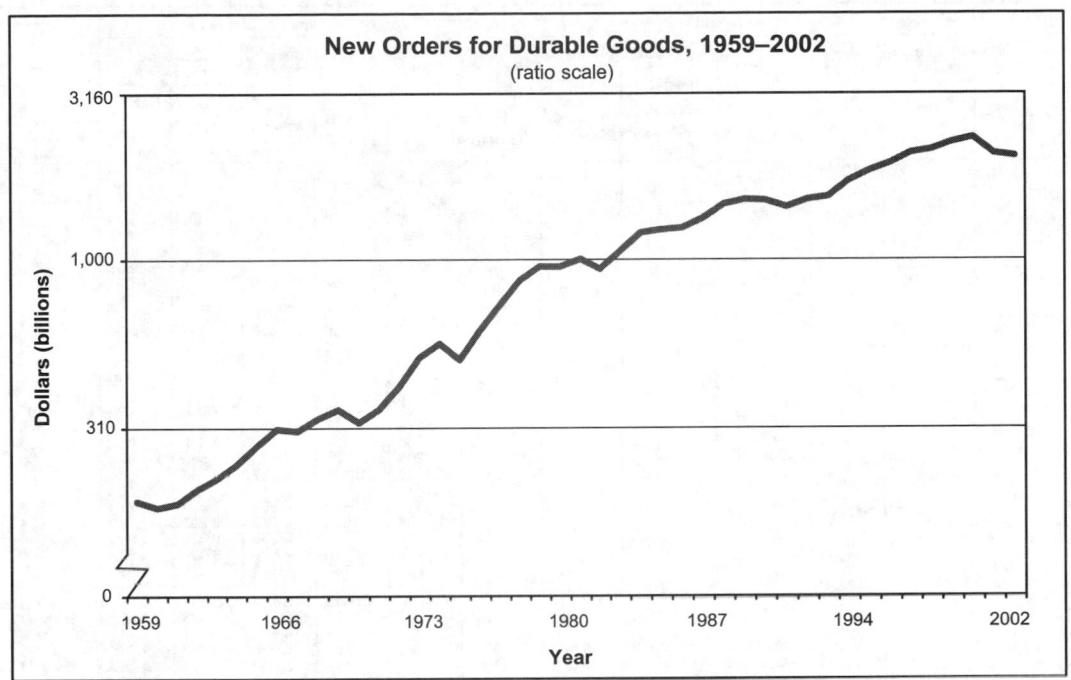

New Orders for Durable Goods, 1959–2002
(ratio scale)

- The value of new orders for durable goods at U.S. manufacturing firms is a sensitive indicator of the business cycle, shown in the graph above. From 2000 to 2002, the annual average of new orders dropped 12.3 percent, exceeding the severe decline from 1974 to 1975. (Table 17-6)

- The value of durable manufacturers' inventories dropped 7.7 percent from the end of 2000 to the end of 2002. By stage of processing, the greatest percentage declines were in holdings of materials and supplies and work in process; finished goods stocks were down a relatively mild 4.9 percent. (Table 17-5)

- Between the end of 2000 and the end of 2002, order backlogs for nondefense capital goods declined 19.9 percent, but defense order backlogs rose 7.5 percent. (Table 17-7)

- As a percentage of the total supply of petroleum and products (domestic production plus net imports), net imports rose from 5.5 percent in 1949 to 58.0 percent in 2002. (Table 17-1)

- From 2000 to 2002, the value of construction put in place declined in a few sectors related to capital spending—office, commercial, and manufacturing—but the construction sector as a whole continued to increase because of increases in residential and government spending. (Tables 17-2 and 17-3)

- The latest recession saw a very modest 3 percent decline in unit sales of cars and light trucks. Previous recessions in vehicle sales were far more severe: 31 percent from 1978 to 1982, and 20 percent from 1988 to 1991. (Table 17-8)

- Sales by electronic shopping and mail-order grew from 1.9 percent of total retail sales in 1992 to 3.6 percent in 2000, leveling off at that rate in 2001 and 2002. (Table 17-9) E-commerce sales have been reported separately only since late 1999. Between the fourth quarter of 1999 and the fourth quarter of 2002, E-commerce grew from 0.7 percent of total retail sales to 1.6 percent. (See Notes and Definitions.)

- E-commerce is still a small fraction of total revenues for surveyed service industries as a whole. The exceptions are the travel and reservation business, online information services, and couriers and messengers. Growth in services revenues slowed in 2001 and so did the growth of the E-commerce share. (Tables 17-14 and 17-15)

Table 17-1. Petroleum and Petroleum Products—Imports, Domestic Production, and Stocks

(Not seasonally adjusted.)

	Imports						Supply (thousands of barrels per day)					Stocks (end of period, millions of barrels)		
	Total energy-related petroleum products		Crude petroleum				Petroleum and products			Domestic production		Crude oil and petroleum products	Crude petroleum	
Year and month	Quantity (thousands of barrels)	Value (millions of dollars)	Quantity (thousands of barrels)		Value (millions of dollars)	Unit price (dollars per barrel)	Exports	Imports	Net imports	Crude oil	Natural gas plant liquids		Total	Strategic petroleum reserve
			Total	Average per day										
1949	...	...	...	...	...	...	327	645	318	5 046	430	603	253	0
1950	...	...	...	...	...	...	305	850	545	5 407	499	583	248	0
1951	...	...	...	...	...	...	422	844	422	6 158	561	634	256	0
1952	...	...	...	...	...	...	432	952	520	6 256	611	674	272	0
1953	...	...	...	...	...	...	402	1 034	633	6 458	654	726	274	0
1954	...	...	...	...	...	...	355	1 052	696	6 342	691	715	258	0
1955	...	...	...	...	...	...	368	1 248	880	6 807	771	715	266	0
1956	...	...	...	...	...	...	430	1 436	1 006	7 151	800	780	266	0
1957	...	...	...	...	...	...	568	1 574	1 007	7 170	808	841	282	0
1958	...	...	...	...	...	...	276	1 700	1 425	6 710	808	789	263	0
1959	...	...	...	...	...	...	211	1 780	1 569	7 054	879	809	257	0
1960	...	...	...	...	...	...	202	1 815	1 613	7 035	929	785	240	0
1961	...	...	...	...	...	...	174	1 917	1 743	7 183	991	825	245	0
1962	...	...	...	...	...	...	168	2 082	1 913	7 332	1 021	834	252	0
1963	...	...	...	...	...	...	208	2 123	1 915	7 542	1 098	836	237	0
1964	...	...	...	...	...	...	202	2 259	2 057	7 614	1 154	839	230	0
1965	...	...	...	...	...	...	187	2 468	2 281	7 804	1 210	836	220	0
1966	...	...	...	...	...	...	198	2 573	2 375	8 295	1 284	874	238	0
1967	...	...	...	...	...	...	307	2 537	2 230	8 810	1 409	944	249	0
1968	...	...	...	...	...	...	231	2 840	2 609	9 096	1 504	1 000	272	0
1969	...	...	...	...	...	...	233	3 166	2 933	9 238	1 590	980	265	0
1970	...	...	...	...	...	...	259	3 419	3 161	9 637	1 660	1 018	276	0
1971	...	...	...	...	...	...	224	3 926	3 701	9 463	1 693	1 044	260	0
1972	...	...	...	...	...	...	222	4 741	4 519	9 441	1 744	959	246	0
1973	...	...	1 392 970	3 816	4 593	3.30	231	6 256	6 025	9 208	1 738	1 008	242	0
1974	...	...	1 367 081	3 745	15 269	11.17	221	6 112	5 892	8 774	1 688	1 074	265	0
1975	...	...	1 584 730	4 342	18 374	11.59	209	6 056	5 846	8 375	1 633	1 133	271	0
1976	...	...	2 050 480	5 618	25 480	12.43	223	7 313	7 090	8 132	1 604	1 112	285	0
1977	...	...	2 519 806	6 904	33 583	13.33	243	8 807	8 565	8 245	1 618	1 312	348	7
1978	...	...	2 392 350	6 554	32 140	13.43	362	8 363	8 002	8 707	1 567	1 278	376	67
1979	...	...	2 467 315	6 760	46 100	18.68	471	8 456	7 985	8 552	1 584	1 341	430	91
1980	...	...	1 977 247	5 417	62 014	31.36	544	6 909	6 365	8 597	1 573	1 392	466	108
1981	...	...	1 763 072	4 830	61 940	35.13	595	5 996	5 401	8 572	1 609	1 484	594	230
1982	...	...	1 420 753	3 892	47 445	33.39	815	5 113	4 298	8 649	1 550	1 430	644	294
1983	...	...	1 293 819	3 545	38 184	29.51	739	5 051	4 312	8 688	1 559	1 454	723	379
1984	...	...	1 319 683	3 616	36 529	27.68	722	5 437	4 715	8 879	1 630	1 556	796	451
1985	...	...	1 260 856	3 454	33 034	26.20	781	5 067	4 286	8 971	1 609	1 519	814	493
1986	...	...	1 634 567	4 478	22 720	13.90	785	6 224	5 439	8 680	1 551	1 593	843	512
1987	...	...	1 744 977	4 781	29 321	16.80	764	6 678	5 914	8 349	1 595	1 607	890	541
1988	...	...	1 887 860	5 172	25 844	13.69	815	7 402	6 587	8 140	1 625	1 597	890	560
1989	...	...	2 146 552	5 881	35 400	16.49	859	8 061	7 202	7 613	1 546	1 581	921	580
1990	...	...	2 216 604	6 073	43 785	19.75	857	8 018	7 161	7 355	1 559	1 621	908	586
1991	2 828 953	50 646	2 146 064	5 880	37 463	17.46	1 001	7 627	6 626	7 417	1 659	1 617	893	569
1992	2 947 582	50 537	2 294 570	6 269	38 553	16.80	950	7 888	6 938	7 171	1 697	1 592	893	575
1993	3 257 008	50 210	2 543 374	6 968	38 469	15.13	1 003	8 620	7 618	6 847	1 736	1 647	922	587
1994	3 416 045	49 533	2 704 196	7 409	38 479	14.23	942	8 996	8 054	6 662	1 727	1 653	929	592
1995	3 361 882	53 835	2 767 312	7 582	43 750	15.81	949	8 835	7 886	6 560	1 762	1 563	895	592
1996	3 622 385	70 199	2 893 647	7 906	54 931	18.98	981	9 478	8 498	6 465	1 830	1 507	850	566
1997	3 802 574	69 288	3 069 430	8 409	54 226	17.67	1 003	10 162	9 158	6 452	1 817	1 560	868	563
1998	4 088 027	49 132	3 242 711	8 884	37 252	11.49	945	10 708	9 764	6 252	1 759	1 647	895	571
1999	4 081 181	65 931	3 228 092	8 844	50 890	15.76	940	10 852	9 912	5 881	1 850	1 493	852	567
2000	4 314 825	117 057	3 399 239	9 288	89 876	26.44	1 040	11 459	10 419	5 822	1 911	1 468	826	541
2001	4 475 026	100 792	3 471 067	9 510	74 293	21.40	971	11 871	10 900	5 801	1 868	1 586	862	550
2002	4 337 075	100 526	3 418 021	9 364	77 283	22.59	984	11 530	10 546	5 746	1 880	1 548	877	599
2001														
January	407 653	10 329	284 112	9 165	6 588	23.19	954	12 555	11 601	5 799	1 398	1 479	836	542
February	343 372	8 706	247 331	8 833	5 898	23.85	1 004	11 643	10 639	5 780	1 732	1 473	824	542
March	381 192	9 085	298 120	9 617	6 781	22.75	938	12 132	11 194	5 880	1 833	1 484	851	542
April	396 417	9 252	306 008	10 200	6 627	21.66	942	12 653	11 711	5 863	1 831	1 522	873	542
May	393 691	9 565	306 813	9 897	6 948	22.65	1 069	12 529	11 461	5 829	1 912	1 555	872	543
June	371 745	8 918	288 550	9 618	6 663	23.09	976	11 732	10 756	5 766	1 908	1 563	852	543
July	370 199	8 438	301 636	9 730	6 735	22.33	879	11 760	10 881	5 749	1 899	1 568	857	544
August	371 249	8 510	293 215	9 459	6 492	22.14	1 048	11 622	10 573	5 725	1 955	1 548	852	544
September	344 231	8 200	270 713	9 024	6 232	23.02	825	11 818	10 993	5 709	2 034	1 579	854	545
October	385 580	7 827	311 803	10 058	6 197	19.88	946	11 379	10 432	5 746	2 025	1 577	858	545
November	356 776	6 279	281 316	9 377	4 781	17.00	960	11 628	10 669	5 881	2 001	1 588	860	547
December	352 921	5 685	281 450	9 079	4 350	15.46	1 109	10 994	9 885	5 887	1 889	1 586	862	550
2002														
January	369 816	6 220	295 494	9 532	4 813	16.29	861	11 088	10 228	5 848	1 827	1 591	875	555
February	310 404	5 321	246 411	8 800	4 086	16.58	1 175	10 904	9 729	5 871	1 900	1 576	887	560
March	335 337	6 755	267 037	8 614	5 145	19.27	853	11 198	10 345	5 883	1 901	1 573	895	561
April	377 653	8 748	296 134	9 871	6 671	22.53	890	11 765	10 876	5 859	1 925	1 588	891	567
May	379 179	9 181	296 505	9 565	7 041	23.75	910	11 769	10 859	5 924	1 936	1 611	898	571
June	347 732	8 267	270 677	9 023	6 321	23.35	880	11 753	10 873	5 915	1 870	1 616	894	576
July	366 643	8 880	290 855	9 382	6 903	23.73	839	11 624	10 785	5 770	1 846	1 611	883	579
August	375 036	9 380	296 068	9 551	7 276	24.58	1 138	11 890	10 752	5 811	1 937	1 596	878	582
September	343 765	8 932	272 653	9 088	6 951	25.49	1 015	11 075	10 059	5 411	1 898	1 574	858	587
October	389 617	10 472	315 720	10 185	8 288	26.25	962	11 893	10 931	5 363	1 875	1 573	881	590
November	370 416	9 171	286 298	9 543	6 927	24.19	1 026	12 268	11 242	5 597	1 891	1 578	884	596
December	371 477	9 198	284 170	9 167	6 862	24.15	1 272	11 100	9 828	5 699	1 760	1 548	877	599

. . . = Not available.

Table 17-2. New Construction Put in Place

(Billions of dollars, monthly data are at seasonally adjusted annual rates.)

| Year and month | Total | Private | | | | | | | | | | | |
| | | Total[1] | Residential | Office | Commercial | | Health care | Educational | Amuse-ment and recreation | Transpor-tation | Communi-cation | Power | Manu-facturing |
					Total[1]	Multi-retail							
1964	75.1	54.9	30.5	...	...	...	...	...	...	...	...	...	...
1965	81.9	60.0	30.2	...	...	...	...	...	...	...	...	...	...
1966	85.8	61.9	28.6	...	...	...	...	...	...	...	...	...	...
1967	87.2	61.8	28.7	...	...	...	...	...	...	...	...	...	...
1968	96.8	69.4	34.2	...	...	...	...	...	...	...	...	...	...
1969	104.9	77.2	37.2	...	...	...	...	...	...	...	...	...	...
1970	105.9	78.0	35.9	...	...	...	...	...	...	...	...	...	...
1971	122.4	92.7	48.5	...	...	...	...	...	...	...	...	...	...
1972	139.1	109.1	60.7	...	...	...	...	...	...	...	...	...	...
1973	153.8	121.4	65.1	...	...	...	...	...	...	...	...	...	...
1974	155.2	117.0	56.0	...	...	...	...	...	...	...	...	...	...
1975	152.6	109.3	51.6	...	...	...	...	...	...	...	...	...	...
1976	172.1	128.2	68.3	...	...	...	...	...	...	...	...	...	...
1977	200.5	157.4	92.0	...	...	...	...	...	...	...	...	...	...
1978	239.9	189.7	109.8	...	...	...	...	...	...	...	...	...	...
1979	272.9	216.2	116.4	...	...	...	...	...	...	...	...	...	...
1980	273.9	210.3	100.4	...	...	...	...	...	...	...	...	...	...
1981	289.1	224.4	99.2	...	...	...	...	...	...	...	...	...	...
1982	279.3	216.3	84.7	...	...	...	...	...	...	...	...	...	...
1983	311.9	248.4	125.8	...	...	...	...	...	...	...	...	...	...
1984	370.2	300.0	155.0	...	...	...	...	...	...	...	...	...	...
1985	403.4	325.6	160.5	...	...	...	...	...	...	...	...	...	...
1986	433.5	348.9	190.7	...	...	...	...	...	...	...	...	...	...
1987	446.6	356.0	199.7	...	...	...	...	...	...	...	...	...	...
1988	462.0	367.3	204.5	...	...	...	...	...	...	...	...	...	...
1989	477.5	379.3	204.3	...	...	...	...	...	...	...	...	...	...
1990	476.8	369.3	191.1	...	...	...	...	...	...	...	...	...	...
1991	432.6	322.5	166.3	...	...	...	...	...	...	...	...	...	...
1992	463.7	347.8	199.4	...	...	...	...	...	...	...	...	...	...
1993	491.0	375.1	225.1	20.0	34.4	11.5	14.9	4.8	4.6	4.7	9.8	23.6	23.4
1994	539.2	419.0	258.6	20.4	39.6	12.2	15.4	5.0	5.1	4.7	10.1	21.0	28.8
1995	557.8	427.9	247.4	23.0	44.1	12.0	15.3	5.7	5.9	4.8	11.1	22.0	35.4
1996	615.9	476.6	281.1	26.5	49.4	13.3	15.4	7.0	7.0	5.8	11.8	17.4	38.1
1997	653.4	502.7	289.0	32.8	53.1	12.2	17.4	8.8	8.5	6.2	12.5	16.4	37.6
1998	705.7	551.4	314.6	40.4	55.7	13.3	17.7	9.8	8.6	7.3	12.5	21.1	40.5
1999	766.1	596.3	350.6	45.1	59.4	15.2	18.4	9.8	9.6	0.5	18.4	21.1	32.6
2000	828.8	642.6	374.5	52.4	64.1	5.1	19.5	11.7	8.8	6.9	18.8	28.0	31.8
2001	852.6	652.5	388.2	49.7	63.6	5.1	19.5	12.8	7.8	7.1	19.6	30.0	29.5
2002	860.9	650.5	421.5	35.1	58.2	6.0	22.2	13.0	7.4	7.0	18.1	31.8	16.6
2000													
January	813.3	627.8	383.9	42.6	61.2	14.3	18.4	10.4	9.2	4.9	19.4	23.9	29.0
February	821.5	645.2	383.7	47.6	65.1	16.2	17.8	10.9	9.5	7.2	16.8	29.4	31.5
March	838.1	649.5	387.3	49.3	63.2	14.9	18.2	11.3	9.8	7.2	18.1	26.8	31.1
April	829.2	641.6	382.3	50.7	62.1	13.9	18.8	10.8	9.2	7.0	17.1	25.8	31.6
May	830.6	647.7	378.4	52.6	62.8	14.2	19.2	12.2	9.3	7.3	18.0	27.0	34.3
June	821.8	640.2	375.9	51.9	63.4	14.3	19.7	11.5	8.8	7.1	18.9	23.2	32.6
July	813.1	632.8	366.1	52.1	63.2	14.4	19.7	12.0	8.7	7.0	17.7	28.0	31.6
August	832.8	643.0	367.5	54.8	66.3	15.1	20.0	12.6	9.0	6.9	17.5	29.7	32.1
September	840.4	648.3	367.5	56.3	66.2	15.0	20.0	12.0	8.5	7.0	22.2	30.6	31.5
October	842.7	650.9	373.0	54.9	66.3	15.7	20.8	12.2	7.9	7.0	17.9	31.5	32.5
November	838.0	648.6	369.4	56.6	64.1	15.2	20.6	12.2	8.0	6.9	19.9	32.4	32.6
December	831.4	642.8	369.6	58.2	64.0	15.9	20.0	11.8	7.4	7.0	22.2	26.9	30.9
2001													
January	836.0	644.1	372.2	57.6	63.3	16.3	20.3	12.3	7.3	7.2	20.9	22.8	35.4
February	835.6	642.4	378.5	55.2	63.8	16.8	19.6	12.0	7.4	7.2	20.6	21.0	32.5
March	848.3	647.1	377.0	56.5	63.9	16.3	20.5	12.2	7.8	7.4	18.1	25.2	33.8
April	855.8	650.7	380.3	54.3	65.5	17.3	19.6	12.1	7.7	7.5	20.7	26.2	32.5
May	862.5	655.6	383.8	51.4	64.3	16.7	20.0	12.1	7.9	7.5	22.8	30.5	30.7
June	867.1	661.3	387.9	53.9	64.0	16.5	19.4	12.7	8.4	7.3	19.4	31.9	31.0
July	865.2	662.4	394.9	50.8	65.3	16.6	19.2	12.6	7.8	7.1	19.0	29.1	30.7
August	855.0	657.0	394.7	46.8	63.6	15.9	18.8	13.0	7.8	7.1	20.0	30.6	29.4
September	848.0	654.4	396.1	44.3	63.0	16.5	19.0	13.6	7.7	6.5	19.6	30.9	29.1
October	850.5	650.7	392.9	44.9	62.9	15.8	19.6	14.0	8.1	6.5	18.3	33.7	25.9
November	846.8	647.4	397.9	42.3	62.7	15.9	18.8	13.9	8.2	6.4	18.4	33.0	22.5
December	854.3	652.5	397.9	40.0	62.3	16.1	19.5	14.0	7.8	7.0	17.9	41.3	22.6
2002													
January	863.7	653.0	399.2	39.7	63.4	17.4	20.1	13.6	7.8	6.8	19.5	40.2	21.4
February	868.7	654.6	409.5	37.9	60.6	16.0	20.0	13.6	7.8	6.9	20.8	37.4	19.8
March	858.1	655.1	411.7	36.3	62.3	15.9	20.2	13.6	7.4	7.2	18.2	39.6	18.5
April	863.6	657.8	415.4	37.5	61.4	17.0	20.9	14.1	7.6	7.2	18.4	35.8	17.9
May	861.5	650.1	417.3	35.8	58.8	15.2	21.8	13.7	7.5	7.2	18.4	31.0	17.7
June	855.0	646.9	420.1	34.3	57.7	15.0	23.1	12.4	7.7	7.0	19.2	28.8	17.0
July	858.7	648.2	423.9	34.7	55.4	13.9	22.6	12.3	7.4	6.9	18.6	31.5	16.1
August	848.6	638.1	423.6	33.9	56.6	14.8	22.4	12.3	7.5	7.3	17.4	23.5	15.1
September	854.9	641.5	425.7	33.6	57.8	15.9	22.7	12.5	7.1	7.0	16.4	26.0	14.2
October	861.9	651.1	429.9	33.5	57.4	15.2	23.8	13.0	7.6	7.0	17.4	28.3	14.6
November	870.0	656.4	434.4	33.2	56.9	15.7	24.6	13.3	6.9	6.9	16.5	30.7	14.6
December	872.1	658.2	441.5	32.1	52.3	14.0	23.3	12.7	6.6	6.7	16.8	34.3	13.9

[1]Includes categories not shown separately.
. . . = Not available.

Table 17-2. New Construction Put in Place—Continued

(Billions of dollars, monthly data are at seasonally adjusted annual rates.)

Year and month	Total	Public													Federal
		State and local													
		Total[1]	Residential	Office	Health care	Educa-tional	Public safety	Amuse-ment and recreation	Transpor-tation	Power	Highway and street	Sewage and waste disposal	Water supply	
1964	20.2	16.5	...	...	...	...	...	...	...	...	...	...	...	3.7
1965	21.9	18.0	...	...	...	...	...	...	...	...	...	...	...	3.9
1966	23.8	20.0	...	...	...	...	...	...	...	...	...	...	...	3.8
1967	25.4	22.1	...	...	...	...	...	...	...	...	...	...	...	3.3
1968	27.4	24.2	...	...	...	...	...	...	...	...	...	...	...	3.2
1969	27.8	24.6	...	...	...	...	...	...	...	...	...	...	...	3.2
1970	27.9	24.8	...	...	...	...	...	...	...	...	...	...	...	3.1
1971	29.7	25.9	...	...	...	...	...	...	...	...	...	...	...	3.8
1972	30.0	25.8	...	...	...	...	...	...	...	...	...	...	...	4.2
1973	32.3	27.6	...	...	...	...	...	...	...	...	...	...	...	4.7
1974	38.1	33.0	...	...	...	...	...	...	...	...	...	...	...	5.1
1975	43.3	37.2	...	...	...	...	...	...	...	...	...	...	...	6.1
1976	44.0	37.2	...	...	...	...	...	...	...	...	...	...	...	6.8
1977	43.1	36.0	...	...	...	...	...	...	...	...	...	...	...	7.1
1978	50.1	42.0	...	...	...	...	...	...	...	...	...	...	...	8.1
1979	56.6	48.1	...	...	...	...	...	...	...	...	...	...	...	8.6
1980	63.6	54.0	...	...	...	...	...	...	...	...	...	...	...	9.6
1981	64.7	54.3	...	...	...	...	...	...	...	...	...	...	...	10.4
1982	63.1	53.1	...	...	...	...	...	...	...	...	...	...	...	10.0
1983	63.5	52.9	...	...	...	...	...	...	...	...	...	...	...	10.6
1984	70.2	59.0	...	...	...	...	...	...	...	...	...	...	...	11.2
1985	77.8	65.8	...	...	...	...	...	...	...	...	...	...	...	12.0
1986	84.6	72.2	...	...	...	...	...	...	...	...	...	...	...	12.4
1987	90.6	76.6	...	...	...	...	...	...	...	...	...	...	...	14.1
1988	94.7	82.5	...	...	...	...	...	...	...	...	...	...	...	12.3
1989	98.2	86.0	...	...	...	...	...	...	...	...	...	...	...	12.2
1990	107.5	95.4	...	...	...	...	...	...	...	...	...	...	...	12.1
1991	110.1	97.3	...	...	...	...	...	...	...	...	...	...	...	12.8
1992	115.8	101.5	...	...	...	...	...	...	...	...	...	...	...	14.4
1993	116.0	101.5	3.7	3.2	2.7	19.2	5.2	4.9	8.8	3.2	34.4	8.9	5.1	14.4
1994	120.2	105.8	3.4	3.6	2.9	20.5	5.4	5.6	8.6	2.8	37.3	8.7	4.7	14.4
1995	129.9	114.2	4.0	3.9	3.2	25.7	5.9	6.1	9.0	2.9	37.6	8.4	4.7	15.8
1996	139.3	123.9	4.2	4.4	3.4	28.6	6.7	6.1	10.0	2.5	39.5	9.8	5.6	15.3
1997	150.7	136.6	4.3	4.6	3.5	33.8	6.7	6.9	9.7	3.1	43.0	10.5	6.5	14.1
1998	154.3	140.0	4.3	4.6	2.9	35.0	7.6	7.7	10.2	2.5	44.8	9.9	6.7	14.3
1999	169.7	155.7	4.6	4.5	3.2	41.1	7.9	9.2	11.3	3.2	49.2	10.5	7.0	14.0
2000	186.1	172.0	4.2	6.3	4.0	45.7	8.2	10.6	14.3	3.9	53.1	10.3	7.0	14.2
2001	200.1	185.0	4.6	6.8	3.6	50.0	7.4	11.2	15.2	4.1	59.0	10.3	8.4	15.1
2002	210.4	194.1	4.6	7.4	4.1	56.1	6.9	10.7	16.0	4.0	59.9	11.1	8.5	16.3
2000														
January	185.5	171.9	4.2	6.0	3.4	44.2	7.7	9.7	12.5	2.3	61.4	10.5	7.1	13.5
February	176.3	161.9	4.1	6.6	3.4	45.2	7.7	9.9	13.5	3.5	47.2	10.7	7.2	14.4
March	188.6	173.6	4.5	5.9	3.7	45.6	7.8	10.2	13.6	5.2	57.4	10.5	6.8	15.0
April	187.6	173.6	4.4	6.2	3.8	44.0	8.2	10.3	13.8	3.9	56.6	12.1	7.0	14.1
May	182.9	169.4	4.1	6.2	4.5	45.3	8.2	10.9	13.8	3.3	51.0	10.5	7.3	13.5
June	181.6	167.1	4.3	6.3	4.1	46.1	8.4	10.5	13.8	3.1	47.9	11.0	6.8	14.5
July	180.3	167.2	4.1	5.9	4.3	44.6	8.5	10.2	14.1	3.5	51.6	9.7	6.3	13.1
August	189.7	175.0	4.3	6.5	4.3	45.9	8.6	10.8	14.6	3.7	55.1	9.9	7.2	14.7
September	192.1	178.1	4.1	6.7	4.3	46.5	8.7	10.7	14.2	4.6	56.2	9.8	7.1	14.0
October	191.8	176.9	4.4	6.8	4.1	46.3	8.5	11.3	16.5	4.4	52.2	9.9	7.3	14.9
November	189.4	175.1	4.4	6.5	4.1	46.2	8.0	12.3	15.1	5.0	51.8	9.7	7.2	14.3
December	188.6	174.4	4.0	6.0	3.5	49.3	7.9	11.0	15.6	3.8	52.4	9.8	6.9	14.2
2001														
January	192.0	176.3	4.6	6.7	3.9	46.3	7.9	11.5	15.4	4.7	53.6	10.2	7.0	15.6
February	193.2	178.0	4.6	6.7	3.7	45.5	7.7	11.7	15.3	4.1	55.8	10.7	7.4	15.3
March	201.1	186.1	4.4	7.3	3.4	47.2	7.7	11.3	15.9	4.5	61.5	10.1	8.1	15.0
April	205.1	190.1	4.7	7.2	3.6	48.8	8.4	11.7	15.9	3.3	62.0	10.9	8.6	15.1
May	206.9	191.6	4.7	7.5	3.6	49.0	7.8	11.9	16.6	3.8	63.5	10.4	8.3	15.2
June	205.8	190.5	4.7	7.3	3.5	48.0	7.2	11.8	15.6	3.8	64.5	10.4	9.1	15.2
July	202.8	188.3	4.3	6.8	3.5	51.7	7.2	10.7	14.5	4.7	61.6	9.8	9.0	14.5
August	198.0	182.9	4.4	6.4	3.7	52.1	6.9	10.5	14.2	4.8	56.9	10.3	8.5	15.1
September	193.6	178.2	4.4	6.5	3.4	51.7	7.0	10.1	14.5	4.4	53.2	10.1	8.8	15.4
October	199.9	184.2	4.4	6.4	3.6	53.3	7.1	11.5	14.3	3.5	57.1	10.3	8.1	15.7
November	199.5	185.3	4.7	6.3	3.6	52.5	7.2	10.7	15.1	3.6	58.3	10.8	8.5	14.1
December	201.9	186.8	4.9	6.5	3.8	52.4	7.0	10.7	15.4	4.0	58.7	10.5	8.4	15.0
2002														
January	210.7	195.6	4.8	7.1	4.0	53.4	7.5	10.8	15.2	3.2	65.2	11.3	8.1	15.1
February	214.2	197.4	4.9	7.0	3.6	54.5	7.3	10.9	15.6	3.4	65.5	11.9	8.3	16.7
March	203.0	186.9	4.6	7.1	3.8	53.1	6.8	11.2	16.5	3.1	57.1	11.1	8.2	16.1
April	205.7	189.6	4.7	7.3	4.0	56.4	6.8	10.5	15.4	4.4	55.7	11.1	8.5	16.1
May	211.5	195.0	4.5	7.4	3.9	57.7	6.7	10.6	16.4	4.2	58.7	11.3	9.1	16.5
June	208.1	192.0	4.7	7.6	4.0	55.7	7.1	10.3	16.1	3.7	58.7	10.9	8.8	16.1
July	210.5	194.0	5.0	7.7	4.2	56.6	6.7	10.5	16.2	3.4	60.2	10.8	8.1	16.5
August	210.5	194.0	4.7	7.7	4.2	56.5	7.0	10.6	16.2	3.5	59.5	11.0	8.4	16.4
September	213.3	197.3	4.6	7.3	4.5	57.1	6.9	11.5	15.9	3.8	61.3	11.1	8.8	16.0
October	210.8	193.8	4.2	7.7	4.3	57.3	6.7	10.9	16.0	4.6	57.5	10.8	8.8	17.0
November	213.6	197.0	4.3	7.6	4.4	57.4	6.8	10.3	16.8	5.9	59.1	10.8	8.6	16.6
December	213.8	197.2	4.2	8.0	4.7	56.5	6.8	10.7	15.8	4.5	62.2	10.9	8.7	16.7

[1]Includes categories not shown separately.
. . . = Not available.

Table 17-3. Housing Starts and Building Permits; Home Sales and Prices

Year and month	Housing starts and building permits									Manufacturers' shipments of manufactured homes (thousands)		New home sales and prices		
	New private housing units (thousands)											Seasonally adjusted		Median sales price (dollars)
	Started (not seasonally adjusted)			Seasonally adjusted annual rate								Sold (thousands, annual rate)	For sale, end-of-period (thousands)	
				Started			Authorized by building permits[2]			Not seasonally adjusted	Seasonally adjusted annual rate			
	Total[1]	One-family structures	5 units or more	Total[1]	One-family structures	5 units or more	Total[1]	One-family structures	5 units or more					
1959	1 517	1 234	...	1 517	1 234	...	1 208	938	193	121	121	...	...	...
1960	1 252	995	...	1 252	995	...	998	746	187	104	104	...	...	...
1961	1 313	974	...	1 313	974	...	1 064	723	274	90	90	...	...	...
1962	1 463	991	...	1 463	991	...	1 187	716	383	118	118	...	...	...
1963	1 603	1 012	...	1 603	1 012	...	1 335	750	466	151	151	560	264	18 000
1964	1 529	970	450	1 529	970	450	1 286	720	465	191	191	565	250	18 900
1965	1 473	964	422	1 473	964	422	1 241	710	446	217	217	575	226	20 000
1966	1 165	779	325	1 165	779	325	972	563	348	217	217	461	194	21 400
1967	1 292	844	376	1 292	844	376	1 141	651	418	240	240	487	187	22 700
1968	1 508	899	527	1 508	899	527	1 353	695	574	318	318	490	213	24 700
1969	1 467	811	571	1 467	811	571	1 322	625	612	413	413	448	222	25 600
1970	1 434	813	536	1 434	813	536	1 352	647	617	401	401	485	220	23 400
1971	2 052	1 151	781	2 052	1 151	781	1 925	906	886	492	492	656	287	25 200
1972	2 357	1 309	906	2 357	1 309	906	2 219	1 033	1 037	576	576	718	409	27 600
1973	2 045	1 132	795	2 045	1 132	795	1 820	882	820	567	567	634	418	32 500
1974	1 338	888	382	1 338	888	382	1 074	644	366	329	329	519	346	35 900
1975	1 160	892	204	1 160	892	204	939	676	200	213	213	549	313	39 300
1976	1 538	1 162	289	1 538	1 162	289	1 296	894	310	246	246	646	353	44 200
1977	1 987	1 451	414	1 987	1 451	414	1 690	1 126	443	277	277	819	402	48 800
1978	2 020	1 433	462	2 020	1 433	462	1 800	1 183	487	276	276	817	414	55 700
1979	1 745	1 194	429	1 745	1 194	429	1 552	982	445	277	277	709	397	62 900
1980	1 292	852	330	1 292	852	330	1 191	710	366	222	222	545	337	64 600
1981	1 084	705	288	1 084	705	288	986	564	319	241	241	436	275	68 900
1982	1 062	663	320	1 062	663	320	1 000	546	366	240	240	412	253	69 300
1983	1 703	1 068	522	1 703	1 068	522	1 605	902	570	296	296	623	301	75 300
1984	1 750	1 084	544	1 750	1 084	544	1 682	922	617	296	296	639	353	79 900
1985	1 742	1 072	576	1 742	1 072	576	1 733	957	657	284	284	688	346	84 300
1986	1 805	1 179	542	1 805	1 179	542	1 769	1 078	584	244	244	750	357	92 000
1987	1 620	1 146	409	1 620	1 146	409	1 535	1 024	421	233	233	671	366	104 500
1988	1 488	1 081	348	1 488	1 081	348	1 456	994	386	218	218	676	368	112 500
1989	1 376	1 003	318	1 376	1 003	318	1 338	932	340	198	198	650	365	120 000
1990	1 193	895	260	1 193	895	260	1 111	794	263	188	188	534	321	122 900
1991	1 014	840	138	1 014	840	138	949	754	152	171	171	509	284	120 000
1992	1 200	1 030	139	1 200	1 030	139	1 095	911	138	210	210	610	265	121 500
1993	1 288	1 126	133	1 288	1 126	133	1 199	986	160	254	254	666	293	126 500
1994	1 457	1 198	224	1 457	1 198	224	1 372	1 068	241	304	304	670	336	130 000
1995	1 354	1 076	244	1 354	1 076	244	1 332	997	272	340	340	667	370	133 900
1996	1 477	1 161	271	1 477	1 161	271	1 426	1 070	290	363	362	757	322	140 000
1997	1 474	1 134	296	1 474	1 134	296	1 441	1 062	310	354	354	804	281	146 000
1998	1 617	1 271	303	1 617	1 271	303	1 612	1 188	356	373	373	886	294	152 500
1999	1 641	1 302	307	1 641	1 302	307	1 664	1 247	351	348	348	880	308	161 000
2000	1 569	1 231	299	1 569	1 231	299	1 592	1 198	329	250	250	877	298	169 000
2001	1 603	1 273	293	1 603	1 273	293	1 637	1 236	335	193	193	908	308	175 200
2002	1 705	1 359	308	1 705	1 359	308	1 748	1 333	341	168	168	973	339	187 500
2001														
January	106	84	20	1 600	1 275	286	1 699	1 251	387	13	167	936	296	171 300
February	108	86	21	1 625	1 280	319	1 656	1 242	345	13	180	963	296	160 100
March	133	104	26	1 590	1 218	329	1 659	1 232	358	16	182	939	292	166 300
April	151	122	25	1 649	1 311	295	1 666	1 259	342	16	188	909	294	175 200
May	154	126	26	1 605	1 285	292	1 665	1 240	356	18	191	885	295	175 300
June	155	126	25	1 636	1 295	287	1 626	1 252	293	18	200	882	301	179 400
July	155	120	30	1 670	1 298	331	1 598	1 235	301	15	196	880	305	175 000
August	142	115	24	1 567	1 286	255	1 615	1 241	309	20	199	866	308	173 700
September	133	105	24	1 562	1 243	273	1 565	1 192	319	17	203	853	310	166 400
October	140	110	26	1 540	1 240	266	1 566	1 185	321	20	202	871	308	171 300
November	121	91	27	1 602	1 244	320	1 651	1 229	360	16	199	924	308	168 100
December	105	84	20	1 568	1 285	266	1 680	1 251	356	13	199	979	308	180 200
2002														
January	110	85	21	1 681	1 307	306	1 679	1 294	313	14	194	876	310	187 100
February	120	99	18	1 817	1 491	282	1 773	1 391	316	13	186	949	313	191 100
March	138	110	25	1 651	1 284	319	1 681	1 281	329	14	171	917	316	183 400
April	149	122	24	1 587	1 275	285	1 662	1 279	313	15	176	916	324	187 100
May	166	134	28	1 752	1 389	326	1 721	1 286	366	16	173	981	328	181 000
June	160	130	26	1 709	1 359	303	1 746	1 309	355	15	171	959	328	190 600
July	156	125	28	1 666	1 329	306	1 742	1 312	360	14	169	961	331	175 500
August	147	111	33	1 630	1 249	350	1 704	1 319	312	16	166	1 025	332	178 900
September	156	124	28	1 810	1 449	324	1 803	1 372	340	14	162	1 057	333	177 500
October	147	119	25	1 653	1 366	254	1 813	1 390	352	16	156	1 005	336	189 200
November	133	103	28	1 760	1 403	323	1 764	1 377	317	12	150	1 022	338	181 200
December	123	97	23	1 815	1 462	318	1 907	1 420	410	9	144	1 052	339	197 600

[1]Includes structures with 2 to 4 units, not shown separately.
[2]Data beginning with 1994 cover 19,000 permit issuing places; 1984–1993: 17,000 places; 1978–1983: 16,000 places; 1972–1977: 14,000 places; 1971: 13,000 places.
... = Not available.

Table 17-4. Manufacturers' Shipments

(Millions of dollars, adjusted for trading-day and calendar-month variation, but without seasonal adjustment.)

Classification basis, year and month	Total	NAICS durable goods industries										
		Total¹	Nonmetallic mineral products	Primary metals		Fabricated metal products	Machinery	Computers and electronic products	Electrical equipment, appliances and components	Transportation equipment	
				Total	Iron and steel mills					Total	Motor vehicles and parts
SIC Basis²											
1958	326 971	162 632	9 543	26 541	15 533	21 359		41 129		39 223	20 411
1959	363 437	187 168	11 052	31 381	18 251	23 723		47 386		45 502	26 239
1960	370 535	190 440	10 879	31 307	18 140	23 947		48 426		47 631	29 263
1961	371 067	187 217	10 782	30 610	17 196	23 701		49 376		44 221	25 222
1962	400 294	206 958	11 298	32 543	18 073	26 162		53 993		52 146	31 979
1963	420 690	219 058	12 000	34 398	18 954	26 847		56 450		56 379	35 328
1964	447 968	235 327	12 652	38 876	21 625	28 866		62 425		58 151	36 557
1965	491 938	266 318	13 652	43 975	23 965	32 378		71 268		68 213	45 162
1966	538 436	295 405	14 301	47 943	24 551	36 775		83 483		72 500	45 058
1967	557 836	302 795	14 116	45 139	23 123	40 054		86 946		72 535	40 337
1968	602 744	331 490	15 465	48 717	24 908	43 638		90 742		83 527	49 465
1969	642 013	352 836	16 499	53 534	26 412	46 104		98 144		85 175	50 943
1970	633 663	337 876	16 454	51 995	25 189	44 210		98 301		74 539	42 538
1971	670 877	359 089	18 220	51 585	25 791	45 478		98 822		88 857	58 247
1972	756 321	407 844	20 875	58 490	28 712	51 487		113 658		94 706	63 923
1973	875 173	475 621	23 141	72 791	36 301	58 804		132 776		110 587	74 799
1974	1 017 477	530 074	25 503	95 686	49 718	67 212		151 725		108 244	68 631
1975	1 039 065	523 178	26 233	80 890	42 281	68 411		152 422		113 503	70 033
1976	1 185 563	607 475	29 618	93 082	46 764	77 560		170 998		141 028	95 380
1977	1 358 416	710 017	34 209	103 267	50 670	89 938		200 594		166 954	117 747
1978	1 522 858	812 776	40 238	118 175	59 228	101 245		232 598		188 773	131 999
1979	1 727 234	911 124	44 287	137 488	67 414	113 494		269 375		201 623	131 378
1980	1 852 689	929 027	44 473	134 057	61 612	116 071		293 428		186 516	104 560
1981	2 017 544	1 004 725	46 220	142 072	70 254	123 535		323 186		205 223	116 981
1982	1 960 214	950 541	43 515	104 874	46 928	119 236		312 501		201 347	112 270
1983	2 070 564	1 025 770	47 697	109 240	46 398	123 083		314 584		245 392	148 296
1984	2 288 184	1 175 276	53 101	120 315	51 978	138 107		373 437		284 593	181 993
1985	2 334 456	1 215 352	55 821	112 265	48 904	143 268		382 359		307 380	193 445
1986	2 335 881	1 238 859	59 254	107 865	45 718	143 063		378 385		322 688	198 811
1987	2 475 906	1 297 532	61 477	120 248	51 815	147 367		388 958		332 936	205 923
1988	2 695 432	1 421 501	63 145	149 837	64 294	159 505		431 666		354 849	222 353
1989	2 840 375	1 477 900	63 729	155 718	64 783	164 073		450 810		369 675	233 232
1990	2 912 228	1 485 313	63 728	148 787	62 826	165 064		455 265		370 328	217 295
1991	2 878 167	1 451 998	59 957	136 378	57 267	159 760		446 786		367 235	209 210
1992	3 004 727	1 541 866	62 521	138 287	58 449	166 532		475 426		399 270	238 384
NAICS Basis											
1992	2 904 024	1 518 862	61 902	123 789	55 947	170 403	186 589	273 728	81 813	433 611	279 197
1993	3 020 497	1 604 544	64 957	126 988	59 632	177 967	201 076	286 457	87 646	453 437	310 178
1994	3 238 112	1 764 061	70 598	142 976	67 087	194 113	224 920	320 769	95 531	494 745	364 840
1995	3 479 677	1 902 815	74 865	160 774	72 019	212 444	246 277	370 679	101 051	508 271	379 551
1996	3 597 188	1 978 597	81 308	157 638	71 814	222 995	257 459	399 516	105 283	516 030	387 394
1997	3 834 699	2 147 384	86 465	168 118	76 900	242 812	270 687	439 380	112 116	575 307	421 573
1998	3 899 813	2 231 588	92 501	166 109	75 871	253 720	280 651	443 768	116 024	612 882	439 590
1999	4 031 887	2 326 736	96 153	156 648	70 087	257 071	276 904	467 059	118 313	676 328	498 716
2000	4 208 584	2 373 688	97 329	156 598	70 470	268 213	291 548	510 639	125 443	639 861	471 180
2001	3 970 499	2 174 406	94 861	138 246	60 559	253 113	266 554	429 471	114 068	602 495	427 175
2002	3 891 753	2 131 404	88 222	135 930	61 999	252 232	255 651	392 026	103 673	624 129	450 136
2001											
January	305 679	163 326	6 851	11 516	5 004	19 657	20 946	34 204	8 764	40 785	30 476
February	333 248	183 561	7 349	12 095	5 265	21 220	23 093	37 895	10 122	49 244	35 588
March	363 113	206 744	7 770	12 481	5 478	22 264	26 289	46 439	11 120	56 707	40 610
April	325 171	175 745	7 958	11 735	5 096	20 908	22 936	32 608	9 527	47 520	35 357
May	345 873	189 442	8 575	12 438	5 497	22 183	23 618	33 349	10 052	55 510	40 718
June	355 733	201 696	8 553	12 153	5 339	22 165	24 716	41 677	10 862	56 887	39 218
July	298 350	154 278	8 150	10 712	4 754	19 723	19 922	29 523	8 316	35 803	24 015
August	339 998	183 825	8 853	12 066	5 303	22 514	21 757	30 676	9 393	54 156	39 572
September	336 359	185 059	7 993	11 221	4 873	21 128	21 767	38 141	9 745	51 312	34 433
October	332 969	180 359	8 623	11 761	5 199	22 075	21 282	31 440	8 791	52 617	39 270
November	317 986	173 945	7 648	10 709	4 614	20 484	19 662	32 553	8 374	52 141	36 671
December	316 020	176 426	6 538	9 359	4 137	18 792	20 566	40 966	9 002	49 813	31 247
2002											
January	293 487	157 567	7 112	10 711	4 771	19 212	18 194	27 436	7 317	46 965	35 484
February	306 553	169 535	7 132	10 769	4 732	19 971	20 534	29 959	8 174	51 072	36 889
March	336 551	189 501	6 973	11 597	5 139	21 053	23 459	37 547	9 363	56 011	38 421
April	321 818	177 397	7 538	11 877	5 300	21 317	21 810	29 148	8 602	53 887	40 794
May	335 139	185 469	7 796	12 232	5 486	21 977	23 019	30 566	8 960	57 073	42 900
June	341 904	191 627	7 634	11 759	5 401	21 890	23 961	36 830	9 407	55 655	39 317
July	298 864	155 915	7 433	10 793	5 018	20 308	19 715	28 463	7 854	38 539	26 652
August	333 948	182 062	8 066	11 949	5 532	22 421	20 843	30 803	8 573	55 230	41 611
September	343 319	190 546	7 649	11 640	5 457	21 987	22 454	38 158	9 467	55 279	38 900
October	341 009	185 688	7 871	12 137	5 638	22 500	21 121	31 812	8 556	57 338	43 837
November	322 601	174 969	6 888	10 744	4 927	20 457	19 926	33 356	8 623	51 395	36 164
December	316 560	171 128	6 130	9 722	4 598	19 139	20 615	37 948	8 777	45 685	29 167

¹Includes categories not shown separately.
²Data are for roughly similar categories in SIC classification system.

Table 17-4. Manufacturers' Shipments—*Continued*

(Millions of dollars, adjusted for trading-day and calendar-month variation, but without seasonal adjustment.)

Classification basis, year and month	Total [1]	Food products	Beverage and tobacco products [3]	Textiles	Textile products	Apparel	Paper products	Basic chemicals	Petroleum and coal products	Plastics and rubber products
SIC Basis [2]										
1958	164 339	59 738	3 868	12 417		...	12 707	23 093	15 188	7 310
1959	176 269	60 781	4 049	14 067		...	14 077	26 358	15 806	8 395
1960	180 095	62 468	4 367	13 791		...	14 308	26 509	16 349	8 483
1961	183 850	64 542	4 487	14 016		...	14 524	27 175	16 359	8 511
1962	193 336	66 935	4 531	15 185		...	15 382	29 266	16 716	9 335
1963	201 632	68 469	4 521	15 744		...	16 192	31 682	17 506	10 076
1964	212 641	71 594	4 653	17 000		...	17 019	34 148	17 855	10 749
1965	225 620	74 250	4 649	18 299		...	18 394	37 289	18 588	11 966
1966	243 031	79 665	4 772	19 600		...	20 211	40 569	19 857	13 181
1967	255 041	83 961	4 903	19 816		...	20 777	42 037	21 435	13 908
1968	271 254	87 328	4 937	21 970		...	22 093	45 491	22 548	15 585
1969	289 177	93 385	4 992	22 978		...	24 188	48 096	23 721	16 935
1970	295 787	98 535	5 350	22 614		...	24 573	49 195	24 200	16 754
1971	311 788	103 637	5 528	24 034		...	25 182	51 681	26 198	18 409
1972	348 477	115 054	5 919	28 065		...	28 004	58 130	27 918	21 662
1973	399 552	135 585	6 341	31 073		...	32 495	66 003	33 903	25 191
1974	487 403	161 884	7 139	32 790		...	41 514	85 387	57 229	28 828
1975	515 887	172 054	8 058	31 065		...	41 497	91 710	67 496	28 128
1976	578 088	180 830	8 786	36 387		...	47 939	106 467	80 022	32 880
1977	648 399	192 913	9 051	40 550		...	51 881	120 905	94 702	40 944
1978	710 082	215 989	9 951	42 281		...	56 777	132 262	100 967	44 823
1979	816 110	235 976	10 602	45 137		...	64 067	151 887	144 156	48 694
1980	923 662	256 191	12 194	47 256		...	72 553	168 220	192 969	49 157
1981	1 012 819	272 140	13 130	50 260		...	79 970	186 909	217 681	55 178
1982	1 009 673	280 529	16 061	47 516		...	79 698	176 254	203 404	57 307
1983	1 044 794	289 314	16 268	53 733		...	84 817	189 552	187 788	62 870
1984	1 112 908	304 584	17 473	56 336		...	95 525	205 963	184 488	72 938
1985	1 119 104	308 606	18 559	54 605		...	94 679	204 790	176 574	75 590
1986	1 097 022	318 203	19 146	57 188		...	99 865	205 711	122 605	78 379
1987	1 178 374	329 725	20 757	62 787		...	108 989	229 546	130 414	86 634
1988	1 273 931	354 084	23 809	64 627		...	122 882	261 238	131 682	95 485
1989	1 362 475	380 160	25 875	67 265		...	131 896	283 196	146 487	101 236
1990	1 426 915	391 728	29 856	65 533		...	132 424	292 802	173 389	105 250
1991	1 426 169	397 893	31 943	65 440		...	130 131	298 545	159 144	105 804
1992	1 462 861	406 964	35 198	70 753		...	133 201	305 420	150 227	113 593
NAICS Basis										
1992	1 385 162	358 494	85 687	52 923	24 763	61 535	127 122	319 501	150 095	113 827
1993	1 415 953	373 612	79 227	55 375	25 623	63 210	126 982	330 760	144 731	122 807
1994	1 474 051	379 786	83 434	58 607	27 233	64 894	136 922	350 098	143 339	134 288
1995	1 576 862	393 204	88 945	59 885	27 976	65 214	166 051	376 995	151 431	145 084
1996	1 618 591	404 173	94 033	59 796	28 515	64 237	152 860	385 919	174 181	149 773
1997	1 687 315	421 737	96 971	58 707	31 052	68 018	150 296	415 617	177 394	159 161
1998	1 668 225	428 479	102 359	57 416	31 137	64 932	154 984	416 742	137 957	163 736
1999	1 705 151	426 001	106 920	54 306	32 689	62 305	156 915	420 321	162 620	171 885
2000	1 834 896	435 229	111 692	52 112	33 654	60 339	165 298	449 159	235 134	178 236
2001	1 796 093	451 385	118 786	45 681	31 971	54 598	155 845	438 410	219 074	170 717
2002	1 760 349	450 183	109 832	43 170	34 232	53 621	151 530	424 143	206 879	178 383
2001										
January	142 353	34 765	8 532	3 634	2 375	4 234	13 108	35 218	18 573	13 174
February	149 687	36 171	9 199	3 982	2 675	5 101	13 694	37 348	17 973	14 383
March	156 369	38 451	9 799	4 230	2 791	4 952	13 747	40 170	17 508	15 085
April	149 426	36 223	9 287	3 746	2 655	4 470	13 085	37 096	19 522	14 468
May	156 431	37 550	11 089	3 905	2 666	4 167	13 111	38 692	21 177	15 105
June	154 037	38 005	10 525	4 229	2 873	4 394	13 191	37 961	19 097	14 834
July	144 072	35 650	10 145	3 388	2 693	4 432	12 568	34 684	18 170	13 780
August	156 173	38 838	11 221	4 010	2 854	5 053	13 363	36 750	19 696	14 999
September	151 300	39 205	9 633	4 063	2 776	4 746	12 588	35 931	18 923	14 205
October	152 610	39 517	10 620	3 819	2 682	5 024	13 300	35 697	17 460	14 800
November	144 041	39 003	9 317	3 415	2 563	4 345	12 341	34 585	15 673	13 429
December	139 594	38 007	9 419	3 260	2 368	3 680	11 749	34 278	15 302	12 455
2002										
January	135 920	35 962	8 840	3 065	2 255	3 941	12 108	33 366	14 753	13 404
February	137 018	36 727	8 507	3 493	2 739	4 596	11 655	32 811	14 276	13 856
March	147 050	38 627	9 596	3 832	2 915	4 412	12 135	35 930	15 604	14 923
April	144 421	35 993	9 033	3 726	2 970	4 309	12 184	35 580	16 440	15 561
May	149 670	37 379	10 083	3 751	2 949	4 126	12 630	36 496	17 655	15 992
June	150 277	36 902	9 760	3 898	3 147	4 345	12 446	37 908	17 698	15 407
July	142 949	35 194	9 424	3 440	2 840	4 734	12 593	33 238	18 290	14 662
August	151 886	38 096	9 654	3 788	3 091	5 038	13 733	34 560	18 872	15 549
September	152 773	38 286	9 103	3 857	2 987	4 830	13 257	37 149	18 589	15 122
October	155 321	39 765	8 978	3 691	2 928	4 918	13 539	36 471	19 114	15 916
November	147 632	38 935	8 601	3 538	2 833	4 645	12 486	34 931	17 586	14 366
December	145 432	38 317	8 253	3 091	2 578	3 727	12 764	35 703	18 002	13 625

[1]Includes categories not shown separately.
[2]Data are for roughly similar categories in SIC classification system.
[3]SIC tobacco only, 1958–1992.
. . . = Not available.

Table 17-4. Manufacturers' Shipments—*Continued*

(Millions of dollars, seasonally adjusted.)

Classification basis, year and month	Total	NAICS durable goods industries										
		Total¹	Nonmetallic mineral products	Primary metals Total	Primary metals Iron and steel mills	Fabricated metal products	Machinery	Computers and electronic products	Electrical equipment, appliances and components	Transportation equipment Total	Transportation equipment Motor vehicles and parts
SIC Basis [2]											
1958	326 971	162 632	9 543	26 541	15 533	21 359		41 129		39 223	20 411
1959	363 437	187 168	11 052	31 381	18 251	23 723		47 386		45 502	26 239
1960	370 535	190 440	10 879	31 307	18 140	23 947		48 426		47 631	29 263
1961	371 067	187 217	10 782	30 610	17 196	23 701		49 376		44 221	25 222
1962	400 294	206 958	11 298	32 543	18 073	26 162		53 993		52 146	31 979
1963	420 690	219 058	12 000	34 398	18 954	26 847		56 450		56 379	35 328
1964	447 968	235 327	12 652	38 876	21 625	28 866		62 425		58 151	36 557
1965	491 938	266 318	13 652	43 975	23 965	32 378		71 268		68 213	45 162
1966	538 436	295 405	14 301	47 943	24 551	36 775		83 483		72 500	45 058
1967	557 836	302 795	14 116	45 139	23 123	40 054		86 946		72 535	40 337
1968	602 744	331 490	15 465	48 717	24 908	43 638		90 742		83 527	49 465
1969	642 013	352 836	16 499	53 534	26 412	46 104		98 144		85 175	50 943
1970	633 663	337 876	16 454	51 995	25 189	44 210		98 301		74 539	42 538
1971	670 877	359 089	18 220	51 585	25 791	45 478		98 822		88 857	58 247
1972	756 321	407 844	20 875	58 490	28 712	51 487		113 658		94 706	63 923
1973	875 173	475 621	23 141	72 791	36 301	58 804		132 776		110 587	74 799
1974	1 017 477	530 074	25 503	95 686	49 718	67 212		151 725		108 244	68 631
1975	1 039 065	523 178	26 233	80 890	42 281	68 411		152 422		113 503	70 033
1976	1 185 563	607 475	29 618	93 082	46 764	77 560		170 998		141 028	95 380
1977	1 358 416	710 017	34 209	103 267	50 670	89 938		200 594		166 954	117 747
1978	1 522 858	812 776	40 238	118 175	59 228	101 245		232 598		188 773	131 999
1979	1 727 234	911 124	44 287	137 488	67 414	113 494		269 375		201 623	131 378
1980	1 852 689	929 027	44 473	134 057	61 612	116 071		293 428		186 516	104 560
1981	2 017 544	1 004 725	46 220	142 072	70 254	123 535		323 186		205 223	116 981
1982	1 960 214	950 541	43 515	104 874	46 928	119 236		312 501		201 347	112 270
1983	2 070 564	1 025 770	47 697	109 240	46 398	123 083		314 584		245 392	148 296
1984	2 288 184	1 175 276	53 101	120 315	51 978	138 107		373 437		284 593	181 993
1985	2 334 456	1 215 352	55 821	112 265	48 904	143 268		382 359		307 380	193 445
1986	2 335 881	1 238 859	59 254	107 865	45 718	143 063		378 385		322 688	198 811
1987	2 475 906	1 297 532	61 477	120 248	51 815	147 367		388 958		332 936	205 923
1988	2 695 432	1 421 501	63 145	149 837	64 294	159 505		431 666		354 849	222 353
1989	2 840 375	1 477 900	63 729	155 718	64 783	164 073		450 810		369 675	233 232
1990	2 912 228	1 485 313	63 728	148 787	62 826	165 064		455 265		370 328	217 295
1991	2 878 167	1 451 998	59 957	136 378	57 267	159 760		446 786		367 235	209 210
1992	3 004 727	1 541 866	62 521	138 287	58 449	166 532		475 426		399 270	238 384
NAICS Basis											
1992	2 904 024	1 518 862	61 902	123 789	55 947	170 403	186 589	273 728	81 813	433 611	279 197
1993	3 020 497	1 604 544	64 957	126 988	59 632	177 967	201 076	286 457	87 646	453 437	310 178
1994	3 238 112	1 764 061	70 598	142 976	67 087	194 113	224 920	320 769	95 531	494 745	364 840
1995	3 479 677	1 902 815	74 865	160 774	72 019	212 444	246 277	370 679	101 051	508 271	379 551
1996	3 597 188	1 978 597	81 308	157 638	71 814	222 995	257 459	399 516	105 283	516 030	387 394
1997	3 834 699	2 147 384	86 465	168 118	76 900	242 812	270 687	439 380	112 116	575 307	421 573
1998	3 899 813	2 231 588	92 501	166 109	75 871	253 720	280 651	443 768	116 024	612 882	439 590
1999	4 031 887	2 326 736	96 153	156 648	70 087	257 071	276 904	467 059	118 313	676 328	498 716
2000	4 208 584	2 373 688	97 329	156 598	70 470	268 213	291 548	510 639	125 443	639 861	471 180
2001	3 970 499	2 174 406	94 861	138 246	60 559	253 113	266 554	429 471	114 068	602 495	427 175
2002	3 891 753	2 131 404	88 222	135 930	61 999	252 232	255 651	392 026	103 673	624 129	450 136
2001											
January	337 854	185 234	7 710	11 818	5 091	21 346	24 715	41 502	10 191	45 078	31 633
February	346 666	190 625	7 964	12 037	5 197	21 656	24 227	41 479	10 466	49 435	35 117
March	341 604	189 042	7 904	11 880	5 211	21 592	23 553	40 356	10 264	50 562	36 640
April	331 953	181 019	7 895	11 480	4 974	20 979	22 587	37 146	9 902	48 033	34 813
May	339 304	185 914	8 091	11 823	5 229	21 456	22 953	36 076	10 057	52 013	37 334
June	332 049	183 037	7 996	11 625	5 091	21 021	22 062	35 959	9 770	51 609	36 074
July	330 794	181 368	8 022	11 638	5 100	20 987	22 193	34 241	9 285	51 826	37 053
August	330 109	179 538	7 997	11 556	5 060	21 145	22 560	32 674	9 324	50 872	36 061
September	320 363	173 800	7 707	11 157	4 893	20 610	20 734	32 826	8 706	49 192	34 152
October	321 926	174 705	7 924	11 203	4 941	20 884	21 408	32 526	8 850	49 165	34 790
November	320 132	175 491	7 826	11 104	4 872	20 771	20 937	32 366	8 536	51 450	36 558
December	321 916	177 210	7 813	10 865	4 830	20 662	20 286	33 845	8 806	52 557	37 156
2002											
January	323 837	178 520	7 908	11 017	4 890	20 912	21 844	33 355	8 537	51 996	36 906
February	320 087	177 021	7 792	10 772	4 699	20 520	22 394	32 819	8 518	51 398	36 562
March	318 481	174 615	7 209	11 114	4 938	20 504	21 093	32 725	8 641	50 428	35 349
April	325 938	180 692	7 393	11 509	5 123	21 298	21 261	32 937	8 878	54 022	39 484
May	325 999	179 898	7 322	11 533	5 190	21 094	22 169	32 639	8 894	52 665	38 493
June	322 827	176 479	7 235	11 404	5 217	21 025	21 329	32 222	8 554	51 672	37 417
July	328 367	181 527	7 236	11 563	5 303	21 359	21 658	32 855	8 688	54 583	39 715
August	326 168	178 881	7 345	11 584	5 369	21 273	21 553	32 653	8 550	52 525	38 783
September	326 165	178 199	7 283	11 452	5 377	21 242	21 285	32 928	8 514	52 541	37 964
October	329 349	179 936	7 202	11 578	5 384	21 285	21 324	33 002	8 645	53 530	39 131
November	326 527	177 483	7 185	11 279	5 271	20 928	21 188	33 064	8 737	51 373	36 716
December	323 362	172 894	7 234	11 162	5 286	20 899	20 857	31 916	8 554	48 395	34 385

[1] Includes categories not shown separately.
[2] Data are for roughly similar categories in SIC classification system.

Table 17-4. Manufacturers' Shipments—*Continued*

(Millions of dollars, seasonally adjusted.)

Classification basis, year and month	Total [1]	Food products	Beverage and tobacco products [3]	Textiles	Textile products	Apparel	Paper products	Basic chemicals	Petroleum and coal products	Plastics and rubber products
SIC Basis [2]										
1958	164 339	59 738	3 868	12 417		...	12 707	23 093	15 188	7 310
1959	176 269	60 781	4 049	14 067		...	14 077	26 358	15 806	8 395
1960	180 095	62 468	4 367	13 791		...	14 308	26 509	16 349	8 483
1961	183 850	64 542	4 487	14 016		...	14 524	27 175	16 359	8 511
1962	193 336	66 935	4 531	15 185		...	15 382	29 266	16 716	9 335
1963	201 632	68 469	4 521	15 744		...	16 192	31 682	17 506	10 076
1964	212 641	71 594	4 653	17 000		...	17 019	34 148	17 855	10 749
1965	225 620	74 250	4 649	18 299		...	18 394	37 289	18 588	11 966
1966	243 031	79 665	4 772	19 600		...	20 211	40 569	19 857	13 181
1967	255 041	83 961	4 903	19 816		...	20 777	42 037	21 435	13 908
1968	271 254	87 328	4 937	21 970		...	22 093	45 491	22 548	15 585
1969	289 177	93 385	4 992	22 978		...	24 188	48 096	23 721	16 935
1970	295 787	98 535	5 350	22 614		...	24 573	49 195	24 200	16 754
1971	311 788	103 637	5 528	24 034		...	25 182	51 681	26 198	18 409
1972	348 477	115 054	5 919	28 065		...	28 004	58 130	27 918	21 662
1973	399 552	135 585	6 341	31 073		...	32 495	66 003	33 903	25 191
1974	487 403	161 884	7 139	32 790		...	41 514	85 387	57 229	28 828
1975	515 887	172 054	8 058	31 065		...	41 497	91 710	67 496	28 128
1976	578 088	180 830	8 786	36 387		...	47 939	106 467	80 022	32 880
1977	648 399	192 913	9 051	40 550		...	51 881	120 905	94 702	40 944
1978	710 082	215 989	9 951	42 281		...	56 777	132 262	100 967	44 823
1979	816 110	235 976	10 602	45 137		...	64 957	151 887	144 156	48 694
1980	923 662	256 191	12 194	47 256		...	72 553	168 220	192 969	49 157
1981	1 012 819	272 140	13 130	50 260		...	79 970	186 909	217 681	55 178
1982	1 009 673	280 529	16 061	47 516		...	79 698	176 254	203 404	57 307
1983	1 044 794	289 314	16 268	53 733		...	84 817	189 552	187 788	62 870
1984	1 112 908	304 584	17 473	56 336		...	95 525	205 963	184 488	72 938
1985	1 119 104	308 606	18 559	54 605		...	94 679	204 790	176 574	75 590
1986	1 097 022	318 203	19 146	57 188		...	99 865	205 711	122 605	78 379
1987	1 178 374	329 725	20 757	62 787		...	108 989	229 546	130 414	86 634
1988	1 273 931	354 084	23 809	64 627		...	122 882	261 238	131 682	95 485
1989	1 362 475	380 160	25 875	67 265		...	131 896	283 196	146 487	101 236
1990	1 426 915	391 728	29 856	65 533		...	132 424	292 802	173 389	105 250
1991	1 426 169	397 893	31 943	65 440		...	130 131	298 545	159 144	105 804
1992	1 462 861	406 964	35 198	70 753		...	133 201	305 420	150 227	113 593
NAICS Basis										
1992	1 385 162	358 494	85 687	52 923	24 763	61 535	127 122	319 501	150 095	113 827
1993	1 415 953	373 612	79 227	55 375	25 623	63 210	126 982	330 760	144 731	122 807
1994	1 474 051	379 786	83 434	58 607	27 233	64 894	136 922	350 098	143 339	134 288
1995	1 576 862	393 204	88 945	59 885	27 976	65 214	166 051	376 995	151 431	145 084
1996	1 618 591	404 173	94 033	59 796	28 515	64 237	152 860	385 919	174 181	149 773
1997	1 687 315	421 737	96 971	58 707	31 052	68 018	150 296	415 617	177 394	159 161
1998	1 668 225	428 479	102 359	57 416	31 137	64 932	154 984	416 742	137 957	163 736
1999	1 705 151	426 001	106 920	54 306	32 689	62 305	156 915	420 321	162 620	171 885
2000	1 834 896	435 229	111 692	52 112	33 654	60 339	165 298	449 159	235 134	178 236
2001	1 796 093	451 385	118 786	45 681	31 971	54 598	155 845	438 410	219 074	170 717
2002	1 760 349	450 183	109 832	43 170	34 232	53 621	151 530	424 143	206 879	178 383
2001										
January	152 620	36 832	9 278	4 120	2 784	4 779	13 427	37 190	20 614	14 097
February	156 041	37 177	9 724	4 088	2 750	4 863	13 961	39 041	20 140	14 752
March	152 562	37 542	9 792	3 950	2 666	4 844	13 660	37 732	18 512	14 384
April	150 934	37 657	9 316	3 835	2 594	4 702	13 406	36 773	19 410	14 046
May	153 390	37 722	10 537	3 883	2 627	4 598	13 099	37 268	19 980	14 227
June	149 012	37 788	9 985	3 831	2 642	4 499	12 874	35 920	18 233	14 083
July	149 426	37 960	9 962	3 767	2 672	4 296	12 828	36 559	17 792	14 515
August	150 571	38 123	10 747	3 776	2 668	4 469	12 766	36 622	18 002	14 328
September	146 563	37 820	9 543	3 711	2 655	4 382	12 475	35 272	17 824	14 085
October	147 221	37 712	10 604	3 687	2 647	4 449	12 715	35 651	16 695	14 141
November	144 641	37 713	9 509	3 497	2 648	4 295	12 489	35 631	16 036	14 033
December	144 706	37 770	9 795	3 572	2 656	4 461	12 159	35 052	16 302	14 126
2002										
January	145 317	37 889	9 625	3 522	2 667	4 401	12 516	34 975	16 443	14 328
February	143 066	37 803	9 038	3 588	2 818	4 417	11 914	34 345	16 101	14 309
March	143 866	37 706	9 615	3 582	2 781	4 314	12 147	33 949	16 595	14 268
April	145 246	37 341	9 012	3 786	2 888	4 555	12 391	34 853	16 471	15 023
May	146 101	37 523	9 511	3 666	2 906	4 544	12 539	35 094	16 338	14 977
June	146 348	36 887	9 314	3 599	2 877	4 444	12 325	36 231	16 833	14 808
July	146 840	37 320	9 145	3 766	2 856	4 583	12 674	34 729	17 560	15 161
August	147 287	37 524	9 163	3 578	2 855	4 457	13 241	34 784	17 523	15 012
September	147 966	37 155	9 054	3 522	2 871	4 480	12 927	36 340	17 529	14 924
October	149 413	37 664	8 972	3 597	2 883	4 393	13 040	36 171	18 287	15 205
November	149 044	37 652	8 761	3 590	2 915	4 568	12 724	36 356	18 185	15 173
December	150 468	37 850	8 592	3 406	2 896	4 468	13 137	36 412	19 286	15 305

[1] Includes categories not shown separately.
[2] Data are for roughly similar categories in SIC classification system.
[3] SIC tobacco only, 1958–1992.
... = Not available.

Table 17-4. Manufacturers' Shipments—Continued

(Millions of dollars, seasonally adjusted.)

Classification basis, year and month	Construction supplies	Information technology industries	By topical categories						
			Capital goods				Consumer goods		
			Total	Nondefense		Defense	Total	Durable	Nondurable
				Total	Excluding aircraft and parts				
SIC Basis [2]									
1958	23 286	...	46 552	...	...	...	...	...	...
1959	26 278	...	51 234	...	...	...	...	...	...
1960	25 886	...	52 171						
1961	25 498	...	53 762	...	...	...	...	...	...
1962	27 019	...	58 711	...	...	...	...	...	...
1963	28 545	...	61 186	...	...	...	...	...	...
1964	30 692	...	64 837	...	...	...	...	...	...
1965	33 287	...	71 621						
1966	35 643	...	84 792	...		...	...	...	...
1967	36 210	...	94 101				...	...	...
1968	39 621	...	99 702	72 405	...	27 297	...	...	...
1969	42 493	...	105 773	79 568	...	26 205	...	...	...
1970	41 945	...	102 285	78 907	...	23 378	...	...	...
1971	45 559	...	98 643	79 148	...	19 495	...	...	...
1972	54 119	...	107 198	87 762	...	19 436	...	...	...
1973	62 228	...	124 912	103 997	...	20 915	...	...	...
1974	69 146	...	143 828	122 674	...	21 154	...	...	...
1975	66 984	...	149 687	126 363	...	23 324	...	...	...
1976	77 948	...	162 172	135 540	...	26 632	...	...	...
1977	91 883	...	185 541	155 956	...	29 585	...	...	...
1978	106 017	...	217 165	186 427	...	30 738	...	...	...
1979	118 024	...	254 754	222 069	...	32 685	...	...	...
1980	118 429	...	287 132	246 797	...	40 335	...	...	...
1981	122 844	...	317 628	269 774	...	47 854	...	...	...
1982	115 777	...	312 298	252 098	...	60 200	...	...	...
1983	127 781	...	316 125	242 297	...	73 828	...	...	...
1984	141 230	...	361 205	278 900	...	82 305	...	...	...
1985	147 103	...	388 763	293 420	...	95 343	...	...	...
1986	154 113	...	396 158	289 969	...	106 189	...	...	...
1987	164 865	...	404 738	295 334	...	109 404	...	...	...
1988	175 594	...	438 089	333 402	...	104 687	...	...	...
1989	180 083	...	450 863	350 870	...	99 993	...	...	...
1990	180 604	...	473 175	370 804	...	102 371	...	...	...
1991	171 876	...	467 419	369 796	...	97 623	...	...	...
1992	184 498	...	481 257	389 448	...	91 809	...	...	...
NAICS Basis									
1992	281 232	236 015	566 268	471 485	435 696	94 783	1 108 692	263 323	845 369
1993	303 391	241 680	580 859	493 875	463 753	86 984	1 138 467	285 651	852 816
1994	332 734	264 092	616 435	538 203	512 327	78 232	1 203 162	325 995	877 167
1995	353 198	291 885	666 167	590 578	565 729	75 589	1 267 611	335 036	932 575
1996	371 401	311 028	704 635	630 932	605 295	73 703	1 304 283	339 730	964 553
1997	399 880	349 846	779 232	702 971	665 074	76 261	1 369 992	371 669	998 323
1998	418 756	362 564	821 736	747 046	695 717	74 690	1 364 326	385 918	978 408
1999	434 138	374 384	839 754	768 799	713 042	70 955	1 438 519	426 337	1 012 182
2000	444 812	399 751	875 396	808 345	757 617	67 051	1 514 377	405 308	1 109 069
2001	424 517	353 237	801 999	727 980	677 991	74 019	1 493 707	380 734	1 112 973
2002	419 040	319 391	753 048	673 223	634 549	79 825	1 472 647	396 590	1 076 057
2001									
January	35 158	32 227	71 059	65 334	61 925	5 725	123 355	27 092	94 053
February	35 842	32 769	72 427	66 787	62 081	5 640	126 615	31 033	95 483
March	35 484	32 641	70 961	65 399	61 314	5 562	125 907	36 195	93 589
April	35 029	30 692	67 595	61 953	58 474	5 642	124 622	31 145	93 630
May	36 357	30 295	68 881	62 859	58 574	6 022	128 326	34 544	95 765
June	35 685	29 805	68 060	61 716	57 038	6 344	124 065	34 072	92 488
July	35 446	28 972	66 150	59 780	55 742	6 370	125 043	23 166	92 455
August	35 762	27 541	65 076	58 700	54 684	6 376	126 763	34 656	94 073
September	34 814	27 279	63 281	56 880	52 826	6 401	122 222	31 824	91 297
October	35 194	26 959	63 238	56 947	53 094	6 291	123 004	34 493	91 656
November	34 882	26 671	62 741	56 469	52 190	6 272	122 057	32 742	89 704
December	34 673	28 297	64 390	57 291	52 875	7 099	123 236	29 772	90 076
2002									
January	35 136	27 212	64 136	57 369	53 610	6 767	122 938	30 821	89 880
February	34 719	26 966	63 811	57 547	53 929	6 264	120 766	32 373	88 095
March	34 266	26 728	63 154	56 453	52 527	6 701	119 830	34 053	88 872
April	35 129	27 027	62 990	56 596	53 047	6 394	122 494	34 685	88 383
May	35 081	26 803	63 580	57 091	53 894	6 489	122 631	36 010	88 997
June	34 838	26 558	62 626	55 880	52 955	6 746	121 871	34 316	89 320
July	35 207	26 857	63 854	57 116	53 652	6 738	124 265	25 250	89 443
August	35 121	26 644	62 552	56 092	53 487	6 460	123 038	35 273	89 467
September	35 001	26 630	62 853	55 985	52 787	6 868	123 264	34 217	90 267
October	34 946	26 617	63 163	56 443	53 328	6 720	124 914	37 118	91 130
November	34 871	26 649	62 837	55 680	52 844	7 157	123 487	32 868	90 655
December	34 933	25 697	60 981	54 373	51 662	6 608	124 339	29 606	91 867

[2]Data are for roughly similar categories in SIC classification system.
... = Not available.

Table 17-5. Manufacturers' Inventories

(Current cost basis, end of period; seasonally adjusted, except as noted; millions of dollars.)

Classification basis, year and month	Total, not seasonally adjusted[1]	Total	NAICS durable goods industries Total[1]	Non-metallic mineral products	Primary metals Total	Iron and steel mills	Fabricated metal products	Machinery	Computers and electronic products	Electrical equipment, appliances and components	Transportation equipment Total	Motor vehicles and parts	Materials and supplies	Work in progress	Finished goods
SIC Basis[2]															
1958	49 995	50 203	30 194	1 217	5 153	3 287	4 186	8 630			6 650	1 815	9 970	12 408	7 816
1959	52 671	52 913	32 012	1 351	5 109	3 109	4 244	9 682			6 943	2 211	10 709	13 086	8 217
1960	53 580	53 786	32 337	1 429	5 488	3 385	4 292	9 804			6 415	2 080	10 306	12 809	9 222
1961	54 730	54 871	32 496	1 439	5 792	3 684	4 269	9 890			6 207	2 082	10 246	13 211	9 039
1962	58 060	58 172	34 565	1 460	5 702	3 494	4 387	11 212			6 628	2 334	10 794	14 124	9 647
1963	59 922	60 029	35 776	1 498	5 749	3 459	4 534	11 352			7 111	2 463	11 053	14 835	9 888
1964	63 293	63 410	38 421	1 590	5 953	3 560	5 011	12 573			7 707	2 899	11 946	16 158	10 317
1965	68 028	68 207	42 189	1 669	6 199	3 617	5 696	14 340			8 430	3 289	13 298	18 055	10 836
1966	77 745	77 986	49 852	1 784	7 031	4 075	6 347	17 242			10 454	3 470	15 464	21 908	12 480
1967	84 388	84 646	54 896	1 827	7 553	4 417	6 729	18 279			12 852	3 516	16 423	24 933	13 540
1968	90 235	90 560	58 732	1 918	7 547	4 207	7 506	18 925			14 413	3 879	17 344	27 213	14 175
1969	97 749	98 145	64 598	2 051	8 066	4 451	7 666	21 480			15 942	4 067	18 636	30 282	15 680
1970	101 246	101 599	66 651	2 239	8 995	4 990	7 907	22 910			14 648	4 178	19 149	29 745	17 757
1971	102 267	102 567	66 136	2 302	9 084	4 926	8 098	22 402			13 799	4 173	19 679	28 550	17 907
1972	107 900	108 121	70 067	2 430	9 617	5 387	8 408	23 670			14 775	4 670	20 807	30 713	18 547
1973	124 327	124 499	81 192	2 712	10 034	5 302	9 864	28 943			16 458	5 708	25 944	35 490	19 758
1974	157 595	157 625	101 493	3 403	13 447	6 820	13 387	36 420			19 197	6 688	35 070	42 530	23 893
1975	159 844	159 708	102 590	3 594	15 742	8 597	13 091	35 266			19 620	6 101	33 903	43 227	25 460
1976	174 867	174 636	111 988	3 841	17 699	10 035	14 304	37 839			20 886	7 814	37 457	46 074	28 457
1977	188 435	188 378	120 877	4 095	18 261	10 004	15 527	41 204			22 423	9 078	40 186	50 226	30 465
1978	209 113	211 691	138 181	4 710	19 420	10 719	17 296	48 249			26 170	10 357	45 198	58 848	34 135
1979	239 101	242 157	160 734	5 183	22 446	12 012	19 145	57 030			31 638	10 978	52 670	69 325	38 739
1980	261 700	265 215	174 788	5 674	23 055	12 153	19 532	62 796			35 900	9 864	55 173	76 945	42 670
1981	279 453	283 413	186 443	6 106	25 794	13 359	20 209	67 260			37 527	9 047	57 998	80 998	47 447
1982	307 212	311 852	200 444	6 506	24 174	12 556	21 440	73 008			43 005	8 534	59 136	86 707	54 601
1983	307 675	312 379	199 854	6 628	22 308	11 065	21 752	71 508			43 791	10 433	60 325	86 899	52 630
1984	334 236	339 516	221 330	7 042	22 444	11 087	23 330	80 396			50 770	11 680	66 031	98 251	57 048
1985	329 555	334 749	218 193	7 040	19 974	9 709	22 880	77 075			52 634	11 809	63 904	98 162	56 127
1986	317 567	322 654	211 997	7 093	18 436	8 567	22 094	71 041			53 363	11 445	61 331	97 000	53 666
1987	332 619	338 109	220 799	7 154	19 076	8 620	22 920	73 000			56 461	11 937	63 562	102 393	54 844
1988	363 300	369 374	242 468	7 496	22 422	10 495	24 950	79 352			63 202	12 310	69 611	112 958	59 899
1989	384 539	391 212	257 513	7 792	22 838	10 942	25 427	83 965			70 968	12 503	72 435	122 251	62 827
1990	397 850	405 073	263 209	8 205	22 560	11 045	25 044	82 586			77 640	13 504	73 559	124 130	65 520
1991	383 509	390 950	250 019	7 928	20 703	10 236	23 922	78 861			73 019	13 163	70 834	114 960	64 225
1992	374 906	382 510	238 105	8 006	19 981	9 809	23 815	77 797			63 290	13 081	69 459	104 424	64 222
NAICS Basis															
1992	369 673	379 183	238 416	8 001	17 945	9 676	26 114	36 282	44 545	12 215	66 743	17 008	69 823	104 341	64 252
1993	370 775	380 102	239 040	7 577	17 951	9 648	26 302	37 124	43 960	12 451	64 662	18 143	72 752	102 114	64 174
1994	390 540	400 335	253 444	7 828	20 078	10 474	28 209	40 901	47 092	13 748	65 241	20 155	78 680	106 676	68 088
1995	414 909	425 217	267 696	8 432	21 407	11 308	30 315	44 662	53 639	14 160	63 491	20 764	85 612	106 777	75 307
1996	420 680	430 816	272 787	8 733	21 716	11 686	31 308	45 384	50 947	13 928	68 427	21 177	86 365	110 651	75 771
1997	433 451	443 804	281 249	8 996	22 461	12 253	32 446	45 918	55 302	14 075	69 085	20 774	92 364	109 991	78 894
1998	438 845	449 231	290 874	9 015	22 023	12 358	32 866	47 115	52 164	14 005	80 153	21 233	93 614	115 328	81 932
1999	452 803	463 646	296 645	9 412	22 034	12 065	33 453	47 411	55 134	13 989	79 758	22 596	97 835	114 230	84 580
2000	470 084	481 396	306 682	9 030	21 922	12 304	34 745	50 535	65 775	15 006	71 717	22 789	106 018	111 270	89 394
2001	441 527	452 236	283 722	9 583	19 270	10 376	32 762	45 836	56 967	13 959	69 560	20 107	96 251	102 304	85 167
2002	433 756	444 188	271 789	9 459	18 899	10 774	31 788	43 479	51 384	12 690	68 030	20 764	89 408	97 383	84 998
2001															
January	482 664	484 302	308 955	9 979	21 951	12 157	34 956	50 679	67 395	15 011	71 829	22 691	107 472	111 119	90 364
February	486 843	483 449	308 575	9 962	21 867	12 077	34 891	50 385	67 938	15 090	71 219	22 541	106 773	110 848	90 954
March	477 099	479 856	304 997	10 061	21 571	11 892	34 725	50 377	65 981	15 048	70 269	22 008	105 200	109 803	89 994
April	480 943	479 555	304 845	10 045	21 468	11 854	34 817	50 084	65 461	15 020	71 113	22 336	104 434	110 160	90 251
May	480 229	477 196	302 996	9 969	21 083	11 593	34 718	49 500	65 173	14 857	70 879	22 005	104 353	108 784	89 859
June	469 540	473 171	300 201	9 987	20 640	11 370	34 391	49 144	64 655	14 665	69 782	21 759	102 834	107 600	89 767
July	472 116	470 341	297 836	9 959	20 390	11 239	34 148	48 466	64 012	14 334	69 701	21 468	101 806	107 248	88 782
August	470 631	466 811	295 228	9 804	20 085	11 068	34 034	47 957	62 998	14 349	69 412	21 265	100 608	106 454	88 166
September	462 767	462 863	291 832	9 842	19 942	11 032	33 852	47 479	60 333	14 228	69 580	20 990	98 885	105 666	87 281
October	463 866	460 340	290 197	9 783	19 737	10 839	33 735	46 988	59 475	14 250	69 908	20 833	98 294	105 286	86 617
November	458 788	456 419	287 373	9 718	19 508	10 610	33 330	46 312	59 314	14 102	68 991	20 339	97 755	103 942	85 676
December	441 527	452 236	283 722	9 583	19 270	10 376	32 762	45 836	56 967	13 959	69 560	20 107	96 251	102 304	85 167
2002															
January	447 325	448 919	281 384	9 458	18 991	10 236	32 583	45 375	56 757	13 788	68 726	19 795	95 378	101 949	84 057
February	449 335	446 363	279 546	9 363	18 798	10 088	32 349	45 070	55 999	13 686	68 672	19 607	94 427	101 379	83 740
March	442 965	445 444	276 976	9 336	18 530	10 056	32 213	44 950	55 419	13 556	67 227	19 783	94 673	98 423	83 880
April	445 869	444 605	275 800	9 294	18 480	9 994	32 146	44 496	55 084	13 530	67 046	20 112	94 461	97 285	84 054
May	445 716	442 917	274 439	9 241	18 364	9 952	31 850	44 227	54 440	13 439	66 947	20 193	93 277	97 207	83 955
June	439 083	442 415	273 396	9 325	18 487	10 063	31 755	43 786	53 342	13 372	67 288	20 384	92 365	97 240	83 791
July	444 107	442 605	272 636	9 297	18 501	10 148	31 778	43 696	53 342	13 306	66 671	20 595	91 752	96 624	84 260
August	446 323	442 827	271 941	9 372	18 633	10 342	31 870	43 498	52 812	13 191	66 551	20 395	91 445	96 186	84 310
September	443 808	443 595	271 364	9 348	18 610	10 480	31 921	43 337	52 607	13 078	66 344	20 756	90 965	95 875	84 524
October	447 245	443 545	270 836	9 403	18 667	10 564	31 858	43 182	52 303	12 934	66 541	20 737	90 730	95 397	84 709
November	444 506	442 499	269 774	9 406	18 822	10 724	31 872	43 091	52 116	12 894	65 602	20 612	89 740	95 051	84 983
December	433 756	444 188	271 789	9 459	18 899	10 774	31 788	43 479	51 384	12 690	68 030	20 764	89 408	97 383	84 998

[1] Includes categories not shown separately.
[2] Data are for roughly similar categories in SIC classification system. Data prior to 1982 are not comparable to subsequent periods due to change in inventory valuation methods; see Notes and Definitions.

Table 17-5. Manufacturers' Inventories—*Continued*

(Current cost basis, end of period; seasonally adjusted, except as noted; millions of dollars.)

Classification basis, year and month	Total [1]	NAICS nondurable goods industries										Nondurables total by stage of fabrication		
		Food products	Beverage and tobacco products [4]	Textiles	Textile products	Apparel	Paper products	Basic chemicals	Petroleum and coal products	Plastics and rubber products		Materials and supplies	Work in process	Finished goods
SIC Basis [1]														
1958	20 009	5 302	1 982	2 148		...	1 430	2 995	1 634	1 033		8 676	2 827	8 506
1959	20 901	5 338	2 082	2 238		...	1 506	3 189	1 700	1 130		9 094	2 942	8 865
1960	21 449	5 492	2 193	2 301		...	1 543	3 298	1 667	1 163		9 097	2 947	9 405
1961	22 375	5 877	2 410	2 418		...	1 576	3 401	1 715	1 172		9 505	3 108	9 762
1962	23 607	6 198	2 404	2 585		...	1 702	3 659	1 786	1 277		9 836	3 304	10 467
1963	24 253	6 449	2 314	2 621		...	1 761	3 775	1 776	1 336		10 009	3 420	10 824
1964	24 989	6 629	2 306	2 682		...	1 783	3 959	1 760	1 430		10 167	3 531	11 291
1965	26 018	6 485	2 279	2 868		...	1 938	4 392	1 761	1 549		10 487	3 825	11 706
1966	28 134	6 973	2 206	3 045		...	2 170	4 951	1 808	1 771		11 197	4 226	12 711
1967	29 750	7 484	2 275	3 181		...	2 236	5 306	1 961	1 840		11 760	4 431	13 559
1968	31 828	8 009	2 218	3 610		...	2 309	5 542	2 035	2 018		12 328	4 852	14 648
1969	33 547	8 329	2 188	3 670		...	2 399	6 173	2 085	2 215		12 753	5 120	15 674
1970	34 948	8 738	2 052	3 676		...	2 735	6 749	2 161	2 386		13 168	5 271	16 509
1971	36 431	9 258	2 099	3 866		...	2 828	6 923	2 260	2 453		13 686	5 678	17 067
1972	38 054	9 673	2 355	4 056		...	2 896	7 079	2 142	2 695		14 677	5 998	17 379
1973	43 307	11 627	2 426	4 592		...	3 317	7 553	2 476	3 103		18 147	6 729	18 431
1974	56 132	14 625	3 024	5 044		...	4 816	11 579	3 945	4 023		23 744	8 189	24 199
1975	57 118	14 467	3 290	4 794		...	4 849	12 073	4 426	4 085		23 565	8 834	24 719
1976	62 648	15 695	3 416	5 232		...	5 299	13 319	4 711	4 581		25 847	9 929	26 872
1977	67 501	16 329	3 511	5 649		...	5 667	14 633	5 439	5 116		27 387	10 961	29 153
1978	73 510	18 073	3 669	5 935		...	6 114	16 018	5 330	5 801		29 619	12 085	31 806
1979	81 423	19 879	3 517	6 148		...	6 926	17 690	7 458	6 399		32 814	13 910	34 699
1980	90 427	21 710	3 721	6 648		...	7 802	20 066	9 693	6 435		36 606	15 884	37 937
1981	96 970	21 483	4 436	6 896		...	8 593	22 438	10 420	6 968		38 165	16 194	42 611
1982	111 408	23 016	6 873	6 723		...	9 022	24 448	17 009	7 748		44 039	18 612	48 757
1983	112 525	23 609	6 746	7 514		...	9 192	24 698	14 843	8 070		44 816	18 691	49 018
1984	118 186	24 182	6 533	7 827		...	10 299	26 420	14 260	8 904		45 692	19 328	53 166
1985	116 556	24 015	5 943	7 439		...	10 140	26 119	13 975	9 213		44 106	19 442	53 008
1986	110 657	23 884	5 449	7 191		...	10 254	25 743	8 791	9 285		42 335	18 124	50 198
1987	117 310	24 860	5 331	7 939		...	11 163	26 585	9 973	10 065		45 319	19 270	52 721
1988	126 906	27 122	5 286	8 384		...	12 495	29 792	9 196	11 367		49 396	20 559	56 951
1989	133 699	28 459	5 570	8 721		...	13 404	31 725	10 743	11 533		50 674	21 653	61 372
1990	141 864	29 714	5 974	8 732		...	13 640	34 001	13 432	12 292		52 645	22 817	66 402
1991	140 931	30 099	6 342	8 484		...	13 796	34 529	11 671	12 121		53 011	22 815	65 105
1992	144 405	30 996	6 668	8 710		...	14 010	35 720	11 350	12 541		54 007	23 532	66 866
NAICS Basis														
1992	140 767	26 445	11 667	6 468	3 516	8 919	13 451	37 544	11 664	12 660		53 126	23 438	64 203
1993	141 062	26 621	11 315	6 840	3 643	10 093	13 463	37 823	10 476	12 845		54 231	23 426	63 405
1994	146 891	27 560	10 979	7 192	3 932	10 491	13 736	38 863	11 308	14 297		57 114	24 491	65 286
1995	157 521	29 268	11 442	7 624	4 112	10 487	16 585	42 021	11 490	15 310		60 699	25 842	70 980
1996	158 029	29 585	12 383	7 238	4 093	8 787	15 260	43 329	12 780	15 801		59 066	26 500	72 463
1997	162 555	29 948	13 801	6 889	4 546	9 669	15 166	45 246	12 189	16 175		60 121	28 527	73 907
1998	158 357	29 211	13 909	6 934	4 222	9 481	14 793	45 502	9 703	16 193		58 139	27 075	73 143
1999	167 001	30 478	13 812	6 897	4 426	9 814	15 136	48 391	12 198	17 238		60 951	28 786	77 264
2000	174 714	31 750	14 023	6 479	4 928	9 513	15 306	52 236	13 824	18 035		61 268	30 065	83 381
2001	168 514	31 801	14 579	5 620	4 876	7 639	15 051	50 645	13 479	16 793		59 499	28 503	80 512
2002	172 399	32 497	14 481	4 947	4 920	7 042	14 714	50 974	15 449	19 313		59 071	30 418	82 910
2001														
January	175 347	31 755	13 996	6 462	4 924	9 565	15 300	52 741	13 831	18 113		61 961	29 841	83 545
February	174 874	31 730	14 028	6 429	4 933	9 459	15 346	52 327	13 906	18 065		61 714	29 697	83 463
March	174 859	31 781	14 224	6 357	4 931	9 313	15 118	52 599	13 807	18 008		61 817	29 562	83 480
April	174 710	31 939	14 252	6 348	4 926	9 202	15 066	52 429	13 971	17 943		61 543	29 561	83 606
May	174 200	32 075	14 314	6 278	4 852	9 086	15 025	52 264	14 085	17 611		61 632	29 514	83 054
June	172 970	32 107	14 240	6 177	4 831	8 960	14 996	51 731	14 007	17 449		61 248	29 034	82 688
July	172 505	32 227	14 518	6 078	4 776	8 727	14 949	51 606	13 877	17 282		61 520	28 878	82 107
August	171 583	32 084	14 531	5 993	4 791	8 529	14 860	51 051	14 049	17 148		60 867	29 064	81 652
September	171 031	31 930	14 523	5 928	4 794	8 290	14 975	51 215	13 994	17 082		60 587	29 322	81 122
October	170 143	31 593	14 429	5 816	4 825	8 072	15 007	51 590	13 551	16 989		60 498	28 634	81 011
November	169 046	31 761	14 434	5 740	4 846	7 887	15 072	50 941	13 310	16 924		60 359	28 337	80 350
December	168 514	31 801	14 579	5 620	4 876	7 639	15 051	50 645	13 479	16 793		59 499	28 503	80 512
2002														
January	167 535	31 901	14 641	5 412	4 811	7 447	14 934	50 594	13 056	16 658		58 873	28 831	79 831
February	166 817	31 865	14 560	5 364	4 771	7 289	14 889	50 455	13 277	16 560		58 996	28 834	78 987
March	168 468	31 702	14 716	5 276	4 740	7 141	14 801	50 215	14 062	18 199		59 355	29 123	79 990
April	168 805	32 069	14 524	5 121	4 794	7 049	14 646	50 294	14 480	18 125		59 557	29 170	80 078
May	168 478	32 077	14 605	5 097	4 835	6 932	14 550	50 134	14 378	18 189		59 308	29 426	79 744
June	169 019	32 280	14 713	5 049	4 863	6 942	14 638	49 977	14 502	18 216		59 234	29 761	80 024
July	169 969	32 344	14 501	5 026	4 923	6 954	14 487	50 570	14 902	18 328		59 509	30 216	80 244
August	170 886	32 478	14 566	5 054	4 930	6 952	14 451	51 220	14 871	18 465		59 390	30 996	80 500
September	172 231	32 570	14 757	5 002	4 947	7 007	14 566	51 317	15 168	19 116		59 560	31 158	81 513
October	172 709	32 654	14 607	4 979	4 931	7 017	14 624	51 422	15 195	19 228		59 597	31 037	82 075
November	172 725	32 774	14 443	4 891	4 898	6 999	14 715	51 824	14 813	19 294		60 036	30 831	81 858
December	172 399	32 497	14 481	4 947	4 920	7 042	14 714	50 974	15 449	19 313		59 071	30 418	82 910

[1]Includes categories not shown separately.
[2]Data are for roughly similar categories in SIC classification system. Data prior to 1982 are not comparable to subsequent periods due to change in inventory valuation methods; see Notes and Definitions.
[4]SIC tobacco only, 1958–1992.
. . . = Not available.

Table 17-5. Manufacturers' Inventories—*Continued*

(Current cost basis, end of period; seasonally adjusted; millions of dollars.)

Classification basis, year and month	Construction supplies	Information technology industries	By topical categories						
			Capital goods				Consumer goods		
			Total	Nondefense		Defense	Total	Durable	Nondurable
				Total	Excluding aircraft and parts				
SIC Basis [1]									
1958	3 762	...	11 381	...	...	...	...	...	...
1959	3 978	...	11 959	...	...	...	...	...	...
1960	4 079	...	11 737	...	...	...	...	...	...
1961	4 092	...	11 651	...	...	...	...	...	...
1962	4 223	...	12 960	...	...	...	...	...	...
1963	4 295	...	13 180	...	...	...	...	...	...
1964	4 551	...	14 267	...	...	...	...	...	...
1965	4 868	...	15 843	...	...	...	...	...	...
1966	5 325	...	19 791	...	...	...	...	...	...
1967	5 431	...	23 499	...	...	...	...	...	...
1968	5 805	...	25 709	18 158	...	7 551	...	...	...
1969	6 378	...	28 652	20 883	...	7 769	...	...	...
1970	6 867	...	27 859	22 810	...	5 049	...	...	...
1971	7 145	...	26 587	22 455	...	4 132	...	...	...
1972	7 603	...	27 667	23 337	...	4 330	...	...	...
1973	8 696	...	32 032	27 460	...	4 572	...	...	...
1974	11 076	...	39 605	34 583	...	5 022	...	...	...
1975	11 267	...	40 181	34 289	...	5 892	...	...	...
1976	12 540	...	41 046	34 449	...	6 597	...	...	...
1977	13 509	...	44 014	37 781	...	6 233	...	...	...
1978	15 100	...	52 237	46 660	...	0 577	...	...	...
1979	16 908	...	63 816	55 393	...	8 423	...	...	...
1980	17 513	...	74 531	63 692	...	10 839	...	...	...
1981	18 328	...	81 112	67 616	...	13 496	...	...	...
1982	18 580	...	92 601	73 748	...	18 853	...	...	...
1983	19 309	...	89 562	68 420	...	21 142	...	...	...
1984	20 552	...	102 615	75 466	...	27 149	...	...	...
1985	20 555	...	102 843	71 763	...	31 080	...	...	...
1986	20 348	...	99 104	67 631	...	31 473	...	...	...
1987	21 158	...	103 167	68 734	...	34 433	...	...	...
1988	22 925	...	114 207	77 448	...	36 759	...	...	...
1989	23 326	...	124 850	86 897	...	37 953	...	...	...
1990	23 714	...	128 997	90 894	...	38 103	...	...	...
1991	22 509	...	121 629	88 958	...	32 671	...	...	...
1992	22 779	...	110 261	84 351	...	25 910	...	...	...
NAICS Basis									
1992	36 752	40 240	121 038	97 454	79 005	23 584	104 422	21 924	82 498
1993	38 287	39 189	118 923	97 182	79 641	21 741	105 963	22 940	83 023
1994	40 873	41 588	123 825	103 433	85 827	20 392	110 851	25 198	85 653
1995	43 390	46 924	130 064	111 623	94 733	18 441	117 983	26 765	91 218
1996	44 073	43 617	133 152	115 321	93 556	17 831	117 946	26 261	91 685
1997	45 651	48 222	137 904	122 676	98 958	15 228	121 143	26 314	94 829
1998	46 410	45 522	145 575	127 230	97 520	18 345	118 752	26 204	92 548
1999	48 395	46 389	146 819	126 400	99 794	20 419	125 620	27 438	98 182
2000	50 384	53 085	149 608	131 918	110 481	17 690	132 234	28 657	103 577
2001	47 347	48 688	141 812	123 620	101 960	18 192	129 602	26 881	102 721
2002	47 267	43 592	131 053	112 905	93 598	18 148	132 444	27 524	104 920
2001									
January	50 501	54 648	151 512	133 604	112 023	17 908	132 541	28 711	103 830
February	50 364	55 280	151 760	134 061	112 653	17 699	132 224	28 749	103 475
March	50 078	53 868	150 368	132 947	111 361	17 421	132 015	28 485	103 530
April	50 228	53 795	150 701	132 646	110 734	18 055	132 216	28 679	103 537
May	50 088	53 771	150 305	132 278	110 275	18 027	132 151	28 414	103 737
June	49 917	53 365	148 833	131 271	109 370	17 562	131 779	28 408	103 371
July	49 623	53 037	147 969	130 428	108 391	17 541	131 786	28 294	103 492
August	49 242	52 725	147 192	129 677	107 615	17 515	131 276	27 918	103 358
September	49 056	50 808	145 132	127 414	105 087	17 718	131 111	27 783	103 328
October	48 728	50 626	144 631	126 946	104 500	17 685	130 093	27 581	102 512
November	48 106	50 872	144 124	126 088	104 138	18 036	129 330	27 255	102 075
December	47 347	48 688	141 812	123 620	101 960	18 192	129 602	26 881	102 721
2002									
January	47 324	48 640	140 865	122 732	100 968	18 133	128 941	26 837	102 104
February	46 959	48 012	140 137	121 945	100 052	18 192	128 854	26 682	102 172
March	46 955	47 215	137 754	119 668	99 055	18 086	129 569	26 906	102 663
April	46 717	47 106	136 573	118 574	98 520	17 999	130 375	27 113	103 262
May	46 604	46 408	135 261	117 534	97 557	17 727	130 218	27 208	103 010
June	46 630	45 567	134 477	116 530	96 417	17 947	130 668	27 364	103 304
July	46 619	45 488	132 994	115 825	96 187	17 169	131 613	27 641	103 972
August	46 811	45 160	132 524	114 915	95 401	17 609	132 048	27 425	104 623
September	46 829	44 291	131 126	113 560	94 478	17 566	132 986	27 661	105 325
October	47 021	44 082	130 322	112 792	93 865	17 530	132 873	27 663	105 210
November	47 184	44 101	129 725	112 243	93 767	17 482	132 896	27 582	105 314
December	47 267	43 592	131 053	112 905	93 598	18 148	132 444	27 524	104 920

[2]Data are for roughly similar categories in SIC classification system. Data prior to 1982 are not comparable to subsequent periods due to change in inventory valuation methods; see Notes and Definitions.
. . . = Not available.

Table 17-6. Manufacturers' New Orders

(Net, millions of dollars, seasonally adjusted.)

Classification basis, year and month	Total [1]	NAICS durable goods industries											
		Total [1]	Primary metals			Fabricated metal products	Machinery	Computers and electronic products	Electrical equipment, appliances and components	Transportation equipment			
			Total [1]	Iron and steel mills	Aluminum and nonferrous metal products					Total [1]	Motor vehicles and parts	Non-defense aircraft and parts	Defense aircraft and parts
SIC Basis [2]													
1959	368 255	191 744	34 503	21 009	...	24 102		49 044		44 712	...	...	
1960	362 759	183 455	26 354	13 603	...	23 410		47 245		47 481	...	...	
1961	373 400	189 032	32 069	18 647	...	24 225		49 867		43 138	...	...	
1962	401 255	208 351	31 179	16 635	...	26 364		54 722		53 728	...	...	
1963	426 084	224 048	34 780	19 122	...	27 903		58 745		57 625	...	...	
1964	459 210	246 088	41 521	23 758	...	30 360		66 005		61 607	...	...	
1965	505 792	279 432	43 380	22 590	...	33 998		76 429		73 803	...	...	
1966	556 494	313 954	49 111	25 134	...	38 501		89 417		80 607	...	...	
1967	564 616	309 632	45 100	23 435	...	41 618		87 944		75 979	...	...	
1968	607 127	336 614	48 089	24 416	...	45 158		91 468		85 893	...	...	
1969	648 289	358 509	54 880	27 247	...	47 446		102 664		83 945	...	...	
1970	624 541	328 079	51 793	25 521	...	43 990		96 439		67 380	...	17 417	
1971	671 134	358 856	51 284	25 571	...	44 305		98 525		89 900	...	22 459	
1972	770 056	420 455	61 447	30 996	...	52 879		119 643		96 501	...	20 963	
1973	912 279	511 525	78 395	39 413	...	64 733		147 437		118 194	...	26 669	
1974	1 047 811	562 339	98 831	51 047	...	74 281		164 985		114 081	...	29 934	
1975	1 022 133	503 485	75 034	38 611	...	64 349		147 473		109 050	...	26 869	
1976	1 194 759	615 680	94 491	47 212	...	76 372		174 459		143 502	...	31 851	
1977	1 382 309	732 422	105 689	52 103	...	92 028		206 245		175 446	...	40 625	
1978	1 579 715	867 335	124 741	62 648	...	105 182		246 832		213 539	...	54 600	
1979	1 771 603	953 796	139 783	66 968	...	117 428		281 974		223 226	...	67 818	
1980	1 877 053	952 701	134 416	62 473	...	116 195		295 085		202 584	...	72 514	
1981	2 015 982	1 003 845	137 286	67 457	...	123 245		324 629		203 482	...	63 530	
1982	1 944 671	936 764	98 445	43 013	...	113 399		296 904		209 325	...	73 365	
1983	2 106 726	1 057 677	113 884	49 123	...	122 760		321 010		261 359	...	86 952	
1984	2 314 256	1 201 964	118 354	50 719	...	141 650		377 650		295 202	...	91 620	
1985	2 346 410	1 228 268	112 276	49 079	...	142 300		381 747		311 482	...	100 889	
1986	2 340 899	1 243 761	108 218	46 408	...	143 541		372 849		327 541	...	107 993	
1987	2 510 890	1 329 712	125 989	54 763	...	150 716		394 381		348 224	...	114 835	
1988	2 737 716	1 464 916	152 578	64 002	...	158 170		439 266		389 635	...	137 443	
1989	2 872 514	1 512 664	152 814	62 752	...	160 037		449 533		411 434	...	153 430	
1990	2 931 275	1 507 001	149 338	63 369	...	163 285		454 642		395 737	...	150 329	
1991	2 866 841	1 438 187	134 657	56 366	...	158 401		441 109		363 366	...	132 645	
1992	2 977 116	1 515 694	136 849	58 002	...	165 793		476 574		377 147	...	110 830	
NAICS Basis [3]													
1992	...	...	...	...	...	...	...	...	...	...	...	...	...
1993	2 960 015	1 544 062	128 895	62 580	53 733	175 990	202 848	248 104	88 263	427 966	311 928	38 427	32 569
1994	3 199 686	1 725 635	146 503	67 619	64 594	196 567	232 226	274 776	96 919	487 253	367 306	39 309	31 524
1995	3 426 503	1 849 641	159 957	72 660	72 264	214 488	251 307	311 275	101 409	508 133	378 886	57 454	27 736
1996	3 567 384	1 948 793	158 066	71 301	70 657	227 447	258 405	327 288	104 837	552 024	385 712	72 094	32 520
1997	3 779 835	2 092 520	171 407	78 577	74 974	247 839	272 998	363 635	113 411	581 780	422 427	85 797	23 280
1998	3 808 143	2 139 918	160 743	72 378	71 274	253 847	278 100	372 433	115 711	600 205	440 934	84 150	23 854
1999	3 957 242	2 252 091	156 968	70 924	68 469	258 116	278 277	402 216	120 774	660 215	499 527	81 619	25 717
2000	4 161 472	2 326 576	153 625	68 181	67 122	270 021	294 608	436 415	126 196	663 326	468 470	99 249	31 326
2001	3 875 329	2 079 236	136 291	59 573	60 025	248 872	260 392	363 049	110 628	591 756	425 580	74 121	37 311
2002	3 800 930	2 040 581	134 089	61 884	56 545	249 408	244 559	325 378	103 013	617 098	450 183	65 295	40 087
2001													
January	329 725	177 105	11 646	4 992	5 326	21 392	24 285	35 710	9 829	43 710	31 439	6 458	1 303
February	336 429	180 388	11 866	5 000	5 470	20 900	23 978	34 327	10 311	47 738	34 944	7 082	2 020
March	335 606	183 044	11 694	5 086	5 245	21 332	22 298	33 425	9 769	55 041	36 487	8 967	1 544
April	324 196	173 262	11 326	4 855	5 047	20 693	21 406	30 201	9 436	49 998	35 092	8 148	1 684
May	329 977	176 587	11 799	5 160	5 151	20 750	22 221	30 233	9 491	50 992	37 103	6 489	3 247
June	323 822	174 810	11 773	5 256	5 081	21 107	21 719	30 020	9 326	50 150	35 970	8 195	2 260
July	322 134	172 708	11 460	5 049	5 014	20 695	21 470	28 902	9 255	49 557	36 797	6 077	2 345
August	322 352	171 781	11 309	4 843	5 017	21 014	22 096	28 515	9 070	48 408	35 909	6 646	1 662
September	308 285	161 722	11 004	4 921	4 730	20 065	20 929	26 580	8 328	44 263	34 004	3 647	2 420
October	321 856	174 635	10 609	4 606	4 673	20 210	20 036	27 954	8 454	56 539	34 460	3 820	14 274
November	310 512	165 871	10 860	4 769	4 760	20 192	20 796	28 628	8 808	46 169	36 436	3 279	2 529
December	313 808	169 102	10 834	4 939	4 491	20 371	20 539	29 651	8 503	48 768	37 158	4 857	1 864
2002													
January	311 730	166 413	10 716	4 829	4 524	20 307	20 879	27 281	8 139	47 981	36 816	4 570	2 722
February	317 675	174 609	10 721	4 794	4 656	20 180	21 013	27 783	8 623	55 776	36 589	6 957	4 233
March	313 271	169 405	10 869	5 026	4 570	20 621	19 675	27 155	8 300	52 927	35 541	6 293	5 299
April	317 606	172 360	11 542	5 380	4 787	21 159	20 718	27 801	9 077	51 484	39 629	5 028	1 694
May	318 297	172 196	11 611	5 450	4 861	21 357	21 147	27 978	9 042	50 282	38 679	5 414	2 027
June	310 680	164 332	11 278	5 221	4 746	20 539	19 390	27 355	8 766	47 071	37 508	2 483	2 595
July	324 427	177 587	11 295	5 205	4 789	21 380	21 357	27 314	8 222	57 496	39 953	6 893	6 313
August	323 955	176 668	11 536	5 447	4 775	20 638	20 574	26 792	8 528	58 218	38 357	9 378	3 125
September	313 949	165 983	11 336	5 319	4 689	20 947	20 423	26 577	8 677	47 549	37 777	2 810	3 135
October	320 000	170 587	11 549	5 357	4 856	21 294	20 931	26 509	8 619	50 737	38 790	4 932	2 705
November	317 869	168 825	10 769	4 911	4 575	20 643	20 340	26 895	8 532	50 663	36 863	5 288	3 129
December	316 944	166 476	10 853	4 998	4 660	20 346	20 454	26 978	8 519	48 260	34 467	5 513	3 444

[1]Includes categories not shown separately.
[2]Data are for roughly similar categories in SIC classification system.
[3]Data excludes semiconductors. See Notes and Definitions.
. . . = Not available.

Table 17-6. Manufacturers' New Orders—*Continued*

(Net, millions of dollars, seasonally adjusted.)

Classification basis, year and month	Construction supplies	Information technology industries	By topical categories							
			Capital goods				Consumer goods			
			Total	Nondefense		Defense	Total	Durable	Nondurable	
				Total	Excluding aircraft and parts					

SIC Basis [2]									
1959	...	...	...	...	...	...	...	...	...
1960	...	...	...	...	...	...	...	...	...
1961	...	...	...	...	...	...	...	...	...
1962	...	...	...	...	...	...	...	...	...
1963	...	...	...	...	...	...	...	...	...
1964	...	...	...	...	...	...	...	...	...
1965	...	...	...	...	...	...	...	...	...
1966	...	...	...	...	...	...	...	...	...
1967	...	...	...	...	...	...	...	...	...
1968	...	...	...	...	...	...	...	...	...
1969	...	...	...	84 549	...	23 790	...	...	...
1970	...	...	...	72 866	...	21 311	...	...	...
1971	...	...	...	80 185	...	18 787	...	...	...
1972	...	...	...	92 943	...	20 467	...	...	...
1973	...	...	...	119 108	...	23 409	...	...	...
1974	...	...	...	139 131	...	26 033	...	...	...
1975	...	...	...	118 635	...	24 765	...	...	...
1976	...	...	...	137 875	...	30 616	...	...	...
1977	...	...	...	164 168	...	34 624	...	...	...
1978	...	...	...	211 056	...	41 511	...	...	...
1979	...	...	...	253 844	...	33 795	...	...	...
1980	...	...	...	253 619	...	58 256	...	...	...
1981	...	...	...	261 666	...	58 881	...	...	...
1982	...	...	...	230 555	...	81 415	...	...	...
1983	...	...	...	235 489	...	96 105	...	...	...
1984	...	...	...	284 022	...	103 504	...	...	...
1985	...	...	...	294 544	...	109 505	...	...	...
1986	...	...	...	287 786	...	111 879	...	...	...
1987	...	...	...	313 127	...	111 639	...	...	...
1988	...	...	...	373 294	...	102 728	...	...	...
1989	...	...	...	395 855	...	93 398	...	...	...
1990	...	...	...	399 966	...	96 638	...	...	...
1991	...	...	...	365 655	...	87 213	...	...	...
1992	...	...	...	378 293	...	76 155	...	...	...
NAICS Basis [3]									
1992				...		...			
1993	304 264	239 387	561 097	488 166	466 433	72 931	1 139 096	286 280	852 816
1994	335 962	265 010	616 252	542 094	523 461	74 158	1 203 225	326 058	877 167
1995	355 161	297 605	680 857	612 132	576 769	68 725	1 268 660	336 085	932 575
1996	373 536	310 074	737 268	648 797	607 174	88 471	1 305 517	340 964	964 553
1997	403 860	352 700	792 859	728 362	676 119	64 497	1 372 919	374 596	998 323
1998	419 330	365 723	809 727	745 600	698 279	64 127	1 364 268	385 860	978 408
1999	435 034	389 160	840 603	772 703	728 089	67 900	1 440 903	428 721	1 012 182
2000	446 702	409 500	910 933	831 335	767 754	79 598	1 515 799	406 730	1 109 069
2001	420 300	350 726	783 060	700 027	665 899	83 033	1 491 143	378 170	1 112 973
2002	418 315	314 473	727 158	647 894	617 878	79 264	1 471 270	395 213	1 076 057
2001									
January	34 883	33 337	69 960	65 931	63 579	4 029	123 264	29 211	94 053
February	35 099	33 089	70 528	64 798	61 394	5 730	126 621	31 138	95 483
March	35 459	32 703	72 793	64 444	59 280	8 349	124 513	30 924	93 589
April	34 694	30 262	66 155	60 890	56 729	5 265	123 905	30 275	93 630
May	35 602	29 217	66 252	60 154	56 889	6 098	128 074	32 309	95 765
June	35 829	28 897	64 325	59 356	55 454	4 969	123 671	31 183	92 488
July	35 294	28 477	62 905	56 595	54 268	6 310	125 235	32 780	92 455
August	35 770	27 828	62 611	57 089	53 939	5 522	126 810	32 737	94 073
September	34 017	25 290	58 023	51 986	50 557	6 037	122 223	30 926	91 297
October	34 519	26 778	69 788	51 461	50 657	18 327	122 627	30 971	91 656
November	34 410	27 249	60 082	53 991	52 881	6 091	122 178	32 474	89 704
December	34 367	28 445	61 403	55 174	52 772	6 229	123 506	33 430	90 076
2002									
January	35 096	26 147	57 097	52 933	51 818	4 164	122 911	33 031	89 880
February	34 903	26 818	64 721	56 194	53 592	8 527	120 462	32 367	88 095
March	34 131	25 517	61 370	51 840	49 419	9 530	119 698	30 826	88 872
April	35 239	26 528	59 612	54 128	52 243	5 484	122 460	34 077	88 383
May	35 324	27 149	60 934	55 528	53 010	5 406	122 468	33 471	88 997
June	34 269	26 259	57 222	50 855	50 534	6 367	121 557	32 237	89 320
July	35 237	26 376	61 817	56 065	52 435	5 752	124 140	34 697	89 443
August	34 821	26 239	66 351	58 967	52 620	7 384	122 575	33 108	89 467
September	35 013	26 599	59 558	51 702	50 357	7 856	123 545	33 278	90 267
October	35 125	25 462	59 764	54 829	52 422	4 935	125 076	33 946	91 130
November	34 734	26 281	60 703	54 439	51 784	6 264	123 240	32 585	90 655
December	34 587	26 037	61 582	53 807	50 752	7 775	124 248	32 381	91 867

[2]Data are for roughly similar categories in SIC classification system.
... = Not available.

Table 17-7. Manufacturers' Unfilled Orders, Durable Goods Industries

(End of period, millions of dollars, seasonally adjusted.)

Classification basis, year and month	Not seasonally adjusted, total	Seasonally adjusted, NAICS industries							
		Total [1]	Primary metals			Fabricated metal products	Machinery	Computers and electronic products	Electrical equipment, appliances and components
			Total [1]	Iron and steel mills	Aluminum and nonferrous metal products				
SIC Basis [2]									
1958	44 090	43 807	5 019	3 521	1 151	4 222		10 539	
1959	48 666	48 369	8 018	6 143	1 382	4 615		12 228	
1960	41 681	41 650	3 334	1 877	1 156	4 079		11 028	
1961	43 496	43 582	4 791	3 314	1 131	4 634		11 540	
1962	44 889	45 170	3 518	1 957	1 169	4 858		12 282	
1963	49 879	50 346	3 952	2 170	1 319	5 955		14 602	
1964	60 640	61 315	6 686	4 386	1 696	7 484		18 203	
1965	73 754	74 459	6 086	3 003	2 238	9 111		23 395	
1966	92 303	93 002	7 267	3 601	2 753	10 814		29 339	
1967	99 140	99 735	7 228	3 921	2 572	12 346		30 296	
1968	104 263	104 393	6 591	3 416	2 472	13 813		30 969	
1969	109 936	110 161	7 991	4 283	2 876	15 128		35 490	
1970	100 139	100 412	7 796	4 617	2 663	14 877		33 618	
1971	99 906	100 225	7 478	4 380	2 552	13 688		33 318	
1972	112 517	113 034	10 470	6 681	3 116	15 077		39 344	
1973	148 421	149 204	16 129	9 794	4 962	21 019		54 070	
1974	180 686	181 519	19 225	11 054	5 952	28 100		67 403	
1975	160 993	161 664	13 266	7 345	4 015	24 008		62 437	
1976	169 198	169 857	14 684	7 776	4 891	22 810		65 905	
1977	191 603	193 323	17 298	9 435	5 483	25 152		72 025	
1978	246 162	248 281	23 969	12 932	7 393	29 137		86 452	
1979	288 834	291 321	26 320	12 485	9 457	33 131		99 105	
1980	312 508	315 202	26 815	13 418	10 096	33 296		100 730	
1981	311 628	314 707	22 024	10 589	8 784	33 036		102 123	
1982	297 851	300 798	15 500	6 574	7 418	27 117		86 503	
1983	329 758	333 114	20 400	9 431	9 594	26 752		93 145	
1984	356 446	359 651	18 362	8 103	8 694	30 254		97 433	
1985	369 362	372 097	18 331	8 248	8 361	29 197		96 882	
1986	374 264	376 699	18 590	8 897	7 783	29 633		91 209	
1987	406 444	408 688	24 340	11 828	10 300	32 973		96 609	
1988	449 859	452 150	27 079	11 508	12 974	31 661		104 285	
1989	484 623	487 098	24 120	9 479	11 824	27 629		102 985	
1990	506 311	509 124	24 768	10 120	11 258	25 859		102 373	
1991	492 500	495 802	23 075	9 290	10 609	24 516		96 800	
1992	466 328	469 381	21 636	8 897	9 925	23 725		97 999	
NAICS Basis [3]									
1992	447 770	450 965	18 794	9 300	7 054	29 714	40 867	84 591	12 123
1993	422 314	425 665	20 862	12 434	10 404	27 756	42 638	81 251	12 769
1994	430 982	434 594	24 378	12 908	10 765	30 259	49 963	82 526	14 232
1995	443 497	447 338	23 456	13 423	11 366	32 338	55 209	89 001	14 593
1996	484 865	488 815	23 774	12 781	10 494	36 898	56 213	88 150	14 096
1997	508 480	513 166	27 158	14 495	11 774	42 091	58 748	91 119	15 432
1998	491 858	496 471	21 611	10 821	8 313	42 220	56 168	95 000	15 078
1999	500 749	505 941	22 004	11 711	9 629	43 301	57 749	113 968	17 551
2000	544 517	550 005	18 940	9 336	6 895	45 068	61 040	130 738	18 242
2001	512 520	517 590	16 934	8 323	5 857	40 680	54 598	127 441	14 665
2002	480 679	485 816	15 042	8 213	6 006	37 752	43 544	119 674	13 999
2001									
January	552 923	548 893	18 768	9 237	6 876	45 114	60 610	131 963	17 880
February	551 661	545 392	18 597	9 040	6 674	44 358	60 361	131 547	17 725
March	553 716	545 889	18 411	8 915	6 588	44 098	59 106	131 111	17 230
April	551 409	543 969	18 257	8 796	6 399	43 812	57 925	130 003	16 764
May	545 351	539 916	18 233	8 727	6 270	43 106	57 193	129 434	16 198
June	538 268	536 942	18 381	8 892	6 415	43 192	56 850	128 748	15 754
July	533 593	533 097	18 203	8 841	6 361	42 900	56 127	128 224	15 724
August	526 347	529 716	17 956	8 624	6 104	42 769	55 663	128 441	15 470
September	516 244	522 186	17 803	8 652	6 142	42 224	55 858	126 743	15 092
October	517 962	526 610	17 209	8 317	5 831	41 550	54 486	126 665	14 696
November	511 804	521 246	16 965	8 214	5 779	40 971	54 345	127 183	14 968
December	512 520	517 590	16 934	8 323	5 857	40 680	54 598	127 441	14 665
2002									
January	513 565	510 293	16 633	8 262	5 790	40 075	53 633	126 177	14 267
February	517 782	512 426	16 582	8 357	5 940	39 735	52 252	125 686	14 372
March	519 462	512 007	16 337	8 445	6 070	39 852	50 834	124 907	14 031
April	516 015	508 336	16 370	8 702	6 348	39 713	50 291	124 432	14 230
May	511 206	505 261	16 448	8 962	6 671	39 976	49 269	124 398	14 378
June	499 512	497 705	16 322	8 966	6 709	39 490	47 330	124 122	14 590
July	499 609	498 562	16 054	8 868	6 636	39 511	47 029	123 378	14 124
August	498 174	501 299	16 006	8 946	6 733	38 876	46 050	122 467	14 102
September	488 171	494 297	15 890	8 888	6 659	38 581	45 188	121 330	14 265
October	481 835	490 267	15 861	8 861	6 610	38 590	44 795	120 156	14 239
November	477 626	487 009	15 351	8 501	6 244	38 305	43 947	119 387	14 034
December	480 679	485 816	15 042	8 213	6 006	37 752	43 544	119 674	13 999

[1] Includes categories not shown separately.
[2] Data are for roughly similar categories in SIC classification system.
[3] Data excludes semiconductors. See Notes and Definitions.

Table 17-7. Manufacturers' Unfilled Orders, Durable Goods Industries—*Continued*

(End of period, millions of dollars, seasonally adjusted.)

Classification basis, year and month	Transportation equipment				By topical categories						
	Not seasonally adjusted, total [1]	Motor vehicles and parts	Non-defense aircraft and parts	Defense aircraft and parts	Construction materials and supplies	Information technology industries	Capital goods				Consumer durable goods
							Total	Nondefense		Defense	
								Total	Excl. aircraft and parts		
SIC Basis [2]											
1958	19 094	...	...		3 149	...	...	...	...	...	967
1959	18 342	...	...		3 642	...	...	...	...	...	1 162
1960	18 217	...	...		3 094	...	...	...	...	...	1 067
1961	17 202	...	...		3 449	...	...	...	...	...	1 245
1962	18 844	...	...		3 480	...	...	...	...	...	1 153
1963	20 151	...	...		4 127	...	...	...	...	...	1 478
1964	23 664	...	...		5 182	...	...	...	...	...	1 620
1965	29 262	...	...		5 823	...	...	...	...	...	1 940
1966	37 376	...	...		6 728	...	...	...	...	...	2 109
1967	40 807	...	...		7 521	...	...	...	...	...	1 849
1968	43 023	...	...		8 205	...	...	47 608	...	23 152	2 129
1969	41 812	...	...		8 873	...	...	52 591	...	20 809	1 967
1970	34 720	...	26 198		8 880	...	...	46 544	...	18 804	2 078
1971	35 793	...	26 259		8 073	...	...	47 576	...	18 158	2 292
1972	37 627	...	26 151		8 810	...	...	52 781	...	19 261	2 914
1973	45 248	...	27 842		12 311	...	...	67 947	...	21 756	3 471
1974	51 118	...	30 506		15 125	...	...	84 495	...	26 558	2 582
1975	46 633	...	28 244		12 694	...	...	76 773	...	27 936	2 740
1976	49 078	...	29 421		11 592	...	...	79 121	...	31 826	2 862
1977	57 101	...	37 325		12 821	...	...	87 652	...	36 692	4 135
1978	81 782	...	54 417		14 408	...	...	112 277	...	47 425	4 864
1979	103 555	...	74 034		15 360	...	...	144 114	...	48 656	4 754
1980	119 700	...	88 051		15 410	...	...	150 973	...	66 636	4 388
1981	118 008	...	86 794		15 213	...	...	142 802	...	77 793	4 729
1982	125 879	...	93 703		11 981	...	...	121 082	...	99 052	4 860
1983	141 637	...	105 504		12 673	...	...	114 280	...	121 177	5 810
1984	152 189	...	117 923		13 102	...	...	119 424	...	142 324	5 603
1985	156 155	...	127 282		13 124	...	...	120 687	...	156 188	5 253
1986	161 145	...	133 565		13 677	...	...	118 429	...	161 705	5 815
1987	176 588	...	144 987		14 140	...	...	136 171	...	163 786	5 842
1988	211 575	...	174 721		14 557	...	...	176 069	...	161 878	5 703
1989	253 517	...	217 557		13 992	...	...	221 152	...	155 314	5 854
1990	279 082	...	242 208		14 021	...	...	250 314	...	149 844	5 215
1991	275 260	...	242 798		14 828	...	...	246 093	...	139 666	5 498
1992	253 076	...	222 194		14 706	...	...	234 817	...	124 047	5 047
NAICS Basis [3]											
1992	258 145	11 577	127 426	49 634	20 900	80 330	318 887	179 454	92 301	139 433	6 437
1993	232 674	13 337	110 787	46 684	21 774	78 044	299 110	173 715	95 048	125 395	7 133
1994	225 182	15 835	100 940	44 758	25 096	79 122	299 000	177 625	106 301	121 375	7 215
1995	225 044	15 133	109 271	42 482	27 158	85 022	314 009	199 417	117 634	114 592	8 211
1996	261 038	13 433	130 353	45 428	29 439	84 288	346 760	217 350	119 704	129 410	9 401
1997	267 511	14 310	143 399	41 115	33 596	87 414	360 764	243 059	131 164	117 705	12 383
1998	254 834	15 620	137 611	38 044	34 228	90 748	348 802	241 553	133 730	107 249	12 288
1999	238 721	16 396	126 662	35 973	35 155	105 777	350 161	245 884	149 249	104 277	14 694
2000	262 186	13 708	138 665	42 994	37 187	115 551	385 821	268 922	159 582	116 899	16 007
2001	251 447	12 126	122 521	52 552	32 804	112 975	366 787	240 676	147 164	126 111	13 419
2002	244 416	12 190	111 273	57 759	32 035	107 999	340 981	215 338	130 428	125 643	11 962
2001											
January	265 043	13 514	138 358	42 207	36 912	116 661	384 722	269 519	161 236	115 203	15 916
February	262 749	13 341	137 550	42 188	36 169	116 981	382 823	267 530	160 549	115 293	15 922
March	268 982	13 188	139 173	41 719	36 144	117 043	384 655	266 575	158 515	118 080	14 528
April	269 441	13 467	140 500	41 436	35 809	116 613	383 215	265 512	156 770	117 703	13 811
May	267 094	13 236	139 275	42 381	35 054	115 535	380 586	262 807	155 085	117 779	13 559
June	264 173	13 132	139 204	42 233	35 198	114 627	376 851	260 447	153 501	116 404	13 165
July	260 260	12 876	137 757	42 189	35 046	114 132	373 606	257 262	152 027	116 344	13 357
August	256 422	12 724	136 768	41 420	35 054	114 419	371 141	255 651	151 282	115 490	13 404
September	251 408	12 576	132 902	41 211	34 257	112 430	365 883	250 757	149 013	115 126	13 405
October	256 801	12 246	129 448	53 220	33 582	112 249	372 433	245 271	146 576	127 162	13 028
November	251 126	12 124	125 077	53 201	33 110	112 827	369 774	242 793	147 267	126 981	13 149
December	251 447	12 126	122 521	52 552	32 804	112 975	366 787	240 676	147 164	126 111	13 419
2002											
January	251 279	12 036	120 095	52 518	32 764	111 910	359 748	236 240	145 372	123 508	13 392
February	255 258	12 063	119 826	54 023	32 948	111 762	360 658	234 887	145 035	125 771	13 088
March	259 866	12 255	119 134	56 431	32 813	110 551	358 874	230 274	141 927	128 600	12 956
April	256 374	12 400	117 419	55 305	32 923	110 052	355 496	227 806	141 123	127 690	12 922
May	252 826	12 586	116 543	54 386	33 166	110 398	352 850	226 243	140 239	126 607	12 759
June	246 576	12 677	113 011	54 008	32 597	110 099	347 446	221 218	137 818	126 228	12 445
July	247 920	12 915	113 347	57 096	32 627	109 618	345 409	220 167	136 601	125 242	12 320
August	251 835	12 489	117 074	57 366	32 327	109 213	349 208	223 042	135 734	126 166	11 857
September	246 387	12 302	113 640	57 331	32 339	109 182	345 913	218 759	133 304	127 154	12 138
October	241 973	11 961	112 317	57 096	32 518	108 027	342 514	217 145	132 398	125 369	12 300
November	240 651	12 108	111 604	57 050	32 381	107 659	340 380	215 904	131 338	124 476	12 053
December	244 416	12 190	111 273	57 759	32 035	107 999	340 981	215 338	130 428	125 643	11 962

[1]Includes categories not shown separately.
[2]Data are for roughly similar categories in SIC classification system.
[3]Data excludes semiconductors. See Notes and Definitions.
. . . = Not available.

Table 17-8. Motor Vehicle Sales and Inventories

Year and month	Retail sales of new passenger cars						Retail inventories of new domestic passenger cars (thousands of units, end of period)		
	Thousands of units, not seasonally adjusted			Millions of units, seasonally adjusted annual rate			Not seasonally adjusted	Seasonally adjusted	Inventory to sales ratio
	Total	Domestic	Imports	Total	Domestic	Imports			
1967	8 347	7 568	779	8.3	7.6	0.8	...	...	...
1968	9 655	8 625	1 030	9.7	8.6	1.0	...	...	...
1969	9 582	8 464	1 117	9.6	8.5	1.1	...	...	...
1970	8 403	7 119	1 283	8.4	7.1	1.3	...	...	...
1971	10 228	8 662	1 566	10.2	8.7	1.6	...	...	...
1972	10 873	9 253	1 621	10.9	9.3	1.6	1 311	1 379	1.7
1973	11 350	9 589	1 762	11.4	9.6	1.8	1 600	1 654	2.5
1974	8 774	7 362	1 412	8.8	7.4	1.4	1 672	1 730	3.4
1975	8 538	6 951	1 587	8.5	7.0	1.6	1 419	1 468	2.2
1976	9 994	8 492	1 502	10.0	8.5	1.5	1 465	1 494	1.9
1977	11 046	8 971	2 075	11.0	9.0	2.1	1 731	1 743	2.3
1978	11 164	9 164	2 000	11.2	9.2	2.0	1 729	1 731	2.3
1979	10 559	8 230	2 329	10.6	8.2	2.3	1 691	1 667	2.4
1980	8 982	6 581	2 400	9.0	6.6	2.4	1 448	1 440	2.6
1981	8 534	6 209	2 326	8.5	6.2	2.3	1 471	1 495	3.6
1982	7 979	5 758	2 221	8.0	5.8	2.2	1 126	1 127	2.2
1983	9 179	6 793	2 386	9.2	6.8	2.4	1 352	1 350	2.0
1984	10 390	7 952	2 439	10.4	8.0	2.4	1 415	1 411	2.1
1985	10 978	8 205	2 774	11.0	8.2	2.8	1 630	1 619	2.5
1986	11 406	8 215	3 191	11.4	8.2	3.2	1 499	1 515	2.0
1987	10 171	7 081	3 090	10.2	7.1	3.1	1 680	1 716	2.8
1988	10 546	7 539	3 006	10.5	7.5	3.0	1 601	1 601	2.3
1989	9 777	7 078	2 699	9.8	7.1	2.7	1 669	1 687	3.1
1990	9 300	6 897	2 403	9.3	6.9	2.4	1 408	1 418	2.6
1991	8 175	6 137	2 038	8.2	6.1	2.0	1 283	1 296	2.6
1992	8 214	6 277	1 938	8.2	6.3	1.9	1 276	1 288	2.3
1993	8 518	6 734	1 784	8.5	6.7	1.8	1 365	1 378	2.4
1994	8 990	7 255	1 735	9.0	7.3	1.7	1 437	1 449	2.3
1995	8 636	7 129	1 507	8.7	7.2	1.5	1 619	1 582	2.5
1996	8 527	7 254	1 273	8.5	7.3	1.3	1 363	1 354	2.3
1997	8 273	6 906	1 366	8.3	6.9	1.4	1 330	1 264	2.3
1998	8 142	6 764	1 378	8.1	6.8	1.4	1 324	1 288	2.1
1999	8 697	6 982	1 715	8.7	7.0	1.7	1 368	1 332	2.2
2000	8 852	6 833	2 019	8.9	6.8	2.0	1 377	1 341	2.6
2001	8 422	6 323	2 099	8.5	6.4	2.1	956	918	2.1
2002	8 102	5 871	2 231	8.1	5.9	2.2	1 148	1 168	2.3
2000									
January	622	483	139	9.5	7.4	2.0	1 416	1 312	2.1
February	769	609	160	9.6	7.6	2.1	1 399	1 239	2.0
March	836	654	182	9.0	7.0	2.0	1 430	1 244	2.1
April	775	606	169	8.9	6.9	2.0	1 388	1 235	2.2
May	834	653	181	8.8	6.8	2.0	1 348	1 229	2.2
June	841	656	185	8.8	6.8	2.0	1 358	1 263	2.2
July	744	567	177	8.8	6.7	2.0	1 162	1 327	2.4
August	806	615	191	8.8	6.9	1.9	1 174	1 328	2.3
September	748	576	172	9.0	6.9	2.1	1 223	1 339	2.3
October	665	512	153	8.5	6.5	2.0	1 299	1 352	2.5
November	601	456	145	8.3	6.4	2.0	1 390	1 350	2.5
December	611	446	165	8.2	6.1	2.0	1 377	1 341	2.6
2001									
January	592	449	142	8.8	6.8	2.0	1 417	1 283	2.3
February	701	551	150	8.9	6.9	2.0	1 336	1 208	2.1
March	789	602	187	8.3	6.3	2.0	1 322	1 181	2.2
April	690	520	170	8.3	6.2	2.1	1 247	1 174	2.3
May	815	623	191	8.3	6.3	2.0	1 189	1 157	2.2
June	811	621	190	8.4	6.3	2.1	1 147	1 131	2.1
July	667	492	175	8.1	6.1	2.0	958	1 138	2.3
August	727	526	201	8.0	5.9	2.1	986	1 142	2.3
September	640	481	159	7.8	5.8	2.0	963	1 112	2.3
October	813	627	186	10.2	7.8	2.4	858	911	1.4
November	603	437	166	8.4	6.2	2.3	919	881	1.7
December	574	393	181	7.6	5.4	2.2	956	918	2.1
2002									
January	526	365	161	7.7	5.4	2.2	1 065	950	2.1
February	625	456	169	7.9	5.7	2.2	1 139	1 004	2.1
March	742	539	202	8.1	5.9	2.3	1 147	1 009	2.1
April	718	531	187	8.5	6.2	2.3	1 163	1 028	2.0
May	758	560	199	7.8	5.7	2.1	1 169	1 068	2.3
June	761	560	202	8.0	5.7	2.2	1 170	1 107	2.3
July	741	540	201	8.8	6.5	2.3	1 000	1 180	2.2
August	830	606	224	8.7	6.6	2.2	949	1 191	2.2
September	602	432	171	7.9	5.5	2.4	1 004	1 210	2.6
October	605	442	163	7.3	5.3	2.0	1 108	1 234	2.8
November	571	399	172	7.9	5.6	2.3	1 205	1 237	2.7
December	625	442	183	8.4	6.1	2.3	1 148	1 168	2.3

. . . = Not available.

Table 17-8. Motor Vehicle Sales and Inventories—*Continued*

Year and month	Retail sales of new trucks and buses								Unit sales of cars and light trucks (millions of units, seasonally adjusted annual rate)		
	Thousands of units, not seasonally adjusted				Millions of units, seasonally adjusted annual rate						
	Total	0–10,000 pounds		10,001 pounds and over	Total	0–10,000 pounds		10,001 pounds and over	Total	Domestic	Imports
		Domestic	Imports			Domestic	Imports				
1967	...	1 193.8	...	329.7	...	1.2	...	0.3	...	8.8	...
1968	...	1 464.2	...	343.3	...	1.5	...	0.3	...	10.1	...
1969	...	1 551.1	...	384.5	...	1.6	...	0.4	...	10.0	...
1970	...	1 408.5	...	337.3	...	1.4	...	0.3	...	8.5	...
1971	...	1 693.0	...	338.9	...	1.7	...	0.3	...	10.4	...
1972	...	2 122.5	...	437.4	...	2.1	...	0.4	...	11.4	...
1973	...	2 509.4	...	495.7	...	2.5	...	0.5	...	12.1	...
1974	...	2 180.1	...	423.9	...	2.2	...	0.4	...	9.5	...
1975	...	2 052.6	...	298.3	...	2.1	...	0.3	...	9.0	...
1976	3 300.5	2 738.3	237.5	324.7	3.3	2.7	0.2	0.3	13.0	11.2	1.7
1977	3 813.0	3 112.8	323.1	377.1	3.8	3.1	0.3	0.4	14.5	12.1	2.4
1978	4 256.8	3 481.1	335.9	439.8	4.2	3.5	0.3	0.4	15.0	12.6	2.3
1979	3 589.7	2 730.2	469.4	390.1	3.6	2.7	0.5	0.4	13.8	11.0	2.8
1980	2 487.4	1 731.1	484.6	271.7	2.5	1.7	0.5	0.3	11.2	8.3	2.9
1981	2 255.6	1 581.7	447.6	226.3	2.3	1.6	0.4	0.2	10.6	7.8	2.8
1982	2 562.8	1 967.5	410.4	184.9	2.6	2.0	0.4	0.2	10.4	7.7	2.6
1983	3 117.3	2 465.2	463.3	188.8	3.1	2.5	0.5	0.2	12.1	9.3	2.8
1984	4 093.1	3 207.2	607.7	278.2	4.1	3.2	0.6	0.3	14.2	11.2	3.0
1985	4 741.7	3 618.4	828.3	295.0	4.8	3.6	0.8	0.3	15.4	11.8	3.6
1986	4 912.1	3 671.4	967.2	273.5	4.9	3.7	1.0	0.3	16.1	11.9	4.2
1987	5 000.6	3 786.1	912.2	302.3	5.0	3.8	0.9	0.3	14.9	10.9	4.0
1988	5 242.4	4 195.8	697.9	348.7	5.2	4.2	0.7	0.3	15.4	11.7	3.7
1989	5 067.8	4 107.0	630.3	330.5	5.1	4.1	0.6	0.3	14.5	11.2	3.3
1990	4 848.4	3 947.4	602.7	298.3	4.9	4.0	0.6	0.3	13.9	10.8	3.0
1991	4 365.8	3 594.8	528.8	242.2	4.4	3.6	0.5	0.2	12.3	9.7	2.6
1992	4 903.3	4 232.7	395.9	274.7	4.9	4.2	0.4	0.3	12.8	10.5	2.3
1993	5 681.1	4 980.9	364.5	335.7	5.7	5.0	0.4	0.3	13.9	11.7	2.1
1994	6 422.4	5 638.0	396.3	388.1	6.4	5.6	0.4	0.4	15.0	12.9	2.1
1995	6 481.4	5 662.7	390.5	428.2	6.5	5.7	0.4	0.4	14.8	12.9	1.9
1996	6 929.3	6 087.6	430.9	410.8	6.9	6.1	0.4	0.4	15.0	13.3	1.7
1997	7 225.8	6 225.7	571.2	428.9	7.2	6.2	0.6	0.4	15.1	13.1	1.9
1998	7 821.6	6 651.0	646.2	524.4	7.8	6.6	0.6	0.5	15.4	13.4	2.0
1999	8 717.1	7 309.6	762.8	644.7	8.7	7.3	0.8	0.6	16.8	14.3	2.5
2000	8 964.8	7 545.5	840.8	578.5	9.0	7.5	0.8	0.6	17.2	14.4	2.9
2001	9 050.1	7 629.4	977.8	442.9	9.0	7.6	1.0	0.4	17.0	13.9	3.1
2002	9 035.4	7 572.1	1 060.9	402.4	9.0	7.6	1.1	0.4	16.7	13.4	3.3
2000											
January	617.3	516.4	58.5	42.4	9.2	7.7	0.8	0.6	18.0	15.1	2.9
February	770.2	656.0	64.9	49.3	9.8	8.3	0.9	0.6	18.7	15.8	2.9
March	877.2	744.5	70.5	62.2	9.3	7.9	0.8	0.7	17.7	14.9	2.8
April	764.4	642.7	68.0	53.7	9.0	7.5	0.9	0.6	17.3	14.4	2.9
May	831.0	699.2	76.0	55.8	9.0	7.5	0.9	0.6	17.2	14.3	2.9
June	821.8	687.8	73.8	60.2	8.8	7.3	0.9	0.6	17.0	14.1	2.9
July	724.5	607.3	71.8	45.4	8.7	7.3	0.9	0.6	16.9	14.0	2.9
August	776.2	649.8	77.9	48.5	8.9	7.6	0.8	0.6	17.2	14.5	2.7
September	758.4	646.3	70.9	41.2	9.7	8.3	0.8	0.5	18.2	15.2	3.0
October	702.4	593.2	66.1	43.1	8.8	7.4	0.8	0.5	16.8	13.9	2.9
November	661.0	555.3	68.4	37.3	8.3	6.9	0.9	0.5	16.1	13.3	2.8
December	660.4	547.0	74.0	39.4	8.2	6.9	0.8	0.5	15.9	13.0	2.9
2001											
January	604.1	504.8	64.3	35.0	8.7	7.3	0.9	0.5	17.0	14.1	2.9
February	680.0	577.5	67.2	35.3	8.7	7.3	0.9	0.5	17.1	14.2	2.9
March	838.6	714.2	81.0	43.4	8.9	7.5	0.9	0.5	16.7	13.8	2.9
April	687.5	575.5	74.2	37.8	8.4	7.0	1.0	0.4	16.3	13.2	3.1
May	820.5	690.8	86.2	43.5	8.5	7.1	0.9	0.5	16.3	13.4	2.9
June	841.1	714.5	85.1	41.5	9.0	7.6	1.0	0.4	17.0	13.9	3.0
July	707.9	592.6	80.5	34.8	8.7	7.3	1.0	0.4	16.4	13.4	3.0
August	751.7	619.6	95.1	37.0	8.7	7.3	1.0	0.4	16.3	13.2	3.0
September	672.4	566.5	75.3	30.6	8.6	7.3	0.9	0.4	16.0	13.1	3.0
October	939.7	804.7	94.9	40.1	11.4	9.7	1.2	0.5	21.1	17.5	3.6
November	744.9	630.4	83.9	30.6	9.6	8.1	1.0	0.4	17.6	14.3	3.3
December	761.7	638.3	90.1	33.3	9.2	7.8	1.0	0.4	16.4	13.1	3.3
2002											
January	603.9	498.0	78.9	27.0	8.6	7.2	1.1	0.4	15.9	12.6	3.3
February	704.0	600.7	75.8	27.5	9.0	7.6	1.0	0.4	16.5	13.3	3.3
March	798.8	672.9	92.4	33.5	8.8	7.3	1.1	0.4	16.6	13.2	3.3
April	754.3	633.1	83.9	37.3	9.1	7.6	1.1	0.4	17.2	13.8	3.3
May	780.0	651.5	90.1	38.4	8.2	6.8	1.0	0.4	15.6	12.5	3.1
June	802.7	678.9	89.9	33.9	8.7	7.2	1.1	0.4	16.3	13.0	3.3
July	811.3	679.7	97.8	33.8	9.7	8.1	1.2	0.4	18.1	14.6	3.4
August	905.2	759.6	108.7	36.9	10.3	8.8	1.0	0.4	18.6	15.4	3.2
September	648.9	539.4	75.5	34.0	8.8	7.3	1.0	0.4	16.2	12.8	3.4
October	726.5	607.0	82.1	37.4	8.5	7.1	1.0	0.4	15.3	12.4	2.9
November	657.0	538.6	87.7	30.7	8.5	7.0	1.1	0.4	15.9	12.6	3.4
December	842.8	712.7	98.1	32.0	10.2	8.7	1.1	0.4	18.2	14.8	3.4

. . . = Not available.

Table 17-9. Retail and Food Services Sales

(All retail and food services establishments; millions of dollars, not seasonally adjusted.)

Classification basis, year and month	Retail and food services, total [1]	Retail (NAICS industry categories)											Food services and drinking places
		Department store type goods, total [2]	Motor vehicles and parts	Furniture and home furnishings	Electronics and appliances	Building materials and garden	Food and beverages	Health and personal care	Gasoline	Clothing and accessories	General merchandise	Nonstore retailers	
SIC Basis [3]													
1967	297 084	...	56 094	13 605	...	13 435	70 456	11 359	22 362	17 900	40 124	...	22 518
1968	329 336	...	64 314	15 257	...	15 602	75 899	12 378	24 750	19 707	44 019	...	25 279
1969	352 457	...	67 745	16 152	...	17 175	81 258	13 200	26 301	21 384	46 559	...	27 173
1970	374 989	...	65 241	17 043	...	18 080	89 990	14 567	28 903	22 095	49 163	...	30 476
1971	413 969	...	80 718	18 183	...	20 924	94 002	15 143	30 620	24 178	54 365	...	32 321
1972	458 267	...	92 335	21 199	...	24 123	100 589	16 139	33 072	26 367	59 656	...	35 738
1973	511 570	...	104 893	24 244	...	27 466	111 817	17 190	36 942	29 109	65 825	...	40 290
1974	541 686	...	97 551	25 982	...	27 347	126 312	18 595	43 054	30 077	69 540	...	44 606
1975	587 704	...	107 348	27 046	...	27 299	138 665	19 995	47 603	32 398	73 759	...	51 067
1976	655 859	...	130 169	30 300	...	33 259	148 218	21 710	52 037	34 706	79 500	...	57 331
1977	722 109	...	150 129	33 308	...	38 913	158 444	23 381	56 638	37 165	87 824	...	63 370
1978	804 019	...	168 065	36 832	...	45 170	175 425	25 607	59 889	42 649	97 215	...	71 828
1979	896 561	...	178 641	42 417	...	51 016	197 985	28 455	73 521	46 070	103 817	...	82 110
1980	956 921	...	164 149	44 238	...	50 794	220 224	30 951	94 093	49 296	108 955	...	90 058
1981	1 038 163	...	181 903	46 900	...	52 230	236 188	33 999	103 072	53 998	120 534	...	98 118
1982	1 068 747	...	192 440	46 761	...	50 994	246 122	36 440	97 440	55 570	124 624	...	104 593
1983	1 170 163	...	229 979	54 691	...	58 739	256 018	40 591	102 927	60 192	135 959	...	113 281
1984	1 286 914	...	273 320	61 432	...	67 077	271 909	44 011	107 565	64 341	150 283	...	121 321
1985	1 375 027	...	303 199	68 287	...	71 196	285 062	46 994	113 341	70 195	158 636	...	127 949
1986	1 449 636	...	326 138	75 714	...	77 104	297 019	50 546	102 093	75 626	169 397	...	139 415
1987	1 541 299	...	342 896	78 072	...	83 454	309 461	54 142	104 769	79 322	181 970	...	153 461
1988	1 656 202	...	372 570	85 390	...	91 056	325 493	57 842	110 341	85 307	192 521	...	167 993
1989	1 758 971	...	386 011	91 301	...	92 379	347 045	63 343	122 882	92 341	206 306	...	177 829
1990	1 844 611	...	387 605	91 545	...	94 640	368 333	70 558	138 504	95 819	215 514	...	190 149
1991	1 855 937	...	372 647	91 676	...	91 496	374 523	75 540	137 295	97 441	226 730	...	194 424
1992	1 951 589	...	406 935	96 947	...	100 838	377 099	77 788	136 950	104 212	246 420	...	200 164
NAICS Basis													
1992	2 062 495	536 894	427 609	54 994	42 763	160 171	371 451	90 794	156 556	120 346	247 968	81 299	203 415
1993	2 202 443	574 126	481 949	57 935	48 760	171 733	375 440	93 623	162 587	124 989	266 088	88 319	216 051
1994	2 381 946	619 580	550 095	62 766	57 413	190 817	385 265	97 299	171 416	129 327	285 278	98 518	225 629
1995	2 501 956	653 010	588 013	65 528	64 919	199 068	391 312	102 469	181 294	131 605	300 589	105 435	233 625
1996	2 655 590	685 254	635 251	69 415	68 515	212 759	402 020	110 199	194 601	136 860	315 398	119 512	242 896
1997	2 778 359	715 682	660 682	74 092	70 211	229 489	410 288	119 055	199 856	140 565	331 454	127 385	258 040
1998	2 917 597	762 646	699 457	78 574	75 981	243 490	421 579	130 228	191 749	149 442	351 872	133 320	272 646
1999	3 164 346	823 097	779 763	85 218	81 921	262 958	442 503	143 744	211 271	160 019	381 542	149 658	285 922
2000	3 377 968	872 276	816 630	91 662	86 361	276 163	460 481	156 976	246 753	167 882	406 208	176 178	306 276
2001	3 471 600	893 866	840 510	91 428	85 239	287 360	480 530	167 567	245 404	167 241	430 363	173 316	318 285
2002	3 580 012	935 176	852 689	94 978	90 096	300 932	490 795	180 180	240 873	171 874	455 674	180 805	334 605
2000													
January	242 833	57 931	60 143	6 693	6 931	18 488	35 252	12 087	17 598	9 467	26 073	13 631	22 864
February	257 393	61 082	68 416	7 048	6 832	19 463	34 618	12 292	18 198	11 196	27 307	14 037	23 644
March	287 354	68 366	76 751	7 696	7 086	23 972	37 717	13 113	20 705	12 852	31 332	15 052	25 970
April	271 997	66 943	67 513	7 194	6 396	23 995	37 623	12 572	19 643	13 136	31 331	12 848	25 536
May	292 099	70 525	74 730	7 701	6 681	27 538	39 014	13 397	21 061	13 763	33 143	13 553	26 299
June	289 502	69 102	74 757	7 552	6 658	26 054	38 870	12 974	22 051	12 969	32 681	13 463	26 399
July	278 910	67 343	68 968	7 551	6 608	23 679	39 591	12 676	22 030	12 506	31 685	12 348	26 881
August	292 060	73 530	73 747	8 025	7 142	24 394	39 179	13 175	21 853	14 604	33 444	14 036	26 632
September	276 792	68 793	67 685	7 576	6 809	22 714	38 116	12 744	21 327	13 391	31 277	14 341	25 690
October	278 524	69 624	65 656	7 711	6 532	23 670	37 926	13 203	21 304	13 387	32 814	15 823	25 897
November	283 511	82 166	60 237	8 353	7 636	21 671	38 926	13 179	20 429	15 671	39 791	17 061	24 527
December	326 993	116 871	58 027	8 562	11 050	20 525	43 649	15 564	20 554	24 940	55 330	19 985	25 937
2001													
January	257 269	61 635	61 093	7 055	6 752	19 276	37 454	13 426	19 473	10 087	28 718	16 188	24 115
February	254 121	61 619	63 363	6 810	6 303	18 978	35 729	12 962	18 415	11 481	28 617	14 129	23 948
March	287 525	69 077	73 473	7 590	6 706	22 744	39 606	14 085	20 268	13 076	32 396	15 597	27 142
April	282 249	68 243	69 215	6 966	5 908	26 865	38 424	13 554	21 155	13 350	33 522	13 668	26 004
May	304 224	71 886	76 473	7 564	6 312	29 746	41 230	14 319	23 322	13 797	35 162	13 550	27 515
June	295 848	70 425	74 858	7 504	6 528	27 365	40 504	13 743	22 753	12 940	34 376	12 706	27 687
July	287 002	68 761	71 098	7 465	6 536	25 494	40 706	13 602	21 615	12 572	33 381	12 449	27 742
August	303 241	76 720	75 608	7 967	7 087	25 509	41 277	14 127	22 184	14 781	36 211	13 854	28 454
September	269 622	67 263	62 942	7 099	6 345	22 594	39 460	13 028	20 922	12 292	32 617	12 614	25 787
October	300 391	71 342	82 026	7 617	6 552	25 369	40 061	14 388	19 961	13 209	34 879	15 157	26 498
November	295 703	85 602	67 342	8 502	8 168	22 844	40 996	14 072	17 984	15 310	42 418	15 842	25 680
December	334 405	121 293	63 019	9 289	12 042	20 576	45 083	16 261	17 352	24 546	58 066	17 562	27 713
2002													
January	263 642	64 759	62 630	7 158	7 124	20 035	39 474	14 552	16 990	10 345	30 530	15 272	25 221
February	261 043	65 523	64 990	7 114	6 727	19 430	36 985	14 012	16 176	11 739	31 408	13 809	25 232
March	294 166	74 799	72 143	7 803	7 110	22 951	41 557	15 053	19 209	13 963	36 597	15 036	28 378
April	294 252	70 741	73 254	7 418	6 408	29 040	38 593	14 881	20 375	13 201	34 934	14 415	27 666
May	310 806	76 542	74 725	8 030	6 953	30 609	42 554	15 448	21 440	14 156	38 080	14 429	29 107
June	299 179	73 837	73 764	7 556	7 015	28 007	40 844	14 454	20 872	13 196	37 038	12 982	28 855
July	306 129	72 133	79 518	7 724	6 963	27 416	42 015	14 925	21 966	12 803	35 499	13 636	29 045
August	318 526	79 999	82 958	8 270	7 489	26 412	42 196	15 111	22 111	15 002	38 308	14 203	29 964
September	283 660	70 194	68 296	7 547	6 821	24 760	39 234	14 434	20 413	12 418	33 847	14 014	27 181
October	298 773	75 626	69 652	7 968	7 032	26 687	40 733	15 315	21 298	13 399	37 122	16 063	27 949
November	301 391	87 844	63 817	8 909	8 310	23 771	41 917	14 875	19 993	15 816	43 428	16 710	27 377
December	348 445	123 179	66 942	9 481	12 144	21 814	44 693	17 120	20 030	25 296	58 883	20 236	28 630

[1] Include store categories not shown separately.
[2] Furniture, home furnishings, electronics, appliances, clothing, sporting goods, hobby, book, music, general merchandise, office supplies, stationery, and gifts.
[3] Data are for roughly similar categories in SIC classification system.
. . . = Not available.

Table 17-9. Retail and Food Services Sales—*Continued*

(All retail and food services establishments; millions of dollars, not seasonally adjusted.)

Classification basis, year and month	Total	Retail (NAICS industry categories) Total	Department store type goods [2]	Motor vehicles and parts	Furniture and home furnishings	Electronics and appliances	Building materials and garden	Food and beverages Total	Groceries	Beer, wine, and liquor	Health and personal care	Gasoline
SIC Basis [3]												
1967	297 084	...	...	56 094	13 605	...	13 435	70 456	65 036	6 652	11 359	22 362
1968	329 336	...	...	64 314	15 257	...	15 602	75 899	69 873	7 258	12 378	24 750
1969	352 457	...	...	67 745	16 152	...	17 175	81 258	74 836	7 739	13 200	26 301
1970	374 989	...	...	65 241	17 043	...	18 080	89 990	82 556	8 412	14 567	28 903
1971	413 969	...	...	80 718	18 183	...	20 924	94 002	86 419	9 294	15 143	30 620
1972	458 267	...	...	92 335	21 199	...	24 123	100 589	92 856	9 814	16 139	33 072
1973	511 570	...	...	104 893	24 244	...	27 466	111 817	103 555	10 288	17 190	36 942
1974	541 686	...	...	97 551	25 982	...	27 347	126 312	117 182	11 087	18 595	43 054
1975	587 704	...	...	107 348	27 046	...	27 299	138 665	129 087	11 896	19 995	47 603
1976	655 859	...	...	130 169	30 300	...	33 259	148 218	137 992	12 442	21 710	52 037
1977	722 109	...	...	150 129	33 308	...	38 913	158 444	148 116	13 031	23 381	56 638
1978	804 019	...	...	168 065	36 832	...	45 170	175 425	164 234	13 630	25 607	59 889
1979	896 561	...	...	178 641	42 417	...	51 016	197 985	185 318	15 194	28 455	73 521
1980	956 921	...	...	164 149	44 238	...	50 794	220 224	205 630	16 882	30 951	94 093
1981	1 038 163	...	...	181 903	46 900	...	52 230	236 188	220 580	17 702	33 999	103 072
1982	1 068 747	...	...	192 440	46 761	...	50 994	246 122	230 696	18 146	36 440	97 440
1983	1 170 163	...	...	229 979	54 691	...	58 739	256 018	240 402	19 121	40 591	102 927
1984	1 286 914	...	...	273 320	61 432	...	67 077	271 909	258 465	18 273	44 011	107 565
1985	1 375 027	...	...	303 199	68 287	...	71 196	285 062	269 546	19 532	46 994	113 341
1986	1 449 636	...	...	326 138	75 714	...	77 104	297 019	280 833	19 929	50 546	102 093
1987	1 541 299	...	...	342 896	78 072	...	83 454	309 461	290 979	19 826	54 142	104 769
1988	1 656 202	...	...	372 570	85 390	...	91 056	325 493	307 173	19 638	57 842	110 341
1989	1 758 971	...	...	386 011	91 301	...	92 379	347 045	328 072	20 099	63 343	122 882
1990	1 844 611	...	...	387 605	91 545	...	94 640	368 333	348 243	21 722	70 558	138 504
1991	1 855 937	...	...	372 647	91 676	...	91 496	374 523	354 331	22 454	75 540	137 295
1992	1 951 589	...	...	406 935	96 947	...	100 838	377 099	358 148	21 698	77 788	136 950
NAICS Basis												
1992	2 062 495	1 859 080	536 894	427 609	54 994	42 763	160 171	371 451	337 925	21 825	90 794	156 556
1993	2 202 443	1 986 392	574 126	481 949	57 935	48 760	171 733	375 440	341 855	21 675	93 623	162 587
1994	2 381 946	2 156 317	619 580	550 095	62 766	57 413	190 817	385 265	351 056	22 240	97 299	171 416
1995	2 501 956	2 268 331	653 010	588 013	65 528	64 919	199 068	391 312	356 932	22 145	102 469	181 294
1996	2 655 590	2 412 694	685 254	635 251	69 415	68 515	212 759	402 020	366 075	23 300	110 199	194 601
1997	2 778 359	2 520 319	715 682	660 682	74 092	70 211	229 489	410 288	373 072	24 222	119 055	199 856
1998	2 917 597	2 644 951	762 646	699 457	78 574	75 981	243 490	421 579	382 426	25 697	130 228	191 749
1999	3 164 346	2 878 424	823 097	779 763	85 218	81 921	262 958	442 503	401 912	26 921	143 744	211 271
2000	3 377 968	3 071 692	872 276	816 630	91 662	86 361	276 163	460 481	416 727	29 076	156 976	246 753
2001	3 471 600	3 153 315	893 866	840 510	91 428	85 239	287 360	480 530	434 375	30 364	167 567	245 404
2002	3 580 012	3 245 407	935 176	852 689	94 978	90 096	300 932	490 795	442 971	31 324	180 180	240 873
2000												
January	276 101	251 113	70 118	69 202	7 487	7 229	23 399	36 844	33 377	2 296	12 512	19 467
February	279 351	254 251	71 072	70 320	7 595	7 298	23 019	37 182	33 650	2 339	12 556	20 220
March	283 155	257 619	72 220	70 005	7 658	7 260	24 433	37 817	34 265	2 362	12 793	20 582
April	278 740	253 280	72 029	67 883	7 735	7 344	22 627	38 289	34 715	2 350	12 815	19 922
May	279 083	253 747	72 679	67 344	7 724	7 226	22 825	38 129	34 516	2 396	12 982	20 001
June	279 975	254 591	72 150	67 516	7 683	7 080	22 770	38 523	34 872	2 422	13 013	20 532
July	281 400	255 775	72 833	67 640	7 761	7 082	22 795	38 495	34 805	2 444	13 109	20 744
August	280 906	255 470	72 958	67 270	7 739	7 170	22 881	38 578	34 876	2 473	13 215	20 366
September	285 205	259 489	74 175	68 936	7 715	7 282	22 803	38 651	34 928	2 475	13 345	20 888
October	283 723	257 980	73 581	67 224	7 734	7 132	22 951	38 903	35 143	2 502	13 459	21 198
November	283 019	257 336	73 270	66 497	7 628	7 043	22 935	38 855	35 095	2 523	13 503	21 482
December	283 585	258 031	72 994	66 384	7 207	7 003	23 588	39 055	35 455	2 397	13 617	21 168
2001												
January	286 382	259 853	74 186	67 587	7 710	7 009	23 422	39 211	35 395	2 542	13 562	21 446
February	286 090	259 745	73 666	67 858	7 600	6 992	23 751	39 511	35 724	2 500	13 716	21 167
March	284 234	257 908	73 008	67 473	7 560	6 921	23 582	39 524	35 715	2 494	13 795	20 087
April	286 958	260 744	73 392	68 412	7 531	6 867	24 264	39 658	35 886	2 495	13 677	21 369
May	289 014	262 608	73 623	69 083	7 556	6 858	24 258	39 934	36 109	2 513	13 902	21 981
June	287 792	261 348	73 620	68 929	7 626	6 949	24 045	39 971	36 119	2 527	13 896	21 126
July	288 146	261 522	74 787	68 604	7 704	7 072	23 984	40 091	36 208	2 519	14 008	20 315
August	289 550	262 605	75 154	68 786	7 639	7 090	23 959	40 301	36 445	2 519	14 099	20 408
September	284 550	258 370	73 955	66 387	7 426	6 941	23 419	40 611	36 752	2 537	13 934	20 964
October	301 990	275 571	74 910	81 927	7 527	7 071	24 042	40 745	36 899	2 552	14 359	19 647
November	293 741	267 212	75 965	73 711	7 722	7 457	24 084	40 720	36 805	2 585	14 345	18 831
December	293 309	265 679	77 296	71 709	7 826	7 567	23 968	40 704	36 797	2 569	14 403	18 285
2002												
January	292 393	264 799	77 038	69 254	7 797	7 430	24 421	40 848	36 960	2 587	14 684	18 711
February	293 878	266 120	77 912	69 721	7 949	7 490	24 439	40 866	36 913	2 613	14 796	18 572
March	293 579	265 947	77 468	69 270	7 874	7 464	24 579	40 842	36 891	2 615	14 686	19 152
April	297 827	270 022	78 172	69 830	7 883	7 429	25 452	40 713	36 760	2 612	15 092	20 355
May	293 870	266 228	77 352	67 401	7 919	7 499	25 163	40 842	36 870	2 609	14 940	20 037
June	298 026	270 093	78 067	70 685	7 846	7 544	25 112	40 875	36 877	2 624	14 963	19 992
July	300 842	272 941	77 521	73 409	7 747	7 450	24 888	40 970	36 973	2 613	15 030	20 529
August	302 449	274 576	77 878	74 620	7 891	7 373	25 136	40 913	36 919	2 606	15 096	20 323
September	298 239	270 361	77 480	70 877	7 936	7 454	25 217	40 855	36 873	2 598	15 258	20 372
October	299 924	272 197	78 988	70 428	7 905	7 593	25 110	41 034	37 060	2 588	15 269	20 942
November	301 630	273 522	78 562	71 262	8 019	7 449	25 398	41 523	37 521	2 589	15 194	20 935
December	305 816	277 100	78 641	74 969	7 954	7 545	25 281	40 743	36 688	2 634	15 191	21 263

[2]Furniture, home furnishings, electronics, appliances, clothing, sporting goods, hobby, book, music, general merchandise, office supplies, stationery, and gifts.
[3]Data are for roughly similar categories in SIC classification system.
... = Not available.

Table 17-9. Retail and Food Services Sales—*Continued*

(All retail and food services establishments; millions of dollars, not seasonally adjusted.)

Classification basis, year and month	Clothing and accessories Total [1]	Men's clothing	Women's clothing	Family clothing [4]	Shoes	Sporting goods, hobby, book, and music	General merchandise Total	Department stores [5]	Other general merchandise	Miscel-laneous store retailers	Nonstore retailers Total [1]	Electronic shopping and mail-order	Food services and drinking places
SIC Basis [3]													
1967	17 900	3 519	6 812	3 569	3 606	...	40 124	29 183	...	...	...	...	22 518
1968	19 707	3 916	7 435	3 897	4 062	...	44 019	32 431	...	...	...	...	25 279
1969	21 384	4 382	7 842	4 204	4 577	...	46 559	34 754	...	...	...	...	27 173
1970	22 095	4 544	8 239	4 363	4 458	...	49 163	36 167	...	...	...	...	30 476
1971	24 178	4 903	9 222	5 046	4 524	...	54 365	40 472	...	...	...	...	32 321
1972	26 367	5 684	9 739	5 525	4 884	...	59 656	44 451	...	...	...	...	35 738
1973	29 109	6 193	10 732	5 959	5 600	...	65 825	49 342	...	...	...	...	40 290
1974	30 077	6 190	11 338	6 360	5 405	...	69 540	52 059	...	...	...	...	44 606
1975	32 398	6 619	12 438	6 725	5 751	...	73 759	55 702	...	...	...	...	51 067
1976	34 706	6 815	13 426	7 201	8 249	...	79 500	61 500	...	...	...	...	57 331
1977	37 165	7 042	12 537	7 972	7 058	...	87 824	68 856	...	...	...	...	63 370
1978	42 649	7 537	15 995	8 559	8 305	...	97 215	76 137	...	...	...	...	71 828
1979	46 070	7 763	17 030	9 397	9 693	...	103 817	81 161	...	...	...	...	82 110
1980	49 296	7 664	17 592	10 843	10 530	...	108 955	85 464	...	...	...	...	90 058
1981	53 998	7 910	19 060	12 251	11 821	...	120 534	95 638	...	...	...	...	98 118
1982	55 570	7 803	20 017	13 660	11 419	...	124 624	99 841	...	...	...	...	104 593
1983	60 192	7 958	21 847	15 384	11 949	...	135 959	108 637	...	...	...	...	113 281
1984	64 341	8 206	23 764	16 443	12 306	...	150 283	120 487	...	...	...	...	121 321
1985	70 195	8 458	26 149	17 827	13 054	...	158 636	126 412	...	...	...	...	127 949
1986	75 626	8 646	28 600	19 336	13 947	...	169 397	134 486	...	...	...	...	139 415
1987	79 322	9 017	29 208	21 472	14 594	...	181 970	144 017	...	...	...	...	153 461
1988	85 307	9 826	30 567	23 902	15 444	...	192 521	151 523	...	...	...	...	167 993
1989	92 341	10 507	32 231	26 375	17 290	...	206 306	160 524	...	...	...	...	177 829
1990	95 819	10 450	32 812	28 398	18 043	...	215 514	165 808	...	...	...	...	190 149
1991	97 441	10 435	32 865	30 521	17 504	...	226 730	172 922	...	...	...	...	194 424
1992	104 212	10 197	35 750	33 222	18 122	...	246 420	186 423	...	...	...	...	200 164
NAICS Basis													
1992	120 346	10 185	31 840	33 159	18 148	49 296	247 968	177 089	70 879	55 833	81 299	35 252	203 415
1993	124 989	9 968	32 377	35 311	18 528	52 368	266 088	187 685	78 403	62 601	88 319	40 725	216 051
1994	129 327	10 039	30 611	38 118	19 361	57 538	285 278	198 945	86 333	70 585	98 518	47 093	225 629
1995	131 605	9 322	28 723	40 014	19 759	60 922	300 589	205 920	94 669	77 177	105 435	52 741	233 625
1996	136 860	9 554	28 266	42 275	20 604	64 055	315 398	212 203	103 195	84 109	119 512	61 174	242 896
1997	140 565	10 077	27 851	45 259	20 788	65 573	331 454	220 108	111 346	91 669	127 385	70 136	258 040
1998	149 442	10 621	28 690	49 472	21 539	69 456	351 872	223 653	128 219	99 803	133 320	79 489	272 646
1999	160 019	10 540	30 219	53 800	21 968	74 045	381 542	231 048	150 494	105 782	149 658	92 611	285 922
2000	167 882	10 818	32 547	56 435	22 135	77 921	406 208	233 628	172 580	108 477	176 178	110 310	306 276
2001	167 241	10 318	33 070	56 733	22 006	79 382	430 363	230 207	200 156	104 975	173 316	109 463	318 285
2002	171 874	9 926	34 331	59 355	21 785	82 004	455 674	225 912	229 762	104 507	180 805	116 705	334 605
2000													
January	13 356	868	2 407	3 151	1 837	6 125	32 385	19 383	13 002	9 345	13 762	8 644	24 988
February	13 590	883	2 523	3 490	1 830	6 457	32 625	19 081	13 544	9 378	14 011	8 603	25 100
March	13 918	894	2 741	4 287	1 887	6 506	33 306	19 329	13 977	9 281	14 060	8 933	25 536
April	13 750	880	2 662	4 347	1 820	6 629	32 928	19 225	13 703	9 282	14 076	9 047	25 460
May	14 038	915	2 746	4 393	1 833	6 675	33 524	19 523	14 001	8 933	14 346	8 953	25 336
June	13 788	879	2 693	4 340	1 806	6 578	33 520	19 258	14 262	8 873	14 715	9 205	25 384
July	13 844	919	2 766	4 249	1 813	6 683	33 950	19 382	14 568	8 982	14 690	9 223	25 625
August	14 072	905	2 772	4 962	1 848	6 523	33 981	19 299	14 682	8 810	14 865	9 288	25 436
September	14 483	930	2 852	4 468	1 876	6 623	34 539	19 598	14 941	9 070	15 154	9 421	25 716
October	14 244	909	2 812	4 642	1 862	6 480	34 436	19 371	15 065	9 051	15 168	9 452	25 743
November	14 223	909	2 776	5 809	1 854	6 345	34 532	19 615	14 917	8 912	15 381	9 604	25 683
December	14 106	896	2 709	8 297	1 841	6 351	34 903	19 742	15 161	8 722	15 927	9 818	25 554
2001													
January	14 146	918	2 759	3 271	1 846	6 347	35 620	20 001	15 619	8 619	15 174	9 230	26 529
February	14 259	911	2 799	3 557	1 819	6 669	34 756	19 187	15 569	8 775	14 691	9 055	26 345
March	14 018	897	2 752	4 339	1 828	6 576	34 495	18 763	15 732	9 042	14 835	9 232	26 326
April	13 973	823	2 740	4 497	1 853	6 550	35 115	18 946	16 169	8 726	14 602	9 143	26 214
May	13 933	881	2 715	4 512	1 855	6 520	35 311	19 058	16 253	9 005	14 267	9 149	26 406
June	13 825	869	2 711	4 394	1 810	6 532	35 316	19 017	16 299	8 868	14 265	9 222	26 444
July	14 032	855	2 753	4 400	1 884	6 592	36 014	19 345	16 669	8 868	14 238	9 163	26 624
August	14 060	870	2 800	5 074	1 875	6 731	36 199	19 338	16 861	8 793	14 540	9 306	26 945
September	13 408	803	2 713	4 198	1 762	6 548	36 404	19 245	17 159	8 553	13 775	8 546	26 180
October	13 942	857	2 817	4 619	1 803	6 670	36 568	19 149	17 419	8 663	14 410	9 230	26 419
November	13 772	834	2 752	5 577	1 821	6 860	36 883	19 262	17 621	8 636	14 191	9 156	26 529
December	14 171	842	2 800	8 295	1 845	6 734	37 530	19 277	18 253	8 537	14 245	9 254	27 630
2002													
January	14 237	827	2 866	3 342	1 863	6 869	37 358	19 264	18 094	8 630	14 560	9 539	27 594
February	14 495	852	2 910	3 571	1 908	6 830	37 721	19 256	18 465	8 718	14 523	9 647	27 758
March	14 382	849	2 869	4 688	1 841	6 872	37 556	19 082	18 474	8 579	14 691	9 500	27 632
April	14 501	843	2 914	4 376	1 869	6 739	38 311	19 446	18 865	8 725	14 992	9 682	27 805
May	14 071	815	2 814	4 609	1 809	6 861	37 657	18 821	18 836	8 664	15 174	9 776	27 642
June	14 333	825	2 880	4 576	1 821	6 740	38 236	19 060	19 176	8 794	14 973	9 614	27 933
July	14 106	824	2 801	4 644	1 776	6 811	38 019	18 847	19 172	8 716	15 266	9 807	27 901
August	14 200	812	2 814	5 387	1 770	6 807	38 179	18 868	19 311	8 843	15 195	9 827	27 873
September	13 860	808	2 764	4 328	1 720	6 864	37 925	18 577	19 348	8 816	14 927	9 627	27 878
October	14 535	822	2 811	5 189	1 793	6 883	38 608	18 931	19 677	8 720	15 170	9 692	27 727
November	14 409	818	2 878	6 008	1 810	6 906	38 447	18 437	20 010	8 565	15 415	9 837	28 108
December	14 512	819	2 943	8 637	1 802	6 811	38 434	18 270	20 164	8 610	15 787	9 934	28 716

[1] Include store categories not shown separately.
[3] Data are for roughly similar categories in SIC classification system.
[4] Not seasonally adjusted.
[5] Excluding leased departments.
. . . = Not available.

Table 17-10. Retail Inventories

(All retail stores; end of period, millions of dollars.)

Classification basis, year and month	Not seasonally adjusted			Seasonally adjusted (NAICS industry categories)								
	Total	Excluding motor vehicles and parts	Motor vehicles and parts	Total	Excluding motor vehicles and parts	Motor vehicles and parts	Furniture, home furnishings, electronics, and appliances	Building materials and garden	Food and beverages	Clothing and accessories	General merchandise Total	Department stores [1]
SIC Basis [2]												
1967	...	...	...	...	...	...	...	...	...	...	...	...
1968	...	...	...	...	...	...	...	...	...	...	...	...
1969	...	...	...	...	...	...	...	...	...	...	...	...
1970	...	...	...	...	...	...	...	...	...	...	...	...
1971	...	...	...	...	...	...	...	...	...	...	...	...
1972	53 791	42 126	11 665	55 079	43 224	11 855	4 414	4 268	5 981	5 200	11 743	8 214
1973	61 835	47 565	14 270	63 237	48 881	14 356	4 800	4 844	6 946	5 791	13 137	9 016
1974	69 644	52 874	16 770	71 067	54 330	16 737	5 439	5 131	8 043	6 071	13 647	9 632
1975	70 273	53 795	16 478	71 744	55 397	16 347	5 717	5 474	8 069	6 029	13 521	9 848
1976	77 617	58 994	18 623	79 273	60 853	18 420	6 115	6 481	8 709	6 516	14 886	11 037
1977	87 411	65 269	22 142	89 444	67 565	21 879	6 610	7 502	9 362	7 646	17 307	13 145
1978	100 242	74 752	25 490	102 694	77 506	25 188	7 876	8 397	10 193	8 914	19 853	14 829
1979	108 408	81 152	27 256	111 098	84 165	26 933	8 681	8 981	11 343	9 514	21 033	15 686
1980	117 857	92 190	25 667	121 078	95 525	25 553	9 207	9 685	13 390	10 929	23 171	16 814
1981	129 073	100 936	28 137	132 719	104 693	28 026	9 795	10 180	14 649	12 234	25 951	19 279
1982	130 797	102 360	28 437	134 628	106 276	28 352	9 714	10 203	15 248	12 392	26 548	19 645
1983	143 513	110 483	33 030	147 833	114 914	32 919	11 217	11 716	16 282	13 466	28 651	21 196
1984	162 773	123 493	39 280	167 812	128 808	39 004	12 433	12 890	17 624	14 641	34 392	25 750
1985	176 941	130 542	46 399	181 881	136 083	45 798	13 762	13 683	19 283	15 689	34 683	25 525
1986	181 651	135 461	46 190	186 510	141 264	45 246	14 340	14 033	19 612	16 067	35 743	26 412
1987	203 210	145 410	57 800	207 836	151 675	56 161	15 050	14 868	19 898	17 280	38 285	28 450
1988	214 824	153 909	60 915	219 047	160 140	58 907	16 311	16 157	21 601	18 079	39 179	29 987
1989	233 143	166 707	66 436	237 234	173 162	64 072	17 280	17 122	23 543	19 422	43 107	33 678
1990	236 152	170 635	65 517	239 815	176 708	63 107	17 442	17 015	25 038	19 690	42 377	33 387
1991	239 478	176 344	63 134	243 389	182 508	60 881	17 649	16 718	25 580	20 263	45 764	36 110
1992	248 198	181 697	66 501	252 185	188 051	64 134	17 934	17 234	25 738	22 249	48 630	38 033
NAICS Basis												
1992	263 182	189 658	73 524	267 931	196 676	71 255	16 483	25 300	27 323	27 448	49 783	38 333
1993	281 052	201 472	79 580	286 026	208 928	77 098	18 399	26 944	27 412	28 165	53 700	40 854
1994	307 023	216 567	90 456	312 162	224 485	87 677	20 661	29 506	28 053	29 573	56 830	42 136
1995	324 410	226 340	98 070	329 644	234 538	95 106	22 032	31 138	28 628	29 354	59 691	43 596
1996	335 257	233 374	101 883	340 552	241 660	98 892	22 434	32 359	29 595	29 830	60 611	44 124
1997	345 657	239 724	105 933	350 901	248 138	102 763	22 260	33 856	29 826	31 133	60 735	44 309
1998	359 587	251 780	107 807	365 085	260 486	104 599	22 840	36 314	31 054	32 360	61 675	43 525
1999	388 879	267 062	121 817	394 311	275 904	118 407	24 159	38 867	33 099	33 585	64 525	44 031
2000	412 144	276 922	135 222	417 786	286 002	131 784	25 582	40 641	32 938	36 398	65 256	42 928
2001	399 880	273 980	125 900	405 571	282 665	122 906	24 328	40 699	34 186	35 187	65 221	40 700
2002	431 121	281 124	149 997	436 317	289 851	146 466	26 453	43 288	34 268	36 061	66 344	37 564
2000												
January	386 182	263 677	122 505	394 078	274 705	119 373	23 970	38 951	33 015	32 858	64 813	44 021
February	390 830	267 359	123 471	395 623	276 161	119 462	24 149	39 222	33 034	33 295	65 032	44 101
March	399 277	273 571	125 706	397 613	277 401	120 212	24 617	39 266	33 058	33 720	64 606	43 593
April	402 125	274 426	127 699	399 094	277 306	121 788	24 501	39 765	33 102	33 932	64 500	43 427
May	401 987	274 454	127 533	403 505	279 792	123 713	24 711	39 980	33 276	34 511	64 705	43 490
June	402 234	273 179	129 055	407 948	280 689	127 259	25 243	40 314	32 732	34 375	65 039	43 484
July	392 745	274 771	117 974	406 745	280 774	125 971	25 166	40 522	32 641	34 824	64 657	42 985
August	399 445	280 322	119 123	412 074	282 657	129 417	25 454	40 807	32 676	35 263	64 722	42 950
September	410 276	289 474	120 802	411 753	282 371	129 382	24 944	40 911	32 860	35 246	64 700	42 804
October	435 289	308 052	127 237	414 440	284 283	130 157	25 295	40 745	32 875	35 817	65 164	43 228
November	445 310	312 818	132 492	417 274	285 714	131 560	25 950	41 018	32 725	36 013	65 099	43 109
December	412 144	276 922	135 222	417 786	286 002	131 784	25 582	40 641	32 938	36 398	65 256	42 928
2001												
January	410 215	275 052	135 163	418 174	286 502	131 672	25 523	40 860	33 144	36 224	65 670	43 020
February	411 235	277 381	133 854	415 880	286 489	129 391	24 981	40 736	33 415	36 367	65 976	43 037
March	417 997	283 138	134 859	416 218	287 057	129 161	25 211	40 675	33 530	36 321	67 126	43 498
April	419 123	283 507	135 616	416 516	286 844	129 672	25 144	40 663	33 772	36 040	66 795	43 297
May	415 535	280 936	134 599	416 918	286 445	130 473	24 817	40 857	33 770	35 907	67 057	43 244
June	410 358	277 928	132 430	416 088	285 617	130 471	24 497	40 684	33 900	36 089	67 116	43 079
July	402 453	278 063	124 390	416 937	284 311	132 626	24 235	40 286	33 945	35 810	66 431	42 295
August	407 342	283 439	123 903	420 198	285 696	134 502	24 202	40 652	34 042	35 845	67 052	42 632
September	417 731	292 520	125 211	419 382	285 124	134 258	23 969	40 755	34 043	36 057	66 625	42 540
October	429 029	309 441	119 588	407 895	285 610	122 285	24 160	40 855	34 185	36 236	66 586	41 979
November	432 532	310 218	122 314	404 842	283 366	121 476	24 295	40 667	34 286	35 456	65 817	41 261
December	399 880	273 980	125 900	405 571	282 665	122 906	24 328	40 699	34 186	35 187	65 221	40 700
2002												
January	400 412	271 745	128 667	408 259	282 807	125 452	24 892	41 018	33 981	35 247	64 525	39 893
February	406 554	273 731	132 823	410 708	282 508	128 200	25 024	41 113	33 955	34 749	64 859	40 012
March	412 674	278 540	134 134	410 401	282 004	128 397	25 174	41 570	33 827	34 512	64 196	39 237
April	414 211	279 034	135 177	411 707	282 433	129 274	25 213	41 855	33 841	34 771	64 098	38 794
May	415 200	277 898	137 302	416 594	283 592	133 002	25 662	41 743	33 817	34 774	64 580	38 637
June	412 835	276 342	136 493	418 653	284 223	134 430	25 580	41 816	33 795	35 129	64 342	38 409
July	408 641	279 567	129 074	423 351	285 765	137 586	25 909	41 774	33 691	35 413	65 185	38 603
August	409 384	283 098	126 286	423 594	285 665	137 929	25 911	41 735	33 956	35 448	65 109	38 264
September	425 816	295 156	130 660	428 436	287 618	140 818	26 304	42 293	34 290	35 706	65 166	38 006
October	451 108	310 293	140 815	431 093	286 538	144 555	26 302	42 942	33 650	35 551	65 097	37 460
November	462 680	315 157	147 523	434 693	288 090	146 603	26 432	42 844	33 871	35 627	66 124	37 764
December	431 121	281 124	149 997	436 317	289 851	146 466	26 453	43 288	34 268	36 061	66 344	37 564

[1]Excluding leased departments.
[2]Data are for roughly similar categories in SIC classification system.
. . . = Not available.

Table 17-11. Merchant Wholesalers—Sales and Inventories

(Millions of dollars.)

Classification basis, year, and month	Not seasonally adjusted						Seasonally adjusted					
	Sales			Inventories (current cost, end of period)			Sales			Inventories (current cost, end of period)		
	Total	Durable goods establish-ments	Nondurable goods establish-ments	Total	Durable goods establish-ments	Nondurable goods establish-ments	Total	Durable goods establish-ments	Nondurable goods establish-ments	Total	Durable goods establish-ments	Nondurable goods establish-ments
SIC Basis[1]												
1972	358 388	168 879	189 509	...	...	...	358 388	168 879	189 509	...	...	...
1973	457 378	208 554	248 824	...	...	...	457 378	208 554	248 824	...	...	...
1974	575 786	255 863	319 923	...	...	...	575 786	255 863	319 923	...	...	...
1975	559 606	235 723	323 883	...	...	...	559 606	235 723	323 883	...	...	...
1976	608 381	263 605	344 776	...	...	...	608 381	263 605	344 776	...	...	...
1977	673 633	304 721	368 912	...	...	...	673 633	304 721	368 912	...	...	...
1978	796 961	372 176	424 785	...	...	...	796 961	372 176	424 785	...	...	...
1979	948 614	436 254	512 360	...	...	...	948 614	436 254	512 360	...	...	...
1980	1 117 187	486 509	630 678	124 015	78 849	45 166	1 117 187	486 509	630 678	122 631	79 372	43 259
1981	1 214 156	525 607	688 549	130 709	85 371	45 338	1 214 156	525 607	688 549	129 654	85 856	43 798
1982	1 142 535	480 318	662 217	128 514	84 806	43 708	1 142 535	480 318	662 217	127 428	85 222	42 206
1983	1 190 705	523 080	667 625	131 306	84 709	46 597	1 190 705	523 080	667 625	130 075	85 180	44 895
1984	1 346 392	622 361	724 031	143 458	94 895	48 563	1 346 392	622 361	724 031	142 452	95 474	46 978
1985	1 361 507	651 864	709 643	148 403	96 659	51 744	1 361 507	651 864	709 643	147 409	97 371	50 038
1986	1 379 514	681 691	697 823	154 081	101 369	52 712	1 379 514	681 691	697 823	153 574	102 349	51 225
1987	1 475 613	730 592	745 021	164 310	106 820	57 490	1 475 613	730 592	745 021	163 903	108 112	55 791
1988	1 614 249	801 751	812 498	179 828	115 613	64 215	1 614 249	801 751	812 498	178 801	117 045	61 756
1989	1 725 123	851 550	873 573	187 897	120 701	67 196	1 725 123	851 550	873 573	187 009	122 237	64 772
1990	1 794 072	880 767	913 305	196 881	124 839	72 042	1 794 072	880 767	913 305	195 833	126 461	69 372
1991	1 779 673	860 138	919 535	201 777	125 921	75 856	1 779 673	860 138	919 535	200 448	127 399	73 049
1992	1 849 798	908 917	940 881	209 675	130 044	79 631	1 849 798	908 917	940 881	208 302	131 509	76 793
NAICS Basis												
1992	1 731 623	832 807	898 816	194 708	117 929	76 779	1 731 623	832 807	898 816	193 706	119 591	74 115
1993	1 809 990	909 079	900 911	203 031	123 362	79 669	1 809 990	909 079	900 911	201 939	125 178	76 761
1994	1 933 598	1 004 153	929 445	219 892	136 039	83 853	1 933 598	1 004 153	929 445	218 856	138 085	80 771
1995	2 114 720	1 106 797	1 007 923	236 344	147 576	88 768	2 114 720	1 106 797	1 007 923	235 128	149 926	85 202
1996	2 239 784	1 156 617	1 083 167	238 510	150 494	88 016	2 239 784	1 156 617	1 083 167	237 828	152 850	84 978
1997	2 334 495	1 223 777	1 110 718	256 297	161 884	94 413	2 334 495	1 223 777	1 110 718	255 427	164 329	91 098
1998	2 379 824	1 265 755	1 114 069	269 241	171 639	97 602	2 379 824	1 265 755	1 114 069	268 385	174 282	94 103
1999	2 541 564	1 354 588	1 186 976	286 175	182 048	104 127	2 541 564	1 354 588	1 186 976	285 167	184 760	100 407
2000	2 742 593	1 422 583	1 320 010	303 879	191 173	112 706	2 742 593	1 422 583	1 320 010	302 495	194 016	108 479
2001	2 708 666	1 350 272	1 358 394	289 459	173 111	116 348	2 708 666	1 350 272	1 358 394	287 556	175 671	111 885
2002	2 751 001	1 338 776	1 412 225	290 763	171 251	119 512	2 751 001	1 338 776	1 412 225	288 847	173 810	115 037
1999												
January	180 788	94 161	86 627	272 518	173 737	98 781	199 837	106 535	93 302	268 718	174 569	94 149
February	184 707	98 797	85 910	273 051	175 593	97 458	202 752	109 408	93 344	270 898	175 516	95 382
March	220 680	119 170	101 510	272 631	175 977	96 654	205 012	109 674	95 338	271 746	176 028	95 718
April	207 781	110 552	97 229	273 104	176 650	96 454	205 884	109 774	96 110	271 857	175 047	96 810
May	207 225	108 737	98 488	270 448	177 602	92 846	210 061	111 753	98 308	272 342	176 373	95 969
June	221 776	119 335	102 441	269 978	177 902	92 076	211 400	112 259	99 141	272 666	177 160	95 506
July	210 098	112 435	97 663	274 235	180 703	93 532	212 358	113 495	98 863	275 453	178 461	96 992
August	217 901	116 674	101 227	272 262	178 663	93 599	214 035	113 524	100 511	276 389	178 319	98 070
September	221 392	119 465	101 927	274 493	178 969	95 524	215 901	114 392	101 509	278 115	179 753	98 362
October	221 626	118 782	102 844	283 573	180 885	102 688	218 491	116 120	102 371	280 821	181 354	99 467
November	220 777	116 403	104 374	286 659	182 690	103 969	220 956	117 166	103 790	284 221	183 997	100 224
December	226 813	120 077	106 736	286 175	182 048	104 127	222 909	118 997	103 912	285 167	184 760	100 407
2000												
January	203 279	105 267	98 012	291 671	184 961	106 710	224 414	119 279	105 135	287 918	185 875	102 043
February	213 368	111 512	101 856	291 610	187 281	104 329	223 157	117 612	105 545	289 645	187 245	102 400
March	242 530	128 029	114 501	292 564	188 186	104 378	226 469	118 421	108 048	291 680	188 262	103 418
April	217 105	112 955	104 150	295 024	191 701	103 323	227 252	118 831	108 421	294 039	190 066	103 973
May	237 428	123 114	114 314	293 441	192 554	100 887	227 163	119 061	108 102	295 790	191 477	104 313
June	240 991	126 618	114 373	295 002	194 300	100 702	230 462	119 300	111 162	297 929	193 546	104 383
July	220 291	114 000	106 291	297 257	196 163	101 094	229 378	118 559	110 819	298 475	193 685	104 790
August	240 190	125 987	114 203	295 571	194 688	100 883	228 776	118 815	109 961	299 345	194 167	105 178
September	230 418	120 963	109 455	296 444	193 105	103 339	230 791	119 003	111 788	299 739	193 746	105 993
October	241 800	125 495	116 305	304 113	193 814	110 299	232 045	119 297	112 748	301 185	194 188	106 997
November	230 256	117 231	113 025	305 627	193 596	112 031	231 213	118 402	112 811	302 989	194 861	108 128
December	224 937	111 412	113 525	303 879	191 173	112 706	233 636	117 185	116 451	302 495	194 016	108 479
2001												
January	223 965	109 262	114 703	305 759	193 284	112 475	232 493	116 615	115 878	302 009	194 330	107 679
February	211 581	105 210	106 371	303 688	193 495	110 193	231 493	116 308	115 185	302 055	193 600	108 455
March	238 515	121 764	116 751	302 473	192 377	110 096	228 323	115 671	112 652	301 917	192 695	109 222
April	222 832	111 391	111 441	303 046	193 421	109 625	227 535	113 997	113 538	302 431	191 921	110 510
May	237 667	118 307	119 360	300 282	191 811	108 471	226 939	113 909	113 030	303 007	190 868	112 139
June	227 831	115 634	112 197	298 023	188 536	109 487	223 661	111 826	111 835	300 842	187 728	113 114
July	222 604	111 562	111 042	296 395	188 098	108 297	224 892	112 168	112 724	297 720	185 636	112 084
August	236 239	118 915	117 324	292 974	184 334	108 640	225 889	112 421	113 468	296 867	183 705	113 162
September	217 488	108 610	108 878	292 704	181 797	110 907	224 719	110 318	114 401	295 789	182 312	113 477
October	236 486	117 173	119 313	296 063	181 262	114 801	221 109	108 662	112 447	293 145	181 617	111 528
November	220 684	108 894	111 790	292 356	176 714	115 642	221 293	109 786	111 507	289 874	177 869	112 005
December	212 774	103 550	109 224	289 459	173 111	116 348	221 152	109 397	111 755	287 556	175 671	111 885
2002												
January	214 244	102 838	111 406	290 829	173 686	117 143	222 112	109 727	112 385	286 905	174 637	112 268
February	204 534	100 130	104 404	285 905	172 847	113 058	224 199	111 181	113 018	284 463	172 747	111 716
March	226 710	111 983	114 727	285 298	172 040	113 258	223 530	109 634	113 896	284 642	172 163	112 479
April	230 318	113 099	117 219	283 146	172 966	110 180	227 173	111 649	115 524	282 779	171 389	111 390
May	236 555	115 979	120 576	279 623	171 597	108 026	227 446	112 108	115 338	282 853	170 864	111 989
June	226 370	113 159	113 211	281 019	171 765	109 254	228 575	112 312	116 263	283 920	171 122	112 798
July	234 510	115 094	119 416	284 385	174 439	109 946	229 714	112 105	117 609	286 083	172 335	113 748
August	237 904	116 468	121 436	282 668	173 476	109 192	232 373	112 745	119 628	286 685	173 202	113 483
September	230 444	113 603	116 841	284 324	172 541	111 783	231 752	111 647	120 105	287 186	173 216	113 970
October	248 546	120 106	128 440	288 730	172 378	116 352	231 615	110 707	120 908	285 890	172 806	113 084
November	228 956	108 375	120 581	288 743	172 059	116 684	234 619	111 574	123 045	286 317	173 289	113 028
December	231 910	107 942	123 968	290 763	171 251	119 512	233 732	110 678	123 054	288 847	173 810	115 037

[1]Data are for roughly similar categories in SIC classification system.
. . . = Not available.

Table 17-12. Selected Service Industries—Receipts of Taxable Firms, 1986–1998, by SIC Industry

(By kind of business and SIC code, millions of dollars.)

Year	Arrangement of passenger transportation (472)	Real estate agents and managers (653)	Hotels, rooming houses, camps and other lodging places, except on membership basis (70, ex. 704)	Personal services (72)	Business services (73)	Automotive repair, services, and parking (75)	Miscellaneous repair services (76)	Motion pictures (78)
1986	7 465	48 360	47 634	39 587	170 250	53 867	22 478	23 740
1987	8 196	52 919	53 630	43 247	188 856	58 278	24 599	27 754
1988	9 521	58 980	58 637	48 329	223 369	66 053	27 659	31 746
1989	11 041	62 325	61 229	51 832	251 648	70 961	30 064	36 173
1990	12 276	63 023	64 225	54 736	280 699	73 722	32 848	39 982
1991	11 438	63 180	65 284	54 620	287 214	71 542	32 401	42 838
1992	11 926	73 115	71 038	59 597	309 439	78 511	35 238	45 662
1993	12 396	79 206	74 149	62 597	337 403	84 324	36 772	49 799
1994	13 125	80 947	79 555	66 105	375 067	91 865	40 683	53 504
1995	14 192	82 667	84 093	70 607	425 075	99 227	44 870	57 184
1996	15 354	90 186	88 961	73 905	484 242	106 638	46 101	60 279
1997	16 461	99 854	94 139	77 712	548 434	111 444	47 895	62 865
1998	17 038	108 639	100 650	82 798	638 500	119 978	52 365	66 229

Year	Amusement and recreation services (79)	Health services (80)	Legal services (81)	Vocational schools (824)	Social services (83)	Museums, art galleries, and botanical and zoological gardens (84)	Engineering, accounting, research, management and related services (87)
1986	33 984	173 885	63 390	3 327	. . .	. . .	127 885
1987	36 646	196 212	72 115	3 400	. . .	. . .	139 897
1988	41 272	221 741	81 636	4 263	. . .	. . .	160 446
1989	44 530	241 558	89 144	4 577	. . .	. . .	183 528
1990	50 126	271 212	97 640	4 519	15 509	144	198 395
1991	51 654	293 907	100 027	4 183	16 365	154	202 696
1992	57 699	321 653	108 443	4 429	18 201	192	215 624
1993	63 651	335 108	112 145	4 507	20 146	222	222 853
1994	68 453	351 419	114 603	4 710	22 498	231	235 447
1995	77 452	376 279	116 000	5 285	24 858	247	263 835
1996	85 733	398 353	124 659	6 190	27 694	273	292 260
1997	92 837	420 361	133 015	7 031	30 150	322	321 079
1998	97 512	444 727	141 827	8 268	31 970	388	360 823

. . . = Not available.

Table 17-13. Selected Service Industries—Revenue of Tax-Exempt Firms, 1986–1998, by SIC Industry

(By kind of business and SIC code, millions of dollars.)

Year	Camps and member- ship lodging (703, 704)	Selected amuse- ment and recreation services (792, 7991, 7997, 7999)	Health services (80)	Legal aid societies and similar legal services (81)	Libraries (823)	Vocational schools (824)	Social services (83)	Museums, art galleries, and botanical and zoological gardens (84)	Selected membership organizations (86 [pt])	Research, develop- ment, and testing services (873)	Commer- cial, physical, and biological research (8731)	Non- commercial research organizations (8733)	Manage- ment and public relations services (874, ex. 8744)
1986	...	5 070	...	563	...	...	...	...	...	7 125	...	...	791
1987	...	5 858	...	665	...	...	...	...	...	8 304	...	...	902
1988	...	6 506	...	775	...	...	...	...	...	9 014	...	...	1 201
1989	...	7 163	...	944	...	...	...	...	...	9 975	...	...	1 494
1990	798	7 922	267 858	1 088	476	507	45 255	2 871	31 458	11 035	...	...	1 933
1991	782	8 160	298 168	1 162	481	486	49 055	3 048	33 288	11 463	...	...	2 150
1992	808	8 993	324 416	1 161	527	549	53 673	3 199	36 256	12 534	...	...	2 246
1993	817	10 279	345 081	1 190	606	569	59 052	3 615	39 426	13 180	...	...	2 588
1994	836	11 560	363 112	1 241	655	612	63 493	3 972	41 907	13 919	...	...	3 119
1995	846	12 778	385 210	1 278	730	696	70 303	4 295	45 873	14 493	5 951	7 688	3 732
1996	877	13 299	401 047	1 259	754	772	75 240	4 729	48 897	14 906	5 703	8 293	4 821
1997	929	14 600	414 990	1 446	850	871	83 235	6 231	51 098	16 839	5 950	9 953	6 583
1998	993	15 360	436 078	1 599	934	943	90 458	6 566	55 955	18 732	6 770	10 753	7 761

. . . = Not available.

Table 17-14. Selected Service Industries—Revenue, 1998–2001, by NAICS Industry

(Millions of dollars.)

NAICS code	Kind of business	1998	1999	2000	2001
	Total for selected service industries	3 706 084	4 021 753	4 370 743	4 492 646
484	Truck transportation	173 458	187 228	198 792	194 929
492	Couriers and messengers	46 947	49 652	55 265	55 914
493	Warehousing and storage	12 073	12 565	13 101	13 595
51	Information	694 293	774 394	853 285	878 302
511	Publishing industries	202 876	220 631	235 193	235 073
512	Motion picture and sound recording industries	60 592	65 051	68 160	69 366
513	Broadcasting and telecommunications	382 429	426 755	471 278	489 184
514	Information services and data processing services	48 396	61 958	78 653	84 680
5231	Securities and commodity contracts intermediation and brokerage	168 331	203 419	239 193	201 377
532	Rental and leasing services	90 073	98 173	106 287	104 091
54	Professional, scientific, and technical services (except notaries and landscape architectural services)	745 427	812 941	895 736	937 176
56	Administrative and support and waste management and remediation services (except landscaping services)	353 731	392 907	430 915	432 595
561	Administrative and support services	310 374	344 996	381 240	383 539
562	Waste management and remediation services	43 357	47 912	49 675	49 056
62	Health care and social assistance	963 848	1 005 584	1 063 990	1 148 678
621	Ambulatory health care services	399 518	417 226	443 730	480 191
622	Hospitals	397 373	413 035	430 329	462 215
623	Nursing and residential care facilities	100 138	102 336	108 638	116 066
624	Social assistance	66 820	72 987	81 293	90 206
71	Arts, entertainment, and recreation	123 968	131 519	139 831	146 518
711	Performing arts, spectator sports, and related industries	50 337	53 319	56 800	59 107
712	Museums, historical sites, and similar institutions	7 222	7 671	8 291	8 224
713	Amusement, gambling, and recreation industries	66 409	70 529	74 740	79 187
81	Other services (except public administration, religious, labor, and political organizations, and private households)	333 934	353 370	374 348	379 473
811	Repair and maintenance	133 797	139 734	146 172	152 593
812	Personal and laundry services	88 436	94 009	99 709	102 423
813	Religious, grantmaking, civic, professional, and similar organizations (except religious, labor, and political organizations)	111 702	119 627	128 467	124 457

Table 17-15. Selected Service Industries—Revenue [1]—Total and E-Commerce, 1998–2001, by NAICS Industry

(Millions of dollars, percent.)

NAICS code	Description	Value of revenue, 2000		Value of revenue, 2001	
		Total	E-commerce revenue	Total	E-commerce revenue
	Total for selected service industries	4 647 156	37 312	4 759 796	37 261
	Selected transportation and warehousing	237 251	3 691	234 436	3 930
484	Truck transportation	171 691	1 158	167 800	1 357
492	Couriers and messengers	52 773	2 453	53 363	2 482
493	Warehousing and storage	12 787	B	13 273	B
51	Information	845 665	9 305	870 204	10 438
511	Publishing industries	233 327	4 748	233 110	4 941
513	Broadcasting and telecommunications	469 707	1 880	487 538	2 516
51419	Online information services	31 438	1 997	32 390	1 850
	Selected finance	338 071	5 976	293 981	3 754
5231	Securities and commodity contracts intermediation and brokerage	232 798	5 664	195 667	3 570
532	Rental and leasing services	100 847	B	98 508	B
	Selected professional, scientific, and technical services	806 789	5 550	843 847	5 309
5415	Computer systems design and related services	175 495	3 541	174 574	3 609
	Selected administrative and support and waste management and remediation services	411 236	9 680	411 947	9 599
5615	Travel arrangement and reservation services	26 306	6 185	26 054	6 272
62	Health care and social assistance services	1 027 439	B	1 109 519	B
71	Arts, entertainment, and recreation services	122 117	B	128 904	B
72	Accommodation and food services	435 365	B	442 274	B
	Selected other services	322 376	554	326 176	656
811	Repair and maintenance	125 032	256	130 868	214
813	Religious, grantmaking, civic, professional, and similar organizations	128 467	267	124 457	383

NAICS code	Description	E-commerce as percent of total revenue			
		1998	1999	2000	2001
	Total for selected service industries	0.4	0.6	0.8	0.8
	Selected transportation and warehousing	1.2	1.4	1.6	1.7
484	Truck transportation	0.4	0.4	0.7	0.8
492	Couriers and messengers	4.1	4.8	4.6	4.7
493	Warehousing and storage	B	B	B	B
51	Information	0.4	0.7	1.1	1.2
511	Publishing industries	0.8	1.4	2.0	2.1
513	Broadcasting and telecommunications	0.1	0.2	0.4	0.5
51419	Online information services	3.6	5.1	6.4	5.7
	Selected finance	0.9	1.4	1.8	1.3
5231	Securities and commodity contracts intermediation and brokerage	1.3	1.9	2.4	1.8
532	Rental and leasing services	B	B	B	B
	Selected professional, scientific, and technical services	0.4	0.6	0.7	0.6
5415	Computer systems design and related services	1.3	1.9	2.0	2.1
	Selected administrative and support and waste management and remediation services	1.4	1.9	2.4	2.3
5615	Travel arrangement and reservation services	18.2	21.1	23.5	24.1
62	Health care and social assistance services	B	B	B	B
71	Arts, entertainment, and recreation services	B	B	B	B
72	Accommodation and food services	B	B	B	B
	Selected other services	0.1	0.1	0.2	0.2
811	Repair and maintenance	0.1	0.1	0.2	0.2
813	Religious, grantmaking, civic, professional, and similar organizations	0.1	0.1	0.2	0.3

[1] Includes data only for businesses with paid employees, except for accommodation and food services, which also includes businesses with and without paid employees. Note that accommodation and food services were not included in Table 17-14.
B = Data do not meet publication standards because of high sampling variability or poor response quality. Unpublished estimates derived from this table by subtraction should be used with caution and not be attributed to the U.S. Census Bureau.

NOTES AND DEFINITIONS

TABLE 17-1
PETROLEUM AND PETROLEUM PRODUCTS— IMPORTS, DOMESTIC PRODUCTION, AND STOCKS

SOURCES: IMPORTS: U.S. DEPARTMENT OF COMMERCE, BUREAU OF THE CENSUS (SEE NOTES AND DEFINITIONS TO TABLES 7-8 THROUGH 7-11); SUPPLY (NET IMPORTS AND DOMESTIC PRODUCTION) AND STOCKS: U.S. DEPARTMENT OF ENERGY, ENERGY INFORMATION ADMINISTRATION.

Notes on the data

The import data in columns 1 through 6 of this table are those published as Exhibit 17: "Imports of Energy-related Petroleum Products, including Crude Petroleum" of the monthly Census-BEA foreign trade press release. *Total energy-related petroleum products* includes the following Standard International Trade Classification (SITC) commodity groupings: crude oil, petroleum preparations, and liquefied propane and butane gas.

The data in columns 7 through 11, on exports, imports, and net imports (imports minus exports) of petroleum and products and domestic production of crude oil and natural gas plant liquids, all expressed as thousands of barrels per day, and in columns 12 through 14 depicting stocks of crude oil in millions of barrels, are derived from the Department of Energy's weekly petroleum supply reporting system and are published in the Energy Information Administration publications "Petroleum Supply Monthly" and *Monthly Energy Review*. Stock totals are as of the end of the period. Geographic coverage includes the 50 states and the District of Columbia.

Data availability

Data on supply and stocks are available from the Energy Information Administration Internet site at <http://www.eia.doe.gov>. See the Notes and Definitions to Tables 7-8 through 7-11 for availability of import data.

TABLE 17-2
CONSTRUCTION PUT IN PLACE

SOURCE: U.S. DEPARTMENT OF COMMERCE, BUREAU OF THE CENSUS

The Census Bureau's estimates of the value of new construction put in place are intended to provide monthly estimates of the total dollar value of construction work done in the United States.

Definitions and notes on the data

The estimates cover all construction work done each month on new residential and nonresidential buildings and structures, public construction, and improvements to existing buildings and structures. Included are the cost of labor, materials, and equipment rental; cost of architectural and engineering work; overhead costs assigned to the project; interest and taxes paid during construction; and contractor's profits.

The total value put-in-place for a given period is the sum of the value of work done on all projects underway during this period, regardless of when work on each individual project was started or when payment was made to the contractors. For some categories, estimates are derived by distributing the total construction cost of the project by means of historic construction progress patterns. For some categories, published estimates do represent payments made during a period.

The statistics on the value of construction put in place result from direct measurement and indirect estimation. A series results from direct measurement when it is based on reports of the actual value of construction progress or construction expenditures obtained from a complete census or a sample survey. All other series are developed by indirect estimation using related construction statistics. On an annual basis, the estimates for series directly measured monthly, quarterly, or annually accounted for about 71 percent of total construction in 1998 (private multifamily residential, private residential improvements, private nonresidential buildings, farm nonresidential construction, public utility construction, all other private construction, and virtually all of public construction). On a monthly basis, directly measured data are available for about 55 percent of the value-in-place estimates.

Beginning in 1993, the Construction Expenditures Branch of the Manufacturing and Construction Division began collecting these data using a new classification system, basing project types on their end usage instead of building/nonbuilding types. Data collection on this system for federal construction began in January 2002.

With the changes in project classifications, data presented in these tables for 1993 to date are not directly comparable with data for previous years, except at aggregate levels. For that reason, *Business Statistics* shows earlier historical data only at those aggregate levels. Although some categories, such as lodging, office, education, or religion seem identical in definition to previously published data, there have been changes within the classifications that make these values incomparable. For example, private medical office buildings were classified as "office" buildings previously, but under the new classification these buildings are in "health care."

The seasonally adjusted data are obtained by removing normal seasonal movement from the unadjusted data to bring out underlying trends and business cycles, using the Census X-12-ARIMA method. Seasonal adjustment accounts for month-to-month variations resulting from normal or average changes in any phenomena affecting the data such as weather conditions, the differing lengths of months, and the varying number of holidays, weekdays and weekends within each month. It does not adjust for abnormal conditions within each month or for year-to-year variations in weather. The seasonally adjusted annual rate is the seasonally adjusted monthly rate multiplied by 12.

Residential includes new houses, town houses, apartments, and condominiums for sale or rent, built by the owner or for the owner on contract. It includes improvements inside and outside residential structures, such remodeling, additions, major replacements, and addition of swimming pools and garages. Manufactured housing, houseboats, and maintenance and repair work are not included.

Office includes general office buildings, administration buildings, professional buildings, and financial institution buildings. Office buildings at manufacturing sites are classified as *manufacturing*, but office buildings owned by manufacturing companies but not at such a site are included in the *office* category. In the state and local government category, *office* includes capitols, city halls, courthouses, and similar buildings.

Commercial includes buildings and structures used by the retail, wholesale, farm, and selected service industries. One of the subgroups of this category is *multi-retail*, which includes department and variety stores, shopping centers and malls, and warehouse-type retail stores.

Health care includes hospitals, medical buildings, nursing homes, adult day-care centers, and similar institutions.

Educational includes schools at all levels, higher education, trade schools, libraries, museums, and similar institutions.

Amusement and recreation includes theme and amusement parks, sports structures not located at an educational institution, fitness centers and health clubs, neighborhood centers, camps, movie theaters, etc.

Transportation includes airport facilities, rail facilities, track, and bridges, bus, rail, maritime, and air terminals, docks, marinas, etc.

Communication includes telephone, television, and radio distribution and maintenance structures.

Power includes electricity production and distribution and gas and crude oil transmission, storage, and distribution.

Manufacturing includes all buildings and structures at

manufacturing sites, but not the installation of production machinery or special-purpose equipment.

Included in *total private construction*, but not shown separately in these pages, are lodging facilities (hotels and motels), religious structures, and private public safety, sewage and waste disposal, water supply, highway and street, and conservation and development spending.

Included in *total state and local construction*, but not shown separately in these pages, are state and local construction of commercial buildings, conservation and development (dam, levee, jetty, and dredging), lodging, religious, and communication.

Public safety includes correctional facilities, policy and sheriffs' stations, fire stations, etc.

Highway and street includes pavement, lighting, retaining wall, bridges, tunnels, toll facilities, and maintenance and rest facilities.

Sewage and waste disposal includes sewage systems, solid waste disposal, and recycling.

Water supply includes water supply, transmission, and storage facilities.

Among the data sources for construction expenditures are the Census Bureau's Survey of Construction, Building Permits Survey, Consumer Expenditure Survey (conducted for the Bureau of Labor Statistics), Annual Capital Expenditures Survey, and Construction Progress Reporting Survey; also, data from the F.W. Dodge Division of the McGraw-Hill Information Systems Company, the U.S. Department of Agriculture, and utility regulatory agencies.

Data availability

Data are released monthly in a press release. The release, more detailed data, and a discussion of methodologies can be found on the Census Web site, <http://www.census.gov/constructionspending>.

TABLE 17-3
HOUSING STARTS AND BUILDING PERMITS; HOME SALES AND PRICES

Sources: *U.S. Department of Commerce, Bureau of the Census*

These data are mainly found in two major Bureau of the Census reports, "New Residential Construction" and "New Residential Sales." They cover new housing units intended for occupancy and maintained by the occupants, excluding hotels, motels, and group residential structures.

Manufactured home units are reported in a separate survey.

Definitions

A *housing unit* is a house, an apartment, a group of rooms or a single room intended for occupancy as separate living quarters, that is, the occupants live separately from any other individuals in the building and the unit has a direct access from the outside of the building or through a common hall. Each apartment unit in an apartment building is counted as one housing unit. As of January 2000, a previous requirement that the residents must have the capability to eat separately has been eliminated. Based on the old definition some senior housing projects were excluded from the multifamily housing statistics because they did not have their own eating facilities. Housing starts exclude group quarters such as dormitories or rooming houses, transient accommodations such as motels, and manufactured homes. Publicly owned housing units are excluded, but units in structures built by private developers with subsidies or for sale to local public housing authorities are both classified as private housing.

The *start* of construction of a privately owned housing unit is when excavation begins for the footings or foundation of a building intended primarily as a housekeeping residential structure and designed for nontransient occupancy. All housing units in a multifamily building are defined as being started when excavation for the building has begun.

One-family structures include fully detached, semi-detached, row houses, and town houses. In the case of attached units, each must be separated from the adjacent unit by a ground-to-roof wall to be classified as a one-unit structure and must not share facilities such as heating or water supply. Units built one on top of another and those built side-by-side which do not have a ground-to-roof wall and/or have common facilities are classified by the number of units in the structure.

Apartment buildings are defined as buildings containing *five units or more*. The type of ownership is not the criterion—a condominium apartment building is classified not as one-family but as a multifamily structure.

A *manufactured home* is a movable dwelling, 8 feet or more wide and 40 feet or more long, designed to be towed on its own chassis, with transportation gear integral to the unit when it leaves the factory, and without need of a permanent foundation. Multiwides and expandable manufactured homes are included. Excluded are travel trailers, motor homes, and modular housing. The shipments figures are based on reports submitted by manufacturers on the number of homes actually shipped during the survey month. Shipments to dealers may not necessarily be placed for residential use in the same

month as they are shipped. The number of manufactured "homes" used for nonresidential purposes (for example, offices) is not known.

Units authorized by building permits represent the approximately 97 percent of housing in permit-requiring areas.

The *start* occurs when excavation begins for the footing or foundation. Starts are estimated for all areas, regardless of whether permits are required.

New home *sales* are reported only for new single-family residential structures. The sales transaction must intend to include both the house and the land. Excluded are houses built for rent, houses built by the owner, and houses built by a contractor on the owner's land. A sale is reported when a deposit is taken or a sales agreement signed, which can occur prior to a permit being issued.

A house is *for sale* when a permit to build has been issued (or work begun in nonpermit areas) and a sales contract has not been signed nor a deposit accepted.

The *sales price* used in this survey is the price agreed upon between the purchaser and the seller at the time the first sales contract is signed or deposit made. It includes the price of the improved lot. The *median sales price* is the sales price of the house that falls on the middle point of a distribution by price of the total number of houses sold. Half of the houses sold have a sales price less than the median; half have a greater price. Changes in the *sales price* data reflect changes in the distribution of houses by region, size, etc., as well as changes in the prices of houses with identical characteristics.

Notes on the data

Monthly permit authorizations are based on data collected by a mail survey from a sample of 8,500 permit-issuing places, selected from a universe of 19,000 such places in the United States. Data for 1984 through 1993 represented 17,000 places; data for 1978 through 1983 are for 16,000 places; data for 1972 through 1977 are for 14,000 places; data for 1971 are for 13,000 places.

Housing starts and sales data are obtained from the Survey of Construction, in which Census field representatives sample both permit-issuing and non-permit-issuing places.

Effective with the data for April 2001 the Census Bureau made changes to the methodology used for new home sales, including discontinuing an adjustment for construction in areas where building permitgs are required without a permit being issued. It was believed that such unauthorized construction has virtually ceased. The upward adjustment was not phased out but dropped completely in revised estimates as of January 1999. The total effect of these changes was to lower the number of sales by about 2.9 percent relative to those published for earlier years.

Data availability and references

Housing start and building permit data have been collected by the Bureau of the Census monthly since 1959.

The monthly report for New Residential Construction (permits, starts, and completions) is issued around the middle of the following month. The monthly report and associated descriptions and historical data can be found at <http://www.census.gov/newresconst>.

The monthly report for New Residential Sales (sales, houses for sale, and prices) is issued toward the end of the following month. The monthly report and associated descriptions and historical data can be found at <http://www.census.gov/newhomesales>.

The manufactured housing data and background information can be accessed through <http://www.manufacturedhousing.org/statistics>.

TABLES 17-4 THROUGH 17-7
MANUFACTURERS' SHIPMENTS, INVENTORIES, AND ORDERS

Source: U.S. Department of Commerce, Bureau of the Census.

These data are from the Bureau of the Census monthly M3 survey, a sample-based survey intended to provide measures of changes in the value of domestic manufacturing activity and indications of future production commitments. The sample includes most companies with $500 million or more in annual shipments and a selection of smaller ones. Currently, reported monthly data represent approximately 60 percent of shipments at the total manufacturing level.

One important technology industry, semiconductors, is represented in the shipments and inventories data in this report but not in new or unfilled orders. This affects the new and unfilled orders totals for Computers and electronic products, Durable goods industries, and total manufacturing. Based on recent shipments data, semiconductors account for about 15 percent of Computers and electronic products, 3 percent of Durable goods industries, and 1.5 percent of total manufacturing. Because semiconductors are intermediate materials and components rather than finished final products, the absence of these data does not distort new and unfilled orders data for important final demand categories such as Capital goods and Information technology.

The Census Bureau now compiles this survey on the NAICS classification system, and has restated historical data on the NAICS basis back to January 1992. To allow the user to observe the difference between levels of activity implied by the two systems, and to "link" the new data to older data if a longer time series is required, *Business Statistics* is republishing, on the same page with the new data, the previous SIC-based annual data up through 1992, providing an overlap with the new data in that year. Link factors can be calculated as the ratio of the 1992 NAICS value to the value of the most closely related SIC category. The SIC values multiplied by these link factors will yield a roughly comparable series without discontinuity. Where overlapping 1992 values are not available, as in the case of new orders, the link factor calculated on shipments can be used for a fairly rough approximation.

Classification changes in NAICS

There were three major changes from SIC to NAICS affecting the level and trend of manufacturing as a whole: publishing was moved out of manufacturing to the new information industry; some research and development activities were moved out of aerospace manufacturing; and logging was moved out of manufacturing to the agriculture, forestry, fishing, and hunting group. A few relatively small activities, of which the largest are dental labs and retail bakeries, have been shifted into manufacturing based on similarity of production process.

In addition, there was a major rearrangement of industries within manufacturing, which should yield groupings that are more relevant in today's economy. Three new industry groups—NAICS 333, Machinery; 334, Computers and Electronic Products; and 335, Electrical Equipment, Appliances and Components have been constituted, mainly from individual industries that were previously represented in SIC 35, Industrial Machinery (which included computers); SIC 36, Electronic and Electric Equipment; and SIC 38, Instruments. Other notable features in NAICS are moving beverages out of the food group into a new Beverages and Tobacco group and replacement of the old textile mill products group with two new groups, textile mills and textile products.

In many cases, the changes are so pervasive that it is not possible to match major SIC and NAICS industries. In Tables 17-4 through 17-7, SIC industries for 1992 and earlier years have been roughly aligned with the new NAICS categories, but a comparison of the old with the new data for 1992 indicates that in many cases, even after this alignment, the old and new industry groupings are still substantially different.

Definitions and notes on the data

Shipments. The value of shipments data represent net selling values, f.o.b. (free on board) plant, after discounts and allowances and excluding freight charges and excise taxes. For multi-establishment companies, the M3 reports typically are company- or division-level reports that encompass groups of plants or products. The data reported are usually net sales and receipts from customers and do not include the value of interplant transfers. The reported sales are used to calculate month-to-month changes that bring forward the estimates for the entire industry (i.e., estimates of the statistical "universe") that have been developed from the Annual Survey of Manufactures (ASM). The value of products made elsewhere under contract from materials owned by the plant is also included in shipments, as well as receipts for contract work performed for others, resales, miscellaneous activities such as the sale of scrap and refuse, and installation and repair work performed by employees of the plant.

Inventories. Inventories in the M3 survey are collected on a current cost or pre-LIFO basis. Because different inventory valuation methods are reflected in the reported data, the estimates differ slightly from replacement cost estimates. Companies using the LIFO (last in, first out) method for valuing inventories report their pre-LIFO value; that is, the adjustment to their base-period prices is excluded. In the ASM, inventories are collected according to this same definition. However, there are discontinuities in the historical data in both surveys. Inventory data prior to 1982 are not comparable to later years because of changes in valuation methods. Until 1982, respondents were asked in the ASM to report their inventories at book values; that is, according to whatever method they used for tax purposes (LIFO, FIFO [first in, first out], and so forth.) Because of this, the value of aggregate inventories for an industry was not precise. The change in instructions for reporting current cost inventories was carried to the monthly survey beginning in January 1987. The data for 1982 to 1987 were redefined (but not re-collected by survey) on a pre-LIFO or current cost basis.

Inventory data are requested from respondents by three stages of fabrication: finished goods, work in process, and raw materials and supplies. There are several limitations to the quality of these data for two reasons. First, response to the stage of fabrication inquiries is lower than for total inventories because not all companies keep their data monthly at this level of detail. Second, a product considered to be a finished good in one industry, such as steel mill shapes, may be reported as a raw material in another industry, such as stamping plants. (For some purposes this is an advantage rather than a problem. When a factory accumulates inventory that it considers to be raw materials, it can be expected that that accumulation is intentional. But when a factory—whether a materials-making or a final-product producer—has a buildup of finished goods inventories, it may indicate involuntary accumulation as a result of sales falling short of expectations. Hence, the two types of accumulation can have different economic interpretations—even if they represent identical types of goods.) Like total inventories, stage of fabrication inventories are also benchmarked to the ASM data, but the stage of fabrication data are benchmarked at the major group level, as opposed to the level of total inventories which is benchmarked at the individual industry level.

New orders, as reported in the monthly survey, are net of order cancellations and include orders received and filled during the month as well as orders received for future delivery. They also include the value of contract changes that increase or decrease the value of the unfilled orders to which they relate. Orders are defined to include those supported by binding legal documents such as signed contracts, letters of award, or letters of intent, although in some industries this definition may not be strictly applicable.

Unfilled orders include new orders (as defined above) that have not been reflected as shipments. Generally, unfilled orders at the end of the reporting period are equal to unfilled orders at the beginning of the period plus net new orders received less net shipments.

Series are adjusted for seasonal variation and variation in the number of trading days in the month using the X-12-ARIMA version of the Census Bureau's seasonal adjustment program.

Benchmarking and revisions

Each year the M3 series are benchmarked and seasonal adjustment factors recalculated. In the latest benchmark, published in August 2003, and available on the Census Internet site, the data were benchmarked to the 2000 and 2001 Annual Surveys of Manufactures (ASM), new orders were adjusted to be consistent with the benchmarked shipments and inventory data, and other corrections were made; also, the seasonal adjustment factors were updated for all series.

Data availability and references

Data have been collected monthly since 1958.

An Advance Report on Durable Goods Manufacturers' Shipments, Inventories and Orders is available as a press release about 17 working days after the end of each month. It includes seasonally and not seasonally adjusted estimates of shipments, new orders, unfilled orders, and inventories for durable goods industries.

The Manufacturers' Shipments, Inventories, and Orders reports are released early in the following month. Content includes revisions to the advance durable goods data, estimates for nondurable goods industries, tabulations by market category, and ratios of shipments to inventories and to unfilled orders. Revisions may affect selected data for the two previous months.

Press releases, historical data, descriptions of the survey, and extensive documentation of the new NAICS including comparisons with the SIC are available on the Census Bureau Internet site at <http://www.census.gov>.

TABLE 17-8
MOTOR VEHICLE SALES AND INVENTORIES

Retail sales and inventories of cars, trucks, and buses. These estimates are prepared by the Bureau of Economic Analysis based on data from the American Automobile Manufacturers Association, Ward's Automotive Reports, and other sources. Data are available in BEA press releases and on the STAT-USA subscription Internet site at <http://www.stat-usa.gov>.

TABLES 17-9 AND 17-10
RETAIL SALES AND INVENTORIES

SOURCE: U.S. DEPARTMENT OF COMMERCE, BUREAU OF THE CENSUS

Each month the Bureau of the Census prepares estimates of retail sales and inventories by kind of business based on a mail-out/mail-back survey of a sample of companies with one or more establishments that sell merchandise and related services to final consumers.

Retail sales and inventories are now compiled using the new NAICS classification system, replacing the old SIC. Historical data have been restated on the NAICS basis back to January 1992. To allow the user to observe the difference between levels of activity implied by the two systems, and to "link" the new data to older data if a longer time series is required, *Business Statistics* is republishing, on the same page with the new data, the previous SIC-based annual data up through 1992, providing an overlap with the new data in that year.

Classification changes in NAICS

• In NAICS, Eating and Drinking Places and Mobile Food Services have been reclassified out of retail into Sector 72, Accommodation and Food Services, which also includes hotels. The retail sales survey still collects and publishes sales data for food services and drinking places, but no longer includes them in the "retail" total.
• Some activities such as retail bakeries are shifted to manufacturing, based on use of the same production processes.
• Partly offsetting these losses, a significant number of businesses are shifted from wholesale to retail trade, including a number of sellers of lumber; construction and lawn equipment; electrical, plumbing, and farm supplies; computers; and office supplies. Establishments which are designed to attract walk-in customers and which use mass-media advertising are now classified as

retail, even if they also serve business and institutional clients.

Data are published under the new NAICS system for a new group consisting of sporting goods, hobby, book and music stores. In addition, total sales of nonstore retailers and a subgroup of nonstores—electronic shopping and mail order houses—are now published. (Store retailers operate fixed point-of-sale locations designed to attract walk-in customers, display merchandise, use mass-media advertising, and may provide after-sales services. Nonstore retailers, on the other hand, sell by "infomercials," paper and electronic catalogs, door-to-door and in-home selling, portable stalls, or vending machines.)

Subtotals of durable and nondurable goods are no longer published. They were always quite imprecise for retail sales, since general merchandise (including department) stores were included in nondurables and yet obviously sold substantial quantities of durable goods.

For further information see Chapter 14.

Special note on retail E-commerce

Beginning with the fourth quarter of 1999, the Census Bureau has conducted a quarterly survey of retail E-commerce sales. (The monthly survey does not report electronic shopping separately but combines it with mail-order.) These data are mentioned in the "bulleted" text at the beginning of this chapter, but have not yet supplied a long enough history for a data page in *Business Statistics*. The quarterly release is issued around the 20th of February, May, August, and November, and is available on the Census Bureau Internet site.

Definitions

Sales is the value of merchandise sold for cash or credit at retail or wholesale. Services that are incidental to the sale of merchandise and excise taxes that are paid by the manufacturer or wholesaler and passed along to the retailer are also included. Sales are net, after deductions for refunds and merchandise returns. Sales exclude sales taxes collected directly from customers and paid directly to a local, state, or federal tax agency. The sales estimates include only sales by establishments primarily engaged in retail trade, and are not intended to measure the total sales for a given commodity or merchandise line.

Inventories is the value of stocks of goods held for sale through retail stores, valued at cost, as of the last day of the report period. Stocks may be held either at the store or at warehouses that maintain supplies primarily intended for distribution to retail stores within the organization.

Inventory data prior to 1980 are not comparable to later years due to changes in valuation methods. Prior to 1980, inventories are book values of merchandise on hand at the end of the period and are valued according to the valuation method used by each respondent. Thus the aggregates are a mixture of LIFO (last-in-first-out) and non-LIFO values. Beginning with 1980, inventories are valued using methods other than LIFO in order to better reflect the current costs of goods held as inventory.

Leased departments are operations of one company conducted within the establishment or another company, such as jewelry counters or optical centers within department stores. The values for sales and inventories at department stores in Tables 17-9 and 17-10 exclude sales of leased departments.

Department store type goods (also referred to as GAFO) represents sales at general merchandise stores and at other stores that sell merchandise normally sold in department stores—clothing and accessories, furniture and home furnishings, electronics, appliances, sporting goods, hobby, book, music, office supplies, stationery, and gifts.

Notes on the data

The new NAICS-based data have been benchmarked to the 1997 Economic Census and the 1999, 2000, and 2001 Annual Retail Trade Surveys. Each year, the monthly series are benchmarked to the latest annual survey and new factors to adjust for seasonal, trading-day, and holiday variations are incorporated, using the Census X-12-ARIMA program.

The survey sample is stratified by kind of business and estimated sales. All firms with sales above applicable size cutoffs are included. Firms are selected randomly from the remaining strata. The sample used for the end-of-month inventory estimates is a subsample of the monthly sales sample, about one-third of the size of the sales sample.

New samples, designed to produce NAICS estimates, were introduced with the 1999 Annual Retail Trade Survey and the March 2001 monthly survey.

Data availability and references

An *Advance Monthly Retail Sales* report is released about nine working days after the close of the reference month, based on responses from a sub-sample of the complete retail sample.

Revised and more complete monthly *Retail Trade, Sales, and Inventories* reports are released six weeks after the close of the reference month. They contain preliminary figures for the current month and final figures for the prior 12 months. Statistics include retail sales, inventories, and ratios of inventories to sales. Data are both seasonally adjusted and unadjusted.

The *Annual Benchmark Report for Retail Trade* is released each spring. It includes updated seasonal adjustment factors; revised and benchmarked monthly estimates of sales and inventories; monthly data for the most recent 10 years; detailed annual estimates and ratios for the United States by kind of business; and comparable prior-year statistics and year-to-year changes. Data and documentation are available on the Bureau of the Census Internet site at <http://www.census.gov>.

TABLE 17-11
MERCHANT WHOLESALERS: SALES AND INVENTORIES

Source: U.S. Department of Commerce, Bureau of the Census

These data are based on a monthly mail-out/mail-back sample survey conducted by the Bureau of the Census.

These data are now based on the new NAICS classification system, replacing the old SIC. Historical data have been restated on the NAICS basis back to January 1992. To allow the user to observe the difference between levels of activity implied by the two systems, and to "link" the new data to older data if a longer time series is required, *Business Statistics* is republishing, on the same page with the new data, the previous SIC-based annual data up through 1992, providing an overlap with the new data in that year.

Classification changes in NAICS

NAICS shifts a significant number of businesses from wholesale to retail, an important new criterion being whether or not the establishment is intended to solicit walk-in traffic. If it is and uses mass-media advertising, it is now classified as retail, even if it also serves business and institutional clients. (See notes on retail trade, above, for the major categories involved in this shift.)

Definitions

Merchant wholesalers include merchant wholesalers that take title of the goods they sell, and jobbers, industrial distributors, exporters, and importers. Excluded are non-merchant wholesalers such as manufacturer sales branches and offices; agents, merchandise or commodity brokers; and commission merchants.

Notes on the data

Inventory data prior to 1980 are not comparable to later years because of changes in valuation methods and are not included in this book. Prior to 1980, inventories are book values of stocks on hand at the end of the period and are valued according to the valuation method used by each respondent. Thus the aggregates are a mixture of LIFO (last-in-first-out) and non-LIFO values. Beginning with 1980 inventories are valued using methods other than LIFO in order to better reflect the current costs of goods held as inventory.

A survey has been conducted monthly since 1946. New samples are drawn every 5 years, most recently in 2001. The samples are updated every quarter to add new businesses and drop companies that are no longer active.

Data availability and references

Monthly Wholesale Trade, Sales and Inventories reports are released six weeks after the close of the reference month. They contain preliminary current-month figures and final figures for the previous month. Statistics include sales, inventories, and stock/sale ratios, along with standard errors. Data are both seasonally adjusted and unadjusted.

The *Annual Benchmark Report for Wholesale Trade* is released each spring. It contains estimated annual sales, monthly and year-end inventories, inventory/sales ratios, purchases, gross margins, and gross margin/sales ratios by kind of business. Annual estimates are benchmarked to the most recent census of wholesale trade. This report also presents the results of a benchmarking operation that revises monthly sales and inventories estimates. Estimates are both seasonally adjusted and unadjusted. Data and documentation are available on the Bureau of the Census Internet site at <http://www.census.gov>.

TABLES 17-12 THROUGH 17-15
SELECTED SERVICE INDUSTRIES—
RECEIPTS AND REVENUE

SOURCE: U.S. DEPARTMENT OF COMMERCE, BUREAU OF THE CENSUS

The Census Service Annual Survey provides, for selected service industries, annual estimates of operating receipts of taxable firms, and revenues of private, nonprofit firms that are exempt from federal income taxation. The survey is based on a sample of establishments.
For the years 1986 through 1998, the data were collected using the old Standard Industrial Classification System (SIC), and were tabulated separately for taxable and nontaxable firms. Data from 1999 through 2001 were collected using the North American Industry Classification System (NAICS), and the data for each industry include both taxable and nontaxable firms.

See Chapter 14 for information on comparability of industries in the new and old classification systems.

Notes on the data

In the SIC estimates for 1986–1998, separate estimates were developed for taxable and nontaxable firms in camps and membership lodging; selected amusement and recreation services; selected health services; legal services; libraries; vocational schools; social services; museums, art galleries, botanical gardens, and zoos; research, development, and testing services; and selected management and public relations services. Firms considered tax-exempt include membership lodging, membership organizations, and noncommercial research organizations. Firms in all remaining SICs were defined to be taxable. For tax-exempt firms, employer firms only were sampled; for all other kinds of business, data represent combined estimates for employer and nonemployer firms. Government-operated hospitals were included, while all other government establishments were excluded.

In Table 17-15, total and e-commerce revenues are reported for the service industries represented in Table 17-14 and also for NAICS industry 72, Accommodation and food services, which is not represented in Table 17-14.

Data availability

Data are published annually as *Current Business Reports, Service Annual Survey*. They are available on the Bureau of the Census Internet site at <http://www.census.gov>.

PART C

HISTORICAL DATA

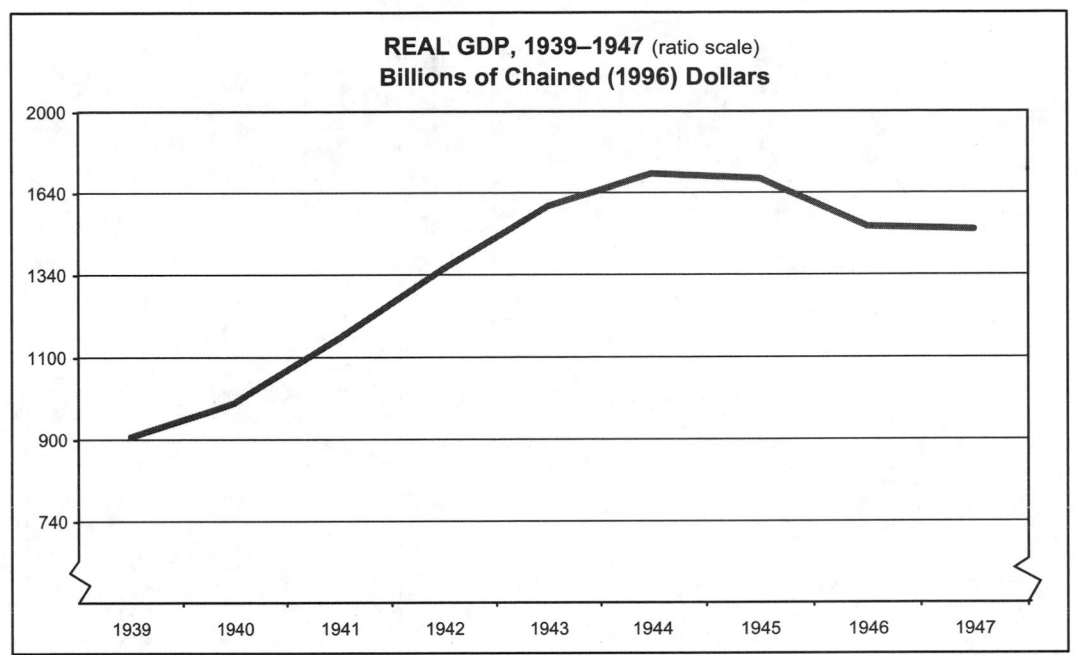

REAL GDP, 1939–1947 (ratio scale)
Billions of Chained (1996) Dollars

- Real GDP grew 89.7 percent from 1939 to its wartime peak in 1944, an annual rate of 13.7 percent. It fell back during the subsequent demobilization, but in 1947 was still 65.5 percent above the 1939 level, representing growth from 1939 at an annual rate of 6.5 percent. Government military spending drove the wartime expansion but declined rapidly after 1945.

- Real investment spending declined during the war but recovered at the war's end to more than double the 1939 level. Consumption spending was maintained in real terms during the wartime period and rose at the war's end.

- Civilian employment rose by 8.7 million from 1939 to 1944, despite the withdrawal of members of the Armed Forces from the civilian population base. The rise in payroll jobs was even greater—11.4 million jobs, as workers left agricultural, household service, and other less-productive employment for jobs manufacturing armaments.

- Unemployment fell to 1.2 percent of the labor force in 1944. When the demobilization ended, unemployment had increased only to 3.9 percent, compared with 17.2 percent (excluding work relief) in 1939.

- Prices increased through the early part of the war, leveled off under the impact of price controls and rationing in 1944 and 1945, then rose again when the controls were lifted.

- Worker incomes increased during the wartime boom as employment, average hours, and hourly wages all rose. Consumption spending opportunities were limited by rationing and production controls; for example, passenger cars were simply not produced, as the assembly lines were converted to build military vehicles. This, combined with intensive "war bond" drives, contributed to a huge increase in personal saving, which peaked at 39 percent of disposable income in 1944. By 1947, the personal saving rate had returned to exactly its 1939 level of 4.7 percent.

Table 18-1. Selected Aggregate Economic Data, 1939–1947

Classification	1939	1940	1941	1942	1943	1944	1945	1946	1947
BILLIONS OF CURRENT DOLLARS									
Gross domestic product, total	92.0	101.3	126.7	161.8	198.4	219.7	223.0	222.3	244.4
Personal consumption expenditures, total	67.2	71.2	81.0	88.9	99.7	108.5	119.8	144.2	162.3
Durable goods	6.7	7.8	9.7	6.9	6.5	6.7	8.0	15.8	20.4
Nondurable goods	35.1	37.0	42.9	50.8	58.6	64.3	71.9	82.7	90.9
Services	25.4	26.4	28.5	31.3	34.6	37.4	40.0	45.8	51.0
Gross private domestic fixed investment, total	9.1	11.2	13.8	8.5	6.9	8.7	12.3	25.1	35.5
Nonresidential, total	6.1	7.7	9.7	6.3	5.4	7.4	10.6	17.3	23.5
Structures	2.2	2.6	3.3	2.2	1.8	2.4	3.3	7.4	8.1
Equipment and software	3.9	5.2	6.4	4.1	3.7	5.0	7.3	9.9	15.3
Residential	3.0	3.5	4.1	2.2	1.4	1.4	1.7	7.8	12.1
Change in private inventories	0.2	2.4	4.3	1.9	-0.7	-0.9	-1.5	6.0	-0.6
Net exports of goods and services	0.8	1.4	1.0	-0.3	-2.4	-2.2	-0.9	7.1	10.8
Exports	3.9	4.8	5.4	4.3	3.9	4.8	6.7	14.1	18.7
Imports	3.1	3.4	4.4	4.6	6.3	6.9	7.5	7.0	7.9
Government consumption expenditures and gross investment, total	14.7	15.1	26.6	62.8	94.9	105.5	93.2	39.8	36.4
Federal	5.9	6.4	17.9	54.1	86.5	97.0	84.2	29.0	22.6
State and local	8.9	8.7	8.7	8.7	8.5	8.5	9.0	10.8	13.9
Gross national product	92.5	101.7	127.2	162.2	198.8	220.1	223.4	223.0	245.6
National income, total	72.9	81.1	104.3	137.6	171.4	184.3	183.3	182.3	198.6
Compensation of employees	48.1	52.2	64.8	85.3	109.6	121.3	123.3	119.6	130.1
Proprietors income with IVA and CCAdj									
Farm	4.4	4.5	6.4	10.1	12.0	12.0	12.4	14.8	15.1
Nonfarm	7.3	8.4	10.9	14.0	17.0	18.3	19.3	21.7	20.5
Rental income of persons with CCAdj	3.3	3.4	4.0	5.0	5.6	5.9	6.1	7.0	7.0
Corporate profits with IVA and CCAdj	6.2	9.5	15.0	20.0	24.5	24.6	20.1	17.4	23.5
Net interest	3.5	3.2	3.2	3.1	2.7	2.3	2.1	1.8	2.4
Personal income, total	73.1	78.6	96.3	123.8	152.4	166.3	171.9	179.5	192.1
Less: Personal tax and nontax payments	1.7	1.9	2.5	5.1	17.0	18.0	19.8	17.5	20.1
Equals: Disposable Personal Income (DPI)	71.4	76.7	93.8	118.7	135.4	148.3	152.1	162.0	172.1
Less: personal outlays	68.0	72.2	82.1	89.7	100.4	109.3	120.8	145.6	164.0
Equals: personal saving	3.4	4.5	11.7	29.0	34.9	39.0	31.4	16.3	8.1
As a percentage of DPI	4.7	5.9	12.4	24.4	25.8	26.3	20.6	10.1	4.7
BILLIONS OF CHAINED (1996) DOLLARS									
Real gross domestic product, total	903.5	980.7	1 148.8	1 360.0	1 583.7	1 714.1	1 693.3	1 505.5	1 495.1
Personal consumption expenditures	689.0	724.9	776.7	758.3	779.1	801.7	851.8	956.9	976.4
Gross private domestic investment	79.6	110.9	135.4	71.6	42.3	52.2	69.0	175.0	168.6
Exports	31.4	35.7	36.7	24.1	20.1	21.6	30.5	66.5	75.9
Imports	36.9	37.8	46.5	42.2	53.2	55.7	59.2	49.1	46.6
Government	179.7	182.4	303.0	711.1	1 059.9	1 195.6	1 041.0	359.7	307.1
Disposable personal income	732.3	781.1	899.0	1 012.4	1 057.9	1 096.1	1 081.5	1 074.4	1 035.2
CHAIN-TYPE PRICE INDEXES, 1996 = 100									
Gross domestic product	10.2	10.3	11.0	11.9	12.5	12.8	13.2	14.7	16.3
Personal consumption expenditures	9.8	9.8	10.4	11.7	12.8	13.5	14.1	15.1	16.6
CONSUMER AND PRODUCER PRICE INDEXES									
Consumer prices, all items; 1982-1984 = 100:									
All urban consumers (CPI-U)	13.9	14.0	14.7	16.3	17.3	17.6	18.0	19.5	22.3
Urban wage earners and clerical workers (CPI-W)	14.0	14.1	14.8	16.4	17.4	17.7	18.1	19.6	22.5
Producer prices, 1982 =100:									
All commodities	13.3	13.5	15.1	17.0	17.8	17.9	18.2	20.8	25.6
Farm products	16.5	17.1	20.8	26.7	30.9	31.2	32.4	37.5	45.1
Industrial commodities	13.9	14.1	15.1	16.2	16.5	16.7	17.0	18.6	22.7
EMPLOYMENT STATUS OF THE CIVILIAN NONINSTITUTIONAL POPULATION, 14 and over (Thousands of persons)									
Civilian noninstitutional population	. . .	99 840	99 900	98 640	94 640	93 220	94 090	103 070	106 018
Civilian labor force	55 230	55 640	55 910	56 410	55 540	54 630	53 860	57 520	60 168
Participation rate, percent	. . .	55.7	56.0	57.2	58.7	58.6	57.2	55.8	56.8
Employment, total	45 750	47 520	50 350	53 750	54 470	53 960	52 820	55 250	57 812
Ratio, employment to population, percent	. . .	47.6	50.4	54.5	57.6	57.9	56.1	53.6	54.5
Agricultural	9 610	9 540	9 100	9 250	9 080	8 950	8 580	8 320	8 256
Nonagricultural	36 140	37 980	41 250	44 500	45 390	45 010	44 240	46 930	49 557
Unemployment	9 480	8 120	5 560	2 660	1 070	670	1 040	2 270	2 356
Percent of civilian labor force	17.2	14.6	9.9	4.7	1.9	1.2	1.9	3.9	3.9

. . . = Not available.

Table 18-1. Selected Aggregate Economic Data, 1939–1947—*Continued*

Classification	1939	1940	1941	1942	1943	1944	1945	1946	1947
NONFARM PAYROLL EMPLOYMENT (NAICS) (Thousands of persons)									
Total	30 645	32 407	36 600	40 213	42 574	42 006	40 510	41 759	43 945
Private, total	26 606	28 156	31 874	34 621	36 353	35 819	34 428	36 054	38 379
Goods–producing, total	11 511	12 378	14 940	17 275	18 738	17 981	16 308	16 122	17 314
Natural resources and mining	856	927	967	1 010	958	926	864	885	976
Construction	1 205	1 352	1 852	2 234	1 627	1 152	1 190	1 724	2 051
Manufacturing, total	9 450	10 099	12 121	14 030	16 153	15 903	14 255	13 513	14 287
Durable goods	4 654	5 261	6 778	8 502	10 583	10 372	8 732	7 535	8 079
Nondurable goods, total	4 796	4 839	5 343	5 528	5 570	5 531	5 523	5 978	6 208
Private service–providing, total	15 094	15 778	16 934	17 347	17 615	17 839	18 121	19 932	21 064
Trade, transportation, and utilities, total	6 739	7 043	7 550	7 607	7 628	7 805	8 048	8 945	9 452
Wholesale trade	1 508	1 571	1 679	1 635	1 566	1 585	1 672	1 962	2 116
Retail trade	3 158	3 324	3 552	3 552	3 479	3 516	3 624	4 118	4 393
Information	1 141	1 196	1 342	1 470	1 605	1 635	1 581	1 594	1 658
Financial activities	1 386	1 424	1 466	1 455	1 431	1 414	1 435	1 619	1 674
Professional and business services	1 976	2 073	2 265	2 410	2 518	2 523	2 495	2 666	2 828
Education and health services	1 405	1 470	1 566	1 632	1 660	1 667	1 698	1 885	2 015
Leisure and hospitality	1 896	1 995	2 130	2 133	2 122	2 142	2 200	2 485	2 650
Other services	553	578	616	641	652	654	664	737	788
Government, total	4 040	4 251	4 726	5 592	6 222	6 187	6 082	5 705	5 567
Federal, total	950	1 045	1 406	2 322	3 047	3 071	2 945	2 365	1 985
Department of Defense, total	132	182	375	920	1 361	1 352	1 234	746	499
Service–providing	19 134	20 029	21 660	22 938	23 837	24 026	24 203	25 637	26 631
Manufacturing, production workers									
Total (thousands)	8 163	8 737	10 641	12 447	14 407	14 031	12 445	11 781	12 453
Average weekly hours (Number of hours per week)	37.7	38.2	40.7	43.2	45.1	45.4	43.6	40.4	40.5
Index of aggregate weekly hours (2002 =100)	70.5	76.4	99.2	123.1	148.8	145.6	124.3	108.9	115.3
Average hourly earnings (dollars)	0.5	0.5	0.6	0.7	0.9	0.9	0.9	1.0	1.1
Average weekly earnings (dollars)	18.5	20.2	24.8	32.0	38.8	41.3	39.2	38.4	44.6
INDEXES OF INDUSTRIAL PRODUCTION (1997 = 100)									
Total	9.5	11.0	13.8	15.9	19.3	20.7	17.8	15.3	17.2
Products	9.3	10.4	13.2	15.0	18.6	20.3	17.2	14.9	16.7
Consumer goods	12.6	13.4	16.0	14.8	15.1	15.8	16.3	19.5	20.7
Materials	9.6	11.6	14.5	16.7	19.7	20.7	18.2	15.5	17.5
Manufacturing (SIC)	8.8	10.3	13.2	15.4	19.2	20.7	17.3	14.4	16.1

NOTES AND DEFINITIONS

TABLE 18-1
SELECTED AGGREGATE ECONOMIC DATA, 1939–1947

For all these data, the sources, definitions, and availability are generally the same as for the identically titled series in Part A. Specific references to the appropriate chapter's Notes and Definitions are given below for each set of data, and differences in definitions where they exist are noted (data on labor force, employment, and unemployment).

Gross domestic product and its components in current and constant dollars, gross national product, national income and its components, and chain-type price indexes: Chapter 1.

Personal income and its disposition and disposable personal income: Chapter 4.

Consumer and producer price indexes: Chapter 8.

Civilian noninstitutional population, labor force, employment, and unemployment are as defined in the Notes and Definitions to Chapter 10 *except* that all the data for 1939 through 1947 in Chapter 18 pertain to persons 14 years of age and over. The data in Chapter 10 from 1947 to date are for persons 16 and over. The differences made by this difference in definitions can be observed in the two different sets of data for the overlap year 1947. Note that in that year the unemployment rates are the same—3.9 percent—but the labor force participation rate and the employment/population ratio are higher when the 14- and 15-year-olds are excluded. Data are from the Bureau of Labor Statistics, as published on their Web site and in the Appendix to the *Economic Report of the President*, February 2003.

Nonfarm employment and its components, and number, hours, and earnings for manufacturing production workers: Chapter 10. Note that because age is not specified in the Current Employment Survey, these data include any workers under 16 and always have done so.

Business cycle status and the duration of World War II

See the Notes and Definitions to Table 1-11 for the business cycle peaks and troughs occurring in this period. Note that the entire pre-war and wartime period from June 1938 to February 1945 is construed as a business cycle expansion. (Also note that the June 1938 trough is not the one marking the end of the Great Depression–which ended in March 1933–but the one marking the end of a 13-month recession in 1937–38.)

World War II broke out in Europe in September 1939. The United States entered the war when attacked by Japan in December 1941. The end of the "wartime" expansion precedes the end of the war, as the European war ended in May 1945 and the Pacific war in August 1945. A brief "demobilization" recession occurred from February to October 1945, followed by the first postwar expansion which lasted from October 1945 to November 1948.

Table 19-1. Gross Domestic Product

(Billions of dollars, quarterly data are at seasonally adjusted annual rates.)

Year and quarter	Gross domestic product	Personal consump-tion expen-ditures	Gross private domestic investment				Exports and imports of goods and services			Government consumption expenditures and gross investment			Adden-dum: Final sales of domestic product
			Total	Fixed investment		Change in private inventories	Net exports	Exports	Imports	Total	Federal	State and local	
				Nonresi-dential	Residen-tial								
1946													
1st quarter	210.6	134.9	25.0	13.6	5.9	5.5	6.5	13.0	6.6	44.2	34.3	9.9	205.0
2nd quarter	218.4	140.1	32.0	16.1	7.4	8.5	7.3	14.2	7.0	39.1	28.7	10.4	210.0
3rd quarter	228.2	148.9	33.1	18.7	8.7	5.7	8.4	15.4	7.0	37.8	26.7	11.1	222.5
4th quarter	232.0	153.1	34.5	20.9	9.3	4.3	6.3	13.6	7.3	38.1	26.2	11.9	227.7
1947													
1st quarter	237.5	156.5	33.7	22.8	10.4	0.5	10.8	18.3	7.5	36.5	23.4	13.1	237.0
2nd quarter	240.7	160.5	32.4	23.2	10.4	-1.2	11.2	19.4	8.2	36.6	23.1	13.5	241.9
3rd quarter	244.9	164.0	32.7	23.3	12.3	-2.9	11.7	19.4	7.7	36.4	22.3	14.1	247.8
4th quarter	254.7	168.2	41.0	24.5	15.1	1.5	9.2	17.6	8.3	36.2	21.5	14.8	253.2
1948													
1st quarter	260.8	170.9	45.0	26.2	15.2	3.6	7.2	16.9	9.6	37.7	22.4	15.3	257.1
2nd quarter	267.7	174.7	48.1	26.0	16.3	5.9	5.2	15.2	10.0	39.8	23.7	16.1	261.9
3rd quarter	274.3	177.6	50.3	27.0	16.1	7.2	4.9	15.4	10.5	41.5	24.6	16.9	267.1
4th quarter	275.6	178.4	49.1	28.1	15.0	6.0	4.4	14.6	10.1	43.6	26.0	17.6	269.6
1949													
1st quarter	270.4	177.3	40.9	26.6	14.0	0.4	6.4	16.0	9.6	45.7	27.5	18.2	270.0
2nd quarter	266.6	178.0	34.0	25.5	13.7	-5.1	6.2	15.6	9.4	47.4	28.5	18.9	271.7
3rd quarter	268.0	178.3	37.3	24.1	14.5	-1.3	5.1	14.0	8.9	47.3	27.6	19.7	269.3
4th quarter	265.6	180.8	35.2	23.5	16.3	-4.7	2.9	12.0	9.1	46.7	26.8	19.9	270.3
1950													
1st quarter	275.7	183.5	44.4	24.2	18.1	2.0	2.1	11.6	9.5	45.7	25.5	20.2	273.7
2nd quarter	285.1	187.4	49.9	26.6	20.4	2.8	1.6	11.8	10.2	46.2	25.7	20.5	282.3
3rd quarter	302.5	201.1	56.1	29.6	22.3	4.2	-0.8	12.2	13.0	46.0	24.9	21.2	298.3
4th quarter	313.9	198.5	65.9	30.6	21.3	14.0	-0.2	13.5	13.7	49.7	27.9	21.8	299.8
1951													
1st quarter	329.3	209.6	62.1	30.9	20.8	10.4	0.1	15.0	14.9	57.6	35.2	22.3	318.9
2nd quarter	336.9	205.3	64.8	31.8	18.2	14.8	1.9	17.0	15.2	64.9	41.8	23.1	322.1
3rd quarter	343.7	207.9	59.4	32.5	17.2	9.7	3.7	18.0	14.3	72.8	49.2	23.7	334.0
4th quarter	348.1	211.8	54.4	32.2	17.5	4.7	4.1	18.1	14.0	77.9	53.9	23.9	343.4
1952													
1st quarter	351.5	213.2	55.2	32.4	18.0	4.7	3.6	18.6	15.0	79.4	55.4	24.0	346.7
2nd quarter	352.4	217.4	49.9	32.9	18.5	-1.5	1.8	16.5	14.6	83.3	58.5	24.8	353.9
3rd quarter	358.8	220.0	53.9	29.8	18.5	5.6	-0.1	15.1	15.3	85.1	60.5	24.7	353.3
4th quarter	371.8	228.2	57.2	32.5	19.4	5.3	-1.1	15.2	16.3	87.6	62.4	25.2	366.5
1953													
1st quarter	378.9	231.8	57.9	34.3	19.7	3.9	-0.8	15.0	15.8	90.0	63.9	26.0	375.0
2nd quarter	382.5	233.6	58.2	34.8	19.8	3.6	-1.4	15.1	16.4	92.1	66.2	25.9	378.9
3rd quarter	381.7	234.4	57.4	35.9	19.2	2.3	-0.7	15.7	16.3	90.6	64.0	26.6	379.4
4th quarter	376.6	233.9	52.3	35.4	18.9	-2.0	-0.4	15.1	15.5	90.7	63.6	27.2	378.6
1954													
1st quarter	376.0	236.0	51.6	34.5	19.0	-2.0	-0.4	14.3	14.8	88.9	60.8	28.1	377.9
2nd quarter	376.7	238.8	51.2	34.3	20.3	-3.4	0.2	16.3	16.2	86.5	57.7	28.8	380.1
3rd quarter	381.5	241.2	54.7	35.0	21.8	-2.1	0.5	15.8	15.3	85.2	55.4	29.8	383.6
4th quarter	390.1	245.9	57.8	34.9	23.2	-0.3	1.1	16.5	15.5	85.3	55.2	30.1	390.4
1955													
1st quarter	403.1	252.1	64.2	35.4	25.0	3.8	1.0	17.2	16.2	85.7	54.6	31.1	399.3
2nd quarter	411.4	257.1	68.1	37.9	25.6	4.6	-0.3	16.8	17.1	86.4	54.7	31.7	406.8
3rd quarter	419.9	261.3	70.0	40.4	25.2	4.3	0.6	18.1	17.4	88.0	55.9	32.2	415.6
4th quarter	426.4	265.3	73.9	42.5	24.2	7.2	0.1	18.3	18.1	87.1	54.4	32.8	419.2
1956													
1st quarter	428.8	266.9	73.0	42.8	23.7	6.4	0.3	19.3	18.9	88.6	54.7	33.9	422.4
2nd quarter	434.7	269.6	71.4	43.9	23.9	3.6	1.8	20.8	19.0	91.9	57.1	34.7	431.1
3rd quarter	439.7	272.8	72.5	45.4	23.5	3.6	2.5	21.7	19.3	92.0	56.5	35.5	436.2
4th quarter	448.6	278.2	71.2	45.9	23.0	2.2	4.4	23.0	18.5	94.8	58.6	36.2	446.4
1957													
1st quarter	457.6	282.5	71.8	47.0	22.6	2.2	4.7	24.8	20.1	98.6	61.0	37.5	455.4
2nd quarter	459.6	284.8	71.9	47.1	22.2	2.7	4.0	24.3	20.3	98.8	60.5	38.4	456.9
3rd quarter	466.8	289.4	73.2	48.4	22.0	2.8	3.9	23.6	19.8	100.3	61.2	39.1	464.0
4th quarter	462.0	291.1	64.9	47.5	21.9	-4.5	3.3	22.9	19.6	102.7	62.7	40.0	466.5
1958													
1st quarter	454.6	290.8	60.5	43.6	20.9	-4.0	1.0	20.4	19.5	102.3	61.3	41.0	458.6
2nd quarter	458.9	293.8	58.7	42.0	21.0	-4.2	0.4	20.4	20.1	106.0	64.0	42.0	463.1
3rd quarter	472.4	298.9	65.5	41.4	22.5	1.5	0.7	20.5	19.7	107.3	64.2	43.2	470.9
4th quarter	485.8	302.8	73.2	43.0	24.9	5.2	-0.4	20.5	20.8	110.2	66.1	44.1	480.6
1959													
1st quarter	496.1	310.4	76.2	44.5	27.8	3.9	-1.7	19.7	21.4	111.3	66.4	44.9	492.3
2nd quarter	509.2	316.5	82.2	46.1	28.8	7.3	-2.5	20.0	22.5	113.1	67.9	45.1	502.0
3rd quarter	510.2	321.7	76.5	47.8	28.3	0.4	-1.1	21.8	22.9	113.1	67.9	45.2	509.8
4th quarter	514.2	323.9	79.3	47.7	27.5	4.1	-1.4	21.1	22.5	112.4	67.4	45.0	510.1
1960													
1st quarter	527.9	327.4	89.1	49.5	28.4	11.2	0.9	24.2	23.3	110.5	64.2	46.3	516.7
2nd quarter	527.1	333.3	79.7	50.3	26.1	3.2	1.7	25.2	23.5	112.4	64.8	47.6	523.8
3rd quarter	529.9	333.3	78.7	49.0	25.3	4.3	3.0	25.9	22.9	115.0	66.5	48.5	525.6
4th quarter	524.6	335.2	68.1	48.6	25.3	-5.8	4.0	25.8	21.7	117.3	68.0	49.2	530.4

Table 19-1. Gross Domestic Product—Continued

(Billions of dollars, quarterly data are at seasonally adjusted annual rates.)

Year and quarter	Gross domestic product	Personal consumption expenditures	Gross private domestic investment Total	Fixed investment Nonresidential	Fixed investment Residential	Change in private inventories	Net exports	Exports	Imports	Government Total	Government Federal	State and local	Addendum: Final sales of domestic product
1961													
1st quarter	528.9	335.7	70.3	47.5	25.3	-2.5	4.4	26.1	21.7	118.5	67.4	51.1	531.5
2nd quarter	539.9	340.6	75.8	48.5	25.5	1.8	3.3	25.2	21.9	120.3	69.1	51.2	538.1
3rd quarter	550.3	343.5	82.3	48.7	26.9	6.7	2.8	26.1	23.3	121.7	69.7	52.0	543.7
4th quarter	563.4	350.8	84.2	50.4	27.8	6.0	2.9	26.8	23.9	125.5	71.7	53.9	557.5
1962													
1st quarter	576.8	356.0	89.4	51.6	28.4	9.4	2.3	26.6	24.3	129.2	75.0	54.2	567.4
2nd quarter	583.9	361.6	87.9	53.2	29.2	5.4	3.2	28.1	24.9	131.2	76.4	54.8	578.4
3rd quarter	591.0	365.6	89.3	53.9	29.2	6.2	2.9	28.0	25.1	133.3	77.7	55.6	584.8
4th quarter	594.4	371.8	86.0	53.5	29.1	3.4	1.5	27.0	25.6	135.1	78.5	56.6	591.0
1963													
1st quarter	603.4	375.4	90.5	53.4	30.2	6.9	2.0	27.2	25.2	135.5	77.4	58.1	596.6
2nd quarter	612.1	379.5	92.2	55.1	32.2	4.8	3.7	29.6	25.9	136.7	77.7	59.0	607.3
3rd quarter	624.9	386.5	95.0	56.8	32.5	5.7	3.1	29.8	26.7	140.3	79.6	60.7	619.1
4th quarter	634.3	391.1	97.4	58.7	33.7	5.1	4.4	31.1	26.8	141.4	79.4	62.0	629.3
1964													
1st quarter	650.4	400.7	100.7	60.1	35.4	5.1	5.9	32.9	27.0	143.1	79.9	63.2	645.3
2nd quarter	659.6	408.6	100.6	62.0	34.2	4.5	4.9	32.6	27.7	145.5	80.5	65.0	655.2
3rd quarter	671.2	417.5	102.5	64.1	33.7	4.7	5.4	33.9	28.4	145.8	79.8	66.0	666.5
4th quarter	676.3	420.1	104.5	65.7	33.8	5.0	5.7	35.0	29.3	146.0	79.0	67.0	671.3
1965													
1st quarter	696.5	430.9	115.7	70.2	33.9	11.5	3.0	31.5	28.5	146.9	78.6	68.3	684.9
2nd quarter	709.0	437.9	115.8	73.1	34.2	8.6	4.7	36.3	31.7	150.6	80.2	70.4	700.5
3rd quarter	726.2	447.2	119.6	76.1	34.3	9.3	3.7	35.7	32.0	155.7	82.7	73.0	716.9
4th quarter	748.7	461.3	121.8	79.7	34.5	7.6	4.1	38.0	33.9	161.6	86.9	74.7	741.2
1966													
1st quarter	772.3	471.8	131.8	83.1	34.8	13.9	3.2	38.2	35.0	165.5	88.8	76.7	758.4
2nd quarter	781.5	477.0	130.7	85.2	33.2	12.3	2.0	38.2	36.2	171.8	93.2	78.6	769.2
3rd quarter	794.8	486.2	130.2	86.4	31.9	11.9	0.8	39.0	38.2	177.7	97.0	80.6	782.9
4th quarter	808.6	492.0	132.6	86.9	29.2	16.5	1.5	40.4	38.8	182.4	98.7	83.7	792.1
1967													
1st quarter	819.3	496.3	129.3	85.5	28.3	15.4	2.3	41.7	39.4	191.4	105.3	86.1	803.9
2nd quarter	823.9	505.5	123.7	85.7	31.6	6.3	2.1	41.1	39.0	192.7	105.2	87.5	817.6
3rd quarter	838.7	512.7	128.5	85.9	33.4	9.3	1.1	40.7	39.5	196.3	107.3	89.0	829.4
4th quarter	854.4	520.3	132.9	88.4	36.0	8.4	0.2	41.9	41.7	201.0	109.4	91.6	846.0
1968													
1st quarter	881.4	538.1	137.2	91.9	36.9	8.4	-1.2	43.2	44.4	207.4	112.6	94.7	873.0
2nd quarter	905.7	551.9	143.4	91.2	38.2	14.1	-0.6	44.8	45.4	211.0	113.3	97.7	891.7
3rd quarter	920.9	568.0	139.7	93.1	38.9	7.7	-1.3	47.0	48.2	214.4	114.4	100.0	913.2
4th quarter	937.8	576.9	144.4	97.5	40.9	6.0	-1.9	46.2	48.2	218.5	115.8	102.7	931.8
1969													
1st quarter	961.9	588.9	155.7	101.0	43.2	11.5	-1.9	41.9	43.8	219.1	114.3	104.8	950.4
2nd quarter	977.0	600.2	155.7	103.0	43.4	9.2	-1.8	50.9	52.7	222.9	115.2	107.7	967.8
3rd quarter	997.2	610.5	160.3	106.9	43.2	10.2	-1.3	51.0	52.4	227.6	117.8	109.8	987.0
4th quarter	1 005.3	622.5	154.1	107.6	40.7	5.8	0.1	53.2	53.1	228.7	117.1	111.6	999.5
1970													
1st quarter	1 018.2	633.7	150.6	108.1	40.7	1.8	1.1	54.7	53.5	232.7	117.5	115.2	1 016.3
2nd quarter	1 034.4	643.8	153.9	109.4	39.4	5.1	2.4	57.6	55.2	234.2	115.9	118.4	1 029.3
3rd quarter	1 051.9	655.8	156.0	110.6	40.4	5.1	0.9	57.3	56.4	239.2	115.9	123.2	1 046.9
4th quarter	1 054.2	662.5	148.9	107.9	45.0	-4.0	0.4	58.3	57.9	242.4	116.3	126.1	1 058.2
1971													
1st quarter	1 099.9	681.7	171.3	110.5	48.6	12.3	0.8	59.5	58.7	246.1	116.6	129.4	1 087.6
2nd quarter	1 120.6	695.7	178.9	113.4	54.6	10.9	-3.8	59.5	63.3	249.8	117.3	132.5	1 109.7
3rd quarter	1 140.8	708.0	183.4	114.8	58.3	10.2	-3.1	62.4	65.5	252.5	118.0	134.5	1 130.6
4th quarter	1 153.1	724.3	179.1	117.9	61.5	-0.3	-6.0	56.0	61.9	255.7	118.3	137.4	1 153.4
1972													
1st quarter	1 192.5	741.7	193.1	123.3	66.6	3.2	-8.6	63.5	72.2	266.3	125.7	140.6	1 189.2
2nd quarter	1 227.5	759.9	206.5	126.3	68.2	12.0	-8.3	63.1	71.4	269.5	127.6	141.9	1 215.5
3rd quarter	1 252.0	778.2	212.4	129.1	69.6	13.7	-7.9	66.2	74.1	269.4	124.0	145.4	1 238.3
4th quarter	1 289.7	803.1	218.5	136.7	74.3	7.5	-7.1	72.1	79.2	275.1	125.3	149.9	1 282.2
1973													
1st quarter	1 338.4	827.9	232.6	144.2	77.9	10.6	-4.4	81.0	85.4	282.4	128.2	154.2	1 327.8
2nd quarter	1 374.4	843.1	246.1	152.1	75.8	18.2	-1.1	88.3	89.5	286.4	128.8	157.6	1 356.2
3rd quarter	1 394.1	861.9	241.8	157.0	75.0	9.8	3.2	94.3	91.1	287.2	125.5	161.7	1 384.3
4th quarter	1 435.3	877.2	257.6	159.8	72.7	25.0	4.7	103.4	98.7	295.7	128.9	166.8	1 410.3
1974													
1st quarter	1 450.0	895.4	244.1	162.6	69.0	12.5	4.3	114.6	110.3	306.2	132.5	173.7	1 437.4
2nd quarter	1 487.6	923.6	252.3	167.4	67.5	17.4	-5.6	123.8	129.4	317.4	135.6	181.8	1 470.2
3rd quarter	1 514.8	951.4	245.5	172.5	67.4	5.6	-9.1	124.5	133.6	327.0	139.2	187.9	1 509.3
4th quarter	1 551.6	959.2	255.9	175.4	60.0	20.4	-2.2	134.4	136.6	338.8	145.5	193.2	1 531.2
1975													
1st quarter	1 567.2	984.4	218.7	171.1	57.7	-10.0	13.1	138.0	124.9	350.9	148.1	202.8	1 577.2
2nd quarter	1 603.1	1 013.7	216.8	170.8	59.9	-14.0	16.6	131.8	115.2	356.1	150.6	205.5	1 617.1
3rd quarter	1 659.9	1 047.2	237.7	174.5	64.6	-1.4	11.6	133.7	122.1	363.3	152.4	210.9	1 661.3
4th quarter	1 710.5	1 076.0	247.7	178.6	68.7	0.3	12.9	141.7	128.7	373.9	157.2	216.7	1 710.2

Table 19-1. Gross Domestic Product—*Continued*

(Billions of dollars, quarterly data are at seasonally adjusted annual rates.)

Year and quarter	Gross domestic product	Personal consumption expenditures	Gross private domestic investment Total	Fixed investment Nonresidential	Fixed investment Residential	Change in private inventories	Net exports	Exports	Imports	Government Total	Government Federal	Government State and local	Addendum: Final sales of domestic product
1976													
1st quarter	1 770.3	1 111.1	274.8	183.9	76.2	14.7	4.2	143.1	138.9	380.3	157.1	223.2	1 755.6
2nd quarter	1 803.1	1 131.1	291.5	188.4	80.7	22.5	-1.1	146.0	147.1	381.5	158.6	222.9	1 780.7
3rd quarter	1 837.0	1 160.8	296.6	195.1	80.6	20.8	-5.0	150.9	155.8	384.6	160.9	223.7	1 816.2
4th quarter	1 885.3	1 196.1	305.0	202.0	92.5	10.5	-7.2	155.4	162.7	391.5	165.6	225.9	1 874.8
1977													
1st quarter	1 939.1	1 231.6	326.7	214.3	97.6	14.8	-21.6	154.8	176.4	402.4	170.3	232.1	1 924.3
2nd quarter	2 006.6	1 260.3	355.1	224.0	111.7	19.5	-21.7	161.3	183.0	413.0	175.4	237.6	1 987.2
3rd quarter	2 067.5	1 291.9	378.2	232.3	115.0	30.9	-21.1	161.8	182.9	418.5	177.1	241.4	2 036.6
4th quarter	2 112.4	1 329.9	385.4	244.3	116.9	24.1	-30.3	157.1	187.4	427.4	181.4	246.0	2 088.2
1978													
1st quarter	2 150.4	1 359.8	396.2	249.7	121.1	25.5	-39.3	164.0	203.3	433.7	184.0	249.7	2 125.0
2nd quarter	2 276.6	1 419.0	429.3	274.5	130.5	24.3	-23.3	185.6	208.8	451.6	190.0	261.6	2 252.4
3rd quarter	2 338.5	1 452.1	448.8	288.1	135.8	25.0	-24.6	190.5	215.1	462.1	193.4	268.7	2 313.5
4th quarter	2 418.0	1 490.6	469.7	302.1	139.1	28.5	-17.3	204.5	221.8	475.0	200.0	275.0	2 389.5
1979													
1st quarter	2 470.9	1 531.5	478.5	316.0	138.6	23.9	-19.2	210.7	229.8	480.1	203.0	277.1	2 447.1
2nd quarter	2 529.3	1 566.9	490.9	322.6	140.9	27.4	-23.4	219.7	243.1	494.9	208.7	286.3	2 501.9
3rd quarter	2 601.5	1 620.1	495.9	340.3	143.5	12.1	-24.4	232.9	257.3	509.9	212.7	297.2	2 589.4
4th quarter	2 663.8	1 666.5	497.3	347.5	141.2	8.6	-29.0	251.5	280.5	529.0	222.2	306.8	2 655.3
1980													
1st quarter	2 732.9	1 716.0	504.3	359.8	134.5	9.9	-37.2	267.1	304.3	549.8	232.8	317.0	2 723.0
2nd quarter	2 736.9	1 719.3	468.2	349.3	111.2	7.8	-16.7	275.9	292.6	566.2	244.4	321.8	2 729.2
3rd quarter	2 793.6	1 777.1	441.7	359.6	115.9	-33.9	3.3	282.5	279.2	571.6	245.5	326.0	2 827.5
4th quarter	2 918.8	1 839.2	497.2	375.0	131.3	-9.1	-8.9	290.3	299.2	591.3	258.4	332.9	2 927.9
1981													
1st quarter	3 052.6	1 893.1	562.4	391.7	132.0	38.8	-17.0	302.8	319.7	614.1	268.2	345.9	3 013.8
2nd quarter	3 086.2	1 926.7	549.4	408.9	128.9	11.7	-16.4	305.5	322.0	626.5	280.5	346.0	3 074.5
3rd quarter	3 183.5	1 970.5	590.7	426.6	120.2	44.0	-10.2	299.7	309.9	632.5	283.3	349.3	3 139.5
4th quarter	3 203.1	1 986.4	580.7	446.3	109.6	24.8	-16.3	303.2	319.4	652.3	295.3	357.1	3 178.3
1982													
1st quarter	3 193.8	2 023.0	525.2	441.9	104.8	-21.5	-17.2	292.3	309.5	662.7	300.6	362.1	3 215.2
2nd quarter	3 248.9	2 048.8	529.2	430.6	102.8	-4.2	-5.0	294.2	299.1	675.8	307.0	368.8	3 253.0
3rd quarter	3 278.6	2 093.7	526.3	418.2	102.3	5.8	-30.3	279.0	309.3	688.9	314.7	374.2	3 272.8
4th quarter	3 315.6	2 151.7	483.5	410.5	112.8	-39.8	-29.7	265.1	294.9	710.1	328.9	381.3	3 355.4
1983													
1st quarter	3 378.5	2 188.4	495.7	399.9	130.9	-35.1	-24.6	270.6	295.3	719.1	334.2	384.9	3 413.6
2nd quarter	3 489.6	2 260.0	543.7	403.2	148.2	-7.7	-45.5	272.5	318.0	731.3	343.4	387.9	3 497.2
3rd quarter	3 582.9	2 319.4	578.0	419.6	162.6	-4.2	-65.2	278.2	343.4	750.7	355.8	394.9	3 587.1
4th quarter	3 688.8	2 377.9	639.5	447.0	168.5	23.9	-71.3	286.7	358.0	742.7	344.4	398.3	3 664.8
1984													
1st quarter	3 813.4	2 427.1	709.3	460.7	175.6	73.0	-94.3	293.7	388.0	771.2	361.5	409.8	3 740.4
2nd quarter	3 909.4	2 481.4	736.0	485.2	181.4	69.3	-103.5	303.0	406.5	795.5	376.2	419.3	3 840.0
3rd quarter	3 974.7	2 517.1	753.2	501.1	180.8	71.3	-103.1	306.5	409.6	807.5	377.2	430.2	3 903.4
4th quarter	4 033.5	2 568.0	743.6	514.3	181.3	48.0	-107.1	309.2	416.4	829.0	390.6	438.4	3 985.5
1985													
1st quarter	4 109.7	2 632.9	721.1	521.5	183.4	16.2	-91.4	305.9	397.3	847.1	399.3	447.9	4 093.5
2nd quarter	4 170.1	2 682.1	734.2	529.8	182.8	21.7	-114.7	303.9	418.6	868.4	408.2	460.2	4 148.5
3rd quarter	4 252.9	2 749.8	727.7	523.8	187.7	16.3	-117.2	297.0	414.2	892.5	421.0	471.5	4 236.6
4th quarter	4 319.3	2 785.6	762.3	535.3	193.9	33.1	-133.6	305.3	438.9	905.1	425.1	480.0	4 286.2
1986													
1st quarter	4 375.3	2 825.1	764.0	529.1	204.5	30.3	-127.1	312.0	439.0	913.2	421.8	491.4	4 344.9
2nd quarter	4 415.2	2 857.0	754.2	520.2	218.3	15.7	-129.2	314.2	443.4	933.2	434.8	498.4	4 399.6
3rd quarter	4 483.4	2 928.6	733.6	516.6	224.1	-7.0	-138.5	320.1	458.6	959.7	452.0	507.7	4 490.4
4th quarter	4 537.5	2 970.0	737.1	524.3	225.6	-12.7	-132.8	334.9	467.7	963.2	446.1	517.1	4 550.3
1987													
1st quarter	4 612.3	3 011.4	762.6	509.3	225.3	28.0	-139.4	337.5	476.8	977.6	452.1	525.5	4 584.3
2nd quarter	4 695.8	3 081.5	766.4	520.7	229.2	16.5	-144.7	356.8	501.5	992.6	459.7	532.9	4 679.3
3rd quarter	4 770.2	3 145.5	765.3	536.9	227.4	1.0	-142.8	373.7	516.5	1 002.2	461.5	540.7	4 769.2
4th quarter	4 891.6	3 182.9	831.6	540.1	228.4	63.1	-142.2	394.5	536.7	1 019.3	468.5	550.8	4 828.5
1988													
1st quarter	4 957.0	3 259.8	797.7	551.1	229.6	17.0	-121.0	421.0	542.0	1 020.5	461.2	559.3	4 940.0
2nd quarter	5 066.5	3 319.5	819.2	566.3	233.3	19.7	-103.4	441.9	545.3	1 031.2	460.0	571.2	5 046.9
3rd quarter	5 151.5	3 387.0	825.7	571.8	235.7	18.2	-96.3	455.8	552.1	1 035.1	457.2	578.0	5 133.3
4th quarter	5 258.3	3 460.1	842.0	584.5	238.4	19.1	-104.4	469.0	573.5	1 060.7	472.2	588.5	5 239.2
1989													
1st quarter	5 379.0	3 511.8	881.2	596.0	237.0	48.2	-84.2	492.0	576.2	1 070.3	470.4	599.8	5 330.8
2nd quarter	5 461.7	3 572.9	875.4	607.1	232.3	36.0	-81.4	512.5	594.0	1 094.8	482.6	612.2	5 425.6
3rd quarter	5 527.5	3 626.9	868.3	628.1	230.2	10.0	-79.6	509.4	589.0	1 111.9	490.0	621.9	5 517.5
4th quarter	5 588.0	3 675.1	866.7	622.3	227.8	16.6	-77.6	522.0	599.6	1 123.9	487.2	636.8	5 571.4
1990													
1st quarter	5 720.8	3 754.8	881.6	633.6	234.1	13.9	-74.2	541.6	615.8	1 158.5	502.0	656.5	5 706.8
2nd quarter	5 800.0	3 806.2	883.0	625.1	224.2	33.7	-60.7	554.6	615.3	1 171.4	506.9	664.6	5 766.3
3rd quarter	5 844.9	3 871.6	869.4	635.4	212.1	21.9	-78.8	555.3	634.1	1 182.7	505.8	676.9	5 823.1
4th quarter	5 847.3	3 893.4	812.8	627.2	196.9	-11.3	-72.1	577.1	649.2	1 213.1	519.1	694.0	5 858.6

Table 19-1. Gross Domestic Product—Continued

(Billions of dollars, quarterly data are at seasonally adjusted annual rates.)

Year and quarter	Gross domestic product	Personal consump- tion expen- ditures	Gross private domestic investment Total	Fixed investment Nonresi- dential	Fixed investment Residen- tial	Change in private inventories	Net exports	Exports	Imports	Total	Federal	State and local	Adden- dum: Final sales of domestic product
1991													
1st quarter	5 886.3	3 904.6	786.5	616.8	185.0	-15.3	-33.4	577.1	610.5	1 228.6	530.3	698.3	5 901.6
2nd quarter	5 962.0	3 958.6	780.5	611.7	186.6	-17.7	-12.6	602.5	615.1	1 235.5	532.2	703.3	5 979.7
3rd quarter	6 015.9	3 998.2	801.5	605.9	194.5	1.0	-22.3	602.3	624.5	1 238.4	526.9	711.5	6 014.8
4th quarter	6 080.7	4 023.6	832.1	601.1	200.0	31.1	-14.5	624.5	639.0	1 239.5	520.1	719.4	6 049.6
1992													
1st quarter	6 183.6	4 123.1	810.9	600.1	211.8	-1.0	-7.7	629.5	637.3	1 257.3	527.1	730.2	6 184.5
2nd quarter	6 276.6	4 171.5	867.2	621.5	223.9	21.8	-27.1	633.4	660.5	1 265.1	530.5	734.5	6 254.8
3rd quarter	6 345.8	4 225.7	878.7	633.0	226.6	19.1	-36.4	637.2	673.6	1 277.8	540.6	737.2	6 326.7
4th quarter	6 469.8	4 318.3	909.8	649.9	239.7	20.2	-40.1	647.0	687.1	1 281.8	539.9	741.9	6 449.6
1993													
1st quarter	6 521.6	4 350.6	938.0	659.3	242.7	36.1	-46.5	646.4	692.9	1 279.5	528.9	750.5	6 485.5
2nd quarter	6 596.7	4 421.3	943.6	675.2	244.1	24.3	-57.3	660.6	717.9	1 289.1	525.3	763.9	6 572.4
3rd quarter	6 655.5	4 488.2	943.0	683.2	252.9	7.0	-72.0	646.4	718.3	1 296.2	526.9	769.3	6 648.5
4th quarter	6 795.5	4 558.7	995.8	711.4	267.3	17.0	-66.2	678.8	744.9	1 307.1	528.0	779.1	6 778.5
1994													
1st quarter	6 887.8	4 613.8	1 042.0	721.7	276.4	43.8	-71.3	683.8	755.1	1 303.3	515.8	787.5	6 844.0
2nd quarter	7 015.7	4 677.5	1 106.4	738.2	288.4	79.8	-84.2	714.5	798.7	1 316.1	515.9	800.2	6 936.0
3rd quarter	7 096.0	4 753.0	1 094.0	752.7	289.3	52.0	-99.1	736.1	835.2	1 348.1	532.5	815.6	7 044.0
4th quarter	7 217.7	4 821.3	1 146.1	781.8	289.8	74.6	-93.8	765.8	859.6	1 344.0	520.0	824.0	7 143.1
1995													
1st quarter	7 297.5	4 868.6	1 162.8	812.5	287.6	62.7	-94.5	787.7	882.2	1 360.6	523.4	837.1	7 234.8
2nd quarter	7 342.6	4 943.7	1 133.1	820.3	276.9	35.8	-109.0	802.5	911.5	1 374.9	525.5	849.4	7 306.8
3rd quarter	7 432.8	5 005.2	1 123.5	825.2	284.9	13.4	-74.2	834.1	908.3	1 378.3	525.0	853.3	7 419.4
4th quarter	7 529.3	5 058.4	1 155.6	842.3	293.1	20.2	-59.3	850.0	909.3	1 374.5	512.3	862.2	7 509.1
1996													
1st quarter	7 629.6	5 130.5	1 172.4	865.1	300.5	6.8	-75.8	853.3	929.1	1 402.6	530.6	872.0	7 622.8
2nd quarter	7 782.7	5 218.0	1 231.5	885.4	316.3	29.8	-89.8	864.7	954.5	1 423.0	537.2	885.7	7 752.9
3rd quarter	7 859.0	5 263.7	1 282.6	913.6	319.0	50.0	-110.6	865.6	976.1	1 423.4	529.1	894.3	7 809.0
4th quarter	7 981.4	5 337.9	1 284.3	933.7	317.2	33.5	-79.7	913.1	992.8	1 438.9	529.4	909.4	7 947.9
1997													
1st quarter	8 124.2	5 429.9	1 324.2	955.5	320.0	48.8	-89.2	927.8	1 017.1	1 459.2	529.2	930.0	8 075.4
2nd quarter	8 279.8	5 470.8	1 397.7	984.3	325.7	87.7	-75.0	966.8	1 041.7	1 486.3	543.4	942.9	8 192.1
3rd quarter	8 390.9	5 575.9	1 405.7	1 026.0	329.8	49.9	-88.6	988.7	1 077.3	1 498.0	541.3	956.6	8 341.1
4th quarter	8 478.6	5 640.6	1 434.5	1 031.8	337.5	65.1	-104.6	982.4	1 087.0	1 508.2	538.9	969.3	8 413.5
1998													
1st quarter	8 627.8	5 719.9	1 528.7	1 074.8	347.2	106.7	-122.6	974.1	1 096.7	1 501.8	526.1	975.8	8 521.1
2nd quarter	8 697.3	5 820.0	1 498.4	1 099.9	357.6	40.9	-154.9	959.2	1 114.1	1 533.8	542.9	990.9	8 656.4
3rd quarter	8 816.5	5 895.1	1 538.6	1 098.6	370.5	69.5	-165.3	946.7	1 112.0	1 548.1	539.5	1 008.6	8 747.0
4th quarter	8 984.5	5 989.1	1 589.3	1 131.7	382.2	75.4	-164.1	979.7	1 143.8	1 570.3	548.4	1 021.9	8 909.1
1999													
1st quarter	9 092.7	6 076.6	1 618.0	1 150.0	393.3	74.7	-196.4	959.2	1 155.6	1 594.6	550.0	1 044.5	9 018.0
2nd quarter	9 171.7	6 195.6	1 597.8	1 167.7	402.4	27.7	-241.8	970.2	1 212.0	1 620.1	556.1	1 064.0	9 144.0
3rd quarter	9 316.5	6 299.4	1 637.9	1 184.5	406.5	46.8	-274.6	996.8	1 271.4	1 653.9	569.0	1 084.8	9 269.7
4th quarter	9 516.4	6 414.5	1 693.2	1 191.9	412.5	88.9	-286.7	1 031.2	1 317.9	1 695.4	584.9	1 110.5	9 427.5
2000													
1st quarter	9 649.5	6 552.2	1 711.4	1 236.6	428.0	46.8	-330.6	1 055.9	1 386.5	1 716.5	575.7	1 140.8	9 602.6
2nd quarter	9 820.7	6 638.7	1 786.3	1 268.3	428.8	89.2	-353.2	1 098.0	1 451.1	1 748.8	598.5	1 150.3	9 731.5
3rd quarter	9 874.8	6 736.1	1 766.4	1 283.4	421.8	61.1	-384.9	1 130.9	1 515.8	1 757.2	589.7	1 167.4	9 813.6
4th quarter	9 953.6	6 808.0	1 757.4	1 274.8	425.6	57.1	-393.2	1 119.8	1 513.0	1 781.4	592.9	1 188.5	9 896.6
2001													
1st quarter	10 028.1	6 904.7	1 671.1	1 258.3	440.0	-27.2	-372.7	1 100.0	1 472.8	1 825.0	613.3	1 211.7	10 055.3
2nd quarter	10 049.9	6 959.8	1 597.2	1 210.0	444.2	-57.1	-365.7	1 059.7	1 425.3	1 858.5	624.8	1 233.7	10 107.0
3rd quarter	10 097.7	6 983.7	1 574.9	1 188.1	447.4	-60.6	-312.6	1 005.8	1 318.4	1 851.7	627.4	1 224.3	10 158.3
4th quarter	10 152.9	7 099.9	1 500.7	1 149.8	447.4	-96.5	-344.5	971.1	1 315.6	1 896.8	646.9	1 249.8	10 249.4
2002													
1st quarter	10 313.1	7 174.2	1 559.4	1 126.8	462.6	-29.9	-360.1	977.5	1 337.5	1 939.5	672.0	1 267.5	10 343.0
2nd quarter	10 376.9	7 254.7	1 588.0	1 115.8	468.7	3.4	-425.6	1 018.1	1 443.7	1 959.8	688.2	1 271.6	10 373.5
3rd quarter	10 506.2	7 360.7	1 597.3	1 109.8	469.9	17.6	-432.9	1 038.6	1 471.5	1 981.1	697.7	1 283.3	10 488.7
4th quarter	10 588.8	7 425.4	1 628.1	1 117.1	486.5	24.5	-476.0	1 025.4	1 501.4	2 011.3	716.9	1 294.4	10 564.3

Table 19-2. Real Gross Domestic Product

(Billions of chained [1996] dollars, quarterly data are at seasonally adjusted annual rates.)

Year and quarter	Gross domestic product	Personal consumption expenditures	Gross private domestic investment				Exports and imports of goods and services			Government consumption expenditures and gross investment			Addendum: Final sales of domestic product
			Total	Fixed investment		Change in private inventories	Net exports	Exports	Imports	Total	Federal	State and local	
				Nonresidential	Residential								
1987													
1st quarter	6 013.3	4 049.7	863.4	554.0	291.3	33.9	-161.3	383.6	544.9	1 278.4	588.6	690.7	5 985.4
2nd quarter	6 077.2	4 101.5	863.9	566.8	294.1	17.3	-159.5	399.3	558.9	1 289.1	597.3	692.8	6 066.8
3rd quarter	6 128.1	4 147.0	860.5	585.1	289.3	-2.1	-153.2	416.7	569.9	1 292.4	598.2	695.1	6 138.7
4th quarter	6 234.4	4 155.3	929.3	584.0	288.0	69.3	-150.8	432.2	583.0	1 310.0	607.0	704.0	6 164.1
1988													
1st quarter	6 275.9	4 228.0	884.6	590.5	287.0	17.2	-124.2	456.1	580.3	1 300.1	589.6	711.3	6 263.0
2nd quarter	6 349.8	4 256.8	902.5	603.4	289.0	18.9	-104.4	468.8	573.2	1 302.4	583.2	720.0	6 334.0
3rd quarter	6 382.3	4 291.6	907.5	606.7	290.2	18.5	-108.8	477.3	586.1	1 300.3	578.3	722.8	6 365.9
4th quarter	6 465.2	4 341.4	916.7	613.8	290.8	18.9	-111.2	491.8	603.0	1 327.2	596.5	731.5	6 447.5
1989													
1st quarter	6 543.8	4 357.1	952.7	623.1	287.0	51.5	-85.2	510.5	595.7	1 319.3	583.0	737.1	6 492.7
2nd quarter	6 579.4	4 374.8	941.1	632.2	277.9	38.9	-76.2	530.8	606.9	1 340.6	596.0	745.3	6 542.8
3rd quarter	6 610.6	4 413.4	929.3	651.1	274.5	10.2	-81.5	530.8	612.3	1 353.5	601.7	752.7	6 605.8
4th quarter	6 633.5	4 429.4	922.9	641.6	269.9	17.9	-74.7	545.5	620.2	1 360.4	598.3	762.9	6 620.4
1990													
1st quarter	6 716.3	4 466.0	934.0	650.0	275.2	15.7	-62.3	565.8	628.1	1 381.2	607.8	774.1	6 705.8
2nd quarter	6 731.7	4 478.8	933.0	639.4	262.5	36.3	-61.7	577.6	639.3	1 384.7	608.7	776.7	6 697.6
3rd quarter	6 719.4	4 495.6	912.6	645.4	247.2	24.1	-67.6	572.8	640.4	1 384.8	603.1	782.2	6 699.2
4th quarter	6 664.2	4 457.7	849.6	632.1	229.2	-9.9	-34.6	586.5	621.0	1 398.6	607.8	791.3	6 680.0
1991													
1st quarter	6 631.4	4 437.5	815.1	616.2	214.7	-15.5	-18.2	584.5	602.7	1 404.7	612.6	792.6	6 652.5
2nd quarter	6 668.5	4 469.9	808.8	611.9	215.6	-19.6	-10.7	613.3	623.9	1 408.9	613.4	796.0	6 692.5
3rd quarter	6 684.9	4 484.3	829.8	607.7	223.4	-1.3	-23.9	616.9	640.8	1 403.0	602.7	800.6	6 689.2
4th quarter	6 720.9	4 474.8	864.2	604.6	230.6	32.4	-10.4	638.3	648.7	1 397.0	591.0	806.3	6 692.0
1992													
1st quarter	6 783.3	4 544.8	843.8	603.6	245.0	0.0	-6.7	643.9	650.6	1 407.6	591.8	816.1	6 788.9
2nd quarter	6 846.8	4 566.7	901.8	626.1	256.6	24.9	-23.0	647.1	670.1	1 405.7	591.1	814.9	6 827.1
3rd quarter	6 899.7	4 600.5	912.1	637.6	257.9	21.4	-22.0	650.8	672.9	1 413.1	598.3	815.1	6 882.7
4th quarter	6 990.6	4 665.9	941.6	655.0	269.2	22.0	-27.3	662.2	689.5	1 413.7	599.1	814.9	6 972.4
1993													
1st quarter	6 988.7	4 674.9	964.8	661.7	269.5	36.2	-44.4	661.4	705.8	1 396.4	579.6	817.1	6 953.6
2nd quarter	7 031.2	4 721.5	967.0	676.6	268.6	23.4	-51.7	674.4	726.1	1 398.0	572.2	826.1	7 008.8
3rd quarter	7 062.0	4 776.9	964.1	684.2	275.7	4.7	-72.3	660.8	733.1	1 398.4	568.9	829.7	7 057.9
4th quarter	7 168.7	4 822.3	1 015.6	711.8	290.1	15.7	-67.9	694.3	762.2	1 402.2	567.3	835.1	7 154.8
1994													
1st quarter	7 229.4	4 866.6	1 057.3	720.0	296.5	47.8	-80.1	696.7	776.8	1 388.0	550.9	837.3	7 187.1
2nd quarter	7 330.2	4 907.9	1 118.5	734.1	307.5	85.8	-86.2	725.1	811.3	1 390.4	545.2	845.4	7 250.2
3rd quarter	7 370.2	4 944.5	1 101.8	747.2	305.2	56.3	-92.2	742.4	834.6	1 417.5	563.2	854.4	7 318.5
4th quarter	7 461.1	4 993.6	1 150.5	777.1	301.8	77.4	-87.7	767.1	854.8	1 404.5	546.1	858.5	7 387.2
1995													
1st quarter	7 488.7	5 011.6	1 162.4	806.4	295.8	62.2	-92.5	780.6	873.1	1 407.3	544.1	863.3	7 427.3
2nd quarter	7 503.3	5 059.6	1 128.5	811.4	283.5	32.5	-97.5	788.9	886.4	1 414.0	544.3	869.7	7 469.6
3rd quarter	7 561.4	5 099.2	1 119.1	816.7	290.4	9.0	-67.3	821.9	889.1	1 410.8	540.4	870.4	7 549.7
4th quarter	7 621.9	5 132.1	1 152.4	835.5	297.3	18.0	-56.4	841.4	897.8	1 393.5	517.1	876.4	7 602.5
1996													
1st quarter	7 676.4	5 174.3	1 172.3	861.6	303.6	5.6	-75.0	846.1	921.1	1 404.8	529.1	875.7	7 669.6
2nd quarter	7 802.9	5 229.5	1 233.4	885.6	318.1	30.3	-90.4	860.1	950.4	1 430.4	540.2	890.2	7 773.4
3rd quarter	7 841.9	5 254.3	1 281.4	914.3	317.3	51.2	-115.9	867.0	982.9	1 422.0	529.5	892.5	7 792.1
4th quarter	7 931.3	5 291.9	1 283.7	936.2	314.0	32.9	-74.6	923.5	998.1	1 430.6	527.6	903.0	7 897.6
1997													
1st quarter	8 016.4	5 350.7	1 325.4	960.8	314.7	49.3	-94.0	940.3	1 034.3	1 434.6	521.7	912.8	7 966.4
2nd quarter	8 131.9	5 375.7	1 400.6	992.7	318.7	88.3	-100.6	979.2	1 079.8	1 457.0	534.8	922.2	8 043.2
3rd quarter	8 216.6	5 462.1	1 408.6	1 037.0	320.3	51.3	-119.6	1 004.2	1 123.8	1 464.8	533.4	931.4	8 164.9
4th quarter	8 272.9	5 507.1	1 438.5	1 047.0	324.9	66.1	-139.2	1 002.1	1 141.2	1 465.3	528.4	936.8	8 206.3
1998													
1st quarter	8 396.3	5 576.3	1 543.3	1 099.5	333.0	113.1	-180.8	1 003.4	1 184.2	1 456.1	515.0	940.8	8 286.6
2nd quarter	8 442.9	5 660.2	1 516.8	1 132.3	340.5	42.0	-223.1	993.1	1 216.2	1 482.6	530.1	952.4	8 397.2
3rd quarter	8 528.5	5 713.7	1 559.7	1 136.6	349.5	71.8	-241.2	987.6	1 228.9	1 489.9	524.9	964.7	8 454.9
4th quarter	8 667.9	5 784.7	1 612.1	1 175.4	357.4	80.0	-239.2	1 025.6	1 264.8	1 504.8	531.7	972.8	8 588.5
1999													
1st quarter	8 733.2	5 851.4	1 640.3	1 197.5	364.1	80.0	-283.2	1 007.5	1 290.7	1 515.9	527.2	988.3	8 654.3
2nd quarter	8 775.5	5 932.8	1 625.0	1 220.4	368.4	31.2	-319.6	1 018.1	1 337.7	1 526.7	530.6	995.7	8 741.0
3rd quarter	8 886.9	6 000.1	1 663.4	1 243.3	369.2	47.6	-339.6	1 044.1	1 383.7	1 546.5	540.1	1 006.0	8 833.6
4th quarter	9 040.1	6 073.6	1 717.8	1 252.4	371.7	92.2	-339.5	1 075.6	1 415.2	1 573.2	553.0	1 019.8	8 946.6
2000													
1st quarter	9 097.4	6 151.9	1 727.8	1 297.1	379.1	45.3	-368.8	1 095.8	1 464.6	1 568.3	533.8	1 033.8	9 042.9
2nd quarter	9 205.7	6 198.2	1 798.1	1 329.1	376.2	91.5	-394.6	1 133.9	1 528.5	1 586.1	554.0	1 031.8	9 111.1
3rd quarter	9 218.7	6 256.8	1 770.3	1 340.7	367.2	63.1	-413.1	1 165.5	1 578.6	1 582.2	543.7	1 037.8	9 150.4
4th quarter	9 243.8	6 288.8	1 755.2	1 329.9	367.2	59.9	-418.5	1 153.7	1 572.2	1 593.4	546.4	1 046.3	9 179.8
2001													
1st quarter	9 229.9	6 326.0	1 661.8	1 311.4	374.5	-26.9	-404.5	1 135.8	1 540.3	1 615.7	559.0	1 056.2	9 243.8
2nd quarter	9 193.1	6 348.0	1 583.5	1 261.0	374.0	-58.3	-414.8	1 098.8	1 513.6	1 638.0	567.2	1 070.2	9 234.3
3rd quarter	9 186.4	6 370.9	1 562.7	1 241.7	374.3	-61.8	-419.0	1 048.0	1 467.0	1 633.3	568.9	1 064.1	9 230.5
4th quarter	9 248.8	6 464.0	1 490.3	1 206.4	371.0	-98.4	-425.3	1 021.8	1 447.2	1 674.5	587.2	1 087.1	9 324.9
2002													
1st quarter	9 363.2	6 513.8	1 554.0	1 188.4	383.6	-28.9	-446.6	1 030.6	1 477.1	1 697.3	597.8	1 099.3	9 379.4
2nd quarter	9 392.4	6 542.4	1 583.9	1 181.1	386.1	4.9	-487.4	1 065.5	1 552.9	1 703.3	608.7	1 094.7	9 377.9
3rd quarter	9 485.6	6 609.9	1 598.0	1 178.7	387.1	18.8	-488.0	1 077.7	1 565.7	1 715.6	615.1	1 100.6	9 457.2
4th quarter	9 518.2	6 637.9	1 622.4	1 185.3	395.9	25.8	-532.2	1 061.6	1 593.8	1 735.0	631.4	1 104.0	9 483.1

Table 19-3. Chain-Type Quantity Indexes for Gross Domestic Product and Domestic Purchases

(Index numbers, 1996 = 100.)

Year and quarter	Gross domestic product	Personal consumption expenditures		Private fixed investment			Exports and imports of goods and services		Government consumption expenditures and gross investment			Gross domestic purchases
		Total	Excluding food and energy	Total	Nonresidential	Residential	Exports	Imports	Total	Federal	State and local	
1947												
1st quarter	19.0	18.4	...	15.0	12.4	24.5	9.2	5.0	21.5	32.2	15.0	18.3
2nd quarter	19.1	18.7	...	14.6	12.2	23.3	9.1	5.1	21.6	32.2	15.2	18.4
3rd quarter	19.1	18.7	...	15.1	11.9	26.8	8.7	4.5	21.8	32.1	15.6	18.5
4th quarter	19.4	18.8	...	16.4	12.3	32.0	7.7	4.8	21.5	31.0	15.8	19.0
1948												
1st quarter	19.7	18.8	...	16.9	13.1	31.6	7.4	5.4	21.9	32.1	15.8	19.4
2nd quarter	20.0	19.1	...	16.9	12.6	33.5	6.7	5.6	22.9	34.0	16.3	19.9
3rd quarter	20.1	19.1	...	16.7	12.7	32.4	6.8	5.9	23.4	34.6	16.5	20.0
4th quarter	20.1	19.3	...	16.5	13.0	30.0	6.6	5.8	24.4	36.6	17.0	20.0
1949												
1st quarter	19.8	19.3	...	15.6	12.4	27.8	7.4	5.6	25.0	37.1	17.6	19.6
2nd quarter	19.8	19.6	...	15.1	11.9	27.3	7.3	5.5	26.1	38.5	18.7	19.5
3rd quarter	20.0	19.6	...	15.1	11.3	29.6	6.7	5.3	26.4	38.1	19.4	19.8
4th quarter	19.8	19.9	...	15.6	11.1	33.2	5.8	5.4	25.8	36.2	19.8	19.8
1950												
1st quarter	20.6	20.2	...	16.6	11.4	37.0	5.7	5.5	25.4	34.4	20.3	20.6
2nd quarter	21.2	20.5	...	18.1	12.4	40.6	5.8	5.8	25.8	35.1	20.5	21.3
3rd quarter	22.1	21.6	...	19.5	13.5	42.9	5.9	7.2	25.3	33.9	20.5	22.3
4th quarter	22.5	21.0	...	19.1	13.5	40.8	6.4	7.2	26.9	37.9	20.5	22.6
1951												
1st quarter	22.7	21.4	...	18.4	13.2	38.7	6.7	7.2	29.7	45.1	20.3	22.8
2nd quarter	23.1	20.8	...	17.5	13.4	33.5	7.4	7.0	33.8	54.8	20.7	23.1
3rd quarter	23.6	21.1	...	17.2	13.5	31.3	7.5	6.4	37.6	64.2	20.8	23.4
4th quarter	23.6	21.2	...	17.1	13.2	31.6	7.5	6.2	39.6	69.4	20.7	23.4
1952												
1st quarter	23.9	21.3	...	17.3	13.3	32.5	7.8	6.9	41.1	73.2	20.8	23.8
2nd quarter	23.9	21.7	...	17.5	13.4	33.0	7.0	6.9	42.5	76.1	21.2	23.9
3rd quarter	24.0	21.8	...	16.4	12.2	32.7	6.4	7.3	42.9	78.1	20.6	24.2
4th quarter	24.8	22.5	...	17.7	13.3	34.5	6.5	8.0	43.7	79.3	21.1	25.1
1953												
1st quarter	25.3	22.8	...	18.4	14.1	35.0	6.4	7.8	45.1	82.2	21.6	25.5
2nd quarter	25.5	23.0	...	18.5	14.1	35.1	6.4	8.2	46.1	84.9	21.5	25.8
3rd quarter	25.3	22.9	...	18.5	14.5	33.8	6.7	8.2	45.5	82.5	22.1	25.6
4th quarter	24.9	22.8	...	18.3	14.3	33.5	6.4	7.7	45.4	81.3	22.7	25.2
1954												
1st quarter	24.8	22.8	...	18.0	13.9	33.8	6.2	7.3	44.1	76.7	23.5	25.0
2nd quarter	24.8	23.1	...	18.3	13.7	36.0	7.0	8.0	42.6	72.8	23.5	25.0
3rd quarter	25.1	23.4	...	19.1	14.1	38.2	6.8	7.5	41.6	69.1	24.2	25.3
4th quarter	25.6	23.9	...	19.5	14.1	40.6	7.1	7.6	41.3	68.3	24.3	25.7
1955												
1st quarter	26.3	24.4	...	20.3	14.3	43.7	7.4	8.0	41.2	66.6	25.4	26.5
2nd quarter	26.8	24.9	...	21.1	15.2	44.3	7.2	8.4	40.8	64.9	25.7	27.0
3rd quarter	27.1	25.2	...	21.6	16.0	43.4	7.7	8.6	41.1	65.7	25.7	27.3
4th quarter	27.3	25.5	...	21.6	16.4	41.5	7.7	8.9	40.2	63.2	25.8	27.5
1956												
1st quarter	27.2	25.6	...	21.2	16.1	40.4	8.1	9.3	40.2	62.8	26.1	27.3
2nd quarter	27.4	25.7	...	21.3	16.4	40.2	8.6	9.2	41.0	64.4	26.4	27.5
3rd quarter	27.3	25.7	...	21.3	16.5	39.4	8.9	9.3	40.6	63.2	26.5	27.4
4th quarter	27.8	26.1	...	21.2	16.5	38.8	9.3	8.9	41.7	65.6	26.8	27.7
1957												
1st quarter	27.9	26.2	...	21.2	16.6	38.2	9.9	9.6	42.5	66.6	27.4	27.9
2nd quarter	27.9	26.3	...	21.0	16.6	37.3	9.7	9.7	42.2	65.7	27.7	27.9
3rd quarter	28.1	26.5	...	21.2	16.9	36.8	9.4	9.5	42.6	66.0	28.1	28.2
4th quarter	27.9	26.5	...	20.8	16.4	36.7	9.1	9.5	43.4	66.9	28.8	27.9
1958												
1st quarter	27.1	26.2	...	19.5	15.3	35.3	8.2	9.6	42.9	64.5	29.6	27.3
2nd quarter	27.3	26.4	...	18.9	14.6	35.4	8.2	10.0	44.0	66.6	30.0	27.5
3rd quarter	27.9	26.8	...	19.2	14.3	38.0	8.2	9.9	44.2	66.2	30.6	28.1
4th quarter	28.5	27.1	...	20.4	14.9	42.0	8.2	10.5	45.1	67.7	31.2	28.8
1959												
1st quarter	29.1	27.6	22.8	21.6	15.4	46.8	7.9	10.6	45.8	69.2	31.4	29.5
2nd quarter	29.9	28.0	23.2	22.3	15.8	48.5	8.1	11.2	46.7	71.3	31.5	30.3
3rd quarter	29.8	28.3	23.5	22.6	16.3	47.6	8.7	11.4	47.0	72.0	31.5	30.2
4th quarter	29.9	28.4	23.5	22.3	16.3	46.2	8.4	11.1	46.6	71.2	31.3	30.3
1960												
1st quarter	30.6	28.6	23.8	23.1	16.9	47.5	9.6	11.5	45.6	68.0	31.9	30.9
2nd quarter	30.5	29.0	24.1	22.6	17.1	43.6	10.0	11.5	46.2	68.3	32.7	30.7
3rd quarter	30.5	28.9	24.1	22.0	16.7	42.3	10.2	11.2	46.8	69.1	33.1	30.7
4th quarter	30.1	28.9	24.1	21.9	16.7	42.2	10.2	10.7	47.3	69.8	33.5	30.2

. . . = Not available.

Table 19-3. Chain-Type Quantity Indexes for Gross Domestic Product and Domestic Purchases—*Continued*

(Index numbers, 1996 = 100.)

Year and quarter	Gross domestic product	Personal consumption expenditures		Private fixed investment			Exports and imports of goods and services		Government consumption expenditures and gross investment			Gross domestic purchases
	Gross domestic product	Total	Excluding food and energy	Total	Nonresi-dential	Residen-tial	Exports	Imports	Total	Federal	State and local	
1961												
1st quarter	30.3	28.9	24.1	21.6	16.3	42.4	10.3	10.6	47.9	69.5	34.6	30.4
2nd quarter	30.9	29.3	24.4	21.9	16.6	42.5	9.8	10.8	48.3	71.1	34.4	31.0
3rd quarter	31.4	29.5	24.7	22.5	16.8	44.8	10.2	11.5	48.8	71.8	34.7	31.6
4th quarter	32.0	30.1	25.3	23.2	17.3	46.3	10.4	11.7	50.0	73.5	35.6	32.2
1962												
1st quarter	32.6	30.4	25.6	23.7	17.7	47.2	10.3	12.1	50.9	76.1	35.4	32.8
2nd quarter	32.9	30.7	26.1	24.4	18.2	48.6	11.0	12.4	51.5	77.2	35.6	33.1
3rd quarter	33.2	31.0	26.3	24.6	18.5	48.6	11.0	12.5	52.1	78.1	36.1	33.5
4th quarter	33.3	31.4	26.8	24.5	18.4	48.5	10.6	12.7	52.3	78.1	36.5	33.6
1963												
1st quarter	33.7	31.6	27.0	24.8	18.3	50.3	10.6	12.4	52.0	76.3	37.2	34.0
2nd quarter	34.2	31.9	27.3	25.9	18.9	53.9	11.6	12.7	52.3	76.6	37.5	34.3
3rd quarter	34.8	32.4	27.8	26.6	19.5	54.9	11.7	13.0	53.9	78.9	38.5	35.0
4th quarter	35.1	32.7	28.1	27.5	20.1	56.6	12.2	12.9	53.4	76.9	39.0	35.2
1964												
1st quarter	35.8	33.3	28.7	28.5	20.6	60.0	12.9	12.9	53.7	76.7	39.6	35.9
2nd quarter	36.3	33.9	29.2	28.4	21.1	57.0	12.8	13.2	54.4	77.1	40.5	36.3
3rd quarter	36.8	34.5	29.8	28.0	21.0	56.1	13.2	13.0	53.9	75.2	41.0	36.8
4th quarter	36.9	34.6	29.8	29.1	22.3	55.1	13.4	13.9	53.9	74.5	41.4	36.9
1965												
1st quarter	37.8	35.4	30.6	30.4	23.8	55.3	11.8	13.4	53.8	73.8	41.8	38.0
2nd quarter	38.3	35.8	30.9	31.3	24.7	55.7	13.7	15.0	55.0	75.0	42.8	38.4
3rd quarter	39.1	36.4	31.5	32.1	25.6	55.9	13.4	15.1	56.3	76.6	44.0	39.3
4th quarter	40.0	37.4	32.3	32.9	26.7	54.7	14.4	15.8	57.5	78.6	44.7	40.2
1966												
1st quarter	41.0	38.0	33.0	34.1	27.9	55.9	14.2	16.2	58.5	80.5	45.3	41.2
2nd quarter	41.1	38.1	33.0	33.6	28.3	51.5	14.1	16.6	60.3	84.6	45.6	41.5
3rd quarter	41.4	38.5	33.5	33.6	28.6	49.8	14.2	17.6	61.2	86.0	46.1	41.8
4th quarter	41.8	38.7	33.7	32.6	28.6	44.6	14.4	17.8	62.5	87.4	47.3	42.2
1967												
1st quarter	42.1	38.9	33.9	31.8	27.9	43.2	14.6	18.0	65.1	93.4	47.9	42.6
2nd quarter	42.1	39.4	34.4	32.6	27.9	48.1	14.5	17.9	64.8	92.2	48.1	42.5
3rd quarter	42.4	39.6	34.7	33.0	27.7	50.5	14.3	18.1	65.2	92.9	48.3	42.9
4th quarter	42.7	39.9	34.8	34.0	28.3	53.5	14.7	19.1	65.7	93.0	49.2	43.3
1968												
1st quarter	43.6	40.8	35.7	34.8	29.2	53.8	15.0	20.2	66.9	94.6	50.1	44.2
2nd quarter	44.4	41.4	36.3	34.6	28.7	55.2	15.3	20.5	67.2	93.9	51.0	45.0
3rd quarter	44.7	42.2	37.0	35.1	29.0	56.2	16.2	21.8	67.4	93.3	51.7	45.3
4th quarter	44.9	42.4	37.2	36.0	29.9	56.9	15.9	21.6	67.6	93.0	52.1	45.5
1969												
1st quarter	45.5	42.9	37.6	37.1	30.8	58.9	14.2	19.5	67.3	91.9	52.4	46.2
2nd quarter	45.7	43.1	37.9	37.3	31.1	58.3	17.2	23.4	67.2	91.1	52.8	46.3
3rd quarter	45.9	43.3	38.1	37.9	32.0	57.8	17.0	23.1	67.1	90.6	52.9	46.6
4th quarter	45.7	43.7	38.4	36.9	31.8	53.6	17.3	22.8	66.3	88.8	52.8	46.3
1970												
1st quarter	45.7	43.9	38.5	36.8	31.6	53.7	17.7	22.8	65.8	86.6	53.3	46.2
2nd quarter	45.7	44.1	38.7	36.0	31.4	50.1	18.3	23.2	65.2	84.5	53.6	46.3
3rd quarter	46.1	44.5	39.0	36.6	31.6	52.8	18.3	23.2	65.5	83.2	54.8	46.7
4th quarter	45.7	44.4	38.8	36.7	30.4	58.3	18.6	23.5	65.4	82.5	55.1	46.2
1971												
1st quarter	46.9	45.3	39.8	37.5	30.7	61.5	18.4	23.2	64.6	80.0	55.4	47.4
2nd quarter	47.2	45.7	40.2	39.0	31.1	67.7	18.4	25.0	64.4	78.8	55.8	47.9
3rd quarter	47.5	46.0	40.7	39.7	31.2	71.0	19.4	25.6	64.1	77.9	56.0	48.2
4th quarter	47.7	46.8	41.5	40.8	31.8	73.7	17.3	23.8	64.0	76.3	56.7	48.4
1972												
1st quarter	48.6	47.4	42.2	42.6	32.9	78.7	19.3	27.3	64.8	78.1	56.9	49.4
2nd quarter	49.7	48.3	42.9	43.4	33.5	80.2	19.0	26.3	64.8	78.6	56.7	50.5
3rd quarter	50.2	49.0	43.6	43.9	34.0	80.4	19.9	26.9	63.8	75.2	57.2	50.9
4th quarter	51.1	50.2	44.7	45.9	35.8	83.3	21.2	28.1	63.9	74.3	58.0	51.8
1973												
1st quarter	52.4	51.1	45.9	47.9	37.5	86.1	23.1	29.4	64.3	74.8	58.3	53.0
2nd quarter	52.9	51.0	46.1	48.3	39.0	81.7	24.1	28.5	64.1	74.1	58.4	53.3
3rd quarter	52.7	51.2	46.2	48.1	39.6	78.2	24.3	27.7	63.2	70.8	59.0	52.9
4th quarter	53.1	51.1	46.3	47.6	39.9	74.5	25.3	27.9	63.9	71.5	59.7	53.2
1974												
1st quarter	52.7	50.6	46.2	46.5	39.9	69.0	26.2	27.0	64.7	72.4	60.5	52.6
2nd quarter	52.9	50.8	46.3	45.8	39.8	66.0	27.3	28.4	65.3	72.6	61.2	52.7
3rd quarter	52.3	51.0	46.3	45.0	39.3	63.8	25.9	27.9	65.0	72.1	61.1	52.3
4th quarter	52.0	50.2	45.2	42.5	38.2	55.4	26.6	27.7	65.2	72.8	61.1	51.8

Table 19-3. Chain-Type Quantity Indexes for Gross Domestic Product and Domestic Purchases—*Continued*

(Index numbers, 1996 = 100.)

Year and quarter	Gross domestic product	Personal consumption expenditures		Private fixed investment			Exports and imports of goods and services		Government consumption expenditures and gross investment			Gross domestic purchases
		Total	Excluding food and energy	Total	Nonresidential	Residential	Exports	Imports	Total	Federal	State and local	
1975												
1st quarter	51.3	50.6	45.8	39.9	35.9	52.0	26.6	24.9	66.2	72.4	62.8	50.7
2nd quarter	51.8	51.5	46.4	39.3	34.9	53.1	25.5	22.9	66.0	72.7	62.4	51.1
3rd quarter	52.7	52.2	47.3	40.3	35.2	56.8	25.9	24.8	66.2	72.2	63.1	52.2
4th quarter	53.3	52.8	48.1	41.1	35.6	59.3	27.3	26.1	66.7	72.5	63.7	52.8
1976												
1st quarter	54.6	53.9	49.1	42.7	36.2	65.4	27.2	27.8	67.0	71.7	64.6	54.4
2nd quarter	55.1	54.4	49.4	43.5	36.7	67.3	27.5	29.0	66.3	71.7	63.6	55.0
3rd quarter	55.3	55.0	49.9	43.9	37.5	66.2	28.2	30.1	66.0	71.5	63.2	55.3
4th quarter	55.8	55.7	50.6	46.2	38.2	74.6	28.6	31.1	66.0	71.7	63.1	55.8
1977												
1st quarter	56.5	56.4	51.3	47.9	39.7	76.8	28.1	32.6	66.5	72.0	63.6	56.8
2nd quarter	57.5	56.7	51.9	50.6	40.9	85.6	28.9	32.9	67.2	73.2	64.0	57.7
3rd quarter	58.5	57.3	52.6	51.2	41.7	85.4	29.1	32.4	67.2	73.4	63.9	58.7
4th quarter	58.6	58.1	53.5	52.1	43.1	84.2	28.1	32.9	67.1	73.0	64.1	59.0
1978												
1st quarter	58.7	58.4	53.8	52.5	43.4	84.7	28.8	35.1	67.3	73.3	64.1	59.4
2nd quarter	61.0	59.7	55.4	56.1	46.9	88.7	31.8	35.2	69.1	74.9	66.0	61.2
3rd quarter	61.6	60.0	55.7	57.6	48.4	89.9	32.2	35.7	69.6	75.2	66.8	61.8
4th quarter	62.4	60.5	56.1	58.7	49.9	89.7	33.4	36.2	70.3	75.9	67.4	62.5
1979												
1st quarter	62.6	60.9	56.4	59.3	51.1	87.6	33.4	36.1	69.7	76.0	66.3	62.6
2nd quarter	62.6	60.8	56.6	58.9	51.0	86.0	33.5	36.3	70.4	76.8	67.0	62.7
3rd quarter	63.1	61.4	57.3	60.0	52.7	84.9	34.7	35.7	70.5	76.7	67.2	62.8
4th quarter	63.3	61.6	57.4	59.4	52.8	81.6	36.8	36.5	71.1	77.1	68.0	62.8
1980												
1st quarter	63.5	61.5	57.3	58.7	53.4	75.8	37.9	36.5	72.1	79.3	68.3	62.9
2nd quarter	62.2	60.1	55.8	53.4	50.7	61.2	38.6	33.9	72.3	81.2	67.4	61.0
3rd quarter	62.1	60.7	56.7	54.0	51.1	62.3	38.5	31.4	71.4	80.3	66.5	60.5
4th quarter	63.2	61.5	57.7	56.3	52.2	68.9	38.2	33.1	71.3	80.5	66.2	61.9
1981												
1st quarter	64.4	61.7	58.1	56.7	53.0	67.7	38.9	34.5	72.3	82.1	66.7	63.3
2nd quarter	64.0	61.8	57.9	56.9	54.0	65.1	39.1	34.6	72.4	84.6	65.4	62.8
3rd quarter	64.7	62.1	58.5	56.9	55.3	60.0	38.3	34.2	72.3	84.6	65.2	63.6
4th quarter	64.0	61.6	57.7	56.7	56.7	53.9	38.6	35.2	72.8	85.1	65.7	63.0
1982												
1st quarter	62.9	61.9	58.1	55.1	55.4	50.8	37.0	34.2	72.7	85.2	65.5	62.0
2nd quarter	63.2	62.1	58.2	53.1	53.4	49.2	37.3	33.6	73.1	86.0	65.6	62.1
3rd quarter	62.9	62.5	58.8	51.5	51.6	48.6	35.6	35.2	73.6	87.4	65.6	62.4
4th quarter	62.9	63.6	59.9	51.7	50.6	53.3	34.0	33.8	74.8	89.9	66.0	62.4
1983												
1st quarter	63.6	64.2	60.6	52.7	49.7	61.5	34.6	34.6	75.2	90.8	66.1	63.2
2nd quarter	65.1	65.5	62.2	54.9	50.4	69.5	34.7	37.2	75.8	92.6	65.9	65.1
3rd quarter	66.3	66.5	63.1	58.1	52.6	75.8	35.2	40.1	77.2	95.2	66.5	66.6
4th quarter	67.7	67.6	64.5	61.3	56.1	77.9	35.9	42.1	75.9	91.9	66.4	68.1
1984												
1st quarter	69.1	68.4	65.5	63.3	57.9	80.7	36.8	45.5	76.7	92.7	67.4	70.0
2nd quarter	70.3	69.3	66.4	66.0	60.7	82.7	37.7	47.4	78.4	95.7	68.2	71.3
3rd quarter	70.9	69.8	66.9	67.3	62.7	81.6	38.5	48.6	79.0	95.4	69.3	72.0
4th quarter	71.5	70.7	68.0	68.5	64.3	81.2	39.2	50.0	80.5	98.2	70.0	72.6
1985												
1st quarter	72.1	71.7	69.2	69.2	65.0	81.8	39.2	48.9	81.4	99.5	70.7	73.0
2nd quarter	72.6	72.4	70.0	69.8	65.9	81.3	39.0	51.3	83.0	101.7	72.0	74.0
3rd quarter	73.7	73.7	71.6	69.4	64.9	82.9	38.5	50.8	85.0	105.0	73.2	75.0
4th quarter	74.3	74.0	71.7	70.7	66.1	84.7	39.6	52.8	85.4	105.0	73.8	75.8
1986												
1st quarter	75.0	74.6	72.4	70.8	65.2	88.3	40.7	52.7	86.1	104.4	75.3	76.3
2nd quarter	75.3	75.4	73.3	70.7	63.7	93.4	41.2	54.9	87.8	107.5	76.1	76.8
3rd quarter	76.0	76.8	75.0	70.2	62.7	94.6	42.2	56.4	89.8	111.8	76.8	77.6
4th quarter	76.4	77.3	75.4	70.7	63.4	94.1	43.8	56.9	89.4	110.1	77.2	77.9
1987												
1st quarter	77.0	77.3	75.5	69.0	61.6	93.0	43.9	56.6	89.9	110.7	77.6	78.4
2nd quarter	77.8	78.3	76.5	70.4	63.0	93.9	45.7	58.0	90.7	112.4	77.8	79.1
3rd quarter	78.4	79.2	77.7	71.6	65.1	92.4	47.7	59.2	90.9	112.5	78.1	79.7
4th quarter	79.8	79.3	77.7	71.4	64.9	91.9	49.4	60.5	92.1	114.2	79.1	81.0
1988												
1st quarter	80.3	80.7	79.1	71.9	65.7	91.6	52.2	60.3	91.4	110.9	79.9	81.1
2nd quarter	81.3	81.3	79.5	73.1	67.1	92.2	53.6	59.5	91.6	109.7	80.9	81.8
3rd quarter	81.7	81.9	80.1	73.5	67.5	92.6	54.6	60.9	91.5	108.8	81.2	82.3
4th quarter	82.8	82.9	81.2	74.2	68.3	92.8	56.3	62.6	93.3	112.2	82.2	83.3

Table 19-3. Chain-Type Quantity Indexes for Gross Domestic Product and Domestic Purchases—*Continued*

(Index numbers, 1996 = 100.)

Year and quarter	Gross domestic product	Personal consumption expenditures		Private fixed investment			Exports and imports of goods and services		Government consumption expenditures and gross investment			Gross domestic purchases
		Total	Excluding food and energy	Total	Nonresidential	Residential	Exports	Imports	Total	Federal	State and local	
1989												
1st quarter	83.8	83.2	81.5	74.7	69.3	91.6	58.4	61.9	92.8	109.7	82.8	83.9
2nd quarter	84.2	83.5	82.1	74.8	70.3	88.7	60.7	63.0	94.3	112.1	83.7	84.3
3rd quarter	84.6	84.3	82.9	76.1	72.4	87.6	60.7	63.6	95.2	113.2	84.5	84.7
4th quarter	84.9	84.6	82.9	75.0	71.3	86.2	62.4	64.4	95.7	112.5	85.7	84.9
1990												
1st quarter	86.0	85.3	84.0	76.1	72.3	87.8	64.7	65.2	97.1	114.3	87.0	85.8
2nd quarter	86.2	85.5	84.0	74.2	71.1	83.8	66.1	66.4	97.4	114.5	87.2	86.0
3rd quarter	86.0	85.8	84.2	73.6	71.8	78.9	65.5	66.5	97.4	113.5	87.9	85.9
4th quarter	85.3	85.1	83.7	71.1	70.3	73.2	67.1	64.5	98.4	114.3	88.9	84.7
1991												
1st quarter	84.9	84.7	83.3	68.7	68.5	68.5	66.9	62.6	98.8	115.2	89.0	84.1
2nd quarter	85.4	85.4	83.7	68.4	68.0	68.8	70.2	64.8	99.1	115.4	89.4	84.5
3rd quarter	85.6	85.6	84.1	68.6	67.6	71.3	70.6	66.5	98.7	113.4	89.9	84.9
4th quarter	86.0	85.4	84.1	68.9	67.2	73.6	73.0	67.4	98.2	111.2	90.6	85.1
1992												
1st quarter	86.8	86.8	85.7	69.9	67.1	78.2	73.7	67.6	99.0	111.3	91.7	85.9
2nd quarter	87.6	87.2	86.2	72.7	69.6	81.9	74.0	69.6	98.9	111.2	91.5	86.9
3rd quarter	88.3	07.0	07.0	73.8	70.9	82.3	74.5	69.9	99.4	112.6	91.6	87.6
4th quarter	89.5	89.1	88.1	76.1	72.8	85.9	75.8	71.6	99.4	112.7	91.5	88.8
1993												
1st quarter	89.5	89.3	88.2	76.7	73.6	86.0	75.7	73.3	98.2	109.0	91.8	89.0
2nd quarter	90.0	90.2	89.2	77.9	75.2	85.7	77.2	75.4	98.3	107.6	92.8	89.6
3rd quarter	90.4	91.2	90.2	79.1	76.1	88.0	75.6	76.1	98.3	107.0	93.2	90.3
4th quarter	91.8	92.1	91.2	82.5	79.1	92.6	79.4	79.1	98.6	106.7	93.8	91.6
1994												
1st quarter	92.5	92.9	92.1	83.7	80.1	94.6	79.7	80.7	97.6	103.6	94.0	92.5
2nd quarter	93.8	93.7	92.9	85.8	81.6	98.2	83.0	84.2	97.8	102.6	95.0	93.9
3rd quarter	94.3	94.4	93.8	86.7	83.1	97.4	84.9	86.7	99.7	105.9	96.0	94.4
4th quarter	95.5	95.3	94.9	88.9	86.4	96.3	87.8	88.8	98.8	102.7	96.4	95.5
1995												
1st quarter	95.9	95.7	95.3	90.9	89.7	94.4	89.3	90.7	99.0	102.4	97.0	95.9
2nd quarter	96.0	96.6	96.2	90.3	90.2	90.5	90.3	92.0	99.4	102.4	97.7	96.2
3rd quarter	96.8	97.4	97.0	91.3	90.8	92.7	94.0	92.3	99.2	101.7	97.8	96.5
4th quarter	97.6	98.0	97.7	93.4	92.9	94.9	96.3	93.2	98.0	97.3	98.4	97.2
1996												
1st quarter	98.3	98.8	98.5	96.1	95.8	96.9	96.8	95.6	98.8	99.5	98.4	98.1
2nd quarter	99.9	99.9	99.8	99.3	98.5	101.6	98.4	98.7	100.6	101.6	100.0	99.9
3rd quarter	100.4	100.3	100.5	101.6	101.7	101.3	99.2	102.1	100.0	99.6	100.2	100.7
4th quarter	101.5	101.0	101.2	103.1	104.1	100.2	105.6	103.6	100.6	99.3	101.4	101.3
1997												
1st quarter	102.6	102.2	102.6	105.2	106.8	100.5	107.6	107.4	100.9	98.2	102.5	102.6
2nd quarter	104.1	102.6	103.1	108.1	110.4	101.7	112.0	112.1	102.5	100.6	103.6	104.2
3rd quarter	105.2	104.3	105.1	111.9	115.3	102.3	114.9	116.7	103.0	100.3	104.6	105.5
4th quarter	105.9	105.2	106.1	113.1	116.4	103.7	114.6	118.5	103.1	99.4	105.2	106.4
1998												
1st quarter	107.5	106.5	107.6	118.0	122.2	106.3	114.8	123.0	102.4	96.9	105.7	108.5
2nd quarter	108.1	108.1	109.1	121.3	125.9	108.7	113.6	126.3	104.3	99.7	107.0	109.6
3rd quarter	109.2	109.1	110.1	122.5	126.4	111.6	113.0	127.6	104.8	98.7	108.4	110.9
4th quarter	110.9	110.5	111.8	126.3	130.7	114.1	117.3	131.3	105.8	100.0	109.3	112.6
1999												
1st quarter	111.8	111.7	113.3	128.7	133.1	116.2	115.3	134.0	106.6	99.2	111.0	113.9
2nd quarter	112.3	113.3	114.9	130.9	135.7	117.6	116.5	138.9	107.4	99.8	111.8	114.9
3rd quarter	113.7	114.6	116.3	132.8	138.2	117.9	119.4	143.7	108.8	101.6	113.0	116.5
4th quarter	115.7	116.0	117.7	133.8	139.3	118.6	123.1	146.9	110.6	104.0	114.5	118.4
2000												
1st quarter	116.4	117.5	119.6	138.0	144.2	121.0	125.4	152.1	110.3	100.4	116.1	119.5
2nd quarter	117.8	118.3	120.2	140.3	147.8	120.1	129.7	158.7	111.6	104.2	115.9	121.1
3rd quarter	118.0	119.5	121.6	140.3	149.1	117.2	133.3	163.9	111.3	102.3	116.6	121.5
4th quarter	118.3	120.1	122.1	139.5	147.9	117.2	132.0	163.2	112.1	102.8	117.5	121.9
2001												
1st quarter	118.1	120.8	122.9	138.7	145.8	119.6	129.9	159.9	113.6	105.2	118.6	121.6
2nd quarter	117.7	121.2	123.8	134.7	140.2	119.4	125.7	157.2	115.2	106.7	120.2	121.2
3rd quarter	117.6	121.6	124.4	133.2	138.1	119.5	119.9	152.3	114.9	107.0	119.5	121.2
4th quarter	118.4	123.4	126.6	130.2	134.1	118.4	116.9	150.3	117.8	110.5	122.1	122.1
2002												
1st quarter	119.8	124.4	127.2	130.0	132.1	122.4	117.9	153.4	119.4	112.5	123.5	123.7
2nd quarter	120.2	124.9	128.0	129.7	131.3	123.3	121.9	161.2	119.8	114.5	123.0	124.5
3rd quarter	121.4	126.2	129.6	129.6	131.1	123.6	123.3	162.6	120.7	115.7	123.6	125.7
4th quarter	121.8	126.7	129.7	131.0	131.8	126.4	121.4	165.5	122.0	118.8	124.0	126.6

Table 19-4. Chain-Type Price Indexes for Gross Domestic Product and Domestic Purchases

(Index numbers, 1996 = 100.)

Year and quarter	Gross domestic product	Personal consumption expenditures		Private fixed investment			Exports and imports of goods and services		Government consumption expenditures and gross investment			Gross domestic purchases
	Gross domestic product	Total	Excluding food and energy	Total	Nonresidential	Residential	Exports	Imports	Total	Federal	State and local	Gross domestic purchases
1947												
1st quarter	15.9	16.3	. . .	18.3	20.5	13.6	22.6	15.6	11.9	13.6	9.8	15.6
2nd quarter	16.2	16.4	. . .	19.1	21.2	14.4	24.3	16.7	11.9	13.5	10.0	15.8
3rd quarter	16.4	16.7	. . .	19.5	21.7	14.7	25.5	17.6	11.8	13.1	10.2	16.0
4th quarter	16.8	17.1	. . .	20.0	22.1	15.1	26.1	18.2	11.9	13.0	10.5	16.4
1948												
1st quarter	17.0	17.3	. . .	20.2	22.3	15.3	26.3	18.6	12.1	13.1	10.9	16.6
2nd quarter	17.2	17.5	. . .	20.6	22.9	15.5	26.1	18.7	12.2	13.1	11.1	16.8
3rd quarter	17.5	17.8	. . .	21.2	23.7	15.9	25.8	18.5	12.5	13.3	11.5	17.1
4th quarter	17.5	17.7	. . .	21.5	24.1	15.9	25.4	18.2	12.6	13.3	11.7	17.1
1949												
1st quarter	17.4	17.6	. . .	21.4	23.9	16.1	25.0	17.8	12.9	13.9	11.6	17.0
2nd quarter	17.3	17.5	. . .	21.4	23.9	16.0	24.5	17.6	12.8	13.9	11.4	16.9
3rd quarter	17.2	17.4	. . .	21.2	23.8	15.7	24.1	17.5	12.6	13.6	11.4	16.8
4th quarter	17.2	17.4	. . .	21.1	23.6	15.7	23.8	17.6	12.7	13.9	11.3	16.8
1950												
1st quarter	17.1	17.3	. . .	21.1	23.6	15.7	23.4	18.0	12.6	13.9	11.2	16.8
2nd quarter	17.2	17.4	. . .	21.4	23.9	16.1	23.5	18.3	12.6	13.7	11.3	16.9
3rd quarter	17.5	17.8	. . .	22.0	24.4	16.7	23.7	18.9	12.8	13.8	11.6	17.2
4th quarter	17.8	18.1	. . .	22.4	25.2	16.6	24.2	19.8	13.0	13.8	11.9	17.5
1951												
1st quarter	18.4	18.7	. . .	23.2	26.1	17.2	25.6	21.4	13.7	14.7	12.4	18.2
2nd quarter	18.5	18.8	. . .	23.6	26.5	17.4	26.5	22.6	13.5	14.3	12.6	18.3
3rd quarter	18.6	18.8	. . .	23.7	26.8	17.5	27.3	23.2	13.6	14.4	12.8	18.3
4th quarter	18.8	19.1	. . .	24.0	27.0	17.6	27.7	23.4	13.8	14.6	13.0	18.5
1952												
1st quarter	18.8	19.2	. . .	24.1	27.2	17.7	27.1	22.4	13.6	14.2	13.0	18.5
2nd quarter	18.9	19.2	. . .	24.2	27.2	17.9	27.0	22.0	13.8	14.4	13.2	18.6
3rd quarter	19.1	19.3	. . .	24.3	27.2	18.1	26.9	21.6	13.9	14.6	13.4	18.7
4th quarter	19.1	19.3	. . .	24.2	27.2	17.9	26.9	21.3	14.1	14.8	13.4	18.8
1953												
1st quarter	19.2	19.4	. . .	24.2	27.2	18.0	27.0	21.1	14.0	14.6	13.5	18.8
2nd quarter	19.2	19.4	. . .	24.4	27.4	18.0	27.0	20.9	14.0	14.6	13.5	18.8
3rd quarter	19.3	19.5	. . .	24.5	27.6	18.1	26.9	20.8	14.0	14.6	13.5	18.9
4th quarter	19.3	19.6	. . .	24.5	27.6	18.1	26.8	20.8	14.1	14.7	13.5	19.0
1954												
1st quarter	19.4	19.7	. . .	24.5	27.7	18.0	26.6	21.1	14.2	14.9	13.5	19.1
2nd quarter	19.5	19.7	. . .	24.6	27.8	18.0	26.6	21.2	14.3	14.9	13.8	19.1
3rd quarter	19.5	19.7	. . .	24.6	27.6	18.2	26.5	21.2	14.4	15.0	13.8	19.1
4th quarter	19.5	19.6	. . .	24.6	27.6	18.2	26.5	21.2	14.5	15.2	13.9	19.1
1955												
1st quarter	19.6	19.7	. . .	24.6	27.6	18.3	26.6	21.1	14.6	15.4	13.8	19.2
2nd quarter	19.7	19.7	. . .	24.8	27.7	18.5	26.7	21.0	14.9	15.8	13.9	19.3
3rd quarter	19.8	19.8	. . .	25.1	28.2	18.6	26.9	21.0	15.1	16.0	14.1	19.4
4th quarter	19.9	19.9	. . .	25.4	28.8	18.6	27.1	21.1	15.2	16.2	14.3	19.6
1956												
1st quarter	20.1	19.9	. . .	26.0	29.6	18.7	27.3	21.2	15.5	16.4	14.6	19.8
2nd quarter	20.3	20.1	. . .	26.2	29.8	19.0	27.6	21.4	15.8	16.7	14.8	19.9
3rd quarter	20.5	20.3	. . .	26.7	30.6	19.1	27.9	21.5	15.9	16.8	15.1	20.2
4th quarter	20.7	20.4	. . .	26.9	31.0	19.0	28.2	21.6	16.0	16.8	15.2	20.3
1957												
1st quarter	20.9	20.6	. . .	27.1	31.5	18.9	28.6	21.8	16.3	17.2	15.4	20.5
2nd quarter	21.1	20.7	. . .	27.3	31.7	19.0	28.8	21.8	16.4	17.3	15.6	20.6
3rd quarter	21.2	20.9	. . .	27.5	31.9	19.1	28.9	21.7	16.6	17.4	15.7	20.8
4th quarter	21.3	21.0	. . .	27.6	32.2	19.0	28.9	21.5	16.7	17.6	15.6	20.9
1958												
1st quarter	21.5	21.2	. . .	27.3	31.8	18.9	28.6	21.0	16.8	17.9	15.6	21.1
2nd quarter	21.6	21.3	. . .	27.5	32.0	19.0	28.5	20.8	17.0	18.1	15.7	21.2
3rd quarter	21.7	21.3	. . .	27.5	32.1	19.0	28.5	20.7	17.1	18.2	15.8	21.2
4th quarter	21.7	21.3	. . .	27.6	32.2	19.0	28.4	20.6	17.2	18.3	15.9	21.3
1959												
1st quarter	21.8	21.5	21.9	27.6	32.2	19.0	28.5	20.9	17.1	18.0	16.1	21.3
2nd quarter	21.8	21.6	22.0	27.7	32.4	19.0	28.4	20.9	17.0	17.9	16.1	21.4
3rd quarter	21.9	21.7	22.1	27.8	32.6	19.0	28.5	20.9	16.9	17.7	16.1	21.4
4th quarter	22.0	21.8	22.3	27.8	32.6	19.0	28.8	21.1	17.0	17.8	16.2	21.5
1960												
1st quarter	22.0	21.8	22.3	27.9	32.6	19.1	28.9	21.1	17.0	17.8	16.3	21.6
2nd quarter	22.1	22.0	22.4	27.9	32.7	19.1	28.8	21.1	17.1	17.8	16.4	21.7
3rd quarter	22.2	22.0	22.5	27.9	32.6	19.1	29.0	21.2	17.3	18.1	16.5	21.8
4th quarter	22.3	22.2	22.6	27.8	32.5	19.2	28.9	21.2	17.4	18.3	16.5	21.9

. . . = Not available.

Table 19-4. Chain-Type Price Indexes for Gross Domestic Product and Domestic Purchases—*Continued*

(Index numbers, 1996 = 100.)

Year and quarter	Gross domestic product	Personal consumption expenditures		Private fixed investment			Exports and imports of goods and services		Government consumption expenditures and gross investment			Gross domestic purchases
		Total	Excluding food and energy	Total	Nonresi-dential	Residen-tial	Exports	Imports	Total	Federal	State and local	
1961												
1st quarter	22.4	22.2	22.6	27.8	32.5	19.1	29.0	21.2	17.4	18.2	16.6	21.9
2nd quarter	22.4	22.2	22.7	27.8	32.4	19.2	29.4	21.2	17.5	18.3	16.7	21.9
3rd quarter	22.5	22.3	22.8	27.8	32.4	19.2	29.3	21.1	17.5	18.2	16.9	22.0
4th quarter	22.5	22.3	22.8	27.8	32.4	19.2	29.5	21.1	17.6	18.3	17.0	22.0
1962												
1st quarter	22.6	22.4	22.9	27.8	32.4	19.2	29.5	20.9	17.8	18.5	17.2	22.1
2nd quarter	22.7	22.5	23.0	27.8	32.5	19.2	29.2	20.9	17.9	18.6	17.3	22.2
3rd quarter	22.8	22.5	23.1	27.8	32.4	19.2	29.2	20.8	18.0	18.7	17.3	22.3
4th quarter	22.8	22.6	23.1	27.8	32.4	19.2	29.2	21.0	18.1	18.9	17.4	22.3
1963												
1st quarter	22.9	22.7	23.2	27.8	32.4	19.2	29.3	21.1	18.3	19.1	17.6	22.4
2nd quarter	23.0	22.7	23.2	27.8	32.4	19.1	29.3	21.2	18.4	19.1	17.7	22.5
3rd quarter	23.0	22.8	23.3	27.7	32.4	18.9	29.2	21.4	18.3	19.0	17.7	22.5
4th quarter	23.1	22.9	23.4	27.7	32.4	19.0	29.2	21.5	18.6	19.4	17.9	22.6
1964												
1st quarter	23.2	23.0	23.5	27.6	32.4	18.8	29.3	21.7	18.7	19.6	17.9	22.7
2nd quarter	23.3	23.0	23.6	27.0	32.6	19.1	29.2	21.8	18.8	19.6	18.0	22.8
3rd quarter	23.4	23.1	23.6	27.9	32.6	19.2	29.5	21.8	19.0	19.9	18.1	22.9
4th quarter	23.5	23.2	23.7	28.2	32.8	19.6	29.8	21.8	19.0	19.9	18.2	23.0
1965												
1st quarter	23.6	23.3	23.8	28.2	32.8	19.6	30.5	22.0	19.2	20.0	18.4	23.1
2nd quarter	23.7	23.4	23.9	28.3	32.9	19.6	30.4	21.9	19.3	20.1	18.5	23.2
3rd quarter	23.8	23.5	24.0	28.3	33.0	19.6	30.4	22.1	19.5	20.3	18.6	23.3
4th quarter	24.0	23.5	24.0	28.7	33.2	20.1	30.3	22.3	19.8	20.8	18.8	23.5
1966												
1st quarter	24.1	23.7	24.1	28.5	33.1	19.8	30.8	22.4	19.9	20.7	19.0	23.6
2nd quarter	24.3	23.9	24.3	29.0	33.5	20.6	31.1	22.6	20.0	20.7	19.4	23.8
3rd quarter	24.6	24.1	24.5	29.0	33.5	20.4	31.4	22.6	20.4	21.2	19.6	24.0
4th quarter	24.8	24.3	24.7	29.4	33.9	20.9	32.0	22.7	20.5	21.2	19.9	24.2
1967												
1st quarter	24.9	24.4	24.8	29.5	34.0	20.9	32.6	22.7	20.7	21.2	20.2	24.3
2nd quarter	25.1	24.5	25.0	29.7	34.2	21.0	32.5	22.6	20.9	21.4	20.4	24.5
3rd quarter	25.3	24.7	25.2	29.9	34.4	21.1	32.5	22.6	21.2	21.7	20.7	24.7
4th quarter	25.6	24.9	25.5	30.2	34.8	21.5	32.7	22.7	21.5	22.1	20.9	25.0
1968												
1st quarter	25.9	25.2	25.8	30.5	35.0	21.9	32.9	22.8	21.8	22.4	21.3	25.2
2nd quarter	26.2	25.4	26.0	30.8	35.4	22.1	33.6	23.0	22.1	22.7	21.5	25.5
3rd quarter	26.4	25.7	26.3	31.0	35.7	22.1	33.1	23.0	22.4	23.0	21.7	25.8
4th quarter	26.8	26.0	26.6	31.7	36.2	23.0	33.4	23.2	22.7	23.4	22.2	26.1
1969												
1st quarter	27.0	26.2	26.9	32.1	36.5	23.4	33.8	23.3	22.9	23.4	22.5	26.4
2nd quarter	27.4	26.6	27.2	32.4	36.8	23.8	33.9	23.4	23.3	23.8	22.9	26.7
3rd quarter	27.8	26.9	27.5	32.7	37.2	23.9	34.3	23.6	23.8	24.4	23.3	27.1
4th quarter	28.2	27.2	27.8	33.1	37.7	24.2	35.2	24.2	24.2	24.8	23.8	27.5
1970												
1st quarter	28.5	27.5	28.1	33.4	38.1	24.2	35.3	24.4	24.8	25.5	24.3	27.9
2nd quarter	28.9	27.9	28.4	34.1	38.7	25.1	36.0	24.7	25.2	25.7	24.8	28.2
3rd quarter	29.2	28.1	28.7	34.0	39.0	24.4	35.9	25.3	25.7	26.2	25.3	28.5
4th quarter	29.6	28.5	29.2	34.4	39.5	24.6	36.0	25.6	26.0	26.5	25.7	28.9
1971												
1st quarter	30.0	28.8	29.5	35.0	40.1	25.3	37.0	26.2	26.8	27.4	26.2	29.3
2nd quarter	30.4	29.1	29.9	35.5	40.6	25.8	37.1	26.3	27.3	28.0	26.7	29.7
3rd quarter	30.7	29.4	30.1	36.0	40.9	26.3	36.8	26.6	27.7	28.4	27.0	30.0
4th quarter	31.0	29.6	30.3	36.3	41.2	26.7	37.1	27.0	28.1	29.1	27.2	30.3
1972												
1st quarter	31.4	29.9	30.6	36.7	41.7	27.1	37.6	27.5	28.9	30.2	27.8	30.8
2nd quarter	31.6	30.1	30.8	37.0	42.0	27.2	37.9	28.2	29.2	30.5	28.1	31.0
3rd quarter	31.9	30.3	31.1	37.3	42.2	27.6	38.1	28.7	29.6	30.9	28.6	31.3
4th quarter	32.3	30.6	31.2	37.9	42.5	28.5	39.0	29.3	30.2	31.7	29.0	31.7
1973												
1st quarter	32.7	31.0	31.5	38.3	42.8	28.9	40.2	30.2	30.8	32.1	29.7	32.1
2nd quarter	33.3	31.6	31.9	38.9	43.4	29.6	42.0	32.5	31.4	32.6	30.3	32.7
3rd quarter	33.9	32.1	32.3	39.8	44.1	30.6	44.5	34.1	31.9	33.3	30.8	33.3
4th quarter	34.5	32.8	32.6	40.3	44.5	31.1	46.9	36.6	32.5	33.9	31.4	33.9
1974												
1st quarter	35.2	33.8	33.2	41.0	45.3	31.8	50.2	42.4	33.3	34.4	32.3	34.8
2nd quarter	36.0	34.7	34.0	42.2	46.8	32.6	51.9	47.3	34.2	35.1	33.4	35.8
3rd quarter	37.1	35.6	34.9	43.9	48.7	33.6	54.9	49.7	35.4	36.2	34.6	36.9
4th quarter	38.2	36.5	35.7	45.7	51.0	34.5	57.8	51.4	36.5	37.6	35.6	37.9

Table 19-4. Chain-Type Price Indexes for Gross Domestic Product and Domestic Purchases—*Continued*

(Index numbers, 1996 = 100.)

Year and quarter	Gross domestic product	Personal consumption expenditures		Private fixed investment			Exports and imports of goods and services		Government consumption expenditures and gross investment			Gross domestic purchases
	Gross domestic product	Total	Excluding food and energy	Total	Nonresidential	Residential	Exports	Imports	Total	Federal	State and local	Gross domestic purchases
1975												
1st quarter	39.1	37.2	36.4	47.3	53.0	35.4	59.4	52.1	37.3	38.4	36.3	38.8
2nd quarter	39.6	37.6	36.9	48.4	54.4	36.0	59.2	52.3	37.9	38.9	37.0	39.3
3rd quarter	40.4	38.3	37.5	49.0	55.0	36.4	59.0	51.1	38.6	39.6	37.6	40.0
4th quarter	41.1	38.9	38.1	49.7	55.8	37.0	59.4	51.2	39.4	40.7	38.2	40.7
1976												
1st quarter	41.5	39.3	38.6	50.2	56.5	37.2	60.2	52.0	39.9	41.1	38.8	41.1
2nd quarter	41.9	39.7	39.1	51.1	57.2	38.3	60.8	52.8	40.4	41.6	39.4	41.6
3rd quarter	42.5	40.3	39.7	51.8	57.9	38.9	61.2	53.8	40.9	42.3	39.7	42.2
4th quarter	43.3	41.0	40.4	52.6	58.8	39.6	62.3	54.3	41.7	43.3	40.2	42.9
1977												
1st quarter	44.0	41.7	41.0	53.8	60.0	40.6	63.0	56.2	42.5	44.4	41.0	43.7
2nd quarter	44.7	42.4	41.7	54.8	61.0	41.7	63.9	57.8	43.2	45.0	41.7	44.5
3rd quarter	45.3	43.1	42.4	56.0	62.0	43.1	63.6	58.6	43.7	45.3	42.4	45.1
4th quarter	46.1	43.7	43.0	57.2	63.1	44.4	63.9	59.2	44.8	46.7	43.1	45.9
1978												
1st quarter	46.9	44.4	43.7	58.3	64.0	45.7	65.2	60.2	45.3	47.2	43.8	46.7
2nd quarter	47.8	45.4	44.5	59.6	65.1	47.0	66.8	61.6	46.0	47.7	44.5	47.6
3rd quarter	48.6	46.2	45.2	60.8	66.2	48.2	67.9	62.6	46.7	48.4	45.2	48.5
4th quarter	49.6	47.1	46.0	62.0	67.4	49.5	70.1	63.7	47.5	49.5	45.8	49.4
1979												
1st quarter	50.6	48.0	46.7	63.3	68.8	50.5	72.2	66.2	48.5	50.2	46.9	50.4
2nd quarter	51.7	49.2	47.5	64.9	70.4	52.2	75.1	69.6	49.5	51.1	48.0	51.6
3rd quarter	52.8	50.4	48.4	66.5	71.9	53.9	76.9	74.8	50.9	52.1	49.7	52.9
4th quarter	53.9	51.7	49.4	67.9	73.2	55.2	78.4	79.8	52.3	54.3	50.7	54.2
1980												
1st quarter	55.1	53.3	50.7	69.5	74.9	56.7	80.7	86.5	53.6	55.2	52.1	55.7
2nd quarter	56.4	54.6	51.9	71.1	76.6	58.0	81.8	89.6	55.0	56.6	53.6	57.1
3rd quarter	57.6	55.9	53.0	72.6	78.2	59.3	84.0	92.1	56.3	57.5	55.1	58.4
4th quarter	59.2	57.1	54.2	74.2	79.9	60.8	86.8	93.6	58.3	60.4	56.5	59.9
1981												
1st quarter	60.7	58.6	55.3	76.2	82.2	62.1	89.0	96.1	59.8	61.5	58.2	61.4
2nd quarter	61.8	59.6	56.3	77.9	84.2	63.1	89.3	96.7	60.8	62.4	59.4	62.5
3rd quarter	63.0	60.6	57.5	79.3	85.8	63.9	89.5	94.2	61.6	63.1	60.2	63.6
4th quarter	64.1	61.6	58.6	80.8	87.6	64.8	89.8	94.4	63.0	65.3	61.1	64.7
1982												
1st quarter	65.0	62.4	59.5	81.9	88.6	65.8	90.3	94.1	64.1	66.4	62.1	65.6
2nd quarter	65.8	63.0	60.3	82.9	89.7	66.8	90.3	92.4	65.0	67.2	63.1	66.3
3rd quarter	66.8	64.0	61.2	83.4	90.2	67.3	89.6	91.3	65.8	67.7	64.1	67.2
4th quarter	67.4	64.6	62.1	83.5	90.3	67.6	89.1	90.6	66.8	68.8	64.9	67.8
1983												
1st quarter	68.0	65.1	62.9	83.1	89.5	68.0	89.5	88.7	67.2	69.3	65.4	68.2
2nd quarter	68.6	65.9	63.6	82.8	89.0	68.1	89.8	88.7	67.8	69.8	66.1	68.8
3rd quarter	69.2	66.6	64.3	82.7	88.7	68.5	90.4	88.9	68.4	70.3	66.7	69.4
4th quarter	69.8	67.2	65.0	82.8	88.6	69.1	91.3	88.3	68.9	70.5	67.3	69.8
1984												
1st quarter	70.6	67.8	65.6	82.9	88.5	69.5	91.4	88.6	70.7	73.4	68.4	70.7
2nd quarter	71.2	68.4	66.3	83.3	88.9	70.0	92.0	89.1	71.4	73.9	69.1	71.3
3rd quarter	71.7	68.9	66.8	83.5	88.9	70.7	91.1	87.5	71.9	74.4	69.7	71.7
4th quarter	72.2	69.4	67.4	83.8	89.0	71.3	90.1	86.4	72.5	74.9	70.3	72.2
1985												
1st quarter	73.0	70.1	68.2	84.1	89.3	71.6	89.2	84.4	73.2	75.5	71.1	72.8
2nd quarter	73.5	70.8	68.9	84.2	89.3	71.8	89.1	84.7	73.6	75.6	71.8	73.3
3rd quarter	73.9	71.2	69.5	84.5	89.7	72.3	88.3	84.7	73.8	75.4	72.4	73.7
4th quarter	74.4	71.9	70.2	85.1	90.0	73.1	88.2	86.3	74.5	76.2	73.0	74.4
1986												
1st quarter	74.7	72.3	70.8	85.5	90.2	74.0	87.6	86.5	74.6	76.0	73.3	74.7
2nd quarter	75.0	72.3	71.4	86.1	90.9	74.7	87.3	83.8	74.8	76.1	73.6	74.9
3rd quarter	75.5	72.9	72.1	87.0	91.6	75.7	86.9	84.4	75.1	76.1	74.2	75.4
4th quarter	76.1	73.4	72.8	87.5	92.0	76.5	87.6	85.3	75.8	76.2	75.3	75.9
1987												
1st quarter	76.7	74.4	73.6	87.8	91.9	77.3	88.0	87.5	76.5	76.8	76.1	76.8
2nd quarter	77.3	75.1	74.4	87.9	91.9	77.9	89.4	89.8	77.0	77.0	76.9	77.4
3rd quarter	77.8	75.9	75.1	88.1	91.8	78.6	89.7	90.7	77.6	77.2	77.8	78.0
4th quarter	78.5	76.6	76.0	88.8	92.5	79.3	91.3	92.1	77.8	77.2	78.3	78.6
1988												
1st quarter	79.0	77.1	76.6	89.6	93.3	80.0	92.3	93.4	78.5	78.2	78.6	79.2
2nd quarter	79.8	78.0	77.5	90.2	93.9	80.7	94.3	95.1	79.2	78.9	79.4	80.0
3rd quarter	80.7	78.9	78.4	90.6	94.3	81.2	95.5	94.2	79.6	79.1	80.0	80.8
4th quarter	81.4	79.7	79.3	91.5	95.2	82.0	95.4	95.1	79.9	79.1	80.5	81.5

Table 19-4. Chain-Type Price Indexes for Gross Domestic Product and Domestic Purchases—*Continued*

(Index numbers, 1996 = 100.)

Year and quarter	Gross domestic product	Personal consumption expenditures Total	Excluding food and energy	Private fixed investment Total	Nonresidential	Residential	Exports	Imports	Government consumption expenditures and gross investment Total	Federal	State and local	Gross domestic purchases
1989												
1st quarter	82.2	80.6	80.1	92.0	95.7	82.6	96.4	96.7	81.1	80.7	81.4	82.4
2nd quarter	83.0	81.7	80.8	92.6	96.0	83.6	96.6	97.9	81.7	81.0	82.2	83.3
3rd quarter	83.6	82.2	81.4	93.0	96.5	83.9	96.0	96.2	82.2	81.4	82.6	83.7
4th quarter	84.2	83.0	82.3	93.5	97.0	84.4	95.7	96.7	82.6	81.4	83.5	84.4
1990												
1st quarter	85.2	84.1	83.2	94.0	97.5	85.1	95.7	98.0	83.9	82.6	84.8	85.5
2nd quarter	86.2	85.0	84.2	94.3	97.8	85.4	96.0	96.2	84.6	83.3	85.6	86.3
3rd quarter	87.0	86.1	85.2	94.9	98.5	85.8	97.0	99.0	85.4	83.9	86.5	87.3
4th quarter	87.8	87.3	86.0	95.5	99.2	85.9	98.4	104.5	86.7	85.4	87.7	88.4
1991												
1st quarter	88.8	88.0	87.0	96.2	100.1	86.2	98.7	101.2	87.5	86.6	88.1	89.1
2nd quarter	89.4	88.6	87.8	96.2	100.0	86.5	98.2	98.6	87.7	86.8	88.4	89.5
3rd quarter	90.0	89.2	88.5	96.2	99.7	87.1	97.6	97.4	88.3	87.4	88.9	90.0
4th quarter	90.5	89.9	89.4	95.9	99.4	86.8	97.8	98.5	88.7	88.0	89.2	90.6
1992												
1st quarter	91.2	90.7	90.4	95.8	99.4	86.5	97.8	98.0	89.3	89.1	89.5	91.3
2nd quarter	91.7	91.4	91.1	95.9	99.3	87.3	97.9	98.6	90.0	89.8	90.1	91.8
3rd quarter	92.0	91.9	91.6	96.1	99.3	87.9	97.9	100.1	90.4	90.4	90.4	92.3
4th quarter	92.6	92.6	92.4	96.4	99.2	89.1	97.7	99.7	90.7	90.1	91.0	92.8
1993												
1st quarter	93.3	93.1	92.9	97.0	99.6	90.1	97.7	98.2	91.6	91.3	91.9	93.4
2nd quarter	93.8	93.7	93.6	97.4	99.8	90.9	98.0	98.9	92.2	91.8	92.5	94.0
3rd quarter	94.3	94.0	94.0	97.6	99.9	91.8	97.8	98.0	92.7	92.6	92.7	94.3
4th quarter	94.8	94.5	94.6	97.8	99.9	92.2	97.8	97.7	93.2	93.1	93.3	94.8
1994												
1st quarter	95.3	94.8	94.9	98.4	100.2	93.3	98.2	97.2	93.9	93.6	94.1	95.2
2nd quarter	95.7	95.3	95.5	98.7	100.6	93.8	98.6	98.5	94.7	94.6	94.7	95.7
3rd quarter	96.3	96.1	96.3	99.2	100.7	94.8	99.2	100.1	95.1	94.6	95.5	96.4
4th quarter	96.7	96.6	96.7	99.4	100.6	96.1	99.8	100.6	95.7	95.2	96.0	96.9
1995												
1st quarter	97.5	97.2	97.4	99.8	100.8	97.2	100.9	101.1	96.7	96.2	97.0	97.5
2nd quarter	97.9	97.7	97.9	100.2	101.1	97.7	101.7	102.8	97.2	96.5	97.7	98.0
3rd quarter	98.3	98.2	98.5	100.3	101.0	98.1	101.5	102.2	97.7	97.1	98.0	98.4
4th quarter	98.8	98.6	98.9	100.3	100.8	98.6	101.0	101.3	98.6	99.0	98.4	98.9
1996												
1st quarter	99.4	99.2	99.4	100.0	100.4	99.0	100.8	100.9	99.8	100.3	99.6	99.4
2nd quarter	99.7	99.8	99.8	99.8	100.0	99.4	100.5	100.4	99.5	99.5	99.5	99.7
3rd quarter	100.2	100.2	100.2	100.1	99.9	100.5	99.8	99.3	100.1	99.9	100.2	100.2
4th quarter	100.6	100.9	100.7	100.1	99.7	101.0	98.9	99.4	100.6	100.4	100.7	100.7
1997												
1st quarter	101.4	101.5	101.3	100.0	99.4	101.7	98.7	98.3	101.7	101.4	101.9	101.3
2nd quarter	101.8	101.8	101.9	99.9	99.1	102.2	98.7	96.4	102.0	101.6	102.3	101.5
3rd quarter	102.1	102.1	102.1	99.9	98.9	103.0	98.5	95.8	102.3	101.5	102.7	101.7
4th quarter	102.5	102.4	102.5	99.9	98.6	103.9	98.0	95.2	102.9	102.0	103.5	102.1
1998												
1st quarter	102.8	102.6	102.9	99.3	97.8	104.3	97.1	92.6	103.1	102.1	103.7	102.1
2nd quarter	103.0	102.8	103.3	99.1	97.1	105.1	96.6	91.6	103.5	102.4	104.1	102.3
3rd quarter	103.4	103.2	103.7	98.9	96.7	106.0	95.9	90.5	103.9	102.8	104.6	102.5
4th quarter	103.7	103.5	104.1	98.8	96.3	107.0	95.5	90.4	104.4	103.2	105.1	102.8
1999												
1st quarter	104.1	103.9	104.4	98.9	96.0	108.0	95.2	89.6	105.2	104.4	105.7	103.2
2nd quarter	104.5	104.4	104.8	98.9	95.7	109.2	95.3	90.7	106.1	104.8	106.9	103.7
3rd quarter	104.8	105.0	105.2	98.8	95.3	110.1	95.5	91.9	107.0	105.4	107.9	104.2
4th quarter	105.3	105.6	105.6	98.9	95.2	111.0	95.9	93.2	107.8	105.8	108.9	104.8
2000												
1st quarter	106.1	106.5	106.2	99.5	95.3	112.9	96.4	94.7	109.5	107.9	110.4	105.7
2nd quarter	106.7	107.1	106.7	99.8	95.4	114.0	96.8	95.0	110.3	108.1	111.5	106.3
3rd quarter	107.1	107.7	107.0	100.2	95.7	114.9	97.0	96.0	111.1	108.5	112.5	106.9
4th quarter	107.7	108.3	107.5	100.5	95.9	115.9	97.1	96.3	111.8	108.5	113.6	107.4
2001												
1st quarter	108.7	109.2	108.3	101.0	96.0	117.5	96.9	95.7	113.0	109.7	114.7	108.3
2nd quarter	109.3	109.6	108.6	101.3	96.0	118.8	96.5	94.2	113.5	110.2	115.3	108.8
3rd quarter	109.9	109.6	108.8	101.2	95.7	119.5	96.0	89.9	113.4	110.3	115.1	108.7
4th quarter	109.8	109.8	109.5	101.2	95.3	120.6	95.1	91.0	113.3	110.2	115.0	108.8
2002												
1st quarter	110.1	110.1	109.9	100.8	94.8	120.6	94.9	90.6	114.3	112.4	115.3	109.2
2nd quarter	110.5	110.9	110.4	100.8	94.5	121.4	95.6	93.0	115.1	113.1	116.2	109.8
3rd quarter	110.8	111.4	110.9	100.5	94.2	121.4	96.4	94.1	115.5	113.4	116.6	110.1
4th quarter	111.3	111.9	111.3	101.0	94.3	122.9	96.6	94.3	115.9	113.5	117.2	110.6

Table 19-5. National Income and Disposition of Personal Income

(Billions of dollars, except as noted; quarterly data are at seasonally adjusted annual rates.)

Year and quarter	National income									Disposition of personal income					
	National income	Compensation of employees			Proprietors' income with IVA [1] and CCAdj [2]		Rental income of persons with CCAdj [2]	Corporate profits with IVA [1] and CCAdj [2]	Net interest	Personal income	Less: Personal tax and nontax payments	Equals: Disposable personal income (DPI)	Less: Personal outlays	Equals: Personal saving	Saving as a percentage of DPI
		Total	Wage and salary accruals	Supplements to wages and salaries	Farm	Nonfarm									
1946															
1st quarter	172.4	115.2	107.7	7.5	13.0	21.1	7.4	14.0	1.7	172.4	16.3	156.0	136.1	20.0	12.8
2nd quarter	179.0	117.5	109.6	8.0	13.6	22.1	7.0	17.0	1.8	176.9	17.6	159.3	141.5	17.9	11.2
3rd quarter	186.3	121.4	113.5	7.8	16.1	22.2	6.8	18.0	1.8	182.7	18.1	164.6	150.3	14.2	8.7
4th quarter	191.5	124.4	117.2	7.2	16.6	21.3	6.8	20.5	1.9	185.9	18.0	167.9	154.7	13.2	7.9
1947															
1st quarter	194.2	127.2	119.7	7.5	16.7	20.7	6.8	20.5	2.4	188.5	19.4	169.1	158.2	10.9	6.4
2nd quarter	195.4	128.7	121.5	7.2	13.2	20.3	6.9	23.9	2.4	186.8	19.8	167.1	162.1	5.0	3.0
3rd quarter	198.5	130.1	123.4	6.6	14.8	20.2	7.1	24.0	2.4	194.9	20.0	174.9	165.8	9.1	5.2
4th quarter	206.1	134.3	127.8	6.5	15.7	20.9	7.3	25.6	2.3	198.3	21.1	177.2	169.9	7.3	4.1
1948															
1st quarter	215.4	138.0	131.4	6.6	15.7	22.1	7.5	29.6	2.5	204.3	21.5	182.8	172.9	9.8	5.4
2nd quarter	222.6	139.7	133.2	6.5	18.8	22.8	7.6	31.3	2.4	209.7	19.3	190.4	176.8	13.6	7.2
3rd quarter	227.0	144.5	138.1	6.5	18.5	23.3	7.7	30.5	2.4	215.3	18.6	196.7	179.7	17.0	8.6
4th quarter	228.4	146.0	139.5	6.5	16.9	23.5	7.8	31.9	2.4	215.3	18.8	196.5	180.6	15.9	8.1
1949															
1st quarter	221.2	144.2	136.9	7.2	13.3	23.0	7.6	30.5	2.5	209.3	18.2	191.2	179.4	11.7	6.1
2nd quarter	216.3	142.0	134.6	7.4	12.7	23.1	7.7	28.2	2.6	208.0	17.4	190.6	181.1	9.5	5.0
3rd quarter	216.3	141.1	133.9	7.2	12.1	23.0	7.9	29.4	2.7	207.2	16.7	190.5	180.6	9.9	5.2
4th quarter	213.1	140.5	133.4	7.1	12.4	23.2	8.1	26.2	2.7	208.3	16.2	192.1	183.2	8.9	4.6
1950															
1st quarter	222.2	144.7	137.1	7.6	12.8	23.9	8.4	29.6	2.9	222.6	17.0	205.6	186.1	19.5	9.5
2nd quarter	232.7	150.7	142.9	7.9	12.8	24.5	8.6	33.2	2.9	223.2	18.0	205.3	190.1	15.2	7.4
3rd quarter	248.3	159.1	150.8	8.3	13.7	26.0	8.7	37.8	3.0	232.1	19.3	212.8	203.9	8.8	4.2
4th quarter	260.7	167.0	158.3	8.8	14.9	25.9	9.0	40.9	3.1	241.8	22.9	218.8	201.4	17.4	8.0
1951															
1st quarter	270.2	175.1	165.5	9.6	15.7	27.4	9.1	39.7	3.3	250.4	24.9	225.5	212.5	13.0	5.8
2nd quarter	276.6	180.7	170.8	9.9	15.9	27.5	9.4	39.8	3.4	257.3	26.8	230.5	208.1	22.4	9.7
3rd quarter	281.4	183.9	173.8	10.0	15.9	28.0	9.6	40.4	3.6	260.9	28.2	232.7	210.8	22.0	9.4
4th quarter	286.7	186.6	176.2	10.3	16.6	28.4	9.9	41.7	3.6	266.3	30.1	236.2	214.8	21.5	9.1
1952															
1st quarter	287.6	191.6	181.2	10.4	14.7	28.6	10.1	39.0	3.6	268.5	31.3	237.1	216.3	20.9	8.8
2nd quarter	288.2	192.9	182.4	10.5	15.3	29.0	10.4	36.9	3.7	272.1	32.3	239.8	220.6	19.2	8.0
3rd quarter	293.5	196.4	185.7	10.7	16.7	29.3	10.6	36.7	3.8	278.9	32.7	246.1	223.3	22.8	9.3
4th quarter	303.7	204.3	193.3	11.0	13.7	30.0	10.9	40.9	3.9	284.9	33.5	251.4	231.7	19.6	7.8
1953															
1st quarter	309.0	208.1	196.9	11.2	13.5	30.5	11.2	41.6	4.2	289.5	33.9	255.6	235.6	20.0	7.8
2nd quarter	311.4	211.5	200.1	11.4	13.1	30.3	11.4	40.8	4.3	293.6	33.9	259.6	237.7	22.0	8.5
3rd quarter	309.9	211.6	200.3	11.4	12.4	30.2	11.6	39.6	4.4	293.6	33.7	259.9	238.6	21.3	8.2
4th quarter	302.6	210.1	198.7	11.5	12.8	30.3	11.9	32.7	4.8	293.7	33.5	260.2	238.1	22.1	8.5
1954															
1st quarter	304.3	208.2	196.4	11.9	13.6	30.2	12.2	35.1	5.0	293.2	30.7	262.5	240.2	22.3	8.5
2nd quarter	304.5	207.8	195.9	11.9	12.0	30.8	12.4	36.3	5.1	292.3	30.5	261.8	243.0	18.8	7.2
3rd quarter	308.0	208.4	196.3	12.1	12.5	31.0	12.5	38.2	5.3	294.7	30.6	264.2	245.7	18.5	7.0
4th quarter	316.8	212.7	200.3	12.4	11.9	32.0	12.7	41.9	5.6	300.7	31.0	269.7	250.3	19.4	7.2
1955															
1st quarter	327.7	217.2	204.2	13.0	12.0	33.0	12.7	47.0	5.8	306.3	31.9	274.3	256.6	17.7	6.5
2nd quarter	336.1	223.7	210.3	13.4	11.8	33.6	12.7	48.3	6.0	313.6	33.0	280.6	261.9	18.7	6.7
3rd quarter	342.1	228.7	214.6	14.0	11.3	34.4	12.8	48.8	6.1	321.1	33.9	287.2	266.3	20.9	7.3
4th quarter	348.3	233.7	219.4	14.3	10.8	35.0	12.9	49.9	6.0	326.1	34.8	291.4	270.5	20.9	7.2
1956															
1st quarter	351.0	238.2	223.3	14.9	10.6	35.1	13.0	47.7	6.3	331.1	35.9	295.1	272.3	22.8	7.7
2nd quarter	356.7	242.8	227.5	15.3	11.1	35.5	13.0	47.6	6.6	337.3	36.8	300.5	275.1	25.3	8.4
3rd quarter	360.0	245.9	229.9	16.0	11.8	35.8	13.2	46.7	6.7	342.2	37.5	304.7	278.4	26.2	8.6
4th quarter	367.0	251.7	235.3	16.4	11.6	36.4	13.3	47.4	6.6	349.5	38.5	311.0	283.9	27.1	8.7
1957															
1st quarter	373.0	255.4	238.2	17.2	10.4	37.3	13.5	49.1	7.2	353.3	39.2	314.0	288.4	25.6	8.2
2nd quarter	375.0	257.1	239.6	17.5	11.0	37.6	13.7	48.0	7.5	358.0	39.6	318.4	290.7	27.6	8.7
3rd quarter	378.8	259.8	241.8	18.0	11.8	38.1	13.8	47.4	8.0	362.9	39.9	323.0	295.4	27.6	8.5
4th quarter	373.4	258.3	240.1	18.2	11.9	37.8	14.0	43.5	8.0	363.0	39.5	323.5	297.2	26.3	8.1
1958															
1st quarter	367.9	255.3	237.3	18.0	13.4	37.7	14.3	38.4	8.8	362.5	38.9	323.6	296.9	26.8	8.3
2nd quarter	368.8	254.9	236.9	18.0	13.3	38.0	14.4	38.9	9.3	364.8	38.4	326.4	299.8	26.6	8.2
3rd quarter	379.7	261.0	242.6	18.4	13.0	38.5	14.5	43.1	9.6	373.9	39.6	334.2	304.8	29.4	8.8
4th quarter	392.6	267.3	248.4	18.9	12.6	39.2	14.6	49.1	9.8	378.9	40.0	338.9	308.8	30.1	8.9
1959															
1st quarter	402.7	274.4	254.0	20.5	11.7	39.9	14.6	52.7	9.4	384.8	41.2	343.6	316.6	26.9	7.8
2nd quarter	416.0	281.7	260.5	21.1	10.8	41.1	15.1	57.6	9.7	393.7	42.4	351.3	322.9	28.4	8.1
3rd quarter	411.4	282.4	260.9	21.5	10.3	41.4	15.5	52.1	9.8	395.9	43.1	352.8	328.4	24.3	6.9
4th quarter	415.8	285.7	263.9	21.8	10.9	41.0	15.7	52.4	10.1	401.6	44.2	357.4	330.9	26.5	7.4
1960															
1st quarter	427.9	294.1	270.7	23.4	10.3	40.8	16.0	56.4	10.4	407.8	45.8	362.0	334.6	27.4	7.6
2nd quarter	427.6	296.9	273.4	23.6	11.3	40.6	16.1	52.4	10.3	412.4	46.5	365.9	340.7	25.2	6.9
3rd quarter	428.2	297.7	273.9	23.7	11.8	40.2	16.3	51.4	10.8	414.6	47.0	367.6	340.9	26.7	7.3
4th quarter	426.5	297.1	273.3	23.8	12.4	40.1	16.5	49.2	11.2	416.2	47.0	369.2	343.0	26.3	7.1

[1] Inventory valuation adjustment.
[2] Capital consumption adjustment.

Table 19-5. National Income and Disposition of Personal Income—*Continued*

(Billions of dollars, except as noted; quarterly data are at seasonally adjusted annual rates.)

Year and quarter	National income	National income — Compensation of employees — Total	Wage and salary accruals	Supplements to wages and salaries	Proprietors' income with IVA[1] and CCAdj[2] — Farm	Proprietors' income with IVA[1] and CCAdj[2] — Nonfarm	Rental income of persons with CCAdj[2]	Corporate profits with IVA[1] and CCAdj[2]	Net interest	Disposition of personal income — Personal income	Less: Personal tax and nontax payments	Equals: Disposable personal income (DPI)	Less: Personal outlays	Equals: Personal saving	Saving as a percentage of DPI
1961															
1st quarter	427.9	298.0	273.7	24.3	12.3	41.2	16.7	48.2	11.6	420.0	47.1	372.9	343.5	29.5	7.9
2nd quarter	437.2	302.2	277.6	24.6	11.5	42.0	16.8	52.5	12.2	425.9	47.6	378.4	348.4	30.0	7.9
3rd quarter	446.0	307.2	282.2	25.0	11.9	42.6	17.0	54.7	12.6	433.1	48.1	385.1	351.4	33.7	8.7
4th quarter	458.8	313.9	288.4	25.5	12.6	43.3	17.3	58.5	13.3	442.0	48.8	393.2	358.8	34.4	8.8
1962															
1st quarter	467.8	320.4	293.2	27.2	12.2	43.7	17.5	60.9	13.0	448.0	50.1	397.9	364.0	33.9	8.5
2nd quarter	474.4	326.4	298.7	27.7	11.8	44.3	17.7	60.2	14.0	455.8	51.6	404.2	369.9	34.3	8.5
3rd quarter	479.8	329.2	301.1	28.1	11.9	44.8	18.0	61.4	14.5	461.0	53.0	408.0	374.1	33.9	8.3
4th quarter	486.6	332.7	304.2	28.5	12.3	44.7	18.1	63.7	15.0	466.7	54.3	412.4	380.6	31.8	7.7
1963															
1st quarter	491.5	337.5	307.9	29.6	12.1	44.9	18.3	64.0	14.7	471.4	54.8	416.6	384.5	32.1	7.7
2nd quarter	500.3	342.4	312.3	30.1	11.7	45.4	18.5	67.4	14.9	476.3	55.0	421.3	388.8	32.5	7.7
3rd quarter	508.1	347.5	316.8	30.7	11.7	46.1	18.6	68.8	15.4	483.6	55.3	428.3	396.2	32.1	7.5
4th quarter	517.7	353.6	322.2	31.4	12.3	47.0	18.6	70.4	15.9	492.9	55.9	437.0	401.1	35.8	8.2
1964															
1st quarter	529.1	360.0	328.2	31.9	10.8	48.5	18.6	74.6	16.5	502.0	54.5	447.5	410.8	36.7	8.2
2nd quarter	537.3	367.4	334.8	32.6	10.1	49.8	18.5	74.5	17.1	510.8	50.5	460.3	419.1	41.2	8.9
3rd quarter	547.7	374.7	341.4	33.3	10.4	50.6	18.6	75.6	17.8	520.7	52.4	468.3	428.4	39.9	8.5
4th quarter	554.4	380.7	346.7	34.0	11.8	50.6	18.6	74.7	18.0	529.7	54.0	475.7	431.3	44.4	9.3
1965															
1st quarter	570.9	387.3	352.8	34.6	12.0	51.0	18.9	82.7	19.0	539.6	57.7	481.9	442.2	39.6	8.2
2nd quarter	582.1	394.2	358.8	35.3	12.8	51.7	19.1	84.8	19.5	549.2	59.2	490.1	449.8	40.3	8.2
3rd quarter	593.6	402.3	366.2	36.2	13.3	52.3	19.4	86.1	20.1	563.6	57.8	505.8	459.3	46.5	9.2
4th quarter	611.6	414.2	377.1	37.1	14.0	53.7	19.4	90.2	20.1	577.1	59.1	518.0	473.6	44.5	8.6
1966															
1st quarter	631.8	426.7	385.7	41.0	15.7	54.9	19.8	93.4	21.3	589.0	62.4	526.6	484.3	42.3	8.0
2nd quarter	640.4	437.8	395.9	41.9	13.5	55.1	19.8	92.2	22.1	598.7	66.5	532.2	489.8	42.4	8.0
3rd quarter	651.5	448.9	406.1	42.8	13.5	55.6	20.1	90.5	22.9	612.3	68.9	543.4	499.1	44.3	8.2
4th quarter	663.0	457.1	413.4	43.7	13.7	56.3	20.1	91.7	24.0	625.7	71.6	554.1	505.1	49.0	8.8
1967															
1st quarter	667.7	463.3	418.8	44.5	13.2	57.3	20.3	89.0	24.5	635.7	72.3	563.4	509.6	53.8	9.6
2nd quarter	672.8	469.0	423.5	45.5	12.3	57.9	20.4	87.9	25.3	642.5	72.1	570.4	519.2	51.2	9.0
3rd quarter	686.1	478.7	431.9	46.7	13.0	59.2	20.5	89.2	25.6	656.0	75.1	581.0	526.3	54.7	9.4
4th quarter	700.0	489.6	441.5	48.1	12.5	59.1	20.4	92.3	26.1	667.2	77.2	590.1	533.9	56.1	9.5
1968															
1st quarter	717.8	504.5	454.1	50.3	12.6	60.6	20.2	93.3	26.6	686.8	79.8	607.0	552.2	54.8	9.0
2nd quarter	736.5	517.6	465.9	51.7	12.3	62.3	20.2	97.1	27.1	706.5	82.9	623.5	566.5	57.1	9.2
3rd quarter	752.8	531.4	478.3	53.1	13.0	63.6	20.3	97.2	27.3	724.7	93.1	631.5	583.2	48.3	7.7
4th quarter	767.5	543.9	489.3	54.5	13.3	64.0	20.1	98.5	27.8	739.9	97.1	642.8	592.4	50.4	7.8
1969															
1st quarter	782.4	556.0	499.0	57.0	12.8	64.7	20.3	98.5	30.1	753.8	103.9	649.9	604.9	45.0	6.9
2nd quarter	796.1	569.8	511.3	58.5	13.9	65.0	20.3	95.5	31.6	771.7	107.0	664.7	616.9	47.8	7.2
3rd quarter	812.4	586.5	526.3	60.2	14.5	65.1	20.4	92.9	33.0	791.7	105.5	686.1	627.6	58.6	8.5
4th quarter	819.7	598.2	536.4	61.8	15.4	64.0	20.3	88.0	33.9	806.2	107.1	699.1	639.9	59.2	8.5
1970															
1st quarter	823.7	608.5	545.0	63.5	15.1	64.2	20.2	80.3	35.4	817.1	106.0	711.1	651.4	59.6	8.4
2nd quarter	833.8	614.0	549.0	65.0	13.8	64.7	19.9	83.9	37.4	838.3	107.0	731.2	661.8	69.5	9.5
3rd quarter	846.7	622.1	555.6	66.5	14.5	65.9	20.5	83.7	39.8	850.5	102.2	748.3	674.0	74.3	9.9
4th quarter	845.7	624.1	556.3	67.9	13.9	67.1	20.7	78.7	41.2	858.5	103.1	755.4	680.8	74.6	9.9
1971															
1st quarter	878.7	641.6	570.1	71.5	14.4	68.1	20.6	91.8	42.1	877.6	99.9	777.6	700.2	77.4	10.0
2nd quarter	896.4	653.6	580.2	73.5	14.8	70.3	21.1	93.8	42.8	900.2	102.4	797.9	714.6	83.3	10.4
3rd quarter	910.6	663.9	588.6	75.3	14.5	72.1	21.3	95.9	42.8	912.8	104.0	808.8	727.4	81.4	10.1
4th quarter	929.9	676.3	598.9	77.4	16.0	74.1	21.6	99.1	42.8	929.8	107.2	822.5	744.2	78.4	9.5
1972															
1st quarter	961.4	701.0	617.8	83.2	15.0	75.5	21.9	104.5	43.5	957.6	121.7	835.9	761.9	74.1	8.9
2nd quarter	979.0	715.8	630.4	85.4	17.2	76.5	19.1	105.6	44.7	974.0	125.4	848.7	780.6	68.0	8.0
3rd quarter	1 009.4	729.7	642.3	87.4	19.7	79.3	22.7	110.7	47.2	1 000.9	126.3	874.6	799.4	75.1	8.6
4th quarter	1 051.8	754.0	664.2	89.8	23.1	84.2	22.8	118.2	49.5	1 044.5	129.2	915.3	825.0	90.3	9.9
1973															
1st quarter	1 087.9	781.6	683.2	98.4	23.2	84.5	23.2	125.4	49.9	1 067.1	128.5	938.6	850.4	88.3	9.4
2nd quarter	1 110.2	800.9	700.0	101.0	28.8	83.6	23.3	122.1	51.5	1 096.8	131.2	965.6	866.4	99.1	10.3
3rd quarter	1 136.7	819.8	716.1	103.7	31.5	84.7	22.5	122.6	55.5	1 125.5	136.1	989.4	886.0	103.4	10.5
4th quarter	1 174.9	842.5	735.3	107.3	39.3	85.3	23.5	125.7	58.7	1 164.4	142.0	1 022.4	903.1	119.3	11.7
1974															
1st quarter	1 184.2	860.5	748.1	112.4	30.7	87.8	23.5	118.6	63.0	1 182.0	145.0	1 037.0	920.5	116.6	11.2
2nd quarter	1 199.9	881.3	765.2	116.2	21.8	89.5	22.8	117.0	67.5	1 207.8	151.2	1 056.6	949.0	107.6	10.2
3rd quarter	1 224.8	903.1	783.0	120.1	22.9	92.3	23.0	113.2	70.3	1 244.4	157.3	1 087.2	977.2	109.9	10.1
4th quarter	1 238.8	915.9	792.4	123.5	25.2	91.7	22.7	109.0	74.4	1 268.2	160.0	1 108.2	985.0	123.2	11.1
1975															
1st quarter	1 243.7	919.2	791.8	127.4	20.9	94.1	22.3	110.9	76.4	1 281.0	160.5	1 120.5	1 010.1	110.4	9.9
2nd quarter	1 270.8	931.7	800.2	131.5	21.7	95.8	22.1	123.6	75.8	1 310.9	123.7	1 187.1	1 039.1	148.1	12.5
3rd quarter	1 326.8	957.7	821.2	136.5	25.6	99.3	22.0	145.4	76.8	1 348.4	155.6	1 192.9	1 073.2	119.7	10.0
4th quarter	1 367.6	987.6	845.6	141.9	25.8	103.2	21.7	152.2	77.3	1 386.5	161.4	1 225.1	1 102.3	122.8	10.0

[1]Inventory valuation adjustment.
[2]Capital consumption adjustment.

Table 19-5. National Income and Disposition of Personal Income—*Continued*

(Billions of dollars, except as noted; quarterly data are at seasonally adjusted annual rates.)

Year and quarter	National income	Compensation of employees			Proprietors' income with IVA[1] and CCAdj[2]		Rental income of persons with CCAdj[2]	Corporate profits with IVA[1] and CCAdj[2]	Net interest	Personal income	Less: Personal tax and nontax payments	Equals: Disposable personal income (DPI)	Less: Personal outlays	Equals: Personal saving	Saving as a percentage of DPI
		Total	Wage and salary accruals	Supplements to wages and salaries	Farm	Nonfarm									
1976															
1st quarter	1 416.0	1 022.3	871.1	151.2	21.0	108.8	21.7	164.5	77.7	1 424.6	165.2	1 259.4	1 138.1	121.4	9.6
2nd quarter	1 438.3	1 045.9	889.2	156.7	18.6	113.2	21.0	159.0	80.5	1 453.2	172.1	1 281.1	1 158.7	122.5	9.6
3rd quarter	1 469.3	1 070.8	908.3	162.5	17.6	118.2	21.4	159.4	81.8	1 492.8	179.0	1 313.8	1 189.1	124.7	9.5
4th quarter	1 501.8	1 098.1	929.8	168.3	17.4	122.2	21.8	159.3	83.1	1 530.9	185.7	1 345.2	1 225.2	120.0	8.9
1977															
1st quarter	1 551.1	1 127.0	949.9	177.1	18.4	125.7	21.9	168.6	89.5	1 569.7	191.9	1 377.8	1 261.8	116.0	8.4
2nd quarter	1 612.4	1 164.4	980.8	183.6	15.7	128.7	20.4	190.2	93.0	1 610.4	198.9	1 411.5	1 291.6	119.8	8.5
3rd quarter	1 667.8	1 196.9	1 007.3	189.6	15.1	132.6	19.7	205.9	97.6	1 656.3	201.9	1 454.4	1 324.4	130.1	8.9
4th quarter	1 712.1	1 233.4	1 038.0	195.5	20.6	136.4	19.6	199.1	102.9	1 712.1	211.9	1 500.2	1 363.8	136.4	9.1
1978															
1st quarter	1 750.1	1 269.5	1 064.0	205.5	20.4	139.8	21.6	192.1	106.5	1 755.7	215.6	1 540.0	1 395.8	144.2	9.4
2nd quarter	1 841.5	1 318.3	1 106.3	212.1	22.5	148.4	21.0	219.3	111.9	1 821.0	226.8	1 594.1	1 457.0	137.1	8.6
3rd quarter	1 893.1	1 355.7	1 137.8	217.9	22.2	152.1	23.2	223.7	116.3	1 879.4	240.2	1 639.2	1 492.2	147.1	9.0
4th quarter	1 956.0	1 400.4	1 176.0	224.4	21.0	153.8	23.9	233.7	123.2	1 937.0	251.2	1 685.8	1 532.5	153.3	9.1
1979															
1st quarter	2 007.6	1 445.1	1 210.0	235.0	25.3	156.0	26.0	224.2	131.1	1 996.8	257.8	1 739.1	1 574.9	164.1	9.4
2nd quarter	2 044.8	1 477.5	1 236.1	241.4	23.3	158.6	22.6	224.4	138.3	2 041.2	266.3	1 774.9	1 611.9	163.0	9.2
3rd quarter	2 095.5	1 519.1	1 270.7	248.5	23.9	161.3	22.1	222.5	146.6	2 108.6	279.2	1 829.3	1 667.1	162.2	8.9
4th quarter	2 154.5	1 561.3	1 305.6	255.7	22.4	164.1	27.1	219.0	160.7	2 179.4	289.8	1 889.7	1 715.6	174.0	9.2
1980															
1st quarter	2 206.2	1 602.7	1 338.2	264.5	14.6	165.7	32.1	215.0	176.1	2 248.1	289.1	1 959.0	1 766.7	192.3	9.8
2nd quarter	2 185.1	1 625.2	1 354.6	270.6	4.9	159.5	32.3	183.7	179.6	2 268.8	296.7	1 972.1	1 769.9	202.2	10.3
3rd quarter	2 233.9	1 658.0	1 380.8	277.2	13.3	163.7	28.6	189.8	180.6	2 339.0	306.9	2 032.1	1 828.3	203.8	10.0
4th quarter	2 346.6	1 721.1	1 436.0	285.1	19.7	169.0	32.2	205.4	199.1	2 439.8	323.9	2 115.9	1 891.7	224.2	10.6
1981															
1st quarter	2 428.7	1 773.9	1 474.5	299.4	19.3	173.7	39.6	218.6	203.6	2 510.6	336.2	2 174.4	1 950.3	224.1	10.3
2nd quarter	2 452.2	1 807.6	1 502.1	305.5	19.5	162.4	38.1	211.7	213.0	2 549.5	348.3	2 201.2	1 985.8	215.5	9.8
3rd quarter	2 550.0	1 846.6	1 534.9	311.7	24.5	165.3	38.8	230.9	243.9	2 652.3	362.7	2 289.6	2 031.5	258.1	11.3
4th quarter	2 557.3	1 874.8	1 557.6	317.3	18.1	162.2	42.0	214.6	245.6	2 685.1	358.7	2 326.4	2 049.2	277.2	11.9
1982															
1st quarter	2 560.3	1 898.7	1 573.0	325.7	15.4	155.1	41.6	193.8	255.6	2 709.4	359.0	2 350.4	2 086.6	263.8	11.2
2nd quarter	2 606.6	1 917.4	1 586.8	330.6	14.0	165.5	38.5	206.0	265.2	2 754.0	366.5	2 387.6	2 113.4	274.2	11.5
3rd quarter	2 618.1	1 937.0	1 601.9	335.1	13.1	166.0	40.1	206.5	255.4	2 786.4	357.2	2 429.2	2 159.4	269.9	11.1
4th quarter	2 626.9	1 950.8	1 611.8	339.0	15.3	175.1	38.0	198.7	249.1	2 823.7	363.9	2 459.9	2 218.9	240.9	9.8
1983															
1st quarter	2 678.9	1 977.8	1 629.2	348.6	14.0	175.0	37.6	219.3	255.2	2 853.6	358.4	2 495.2	2 256.6	238.6	9.6
2nd quarter	2 754.6	2 016.0	1 661.4	354.5	8.9	184.1	37.5	250.2	257.8	2 909.2	367.5	2 541.8	2 329.9	211.9	8.3
3rd quarter	2 830.2	2 059.8	1 698.7	361.2	1.2	193.8	34.8	267.7	272.9	2 968.6	353.7	2 614.9	2 392.2	222.7	8.5
4th quarter	2 922.3	2 117.3	1 747.8	369.5	4.6	200.2	37.9	279.3	283.1	3 056.2	364.2	2 692.1	2 454.1	238.0	8.8
1984															
1st quarter	3 049.0	2 182.5	1 793.6	389.0	20.5	215.3	37.1	305.7	287.9	3 152.0	370.0	2 782.0	2 506.0	276.0	9.9
2nd quarter	3 139.4	2 235.1	1 837.6	397.5	22.2	227.0	35.4	314.8	305.0	3 239.9	379.6	2 860.3	2 563.3	297.0	10.4
3rd quarter	3 207.5	2 282.6	1 877.1	405.4	21.2	236.2	40.1	305.7	321.7	3 327.6	393.5	2 934.1	2 601.1	332.9	11.3
4th quarter	3 253.2	2 323.5	1 910.9	412.6	22.7	225.1	45.4	312.8	323.8	3 379.7	405.6	2 974.1	2 654.1	320.0	10.8
1985															
1st quarter	3 315.6	2 366.4	1 946.1	420.3	23.2	243.1	41.7	315.3	325.7	3 447.2	442.4	3 004.9	2 721.3	283.6	9.4
2nd quarter	3 352.4	2 402.7	1 976.0	426.7	21.0	243.0	40.3	319.2	326.3	3 489.3	399.0	3 090.4	2 772.6	317.8	10.3
3rd quarter	3 403.9	2 442.0	2 008.9	433.1	20.0	245.4	37.9	335.5	323.1	3 528.1	432.4	3 095.7	2 842.1	253.5	8.2
4th quarter	3 449.9	2 489.7	2 049.7	440.0	22.0	250.5	36.5	319.8	331.5	3 595.4	440.2	3 155.2	2 879.6	275.6	8.7
1986															
1st quarter	3 487.7	2 522.5	2 075.7	446.8	20.0	251.9	36.6	313.5	343.2	3 650.9	437.9	3 213.0	2 922.5	290.5	9.0
2nd quarter	3 503.5	2 545.8	2 093.4	452.3	20.2	255.5	34.8	302.5	344.7	3 688.2	441.4	3 246.8	2 955.9	291.0	9.0
3rd quarter	3 537.6	2 582.9	2 123.6	459.2	25.9	259.4	30.7	293.2	345.5	3 736.0	451.7	3 284.3	3 028.9	255.4	7.8
4th quarter	3 574.5	2 631.6	2 164.8	466.8	26.0	255.6	26.8	293.7	340.9	3 774.7	468.9	3 305.9	3 071.7	234.2	7.1
1987															
1st quarter	3 665.3	2 681.8	2 207.1	474.7	27.1	267.8	32.7	309.7	346.2	3 852.2	463.7	3 388.5	3 111.8	276.8	8.2
2nd quarter	3 756.0	2 725.9	2 244.2	481.7	29.1	272.1	30.8	342.5	355.6	3 915.3	524.8	3 390.5	3 182.6	207.9	6.1
3rd quarter	3 849.3	2 773.7	2 284.8	488.9	29.1	278.2	37.8	364.3	366.2	3 992.4	502.7	3 489.6	3 247.8	241.9	6.9
4th quarter	3 943.0	2 841.0	2 344.8	496.2	30.8	281.3	41.9	370.0	378.1	4 090.1	520.9	3 569.2	3 284.7	284.5	8.0
1988															
1st quarter	4 023.3	2 888.4	2 379.6	508.8	32.9	296.6	44.9	381.1	379.4	4 156.8	514.5	3 642.3	3 362.2	280.1	7.7
2nd quarter	4 107.3	2 951.8	2 434.7	517.1	26.8	310.4	41.5	400.4	376.4	4 227.7	516.6	3 711.1	3 422.5	288.6	7.8
3rd quarter	4 186.9	3 001.3	2 476.4	524.9	28.0	318.3	40.0	408.5	390.8	4 308.7	519.1	3 789.7	3 490.3	299.3	7.9
4th quarter	4 286.8	3 053.7	2 520.1	533.6	16.5	325.6	50.0	430.2	410.9	4 395.1	528.5	3 866.6	3 565.3	301.3	7.8
1989															
1st quarter	4 350.2	3 097.0	2 555.8	541.2	35.7	330.8	46.6	406.7	433.3	4 517.5	565.3	3 952.2	3 623.3	328.9	8.3
2nd quarter	4 375.0	3 126.6	2 577.3	549.3	31.5	326.3	44.9	397.4	448.3	4 573.5	578.9	3 994.5	3 689.2	305.3	7.6
3rd quarter	4 396.4	3 163.6	2 605.5	558.1	29.2	326.3	37.4	390.0	449.8	4 617.4	588.4	4 029.0	3 746.6	282.4	7.0
4th quarter	4 446.7	3 216.9	2 648.6	568.3	32.1	335.0	33.1	388.6	440.9	4 690.7	601.3	4 089.4	3 798.7	290.7	7.1
1990															
1st quarter	4 552.9	3 284.1	2 701.6	582.6	33.2	343.3	42.1	403.2	447.1	4 800.8	595.7	4 205.1	3 879.2	325.9	7.8
2nd quarter	4 645.0	3 343.4	2 750.4	593.0	31.5	347.2	45.3	427.0	450.5	4 879.3	607.6	4 271.7	3 932.4	339.4	7.9
3rd quarter	4 675.6	3 383.7	2 781.8	601.9	30.9	355.9	53.2	401.9	450.1	4 951.4	617.3	4 334.1	4 001.0	333.1	7.7
4th quarter	4 695.0	3 393.0	2 784.7	608.3	29.0	353.0	55.8	402.2	462.0	4 981.4	618.0	4 363.5	4 024.5	339.0	7.8

[1] Inventory valuation adjustment.
[2] Capital consumption adjustment.

Table 19-5. National Income and Disposition of Personal Income—*Continued*

(Billions of dollars, except as noted; quarterly data are at seasonally adjusted annual rates.)

Year and quarter	National income	Compensation of employees			Proprietors' income with IVA [1] and CCAdj [2]		Rental income of persons with CCAdj [2]	Corporate profits with IVA [1] and CCAdj [2]	Net interest	Personal income	Less: Personal tax and nontax payments	Equals: Disposable personal income (DPI)	Less: Personal outlays	Equals: Personal saving	Saving as a percentage of DPI
		Total	Wage and salary accruals	Supplements to wages and salaries	Farm	Nonfarm									
1991															
1st quarter	4 703.5	3 403.5	2 786.7	616.8	26.5	346.7	53.9	432.9	440.0	4 999.9	600.7	4 399.1	4 035.9	363.2	8.3
2nd quarter	4 737.1	3 436.2	2 810.7	625.5	27.7	355.4	56.4	429.0	432.5	5 064.1	606.5	4 457.5	4 090.5	367.1	8.2
3rd quarter	4 773.0	3 471.0	2 835.7	635.3	23.8	361.3	57.6	428.3	430.9	5 110.1	611.6	4 498.5	4 130.2	368.3	8.2
4th quarter	4 812.6	3 509.0	2 863.7	645.3	27.5	367.9	57.8	434.7	415.7	5 167.4	623.2	4 544.2	4 156.0	388.1	8.5
1992															
1st quarter	4 935.1	3 574.8	2 913.3	661.4	31.4	389.2	59.3	469.8	410.6	5 276.8	614.7	4 662.0	4 255.3	406.7	8.7
2nd quarter	4 995.5	3 625.4	2 952.4	673.0	33.6	399.1	63.8	468.6	405.0	5 352.2	627.3	4 724.9	4 302.9	421.9	8.9
3rd quarter	4 951.9	3 668.0	2 984.0	683.9	33.2	403.5	53.2	401.4	392.7	5 390.7	638.0	4 752.7	4 356.2	396.5	8.3
4th quarter	5 097.2	3 710.9	3 017.4	693.4	32.5	414.9	76.8	472.5	389.6	5 541.8	663.1	4 878.7	4 449.1	429.6	8.8
1993															
1st quarter	5 150.2	3 750.6	3 044.8	705.9	29.5	426.4	84.7	472.4	386.6	5 465.8	644.0	4 821.7	4 481.8	340.0	7.1
2nd quarter	5 232.6	3 795.5	3 077.3	718.2	34.4	430.0	90.3	503.6	378.8	5 595.3	671.0	4 924.2	4 550.5	373.7	7.6
3rd quarter	5 259.4	3 835.1	3 107.0	728.1	22.9	432.5	90.8	508.5	369.5	5 630.3	681.8	4 948.5	4 617.1	331.5	6.7
4th quarter	5 365.5	3 876.3	3 137.4	738.9	33.7	437.9	97.6	557.6	362.4	5 748.5	701.7	5 046.8	4 688.6	358.2	7.1
1994															
1st quarter	5 373.4	3 943.5	3 190.2	753.3	40.6	427.9	98.0	498.8	364.6	5 713.7	695.4	5 018.3	4 744.0	274.3	5.5
2nd quarter	5 525.2	3 994.9	3 233.4	761.5	33.9	445.6	112.0	569.3	369.6	5 860.8	732.2	5 128.6	4 809.1	319.5	6.2
3rd quarter	5 608.7	4 032.8	3 267.7	765.1	27.7	448.1	116.2	598.5	385.4	5 935.3	724.3	5 211.0	4 886.9	324.1	6.2
4th quarter	5 719.9	4 093.6	3 325.9	767.7	25.5	457.0	115.2	626.2	402.5	6 042.4	738.5	5 303.9	4 959.7	344.2	6.5
1995															
1st quarter	5 775.0	4 142.7	3 379.6	763.1	21.4	467.2	116.9	630.0	396.8	6 109.9	751.8	5 358.1	5 012.1	346.0	6.5
2nd quarter	5 833.7	4 178.8	3 417.2	761.6	19.6	471.8	115.1	655.5	392.8	6 163.3	780.5	5 382.8	5 091.3	291.5	5.4
3rd quarter	5 920.0	4 224.3	3 463.6	760.7	20.5	479.2	116.6	692.8	386.7	6 225.9	781.6	5 444.4	5 158.4	285.9	5.3
4th quarter	5 978.1	4 264.1	3 503.8	760.2	27.3	483.9	123.2	696.7	383.0	6 304.6	799.5	5 505.1	5 218.8	286.3	5.2
1996															
1st quarter	6 066.6	4 297.4	3 537.4	760.0	31.1	494.8	128.4	736.7	378.2	6 405.1	830.7	5 574.4	5 292.2	282.2	5.1
2nd quarter	6 177.5	4 367.8	3 604.6	763.2	36.3	510.3	129.0	748.6	385.5	6 509.4	872.5	5 637.0	5 383.9	253.1	4.5
3rd quarter	6 254.5	4 427.8	3 660.9	766.8	38.0	515.5	130.1	755.0	388.1	6 597.1	877.3	5 719.8	5 433.7	286.1	5.0
4th quarter	6 342.9	4 489.4	3 717.6	771.8	31.7	521.4	131.4	775.8	393.3	6 677.9	898.1	5 779.7	5 512.6	267.1	4.6
1997															
1st quarter	6 454.8	4 553.7	3 786.5	767.2	30.6	539.4	130.4	798.5	402.2	6 792.4	935.1	5 857.3	5 609.2	248.1	4.2
2nd quarter	6 555.8	4 607.8	3 845.0	762.8	29.6	546.4	128.9	825.6	417.5	6 879.1	954.9	5 924.2	5 654.1	270.1	4.6
3rd quarter	6 676.4	4 675.8	3 912.7	763.0	29.8	556.2	127.4	858.3	429.0	6 978.6	978.9	5 999.7	5 763.7	236.0	3.9
4th quarter	6 786.7	4 767.9	3 999.7	768.2	28.9	563.8	126.7	852.7	446.8	7 097.9	1 006.3	6 091.6	5 834.3	257.3	4.2
1998															
1st quarter	6 874.1	4 869.4	4 085.1	784.3	24.1	582.9	127.7	787.4	482.8	7 254.8	1 034.0	6 220.8	5 912.9	307.9	4.9
2nd quarter	6 985.5	4 948.9	4 155.8	793.1	24.9	592.6	136.1	769.6	513.2	7 382.8	1 055.4	6 327.4	6 018.2	309.1	4.9
3rd quarter	7 108.9	5 029.8	4 227.7	802.1	25.4	601.6	144.2	781.9	526.0	7 490.7	1 083.7	6 407.0	6 095.6	311.4	4.9
4th quarter	7 197.0	5 110.5	4 299.8	810.6	27.9	615.8	146.5	770.8	525.5	7 575.8	1 108.5	6 467.3	6 189.7	277.6	4.3
1999															
1st quarter	7 343.1	5 216.8	4 395.0	821.9	30.1	629.2	148.9	808.2	509.9	7 655.9	1 125.5	6 530.3	6 276.4	253.9	3.9
2nd quarter	7 405.9	5 260.3	4 432.0	828.3	29.7	644.5	149.9	802.1	519.4	7 722.2	1 142.0	6 580.2	6 400.3	179.9	2.7
3rd quarter	7 475.9	5 329.0	4 492.7	836.3	25.7	657.0	145.8	788.0	530.4	7 807.7	1 167.2	6 640.5	6 507.2	133.3	2.0
4th quarter	7 650.1	5 429.1	4 582.7	846.4	25.4	672.0	152.0	824.7	546.8	7 960.2	1 201.8	6 758.4	6 629.4	129.0	1.9
2000															
1st quarter	7 860.2	5 627.3	4 757.4	869.9	22.3	680.2	151.4	807.6	571.3	8 211.6	1 256.3	6 955.3	6 775.9	179.4	2.6
2nd quarter	7 954.5	5 670.5	4 790.8	879.6	25.0	693.8	146.7	807.3	611.1	8 350.2	1 273.0	7 077.2	6 869.8	207.5	2.9
3rd quarter	8 048.3	5 773.1	4 879.3	893.8	21.7	696.9	144.9	787.7	624.0	8 487.8	1 290.6	7 188.2	6 976.7	211.5	2.9
4th quarter	8 074.8	5 822.7	4 917.8	904.9	21.2	698.1	143.5	749.7	639.6	8 576.6	1 316.7	7 259.8	7 052.1	207.7	2.9
2001															
1st quarter	8 092.1	5 878.9	4 960.4	918.5	19.3	701.9	137.0	706.5	648.5	8 658.1	1 340.6	7 317.5	7 143.9	173.7	2.4
2nd quarter	8 110.1	5 879.3	4 956.9	922.4	18.4	708.2	134.3	721.4	648.6	8 676.2	1 336.1	7 340.0	7 198.5	141.6	1.9
3rd quarter	8 089.1	5 880.4	4 953.7	926.7	19.3	713.1	140.8	687.2	648.3	8 706.2	1 181.9	7 524.2	7 222.0	302.2	4.0
4th quarter	8 196.8	5 860.9	4 931.4	929.4	19.2	712.1	139.3	811.4	653.9	8 700.9	1 309.7	7 391.2	7 329.6	61.5	0.8
2002															
1st quarter	8 268.5	5 908.4	4 957.8	950.7	21.7	726.7	141.3	797.6	672.8	8 803.4	1 136.8	7 666.7	7 396.3	270.4	3.5
2nd quarter	8 328.0	5 963.9	4 997.3	966.6	7.5	740.0	153.5	785.0	678.1	8 914.0	1 121.8	7 792.2	7 477.9	314.3	4.0
3rd quarter	8 349.9	5 988.4	5 007.4	981.0	10.7	748.0	144.1	771.0	687.6	8 958.9	1 099.0	7 859.9	7 583.0	276.9	3.5
4th quarter	8 413.9	6 017.4	5 023.1	994.3	11.7	759.9	130.6	796.1	698.3	9 012.5	1 090.1	7 922.5	7 640.7	281.8	3.6

[1]Inventory valuation adjustment.
[2]Capital consumption adjustment.

Table 19-6. Inventories to Sales Ratios

(Seasonally adjusted, ratio of inventories at end of quarter to monthly rate of sales during the quarter.)

Year and quarter	Total private inventories to final sales of domestic business		Nonfarm inventories to:			
			Final sales of domestic business		Final sales of goods and structures	
	Current dollars	Chained (1996) dollars	Current dollars	Chained (1996) dollars	Current dollars	Chained (1996) dollars
1946						
1st quarter	. . .	. . .	. . .	. . .	. . .	. . .
2nd quarter	. . .	. . .	. . .	. . .	. . .	. . .
3rd quarter	. . .	. . .	. . .	. . .	. . .	. . .
4th quarter	4.55	. . .	2.59	. . .	3.41	. . .
1947						
1st quarter	4.61	3.15	2.62	2.10	3.41	3.39
2nd quarter	4.51	3.10	2.60	2.09	3.37	3.37
3rd quarter	4.55	3.04	2.54	2.06	3.29	3.32
4th quarter	4.72	3.03	2.59	2.08	3.33	3.33
1948						
1st quarter	4.59	3.06	2.64	2.10	3.41	3.36
2nd quarter	4.62	3.09	2.64	2.10	3.42	3.39
3rd quarter	4.58	3.15	2.71	2.14	3.51	3.44
4th quarter	4.51	3.17	2.72	2.14	3.55	3.46
1949						
1st quarter	4.42	3.15	2.68	2.13	3.50	3.45
2nd quarter	4.18	3.07	2.54	2.07	3.34	3.35
3rd quarter	4.17	3.05	2.53	2.07	3.33	3.33
4th quarter	4.05	3.00	2.49	2.01	3.26	3.23
1950						
1st quarter	4.05	2.95	2.47	2.00	3.26	3.21
2nd quarter	4.03	2.90	2.45	1.98	3.23	3.17
3rd quarter	4.04	2.82	2.47	1.93	3.21	3.08
4th quarter	4.47	2.97	2.74	2.08	3.59	3.34
1951						
1st quarter	4.53	2.95	2.77	2.08	3.62	3.35
2nd quarter	4.59	3.04	2.88	2.18	3.79	3.53
3rd quarter	4.49	3.00	2.81	2.17	3.71	3.53
4th quarter	4.46	2.98	2.76	2.16	3.62	3.48
1952						
1st quarter	4.40	2.98	2.76	2.17	3.63	3.51
2nd quarter	4.25	2.93	2.66	2.11	3.51	3.42
3rd quarter	4.24	3.00	2.71	2.16	3.60	3.52
4th quarter	3.97	2.92	2.62	2.11	3.47	3.40
1953						
1st quarter	3.84	2.88	2.58	2.08	3.40	3.32
2nd quarter	3.78	2.88	2.61	2.09	3.43	3.32
3rd quarter	3.79	2.90	2.64	2.10	3.51	3.38
4th quarter	3.78	2.91	2.61	2.09	3.50	3.37
1954						
1st quarter	3.79	2.91	2.60	2.09	3.50	3.39
2nd quarter	3.74	2.88	2.57	2.06	3.45	3.34
3rd quarter	3.70	2.84	2.53	2.02	3.43	3.29
4th quarter	3.62	2.79	2.49	1.99	3.33	3.19
1955						
1st quarter	3.58	2.75	2.47	1.97	3.35	3.20
2nd quarter	3.51	2.74	2.48	1.98	3.31	3.16
3rd quarter	3.46	2.72	2.49	1.98	3.35	3.18
4th quarter	3.45	2.75	2.55	2.01	3.46	3.26
1956						
1st quarter	3.51	2.79	2.61	2.05	3.55	3.34
2nd quarter	3.55	2.78	2.62	2.06	3.57	3.35
3rd quarter	3.53	2.79	2.64	2.08	3.59	3.40
4th quarter	3.49	2.76	2.63	2.06	3.60	3.39
1957						
1st quarter	3.46	2.74	2.60	2.05	3.56	3.37
2nd quarter	3.49	2.76	2.62	2.07	3.60	3.43
3rd quarter	3.48	2.76	2.61	2.07	3.59	3.42
4th quarter	3.46	2.74	2.58	2.05	3.58	3.42
1958						
1st quarter	3.61	2.81	2.60	2.08	3.63	3.49
2nd quarter	3.56	2.78	2.53	2.04	3.56	3.43
3rd quarter	3.55	2.75	2.50	2.01	3.50	3.37
4th quarter	3.49	2.72	2.47	1.99	3.46	3.32
1959						
1st quarter	3.43	2.67	2.44	1.96	3.39	3.25
2nd quarter	3.39	2.66	2.46	1.97	3.42	3.28
3rd quarter	3.32	2.62	2.44	1.96	3.40	3.27
4th quarter	3.33	2.66	2.49	2.00	3.50	3.37
1960						
1st quarter	3.38	2.69	2.53	2.04	3.57	3.43
2nd quarter	3.33	2.68	2.52	2.04	3.55	3.43
3rd quarter	3.37	2.71	2.54	2.06	3.59	3.47
4th quarter	3.31	2.68	2.48	2.02	3.53	3.42

. . . = Not available.

Table 19-6. Inventories to Sales Ratios—*Continued*

(Seasonally adjusted, ratio of inventories at end of quarter to monthly rate of sales during the quarter.)

Year and quarter	Total private inventories to final sales of domestic business		Nonfarm inventories to:			
			Final sales of domestic business		Final sales of goods and structures	
	Current dollars	Chained (1996) dollars	Current dollars	Chained (1996) dollars	Current dollars	Chained (1996) dollars
1961						
1st quarter	3.30	2.67	2.46	2.01	3.53	3.42
2nd quarter	3.24	2.64	2.43	1.99	3.50	3.40
3rd quarter	3.28	2.66	2.44	2.00	3.51	3.42
4th quarter	3.24	2.62	2.41	1.98	3.46	3.37
1962						
1st quarter	3.25	2.64	2.41	2.00	3.47	3.40
2nd quarter	3.21	2.62	2.39	1.99	3.44	3.38
3rd quarter	3.25	2.63	2.41	2.00	3.46	3.40
4th quarter	3.23	2.62	2.40	2.00	3.46	3.41
1963						
1st quarter	3.22	2.64	2.41	2.01	3.47	3.44
2nd quarter	3.17	2.62	2.39	2.00	3.45	3.42
3rd quarter	3.13	2.60	2.37	1.99	3.43	3.41
4th quarter	3.09	2.59	2.37	1.99	3.44	3.41
1964						
1st quarter	3.03	2.55	2.34	1.97	3.38	3.36
2nd quarter	3.00	2.53	2.34	1.97	3.38	3.37
3rd quarter	2.99	2.52	2.34	1.98	3.38	3.37
4th quarter	3.01	2.54	2.36	2.00	3.43	3.43
1965						
1st quarter	3.03	2.55	2.37	2.01	3.44	3.44
2nd quarter	3.04	2.53	2.37	2.01	3.42	3.42
3rd quarter	3.01	2.53	2.36	2.00	3.41	3.41
4th quarter	2.99	2.48	2.33	1.97	3.35	3.35
1966						
1st quarter	3.02	2.49	2.34	1.99	3.36	3.36
2nd quarter	3.06	2.53	2.38	2.04	3.42	3.46
3rd quarter	3.09	2.56	2.42	2.08	3.50	3.54
4th quarter	3.12	2.62	2.48	2.14	3.60	3.66
1967						
1st quarter	3.13	2.66	2.51	2.17	3.66	3.73
2nd quarter	3.13	2.65	2.49	2.16	3.63	3.71
3rd quarter	3.12	2.68	2.51	2.19	3.66	3.77
4th quarter	3.11	2.68	2.52	2.20	3.69	3.80
1968						
1st quarter	3.09	2.65	2.48	2.17	3.61	3.73
2nd quarter	3.09	2.68	2.47	2.19	3.60	3.76
3rd quarter	3.06	2.66	2.45	2.18	3.57	3.74
4th quarter	3.03	2.67	2.45	2.19	3.57	3.77
1969						
1st quarter	3.06	2.68	2.46	2.20	3.58	3.78
2nd quarter	3.08	2.70	2.46	2.22	3.60	3.83
3rd quarter	3.07	2.72	2.49	2.25	3.64	3.88
4th quarter	3.11	2.74	2.52	2.28	3.72	3.96
1970						
1st quarter	3.11	2.73	2.51	2.27	3.72	3.96
2nd quarter	3.11	2.75	2.52	2.28	3.74	4.00
3rd quarter	3.09	2.73	2.52	2.28	3.75	4.00
4th quarter	3.05	2.73	2.51	2.29	3.76	4.03
1971						
1st quarter	3.08	2.73	2.50	2.28	3.76	4.03
2nd quarter	3.07	2.74	2.49	2.28	3.75	4.03
3rd quarter	3.05	2.74	2.48	2.29	3.73	4.03
4th quarter	3.02	2.70	2.44	2.26	3.68	3.99
1972						
1st quarter	2.98	2.66	2.40	2.23	3.61	3.91
2nd quarter	3.00	2.64	2.39	2.21	3.60	3.88
3rd quarter	3.02	2.65	2.41	2.23	3.61	3.90
4th quarter	3.01	2.60	2.37	2.19	3.53	3.82
1973						
1st quarter	3.07	2.55	2.38	2.17	3.53	3.77
2nd quarter	3.19	2.58	2.44	2.19	3.63	3.82
3rd quarter	3.23	2.60	2.46	2.21	3.65	3.86
4th quarter	3.30	2.64	2.55	2.26	3.78	3.94
1974						
1st quarter	3.36	2.67	2.66	2.30	3.97	4.04
2nd quarter	3.41	2.70	2.79	2.33	4.19	4.12
3rd quarter	3.56	2.72	2.89	2.35	4.34	4.18
4th quarter	3.61	2.81	3.01	2.45	4.56	4.43
1975						
1st quarter	3.46	2.77	2.90	2.40	4.39	4.33
2nd quarter	3.42	2.72	2.80	2.34	4.26	4.23
3rd quarter	3.37	2.69	2.76	2.31	4.19	4.18
4th quarter	3.27	2.66	2.69	2.28	4.09	4.11

Table 19-6. Inventories to Sales Ratios—Continued

(Seasonally adjusted, ratio of inventories at end of quarter to monthly rate of sales during the quarter.)

Year and quarter	Total private inventories to final sales of domestic business		Nonfarm inventories to:			
			Final sales of domestic business		Final sales of goods and structures	
	Current dollars	Chained (1996) dollars	Current dollars	Chained (1996) dollars	Current dollars	Chained (1996) dollars
1976						
1st quarter	3.23	2.63	2.68	2.26	4.07	4.07
2nd quarter	3.31	2.66	2.73	2.30	4.16	4.14
3rd quarter	3.27	2.68	2.76	2.31	4.22	4.18
4th quarter	3.22	2.65	2.72	2.30	4.17	4.15
1977						
1st quarter	3.22	2.64	2.73	2.30	4.19	4.15
2nd quarter	3.15	2.62	2.69	2.28	4.11	4.08
3rd quarter	3.14	2.65	2.69	2.29	4.13	4.13
4th quarter	3.18	2.66	2.69	2.29	4.13	4.12
1978						
1st quarter	3.29	2.69	2.74	2.33	4.26	4.23
2nd quarter	3.21	2.60	2.67	2.26	4.07	4.03
3rd quarter	3.22	2.61	2.67	2.26	4.06	4.02
4th quarter	3.25	2.61	2.68	2.27	4.07	4.02
1979						
1st quarter	3.38	2.63	2.74	2.28	4.16	4.07
2nd quarter	3.45	2.66	2.80	2.31	4.27	4.13
3rd quarter	3.42	2.63	2.81	2.28	4.23	4.03
4th quarter	3.44	2.63	2.84	2.27	4.32	4.04
1980						
1st quarter	3.49	2.63	2.92	2.28	4.46	4.06
2nd quarter	3.58	2.70	3.00	2.35	4.64	4.24
3rd quarter	3.52	2.62	2.95	2.30	4.56	4.14
4th quarter	3.45	2.59	2.91	2.27	4.50	4.09
1981						
1st quarter	3.46	2.61	2.94	2.29	4.53	4.10
2nd quarter	3.45	2.62	2.92	2.29	4.53	4.11
3rd quarter	3.41	2.66	2.92	2.31	4.56	4.17
4th quarter	3.39	2.70	2.92	2.35	4.59	4.25
1982						
1st quarter	3.39	2.70	2.89	2.33	4.59	4.25
2nd quarter	3.37	2.70	2.86	2.33	4.55	4.24
3rd quarter	3.33	2.73	2.86	2.35	4.61	4.33
4th quarter	3.21	2.65	2.74	2.27	4.46	4.18
1983						
1st quarter	3.15	2.59	2.66	2.22	4.35	4.10
2nd quarter	3.07	2.54	2.61	2.19	4.26	4.02
3rd quarter	3.02	2.48	2.60	2.17	4.23	3.96
4th quarter	2.99	2.46	2.59	2.16	4.21	3.94
1984						
1st quarter	3.06	2.50	2.64	2.20	4.30	4.00
2nd quarter	3.04	2.50	2.64	2.20	4.29	3.98
3rd quarter	3.04	2.54	2.66	2.23	4.34	4.04
4th quarter	3.03	2.53	2.64	2.23	4.31	4.02
1985						
1st quarter	2.96	2.50	2.57	2.20	4.21	3.97
2nd quarter	2.90	2.50	2.55	2.20	4.19	3.97
3rd quarter	2.83	2.48	2.49	2.17	4.11	3.93
4th quarter	2.85	2.49	2.50	2.18	4.17	3.98
1986						
1st quarter	2.79	2.49	2.45	2.18	4.09	3.96
2nd quarter	2.74	2.48	2.42	2.18	4.06	3.96
3rd quarter	2.68	2.44	2.37	2.14	3.96	3.88
4th quarter	2.64	2.42	2.34	2.12	3.94	3.86
1987						
1st quarter	2.68	2.45	2.37	2.15	4.04	3.97
2nd quarter	2.66	2.42	2.36	2.14	4.03	3.93
3rd quarter	2.62	2.39	2.34	2.12	3.98	3.87
4th quarter	2.68	2.42	2.39	2.16	4.08	3.95
1988						
1st quarter	2.66	2.39	2.37	2.14	4.05	3.91
2nd quarter	2.66	2.37	2.37	2.13	4.05	3.89
3rd quarter	2.66	2.37	2.38	2.14	4.08	3.92
4th quarter	2.65	2.35	2.37	2.13	4.07	3.90
1989						
1st quarter	2.68	2.37	2.40	2.14	4.10	3.90
2nd quarter	2.66	2.37	2.38	2.15	4.08	3.90
3rd quarter	2.61	2.35	2.35	2.13	4.02	3.87
4th quarter	2.62	2.36	2.35	2.14	4.06	3.92
1990						
1st quarter	2.57	2.33	2.31	2.12	3.96	3.85
2nd quarter	2.57	2.36	2.31	2.15	4.01	3.94
3rd quarter	2.60	2.38	2.35	2.16	4.10	3.99
4th quarter	2.60	2.38	2.34	2.16	4.11	4.00

Table 19-6. Inventories to Sales Ratios—*Continued*

(Seasonally adjusted, ratio of inventories at end of quarter to monthly rate of sales during the quarter.)

Year and quarter	Total private inventories to final sales of domestic business		Nonfarm inventories to:			
			Final sales of domestic business		Final sales of goods and structures	
	Current dollars	Chained (1996) dollars	Current dollars	Chained (1996) dollars	Current dollars	Chained (1996) dollars
1991						
1st quarter	2.56	2.39	2.29	2.17	4.05	4.02
2nd quarter	2.48	2.36	2.24	2.14	3.97	4.00
3rd quarter	2.46	2.36	2.23	2.15	3.99	4.03
4th quarter	2.46	2.38	2.24	2.17	4.03	4.06
1992						
1st quarter	2.42	2.34	2.18	2.12	3.93	3.97
2nd quarter	2.41	2.34	2.18	2.12	3.94	3.97
3rd quarter	2.40	2.33	2.16	2.11	3.93	3.95
4th quarter	2.36	2.30	2.13	2.09	3.85	3.89
1993						
1st quarter	2.39	2.33	2.15	2.12	3.90	3.96
2nd quarter	2.37	2.32	2.14	2.12	3.88	3.93
3rd quarter	2.34	2.31	2.12	2.11	3.87	3.93
4th quarter	2.30	2.28	2.09	2.08	3.79	3.85
1994						
1st quarter	2.31	2.29	2.09	2.09	3.80	3.87
2nd quarter	2.32	2.31	2.11	2.10	3.83	3.89
3rd quarter	2.31	2.31	2.11	2.10	3.84	3.88
4th quarter	2.34	2.33	2.13	2.11	3.86	3.89
1995						
1st quarter	2.38	2.34	2.17	2.14	3.93	3.91
2nd quarter	2.38	2.34	2.19	2.15	3.99	3.95
3rd quarter	2.35	2.32	2.16	2.13	3.95	3.92
4th quarter	2.33	2.31	2.15	2.13	3.91	3.88
1996						
1st quarter	2.30	2.28	2.12	2.11	3.85	3.84
2nd quarter	2.28	2.27	2.09	2.09	3.79	3.79
3rd quarter	2.29	2.28	2.09	2.10	3.79	3.80
4th quarter	2.25	2.26	2.06	2.08	3.76	3.77
1997						
1st quarter	2.23	2.26	2.04	2.08	3.70	3.75
2nd quarter	2.22	2.28	2.03	2.10	3.71	3.79
3rd quarter	2.20	2.26	2.02	2.08	3.66	3.73
4th quarter	2.19	2.28	2.01	2.10	3.68	3.76
1998						
1st quarter	2.19	2.31	2.01	2.12	3.67	3.79
2nd quarter	2.16	2.29	1.99	2.11	3.64	3.77
3rd quarter	2.14	2.30	1.99	2.12	3.63	3.79
4th quarter	2.11	2.29	1.97	2.12	3.57	3.74
1999						
1st quarter	2.12	2.31	1.96	2.13	3.58	3.77
2nd quarter	2.12	2.29	1.96	2.11	3.57	3.74
3rd quarter	2.13	2.29	1.98	2.11	3.62	3.75
4th quarter	2.14	2.29	1.99	2.12	3.64	3.75
2000						
1st quarter	2.15	2.28	2.00	2.12	3.63	3.73
2nd quarter	2.16	2.30	2.01	2.14	3.68	3.78
3rd quarter	2.17	2.31	2.03	2.15	3.72	3.81
4th quarter	2.19	2.33	2.04	2.17	3.77	3.86
2001						
1st quarter	2.16	2.30	2.01	2.14	3.70	3.79
2nd quarter	2.12	2.29	1.97	2.13	3.65	3.77
3rd quarter	2.07	2.27	1.93	2.11	3.60	3.75
4th quarter	1.99	2.21	1.85	2.04	3.44	3.64
2002						
1st quarter	1.97	2.18	1.83	2.02	3.42	3.60
2nd quarter	1.98	2.19	1.84	2.02	3.49	3.64
3rd quarter	1.98	2.17	1.84	2.01	3.48	3.61
4th quarter	1.98	2.18	1.84	2.02	3.51	3.64

Table 19-7. Federal Government Current Receipts and Expenditures

(National Income and Product Accounts, calendar years, billions of dollars, quarterly data are at seasonally adjusted annual rates.)

Year and quarter	Current receipts					Current expenditures						Current surplus or deficit (-), national income and product accounts		
	Total	Personal tax and nontax receipts	Corporate profits tax accruals	Indirect business tax and nontax accruals	Contributions for social insurance	Total	Consumption expenditures	Transfer payments (net)	Grants in-aid to state and local governments	Net interest paid	Subsidies less surplus of government enterprises	Total	Social insurance funds	Other
1946														
1st quarter	35.2	15.3	5.8	7.6	6.5	49.3	29.5	12.6	0.9	3.9	2.5	-14.0	. . .	. . .
2nd quarter	38.9	16.5	7.6	7.9	6.9	45.5	27.2	11.2	0.8	4.0	2.0	-6.6	. . .	. . .
3rd quarter	41.7	17.1	10.0	8.1	6.6	42.6	26.1	10.3	1.1	4.1	0.9	-0.9	. . .	. . .
4th quarter	42.1	17.0	11.2	8.1	5.8	41.1	25.3	9.6	1.3	4.2	0.8	0.9	. . .	. . .
1947														
1st quarter	43.4	18.2	10.9	8.1	6.2	37.5	21.8	9.4	1.4	4.2	0.7	5.9	. . .	. . .
2nd quarter	42.5	18.5	10.4	7.8	5.8	37.2	21.5	9.2	1.7	4.2	0.6	5.2	. . .	. . .
3rd quarter	41.6	18.7	10.2	7.7	5.0	39.7	20.5	12.8	1.6	4.2	0.5	1.9	. . .	. . .
4th quarter	43.8	19.8	11.1	8.2	4.6	35.8	19.5	10.0	1.6	4.3	0.5	7.9	. . .	. . .
1948														
1st quarter	44.0	20.1	11.5	7.8	4.6	36.4	19.5	10.5	1.6	4.3	0.5	7.7	. . .	. . .
2nd quarter	42.5	17.8	12.1	8.2	4.3	37.5	20.9	10.2	1.7	4.3	0.4	5.0	. . .	. . .
3rd quarter	41.6	17.1	11.9	8.2	4.4	40.3	21.7	11.9	1.8	4.3	0.7	1.3	. . .	. . .
4th quarter	41.4	17.3	11.5	8.2	4.3	41.2	22.5	11.6	1.9	4.3	1.0	0.1	. . .	. . .
1949														
1st quarter	39.9	16.5	10.4	8.1	5.0	43.4	23.7	12.8	1.7	4.4	0.7	-3.5	. . .	. . .
2nd quarter	37.9	15.7	9.1	8.2	4.9	44.5	24.3	13.5	1.7	4.4	0.5	-6.6	. . .	. . .
3rd quarter	37.4	15.0	9.5	8.3	4.6	44.0	23.0	13.8	2.1	4.4	0.7	-6.5	. . .	. . .
4th quarter	36.2	14.5	9.3	8.0	4.3	42.4	22.1	13.2	1.9	4.5	0.7	-6.2	. . .	. . .
1950														
1st quarter	41.4	15.2	13.0	8.0	5.1	49.8	22.0	20.5	1.9	4.5	0.9	-8.4	. . .	. . .
2nd quarter	45.5	16.1	15.6	8.7	5.1	42.8	22.0	13.4	1.9	4.5	1.0	2.7	. . .	. . .
3rd quarter	51.8	17.5	19.1	10.0	5.3	38.3	20.6	10.3	1.9	4.6	0.9	13.5	. . .	. . .
4th quarter	56.5	21.1	20.9	9.0	5.6	42.4	23.6	11.1	1.9	4.6	1.3	14.1	. . .	. . .
1951														
1st quarter	64.5	22.8	25.3	10.1	6.4	47.3	28.8	10.6	2.0	4.6	1.3	17.2	. . .	. . .
2nd quarter	61.6	24.8	21.4	9.0	6.5	51.6	32.6	11.0	2.1	4.6	1.3	10.0	. . .	. . .
3rd quarter	60.9	26.1	19.4	9.1	6.3	55.5	37.4	11.3	1.9	4.6	1.1	5.3	. . .	. . .
4th quarter	64.6	28.0	20.7	9.5	6.4	58.7	38.8	11.3	2.1	4.7	1.2	5.9	. . .	. . .
1952														
1st quarter	64.7	29.1	19.0	10.0	6.7	57.9	40.8	9.4	2.0	4.7	1.0	6.9	. . .	. . .
2nd quarter	64.8	30.0	17.9	10.4	6.6	61.4	43.8	10.1	2.1	4.6	0.9	3.4	. . .	. . .
3rd quarter	65.3	30.5	17.8	10.4	6.6	64.2	45.3	11.1	2.3	4.7	0.9	1.1	. . .	. . .
4th quarter	68.4	31.3	19.7	10.7	6.8	64.9	46.9	10.2	2.3	4.7	0.8	3.5	. . .	. . .
1953														
1st quarter	70.1	31.6	20.8	11.0	6.8	65.8	47.7	10.6	1.8	4.7	0.9	4.3	. . .	. . .
2nd quarter	70.5	31.6	20.9	11.2	6.8	67.8	49.2	10.6	2.7	4.7	0.6	2.6	. . .	. . .
3rd quarter	69.5	31.3	20.4	11.0	6.9	66.1	47.6	10.5	2.3	4.8	0.8	3.4	. . .	. . .
4th quarter	64.3	31.0	15.9	10.6	6.7	67.6	48.8	11.1	2.3	4.8	0.4	-3.2	. . .	. . .
1954														
1st quarter	61.6	28.2	15.7	10.0	7.8	65.0	45.9	11.6	2.4	4.9	0.3	-3.4	. . .	. . .
2nd quarter	61.7	28.0	16.2	9.9	7.7	63.7	43.6	12.0	2.3	4.9	0.9	-2.0	. . .	. . .
3rd quarter	62.3	28.0	17.1	9.5	7.7	63.7	43.1	12.8	2.4	4.9	0.6	-1.4	. . .	. . .
4th quarter	64.4	28.4	18.4	9.7	7.8	64.4	43.3	13.5	2.3	4.9	0.4	0.0	. . .	. . .
1955														
1st quarter	68.3	29.1	20.4	10.3	8.5	64.8	43.3	13.9	2.3	4.8	0.6	3.5	. . .	. . .
2nd quarter	70.3	30.1	20.7	10.8	8.7	63.6	42.8	13.4	2.4	4.7	0.8	6.7	. . .	. . .
3rd quarter	72.0	31.0	21.2	10.9	8.9	67.2	45.3	13.5	2.5	4.8	0.5	4.8	. . .	. . .
4th quarter	73.7	31.9	22.0	10.9	8.9	66.0	44.4	13.5	2.4	5.0	0.7	7.7	. . .	. . .
1956														
1st quarter	74.2	32.8	21.0	10.9	9.5	65.7	43.9	13.7	2.4	5.0	0.8	8.5	. . .	. . .
2nd quarter	75.6	33.6	21.4	10.9	9.6	68.9	46.2	14.1	2.5	5.2	1.0	6.6	. . .	. . .
3rd quarter	75.4	34.3	20.1	11.4	9.6	67.7	43.9	14.4	2.6	5.3	1.4	7.7	. . .	. . .
4th quarter	78.2	35.2	21.2	12.0	9.8	71.0	46.3	14.6	2.7	5.7	1.7	7.2	. . .	. . .
1957														
1st quarter	80.4	35.8	21.7	11.9	11.0	74.4	49.1	15.1	2.9	5.5	1.7	6.0	. . .	. . .
2nd quarter	79.9	36.1	20.8	11.9	11.0	75.6	49.0	16.5	2.8	5.7	1.6	4.3	. . .	. . .
3rd quarter	79.9	36.3	20.4	12.0	11.1	75.6	49.0	16.3	2.9	5.8	1.5	4.3	. . .	. . .
4th quarter	77.1	35.9	18.6	11.6	10.9	78.7	50.7	17.5	3.1	6.0	1.4	-1.6	. . .	. . .
1958														
1st quarter	73.6	35.2	16.0	11.4	10.9	76.9	49.2	18.6	2.9	5.4	1.5	-3.3	-1.3	-2.0
2nd quarter	73.5	34.7	16.3	11.6	10.9	81.9	51.9	20.5	3.3	5.2	1.7	-8.4	-3.6	-4.9
3rd quarter	76.7	35.9	18.4	11.4	11.0	83.2	50.6	20.9	3.2	5.5	1.9	-6.5	-3.5	-3.1
4th quarter	80.4	36.3	21.1	11.9	11.1	84.0	52.1	20.2	4.0	5.6	2.0	-3.6	-2.4	-1.2
1959														
1st quarter	84.9	37.2	22.3	12.2	13.3	81.2	50.3	20.3	3.5	5.9	1.3	3.7	-0.6	4.3
2nd quarter	88.7	38.3	24.4	12.5	13.5	83.8	52.7	19.9	3.9	6.2	1.1	4.9	-0.3	5.2
3rd quarter	86.9	38.8	21.9	12.8	13.4	84.4	52.4	20.3	3.8	6.6	1.3	2.5	-0.7	3.2
4th quarter	87.5	39.8	21.4	12.9	13.5	85.7	52.6	21.1	3.8	7.0	1.2	1.8	-1.2	2.9

. . . = Not available.

Table 19-7. Federal Government Current Receipts and Expenditures—*Continued*

(National Income and Product Accounts, calendar years, billions of dollars, quarterly data are at seasonally adjusted annual rates.)

Year and quarter	Current receipts					Current expenditures						Current surplus or deficit (-), national income and product accounts		
	Total	Personal tax and nontax receipts	Corporate profits tax accruals	Indirect business tax and nontax accruals	Contributions for social insurance	Total	Consumption expenditures	Transfer payments (net)	Grants in-aid to state and local governments	Net interest paid	Subsidies less surplus of government enterprises	Total	Social insurance funds	Other
1960														
1st quarter	94.5	41.2	23.7	13.7	16.0	82.9	49.9	20.5	3.9	7.4	1.2	11.6	1.5	10.0
2nd quarter	93.2	41.9	21.7	13.6	16.0	85.1	51.0	21.2	4.0	7.3	1.5	8.1	1.0	7.1
3rd quarter	92.6	42.3	20.7	13.5	16.0	86.1	51.7	22.1	4.0	6.9	1.4	6.5	0.4	6.1
4th quarter	91.1	42.2	19.7	13.4	15.9	89.1	53.5	23.0	4.2	6.7	1.7	2.1	-0.6	2.6
1961														
1st quarter	91.2	42.2	19.4	13.4	16.3	88.9	51.2	24.8	4.2	6.5	2.1	2.4	-1.9	4.3
2nd quarter	93.2	42.5	20.7	13.5	16.4	92.6	53.4	25.6	4.5	6.5	2.6	0.6	-2.5	3.2
3rd quarter	95.0	42.8	22.0	13.7	16.6	92.7	53.3	25.5	4.6	6.6	2.7	2.4	-2.5	4.8
4th quarter	98.3	43.4	23.9	14.2	16.8	93.7	54.8	25.0	4.7	6.6	2.6	4.5	-1.6	6.1
1962														
1st quarter	99.7	44.6	22.3	14.5	18.4	97.5	57.6	25.6	4.9	6.8	2.7	2.3	-0.4	2.6
2nd quarter	101.2	46.0	22.1	14.5	18.6	99.1	59.3	25.1	4.9	6.9	2.9	2.0	-0.1	2.1
3rd quarter	103.6	47.3	22.7	15.0	18.6	100.6	60.0	25.5	5.2	7.3	2.7	3.0	-0.3	3.3
4th quarter	104.8	48.4	22.8	14.9	18.7	102.6	61.0	26.2	5.2	7.4	2.8	2.2	-0.6	2.8
1963														
1st quarter	107.6	48.9	22.9	15.0	20.7	103.6	61.4	27.1	5.3	7.5	2.3	4.0	0.1	3.9
2nd quarter	109.8	49.1	24.5	15.4	20.9	103.7	61.9	26.2	5.5	7.6	2.5	6.2	1.4	4.8
3rd quarter	110.9	49.2	25.2	15.4	21.1	105.2	62.6	26.4	5.8	7.8	2.6	5.7	1.4	4.3
4th quarter	112.4	49.7	25.8	15.6	21.4	107.4	63.7	27.0	6.1	8.0	2.6	5.0	1.4	3.6
1964														
1st quarter	111.0	48.1	25.9	15.7	21.4	109.1	64.0	27.5	6.5	8.2	2.9	1.9	0.8	1.1
2nd quarter	107.3	43.8	26.0	16.0	21.6	110.1	65.0	27.1	6.5	8.3	3.1	-2.7	1.6	-4.3
3rd quarter	110.3	45.4	26.5	16.5	21.8	109.1	64.3	27.1	6.2	8.4	3.2	1.1	1.8	-0.6
4th quarter	112.0	46.9	26.1	17.0	22.0	108.9	63.3	27.3	6.6	8.8	2.8	3.1	2.0	1.1
1965														
1st quarter	117.7	50.6	27.5	17.5	22.2	110.3	63.8	28.1	6.5	8.6	3.2	7.4	1.1	6.3
2nd quarter	119.6	51.9	28.4	16.8	22.4	112.9	65.8	28.0	7.1	8.8	3.2	6.6	2.2	4.5
3rd quarter	118.0	50.4	28.9	15.9	22.8	118.6	67.8	31.2	7.5	8.8	3.3	-0.6	-0.9	0.4
4th quarter	121.8	51.6	30.8	16.2	23.2	122.5	72.1	29.9	7.6	9.3	3.6	-0.7	0.8	-1.6
1966														
1st quarter	130.8	54.4	31.7	15.1	29.6	125.5	72.1	31.2	9.0	9.2	4.0	5.3	6.7	-1.4
2nd quarter	135.7	58.0	31.7	15.9	30.0	131.4	76.8	30.4	10.1	9.6	4.5	4.3	7.0	-2.7
3rd quarter	138.2	59.9	31.4	15.8	31.1	136.6	79.5	31.8	10.5	9.9	4.8	1.6	6.7	-5.0
4th quarter	140.6	62.2	30.9	16.2	31.4	140.9	80.4	34.7	10.7	10.3	4.9	-0.3	5.0	-5.3
1967														
1st quarter	141.5	62.9	29.7	16.1	32.8	150.3	86.7	37.4	11.1	10.5	4.6	-8.8	4.3	-13.1
2nd quarter	142.2	62.7	29.4	16.4	33.7	151.5	87.5	37.8	11.6	10.2	4.4	-9.3	4.9	-14.2
3rd quarter	145.7	65.2	29.6	16.5	34.4	153.2	88.1	38.9	11.6	10.4	4.2	-7.5	5.0	-12.4
4th quarter	150.2	67.0	31.4	16.8	35.1	157.9	90.9	38.9	12.7	10.9	4.5	-7.7	5.4	-13.1
1968														
1st quarter	158.3	68.9	35.2	17.5	36.7	163.1	95.1	40.5	11.8	11.3	4.4	-4.8	5.4	-10.2
2nd quarter	162.9	71.4	35.9	18.1	37.5	160.4	96.2	43.4	13.3	12.0	4.5	-6.5	3.6	-10.0
3rd quarter	173.8	81.1	36.1	18.6	38.1	171.4	97.5	44.6	12.6	12.3	4.5	2.4	3.3	-0.9
4th quarter	178.9	84.5	37.0	18.7	38.7	175.2	99.2	45.6	13.2	12.7	4.6	3.7	3.1	0.6
1969														
1st quarter	188.7	90.8	37.4	18.6	41.9	173.8	96.8	46.1	13.1	13.0	4.8	14.9	5.5	9.5
2nd quarter	191.7	93.4	36.5	19.2	42.7	179.4	99.5	47.5	14.0	13.4	4.9	12.3	5.9	6.5
3rd quarter	189.3	90.8	35.3	19.6	43.6	182.6	101.3	47.5	15.1	13.7	5.1	6.7	6.6	0.1
4th quarter	190.6	92.0	35.1	19.3	44.2	186.1	102.3	48.4	16.1	14.5	5.0	4.5	6.9	-2.4
1970														
1st quarter	185.2	90.6	30.4	19.2	44.9	186.9	101.5	49.8	17.5	14.9	5.7	-1.8	7.2	-8.9
2nd quarter	186.7	91.5	30.5	19.5	45.2	201.4	99.8	59.1	18.8	15.1	6.4	-14.7	-0.7	-14.0
3rd quarter	183.0	86.4	31.5	19.5	45.6	201.6	100.3	58.8	20.1	15.7	6.2	-18.5	1.1	-19.6
4th quarter	182.2	87.2	30.1	19.5	45.4	204.7	99.9	61.8	20.8	15.6	6.6	-22.4	-1.1	-21.3
1971														
1st quarter	187.2	83.7	33.3	20.8	49.3	208.8	102.4	62.8	21.6	15.5	6.6	-21.6	2.0	-23.6
2nd quarter	189.2	85.2	33.9	20.2	49.9	217.6	103.5	69.9	23.2	15.0	6.0	-28.4	-4.4	-24.0
3rd quarter	190.0	86.4	33.1	20.4	50.1	218.5	104.1	69.5	23.5	15.4	6.1	-28.6	-3.3	-25.2
4th quarter	192.9	88.3	33.5	20.5	50.7	221.5	104.7	70.5	24.7	15.5	6.3	-28.6	-3.5	-25.1
1972														
1st quarter	212.0	100.4	35.0	19.8	56.9	231.2	110.2	72.6	25.7	15.7	7.0	-19.2	0.9	-20.1
2nd quarter	215.1	102.5	35.2	19.9	57.5	241.1	111.3	72.4	33.9	15.9	7.4	-26.0	1.6	-27.6
3rd quarter	217.8	103.2	36.3	20.2	58.2	232.2	108.4	72.7	26.8	16.0	8.4	-14.4	2.5	-16.9
4th quarter	225.0	105.5	39.9	20.6	59.0	255.4	109.9	82.6	40.4	16.6	7.9	-30.4	-4.6	-25.8
1973														
1st quarter	241.2	104.7	43.1	21.3	72.2	255.8	111.3	83.6	35.6	18.1	7.2	-14.6	7.2	-21.7
2nd quarter	245.5	107.0	43.5	21.8	73.3	259.4	112.1	86.0	34.7	19.4	7.2	-13.9	6.9	-20.8
3rd quarter	249.1	111.1	42.2	21.2	74.5	258.5	110.5	86.9	33.9	20.7	6.6	-9.5	7.0	-16.4
4th quarter	258.1	116.1	44.3	21.7	76.0	265.0	112.6	89.1	34.9	21.5	7.0	-6.9	6.7	-13.6
1974														
1st quarter	265.3	119.6	42.5	21.6	81.5	274.4	116.7	96.4	34.6	21.7	4.9	-9.1	9.8	-18.9
2nd quarter	274.8	124.9	44.8	22.1	83.1	284.1	117.3	104.1	35.4	22.4	4.3	-9.3	5.0	-14.2
3rd quarter	286.2	129.9	49.3	22.3	84.7	297.3	121.3	109.2	36.8	23.5	5.0	-11.1	2.6	-13.7
4th quarter	283.0	132.1	43.8	22.3	84.8	308.9	126.2	115.1	38.2	23.9	5.6	-25.9	-1.4	-24.5

Table 19-7. Federal Government Current Receipts and Expenditures—*Continued*

(National Income and Product Accounts, calendar years, billions of dollars, quarterly data are at seasonally adjusted annual rates.)

Year and quarter	Current receipts					Current expenditures						Current surplus or deficit (-), national income and product accounts		
	Total	Personal tax and nontax receipts	Corporate profits tax accruals	Indirect business tax and nontax accruals	Contributions for social insurance	Total	Consumption expenditures	Transfer payments (net)	Grants in-aid to state and local governments	Net interest paid	Subsidies less surplus of government enterprises	Total	Social insurance funds	Other
1975														
1st quarter	277.0	132.4	36.9	21.9	85.9	324.0	127.9	124.1	40.7	24.2	7.2	-47.0	-8.3	-38.7
2nd quarter	243.9	94.7	39.5	23.4	86.2	346.2	130.3	137.8	45.8	24.8	7.5	-102.3	-14.2	-88.1
3rd quarter	287.5	125.8	48.4	25.4	87.9	351.2	131.3	139.4	46.5	25.9	8.3	-63.7	-20.3	-43.3
4th quarter	295.9	130.5	49.4	26.1	89.9	360.1	135.2	141.1	47.5	27.6	8.8	-64.2	-18.6	-45.6
1976														
1st quarter	308.5	132.8	55.7	23.1	96.9	362.3	135.0	143.2	48.7	28.6	6.9	-53.8	-13.8	-40.0
2nd quarter	315.3	138.5	54.8	23.7	98.3	364.6	137.3	141.8	49.5	29.4	6.8	-49.3	-11.2	-38.1
3rd quarter	322.7	144.3	54.4	24.1	100.0	375.7	137.6	150.6	50.4	30.1	7.1	-53.0	-16.0	-36.9
4th quarter	328.9	149.9	53.4	24.2	101.4	385.0	142.1	149.4	54.4	31.6	7.5	-56.1	-16.6	-39.5
1977														
1st quarter	343.3	155.1	56.9	24.5	106.8	389.6	145.8	152.1	52.5	31.2	8.1	-46.3	-13.2	-33.1
2nd quarter	357.1	160.8	61.7	25.2	109.4	397.5	150.0	151.9	55.5	31.8	8.3	-40.4	-10.9	-29.5
3rd quarter	364.0	162.4	63.8	26.3	111.5	410.2	152.1	157.4	59.1	32.4	9.3	-46.2	-13.5	-32.7
4th quarter	375.1	171.0	64.0	26.4	113.6	422.8	157.3	158.5	59.2	34.5	13.4	-47.7	-12.9	-34.8
1978														
1st quarter	384.4	173.3	60.8	27.3	123.0	431.6	159.3	161.2	63.5	36.1	11.5	-47.2	-4.1	-43.1
2nd quarter	411.3	182.9	72.9	28.9	126.7	437.3	162.9	160.8	66.1	37.2	10.5	-26.0	0.0	-26.0
3rd quarter	427.6	195.3	73.9	29.2	129.2	447.4	165.0	168.4	65.5	39.3	9.4	-19.8	-4.7	-15.2
4th quarter	445.8	205.0	78.0	30.2	132.5	460.5	169.8	170.8	67.1	41.5	11.3	-14.7	-3.1	-11.5
1979														
1st quarter	461.1	211.5	75.1	29.9	144.6	467.6	173.9	175.3	64.4	44.2	9.6	-6.5	6.1	-12.6
2nd quarter	472.7	219.9	75.4	30.2	147.1	478.9	178.7	178.7	65.0	46.2	10.3	-6.2	6.2	-12.4
3rd quarter	484.4	229.4	74.7	29.9	150.4	496.4	178.1	193.0	67.6	47.4	10.3	-12.1	-2.4	-9.7
4th quarter	494.9	238.5	72.5	30.5	153.3	515.6	189.2	196.7	68.4	50.2	11.1	-20.8	-2.6	-18.1
1980														
1st quarter	508.9	237.9	78.7	32.8	159.5	539.3	196.9	206.2	69.3	55.4	11.6	-30.4	-0.6	-29.9
2nd quarter	505.3	243.8	62.1	39.1	160.4	560.0	208.5	209.2	70.8	59.1	12.5	-54.7	-5.9	-48.9
3rd quarter	524.1	252.4	67.1	41.9	162.7	593.2	210.0	237.9	73.4	58.3	13.6	-69.0	-26.0	-43.1
4th quarter	552.9	266.9	73.4	44.8	167.8	613.7	220.6	241.9	75.8	61.4	13.9	-60.8	-22.7	-38.1
1981														
1st quarter	595.4	278.0	71.9	57.8	187.7	634.8	229.8	243.6	74.4	73.4	13.7	-39.4	-5.9	-33.5
2nd quarter	601.8	288.7	64.1	58.8	190.2	646.1	238.9	244.9	74.5	75.9	12.0	-44.3	-4.9	-39.4
3rd quarter	618.5	301.1	67.2	56.6	193.7	670.3	240.1	263.9	71.9	80.8	13.9	-51.8	-18.5	-33.3
4th quarter	606.8	295.6	59.6	55.9	195.8	686.0	250.8	266.4	69.2	86.1	13.6	-79.2	-20.2	-59.0
1982														
1st quarter	599.2	295.2	48.9	52.0	203.1	700.2	257.1	270.9	68.8	89.1	14.1	-101.0	-17.8	-83.2
2nd quarter	605.4	301.7	50.4	49.0	204.4	712.8	258.3	276.7	70.4	92.6	14.9	-107.4	-24.2	-83.2
3rd quarter	595.8	289.9	50.9	49.2	205.9	740.5	267.4	292.0	69.0	96.8	15.4	-144.7	-37.4	-107.3
4th quarter	597.6	296.0	46.0	49.5	206.1	774.8	278.4	309.6	69.8	97.1	19.9	-177.2	-50.5	-126.6
1983														
1st quarter	603.7	289.9	47.5	49.9	216.4	777.7	281.8	306.4	70.6	97.9	20.9	-173.9	-40.3	-133.6
2nd quarter	629.4	295.7	59.9	54.2	219.6	800.4	288.6	312.3	72.7	101.5	24.1	-170.9	-42.5	-128.4
3rd quarter	623.4	277.8	68.0	54.5	223.0	809.2	297.9	307.0	71.8	107.2	24.9	-185.8	-31.5	-154.3
4th quarter	639.0	285.4	70.0	55.3	228.3	803.9	283.9	312.5	71.2	111.7	24.7	-164.9	-27.4	-137.5
1984														
1st quarter	672.8	288.4	80.7	57.2	246.4	829.9	299.3	310.1	75.4	117.8	27.4	-157.1	-9.7	-147.4
2nd quarter	683.6	295.2	79.4	57.9	251.2	847.2	312.6	312.2	77.4	121.7	23.4	-163.6	-5.8	-157.8
3rd quarter	690.9	307.9	70.0	57.8	255.2	860.9	315.2	315.9	75.1	132.2	22.4	-170.0	-1.9	-168.1
4th quarter	705.0	318.3	70.8	57.5	258.4	886.5	320.8	326.6	78.8	138.1	22.7	-181.5	-4.2	-177.4
1985														
1st quarter	756.7	353.7	75.5	56.7	270.8	904.5	330.4	331.8	79.1	140.8	22.5	-147.8	-0.2	-147.5
2nd quarter	717.9	308.3	74.1	61.4	274.1	917.4	335.0	334.2	80.0	144.7	22.3	-199.5	2.0	-201.4
3rd quarter	754.0	340.8	78.5	56.7	277.9	930.9	342.4	339.7	81.2	144.1	23.5	-177.0	2.1	-179.1
4th quarter	761.2	346.0	76.9	55.2	283.1	945.5	348.1	341.7	83.1	147.8	24.8	-184.3	6.4	-190.8
1986														
1st quarter	771.7	342.4	82.2	54.6	292.5	954.0	347.5	346.9	84.8	149.6	25.2	-182.3	7.9	-190.2
2nd quarter	774.3	345.1	81.2	53.1	294.9	978.4	357.0	355.1	89.0	151.2	26.1	-204.1	7.3	-211.4
3rd quarter	786.3	352.7	81.8	52.9	298.9	994.5	365.7	361.3	91.8	149.2	26.5	-208.2	5.9	-214.0
4th quarter	813.2	365.3	90.1	54.2	303.6	987.2	362.9	360.8	84.9	152.1	26.6	-174.0	9.9	-183.8
1987														
1st quarter	815.4	359.6	91.1	55.1	309.6	997.9	369.8	361.8	82.1	153.9	30.2	-182.5	12.4	-194.8
2nd quarter	884.9	411.6	102.5	57.6	313.3	1 013.7	372.9	366.3	85.8	155.9	32.9	-128.8	12.8	-141.6
3rd quarter	880.5	396.7	109.3	56.9	317.7	1 017.2	372.7	366.7	83.9	160.4	33.7	-136.7	17.4	-154.1
4th quarter	901.1	410.4	109.9	57.8	323.1	1 044.7	383.1	373.8	83.8	168.9	34.8	-143.6	22.8	-166.4
1988														
1st quarter	908.8	404.2	102.3	58.2	344.0	1 056.2	381.8	384.3	89.5	165.0	35.5	-147.4	31.7	-179.2
2nd quarter	920.6	402.5	109.5	57.8	350.8	1 055.0	380.2	383.1	90.0	170.7	30.9	-134.4	39.4	-173.8
3rd quarter	933.5	404.5	113.6	59.5	355.9	1 064.3	377.3	387.7	93.1	174.9	31.3	-130.7	44.0	-174.7
4th quarter	952.6	411.6	119.1	60.2	361.7	1 089.5	391.8	396.3	93.8	177.7	30.0	-136.9	49.7	-186.6

Table 19-7. Federal Government Current Receipts and Expenditures—*Continued*

(National Income and Product Accounts, calendar years, billions of dollars, quarterly data are at seasonally adjusted annual rates.)

Year and quarter	Current receipts					Current expenditures						Current surplus or deficit (-), national income and product accounts		
	Total	Personal tax and nontax receipts	Corporate profits tax accruals	Indirect business tax and nontax accruals	Contributions for social insurance	Total	Consumption expenditures	Transfer payments (net)	Grants in-aid to state and local governments	Net interest paid	Subsidies less surplus of government enterprises	Total	Social insurance funds	Other
1989														
1st quarter	1 000.9	440.9	126.7	62.2	371.1	1 109.7	389.4	408.3	94.9	187.7	29.4	-108.9	46.7	-155.6
2nd quarter	1 004.3	449.9	119.2	61.3	374.0	1 131.7	400.9	413.0	95.6	193.5	28.7	-127.4	46.1	-173.5
3rd quarter	1 009.8	458.6	110.3	63.4	377.4	1 150.3	403.3	423.9	101.4	193.4	28.4	-140.5	44.3	-184.9
4th quarter	1 026.3	469.0	112.7	62.0	382.6	1 169.6	404.8	435.4	101.4	199.5	28.6	-143.3	45.0	-188.3
1990														
1st quarter	1 033.7	464.5	112.2	62.4	394.5	1 205.7	415.5	448.5	106.5	204.7	30.5	-172.0	43.0	-215.0
2nd quarter	1 053.5	473.5	118.5	63.0	398.5	1 224.5	418.2	454.5	110.3	210.0	31.6	-171.0	46.8	-217.8
3rd quarter	1 070.9	478.6	124.4	64.1	403.9	1 235.7	416.4	457.2	112.6	217.6	31.8	-164.8	48.6	-213.4
4th quarter	1 064.8	477.9	117.4	66.2	403.4	1 249.0	429.6	461.0	116.3	209.9	32.3	-184.1	41.1	-225.2
1991														
1st quarter	1 057.5	461.0	107.1	75.9	413.4	1 217.5	443.8	401.2	122.8	220.0	29.9	-160.1	31.3	-191.3
2nd quarter	1 066.2	463.1	109.0	77.8	416.4	1 279.7	441.5	456.8	128.1	225.4	27.5	-213.5	26.4	-239.9
3rd quarter	1 077.2	465.8	111.9	78.9	420.6	1 311.8	437.8	486.6	134.9	224.8	27.7	-234.6	28.3	-262.9
4th quarter	1 088.1	471.0	111.8	81.5	423.8	1 341.3	433.4	509.0	140.6	230.8	27.5	-253.2	23.7	-276.9
1992														
1st quarter	1 100.0	463.1	120.1	80.8	436.0	1 388.3	439.5	548.9	143.2	229.2	27.5	-288.3	11.0	-299.3
2nd quarter	1 117.3	472.1	124.6	79.9	440.7	1 409.2	441.6	562.4	146.2	230.5	28.4	-291.8	8.0	-299.9
3rd quarter	1 111.9	481.4	107.0	79.1	444.4	1 428.4	451.1	565.1	152.4	230.1	29.7	-316.5	9.2	-325.8
4th quarter	1 156.0	501.0	123.4	85.5	446.2	1 449.6	450.9	584.5	154.6	226.8	32.8	-293.5	8.3	-301.8
1993														
1st quarter	1 149.0	486.0	126.7	81.7	454.6	1 449.8	442.1	584.4	155.5	228.7	39.1	-300.8	4.2	-305.0
2nd quarter	1 191.8	507.1	138.6	83.9	462.1	1 458.9	439.6	593.5	157.8	230.3	37.8	-267.2	7.0	-274.2
3rd quarter	1 201.2	515.8	135.9	83.8	465.7	1 476.7	444.4	599.4	163.4	231.0	38.5	-275.5	6.1	-281.6
4th quarter	1 247.3	530.8	152.8	91.5	472.2	1 500.4	444.4	614.0	173.7	230.8	37.4	-253.1	10.3	-263.4
1994														
1st quarter	1 243.7	526.8	138.9	94.4	483.6	1 481.2	437.6	608.1	171.3	229.3	34.9	-237.5	16.3	-253.8
2nd quarter	1 297.6	558.1	153.4	94.5	491.6	1 488.2	435.3	611.6	171.2	236.2	33.8	-190.5	22.3	-212.8
3rd quarter	1 303.5	548.0	163.1	96.1	496.4	1 515.5	447.2	618.0	175.1	242.7	32.4	-212.0	24.8	-236.8
4th quarter	1 329.9	558.4	171.5	95.9	504.1	1 539.3	438.7	636.6	180.4	250.2	33.3	-209.4	27.6	-237.0
1995														
1st quarter	1 348.2	569.4	172.6	94.6	511.6	1 556.4	439.2	641.8	185.1	259.2	31.1	-208.3	21.0	-229.3
2nd quarter	1 385.7	596.3	177.5	95.3	516.6	1 574.6	441.3	648.8	186.3	266.4	31.9	-188.9	19.0	-207.9
3rd quarter	1 391.7	593.3	185.9	90.0	522.5	1 589.3	444.6	655.4	185.2	271.1	32.9	-197.6	19.6	-217.2
4th quarter	1 409.2	608.3	181.3	92.0	527.7	1 582.4	431.8	662.5	181.3	273.3	33.6	-173.2	20.1	-193.3
1996														
1st quarter	1 446.9	637.5	187.3	90.4	531.8	1 623.4	441.8	686.9	185.5	273.9	35.4	-176.5	11.2	-187.6
2nd quarter	1 495.6	674.4	192.0	89.0	540.2	1 632.6	447.0	684.7	194.0	271.5	35.4	-137.0	15.0	-151.9
3rd quarter	1 503.4	675.6	190.9	89.7	547.2	1 633.5	442.9	689.2	193.0	273.7	34.7	-130.1	19.1	-149.2
4th quarter	1 550.5	692.6	192.3	111.3	554.2	1 654.2	449.4	705.8	189.2	275.1	34.8	-103.7	21.6	-125.3
1997														
1st quarter	1 572.7	724.9	194.3	88.5	565.0	1 659.2	451.3	709.3	191.1	273.8	33.7	-86.5	21.3	-107.7
2nd quarter	1 607.8	741.5	198.4	95.6	572.2	1 675.8	461.5	714.1	193.8	274.8	31.7	-68.0	25.8	-93.8
3rd quarter	1 645.5	759.6	209.8	95.9	580.2	1 679.2	457.5	717.1	196.7	277.5	30.4	-33.7	32.1	-65.8
4th quarter	1 676.0	781.3	209.5	94.7	590.5	1 701.0	457.2	729.4	205.6	278.5	30.3	-25.0	42.7	-67.8
1998														
1st quarter	1 708.0	805.8	205.1	96.0	601.1	1 688.4	444.2	727.9	205.2	280.8	30.3	19.6	45.2	-25.6
2nd quarter	1 733.8	825.0	203.4	96.5	608.9	1 700.8	456.5	726.3	206.4	280.0	31.6	33.0	53.4	-20.4
3rd quarter	1 768.9	844.8	208.3	98.6	617.2	1 703.2	449.9	729.7	209.9	279.7	34.0	65.7	60.7	5.0
4th quarter	1 788.2	864.1	200.3	98.5	625.3	1 731.1	461.8	738.5	219.6	273.3	37.9	57.0	72.6	-15.6
1999														
1st quarter	1 823.2	875.0	208.9	97.5	641.8	1 734.5	465.5	739.1	224.9	265.3	39.6	88.7	85.5	3.2
2nd quarter	1 847.1	891.2	211.4	98.2	646.3	1 734.2	461.6	743.2	222.2	264.2	42.8	112.9	91.0	21.9
3rd quarter	1 876.3	911.2	211.7	100.8	652.6	1 758.9	473.4	743.9	234.9	262.1	44.6	117.4	98.8	18.6
4th quarter	1 922.4	935.8	219.9	104.4	662.2	1 793.6	486.0	756.9	242.0	263.7	44.9	128.8	108.4	20.4
2000														
1st quarter	2 009.6	984.5	233.7	107.0	684.5	1 786.4	480.0	758.5	239.4	264.2	44.2	223.2	122.4	100.8
2nd quarter	2 022.9	997.2	230.5	109.5	685.7	1 825.7	501.3	774.6	242.2	264.1	43.5	197.2	111.0	86.2
3rd quarter	2 049.1	1 020.5	222.1	109.8	696.6	1 835.9	494.2	781.3	253.8	263.0	43.6	213.2	120.2	93.0
4th quarter	2 054.1	1 033.6	208.9	110.1	701.5	1 860.3	497.7	803.5	254.6	260.5	44.0	193.8	119.4	74.4
2001														
1st quarter	2 072.9	1 057.9	186.9	112.3	715.8	1 899.1	517.3	816.3	266.8	254.1	44.6	173.8	108.6	65.3
2nd quarter	2 072.3	1 059.8	183.2	112.2	717.1	1 927.8	524.9	832.2	281.9	243.1	45.6	144.4	99.6	44.9
3rd quarter	1 896.0	900.4	168.0	109.5	718.1	1 947.7	527.9	849.3	271.4	233.6	65.5	-51.7	88.5	-140.2
4th quarter	1 992.3	1 025.5	142.9	107.3	716.6	1 971.0	543.6	870.9	289.4	221.6	45.5	21.3	76.4	-55.1
2002														
1st quarter	1 884.7	874.8	170.5	108.4	731.1	2 030.5	566.3	916.9	292.3	208.5	46.6	-145.8	64.1	-209.9
2nd quarter	1 883.7	856.6	180.2	110.2	736.7	2 079.3	581.0	927.6	309.6	214.9	46.3	-195.6	49.7	-245.3
3rd quarter	1 864.1	831.3	181.1	112.4	739.3	2 074.6	589.8	934.1	305.0	205.8	39.9	-210.5	48.1	-258.6
4th quarter	1 860.8	820.5	187.5	111.5	741.4	2 117.4	608.9	948.5	315.8	202.1	42.1	-256.6	46.0	-302.6

Table 19-8. State and Local Government Current Receipts and Expenditures

(National Income and Product Accounts, calendar years, billions of dollars, quarterly data are at seasonally adjusted annual rates.)

Year and quarter	Current receipts						Current expenditures						Current surplus or deficit (-), national income and product accounts		
	Total	Personal tax and nontax receipts	Corporate profits tax accruals	Indirect business tax and nontax accruals	Contributions for social insurance	Federal grants-in-aid	Total	Consumption expenditures	Transfer payments to persons	Net interest paid	Less: dividends received by government	Subsidies less surplus of government enterprises	Total	Social insurance funds	Other
1946															
1st quarter	11.3	1.1	0.3	8.9	0.1	0.9	10.0	8.7	1.3	0.3	. . .	-0.4	1.3	. . .	. . .
2nd quarter	11.6	1.1	0.4	9.2	0.2	0.8	10.2	9.0	1.3	0.3	. . .	-0.4	1.4	. . .	. . .
3rd quarter	12.4	1.1	0.5	9.5	0.2	1.1	10.9	9.4	1.6	0.2	. . .	-0.4	1.5	. . .	. . .
4th quarter	12.9	1.1	0.6	9.7	0.2	1.3	11.4	10.0	1.6	0.2	. . .	-0.4	1.5	. . .	. . .
1947															
1st quarter	13.5	1.2	0.6	10.0	0.2	1.4	11.9	10.4	1.6	0.2	. . .	-0.4	1.5	. . .	. . .
2nd quarter	14.1	1.2	0.6	10.4	0.2	1.7	12.5	10.8	1.9	0.2	. . .	-0.4	1.6	. . .	. . .
3rd quarter	14.5	1.3	0.6	10.8	0.2	1.6	13.4	11.2	2.4	0.2	. . .	-0.4	1.1	. . .	. . .
4th quarter	15.0	1.3	0.6	11.3	0.2	1.6	13.7	11.6	2.3	0.2	. . .	-0.4	1.3	. . .	. . .
1948															
1st quarter	15.5	1.4	0.7	11.7	0.2	1.6	14.5	11.9	2.8	0.2	. . .	-0.4	1.0	. . .	. . .
2nd quarter	16.0	1.5	0.7	12.0	0.2	1.7	14.9	12.2	2.8	0.2	. . .	-0.3	1.1	. . .	. . .
3rd quarter	16.5	1.5	0.7	12.4	0.2	1.8	15.3	12.7	2.7	0.2	. . .	-0.3	1.2	. . .	. . .
4th quarter	16.8	1.5	0.7	12.6	0.2	1.9	15.4	13.1	2.4	0.2	. . .	-0.3	1.4	. . .	. . .
1949															
1st quarter	17.1	1.7	0.7	12.9	0.2	1.7	15.7	13.4	2.5	0.2	. . .	-0.4	1.4	. . .	. . .
2nd quarter	17.3	1.7	0.6	13.2	0.2	1.7	16.0	13.6	2.6	0.2	. . .	-0.4	1.4	. . .	. . .
3rd quarter	18.1	1.7	0.6	13.5	0.2	2.1	16.5	14.0	2.7	0.2	. . .	-0.4	1.6	. . .	. . .
4th quarter	18.2	1.7	0.6	13.8	0.2	1.9	16.9	14.2	2.9	0.2	. . .	-0.4	1.3	. . .	. . .
1950															
1st quarter	18.6	1.8	0.6	14.0	0.2	1.9	17.6	14.7	3.2	0.2	. . .	-0.4	0.9	. . .	. . .
2nd quarter	19.0	1.8	0.7	14.3	0.2	1.9	18.3	14.9	3.7	0.2	. . .	-0.4	0.7	. . .	. . .
3rd quarter	19.7	1.8	0.9	14.9	0.2	1.9	18.0	15.2	3.0	0.2	. . .	-0.4	1.7	. . .	. . .
4th quarter	19.9	1.9	0.9	15.0	0.2	1.9	18.2	15.5	2.9	0.2	. . .	-0.4	1.7	. . .	. . .
1951															
1st quarter	21.0	2.0	1.0	15.6	0.2	2.0	18.3	15.8	2.8	0.2	. . .	-0.5	2.6	. . .	. . .
2nd quarter	20.9	2.0	0.9	15.6	0.2	2.1	18.4	16.1	2.6	0.2	. . .	-0.5	2.4	. . .	. . .
3rd quarter	21.1	2.1	0.8	16.0	0.2	1.9	18.7	16.5	2.6	0.2	. . .	-0.5	2.3	. . .	. . .
4th quarter	21.7	2.1	0.8	16.4	0.2	2.1	19.1	16.8	2.6	0.2	. . .	-0.5	2.7	. . .	. . .
1952															
1st quarter	22.1	2.2	0.8	16.7	0.3	2.0	19.3	16.8	2.8	0.2	. . .	-0.5	2.8	. . .	. . .
2nd quarter	22.6	2.2	0.8	17.2	0.3	2.1	20.3	17.6	3.0	0.2	. . .	-0.5	2.3	. . .	. . .
3rd quarter	23.2	2.2	0.8	17.6	0.3	2.3	20.0	17.4	2.9	0.2	. . .	-0.5	3.2	. . .	. . .
4th quarter	23.8	2.3	0.9	18.1	0.3	2.3	20.4	17.8	2.9	0.2	. . .	-0.5	3.3	. . .	. . .
1953															
1st quarter	23.7	2.3	0.9	18.4	0.3	1.8	20.9	18.3	2.9	0.2	. . .	-0.5	2.8	. . .	. . .
2nd quarter	24.9	2.4	0.9	18.7	0.3	2.7	21.0	18.3	3.0	0.2	. . .	-0.5	3.9	. . .	. . .
3rd quarter	24.9	2.4	0.8	19.0	0.3	2.3	21.4	18.7	3.1	0.2	. . .	-0.6	3.4	. . .	. . .
4th quarter	25.0	2.4	0.7	19.3	0.3	2.3	21.4	18.8	2.9	0.3	. . .	-0.6	3.6	. . .	. . .
1954															
1st quarter	25.4	2.5	0.7	19.5	0.3	2.4	21.9	19.2	3.0	0.3	. . .	-0.6	3.5	. . .	. . .
2nd quarter	25.6	2.6	0.7	19.7	0.3	2.3	22.4	19.7	3.0	0.3	. . .	-0.7	3.2	. . .	. . .
3rd quarter	26.1	2.6	0.8	20.0	0.3	2.4	23.2	20.4	3.1	0.3	. . .	-0.7	3.0	. . .	. . .
4th quarter	26.5	2.6	0.8	20.4	0.3	2.3	23.5	20.7	3.1	0.4	. . .	-0.7	3.0	. . .	. . .
1955															
1st quarter	27.2	2.8	0.9	20.8	0.3	2.3	24.2	21.4	3.2	0.4	. . .	-0.8	3.0	. . .	. . .
2nd quarter	27.7	2.8	0.9	21.2	0.3	2.4	24.5	21.7	3.3	0.4	. . .	-0.8	3.2	. . .	. . .
3rd quarter	28.6	2.9	1.0	21.8	0.3	2.5	24.8	22.0	3.3	0.4	. . .	-0.9	3.7	. . .	. . .
4th quarter	29.1	2.9	1.0	22.4	0.3	2.4	25.3	22.5	3.2	0.4	. . .	-0.9	3.8	. . .	. . .
1956															
1st quarter	29.9	3.2	1.0	23.0	0.4	2.4	25.7	22.9	3.3	0.4	. . .	-0.9	4.2	. . .	. . .
2nd quarter	30.7	3.2	1.1	23.6	0.4	2.5	26.3	23.5	3.2	0.4	. . .	-0.9	4.4	. . .	. . .
3rd quarter	31.4	3.3	1.0	24.1	0.4	2.6	27.0	24.1	3.3	0.4	. . .	-0.9	4.4	. . .	. . .
4th quarter	32.0	3.3	1.1	24.6	0.4	2.7	27.7	24.7	3.4	0.5	. . .	-0.9	4.3	. . .	. . .
1957															
1st quarter	33.0	3.5	1.1	25.1	0.4	2.9	28.3	25.2	3.5	0.5	. . .	-0.9	4.7	. . .	. . .
2nd quarter	33.3	3.5	1.0	25.6	0.4	2.8	29.1	25.9	3.5	0.5	. . .	-0.9	4.2	. . .	. . .
3rd quarter	33.9	3.6	1.0	25.9	0.4	2.9	29.9	26.6	3.6	0.5	. . .	-0.9	4.0	. . .	. . .
4th quarter	34.1	3.6	0.9	26.1	0.4	3.1	30.6	27.2	3.7	0.5	. . .	-0.9	3.5	. . .	. . .
1958															
1st quarter	34.3	3.7	0.9	26.4	0.4	2.9	31.7	28.0	4.0	0.6	. . .	-0.9	2.6	0.0	2.5
2nd quarter	35.1	3.7	0.9	26.8	0.4	3.3	32.6	28.8	4.0	0.6	. . .	-0.9	2.5	0.0	2.4
3rd quarter	35.7	3.7	1.0	27.4	0.4	3.2	33.2	29.4	4.0	0.6	. . .	-0.9	2.5	0.0	2.5
4th quarter	37.4	3.7	1.2	28.1	0.4	4.0	33.9	29.9	4.1	0.7	. . .	-0.9	3.5	0.0	3.5
1959															
1st quarter	37.5	4.0	1.2	28.4	0.4	3.5	34.4	30.4	4.3	0.7	. . .	-1.0	3.0	0.0	3.0
2nd quarter	38.4	4.1	1.3	28.7	0.4	3.9	34.8	30.9	4.3	0.7	. . .	-1.1	3.6	0.0	3.5
3rd quarter	39.4	4.4	1.1	29.7	0.4	3.8	35.3	31.4	4.3	0.7	. . .	-1.2	4.2	0.0	4.1
4th quarter	40.2	4.4	1.1	30.4	0.4	3.8	35.9	31.9	4.4	0.8	. . .	-1.2	4.3	0.0	4.3

. . . = Not available.

Table 19-8. State and Local Government Current Receipts and Expenditures—*Continued*

(National Income and Product Accounts, calendar years, billions of dollars, quarterly data are at seasonally adjusted annual rates.)

Year and quarter	Current receipts						Current expenditures						Current surplus or deficit (-), national income and product accounts		
	Total	Personal tax and nontax receipts	Corporate profits tax accruals	Indirect business tax and nontax accruals	Contributions for social insurance	Federal grants-in-aid	Total	Consumption expenditures	Transfer payments to persons	Net interest paid	Less: dividends received by government	Subsidies less surplus of government enterprises	Total	Social insurance funds	Other
1960															
1st quarter	41.2	4.6	1.4	30.9	0.4	3.9	36.9	32.9	4.4	0.8	. . .	-1.2	4.2	0.0	4.2
2nd quarter	42.0	4.7	1.3	31.7	0.4	4.0	37.9	33.8	4.5	0.8	. . .	-1.3	4.2	0.0	4.1
3rd quarter	42.7	4.7	1.2	32.3	0.5	4.0	38.4	34.3	4.6	0.8	. . .	-1.3	4.3	0.0	4.3
4th quarter	43.5	4.8	1.1	33.0	0.5	4.2	39.1	34.9	4.7	0.8	. . .	-1.3	4.4	0.0	4.4
1961															
1st quarter	44.3	4.9	1.2	33.5	0.5	4.2	40.3	35.9	4.9	0.8	. . .	-1.3	4.0	0.0	4.0
2nd quarter	45.4	5.1	1.2	34.1	0.5	4.5	41.4	36.9	4.9	0.9	. . .	-1.4	4.0	0.0	4.0
3rd quarter	46.4	5.3	1.3	34.7	0.5	4.6	42.0	37.2	5.0	1.0	. . .	-1.3	4.5	0.0	4.5
4th quarter	47.5	5.4	1.4	35.5	0.5	4.7	42.8	37.9	5.1	1.1	. . .	-1.4	4.6	0.0	4.6
1962															
1st quarter	48.6	5.5	1.5	36.2	0.5	4.9	43.7	38.6	5.2	1.2	. . .	-1.3	4.9	0.0	4.9
2nd quarter	49.2	5.6	1.5	36.7	0.5	4.9	44.2	39.2	5.3	1.1	. . .	-1.4	5.0	0.0	5.0
3rd quarter	50.2	5.8	1.5	37.2	0.6	5.2	44.7	39.6	5.3	1.1	. . .	-1.4	5.5	0.0	5.5
4th quarter	50.9	5.8	1.5	37.7	0.6	5.2	45.4	40.3	5.5	1.1	. . .	-1.5	5.5	0.0	5.4
1963															
1st quarter	51.5	5.9	1.5	38.2	0.6	5.3	46.2	41.1	5.6	1.1	. . .	-1.6	5.3	0.0	5.3
2nd quarter	52.6	5.9	1.6	38.9	0.6	5.5	47.1	42.0	5.7	1.1	. . .	-1.6	5.5	0.0	5.4
3rd quarter	54.1	6.1	1.7	39.8	0.6	5.8	48.1	42.8	5.7	1.2	. . .	-1.6	6.0	0.0	6.0
4th quarter	55.2	6.3	1.7	40.5	0.7	6.1	49.3	43.8	5.8	1.3	. . .	-1.6	5.9	0.0	5.9
1964															
1st quarter	56.9	6.5	1.8	41.4	0.7	6.5	50.5	44.9	6.0	1.2	. . .	-1.6	6.3	0.0	6.3
2nd quarter	57.8	6.7	1.8	42.1	0.7	6.5	51.6	45.8	6.1	1.2	. . .	-1.6	6.3	0.0	6.2
3rd quarter	58.8	6.9	1.9	43.2	0.7	6.2	52.4	46.7	6.2	1.1	. . .	-1.7	6.5	0.1	6.4
4th quarter	59.9	7.1	1.8	43.7	0.7	6.6	53.5	47.8	6.4	1.1	. . .	-1.7	6.4	0.1	6.3
1965															
1st quarter	60.9	7.2	1.9	44.6	0.7	6.5	54.7	48.9	6.5	1.1	. . .	-1.7	6.2	0.1	6.1
2nd quarter	62.5	7.2	1.9	45.5	0.8	7.1	56.0	50.1	6.6	1.1	. . .	-1.7	6.5	0.1	6.4
3rd quarter	64.2	7.3	2.0	46.6	0.8	7.5	57.6	51.5	6.7	1.1	. . .	-1.6	6.5	0.1	6.5
4th quarter	65.6	7.5	2.1	47.7	0.8	7.6	58.9	52.7	6.8	1.0	. . .	-1.6	6.8	0.1	6.7
1966															
1st quarter	68.4	8.0	2.3	48.4	0.8	9.0	60.8	54.3	7.0	1.0	. . .	-1.6	7.7	0.1	7.6
2nd quarter	70.8	8.5	2.3	49.1	0.8	10.1	62.8	55.9	7.5	1.0	. . .	-1.6	8.0	0.1	7.9
3rd quarter	72.7	9.0	2.2	50.2	0.8	10.5	64.7	57.6	7.7	1.0	. . .	-1.6	8.0	0.1	7.8
4th quarter	74.2	9.4	2.2	51.1	0.8	10.7	66.9	59.4	8.2	0.9	. . .	-1.6	7.3	0.1	7.2
1967															
1st quarter	75.7	9.4	2.6	51.8	0.9	11.1	68.3	60.7	8.4	0.8	. . .	-1.6	7.4	0.1	7.3
2nd quarter	77.2	9.4	2.6	52.8	0.9	11.6	70.4	62.2	8.9	0.9	. . .	-1.6	6.8	0.1	6.7
3rd quarter	79.6	9.8	2.6	54.7	0.9	11.6	73.3	64.2	9.5	1.0	. . .	-1.4	6.4	0.1	6.2
4th quarter	83.0	10.2	2.7	56.4	0.9	12.7	75.8	66.0	10.1	1.2	. . .	-1.5	7.2	0.1	7.1
1968															
1st quarter	85.3	10.9	3.2	58.4	0.9	11.8	78.2	68.2	10.6	1.0	. . .	-1.6	7.1	0.1	6.9
2nd quarter	89.0	11.5	3.3	60.0	0.9	13.3	80.9	69.9	11.4	1.0	. . .	-1.5	8.1	0.1	8.0
3rd quarter	90.8	12.1	3.3	61.7	1.0	12.6	83.3	72.0	11.7	1.0	. . .	-1.5	7.4	0.1	7.2
4th quarter	93.2	12.6	3.4	63.1	1.0	13.2	86.0	74.3	12.1	1.0	. . .	-1.4	7.3	0.2	7.1
1969															
1st quarter	95.7	13.1	3.8	64.6	1.0	13.1	88.3	76.3	12.6	0.9	. . .	-1.4	7.4	0.1	7.2
2nd quarter	98.7	13.6	3.7	66.4	1.0	14.0	91.0	78.8	12.8	0.8	. . .	-1.4	7.7	0.2	7.6
3rd quarter	102.7	14.7	3.5	68.4	1.0	15.1	94.2	81.4	13.4	0.8	. . .	-1.4	8.4	0.2	8.3
4th quarter	105.8	15.0	3.4	70.2	1.1	16.1	97.6	84.2	14.0	0.8	. . .	-1.5	8.3	0.2	8.1
1970															
1st quarter	109.7	15.4	3.8	72.0	1.1	17.5	101.6	87.6	14.7	0.8	. . .	-1.5	8.1	0.2	7.9
2nd quarter	113.1	15.6	3.7	73.9	1.1	18.8	105.4	90.4	15.6	0.8	. . .	-1.5	7.7	0.2	7.5
3rd quarter	116.7	15.8	3.8	75.8	1.1	20.1	109.5	93.5	16.6	0.9	. . .	-1.5	7.1	0.2	6.9
4th quarter	118.9	15.9	3.6	77.5	1.1	20.8	113.5	96.3	17.5	1.1	. . .	-1.4	5.4	0.2	5.2
1971															
1st quarter	122.8	16.2	4.1	79.8	1.1	21.6	118.0	99.7	18.3	1.3	. . .	-1.4	4.8	0.2	4.6
2nd quarter	127.5	17.2	4.2	81.8	1.2	23.2	121.6	102.3	19.1	1.6	. . .	-1.3	5.9	0.2	5.7
3rd quarter	131.1	17.7	4.4	84.5	1.2	23.5	124.7	104.8	19.6	1.8	. . .	-1.3	6.5	0.2	6.2
4th quarter	135.8	19.0	4.5	86.4	1.2	24.7	127.3	106.7	20.3	2.0	. . .	-1.3	8.5	0.2	8.2
1972															
1st quarter	141.3	21.3	5.0	88.1	1.3	25.7	132.4	109.8	21.2	2.3	. . .	-1.4	8.9	0.2	8.7
2nd quarter	153.4	22.8	5.0	90.3	1.3	33.9	134.8	112.2	21.6	2.4	. . .	-1.5	18.6	0.3	18.3
3rd quarter	148.6	23.1	5.2	92.2	1.3	26.8	138.5	115.3	22.5	2.4	. . .	-1.6	10.1	0.3	9.9
4th quarter	165.8	23.8	5.7	94.4	1.4	40.4	141.1	118.0	22.5	2.2	. . .	-1.6	24.7	0.3	24.4
1973															
1st quarter	163.9	23.8	6.0	97.0	1.4	35.6	145.1	121.5	23.2	1.9	0.0	-1.5	18.8	0.3	18.5
2nd quarter	164.8	24.2	6.1	98.4	1.5	34.7	149.2	125.1	24.0	1.5	0.0	-1.4	15.7	0.3	15.4
3rd quarter	167.1	25.0	5.9	100.8	1.5	33.9	152.5	128.6	24.2	1.2	0.0	-1.4	14.6	0.3	14.3
4th quarter	170.4	25.9	6.1	101.9	1.6	34.9	156.7	132.3	25.0	0.8	0.0	-1.3	13.7	0.3	13.3
1974															
1st quarter	171.2	25.3	6.3	103.3	1.6	34.6	159.5	136.9	23.4	0.4	0.0	-1.1	11.7	0.4	11.3
2nd quarter	176.3	26.2	6.6	106.3	1.6	35.4	165.7	141.8	24.7	0.1	0.0	-0.9	10.6	0.4	10.2
3rd quarter	182.4	27.4	7.3	109.2	1.7	36.8	172.4	147.0	25.9	0.1	0.0	-0.6	10.0	0.4	9.6
4th quarter	184.3	27.9	6.5	110.0	1.7	38.2	179.4	152.4	27.1	0.3	0.0	-0.4	4.9	0.4	4.5

. . . = Not available.

Table 19-8. State and Local Government Current Receipts and Expenditures—*Continued*

(National Income and Product Accounts, calendar years, billions of dollars, quarterly data are at seasonally adjusted annual rates.)

Year and quarter	Current receipts						Current expenditures						Current surplus or deficit (-), national income and product accounts		
	Total	Personal tax and nontax receipts	Corporate profits tax accruals	Indirect business tax and nontax accruals	Contributions for social insurance	Federal grants-in-aid	Total	Consumption expenditures	Transfer payments to persons	Net interest paid	Less: dividends received by government	Subsidies less surplus of government enterprises	Total	Social insurance funds	Other
1975															
1st quarter	188.2	28.1	6.1	111.5	1.8	40.7	187.8	158.2	29.2	0.6	0.0	-0.2	0.5	0.4	0.0
2nd quarter	197.5	29.0	6.6	114.2	1.8	45.8	195.0	163.8	30.5	1.0	0.0	-0.2	2.5	0.5	2.0
3rd quarter	203.9	29.8	8.2	117.5	1.9	46.5	200.4	168.1	31.0	1.5	0.0	-0.2	3.6	0.5	3.1
4th quarter	208.8	30.9	8.5	119.9	2.0	47.5	205.6	171.4	32.6	2.0	0.0	-0.4	3.2	0.5	2.7
1976															
1st quarter	216.3	32.4	9.7	123.6	2.0	48.7	210.8	175.0	33.4	2.7	0.0	-0.3	5.6	0.5	5.0
2nd quarter	221.1	33.6	9.6	126.3	2.1	49.5	214.7	178.4	33.4	3.1	0.0	-0.2	6.5	0.6	5.9
3rd quarter	225.9	34.7	9.7	128.9	2.2	50.4	219.6	181.6	34.7	3.4	0.0	-0.1	6.3	0.6	5.7
4th quarter	234.7	35.9	9.6	132.5	2.3	54.4	223.7	185.3	35.0	3.5	0.0	-0.1	11.0	0.7	10.3
1977															
1st quarter	238.1	36.9	10.5	135.7	2.5	52.5	228.6	189.7	35.7	3.4	0.0	-0.1	9.5	0.8	8.7
2nd quarter	246.1	38.1	11.4	138.4	2.7	55.5	234.4	193.9	37.5	3.2	0.0	-0.1	11.7	0.9	10.8
3rd quarter	254.6	39.4	11.9	141.3	2.9	59.1	238.9	198.8	37.3	2.9	0.0	-0.1	15.7	1.1	14.7
4th quarter	259.2	40.9	11.9	144.1	3.0	59.2	243.6	203.6	37.7	2.5	0.0	-0.1	15.6	1.2	14.4
1978															
1st quarter	265.5	42.3	10.5	146.0	3.2	63.5	248.8	208.0	39.2	1.9	0.1	-0.2	16.8	1.3	15.4
2nd quarter	276.7	44.0	12.4	150.9	3.3	66.1	253.7	211.7	41.0	1.2	0.1	-0.1	23.0	1.4	21.5
3rd quarter	273.9	44.9	12.5	147.6	3.5	65.5	257.8	216.4	41.3	0.5	0.1	0.0	16.1	1.5	14.6
4th quarter	281.1	46.2	13.0	151.2	3.6	67.1	262.1	221.0	41.7	-0.2	0.1	0.1	19.0	1.7	17.3
1979															
1st quarter	282.4	46.2	13.7	154.3	3.8	64.4	268.4	227.1	42.4	-1.0	0.1	0.3	14.0	1.7	12.3
2nd quarter	285.6	46.4	13.8	156.5	3.9	65.0	273.9	230.8	43.5	-1.8	0.1	0.6	11.7	1.8	9.9
3rd quarter	294.9	49.9	13.6	159.9	3.9	67.6	280.8	238.1	44.5	-2.6	0.1	0.8	14.1	1.8	12.3
4th quarter	300.5	51.3	13.2	163.7	4.0	68.4	288.2	244.1	46.9	-3.4	0.1	0.9	12.3	1.8	10.5
1980															
1st quarter	307.3	51.3	16.1	167.0	3.6	69.3	297.1	251.2	49.1	-4.3	0.1	1.0	10.2	1.4	8.8
2nd quarter	308.3	52.9	12.7	168.9	2.9	70.8	302.9	257.8	49.0	-5.0	0.1	1.3	5.4	0.7	4.7
3rd quarter	319.7	54.5	14.0	174.0	3.8	73.4	312.0	263.7	52.4	-5.7	0.1	1.7	7.7	1.5	6.2
4th quarter	331.2	57.0	15.1	179.4	4.0	75.8	319.3	269.2	54.3	-6.4	0.1	2.2	11.9	1.6	10.3
1981															
1st quarter	339.5	58.2	16.9	186.3	3.7	74.4	327.9	276.7	55.6	-6.9	0.1	2.7	11.5	1.3	10.2
2nd quarter	343.0	59.6	15.1	189.9	3.8	74.5	335.0	282.2	57.4	-7.4	0.1	3.0	8.0	1.3	6.7
3rd quarter	347.8	61.7	15.7	194.7	3.9	71.9	340.0	287.2	57.7	-7.7	0.1	3.0	7.7	1.3	6.4
4th quarter	347.5	63.1	14.1	197.2	4.0	69.2	344.7	292.3	57.7	-7.8	0.1	2.6	2.9	1.3	1.6
1982															
1st quarter	351.3	63.8	14.2	200.4	4.0	68.8	352.3	298.9	59.0	-7.9	0.1	2.4	-1.0	1.3	-2.3
2nd quarter	358.3	64.8	14.3	204.9	4.0	70.4	360.0	304.7	61.0	-7.7	0.2	2.2	-1.7	1.2	-3.0
3rd quarter	363.3	67.3	14.4	208.6	4.1	69.0	365.9	309.2	62.1	-7.2	0.2	1.9	-2.6	1.2	-3.8
4th quarter	368.1	67.9	13.3	213.1	4.1	69.8	371.9	314.3	62.6	-6.5	0.2	1.7	-3.8	1.2	-5.0
1983															
1st quarter	372.9	68.5	12.6	217.1	4.0	70.6	380.7	319.4	65.8	-5.5	0.2	1.2	-7.8	1.2	-9.0
2nd quarter	387.8	71.8	15.6	223.8	4.1	72.7	385.0	323.0	66.3	-5.0	0.2	0.8	2.9	1.2	1.7
3rd quarter	399.4	75.9	17.5	230.1	4.1	71.8	389.5	327.0	67.2	-4.9	0.2	0.4	9.9	1.2	8.7
4th quarter	408.4	78.7	17.9	236.3	4.3	71.2	394.0	330.8	68.3	-5.2	0.2	0.2	14.4	1.3	13.1
1984															
1st quarter	425.1	81.6	20.2	243.4	4.5	75.4	402.5	339.0	69.9	-5.9	0.2	-0.3	22.6	1.4	21.2
2nd quarter	435.6	84.4	19.8	249.3	4.7	77.4	409.1	345.8	70.6	-6.5	0.2	-0.8	26.6	1.5	25.1
3rd quarter	436.9	85.6	17.5	253.9	4.8	75.1	416.0	353.2	71.3	-7.0	0.2	-1.3	20.9	1.5	19.5
4th quarter	448.1	87.3	17.7	259.6	4.8	78.8	422.9	359.9	72.8	-7.5	0.2	-2.1	25.3	1.4	23.9
1985															
1st quarter	456.5	88.7	19.9	264.1	4.7	79.1	431.8	367.6	74.9	-8.0	0.2	-2.5	24.7	1.3	23.4
2nd quarter	464.7	90.7	19.5	269.7	4.8	80.0	440.7	375.4	76.4	-8.1	0.2	-2.8	24.0	1.2	22.7
3rd quarter	473.7	91.6	21.0	275.1	4.9	81.2	452.2	385.2	78.1	-7.9	0.2	-3.1	21.5	1.3	20.2
4th quarter	482.0	94.2	20.6	278.9	5.2	83.1	463.1	393.8	79.8	-7.5	0.2	-3.0	18.9	1.5	17.5
1986															
1st quarter	499.3	95.4	21.5	292.1	5.5	84.8	472.7	400.7	81.6	-6.7	0.2	-2.7	26.6	1.6	25.0
2nd quarter	501.1	96.3	22.0	288.1	5.8	89.0	480.7	405.7	83.7	-5.9	0.1	-2.6	20.4	1.8	18.6
3rd quarter	513.2	99.0	22.4	294.0	6.1	91.8	490.6	412.9	85.3	-5.1	0.1	-2.4	22.6	2.0	20.7
4th quarter	518.0	103.5	24.8	298.4	6.4	84.9	504.6	424.1	87.0	-4.2	0.2	-2.2	13.4	2.1	11.3
1987															
1st quarter	517.0	104.1	21.0	303.1	6.7	82.1	511.4	429.0	88.4	-3.5	0.2	-2.4	5.7	2.1	3.6
2nd quarter	539.3	113.3	23.7	309.5	7.0	85.8	520.3	436.0	90.0	-3.0	0.2	-2.5	19.0	2.1	16.8
3rd quarter	539.4	106.1	25.4	316.7	7.3	83.9	527.4	441.5	91.6	-2.8	0.2	-2.8	12.0	2.2	9.8
4th quarter	548.1	110.5	25.5	320.5	7.7	83.8	536.0	449.6	93.2	-3.0	0.2	-3.6	12.1	2.3	9.8
1988															
1st quarter	556.8	110.3	23.9	325.1	8.0	89.5	545.7	457.2	95.4	-2.8	0.2	-3.8	11.1	2.4	8.7
2nd quarter	569.0	114.1	25.8	330.7	8.3	90.0	554.3	464.7	97.4	-3.4	0.2	-4.2	14.6	2.5	12.1
3rd quarter	578.5	114.5	26.6	335.7	8.5	93.1	562.1	471.5	99.6	-4.1	0.2	-4.7	16.4	2.6	13.8
4th quarter	590.4	116.9	27.8	343.3	8.7	93.8	570.2	478.5	102.0	-4.9	0.2	-5.2	20.2	2.6	17.7

Table 19-8. State and Local Government Current Receipts and Expenditures—*Continued*

(National Income and Product Accounts, calendar years, billions of dollars, quarterly data are at seasonally adjusted annual rates.)

Year and quarter	Current receipts						Current expenditures						Current surplus or deficit (-), national income and product accounts		
	Total	Personal tax and nontax receipts	Corporate profits tax accruals	Indirect business tax and nontax accruals	Contributions for social insurance	Federal grants-in-aid	Total	Consumption expenditures	Transfer payments to persons	Net interest paid	Less: dividends received by government	Subsidies less surplus of government enterprises	Total	Social insurance funds	Other
1989															
1st quarter	602.5	124.4	26.7	347.7	8.8	94.9	582.1	489.8	104.4	-6.0	0.2	-5.9	20.5	2.5	17.9
2nd quarter	614.1	129.1	24.7	355.9	8.9	95.6	593.3	498.8	107.4	-6.5	0.2	-6.3	20.8	2.4	18.4
3rd quarter	625.9	129.8	22.6	363.0	9.0	101.4	604.2	506.4	111.1	-6.7	0.2	-6.4	21.7	2.3	19.4
4th quarter	633.1	132.3	23.0	367.2	9.3	101.4	618.8	516.9	114.9	-7.0	0.2	-5.8	14.4	2.1	12.2
1990															
1st quarter	643.3	131.2	21.5	374.6	9.5	106.5	636.1	530.6	118.9	-6.8	0.2	-6.4	7.2	2.0	5.2
2nd quarter	654.3	134.1	22.7	377.4	9.9	110.3	650.5	539.5	124.3	-6.9	0.2	-6.3	3.9	2.0	1.9
3rd quarter	672.8	138.8	23.6	387.5	10.2	112.6	668.3	550.4	130.4	-6.2	0.2	-6.2	4.5	2.0	2.6
4th quarter	683.2	140.1	22.2	394.0	10.5	116.3	688.3	562.5	137.6	-5.3	0.2	-6.3	-5.0	2.0	-7.0
1991															
1st quarter	688.6	139.7	22.7	392.4	11.0	122.8	704.2	568.4	146.6	-4.1	0.2	-6.5	-15.6	2.1	-17.7
2nd quarter	705.7	143.5	23.4	399.4	11.4	128.1	716.3	572.7	153.2	-2.9	0.2	-6.6	-10.6	2.3	-12.9
3rd quarter	725.7	145.8	24.2	409.0	11.8	134.9	730.4	578.6	160.1	-1.5	0.2	-6.6	-4.7	2.4	-7.1
4th quarter	743.8	152.2	24.3	414.4	12.2	140.6	744.1	584.5	166.7	-0.1	0.2	-6.8	-0.3	2.6	-2.9
1992															
1st quarter	751.9	151.6	24.4	420.0	12.6	143.2	757.0	590.8	172.3	1.1	0.2	-6.9	-5.1	2.8	-7.9
2nd quarter	763.2	155.2	25.5	423.3	13.0	146.2	771.7	598.8	177.7	2.4	0.2	-7.0	-8.5	3.0	-11.5
3rd quarter	776.9	156.6	21.8	432.8	13.3	152.4	785.4	605.4	184.0	3.4	0.2	-7.3	-8.5	3.3	-11.8
4th quarter	796.9	162.1	25.8	440.8	13.6	154.6	794.6	611.6	186.5	4.3	0.2	-7.6	2.3	3.5	-1.2
1993															
1st quarter	794.5	158.1	24.3	442.8	13.8	155.5	806.9	619.8	190.4	5.1	0.2	-8.2	-12.4	3.8	-16.3
2nd quarter	814.0	163.9	26.9	451.3	14.1	157.8	818.0	627.1	193.9	5.6	0.2	-8.4	-4.0	4.1	-8.1
3rd quarter	828.2	166.0	26.4	458.2	14.2	163.4	825.8	631.6	197.3	5.9	0.2	-8.8	2.4	4.3	-1.9
4th quarter	856.0	170.9	30.0	467.0	14.4	173.7	836.1	639.5	199.9	5.7	0.2	-8.9	19.9	4.5	15.4
1994															
1st quarter	852.0	168.6	26.5	470.9	14.6	171.3	851.4	650.0	203.2	5.7	0.2	-7.3	0.6	4.6	-4.0
2nd quarter	867.0	174.0	29.4	477.7	14.6	171.2	860.1	658.6	205.3	5.1	0.2	-8.7	6.9	4.7	2.2
3rd quarter	879.8	176.3	31.3	482.6	14.5	175.1	870.6	667.6	208.1	3.9	0.2	-8.8	9.2	4.6	4.6
4th quarter	896.6	180.1	32.6	489.0	14.4	180.4	878.7	674.2	210.9	2.9	0.2	-9.1	17.8	4.5	13.3
1995															
1st quarter	906.8	182.4	30.5	494.7	14.0	185.1	890.8	685.0	214.1	1.3	0.2	-9.4	15.9	4.3	11.6
2nd quarter	914.3	184.2	31.2	498.8	13.8	186.3	899.7	692.6	216.7	0.6	0.2	-9.9	14.6	4.1	10.4
3rd quarter	923.4	188.3	32.9	503.5	13.5	185.2	905.8	697.3	219.1	0.1	0.3	-10.4	17.5	3.9	13.7
4th quarter	927.0	191.3	32.1	509.3	13.2	181.3	913.8	703.8	221.3	0.0	0.3	-11.1	13.3	3.5	9.7
1996															
1st quarter	940.4	193.2	32.4	516.4	12.9	185.5	923.4	712.5	222.6	0.8	0.3	-12.1	17.0	3.2	13.8
2nd quarter	962.2	198.1	33.3	524.2	12.6	194.0	935.0	723.0	223.9	1.0	0.3	-12.6	27.2	2.9	24.3
3rd quarter	966.1	201.7	33.1	526.0	12.3	193.0	943.8	730.6	225.3	1.0	0.3	-12.7	22.3	2.6	19.6
4th quarter	972.9	205.5	33.3	533.0	11.9	189.2	953.6	740.0	225.6	0.8	0.3	-12.5	19.3	2.2	17.1
1997															
1st quarter	988.9	210.2	32.8	543.5	11.4	191.1	965.4	751.9	226.6	-0.2	0.3	-12.5	23.5	1.6	21.9
2nd quarter	999.7	213.4	33.4	548.2	11.0	193.8	973.1	760.0	227.0	-1.0	0.3	-12.5	26.6	1.2	25.4
3rd quarter	1 020.1	219.2	35.4	558.2	10.6	196.7	984.6	770.7	227.9	-1.1	0.3	-12.5	35.5	0.8	34.7
4th quarter	1 036.6	225.0	35.2	560.3	10.4	205.6	998.3	783.2	228.7	-1.2	0.4	-12.1	38.3	0.6	37.6
1998															
1st quarter	1 048.8	228.3	34.8	570.2	10.3	205.2	1 012.1	792.3	230.9	-0.2	0.4	-10.6	36.7	0.7	36.0
2nd quarter	1 058.5	230.5	34.5	577.0	10.2	206.4	1 026.5	803.2	233.3	0.4	0.4	-10.0	32.0	0.7	31.3
3rd quarter	1 077.0	238.9	35.3	582.8	10.1	209.9	1 041.4	814.1	236.5	0.6	0.4	-9.5	35.6	0.6	34.9
4th quarter	1 113.3	244.4	33.8	605.4	10.0	219.6	1 054.9	823.6	240.4	0.7	0.4	-9.5	58.4	0.6	57.9
1999															
1st quarter	1 119.9	250.5	34.3	600.3	9.9	224.9	1 071.6	836.3	245.8	0.1	0.4	-10.3	48.4	0.8	47.5
2nd quarter	1 125.9	250.8	34.6	608.5	9.8	222.2	1 094.6	855.6	250.4	-0.4	0.4	-10.5	31.3	1.0	30.3
3rd quarter	1 151.4	256.0	34.6	616.3	9.6	234.9	1 117.6	874.4	255.3	-1.1	0.4	-10.6	33.8	0.9	32.9
4th quarter	1 179.1	265.9	35.8	625.8	9.5	242.0	1 139.5	892.3	259.5	-1.5	0.4	-10.5	39.6	0.8	38.8
2000															
1st quarter	1 195.9	271.8	37.1	638.1	9.4	239.4	1 163.2	914.0	262.0	-2.4	0.4	-9.9	32.7	0.5	32.2
2nd quarter	1 204.7	275.7	36.8	640.8	9.2	242.2	1 184.5	930.0	267.4	-2.9	0.4	-9.6	20.2	0.2	20.0
3rd quarter	1 225.4	279.1	35.3	648.0	9.1	253.8	1 206.2	945.4	273.8	-3.0	0.4	-9.6	19.2	-0.1	19.2
4th quarter	1 230.8	283.2	33.0	650.9	9.2	254.6	1 231.0	962.2	282.1	-3.1	0.4	-9.8	-0.2	-0.1	-0.1
2001															
1st quarter	1 247.3	282.6	30.4	658.3	9.2	266.8	1 263.8	976.2	292.4	-2.4	0.4	-1.9	-16.5	-0.1	-16.4
2nd quarter	1 261.1	276.3	29.9	663.8	9.2	281.9	1 293.4	990.6	301.5	-2.2	0.4	4.1	-32.3	-0.1	-32.2
3rd quarter	1 253.6	281.6	28.2	663.2	9.3	271.4	1 299.8	1 000.1	308.5	-2.0	0.4	-6.4	-46.2	-0.1	-46.1
4th quarter	1 283.2	284.3	27.7	672.5	9.2	289.4	1 313.3	1 008.2	315.4	-1.8	0.4	-8.1	-30.2	-0.2	-30.0
2002															
1st quarter	1 273.3	262.0	32.0	677.8	9.3	292.3	1 329.1	1 017.7	323.4	-1.9	0.4	-9.6	-55.8	-0.2	-55.6
2nd quarter	1 302.5	265.3	33.5	684.9	9.4	309.6	1 347.6	1 030.6	330.7	-2.0	0.5	-11.2	-45.1	-0.1	-44.9
3rd quarter	1 310.3	267.7	33.7	694.5	9.4	305.0	1 365.0	1 039.6	338.7	-2.0	0.5	-10.8	-54.7	-0.1	-54.6
4th quarter	1 331.6	269.6	34.9	701.8	9.5	315.8	1 384.0	1 050.1	349.5	-1.9	0.5	-13.2	-52.4	-0.1	-52.3

Table 19-9. U.S. International Transactions

(Millions of dollars, seasonally adjusted.)

Year and quarter	Exports of goods, services, and income				Imports of goods, services, and income [1]				Unilateral current transfers, net [2]	U.S.-owned assets abroad, net [3]					
										Total	U.S. official reserve assets, net	U.S. government assets other than official reserve assets, net	U.S. private assets, net		
	Total	Goods	Services	Income receipts	Total	Goods	Services	Income payments					Total	Direct investment	Foreign securities
1960															
1st quarter	7 355	4 685	1 543	1 127	-6 050	-3 812	-1 907	-331	-955	-1 066	159	-237	-988	-664	-266
2nd quarter	7 762	4 916	1 715	1 131	-6 078	-3 858	-1 906	-314	-1 154	-1 156	175	-339	-992	-586	-166
3rd quarter	7 650	5 031	1 453	1 166	-5 925	-3 648	-1 970	-307	-889	-956	740	-160	-1 536	-754	-111
4th quarter	7 791	5 018	1 580	1 193	-5 619	-3 440	-1 892	-287	-1 064	-923	1 071	-365	-1 629	-936	-120
1961															
1st quarter	7 827	5 095	1 481	1 251	-5 599	-3 394	-1 912	-293	-989	-1 320	371	-381	-1 310	-774	-135
2nd quarter	7 773	4 806	1 758	1 209	-5 659	-3 438	-1 922	-299	-1 208	-1 029	-320	471	-1 180	-551	-246
3rd quarter	7 757	5 038	1 468	1 251	-6 026	-3 809	-1 900	-317	-887	-1 928	-212	-486	-1 230	-737	-124
4th quarter	8 047	5 169	1 590	1 288	-6 171	-3 896	-1 939	-336	-1 043	-1 260	768	-513	-1 515	-592	-257
1962															
1st quarter	8 015	5 077	1 666	1 272	-6 256	-3 966	-1 971	-319	-1 113	-1 301	427	-406	-1 322	-545	-196
2nd quarter	8 719	5 336	2 004	1 379	-6 402	-4 080	-1 992	-330	-1 272	-1 461	-163	-381	-917	-716	-308
3rd quarter	8 295	5 331	1 567	1 397	-6 455	-4 116	-2 005	-334	-879	-279	881	8	-1 168	-811	-87
4th quarter	8 315	5 037	1 709	1 569	-6 567	-4 098	-2 126	-343	-1 016	-1 134	390	-306	-1 218	-779	-378
1963															
1st quarter	8 428	5 063	1 849	1 516	-6 478	-4 064	-2 057	-357	-1 107	-1 922	32	-482	-1 472	-980	-522
2nd quarter	9 244	5 599	2 150	1 495	-6 674	-4 226	-2 066	-382	-1 371	-2 631	124	-654	-2 101	-874	-536
3rd quarter	8 832	5 671	1 620	1 541	-6 893	-4 372	-2 122	-399	-918	-887	227	-86	-1 028	-721	-100
4th quarter	9 275	5 939	1 731	1 605	-6 926	-4 386	-2 118	-422	-999	-1 831	-5	-440	-1 386	-908	53
1964															
1st quarter	9 885	6 242	1 922	1 721	-6 982	-4 416	-2 140	-426	-993	-2 086	-51	-288	-1 747	-822	20
2nd quarter	9 975	6 199	2 088	1 688	-7 179	-4 598	-2 142	-439	-1 269	-2 018	303	-386	-1 935	-970	-206
3rd quarter	10 009	6 423	1 851	1 735	-7 349	-4 756	-2 153	-440	-935	-2 255	70	-414	-1 911	-1 018	2
4th quarter	10 299	6 637	1 982	1 680	-7 594	-4 930	-2 186	-478	-1 043	-3 200	-151	-592	-2 457	-949	-494
1965															
1st quarter	9 689	5 768	2 047	1 874	-7 395	-4 711	-2 187	-497	-1 037	-1 576	843	-374	-2 045	-1 606	-198
2nd quarter	11 263	6 876	2 448	1 939	-8 208	-5 428	-2 269	-511	-1 478	-1 270	69	-536	-803	-1 250	-147
3rd quarter	10 625	6 643	2 120	1 862	-8 307	-5 516	-2 263	-528	-1 013	-1 454	42	-254	-1 242	-1 030	-209
4th quarter	11 149	7 174	2 212	1 763	-8 802	-5 855	-2 393	-554	-1 058	-1 416	271	-441	-1 246	-1 125	-205
1966															
1st quarter	11 190	7 242	2 124	1 824	-9 068	-6 012	-2 483	-573	-1 140	-1 465	424	-321	-1 568	-1 115	-437
2nd quarter	11 726	7 169	2 705	1 852	-9 390	-6 195	-2 601	-594	-1 547	-1 967	68	-504	-1 531	-1 373	-115
3rd quarter	11 470	7 290	2 301	1 879	-9 912	-6 576	-2 693	-643	-1 073	-1 681	83	-339	-1 425	-1 314	-115
4th quarter	12 068	7 609	2 487	1 972	-10 098	-6 710	-2 717	-671	-1 194	-2 208	-5	-380	-1 823	-1 616	-53
1967															
1st quarter	12 439	7 751	2 731	1 957	-10 248	-6 708	-2 866	-674	-1 315	-1 203	1 027	-643	-1 587	-1 186	-265
2nd quarter	12 275	7 693	2 666	1 916	-10 136	-6 475	-2 986	-675	-1 472	-2 339	-419	-543	-1 377	-964	-261
3rd quarter	12 134	7 530	2 540	2 064	-10 262	-6 526	-3 059	-677	-1 309	-3 155	-375	-551	-2 229	-1 359	-419
4th quarter	12 506	7 692	2 731	2 083	-10 833	-7 157	-2 955	-721	-1 199	-3 060	-180	-685	-2 195	-1 297	-363
1968															
1st quarter	13 016	7 998	2 816	2 202	-11 571	-7 796	-2 997	-778	-1 249	-1 299	912	-706	-1 505	-981	-449
2nd quarter	13 577	8 324	2 936	2 317	-11 885	-8 051	-2 990	-844	-1 363	-2 427	-135	-632	-1 660	-1 172	-283
3rd quarter	14 195	8 745	3 039	2 411	-12 611	-8 612	-3 129	-870	-1 445	-3 447	-572	-568	-2 307	-1 573	-318
4th quarter	14 126	8 559	3 129	2 438	-12 604	-8 532	-3 185	-887	-1 573	-3 803	-1 075	-368	-2 360	-1 568	-519
1969															
1st quarter	12 921	7 468	2 884	2 569	-11 622	-7 444	-3 174	-1 004	-1 177	-2 595	-45	-406	-2 144	-1 556	-366
2nd quarter	15 492	9 536	3 283	2 673	-13 978	-9 527	-3 303	-1 148	-1 645	-3 428	-298	-632	-2 498	-1 663	-498
3rd quarter	15 439	9 400	3 245	2 794	-14 072	-9 380	-3 368	-1 324	-1 319	-3 361	-685	-703	-1 973	-1 548	-546
4th quarter	16 279	10 010	3 394	2 875	-14 329	-9 456	-3 481	-1 392	-1 593	-2 199	-151	-459	-1 589	-1 192	-139
1970															
1st quarter	16 461	10 258	3 235	2 968	-14 458	-9 587	-3 449	-1 422	-1 383	-2 611	481	-399	-2 693	-1 958	-306
2nd quarter	17 419	10 744	3 645	3 030	-14 861	-9 766	-3 690	-1 405	-1 586	-1 725	1 025	-348	-2 402	-2 144	80
3rd quarter	17 267	10 665	3 625	2 977	-15 141	-10 049	-3 715	-1 377	-1 611	-2 146	802	-423	-2 525	-1 718	-517
4th quarter	17 241	10 802	3 666	2 773	-15 443	-10 464	-3 668	-1 311	-1 576	-1 989	1 040	-419	-2 610	-1 771	-333
1971															
1st quarter	17 980	10 920	4 048	3 012	-15 551	-10 600	-3 724	-1 227	-1 746	-2 747	868	-573	-3 042	-2 033	-408
2nd quarter	18 163	10 878	4 087	3 198	-16 764	-11 614	-3 867	-1 283	-1 808	-2 534	839	-567	-2 806	-1 949	-368
3rd quarter	18 676	11 548	3 972	3 156	-17 460	-12 171	-3 861	-1 428	-1 752	-3 390	1 377	-387	-4 380	-2 308	-346
4th quarter	17 564	9 973	4 251	3 340	-16 639	-11 194	-3 948	-1 497	-2 098	-3 084	-18	-355	-2 711	-1 327	9
1972															
1st quarter	19 757	11 833	4 473	3 451	-19 153	-13 501	-4 173	-1 479	-2 297	-3 585	620	-212	-3 993	-2 187	-476
2nd quarter	19 427	11 618	4 233	3 576	-19 105	-13 254	-4 228	-1 623	-2 011	-2 125	-60	-271	-1 794	-1 481	-318
3rd quarter	20 788	12 351	4 634	3 803	-19 767	-14 022	-4 095	-1 650	-2 306	-3 952	96	-518	-3 530	-2 435	203
4th quarter	22 015	13 579	4 503	3 933	-21 212	-15 020	-4 371	-1 821	-1 933	-4 125	50	-566	-3 609	-1 644	-28
1973															
1st quarter	24 681	15 474	4 579	4 628	-23 000	-16 285	-4 613	-2 102	-1 536	-7 886	213	-572	-7 527	-3 785	55
2nd quarter	27 127	17 112	4 828	5 187	-24 301	-17 168	-4 741	-2 392	-1 953	-4 154	11	-423	-3 742	-2 691	-86
3rd quarter	29 329	18 271	5 145	5 913	-24 841	-17 683	-4 640	-2 518	-1 751	-3 189	-23	-608	-2 558	-2 159	-196
4th quarter	31 912	20 553	5 279	6 080	-26 855	-19 363	-4 849	-2 643	-1 674	-7 646	-43	-1 042	-6 561	-2 718	-445
1974															
1st quarter	34 698	22 614	5 189	6 895	-29 643	-21 952	-4 985	-2 706	-3 443	-5 914	-246	1 389	-7 057	900	-600
2nd quarter	37 295	24 500	5 691	7 104	-34 710	-26 346	-5 359	-3 005	-2 475	-10 318	-358	267	-10 227	-1 790	-272
3rd quarter	37 385	24 629	5 633	7 123	-36 004	-27 368	-5 360	-3 276	-1 676	-7 694	-1 002	-354	-6 338	-4 385	-282
4th quarter	39 105	26 563	6 078	6 464	-36 918	-28 145	-5 675	-3 098	-1 656	-10 818	139	-938	-10 019	-3 776	-699

[1] A minus sign indicates imports of goods or services or income payments.
[2] A minus sign indicates net unilateral transfers to foreigners.
[3] A minus sign indicates financial outflows or increases in U.S. official assets.

Table 19-9. U.S. International Transactions—*Continued*

(Millions of dollars, seasonally adjusted.)

Year and quarter	U.S. private assets, net—Continued / U.S. claims — On unaffiliated foreigners reported by U.S. nonbanking concerns	Reported by U.S. banks, not included elsewhere	Total	Foreign official assets in the United States, net	Total	Direct investment	U.S. Treasury securities and U.S. currency flows	U.S. securities other than U.S. Treasury securities	To unaffiliated foreigners reported by U.S. nonbanking concerns	Reported by U.S. banks, not included elsewhere	Statistical discrepancy [5]	Goods and services	Current account
1960													
1st quarter	38	-96	926	380	546	89	-100	170	-1	388	-210	509	350
2nd quarter	-100	-140	912	435	477	102	-143	118	-50	450	-286	867	530
3rd quarter	-51	-620	381	283	98	93	-99	5	-11	110	-261	866	836
4th quarter	-281	-292	77	377	-300	31	-22	-11	-28	-270	-262	1 266	1 108
1961													
1st quarter	-117	-284	435	438	-3	68	-82	104	73	-166	-354	1 270	1 239
2nd quarter	-164	-219	620	-307	927	86	-38	152	72	655	-497	1 204	906
3rd quarter	-149	-220	934	673	261	58	83	3	14	103	150	797	844
4th quarter	-128	-538	715	-41	756	99	188	66	67	336	-288	924	833
1962													
1st quarter	-186	-395	737	*	737	89	193	145	-14	324	-82	806	646
2nd quarter	-5	112	675	503	172	130	-51	7	-64	150	-259	1 268	1 045
3rd quarter	-181	-89	-277	178	-455	59	-109	-23	16	-398	-405	777	961
4th quarter	17	-78	779	591	188	68	-99	6	-47	260	-377	522	732
1963													
1st quarter	-27	57	1 191	946	245	40	25	14	-36	202	-112	791	843
2nd quarter	-108	-583	1 527	910	617	108	-109	119	69	430	-95	1 457	1 199
3rd quarter	47	-254	205	56	149	105	1	52	11	-20	-339	797	1 021
4th quarter	245	-776	295	75	220	-22	-66	102	80	286	186	1 100	1 350
1964													
1st quarter	-206	-739	462	393	69	87	32	-42	0	-8	-286	1 608	1 910
2nd quarter	-166	-593	630	227	403	109	-108	14	19	369	-139	1 547	1 527
3rd quarter	-532	-363	769	275	494	56	-65	-30	37	496	-239	1 365	1 725
4th quarter	-204	-810	1 781	763	1 018	70	-5	-27	19	961	-243	1 503	1 662
1965													
1st quarter	286	-527	208	-202	410	184	60	57	3	106	111	917	1 257
2nd quarter	165	429	-330	-194	-136	-21	64	-243	63	1	23	1 627	1 577
3rd quarter	-19	16	587	115	472	147	-149	-227	49	652	-438	984	1 305
4th quarter	-91	175	280	421	-141	104	-106	54	63	-256	-153	1 138	1 289
1966													
1st quarter	-159	143	458	-164	622	143	-102	173	68	340	25	871	982
2nd quarter	-68	25	961	-57	1 018	133	-316	518	78	605	217	1 078	789
3rd quarter	-105	109	909	-342	1 251	-37	66	107	195	920	287	322	485
4th quarter	-110	-44	1 332	-111	1 443	187	-4	108	135	1 017	100	669	776
1967													
1st quarter	-107	-29	401	708	-307	169	-6	133	219	-822	-74	908	876
2nd quarter	-69	-83	1 884	1 100	784	174	-61	329	66	276	-212	898	667
3rd quarter	-40	-411	2 513	548	1 965	127	-36	520	164	1 190	79	485	563
4th quarter	-563	28	2 584	1 098	1 486	228	-32	34	135	1 121	2	311	474
1968													
1st quarter	-231	156	1 374	-533	1 907	367	22	855	207	456	-271	21	196
2nd quarter	-567	362	2 192	-2 007	4 199	133	86	1 122	478	2 380	-94	219	329
3rd quarter	-213	-203	2 809	442	2 367	148	-8	1 124	315	788	499	43	139
4th quarter	-101	-82	3 550	1 321	2 229	160	36	1 312	474	247	304	-29	-51
1969													
1st quarter	-132	-90	3 664	-1 117	4 781	359	-125	1 388	90	3 069	-1 191	-266	122
2nd quarter	-21	-316	3 896	-766	4 662	267	-35	365	181	3 884	-337	-11	-131
3rd quarter	141	-20	3 833	1 256	2 577	261	79	396	345	1 496	-520	-103	48
4th quarter	-114	-144	1 311	-672	1 983	376	13	981	176	437	531	467	357
1970													
1st quarter	-366	-63	2 160	2 830	-670	592	16	304	222	-1 804	-169	457	620
2nd quarter	-73	-265	848	694	154	212	-35	374	534	-931	-95	933	972
3rd quarter	-157	-133	1 940	1 411	529	357	1	720	510	-1 059	-309	526	515
4th quarter	0	-506	1 413	1 975	-562	303	99	792	748	-2 504	354	336	222
1971													
1st quarter	-355	-246	3 092	5 178	-2 086	196	179	559	-62	-2 958	-1 028	644	683
2nd quarter	-131	-358	5 154	5 630	-476	140	1 862	196	-34	-2 640	-2 211	-516	-409
3rd quarter	-337	-1 389	8 726	10 367	-1 641	-293	-795	626	79	-1 258	-4 800	-512	-536
4th quarter	-406	-987	5 997	5 704	293	324	-1 270	908	386	-55	-1 740	-918	-1 173
1972													
1st quarter	-248	-1 082	4 367	2 762	1 605	-136	-3	1 059	-14	699	911	-1 368	-1 693
2nd quarter	-185	190	4 277	1 103	3 174	373	-83	961	250	1 673	-463	-1 631	-1 689
3rd quarter	-241	-1 057	6 382	4 740	1 642	310	-12	718	216	410	-1 145	-1 132	-1 285
4th quarter	-380	-1 557	6 437	1 871	4 566	403	59	1 769	363	1 972	-1 182	-1 309	-1 130
1973													
1st quarter	-809	-2 988	10 743	9 937	806	631	-119	1 718	246	-1 670	-3 002	-845	145
2nd quarter	-202	-763	3 056	-403	3 458	835	-185	489	54	2 265	225	31	873
3rd quarter	-502	299	2 168	-772	2 940	539	-205	1 173	454	979	-1 716	1 093	2 737
4th quarter	-870	-2 528	2 423	-2 736	5 159	795	293	662	281	3 128	1 840	1 620	3 383
1974													
1st quarter	-2 113	-5 244	6 514	-1 138	7 652	1 784	336	712	354	4 466	-2 212	866	1 612
2nd quarter	-588	-7 577	9 962	4 434	5 528	539	60	363	390	4 176	246	-1 514	110
3rd quarter	273	-1 944	9 303	3 062	6 241	1 610	400	227	239	3 765	-1 314	-2 466	-295
4th quarter	-793	-4 751	9 563	4 188	5 375	828	1 001	-925	861	3 610	724	-1 179	531

[4] A minus sign indicates financial outflows or decreases in foreign official assets in the United States.
[5] Sum of credits and debits with the sign reversed.
* = Less than $500,000 (+/-).

Table 19-9. U.S. International Transactions—Continued

(Millions of dollars, seasonally adjusted.)

Year and quarter	Exports of goods, services, and income				Imports of goods, services, and income [1]				Unilateral current transfers, net [2]	U.S.-owned assets abroad, net [3]			U.S. private assets, net		
	Total	Goods	Services	Income receipts	Total	Goods	Services	Income payments		Total	U.S. official reserve assets, net	U.S. government assets other than official reserve assets, net	Total	Direct investment	Foreign securities
1975															
1st quarter	40 047	27 480	6 454	6 113	-33 797	-24 980	-5 580	-3 237	-2 043	-10 576	-327	-877	-9 372	-4 022	-1 931
2nd quarter	38 675	25 866	6 807	6 002	-31 284	-22 832	-5 309	-3 143	-2 377	-9 591	-28	-875	-8 688	-3 990	-985
3rd quarter	38 347	26 109	5 886	6 352	-33 078	-24 487	-5 379	-3 212	-1 189	-5 099	-333	-745	-4 021	-1 495	-938
4th quarter	40 868	27 633	6 351	6 884	-34 588	-25 886	-5 729	-2 973	-1 467	-14 436	-161	-977	-13 298	-4 736	-2 393
1976															
1st quarter	41 183	27 575	6 556	7 052	-37 464	-28 176	-5 883	-3 405	-1 153	-12 364	-777	-749	-10 838	-3 923	-2 467
2nd quarter	42 309	28 256	6 660	7 393	-39 494	-30 182	-5 980	-3 332	-1 167	-11 701	-1 580	-914	-9 207	-2 017	-1 405
3rd quarter	43 818	29 056	7 311	7 451	-41 737	-32 213	-6 231	-3 293	-2 165	-10 618	-408	-1 428	-8 782	-3 327	-2 751
4th quarter	44 780	29 858	7 444	7 478	-43 416	-33 657	-6 478	-3 281	-1 201	-16 588	207	-1 124	-15 671	-2 682	-2 262
1977															
1st quarter	44 916	29 668	7 494	7 754	-46 360	-36 585	-6 676	-3 099	-1 243	-1 198	-420	-1 062	284	-1 880	-749
2nd quarter	46 796	30 852	7 901	8 043	-48 401	-38 063	-6 940	-3 398	-1 426	-12 182	-24	-885	-11 273	-3 783	-1 784
3rd quarter	47 125	30 752	7 991	8 382	-48 511	-38 005	-6 894	-3 612	-1 371	-6 297	112	-1 001	-5 408	-2 762	-2 177
4th quarter	45 818	29 544	8 098	8 176	-50 495	-39 254	-7 133	-4 108	-1 185	-15 109	-43	-746	-14 320	-3 466	-749
1978															
1st quarter	48 847	30 470	8 704	9 673	-54 471	-42 487	-7 612	-4 372	-1 396	-15 219	187	-1 009	-14 397	-4 771	-1 115
2nd quarter	54 213	35 674	8 772	9 767	-56 513	-43 419	-7 768	-5 326	-1 477	-5 606	248	-1 257	-4 597	-3 720	-1 094
3rd quarter	56 058	36 523	9 203	10 332	-58 300	-44 422	-8 248	-5 630	-1 425	-9 703	115	-1 394	-8 424	-2 753	-510
4th quarter	61 399	39 408	9 673	12 318	-60 587	-45 674	-8 561	-6 352	-1 491	-30 601	182	-999	-29 784	-4 812	-907
1979															
1st quarter	64 530	41 475	9 664	13 391	-63 492	-47 582	-8 649	-7 261	-1 462	-7 841	-2 446	-1 094	-4 301	-5 465	-908
2nd quarter	68 445	43 885	9 713	14 847	-67 584	-50 778	-8 960	-7 846	-1 552	-15 565	322	-970	-14 917	-7 220	-492
3rd quarter	74 411	47 104	9 936	17 371	-71 856	-54 002	-9 329	-8 525	-1 632	-27 156	2 779	-779	-29 156	-7 166	-2 331
4th quarter	80 577	51 975	10 378	18 224	-78 726	-59 645	-9 751	-9 330	-1 949	-14 353	-649	-904	-12 800	-5 370	-995
1980															
1st quarter	85 274	54 237	10 997	20 040	-86 559	-65 815	-10 335	-10 409	-2 174	-12 662	-2 116	-1 441	-9 105	-5 188	-787
2nd quarter	83 441	55 967	11 491	15 983	-82 734	-62 274	-10 106	-10 354	-1 648	-24 724	502	-1 159	-24 067	-2 659	-1 387
3rd quarter	86 148	55 830	12 543	17 775	-79 906	-59 010	-10 292	-10 604	-1 909	-19 666	-1 109	-1 382	-17 175	-4 156	-944
4th quarter	89 578	58 216	12 554	18 808	-84 577	-62 651	-10 760	-11 166	-2 618	-28 761	-4 279	-1 178	-23 304	-7 219	-450
1981															
1st quarter	94 665	60 317	13 684	20 664	-91 024	-67 004	-11 360	-12 660	-2 678	-21 922	-3 436	-1 361	-17 125	-2 044	-473
2nd quarter	96 294	60 141	14 392	21 761	-92 303	-67 181	-11 447	-13 675	-2 763	-24 158	-905	-1 491	-21 762	-5 709	-1 564
3rd quarter	95 013	58 031	14 835	22 147	-89 787	-64 407	-11 236	-14 144	-3 145	-17 945	-4	-1 268	-16 673	-1 124	-697
4th quarter	94 958	58 555	14 446	21 957	-91 082	-66 475	-11 460	-13 147	-3 117	-49 028	262	-976	-48 314	-745	-2 966
1982															
1st quarter	94 006	55 163	16 032	22 811	-90 336	-63 502	-12 749	-14 085	-3 955	-36 335	-1 089	-800	-34 446	-2 695	-628
2nd quarter	96 060	55 344	16 187	24 529	-88 318	-60 580	-13 096	-14 642	-3 953	-42 754	-1 132	-1 727	-39 895	1 074	-471
3rd quarter	90 925	52 089	16 003	22 833	-90 938	-63 696	-12 794	-14 448	-4 027	-23 547	-794	-2 524	-20 229	903	-3 397
4th quarter	85 993	48 561	15 857	21 575	-86 379	-59 864	-13 109	-13 406	-4 611	-25 246	-1 950	-1 080	-22 217	-3 838	-3 488
1983															
1st quarter	86 146	49 198	16 239	20 709	-85 097	-59 757	-12 951	-12 389	-3 566	-28 890	-787	-1 136	-26 967	-862	-1 549
2nd quarter	87 214	49 340	16 093	21 781	-91 096	-64 783	-13 557	-12 756	-3 951	-2 974	16	-1 263	-1 727	-1 842	-2 813
3rd quarter	89 919	50 324	16 308	23 287	-98 481	-70 370	-14 133	-13 978	-4 339	-12 191	529	-1 171	-11 549	-4 861	-1 308
4th quarter	92 831	52 937	15 671	24 223	-102 822	-73 991	-14 337	-14 494	-5 453	-22 318	-953	-1 436	-19 929	-4 962	-1 093
1984															
1st quarter	96 000	52 991	17 353	25 656	-112 576	-79 740	-16 131	-16 705	-4 354	-8 338	-657	-2 033	-5 648	-1 837	758
2nd quarter	100 257	54 626	18 045	27 586	-119 220	-83 798	-16 885	-18 537	-4 476	-25 718	-566	-1 342	-23 811	-1 967	-764
3rd quarter	102 296	55 893	17 936	28 467	-120 533	-83 918	-17 168	-19 447	-5 147	15 298	-799	-1 392	17 489	-3 209	-1 106
4th quarter	101 361	56 416	17 834	27 111	-121 591	-84 962	-17 564	-19 065	-6 359	-21 618	-1 110	-720	-19 789	-9 396	-3 644
1985															
1st quarter	97 794	54 866	18 227	24 701	-116 249	-80 319	-17 707	-18 223	-5 064	-5 491	-233	-760	-4 498	-2 783	-2 474
2nd quarter	97 437	54 154	18 214	25 069	-120 891	-84 565	-18 276	-18 050	-5 235	-2 340	-356	-1 053	-931	-4 374	-2 219
3rd quarter	94 771	52 836	17 961	23 974	-120 285	-83 909	-18 151	-18 225	-5 789	-5 776	-121	-453	-5 202	-4 698	-1 572
4th quarter	97 612	54 059	18 756	24 797	-126 349	-89 295	-18 732	-18 322	-5 911	-31 146	-3 148	-555	-27 444	-7 073	-1 217
1986															
1st quarter	100 332	53 536	21 052	25 744	-129 342	-89 220	-19 855	-20 267	-5 199	-17 406	-115	-266	-17 025	-9 781	-5 930
2nd quarter	102 206	56 828	20 912	24 466	-131 690	-91 743	-19 066	-20 881	-6 208	-24 945	16	-230	-24 731	-7 298	-1 051
3rd quarter	101 288	55 645	21 969	23 674	-132 879	-92 801	-20 448	-19 630	-6 458	-32 615	280	-1 554	-31 341	-4 975	181
4th quarter	103 275	57 335	22 761	23 179	-136 232	-94 661	-20 778	-20 793	-6 269	-36 753	132	29	-36 914	-1 938	2 529
1987															
1st quarter	104 750	56 696	23 602	24 452	-138 887	-96 023	-21 273	-21 591	-5 128	8 177	1 956	-5	6 226	-6 547	-1 749
2nd quarter	111 642	60 202	24 740	26 700	-146 125	-100 648	-22 537	-22 940	-5 502	-26 738	3 419	-168	-29 989	-7 541	-287
3rd quarter	116 688	64 217	24 986	27 485	-151 111	-104 412	-22 833	-23 866	-5 706	-27 791	32	310	-28 133	-8 795	-1 159
4th quarter	123 968	69 093	25 329	29 546	-158 324	-108 682	-24 146	-25 496	-6 926	-32 943	3 742	868	-37 553	-12 150	-2 056
1988															
1st quarter	134 932	75 655	26 598	32 679	-161 810	-109 963	-24 503	-27 344	-6 074	2 892	1 502	-1 597	2 987	-5 037	-4 504
2nd quarter	139 984	79 542	27 567	32 875	-163 265	-110 836	-24 282	-28 147	-5 615	-23 428	39	-854	-22 613	-2 594	1 318
3rd quarter	143 879	80 941	28 453	34 485	-165 901	-110 901	-24 588	-30 412	-5 902	-49 965	-7 380	1 960	-44 545	-7 791	-1 500
4th quarter	149 068	84 092	28 302	36 674	-172 770	-115 489	-25 157	-32 124	-7 685	-36 074	1 925	3 457	-41 456	-7 105	-3 294
1989															
1st quarter	155 805	86 274	30 576	38 955	-177 206	-117 618	-25 140	-34 448	-6 048	-53 703	-4 000	961	-50 664	-12 136	-2 225
2nd quarter	163 352	91 399	31 110	40 843	-183 220	-121 382	-25 241	-36 597	-5 753	-8 202	-12 095	-306	4 199	-7 686	-6 192
3rd quarter	163 579	90 762	32 316	40 501	-179 692	-118 171	-25 792	-35 729	-6 630	-51 678	-5 996	489	-46 171	-8 704	-9 149
4th quarter	165 556	91 481	33 087	40 988	-181 489	-120 494	-26 306	-34 689	-7 739	-61 803	-3 202	87	-58 688	-14 922	-4 504

[1] A minus sign indicates imports of goods or services or income payments.
[2] A minus sign indicates net unilateral transfers to foreigners.
[3] A minus sign indicates financial outflows or increases in U.S. official assets.

Table 19-9. U.S. International Transactions—*Continued*

(Millions of dollars, seasonally adjusted.)

Year and quarter	U.S.-owned assets abroad, net [4] —Continued / U.S. private assets, net—Continued / U.S. claims: On unaffiliated foreigners reported by U.S. nonbanking concerns	Reported by U.S. banks, not included elsewhere	Foreign-owned assets in the United States, net [4]: Total	Foreign official assets in the United States, net	Other foreign assets in the United States, net: Total	Direct investment	U.S. Treasury securities and U.S. currency flows	U.S. securities other than U.S. Treasury securities	U.S. liabilities: To unaffiliated foreigners reported by U.S. nonbanking concerns	Reported by U.S. banks, not included elsewhere	Statistical discrepancy [5]	Balance on: Goods and services	Current account
1975													
1st quarter	353	-3 772	2 788	3 419	-631	278	892	344	359	-2 504	3 581	3 374	4 207
2nd quarter	112	-3 825	4 371	2 244	2 127	870	10	385	55	807	206	4 532	5 014
3rd quarter	-939	-649	2 991	-1 731	4 722	86	2 424	737	-163	1 638	-1 972	2 129	4 080
4th quarter	-883	-5 286	7 021	3 095	3 926	1 369	764	1 038	68	687	2 602	2 369	4 813
1976													
1st quarter	-747	-3 701	7 769	3 699	4 070	1 471	737	1 036	154	672	2 029	72	2 566
2nd quarter	-999	-4 786	8 453	4 039	4 414	1 086	-91	134	-231	3 516	1 600	-1 246	1 648
3rd quarter	616	-3 320	9 120	2 958	6 162	999	3 325	64	-184	1 958	1 582	-2 077	-84
4th quarter	-1 166	-9 561	12 677	6 997	5 680	790	312	51	-317	4 844	3 748	-2 833	163
1977													
1st quarter	-771	3 684	3 062	5 554	-2 492	980	1 181	749	-98	-5 304	823	-6 099	-2 687
2nd quarter	-1 124	-4 582	14 781	7 888	6 893	965	-799	589	-102	6 240	432	-6 250	-3 031
3rd quarter	1 310	-1 779	14 676	8 257	6 419	1 023	1 651	337	768	2 640	-5 622	-6 156	-2 757
4th quarter	-1 355	-8 750	20 703	15 117	5 586	761	401	763	518	3 143	268	-8 745	-5 862
1978													
1st quarter	-2 241	-6 270	18 684	15 448	3 236	1 356	1 381	396	507	-404	3 555	-10 925	-7 020
2nd quarter	315	-98	1 551	-5 113	6 664	2 313	1 493	1 082	304	1 472	7 832	-6 741	-3 777
3rd quarter	-29	-5 132	17 582	4 903	12 679	2 620	-368	296	912	9 219	-4 212	-6 944	-3 667
4th quarter	-1 898	-22 167	29 220	18 440	10 780	1 608	2 672	480	166	5 854	2 060	-5 154	-679
1979													
1st quarter	-3 854	5 926	2 707	-8 697	11 404	1 554	2 964	409	-296	6 773	5 558	-5 092	-424
2nd quarter	716	-7 921	7 663	-9 775	17 438	3 354	743	524	799	12 018	8 593	-6 140	-691
3rd quarter	-1 826	-17 833	25 349	6 036	19 313	3 382	2 402	166	210	13 153	884	-6 291	923
4th quarter	-50	-6 385	5 134	-1 228	6 362	3 588	951	252	908	663	9 317	-7 043	-98
1980													
1st quarter	-1 927	-1 203	9 582	-7 413	16 995	3 321	4 300	2 435	340	6 599	6 539	-10 916	-3 459
2nd quarter	144	-20 165	11 373	7 731	3 643	5 756	229	496	1 671	-4 509	14 292	-4 922	-941
3rd quarter	365	-12 440	14 930	7 564	7 366	4 713	222	263	1 252	916	403	-929	4 333
4th quarter	-2 605	-13 030	26 726	7 614	19 112	3 128	2 394	2 263	3 590	7 737	-348	-2 641	2 383
1981													
1st quarter	-2 944	-11 664	9 819	5 502	4 317	3 146	2 486	2 357	121	-3 793	11 140	-4 363	963
2nd quarter	513	-15 002	15 364	-3 159	18 523	5 294	1 641	3 512	13	8 063	7 566	-4 095	1 228
3rd quarter	458	-15 310	17 531	-5 992	23 523	5 505	-248	704	1 084	16 478	-1 667	-2 777	2 081
4th quarter	-2 404	-42 199	43 519	8 609	34 910	11 251	2 248	332	-301	21 380	4 750	-4 934	759
1982													
1st quarter	2 220	33 343	27 240	-3 265	30 505	2 154	1 297	1 263	-65	25 856	9 325	-5 056	-285
2nd quarter	-1 095	-39 403	35 260	1 534	33 726	2 945	4 193	2 486	-2 023	26 125	3 653	-2 145	3 789
3rd quarter	3 670	-21 405	18 663	2 694	15 969	2 849	2 091	555	-282	10 756	8 876	-8 398	-4 040
4th quarter	2 028	-16 919	15 424	2 629	12 795	4 685	3 446	1 781	-13	2 896	14 775	-8 555	-4 997
1983													
1st quarter	-4 253	-20 303	16 266	-38	16 304	1 254	3 713	2 873	-2 763	11 227	15 090	-7 271	-2 517
2nd quarter	-590	3 518	16 325	1 612	14 713	3 287	4 616	2 470	-64	4 404	-5 570	-12 907	-7 833
3rd quarter	-1 764	-3 616	20 420	-2 689	23 109	4 059	2 308	1 777	1 311	13 654	4 619	-17 871	-12 901
4th quarter	-4 347	-9 527	35 682	6 960	28 722	1 771	3 452	1 044	1 398	21 057	2 027	-19 720	-15 444
1984													
1st quarter	-3 012	-1 557	23 302	-2 956	26 258	4 858	2 450	1 333	6 092	11 525	5 910	-25 527	-20 930
2nd quarter	-934	-20 146	42 689	-156	42 845	8 625	8 036	362	4 232	21 590	6 411	-28 012	-23 439
3rd quarter	3 987	17 817	7 568	-884	8 452	4 432	6 103	1 447	1 662	-5 192	458	-27 257	-23 384
4th quarter	492	-7 241	44 192	7 136	37 056	6 552	10 512	9 426	4 640	5 926	3 953	-28 276	-26 589
1985													
1st quarter	475	284	18 342	-10 962	29 304	4 913	3 390	9 615	-720	12 106	10 597	-24 933	-23 519
2nd quarter	2 337	3 325	29 334	8 502	20 832	4 376	6 888	7 194	1 724	650	1 619	-30 473	-28 689
3rd quarter	-2 779	3 847	38 263	2 506	35 757	4 839	9 136	11 669	2 801	7 312	-1 265	-31 263	-31 303
4th quarter	-10 375	-8 779	60 179	-1 165	61 344	5 618	6 219	22 484	6 046	20 977	5 528	-35 212	-34 648
1986													
1st quarter	-6 230	4 916	41 489	2 712	38 777	3 431	6 420	18 730	696	9 500	10 042	-34 487	-34 209
2nd quarter	-2 722	-13 660	53 710	15 918	37 792	5 520	4 620	22 752	1 635	3 265	6 851	-33 069	-35 692
3rd quarter	-7 638	-18 909	70 876	15 789	55 087	8 746	-854	17 107	1 947	28 141	-282	-35 635	-38 049
4th quarter	-5 183	-32 322	63 933	1 229	62 704	17 723	-2 277	12 380	-953	35 831	11 975	-35 343	-39 226
1987													
1st quarter	-5 715	20 237	42 247	14 199	28 048	12 883	-2 326	18 372	6 151	-7 032	-11 246	-36 998	-39 265
2nd quarter	712	-22 873	57 331	10 444	46 887	8 593	-731	15 960	5 595	17 470	9 301	-38 243	-39 985
3rd quarter	-1 319	-16 860	83 145	764	82 381	20 763	-1 835	12 676	6 656	44 121	-15 319	-38 042	-40 129
4th quarter	-724	-22 623	65 910	19 980	45 930	16 230	2 649	-4 888	-39	31 978	8 222	-38 406	-41 282
1988													
1st quarter	-3 454	15 982	32 028	24 925	7 103	8 425	6 511	2 423	12 593	-22 849	-2 077	-32 213	-32 952
2nd quarter	-9 954	-11 383	74 531	6 006	68 525	13 717	7 673	9 702	6 742	30 691	-22 325	-28 009	-28 896
3rd quarter	-5 217	-30 037	52 797	-1 974	54 771	13 778	4 743	7 464	6 399	22 387	24 962	-26 095	-27 924
4th quarter	-2 568	-28 489	87 166	10 801	76 365	21 815	7 112	6 764	7 159	33 515	-19 841	-28 252	-31 387
1989													
1st quarter	-9 293	-27 010	66 666	7 700	58 966	18 584	10 961	8 544	6 637	14 240	14 358	-25 908	-27 449
2nd quarter	-5 767	23 844	10 980	-5 115	16 094	15 325	4 789	9 365	12 000	-25 385	22 710	-24 114	-25 621
3rd quarter	-5 924	-22 394	74 068	13 060	61 008	11 519	12 744	10 270	-1 121	27 596	214	-20 885	-22 743
4th quarter	-6 662	-32 600	73 215	-7 142	80 357	22 846	7 024	10 588	4 570	35 329	12 324	-22 232	-23 672

[4]A minus sign indicates financial outflows or decreases in foreign official assets in the United States.
[5]Sum of credits and debits with the sign reversed.

Table 19-9. U.S. International Transactions—*Continued*

(Millions of dollars, seasonally adjusted.)

| Year and quarter | Exports of goods, services, and income | | | | Imports of goods, services, and income [1] | | | | Unilateral current transfers, net [2] | U.S.-owned assets abroad, net [3] | | | U.S. private assets, net | | |
	Total	Goods	Services	Income receipts	Total	Goods	Services	Income payments		Total	U.S. official reserve assets, net	U.S. government assets other than official reserve assets, net	Total	Direct invest-ment	Foreign securities
1990															
1st quarter	171 784	94 998	35 016	41 770	-187 397	-123 382	-28 173	-35 842	-6 540	37 828	-3 177	-756	41 761	-10 391	-8 580
2nd quarter	174 177	96 184	35 988	42 005	-186 593	-122 229	-28 764	-35 600	-7 644	-37 204	371	-796	-36 779	-4 651	-11 037
3rd quarter	176 450	97 211	37 402	41 837	-191 570	-125 038	-29 923	-36 609	-7 339	-43 716	1 739	-338	-45 117	-17 898	-1 037
4th quarter	184 566	99 008	39 428	46 130	-193 723	-127 786	-30 795	-35 142	-5 133	-38 142	-1 091	4 205	-41 255	-4 240	-8 111
1991															
1st quarter	181 195	101 157	37 891	42 147	-184 921	-121 080	-29 801	-34 040	15 004	-10 570	-353	549	-10 766	-14 318	-9 960
2nd quarter	180 564	102 611	40 745	37 208	-182 176	-120 584	-29 660	-31 932	3 780	745	1 014	-423	154	-1 230	-12 021
3rd quarter	181 692	104 283	41 860	35 549	-183 523	-123 171	-29 200	-31 152	-2 812	-15 900	3 877	3 256	-23 034	-9 356	-12 550
4th quarter	184 112	106 032	43 766	34 314	-183 948	-126 185	-29 799	-27 964	-5 224	-38 664	1 225	-459	-39 431	-12 987	-11 142
1992															
1st quarter	185 909	108 005	44 041	33 863	-183 755	-126 756	-29 377	-27 622	-6 847	-11 428	-1 057	-259	-10 112	-20 695	-8 668
2nd quarter	186 380	107 884	44 027	34 469	-190 447	-132 983	-29 084	-28 380	-7 890	-16 235	1 464	-302	-17 397	-10 268	-8 196
3rd quarter	187 709	110 851	44 510	32 348	-193 531	-136 718	-29 823	-26 990	-7 457	-13 570	1 952	-392	-15 130	-5 157	-13 059
4th quarter	188 880	112 891	44 243	31 746	-196 005	-140 071	-29 824	-26 110	-10 960	-33 177	1 542	-715	-34 004	-12 145	-19 243
1993															
1st quarter	190 925	112 053	45 877	32 995	-196 106	-141 057	-29 621	-25 428	-7 741	-21 491	-983	487	-20 995	-14 982	-28 208
2nd quarter	192 634	113 202	46 341	33 091	-204 825	-147 402	-30 264	-27 159	-8 451	-45 843	822	-304	-46 361	-23 264	-29 833
3rd quarter	193 639	112 985	46 580	34 074	-205 599	-148 361	-30 501	-26 737	-9 211	-52 975	-544	-194	-52 237	-13 155	-51 940
4th quarter	199 716	118 703	46 628	34 385	-215 267	-152 574	-31 760	-30 933	-11 709	-80 243	-673	-340	-79 230	-32 550	-36 272
1994															
1st quarter	203 607	118 782	48 214	36 611	-219 109	-155 297	-32 345	-31 467	-7 708	-39 740	-59	399	-40 080	-28 554	-19 540
2nd quarter	211 276	122 210	49 822	39 244	-231 424	-163 784	-32 542	-35 098	-8 277	-43 072	3 537	477	-47 086	-14 932	-9 229
3rd quarter	222 554	128 946	50 505	43 103	-244 192	-171 869	-33 132	-39 191	-9 452	-30 985	-165	-323	-30 497	-17 316	-12 405
4th quarter	231 025	132 921	51 225	46 879	-253 831	-177 740	-33 104	-42 987	-12 146	-62 261	2 033	-943	-63 351	-19 367	-19 135
1995															
1st quarter	241 511	138 330	52 011	51 170	-261 135	-182 830	-33 927	-44 378	-8 812	-64 950	-5 318	-553	-59 079	-19 325	-8 775
2nd quarter	249 001	142 452	52 999	53 550	-271 151	-190 570	-34 600	-45 981	-8 418	-117 959	-2 722	-225	-115 012	-15 078	-27 834
3rd quarter	255 574	146 547	56 269	52 758	-272 181	-188 239	-35 111	-48 831	-8 784	-46 759	-1 893	252	-45 118	-21 772	-41 564
4th quarter	259 555	147 875	57 239	54 441	-271 208	-187 735	-35 784	-47 689	-9 174	-122 706	191	-458	-122 439	-42 573	-44 333
1996															
1st quarter	262 752	150 496	57 265	54 991	-276 829	-193 142	-36 604	-47 083	-10 212	-80 936	17	-210	-80 743	-23 759	-44 043
2nd quarter	266 662	152 791	59 170	54 701	-286 956	-200 825	-37 125	-49 006	-8 462	-68 512	-523	-568	-67 421	-15 096	-30 968
3rd quarter	267 020	151 884	58 481	56 655	-293 453	-203 103	-38 358	-51 992	-8 653	-91 675	7 489	105	-99 269	-23 129	-33 273
4th quarter	280 708	156 942	63 844	59 922	-298 252	-206 043	-38 547	-53 662	-11 535	-172 797	-315	-316	-172 166	-29 898	-41 545
1997															
1st quarter	287 175	162 626	62 352	62 197	-310 602	-212 725	-40 081	-57 796	-8 899	-152 213	4 480	-76	-156 617	-29 544	-23 836
2nd quarter	300 275	170 171	64 165	65 939	-317 518	-218 027	-40 493	-58 998	-9 285	-93 616	-236	-298	-93 082	-24 883	-31 739
3rd quarter	304 962	173 161	64 712	67 089	-325 106	-221 656	-41 723	-61 727	-9 772	-119 283	-730	377	-118 930	-21 217	-51 297
4th quarter	302 490	172 408	64 280	65 802	-328 068	-224 077	-42 141	-61 850	-13 336	-122 489	-4 524	65	-118 030	-29 161	-12 104
1998															
1st quarter	301 310	170 998	64 505	65 807	-331 242	-226 372	-42 772	-62 098	-10 868	-72 938	-444	-80	-72 414	-41 844	-17 951
2nd quarter	297 869	165 511	65 995	66 363	-336 183	-228 721	-44 093	-63 369	-11 171	-137 128	-1 945	-483	-134 700	-44 689	-41 461
3rd quarter	292 139	164 081	64 631	63 427	-337 144	-228 010	-45 297	-63 837	-11 954	-57 020	-2 025	188	-55 183	-20 479	9 283
4th quarter	299 886	169 826	67 009	63 051	-342 895	-234 009	-46 440	-62 446	-14 441	-80 745	-2 369	-47	-78 329	-35 634	-74 075
1999															
1st quarter	299 118	164 235	68 596	66 287	-347 512	-237 825	-47 088	-62 599	-10 899	-84 290	4 068	118	-88 476	-68 498	4 196
2nd quarter	306 214	166 084	70 039	70 091	-364 498	-250 654	-48 608	-65 236	-11 316	-180 642	1 159	-392	-181 409	-50 190	-68 182
3rd quarter	318 820	173 003	71 021	74 796	-386 995	-265 292	-50 162	-71 541	-11 092	-125 226	1 951	-686	-126 491	-64 062	-38 290
4th quarter	331 524	180 643	71 853	79 028	-400 756	-276 216	-50 829	-73 711	-13 449	-113 483	1 569	3 710	-118 762	-42 185	-13 960
2000															
1st quarter	340 457	185 168	72 998	82 291	-423 355	-291 359	-53 525	-78 471	-12 123	-214 667	-554	-127	-213 986	-34 934	-31 042
2nd quarter	354 103	191 175	75 148	87 780	-440 583	-302 905	-54 552	-83 126	-12 646	-108 046	2 020	-570	-109 496	-52 029	-36 671
3rd quarter	359 157	198 821	74 545	85 791	-454 244	-314 622	-56 684	-82 938	-13 480	-86 485	-346	114	-86 253	-39 618	-30 863
4th quarter	363 198	196 830	75 368	91 000	-454 517	-315 531	-56 265	-82 721	-17 435	-160 602	-1 410	-358	-158 834	-32 633	-23 332
2001															
1st quarter	348 355	194 145	75 123	79 087	-440 865	-306 871	-55 837	-78 157	-11 494	-192 224	190	77	-192 491	-14 147	-23 849
2nd quarter	331 765	184 457	74 701	72 607	-420 408	-291 627	-56 987	-71 794	-11 321	-92 213	-1 343	-783	-90 087	-30 809	-48 701
3rd quarter	309 601	172 526	71 374	65 701	-401 981	-278 847	-54 096	-69 038	-11 256	37 353	-3 559	77	40 835	-41 781	13 140
4th quarter	295 222	167 584	67 671	59 967	-368 820	-268 582	-52 555	-47 683	-12 542	-102 853	-199	143	-102 797	-33 224	-25 227
2002															
1st quarter	297 074	165 298	71 144	60 632	-387 864	-271 331	-55 168	-61 365	-15 938	-35 227	390	133	-35 750	-39 083	5 367
2nd quarter	307 616	171 421	72 275	63 920	-416 962	-292 707	-55 877	-68 378	-13 481	-128 567	-1 843	42	-126 766	-35 459	-5 843
3rd quarter	313 939	174 315	73 500	66 124	-422 666	-297 627	-57 168	-67 871	-13 997	29 712	-1 416	-27	31 155	-31 623	21 641
4th quarter	311 015	170 840	75 311	64 864	-424 165	-303 081	-59 186	-61 898	-15 436	-44 902	-812	-180	-43 910	-31 670	-5 364

[1] A minus sign indicates imports of goods or services or income payments.
[2] A minus sign indicates net unilateral transfers to foreigners.
[3] A minus sign indicates financial outflows or increases in U.S. official assets.

Table 19-9. U.S. International Transactions—Continued

(Millions of dollars, seasonally adjusted.)

Year and quarter	U.S.-owned assets abroad, net[4]—Continued / U.S. private assets, net—Continued / U.S. claims / On unaffiliated foreigners reported by U.S. nonbanking concerns	Reported by U.S. banks, not included elsewhere	Total	Foreign official assets in the United States, net	Total	Direct invest-ment	U.S. Treasury securities and U.S. currency flows	U.S. securities other than U.S. Treasury securities	To unaffiliated foreigners reported by U.S. nonbanking concerns	Reported by U.S. banks, not included elsewhere	Statistical discrep-ancy[5]	Goods and services	Current account
1990													
1st quarter	3 019	57 713	-22 824	-6 421	-16 403	15 774	1 709	1 311	12 904	-48 101	7 168	-21 541	-22 153
2nd quarter	-5 069	-16 022	41 215	6 207	35 008	13 773	6 257	2 114	6 713	6 151	15 892	-18 821	-20 060
3rd quarter	-15 514	-10 668	63 231	13 937	49 294	8 313	6 044	-2 874	16 838	20 973	2 779	-20 348	-22 459
4th quarter	-10 260	-18 644	59 949	20 186	39 763	10 635	2 256	1 041	8 678	17 153	-635	-20 145	-14 290
1991													
1st quarter	-40	13 552	8 347	5 569	2 778	4 076	9 539	5 023	-586	-15 274	-8 114	-11 833	11 278
2nd quarter	7 902	5 503	12 678	-4 914	17 591	13 378	15 661	14 872	-2 549	-23 771	-15 664	-6 888	2 168
3rd quarter	3 341	-4 469	33 236	3 854	29 382	-1 354	3 004	10 310	4 761	12 661	-8 907	-6 228	-4 643
4th quarter	-106	-15 196	56 549	12 879	43 670	7 072	6 022	4 939	-4 741	30 378	-13 000	-6 186	-5 060
1992													
1st quarter	7 562	11 689	31 079	20 988	10 091	2 086	1 986	4 569	5 689	-4 239	-14 821	-4 087	-4 693
2nd quarter	-6 620	7 687	50 304	20 879	29 425	5 916	11 331	10 467	3 954	-2 243	-21 937	-10 156	-11 957
3rd quarter	-3 737	6 823	35 469	-7 524	42 993	2 898	11 008	2 531	4 854	21 702	-8 489	-11 180	-13 279
4th quarter	2 408	-5 024	53 809	6 133	47 676	8 922	26 206	12 476	-924	996	-2 433	-12 761	-18 085
1993													
1st quarter	-6 130	28 325	25 099	10 937	14 162	8 060	16 363	9 694	-215	-19 740	10 072	-12 748	-12 922
2nd quarter	-725	7 461	59 038	17 466	41 572	11 386	5 608	15 205	6 531	2 842	7 597	-18 123	-20 642
3rd quarter	5 896	6 962	85 694	19 073	66 621	11 688	9 658	17 782	288	27 205	-11 316	-19 297	-21 171
4th quarter	1 725	-12 133	112 210	24 277	87 933	20 229	11 652	37 411	3 885	14 756	-4 548	-19 003	-27 260
1994													
1st quarter	-2 215	10 229	90 280	10 568	79 712	5 883	15 412	21 070	5 856	31 491	-27 172	-20 646	-23 210
2nd quarter	-20 966	-1 959	58 842	9 455	47 387	5 767	-798	12 352	4 269	25 797	15 666	-24 294	-28 425
3rd quarter	-960	184	81 934	19 358	62 576	13 709	10 361	13 389	-1 620	26 737	-19 463	-25 550	-31 090
4th quarter	-12 195	-12 654	76 933	202	76 731	20 762	32 699	10 160	-7 203	20 313	20 438	-26 698	-34 952
1995													
1st quarter	-2 631	-28 348	97 915	21 956	75 959	9 924	34 410	12 400	17 764	1 461	-4 354	-26 416	-28 436
2nd quarter	-24 580	-47 520	122 149	37 072	85 077	11 888	30 338	15 851	11 864	15 136	26 424	-29 719	-30 568
3rd quarter	13 729	4 489	116 366	39 302	77 064	16 764	37 194	26 218	13 493	-16 605	-43 579	-20 534	-25 391
4th quarter	-31 804	-3 729	102 132	11 550	90 582	19 200	1 902	22 780	16 516	30 184	41 470	-18 405	-20 827
1996													
1st quarter	-15 210	2 269	85 255	51 771	33 484	28 518	13 646	20 356	4 350	-33 386	20 147	-21 985	-24 289
2nd quarter	-22 000	643	101 405	13 503	87 902	16 184	29 514	24 686	15 259	2 259	-3 980	-25 989	-28 756
3rd quarter	-9 090	-33 777	144 109	23 020	121 089	15 257	44 116	29 719	28 925	3 072	-17 176	-31 096	-35 086
4th quarter	-40 033	-60 690	220 326	38 430	181 896	26 542	77 108	28 511	5 202	44 533	-18 302	-23 804	-29 079
1997													
1st quarter	-38 112	-65 125	173 005	27 763	145 242	28 626	32 537	38 490	25 055	20 534	11 740	-27 828	-32 326
2nd quarter	-9 885	-26 575	140 719	-6 019	146 738	23 150	38 750	45 651	6 461	32 726	-20 302	-24 184	-26 528
3rd quarter	-22 173	-24 243	167 223	23 474	143 749	17 865	42 709	52 544	25 550	5 081	-17 702	-25 506	-29 916
4th quarter	-51 590	-25 175	225 860	-26 182	252 042	35 960	41 221	24 724	59 452	90 685	-64 214	-29 530	-38 914
1998													
1st quarter	-7 822	-4 797	79 170	11 072	68 098	19 759	-5 789	63 237	39 833	-48 942	34 759	-33 641	40 800
2nd quarter	-20 363	-28 187	155 055	-10 235	165 290	20 391	24 163	56 146	30 722	33 868	31 738	-41 308	-49 485
3rd quarter	-15 658	-28 329	75 963	-46 640	122 603	23 490	2 195	6 628	14 976	75 314	38 219	-44 595	-56 959
4th quarter	5 639	25 741	113 381	25 900	87 481	115 405	24 634	30 304	-62 391	-20 471	24 980	-43 614	-57 450
1999													
1st quarter	-47 211	23 037	109 283	4 381	104 902	28 759	-10 887	49 157	51 307	-13 434	34 488	-52 082	-59 293
2nd quarter	-27 021	-36 016	247 860	-757	248 617	140 759	-8 355	70 205	16 928	29 080	2 551	-63 139	-69 600
3rd quarter	-13 663	-10 476	156 858	12 625	144 233	50 758	8 382	86 202	-8 777	7 668	47 810	-71 430	-79 267
4th quarter	-9 809	-52 808	226 210	27 294	198 916	69 169	-11 230	93 270	16 789	30 918	-25 735	-74 549	-82 681
2000													
1st quarter	-79 800	-68 210	244 512	22 542	221 970	52 094	-22 046	129 306	72 433	-9 817	65 370	-86 718	-95 021
2nd quarter	-25 287	4 491	242 481	6 548	235 933	91 669	-25 491	87 112	28 796	53 847	-35 114	-91 134	-99 126
3rd quarter	-14 121	-1 651	240 954	12 952	228 002	79 979	-18 253	120 906	16 914	28 456	-45 684	-97 940	-108 567
4th quarter	-19 582	-83 287	298 194	-4 318	302 512	97 534	-10 030	117 994	52 529	44 485	-28 646	-99 598	-108 754
2001													
1st quarter	-43 929	-110 566	313 923	4 290	309 633	44 924	-2 309	129 999	111 565	25 454	-17 428	-93 440	-104 004
2nd quarter	-7 404	-3 173	213 471	-21 197	234 668	63 011	-11 916	113 548	752	69 273	-21 034	-89 456	-99 964
3rd quarter	-101	69 577	24 084	16 702	7 382	14 962	-4 847	64 172	-22 623	-44 282	42 485	-89 043	-103 636
4th quarter	46 437	-90 783	214 051	5 309	208 742	28 682	35 417	98 914	-22 205	67 934	-24 809	-85 882	-86 140
2002													
1st quarter	-1 886	-148	146 813	6 106	140 707	10 607	16 314	74 461	46 771	-7 446	-4 581	-90 057	-106 728
2nd quarter	-16 210	-69 254	221 242	47 552	173 690	-456	21 401	104 187	24 610	23 948	30 438	-104 888	-122 827
3rd quarter	-11 862	52 999	141 478	8 992	132 486	14 199	60 061	45 880	-8 102	20 448	-48 102	-106 980	-122 724
4th quarter	-1 922	-4 954	197 448	32 210	165 238	15 281	19 954	66 964	8 863	54 176	-23 602	-116 116	-128 586

[4]A minus sign indicates financial outflows or decreases in foreign official assets in the United States.
[5]Sum of credits and debits with the sign reversed.

Table 19-10. Productivity and Related Data

(1992 = 100, seasonally adjusted.)

Year and quarter	Business sector								Nonfarm business sector							
	Output per hour of all persons	Output	Hours of all persons	Compensation per hour	Real compensation per hour	Unit labor costs	Unit nonlabor payments	Implicit price deflator	Output per hour of all persons	Output	Hours of all persons	Compensation per hour	Real compensation per hour	Unit labor costs	Unit nonlabor payments	Implicit price deflator
1947																
1st quarter	32.3	20.3	63.0	6.8	40.4	21.0	18.4	20.0	36.8	19.9	54.2	7.2	43.0	19.6	16.8	18.6
2nd quarter	32.7	20.6	62.9	6.9	40.8	21.2	18.3	20.1	37.7	20.4	54.2	7.3	43.1	19.5	17.8	18.9
3rd quarter	32.6	20.7	63.4	7.0	40.2	21.4	19.1	20.6	36.6	19.9	54.3	7.5	43.1	20.5	18.4	19.7
4th quarter	33.0	21.1	63.9	7.2	40.6	21.9	19.7	21.1	38.1	20.9	54.9	7.7	43.0	20.1	18.7	19.6
1948																
1st quarter	33.7	21.4	63.6	7.4	40.4	21.9	20.5	21.3	38.1	21.1	55.2	7.9	43.2	20.7	18.9	20.0
2nd quarter	34.3	21.9	63.6	7.5	40.2	21.7	21.3	21.6	38.2	21.1	55.2	8.0	43.1	20.9	19.3	20.4
3rd quarter	34.1	21.9	64.2	7.7	40.7	22.5	21.2	22.0	38.3	21.3	55.6	8.2	43.3	21.3	19.7	20.7
4th quarter	34.4	21.9	63.8	7.8	42.0	22.8	20.7	22.0	38.6	21.3	55.1	8.3	44.3	21.4	20.1	20.9
1949																
1st quarter	34.3	21.6	62.9	7.7	41.6	22.4	20.8	21.8	39.0	21.1	54.1	8.3	45.0	21.3	19.9	20.8
2nd quarter	34.4	21.5	62.3	7.6	41.1	22.0	20.8	21.6	39.2	20.9	53.2	8.3	44.9	21.1	19.9	20.7
3rd quarter	35.5	21.7	61.3	7.7	42.1	21.7	20.9	21.4	40.3	21.2	52.6	8.3	45.5	20.7	20.5	20.6
4th quarter	35.5	21.5	60.5	7.8	42.7	22.0	20.4	21.4	39.9	20.9	52.4	8.3	45.6	20.9	20.1	20.6
1950																
1st quarter	37.2	22.6	60.7	8.1	44.3	21.7	20.7	21.3	41.4	21.9	52.8	8.5	46.9	20.6	20.6	20.6
2nd quarter	37.5	23.3	62.1	8.1	44.3	21.7	21.0	21.5	41.9	22.7	54.1	8.7	47.4	20.8	20.6	20.7
3rd quarter	38.1	24.3	63.7	8.3	44.3	21.7	22.3	21.9	42.8	23.9	55.9	8.9	47.4	20.7	21.3	20.9
4th quarter	38.3	24.5	64.1	8.5	44.3	22.1	23.0	22.4	42.8	24.1	56.4	9.1	47.8	21.3	21.5	21.4
1951																
1st quarter	38.2	24.7	64.7	8.7	44.1	22.9	23.9	23.3	42.9	24.6	57.3	9.3	47.0	21.7	22.3	22.0
2nd quarter	38.4	25.0	65.1	9.0	44.8	23.4	23.7	23.5	42.8	24.7	57.8	9.5	47.5	22.2	22.3	22.3
3rd quarter	39.6	25.4	64.3	9.1	45.6	23.1	24.1	23.4	43.7	25.0	57.2	9.7	48.2	22.1	22.9	22.4
4th quarter	39.4	25.4	64.5	9.2	45.3	23.4	24.3	23.7	43.8	25.0	57.2	9.8	48.2	22.4	22.9	22.6
1952																
1st quarter	39.6	25.7	64.8	9.3	45.7	23.5	23.7	23.6	43.9	25.3	57.6	9.9	48.7	22.6	22.6	22.6
2nd quarter	40.0	25.6	64.2	9.5	46.4	23.8	23.2	23.6	44.1	25.3	57.4	10.0	48.9	22.7	22.1	22.5
3rd quarter	40.1	25.8	64.4	9.6	46.7	24.0	23.5	23.8	43.8	25.3	57.8	10.1	49.0	23.0	22.3	22.8
4th quarter	40.6	26.8	66.0	9.8	47.8	24.2	23.2	23.9	44.7	26.5	59.3	10.4	50.2	23.2	22.6	22.9
1953																
1st quarter	41.2	27.3	66.3	10.0	48.8	24.3	23.1	23.9	44.9	27.0	60.0	10.5	51.0	23.3	22.6	23.1
2nd quarter	41.6	27.6	66.2	10.1	49.1	24.3	23.0	23.8	45.1	27.1	60.1	10.6	51.4	23.5	22.5	23.2
3rd quarter	41.6	27.3	65.6	10.3	49.6	24.7	22.7	24.0	45.4	27.0	59.5	10.7	51.8	23.7	22.4	23.2
4th quarter	41.5	26.8	64.5	10.3	49.5	24.8	22.7	24.0	45.1	26.4	58.5	10.8	52.1	24.0	21.9	23.2
1954																
1st quarter	41.5	26.6	64.1	10.3	49.7	24.9	22.6	24.1	45.2	26.1	57.7	10.9	52.5	24.1	22.0	23.4
2nd quarter	42.1	26.6	63.2	10.5	50.5	25.0	22.4	24.0	45.6	26.1	57.3	10.9	52.6	24.0	22.3	23.4
3rd quarter	42.7	26.9	63.0	10.5	50.8	24.7	23.0	24.1	46.4	26.4	57.0	11.0	53.2	23.8	22.6	23.4
4th quarter	43.3	27.5	63.4	10.7	51.7	24.6	23.1	24.1	46.8	27.0	57.8	11.1	53.9	23.8	22.9	23.5
1955																
1st quarter	44.0	28.4	64.6	10.6	51.4	24.2	24.2	24.2	47.8	28.0	58.7	11.2	54.2	23.5	23.7	23.6
2nd quarter	44.3	28.9	65.3	10.8	52.2	24.3	24.1	24.2	47.9	28.5	59.5	11.3	54.9	23.7	23.7	23.7
3rd quarter	44.2	29.3	66.3	10.8	52.2	24.4	24.4	24.4	48.1	28.9	60.1	11.5	55.5	23.9	24.0	23.9
4th quarter	43.9	29.4	67.0	10.9	52.6	24.9	24.3	24.7	47.8	29.1	60.8	11.6	56.0	24.3	23.9	24.1
1956																
1st quarter	43.8	29.3	66.8	11.2	54.0	25.6	23.7	24.9	47.3	28.9	61.2	11.8	56.9	24.9	23.3	24.3
2nd quarter	44.0	29.5	67.0	11.4	54.7	26.0	23.4	25.0	47.4	29.1	61.3	12.0	57.6	25.3	23.1	24.5
3rd quarter	44.0	29.3	66.8	11.5	54.7	26.3	23.8	25.3	47.4	29.0	61.1	12.2	57.9	25.7	23.2	24.8
4th quarter	44.9	29.9	66.6	11.8	55.5	26.3	23.9	25.4	47.9	29.4	61.4	12.4	58.3	25.9	23.3	25.0
1957																
1st quarter	45.1	30.0	66.5	12.0	56.1	26.7	24.3	25.8	48.5	29.8	61.4	12.6	58.7	26.0	24.0	25.3
2nd quarter	45.2	29.9	66.2	12.2	56.2	26.9	24.3	26.0	48.3	29.6	61.3	12.7	58.8	26.3	23.8	25.4
3rd quarter	45.7	30.2	66.1	12.3	56.2	26.9	24.7	26.1	49.0	29.9	61.0	12.9	59.0	26.3	24.2	25.5
4th quarter	46.1	29.8	64.6	12.5	56.9	27.1	24.3	26.0	49.2	29.4	59.7	13.1	59.6	26.6	23.9	25.6
1958																
1st quarter	45.7	28.7	62.8	12.6	56.8	27.6	24.2	26.3	48.5	28.3	58.4	13.1	59.1	27.0	23.4	25.7
2nd quarter	46.4	28.9	62.3	12.6	56.6	27.3	24.8	26.4	49.4	28.4	57.5	13.2	59.2	26.8	24.0	25.8
3rd quarter	47.2	29.6	62.7	12.9	57.7	27.3	25.3	26.5	50.3	29.3	58.2	13.4	60.1	26.6	24.5	25.9
4th quarter	47.7	30.4	63.7	13.0	58.1	27.2	25.8	26.7	51.1	30.2	59.1	13.5	60.6	26.5	25.1	26.0
1959																
1st quarter	48.2	31.2	64.7	13.2	58.8	27.3	25.6	26.6	51.3	30.9	60.2	13.7	61.0	26.6	25.2	26.1
2nd quarter	48.5	32.1	66.2	13.2	58.8	27.2	25.7	26.6	52.0	31.9	61.4	13.8	61.5	26.6	25.3	26.1
3rd quarter	48.8	32.0	65.6	13.4	59.3	27.4	25.4	26.7	52.0	31.8	61.2	13.9	61.6	26.7	25.2	26.1
4th quarter	49.0	32.1	65.5	13.5	59.7	27.7	25.2	26.8	52.0	31.8	61.2	14.0	61.9	27.0	25.0	26.3
1960																
1st quarter	50.3	32.9	65.4	13.9	61.2	27.6	25.5	26.9	53.1	32.7	61.6	14.3	63.1	27.0	25.2	26.3
2nd quarter	49.3	32.5	66.0	13.8	60.6	28.1	25.0	27.0	52.3	32.3	61.6	14.4	63.1	27.5	24.4	26.4
3rd quarter	49.4	32.6	65.9	13.8	60.5	28.0	25.3	27.0	52.5	32.2	61.3	14.5	63.5	27.6	24.5	26.5
4th quarter	49.1	31.9	65.1	14.0	60.7	28.4	24.6	27.0	51.8	31.4	60.7	14.6	63.4	28.1	23.9	26.6
1961																
1st quarter	49.6	32.1	64.7	14.1	61.2	28.4	24.8	27.1	52.5	31.7	60.3	14.7	63.9	28.0	24.2	26.6
2nd quarter	51.3	32.8	63.9	14.4	62.6	28.1	25.5	27.1	54.1	32.5	60.1	14.9	64.8	27.6	25.0	26.7
3rd quarter	51.9	33.4	64.4	14.5	62.8	28.0	25.8	27.2	54.8	33.1	60.5	15.0	65.0	27.5	25.3	26.7
4th quarter	52.5	34.1	65.0	14.7	63.4	28.0	26.0	27.3	55.3	33.9	61.2	15.2	65.4	27.4	25.5	26.7
1962																
1st quarter	52.9	34.8	65.7	14.8	63.8	28.0	26.3	27.4	56.3	34.6	61.5	15.4	66.2	27.3	25.9	26.8
2nd quarter	53.2	35.2	66.1	15.0	64.3	28.2	26.1	27.4	56.1	34.9	62.2	15.5	66.4	27.6	25.7	26.9
3rd quarter	54.0	35.5	65.7	15.1	64.6	28.0	26.5	27.5	56.8	35.3	62.1	15.6	66.7	27.5	26.1	27.0
4th quarter	54.5	35.5	65.2	15.3	65.3	28.1	26.4	27.5	57.2	35.3	61.7	15.7	67.1	27.5	26.0	27.0
1963																
1st quarter	54.8	36.0	65.7	15.4	65.4	28.1	26.6	27.5	57.6	35.7	62.1	15.9	67.6	27.6	26.1	27.1
2nd quarter	55.2	36.5	66.1	15.5	65.6	28.0	26.7	27.6	58.1	36.3	62.4	16.0	67.8	27.5	26.3	27.1
3rd quarter	56.4	37.3	66.1	15.7	66.2	27.8	27.2	27.6	59.3	37.1	62.6	16.2	68.1	27.2	26.8	27.1
4th quarter	56.5	37.6	66.5	15.9	66.7	28.1	27.2	27.8	59.3	37.4	63.1	16.3	68.7	27.5	26.7	27.2

Table 19-10. Productivity and Related Data—*Continued*

(1992 = 100, seasonally adjusted.)

Year and quarter	Nonfinancial corporations										Manufacturing					
	Output per hour of all employees	Output	Employee hours	Compensation per hour	Real compensation per hour	Unit costs Total	Labor costs	Non-labor costs	Implicit price deflator	Unit profits	Output per hour of all persons	Output	Hours of all persons	Compensation per hour	Real compensation per hour	Unit labor costs
1947																
1st quarter	...	...	...	...	...	...	...	...	...	...	...	...	...	...	...	...
2nd quarter	...	...	...	...	...	...	...	...	...	...	...	...	...	...	...	...
3rd quarter	...	...	...	...	...	...	...	...	...	...	...	...	...	...	...	...
4th quarter	...	...	...	...	...	...	...	...	...	...	...	...	...	...	...	...
1948																
1st quarter	...	...	...	...	...	...	...	...	...	...	...	...	...	...	...	...
2nd quarter	...	...	...	...	...	...	...	...	...	...	...	...	...	...	...	...
3rd quarter	...	...	...	...	...	...	...	...	...	...	...	...	...	...	...	...
4th quarter	...	...	...	...	...	...	...	...	...	...	...	...	...	...	...	...
1949																
1st quarter	...	...	...	...	...	...	...	...	...	...	33.4	27.4	82.1	8.2	44.6	24.7
2nd quarter	...	...	...	...	...	...	...	...	...	...	33.5	26.3	78.5	8.3	44.9	24.7
3rd quarter	...	...	...	...	...	...	...	...	...	...	33.7	26.5	78.5	8.3	45.2	24.6
4th quarter	...	...	...	...	...	...	...	...	...	...	33.4	25.8	77.3	8.2	45.1	24.6
1950																
1st quarter	...	...	...	...	...	...	...	...	...	...	33.4	26.6	79.6	8.4	46.2	25.2
2nd quarter	...	...	...	...	...	...	...	...	...	...	34.1	28.4	83.3	8.6	46.7	25.1
3rd quarter	...	...	...	...	...	...	...	...	...	...	34.5	30.5	88.4	8.7	46.4	25.1
4th quarter	...	...	...	...	...	...	...	...	...	...	34.0	30.8	90.6	9.0	47.3	26.5
1951																
1st quarter	...	...	...	...	...	...	...	...	...	...	33.9	31.4	92.6	9.2	46.5	27.2
2nd quarter	...	...	...	...	...	...	...	...	...	...	33.7	31.5	93.3	9.5	47.3	28.1
3rd quarter	...	...	...	...	...	...	...	...	...	...	33.6	30.7	91.4	9.7	48.3	28.9
4th quarter	...	...	...	...	...	...	...	...	...	...	34.0	30.9	90.9	9.8	48.3	28.9
1952																
1st quarter	...	...	...	...	...	...	...	...	...	...	34.5	31.9	92.3	10.0	48.8	28.8
2nd quarter	...	...	...	...	...	...	...	...	...	...	34.8	31.7	91.3	10.1	49.4	29.0
3rd quarter	...	...	...	...	...	...	...	...	...	...	35.4	32.7	92.4	10.2	49.5	28.8
4th quarter	...	...	...	...	...	...	...	...	...	...	36.2	35.2	97.3	10.5	50.8	28.9
1953																
1st quarter	...	...	...	...	...	...	...	...	...	...	36.1	35.9	99.3	10.6	51.4	29.3
2nd quarter	...	...	...	...	...	...	...	...	...	...	36.2	36.3	100.1	10.7	51.7	29.5
3rd quarter	...	...	...	...	...	...	...	...	...	...	36.7	36.1	98.3	10.8	52.0	29.4
4th quarter	...	...	...	...	...	...	...	...	...	...	36.4	34.4	94.5	10.9	52.6	30.0
1954																
1st quarter	...	...	...	...	...	...	...	...	...	...	36.5	33.3	91.3	11.1	53.2	30.3
2nd quarter	...	...	...	...	...	...	...	...	...	...	37.1	33.2	89.5	11.2	53.7	30.1
3rd quarter	...	...	...	...	...	...	...	...	...	...	37.6	33.2	88.2	11.2	54.3	29.9
4th quarter	...	...	...	...	...	...	...	...	...	...	38.0	34.0	89.5	11.4	55.3	30.1
1955																
1st quarter	...	...	...	...	...	...	...	...	...	...	38.6	35.5	92.0	11.5	55.5	29.7
2nd quarter	...	...	...	...	...	...	...	...	...	...	38.9	36.8	94.6	11.5	55.8	29.7
3rd quarter	...	...	...	...	...	...	...	...	...	...	38.9	36.9	95.0	11.7	56.7	30.2
4th quarter	...	...	...	...	...	...	...	...	...	...	38.8	37.5	96.6	11.9	57.4	30.7
1956																
1st quarter	...	...	...	...	...	...	...	...	...	...	38.5	37.3	96.7	12.0	57.8	31.1
2nd quarter	...	...	...	...	...	...	...	...	...	...	38.6	37.1	95.9	12.3	58.8	31.8
3rd quarter	...	...	...	...	...	...	...	...	...	...	38.5	36.3	94.5	12.6	59.7	32.7
4th quarter	...	...	...	...	...	...	...	...	...	...	38.0	37.6	96.7	12.8	60.1	32.9
1957																
1st quarter	...	...	...	...	...	...	...	...	...	...	39.2	38.0	96.8	12.9	60.2	32.9
2nd quarter	...	...	...	...	...	...	...	...	...	...	39.3	37.4	95.4	13.1	60.4	33.3
3rd quarter	...	...	...	...	...	...	...	...	...	...	39.8	37.5	94.2	13.3	60.8	33.3
4th quarter	...	...	...	...	...	...	...	...	...	...	39.3	36.0	91.5	13.4	61.0	34.1
1958																
1st quarter	50.3	24.0	49.6	14.2	63.8	26.9	28.2	23.4	28.2	42.9	38.8	34.0	87.5	13.5	60.7	34.7
2nd quarter	51.4	24.9	48.4	14.3	64.0	26.8	27.9	23.9	28.2	43.7	39.5	33.5	84.7	13.7	61.1	34.6
3rd quarter	52.3	25.7	49.0	14.5	65.0	26.6	27.7	23.5	28.4	48.2	40.6	35.0	86.2	13.9	62.2	34.2
4th quarter	53.4	26.7	50.1	14.6	65.5	26.2	27.4	23.0	28.6	53.9	41.2	36.3	88.1	14.0	62.8	34.1
1959																
1st quarter	53.8	27.7	51.5	14.7	65.7	26.0	27.3	22.5	28.6	56.3	41.2	37.6	91.4	14.1	62.9	34.2
2nd quarter	54.9	29.0	52.7	14.9	66.3	25.7	27.1	21.9	28.5	59.5	41.6	39.1	93.9	14.2	63.4	34.2
3rd quarter	54.3	28.4	52.3	15.0	66.6	26.4	27.7	22.9	28.6	52.7	40.4	37.3	92.4	14.3	63.6	35.5
4th quarter	54.6	28.7	52.5	15.2	66.9	26.5	27.8	23.1	28.7	51.9	40.5	37.4	92.2	14.4	63.6	35.6
1960																
1st quarter	55.6	29.7	53.4	15.4	67.9	26.4	27.7	22.8	28.8	54.6	42.1	39.9	94.7	14.7	64.8	34.9
2nd quarter	55.0	29.4	53.4	15.5	68.0	26.8	28.2	23.2	28.8	50.1	41.7	38.9	93.2	14.8	65.0	35.6
3rd quarter	55.3	29.3	53.0	15.6	68.2	26.9	28.2	23.5	28.8	49.3	41.6	38.1	91.6	14.9	65.1	35.7
4th quarter	55.7	29.0	52.1	15.8	68.5	27.1	28.3	23.9	28.8	46.8	41.7	37.1	88.9	15.1	65.5	36.1
1961																
1st quarter	55.8	28.8	51.6	15.9	68.9	27.3	28.5	24.3	28.9	45.5	41.4	36.4	87.8	15.1	65.7	36.6
2nd quarter	57.2	29.7	51.9	16.0	69.7	26.8	28.1	23.8	28.9	49.9	42.5	37.8	89.0	15.3	66.2	35.9
3rd quarter	57.7	30.3	52.6	16.2	69.9	26.8	28.0	23.7	28.9	51.3	43.3	39.0	90.1	15.3	66.3	35.4
4th quarter	58.6	31.3	53.4	16.3	70.6	26.7	27.9	23.4	29.0	54.1	43.9	40.4	91.9	15.5	66.8	35.2
1962																
1st quarter	59.3	31.9	53.8	16.5	71.1	26.7	27.9	23.3	29.1	55.6	44.1	40.9	92.5	15.7	67.6	35.6
2nd quarter	59.2	32.3	54.6	16.7	71.4	26.8	28.1	23.4	29.1	53.5	43.8	41.1	93.9	15.8	67.8	36.1
3rd quarter	59.7	32.7	54.8	16.8	71.6	26.8	28.1	23.6	29.2	54.1	44.1	41.4	93.8	15.9	68.0	36.1
4th quarter	60.5	33.1	54.8	16.9	72.2	26.8	28.0	23.5	29.2	55.4	44.5	41.6	93.5	16.1	68.5	36.1
1963																
1st quarter	60.8	33.5	55.1	17.0	72.4	26.8	28.0	23.5	29.2	55.4	45.0	42.1	93.7	16.2	68.7	36.0
2nd quarter	61.5	34.3	55.7	17.1	72.6	26.6	27.8	23.2	29.2	58.0	45.7	43.1	94.3	16.3	69.0	35.5
3rd quarter	62.1	34.8	56.0	17.3	72.9	26.6	27.8	23.3	29.3	58.5	45.7	43.3	94.6	16.4	69.1	35.8

... = Not available.

Table 19-10. Productivity and Related Data—Continued

(1992 = 100, seasonally adjusted.)

Year and quarter	Business sector								Nonfarm business sector							
	Output per hour of all persons	Output	Hours of all persons	Compensation per hour	Real compensation per hour	Unit labor costs	Unit nonlabor payments	Implicit price deflator	Output per hour of all persons	Output	Hours of all persons	Compensation per hour	Real compensation per hour	Unit labor costs	Unit nonlabor payments	Implicit price deflator
1964																
1st quarter	57.3	38.5	67.2	16.0	66.9	27.9	27.7	27.8	60.0	38.5	64.2	16.3	68.4	27.2	27.4	27.3
2nd quarter	57.5	39.0	67.9	16.1	67.3	28.0	27.6	27.8	60.4	39.0	64.5	16.5	69.0	27.3	27.5	27.4
3rd quarter	58.0	39.6	68.2	16.3	68.0	28.1	27.6	27.9	60.8	39.5	64.9	16.7	69.8	27.5	27.5	27.5
4th quarter	57.7	39.6	68.7	16.5	68.3	28.5	27.3	28.1	60.2	39.5	65.6	16.9	70.0	28.0	26.9	27.6
1965																
1st quarter	58.7	40.8	69.5	16.6	68.7	28.3	28.1	28.2	61.1	40.7	66.6	16.9	70.0	27.7	27.8	27.7
2nd quarter	58.8	41.4	70.4	16.7	68.6	28.4	28.2	28.3	61.5	41.3	67.2	17.0	70.1	27.7	27.8	27.8
3rd quarter	60.1	42.3	70.3	16.9	69.3	28.1	28.9	28.4	62.6	42.2	67.4	17.2	70.6	27.5	28.5	27.9
4th quarter	61.1	43.4	71.0	17.1	69.7	28.0	29.5	28.5	63.7	43.3	68.0	17.5	71.2	27.4	28.9	28.0
1966																
1st quarter	62.2	44.6	71.7	17.5	70.7	28.1	29.7	28.7	64.7	44.6	69.0	17.8	71.8	27.5	29.1	28.0
2nd quarter	61.8	44.7	72.2	17.8	71.3	28.8	29.1	28.9	64.3	44.8	69.7	18.0	72.3	28.1	28.8	28.3
3rd quarter	61.9	44.8	72.4	18.1	71.8	29.2	29.2	29.2	64.3	45.0	70.0	18.3	72.7	28.5	28.8	28.6
4th quarter	62.5	45.1	72.2	18.4	72.4	29.4	29.5	29.4	64.7	45.2	69.8	18.6	73.1	28.7	29.3	28.9
1967																
1st quarter	63.1	45.5	72.1	18.6	72.9	29.4	29.8	29.5	65.3	45.5	69.7	18.8	74.0	28.8	29.5	29.1
2nd quarter	63.6	45.4	71.4	18.9	73.8	29.7	29.6	29.7	65.6	45.4	69.2	19.1	74.7	29.2	29.3	29.2
3rd quarter	63.6	45.7	71.8	19.1	73.9	30.1	29.8	30.0	65.8	45.7	69.5	19.4	75.0	29.5	29.5	29.5
4th quarter	63.7	46.0	72.2	19.3	73.9	30.4	30.1	30.2	66.0	46.1	69.9	19.7	75.1	29.8	29.7	29.7
1968																
1st quarter	65.0	47.1	72.4	19.9	75.3	30.6	30.5	30.6	67.3	47.2	70.1	20.2	76.4	30.0	30.2	30.1
2nd quarter	65.7	48.0	73.1	20.2	75.9	30.8	31.0	30.9	67.9	48.1	70.9	20.5	76.8	30.2	30.8	30.4
3rd quarter	65.7	48.3	73.5	20.6	76.2	31.4	30.6	31.1	67.8	48.4	71.4	20.8	77.0	30.7	30.4	30.6
4th quarter	65.6	48.5	73.9	21.0	76.8	32.0	30.6	31.5	67.7	48.6	71.8	21.2	77.6	31.4	30.3	31.0
1969																
1st quarter	65.8	49.3	75.0	21.1	76.2	32.1	31.4	31.8	68.3	49.5	72.5	21.5	77.7	31.5	31.0	31.3
2nd quarter	65.7	49.4	75.1	21.7	77.0	32.9	31.1	32.3	67.7	49.5	73.1	21.9	77.7	32.3	30.6	31.7
3rd quarter	65.9	49.6	75.3	22.1	77.5	33.6	31.0	32.6	67.7	49.8	73.5	22.3	78.0	32.9	30.6	32.0
4th quarter	65.7	49.2	74.9	22.6	78.0	34.4	30.6	33.0	67.4	49.4	73.3	22.7	78.4	33.7	30.1	32.4
1970																
1st quarter	66.0	49.2	74.6	23.0	78.3	34.9	30.6	33.3	67.6	49.3	73.0	23.1	78.6	34.2	30.2	32.7
2nd quarter	66.8	49.3	73.8	23.3	78.2	34.9	31.7	33.7	68.7	49.4	72.0	23.5	78.8	34.2	31.4	33.2
3rd quarter	68.0	49.9	73.3	23.8	78.9	34.9	32.2	33.9	69.8	50.0	71.6	23.9	79.3	34.3	31.8	33.4
4th quarter	67.7	49.1	72.5	24.1	78.8	35.6	32.3	34.4	69.2	49.2	71.0	24.2	79.1	35.0	32.0	33.9
1971																
1st quarter	69.7	50.8	72.9	24.6	79.6	35.2	34.0	34.8	71.4	50.9	71.3	24.7	80.0	34.6	33.5	34.2
2nd quarter	69.8	51.1	73.2	24.8	79.9	35.6	34.4	35.2	71.6	51.2	71.5	25.1	80.5	35.0	34.0	34.6
3rd quarter	70.6	51.6	73.1	25.3	80.4	35.8	35.0	35.5	72.2	51.7	71.6	25.4	80.9	35.2	34.6	35.0
4th quarter	69.9	51.6	73.9	25.5	80.5	36.4	34.5	35.7	71.5	51.7	72.4	25.6	80.9	35.8	33.9	35.1
1972																
1st quarter	70.7	53.0	74.9	26.0	81.5	36.8	34.8	36.1	72.6	53.2	73.3	26.2	82.1	36.1	34.4	35.5
2nd quarter	72.3	54.5	75.4	26.4	82.0	36.5	35.9	36.3	74.0	54.7	73.9	26.5	82.6	35.9	35.2	35.6
3rd quarter	72.5	55.1	76.0	26.6	82.3	36.7	36.3	36.6	74.4	55.3	74.3	26.9	83.0	36.1	35.3	35.8
4th quarter	73.4	56.2	76.6	27.2	83.3	37.1	36.6	36.9	75.0	56.4	75.1	27.4	83.9	36.6	35.2	36.1
1973																
1st quarter	74.8	58.1	77.6	28.0	84.4	37.5	37.0	37.3	76.7	58.5	76.2	28.2	84.8	36.7	35.5	36.3
2nd quarter	74.9	58.7	78.4	28.5	84.0	38.0	37.8	37.9	76.8	59.1	77.0	28.6	84.4	37.3	35.6	36.7
3rd quarter	74.0	58.3	78.9	29.1	84.0	39.3	37.6	38.7	76.1	59.0	77.5	29.2	84.3	38.4	35.0	37.1
4th quarter	74.2	58.8	79.3	29.7	83.6	40.0	38.8	39.5	75.6	58.9	77.9	29.8	84.1	39.4	35.5	38.0
1974																
1st quarter	73.3	58.1	79.3	30.2	82.8	41.3	38.7	40.3	75.5	58.6	77.5	30.5	83.6	40.4	36.0	38.8
2nd quarter	73.6	58.2	79.1	31.2	83.2	42.4	39.5	41.3	75.3	58.6	77.7	31.4	83.6	41.6	37.9	40.3
3rd quarter	72.8	57.3	78.7	32.2	83.4	44.2	40.0	42.7	74.5	57.7	77.5	32.3	83.7	43.3	38.3	41.5
4th quarter	73.3	56.8	77.5	32.9	82.8	44.9	42.4	44.0	75.1	57.2	76.2	33.1	83.3	44.1	40.4	42.7
1975																
1st quarter	74.3	55.8	75.1	33.9	83.5	45.6	44.1	45.0	75.7	55.9	73.8	34.0	83.8	44.9	42.7	44.1
2nd quarter	75.6	56.3	74.5	34.6	84.2	45.7	45.5	45.6	77.0	56.3	73.1	34.7	84.5	45.1	44.2	44.8
3rd quarter	76.5	57.5	75.2	35.1	83.7	45.9	47.4	46.4	77.9	57.4	73.8	35.3	84.3	45.4	45.6	45.5
4th quarter	76.6	58.4	76.3	35.8	84.0	46.8	47.9	47.2	77.9	58.4	75.0	36.0	84.3	46.2	46.0	46.1
1976																
1st quarter	77.7	60.2	77.4	36.7	85.0	47.2	48.3	47.6	79.2	60.4	76.2	36.8	85.2	46.4	47.0	46.6
2nd quarter	78.4	60.8	77.5	37.5	86.0	47.8	48.4	48.0	80.0	61.0	76.2	37.6	86.3	46.9	47.4	47.1
3rd quarter	78.4	61.1	77.9	38.2	86.4	48.7	48.6	48.7	80.1	61.3	76.5	38.4	86.8	47.9	47.6	47.8
4th quarter	79.0	61.7	78.1	39.1	87.2	49.6	49.5	49.5	80.4	61.9	76.9	39.2	87.4	48.8	48.6	48.7
1977																
1st quarter	79.4	62.6	78.9	39.8	87.1	50.1	50.5	50.3	80.8	62.8	77.8	39.9	87.3	49.4	49.4	49.4
2nd quarter	79.4	64.0	80.6	40.4	86.9	50.9	51.4	51.1	81.1	64.3	79.3	40.7	87.4	50.1	50.5	50.3
3rd quarter	80.4	65.4	81.3	41.3	87.6	51.3	52.2	51.7	82.0	65.7	80.1	41.5	88.0	50.6	51.6	51.0
4th quarter	79.6	65.4	82.1	42.0	87.8	52.7	52.5	52.7	80.9	65.4	80.9	42.2	88.2	52.2	51.3	51.9
1978																
1st quarter	79.3	65.4	82.5	43.2	88.9	54.5	51.8	53.5	80.9	65.7	81.2	43.5	89.5	53.7	50.3	52.5
2nd quarter	80.8	68.5	84.8	43.9	88.6	54.4	54.9	54.6	82.5	69.0	83.6	44.2	89.1	53.6	53.3	53.5
3rd quarter	80.9	69.2	85.5	44.8	88.7	55.3	56.0	55.6	82.5	69.5	84.3	45.1	89.2	54.6	54.4	54.6
4th quarter	81.2	70.2	86.4	45.9	89.1	56.5	57.1	56.7	83.0	70.8	85.3	46.1	89.6	55.6	55.7	55.6
1979																
1st quarter	80.8	70.3	87.0	47.2	89.6	58.4	56.8	57.8	82.3	70.7	85.9	47.4	90.0	57.6	54.8	56.6
2nd quarter	80.6	70.3	87.3	48.2	89.2	59.9	58.2	59.3	81.9	70.7	86.3	48.4	89.6	59.1	56.4	58.1
3rd quarter	80.5	70.9	88.1	49.3	88.9	61.2	59.2	60.5	81.8	71.2	87.0	49.5	89.2	60.5	57.3	59.3
4th quarter	80.3	71.0	88.4	50.4	88.7	62.8	59.6	61.6	81.7	71.3	87.2	50.7	89.2	62.1	57.9	60.5
1980																
1st quarter	80.8	71.0	88.0	52.0	88.7	64.4	60.8	63.1	82.0	71.4	87.0	52.2	89.0	63.6	59.7	62.2
2nd quarter	79.9	69.0	86.4	53.4	89.0	66.9	64.0	64.5	81.1	69.3	85.4	53.6	89.3	66.1	60.3	64.0
3rd quarter	80.0	68.8	86.0	54.8	89.1	68.5	61.5	65.9	81.5	69.2	85.0	55.0	89.6	67.5	60.4	65.0
4th quarter	80.6	70.4	87.3	56.0	89.0	69.5	64.0	67.5	82.1	70.8	86.2	56.3	89.6	68.6	62.2	66.3

Table 19-10. Productivity and Related Data—Continued

(1992 = 100, seasonally adjusted.)

Year and quarter	Nonfinancial corporations										Manufacturing					
	Output per hour of all employees	Output	Employee hours	Compensation per hour	Real compensation per hour	Total	Labor costs	Non-labor costs	Implicit price deflator	Unit profits	Output per hour of all persons	Output	Hours of all persons	Compensation per hour	Real compensation per hour	Unit labor costs
1964																
1st quarter	63.8	36.0	56.4	17.7	74.3	26.5	27.8	23.1	29.5	61.3	46.9	44.5	95.0	16.8	70.4	35.8
2nd quarter	63.9	36.6	57.2	17.9	74.7	26.6	27.9	23.2	29.5	60.3	47.4	45.5	96.1	17.0	71.0	35.8
3rd quarter	64.6	37.3	57.8	18.1	75.4	26.7	28.0	23.2	29.5	60.1	47.6	46.1	97.0	17.2	71.6	36.1
4th quarter	64.1	37.5	58.5	18.1	75.3	27.0	28.3	23.5	29.7	58.9	47.8	46.6	97.5	17.2	71.5	36.0
1965																
1st quarter	65.3	38.9	59.5	18.3	75.5	26.7	27.9	23.3	29.8	64.1	48.2	48.3	100.3	17.3	71.4	35.8
2nd quarter	65.4	39.4	60.2	18.4	75.6	26.8	28.1	23.2	30.0	64.8	48.6	49.1	101.0	17.4	71.4	35.7
3rd quarter	65.9	40.1	60.9	18.6	76.1	26.8	28.2	23.1	30.0	64.7	48.8	50.0	102.4	17.4	71.5	35.7
4th quarter	66.5	41.2	62.0	18.8	76.7	26.8	28.3	23.0	30.1	65.8	48.6	50.6	104.2	17.6	71.7	36.2
1966																
1st quarter	66.6	42.0	63.1	19.0	76.8	27.0	28.5	22.7	30.4	67.1	48.7	51.9	106.7	17.8	72.0	36.6
2nd quarter	66.7	42.6	63.8	19.3	77.5	27.4	29.0	23.0	30.6	65.2	48.8	53.0	108.6	18.1	72.4	37.0
3rd quarter	66.6	42.9	64.4	19.7	78.1	27.8	29.5	23.3	30.8	63.1	49.2	53.8	109.4	18.3	72.8	37.3
4th quarter	66.9	43.3	64.8	19.9	78.5	28.1	29.8	23.6	31.1	63.4	49.6	54.5	109.8	18.6	73.2	37.5
1967																
1st quarter	67.1	43.3	64.6	20.2	79.2	28.4	30.1	24.0	31.2	61.0	50.0	54.4	108.8	18.8	73.8	37.6
2nd quarter	67.6	43.5	64.3	20.4	79.8	28.7	30.2	24.4	31.3	59.9	50.5	54.3	107.5	19.0	74.4	37.7
3rd quarter	67.7	43.8	64.7	20.7	80.0	29.0	30.6	24.9	31.6	59.9	50.9	54.7	107.4	19.4	74.8	38.1
4th quarter	68.3	44.6	65.3	21.0	80.1	29.2	30.7	25.2	31.9	61.2	52.0	56.3	108.2	19.6	74.9	37.7
1968																
1st quarter	69.2	45.3	65.5	21.6	81.7	29.7	31.2	25.7	32.3	60.1	52.4	57.0	108.7	20.1	76.3	38.4
2nd quarter	70.0	46.3	66.2	21.9	82.3	29.9	31.3	26.0	32.5	61.1	52.7	57.6	109.2	20.6	77.1	39.0
3rd quarter	70.3	47.0	67.0	22.3	82.4	30.3	31.7	26.4	32.8	59.9	52.5	57.7	109.9	20.8	76.8	39.5
4th quarter	70.5	47.6	67.5	22.7	83.0	30.8	32.2	26.8	33.2	60.0	53.0	58.5	110.4	21.2	77.5	40.0
1969																
1st quarter	70.2	48.0	68.4	23.0	82.9	31.2	32.7	27.3	33.6	58.7	53.6	59.4	110.8	21.6	77.9	40.3
2nd quarter	70.2	48.4	69.0	23.4	83.2	31.9	33.4	28.0	33.9	56.1	53.3	59.3	111.2	21.9	77.9	41.1
3rd quarter	70.1	48.8	69.6	23.8	83.6	32.6	34.0	28.6	34.3	53.5	53.6	59.7	111.4	22.4	78.5	41.7
4th quarter	69.8	48.6	69.6	24.3	84.0	33.4	34.8	29.4	·34.7	49.5	53.6	59.1	110.2	22.8	78.8	42.5
1970																
1st quarter	69.3	47.9	69.2	24.7	83.9	34.3	35.7	30.6	35.1	44.2	52.8	57.3	108.4	23.1	78.6	43.8
2nd quarter	70.1	48.0	68.5	25.1	84.0	34.6	35.8	31.5	35.6	46.6	53.8	56.8	105.6	23.6	79.1	43.8
3rd quarter	71.2	48.4	68.0	25.6	84.8	34.8	35.9	32.1	35.7	45.1	54.6	56.6	103.6	24.0	79.6	43.9
4th quarter	70.9	47.5	67.0	25.9	84.6	35.6	36.4	33.3	36.1	41.8	55.5	55.4	99.9	24.3	79.4	43.8
1971																
1st quarter	72.8	49.1	67.4	26.3	85.4	35.3	36.2	33.1	36.5	49.5	56.7	57.1	100.6	24.8	80.4	43.7
2nd quarter	72.9	49.5	67.9	26.7	85.9	35.7	36.6	33.3	36.9	49.9	57.5	57.8	100.5	25.1	80.6	43.6
3rd quarter	73.7	50.0	67.9	27.1	86.3	36.0	36.8	33.7	37.2	50.1	58.1	58.1	100.0	25.3	80.5	43.6
4th quarter	73.8	50.9	68.9	27.3	86.3	36.1	37.0	33.6	37.4	51.3	59.1	59.6	100.9	25.5	80.6	43.2
1972																
1st quarter	74.4	52.2	70.1	27.9	87.3	36.3	37.4	33.2	37.7	52.9	59.8	61.6	102.9	26.0	81.5	43.4
2nd quarter	74.9	53.3	71.2	28.2	87.7	36.6	37.6	33.8	37.9	51.9	59.9	62.8	104.7	26.3	81.8	43.8
3rd quarter	75.4	54.1	71.7	28.5	88.1	36.7	37.9	33.5	38.2	54.3	60.2	63.4	105.2	26.6	82.1	44.1
4th quarter	76.3	55.6	72.9	29.2	89.1	36.9	38.2	33.5	38.6	57.0	61.1	65.6	107.4	27.0	82.6	44.2
1973																
1st quarter	77.0	56.9	73.9	29.8	89.7	37.3	38.7	33.7	39.1	58.2	61.3	67.1	109.4	27.7	83.5	45.3
2nd quarter	76.1	56.9	74.7	30.3	89.5	38.5	39.9	34.7	39.8	54.7	61.4	67.7	110.4	28.2	83.1	46.0
3rd quarter	75.8	56.9	75.1	31.0	89.7	39.5	40.9	35.6	40.7	53.8	61.9	68.3	110.4	28.7	83.1	46.4
4th quarter	75.4	57.1	75.8	31.6	89.2	40.5	42.0	36.3	41.7	55.4	61.2	68.2	111.4	29.3	82.6	47.8
1974																
1st quarter	74.7	56.6	75.7	32.3	88.4	41.7	43.2	37.8	42.5	50.5	60.0	66.0	110.0	30.1	82.4	50.2
2nd quarter	75.1	56.7	75.5	33.2	88.6	42.9	44.3	39.3	43.5	49.9	61.0	66.4	108.8	31.2	83.1	51.1
3rd quarter	74.3	56.0	75.4	34.2	88.6	44.7	46.0	41.3	45.0	48.2	61.7	66.9	108.4	32.1	83.3	52.0
4th quarter	73.8	54.6	74.0	35.0	88.0	46.5	47.4	43.8	46.6	48.1	62.3	65.1	104.5	33.3	83.7	53.4
1975																
1st quarter	75.0	53.3	71.1	36.0	88.7	47.4	48.0	45.7	47.7	51.6	62.1	60.5	97.3	34.4	84.8	55.4
2nd quarter	77.1	54.2	70.3	36.6	89.2	47.1	47.5	46.1	48.3	60.3	63.7	60.9	95.6	35.2	85.6	55.2
3rd quarter	78.5	56.0	71.3	37.3	89.0	47.0	47.5	45.8	49.1	71.4	65.4	63.4	96.9	35.8	85.5	54.8
4th quarter	78.4	56.8	72.5	38.0	89.1	47.8	48.5	46.0	49.9	72.4	65.8	65.3	99.2	36.4	85.3	55.3
1976																
1st quarter	79.5	58.7	73.9	38.8	89.9	47.7	48.8	44.9	50.2	76.8	66.1	67.0	101.3	37.2	86.3	56.4
2nd quarter	79.6	59.2	74.4	39.5	90.8	48.6	49.7	45.6	50.6	72.1	66.5	67.6	101.7	38.0	87.3	57.2
3rd quarter	80.0	59.8	74.8	40.5	91.4	49.3	50.6	46.0	51.2	71.1	67.1	68.5	102.0	38.8	87.8	57.8
4th quarter	79.9	60.1	75.2	41.3	92.0	50.4	51.7	46.9	52.0	69.4	68.1	69.8	102.4	39.6	88.3	58.2
1977																
1st quarter	80.2	61.1	76.2	41.9	91.6	51.0	52.2	47.7	52.7	71.4	69.0	71.6	103.8	40.5	88.7	58.7
2nd quarter	81.5	63.4	77.8	42.7	91.9	51.0	52.4	47.1	53.4	79.9	69.7	74.0	106.1	41.3	88.8	59.2
3rd quarter	82.9	65.3	78.8	43.6	92.4	51.0	52.5	46.8	53.9	84.9	70.1	75.0	106.9	42.3	89.6	60.3
4th quarter	81.9	65.3	79.8	44.4	92.8	52.6	54.2	48.2	55.0	81.0	69.8	75.2	107.8	43.0	89.9	61.6
1978																
1st quarter	81.3	65.3	80.3	45.3	93.3	54.1	55.7	49.5	55.8	74.2	69.5	75.2	108.2	43.9	90.4	63.1
2nd quarter	82.4	68.2	82.8	46.2	93.1	54.3	56.1	49.4	56.9	85.3	70.4	77.8	110.6	44.5	89.7	63.2
3rd quarter	82.2	68.8	83.7	47.2	93.4	55.4	57.4	50.0	57.9	84.4	70.7	78.7	111.4	45.5	90.0	64.3
4th quarter	82.5	69.9	84.8	48.4	93.9	56.6	58.6	51.0	59.0	85.6	70.6	79.5	112.5	46.6	90.6	66.0
1979																
1st quarter	82.0	70.2	85.6	49.4	93.8	58.1	60.3	52.4	60.0	80.4	69.9	79.4	113.6	47.6	90.5	68.2
2nd quarter	81.7	70.1	85.8	50.6	93.6	59.9	61.9	54.3	61.4	78.2	70.2	79.0	112.6	49.1	90.8	70.0
3rd quarter	81.2	70.1	86.4	51.7	93.2	61.6	63.6	56.0	62.7	74.7	69.4	78.3	112.9	50.1	90.4	72.2
4th quarter	81.2	70.3	86.6	52.9	93.0	63.1	65.1	57.7	64.0	73.4	69.6	78.0	112.0	51.5	90.5	73.9
1980																
1st quarter	81.1	70.2	86.6	54.3	92.6	65.2	66.9	60.5	65.7	71.7	70.1	78.0	111.4	52.9	90.3	75.5
2nd quarter	80.5	68.3	84.8	55.8	92.9	68.0	69.3	64.5	67.4	61.2	69.6	74.3	106.7	54.8	91.3	78.7
3rd quarter	81.1	68.3	84.3	57.2	93.0	69.5	70.5	66.7	69.2	66.7	69.8	73.2	105.0	56.5	91.9	80.9
4th quarter	81.7	70.0	85.7	58.6	93.1	70.9	71.7	68.6	71.2	75.1	70.6	75.8	107.3	58.0	92.2	82.2

Table 19-10. Productivity and Related Data—Continued

(1992 = 100, seasonally adjusted.)

Year and quarter	Business sector								Nonfarm business sector							
	Output per hour of all persons	Output	Hours of all persons	Compensation per hour	Real compensation per hour	Unit labor costs	Unit nonlabor payments	Implicit price deflator	Output per hour of all persons	Output	Hours of all persons	Compensation per hour	Real compensation per hour	Unit labor costs	Unit nonlabor payments	Implicit price deflator
1981																
1st quarter	82.1	72.0	87.8	57.5	88.9	70.0	68.0	69.3	83.3	72.3	86.7	57.8	89.4	69.4	66.4	68.3
2nd quarter	81.4	71.3	87.6	58.5	88.9	71.9	68.1	70.5	82.2	71.3	86.7	58.9	89.4	71.6	66.5	69.7
3rd quarter	82.4	72.3	87.7	59.8	89.1	72.6	70.9	72.0	83.1	72.0	86.7	60.2	89.6	72.5	69.1	71.3
4th quarter	81.6	71.1	87.1	60.9	89.2	74.7	70.4	73.1	82.3	70.8	86.1	61.3	89.7	74.5	69.3	72.6
1982																
1st quarter	81.1	69.5	85.7	62.5	90.4	77.0	68.7	74.0	81.8	69.3	84.7	62.9	90.9	76.8	67.7	73.5
2nd quarter	81.4	69.9	85.8	63.2	90.5	77.6	70.2	74.9	82.1	69.7	84.9	63.5	90.9	77.3	69.3	74.4
3rd quarter	81.5	69.4	85.2	64.1	90.3	78.7	70.9	75.8	82.2	69.2	84.2	64.5	90.9	78.5	69.8	75.3
4th quarter	82.4	69.5	84.3	65.0	90.6	78.9	72.1	76.4	83.0	69.2	83.4	65.4	91.1	78.8	71.4	76.1
1983																
1st quarter	83.1	70.4	84.8	65.5	90.8	78.9	73.5	76.9	84.0	70.4	83.9	66.0	91.4	78.6	72.7	76.4
2nd quarter	84.6	72.6	85.8	66.0	90.4	78.0	76.5	77.5	85.9	73.0	85.0	66.4	90.9	77.3	76.2	76.9
3rd quarter	84.8	74.1	87.4	66.4	90.1	78.3	77.7	78.1	86.7	75.0	86.5	66.9	90.8	77.1	77.9	77.4
4th quarter	85.4	76.0	89.0	67.3	90.5	78.8	78.6	78.7	87.0	76.8	88.3	67.6	90.9	77.7	78.5	78.0
1984																
1st quarter	86.1	78.0	90.6	68.0	90.2	78.9	79.8	79.3	87.2	78.4	89.9	68.3	90.7	78.4	78.7	78.5
2nd quarter	86.9	79.7	91.7	68.7	90.4	79.1	80.8	79.8	87.8	79.9	91.0	69.1	90.9	78.7	79.7	79.1
3rd quarter	87.0	80.3	92.3	69.6	90.9	80.0	80.8	80.3	87.9	80.5	91.6	70.0	91.3	79.6	79.8	79.7
4th quarter	87.3	80.9	92.7	70.4	91.1	80.6	81.0	80.8	88.1	81.0	92.0	70.7	91.6	80.3	80.1	80.2
1985																
1st quarter	87.5	81.7	93.4	71.2	91.4	81.4	81.7	81.5	88.1	81.7	92.8	71.5	91.8	81.2	80.8	81.0
2nd quarter	87.8	82.3	93.8	71.9	91.5	81.9	82.2	82.0	88.3	82.4	93.3	72.1	91.8	81.7	81.6	81.7
3rd quarter	89.2	83.8	93.9	73.0	92.4	81.8	83.1	82.3	89.4	83.6	93.5	73.2	92.6	81.9	82.8	82.2
4th quarter	89.6	84.5	94.3	74.3	93.0	82.9	82.6	82.8	89.8	84.5	94.1	74.4	93.2	82.8	82.1	82.6
1986																
1st quarter	90.6	85.3	94.2	75.2	93.7	83.0	82.9	83.0	91.0	85.4	93.9	75.4	94.0	82.9	82.7	82.8
2nd quarter	91.2	85.7	93.9	75.9	95.1	83.2	83.2	83.2	91.7	85.8	93.6	76.1	95.4	83.0	83.0	83.0
3rd quarter	91.6	86.5	94.5	76.6	95.4	83.6	83.4	83.5	92.0	86.6	94.2	76.8	95.7	83.5	82.8	83.3
4th quarter	91.4	86.9	95.2	77.8	96.3	85.2	82.4	84.2	91.8	87.1	94.9	78.1	96.6	85.0	81.8	83.9
1987																
1st quarter	90.9	87.6	96.4	78.0	95.4	85.8	82.7	84.6	91.3	87.7	96.2	78.2	95.7	85.7	82.2	84.4
2nd quarter	91.5	88.7	96.9	78.8	95.4	86.1	83.8	85.3	91.9	88.9	96.7	79.0	95.7	86.0	83.4	85.0
3rd quarter	91.6	89.3	97.5	79.7	95.6	87.0	84.1	85.9	91.9	89.4	97.3	79.9	95.8	87.0	83.6	85.7
4th quarter	92.4	91.0	98.4	80.8	96.1	87.4	84.7	86.4	92.7	91.1	98.3	80.9	96.2	87.3	84.2	86.2
1988																
1st quarter	92.8	91.5	98.6	81.8	96.6	88.1	84.7	86.9	93.0	91.6	98.5	81.9	96.7	88.1	84.1	86.7
2nd quarter	92.9	92.8	99.9	83.1	97.1	89.4	84.9	87.8	93.2	93.1	99.8	83.1	97.2	89.1	84.7	87.5
3rd quarter	93.1	93.1	100.0	84.1	97.2	90.3	86.3	88.8	93.5	93.6	100.1	84.0	97.2	89.9	85.8	88.4
4th quarter	93.3	94.4	101.2	84.6	96.9	90.7	87.5	89.5	94.0	95.2	101.2	84.6	96.9	90.0	87.6	89.1
1989																
1st quarter	93.6	95.7	102.2	84.6	96.0	90.4	90.3	90.4	93.8	95.9	102.3	84.6	96.0	90.2	89.5	90.0
2nd quarter	93.9	96.1	102.3	85.2	95.1	90.7	92.4	91.3	94.0	96.3	102.5	85.0	95.0	90.5	91.9	91.0
3rd quarter	93.9	96.4	102.6	85.9	95.2	91.4	92.7	91.9	94.1	96.6	102.7	85.8	95.1	91.1	92.4	91.6
4th quarter	94.2	96.8	102.8	87.0	95.7	92.3	92.8	92.5	94.4	97.0	102.8	87.0	95.6	92.1	92.2	92.2
1990																
1st quarter	95.0	98.2	103.4	88.4	95.6	93.1	94.0	93.4	95.0	98.4	103.5	88.2	95.4	92.8	93.5	93.0
2nd quarter	95.5	98.2	102.8	90.3	96.9	94.5	94.2	94.4	95.6	98.5	103.0	90.0	96.6	94.2	93.8	94.1
3rd quarter	95.8	97.7	102.0	91.7	96.8	95.8	94.3	95.2	95.7	97.9	102.3	91.5	96.5	95.6	93.9	94.9
4th quarter	94.9	96.5	101.7	92.4	96.0	97.4	93.8	96.1	94.9	96.6	101.8	92.3	95.9	97.2	93.7	95.9
1991																
1st quarter	95.1	95.7	100.6	93.0	96.2	97.8	96.1	97.1	95.2	95.8	100.6	92.9	96.1	97.6	96.1	97.1
2nd quarter	96.3	96.4	100.1	94.6	97.4	98.3	97.0	97.8	96.5	96.5	100.1	94.6	97.3	98.1	97.0	97.7
3rd quarter	96.6	96.6	100.0	95.6	97.8	99.0	97.4	98.4	96.8	96.8	100.0	95.6	97.8	98.8	97.8	98.4
4th quarter	97.4	97.2	99.8	96.8	98.3	99.4	97.8	98.8	97.5	97.3	99.8	96.7	98.3	99.3	97.9	98.8
1992																
1st quarter	99.2	98.5	99.3	98.7	99.7	99.5	99.3	99.4	99.1	98.5	99.3	98.6	99.6	99.5	99.2	99.4
2nd quarter	99.8	99.6	99.8	99.3	99.6	99.5	100.2	99.8	99.8	99.6	99.8	99.4	99.7	99.6	100.1	99.8
3rd quarter	99.6	99.8	100.3	100.6	100.3	101.0	98.5	100.1	99.5	99.8	100.3	100.6	100.3	101.0	98.4	100.1
4th quarter	101.5	102.1	100.6	101.4	100.4	100.0	102.0	100.7	101.5	102.2	100.6	101.4	100.4	99.9	102.2	100.7
1993																
1st quarter	100.3	101.7	101.4	101.7	100.1	101.4	101.5	101.4	100.3	101.8	101.6	101.5	99.9	101.2	102.0	101.5
2nd quarter	100.1	102.5	102.4	102.3	100.0	102.2	101.6	101.9	100.0	102.6	102.6	102.0	99.7	102.0	101.8	101.9
3rd quarter	100.2	103.1	102.9	102.7	99.9	102.5	102.1	102.3	100.4	103.6	103.2	102.4	99.7	102.0	102.9	102.3
4th quarter	101.2	105.1	103.8	103.0	99.6	101.7	104.9	102.9	101.2	105.3	104.1	102.7	99.3	101.5	105.2	102.9
1994																
1st quarter	101.6	106.0	104.3	104.3	100.6	102.7	104.3	103.3	101.5	105.9	104.4	104.1	100.4	102.6	104.3	103.2
2nd quarter	101.7	107.9	106.2	104.1	99.8	102.3	105.9	103.7	101.8	108.0	106.1	104.0	99.8	102.2	106.3	103.7
3rd quarter	101.4	108.5	107.0	104.2	99.1	102.7	107.1	104.3	101.5	108.5	107.0	104.1	99.1	102.6	107.9	104.5
4th quarter	102.1	110.1	107.9	104.9	99.4	102.7	108.3	104.8	102.3	110.3	107.8	104.9	99.4	102.5	109.1	104.9
1995																
1st quarter	101.8	110.5	108.5	105.4	99.2	103.5	108.9	105.5	102.2	110.8	108.4	105.3	99.2	103.1	110.0	105.6
2nd quarter	102.1	110.8	108.4	106.2	99.2	104.0	109.1	105.9	102.5	111.1	108.4	106.2	99.2	103.6	110.3	106.0
3rd quarter	102.2	111.8	109.3	106.9	99.4	104.5	109.3	106.3	102.7	112.2	109.2	106.9	99.4	104.1	110.3	106.3
4th quarter	103.1	112.9	109.5	107.7	99.7	104.5	110.2	106.6	103.5	113.3	109.5	107.7	99.7	104.1	110.8	106.5
1996																
1st quarter	104.2	114.0	109.5	108.3	99.5	104.0	112.3	107.0	104.5	114.4	109.5	108.3	99.5	103.7	112.6	106.9
2nd quarter	105.3	116.1	110.3	109.5	99.7	104.0	113.6	107.5	105.5	116.4	110.4	109.4	99.7	103.7	113.7	107.3
3rd quarter	105.3	116.8	111.0	110.4	100.0	104.9	113.2	108.0	105.4	117.2	111.1	110.3	99.9	104.6	113.3	107.7
4th quarter	105.7	118.4	112.0	111.3	100.1	105.3	113.6	108.4	105.9	118.7	112.2	111.2	99.9	105.0	114.1	108.3
1997																
1st quarter	106.1	119.9	113.1	111.9	100.1	105.5	115.2	109.1	106.1	120.2	113.2	111.8	99.9	105.3	115.8	109.1
2nd quarter	107.1	122.0	113.9	112.2	100.1	104.8	117.9	109.6	107.2	122.2	114.0	112.1	100.0	104.6	118.7	109.7
3rd quarter	108.1	123.5	114.2	113.5	100.8	105.0	118.3	109.9	108.0	123.6	114.4	113.2	100.5	104.8	119.3	110.1
4th quarter	108.3	124.4	115.0	115.2	101.8	106.5	116.6	110.2	108.2	124.7	115.2	115.0	101.6	106.2	117.6	110.4

Table 19-10. Productivity and Related Data—*Continued*

(1992 = 100, seasonally adjusted.)

Year and quarter	Nonfinancial corporations										Manufacturing					
	Output per hour of all employees	Output	Employee hours	Compensation per hour	Real compensation per hour	Unit costs			Implicit price deflator	Unit profits	Output per hour of all persons	Output	Hours of all persons	Compensation per hour	Real compensation per hour	Unit labor costs
						Total	Labor costs	Non-labor costs								
1981																
1st quarter	82.0	70.9	86.5	59.7	92.4	72.6	72.9	71.7	73.2	80.3	70.3	75.7	107.7	58.9	91.2	83.9
2nd quarter	82.3	71.3	86.6	61.0	92.7	74.0	74.1	73.7	74.5	80.2	70.6	76.3	107.9	60.4	91.8	85.5
3rd quarter	83.5	72.5	86.8	62.3	92.9	74.9	74.6	75.6	76.1	89.1	71.1	76.4	107.4	61.7	91.9	86.8
4th quarter	82.6	71.3	86.3	63.3	92.7	77.1	76.7	78.2	77.3	80.0	70.7	74.2	105.0	63.1	92.3	89.2
1982																
1st quarter	82.7	70.5	85.2	64.6	93.5	78.8	78.2	80.3	78.4	74.2	72.3	73.6	101.8	64.9	93.9	89.8
2nd quarter	83.6	70.4	84.3	65.7	94.1	79.5	78.6	81.8	79.3	77.9	74.4	73.6	98.9	66.8	95.6	89.8
3rd quarter	83.7	69.9	83.5	66.7	93.9	80.5	79.7	82.7	80.2	77.7	75.3	72.7	96.5	67.9	95.6	90.1
4th quarter	83.6	69.1	82.7	67.2	93.7	81.5	80.5	84.2	80.5	70.0	75.0	71.0	94.7	68.3	95.2	91.1
1983																
1st quarter	84.6	70.3	83.1	67.6	93.6	80.7	79.9	82.8	80.5	78.5	75.8	72.3	95.4	68.6	95.0	90.4
2nd quarter	85.9	72.4	84.3	68.1	93.2	79.9	79.3	81.7	80.8	89.7	76.3	74.5	97.7	68.6	93.9	89.9
3rd quarter	86.5	74.3	85.9	68.5	92.9	79.7	79.2	81.2	81.2	96.7	77.2	77.3	100.1	68.8	93.3	89.0
4th quarter	86.7	76.2	87.8	69.4	93.4	80.2	80.0	80.6	81.8	98.9	77.4	79.4	102.6	69.3	93.2	89.5
1984																
1st quarter	87.5	78.4	89.5	69.9	92.8	79.9	79.9	80.2	82.5	109.6	78.6	82.1	104.5	69.9	92.7	88.9
2nd quarter	88.2	80.0	90.7	70.8	93.1	80.4	80.3	80.7	83.0	110.7	79.2	83.6	105.6	70.6	92.9	89.2
3rd quarter	88.3	80.8	91.4	71.7	93.6	81.3	81.2	81.7	83.5	106.9	80.0	84.5	105.6	71.7	93.6	89.6
4th quarter	88.7	81.8	92.2	72.4	93.8	81.7	81.6	81.9	83.8	107.2	80.1	84.5	105.6	72.6	94.0	90.7
1985																
1st quarter	88.8	82.4	92.8	73.1	93.9	82.3	82.3	82.1	84.2	105.3	80.7	85.0	105.4	73.8	94.7	91.5
2nd quarter	89.4	83.2	93.1	73.9	94.0	82.7	82.6	82.9	84.4	102.3	82.3	86.0	104.5	74.5	94.8	90.5
3rd quarter	90.8	84.8	93.3	74.8	94.5	82.2	82.3	81.9	84.5	109.3	82.8	86.3	104.2	75.4	95.4	91.1
4th quarter	90.7	85.0	93.7	75.9	95.1	83.5	83.7	82.8	84.9	100.0	83.4	86.8	104.1	76.6	96.0	91.9
1986																
1st quarter	91.3	85.8	93.9	76.7	95.5	84.2	84.0	85.1	85.0	93.0	84.7	87.9	103.8	77.4	96.5	91.3
2nd quarter	91.2	85.3	93.6	77.4	96.9	85.0	84.8	85.4	85.3	88.5	85.7	88.3	103.0	77.9	97.6	91.0
3rd quarter	91.5	85.7	93.7	78.3	97.5	85.7	85.6	86.2	85.7	85.4	86.1	88.4	102.7	78.8	98.1	91.5
4th quarter	92.5	86.8	93.8	79.6	98.5	86.1	86.1	86.1	86.0	85.1	87.0	89.4	102.7	79.7	98.6	91.5
1987																
1st quarter	93.3	88.2	94.5	80.6	98.6	86.1	86.4	85.4	86.5	90.1	87.2	89.8	103.0	80.2	98.1	92.0
2nd quarter	94.6	90.0	95.1	81.3	98.5	85.8	86.0	85.4	86.7	97.0	88.3	90.9	103.0	80.4	97.3	91.0
3rd quarter	95.3	91.7	96.2	81.9	98.2	85.6	85.9	84.9	87.2	103.9	88.5	92.0	104.0	80.9	97.0	91.4
4th quarter	95.6	93.0	97.2	82.9	98.6	86.4	86.7	85.6	87.6	101.1	89.1	93.8	105.3	81.3	96.7	91.2
1988																
1st quarter	95.7	94.3	98.5	82.8	97.8	86.3	86.5	85.9	88.0	106.2	89.4	94.8	105.9	82.7	97.7	92.4
2nd quarter	96.0	95.4	99.4	84.0	98.1	87.2	87.5	86.5	88.8	106.5	90.1	95.8	106.4	83.5	97.6	92.6
3rd quarter	95.7	95.8	100.1	84.7	98.0	88.4	88.6	87.9	90.0	107.3	90.5	96.5	106.7	84.3	97.5	93.2
4th quarter	96.4	97.7	101.3	85.2	97.6	88.6	88.4	89.1	90.6	112.1	90.7	97.3	107.3	85.5	98.0	94.2
1989																
1st quarter	95.2	97.4	102.3	85.5	97.0	90.4	89.9	91.8	91.3	101.2	90.5	97.7	107.8	86.0	97.5	95.0
2nd quarter	94.5	97.0	102.7	85.8	95.9	91.7	90.8	94.1	92.3	98.7	90.4	97.1	107.4	85.8	95.9	95.0
3rd quarter	94.7	97.4	102.9	86.4	95.8	92.5	91.2	96.0	92.9	97.2	89.6	95.9	107.0	86.7	96.2	96.7
4th quarter	94.7	97.7	103.2	87.6	96.4	93.6	92.5	96.4	93.4	92.1	90.5	95.9	106.0	88.0	96.8	97.3
1990																
1st quarter	94.6	98.1	103.7	88.7	96.0	94.5	93.8	96.5	94.5	94.7	91.9	97.2	105.7	88.8	96.1	96.6
2nd quarter	95.6	99.0	103.5	90.4	97.0	95.1	94.5	96.5	95.5	100.2	92.2	97.6	105.8	90.4	97.0	98.0
3rd quarter	95.6	98.4	102.9	91.8	96.8	96.7	96.0	98.6	96.3	92.5	93.6	98.0	104.7	91.4	96.5	97.7
4th quarter	96.1	97.8	101.8	92.6	96.2	97.5	96.4	100.4	96.9	89.9	93.7	96.5	103.0	92.5	96.1	98.7
1991																
1st quarter	96.7	97.1	100.3	93.4	96.5	98.0	96.5	102.1	97.7	93.4	93.3	94.0	100.8	93.7	96.9	100.5
2nd quarter	97.6	97.3	99.7	94.9	97.6	98.5	97.2	102.2	98.1	93.3	94.1	94.3	100.3	95.0	97.7	101.0
3rd quarter	97.9	97.7	99.7	95.8	98.0	99.1	97.9	102.3	98.5	92.7	95.8	96.3	100.5	96.3	98.4	100.4
4th quarter	98.4	98.0	99.6	97.0	98.5	99.4	98.5	101.6	98.8	92.5	96.8	96.9	100.2	97.3	98.8	100.5
1992																
1st quarter	99.7	99.0	99.3	98.8	99.7	99.4	99.0	100.2	99.2	97.3	98.2	97.7	99.5	98.4	99.4	100.2
2nd quarter	99.6	99.6	100.0	99.4	99.7	99.7	99.8	99.3	99.8	100.8	99.6	99.7	100.1	99.6	99.9	100.0
3rd quarter	100.0	100.1	100.1	100.6	100.3	100.8	100.6	101.3	100.2	94.6	100.9	100.8	99.9	100.7	100.4	99.8
4th quarter	100.7	101.3	100.6	101.2	100.2	100.2	100.5	99.3	100.8	107.2	101.3	101.7	100.4	101.2	100.2	99.9
1993																
1st quarter	99.5	100.8	101.3	101.3	99.7	101.5	101.8	100.7	101.6	102.5	101.8	102.6	100.8	101.5	99.9	99.7
2nd quarter	100.7	102.6	101.9	102.0	99.7	100.8	101.3	99.7	101.8	112.2	101.7	102.9	101.2	102.3	100.0	100.6
3rd quarter	100.8	103.4	102.6	102.3	99.5	101.2	101.5	100.4	102.1	112.2	101.5	103.1	101.5	103.1	100.3	101.5
4th quarter	101.8	105.4	103.5	102.5	99.1	100.6	100.7	100.2	102.7	125.4	102.5	104.6	102.0	104.0	100.6	101.5
1994																
1st quarter	102.9	107.1	104.1	104.0	100.3	101.6	101.1	103.1	103.2	119.6	103.6	105.9	102.2	105.1	101.3	101.5
2nd quarter	102.9	108.9	105.9	103.9	99.7	100.8	101.0	100.1	103.4	131.4	104.9	108.1	103.0	105.2	100.9	100.3
3rd quarter	102.9	110.1	107.0	104.0	99.0	101.1	101.1	101.0	103.9	134.8	105.2	109.4	104.0	105.8	100.7	100.5
4th quarter	103.7	112.3	108.3	104.7	99.1	101.0	101.0	100.9	104.3	140.5	106.2	111.6	105.1	106.5	100.9	100.3
1995																
1st quarter	103.0	112.5	109.2	105.1	99.0	102.1	102.0	102.3	104.8	134.2	107.6	113.1	105.1	106.8	100.6	99.2
2nd quarter	103.5	113.2	109.3	105.8	98.9	102.3	102.2	102.8	105.1	134.5	108.6	112.9	104.0	107.8	100.7	99.2
3rd quarter	104.6	115.0	109.9	106.4	99.0	101.7	101.7	101.6	105.3	143.6	109.4	113.4	103.7	108.4	100.8	99.1
4th quarter	105.4	116.0	110.1	107.1	99.2	101.7	101.6	102.0	105.3	143.3	110.3	114.1	103.4	108.6	100.6	98.4
1996																
1st quarter	106.3	117.0	110.0	107.7	98.9	101.3	101.3	101.3	105.5	150.5	111.3	114.2	102.6	108.4	99.6	97.4
2nd quarter	107.3	119.1	111.0	108.8	99.1	101.2	101.4	100.7	105.5	151.8	112.1	116.2	103.7	109.1	99.3	97.3
3rd quarter	107.8	120.7	112.0	109.4	99.1	101.2	101.5	100.3	105.5	151.9	113.5	118.1	104.0	109.7	99.3	96.6
4th quarter	108.4	122.9	113.4	109.7	98.6	100.9	101.2	100.2	105.5	154.6	114.4	119.3	104.3	110.3	99.2	96.4
1997																
1st quarter	107.5	123.8	115.2	109.5	97.9	101.6	101.9	100.6	106.1	154.8	115.4	121.3	105.1	110.3	98.7	95.6
2nd quarter	107.6	125.7	116.8	109.9	97.7	101.7	101.7	101.5	106.2	155.4	116.4	122.8	105.5	110.6	98.7	95.0
3rd quarter	108.8	128.2	117.8	110.2	97.9	101.2	101.3	101.0	106.2	160.5	118.7	124.9	105.2	111.6	99.1	94.0
4th quarter	109.5	130.2	118.9	111.8	98.7	101.7	102.1	100.6	106.3	156.8	119.8	127.0	106.0	113.3	100.1	94.6

Table 19-10. Productivity and Related Data—*Continued*

(1992 = 100, seasonally adjusted.)

Year and quarter	Business sector								Nonfarm business sector							
	Output per hour of all persons	Output	Hours of all persons	Compensation per hour	Real compensation per hour	Unit labor costs	Unit nonlabor payments	Implicit price deflator	Output per hour of all persons	Output	Hours of all persons	Compensation per hour	Real compensation per hour	Unit labor costs	Unit nonlabor payments	Implicit price deflator
1998																
1st quarter	109.6	126.7	115.6	117.3	103.5	107.0	115.9	110.3	109.5	127.0	116.0	117.0	103.2	106.8	117.1	110.5
2nd quarter	109.6	127.3	116.2	118.8	104.5	108.4	113.9	110.4	109.6	127.7	116.5	118.5	104.3	108.1	115.1	110.6
3rd quarter	110.2	128.7	116.8	120.2	105.2	109.0	113.5	110.7	110.2	129.0	117.1	119.9	105.0	108.8	114.7	111.0
4th quarter	111.5	131.3	117.8	121.4	105.9	108.9	114.1	110.8	111.4	131.6	118.2	121.1	105.6	108.7	115.3	111.1
1999																
1st quarter	112.3	132.4	117.9	123.9	107.6	110.3	112.7	111.2	112.0	132.7	118.4	123.3	107.1	110.0	114.1	111.5
2nd quarter	112.1	133.0	118.7	123.9	106.9	110.6	113.0	111.5	111.8	133.3	119.3	123.4	106.4	110.4	114.6	111.9
3rd quarter	113.1	134.9	119.4	125.0	107.0	110.6	113.9	111.8	112.7	135.3	120.0	124.4	106.5	110.4	115.6	112.3
4th quarter	114.7	137.7	120.1	126.5	107.5	110.3	115.2	112.1	114.5	138.0	120.6	126.2	107.2	110.2	116.9	112.6
2000																
1st quarter	114.8	138.4	120.6	131.1	110.3	114.1	110.4	112.8	114.6	138.7	121.0	130.8	110.1	114.2	112.0	113.4
2nd quarter	116.6	140.3	120.3	131.9	110.1	113.1	113.8	113.4	116.1	140.5	121.0	131.4	109.7	113.1	115.3	113.9
3rd quarter	116.8	140.4	120.2	134.6	111.4	115.3	111.0	113.7	116.4	140.6	120.8	134.2	111.0	115.3	112.6	114.3
4th quarter	117.5	140.7	119.7	135.9	111.7	115.6	111.9	114.3	117.0	141.0	120.5	135.3	111.2	115.6	113.3	114.8
2001																
1st quarter	117.4	140.4	119.6	137.4	111.9	117.1	112.0	115.2	116.9	140.7	120.3	136.7	111.3	117.0	113.5	115.7
2nd quarter	117.8	139.4	118.3	138.2	111.6	117.3	113.3	115.8	117.4	139.7	119.0	137.4	111.0	117.1	114.9	116.3
3rd quarter	118.8	139.1	117.1	139.1	112.1	117.1	115.1	116.4	118.3	139.4	117.8	138.2	111.4	116.8	116.8	116.8
4th quarter	121.3	140.3	115.6	139.8	112.8	115.2	117.0	115.9	120.7	140.4	116.3	138.9	112.1	115.1	119.0	116.5
2002																
1st quarter	123.9	142.3	114.9	141.0	113.4	113.8	119.7	116.0	123.4	142.5	115.5	140.2	112.8	113.6	121.5	116.4
2nd quarter	124.1	142.5	114.8	142.4	113.5	114.7	118.8	116.2	123.7	142.9	115.5	141.5	112.9	114.4	121.2	116.8
3rd quarter	125.9	144.4	114.6	143.1	113.5	113.6	120.9	116.3	125.5	144.7	115.3	142.2	112.8	113.3	123.1	116.9
4th quarter	126.4	145.0	114.7	143.7	113.4	113.7	122.1	116.8	126.0	145.3	115.3	142.8	112.7	113.3	124.3	117.3

Table 19-10. Productivity and Related Data—*Continued*

(1992 = 100, seasonally adjusted.)

Year and quarter	Nonfinancial corporations										Manufacturing					
	Output per hour of all employees	Output	Em-ployee hours	Compensation per hour	Real compensation per hour	Unit costs			Implicit price deflator	Unit profits	Output per hour of all persons	Output	Hours of all persons	Compensation per hour	Real compensation per hour	Unit labor costs
						Total	Labor costs	Non-labor costs								
1998																
1st quarter	109.8	131.2	119.5	113.7	100.3	103.1	103.6	101.7	106.5	143.8	121.3	128.3	105.8	115.5	101.9	95.2
2nd quarter	111.1	133.1	119.8	115.3	101.5	103.3	103.8	101.9	106.4	140.4	122.3	129.0	105.5	117.0	102.9	95.7
3rd quarter	112.6	135.6	120.4	116.6	102.1	103.1	103.6	101.8	106.7	144.9	124.3	130.0	104.5	118.2	103.5	95.1
4th quarter	113.1	137.3	121.4	117.7	102.6	103.9	104.1	103.3	106.7	137.7	125.5	131.8	105.0	119.0	103.8	94.8
1999																
1st quarter	114.2	139.3	122.0	120.1	104.3	104.2	105.1	101.6	107.0	137.1	128.0	133.4	104.3	120.6	104.8	94.3
2nd quarter	114.3	140.3	122.8	120.3	103.7	104.5	105.2	102.7	107.2	135.6	128.8	134.6	104.5	120.9	104.3	93.9
3rd quarter	114.7	141.7	123.6	121.1	103.6	105.3	105.6	104.5	107.2	127.7	129.8	135.8	104.7	122.6	104.9	94.4
4th quarter	115.6	144.0	124.5	122.6	104.2	105.7	106.0	104.6	107.4	126.0	132.1	137.3	103.9	124.2	105.5	94.0
2000																
1st quarter	117.7	147.3	125.2	126.8	106.7	106.9	107.8	104.5	108.0	119.5	133.6	138.3	103.5	131.4	110.6	98.4
2nd quarter	118.2	147.9	125.1	127.7	106.6	107.5	108.0	106.3	108.5	118.8	134.9	139.8	103.6	129.3	107.9	95.9
3rd quarter	119.4	149.4	125.1	130.3	107.8	108.6	109.1	107.1	108.6	109.5	135.4	139.3	102.9	132.2	109.4	97.7
4th quarter	119.4	149.2	124.9	131.6	108.1	109.8	110.2	108.9	108.9	98.6	135.9	137.6	101.3	131.5	108.0	96.8
2001																
1st quarter	118.7	147.9	124.7	131.2	106.8	110.8	110.6	111.6	109.3	93.1	135.1	134.8	99.8	132.0	107.5	97.7
2nd quarter	120.0	147.8	123.1	132.6	107.1	111.3	110.4	113.5	109.9	95.4	136.1	133.1	97.8	133.6	107.9	98.2
3rd quarter	121.3	147.7	121.7	133.8	107.8	111.7	110.3	115.5	110.5	97.9	137.9	131.2	95.1	135.0	108.8	97.9
4th quarter	124.5	149.6	120.2	134.7	108.7	109.8	108.2	114.1	109.6	107.6	140.6	129.7	92.3	136.7	110.3	97.2
2002																
1st quarter	126.0	150.8	119.7	135.9	109.4	109.5	107.9	114.0	109.4	107.6	144.0	130.4	90.6	138.3	111.3	96.1
2nd quarter	127.7	152.8	119.6	137.3	109.5	109.4	107.5	114.5	109.3	107.8	145.9	131.5	90.2	140.5	112.0	96.3
3rd quarter	128.7	153.4	119.2	138.2	109.7	109.6	107.4	115.4	109.1	104.6	147.7	132.0	89.4	141.3	112.1	95.7
4th quarter	129.9	154.5	118.9	139.2	109.9	109.3	107.1	115.2	109.4	110.1	147.9	131.1	88.6	142.4	112.4	96.3

NOTES AND DEFINITIONS

TABLES 19-1 THROUGH 19-8
SELECTED NATIONAL INCOME AND PRODUCT ACCOUNT DATA

See the Notes and Definitions for Tables 1-1 through 1-10. For *Disposition of Personal Income*, see the Notes and Definitions for Tables 4-1 through 4-4. For *Inventories to Sales Ratios*, see the Notes and Definitions for Table 5-7. For *Federal and State and Local Government Current Receipts and Expenditures*, see the Notes and Definitions for Tables 6-1 and 6-2.

TABLE 19-9
U.S. INTERNATIONAL TRANSACTIONS

See the Notes and Definitions for Table 7-6.

TABLE 19-10
PRODUCTIVITY AND RELATED DATA

See the Notes and Definitions for Table 9-3.

Table 20-1. Industrial Production and Capacity Utilization

(Seasonally adjusted.)

Year and month	Total industry	Manufac-turing (SIC)	Market groups								Capacity utilization (output as percentage of capacity)	
			Consumer goods			Business equipment	Defense and space equipment	Construction supplies	Business supplies	Materials	Total industry	Manufac-turing (SIC)
			Total	Durable	Nondurable							
1947	17.2	16.1	20.7	14.7	23.6	9.3	9.3	24.5	14.0	17.5	. . .	. . .
1948	18.0	16.7	21.3	15.3	24.3	9.7	11.0	26.3	14.6	18.3	. . .	82.5
1949	17.0	15.8	21.2	14.5	24.5	8.4	11.5	24.1	14.4	16.7	. . .	74.2
1950	19.7	18.3	24.2	19.4	26.5	9.0	13.5	29.0	16.1	20.0	. . .	82.8
1951	21.3	19.8	24.0	16.8	27.5	11.0	33.1	30.1	17.0	22.1	. . .	85.8
1952	22.1	20.6	24.5	16.3	28.6	12.5	46.6	29.9	16.9	22.4	. . .	85.4
1953	24.0	22.5	26.0	19.1	29.4	13.0	55.7	32.1	18.0	24.9	. . .	89.3
1954	22.7	21.0	25.8	17.7	29.7	11.4	49.1	31.6	18.3	23.0	. . .	80.1
1955	25.6	23.7	28.8	21.8	32.0	12.4	44.9	36.4	20.5	27.2	. . .	87.0
1956	26.7	24.6	29.9	21.1	34.1	14.4	43.9	37.4	21.7	27.9	. . .	86.1
1957	27.1	24.9	30.6	21.1	35.2	14.9	45.9	36.9	22.0	27.8	. . .	83.6
1958	25.4	23.2	30.3	18.7	36.2	12.6	46.0	35.6	21.8	25.1	. . .	75.0
1959	28.4	26.1	33.3	22.2	38.7	14.2	48.6	39.9	23.7	28.9	. . .	81.6
1960	29.0	26.6	34.6	23.4	39.9	14.5	49.9	39.0	24.5	29.3	. . .	80.1
1961	29.2	26.7	35.3	23.1	41.3	14.1	50.7	39.4	25.3	29.3	. . .	77.3
1962	31.6	29.1	37.7	26.1	43.2	15.3	58.7	41.7	26.8	31.9	. . .	81.4
1963	33.5	30.9	39.7	28.3	45.1	16.1	63.3	43.7	28.6	34.0	. . .	83.5
1964	35.8	33.0	42.0	30.4	47.4	18.0	61.3	46.3	30.6	36.7	. . .	85.6
1965	39.3	36.5	45.3	35.6	49.4	20.6	67.8	49.2	32.6	41.0	. . .	89.5
1966	42.8	39.9	47.6	37.8	51.8	23.9	79.7	51.3	35.1	44.6	. . .	91.1
1967	43.7	40.6	48.7	36.3	54.4	24.4	90.9	52.6	37.0	44.2	87.0	87.2
1947												
January	17.0	15.9	20.5	13.8	23.9	8.9	9.6	23.3	13.9	17.2	. . .	. . .
February	17.1	16.0	20.5	14.3	23.5	9.0	9.5	24.0	13.9	17.4	. . .	. . .
March	17.2	16.0	20.5	14.6	23.5	9.1	9.3	24.3	13.9	17.9	. . .	. . .
April	17.1	16.1	20.5	14.7	23.3	9.2	9.4	24.5	14.1	17.5	. . .	. . .
May	17.2	15.9	20.3	14.5	23.1	9.3	9.2	24.8	14.0	17.6	. . .	. . .
June	17.2	15.9	20.3	14.7	23.1	9.3	9.2	24.8	13.9	17.4	. . .	. . .
July	17.1	15.8	20.4	14.4	23.3	9.2	9.1	24.2	13.9	17.2	. . .	. . .
August	17.2	15.9	20.6	14.2	23.6	9.3	9.1	24.6	13.8	17.2	. . .	. . .
September	17.3	16.0	20.8	14.7	23.7	9.5	9.1	24.8	13.9	17.4	. . .	. . .
October	17.5	16.2	21.1	14.9	24.1	9.5	9.4	24.7	13.9	17.6	. . .	. . .
November	17.7	16.5	21.4	15.4	24.3	9.5	9.5	25.2	14.2	18.0	. . .	. . .
December	17.8	16.5	21.5	15.6	24.3	9.6	9.7	25.3	14.5	17.8	. . .	. . .
1948												
January	17.9	16.6	21.3	15.4	24.2	9.7	9.8	26.4	14.4	17.8	. . .	84.4
February	17.9	16.6	21.4	15.2	24.4	9.6	10.2	26.1	14.6	17.9	. . .	84.0
March	17.7	16.6	21.2	15.3	24.1	9.7	10.4	26.2	14.5	17.8	. . .	83.4
April	17.7	16.5	21.3	15.2	24.4	9.6	10.6	26.1	14.5	17.6	. . .	82.8
May	18.0	16.7	21.3	14.9	24.4	9.6	10.4	26.3	14.5	18.6	. . .	83.3
June	18.3	16.9	21.6	15.5	24.6	9.7	10.8	26.0	14.6	18.6	. . .	83.6
July	18.3	16.9	21.6	15.9	24.3	9.8	11.0	26.7	14.5	18.7	. . .	83.4
August	18.2	16.8	21.4	15.6	24.1	9.8	11.2	26.6	14.7	18.5	. . .	82.7
September	18.1	16.7	21.3	15.2	24.2	9.7	11.5	26.2	14.6	18.5	. . .	81.5
October	18.2	16.8	21.5	15.7	24.3	9.6	11.7	26.8	14.6	18.6	. . .	81.7
November	18.0	16.6	21.3	15.1	24.3	9.5	12.0	26.0	14.7	18.4	. . .	80.2
December	17.8	16.5	21.0	14.5	24.2	9.4	12.0	25.8	14.7	18.3	. . .	79.3
1949												
January	17.6	16.2	20.8	14.1	24.0	9.2	11.8	25.1	14.4	17.9	. . .	77.9
February	17.5	16.1	20.7	13.9	24.1	9.2	11.8	24.6	14.2	17.8	. . .	76.9
March	17.1	15.9	20.9	13.8	24.3	9.0	11.7	24.3	14.2	17.1	. . .	75.9
April	17.0	15.6	20.8	13.9	24.2	8.8	11.5	23.9	14.2	16.9	. . .	74.2
May	16.8	15.5	20.8	13.8	24.3	8.6	11.7	23.6	14.3	16.4	. . .	73.2
June	16.8	15.5	21.1	14.1	24.4	8.5	11.8	23.6	14.3	16.2	. . .	73.1
July	16.7	15.6	21.3	14.6	24.5	8.3	11.7	23.3	14.3	16.1	. . .	73.1
August	16.9	15.7	21.5	14.8	24.7	8.3	11.5	23.5	14.3	16.4	. . .	73.6
September	17.1	16.0	21.8	15.3	24.8	8.2	11.3	24.3	14.6	16.7	. . .	74.8
October	16.4	15.4	21.9	15.6	24.9	7.9	11.0	23.5	14.7	15.0	. . .	71.7
November	16.9	15.5	21.5	14.7	24.8	7.6	11.0	24.3	14.7	16.3	. . .	72.0
December	17.2	15.9	21.3	14.5	24.7	7.6	10.8	25.3	14.7	17.1	. . .	73.6
1950												
January	17.5	16.3	22.2	16.2	25.1	7.8	10.8	25.0	14.9	17.3	. . .	74.9
February	17.5	16.4	22.2	16.2	25.1	8.0	10.8	26.0	15.3	17.0	. . .	75.4
March	18.1	16.7	22.7	16.9	25.5	8.1	10.9	26.6	15.3	18.1	. . .	76.4
April	18.7	17.4	23.3	18.1	25.9	8.3	11.1	28.0	15.6	18.9	. . .	79.2
May	19.1	17.8	23.8	19.0	26.1	8.7	11.5	28.2	15.7	19.4	. . .	81.0
June	19.7	18.4	24.5	20.6	26.3	9.0	11.9	29.2	15.9	20.2	. . .	83.1
July	20.3	19.0	25.2	21.5	26.8	9.3	12.5	30.0	16.3	20.7	. . .	85.5
August	21.0	19.7	26.0	22.1	27.8	9.9	13.8	30.6	16.7	21.3	. . .	88.4
September	20.8	19.5	25.4	21.1	27.4	9.6	15.2	30.6	16.5	21.5	. . .	87.2
October	21.0	19.6	25.2	20.7	27.2	9.8	16.4	30.9	16.8	21.8	. . .	87.5
November	20.9	19.6	25.1	20.3	27.3	9.9	17.5	31.0	16.8	21.6	. . .	87.0
December	21.3	19.9	25.5	20.1	28.1	10.1	19.0	31.0	17.1	21.9	. . .	88.1
1951												
January	21.4	20.0	25.6	19.7	28.4	10.2	21.1	31.3	17.3	21.7	. . .	88.3
February	21.5	20.1	25.6	19.8	28.4	10.3	24.4	31.0	17.0	21.8	. . .	88.3
March	21.6	20.2	25.2	19.6	27.9	10.5	27.7	31.1	17.3	22.3	. . .	88.4
April	21.6	20.2	24.8	18.7	27.7	10.7	30.3	31.0	17.7	22.4	. . .	88.2
May	21.6	20.1	24.3	17.8	27.5	10.8	31.3	30.7	17.5	22.6	. . .	87.4
June	21.5	20.0	24.0	16.9	27.4	11.0	33.0	30.5	17.2	22.7	. . .	86.6
July	21.1	19.6	23.2	15.1	27.2	11.1	34.9	29.8	17.1	22.3	. . .	84.9
August	20.9	19.4	22.7	14.1	26.9	11.2	36.0	29.6	16.9	21.9	. . .	83.6
September	21.1	19.5	22.9	14.7	26.9	11.4	37.2	29.6	16.8	22.1	. . .	83.7
October	21.0	19.4	22.8	14.6	26.9	11.6	38.7	29.3	16.4	21.7	. . .	83.1
November	21.2	19.6	23.2	14.9	27.2	11.8	41.0	29.1	16.5	21.8	. . .	83.6
December	21.3	19.8	23.3	15.1	27.4	12.0	41.8	29.2	16.5	21.9	. . .	83.9

. . . = Not available.

Table 20-1. Industrial Production and Capacity Utilization—*Continued*

(Seasonally adjusted.)

Year and month	Total industry	Manufac-turing (SIC)	Consumer goods Total	Durable	Nondurable	Business equipment	Defense and space equipment	Construction supplies	Business supplies	Materials	Capacity utilization Total industry	Manufac-turing (SIC)
1952												
January	21.6	19.9	23.5	15.0	27.7	12.3	42.5	29.6	16.6	22.4	. . .	84.4
February	21.7	20.1	23.7	15.0	28.0	12.4	43.0	29.8	16.6	22.2	. . .	84.6
March	21.8	20.2	23.8	15.3	28.0	12.5	43.1	29.6	16.6	22.2	. . .	84.7
April	21.6	20.0	23.8	15.2	28.1	12.5	43.6	29.1	16.5	21.7	. . .	83.6
May	21.4	19.9	23.8	15.6	27.8	12.6	45.0	28.7	16.4	21.4	. . .	83.1
June	21.2	19.7	24.4	15.8	28.8	12.6	46.4	28.5	16.8	20.2	. . .	81.9
July	20.8	19.3	24.0	14.3	28.9	12.0	46.6	28.5	16.9	19.8	. . .	79.8
August	22.2	20.7	24.5	15.7	28.9	12.2	47.4	30.4	17.0	22.3	. . .	85.1
September	23.0	21.4	25.1	17.3	28.9	12.5	48.2	30.7	17.3	23.8	. . .	87.7
October	23.2	21.7	25.5	17.9	29.2	12.7	49.7	31.1	17.5	23.6	. . .	88.8
November	23.7	22.1	26.0	19.0	29.5	12.8	50.8	31.7	17.7	24.3	. . .	90.2
December	23.8	22.3	26.0	19.1	29.4	13.0	52.3	31.8	17.6	24.4	. . .	90.5
1953												
January	23.9	22.4	26.3	19.8	29.4	13.0	53.1	32.3	17.3	24.3	. . .	90.5
February	24.0	22.6	26.5	20.0	29.6	13.1	54.2	32.8	17.7	24.8	. . .	91.1
March	24.2	22.8	26.5	20.2	29.4	13.2	55.3	32.9	18.1	25.1	. . .	91.4
April	24.3	22.9	26.4	20.0	29.6	13.2	56.0	33.0	18.2	25.4	. . .	91.5
May	24.5	23.0	26.5	20.1	29.7	13.1	57.0	32.3	18.3	25.9	. . .	91.7
June	24.4	22.8	26.1	19.4	29.6	13.0	57.3	32.1	18.3	25.9	. . .	90.7
July	24.7	22.9	26.2	19.2	29.5	13.2	57.8	32.5	18.3	26.2	. . .	91.0
August	24.5	22.9	26.0	19.1	29.4	13.2	57.4	32.4	18.3	25.5	. . .	90.6
September	24.0	22.4	25.7	18.3	29.2	13.0	57.3	31.8	18.2	24.9	. . .	88.3
October	23.8	22.2	25.7	18.1	29.3	13.0	56.8	31.9	18.1	24.1	. . .	87.2
November	23.3	21.6	25.3	17.5	29.1	12.6	53.1	31.3	18.0	23.5	. . .	84.7
December	22.7	21.1	24.9	16.9	28.8	12.4	53.5	30.6	17.7	22.9	. . .	82.3
1954												
January	22.5	20.9	25.0	16.6	29.2	12.0	52.5	31.2	17.7	22.7	. . .	81.3
February	22.6	20.8	25.3	17.0	29.3	11.9	52.1	31.3	17.9	22.6	. . .	80.8
March	22.5	20.8	25.3	17.0	29.4	11.7	51.4	31.0	17.9	22.4	. . .	80.2
April	22.3	20.6	25.3	17.2	29.2	11.5	50.5	31.0	18.0	22.4	. . .	79.4
May	22.5	20.8	25.5	17.5	29.3	11.5	49.7	31.4	17.9	22.7	. . .	79.8
June	22.5	20.8	25.6	17.7	29.4	11.3	49.0	30.7	18.1	22.9	. . .	79.9
July	22.6	20.8	25.7	17.5	29.7	11.3	48.8	30.6	17.9	23.0	. . .	79.4
August	22.5	20.7	25.8	17.6	29.7	11.2	47.8	30.5	18.0	22.9	. . .	78.8
September	22.6	20.8	26.0	17.7	30.0	11.1	47.3	32.0	18.5	22.7	. . .	79.2
October	22.8	21.1	26.1	18.0	30.1	11.1	46.8	33.1	18.7	23.2	. . .	79.7
November	23.2	21.4	26.6	18.5	30.6	11.3	46.6	33.4	19.0	23.7	. . .	80.9
December	23.5	21.7	27.1	19.2	30.8	11.3	45.9	33.7	19.3	24.1	. . .	81.8
1955												
January	24.0	22.3	27.7	20.5	31.0	11.4	45.6	34.1	19.4	24.9	. . .	83.5
February	24.3	22.5	27.8	20.8	31.0	11.6	45.6	34.6	19.6	25.5	. . .	84.1
March	24.9	23.0	28.3	21.3	31.5	11.7	45.3	35.8	20.2	26.2	. . .	85.8
April	25.2	23.4	28.5	21.7	31.7	12.1	45.3	36.0	20.1	26.7	. . .	86.7
May	25.6	23.8	28.9	22.2	31.9	12.3	45.3	36.2	20.4	27.2	. . .	87.9
June	25.6	23.8	28.7	21.8	31.8	12.4	44.8	36.8	20.6	27.3	. . .	87.6
July	25.8	23.9	28.8	22.1	31.8	12.4	44.7	36.9	20.5	27.6	. . .	87.7
August	25.8	23.9	28.9	22.1	31.8	12.5	44.4	36.9	20.4	27.6	. . .	87.3
September	26.0	24.0	29.0	22.2	32.1	12.6	44.6	37.1	20.8	27.9	. . .	87.5
October	26.4	24.4	29.6	22.3	32.9	13.2	44.4	37.1	21.0	28.2	. . .	88.4
November	26.5	24.4	29.6	22.1	33.2	13.2	44.3	37.5	21.3	28.1	. . .	88.3
December	26.6	24.7	29.8	22.0	33.5	13.5	44.4	37.7	21.2	28.3	. . .	89.0
1956												
January	26.7	24.6	29.8	21.8	33.6	13.6	43.9	38.3	21.4	28.4	. . .	88.2
February	26.5	24.5	29.8	21.4	33.7	13.8	43.5	38.2	21.4	27.9	. . .	87.4
March	26.5	24.5	29.7	21.4	33.7	13.9	42.6	38.1	21.5	27.8	. . .	87.0
April	26.7	24.8	29.8	21.7	33.7	14.3	42.9	37.9	21.8	28.0	. . .	87.8
May	26.5	24.5	29.7	21.2	33.8	14.3	43.0	37.4	21.6	27.5	. . .	86.3
June	26.2	24.3	29.6	20.7	33.9	14.3	43.0	37.0	21.5	27.1	. . .	85.3
July	25.4	23.3	29.7	20.7	34.0	14.3	43.0	35.1	21.7	24.9	. . .	81.5
August	26.5	24.4	29.8	20.7	34.3	14.5	43.5	36.9	21.7	27.2	. . .	84.9
September	27.1	24.8	29.8	20.4	34.3	14.6	43.9	37.8	21.7	28.6	. . .	86.0
October	27.3	25.0	30.0	20.7	34.5	14.7	45.1	37.6	21.9	29.1	. . .	86.5
November	27.1	25.0	29.9	20.4	34.4	14.9	45.8	37.2	21.9	28.4	. . .	85.8
December	27.5	25.3	30.1	21.2	34.4	15.1	46.8	37.9	22.0	29.0	. . .	86.8
1957												
January	27.4	25.2	30.3	21.3	34.5	15.3	47.0	37.4	22.1	28.4	. . .	86.2
February	27.6	25.6	30.7	21.7	34.9	15.6	47.2	38.5	22.1	28.6	. . .	87.0
March	27.6	25.5	30.8	21.6	35.1	15.6	47.2	37.9	22.0	28.5	. . .	86.4
April	27.2	25.1	30.4	21.0	35.0	15.3	47.3	37.1	22.0	28.1	. . .	85.0
May	27.1	25.0	30.5	20.9	35.1	15.0	46.6	36.9	22.2	28.0	. . .	84.2
June	27.2	25.2	30.6	21.2	35.2	15.0	46.8	37.2	22.0	28.1	. . .	84.6
July	27.4	25.2	30.8	21.0	35.5	15.1	46.3	37.2	22.1	28.3	. . .	84.3
August	27.4	25.2	30.9	21.6	35.4	15.1	46.4	36.9	22.1	28.3	. . .	84.2
September	27.1	25.0	30.9	21.5	35.4	14.9	45.4	36.7	22.1	28.0	. . .	83.2
October	26.7	24.5	30.4	20.7	35.2	14.5	44.4	36.3	21.8	27.5	. . .	81.4
November	26.1	24.0	30.4	20.7	35.0	14.1	42.9	35.9	21.6	26.5	. . .	79.4
December	25.6	23.5	30.2	19.7	35.3	13.7	42.5	35.3	21.5	25.7	. . .	77.5

. . . = Not available.

Table 20-1. Industrial Production and Capacity Utilization—*Continued*

(Seasonally adjusted.)

Year and month	Total industry	Manufac-turing (SIC)	Consumer goods			Business equipment	Defense and space equipment	Construction supplies	Business supplies	Materials	Capacity utilization (output as percentage of capacity)	
			Total	Durable	Nondurable						Total industry	Manufac-turing (SIC)
1958												
January	25.1	23.0	29.8	19.0	35.2	13.4	43.0	34.8	21.5	24.9	. . .	75.7
February	24.6	22.5	29.6	18.3	35.3	12.9	43.4	33.7	21.4	24.1	. . .	73.8
March	24.3	22.2	29.3	17.7	35.3	12.6	44.2	33.5	21.4	23.5	. . .	72.7
April	23.9	21.9	29.0	17.0	35.2	12.4	44.9	33.1	21.3	22.9	. . .	71.3
May	24.1	22.1	29.4	17.6	35.5	12.1	45.4	34.2	21.2	23.2	. . .	71.9
June	24.8	22.8	30.0	18.1	36.1	12.1	46.7	35.6	21.5	24.2	. . .	73.9
July	25.1	23.0	30.5	18.4	36.6	12.2	46.8	35.4	21.5	24.8	. . .	74.3
August	25.6	23.5	30.6	18.7	36.6	12.4	47.2	36.9	21.8	25.6	. . .	75.7
September	25.9	23.7	30.2	17.4	36.8	12.5	47.5	37.0	22.1	26.2	. . .	76.2
October	26.2	23.8	30.5	18.3	36.8	12.6	47.5	37.0	22.4	26.6	. . .	76.4
November	26.9	24.7	32.0	21.4	37.2	12.9	47.9	38.4	22.6	27.4	. . .	79.1
December	27.0	24.8	32.1	21.5	37.3	13.0	47.9	37.9	22.4	27.4	. . .	79.0
1959												
January	27.4	25.2	32.5	21.6	37.8	13.2	48.1	38.7	23.0	27.9	. . .	80.2
February	27.9	25.7	32.7	21.7	38.2	13.4	47.7	39.7	23.2	28.8	. . .	81.4
March	28.3	26.1	32.7	22.1	38.0	13.5	47.9	40.7	23.4	29.5	. . .	82.5
April	28.9	26.6	33.3	22.2	38.6	13.9	48.2	41.9	23.4	30.3	. . .	84.0
May	29.4	27.0	33.4	22.7	38.6	14.4	48.5	42.3	23.4	31.1	. . .	84.9
June	29.4	27.0	33.3	22.9	38.3	14.7	48.7	42.1	23.7	30.9	. . .	84.8
July	28.7	26.5	33.7	23.3	38.6	14.7	48.9	40.4	23.9	29.1	. . .	83.0
August	27.7	25.5	33.7	22.7	39.1	14.6	48.6	37.9	23.9	26.9	. . .	79.5
September	27.7	25.4	33.6	22.0	39.3	14.5	48.9	37.5	24.0	26.8	. . .	79.0
October	27.5	25.2	33.5	22.5	38.8	14.4	48.8	37.6	24.0	26.6	. . .	78.2
November	27.6	25.4	32.7	19.7	39.4	14.1	48.7	36.9	23.9	27.0	. . .	78.5
December	29.4	27.1	33.8	22.2	39.5	14.4	49.1	41.9	24.2	30.6	. . .	83.6
1960												
January	30.1	27.9	34.9	24.7	39.7	14.9	49.5	41.6	24.5	31.5	. . .	85.6
February	29.9	27.6	34.5	24.3	39.3	15.0	49.7	41.2	24.4	31.1	. . .	84.6
March	29.6	27.3	34.5	23.8	39.6	15.0	50.0	39.9	24.4	30.5	. . .	83.2
April	29.4	27.1	34.8	23.8	40.0	14.8	49.7	39.9	24.8	29.8	. . .	82.3
May	29.3	26.9	35.0	24.0	40.2	14.9	50.3	39.5	24.9	29.6	. . .	81.5
June	29.0	26.6	34.7	23.8	40.0	14.7	49.0	38.8	24.6	29.1	. . .	80.2
July	28.9	26.6	34.4	22.9	40.0	14.5	50.2	39.2	24.7	29.1	. . .	79.7
August	28.8	26.4	34.5	23.1	40.0	14.3	50.4	38.2	24.5	29.0	. . .	79.1
September	28.5	26.2	34.3	22.9	39.9	14.2	50.3	37.9	24.4	28.5	. . .	77.9
October	28.5	26.1	34.7	23.1	40.3	14.1	49.8	37.9	24.4	28.4	. . .	77.5
November	28.1	25.6	34.1	22.4	39.9	14.1	50.0	37.5	24.4	27.7	. . .	75.8
December	27.5	25.2	33.8	21.6	39.9	13.7	49.2	37.0	24.0	26.9	. . .	74.3
1961												
January	27.6	25.2	33.5	20.8	40.0	13.8	49.7	36.7	24.4	27.2	. . .	74.1
February	27.5	25.1	33.7	20.7	40.3	13.7	49.4	36.6	24.4	26.9	. . .	73.5
March	27.7	25.3	33.7	20.7	40.3	13.7	49.3	37.5	24.7	27.2	. . .	73.9
April	28.3	25.9	34.5	22.2	40.6	13.8	49.4	38.4	24.8	28.0	. . .	75.4
May	28.7	26.3	34.9	22.9	40.9	13.9	49.4	38.6	24.9	28.9	. . .	76.4
June	29.1	26.7	35.3	23.7	41.1	14.0	49.4	39.4	25.1	29.3	. . .	77.3
July	29.5	27.0	35.6	24.1	41.3	14.0	49.7	40.0	25.4	29.7	. . .	78.1
August	29.7	27.4	35.9	24.1	41.6	14.1	50.0	40.5	25.5	30.3	. . .	79.0
September	29.7	27.2	35.3	22.8	41.4	14.3	51.1	40.8	25.4	30.3	. . .	78.2
October	30.3	27.7	36.2	24.0	42.1	14.3	52.2	41.1	25.8	30.9	. . .	79.6
November	30.7	28.2	36.9	25.1	42.5	14.7	53.5	40.8	26.0	31.3	. . .	80.8
December	31.0	28.6	37.0	25.6	42.5	14.7	54.4	41.1	26.3	31.7	. . .	81.6
1962												
January	30.7	28.2	36.7	25.0	42.4	14.7	55.1	39.2	26.3	31.5	. . .	80.2
February	31.2	28.7	36.9	25.2	42.6	14.9	56.0	41.5	26.5	32.0	. . .	81.4
March	31.4	28.9	37.2	25.5	42.9	15.1	56.8	42.0	26.4	32.0	. . .	81.9
April	31.5	29.0	37.5	26.1	42.9	15.2	57.3	41.4	26.4	32.0	. . .	81.7
May	31.4	28.9	37.7	26.3	43.2	15.2	57.7	41.4	26.9	31.6	. . .	81.3
June	31.4	28.8	37.5	25.9	43.1	15.3	58.2	41.7	26.8	31.5	. . .	80.9
July	31.7	29.1	38.1	26.4	43.6	15.5	59.4	41.5	26.8	31.7	. . .	81.5
August	31.7	29.2	37.7	26.1	43.2	15.6	60.2	42.3	26.9	31.8	. . .	81.4
September	31.9	29.4	37.9	26.4	43.5	15.6	60.3	42.8	27.2	32.1	. . .	81.8
October	31.9	29.3	37.8	26.5	43.3	15.7	60.5	42.1	27.2	32.1	. . .	81.4
November	32.1	29.6	38.1	26.5	43.5	15.7	61.1	42.2	27.3	32.4	. . .	81.8
December	32.1	29.6	38.2	26.7	43.7	15.6	61.4	42.6	27.2	32.2	. . .	81.7
1963												
January	32.3	29.8	38.7	27.0	44.3	15.5	64.2	41.5	27.4	32.3	. . .	81.9
February	32.7	30.0	39.1	27.3	44.8	15.7	63.8	41.6	27.6	32.8	. . .	82.4
March	32.9	30.2	39.3	27.4	45.0	15.6	63.4	42.1	27.4	33.3	. . .	82.6
April	33.2	30.6	39.5	27.6	45.2	15.8	63.4	43.5	28.3	33.6	. . .	83.5
May	33.6	30.9	39.5	28.0	45.0	15.7	63.4	44.5	28.6	34.4	. . .	84.0
June	33.7	31.0	39.8	28.5	45.1	15.8	63.3	44.3	28.4	34.5	. . .	83.9
July	33.5	30.9	39.7	28.5	44.9	16.0	62.7	44.2	28.6	34.2	. . .	83.3
August	33.6	31.0	40.0	28.5	45.4	16.4	62.9	44.3	28.8	33.8	. . .	83.5
September	33.9	31.2	40.1	29.1	45.2	16.4	63.2	44.0	29.1	34.5	. . .	83.8
October	34.2	31.5	40.4	29.1	45.6	16.7	63.2	44.6	29.3	34.7	. . .	84.3
November	34.3	31.6	40.4	29.4	45.6	16.8	62.9	45.2	29.6	34.9	. . .	84.3
December	34.3	31.6	40.7	29.5	46.0	16.7	63.1	44.5	29.4	34.7	. . .	84.0

. . . = Not available.

Table 20-1. Industrial Production and Capacity Utilization—Continued
(Seasonally adjusted.)

Year and month	Total industry	Manufacturing (SIC)	Consumer goods			Business equipment	Defense and space equipment	Construction supplies	Business supplies	Materials	Capacity utilization (output as percentage of capacity)	
			Total	Durable	Nondurable						Total industry	Manufacturing (SIC)
1964												
January	34.6	31.9	41.0	29.5	46.4	17.2	62.5	44.8	29.7	35.0	. . .	84.5
February	34.8	32.1	41.0	29.7	46.2	17.1	61.9	45.9	29.9	35.5	. . .	84.7
March	34.8	32.1	40.8	29.5	46.1	17.3	61.8	46.1	30.1	35.5	. . .	84.4
April	35.4	32.7	41.8	30.2	47.2	17.7	61.6	46.3	30.5	36.0	. . .	85.6
May	35.6	32.8	42.1	30.4	47.6	17.9	60.6	46.5	30.8	36.3	. . .	85.6
June	35.7	32.9	42.0	30.7	47.3	18.0	60.2	46.2	30.8	36.5	. . .	85.4
July	35.9	33.1	42.6	31.2	47.9	18.2	60.1	47.0	30.8	36.6	. . .	85.9
August	36.2	33.3	42.6	31.5	47.6	18.2	60.4	46.6	30.7	37.3	. . .	86.1
September	36.3	33.5	42.1	30.7	47.4	18.4	60.8	46.2	30.7	37.9	. . .	86.2
October	35.8	33.0	41.2	27.5	48.0	18.2	61.2	46.4	30.8	37.2	. . .	84.6
November	36.9	34.0	42.8	31.3	48.1	18.8	61.8	47.5	31.0	38.3	. . .	86.8
December	37.3	34.6	43.7	33.1	48.4	19.2	62.3	46.9	31.3	38.8	. . .	88.0
1965												
January	37.7	35.0	44.3	33.7	49.1	19.1	63.0	47.2	31.6	39.2	. . .	88.6
February	38.0	35.2	44.4	34.1	49.0	19.5	63.7	48.4	31.7	39.4	. . .	88.7
March	38.5	35.7	44.8	35.1	49.0	19.7	64.8	48.8	32.0	40.0	. . .	89.3
April	38.6	35.9	44.7	35.0	48.9	19.9	65.6	48.1	32.0	40.4	. . .	89.3
May	38.9	36.2	45.0	35.3	49.2	20.2	67.0	48.6	32.4	40.6	. . .	89.4
June	39.2	36.4	45.1	35.6	49.2	20.5	67.9	48.7	32.5	41.0	. . .	89.5
July	39.6	36.9	45.1	35.8	49.1	20.8	68.9	50.0	32.5	41.4	. . .	90.3
August	39.8	37.0	45.1	35.5	49.2	20.8	69.5	49.5	32.8	41.8	. . .	89.9
September	39.9	37.1	45.7	36.1	49.8	21.2	69.6	49.1	32.8	41.5	. . .	89.6
October	40.3	37.4	46.0	36.5	50.0	21.5	70.5	49.8	33.2	41.9	. . .	89.8
November	40.4	37.5	46.2	36.7	50.3	21.9	71.1	50.5	33.4	41.8	. . .	89.6
December	41.0	38.1	46.5	37.5	50.3	22.4	71.8	51.6	33.9	42.2	. . .	90.5
1966												
January	41.4	38.5	46.7	37.6	50.5	22.8	73.4	51.5	33.9	42.8	. . .	90.9
February	41.6	38.7	46.9	37.5	50.8	22.8	74.5	51.1	34.3	43.3	. . .	90.9
March	42.2	39.2	47.2	37.8	51.2	23.2	75.1	52.1	34.6	44.1	. . .	91.6
April	42.3	39.5	47.4	38.5	51.1	23.4	76.7	52.1	34.3	44.0	. . .	91.5
May	42.7	39.7	47.4	37.9	51.4	23.7	78.1	52.3	34.8	44.5	. . .	91.6
June	42.9	39.9	47.6	37.9	51.7	23.9	79.2	51.6	35.3	44.8	. . .	91.5
July	43.1	40.1	47.5	37.2	52.0	24.3	80.3	52.1	35.7	44.9	. . .	91.4
August	43.1	40.2	47.3	36.6	52.1	24.4	81.4	50.5	35.5	45.2	. . .	91.1
September	43.5	40.5	47.5	36.8	52.2	24.7	82.5	50.5	35.7	45.7	. . .	91.2
October	43.8	40.9	48.5	38.7	52.6	24.6	83.7	50.6	35.7	45.9	. . .	91.6
November	43.5	40.5	48.2	37.6	52.9	24.3	85.3	50.6	35.8	45.2	. . .	90.1
December	43.6	40.7	48.1	37.2	53.0	24.6	86.1	50.5	35.9	45.2	. . .	90.0
1967												
January	43.8	40.8	48.6	36.2	54.2	24.4	87.6	51.9	36.6	45.0	89.4	89.8
February	43.3	40.3	47.9	35.2	53.8	24.5	88.6	51.4	36.4	44.1	88.0	88.4
March	43.1	40.1	48.1	35.6	53.8	24.4	89.6	51.5	36.4	43.3	87.1	87.5
April	43.5	40.4	48.9	35.8	54.9	24.4	90.4	51.4	36.8	43.7	87.5	87.7
May	43.1	40.1	47.9	35.3	53.7	24.5	91.1	52.2	36.2	43.3	86.4	86.6
June	43.1	40.0	48.1	35.0	54.2	24.4	90.9	52.5	36.4	43.2	86.0	86.1
July	43.0	39.9	48.0	35.4	53.8	23.9	91.4	52.7	36.5	43.2	85.4	85.3
August	43.8	40.6	48.5	35.8	54.3	24.3	91.5	53.3	37.4	44.4	86.6	86.5
September	43.8	40.6	48.6	35.7	54.5	24.2	91.8	53.7	37.6	44.2	86.1	86.1
October	44.1	41.0	49.2	36.4	55.1	24.0	92.5	53.4	37.8	44.7	86.4	86.4
November	44.8	41.7	50.3	38.4	55.6	24.6	92.7	53.8	37.9	45.2	87.3	87.5
December	45.2	42.1	51.1	39.9	55.9	24.9	92.7	53.7	37.9	45.8	87.8	88.0
1968												
January	45.2	42.0	50.4	38.8	55.6	25.0	92.3	54.1	38.0	46.0	87.4	87.4
February	45.4	42.2	50.7	39.4	55.6	25.0	93.4	54.7	38.3	46.0	87.3	87.4
March	45.5	42.3	51.0	39.3	56.2	25.2	91.5	54.8	38.3	46.2	87.3	87.1
April	45.6	42.3	50.9	39.3	56.0	25.1	89.7	55.1	38.7	46.5	87.0	86.8
May	46.1	42.9	51.2	39.8	56.2	25.5	91.0	55.3	39.0	47.2	87.7	87.6
June	46.2	43.0	51.5	40.2	56.4	25.4	91.5	55.3	39.2	47.4	87.6	87.3
July	46.2	42.8	51.4	39.9	56.4	25.2	91.5	55.3	39.2	47.5	87.2	86.7
August	46.3	43.0	52.0	40.4	57.1	25.4	91.7	55.6	39.6	47.1	87.1	86.7
September	46.5	43.1	52.2	40.8	57.2	25.6	91.6	55.2	39.7	47.3	87.0	86.4
October	46.6	43.3	52.5	41.4	57.3	25.9	89.2	55.1	40.0	47.4	86.9	86.6
November	47.2	43.9	53.2	42.3	57.8	25.9	90.1	56.4	40.4	48.1	87.7	87.4
December	47.3	44.0	52.9	42.7	57.1	26.2	89.6	57.5	40.6	48.4	87.6	87.1
1969												
January	47.6	44.2	53.2	42.6	57.6	26.5	89.8	57.9	40.8	48.6	87.8	87.2
February	47.9	44.6	53.6	42.5	58.3	26.5	89.2	58.4	40.7	49.1	88.0	87.6
March	48.3	44.9	54.0	42.8	58.7	26.8	89.5	58.6	42.0	49.4	88.4	87.9
April	48.1	44.7	53.2	41.7	58.1	27.1	88.8	58.1	41.4	49.5	87.8	87.2
May	47.9	44.5	52.8	41.1	57.9	26.9	88.6	57.7	41.8	49.4	87.1	86.5
June	48.4	44.8	53.4	42.5	58.0	27.1	87.4	58.0	42.1	50.1	87.6	86.7
July	48.6	45.1	54.3	42.5	59.4	27.4	87.0	57.5	41.9	50.1	87.8	87.0
August	48.8	45.2	54.2	42.9	59.0	27.3	85.8	57.4	42.0	50.6	87.7	86.8
September	48.8	45.1	53.8	42.5	58.6	27.6	85.3	57.4	41.9	50.7	87.3	86.3
October	48.8	45.2	53.8	42.5	58.5	27.7	84.5	57.6	42.1	50.7	87.1	86.1
November	48.3	44.7	53.4	41.0	58.8	27.0	82.9	57.3	41.8	50.5	85.9	84.9
December	48.2	44.5	53.4	40.8	59.1	26.9	81.9	57.0	42.3	50.2	85.4	84.1

. . . = Not available.

Table 20-1. Industrial Production and Capacity Utilization—*Continued*

(Seasonally adjusted.)

Year and month	Total industry	Manufac-turing (SIC)	Market groups								Capacity utilization (output as percentage of capacity)	
			Consumer goods			Business equipment	Defense and space equipment	Construction supplies	Business supplies	Materials	Total industry	Manufac-turing (SIC)
			Total	Durable	Nondurable							
1970												
January	47.3	43.5	52.6	38.6	59.0	26.6	80.8	55.2	42.3	49.0	83.5	82.0
February	47.3	43.5	53.1	39.2	59.4	26.7	79.4	55.0	42.0	48.7	83.2	81.8
March	47.2	43.4	53.0	39.5	59.1	26.7	77.7	55.5	42.2	48.6	82.8	81.3
April	47.1	43.3	53.2	39.5	59.5	26.7	75.9	56.0	42.0	48.3	82.4	80.7
May	47.0	43.2	53.5	39.6	59.9	26.7	74.3	56.1	41.9	48.1	82.0	80.3
June	46.9	43.0	53.6	40.3	59.6	26.5	73.0	55.8	41.8	47.9	81.5	79.8
July	47.0	43.2	53.8	40.4	59.8	26.4	71.8	56.5	42.0	48.1	81.4	79.8
August	46.9	42.9	52.9	39.2	59.1	26.4	71.2	56.3	41.6	48.7	81.0	79.0
September	46.6	42.5	52.7	38.1	59.4	25.8	70.5	56.1	41.9	48.4	80.2	78.1
October	45.6	41.6	52.0	35.9	59.8	25.0	69.5	55.6	41.8	47.1	78.4	76.1
November	45.4	41.3	51.7	36.0	59.2	24.8	69.0	54.9	41.8	46.8	77.6	75.4
December	46.4	42.4	53.9	40.2	60.1	25.1	68.2	55.5	41.9	47.9	79.2	77.1
1971												
January	46.8	42.8	54.7	41.8	60.4	24.6	68.7	55.5	42.1	48.6	79.6	77.6
February	46.7	42.8	54.7	42.7	59.8	24.7	67.1	55.9	42.5	48.3	79.2	77.4
March	46.6	42.7	54.8	42.7	60.0	24.5	66.5	55.7	42.1	48.4	78.9	77.0
April	46.9	42.9	55.3	43.0	60.6	24.3	66.6	56.2	42.6	48.7	79.2	77.2
May	47.1	43.2	55.3	43.7	60.3	24.2	67.4	56.5	42.7	49.3	79.4	77.6
June	47.3	43.3	55.7	44.0	60.7	24.3	66.4	57.1	42.5	49.5	79.5	77.5
July	47.2	43.4	56.6	44.9	61.6	24.3	65.9	57.6	43.6	48.3	79.0	77.5
August	46.9	42.9	55.9	44.4	60.8	24.7	65.9	56.6	43.1	48.0	78.4	76.4
September	47.7	43.7	56.5	44.3	61.7	25.3	65.2	58.7	43.8	48.9	79.5	77.7
October	48.0	44.4	57.2	45.2	62.4	25.5	64.8	59.5	44.0	49.1	79.8	78.7
November	48.2	44.5	57.7	45.6	62.8	25.6	64.3	59.7	44.5	49.2	80.0	78.7
December	48.8	45.0	58.1	45.8	63.3	25.8	63.3	60.7	44.7	50.2	80.7	79.3
1972												
January	50.0	46.1	59.0	47.2	63.9	26.6	63.2	62.4	45.5	51.7	82.4	81.1
February	50.5	46.5	59.4	47.5	64.4	27.0	63.5	62.7	46.3	52.3	83.1	81.6
March	50.9	46.9	59.4	47.2	64.6	27.3	64.1	63.3	46.8	52.8	83.5	82.0
April	51.4	47.4	60.1	48.6	64.8	27.8	64.3	63.9	46.8	53.3	84.1	82.7
May	51.4	47.4	59.8	48.1	64.6	27.8	63.7	64.4	47.0	53.4	84.0	82.6
June	51.5	47.6	59.7	48.1	64.6	28.0	63.6	64.7	47.5	53.5	83.9	82.7
July	51.5	47.6	60.2	49.1	64.7	28.0	63.7	65.6	47.4	53.1	83.7	82.5
August	52.1	48.2	60.8	49.3	65.4	28.5	63.4	65.8	48.0	53.9	84.5	83.2
September	52.4	48.5	61.0	49.8	65.5	28.8	63.9	66.2	47.9	54.4	84.9	83.6
October	53.1	49.2	61.9	51.0	66.2	29.3	64.1	67.3	48.7	54.9	85.7	84.5
November	53.7	49.8	62.3	52.1	66.1	29.8	65.9	68.1	48.9	55.8	86.5	85.4
December	54.5	50.6	63.0	53.5	66.4	30.2	66.9	68.2	49.2	56.7	87.5	86.5
1973												
January	54.9	51.0	63.0	53.3	66.4	30.8	68.1	69.2	49.5	57.3	87.9	87.0
February	55.7	51.8	63.7	54.2	67.0	31.5	69.4	70.3	50.0	58.1	88.9	88.1
March	55.8	52.0	63.9	54.3	67.3	31.7	69.0	70.6	50.1	58.0	88.7	88.0
April	55.6	51.8	63.2	53.3	66.8	31.8	68.3	70.2	50.0	58.0	88.1	87.4
May	56.0	52.1	63.6	53.2	67.5	32.3	68.6	70.5	50.3	58.4	88.4	87.7
June	56.0	52.1	63.1	53.1	66.8	32.7	69.1	70.7	50.5	58.5	88.2	87.4
July	56.2	52.3	63.0	53.1	66.7	33.0	70.6	71.2	50.6	58.7	88.2	87.4
August	56.1	52.2	62.4	51.3	66.8	33.1	70.8	71.1	50.7	58.7	87.8	86.9
September	56.5	52.6	63.4	53.0	67.3	33.6	70.7	70.6	50.6	59.0	88.2	87.3
October	56.9	53.0	63.6	52.6	67.7	33.9	71.9	71.1	51.1	59.4	88.5	87.6
November	57.1	53.3	63.7	52.6	68.0	34.1	71.3	71.4	51.0	59.8	88.5	87.9
December	57.0	53.3	62.5	51.4	66.9	34.2	70.7	71.9	50.7	60.1	88.0	87.7
1974												
January	56.7	53.0	61.8	48.9	67.3	34.2	70.7	72.7	50.8	59.6	87.3	86.8
February	56.5	52.8	61.6	48.9	67.0	34.1	71.3	71.1	50.5	59.6	86.7	86.2
March	56.6	52.8	61.8	49.0	67.2	34.5	71.2	71.5	50.7	59.4	86.6	86.0
April	56.5	52.7	61.7	48.8	67.1	34.4	71.4	71.1	50.8	59.4	86.4	85.6
May	56.8	53.0	62.1	48.8	67.9	34.8	71.3	71.3	50.9	59.7	86.6	85.8
June	56.8	53.0	62.4	49.5	67.8	34.8	70.2	70.9	51.3	59.4	86.3	85.6
July	56.7	52.8	62.2	49.0	67.8	34.6	71.1	69.3	50.8	59.6	85.9	85.1
August	56.2	52.4	62.1	49.1	67.7	34.6	73.0	68.6	50.7	58.6	84.9	84.2
September	56.2	52.4	61.6	48.9	67.0	35.1	73.1	68.3	50.4	58.7	84.8	84.0
October	55.9	52.0	61.6	48.3	67.3	35.0	74.1	66.8	50.1	58.4	84.2	83.1
November	54.1	50.5	59.9	46.1	65.9	34.4	73.7	65.0	49.0	55.9	81.3	80.5
December	52.2	48.2	58.0	42.2	65.2	33.0	72.9	61.7	48.0	53.7	78.3	76.7
1975												
January	51.6	47.4	56.8	40.6	64.4	32.4	73.9	61.5	47.3	53.4	77.3	75.3
February	50.5	46.1	56.2	39.6	64.0	31.3	70.4	60.0	46.4	52.1	75.4	73.1
March	49.9	45.5	56.4	40.3	63.9	30.7	70.9	58.1	45.8	51.4	74.5	72.0
April	49.9	45.3	57.5	41.6	64.9	30.3	70.4	57.3	45.9	50.9	74.3	71.6
May	49.8	45.3	57.7	42.5	64.6	30.1	73.9	56.8	45.6	50.7	74.0	71.5
June	50.1	45.7	58.5	42.9	65.6	29.9	74.8	56.7	45.7	51.1	74.4	72.0
July	50.6	46.4	59.9	45.0	66.6	30.0	74.3	57.5	46.2	51.3	75.0	72.9
August	51.0	46.7	60.2	45.6	66.7	29.8	73.6	58.1	46.5	52.0	75.5	73.4
September	51.6	47.5	60.9	46.4	67.4	30.2	75.6	58.8	46.6	52.6	76.2	74.4
October	51.7	47.6	60.9	46.2	67.5	30.1	74.7	59.3	46.7	52.9	76.2	74.4
November	51.9	47.7	61.2	46.3	67.8	30.1	71.8	59.1	46.8	53.1	76.3	74.4
December	52.6	48.4	61.8	47.2	68.2	30.6	74.1	58.8	47.3	54.0	77.2	75.4

Table 20-1. Industrial Production and Capacity Utilization—*Continued*

(Seasonally adjusted.)

Year and month	Total industry	Manufac- turing (SIC)	Consumer goods Total	Durable	Nondurable	Business equipment	Defense and space equipment	Construction supplies	Business supplies	Materials	Cap util Total industry	Manufac- turing (SIC)
1976												
January	53.3	49.0	62.7	48.0	69.2	30.9	74.4	60.5	47.8	54.8	78.1	76.2
February	54.0	49.9	63.0	48.7	69.3	31.1	74.5	61.7	48.1	55.8	78.9	77.3
March	54.0	49.9	62.7	48.6	68.8	31.2	74.2	61.2	48.3	56.0	78.8	77.2
April	54.4	50.3	62.9	48.7	69.1	31.7	73.1	62.1	48.6	56.4	79.2	77.7
May	54.6	50.6	63.5	48.7	70.0	31.9	72.0	62.8	48.8	56.4	79.3	77.9
June	54.6	50.6	63.2	48.5	69.7	32.0	71.1	63.2	48.6	56.6	79.1	77.7
July	54.9	50.9	63.6	48.6	70.2	32.3	69.1	64.3	49.3	56.7	79.4	78.1
August	55.2	51.2	63.8	49.4	70.1	32.8	69.1	63.8	49.4	57.2	79.7	78.3
September	55.3	51.3	63.8	48.9	70.3	32.6	68.7	64.0	50.4	57.2	79.7	78.2
October	55.4	51.3	64.3	49.7	70.7	32.9	68.9	64.0	50.7	57.0	79.6	78.1
November	56.2	52.0	65.4	51.3	71.5	33.9	68.3	64.5	50.9	57.7	80.6	78.9
December	56.9	52.6	66.2	52.7	71.8	34.4	67.3	64.7	51.5	58.5	81.4	79.7
1977												
January	56.6	52.5	66.1	52.6	71.7	34.6	66.5	63.7	51.4	58.0	80.8	79.3
February	57.4	53.4	66.8	53.1	72.6	35.3	66.2	64.9	51.7	58.8	81.7	80.4
March	58.2	54.2	66.9	54.5	71.8	35.8	64.6	66.8	52.3	60.0	82.6	81.5
April	58.7	54.8	67.4	55.0	72.3	36.3	65.1	68.2	52.9	60.5	83.2	82.2
May	59.1	55.2	67.3	55.1	72.2	36.9	64.9	69.4	53.4	61.0	83.6	82.6
June	59.5	55.6	67.8	56.1	72.2	37.6	64.7	69.9	53.9	61.2	83.9	83.0
July	59.7	55.7	68.0	56.2	72.6	38.2	64.5	70.0	54.1	61.2	84.0	82.9
August	59.7	56.0	68.0	56.0	72.7	38.4	63.7	70.5	54.4	61.1	83.8	83.1
September	60.0	56.0	68.0	56.3	72.5	38.7	63.7	69.9	54.4	61.5	83.9	83.0
October	60.1	56.2	68.5	56.2	73.4	38.8	58.3	70.0	54.4	61.7	83.9	83.0
November	60.1	56.2	68.5	56.2	73.4	38.8	57.4	70.3	54.4	61.8	83.7	82.8
December	60.3	56.9	69.1	56.6	74.1	39.5	61.5	70.9	54.9	61.2	83.6	83.6
1978												
January	59.6	56.2	67.6	53.8	73.5	38.8	62.4	70.2	54.8	60.7	82.5	82.3
February	59.7	56.3	68.6	54.9	74.3	39.6	58.9	69.8	54.9	60.5	82.5	82.2
March	60.9	57.3	70.0	56.6	75.4	40.6	64.1	70.9	55.7	61.4	83.8	83.5
April	62.1	58.1	70.5	57.7	75.6	41.3	63.6	72.1	55.8	63.3	85.2	84.5
May	62.4	58.4	70.0	56.9	75.3	41.5	63.9	72.4	56.1	64.0	85.4	84.6
June	62.8	58.8	70.4	57.3	75.8	42.1	64.6	72.9	56.7	64.3	85.8	85.1
July	62.8	58.8	70.2	57.4	75.2	42.4	64.5	73.0	56.7	64.3	85.5	84.8
August	63.0	59.0	70.1	57.0	75.4	42.9	65.1	73.0	56.8	64.5	85.5	84.9
September	63.1	59.3	70.2	56.6	75.7	43.4	65.1	73.3	56.8	64.5	85.5	85.0
October	63.6	59.7	69.9	56.7	75.2	44.2	64.9	73.9	57.1	65.2	85.9	85.3
November	64.0	60.2	70.1	56.9	75.4	45.0	64.5	74.7	57.3	65.7	86.3	85.8
December	64.4	60.7	70.3	57.0	75.6	45.7	65.3	75.7	57.8	66.0	86.6	86.3
1979												
January	64.1	60.3	70.3	57.6	75.3	46.2	65.8	74.7	58.0	65.1	85.9	85.5
February	64.4	60.5	69.7	56.9	74.9	46.9	67.1	74.8	58.4	65.7	86.2	85.6
March	64.6	60.8	70.0	56.7	75.4	47.2	66.6	75.0	58.6	65.9	86.3	85.7
April	64.1	60.1	68.9	54.1	75.1	46.5	65.4	74.1	58.5	65.6	85.3	84.4
May	64.5	60.7	69.3	55.5	75.0	47.6	66.3	74.2	58.6	65.9	85.7	85.1
June	64.5	60.8	69.0	55.0	74.8	47.9	66.9	74.7	58.3	65.9	85.5	85.0
July	64.3	60.8	68.3	54.2	74.3	48.2	68.2	74.9	58.3	65.6	85.1	84.7
August	63.9	60.0	67.8	51.9	74.7	47.5	69.2	73.9	58.6	65.2	84.3	83.4
September	63.9	60.1	68.0	53.7	74.1	48.8	69.7	73.9	57.8	64.8	84.2	83.3
October	64.2	60.2	68.1	53.3	74.3	48.0	71.7	74.3	58.3	65.3	84.4	83.2
November	64.1	60.0	67.9	52.5	74.6	47.9	73.3	74.0	58.5	65.2	84.1	82.8
December	64.2	60.2	68.0	52.3	74.8	48.2	74.8	74.7	58.6	65.1	84.0	82.8
1980												
January	64.5	60.5	67.8	51.3	75.1	48.9	76.1	74.8	58.3	65.7	84.3	83.1
February	64.6	60.5	68.0	51.0	75.5	49.3	79.1	73.9	58.3	65.5	84.2	82.9
March	64.4	60.0	67.7	50.4	75.4	48.9	80.1	72.6	58.1	65.5	83.8	82.1
April	63.1	58.9	66.6	48.2	75.0	48.5	81.0	68.9	57.1	63.9	82.0	80.3
May	61.6	57.1	65.2	45.2	74.5	47.7	81.1	66.4	56.0	62.1	79.9	77.7
June	60.8	56.2	64.9	44.7	74.4	47.1	81.8	65.1	55.4	60.9	78.7	76.3
July	60.4	55.7	65.0	44.5	74.6	47.1	82.8	64.6	55.7	60.1	78.1	75.5
August	60.5	56.1	65.3	44.9	74.8	47.0	82.9	65.4	55.9	60.2	78.1	75.7
September	61.5	57.0	65.8	46.9	74.5	47.7	82.9	67.2	56.7	61.4	79.3	76.8
October	62.2	57.8	66.2	47.7	74.7	48.3	83.8	68.2	56.7	62.2	79.9	77.7
November	63.2	58.9	66.6	48.9	74.6	49.1	85.1	69.5	57.4	63.6	81.1	79.0
December	63.6	59.1	66.5	48.1	74.9	49.2	85.1	69.2	58.1	64.3	81.5	79.0
1981												
January	63.2	58.8	66.5	47.9	75.0	49.5	84.6	68.9	58.2	63.5	80.8	78.5
February	63.0	58.6	66.4	47.9	74.8	49.2	84.4	68.8	57.7	63.3	80.4	78.0
March	63.4	58.8	66.4	48.5	74.5	49.5	84.8	69.1	57.6	63.7	80.6	78.0
April	63.1	59.2	66.6	49.2	74.5	50.0	85.2	69.4	58.0	62.8	80.1	78.3
May	63.5	59.5	67.3	49.9	75.1	50.1	86.1	69.4	58.7	63.2	80.4	78.5
June	63.9	59.3	66.8	49.5	74.6	50.0	86.9	68.3	58.9	64.1	80.7	78.0
July	64.3	59.4	67.3	49.8	75.1	50.1	87.9	68.4	59.3	64.6	81.1	78.0
August	64.2	59.4	67.4	49.4	75.5	50.0	88.8	68.2	58.8	64.5	80.8	77.8
September	63.8	59.1	66.7	48.1	75.2	49.8	90.4	67.5	58.8	64.0	80.0	77.1
October	63.3	58.4	67.0	47.8	75.8	49.5	92.6	65.7	58.4	63.1	79.2	76.1
November	62.6	57.7	66.9	47.1	76.0	48.7	95.1	64.7	58.1	62.0	78.1	75.1
December	61.9	56.7	66.1	45.0	76.1	47.9	97.6	63.2	58.0	61.3	77.1	73.6

Table 20-1. Industrial Production and Capacity Utilization—*Continued*

(Seasonally adjusted.)

Year and month	Total industry	Manufac-turing (SIC)	Market groups								Capacity utilization (output as percentage of capacity)	
			Consumer goods			Business equipment	Defense and space equipment	Construction supplies	Business supplies	Materials	Total industry	Manufac-turing (SIC)
			Total	Durable	Nondurable							
1982												
January	60.8	55.5	65.3	43.9	75.5	46.4	97.1	61.5	57.4	60.1	75.5	71.9
February	62.0	57.0	67.0	45.5	77.1	47.8	102.6	63.7	58.5	60.9	76.8	73.7
March	61.6	56.6	66.6	45.3	76.7	47.2	104.3	62.1	58.3	60.5	76.1	73.0
April	61.0	56.3	66.6	46.3	76.1	46.9	105.6	62.1	58.1	59.7	75.3	72.4
May	60.6	56.1	66.6	46.2	76.1	46.7	107.0	62.1	57.6	59.0	74.7	72.1
June	60.4	56.1	66.9	46.5	76.5	45.9	107.1	61.5	57.6	58.8	74.3	71.9
July	60.2	56.0	67.1	46.8	76.5	45.7	108.2	61.1	57.6	58.4	73.9	71.6
August	59.7	55.5	66.9	46.1	76.7	44.6	107.5	61.2	57.6	57.8	73.1	70.9
September	59.4	55.2	66.7	45.4	76.7	44.2	108.9	61.3	57.6	57.4	72.6	70.4
October	58.9	54.6	66.8	44.9	77.2	43.2	109.0	60.4	57.4	56.8	71.9	69.5
November	58.6	54.3	66.7	44.9	76.9	42.8	109.1	60.4	57.4	56.5	71.5	69.0
December	58.2	54.0	65.7	44.9	75.5	43.0	108.4	59.7	57.1	56.1	70.9	68.7
1983												
January	59.2	55.4	67.1	46.8	76.5	43.1	107.1	62.0	57.8	57.2	72.1	70.3
February	58.9	55.3	66.4	46.7	75.5	43.0	105.3	61.3	57.9	57.1	71.7	70.1
March	59.4	55.8	66.6	47.3	75.4	43.4	105.8	62.7	58.6	57.6	72.2	70.8
April	60.2	56.5	68.1	48.3	77.2	43.6	105.0	63.4	59.3	58.3	73.1	71.6
May	60.6	57.3	68.4	49.1	77.1	44.1	105.3	64.6	59.5	58.8	73.6	72.5
June	61.0	57.7	68.7	50.0	77.2	44.5	104.9	65.5	59.8	59.2	74.0	73.1
July	61.9	58.5	69.6	51.0	78.0	45.3	106.2	67.0	60.5	60.2	75.1	74.1
August	62.6	58.9	70.2	51.9	78.5	45.7	106.3	67.2	61.3	61.0	75.9	74.5
September	63.5	60.0	71.0	52.9	79.1	47.1	107.7	67.8	62.3	61.8	77.0	75.9
October	64.0	60.7	70.5	53.5	78.0	47.6	109.5	69.1	62.4	62.7	77.5	76.6
November	64.2	60.9	70.5	53.4	78.0	47.9	109.9	68.9	62.7	63.0	77.7	76.8
December	64.6	61.1	70.6	54.7	77.6	48.4	111.2	69.1	63.0	63.4	78.1	76.9
1984												
January	65.9	62.2	72.1	56.0	79.1	49.6	113.9	69.7	64.1	64.6	79.6	78.3
February	66.1	62.8	71.7	56.0	78.5	50.1	116.2	71.0	64.0	65.0	79.7	78.9
March	66.6	63.3	72.2	56.3	79.0	50.7	117.1	71.0	64.9	65.3	80.2	79.3
April	67.0	63.6	72.4	56.1	79.4	51.2	119.7	71.2	64.8	65.7	80.5	79.6
May	67.4	63.8	72.1	55.6	79.4	51.6	120.7	71.4	65.8	66.2	80.9	79.7
June	67.6	64.2	72.0	55.9	79.1	52.3	122.3	72.2	66.0	66.4	81.0	79.9
July	67.8	64.5	72.1	56.5	78.8	53.1	120.6	71.8	66.4	66.6	81.1	80.1
August	67.9	64.6	71.8	56.9	78.2	53.7	124.7	72.0	66.4	66.5	81.1	80.0
September	67.7	64.4	71.6	56.1	78.3	53.9	127.5	72.1	66.2	66.2	80.7	79.6
October	67.6	64.6	72.0	55.6	79.2	54.1	128.3	72.0	66.6	65.6	80.4	79.6
November	67.8	64.8	72.2	56.4	79.0	54.7	127.4	71.6	66.9	65.8	80.5	79.6
December	67.9	65.0	72.6	57.1	79.3	54.9	129.5	72.7	66.4	65.7	80.4	79.7
1985												
January	67.7	64.7	72.1	56.0	79.1	54.6	129.7	71.2	66.5	65.7	80.0	79.1
February	68.1	64.6	72.6	55.9	80.0	54.4	131.0	71.5	67.2	66.0	80.2	78.8
March	68.1	65.1	72.5	56.4	79.6	54.9	133.6	73.0	67.0	65.8	80.1	79.1
April	68.1	65.0	72.2	55.7	79.5	54.5	134.5	73.2	67.4	65.9	79.9	78.8
May	68.2	65.1	72.3	55.8	79.4	54.7	135.2	73.9	67.7	65.9	79.8	78.7
June	68.2	65.2	72.5	55.7	79.9	54.9	137.3	74.0	67.3	65.8	79.6	78.6
July	67.7	64.8	72.3	55.9	79.5	54.4	136.1	73.9	66.9	65.3	79.0	78.0
August	68.1	65.2	72.6	56.2	79.8	54.6	138.6	73.9	67.5	65.5	79.2	78.3
September	68.4	65.3	73.1	56.2	80.5	54.4	139.5	73.9	68.0	65.8	79.3	78.2
October	68.0	65.0	72.9	55.8	80.4	54.3	141.1	73.9	67.4	65.4	78.8	77.8
November	68.2	65.4	73.1	57.2	80.0	54.8	142.8	74.0	67.6	65.4	78.9	78.1
December	68.0	65.6	73.9	57.2	81.2	54.7	143.7	73.9	68.5	66.3	79.5	78.2
1986												
January	69.3	66.4	74.8	58.8	81.7	54.8	144.4	75.5	69.0	66.5	79.9	79.0
February	68.8	66.1	74.2	58.5	81.0	54.3	142.6	74.9	68.4	66.2	79.2	78.5
March	68.3	65.8	73.9	58.4	80.6	54.3	144.1	74.9	68.1	65.4	78.6	78.1
April	68.4	66.1	74.3	58.1	81.3	53.9	144.3	75.3	68.6	65.4	78.5	78.3
May	68.5	66.2	74.6	58.2	81.8	53.8	145.0	75.8	69.2	65.4	78.6	78.4
June	68.3	66.0	74.8	58.8	81.8	53.3	145.5	74.9	69.8	65.0	78.3	78.0
July	68.7	66.4	75.2	59.4	82.0	53.7	147.3	75.5	69.9	65.4	78.6	78.3
August	68.6	66.5	75.2	59.5	82.0	53.7	146.6	76.3	69.8	65.2	78.4	78.4
September	68.7	66.7	75.3	60.0	81.8	53.7	146.1	76.5	70.1	65.3	78.4	78.5
October	69.0	66.9	75.5	60.2	82.1	53.4	146.1	76.3	70.6	65.8	78.6	78.6
November	69.3	67.2	76.1	61.1	82.5	53.5	147.2	77.2	70.6	66.1	78.9	78.8
December	70.0	67.8	76.7	62.2	82.9	54.1	147.1	77.3	71.6	66.7	79.5	79.4
1987												
January	69.6	67.4	75.7	61.4	81.8	54.3	147.5	77.3	71.0	66.4	78.9	78.8
February	70.6	68.5	76.8	62.4	82.9	55.7	148.5	78.5	71.6	67.3	79.9	79.9
March	70.7	68.6	77.1	62.3	83.3	55.3	148.5	78.8	72.0	67.5	79.9	79.9
April	71.2	69.0	77.1	61.9	83.6	55.7	149.0	79.5	72.8	68.1	80.3	80.2
May	71.6	69.5	77.5	62.3	84.0	56.1	148.5	79.9	73.6	68.4	80.7	80.5
June	72.0	69.9	77.9	61.9	84.8	56.7	147.8	80.5	74.1	68.9	81.0	80.8
July	72.5	70.4	78.3	61.6	85.5	57.1	146.9	80.8	74.5	69.4	81.4	81.2
August	73.0	70.7	78.9	62.2	86.1	57.9	148.0	81.1	74.7	69.8	81.8	81.4
September	73.1	71.0	78.5	62.7	85.2	58.5	148.5	81.8	74.8	70.0	81.9	81.7
October	74.1	72.1	79.7	64.6	86.1	59.7	148.1	82.6	75.5	71.0	82.9	82.8
November	74.5	72.5	79.9	64.7	86.3	60.0	149.0	82.9	75.4	71.6	83.2	83.2
December	74.8	72.8	79.8	64.1	86.6	60.6	149.8	82.8	75.6	72.0	83.5	83.5

Table 20-1. Industrial Production and Capacity Utilization—*Continued*

(Seasonally adjusted.)

Year and month	Total industry	Manufac-turing (SIC)	Market groups								Capacity utilization (output as percentage of capacity)	
			Consumer goods			Business equipment	Defense and space equipment	Construction supplies	Business supplies	Materials	Total industry	Manufac-turing (SIC)
			Total	Durable	Nondurable							
1988												
January	74.8	72.7	80.3	64.0	87.2	60.7	152.7	81.7	76.0	71.7	83.4	83.2
February	75.2	72.9	80.8	64.0	88.1	60.8	150.5	82.3	76.5	72.1	83.8	83.4
March	75.4	73.1	80.8	64.8	87.6	61.2	149.3	82.9	76.4	72.3	83.9	83.6
April	75.7	73.6	81.1	66.1	87.5	61.9	147.6	82.5	76.3	72.7	84.2	84.1
May	75.7	73.6	80.9	66.2	87.1	62.2	147.7	82.7	75.7	72.8	84.1	84.0
June	75.8	73.6	80.9	66.6	86.9	62.5	146.5	81.9	76.0	73.0	84.2	84.0
July	75.9	73.8	81.0	65.0	87.8	62.1	147.6	82.1	76.6	73.3	84.3	84.1
August	76.3	73.9	81.6	65.7	88.4	62.5	146.7	82.0	77.4	73.6	84.7	84.1
September	76.1	74.1	81.1	67.1	87.0	63.1	147.1	81.8	76.7	73.3	84.3	84.3
October	76.5	74.5	81.7	67.6	87.7	63.7	147.9	82.5	77.0	73.5	84.7	84.7
November	76.6	74.7	81.7	68.2	87.3	64.1	147.6	82.6	77.1	73.7	84.8	84.8
December	77.0	75.1	82.1	69.1	87.4	64.1	148.5	83.0	77.4	74.1	85.0	85.1
1989												
January	77.2	75.6	82.1	70.4	86.9	64.8	148.2	84.5	77.4	74.2	85.2	85.6
February	76.8	74.9	82.0	69.6	87.1	64.7	148.3	82.3	77.6	73.6	84.6	84.6
March	77.0	74.8	82.3	68.6	88.0	64.2	147.4	82.4	78.5	74.0	84.7	84.4
April	77.0	74.9	82.2	69.1	87.6	64.8	149.5	81.9	77.8	73.9	84.5	84.2
May	76.5	74.3	81.4	67.7	87.1	63.6	150.4	81.9	77.5	73.7	83.8	83.4
June	76.5	74.4	81.3	66.9	87.3	64.5	150.4	82.2	77.8	73.4	83.7	83.3
July	75.8	73.5	79.6	64.6	85.9	63.8	150.5	81.5	77.1	73.0	82.7	82.2
August	76.5	74.2	80.9	66.8	86.8	64.8	151.0	81.3	77.4	73.4	83.3	82.7
September	76.2	73.9	80.7	67.3	86.2	64.4	150.1	81.7	77.6	73.1	82.8	82.3
October	76.1	73.8	81.0	66.1	87.2	63.7	145.1	81.3	77.5	73.2	82.6	82.0
November	76.3	73.9	81.0	66.2	87.2	64.2	143.0	81.3	77.9	73.4	82.6	81.8
December	76.8	74.0	82.6	67.1	89.1	65.5	146.0	80.6	78.3	73.2	83.0	81.8
1990												
January	76.5	74.0	81.0	63.7	88.3	64.7	146.1	82.5	79.0	73.1	82.4	81.6
February	77.1	75.0	81.8	67.5	87.7	65.6	145.9	83.1	78.9	73.8	83.0	82.5
March	77.4	75.3	82.4	68.7	88.1	66.1	145.1	82.2	79.4	74.0	83.1	82.6
April	77.4	75.2	82.2	67.4	88.4	66.0	144.6	82.0	79.3	74.2	83.0	82.4
May	77.5	75.2	82.0	67.8	88.0	66.6	143.0	81.2	79.8	74.3	82.9	82.2
June	77.7	75.4	82.9	68.8	88.8	66.8	142.5	81.7	79.6	74.3	83.0	82.3
July	77.6	75.3	82.3	67.1	88.7	66.8	142.9	81.0	80.1	74.3	82.7	81.9
August	77.8	75.5	82.4	66.9	88.9	67.0	141.4	80.9	80.0	74.7	82.8	82.0
September	78.0	75.4	83.2	67.4	89.9	66.9	140.4	80.3	80.1	74.6	82.8	81.8
October	77.4	74.9	81.9	65.3	89.0	66.5	141.0	80.1	80.0	74.4	82.1	81.0
November	76.5	74.0	81.1	62.0	89.3	65.0	138.6	79.4	79.6	73.5	81.0	79.9
December	76.0	73.5	80.6	61.0	89.0	64.8	139.6	79.2	79.2	72.7	80.3	79.2
1991												
January	75.7	72.9	81.1	61.4	89.6	64.0	137.9	76.8	78.8	72.4	79.8	78.5
February	75.1	72.5	80.3	59.9	89.1	63.6	136.7	76.0	78.1	72.1	79.1	77.9
March	74.7	71.9	80.3	59.9	89.1	63.8	136.0	75.0	77.1	71.4	78.6	77.2
April	74.9	72.2	80.3	60.9	88.6	63.9	132.3	75.5	77.7	71.7	78.6	77.3
May	75.7	72.7	81.7	62.4	90.1	64.3	129.8	75.9	78.3	72.4	79.3	77.8
June	76.4	73.5	82.9	63.9	91.1	65.2	130.6	76.8	78.9	72.9	80.0	78.5
July	76.4	73.7	82.5	64.9	90.0	65.1	128.9	77.0	78.4	73.4	79.8	78.5
August	76.4	73.8	82.5	64.1	90.3	64.8	130.4	77.5	78.8	73.4	79.8	78.5
September	77.1	74.6	83.6	66.6	90.9	65.6	129.8	77.7	79.2	73.9	80.3	79.2
October	76.9	74.5	83.4	66.4	90.6	65.2	130.1	76.7	78.9	74.0	80.0	78.9
November	76.8	74.3	83.5	66.6	90.6	64.9	129.1	77.5	78.9	73.7	79.8	78.6
December	76.6	74.2	82.5	65.9	89.5	65.2	127.8	77.2	79.0	73.7	79.4	78.4
1992												
January	76.1	73.8	81.6	63.4	89.4	63.9	126.0	77.5	78.8	73.7	78.8	77.8
February	76.8	74.5	82.6	66.0	89.6	65.6	125.7	78.6	79.0	74.0	79.4	78.5
March	77.4	75.2	83.3	67.3	90.1	65.9	125.1	79.0	79.4	74.6	79.9	79.0
April	77.9	75.6	84.1	68.6	90.6	66.6	123.3	79.7	80.0	75.1	80.3	79.3
May	78.2	76.1	84.5	70.7	90.2	67.3	122.7	80.0	80.2	75.3	80.4	79.6
June	78.1	76.2	84.0	69.7	90.0	67.4	122.5	79.9	80.0	75.5	80.3	79.6
July	78.7	76.8	85.0	71.5	90.7	67.9	120.5	80.2	80.6	76.0	80.8	80.1
August	78.5	76.6	85.2	71.0	91.2	67.8	120.6	80.6	80.6	75.3	80.4	79.7
September	78.6	76.6	84.8	70.6	90.7	67.8	120.6	80.4	80.7	75.7	80.3	79.5
October	79.2	77.0	85.9	71.9	91.7	68.1	120.2	80.7	81.2	76.2	80.8	79.8
November	79.6	77.4	86.2	72.7	91.9	68.6	120.2	80.5	81.6	76.6	81.1	80.1
December	79.6	77.3	86.2	73.5	91.5	68.8	120.0	80.8	81.8	76.5	80.9	79.8
1993												
January	79.9	78.0	86.5	74.8	91.4	69.3	119.1	81.2	81.8	76.8	81.1	80.3
February	80.2	78.1	86.8	74.4	91.9	69.1	118.5	81.6	82.3	77.3	81.3	80.3
March	80.3	78.1	86.9	75.1	91.9	69.3	116.9	81.7	83.0	77.2	81.3	80.2
April	80.5	78.5	87.2	75.8	91.9	69.7	117.1	82.1	82.9	77.4	81.3	80.4
May	80.2	78.4	86.5	76.1	90.7	69.9	116.0	83.1	82.6	77.2	80.9	80.2
June	80.4	78.3	86.7	75.7	91.3	69.1	115.0	82.8	82.6	77.6	80.9	79.9
July	80.7	78.6	87.7	76.0	92.5	69.0	115.6	83.6	82.9	77.6	81.1	80.0
August	80.6	78.4	87.6	75.3	92.7	68.6	113.8	83.3	82.8	77.7	80.9	79.6
September	81.0	79.0	87.9	76.9	92.4	69.5	114.4	84.1	83.2	78.0	81.2	80.1
October	81.6	79.5	88.2	79.0	92.0	70.6	114.1	84.9	83.2	78.6	81.6	80.5
November	81.9	79.9	88.4	79.7	91.9	70.8	113.7	85.5	83.2	79.3	81.8	80.7
December	82.4	80.5	88.7	80.4	92.2	71.0	112.7	86.9	83.9	79.9	82.1	81.0

Table 20-1. Industrial Production and Capacity Utilization—*Continued*

(Seasonally adjusted.)

Year and month	Total industry	Manufac-turing (SIC)	Market groups								Capacity utilization (output as percentage of capacity)	
			Consumer goods			Business equipment	Defense and space equipment	Construction supplies	Business supplies	Materials	Total industry	Manufac-turing (SIC)
			Total	Durable	Nondurable							
1994												
January	82.9	80.7	89.7	82.0	92.8	71.3	111.3	86.6	84.6	80.1	82.4	81.1
February	82.9	80.9	89.9	82.1	93.1	70.9	109.6	86.0	84.8	80.4	82.3	81.0
March	83.7	81.8	90.4	82.9	93.6	71.6	110.6	87.7	85.3	81.2	82.8	81.8
April	84.1	82.4	90.5	83.8	93.3	72.3	110.6	88.6	85.4	81.7	83.0	82.2
May	84.6	83.0	91.3	84.4	94.1	72.7	109.5	89.1	85.7	82.3	83.3	82.5
June	85.2	83.3	92.0	85.3	94.8	73.2	108.3	89.2	86.4	82.8	83.6	82.5
July	85.3	83.6	91.6	85.5	94.0	74.0	107.4	90.2	86.2	83.2	83.5	82.6
August	85.8	84.3	92.6	87.0	94.8	73.9	106.1	90.2	86.3	83.8	83.7	82.9
September	85.9	84.5	92.0	87.2	94.0	74.2	107.2	90.7	86.6	84.1	83.6	82.8
October	86.6	85.3	92.9	88.0	94.9	75.1	107.8	91.2	87.2	84.7	84.0	83.3
November	87.2	85.9	93.0	87.7	95.1	75.8	109.0	91.6	87.6	85.5	84.2	83.6
December	88.1	87.0	93.7	88.7	95.7	76.6	109.4	92.5	88.3	86.7	84.8	84.3
1995												
January	88.5	87.4	93.8	89.7	95.4	77.3	109.3	92.8	88.6	87.2	84.8	84.3
February	88.5	87.3	94.1	89.5	96.0	77.5	107.7	91.8	88.6	87.2	84.5	83.9
March	88.5	87.4	93.8	89.3	95.7	78.0	107.8	91.4	88.9	87.2	84.2	83.6
April	88.5	87.3	93.6	89.0	95.5	77.9	107.6	90.4	89.0	87.4	83.8	83.1
May	88.7	87.3	93.9	88.1	96.3	78.0	107.1	90.0	89.3	87.5	83.7	82.8
June	89.0	87.7	94.4	88.8	96.7	78.7	107.8	90.3	89.7	87.6	83.6	82.7
July	88.6	87.1	93.9	87.2	96.6	78.4	106.2	89.9	89.7	87.2	82.8	81.8
August	89.8	88.2	95.4	90.2	97.5	80.2	105.9	90.3	90.7	88.2	83.6	82.3
September	90.2	89.0	95.6	91.6	97.2	81.4	105.1	91.9	90.7	88.6	83.6	82.7
October	90.0	88.8	94.8	90.6	96.4	80.9	104.2	91.8	90.7	88.8	83.0	82.1
November	90.3	89.0	95.2	90.8	96.9	81.4	101.7	92.2	91.4	89.0	82.9	81.8
December	90.7	89.4	95.5	91.3	97.2	82.7	101.2	93.3	91.4	89.3	82.9	81.7
1996												
January	90.1	88.7	94.5	88.7	96.8	82.1	100.2	91.5	91.0	88.9	81.9	80.6
February	91.3	89.8	95.8	90.9	97.8	83.9	102.3	92.5	91.9	89.9	82.6	81.1
March	91.1	89.5	95.2	87.9	98.1	83.2	102.5	93.3	91.8	89.9	82.0	80.4
April	91.9	90.5	96.2	92.7	97.7	84.3	102.2	93.8	91.6	90.8	82.3	80.8
May	92.5	91.2	96.3	93.6	97.5	85.1	102.2	94.8	92.5	91.7	82.5	81.0
June	93.4	92.2	97.2	95.6	97.9	86.3	101.6	96.1	92.9	92.5	82.8	81.4
July	93.2	92.5	96.5	95.8	96.8	87.2	101.8	95.8	92.9	92.5	82.3	81.2
August	93.9	93.1	96.4	95.4	96.9	88.5	102.8	97.0	93.9	93.3	82.5	81.4
September	94.5	93.8	97.3	95.5	98.0	89.3	103.3	97.3	94.2	93.7	82.6	81.5
October	94.5	93.8	96.9	94.0	98.1	89.4	102.3	97.4	94.5	94.0	82.3	81.1
November	95.4	94.7	98.0	95.7	99.0	90.9	101.8	98.5	95.5	94.6	82.7	81.5
December	96.0	95.4	98.1	96.9	98.6	92.7	101.5	97.6	96.0	95.2	82.8	81.7
1997												
January	96.3	95.7	97.9	96.4	98.5	93.3	100.0	97.4	96.9	95.8	82.7	81.5
February	97.7	97.3	98.8	98.0	99.1	95.4	100.2	99.1	97.9	97.3	83.5	82.4
March	97.9	97.8	98.9	98.7	99.0	96.4	99.8	99.2	97.5	97.6	83.4	82.5
April	98.4	98.2	98.5	96.6	99.3	97.4	99.6	99.6	98.9	98.4	83.4	82.4
May	98.8	98.7	98.9	97.7	99.3	98.5	99.6	99.7	99.1	98.6	83.3	82.4
June	99.3	99.4	98.9	99.6	98.6	99.9	99.5	99.7	99.4	99.3	83.3	82.5
July	99.9	99.9	99.0	96.9	99.9	100.1	99.6	99.5	100.4	100.3	83.4	82.5
August	100.9	101.1	100.2	101.0	99.9	102.5	100.1	100.2	100.3	101.0	83.8	82.9
September	101.7	101.9	101.2	102.2	100.7	102.2	100.5	100.4	101.3	102.1	84.0	83.1
October	102.5	102.6	102.5	102.4	102.6	102.9	100.1	101.0	102.7	102.5	84.2	83.1
November	103.2	103.5	102.9	105.3	101.9	105.0	99.7	101.6	102.6	103.3	84.3	83.3
December	103.5	103.9	102.3	105.2	101.2	106.3	101.3	102.6	103.0	103.8	84.1	83.1
1998												
January	104.0	104.9	103.0	105.8	101.8	108.1	102.2	103.3	102.8	104.0	84.0	83.3
February	104.3	105.1	102.7	105.6	101.5	108.8	102.7	103.7	103.1	104.5	83.7	83.0
March	104.6	105.3	103.0	106.3	101.6	108.7	102.3	103.5	104.2	104.8	83.5	82.5
April	105.2	106.0	103.9	107.1	102.6	108.6	102.3	104.0	104.8	105.4	83.5	82.6
May	105.7	106.4	104.1	107.3	102.8	109.0	103.6	105.3	105.8	106.0	83.4	82.3
June	105.3	105.8	102.9	101.9	103.2	109.8	103.8	105.0	106.0	105.4	82.6	81.3
July	105.0	105.5	101.9	97.5	103.5	109.9	104.5	105.9	106.7	105.2	81.9	80.7
August	107.1	108.0	105.1	110.1	103.1	113.4	105.3	105.8	107.0	107.0	83.2	82.1
September	106.9	107.7	104.0	109.2	101.9	113.7	104.8	105.7	107.3	107.1	82.6	81.5
October	107.8	108.9	104.9	111.5	102.3	114.8	106.5	106.6	107.5	108.1	82.9	81.9
November	107.5	108.8	104.0	110.6	101.4	114.7	106.2	106.5	107.7	108.0	82.3	81.4
December	107.5	109.0	103.4	110.7	100.5	114.4	105.3	107.2	107.6	108.6	82.0	81.2
1999												
January	108.2	109.4	104.6	111.1	102.1	114.7	105.3	107.3	108.1	109.0	82.2	81.2
February	108.6	110.1	104.9	111.8	102.2	115.4	106.0	107.2	108.1	109.5	82.1	81.3
March	109.0	110.3	104.7	111.2	102.1	115.2	105.6	106.7	109.0	110.6	82.2	81.1
April	109.2	110.6	104.3	112.0	101.4	116.1	104.6	107.1	109.6	111.0	82.1	81.1
May	110.0	111.6	105.6	113.1	102.6	116.9	103.8	107.1	110.0	111.7	82.3	81.5
June	110.1	111.5	104.6	112.6	101.5	116.7	102.6	107.2	110.3	112.6	82.1	81.1
July	110.6	111.9	104.1	112.8	100.8	117.8	101.5	108.4	111.1	113.8	82.3	81.1
August	111.4	112.9	106.1	115.4	102.5	117.7	101.2	107.9	111.1	114.3	82.6	81.5
September	111.1	112.7	105.0	113.6	101.6	117.9	98.5	108.0	111.8	114.4	82.1	81.0
October	112.3	114.0	106.3	116.7	102.4	118.9	98.0	108.9	112.3	115.5	82.7	81.6
November	112.8	114.8	106.3	115.6	102.7	118.7	95.6	109.5	112.8	117.0	82.8	81.9
December	113.7	115.6	107.1	116.0	103.7	119.3	94.1	110.2	113.7	118.1	83.2	82.1

Table 20-1. Industrial Production and Capacity Utilization—*Continued*

(Seasonally adjusted.)

Year and month	Total industry	Manufac- turing (SIC)	Consumer goods Total	Consumer goods Durable	Consumer goods Nondurable	Business equipment	Defense and space equipment	Construction supplies	Business supplies	Materials	Capacity utilization Total industry	Capacity utilization Manufac- turing (SIC)
2000												
January	113.6	115.6	105.5	118.4	100.6	121.1	93.8	110.6	113.9	118.4	82.8	81.7
February	114.3	116.2	106.8	118.5	102.5	121.5	91.4	110.6	114.4	118.9	83.0	81.8
March	114.8	117.0	106.6	118.1	102.3	123.2	90.9	111.4	115.3	119.5	83.0	82.0
April	115.6	117.8	107.6	119.5	103.2	125.0	89.2	111.3	116.6	120.0	83.3	82.2
May	116.3	118.2	108.2	119.9	103.9	126.4	89.0	110.3	117.3	120.8	83.5	82.2
June	116.4	118.4	108.6	119.9	104.4	126.3	90.1	110.2	116.9	120.8	83.3	82.0
July	115.8	118.1	107.5	116.8	103.9	127.2	91.9	110.8	116.3	120.1	82.7	81.4
August	115.7	117.6	107.8	118.0	103.9	126.2	90.0	109.8	116.3	120.0	82.3	80.8
September	116.2	118.1	108.7	119.1	104.7	127.5	86.4	110.3	116.0	120.3	82.4	80.8
October	115.7	117.6	107.3	116.4	103.8	127.4	91.0	110.0	116.0	120.1	81.8	80.2
November	115.6	117.1	107.5	113.4	105.1	127.0	93.7	109.5	116.3	119.7	81.5	79.6
December	115.3	116.5	108.0	111.8	106.2	126.8	94.1	108.6	116.2	118.7	81.0	79.0
2001												
January	114.2	115.4	106.6	109.2	105.3	126.0	97.8	108.4	115.6	117.4	80.1	78.0
February	113.6	114.8	106.4	109.3	105.0	124.3	97.4	107.6	114.1	116.9	79.5	77.4
March	113.2	114.3	106.1	111.3	103.9	123.4	100.3	107.2	113.3	116.4	79.0	76.9
April	112.8	114.1	106.5	110.7	104.6	122.0	102.0	106.6	112.0	115.9	78.6	76.6
May	112.3	113.5	106.6	111.3	104.5	119.8	102.1	106.3	111.6	115.2	78.1	76.1
June	111.6	112.7	106.3	110.5	104.4	118.1	103.8	105.9	111.2	114.2	77.5	75.4
July	111.1	112.4	106.0	111.8	103.6	117.1	105.1	105.3	110.8	113.7	77.0	75.1
August	110.9	111.8	105.9	110.0	104.0	114.7	104.6	104.2	111.0	114.0	76.7	74.6
September	110.2	111.2	105.4	109.4	103.6	112.8	105.4	103.7	110.0	113.4	76.1	74.1
October	109.9	110.8	105.5	108.3	104.0	111.5	105.0	102.1	110.2	113.3	75.8	73.8
November	109.4	110.5	104.9	110.5	102.6	110.8	104.1	102.2	109.5	112.7	75.3	73.5
December	109.1	110.4	105.4	112.8	102.5	110.1	104.1	102.4	109.4	112.0	75.1	73.4
2002												
January	109.7	111.0	106.3	112.7	103.6	110.0	103.7	101.9	109.2	113.0	75.4	73.7
February	109.9	111.0	106.3	113.7	103.4	109.8	103.3	102.7	109.3	113.4	75.4	73.7
March	110.3	111.4	106.8	113.9	104.0	109.5	103.9	103.9	109.8	113.9	75.6	73.8
April	110.8	111.6	107.0	114.4	104.1	109.4	104.3	103.5	110.7	114.8	75.8	73.9
May	111.0	111.9	106.5	114.9	103.2	109.7	104.5	103.9	111.3	115.3	75.8	74.1
June	111.7	112.6	107.6	116.1	104.4	110.1	105.3	104.0	111.1	116.0	76.2	74.4
July	111.5	112.4	107.5	116.8	103.9	109.0	105.0	102.6	111.6	116.2	76.0	74.3
August	111.5	112.6	107.1	116.8	103.5	109.7	106.1	103.3	111.2	116.1	75.9	74.3
September	111.3	112.5	107.3	117.0	103.6	109.3	107.2	103.4	111.1	115.7	75.7	74.2
October	111.0	111.9	106.7	115.9	103.2	108.8	107.9	103.2	111.7	115.3	75.4	73.7
November	111.2	111.9	106.6	118.8	102.1	109.6	107.1	102.8	111.0	115.9	75.4	73.6
December	110.6	111.3	105.6	116.8	101.5	109.2	109.7	102.1	110.9	115.3	74.9	73.1

Table 20-2. Summary Consumer and Producer Price Indexes

(Seasonally adjusted.)

| Year and month | Consumer Price Index, all urban consumers, 1982–1984 = 100 | | | | | | Producer Price Index, 1982 = 100 | | | | | |
| | All items | All items less food and energy | Food | Energy | Transportation | Medical care | Finished goods | | Intermediate materials, supplies, and components | | Crude materials for further processing | |
							Total	Less food and energy	Total	Less food and energy	Total	Crude nonfood less energy
1947												
January	21.5	...	22.8	...	17.9	13.2	...	...	...	...	...	...
February	21.6	...	23.1	...	17.9	13.3	...	...	...	...	...	...
March	22.0	...	23.8	...	18.1	13.3	...	...	...	...	...	...
April	22.0	...	23.5	...	18.3	13.4	26.0	...	23.1	...	30.7	...
May	22.0	...	23.4	...	18.3	13.5	26.1	...	23.0	...	30.4	...
June	22.1	...	23.5	...	18.4	13.5	26.2	...	23.2	...	30.6	...
July	22.2	...	23.8	...	18.5	13.5	26.2	...	23.2	...	31.0	...
August	22.4	...	24.1	...	18.5	13.6	26.3	...	23.3	...	31.6	...
September	22.8	...	24.8	...	18.7	13.7	26.7	...	23.7	...	32.4	...
October	22.9	...	24.9	...	18.8	13.8	26.8	...	24.0	...	33.7	...
November	23.1	...	25.2	...	19.0	13.8	27.1	...	24.3	...	33.9	...
December	23.4	...	25.7	...	19.1	13.9	27.7	...	24.5	...	35.3	...
1948												
January	23.7	...	26.1	...	19.6	14.0	28.1	...	25.0	...	36.2	...
February	23.7	...	25.9	...	19.5	14.0	27.9	...	24.7	...	34.4	...
March	23.5	...	25.3	...	19.6	14.1	28.0	...	24.8	...	33.5	...
April	23.8	...	26.0	...	19.9	14.3	28.1	...	25.1	...	34.2	...
May	24.0	...	26.3	...	19.9	14.3	28.4	...	25.1	...	35.3	...
June	24.2	...	26.5	...	20.0	14.4	28.6	...	25.4	...	36.2	...
July	24.4	...	26.7	...	21.0	14.5	28.8	...	25.4	...	36.1	...
August	24.4	...	26.5	...	21.3	14.6	28.9	...	25.5	...	35.5	...
September	24.4	...	26.3	...	21.4	14.5	28.8	...	25.5	...	34.9	...
October	24.3	...	26.1	...	21.5	14.6	28.7	...	25.5	...	33.8	...
November	24.2	...	25.7	...	21.6	14.7	28.5	...	25.4	...	33.5	...
December	24.1	...	25.5	...	21.6	14.7	28.5	...	25.2	...	33.0	...
1949												
January	24.0	...	25.4	...	21.6	14.7	28.3	...	25.2	...	32.0	...
February	23.9	...	25.3	...	21.8	14.8	28.0	...	24.8	...	30.9	...
March	23.9	...	25.3	...	21.9	14.8	28.0	...	24.7	...	30.8	...
April	23.9	...	25.3	...	22.0	14.8	27.9	...	24.5	...	30.2	...
May	23.9	...	25.2	...	22.2	14.8	27.8	...	24.3	...	30.1	...
June	23.9	...	25.3	...	22.1	14.8	27.7	...	24.1	...	29.7	...
July	23.7	...	24.8	...	22.2	14.8	27.5	...	24.1	...	29.2	...
August	23.7	...	24.8	...	22.3	14.9	27.4	...	23.9	...	29.2	...
September	23.8	...	25.0	...	22.2	14.9	27.4	...	23.9	...	29.5	...
October	23.7	...	24.8	...	22.3	14.9	27.3	...	23.8	...	29.5	...
November	23.7	...	24.8	...	22.3	14.9	27.2	...	23.7	...	29.6	...
December	23.6	...	24.5	...	22.5	14.9	27.2	...	23.8	...	29.6	...
1950												
January	23.5	...	24.3	...	22.4	14.9	27.2	...	23.8	...	29.6	...
February	23.6	...	24.7	...	22.4	15.0	27.2	...	23.9	...	30.5	...
March	23.6	...	24.6	...	22.4	14.9	27.3	...	24.1	...	30.3	...
April	23.7	...	24.6	...	22.4	15.0	27.3	...	24.2	...	30.5	...
May	23.8	...	24.8	...	22.5	15.0	27.5	...	24.6	...	31.6	...
June	23.9	...	25.1	...	22.5	15.0	27.6	...	24.7	...	32.1	...
July	24.1	...	25.6	...	22.7	15.1	28.0	...	25.3	...	33.3	...
August	24.2	...	25.8	...	22.9	15.1	28.6	...	25.6	...	34.0	...
September	24.3	...	25.8	...	22.9	15.2	28.9	...	26.2	...	34.5	...
October	24.5	...	26.0	...	22.9	15.3	29.0	...	26.7	...	34.5	...
November	24.6	...	26.1	...	23.0	15.3	29.4	...	26.9	...	35.4	...
December	25.0	...	26.9	...	23.2	15.4	30.0	...	27.8	...	36.7	...
1951												
January	25.4	...	27.6	...	23.3	15.4	30.5	...	28.5	...	38.2	...
February	25.8	...	28.5	...	23.6	15.5	30.8	...	28.7	...	39.6	...
March	25.9	...	28.4	...	23.8	15.7	30.9	...	28.8	...	39.1	...
April	25.9	...	28.2	...	23.9	15.7	30.9	...	28.8	...	39.1	...
May	26.0	...	28.3	...	24.0	15.8	31.1	...	28.8	...	38.4	...
June	25.9	...	28.0	...	24.1	15.8	31.0	...	28.7	...	38.1	...
July	25.9	...	27.9	...	24.1	15.8	30.8	...	28.4	...	36.8	...
August	25.9	...	27.8	...	24.2	15.9	30.7	...	28.0	...	36.2	...
September	26.0	...	27.9	...	24.4	15.9	30.6	...	28.0	...	35.9	...
October	26.2	...	28.4	...	24.5	16.0	30.8	...	27.9	...	36.7	...
November	26.3	...	28.6	...	24.8	16.1	30.9	...	27.9	...	36.4	...
December	26.5	...	28.9	...	24.9	16.3	30.9	...	27.8	...	36.6	...
1952												
January	26.5	...	28.9	...	25.0	16.3	30.8	...	27.8	...	35.8	...
February	26.4	...	28.6	...	25.2	16.4	30.7	...	27.7	...	35.5	...
March	26.4	...	28.5	...	25.3	16.5	30.9	...	27.6	...	35.0	...
April	26.5	...	28.7	...	25.5	16.5	30.7	...	27.5	...	34.9	...
May	26.5	...	28.7	...	25.6	16.5	30.7	...	27.5	...	34.8	...
June	26.5	...	28.6	...	25.8	16.8	30.7	...	27.6	...	34.6	...
July	26.7	...	28.9	...	26.0	16.9	30.8	...	27.5	...	34.6	...
August	26.7	...	28.9	...	25.9	16.9	30.7	...	27.6	...	34.7	...
September	26.6	...	28.7	...	26.0	16.9	30.6	...	27.6	...	33.8	...
October	26.7	...	28.8	...	26.1	16.9	30.5	...	27.5	...	33.8	...
November	26.7	...	28.8	...	26.2	16.9	30.4	...	27.4	...	33.7	...
December	26.7	...	28.6	...	26.2	17.0	30.2	...	27.3	...	32.9	...

... = Not available.

Table 20-2. Summary Consumer and Producer Price Indexes—*Continued*

(Seasonally adjusted.)

Year and month	Consumer Price Index, all urban consumers, 1982–1984 = 100						Producer Price Index, 1982 = 100					
							Finished goods		Intermediate materials, supplies, and components		Crude materials for further processing	
	All items	All items less food and energy	Food	Energy	Transportation	Medical care	Total	Less food and energy	Total	Less food and energy	Total	Crude nonfood less energy
1953												
January	26.6	...	28.4	...	26.3	17.0	30.3	...	27.4	...	32.5	...
February	26.6	...	28.3	...	26.2	17.0	30.2	...	27.4	...	32.4	...
March	26.6	...	28.3	...	26.3	17.0	30.3	...	27.5	...	32.4	...
April	26.7	...	28.1	...	26.4	17.1	30.2	...	27.5	...	31.6	...
May	26.7	...	28.2	...	26.4	17.2	30.3	...	27.6	...	31.8	...
June	26.8	...	28.4	...	26.5	17.3	30.4	...	27.7	...	31.4	...
July	26.8	...	28.2	...	26.6	17.3	30.5	...	28.0	...	32.3	...
August	26.9	...	28.3	...	26.7	17.4	30.4	...	27.9	...	31.8	...
September	26.9	...	28.4	...	26.7	17.5	30.4	...	27.9	...	32.0	...
October	27.0	...	28.4	...	26.6	17.5	30.4	...	27.9	...	31.4	...
November	26.9	...	28.1	...	26.3	17.6	30.3	...	27.8	...	31.2	...
December	26.9	...	28.3	...	26.2	17.6	30.4	...	27.8	...	31.7	...
1954												
January	26.9	...	28.5	...	26.5	17.6	30.5	...	27.9	...	32.0	...
February	27.0	...	28.5	...	26.3	17.7	30.4	...	27.9	...	32.0	...
March	26.9	...	28.4	...	26.3	17.7	30.4	...	27.9	...	32.1	...
April	26.9	...	28.4	...	26.4	17.8	30.6	...	27.9	...	32.2	...
May	26.9	...	28.4	...	26.4	17.8	30.6	...	27.9	...	32.1	...
June	26.9	...	28.4	...	26.4	17.8	30.4	...	27.8	...	31.5	...
July	26.9	...	28.4	...	26.0	17.8	30.5	...	27.9	...	31.4	...
August	26.9	...	28.3	...	25.9	17.9	30.4	...	27.9	...	31.3	...
September	26.8	...	28.0	...	25.9	17.9	30.3	...	27.8	...	31.5	...
October	26.7	...	27.9	...	25.4	17.9	30.2	...	27.8	...	31.2	...
November	26.8	...	27.9	...	25.8	18.0	30.3	...	27.9	...	31.4	...
December	26.8	...	27.8	...	25.8	18.0	30.3	...	27.9	...	30.8	...
1955												
January	26.8	...	27.8	...	25.9	18.0	30.4	...	27.9	...	31.1	...
February	26.8	...	28.0	...	25.9	18.1	30.5	...	28.0	...	31.0	...
March	26.8	...	28.0	...	25.9	18.1	30.3	...	28.0	...	30.7	...
April	26.8	...	28.0	...	25.6	18.1	30.4	...	28.1	...	31.0	...
May	26.8	...	27.9	...	25.7	18.2	30.4	...	28.1	...	30.2	...
June	26.7	...	27.7	...	25.8	18.2	30.5	...	28.2	...	30.7	...
July	26.8	...	27.7	...	25.7	18.2	30.4	...	28.4	...	30.4	...
August	26.7	...	27.6	...	25.6	18.3	30.4	...	28.5	...	30.1	...
September	26.9	...	27.8	...	25.7	18.3	30.5	...	28.8	...	30.4	...
October	26.8	...	27.7	...	25.8	18.4	30.6	...	28.9	...	30.4	...
November	26.9	...	27.6	...	26.0	18.5	30.6	...	28.9	...	29.4	...
December	26.9	...	27.6	...	25.8	18.6	30.7	...	29.0	...	29.5	...
1956												
January	26.8	...	27.5	...	25.8	18.6	30.7	...	29.1	...	29.4	...
February	26.9	...	27.5	...	25.8	18.7	30.8	...	29.2	...	29.9	...
March	26.9	...	27.5	...	25.8	18.7	30.9	...	29.4	...	29.8	...
April	26.9	...	27.6	...	25.8	18.8	31.0	...	29.5	...	30.3	...
May	27.0	...	27.8	...	26.0	18.8	31.2	...	29.6	...	30.7	...
June	27.2	...	28.1	...	26.0	18.8	31.4	...	29.6	...	30.5	...
July	27.3	...	28.4	...	26.2	18.9	31.3	...	29.4	...	30.5	...
August	27.3	...	28.2	...	26.3	19.0	31.4	...	29.7	...	31.0	...
September	27.4	...	28.2	...	26.4	19.1	31.6	...	29.8	...	31.0	...
October	27.5	...	28.3	...	27.0	19.1	31.8	...	30.0	...	31.0	...
November	27.5	...	28.4	...	26.9	19.1	31.9	...	30.0	...	31.1	...
December	27.6	...	28.5	...	27.0	19.2	31.9	...	30.1	...	31.7	...
1957												
January	27.7	28.5	28.4	21.3	27.2	19.3	32.1	...	30.3	...	31.3	...
February	27.8	28.6	28.7	21.4	27.4	19.3	32.2	...	30.3	...	31.0	...
March	27.9	28.7	28.6	21.5	27.5	19.4	32.1	...	30.3	...	30.9	...
April	27.9	28.8	28.6	21.6	27.7	19.5	32.3	...	30.2	...	30.8	...
May	28.0	28.8	28.7	21.6	27.6	19.6	32.3	...	30.2	...	30.7	...
June	28.1	28.9	28.9	21.6	27.7	19.7	32.5	...	30.3	...	31.5	...
July	28.2	29.0	29.1	21.5	27.8	19.7	32.6	...	30.3	...	32.0	...
August	28.3	29.0	29.4	21.4	27.8	19.8	32.6	...	30.4	...	32.0	...
September	28.3	29.1	29.2	21.4	27.9	19.8	32.6	...	30.4	...	31.2	...
October	28.3	29.2	29.2	21.4	27.5	19.9	32.7	...	30.3	...	31.0	...
November	28.4	29.3	29.2	21.5	28.3	20.0	32.9	...	30.4	...	31.1	...
December	28.5	29.3	29.2	21.5	28.1	20.1	33.0	...	30.4	...	31.5	...
1958												
January	28.6	29.3	29.8	21.6	28.1	20.2	33.2	...	30.4	...	31.4	...
February	28.7	29.4	29.9	21.3	28.2	20.2	33.2	...	30.3	...	31.9	...
March	28.9	29.5	30.5	21.4	28.3	20.3	33.4	...	30.3	...	32.3	...
April	28.9	29.5	30.6	21.4	28.3	20.4	33.2	...	30.2	...	31.8	...
May	28.9	29.5	30.5	21.5	28.4	20.5	33.2	...	30.3	...	32.4	...
June	28.9	29.6	30.3	21.5	28.4	20.6	33.3	...	30.3	...	32.0	...
July	28.9	29.6	30.2	21.6	28.7	20.7	33.2	...	30.3	...	32.1	...
August	28.9	29.6	30.1	21.7	28.8	20.7	33.2	...	30.4	...	31.9	...
September	28.9	29.7	30.0	21.7	28.9	20.9	33.2	...	30.4	...	31.6	...
October	28.9	29.7	30.0	21.7	28.9	21.0	33.2	...	30.4	...	31.9	...
November	29.0	29.8	30.0	21.4	29.1	21.0	33.2	...	30.5	...	32.1	...
December	29.0	29.9	29.9	21.4	29.2	21.1	33.1	...	30.6	...	31.6	...

. . . = Not available.

Table 20-2. Summary Consumer and Producer Price Indexes—*Continued*

(Seasonally adjusted.)

| Year and month | Consumer Price Index, all urban consumers, 1982–1984 = 100 | | | | | | Producer Price Index, 1982 = 100 | | | | | |
| | | | | | | | Finished goods | | Intermediate materials, supplies, and components | | Crude materials for further processing | |
	All items	All items less food and energy	Food	Energy	Transportation	Medical care	Total	Less food and energy	Total	Less food and energy	Total	Crude nonfood less energy
1959												
January	29.0	29.9	30.0	21.4	29.3	21.1	33.1	...	30.6	...	31.6	...
February	29.0	29.9	29.8	21.6	29.4	21.2	33.2	...	30.7	...	31.4	...
March	29.0	30.0	29.7	21.7	29.6	21.3	33.2	...	30.7	...	31.5	...
April	29.0	30.0	29.5	21.8	29.7	21.3	33.2	...	30.7	...	31.7	...
May	29.0	30.1	29.5	21.8	29.7	21.4	33.3	...	30.9	...	31.5	...
June	29.1	30.2	29.7	21.9	29.8	21.5	33.2	...	30.9	...	31.3	...
July	29.2	30.2	29.6	21.8	29.9	21.5	33.1	...	30.8	...	31.0	...
August	29.2	30.2	29.6	21.9	29.9	21.6	33.0	...	30.8	...	30.7	...
September	29.3	30.3	29.7	21.9	30.0	21.7	33.4	...	30.8	...	30.9	...
October	29.4	30.4	29.7	22.2	30.1	21.7	33.1	...	30.8	...	30.7	...
November	29.4	30.4	29.7	22.2	30.1	21.8	33.0	...	30.9	...	30.5	...
December	29.4	30.5	29.6	22.3	30.1	21.8	33.0	...	30.9	...	30.3	...
1960												
January	29.4	30.5	29.6	22.3	30.0	21.9	33.1	...	30.8	...	30.4	...
February	29.4	30.6	29.5	22.2	30.0	22.0	33.1	...	30.9	...	30.4	...
March	29.4	30.6	29.6	22.3	29.9	22.1	33.4	...	30.9	...	30.7	...
April	29.5	30.6	30.0	22.4	29.9	22.2	33.4	...	30.8	...	30.8	...
May	29.6	30.6	30.0	22.3	29.8	22.2	33.4	...	30.8	...	30.8	...
June	29.6	30.7	30.0	22.4	29.8	22.2	33.4	...	30.9	...	30.4	...
July	29.6	30.6	29.9	22.5	29.8	22.3	33.5	...	30.8	...	30.4	...
August	29.0	30.6	30.0	22.5	29.8	22.3	33.4	...	30.8	...	29.8	...
September	29.6	30.6	30.1	22.6	29.6	22.4	33.4	...	30.8	...	30.0	...
October	29.8	30.8	30.3	22.5	29.6	22.4	33.7	...	30.8	...	30.2	...
November	29.8	30.8	30.5	22.7	29.6	22.5	33.7	...	30.7	...	30.2	...
December	29.8	30.7	30.5	22.6	29.7	22.6	33.6	...	30.7	...	30.3	...
1961												
January	29.8	30.8	30.5	22.7	29.7	22.6	33.6	...	30.6	...	30.4	...
February	29.8	30.8	30.5	22.6	29.8	22.7	33.7	...	30.7	...	30.5	...
March	29.8	30.9	30.5	22.6	29.8	22.7	33.6	...	30.8	...	30.3	...
April	29.8	30.9	30.4	22.2	29.8	22.8	33.4	...	30.7	...	30.2	...
May	29.8	30.9	30.3	22.4	30.0	22.8	33.3	...	30.6	...	29.9	...
June	29.8	31.0	30.2	22.5	30.1	22.9	33.3	...	30.5	...	29.5	...
July	29.9	31.0	30.3	22.5	30.3	22.9	33.3	...	30.5	...	29.7	...
August	29.9	31.1	30.3	22.5	30.4	23.0	33.4	...	30.5	...	30.5	...
September	30.0	31.1	30.3	22.6	30.5	23.1	33.3	...	30.5	...	30.3	...
October	30.0	31.1	30.3	22.4	30.5	23.1	33.3	...	30.4	...	30.3	...
November	30.0	31.2	30.3	22.5	30.4	23.1	33.4	...	30.5	...	30.2	...
December	30.0	31.2	30.3	22.4	30.3	23.2	33.4	...	30.6	...	30.6	...
1962												
January	30.0	31.2	30.4	22.4	30.4	23.2	33.5	...	30.5	...	30.6	...
February	30.1	31.2	30.5	22.6	30.5	23.3	33.6	...	30.6	...	30.5	...
March	30.2	31.3	30.6	22.4	30.5	23.4	33.5	...	30.6	...	30.5	...
April	30.2	31.3	30.7	22.7	30.9	23.4	33.5	...	30.6	...	30.1	...
May	30.2	31.4	30.6	22.7	30.9	23.5	33.4	...	30.6	...	30.1	...
June	30.2	31.4	30.5	22.5	30.9	23.5	33.4	...	30.6	...	29.9	...
July	30.2	31.4	30.4	22.3	30.6	23.6	33.4	...	30.6	...	30.2	...
August	30.3	31.5	30.6	22.4	30.8	23.6	33.5	...	30.6	...	30.5	...
September	30.4	31.5	30.9	22.8	31.0	23.6	33.8	...	30.6	...	31.2	...
October	30.4	31.5	30.8	22.7	30.9	23.7	33.6	...	30.5	...	30.8	...
November	30.4	31.5	30.9	22.7	30.9	23.7	33.6	...	30.5	...	31.0	...
December	30.4	31.6	30.7	22.8	30.9	23.8	33.5	...	30.5	...	30.6	...
1963												
January	30.4	31.5	31.0	22.8	30.6	23.9	33.4	...	30.5	...	30.3	...
February	30.5	31.6	31.1	22.7	30.7	23.9	33.4	...	30.5	...	30.0	...
March	30.5	31.7	31.0	22.7	30.8	23.9	33.3	...	30.5	...	29.6	...
April	30.5	31.7	30.9	22.6	30.8	23.9	33.3	...	30.5	...	29.8	...
May	30.5	31.7	30.9	22.6	30.9	24.0	33.4	...	30.7	...	29.6	...
June	30.6	31.8	31.0	22.5	30.9	24.1	33.5	...	30.7	...	29.9	...
July	30.7	31.8	31.2	22.7	30.9	24.1	33.4	...	30.7	...	30.0	...
August	30.8	31.9	31.2	22.6	31.0	24.2	33.4	...	30.7	...	29.9	...
September	30.7	31.9	31.1	22.5	31.0	24.2	33.4	...	30.7	...	29.8	...
October	30.8	32.0	31.0	22.7	31.2	24.2	33.5	...	30.8	...	29.9	...
November	30.8	32.0	31.2	22.6	31.1	24.3	33.5	...	30.8	...	30.2	...
December	30.9	32.1	31.3	22.6	31.2	24.3	33.4	...	30.8	...	29.4	...
1964												
January	30.9	32.2	31.4	22.8	31.4	24.4	33.5	...	30.8	...	29.8	...
February	30.9	32.2	31.4	22.2	31.3	24.4	33.5	...	30.8	...	29.4	...
March	30.9	32.2	31.4	22.6	31.4	24.4	33.4	...	30.8	...	29.5	...
April	31.0	32.2	31.4	22.5	31.3	24.5	33.5	...	30.8	...	29.5	...
May	31.0	32.2	31.4	22.5	31.3	24.5	33.5	...	30.7	...	29.4	...
June	31.0	32.3	31.4	22.6	31.4	24.6	33.5	...	30.6	...	29.0	...
July	31.0	32.3	31.5	22.5	31.3	24.6	33.5	...	30.7	...	29.2	...
August	31.1	32.3	31.4	22.6	31.4	24.7	33.6	...	30.6	...	29.4	...
September	31.1	32.3	31.6	22.5	31.3	24.7	33.6	...	30.7	...	30.1	...
October	31.1	32.4	31.6	22.5	31.3	24.7	33.6	...	30.8	...	29.8	...
November	31.2	32.5	31.7	22.5	31.4	24.8	33.6	...	30.8	...	29.9	...
December	31.3	32.5	31.7	22.6	31.7	24.8	33.6	...	30.9	...	29.8	...

. . . = Not available.

Table 20-2. Summary Consumer and Producer Price Indexes—*Continued*

(Seasonally adjusted.)

Year and month	Consumer Price Index, all urban consumers, 1982–1984 = 100						Producer Price Index, 1982 = 100					
							Finished goods		Intermediate materials, supplies, and components		Crude materials for further processing	
	All items	All items less food and energy	Food	Energy	Transportation	Medical care	Total	Less food and energy	Total	Less food and energy	Total	Crude nonfood less energy
1965												
January	31.3	32.6	31.6	22.8	31.9	24.8	33.6	. . .	30.9	. . .	29.5	. . .
February	31.3	32.6	31.5	22.7	31.8	24.9	33.7	. . .	30.9	. . .	29.9	. . .
March	31.3	32.6	31.7	22.6	31.8	25.0	33.7	. . .	31.0	. . .	30.0	. . .
April	31.4	32.7	31.8	22.9	31.9	25.0	34.0	. . .	31.1	. . .	30.4	. . .
May	31.5	32.7	32.1	23.0	32.0	25.1	34.1	. . .	31.1	. . .	30.8	. . .
June	31.6	32.7	32.6	23.1	31.9	25.1	34.2	. . .	31.2	. . .	31.6	. . .
July	31.6	32.7	32.5	23.0	31.9	25.3	34.1	. . .	31.2	. . .	31.2	. . .
August	31.6	32.7	32.4	23.0	31.9	25.3	34.2	. . .	31.3	. . .	31.5	. . .
September	31.6	32.8	32.3	23.1	31.9	25.3	34.3	. . .	31.3	. . .	31.4	. . .
October	31.7	32.8	32.5	23.0	31.8	25.4	34.4	. . .	31.3	. . .	31.8	. . .
November	31.8	32.9	32.6	23.1	31.9	25.5	34.5	. . .	31.4	. . .	32.1	. . .
December	31.9	33.0	32.8	23.1	32.0	25.5	34.7	. . .	31.4	. . .	32.7	. . .
1966												
January	31.9	33.0	33.0	23.1	31.9	25.6	34.7	. . .	31.4	. . .	33.1	. . .
February	32.1	33.1	33.5	23.2	32.0	25.6	35.0	. . .	31.6	. . .	33.7	. . .
March	32.2	33.1	33.8	23.2	32.1	25.8	35.0	. . .	31.7	. . .	33.5	. . .
April	32.3	33.3	33.8	23.2	32.2	25.9	35.1	. . .	31.8	. . .	33.3	. . .
May	32.4	33.4	33.7	23.2	32.1	26.0	35.1	. . .	32.0	. . .	33.0	. . .
June	32.4	33.5	33.7	23.3	32.2	26.1	34.9	. . .	32.0	. . .	33.0	. . .
July	32.5	33.6	33.5	23.4	32.5	26.3	35.1	. . .	32.2	. . .	33.4	. . .
August	32.7	33.7	34.0	23.3	32.6	26.4	35.4	. . .	32.3	. . .	33.5	. . .
September	32.8	33.8	34.1	23.4	32.6	26.7	35.6	. . .	32.2	. . .	33.4	. . .
October	32.9	34.0	34.2	23.4	32.7	26.9	35.5	. . .	32.1	. . .	32.9	. . .
November	32.9	34.0	34.1	23.5	32.8	27.1	35.5	. . .	32.2	. . .	32.3	. . .
December	32.9	34.1	34.0	23.5	32.6	27.2	35.4	. . .	32.2	. . .	32.1	. . .
1967												
January	32.9	34.2	33.9	23.6	32.6	27.4	35.4	. . .	32.2	. . .	32.2	. . .
February	33.0	34.2	33.8	23.7	32.8	27.5	35.3	. . .	32.1	. . .	31.5	. . .
March	33.0	34.3	33.8	23.6	32.8	27.6	35.3	. . .	32.1	. . .	31.1	. . .
April	33.1	34.4	33.7	23.9	33.0	27.8	35.3	. . .	32.1	. . .	30.7	. . .
May	33.1	34.5	33.7	23.9	33.1	27.9	35.4	. . .	32.1	. . .	31.1	. . .
June	33.3	34.6	34.0	23.8	33.1	28.1	35.7	. . .	32.2	. . .	31.4	. . .
July	33.4	34.7	34.1	23.8	33.3	28.2	35.7	. . .	32.2	. . .	31.3	. . .
August	33.5	34.9	34.3	23.9	33.4	28.3	35.8	. . .	32.2	. . .	31.3	. . .
September	33.6	35.0	34.3	24.0	33.7	28.5	35.8	. . .	32.3	. . .	31.2	. . .
October	33.7	35.1	34.4	23.9	33.6	28.7	35.9	. . .	32.3	. . .	31.3	. . .
November	33.9	35.2	34.5	24.0	33.9	28.8	35.9	. . .	32.4	. . .	31.1	. . .
December	34.0	35.4	34.6	23.9	33.9	29.0	36.0	. . .	32.6	. . .	31.5	. . .
1968												
January	34.1	35.5	34.6	24.0	34.1	29.1	36.1	. . .	32.6	. . .	31.4	. . .
February	34.2	35.7	34.8	24.1	34.2	29.2	36.2	. . .	32.7	. . .	31.5	. . .
March	34.3	35.8	34.9	24.1	34.2	29.4	36.3	. . .	32.8	. . .	31.6	. . .
April	34.4	35.9	35.0	24.0	34.1	29.5	36.5	. . .	32.8	. . .	31.7	. . .
May	34.5	36.0	35.1	24.1	34.1	29.6	36.5	. . .	32.8	. . .	31.5	. . .
June	34.7	36.2	35.2	24.2	34.3	29.7	36.6	. . .	32.9	. . .	31.3	. . .
July	34.9	36.4	35.3	24.2	34.3	29.9	36.7	. . .	33.0	. . .	31.6	. . .
August	35.0	36.5	35.4	24.3	34.4	30.0	36.8	. . .	33.0	. . .	31.7	. . .
September	35.1	36.7	35.6	24.3	34.4	30.2	37.0	. . .	33.1	. . .	31.9	. . .
October	35.3	36.9	35.9	24.3	34.5	30.4	37.0	. . .	33.2	. . .	32.1	. . .
November	35.4	37.1	35.9	24.4	34.7	30.6	37.1	. . .	33.2	. . .	32.8	. . .
December	35.6	37.2	36.0	24.3	34.5	30.8	37.1	. . .	33.4	. . .	32.4	. . .
1969												
January	35.7	37.3	36.1	24.4	34.7	30.9	37.2	. . .	33.6	. . .	32.6	. . .
February	35.8	37.6	36.1	24.4	35.2	31.2	37.2	. . .	33.7	. . .	32.3	. . .
March	36.1	37.8	36.2	24.7	35.8	31.4	37.4	. . .	33.9	. . .	32.7	. . .
April	36.3	38.1	36.4	24.9	35.8	31.6	37.6	. . .	33.8	. . .	33.1	. . .
May	36.4	38.1	36.6	24.8	35.5	31.8	37.8	. . .	33.9	. . .	34.0	. . .
June	36.6	38.3	37.0	25.0	35.6	31.9	38.0	. . .	34.0	. . .	34.5	. . .
July	36.8	38.5	37.3	24.9	35.6	32.1	38.1	. . .	34.0	. . .	34.1	. . .
August	36.9	38.7	37.5	24.9	35.7	32.2	38.2	. . .	34.2	. . .	34.4	. . .
September	37.1	38.9	37.7	25.0	35.6	32.5	38.3	. . .	34.2	. . .	34.4	. . .
October	37.3	39.1	37.8	25.0	35.9	32.3	38.5	. . .	34.4	. . .	34.8	. . .
November	37.5	39.2	38.2	25.0	36.0	32.5	38.8	. . .	34.6	. . .	35.2	. . .
December	37.7	39.4	38.6	25.1	36.2	32.6	38.9	. . .	34.7	. . .	35.1	. . .
1970												
January	37.9	39.6	38.7	25.1	36.6	32.8	39.1	. . .	35.0	. . .	35.1	. . .
February	38.1	39.8	38.9	25.1	36.7	33.0	39.0	. . .	35.0	. . .	35.2	. . .
March	38.3	40.1	38.9	25.0	36.6	33.2	39.1	. . .	34.9	. . .	35.6	. . .
April	38.5	40.4	39.0	25.5	37.1	33.5	39.1	. . .	35.1	. . .	35.5	. . .
May	38.6	40.5	39.2	25.4	37.2	33.7	39.1	. . .	35.2	. . .	35.0	. . .
June	38.8	40.8	39.2	25.3	37.4	33.9	39.2	. . .	35.3	. . .	35.0	. . .
July	38.9	40.9	39.2	25.5	37.6	34.1	39.2	. . .	35.5	. . .	35.1	. . .
August	39.0	41.1	39.2	25.4	37.5	34.3	39.2	. . .	35.5	. . .	34.7	. . .
September	39.2	41.3	39.4	25.6	37.7	34.5	39.6	. . .	35.6	. . .	35.5	. . .
October	39.4	41.5	39.5	25.9	38.1	34.6	39.6	. . .	35.8	. . .	35.5	. . .
November	39.6	41.8	39.5	26.0	38.5	34.8	39.8	. . .	35.9	. . .	35.1	. . .
December	39.8	42.0	39.5	26.2	38.9	35.1	39.8	. . .	35.9	. . .	34.5	. . .

. . . = Not available.

Table 20-2. Summary Consumer and Price Indexes—Continued

(All urban consumers; 1982–1984 = 100, seasonally adjusted.)

| Year and month | Consumer Price Index, all urban consumers, 1982–1984 = 100 | | | | | | Producer Price Index, 1982 = 100 | | | | | |
| | All items | All items less food and energy | Food | Energy | Transportation | Medical care | Finished goods | | Intermediate materials, supplies, and components | | Crude materials for further processing | |
							Total	Less food and energy	Total	Less food and energy	Total	Crude nonfood less energy
1971												
January	39.9	42.1	39.4	26.3	39.2	35.2	39.9	...	36.0	...	34.8	...
February	39.9	42.2	39.5	26.2	39.4	35.4	40.1	...	36.1	...	35.9	...
March	40.0	42.2	39.8	26.2	39.4	35.6	40.2	...	36.3	...	35.4	...
April	40.1	42.4	40.1	26.1	39.4	35.8	40.3	...	36.3	...	36.0	...
May	40.3	42.6	40.3	26.2	39.4	36.0	40.5	...	36.5	...	36.0	...
June	40.5	42.8	40.5	26.3	39.6	36.2	40.6	...	36.7	...	36.2	...
July	40.6	42.9	40.6	26.3	39.6	36.4	40.4	...	36.9	...	35.9	...
August	40.7	43.0	40.6	26.8	39.7	36.5	40.7	...	37.2	...	35.8	...
September	40.8	43.0	40.6	26.9	39.5	36.7	40.7	...	37.2	...	35.7	...
October	40.9	43.1	40.7	27.0	39.5	36.5	40.7	...	37.1	...	36.4	...
November	41.0	43.2	40.9	26.9	39.4	36.6	40.8	...	37.2	...	37.0	...
December	41.1	43.3	41.3	27.0	39.4	36.7	41.1	...	37.4	...	37.2	...
1972												
January	41.2	43.5	41.1	27.0	39.7	36.8	41.0	...	37.5	...	37.8	...
February	41.4	43.6	41.7	26.8	39.6	36.9	41.3	...	37.7	...	38.1	...
March	41.4	43.6	41.6	26.9	39.6	37.0	41.3	...	37.8	...	38.1	...
April	41.5	43.8	41.6	26.9	39.6	37.1	41.3	...	37.9	...	38.7	...
May	41.6	43.9	41.7	27.0	39.7	37.2	41.5	...	38.0	...	39.3	...
June	41.7	44.0	41.9	27.0	39.7	37.3	41.7	...	38.0	...	39.4	...
July	41.8	44.1	42.1	27.1	39.8	37.3	41.8	...	38.1	...	40.0	...
August	41.9	44.3	42.2	27.3	40.0	37.4	42.0	...	38.2	...	40.3	...
September	42.1	44.3	42.5	27.6	40.2	37.4	42.2	...	38.5	...	40.5	...
October	42.2	44.4	42.8	27.7	40.1	37.8	42.0	...	38.7	...	40.9	...
November	42.4	44.4	43.0	27.9	40.3	37.8	42.3	...	39.0	...	42.0	...
December	42.5	44.6	43.2	27.8	40.4	37.9	42.7	...	39.6	...	43.8	...
1973												
January	42.7	44.6	44.0	27.9	40.4	38.0	43.0	...	39.8	...	45.0	...
February	43.0	44.8	44.6	28.2	40.6	38.1	43.5	...	40.4	...	47.1	...
March	43.4	45.0	45.8	28.3	40.7	38.2	44.4	...	41.1	...	49.3	...
April	43.7	45.1	46.5	28.6	41.0	38.3	44.7	...	41.3	...	50.1	...
May	43.9	45.3	47.1	28.8	41.0	38.5	45.0	...	42.2	...	52.5	...
June	44.2	45.4	47.6	29.2	41.2	38.6	45.5	...	43.0	...	55.0	...
July	44.2	45.5	47.7	29.2	41.2	38.6	45.4	...	42.3	...	52.5	...
August	45.0	45.7	50.5	29.4	41.2	38.7	47.0	...	43.5	...	64.1	...
September	45.2	46.0	50.4	29.4	41.1	38.9	46.9	...	43.0	...	60.9	...
October	45.6	46.3	50.7	30.3	41.4	39.6	46.8	...	43.4	...	58.5	...
November	45.9	46.5	51.4	31.5	41.8	39.7	47.2	...	43.8	...	59.0	...
December	46.3	46.7	51.9	32.5	42.2	39.9	47.6	...	44.8	...	59.1	...
1974												
January	46.8	46.9	52.5	34.1	42.8	40.1	48.8	49.7	45.9	47.5	63.3	86.3
February	47.3	47.2	53.6	35.4	43.4	40.3	49.7	50.0	46.8	48.1	64.3	86.5
March	47.8	47.6	54.2	36.9	44.2	40.7	50.2	50.5	48.1	49.5	62.3	88.3
April	48.1	47.9	54.1	37.6	44.7	41.0	50.7	51.1	49.0	50.9	60.6	89.7
May	48.6	48.5	54.5	38.3	45.3	41.4	51.3	52.2	50.6	52.5	58.3	83.8
June	49.0	49.0	54.5	38.6	45.9	42.1	51.3	53.1	51.5	53.7	55.4	82.9
July	49.3	49.5	54.3	38.9	46.4	42.6	52.7	54.0	53.4	55.2	59.8	84.2
August	40.0	50.2	55.1	39.2	46.8	43.2	53.7	55.0	55.8	57.0	62.9	85.5
September	50.6	50.7	56.2	39.3	47.0	43.7	54.3	55.7	55.9	57.6	60.9	82.5
October	51.0	51.2	56.8	39.2	47.3	44.1	55.3	56.7	57.2	58.2	63.2	80.6
November	51.5	51.6	57.5	39.4	47.6	44.4	56.4	57.4	57.8	58.8	64.2	77.6
December	51.9	52.0	58.2	39.6	47.9	44.8	56.4	57.9	57.8	59.1	61.5	71.6
1975												
January	52.3	52.3	58.4	40.0	48.0	45.3	56.7	58.3	58.0	59.6	59.6	69.8
February	52.6	52.8	58.5	40.3	48.3	45.8	56.6	58.7	57.8	59.8	57.9	69.2
March	52.8	53.0	58.4	40.6	48.7	46.3	56.6	59.0	57.4	59.7	57.1	68.2
April	53.0	53.3	58.3	41.0	48.8	46.7	57.1	59.2	57.5	59.7	59.5	67.7
May	53.1	53.5	58.6	41.3	48.9	47.0	57.4	59.3	57.3	59.7	61.2	68.8
June	53.5	53.8	59.2	41.7	49.4	47.4	57.9	59.5	57.3	59.8	61.5	66.5
July	54.0	54.0	60.3	42.5	50.2	47.8	58.4	59.8	57.5	59.9	62.4	66.5
August	54.2	54.2	60.3	42.8	50.6	48.1	58.9	59.9	58.0	60.1	63.0	67.7
September	54.6	54.5	60.7	43.2	51.4	48.5	59.3	60.2	58.2	60.3	64.5	71.2
October	54.9	54.8	61.3	43.5	51.7	48.9	59.8	60.6	58.8	61.0	65.1	71.5
November	55.3	55.2	61.7	43.9	52.4	48.8	60.0	61.0	59.0	61.4	64.4	71.9
December	55.6	55.5	62.1	44.1	52.6	49.3	60.1	61.4	59.2	61.8	64.0	73.1
1976												
January	55.8	55.9	61.9	44.5	53.0	49.7	60.0	61.7	59.4	62.1	63.0	72.4
February	55.9	56.2	61.3	44.4	53.3	50.2	59.9	61.9	59.6	62.3	62.1	73.8
March	56.0	56.5	60.9	44.1	53.8	50.7	60.0	62.2	59.8	62.6	61.5	74.5
April	56.1	56.7	60.9	43.9	54.0	51.0	60.3	62.3	60.0	62.8	63.9	78.1
May	56.4	57.0	61.1	44.1	54.3	51.4	60.4	62.4	60.3	63.2	63.6	80.6
June	56.7	57.2	61.3	44.4	54.8	51.8	60.5	62.8	60.8	63.6	65.2	82.8
July	57.0	57.6	61.6	44.8	55.1	52.3	60.7	63.1	61.1	63.9	64.8	87.3
August	57.3	57.9	61.8	45.2	55.4	52.6	60.9	63.5	61.3	64.3	63.6	84.1
September	57.6	58.2	62.1	45.7	56.0	53.0	61.1	63.9	61.9	64.7	63.4	84.4
October	57.9	58.5	62.4	46.1	56.6	53.2	61.4	64.1	62.0	65.0	63.0	82.2
November	58.1	58.7	62.3	46.8	57.0	53.9	61.9	64.6	62.4	65.3	63.4	81.8
December	58.4	58.9	62.5	47.5	57.3	54.2	62.4	64.9	62.8	65.6	64.5	81.1

. . . = Not available.

Table 20-2. Summary Consumer and Price Indexes—Continued

(All urban consumers; 1982–1984 = 100, seasonally adjusted.)

| Year and month | Consumer Price Index, all urban consumers, 1982–1984 = 100 | | | | | | Producer Price Index, 1982 = 100 | | | | | |
| | | | | | | | Finished goods | | Intermediate materials, supplies, and components | | Crude materials for further processing | |
	All items	All items less food and energy	Food	Energy	Transportation	Medical care	Total	Less food and energy	Total	Less food and energy	Total	Crude nonfood less energy
1977												
January	58.7	59.3	62.7	48.1	57.8	54.6	62.5	65.1	63.0	65.8	64.3	78.7
February	59.3	59.7	63.9	48.1	58.2	54.9	63.2	65.4	63.3	65.9	65.7	79.7
March	59.6	60.0	64.2	48.4	58.7	55.5	63.7	65.7	63.9	66.4	66.6	81.5
April	60.0	60.3	65.0	48.6	59.0	56.0	64.0	65.9	64.4	66.7	68.3	82.1
May	60.2	60.6	65.3	48.9	59.1	56.5	64.4	66.1	64.9	67.1	67.6	82.5
June	60.5	61.0	65.7	48.9	59.1	57.0	64.6	66.5	64.9	67.4	65.5	79.7
July	60.8	61.2	65.9	49.1	59.0	57.3	64.8	66.8	65.1	67.9	64.7	78.8
August	61.1	61.5	66.2	49.5	58.9	57.7	65.2	67.3	65.4	68.2	63.9	79.2
September	61.3	61.8	66.4	49.8	59.1	58.2	65.5	67.8	65.7	68.7	63.7	79.2
October	61.6	62.0	66.6	50.5	59.3	58.4	65.9	68.2	65.8	68.8	64.0	78.5
November	62.0	62.3	67.1	51.3	59.5	58.6	66.4	68.8	66.3	69.1	65.4	78.4
December	62.3	62.7	67.4	51.6	59.8	59.0	66.7	69.0	66.6	69.4	66.4	80.1
1978												
January	62.7	63.1	67.9	51.1	60.1	59.3	67.0	69.2	66.9	69.8	67.3	80.3
February	63.0	63.4	68.6	50.6	60.2	59.9	67.5	69.5	67.4	70.3	68.4	80.6
March	63.4	63.8	69.5	51.0	60.3	60.2	67.8	69.9	67.8	70.6	69.8	80.3
April	63.9	64.3	70.6	51.4	60.4	60.7	68.6	70.6	68.1	71.1	72.1	82.2
May	64.5	64.7	71.6	51.7	60.7	61.1	69.1	71.1	68.7	71.6	72.8	84.6
June	65.0	65.2	72.7	51.9	61.1	61.5	69.7	71.7	69.2	72.2	74.6	87.4
July	65.5	65.6	73.0	52.1	61.6	61.9	70.3	72.3	69.4	72.5	74.2	89.6
August	65.9	66.1	73.3	52.6	62.0	62.4	70.4	72.8	69.9	73.2	73.7	90.4
September	66.5	66.7	73.6	53.2	62.6	62.8	71.1	73.5	70.5	73.7	75.1	92.3
October	67.1	67.2	74.2	54.1	63.3	63.3	71.4	73.4	71.3	74.5	77.0	94.7
November	67.5	67.6	74.7	54.9	63.9	63.8	72.0	74.1	71.9	75.2	77.4	96.3
December	67.9	68.0	75.1	55.6	64.5	64.1	72.8	74.7	72.4	75.6	78.0	96.8
1979												
January	68.5	68.5	76.4	55.8	64.6	64.8	73.7	75.3	73.1	76.3	80.1	96.4
February	69.2	69.2	77.7	55.9	65.2	65.2	74.4	75.9	73.7	77.0	82.1	99.6
March	69.9	69.8	78.4	57.4	66.4	65.7	75.0	76.4	74.6	77.8	83.8	104.2
April	70.6	70.3	79.0	59.5	67.8	66.1	75.8	77.0	75.7	78.9	84.4	105.1
May	71.4	70.8	79.7	62.0	69.1	66.6	76.2	77.4	76.6	79.6	84.7	106.7
June	72.2	71.3	80.0	64.7	70.5	67.1	76.6	78.0	77.5	80.1	85.6	111.6
July	73.0	71.9	80.5	67.3	71.7	67.7	77.4	78.5	78.7	81.1	86.5	109.4
August	73.7	72.7	80.4	69.7	72.7	68.2	78.2	78.8	79.8	81.8	85.5	106.4
September	74.4	73.3	80.9	71.9	73.5	68.7	79.5	79.7	81.1	82.7	87.9	106.5
October	75.2	74.0	81.5	73.5	74.0	69.2	80.4	80.4	82.4	83.9	88.8	108.9
November	76.0	74.8	82.0	74.8	74.7	69.8	81.4	81.0	83.2	84.5	90.0	111.3
December	76.9	75.7	82.8	76.8	75.8	70.6	82.2	81.7	84.0	85.2	91.2	111.3
1980												
January	78.0	76.7	83.3	79.1	78.0	71.4	83.4	83.3	86.0	87.2	90.9	112.6
February	79.0	77.5	83.4	81.9	79.8	72.3	84.6	84.2	87.6	88.2	92.6	115.3
March	80.1	78.6	84.1	84.5	81.8	73.0	85.5	84.7	88.2	88.6	90.8	111.7
April	80.9	79.5	84.7	85.4	82.2	73.6	86.2	85.5	88.5	88.8	88.3	109.9
May	81.7	80.1	85.2	86.4	82.8	74.2	86.6	85.7	89.0	89.1	89.5	107.2
June	82.5	81.0	85.7	86.5	82.7	74.7	87.3	86.6	89.8	89.8	90.1	106.1
July	82.6	80.8	86.6	86.7	83.1	75.2	88.7	87.7	90.5	90.3	94.6	109.6
August	83.2	81.3	88.0	87.2	83.7	75.6	89.7	88.4	91.5	91.1	99.0	112.4
September	83.9	82.1	89.1	87.5	84.6	76.3	90.1	88.8	91.9	91.4	100.4	116.2
October	84.7	83.0	89.8	88.0	85.3	76.9	90.8	89.6	92.8	92.1	102.2	118.2
November	85.6	83.9	90.8	88.8	86.1	77.3	91.4	90.1	93.5	92.6	103.5	119.8
December	86.4	84.9	91.3	90.7	86.8	77.8	91.8	90.4	94.4	93.7	102.7	119.3
1981												
January	87.2	85.4	91.6	92.1	88.5	78.6	92.8	91.4	95.6	94.7	103.4	113.3
February	88.0	85.9	92.1	95.2	90.7	79.2	93.6	92.0	96.1	94.9	104.2	106.2
March	88.6	86.4	92.6	97.4	91.8	79.9	94.7	92.6	97.1	95.6	103.8	108.9
April	89.1	87.0	92.8	97.6	91.7	80.7	95.7	93.5	98.3	96.6	104.2	111.9
May	89.7	87.8	92.8	97.9	92.2	81.4	96.0	94.0	98.7	97.1	103.8	113.7
June	90.5	88.6	93.2	97.3	92.7	82.3	96.5	94.6	99.0	97.7	104.9	115.5
July	91.5	89.8	93.9	97.3	93.5	83.4	96.7	94.8	99.2	98.4	105.0	116.4
August	92.2	90.7	94.4	97.8	93.9	84.3	96.8	95.3	99.7	98.9	104.0	115.5
September	93.1	91.8	94.8	98.6	94.6	85.1	97.2	95.9	99.7	99.3	102.7	112.6
October	93.4	92.1	95.0	99.2	95.5	85.9	97.6	96.5	99.8	99.5	101.2	110.8
November	93.8	92.5	95.1	100.5	96.2	86.8	97.9	97.0	99.9	99.7	99.7	107.5
December	94.1	93.0	95.3	101.5	96.4	87.5	98.3	97.6	100.0	99.8	98.8	106.0
1982												
January	94.4	93.3	95.6	100.6	96.7	88.2	98.9	98.1	100.4	99.9	99.7	101.2
February	94.7	93.8	96.3	98.0	96.2	88.8	98.8	98.1	100.3	100.0	100.0	100.7
March	94.7	93.9	96.2	96.6	95.8	89.6	98.8	98.7	99.9	99.9	99.7	100.0
April	95.0	94.7	96.4	94.2	94.5	90.5	99.0	99.0	99.7	99.8	100.2	101.1
May	95.9	95.4	97.2	95.7	95.1	91.3	99.0	99.4	99.7	100.1	101.9	102.2
June	97.0	96.1	98.1	98.4	97.2	92.2	99.8	99.9	99.8	100.0	101.8	101.0
July	97.5	96.7	98.2	99.3	98.1	93.0	100.2	100.1	100.0	99.8	100.7	101.4
August	97.7	97.1	98.0	99.8	98.2	93.9	100.6	100.6	99.9	99.7	99.8	100.0
September	97.7	97.2	98.2	100.3	98.0	94.7	100.7	100.8	100.0	100.2	99.2	98.9
October	98.1	97.5	98.2	101.7	98.2	95.5	101.0	101.3	99.9	100.2	98.7	97.7
November	98.0	97.3	98.2	102.5	98.2	96.5	101.4	101.6	100.1	100.2	99.2	96.3
December	97.7	97.2	98.2	102.8	97.7	97.2	101.8	102.2	100.1	100.3	98.8	95.9

Table 20-2. Summary Consumer and Price Indexes—Continued

(All urban consumers; 1982–1984 = 100, seasonally adjusted.)

Year and month	Consumer Price Index, all urban consumers, 1982–1984 = 100						Producer Price Index, 1982 = 100					
							Finished goods		Intermediate materials, supplies, and components		Crude materials for further processing	
	All items	All items less food and energy	Food	Energy	Transportation	Medical care	Total	Less food and energy	Total	Less food and energy	Total	Crude nonfood less energy
1983												
January	97.9	97.6	98.1	99.6	97.6	97.9	101.0	101.8	99.8	100.3	98.8	97.3
February	98.0	98.0	98.2	97.7	96.9	98.8	101.1	102.2	100.0	100.8	100.0	99.8
March	98.1	98.2	98.8	96.8	96.5	99.0	101.0	102.5	99.7	100.8	100.5	102.2
April	98.8	98.6	99.2	98.9	97.8	99.4	101.1	102.4	99.5	100.9	101.2	102.1
May	99.2	98.9	99.5	100.4	98.6	99.9	101.4	102.6	99.8	101.0	100.9	103.4
June	99.4	99.2	99.6	100.6	99.0	100.4	101.6	102.8	100.2	101.3	100.5	104.8
July	99.8	99.8	99.6	100.9	99.6	100.8	101.6	103.1	100.5	101.8	99.5	106.2
August	100.1	100.1	99.7	101.2	100.4	101.4	101.9	103.5	100.9	102.0	102.2	108.4
September	100.4	100.5	100.0	101.0	100.7	101.8	102.2	103.5	101.6	102.3	103.3	109.0
October	100.8	101.0	100.3	100.8	101.1	102.3	102.2	103.6	101.7	102.5	103.2	109.1
November	101.1	101.5	100.3	100.5	101.5	102.8	102.0	103.8	101.8	102.8	102.3	109.9
December	101.4	101.8	100.6	100.0	101.5	103.4	102.3	104.1	101.9	103.1	103.5	111.2
1984												
January	102.1	102.5	102.0	100.2	102.0	104.0	103.0	104.5	102.1	103.4	104.6	111.5
February	102.6	102.8	102.7	101.4	102.2	105.0	103.4	104.7	102.5	103.8	103.8	113.8
March	102.9	103.2	102.9	101.4	102.9	105.2	103.8	105.2	103.0	104.4	105.7	114.8
April	103.3	103.7	102.9	101.7	103.3	105.8	103.9	105.3	103.2	104.5	105.2	115.1
May	103.5	104.1	102.7	101.6	103.7	106.2	103.8	105.3	103.4	104.6	104.5	115.7
June	103.7	104.5	103.1	100.8	103.9	106.7	103.8	105.5	103.6	104.8	103.3	114.1
July	104.1	105.0	103.3	100.5	103.7	107.2	104.0	105.7	103.4	104.9	104.0	112.0
August	104.4	105.4	103.9	100.1	103.8	107.7	103.8	105.9	103.2	105.1	103.3	109.6
September	104.7	105.8	103.8	100.6	104.1	108.1	103.8	106.2	103.1	105.0	102.8	110.5
October	105.1	106.2	104.0	101.1	104.8	108.7	103.6	105.9	103.2	105.1	101.5	108.5
November	105.3	106.4	104.1	100.8	104.9	109.3	104.0	106.2	103.3	105.3	101.9	107.7
December	105.5	106.8	104.5	100.1	104.7	109.8	104.0	106.3	103.2	105.3	101.4	107.3
1985												
January	105.7	107.1	104.7	100.3	105.1	110.2	104.0	106.9	103.1	105.3	99.9	107.4
February	106.3	107.7	105.2	100.3	105.6	110.8	104.1	107.3	102.8	105.3	99.4	107.2
March	106.8	108.1	105.5	101.3	106.3	111.4	104.1	107.6	102.7	105.2	97.6	107.0
April	107.0	108.4	105.4	102.3	106.8	112.0	104.6	107.6	102.9	105.2	96.7	107.4
May	107.2	108.8	105.2	102.2	106.5	112.6	104.9	107.8	103.2	105.3	95.8	105.3
June	107.5	109.1	105.5	102.2	106.5	113.3	104.6	108.2	102.6	105.5	95.2	103.6
July	107.7	109.4	105.5	102.2	106.6	113.9	104.7	108.4	102.3	105.3	94.9	104.3
August	107.9	109.8	105.6	101.2	106.2	114.6	104.5	108.5	102.3	105.3	92.9	103.6
September	108.1	110.0	105.8	101.2	106.2	115.2	103.8	107.9	102.2	105.2	91.8	103.3
October	108.5	110.5	105.8	101.2	106.5	115.8	104.9	108.9	102.3	105.1	94.1	103.7
November	109.0	111.1	106.5	101.8	107.0	116.5	105.5	109.1	102.5	105.1	95.7	103.0
December	109.5	111.4	107.3	102.4	107.5	117.1	106.0	109.1	102.9	105.1	95.5	102.4
1986												
January	109.9	111.9	107.5	102.6	108.0	118.0	105.5	109.3	102.4	105.0	94.2	103.6
February	109.7	112.2	107.3	99.5	107.0	118.8	104.1	109.5	101.2	104.9	90.5	103.5
March	109.1	112.5	107.5	92.6	103.6	119.7	102.8	109.6	99.9	105.0	88.2	103.8
April	108.7	112.9	107.7	87.2	101.0	120.4	102.3	110.1	98.9	104.7	85.6	103.9
May	109.0	113.1	108.2	87.2	101.4	121.2	102.8	110.2	98.7	104.6	86.5	104.1
June	109.4	113.4	108.3	88.8	102.3	121.8	103.1	110.5	98.6	104.7	86.2	104.7
July	109.5	113.8	109.1	85.6	101.1	122.5	102.3	110.7	98.0	104.8	86.4	105.3
August	109.6	114.2	110.1	83.6	100.1	123.2	102.7	110.8	98.0	104.9	86.7	99.7
September	110.0	114.6	110.2	84.4	100.6	124.0	102.9	110.7	98.5	105.1	86.6	100.3
October	110.2	115.0	110.5	82.8	100.5	124.7	103.5	111.8	98.3	105.1	87.4	102.0
November	110.4	115.3	111.1	82.1	100.8	125.5	103.4	112.0	98.3	105.2	87.6	102.8
December	110.8	115.6	111.4	82.5	101.1	126.2	103.6	112.1	98.5	105.3	86.9	104.1
1987												
January	111.4	115.9	111.8	85.4	102.6	126.7	104.1	112.5	99.0	105.6	89.3	105.4
February	111.8	116.2	112.2	87.4	103.5	127.2	104.4	112.3	99.8	105.9	90.2	106.2
March	112.2	116.6	112.4	87.6	103.8	127.8	104.5	112.4	99.9	106.2	90.5	106.5
April	112.7	117.3	112.6	87.6	104.3	128.6	105.1	112.9	100.3	106.5	92.5	107.5
May	113.0	117.7	113.2	87.1	104.4	129.2	105.2	113.0	100.8	107.0	93.8	110.0
June	113.5	117.9	113.9	88.5	105.1	130.0	105.5	113.1	101.4	107.5	94.5	113.2
July	113.8	118.3	113.7	89.2	105.9	130.6	105.7	113.3	101.9	107.9	95.6	115.9
August	114.3	118.7	113.9	90.5	106.6	131.2	105.9	113.6	102.4	108.3	96.5	119.1
September	114.7	119.2	114.3	90.3	106.9	131.9	106.2	113.9	102.6	108.9	96.0	122.8
October	115.0	119.8	114.5	89.6	107.0	132.4	106.0	114.0	103.1	109.6	95.8	126.6
November	115.4	120.1	114.5	90.0	107.3	133.0	106.0	114.2	103.5	110.1	95.1	127.5
December	115.6	120.4	115.1	89.5	107.2	133.5	105.8	114.3	103.8	110.7	94.9	127.9
1988												
January	116.0	120.9	115.6	88.8	107.0	134.4	106.4	115.0	104.1	111.8	94.2	129.4
February	116.2	121.2	115.6	88.7	107.0	135.2	106.3	115.3	104.4	112.2	95.2	131.7
March	116.5	121.7	115.8	88.4	107.0	135.8	106.6	115.6	104.8	112.8	94.1	133.0
April	117.2	122.3	116.4	88.8	107.5	136.7	107.0	115.9	105.5	113.6	95.4	132.1
May	117.5	122.7	116.9	88.5	107.9	137.6	107.2	116.2	106.2	114.3	95.8	130.7
June	118.0	123.2	117.6	88.9	108.3	138.3	107.5	116.6	107.4	114.9	97.0	131.1
July	118.5	123.6	118.8	89.4	108.8	139.1	108.4	117.2	108.3	115.8	96.7	133.2
August	119.0	124.0	119.4	90.1	109.7	139.8	108.8	117.7	108.5	116.3	97.0	134.3
September	119.5	124.7	120.1	89.8	109.9	140.5	109.0	118.1	108.7	116.8	97.0	133.3
October	119.9	125.2	120.3	89.8	110.0	141.4	109.2	118.4	108.6	117.3	96.6	133.6
November	120.3	125.6	120.5	89.8	110.2	142.0	109.6	118.7	108.8	118.0	95.2	136.0
December	120.7	126.0	121.1	89.6	110.4	142.7	110.0	119.2	109.4	118.6	98.1	137.6

Table 20-2. Summary Consumer and Price Indexes—Continued

(All urban consumers; 1982–1984 = 100, seasonally adjusted.)

| Year and month | Consumer Price Index, all urban consumers, 1982–1984 = 100 | | | | | | Producer Price Index, 1982 = 100 | | | | | |
| | | | | | | | Finished goods | | Intermediate materials, supplies, and components | | Crude materials for further processing | |
	All items	All items less food and energy	Food	Energy	Transportation	Medical care	Total	Less food and energy	Total	Less food and energy	Total	Crude nonfood less energy
1989												
January	121.2	126.5	121.6	90.3	110.9	143.8	111.1	119.9	110.8	119.5	102.0	140.6
February	121.6	126.9	122.5	90.8	111.7	144.9	111.9	120.5	111.3	119.9	101.7	140.3
March	122.2	127.4	123.2	91.8	112.4	145.8	112.3	120.7	111.9	120.2	102.9	140.6
April	123.1	127.8	123.9	96.6	115.0	146.6	113.1	120.8	112.5	120.5	104.1	140.3
May	123.7	128.3	124.7	97.4	115.8	147.5	114.0	121.6	112.6	120.6	104.5	139.8
June	124.1	128.8	125.1	96.9	115.7	148.6	114.0	122.2	112.5	120.6	103.2	137.9
July	124.5	129.2	125.6	96.7	115.4	149.6	113.8	122.1	112.2	120.3	103.5	135.9
August	124.5	129.5	125.9	94.9	114.5	150.6	113.4	122.7	111.8	120.2	101.2	136.8
September	124.8	129.9	126.3	93.8	113.9	151.8	114.0	123.1	112.1	120.2	102.5	137.5
October	125.4	130.6	126.8	94.4	114.5	152.8	114.6	123.5	112.2	120.3	102.7	137.9
November	125.9	131.1	127.4	93.9	114.4	154.1	114.8	123.9	112.0	120.0	103.5	134.9
December	126.3	131.6	127.8	94.2	114.7	154.9	115.5	124.2	112.2	119.8	105.1	132.8
1990												
January	127.5	132.1	129.7	98.9	117.0	156.0	117.7	124.5	113.7	120.0	106.7	132.7
February	128.0	132.7	130.8	98.2	117.2	157.1	117.6	124.9	112.8	119.9	106.8	131.6
March	128.6	133.5	131.0	97.6	117.3	158.3	117.5	125.3	112.9	120.2	105.1	133.9
April	128.9	134.0	130.8	97.5	117.7	159.6	117.4	125.5	113.1	120.5	102.7	137.0
May	129.1	134.4	131.1	96.7	117.5	160.8	117.5	126.0	113.1	120.6	103.1	138.0
June	129.9	135.1	132.1	97.3	118.0	162.0	117.6	126.4	112.9	120.4	100.6	137.3
July	130.5	135.8	132.8	97.1	118.5	163.4	117.9	126.6	112.8	120.6	101.0	138.0
August	131.6	136.6	133.2	101.6	120.7	164.8	119.2	127.1	114.0	120.8	110.5	140.1
September	132.5	137.1	133.6	106.5	123.2	165.9	120.7	127.7	115.8	121.5	115.8	139.9
October	133.4	137.6	134.1	110.8	125.6	167.3	121.9	128.0	117.4	122.1	125.8	138.4
November	133.7	138.0	134.5	111.2	126.1	168.7	122.6	128.4	117.7	122.3	117.8	135.7
December	134.2	138.6	134.6	111.0	126.9	169.8	122.0	128.6	116.9	122.1	110.8	133.8
1991												
January	134.7	139.5	135.0	108.5	125.5	171.0	122.6	129.5	116.9	122.4	113.3	134.2
February	134.8	140.2	135.1	104.5	123.9	172.1	121.8	129.8	115.9	122.1	104.1	133.7
March	134.8	140.5	135.3	101.9	122.7	173.2	121.3	130.1	114.7	121.7	100.5	131.8
April	135.1	140.9	136.1	101.2	122.5	174.3	121.3	130.4	114.2	121.5	100.2	131.7
May	135.6	141.3	136.6	102.1	123.2	175.2	121.6	130.6	114.1	121.3	100.9	130.4
June	136.0	141.8	137.4	101.1	123.4	176.4	121.4	130.7	113.9	121.3	99.2	126.1
July	136.2	142.3	136.7	100.7	123.3	177.4	121.1	131.0	113.6	121.1	99.4	125.4
August	136.6	142.9	136.2	101.1	124.0	178.8	121.3	131.3	113.8	121.0	99.1	125.8
September	137.0	143.4	136.4	101.5	124.1	179.9	121.5	131.8	114.0	121.0	98.4	125.7
October	137.2	143.7	136.2	101.6	123.9	180.9	121.9	132.3	114.0	121.1	100.8	125.4
November	137.8	144.2	136.7	102.4	124.5	181.9	122.4	132.5	114.1	121.1	100.7	124.4
December	138.2	144.7	137.0	103.1	125.1	183.1	122.3	132.6	114.0	121.1	98.2	123.4
1992												
January	138.3	145.1	136.6	101.5	124.6	184.3	122.0	133.0	113.4	121.0	97.2	123.4
February	138.6	145.4	137.1	101.2	124.5	185.6	122.3	133.1	113.8	121.3	98.6	125.2
March	139.1	145.9	137.6	101.2	125.0	186.8	122.4	133.4	113.9	121.5	97.1	127.7
April	139.4	146.3	137.5	101.4	125.6	187.9	122.5	133.8	114.1	121.7	98.1	128.4
May	139.7	146.8	137.2	102.0	125.9	188.7	122.9	134.3	114.5	121.8	100.3	129.1
June	140.1	147.1	137.6	103.3	126.4	189.6	123.4	134.1	115.1	122.0	101.6	128.8
July	140.5	147.6	137.4	103.7	126.9	190.6	123.3	134.3	115.2	122.1	101.6	129.6
August	140.8	147.9	138.4	103.5	127.0	191.5	123.4	134.3	115.1	122.3	100.7	130.4
September	141.1	148.1	138.9	103.6	127.0	192.4	123.7	134.6	115.3	122.4	102.8	130.4
October	141.7	148.8	138.9	104.3	128.1	193.5	124.2	134.9	115.3	122.4	102.8	128.9
November	142.1	149.2	138.7	105.1	128.7	194.5	124.1	135.1	115.1	122.4	102.5	128.2
December	142.3	149.6	138.8	105.3	128.9	195.3	124.2	135.2	115.1	122.5	101.3	130.5
1993												
January	142.8	150.1	139.1	105.0	129.2	196.4	124.4	135.6	115.4	122.9	101.7	135.0
February	143.1	150.6	139.6	104.3	129.6	197.4	124.7	135.9	115.9	123.5	101.2	136.8
March	143.3	150.8	139.6	104.9	129.4	198.1	125.0	136.1	116.3	123.8	101.7	137.0
April	143.8	151.4	140.0	104.9	129.6	199.1	125.7	136.5	116.6	124.0	103.2	138.4
May	144.2	151.8	141.0	104.3	129.9	200.5	125.7	136.6	116.3	123.7	105.6	140.3
June	144.3	152.1	140.6	103.9	129.9	201.3	125.2	136.4	116.3	123.7	103.8	140.3
July	144.5	152.3	140.6	103.4	130.1	202.2	125.1	136.6	116.3	123.7	101.6	142.1
August	144.8	152.8	141.1	103.4	130.5	202.8	123.9	134.9	116.2	123.9	100.8	140.4
September	145.0	152.9	141.4	103.0	130.4	203.6	124.1	134.9	116.3	124.0	101.2	140.7
October	145.6	153.4	142.0	105.3	132.0	204.5	124.2	135.0	116.4	124.0	103.7	142.6
November	146.0	153.9	142.3	104.4	132.2	205.1	124.4	135.3	116.5	124.3	103.0	144.1
December	146.3	154.3	142.8	103.7	132.1	205.8	124.4	135.7	116.2	124.5	101.7	145.3
1994												
January	146.3	154.5	142.9	102.8	131.7	206.4	124.8	136.3	116.5	124.7	103.8	148.3
February	146.7	154.8	142.7	104.1	132.3	207.2	125.0	136.3	116.9	124.9	102.1	151.0
March	147.1	155.3	142.7	104.3	132.6	207.9	125.1	136.4	117.1	125.1	103.8	151.5
April	147.2	155.5	143.0	103.7	132.8	209.0	125.1	136.6	117.1	125.3	103.8	150.7
May	147.5	155.9	143.3	102.8	132.4	209.7	125.1	137.0	117.2	125.6	102.2	149.7
June	147.9	156.4	143.8	103.1	133.2	210.5	125.2	137.2	117.8	126.3	102.7	151.2
July	148.4	156.7	144.6	104.5	134.4	211.3	125.7	137.3	118.3	126.7	101.7	155.5
August	149.0	157.1	145.1	106.7	136.0	212.2	126.2	137.6	119.1	127.4	101.6	158.8
September	149.3	157.5	145.3	106.1	136.1	213.1	125.9	137.7	119.6	128.4	99.7	160.5
October	149.4	157.8	145.3	105.7	136.2	214.1	125.5	137.4	120.1	129.3	98.6	161.3
November	149.8	158.2	145.6	106.1	136.7	215.0	126.1	137.6	121.0	130.3	99.8	166.6
December	150.1	158.3	146.8	105.9	137.1	215.9	126.6	137.9	121.5	131.0	101.1	169.9

Table 20-2. Summary Consumer and Price Indexes—*Continued*

(All urban consumers; 1982–1984 = 100, seasonally adjusted.)

Year and month	Consumer Price Index, all urban consumers, 1982–1984 = 100						Producer Price Index, 1982 = 100					
							Finished goods		Intermediate materials, supplies, and components		Crude materials for further processing	
	All items	All items less food and energy	Food	Energy	Transportation	Medical care	Total	Less food and energy	Total	Less food and energy	Total	Crude nonfood less energy
1995												
January	150.5	159.0	146.7	105.7	137.4	216.6	126.9	138.4	122.8	132.6	102.1	174.5
February	150.9	159.4	147.3	105.8	137.9	217.4	127.2	138.7	123.7	133.7	102.9	176.5
March	151.2	159.9	147.1	105.5	138.4	218.1	127.4	139.0	124.3	134.3	102.3	177.8
April	151.8	160.4	148.1	105.6	139.2	218.6	127.7	139.3	125.0	135.2	103.7	180.2
May	152.1	160.7	148.2	105.8	139.7	219.2	127.8	139.7	125.2	135.5	102.4	179.6
June	152.4	161.1	148.3	106.7	140.6	219.9	127.8	139.8	125.5	135.7	103.0	179.5
July	152.6	161.4	148.5	105.8	139.9	220.6	128.0	140.2	125.6	136.1	101.6	176.4
August	152.9	161.8	148.6	105.6	139.4	221.6	127.9	140.2	125.6	136.1	99.7	173.4
September	153.1	162.2	149.1	104.1	139.1	222.4	128.1	140.2	125.5	136.2	102.0	170.9
October	153.5	162.7	149.5	104.4	139.5	223.0	128.4	141.0	125.4	135.8	101.9	166.6
November	153.7	163.0	149.6	103.4	139.1	223.7	128.7	141.3	125.2	135.5	104.1	163.6
December	153.9	163.1	149.9	104.4	139.1	224.3	129.3	141.5	125.4	135.2	106.5	162.3
1996												
January	154.7	163.7	150.4	106.9	140.4	225.2	129.7	141.5	125.5	134.8	109.8	162.6
February	155.0	164.0	150.8	107.1	140.9	225.7	129.7	141.6	125.0	134.4	111.6	162.1
March	155.5	164.4	151.4	108.3	141.5	226.2	130.5	141.6	125.3	134.1	109.8	158.2
April	156.1	164.6	152.0	111.2	142.9	226.8	130.9	141.6	125.7	133.8	114.2	156.7
May	156.4	165.0	151.9	112.0	143.5	227.4	130.9	142.0	126.2	134.0	114.6	157.6
June	156.7	165.4	152.9	110.3	143.4	228.0	131.3	142.2	125.8	133.9	112.2	154.6
July	157.0	165.7	153.4	110.1	143.0	228.6	131.2	142.2	125.5	133.6	114.6	152.2
August	157.2	166.0	153.9	109.7	143.0	229.1	131.6	142.3	125.6	133.6	115.3	152.5
September	157.7	166.5	154.6	109.8	143.6	229.7	131.7	142.2	126.1	134.0	112.7	153.5
October	158.2	166.8	155.5	110.5	143.9	230.3	132.4	142.3	126.0	133.7	111.9	153.3
November	158.7	167.2	156.1	111.8	144.6	231.0	132.5	142.1	125.8	133.7	115.7	153.0
December	159.1	167.4	156.3	113.9	145.7	231.2	132.9	142.3	126.4	133.9	122.5	153.6
1997												
January	159.4	167.8	155.9	115.2	145.6	231.8	133.0	142.5	126.6	134.1	127.5	156.2
February	159.7	168.1	156.5	115.0	145.2	232.2	132.7	142.4	126.5	134.1	116.6	157.6
March	159.8	168.4	156.6	113.0	145.0	233.0	132.6	142.6	126.1	134.2	107.5	158.7
April	159.9	168.9	156.5	111.0	144.3	233.5	131.8	142.6	125.6	134.1	107.8	155.8
May	159.9	169.2	156.6	108.8	143.3	234.1	131.5	142.4	125.4	134.2	109.1	157.0
June	160.2	169.4	156.9	110.0	143.6	234.4	131.3	142.4	125.4	134.2	106.2	156.9
July	160.4	169.7	157.2	109.1	143.3	234.7	130.9	142.2	125.1	134.2	106.2	155.7
August	160.8	169.8	157.7	110.9	144.1	235.1	131.4	142.3	125.3	134.3	106.8	156.8
September	161.2	170.2	158.0	112.4	144.8	235.5	131.6	142.6	125.5	134.3	108.4	155.8
October	161.5	170.6	158.3	111.8	144.7	236.1	131.9	142.6	125.4	134.3	113.4	156.7
November	161.7	170.8	158.6	111.4	143.9	236.9	131.6	142.4	125.6	134.4	115.8	156.5
December	161.8	171.2	158.7	109.8	143.7	237.8	131.4	142.3	125.4	134.4	108.8	154.2
1998												
January	162.0	171.6	159.5	107.5	143.0	238.1	130.7	142.4	124.6	134.3	102.8	150.4
February	162.0	171.9	159.4	105.1	142.4	238.8	130.6	142.6	124.2	134.2	100.8	150.1
March	162.0	172.2	159.7	103.3	141.5	239.4	130.5	143.3	123.7	134.1	99.5	148.7
April	162.2	172.5	159.7	102.4	140.9	240.3	130.7	143.4	123.6	134.0	100.6	147.3
May	162.6	172.9	160.3	103.2	141.2	241.2	130.5	143.5	123.5	133.9	99.6	146.2
June	162.8	173.2	160.2	103.6	141.4	241.8	130.4	143.5	123.1	133.6	97.1	145.9
July	163.2	173.5	160.6	103.3	141.7	242.5	130.7	143.8	123.0	133.5	97.4	143.4
August	163.4	174.0	161.0	102.1	141.6	243.3	130.4	143.8	122.7	133.4	93.6	139.4
September	163.5	174.2	161.1	101.3	141.2	244.1	130.4	144.0	122.3	133.1	91.4	137.6
October	163.9	174.4	162.0	101.5	141.4	244.8	130.9	144.2	122.2	132.7	93.9	134.0
November	164.1	174.8	162.2	101.1	141.3	245.3	130.8	144.3	122.0	132.5	93.6	131.6
December	164.4	175.4	162.4	100.1	140.9	245.9	131.3	145.8	121.3	132.2	90.2	129.4
1999												
January	164.7	175.6	163.1	99.7	140.7	246.5	131.7	145.6	121.2	132.0	91.1	128.9
February	164.6	175.6	163.4	99.1	140.0	247.2	131.2	145.7	120.8	131.8	88.9	130.6
March	164.8	175.7	163.3	100.0	140.6	247.9	131.5	145.7	121.1	131.9	89.3	129.6
April	165.8	176.3	163.4	105.1	143.5	248.7	132.1	145.7	121.8	132.1	91.2	128.8
May	166.0	176.5	163.7	105.0	143.4	249.3	132.3	145.8	122.2	132.4	96.6	130.5
June	166.1	176.7	163.6	104.8	143.1	250.0	132.3	145.8	122.6	132.8	96.9	131.5
July	166.7	177.1	163.8	107.0	144.7	250.9	132.6	145.8	123.3	133.3	97.3	133.5
August	167.1	177.3	164.1	109.6	145.9	251.7	133.5	145.7	124.1	133.6	102.4	136.2
September	167.8	177.8	164.6	111.9	147.1	252.5	134.5	146.5	124.6	133.9	106.7	138.6
October	168.1	178.1	165.1	111.9	147.4	253.1	134.5	146.9	124.9	134.3	104.0	142.5
November	168.4	178.4	165.4	111.5	147.4	254.0	134.9	146.9	125.4	134.5	109.7	144.3
December	168.8	178.7	165.6	113.7	148.7	255.0	135.3	147.0	125.8	134.7	104.3	147.7

Table 20-2. Summary Consumer and Price Indexes—*Continued*

(All urban consumers; 1982–1984 = 100, seasonally adjusted.)

| Year and month | Consumer Price Index, all urban consumers, 1982–1984 = 100 | | | | | | Producer Price Index, 1982 = 100 | | | | | |
| | All items | All items less food and energy | Food | Energy | Transporta-tion | Medical care | Finished goods | | Intermediate materials, supplies, and components | | Crude materials for further processing | |
							Total	Less food and energy	Total	Less food and energy	Total	Crude nonfood less energy
2000												
January	169.3	179.2	165.7	114.6	148.9	255.5	135.1	146.8	126.4	135.1	106.8	150.3
February	169.9	179.4	166.3	118.8	150.0	256.5	136.6	147.3	127.4	135.5	111.1	151.5
March	171.0	180.0	166.5	123.7	153.4	257.7	137.3	147.4	128.4	136.0	113.1	150.9
April	170.9	180.4	166.6	120.3	151.9	258.4	136.9	147.4	128.3	136.5	111.5	149.4
May	171.2	180.7	167.4	120.1	152.1	259.2	137.1	147.8	128.2	136.6	115.0	147.9
June	172.3	181.1	167.4	127.6	155.4	260.3	138.1	147.8	129.3	136.9	124.8	145.4
July	172.7	181.5	168.2	128.0	154.9	261.2	138.3	148.0	129.7	137.1	121.9	143.0
August	172.7	181.9	168.6	124.1	153.4	262.3	138.0	148.2	129.4	136.9	117.5	141.2
September	173.6	182.3	168.9	129.4	155.3	263.3	139.1	148.6	130.2	137.0	125.5	142.3
October	173.9	182.6	169.1	129.6	154.6	264.1	139.5	148.6	130.7	137.1	130.3	141.7
November	174.2	183.1	169.2	129.1	154.9	264.8	140.0	148.8	130.6	136.9	129.0	139.3
December	174.6	183.3	170.1	129.6	154.9	265.7	140.1	149.0	131.0	136.9	141.1	139.4
2001												
January	175.6	183.9	170.4	134.6	155.2	267.1	141.7	149.6	132.1	137.2	165.6	138.8
February	176.0	184.3	171.2	134.1	155.3	268.3	142.0	149.2	131.9	137.4	142.0	136.9
March	176.0	184.8	171.6	131.0	153.9	269.4	141.5	149.5	131.2	137.4	132.5	135.5
April	176.5	185.1	171.9	132.6	155.0	270.3	142.0	149.8	131.0	137.3	133.3	131.8
May	177.4	185.4	172.5	139.1	158.0	271.2	142.3	150.1	131.2	137.3	130.6	130.7
June	177.9	186.0	173.0	138.5	158.0	272.4	141.7	150.1	131.0	137.0	119.9	129.4
July	177.5	186.4	173.6	130.6	154.4	272.9	140.2	150.5	129.4	136.4	113.0	130.4
August	177.5	186.7	173.9	127.6	153.5	274.2	140.7	150.5	129.1	135.9	112.0	128.2
September	178.1	187.1	174.2	131.0	156.0	275.2	141.3	150.7	129.2	135.8	106.9	128.4
October	177.6	187.4	174.9	122.4	152.6	276.3	139.1	149.9	127.6	135.4	97.5	126.2
November	177.4	188.1	174.9	116.2	149.9	277.4	138.3	150.2	126.8	135.1	102.7	126.2
December	177.3	188.4	174.8	112.8	148.8	278.4	137.7	150.4	125.9	134.8	95.6	125.8
2002												
January	177.6	188.7	175.3	114.0	149.1	279.6	137.7	150.2	125.6	134.7	99.9	126.5
February	177.9	189.0	175.8	113.1	148.6	280.4	138.1	150.2	125.5	134.7	98.9	128.2
March	178.5	189.2	176.0	117.2	150.5	281.5	139.2	150.1	126.4	135.0	104.0	128.9
April	179.3	189.7	176.1	121.9	152.8	282.7	139.0	150.3	127.5	135.3	108.5	131.4
May	179.5	190.0	175.9	122.1	152.9	283.9	138.4	150.3	127.1	135.3	109.3	133.9
June	179.8	190.2	175.9	122.9	153.2	284.6	138.6	150.4	127.4	135.6	105.1	137.7
July	180.1	190.5	176.1	123.7	153.8	286.4	138.6	150.0	127.7	135.9	105.9	140.0
August	180.5	191.1	176.0	123.9	154.2	287.1	138.6	149.8	128.2	136.2	107.8	139.5
September	180.9	191.4	176.4	124.4	154.5	288.0	139.0	150.2	128.9	136.4	110.2	139.2
October	181.2	191.6	176.6	126.2	155.2	289.7	140.1	150.7	129.8	136.7	112.6	139.6
November	181.4	191.8	177.0	125.6	154.9	291.2	139.7	150.5	129.7	136.8	116.8	141.5
December	181.6	192.1	177.3	125.1	154.5	292.3	139.3	149.6	129.6	136.7	119.1	141.8

Table 20-3. Summary Labor Force, Employment, and Unemployment

(Thousands of persons, percent, seasonally adjusted, except as noted.)

Year and month	Noninsti-tutional population [1]	Labor force		Employment, thousands of persons					Employ-ment–population ratio, percent	Unemployment		
		Thousands of persons	Participa-tion rate (percent)	By age and sex			By industry			Thousands of persons		Rate, percent
				Men, 20 years and over	Women, 20 years and over	Both sexes, 16–19 years	Agricultural	Nonagri-cultural		Total	Unem-ployed 15 weeks and over	
1948												
January	102 603	60 095	58.6	39 386	14 556	4 119	8 077	49 984	56.6	2 034	311	3.4
February	102 698	60 524	58.9	39 480	14 621	4 095	7 696	50 500	56.7	2 328	283	3.8
March	102 771	60 070	58.5	39 098	14 481	4 092	7 333	50 338	56.1	2 399	292	4.0
April	102 831	60 677	59.0	39 157	15 001	4 133	7 557	50 734	56.7	2 386	324	3.9
May	102 923	59 972	58.3	39 139	14 712	4 003	7 141	50 713	56.2	2 118	329	3.5
June	102 992	60 957	59.2	39 392	15 213	4 138	7 591	51 152	57.0	2 214	322	3.6
July	103 216	61 181	59.3	39 607	15 348	4 013	7 602	51 366	57.1	2 213	295	3.6
August	103 240	60 806	58.9	39 510	14 994	3 952	7 562	50 894	56.6	2 350	332	3.9
September	103 291	60 815	58.9	39 324	15 207	3 982	7 865	50 648	56.6	2 302	298	3.8
October	103 361	60 646	58.7	39 522	14 956	3 909	7 626	50 761	56.5	2 259	324	3.7
November	103 424	60 702	58.7	39 459	15 054	3 904	7 624	50 793	56.5	2 285	282	3.8
December	103 468	61 169	59.1	39 539	15 137	4 064	7 984	50 756	56.8	2 429	305	4.0
1949												
January	103 529	60 771	58.7	39 233	14 991	3 951	7 790	50 385	56.2	2 596	315	4.3
February	103 559	61 057	59.0	39 117	15 117	3 974	8 022	50 186	56.2	2 849	374	4.7
March	103 665	61 073	58.9	39 015	15 069	3 959	8 008	50 035	56.0	3 030	414	5.0
April	103 739	61 007	58.8	38 993	14 978	3 776	7 911	49 836	55.7	3 260	483	5.3
May	103 845	61 259	59.0	38 701	15 066	3 785	8 067	49 485	55.4	3 707	602	6.1
June	103 930	60 948	58.6	38 632	15 003	3 537	7 802	49 370	55.0	3 776	705	6.2
July	104 042	61 301	58.9	38 405	15 244	3 541	8 021	49 189	55.0	4 111	848	6.7
August	104 121	61 590	59.2	38 610	15 181	3 606	7 604	49 793	55.1	4 193	917	6.8
September	104 219	61 633	59.1	38 744	15 129	3 711	7 297	50 287	55.3	4 049	973	6.6
October	104 338	62 185	59.6	38 394	15 260	3 615	6 814	50 455	54.9	4 916	1 000	7.9
November	104 421	62 005	59.4	38 860	15 422	3 727	7 497	50 512	55.6	3 996	1 056	6.4
December	104 524	61 908	59.2	38 908	15 300	3 637	7 379	50 466	55.3	4 063	961	6.6
1950												
January	104 619	61 661	58.9	38 780	15 255	3 600	7 065	50 570	55.1	4 026	947	6.5
February	104 737	61 687	58.9	38 818	15 339	3 594	7 057	50 694	55.1	3 936	947	6.4
March	104 844	61 604	58.8	38 851	15 366	3 511	7 116	50 612	55.1	3 876	912	6.3
April	104 943	62 158	59.2	39 100	15 831	3 652	7 264	51 319	55.8	3 575	920	5.8
May	105 014	62 083	59.1	39 416	15 628	3 605	7 277	51 372	55.8	3 434	890	5.5
June	105 104	62 419	59.4	39 476	15 953	3 623	7 285	51 767	56.2	3 367	868	5.4
July	105 194	62 121	59.1	39 517	15 793	3 691	7 126	51 875	56.1	3 120	769	5.0
August	105 282	62 596	59.5	39 879	16 124	3 794	7 248	52 549	56.8	2 799	633	4.5
September	105 269	62 349	59.2	39 865	15 902	3 808	6 992	52 583	56.6	2 774	648	4.4
October	105 096	62 428	59.4	39 737	16 175	3 891	7 371	52 432	56.9	2 625	545	4.2
November	104 979	62 286	59.3	39 668	16 195	3 834	7 163	52 534	56.9	2 589	507	4.2
December	104 872	62 068	59.2	39 536	16 149	3 744	6 760	52 669	56.7	2 639	482	4.3
1951												
January	104 844	61 941	59.1	39 595	16 279	3 762	6 828	52 808	56.9	2 305	438	3.7
February	104 604	61 778	59.1	39 695	16 257	3 709	6 738	52 923	57.0	2 117	386	3.4
March	104 629	62 526	59.8	40 013	16 557	3 831	6 858	53 543	57.7	2 125	355	3.4
April	104 541	61 808	59.1	39 804	16 426	3 659	6 722	53 167	57.3	1 919	294	3.1
May	104 491	62 044	59.4	39 752	16 581	3 855	6 752	53 436	57.6	1 856	269	3.0
June	104 488	61 615	59.0	39 538	16 368	3 714	6 529	53 091	57.1	1 995	258	3.2
July	104 504	62 106	59.4	39 483	16 898	3 775	6 601	53 555	57.6	1 950	260	3.1
August	104 536	61 927	59.2	39 508	16 665	3 821	6 790	53 204	57.4	1 933	249	3.1
September	104 588	61 780	59.1	39 416	16 504	3 793	6 558	53 155	57.1	2 067	223	3.3
October	104 690	62 204	59.4	39 555	16 674	3 781	6 636	53 374	57.3	2 194	269	3.5
November	104 740	62 014	59.2	39 504	16 669	3 663	6 699	53 137	57.1	2 178	316	3.5
December	104 810	62 457	59.6	39 691	16 946	3 860	7 065	53 432	57.7	1 960	269	3.1
1952												
January	104 862	62 432	59.5	39 714	17 001	3 745	7 148	53 312	57.7	1 972	282	3.2
February	104 868	62 419	59.5	39 772	16 935	3 755	7 020	53 442	57.7	1 957	248	3.1
March	104 860	61 721	58.9	39 580	16 627	3 701	6 468	53 440	57.1	1 813	234	2.9
April	104 906	61 720	58.8	39 542	16 659	3 708	6 525	53 384	57.1	1 811	242	2.9
May	104 996	62 058	59.1	39 588	16 844	3 763	6 334	53 861	57.3	1 863	219	3.0
June	105 118	62 103	59.1	39 558	16 837	3 824	6 529	53 690	57.3	1 884	210	3.0
July	105 246	61 962	58.9	39 496	16 778	3 697	6 334	53 637	57.0	1 991	194	3.2
August	105 346	61 877	58.7	39 289	16 867	3 634	6 174	53 616	56.8	2 087	211	3.4
September	105 436	62 457	59.2	39 386	17 477	3 658	6 537	53 984	57.4	1 936	249	3.1
October	105 591	61 971	58.7	39 451	17 032	3 649	6 363	53 769	56.9	1 839	230	3.0
November	105 706	62 491	59.1	39 549	17 450	3 749	6 509	54 239	57.5	1 743	216	2.8
December	105 812	62 621	59.2	40 011	17 181	3 762	6 361	54 593	57.6	1 667	238	2.7
1953												
January	106 594	63 439	59.5	40 256	17 482	3 862	6 642	54 958	57.8	1 839	268	2.9
February	106 678	63 520	59.5	40 546	17 321	4 017	6 463	55 421	58.0	1 636	208	2.6
March	106 744	63 657	59.6	40 648	17 397	3 965	6 420	55 590	58.1	1 647	213	2.6
April	106 826	63 167	59.1	40 346	17 242	3 856	6 362	55 082	57.5	1 723	180	2.7
May	106 910	62 615	58.6	40 323	16 983	3 713	5 937	55 082	57.1	1 596	176	2.5
June	106 978	63 063	58.9	40 358	17 301	3 797	6 361	55 095	57.4	1 607	213	2.5
July	107 034	63 057	58.9	40 378	17 341	3 678	6 267	55 130	57.4	1 660	168	2.6
August	107 132	62 816	58.6	40 352	17 108	3 691	6 319	54 832	57.1	1 665	177	2.7
September	107 253	62 727	58.5	40 192	17 063	3 651	6 198	54 708	56.8	1 821	178	2.9
October	107 383	62 867	58.5	40 155	17 236	3 502	6 096	54 797	56.7	1 974	190	3.1
November	107 504	62 949	58.6	40 163	16 974	3 601	6 345	54 393	56.5	2 211	259	3.5
December	107 623	62 795	58.3	39 885	16 599	3 493	5 929	54 048	55.7	2 818	309	4.5

[1]Not seasonally adjusted.

Table 20-3. Summary Labor Force, Employment, and Unemployment—*Continued*

(Thousands of persons, percent, seasonally adjusted, except as noted.)

Year and month	Noninstitutional population [1]	Labor force Thousands of persons	Labor force Participation rate (percent)	Men, 20 years and over	Women, 20 years and over	Both sexes, 16–19 years	Agricultural	Nonagricultural	Employment–population ratio, percent	Total	Unemployed 15 weeks and over	Rate, percent
1954												
January	107 763	63 101	58.6	39 834	16 574	3 616	6 073	53 951	55.7	3 077	372	4.9
February	107 880	63 994	59.3	39 899	17 162	3 602	6 590	54 073	56.2	3 331	532	5.2
March	107 987	63 793	59.1	39 497	17 022	3 667	6 395	53 791	55.7	3 607	765	5.7
April	108 080	63 934	59.2	39 613	17 015	3 557	6 142	54 043	55.7	3 749	774	5.9
May	108 184	63 675	58.9	39 467	16 975	3 466	6 210	53 698	55.4	3 767	879	5.9
June	108 267	63 343	58.5	39 476	16 894	3 422	6 162	53 630	55.2	3 551	880	5.6
July	108 344	63 302	58.4	39 467	16 777	3 399	6 222	53 421	55.0	3 659	932	5.8
August	108 440	63 707	58.7	39 582	16 868	3 403	6 087	53 766	55.2	3 854	1 002	6.0
September	108 546	64 209	59.2	39 702	17 133	3 447	6 453	53 829	55.5	3 927	1 017	6.1
October	108 668	63 936	58.8	39 618	17 209	3 443	6 242	54 028	55.5	3 666	1 009	5.7
November	108 798	63 759	58.6	39 745	17 213	3 399	5 934	54 423	55.5	3 402	975	5.3
December	108 892	63 312	58.1	39 763	17 121	3 232	5 848	54 268	55.2	3 196	827	5.0
1955												
January	109 059	63 910	58.6	39 937	17 375	3 441	6 113	54 640	55.7	3 157	882	4.9
February	109 078	63 696	58.4	39 964	17 413	3 350	5 854	54 873	55.7	2 969	826	4.7
March	109 254	63 882	58.5	40 111	17 415	3 438	6 242	54 722	55.8	2 918	816	4.6
April	109 377	64 564	59.0	40 120	17 867	3 528	6 363	55 152	56.2	3 049	811	4.7
May	109 544	64 381	58.8	40 410	17 665	3 559	6 327	55 307	56.3	2 747	734	4.3
June	109 680	64 482	58.8	40 444	17 837	3 500	6 243	55 538	56.3	2 701	668	4.2
July	109 792	65 145	59.3	40 751	18 123	3 639	6 438	56 075	56.9	2 632	640	4.0
August	109 882	65 581	59.7	40 747	18 377	3 673	6 575	56 222	57.1	2 784	535	4.2
September	109 977	65 628	59.7	40 920	18 285	3 745	6 819	56 131	57.2	2 678	558	4.1
October	110 085	65 821	59.8	40 858	18 327	3 806	6 728	56 263	57.2	2 830	572	4.3
November	110 177	66 037	59.9	40 936	18 422	3 899	6 655	56 602	57.4	2 780	564	4.2
December	110 296	66 445	60.2	41 063	18 630	3 991	6 653	57 031	57.7	2 761	581	4.2
1956												
January	110 390	66 419	60.2	41 203	18 691	3 859	6 590	57 163	57.8	2 666	561	4.0
February	110 478	66 124	59.9	41 175	18 582	3 761	6 457	57 061	57.5	2 606	545	3.9
March	110 582	66 175	59.8	41 199	18 496	3 716	6 221	57 190	57.3	2 764	521	4.2
April	110 650	66 264	59.9	41 289	18 629	3 696	6 460	57 154	57.5	2 650	476	4.0
May	110 810	66 722	60.2	41 166	18 844	3 851	6 375	57 486	57.6	2 861	506	4.3
June	110 903	66 702	60.1	41 196	18 748	3 876	6 335	57 485	57.5	2 882	516	4.3
July	111 019	66 752	60.1	41 216	18 718	3 866	6 320	57 480	57.5	2 952	523	4.4
August	111 099	66 673	60.0	41 265	18 864	3 843	6 280	57 692	57.6	2 701	543	4.1
September	111 222	66 714	60.0	41 221	19 019	3 839	6 375	57 704	57.6	2 635	577	3.9
October	111 335	66 546	59.8	41 261	18 928	3 786	6 137	57 838	57.5	2 571	530	3.9
November	111 432	66 657	59.8	41 208	18 846	3 742	5 997	57 799	57.3	2 861	575	4.3
December	111 526	66 700	59.8	41 192	18 859	3 859	5 806	58 104	57.3	2 790	567	4.2
1957												
January	111 626	66 428	59.5	41 168	18 740	3 724	5 790	57 842	57.0	2 796	509	4.2
February	111 711	66 879	59.9	41 341	19 115	3 801	6 125	58 132	57.5	2 622	530	3.9
March	111 824	66 913	59.8	41 500	19 066	3 838	5 963	58 441	57.6	2 509	514	3.7
April	111 933	66 647	59.5	41 345	18 937	3 765	5 836	58 211	57.2	2 600	516	3.9
May	112 031	66 695	59.5	41 334	18 897	3 754	5 999	57 986	57.1	2 710	538	4.1
June	112 172	67 052	59.8	41 411	18 973	3 812	6 002	58 194	57.2	2 856	526	4.3
July	112 317	67 336	60.0	41 472	19 262	3 806	6 401	58 139	57.5	2 796	535	4.2
August	112 421	66 706	59.3	41 243	19 020	3 696	5 898	58 061	56.9	2 747	542	4.1
September	112 554	67 064	59.6	41 213	19 116	3 792	5 728	58 393	57.0	2 943	559	4.4
October	112 710	67 066	59.5	41 069	19 160	3 817	5 875	58 171	56.8	3 020	650	4.5
November	112 874	67 123	59.5	40 853	19 082	3 734	5 686	57 983	56.4	3 454	674	5.1
December	113 013	67 398	59.6	40 884	19 285	3 753	6 037	57 885	56.6	3 476	731	5.2
1958												
January	113 138	67 095	59.3	40 617	19 035	3 568	5 831	57 389	55.9	3 875	879	5.8
February	113 234	67 201	59.3	40 336	18 951	3 611	5 654	57 244	55.5	4 303	1 005	6.4
March	113 337	67 223	59.3	40 180	18 968	3 583	5 561	57 170	55.3	4 492	1 128	6.7
April	113 415	67 647	59.6	40 129	18 969	3 533	5 602	57 029	55.2	5 016	1 387	7.4
May	113 534	67 895	59.8	40 253	18 978	3 643	5 647	57 227	55.4	5 021	1 493	7.4
June	113 647	67 674	59.5	40 208	19 008	3 514	5 510	57 220	55.2	4 944	1 677	7.3
July	113 727	67 824	59.6	40 270	19 039	3 436	5 525	57 220	55.2	5 079	1 796	7.5
August	113 835	68 037	59.8	40 343	19 103	3 566	5 673	57 339	55.4	5 025	1 888	7.4
September	113 977	68 002	59.7	40 564	19 033	3 584	5 453	57 728	55.4	4 821	1 795	7.1
October	114 138	68 045	59.6	40 699	19 091	3 685	5 563	57 912	55.6	4 570	1 708	6.7
November	114 283	67 658	59.2	40 684	19 157	3 629	5 571	57 899	55.5	4 188	1 570	6.2
December	114 429	67 740	59.2	40 666	19 170	3 713	5 521	58 028	55.5	4 191	1 490	6.2
1959												
January	114 582	67 936	59.3	40 769	19 292	3 807	5 481	58 387	55.7	4 068	1 396	6.0
February	114 712	67 649	59.0	40 699	19 167	3 818	5 429	58 255	55.5	3 965	1 277	5.9
March	114 849	68 068	59.3	41 079	19 379	3 809	5 677	58 590	56.0	3 801	1 210	5.6
April	114 986	68 339	59.4	41 419	19 498	3 851	5 893	58 875	56.3	3 571	1 039	5.2
May	115 144	68 178	59.2	41 355	19 565	3 779	5 792	58 907	56.2	3 479	965	5.1
June	115 287	68 278	59.2	41 387	19 658	3 804	5 712	59 137	56.3	3 429	963	5.0
July	115 429	68 539	59.4	41 596	19 595	3 820	5 564	59 447	56.3	3 528	889	5.1
August	115 555	68 432	59.2	41 485	19 568	3 791	5 442	59 402	56.1	3 588	889	5.2
September	115 668	68 545	59.3	41 351	19 531	3 888	5 447	59 323	56.0	3 775	895	5.5
October	115 798	68 821	59.4	41 362	19 702	3 847	5 355	59 556	56.1	3 910	883	5.7
November	115 916	68 533	59.1	41 062	19 594	3 874	5 480	59 050	55.7	4 003	982	5.8
December	116 040	68 994	59.5	41 651	19 717	3 973	5 458	59 883	56.3	3 653	920	5.3

[1] Not seasonally adjusted.

Table 20-3. Summary Labor Force, Employment, and Unemployment—*Continued*

(Thousands of persons, percent, seasonally adjusted, except as noted.)

Year and month	Noninsti-tutional population [1]	Labor force		Employment, thousands of persons					Employ-ment–population ratio, percent	Unemployment		
		Thousands of persons	Participa-tion rate (percent)	By age and sex			By industry			Thousands of persons		Rate, percent
				Men, 20 years and over	Women, 20 years and over	Both sexes, 16–19 years	Agricultural	Nonagri-cultural		Total	Unem-ployed 15 weeks and over	
1960												
January	116 594	68 962	59.1	41 637	19 686	4 024	5 458	59 889	56.0	3 615	915	5.2
February	116 702	68 949	59.1	41 729	19 765	4 126	5 443	60 177	56.2	3 329	841	4.8
March	116 827	68 399	58.5	41 320	19 388	3 965	4 959	59 714	55.4	3 726	959	5.4
April	116 910	69 579	59.5	41 641	20 110	4 208	5 471	60 488	56.4	3 620	896	5.2
May	117 033	69 626	59.5	41 668	20 186	4 203	5 359	60 698	56.4	3 569	797	5.1
June	117 167	69 934	59.7	41 553	20 290	4 325	5 416	60 752	56.5	3 766	854	5.4
July	117 281	69 745	59.5	41 490	20 257	4 162	5 542	60 367	56.2	3 836	921	5.5
August	117 431	69 841	59.5	41 503	20 316	4 076	5 520	60 375	56.1	3 946	927	5.6
September	117 521	70 151	59.7	41 604	20 493	4 170	5 755	60 512	56.4	3 884	982	5.5
October	117 643	69 884	59.4	41 464	20 076	4 092	5 436	60 196	55.8	4 252	1 189	6.1
November	117 829	70 439	59.8	41 543	20 384	4 182	5 513	60 596	56.1	4 330	1 223	6.1
December	118 001	70 395	59.7	41 416	20 332	4 030	5 622	60 156	55.7	4 617	1 142	6.6
1961												
January	118 155	70 447	59.6	41 363	20 325	4 088	5 422	60 354	55.7	4 671	1 328	6.6
February	118 250	70 420	59.6	41 177	20 392	4 019	5 472	60 116	55.5	4 832	1 416	6.9
March	118 358	70 703	59.7	41 273	20 459	4 118	5 406	60 444	55.6	4 853	1 463	6.9
April	118 503	70 267	59.3	41 206	20 145	4 023	5 037	60 337	55.2	4 893	1 598	7.0
May	118 638	70 452	59.4	41 139	20 261	4 049	5 099	60 350	55.2	5 003	1 686	7.1
June	118 767	70 878	59.7	41 349	20 446	4 198	5 220	60 773	55.6	4 885	1 651	6.9
July	118 889	70 536	59.3	41 245	20 252	4 111	5 153	60 455	55.2	4 928	1 830	7.0
August	119 006	70 534	59.3	41 362	20 279	4 211	5 366	60 486	55.3	4 682	1 649	6.6
September	119 107	70 217	59.0	41 400	20 112	4 029	5 021	60 520	55.0	4 676	1 531	6.7
October	119 202	70 492	59.1	41 509	20 338	4 072	5 203	60 716	55.3	4 573	1 481	6.5
November	119 153	70 376	59.1	41 556	20 330	4 195	5 090	60 991	55.5	4 295	1 388	6.1
December	119 214	70 077	58.8	41 534	20 287	4 079	4 992	60 908	55.3	4 177	1 361	6.0
1962												
January	119 300	70 189	58.8	41 547	20 501	4 060	5 094	61 014	55.4	4 081	1 235	5.8
February	119 360	70 409	59.0	41 745	20 693	4 100	5 289	61 249	55.7	3 871	1 244	5.5
March	119 476	70 414	58.9	41 696	20 567	4 230	5 157	61 336	55.7	3 921	1 162	5.6
April	119 702	70 278	58.7	41 647	20 567	4 158	5 009	61 363	55.4	3 906	1 122	5.6
May	119 813	70 551	58.9	41 847	20 558	4 283	4 964	61 724	55.7	3 863	1 134	5.5
June	119 943	70 514	58.8	41 761	20 547	4 362	4 943	61 727	55.6	3 844	1 079	5.5
July	120 128	70 302	58.5	41 071	20 592	4 220	4 840	61 643	55.3	3 819	1 049	5.4
August	120 323	70 981	59.0	41 900	20 841	4 227	4 866	62 102	55.7	4 013	1 081	5.7
September	120 653	71 153	59.0	42 020	20 982	4 190	4 867	62 325	55.7	3 961	1 096	5.6
October	120 856	70 917	58.7	42 086	20 856	4 172	4 816	62 298	55.5	3 803	1 022	5.4
November	121 045	70 871	58.5	41 985	20 794	4 068	4 831	62 016	55.2	4 024	1 051	5.7
December	121 236	70 854	58.4	41 934	20 831	4 182	4 647	62 300	55.2	3 907	1 068	5.5
1963												
January	121 463	71 146	58.6	41 938	20 933	4 201	4 882	62 190	55.2	4 074	1 122	5.7
February	121 633	71 262	58.6	41 876	21 046	4 102	4 652	62 372	55.1	4 238	1 137	5.9
March	121 824	71 423	58.6	42 047	21 162	4 142	4 696	62 655	55.3	4 072	1 087	5.7
April	121 986	71 697	58.8	42 131	21 281	4 230	4 670	62 972	55.5	4 055	1 071	5.7
May	122 162	71 832	58.8	42 145	21 225	4 245	4 729	62 886	55.3	4 217	1 157	5.9
June	122 352	71 626	58.5	42 260	21 105	4 196	4 642	63 007	55.3	3 977	1 067	5.6
July	122 521	71 956	58.7	42 427	21 268	4 210	4 694	63 211	55.4	4 051	1 070	5.6
August	122 667	71 786	58.5	42 400	21 185	4 323	4 604	63 304	55.4	3 878	1 114	5.4
September	122 821	72 131	58.7	42 500	21 317	4 357	4 650	63 524	55.5	3 957	1 069	5.5
October	123 014	72 281	58.8	42 437	21 456	4 401	4 702	63 592	55.5	3 987	1 071	5.5
November	123 192	72 418	58.8	42 415	21 553	4 299	4 694	63 573	55.4	4 151	1 054	5.7
December	123 360	72 188	58.5	42 427	21 481	4 305	4 629	63 584	55.3	3 975	1 007	5.5
1964												
January	123 560	72 356	58.6	42 510	21 462	4 355	4 603	63 724	55.3	4 029	1 057	5.6
February	123 707	72 683	58.8	42 579	21 652	4 520	4 563	64 188	55.6	3 932	1 015	5.4
March	123 857	72 713	58.7	42 600	21 685	4 478	4 366	64 397	55.5	3 950	1 039	5.4
April	124 019	73 274	59.1	42 885	22 110	4 361	4 414	64 942	55.9	3 918	934	5.3
May	124 204	73 395	59.1	43 025	22 103	4 503	4 603	65 028	56.1	3 764	975	5.1
June	124 386	73 032	58.7	42 760	21 995	4 463	4 556	64 662	55.6	3 814	1 047	5.2
July	124 567	73 007	58.6	42 998	21 846	4 555	4 591	64 808	55.7	3 608	1 002	4.9
August	124 731	73 118	58.6	42 963	22 002	4 498	4 573	64 890	55.7	3 655	934	5.0
September	124 920	73 290	58.7	43 009	21 863	4 706	4 619	64 959	55.7	3 712	917	5.1
October	125 108	73 308	58.6	43 023	21 984	4 575	4 550	65 032	55.6	3 726	903	5.1
November	125 291	73 286	58.5	43 171	21 954	4 610	4 496	65 239	55.7	3 551	922	4.8
December	125 468	73 465	58.6	43 109	22 136	4 569	4 322	65 492	55.6	3 651	873	5.0
1965												
January	125 647	73 569	58.6	43 237	22 282	4 478	4 271	65 726	55.7	3 572	793	4.9
February	125 810	73 857	58.7	43 279	22 276	4 572	4 322	65 805	55.7	3 730	919	5.1
March	125 985	73 949	58.7	43 370	22 373	4 696	4 318	66 121	55.9	3 510	796	4.7
April	126 155	74 228	58.8	43 397	22 416	4 820	4 424	66 209	56.0	3 595	796	4.8
May	126 320	74 466	59.0	43 579	22 494	4 961	4 724	66 310	56.2	3 432	736	4.6
June	126 499	74 412	58.8	43 487	22 759	4 779	4 444	66 581	56.1	3 387	786	4.6
July	126 573	74 761	59.1	43 489	22 841	5 130	4 390	67 070	56.5	3 301	683	4.4
August	126 756	74 616	58.9	43 447	22 783	5 132	4 355	67 007	56.3	3 254	733	4.4
September	126 906	74 502	58.7	43 371	22 684	5 231	4 271	67 015	56.2	3 216	732	4.3
October	127 043	74 838	58.9	43 461	22 819	5 415	4 418	67 277	56.4	3 143	672	4.2
November	127 171	74 797	58.8	43 447	22 829	5 448	4 093	67 631	56.4	3 073	645	4.1
December	127 294	75 093	59.0	43 513	22 983	5 566	4 159	67 903	56.6	3 031	659	4.0

[1] Not seasonally adjusted.

Table 20-3. Summary Labor Force, Employment, and Unemployment—*Continued*

(Thousands of persons, percent, seasonally adjusted, except as noted.)

Year and month	Noninstitutional population [1]	Labor force Thousands of persons	Labor force Participation rate (percent)	Men, 20 years and over	Women, 20 years and over	Both sexes, 16–19 years	Agricultural	Nonagricultural	Employment–population ratio, percent	Total	Unemployed 15 weeks and over	Rate, percent
1966												
January	127 394	75 186	59.0	43 495	23 098	5 605	4 077	68 121	56.7	2 988	623	4.0
February	127 514	74 954	58.8	43 528	23 089	5 517	4 078	68 056	56.6	2 820	594	3.8
March	127 626	75 075	58.8	43 576	23 109	5 503	4 069	68 119	56.6	2 887	583	3.8
April	127 744	75 338	59.0	43 679	23 227	5 604	4 108	68 402	56.8	2 828	575	3.8
May	127 879	75 447	59.0	43 710	23 282	5 505	3 930	68 567	56.7	2 950	534	3.9
June	127 983	75 647	59.1	43 662	23 359	5 754	3 967	68 808	56.9	2 872	475	3.8
July	128 102	75 736	59.1	43 574	23 422	5 864	3 920	68 940	56.9	2 876	427	3.8
August	128 240	76 046	59.3	43 636	23 605	5 905	3 921	69 225	57.0	2 900	464	3.8
September	128 359	76 056	59.3	43 718	23 881	5 659	3 952	69 306	57.1	2 798	488	3.7
October	128 494	76 199	59.3	43 776	23 881	5 744	3 912	69 489	57.1	2 798	494	3.7
November	128 627	76 610	59.6	43 804	24 130	5 906	3 945	69 895	57.4	2 770	464	3.6
December	128 730	76 641	59.5	43 820	24 025	5 884	3 906	69 823	57.3	2 912	488	3.8
1967												
January	128 909	76 639	59.5	44 029	23 872	5 770	3 890	69 781	57.1	2 968	489	3.9
February	129 032	76 521	59.3	43 997	23 919	5 690	3 723	69 883	57.0	2 915	459	3.8
March	129 190	76 328	59.1	43 922	23 832	5 685	3 757	69 682	56.8	2 889	436	3.8
April	129 344	76 777	59.4	44 061	24 161	5 660	3 748	70 134	57.1	2 895	428	3.8
May	129 515	76 773	59.3	44 100	24 172	5 572	3 658	70 186	57.0	2 929	417	3.8
June	129 722	77 270	59.6	44 230	24 303	5 745	3 689	70 589	57.3	2 992	422	3.9
July	129 918	77 464	59.6	44 364	24 416	5 740	3 833	70 687	57.4	2 944	412	3.8
August	130 187	77 712	59.7	44 410	24 600	5 757	3 963	70 804	57.4	2 945	441	3.8
September	130 392	77 812	59.7	44 535	24 683	5 636	3 851	71 003	57.4	2 958	448	3.8
October	130 582	78 194	59.9	44 610	24 802	5 639	4 008	71 043	57.5	3 143	472	4.0
November	130 754	78 191	59.8	44 625	24 914	5 586	3 933	71 192	57.5	3 066	490	3.9
December	130 936	78 491	59.9	44 719	25 104	5 650	4 076	71 397	57.6	3 018	485	3.8
1968												
January	131 112	77 578	59.2	44 606	24 581	5 513	3 908	70 792	57.0	2 878	503	3.7
February	131 277	78 230	59.6	44 659	24 881	5 689	3 959	71 270	57.3	3 001	468	3.8
March	131 412	78 256	59.6	44 663	25 019	5 697	3 904	71 475	57.4	2 877	447	3.7
April	131 553	78 270	59.5	44 753	25 072	5 736	3 875	71 686	57.4	2 709	393	3.5
May	131 712	78 847	59.9	44 841	25 513	5 753	3 814	72 293	57.8	2 740	395	3.5
June	131 872	79 120	60.0	44 914	25 466	5 802	3 806	72 376	57.8	2 938	405	3.7
July	132 053	78 970	59.8	44 935	25 347	5 805	3 820	72 267	57.6	2 883	426	3.7
August	132 251	78 811	59.6	44 897	25 201	5 945	3 736	72 307	57.5	2 768	393	3.5
September	132 446	78 858	59.5	44 893	25 445	5 834	3 758	72 414	57.5	2 686	375	3.4
October	132 617	78 913	59.5	44 884	25 475	5 865	3 741	72 483	57.5	2 689	386	3.4
November	132 903	79 209	59.6	44 996	25 674	5 824	3 758	72 736	57.6	2 715	357	3.4
December	133 120	79 463	59.7	45 262	25 712	5 804	3 746	73 032	57.7	2 685	351	3.4
1969												
January	133 324	79 523	59.6	45 154	25 777	5 874	3 704	73 101	57.6	2 718	339	3.4
February	133 465	80 019	60.0	45 339	26 092	5 896	3 770	73 557	57.9	2 692	358	3.4
March	133 639	80 079	59.9	45 305	26 115	5 947	3 668	73 699	57.9	2 712	353	3.4
April	133 821	80 281	60.0	45 262	26 233	6 028	3 629	73 894	57.9	2 758	386	3.4
May	134 027	80 125	59.8	45 278	26 283	5 851	3 706	73 706	57.8	2 713	387	3.4
June	134 213	80 696	60.1	45 313	26 429	6 138	3 663	74 217	58.0	2 816	368	3.5
July	134 414	80 827	60.1	45 305	26 516	6 138	3 548	74 411	58.0	2 868	377	3.5
August	134 597	81 106	60.3	45 513	26 556	6 181	3 613	74 637	58.1	2 856	373	3.5
September	134 774	81 290	60.3	45 447	26 572	6 231	3 551	74 699	58.1	3 040	391	3.7
October	135 012	81 494	60.4	45 488	26 658	6 299	3 517	74 928	58.1	3 049	374	3.7
November	135 239	81 397	60.2	45 505	26 652	6 384	3 477	75 064	58.1	2 856	392	3.5
December	135 489	81 624	60.2	45 577	26 832	6 331	3 409	75 331	58.1	2 884	413	3.5
1970												
January	135 713	81 981	60.4	45 654	26 908	6 218	3 422	75 358	58.0	3 201	431	3.9
February	135 957	82 151	60.4	45 627	26 828	6 243	3 439	75 259	57.9	3 453	470	4.2
March	136 179	82 498	60.6	45 668	26 933	6 262	3 499	75 364	57.9	3 635	534	4.4
April	136 416	82 727	60.6	45 679	27 114	6 137	3 568	75 362	57.9	3 797	602	4.6
May	136 686	82 483	60.3	45 666	26 739	6 159	3 547	75 017	57.5	3 919	591	4.8
June	136 928	82 484	60.2	45 554	26 904	5 955	3 555	74 858	57.3	4 071	657	4.9
July	137 196	82 901	60.4	45 516	27 083	6 127	3 517	75 209	57.4	4 175	662	5.0
August	137 455	82 880	60.3	45 495	27 011	6 118	3 418	75 206	57.2	4 256	705	5.1
September	137 717	82 954	60.2	45 535	26 784	6 179	3 451	75 047	57.0	4 456	788	5.4
October	137 988	83 276	60.4	45 508	27 058	6 119	3 337	75 348	57.0	4 591	771	5.5
November	138 264	83 548	60.4	45 540	27 020	6 090	3 372	75 278	56.9	4 898	871	5.9
December	138 529	83 670	60.4	45 466	27 038	6 090	3 380	75 214	56.7	5 076	1 102	6.1
1971												
January	138 795	83 850	60.4	45 527	27 173	6 164	3 393	75 471	56.8	4 986	1 113	5.9
February	139 021	83 603	60.1	45 455	27 040	6 205	3 288	75 412	56.6	4 903	1 068	5.9
March	139 285	83 575	60.0	45 520	26 967	6 101	3 356	75 232	56.4	4 987	1 098	6.0
April	139 566	83 946	60.1	45 789	26 984	6 214	3 574	75 413	56.6	4 959	1 149	5.9
May	139 826	84 135	60.2	45 917	27 056	6 166	3 449	75 690	56.6	4 996	1 173	5.9
June	140 090	83 706	59.8	45 879	27 013	5 865	3 334	75 423	56.2	4 949	1 167	5.9
July	140 343	84 340	60.1	46 000	27 054	6 251	3 386	75 919	56.5	5 035	1 251	6.0
August	140 596	84 673	60.2	46 041	27 171	6 327	3 395	76 144	56.6	5 134	1 261	6.1
September	140 869	84 731	60.1	46 090	27 390	6 209	3 367	76 322	56.6	5 042	1 239	6.0
October	141 146	84 872	60.1	46 132	27 538	6 248	3 405	76 513	56.6	4 954	1 268	5.8
November	141 393	85 458	60.4	46 209	27 721	6 367	3 410	76 887	56.8	5 161	1 277	6.0
December	141 666	85 625	60.4	46 280	27 791	6 400	3 371	77 100	56.8	5 154	1 283	6.0

[1]Not seasonally adjusted.

Table 20-3. Summary Labor Force, Employment, and Unemployment—*Continued*

(Thousands of persons, percent, seasonally adjusted, except as noted.)

Year and month	Noninsti-tutional population [1]	Labor force		Employment, thousands of persons					Employ-ment population ratio, percent	Unemployment		
		Thousands of persons	Participa-tion rate (percent)	By age and sex			By industry			Thousands of persons		Rate, percent
				Men, 20 years and over	Women, 20 years and over	Both sexes, 16–19 years	Agricultural	Nonagri-cultural		Total	Unem-ployed 15 weeks and over	
1972												
January	142 736	85 978	60.2	46 471	27 956	6 532	3 366	77 593	56.7	5 019	1 257	5.8
February	143 017	86 036	60.2	46 600	28 016	6 492	3 358	77 750	56.7	4 928	1 292	5.7
March	143 263	86 611	60.5	46 821	28 126	6 626	3 438	78 135	56.9	5 038	1 232	5.8
April	143 483	86 614	60.4	46 863	28 114	6 678	3 382	78 273	56.9	4 959	1 203	5.7
May	143 760	86 809	60.4	46 950	28 184	6 753	3 412	78 475	57.0	4 922	1 168	5.7
June	144 033	87 006	60.4	47 147	28 175	6 761	3 402	78 681	57.0	4 923	1 141	5.7
July	144 285	87 143	60.4	47 244	28 225	6 761	3 461	78 769	57.0	4 913	1 154	5.6
August	144 522	87 517	60.6	47 321	28 382	6 875	3 603	78 975	57.1	4 939	1 156	5.6
September	144 761	87 392	60.4	47 394	28 417	6 732	3 568	78 975	57.0	4 849	1 131	5.5
October	144 988	87 491	60.3	47 354	28 438	6 824	3 634	78 982	57.0	4 875	1 123	5.6
November	145 211	87 592	60.3	47 529	28 567	6 894	3 517	79 473	57.2	4 602	1 040	5.3
December	145 446	87 943	60.5	47 747	28 698	6 955	3 596	79 804	57.3	4 543	1 006	5.2
1973												
January	145 720	87 487	60.0	47 701	28 596	6 864	3 456	79 705	57.1	4 326	947	4.9
February	145 943	88 364	60.5	47 884	28 995	7 033	3 415	80 497	57.5	4 452	894	5.0
March	146 230	88 846	60.8	48 117	29 110	7 225	3 469	80 983	57.8	4 394	889	4.9
April	146 459	89 018	60.8	48 098	29 304	7 157	3 407	81 152	57.7	4 459	809	5.0
May	146 719	88 977	60.6	48 068	29 432	7 148	3 376	81 272	57.7	4 329	816	4.9
June	146 981	89 548	60.9	48 244	29 505	7 436	3 509	81 676	58.0	4 363	779	4.9
July	147 233	89 604	60.9	48 452	29 592	7 255	3 540	81 759	57.9	4 305	750	4.8
August	147 471	89 509	60.7	48 353	29 578	7 273	3 425	81 779	57.8	4 305	788	4.8
September	147 731	89 838	60.8	48 408	29 710	7 370	3 342	82 146	57.9	4 350	785	4.8
October	147 980	90 131	60.9	48 631	29 885	7 471	3 424	82 563	58.1	4 144	793	4.6
November	148 219	90 716	61.2	48 764	30 071	7 485	3 593	82 727	58.2	4 396	832	4.8
December	148 479	90 890	61.2	48 902	29 991	7 508	3 658	82 743	58.2	4 489	767	4.9
1974												
January	148 753	91 199	61.3	49 107	29 893	7 555	3 756	82 799	58.2	4 644	799	5.1
February	148 982	91 485	61.4	49 057	30 146	7 551	3 824	82 930	58.2	4 731	829	5.2
March	149 225	91 453	61.3	48 986	30 293	7 540	3 726	83 093	58.2	4 634	849	5.1
April	149 478	91 287	61.1	48 853	30 376	7 440	3 582	83 087	58.0	4 618	889	5.1
May	149 750	91 596	61.2	49 039	30 424	7 428	3 529	83 362	58.0	4 705	880	5.1
June	150 012	91 868	61.2	48 946	30 512	7 483	3 386	83 555	58.0	4 927	926	5.4
July	150 248	92 212	61.4	48 883	30 869	7 397	3 436	83 713	58.0	5 063	924	5.5
August	150 493	92 059	61.2	48 950	30 662	7 425	3 429	83 608	57.8	5 022	960	5.5
September	150 753	92 488	61.4	48 978	30 569	7 504	3 460	83 591	57.7	5 437	1 021	5.9
October	151 009	92 518	61.3	48 959	30 570	7 466	3 431	83 564	57.6	5 523	1 072	6.0
November	151 256	92 766	61.3	48 833	30 424	7 369	3 405	83 221	57.3	6 140	1 128	6.6
December	151 494	92 780	61.2	48 458	30 431	7 255	3 361	82 783	56.9	6 636	1 326	7.2
1975												
January	151 755	93 128	61.4	48 086	30 343	7 198	3 401	82 226	56.4	7 501	1 555	8.1
February	151 990	92 776	61.0	47 927	30 215	7 114	3 361	81 895	56.1	7 520	1 841	8.1
March	152 217	93 165	61.2	47 776	30 334	7 077	3 358	81 829	56.0	7 978	2 074	8.6
April	152 443	93 399	61.3	47 759	30 410	7 020	3 315	81 874	55.9	8 210	2 442	8.8
May	152 704	93 884	61.5	47 835	30 483	7 133	3 560	81 891	56.0	8 433	2 643	9.0
June	152 976	93 575	61.2	47 754	30 618	6 983	3 368	81 987	55.8	8 220	2 843	8.8
July	153 309	94 021	61.3	48 050	30 794	7 050	3 457	82 437	56.0	8 127	2 943	8.6
August	153 580	94 162	61.3	48 239	30 966	7 029	3 429	82 805	56.1	7 928	2 862	8.4
September	153 848	94 202	61.2	48 126	30 979	7 174	3 508	82 771	56.1	7 923	2 906	8.4
October	154 082	94 267	61.2	48 165	31 121	7 084	3 397	82 973	56.1	7 897	2 689	8.4
November	154 338	94 250	61.1	48 203	31 135	7 118	3 331	83 125	56.0	7 794	2 789	8.3
December	154 589	94 409	61.1	48 266	31 268	7 131	3 259	83 406	56.1	7 744	2 868	8.2
1976												
January	154 853	94 934	61.3	48 592	31 595	7 213	3 387	84 013	56.4	7 534	2 713	7.9
February	155 066	94 998	61.3	48 721	31 680	7 271	3 304	84 368	56.5	7 326	2 519	7.7
March	155 306	95 215	61.3	48 836	31 842	7 307	3 296	84 689	56.7	7 230	2 441	7.6
April	155 529	95 746	61.6	49 097	31 951	7 368	3 438	84 978	56.8	7 330	2 210	7.7
May	155 765	95 847	61.5	49 193	32 147	7 454	3 367	85 427	57.0	7 053	2 115	7.4
June	156 027	95 885	61.5	49 010	32 267	7 286	3 310	85 253	56.8	7 322	2 332	7.6
July	156 276	96 583	61.8	49 236	32 334	7 523	3 358	85 735	57.0	7 490	2 316	7.8
August	156 525	96 741	61.8	49 417	32 437	7 369	3 380	85 843	57.0	7 518	2 378	7.8
September	156 779	96 553	61.6	49 485	32 390	7 298	3 278	85 895	56.9	7 380	2 296	7.6
October	156 993	96 704	61.6	49 524	32 412	7 338	3 316	85 958	56.9	7 430	2 292	7.7
November	157 235	97 254	61.9	49 561	32 753	7 320	3 263	86 371	57.0	7 620	2 354	7.8
December	157 438	97 348	61.8	49 599	32 914	7 290	3 251	86 552	57.0	7 545	2 375	7.8
1977												
January	157 688	97 208	61.6	49 738	32 872	7 318	3 185	86 743	57.0	7 280	2 200	7.5
February	157 913	97 785	61.9	49 838	32 997	7 507	3 222	87 120	57.2	7 443	2 174	7.6
March	158 131	98 115	62.0	50 031	33 246	7 531	3 212	87 596	57.4	7 307	2 057	7.4
April	158 371	98 330	62.1	50 185	33 470	7 616	3 313	87 958	57.6	7 059	1 936	7.2
May	158 657	98 665	62.2	50 280	33 851	7 623	3 432	88 322	57.8	6 911	1 928	7.0
June	158 929	99 093	62.4	50 544	33 678	7 737	3 340	88 619	57.9	7 134	1 918	7.2
July	159 185	98 913	62.1	50 597	33 749	7 738	3 247	88 837	57.8	6 829	1 907	6.9
August	159 430	99 366	62.3	50 745	33 809	7 887	3 260	89 181	58.0	6 925	1 836	7.0
September	159 674	99 453	62.3	50 825	34 218	7 659	3 201	89 501	58.1	6 751	1 853	6.8
October	159 915	99 815	62.4	51 046	34 187	7 819	3 272	89 780	58.2	6 763	1 789	6.8
November	160 129	100 576	62.8	51 316	34 536	7 909	3 375	90 386	58.6	6 815	1 804	6.8
December	160 377	100 491	62.7	51 492	34 668	7 945	3 320	90 785	58.7	6 386	1 717	6.4

[1] Not seasonally adjusted.

Table 20-3. Summary Labor Force, Employment, and Unemployment—*Continued*

(Thousands of persons, percent, seasonally adjusted, except as noted.)

Year and month	Noninsti-tutional population [1]	Labor force		Employment, thousands of persons					Employ-ment population ratio, percent	Unemployment		
		Thousands of persons	Participa-tion rate (percent)	By age and sex			By industry			Thousands of persons		Rate, percent
				Men, 20 years and over	Women, 20 years and over	Both sexes, 16–19 years	Agricultural	Nonagri-cultural		Total	Unem-ployed 15 weeks and over	
1978												
January	160 617	100 873	62.8	51 542	34 948	7 894	3 434	90 950	58.8	6 489	1 643	6.4
February	160 831	100 837	62.7	51 578	35 118	7 823	3 320	91 199	58.8	6 318	1 584	6.3
March	161 038	101 092	62.8	51 635	35 310	7 810	3 351	91 404	58.8	6 337	1 531	6.3
April	161 263	101 574	63.0	51 912	35 546	7 936	3 349	92 045	59.2	6 180	1 502	6.1
May	161 518	101 896	63.1	52 050	35 597	8 122	3 325	92 444	59.3	6 127	1 420	6.0
June	161 795	102 371	63.3	52 240	35 828	8 275	3 483	92 860	59.5	6 028	1 352	5.9
July	162 034	102 399	63.2	52 190	35 764	8 136	3 441	92 649	59.3	6 309	1 373	6.2
August	162 259	102 511	63.2	52 228	35 856	8 347	3 401	93 030	59.4	6 080	1 242	5.9
September	162 502	102 795	63.3	52 284	36 274	8 112	3 400	93 270	59.5	6 125	1 308	6.0
October	162 783	103 080	63.3	52 448	36 525	8 160	3 409	93 724	59.7	5 947	1 319	5.8
November	163 017	103 562	63.5	52 802	36 559	8 124	3 284	94 201	59.8	6 077	1 242	5.9
December	163 272	103 809	63.6	52 807	36 686	8 088	3 396	94 185	59.8	6 228	1 269	6.0
1979												
January	163 516	104 057	63.6	53 072	36 697	8 179	3 305	94 643	59.9	6 109	1 250	5.9
February	163 726	104 502	63.8	53 233	36 904	8 192	3 373	94 956	60.1	6 173	1 297	5.9
March	164 027	104 589	63.8	53 120	37 159	8 201	3 368	95 112	60.0	6 109	1 365	5.8
April	164 162	104 172	63.5	53 085	36 944	8 074	3 291	94 812	59.8	6 069	1 272	5.8
May	164 459	104 171	63.3	53 178	37 134	8 019	3 272	95 059	59.8	5 840	1 239	5.6
June	164 721	104 638	63.5	53 309	37 221	8 149	3 331	95 348	59.9	5 959	1 171	5.7
July	164 970	105 002	63.6	53 384	37 514	8 108	3 335	95 671	60.0	5 996	1 123	5.7
August	165 198	105 096	63.6	53 336	37 548	7 892	3 374	95 402	59.8	6 320	1 203	6.0
September	165 431	105 530	63.8	53 510	37 798	8 032	3 371	95 969	60.0	6 190	1 172	5.9
October	165 813	105 700	63.7	53 478	37 931	7 995	3 325	96 079	59.9	6 296	1 219	6.0
November	166 051	105 812	63.7	53 435	38 065	8 074	3 436	96 138	60.0	6 238	1 239	5.9
December	166 300	106 258	63.9	53 555	38 259	8 119	3 400	96 533	60.1	6 325	1 277	6.0
1980												
January	166 544	106 562	64.0	53 501	38 367	8 011	3 316	96 563	60.0	6 683	1 353	6.3
February	166 759	106 697	64.0	53 686	38 389	7 920	3 397	96 598	60.0	6 702	1 358	6.3
March	166 984	106 442	63.7	53 353	38 406	7 954	3 418	96 295	59.7	6 729	1 457	6.3
April	167 197	106 591	63.8	53 035	38 427	7 771	3 326	95 907	59.4	7 358	1 694	6.9
May	167 407	106 929	63.9	52 915	38 335	7 695	3 382	95 563	59.1	7 984	1 740	7.5
June	167 643	106 780	63.7	52 712	38 312	7 658	3 296	95 386	58.9	8 098	1 760	7.6
July	167 932	107 159	63.8	52 733	38 374	7 689	3 319	95 477	58.8	8 363	1 995	7.8
August	168 103	107 105	63.7	52 815	38 511	7 498	3 234	95 590	58.8	8 281	2 162	7.7
September	168 297	107 098	63.6	52 866	38 595	7 616	3 443	95 634	58.9	8 021	2 309	7.5
October	168 503	107 405	63.7	53 094	38 620	7 603	3 372	95 945	58.9	8 088	2 306	7.5
November	168 695	107 568	63.8	53 210	38 795	7 540	3 396	96 149	59.0	8 023	2 329	7.5
December	168 883	107 352	63.6	53 333	38 737	7 564	3 492	96 142	59.0	7 718	2 406	7.2
1981												
January	169 104	108 026	63.9	53 392	39 042	7 521	3 429	96 526	59.1	8 071	2 389	7.5
February	169 280	108 242	63.9	53 445	39 280	7 466	3 345	96 846	59.2	8 051	2 344	7.4
March	169 453	108 553	64.1	53 662	39 464	7 445	3 365	97 206	59.4	7 982	2 276	7.4
April	169 641	108 925	64.2	53 886	39 628	7 542	3 529	97 527	59.6	7 869	2 231	7.2
May	169 829	109 222	64.3	53 879	39 759	7 410	3 369	97 679	59.5	8 174	2 221	7.5
June	170 042	108 396	63.7	53 576	39 682	7 040	3 334	96 964	59.0	8 098	2 250	7.5
July	170 246	108 556	63.8	53 814	39 683	7 196	3 296	97 397	59.1	7 863	2 166	7.2
August	170 399	108 725	63.8	53 718	39 723	7 248	3 379	97 310	59.1	8 036	2 241	7.4
September	170 593	108 294	63.5	53 625	39 342	7 097	3 361	96 703	58.7	8 230	2 261	7.6
October	170 809	109 024	63.8	53 482	39 843	7 053	3 412	96 966	58.8	8 646	2 303	7.9
November	170 996	109 236	63.9	53 335	39 908	6 964	3 415	96 792	58.6	9 029	2 345	8.3
December	171 166	108 912	63.6	53 149	39 708	6 788	3 227	96 418	58.2	9 267	2 374	8.5
1982												
January	171 335	109 089	63.7	53 103	39 821	6 768	3 393	96 299	58.2	9 397	2 409	8.6
February	171 489	109 467	63.8	53 172	39 859	6 731	3 375	96 387	58.2	9 705	2 758	8.9
March	171 667	109 567	63.8	53 054	39 936	6 682	3 372	96 300	58.1	9 895	2 965	9.0
April	171 844	109 820	63.9	53 081	39 848	6 647	3 351	96 225	57.9	10 244	3 086	9.3
May	172 026	110 451	64.2	53 234	40 121	6 761	3 434	96 682	58.2	10 335	3 276	9.4
June	172 190	110 081	63.9	52 933	40 219	6 391	3 331	96 212	57.8	10 538	3 451	9.6
July	172 364	110 342	64.0	52 896	40 228	6 369	3 402	96 091	57.7	10 849	3 555	9.8
August	172 511	110 514	64.1	52 797	40 336	6 500	3 408	96 225	57.8	10 881	3 696	9.8
September	172 690	110 721	64.1	52 760	40 275	6 469	3 385	96 119	57.6	11 217	3 889	10.1
October	172 881	110 744	64.1	52 624	40 105	6 486	3 489	95 726	57.4	11 529	4 185	10.4
November	173 058	111 050	64.2	52 537	40 111	6 464	3 510	95 602	57.3	11 938	4 485	10.8
December	173 199	111 083	64.1	52 497	40 164	6 371	3 414	95 618	57.2	12 051	4 662	10.8
1983												
January	173 354	110 695	63.9	52 487	40 268	6 406	3 439	95 722	57.2	11 534	4 668	10.4
February	173 505	110 634	63.8	52 453	40 336	6 300	3 382	95 707	57.1	11 545	4 641	10.4
March	173 656	110 587	63.7	52 615	40 368	6 196	3 360	95 819	57.1	11 408	4 612	10.3
April	173 794	110 828	63.8	52 814	40 542	6 204	3 341	96 219	57.3	11 268	4 370	10.2
May	173 953	110 796	63.7	52 922	40 538	6 182	3 328	96 314	57.3	11 154	4 538	10.1
June	174 125	111 879	64.3	53 515	40 695	6 423	3 462	97 171	57.8	11 246	4 470	10.1
July	174 306	111 756	64.1	53 835	41 041	6 332	3 481	97 727	58.1	10 548	4 329	9.4
August	174 440	112 231	64.3	53 837	41 314	6 457	3 502	98 106	58.2	10 623	4 070	9.5
September	174 602	112 298	64.3	53 983	41 650	6 383	3 347	98 669	58.2	10 282	3 854	9.2
October	174 779	111 926	64.0	54 146	41 597	6 296	3 303	98 736	58.4	9 887	3 648	8.8
November	174 951	112 228	64.1	54 499	41 788	6 442	3 291	99 438	58.7	9 499	3 535	8.5
December	175 121	112 327	64.1	54 662	41 852	6 482	3 332	99 664	58.8	9 331	3 379	8.3

[1]Not seasonally adjusted.

Table 20-3. Summary Labor Force, Employment, and Unemployment—*Continued*

(Thousands of persons, percent, seasonally adjusted, except as noted.)

Year and month	Noninsti-tutional population [1]	Labor force		Employment, thousands of persons					Employ-ment population ratio, percent	Unemployment		
		Thousands of persons	Participa-tion rate (percent)	By age and sex			By industry			Thousands of persons		Rate, percent
				Men, 20 years and over	Women, 20 years and over	Both sexes, 16–19 years	Agricultural	Nonagri-cultural		Total	Unem-ployed 15 weeks and over	
1984												
January	175 533	112 209	63.9	54 975	41 812	6 414	3 293	99 908	58.8	9 008	3 254	8.0
February	175 679	112 615	64.1	55 213	42 196	6 415	3 353	100 471	59.1	8 791	2 991	7.8
March	175 824	112 713	64.1	55 281	42 328	6 358	3 233	100 734	59.1	8 746	2 881	7.8
April	175 969	113 098	64.3	55 373	42 512	6 451	3 291	101 045	59.3	8 762	2 858	7.7
May	176 123	113 649	64.5	55 661	43 071	6 461	3 343	101 850	59.7	8 456	2 884	7.4
June	176 284	113 817	64.6	55 996	42 944	6 651	3 383	102 208	59.9	8 226	2 612	7.2
July	176 440	113 972	64.6	55 921	42 979	6 535	3 344	102 091	59.8	8 537	2 638	7.5
August	176 583	113 682	64.4	55 930	42 885	6 348	3 286	101 877	59.6	8 519	2 604	7.5
September	176 763	113 857	64.4	56 095	42 967	6 428	3 393	102 097	59.7	8 367	2 538	7.3
October	176 956	114 019	64.4	56 183	43 052	6 403	3 194	102 444	59.7	8 381	2 526	7.4
November	177 135	114 170	64.5	56 274	43 244	6 454	3 394	102 578	59.8	8 198	2 438	7.2
December	177 306	114 581	64.6	56 313	43 472	6 438	3 385	102 838	59.9	8 358	2 401	7.3
1985												
January	177 384	114 725	64.7	56 184	43 509	6 529	3 317	102 985	59.9	8 423	2 284	7.3
February	177 516	114 876	64.7	56 216	43 787	6 552	3 317	103 238	60.0	8 321	2 389	7.2
March	177 667	115 328	64.9	56 356	44 035	6 598	3 250	103 739	60.2	8 339	2 394	7.2
April	177 799	115 331	64.9	56 374	44 000	6 562	3 306	103 630	60.1	8 395	2 393	7.3
May	177 944	115 234	64.8	56 531	43 905	6 496	3 280	103 652	60.1	8 302	2 292	7.2
June	178 096	114 965	64.6	56 288	43 958	6 259	3 161	103 344	59.8	8 460	2 310	7.4
July	178 263	115 320	64.7	56 435	43 975	6 397	3 143	103 664	59.9	8 513	2 329	7.4
August	178 405	115 291	64.6	56 655	44 103	6 337	3 121	103 974	60.0	8 196	2 258	7.1
September	178 572	115 905	64.9	56 845	44 395	6 417	3 064	104 593	60.3	8 248	2 242	7.1
October	178 770	116 145	65.0	56 969	44 565	6 313	3 051	104 796	60.3	8 298	2 295	7.1
November	178 940	116 135	64.9	56 972	44 617	6 418	3 062	104 945	60.4	8 128	2 207	7.0
December	179 112	116 354	65.0	56 995	44 889	6 332	3 141	105 075	60.4	8 138	2 208	7.0
1986												
January	179 670	116 682	64.9	57 637	44 944	6 306	3 287	105 600	60.6	7 795	2 089	6.7
February	179 821	116 882	65.0	57 269	44 804	6 407	3 083	105 397	60.3	8 402	2 308	7.2
March	179 985	117 220	65.1	57 353	44 960	6 524	3 200	105 637	60.5	8 383	2 261	7.2
April	180 148	117 316	65.1	57 358	45 081	6 513	3 153	105 799	60.5	8 364	2 162	7.1
May	180 311	117 528	65.2	57 287	45 289	6 513	3 150	105 939	60.5	8 439	2 232	7.2
June	180 503	118 084	65.4	57 471	45 621	6 484	3 193	106 383	60.7	8 508	2 320	7.2
July	180 682	118 129	65.4	57 514	45 837	6 459	3 141	106 669	60.8	8 319	2 269	7.0
August	180 828	118 150	65.3	57 597	45 926	6 492	3 082	106 933	60.8	8 135	2 276	6.9
September	180 997	118 395	65.4	57 630	45 972	6 483	3 171	106 914	60.8	8 310	2 318	7.0
October	181 186	118 516	65.4	57 660	46 046	6 567	3 128	107 145	60.9	8 243	2 188	7.0
November	181 363	118 634	65.4	57 941	46 070	6 464	3 220	107 255	60.9	8 159	2 202	6.9
December	181 547	118 611	65.3	58 185	46 132	6 411	3 148	107 580	61.0	7 883	2 161	6.6
1987												
January	181 827	118 845	65.4	58 264	46 219	6 470	3 143	107 810	61.0	7 892	2 168	6.6
February	181 998	119 122	65.5	58 279	46 444	6 534	3 208	108 049	61.1	7 865	2 117	6.6
March	182 179	119 270	65.5	58 362	46 549	6 497	3 214	108 194	61.2	7 862	2 070	6.6
April	182 344	119 336	65.4	58 503	46 746	6 545	3 246	108 548	61.3	7 542	2 091	6.3
May	182 533	120 008	65.7	58 713	47 052	6 669	3 345	109 089	61.6	7 574	2 104	6.3
June	182 703	119 644	65.5	58 581	47 102	6 563	3 218	109 030	61.4	7 398	2 087	6.2
July	182 885	119 902	65.6	58 740	47 229	6 665	3 235	109 399	61.6	7 268	1 921	6.1
August	183 002	120 318	65.7	58 810	47 322	6 925	3 112	109 945	61.8	7 261	1 878	6.0
September	183 161	120 011	65.5	58 964	47 285	6 660	3 189	109 720	61.6	7 102	1 866	5.9
October	183 311	120 509	65.7	59 073	47 533	6 676	3 219	110 063	61.8	7 227	1 794	6.0
November	183 470	120 540	65.7	59 210	47 622	6 673	3 145	110 360	61.9	7 035	1 797	5.8
December	183 620	120 729	65.7	59 217	47 781	6 795	3 213	110 580	62.0	6 936	1 767	5.7
1988												
January	183 822	120 969	65.8	59 346	47 862	6 808	3 247	110 769	62.0	6 953	1 714	5.7
February	183 969	121 156	65.9	59 535	47 919	6 773	3 201	111 026	62.1	6 929	1 738	5.7
March	184 111	120 913	65.7	59 393	48 090	6 554	3 169	110 868	61.9	6 876	1 744	5.7
April	184 232	121 251	65.8	59 832	48 147	6 671	3 224	111 426	62.2	6 601	1 563	5.4
May	184 374	121 071	65.7	59 644	47 946	6 702	3 121	111 171	62.0	6 779	1 647	5.6
June	184 562	121 473	65.8	59 751	48 146	7 030	3 111	111 816	62.3	6 546	1 531	5.4
July	184 729	121 665	65.9	59 888	48 186	6 986	3 060	112 000	62.3	6 605	1 601	5.4
August	184 830	122 125	66.1	59 877	48 467	6 938	3 119	112 163	62.4	6 843	1 639	5.6
September	184 962	121 960	65.9	59 980	48 511	6 865	3 165	112 191	62.4	6 604	1 569	5.4
October	185 114	122 206	66.0	60 023	48 859	6 756	3 231	112 407	62.5	6 568	1 562	5.4
November	185 244	122 637	66.2	60 042	49 254	6 804	3 241	112 859	62.7	6 537	1 468	5.3
December	185 402	122 622	66.1	60 059	49 257	6 788	3 194	112 910	62.6	6 518	1 490	5.3
1989												
January	185 644	123 390	66.5	60 477	49 529	6 702	3 287	113 421	62.9	6 682	1 480	5.4
February	185 777	123 135	66.3	60 588	49 497	6 691	3 234	113 542	62.9	6 359	1 304	5.2
March	185 897	123 227	66.3	60 795	49 503	6 724	3 198	113 824	62.9	6 205	1 353	5.0
April	186 024	123 565	66.4	60 764	49 565	6 768	3 162	113 935	62.9	6 468	1 397	5.2
May	186 181	123 474	66.3	60 795	49 583	6 721	3 125	113 974	62.9	6 375	1 348	5.2
June	186 329	123 995	66.5	61 054	49 542	6 822	3 068	114 350	63.0	6 577	1 300	5.3
July	186 483	123 967	66.5	60 947	49 693	6 832	3 227	114 245	63.0	6 495	1 435	5.2
August	186 598	124 166	66.5	60 915	49 804	6 936	3 284	114 371	63.1	6 511	1 302	5.2
September	186 726	123 944	66.4	60 668	50 015	6 671	3 219	114 135	62.8	6 590	1 360	5.3
October	186 871	124 211	66.5	60 958	49 871	6 752	3 215	114 366	62.9	6 630	1 392	5.3
November	187 017	124 637	66.6	60 958	50 221	6 733	3 132	114 780	63.0	6 725	1 418	5.4
December	187 165	124 497	66.5	61 068	50 116	6 646	3 188	114 642	63.0	6 667	1 375	5.4

[1] Not seasonally adjusted.

Table 20-3. Summary Labor Force, Employment, and Unemployment—*Continued*

(Thousands of persons, percent, seasonally adjusted, except as noted.)

Year and month	Noninsti- tutional population [1]	Labor force		Employment, thousands of persons					Employ- ment population ratio, percent	Unemployment		
		Thousands of persons	Participa- tion rate (percent)	By age and sex			By industry			Thousands of persons		Rate, percent
				Men, 20 years and over	Women, 20 years and over	Both sexes, 16–19 years	Agricultural	Nonagri- cultural		Total	Unem- ployed 15 weeks and over	
1990												
January	188 413	125 833	66.8	61 742	50 436	6 903	3 210	115 871	63.2	6 752	1 412	5.4
February	188 516	125 710	66.7	61 805	50 438	6 816	3 188	115 871	63.2	6 651	1 350	5.3
March	188 630	125 801	66.7	61 832	50 463	6 908	3 260	115 943	63.2	6 598	1 331	5.2
April	188 778	125 649	66.6	61 579	50 457	6 816	3 231	115 621	63.0	6 797	1 376	5.4
May	188 913	125 893	66.6	61 778	50 646	6 727	3 266	115 885	63.1	6 742	1 415	5.4
June	189 058	125 573	66.4	61 762	50 550	6 671	3 245	115 738	62.9	6 590	1 436	5.2
July	189 188	125 732	66.5	61 683	50 514	6 613	3 192	115 618	62.8	6 922	1 534	5.5
August	189 342	125 990	66.5	61 715	50 635	6 452	3 197	115 605	62.7	7 188	1 607	5.7
September	189 528	125 892	66.4	61 608	50 587	6 329	3 206	115 318	62.5	7 368	1 695	5.9
October	189 710	125 995	66.4	61 606	50 616	6 314	3 270	115 266	62.5	7 459	1 689	5.9
November	189 872	126 070	66.4	61 545	50 541	6 220	3 189	115 117	62.3	7 764	1 831	6.2
December	190 017	126 142	66.4	61 506	50 530	6 205	3 245	114 996	62.2	7 901	1 804	6.3
1991												
January	190 163	125 955	66.2	61 383	50 472	6 085	3 208	114 732	62.0	8 015	1 866	6.4
February	190 271	126 020	66.2	61 117	50 523	6 115	3 270	114 485	61.9	8 265	1 955	6.6
March	190 381	126 238	66.3	61 144	50 422	6 086	3 177	114 475	61.8	8 586	2 137	6.8
April	190 517	126 548	66.4	61 280	50 760	6 069	3 241	114 868	62.0	8 439	2 206	6.7
May	190 650	126 176	66.2	61 052	50 457	5 931	3 275	114 165	61.6	8 736	2 252	6.9
June	190 800	126 331	66.2	61 147	50 585	5 907	3 300	114 339	61.7	8 692	2 533	6.9
July	190 946	126 154	66.1	61 179	50 636	5 753	3 319	114 249	61.6	8 586	2 388	6.8
August	191 116	126 150	66.0	61 122	50 601	5 761	3 313	114 171	61.5	8 666	2 460	6.9
September	191 302	126 650	66.2	61 279	50 864	5 785	3 319	114 609	61.6	8 722	2 497	6.9
October	191 497	126 642	66.1	61 174	50 811	5 815	3 289	114 511	61.5	8 842	2 638	7.0
November	191 657	126 701	66.1	61 201	50 759	5 810	3 296	114 474	61.4	8 931	2 718	7.0
December	191 798	126 664	66.0	61 074	50 728	5 664	3 146	114 320	61.2	9 198	2 892	7.3
1992												
January	191 953	127 261	66.3	61 116	51 095	5 767	3 155	114 823	61.5	9 283	3 060	7.3
February	192 067	127 207	66.2	61 062	51 033	5 658	3 239	114 514	61.3	9 454	3 182	7.4
March	192 204	127 604	66.4	61 363	51 204	5 577	3 236	114 908	61.5	9 460	3 196	7.4
April	192 354	127 841	66.5	61 468	51 323	5 635	3 245	115 181	61.6	9 415	3 130	7.4
May	192 503	128 119	66.6	61 513	51 245	5 617	3 213	115 162	61.5	9 744	3 444	7.6
June	192 663	128 459	66.7	61 537	51 383	5 499	3 297	115 122	61.5	10 040	3 758	7.8
July	192 826	128 563	66.7	61 641	51 458	5 614	3 285	115 428	61.6	9 850	3 614	7.7
August	193 018	128 613	66.6	61 681	51 386	5 759	3 279	115 547	61.6	9 787	3 579	7.6
September	193 229	128 501	66.5	61 663	51 359	5 698	3 274	115 446	61.4	9 781	3 504	7.6
October	193 442	128 026	66.2	61 550	51 373	5 705	3 254	115 374	61.3	9 398	3 505	7.3
November	193 621	128 441	66.3	61 644	51 535	5 697	3 207	115 669	61.4	9 565	3 397	7.4
December	193 784	128 554	66.3	61 721	51 524	5 752	3 259	115 738	61.4	9 557	3 651	7.4
1993												
January	193 962	128 400	66.2	61 895	51 505	5 675	3 222	115 853	61.4	9 325	3 346	7.3
February	194 108	128 458	66.2	61 963	51 573	5 739	3 125	116 150	61.4	9 183	3 190	7.1
March	194 248	128 598	66.2	62 007	51 808	5 727	3 119	116 423	61.5	9 056	3 115	7.0
April	194 398	128 584	66.1	62 032	51 732	5 710	3 074	116 400	61.5	9 110	3 014	7.1
May	194 549	129 264	66.4	62 309	51 996	5 810	3 100	117 015	61.7	9 149	3 101	7.1
June	194 719	129 411	66.5	62 409	52 183	5 698	3 108	117 182	61.8	9 121	3 141	7.0
July	194 882	129 397	66.4	62 497	52 088	5 882	3 126	117 341	61.8	8 930	3 046	6.9
August	195 063	129 619	66.4	62 634	52 294	5 928	3 026	117 830	62.0	8 763	3 026	6.8
September	195 259	129 268	66.2	62 437	52 241	5 876	3 174	117 380	61.7	8 714	3 042	6.7
October	195 444	129 573	66.3	62 614	52 379	5 830	3 084	117 739	61.8	8 750	3 029	6.8
November	195 625	129 711	66.3	62 732	52 531	5 906	3 157	118 012	61.9	8 542	2 986	6.6
December	195 794	129 941	66.4	62 760	52 813	5 891	3 116	118 348	62.0	8 477	2 968	6.5
1994												
January	195 953	130 596	66.6	62 798	53 052	6 116	3 302	118 664	62.2	8 630	3 060	6.6
February	196 090	130 669	66.6	62 708	53 266	6 112	3 339	118 747	62.3	8 583	3 118	6.6
March	196 213	130 400	66.5	62 780	53 099	6 051	3 354	118 576	62.1	8 470	3 055	6.5
April	196 363	130 621	66.5	62 906	53 274	6 110	3 428	118 862	62.3	8 331	2 921	6.4
May	196 510	130 779	66.6	63 116	53 624	6 124	3 409	119 455	62.5	7 915	2 836	6.1
June	196 693	130 561	66.4	63 041	53 393	6 200	3 299	119 335	62.3	7 927	2 735	6.1
July	196 859	130 652	66.4	63 034	53 531	6 141	3 333	119 373	62.3	7 946	2 822	6.1
August	197 043	131 275	66.6	63 294	53 744	6 304	3 451	119 891	62.6	7 933	2 750	6.0
September	197 248	131 421	66.6	63 631	53 991	6 065	3 430	120 257	62.7	7 734	2 746	5.9
October	197 430	131 744	66.7	63 818	54 071	6 223	3 490	120 622	62.9	7 632	2 955	5.8
November	197 607	131 891	66.7	64 080	54 168	6 268	3 574	120 942	63.0	7 375	2 666	5.6
December	197 765	131 951	66.7	64 359	54 054	6 308	3 577	121 144	63.1	7 230	2 488	5.5
1995												
January	197 753	132 038	66.8	64 185	54 087	6 391	3 519	121 144	63.0	7 375	2 396	5.6
February	197 886	132 115	66.8	64 378	54 226	6 324	3 620	121 308	63.1	7 187	2 345	5.4
March	198 007	132 108	66.7	64 321	54 141	6 493	3 634	121 321	63.1	7 153	2 287	5.4
April	198 148	132 590	66.9	64 165	54 366	6 414	3 566	121 379	63.1	7 645	2 473	5.8
May	198 286	131 851	66.5	63 829	54 272	6 320	3 349	121 072	62.7	7 430	2 577	5.6
June	198 453	131 949	66.5	63 992	54 020	6 510	3 461	121 061	62.7	7 427	2 266	5.6
July	198 615	132 343	66.6	63 962	54 476	6 378	3 379	121 437	62.8	7 527	2 311	5.7
August	198 801	132 336	66.6	63 875	54 434	6 543	3 374	121 478	62.8	7 484	2 391	5.7
September	199 005	132 611	66.6	64 179	54 507	6 447	3 285	121 848	62.9	7 478	2 306	5.6
October	199 192	132 716	66.6	64 272	54 692	6 424	3 438	121 950	62.9	7 328	2 272	5.5
November	199 355	132 614	66.5	63 931	54 850	6 407	3 338	121 850	62.8	7 426	2 339	5.6
December	199 508	132 511	66.4	64 041	54 674	6 373	3 352	121 736	62.7	7 423	2 331	5.6

[1]Not seasonally adjusted.

Table 20-3. Summary Labor Force, Employment, and Unemployment—*Continued*

(Thousands of persons, percent, seasonally adjusted, except as noted.)

Year and month	Noninsti-tutional population [1]	Labor force — Thousands of persons	Labor force — Participa-tion rate (percent)	Men, 20 years and over	Women, 20 years and over	Both sexes, 16–19 years	Agricultural	Nonagri-cultural	Employ-ment population ratio, percent	Total	Unem-ployed 15 weeks and over	Rate, percent
1996												
January	199 634	132 616	66.4	64 180	54 580	6 365	3 483	121 642	62.7	7 491	2 371	5.6
February	199 773	132 952	66.6	64 398	54 844	6 397	3 547	122 092	62.9	7 313	2 307	5.5
March	199 921	133 180	66.6	64 506	54 994	6 362	3 489	122 373	63.0	7 318	2 454	5.5
April	200 101	133 409	66.7	64 481	55 067	6 446	3 406	122 588	63.0	7 415	2 455	5.6
May	200 278	133 667	66.7	64 683	55 034	6 527	3 473	122 771	63.0	7 423	2 403	5.6
June	200 459	133 697	66.7	64 940	55 177	6 485	3 424	123 178	63.2	7 095	2 355	5.3
July	200 641	134 284	66.9	65 068	55 362	6 517	3 433	123 514	63.3	7 337	2 297	5.5
August	200 847	134 054	66.7	65 216	55 525	6 431	3 395	123 777	63.3	6 882	2 267	5.1
September	201 061	134 515	66.9	65 169	55 669	6 698	3 448	124 088	63.4	6 979	2 220	5.2
October	201 273	134 921	67.0	65 460	55 750	6 680	3 463	124 427	63.5	7 031	2 268	5.2
November	201 463	135 007	67.0	65 320	55 896	6 555	3 356	124 415	63.4	7 236	2 159	5.4
December	201 636	135 113	67.0	65 435	55 849	6 576	3 445	124 415	63.4	7 253	2 124	5.4
1997												
January	202 285	135 456	67.0	65 679	56 024	6 595	3 449	124 849	63.4	7 158	2 162	5.3
February	202 389	135 400	66.9	65 758	55 955	6 585	3 353	124 945	63.4	7 102	2 140	5.2
March	202 513	135 891	67.1	65 974	56 270	6 647	3 419	125 472	63.6	7 000	2 110	5.2
April	202 674	136 016	67.1	66 092	56 347	6 704	3 462	125 681	63.7	6 873	2 176	5.1
May	202 832	136 119	67.1	66 328	56 446	6 690	3 437	126 027	63.8	6 655	2 121	4.9
June	203 000	136 211	67.1	66 308	56 573	6 531	3 409	126 003	63.7	6 799	2 085	5.0
July	203 166	136 477	67.2	66 422	56 785	6 615	3 422	126 400	63.9	6 655	2 119	4.9
August	203 364	136 618	67.2	66 508	56 852	6 650	3 359	126 651	63.9	6 608	2 004	4.8
September	203 570	136 675	67.1	66 483	56 931	6 605	3 392	126 627	63.9	6 656	2 074	4.9
October	203 767	136 633	67.1	66 511	56 982	6 686	3 312	126 867	63.9	6 454	1 950	4.7
November	203 941	136 961	67.2	66 765	57 039	6 849	3 386	127 267	64.1	6 308	1 817	4.6
December	204 098	137 155	67.2	66 643	57 219	6 817	3 405	127 274	64.0	6 476	1 901	4.7
1998												
January	204 238	137 095	67.1	66 750	56 941	7 035	3 299	127 389	64.0	6 368	1 833	4.6
February	204 400	137 112	67.1	66 856	56 992	6 959	3 284	127 522	64.0	6 306	1 809	4.6
March	204 547	137 236	67.1	66 721	57 080	7 014	3 146	127 650	64.0	6 422	1 772	4.7
April	204 731	137 150	67.0	67 151	57 074	6 985	3 334	127 852	64.1	5 941	1 476	4.3
May	204 899	137 372	67.0	67 164	57 155	7 007	3 360	127 959	64.1	6 047	1 490	4.4
June	205 085	137 455	67.0	67 054	57 156	7 033	3 380	127 874	64.0	6 212	1 613	4.5
July	205 270	137 588	67.0	67 119	57 192	7 018	3 455	127 913	64.0	6 259	1 577	4.5
August	205 479	137 570	67.0	66 985	57 332	7 074	3 509	127 970	63.9	6 179	1 626	4.5
September	205 699	138 286	67.2	67 254	57 520	7 212	3 500	128 399	64.2	6 300	1 688	4.6
October	205 919	138 279	67.2	67 433	57 529	7 036	3 593	128 389	64.1	6 280	1 582	4.5
November	206 104	138 381	67.1	67 591	57 638	7 052	3 375	128 897	64.2	6 100	1 590	4.4
December	206 270	138 634	67.2	67 548	57 840	7 214	3 246	129 320	64.3	6 032	1 559	4.4
1999												
January	206 719	139 045	67.3	67 688	58 306	7 092	3 233	129 802	64.4	5 967	1 486	4.3
February	206 873	138 916	67.2	67 514	58 123	7 229	3 246	129 647	64.2	6 056	1 552	4.4
March	207 036	138 716	67.0	67 673	58 126	7 155	3 238	129 656	64.2	5 773	1 468	4.2
April	207 236	138 977	67.1	67 564	58 262	7 153	3 336	129 615	64.2	6 008	1 475	4.3
May	207 427	139 077	67.0	67 515	58 428	7 331	3 335	129 937	64.2	5 812	1 500	4.2
June	207 632	139 383	67.1	67 699	58 693	7 037	3 386	129 982	64.3	5 958	1 636	4.3
July	207 828	139 465	67.1	67 726	58 521	7 193	3 346	130 146	64.2	6 033	1 509	4.3
August	208 038	139 377	67.0	67 723	58 677	7 117	3 234	130 366	64.2	5 837	1 452	4.2
September	208 265	139 636	67.0	67 901	58 717	7 090	3 173	130 434	64.2	5 926	1 472	4.2
October	208 483	139 768	67.0	67 826	58 902	7 232	3 229	130 758	64.3	5 794	1 437	4.1
November	208 666	140 025	67.1	68 083	58 986	7 198	3 343	130 989	64.4	5 738	1 382	4.1
December	208 832	140 174	67.1	68 212	59 029	7 251	3 260	131 257	64.4	5 677	1 372	4.0

[1] Not seasonally adjusted.

Table 20-3. Summary Labor Force, Employment, and Unemployment—*Continued*

(Thousands of persons, percent, seasonally adjusted, except as noted.)

Year and month	Noninstitutional population [1]	Labor force Thousands of persons	Labor force Participation rate (percent)	Men, 20 years and over	Women, 20 years and over	Both sexes, 16–19 years	Agricultural	Nonagricultural	Employment population ratio, percent	Total	Unemployed 15 weeks and over	Rate, percent
2000												
January	211 410	142 283	67.3	69 435	59 878	7 301	2 611	133 912	64.6	5 674	1 375	4.0
February	211 576	142 423	67.3	69 546	59 887	7 209	2 728	133 901	64.6	5 786	1 304	4.1
March	211 772	142 391	67.2	69 502	59 975	7 222	2 578	134 004	64.5	5 713	1 305	4.0
April	212 018	142 795	67.4	69 548	60 374	7 402	2 505	134 778	64.8	5 483	1 253	3.8
May	212 242	142 349	67.1	69 358	59 954	7 276	2 481	134 118	64.3	5 773	1 319	4.1
June	212 466	142 624	67.1	69 616	60 069	7 277	2 446	134 515	64.5	5 671	1 251	4.0
July	212 677	142 252	66.9	69 509	60 003	6 996	2 401	134 217	64.2	5 763	1 344	4.1
August	212 916	142 508	66.9	69 785	59 700	7 126	2 437	134 309	64.2	5 864	1 388	4.1
September	213 163	142 554	66.9	69 719	60 075	7 110	2 388	134 483	64.2	5 645	1 304	4.0
October	213 405	142 636	66.8	69 745	60 224	7 098	2 316	134 820	64.2	5 559	1 344	3.9
November	213 540	142 965	66.9	69 894	60 233	7 129	2 342	134 942	64.3	5 676	1 327	4.0
December	213 736	143 279	67.0	69 931	60 495	7 182	2 389	135 205	64.4	5 659	1 328	3.9
2001												
January	213 888	143 797	67.2	70 088	60 642	7 114	2 349	135 407	64.4	5 951	1 367	4.1
February	214 110	143 638	67.1	70 007	60 606	7 037	2 359	135 249	64.3	5 990	1 494	4.2
March	214 305	143 871	67.1	69 906	60 900	6 990	2 340	135 320	64.3	6 108	1 505	4.2
April	214 525	143 624	66.9	69 957	60 551	6 861	2 335	134 989	64.0	6 271	1 483	4.4
May	214 732	143 280	66.7	69 815	60 528	6 708	2 357	134 699	63.8	6 244	1 489	4.4
June	214 950	143 395	66.7	69 676	60 403	6 803	2 092	134 725	63.7	6 526	1 542	4.6
July	215 180	143 616	66.7	69 793	60 456	6 788	2 297	134 859	63.7	6 610	1 651	4.6
August	215 420	143 331	66.5	69 548	60 297	6 371	2 314	133 967	63.3	7 075	1 852	4.9
September	215 665	144 042	66.8	69 943	60 256	6 651	2 327	134 565	63.5	7 183	1 973	5.0
October	215 903	144 128	66.8	69 598	60 155	6 611	2 315	134 141	63.2	7 758	2 109	5.4
November	216 117	144 296	66.8	69 437	60 146	6 595	2 228	134 011	63.0	8 078	2 360	5.6
December	216 315	144 379	66.7	69 543	60 093	6 411	2 289	133 770	62.9	8 312	2 455	5.8
2002												
January	216 506	143 826	66.4	69 351	60 058	6 374	2 360	133 359	62.7	8 035	2 561	5.6
February	216 663	144 510	66.7	69 591	60 441	6 417	2 373	134 046	63.0	8 060	2 609	5.6
March	216 823	144 367	66.6	69 517	60 161	6 503	2 348	133 710	62.8	8 224	2 685	5.7
April	217 006	144 763	66.7	69 627	60 237	6 353	2 375	133 782	62.8	8 567	2 810	5.9
May	217 198	144 911	66.7	69 918	60 262	6 325	2 270	134 236	62.8	8 424	2 911	5.8
June	217 407	144 852	66.6	69 739	60 320	6 339	2 191	134 087	62.7	8 469	3 045	5.8
July	217 630	144 786	66.5	69 792	60 262	6 325	2 341	134 094	62.6	8 443	2 955	5.8
August	217 866	145 123	66.6	69 895	60 581	6 235	2 146	134 639	62.8	8 366	2 891	5.8
September	218 107	145 634	66.8	70 213	60 675	6 414	2 288	135 127	63.0	8 321	3 019	5.7
October	218 340	145 393	66.6	69 921	60 668	6 397	2 421	134 666	62.7	8 405	3 099	5.8
November	218 548	145 180	66.4	69 617	60 697	6 179	2 296	134 269	62.5	8 637	3 143	5.9
December	218 741	145 150	66.4	69 600	60 676	6 141	2 345	134 098	62.4	8 711	3 296	6.0

[1] Not seasonally adjusted.

Table 20-4. Nonfarm Payroll Employment, Hours, and Earnings

(Wage and salary workers on nonfarm payrolls, seasonally adjusted.)

Year and month	All wage and salary workers, (thousands)					Production or nonsupervisory workers on private payrolls							
	Total	Private				Number (thousands)		Average hours per week		Average hourly earnings, dollars		Average weekly earnings, dollars	
		Total	Goods–producing		Service–providing	Total private	Manufacturing	Total private	Manufacturing	Total private	Manufacturing	Total private	Manufacturing
			Total	Manufacturing									
1946													
January	39 839	34 054	15 031	12 719	24 808	...	10 990	...	40.9	...	0.86	...	35.17
February	39 250	33 472	14 308	11 922	24 942	...	10 292	...	40.4	...	0.85	...	34.34
March	40 192	34 434	15 017	12 545	25 175	...	10 989	...	40.6	...	0.89	...	36.13
April	40 908	35 147	15 439	13 200	25 469	...	11 616	...	40.4	...	0.92	...	37.17
May	41 348	35 616	15 875	13 389	25 473	...	11 758	...	39.8	...	0.93	...	37.01
June	41 732	36 052	16 206	13 598	25 526	...	11 905	...	40.0	...	0.94	...	37.60
July	42 153	36 471	16 461	13 771	25 692	...	12 065	...	40.2	...	0.96	...	38.59
August	42 642	36 961	16 728	13 981	25 914	...	12 241	...	40.6	...	0.98	...	39.79
September	42 908	37 239	16 912	14 135	25 996	...	12 311	...	40.4	...	0.99	...	40.00
October	43 094	37 430	17 002	14 182	26 092	...	12 302	...	40.4	...	1.00	...	40.40
November	43 396	37 757	17 157	14 310	26 239	...	12 421	...	40.3	...	1.02	...	41.11
December	43 379	37 751	17 164	14 301	26 215	...	12 419	...	40.5	...	1.02	...	41.31
1947													
January	43 545	37 926	17 213	14 328	26 332	...	12 445	...	40.5	...	1.03	...	41.72
February	43 563	37 957	17 200	14 278	26 363	...	12 487	...	40.4	...	1.04	...	42.02
March	43 605	38 017	17 196	14 259	26 409	...	12 518	...	40.3	...	1.06	...	42.72
April	43 491	37 933	17 178	14 240	26 313	...	12 531	...	40.5	...	1.06	...	42.93
May	43 637	38 086	17 176	14 189	26 461	...	12 449	...	40.4	...	1.08	...	43.63
June	43 808	38 284	17 253	14 200	26 555	...	12 389	...	40.4	...	1.10	...	44.44
July	43 742	38 218	17 106	14 076	26 636	...	12 265	...	40.4	...	1.10	...	44.44
August	43 958	38 439	17 280	14 200	26 678	...	12 370	...	40.0	...	1.11	...	44.40
September	44 201	38 662	17 398	14 315	26 803	...	12 430	...	40.5	...	1.11	...	44.96
October	44 415	38 849	17 499	14 393	26 916	...	12 464	...	40.5	...	1.13	...	45.77
November	44 486	38 901	17 517	14 414	26 969	...	12 494	...	40.5	...	1.14	...	46.17
December	44 578	38 973	17 563	14 428	27 015	...	12 526	...	40.8	...	1.16	...	47.33
1948													
January	44 686	39 062	17 625	14 438	27 061	...	12 520	...	40.5	...	1.16	...	46.98
February	44 537	38 922	17 447	14 339	27 090	...	12 437	...	40.2	...	1.16	...	46.63
March	44 680	39 057	17 544	14 364	27 136	...	12 489	...	40.4	...	1.16	...	46.86
April	44 369	38 726	17 302	14 183	27 067	...	12 304	...	40.1	...	1.17	...	46.92
May	44 795	39 114	17 508	14 235	27 287	...	12 344	...	40.2	...	1.18	...	47.44
June	45 032	39 296	17 633	14 318	27 399	...	12 402	...	40.3	...	1.19	...	47.96
July	45 160	39 386	17 649	14 359	27 511	...	12 417	...	40.2	...	1.21	...	48.64
August	45 175	39 384	17 655	14 353	27 520	...	12 397	...	40.2	...	1.23	...	49.45
September	45 294	39 489	17 741	14 441	27 553	...	12 450	...	40.1	...	1.24	...	49.72
October	45 250	39 421	17 683	14 390	27 567	...	12 364	...	39.8	...	1.25	...	49.75
November	45 194	39 325	17 599	14 292	27 595	...	12 302	...	39.8	...	1.26	...	50.15
December	45 028	39 140	17 417	14 086	27 611	...	12 127	...	39.6	...	1.26	...	49.90
1949													
January	44 675	38 781	17 170	13 867	27 505	...	11 905	...	39.4	...	1.26	...	49.64
February	44 500	38 607	17 019	13 734	27 481	...	11 792	...	39.4	...	1.26	...	49.64
March	44 238	38 323	16 848	13 581	27 390	...	11 654	...	39.1	...	1.26	...	49.27
April	44 230	38 282	16 685	13 439	27 545	...	11 517	...	38.8	...	1.25	...	48.50
May	43 982	38 020	16 492	13 269	27 490	...	11 352	...	38.9	...	1.25	...	48.63
June	43 739	37 783	16 351	13 178	27 388	...	11 266	...	39.0	...	1.26	...	49.14
July	43 530	37 568	16 222	13 067	27 308	...	11 168	...	39.2	...	1.26	...	49.39
August	43 621	37 636	16 327	13 158	27 294	...	11 251	...	39.2	...	1.25	...	49.00
September	43 784	37 794	16 403	13 225	27 381	...	11 284	...	39.4	...	1.25	...	49.25
October	42 950	36 980	15 739	12 891	27 211	...	10 940	...	39.6	...	1.24	...	49.10
November	43 244	37 294	16 040	12 882	27 204	...	10 964	...	39.1	...	1.24	...	48.48
December	43 516	37 564	16 217	13 062	27 299	...	11 173	...	39.4	...	1.25	...	49.25
1950													
January	43 530	37 596	16 255	13 161	27 275	...	11 258	...	39.6	...	1.27	...	50.29
February	43 298	37 372	16 035	13 169	27 263	...	11 262	...	39.7	...	1.26	...	50.02
March	43 952	37 874	16 482	13 290	27 470	...	11 362	...	39.7	...	1.28	...	50.82
April	44 376	38 282	16 718	13 471	27 658	...	11 528	...	40.3	...	1.29	...	51.99
May	44 717	38 674	17 080	13 780	27 637	...	11 855	...	40.3	...	1.30	...	52.39
June	45 084	39 062	17 288	13 923	27 796	...	11 979	...	40.6	...	1.30	...	52.78
July	45 453	39 363	17 464	14 072	27 989	...	12 107	...	40.9	...	1.31	...	53.58
August	46 187	40 000	17 917	14 461	28 270	...	12 476	...	41.3	...	1.33	...	54.93
September	46 442	40 214	18 040	14 561	28 402	...	12 519	...	40.8	...	1.33	...	54.26
October	46 712	40 463	18 249	14 737	28 463	...	12 659	...	41.1	...	1.36	...	55.90
November	46 778	40 516	18 288	14 762	28 490	...	12 682	...	41.0	...	1.37	...	56.17
December	46 855	40 541	18 283	14 782	28 572	...	12 710	...	40.9	...	1.39	...	56.85
1951													
January	47 289	40 937	18 518	14 950	28 771	...	12 816	...	41.0	...	1.40	...	57.40
February	47 577	41 195	18 666	15 076	28 911	...	12 929	...	40.9	...	1.41	...	57.67
March	47 871	41 461	18 754	15 125	29 117	...	12 936	...	41.0	...	1.42	...	58.22
April	47 856	41 405	18 810	15 166	29 046	...	12 960	...	41.0	...	1.43	...	58.63
May	47 952	41 535	18 829	15 164	29 123	...	12 941	...	41.0	...	1.44	...	59.04
June	48 067	41 568	18 826	15 176	29 241	...	12 934	...	40.9	...	1.45	...	59.31
July	48 061	41 523	18 747	15 110	29 314	...	12 848	...	40.6	...	1.45	...	58.87
August	48 008	41 489	18 709	15 061	29 299	...	12 772	...	40.4	...	1.46	...	58.98
September	47 955	41 403	18 622	14 996	29 333	...	12 659	...	40.4	...	1.46	...	58.98
October	48 009	41 432	18 630	14 973	29 379	...	12 615	...	40.3	...	1.47	...	59.24
November	48 149	41 523	18 617	14 999	29 532	...	12 628	...	40.4	...	1.48	...	59.79
December	48 308	41 620	18 698	15 045	29 610	...	12 667	...	40.7	...	1.49	...	60.64

. . . = Not available.

Table 20-4. Nonfarm Payroll Employment, Hours, and Earnings—*Continued*

(Wage and salary workers on nonfarm payrolls, seasonally adjusted.)

Year and month	All wage and salary workers, (thousands)					Production or nonsupervisory workers on private payrolls							
	Total	Private				Number (thousands)		Average hours per week		Average hourly earnings, dollars		Average weekly earnings, dollars	
		Total	Goods–producing		Service–providing	Total private	Manufac-turing	Total private	Manufac-turing	Total private	Manufac-turing	Total private	Manufac-turing
			Total	Manufac-turing									
1952													
January	48 299	41 710	18 719	15 067	29 580	...	12 675	...	40.8	...	1.49	...	60.79
February	48 522	41 872	18 813	15 105	29 709	...	12 689	...	40.8	...	1.49	...	60.79
March	48 504	41 842	18 775	15 127	29 729	...	12 695	...	40.6	...	1.51	...	61.31
April	48 616	41 954	18 806	15 162	29 810	...	12 713	...	40.3	...	1.51	...	60.85
May	48 645	41 951	18 784	15 143	29 861	...	12 676	...	40.5	...	1.51	...	61.16
June	48 286	41 574	18 419	14 828	29 867	...	12 353	...	40.6	...	1.51	...	61.31
July	48 144	41 407	18 268	14 707	29 876	...	12 233	...	40.2	...	1.50	...	60.30
August	48 922	42 204	18 928	15 279	29 994	...	12 764	...	40.7	...	1.53	...	62.27
September	49 319	42 585	19 206	15 553	30 113	...	13 007	...	41.1	...	1.55	...	63.71
October	49 598	42 782	19 312	15 690	30 286	...	13 122	...	41.2	...	1.56	...	64.27
November	49 816	43 015	19 473	15 843	30 343	...	13 262	...	41.2	...	1.58	...	65.10
December	50 164	43 229	19 610	15 973	30 554	...	13 375	...	41.2	...	1.58	...	65.10
1953													
January	50 145	43 351	19 721	16 067	30 424	...	13 447	...	41.1	...	1.59	...	65.35
February	50 339	43 542	19 841	16 158	30 498	...	13 529	...	41.0	...	1.61	...	66.01
March	50 474	43 690	19 909	16 270	30 565	...	13 620	...	41.2	...	1.61	...	66.33
April	50 432	43 662	19 908	16 293	30 524	...	13 629	...	40.9	...	1.62	...	66.26
May	50 491	43 774	19 930	16 341	30 561	...	13 645	...	41.0	...	1.62	...	66.42
June	50 522	43 788	19 909	16 343	30 613	...	13 636	...	40.9	...	1.63	...	66.67
July	50 536	43 813	19 910	16 353	30 626	...	13 653	...	40.7	...	1.64	...	66.75
August	50 487	43 733	19 834	16 278	30 653	...	13 564	...	40.7	...	1.64	...	66.75
September	50 365	43 616	19 726	16 151	30 639	...	13 419	...	40.1	...	1.65	...	66.17
October	50 242	43 478	19 578	15 981	30 664	...	13 244	...	40.1	...	1.65	...	66.17
November	49 906	43 157	19 315	15 728	30 591	...	12 990	...	40.0	...	1.65	...	66.00
December	49 702	42 959	19 173	15 581	30 529	...	12 847	...	39.7	...	1.65	...	65.51
1954													
January	49 467	42 707	18 963	15 440	30 504	...	12 706	...	39.5	...	1.65	...	65.18
February	49 381	42 598	18 880	15 307	30 501	...	12 593	...	39.7	...	1.65	...	65.51
March	49 158	42 362	18 748	15 197	30 410	...	12 493	...	39.6	...	1.65	...	65.34
April	49 177	42 371	18 602	15 065	30 575	...	12 361	...	39.7	...	1.65	...	65.51
May	48 965	42 136	18 476	14 974	30 489	...	12 282	...	39.7	...	1.67	...	66.30
June	48 896	42 050	18 400	14 910	30 496	...	12 220	...	39.7	...	1.67	...	66.30
July	48 834	41 966	18 280	14 799	30 554	...	12 121	...	39.7	...	1.66	...	65.90
August	48 825	41 933	18 251	14 772	30 574	...	12 089	...	39.8	...	1.66	...	66.07
September	48 881	41 987	18 261	14 805	30 620	...	12 104	...	39.9	...	1.66	...	66.23
October	48 944	42 044	18 321	14 841	30 623	...	12 142	...	39.7	...	1.67	...	66.30
November	49 179	42 215	18 438	14 913	30 741	...	12 206	...	40.1	...	1.68	...	67.37
December	49 331	42 374	18 508	14 967	30 823	...	12 254	...	40.1	...	1.68	...	67.37
1955													
January	49 497	42 544	18 609	15 034	30 888	...	12 309	...	40.4	...	1.69	...	68.28
February	49 644	42 721	18 726	15 138	30 918	...	12 408	...	40.6	...	1.70	...	69.02
March	49 963	43 025	18 910	15 258	31 053	...	12 524	...	40.7	...	1.71	...	69.60
April	50 246	43 287	19 067	15 375	31 179	...	12 626	...	40.8	...	1.71	...	69.77
May	50 512	43 521	19 223	15 493	31 289	...	12 731	...	41.1	...	1.73	...	71.10
June	50 790	43 770	19 331	15 585	31 459	...	12 810	...	40.8	...	1.73	...	70.58
July	50 985	43 936	19 376	15 614	31 609	...	12 818	...	40.7	...	1.75	...	71.23
August	51 112	44 089	19 432	15 679	31 680	...	12 866	...	40.7	...	1.76	...	71.63
September	51 262	44 195	19 427	15 668	31 835	...	12 830	...	40.7	...	1.77	...	72.04
October	51 431	44 313	19 482	15 740	31 949	...	12 896	...	41.0	...	1.77	...	72.57
November	51 592	44 509	19 554	15 813	32 038	...	12 967	...	41.1	...	1.78	...	73.16
December	51 805	44 673	19 608	15 859	32 197	...	13 009	...	40.9	...	1.78	...	72.80
1956													
January	51 975	44 808	19 665	15 882	32 310	...	13 011	...	40.8	...	1.78	...	72.62
February	52 167	44 955	19 731	15 889	32 436	...	12 986	...	40.7	...	1.79	...	72.85
March	52 295	45 043	19 691	15 829	32 604	...	12 905	...	40.6	...	1.80	...	73.08
April	52 375	45 099	19 811	15 909	32 564	...	12 970	...	40.5	...	1.82	...	73.71
May	52 506	45 139	19 825	15 893	32 681	...	12 925	...	40.4	...	1.83	...	73.93
June	52 583	45 216	19 905	15 835	32 678	...	12 836	...	40.3	...	1.83	...	73.75
July	51 954	44 549	19 390	15 468	32 564	...	12 435	...	40.3	...	1.82	...	73.35
August	52 632	45 181	19 922	15 893	32 710	...	12 860	...	40.3	...	1.85	...	74.56
September	52 600	45 119	19 860	15 863	32 740	...	12 822	...	40.5	...	1.87	...	75.74
October	52 781	45 262	19 918	15 937	32 863	...	12 908	...	40.6	...	1.88	...	76.33
November	52 822	45 269	19 886	15 916	32 936	...	12 864	...	40.4	...	1.88	...	75.95
December	52 930	45 346	19 926	15 957	33 004	...	12 882	...	40.6	...	1.91	...	77.55
1957													
January	52 888	45 268	19 833	15 970	33 055	...	12 881	...	40.4	...	1.90	...	76.76
February	53 098	45 452	19 933	15 998	33 165	...	12 885	...	40.5	...	1.91	...	77.36
March	53 156	45 484	19 936	15 994	33 220	...	12 855	...	40.4	...	1.92	...	77.57
April	53 238	45 537	19 887	15 970	33 351	...	12 811	...	40.0	...	1.91	...	76.40
May	53 149	45 436	19 834	15 931	33 315	...	12 762	...	40.0	...	1.92	...	76.80
June	53 066	45 364	19 777	15 873	33 289	...	12 697	...	40.0	...	1.92	...	76.80
July	53 122	45 368	19 735	15 854	33 387	...	12 669	...	40.0	...	1.93	...	77.20
August	53 128	45 371	19 728	15 867	33 400	...	12 673	...	40.0	...	1.94	...	77.60
September	52 932	45 183	19 545	15 710	33 387	...	12 528	...	39.7	...	1.95	...	77.42
October	52 765	44 997	19 421	15 599	33 344	...	12 437	...	39.4	...	1.96	...	77.22
November	52 557	44 788	19 260	15 466	33 297	...	12 301	...	39.2	...	1.96	...	76.83
December	52 385	44 539	19 111	15 332	33 274	...	12 170	...	39.1	...	1.95	...	76.25

. . . = Not available.

Table 20-4. Nonfarm Payroll Employment, Hours, and Earnings—*Continued*

(Wage and salary workers on nonfarm payrolls, seasonally adjusted.)

Year and month	All wage and salary workers, (thousands)					Production or nonsupervisory workers on private payrolls							
	Total	Private				Number (thousands)		Average hours per week		Average hourly earnings, dollars		Average weekly earnings, dollars	
		Total	Goods–producing		Service–providing	Total private	Manufac-turing	Total private	Manufac-turing	Total private	Manufac-turing	Total private	Manufac-turing
			Total	Manufac-turing									
1958													
January	52 077	44 256	18 902	15 130	33 175	...	11 969	...	38.9	...	1.95	...	75.86
February	51 576	43 744	18 529	14 908	33 047	...	11 757	...	38.7	...	1.95	...	75.47
March	51 300	43 452	18 335	14 670	32 965	...	11 532	...	38.8	...	1.96	...	76.05
April	51 026	43 158	18 120	14 506	32 906	...	11 373	...	38.9	...	1.96	...	76.24
May	50 913	43 019	18 008	14 414	32 905	...	11 294	...	38.9	...	1.97	...	76.63
June	50 912	42 986	17 984	14 408	32 928	...	11 300	...	39.1	...	1.98	...	77.42
July	51 037	43 065	18 038	14 450	32 999	...	11 349	...	39.3	...	1.98	...	77.81
August	51 233	43 221	18 147	14 524	33 086	...	11 412	...	39.5	...	2.01	...	79.40
September	51 506	43 490	18 331	14 658	33 175	...	11 556	...	39.5	...	2.00	...	79.00
October	51 485	43 454	18 218	14 503	33 267	...	11 394	...	39.6	...	2.00	...	79.20
November	51 943	43 915	18 610	14 827	33 333	...	11 702	...	39.9	...	2.03	...	81.00
December	52 088	43 988	18 592	14 877	33 496	...	11 743	...	39.9	...	2.04	...	81.40
1959													
January	52 481	44 376	18 796	14 998	33 685	...	11 849	...	40.2	...	2.04	...	82.01
February	52 687	44 571	18 890	15 115	33 797	...	11 950	...	40.3	...	2.05	...	82.62
March	53 016	44 884	19 069	15 259	33 947	...	12 078	...	40.4	...	2.07	...	83.63
April	53 320	45 178	19 269	15 385	34 051	...	12 185	...	40.5	...	2.08	...	84.24
May	53 549	45 396	19 378	15 487	34 171	...	12 277	...	40.7	...	2.08	...	84.66
June	53 678	45 535	19 462	15 554	34 216	...	12 330	...	40.6	...	2.09	...	84.85
July	53 803	45 630	19 529	15 623	34 274	...	12 366	...	40.3	...	2.09	...	84.23
August	53 337	45 156	19 049	15 202	34 288	...	11 936	...	40.4	...	2.07	...	83.63
September	53 428	45 189	19 052	15 254	34 376	...	11 984	...	40.4	...	2.08	...	84.03
October	53 359	45 094	18 925	15 158	34 434	...	11 864	...	40.1	...	2.07	...	83.01
November	53 635	45 351	19 108	15 300	34 527	...	11 991	...	39.9	...	2.07	...	82.59
December	54 175	45 807	19 425	15 573	34 750	...	12 254	...	40.3	...	2.11	...	85.03
1960													
January	54 274	45 967	19 491	15 687	34 783	...	12 362	...	40.6	...	2.13	...	86.48
February	54 513	46 187	19 605	15 765	34 908	...	12 434	...	40.3	...	2.14	...	86.24
March	54 458	45 933	19 373	15 707	35 085	...	12 362	...	40.0	...	2.14	...	85.60
April	54 812	46 278	19 446	15 654	35 366	...	12 299	...	40.0	...	2.14	...	85.60
May	54 472	46 040	19 374	15 575	35 098	...	12 218	...	40.1	...	2.14	...	85.81
June	54 347	45 915	19 240	15 466	35 107	...	12 102	...	39.9	...	2.14	...	85.39
July	54 303	45 861	19 170	15 413	35 133	...	12 047	...	39.9	...	2.14	...	85.39
August	54 272	45 800	19 105	15 360	35 167	...	11 986	...	39.7	...	2.15	...	85.36
September	54 228	45 734	19 057	15 330	35 171	...	11 956	...	39.4	...	2.16	...	85.10
October	54 144	45 642	18 952	15 231	35 192	...	11 846	...	39.7	...	2.16	...	85.75
November	53 962	45 446	18 799	15 112	35 163	...	11 726	...	39.3	...	2.15	...	84.50
December	53 743	45 146	18 548	14 947	35 195	...	11 556	...	38.4	...	2.16	...	82.94
1961													
January	53 683	45 119	18 508	14 863	35 175	...	11 473	...	39.3	...	2.16	...	84.89
February	53 556	44 969	18 418	14 801	35 138	...	11 414	...	39.4	...	2.16	...	85.10
March	53 662	45 051	18 438	14 802	35 224	...	11 410	...	39.5	...	2.16	...	85.32
April	53 626	44 997	18 432	14 825	35 194	...	11 444	...	39.5	...	2.18	...	86.11
May	53 783	45 119	18 523	14 932	35 260	...	11 544	...	39.7	...	2.19	...	86.94
June	53 977	45 209	18 618	14 981	35 359	...	11 593	...	40.0	...	2.20	...	88.00
July	54 124	45 400	18 640	15 029	35 484	...	11 639	...	40.0	...	2.21	...	88.40
August	54 299	45 535	18 725	15 093	35 574	...	11 701	...	40.1	...	2.22	...	89.02
September	54 387	45 591	18 730	15 080	35 657	...	11 679	...	39.5	...	2.20	...	86.90
October	54 521	45 716	18 805	15 143	35 716	...	11 731	...	40.3	...	2.23	...	89.87
November	54 743	45 931	18 927	15 259	35 816	...	11 842	...	40.7	...	2.23	...	90.76
December	54 871	46 035	18 981	15 309	35 890	...	11 872	...	40.4	...	2.24	...	90.50
1962													
January	54 891	46 040	18 936	15 322	35 955	...	11 865	...	40.0	...	2.25	...	90.00
February	55 187	46 309	19 109	15 411	36 078	...	11 950	...	40.4	...	2.26	...	91.30
March	55 276	46 375	19 109	15 451	36 167	...	11 970	...	40.6	...	2.26	...	91.76
April	55 601	46 679	19 258	15 524	36 343	...	12 034	...	40.6	...	2.26	...	91.76
May	55 626	46 668	19 253	15 513	36 373	...	12 011	...	40.6	...	2.27	...	92.16
June	55 644	46 644	19 186	15 518	36 458	...	12 006	...	40.5	...	2.26	...	91.53
July	55 746	46 720	19 248	15 522	36 498	...	12 004	...	40.5	...	2.27	...	91.94
August	55 838	46 775	19 251	15 517	36 587	...	11 990	...	40.5	...	2.28	...	92.34
September	55 977	46 888	19 305	15 568	36 672	...	12 033	...	40.5	...	2.28	...	92.34
October	56 041	46 927	19 301	15 569	36 740	...	12 034	...	40.3	...	2.29	...	92.29
November	56 055	46 910	19 260	15 530	36 795	...	11 977	...	40.5	...	2.29	...	92.75
December	56 027	46 901	19 219	15 520	36 808	...	11 961	...	40.3	...	2.29	...	92.29
1963													
January	56 116	46 912	19 257	15 545	36 859	...	11 974	...	40.5	...	2.30	...	93.15
February	56 231	47 000	19 228	15 542	37 003	...	11 965	...	40.5	...	2.31	...	93.56
March	56 322	47 077	19 233	15 564	37 089	...	11 990	...	40.5	...	2.32	...	93.96
April	56 580	47 316	19 343	15 602	37 237	...	12 029	...	40.5	...	2.32	...	93.96
May	56 616	47 328	19 399	15 641	37 217	...	12 066	...	40.5	...	2.33	...	94.37
June	56 658	47 356	19 371	15 624	37 287	...	12 050	...	40.7	...	2.34	...	95.24
July	56 795	47 461	19 423	15 646	37 372	...	12 080	...	40.6	...	2.35	...	95.41
August	56 910	47 542	19 437	15 644	37 473	...	12 060	...	40.6	...	2.34	...	95.00
September	57 078	47 661	19 483	15 674	37 595	...	12 088	...	40.6	...	2.36	...	95.82
October	57 284	47 805	19 517	15 714	37 767	...	12 131	...	40.7	...	2.36	...	96.05
November	57 255	47 771	19 456	15 675	37 799	...	12 072	...	40.7	...	2.37	...	96.46
December	57 360	47 863	19 493	15 712	37 867	...	12 108	...	40.6	...	2.38	...	96.63

. . . = Not available.

Table 20-4. Nonfarm Payroll Employment, Hours, and Earnings—Continued

(Wage and salary workers on nonfarm payrolls, seasonally adjusted.)

Year and month	All wage and salary workers, (thousands)					Production or nonsupervisory workers on private payrolls							
		Private				Number (thousands)		Average hours per week		Average hourly earnings, dollars		Average weekly earnings, dollars	
	Total	Total	Goods–producing		Service–providing	Total private	Manufac-turing	Total private	Manufac-turing	Total private	Manufac-turing	Total private	Manufac-turing
			Total	Manufac-turing									
1964													
January	57 487	47 925	19 406	15 715	38 081	39 914	12 132	38.2	40.1	2.50	2.38	95.50	95.44
February	57 752	48 171	19 570	15 742	38 182	40 123	12 165	38.5	40.7	2.50	2.38	96.25	96.87
March	57 898	48 287	19 587	15 770	38 311	40 171	12 190	38.5	40.6	2.50	2.38	96.25	96.63
April	57 923	48 279	19 593	15 785	38 330	40 208	12 211	38.6	40.7	2.52	2.40	97.27	97.68
May	58 089	48 419	19 630	15 812	38 459	40 332	12 231	38.6	40.8	2.52	2.40	97.27	97.92
June	58 221	48 552	19 682	15 839	38 539	40 448	12 255	38.6	40.8	2.53	2.41	97.66	98.33
July	58 412	48 735	19 740	15 887	38 672	40 624	12 309	38.5	40.8	2.53	2.41	97.41	98.33
August	58 620	48 888	19 810	15 948	38 810	40 770	12 354	38.5	40.9	2.55	2.42	98.18	98.98
September	58 903	49 117	19 943	16 073	38 960	41 026	12 479	38.5	40.9	2.55	2.44	98.18	99.80
October	58 794	48 949	19 723	15 821	39 071	40 827	12 224	38.5	40.7	2.55	2.40	98.18	97.68
November	59 217	49 338	20 026	16 096	39 191	41 157	12 477	38.6	41.0	2.56	2.42	98.82	99.22
December	59 420	49 523	20 111	16 176	39 309	41 308	12 551	38.7	41.2	2.58	2.44	99.85	100.53
1965													
January	59 583	49 646	20 173	16 245	39 410	41 453	12 603	38.7	41.3	2.58	2.45	99.85	101.19
February	59 800	49 826	20 216	16 291	39 584	41 583	12 644	38.7	41.3	2.59	2.46	100.23	101.60
March	60 003	49 993	20 292	16 353	39 711	41 675	12 701	38.7	41.3	2.60	2.47	100.62	102.01
April	60 258	50 207	20 317	16 418	39 941	41 886	12 752	38.7	41.2	2.60	2.47	100.62	101.76
May	60 492	50 398	20 444	16 477	40 048	42 044	12 792	38.8	41.3	2.62	2.49	101.66	102.84
June	60 690	50 562	20 522	16 554	40 168	42 183	12 854	38.6	41.2	2.62	2.49	101.13	102.59
July	60 963	50 762	20 611	16 669	40 352	42 364	12 962	38.6	41.2	2.63	2.49	101.52	102.59
August	61 228	50 957	20 726	16 732	40 502	42 537	12 994	38.5	41.1	2.64	2.50	101.64	102.75
September	61 490	51 152	20 808	16 802	40 682	42 726	13 046	38.6	41.1	2.65	2.51	102.29	103.16
October	61 718	51 340	20 895	16 864	40 823	42 870	13 100	38.5	41.2	2.66	2.52	102.41	103.82
November	61 997	51 561	21 021	16 962	40 976	43 045	13 175	38.6	41.3	2.67	2.52	103.06	104.08
December	62 321	51 822	21 151	17 051	41 170	43 270	13 243	38.6	41.3	2.68	2.53	103.45	104.49
1966													
January	62 528	51 987	21 214	17 143	41 314	43 401	13 301	38.6	41.5	2.68	2.54	103.45	105.41
February	62 796	52 185	21 315	17 288	41 481	43 552	13 426	38.7	41.7	2.69	2.56	104.10	106.75
March	63 191	52 499	21 515	17 400	41 676	43 801	13 508	38.7	41.6	2.70	2.56	104.49	106.50
April	63 436	52 677	21 568	17 517	41 868	43 959	13 598	38.7	41.8	2.71	2.58	104.88	107.84
May	63 711	52 890	21 675	17 625	42 036	44 138	13 678	38.5	41.5	2.72	2.58	104.72	107.07
June	64 110	53 208	21 846	17 733	42 264	44 390	13 753	38.5	41.4	2.72	2.58	104.72	106.81
July	64 301	53 327	21 872	17 760	42 429	44 484	13 758	38.4	41.2	2.74	2.60	105.22	107.12
August	64 507	53 501	21 972	17 882	42 535	44 596	13 843	38.4	41.4	2.75	2.61	105.60	108.05
September	64 645	53 582	21 948	17 886	42 697	44 659	13 841	38.3	41.2	2.76	2.63	105.71	108.36
October	64 854	53 727	21 991	17 956	42 863	44 789	13 906	38.4	41.3	2.77	2.64	106.37	109.03
November	65 019	53 816	21 988	17 981	43 031	44 834	13 918	38.3	41.2	2.78	2.65	106.47	109.18
December	65 199	53 943	22 008	17 998	43 191	44 916	13 906	38.2	40.9	2.78	2.64	106.20	107.98
1967													
January	65 407	54 092	22 057	18 033	43 350	45 050	13 925	38.3	41.1	2.79	2.65	106.86	108.92
February	65 427	54 074	21 987	17 978	43 440	44 967	13 853	37.9	40.4	2.81	2.67	106.50	107.87
March	65 530	54 133	21 919	17 940	43 611	44 991	13 797	37.9	40.5	2.81	2.67	106.50	108.14
April	65 467	54 032	21 842	17 878	43 625	44 871	13 712	37.8	40.4	2.82	2.68	106.60	108.27
May	65 618	54 144	21 779	17 832	43 839	44 961	13 664	37.8	40.4	2.83	2.69	106.97	108.68
June	65 750	54 216	21 761	17 812	43 989	45 004	13 632	37.8	40.4	2.84	2.69	107.35	108.68
July	65 887	54 343	21 772	17 784	44 115	45 105	13 602	37.8	40.5	2.86	2.71	108.11	109.76
August	66 142	54 552	21 887	17 905	44 255	45 267	13 681	37.8	40.6	2.87	2.73	108.49	110.84
September	66 163	54 540	21 775	17 794	44 388	45 236	13 559	37.8	40.6	2.88	2.73	108.86	110.84
October	66 225	54 583	21 779	17 800	44 446	45 278	13 587	37.8	40.6	2.89	2.74	109.24	111.24
November	66 703	55 008	21 996	17 985	44 707	45 701	13 777	37.9	40.6	2.91	2.75	110.29	111.65
December	66 900	55 165	22 037	18 025	44 863	45 800	13 782	37.7	40.7	2.92	2.77	110.08	112.74
1968													
January	66 805	55 011	21 917	18 040	44 888	45 655	13 798	37.6	40.4	2.94	2.81	110.54	113.52
February	67 214	55 395	22 117	18 054	45 097	45 980	13 793	37.8	40.8	2.95	2.82	111.51	115.06
March	67 296	55 454	22 119	18 067	45 177	46 041	13 803	37.7	40.8	2.97	2.84	111.97	115.87
April	67 555	55 677	22 207	18 131	45 348	46 239	13 858	37.6	40.3	2.98	2.85	112.05	114.86
May	67 652	55 747	22 255	18 190	45 397	46 267	13 900	37.7	40.9	3.00	2.87	113.10	117.38
June	67 904	55 917	22 264	18 228	45 640	46 402	13 921	37.8	40.9	3.01	2.88	113.78	117.79
July	68 126	56 108	22 329	18 265	45 797	46 562	13 953	37.7	40.8	3.03	2.89	114.23	117.91
August	68 328	56 286	22 350	18 254	45 978	46 669	13 903	37.7	40.7	3.03	2.89	114.23	117.62
September	68 487	56 420	22 390	18 252	46 097	46 792	13 914	37.7	40.9	3.06	2.92	115.36	119.43
October	68 720	56 619	22 419	18 293	46 301	46 989	13 974	37.7	41.0	3.07	2.94	115.74	120.54
November	68 985	56 878	22 512	18 346	46 473	47 244	14 028	37.5	40.9	3.09	2.96	115.88	121.06
December	69 245	57 100	22 617	18 410	46 628	47 384	14 044	37.5	40.7	3.11	2.97	116.63	120.88
1969													
January	69 438	57 229	22 644	18 432	46 794	47 528	14 086	37.7	40.8	3.12	2.99	117.62	121.99
February	69 698	57 474	22 755	18 502	46 943	47 697	14 134	37.5	40.4	3.14	3.00	117.75	121.20
March	69 906	57 677	22 813	18 558	47 093	47 852	14 169	37.6	40.8	3.15	3.01	118.44	122.81
April	70 072	57 827	22 815	18 554	47 257	47 959	14 144	37.7	41.0	3.17	3.03	119.51	124.23
May	70 328	58 044	22 899	18 608	47 429	48 112	14 161	37.6	40.7	3.19	3.04	119.94	123.73
June	70 636	58 277	22 981	18 640	47 655	48 330	14 206	37.5	40.7	3.20	3.05	120.00	124.14
July	70 730	58 390	22 990	18 642	47 740	48 434	14 194	37.5	40.6	3.22	3.08	120.75	125.05
August	71 005	58 632	23 111	18 767	47 894	48 616	14 287	37.5	40.6	3.24	3.10	121.50	125.86
September	70 918	58 539	22 988	18 620	47 930	48 524	14 159	37.5	40.6	3.26	3.12	122.25	126.67
October	71 119	58 689	22 976	18 613	48 143	48 669	14 174	37.4	40.5	3.28	3.13	122.67	126.77
November	71 088	58 640	22 840	18 467	48 248	48 589	14 035	37.5	40.5	3.29	3.14	123.38	127.17
December	71 240	58 763	22 884	18 485	48 356	48 638	14 013	37.5	40.6	3.30	3.15	123.75	127.89

Table 20-4. Nonfarm Payroll Employment, Hours, and Earnings—*Continued*

(Wage and salary workers on nonfarm payrolls, seasonally adjusted.)

Year and month	All wage and salary workers, (thousands)					Production or nonsupervisory workers on private payrolls							
	Total	Private				Number (thousands)		Average hours per week		Average hourly earnings, dollars		Average weekly earnings, dollars	
		Total	Goods–producing		Service–providing	Total private	Manufac-turing	Total private	Manufac-turing	Total private	Manufac-turing	Total private	Manufac-turing
			Total	Manufac-turing									
1970													
January	71 176	58 680	22 726	18 424	48 450	48 564	13 964	37.3	40.4	3.31	3.16	123.46	127.66
February	71 302	58 784	22 747	18 361	48 555	48 600	13 897	37.3	40.2	3.33	3.17	124.21	127.43
March	71 453	58 850	22 738	18 360	48 715	48 690	13 917	37.2	40.1	3.35	3.19	124.62	127.92
April	71 348	58 643	22 552	18 207	48 796	48 479	13 785	37.0	39.8	3.36	3.19	124.32	126.96
May	71 122	58 454	22 336	18 029	48 786	48 287	13 616	37.0	39.8	3.38	3.22	125.06	128.16
June	71 028	58 361	22 241	17 930	48 787	48 226	13 554	36.9	39.8	3.39	3.24	125.09	128.95
July	71 055	58 358	22 195	17 877	48 860	48 242	13 527	37.0	40.0	3.41	3.25	126.17	130.00
August	70 932	58 221	22 105	17 779	48 827	48 089	13 449	37.0	39.8	3.43	3.26	126.91	129.75
September	70 949	58 208	21 988	17 692	48 961	48 101	13 401	36.8	39.6	3.45	3.29	126.96	130.28
October	70 519	57 726	21 477	17 173	49 042	47 619	12 905	36.8	39.5	3.46	3.26	127.33	128.77
November	70 409	57 579	21 345	17 024	49 064	47 466	12 781	36.7	39.5	3.47	3.26	127.35	128.77
December	70 790	57 945	21 673	17 309	49 117	47 778	13 062	36.8	39.5	3.50	3.32	128.80	131.14
1971													
January	70 866	57 988	21 594	17 280	49 272	47 859	13 069	36.8	39.9	3.52	3.36	129.54	134.06
February	70 805	57 928	21 514	17 216	49 291	47 779	13 033	36.7	39.7	3.54	3.39	129.92	134.58
March	70 859	57 951	21 491	17 154	49 368	47 819	12 984	36.7	39.8	3.56	3.39	130.65	134.92
April	71 037	58 092	21 552	17 149	49 485	47 966	12 993	36.8	39.9	3.57	3.41	131.38	136.06
May	71 247	58 277	21 645	17 225	49 602	48 153	13 081	36.7	40.0	3.60	3.43	132.12	137.20
June	71 253	58 245	21 568	17 139	49 685	48 109	13 012	36.8	39.9	3.62	3.45	133.22	137.66
July	71 316	58 305	21 564	17 126	49 752	48 167	13 001	36.7	40.0	3.63	3.46	133.22	138.40
August	71 368	58 327	21 570	17 115	49 798	48 164	12 993	36.7	39.8	3.66	3.48	134.32	138.50
September	71 620	58 552	21 650	17 154	49 970	48 362	13 038	36.7	39.7	3.67	3.48	134.69	138.16
October	71 642	58 527	21 604	17 126	50 038	48 305	13 027	36.8	39.9	3.68	3.50	135.42	139.65
November	71 844	58 696	21 684	17 166	50 160	48 442	13 064	36.9	40.0	3.69	3.49	136.16	139.60
December	72 108	58 918	21 741	17 202	50 367	48 613	13 078	36.9	40.2	3.73	3.55	137.64	142.71
1972													
January	72 445	59 179	21 865	17 283	50 580	49 035	13 173	36.9	40.2	3.80	3.57	140.22	143.51
February	72 652	59 354	21 915	17 361	50 737	49 143	13 235	36.9	40.4	3.82	3.61	140.96	145.84
March	72 945	59 616	22 036	17 447	50 909	49 437	13 316	36.9	40.4	3.84	3.63	141.70	146.65
April	73 163	59 805	22 099	17 508	51 064	49 561	13 373	36.9	40.5	3.86	3.65	142.43	147.83
May	73 467	60 051	22 222	17 602	51 245	49 745	13 451	36.8	40.5	3.87	3.67	142.42	148.64
June	73 760	60 355	22 282	17 641	51 478	49 997	13 475	36.9	40.6	3.88	3.68	143.17	149.41
July	73 709	60 227	22 162	17 556	51 547	49 842	13 387	36.8	40.5	3.90	3.69	143.52	149.45
August	74 137	60 607	22 400	17 741	51 737	50 156	13 562	36.8	40.6	3.92	3.73	144.26	151.44
September	74 268	60 693	22 456	17 774	51 812	50 224	13 572	36.9	40.6	3.94	3.75	145.39	152.25
October	74 672	61 066	22 613	17 893	52 059	50 552	13 681	37.0	40.7	3.97	3.78	146.89	153.85
November	74 965	61 322	22 688	18 005	52 277	50 790	13 783	36.9	40.7	3.98	3.79	146.86	154.25
December	75 270	61 586	22 772	18 158	52 498	51 054	13 902	36.8	40.6	4.01	3.83	147.57	155.50
1973													
January	75 620	61 930	22 955	18 276	52 665	51 349	14 006	36.8	40.4	4.03	3.86	148.30	155.94
February	76 017	62 306	23 160	18 410	52 857	51 686	14 127	36.9	40.9	4.04	3.87	149.08	158.28
March	76 286	62 541	23 262	18 493	53 024	51 901	14 181	37.0	40.9	4.06	3.88	150.22	158.69
April	76 456	62 679	23 316	18 530	53 140	51 982	14 192	36.9	40.8	4.08	3.91	150.55	159.53
May	76 646	62 829	23 382	18 564	53 264	52 082	14 217	36.9	40.7	4.10	3.93	151.29	159.95
June	76 886	63 014	23 485	18 606	53 401	52 234	14 253	36.9	40.7	4.12	3.95	152.03	160.77
July	76 911	63 046	23 522	18 598	53 389	52 238	14 232	36.9	40.7	4.15	3.98	153.14	161.99
August	77 166	63 262	23 559	18 629	53 607	52 393	14 251	36.9	40.6	4.16	4.00	153.50	162.40
September	77 281	63 389	23 548	18 609	53 733	52 410	14 213	36.8	40.7	4.19	4.03	154.19	164.02
October	77 605	63 628	23 641	18 702	53 964	52 655	14 289	36.7	40.6	4.21	4.05	154.51	164.43
November	77 909	63 874	23 710	18 773	54 190	52 847	14 342	36.9	40.6	4.23	4.07	156.09	165.24
December	78 035	63 965	23 779	18 820	54 256	52 954	14 386	36.7	40.6	4.25	4.09	155.98	166.05
1974													
January	78 104	64 014	23 709	18 788	54 395	52 896	14 340	36.6	40.5	4.26	4.10	155.92	166.05
February	78 253	64 118	23 718	18 727	54 535	52 971	14 269	36.6	40.4	4.29	4.13	157.01	166.85
March	78 295	64 143	23 687	18 700	54 608	52 951	14 223	36.6	40.4	4.31	4.15	157.75	167.66
April	78 384	64 193	23 670	18 702	54 714	53 003	14 225	36.4	39.5	4.34	4.16	157.98	164.32
May	78 547	64 326	23 635	18 688	54 912	53 095	14 199	36.5	40.3	4.39	4.25	160.24	171.28
June	78 602	64 363	23 591	18 690	55 011	53 107	14 197	36.5	40.2	4.43	4.30	161.70	172.86
July	78 634	64 346	23 462	18 656	55 172	53 044	14 152	36.5	40.1	4.45	4.33	162.43	173.63
August	78 619	64 291	23 396	18 570	55 223	53 025	14 089	36.5	40.2	4.49	4.38	163.89	176.08
September	78 614	64 192	23 274	18 492	55 340	52 915	14 025	36.4	40.0	4.53	4.42	164.89	176.80
October	78 627	64 143	23 118	18 364	55 509	52 836	13 884	36.3	40.0	4.56	4.48	165.53	179.20
November	78 259	63 727	22 773	18 077	55 486	52 413	13 607	36.1	39.5	4.57	4.49	164.98	177.36
December	77 657	63 098	22 303	17 693	55 354	51 856	13 259	36.1	39.3	4.60	4.52	166.06	177.64
1975													
January	77 297	62 673	21 974	17 344	55 323	51 439	12 933	36.1	39.2	4.61	4.54	166.42	177.97
February	76 919	62 172	21 512	17 004	55 407	50 934	12 622	35.9	38.9	4.63	4.58	166.22	178.16
March	76 649	61 895	21 274	16 853	55 375	50 666	12 483	35.7	38.8	4.66	4.63	166.36	179.64
April	76 463	61 668	21 109	16 759	55 354	50 439	12 407	35.8	39.0	4.66	4.63	166.83	180.57
May	76 623	61 796	21 097	16 746	55 526	50 558	12 406	35.9	39.0	4.68	4.65	168.01	181.35
June	76 519	61 735	21 018	16 690	55 501	50 537	12 371	35.9	39.2	4.72	4.68	169.45	183.46
July	76 768	61 907	20 981	16 678	55 787	50 726	12 374	35.9	39.4	4.73	4.71	169.81	185.57
August	77 154	62 284	21 176	16 824	55 978	51 070	12 538	36.1	39.7	4.77	4.75	172.20	188.58
September	77 232	62 408	21 284	16 904	55 948	51 183	12 617	36.1	39.8	4.79	4.78	172.92	190.24
October	77 535	62 635	21 384	16 984	56 151	51 376	12 687	36.1	39.9	4.81	4.80	173.64	191.52
November	77 679	62 776	21 442	17 025	56 237	51 458	12 700	36.1	39.9	4.85	4.83	175.09	192.72
December	78 017	63 071	21 602	17 140	56 415	51 759	12 811	36.2	40.2	4.87	4.86	176.29	195.37

Table 20-4. Nonfarm Payroll Employment, Hours, and Earnings—*Continued*

(Wage and salary workers on nonfarm payrolls, seasonally adjusted.)

Year and month	All wage and salary workers, (thousands)					Production or nonsupervisory workers on private payrolls							
	Total	Private				Number (thousands)		Average hours per week		Average hourly earnings, dollars		Average weekly earnings, dollars	
		Total	Goods–producing		Service–providing	Total private	Manufac-turing	Total private	Manufac-turing	Total private	Manufac-turing	Total private	Manufac-turing
			Total	Manufac-turing									
1976													
January	78 506	63 537	21 799	17 287	56 707	52 182	12 945	36.3	40.3	4.89	4.90	177.51	197.47
February	78 817	63 836	21 893	17 384	56 924	52 430	13 030	36.3	40.4	4.93	4.94	178.96	199.58
March	79 049	64 062	21 980	17 470	57 069	52 615	13 092	36.0	40.2	4.95	4.98	178.20	200.20
April	79 293	64 308	22 050	17 541	57 243	52 810	13 160	36.0	39.6	4.97	4.98	178.92	197.21
May	79 311	64 340	21 988	17 513	57 323	52 802	13 130	36.1	40.3	5.01	5.04	180.86	203.11
June	79 376	64 413	21 982	17 521	57 394	52 830	13 121	36.1	40.2	5.03	5.07	181.58	203.81
July	79 546	64 553	21 988	17 524	57 558	52 973	13 124	36.1	40.3	5.06	5.11	182.67	205.93
August	79 704	64 697	22 038	17 596	57 666	53 072	13 195	36.0	40.2	5.11	5.16	183.96	207.43
September	79 892	64 921	22 142	17 665	57 750	53 268	13 253	36.0	40.2	5.14	5.20	185.04	209.04
October	79 905	64 877	22 037	17 548	57 868	53 165	13 109	35.9	40.0	5.16	5.19	185.24	207.60
November	80 237	65 164	22 207	17 682	58 030	53 362	13 199	35.9	40.1	5.20	5.25	186.68	210.53
December	80 448	65 373	22 261	17 719	58 187	53 543	13 230	35.9	39.9	5.22	5.29	187.40	211.07
1977													
January	80 692	65 636	22 320	17 803	58 372	53 756	13 305	35.6	39.4	5.25	5.35	186.90	210.79
February	80 987	65 931	22 478	17 843	58 509	54 016	13 331	36.0	40.2	5.29	5.36	190.44	215.47
March	81 391	66 341	22 672	17 941	58 719	54 390	13 424	35.9	40.3	5.32	5.40	190.99	217.62
April	81 730	66 655	22 807	18 024	58 923	54 670	13 490	36.0	40.4	5.36	5.45	192.96	220.18
May	82 089	66 957	22 919	18 107	59 170	54 940	13 567	36.0	40.5	5.39	5.49	194.04	222.35
June	82 488	67 281	23 046	18 192	59 442	55 195	13 622	36.0	40.5	5.42	5.54	195.12	224.37
July	82 836	67 537	23 106	18 259	59 730	55 395	13 670	35.9	40.4	5.45	5.58	195.66	225.43
August	83 074	67 746	23 124	18 276	59 950	55 543	13 679	35.9	40.4	5.47	5.61	196.37	226.64
September	83 532	68 129	23 244	18 334	60 288	55 859	13 714	35.9	40.4	5.50	5.65	197.45	228.26
October	83 794	68 331	23 279	18 356	60 515	56 004	13 722	36.0	40.6	5.55	5.69	199.80	231.01
November	84 173	68 658	23 371	18 419	60 802	56 281	13 771	35.9	40.5	5.58	5.72	200.32	231.66
December	84 408	68 870	23 371	18 531	61 037	56 466	13 861	35.8	40.4	5.60	5.75	200.48	232.30
1978													
January	84 595	68 984	23 374	18 593	61 221	56 547	13 917	35.3	39.5	5.65	5.83	199.45	230.29
February	84 948	69 277	23 453	18 639	61 495	56 768	13 950	35.6	39.9	5.68	5.86	202.21	233.81
March	85 461	69 730	23 649	18 699	61 812	57 176	13 992	35.8	40.5	5.72	5.88	204.78	238.14
April	86 163	70 366	24 008	18 772	62 155	57 709	14 037	35.8	40.4	5.78	5.93	206.92	239.57
May	86 509	70 675	24 082	18 848	62 427	57 941	14 096	35.8	40.4	5.81	5.96	208.00	240.78
June	86 951	71 099	24 238	18 919	62 713	58 263	14 129	35.9	40.6	5.86	6.01	210.37	244.01
July	87 205	71 304	24 300	18 951	62 905	58 422	14 152	35.9	40.6	5.89	6.06	211.45	246.04
August	87 481	71 590	24 374	19 006	63 107	58 626	14 187	35.8	40.5	5.92	6.09	211.94	246.65
September	87 618	71 799	24 444	19 068	63 174	58 819	14 241	35.8	40.5	5.96	6.15	213.37	249.08
October	87 954	72 096	24 548	19 142	63 406	59 017	14 291	35.8	40.5	6.02	6.20	215.52	251.10
November	88 391	72 497	24 678	19 257	63 713	59 377	14 388	35.7	40.6	6.05	6.26	215.99	254.16
December	88 674	72 763	24 758	19 334	63 916	59 599	14 459	35.7	40.5	6.09	6.31	217.41	255.56
1979													
January	88 811	72 874	24 740	19 388	64 071	59 659	14 497	35.6	40.4	6.13	6.36	218.23	256.94
February	89 054	73 107	24 784	19 409	64 270	59 840	14 501	35.7	40.5	6.17	6.40	220.27	259.20
March	89 480	73 524	24 998	19 453	64 482	60 216	14 526	35.8	40.6	6.21	6.45	222.32	261.87
April	89 418	73 441	24 958	19 450	64 460	60 067	14 515	35.3	39.3	6.21	6.43	219.21	252.70
May	89 790	73 800	25 071	19 509	64 719	60 368	14 551	35.6	40.2	6.27	6.52	223.21	262.10
June	90 108	74 063	25 161	19 553	64 947	60 583	14 566	35.6	40.2	6.31	6.56	224.64	263.71
July	90 214	74 064	25 163	19 531	65 051	60 558	14 536	35.6	40.2	6.35	6.59	226.06	264.92
August	90 296	74 067	25 059	19 406	65 237	60 516	14 397	35.6	40.1	6.39	6.63	227.48	265.86
September	90 323	74 195	25 088	19 442	65 235	60 629	14 440	35.6	40.1	6.44	6.67	229.26	267.47
October	90 480	74 344	25 038	19 390	65 442	60 746	14 384	35.6	40.2	6.46	6.71	229.98	269.74
November	90 574	74 401	24 947	19 299	65 627	60 778	14 295	35.6	40.1	6.50	6.74	231.40	270.27
December	90 669	74 489	24 970	19 301	65 699	60 860	14 300	35.5	40.1	6.56	6.80	232.88	272.68
1980													
January	90 800	74 599	24 949	19 282	65 851	60 896	14 241	35.4	40.0	6.56	6.82	232.22	272.80
February	90 879	74 653	24 874	19 219	66 005	60 964	14 170	35.4	40.1	6.62	6.88	234.35	275.89
March	90 991	74 695	24 818	19 217	66 173	60 987	14 165	35.3	39.9	6.69	6.95	236.16	277.31
April	90 846	74 263	24 507	18 973	66 339	60 540	13 914	35.2	39.8	6.71	6.97	236.19	277.41
May	90 415	73 961	24 234	18 726	66 181	60 194	13 632	35.1	39.3	6.75	7.02	236.93	275.89
June	90 095	73 654	23 968	18 490	66 127	59 892	13 405	35.0	39.2	6.81	7.10	238.35	278.32
July	89 832	73 414	23 698	18 276	66 134	59 693	13 227	34.9	39.1	6.85	7.16	239.07	279.96
August	90 092	73 682	23 860	18 414	66 232	59 908	13 349	35.1	39.5	6.90	7.24	242.19	285.98
September	90 205	73 875	23 931	18 445	66 274	60 075	13 396	35.1	39.6	6.94	7.30	243.59	289.08
October	90 485	74 099	24 012	18 506	66 473	60 239	13 437	35.2	39.8	7.01	7.38	246.75	293.72
November	90 741	74 350	24 123	18 601	66 618	60 449	13 528	35.3	39.9	7.08	7.47	249.92	298.05
December	90 936	74 563	24 182	18 640	66 754	60 606	13 550	35.3	40.1	7.12	7.52	251.34	301.55
1981													
January	91 031	74 671	24 152	18 639	66 879	60 710	13 545	35.4	40.1	7.18	7.58	254.17	303.96
February	91 098	74 752	24 118	18 613	66 980	60 736	13 518	35.2	39.8	7.22	7.62	254.14	303.28
March	91 202	74 910	24 203	18 647	66 999	60 875	13 550	35.3	40.0	7.28	7.68	256.98	307.20
April	91 276	75 016	24 151	18 711	67 125	60 973	13 594	35.3	40.1	7.32	7.76	258.40	311.18
May	91 286	75 088	24 148	18 766	67 138	60 973	13 633	35.3	40.2	7.36	7.81	259.81	313.96
June	91 482	75 323	24 290	18 789	67 192	61 134	13 632	35.2	40.0	7.41	7.85	260.83	314.00
July	91 594	75 419	24 302	18 785	67 292	61 222	13 629	35.2	39.9	7.45	7.89	262.24	314.81
August	91 558	75 448	24 258	18 748	67 300	61 216	13 573	35.2	40.0	7.52	7.97	264.70	318.80
September	91 471	75 440	24 210	18 712	67 261	61 235	13 565	35.0	39.6	7.56	8.03	264.60	317.99
October	91 371	75 302	24 051	18 566	67 320	61 066	13 399	35.1	39.6	7.58	8.06	266.06	319.18
November	91 162	75 084	23 875	18 409	67 287	60 817	13 235	35.1	39.4	7.63	8.08	267.81	318.35
December	90 884	74 811	23 656	18 223	67 228	60 511	13 033	34.9	39.2	7.63	8.09	266.29	317.13

Table 20-4. Nonfarm Payroll Employment, Hours, and Earnings—*Continued*

(Wage and salary workers on nonfarm payrolls, seasonally adjusted.)

Year and month	All wage and salary workers, (thousands)					Production or nonsupervisory workers on private payrolls								
		Private				Number (thousands)		Average hours per week		Average hourly earnings, dollars		Average weekly earnings, dollars	
	Total	Total	Goods–producing		Service– providing	Total private	Manufac- turing	Total private	Manufac- turing	Total private	Manufac- turing	Total private	Manufac- turing
			Total	Manufac- turing									
1982													
January	90 557	74 516	23 362	18 047	67 195	60 206	12 874	34.1	37.3	7.71	8.26	262.91	308.10
February	90 551	74 540	23 361	17 981	67 190	60 277	12 831	35.1	39.6	7.72	8.21	270.97	325.12
March	90 422	74 398	23 214	17 857	67 208	60 140	12 727	34.9	39.1	7.75	8.24	270.48	322.18
April	90 141	74 131	22 996	17 683	67 145	59 867	12 566	34.8	39.1	7.76	8.28	270.05	323.75
May	90 096	74 093	22 884	17 588	67 212	59 840	12 506	34.8	39.1	7.82	8.33	272.14	325.70
June	89 853	73 837	22 643	17 430	67 210	59 589	12 365	34.8	39.2	7.84	8.37	272.83	328.10
July	89 510	73 620	22 434	17 278	67 076	59 411	12 261	34.8	39.2	7.88	8.40	274.22	329.28
August	89 352	73 422	22 268	17 160	67 084	59 203	12 153	34.7	39.0	7.93	8.43	275.17	328.77
September	89 171	73 248	22 146	17 074	67 025	59 069	12 104	34.8	39.0	7.93	8.45	275.96	329.55
October	88 894	72 938	21 879	16 853	67 015	58 750	11 880	34.6	38.9	7.95	8.44	275.07	328.32
November	88 770	72 793	21 736	16 722	67 034	58 613	11 766	34.6	39.0	7.97	8.46	275.76	329.94
December	88 756	72 775	21 688	16 690	67 068	58 585	11 746	34.7	39.0	8.01	8.49	277.95	331.11
1983													
January	88 981	72 958	21 757	16 705	67 224	58 813	11 783	34.8	39.3	8.05	8.52	280.14	334.84
February	88 903	72 899	21 676	16 706	67 227	58 792	11 794	34.5	39.3	8.09	8.59	279.11	337.59
March	89 076	73 071	21 649	16 711	67 427	58 958	11 817	34.7	39.6	8.09	8.59	280.72	340.16
April	89 352	73 362	21 729	16 794	67 623	59 201	11 894	34.8	39.7	8.12	8.61	282.58	341.82
May	89 629	73 624	21 829	16 885	67 800	59 444	11 987	34.9	40.0	8.16	8.64	284.78	345.60
June	90 007	73 987	21 949	16 960	68 058	59 806	12 054	34.9	40.1	8.18	8.66	285.48	347.27
July	90 425	74 414	22 103	17 059	68 322	60 189	12 155	34.9	40.3	8.22	8.71	286.88	351.01
August	90 117	74 101	22 207	17 118	67 910	59 820	12 200	34.9	40.3	8.19	8.71	285.83	351.01
September	91 231	75 189	22 381	17 255	68 850	60 849	12 318	35.0	40.6	8.25	8.76	288.75	355.66
October	91 502	75 516	22 546	17 367	68 956	61 095	12 408	35.2	40.6	8.30	8.80	292.16	357.28
November	91 854	75 857	22 698	17 479	69 156	61 378	12 503	35.1	40.6	8.31	8.84	291.68	358.90
December	92 210	76 202	22 803	17 551	69 407	61 664	12 553	35.1	40.5	8.32	8.87	292.03	359.24
1984													
January	92 657	76 647	22 942	17 630	69 715	61 906	12 617	35.1	40.6	8.37	8.91	293.79	361.75
February	93 136	77 111	23 146	17 728	69 990	62 329	12 703	35.3	41.1	8.36	8.92	295.11	366.61
March	93 411	77 381	23 209	17 806	70 202	62 516	12 768	35.1	40.7	8.40	8.96	294.84	364.67
April	93 774	77 699	23 305	17 872	70 469	62 801	12 814	35.2	40.8	8.44	8.98	297.09	366.38
May	94 082	77 979	23 389	17 916	70 693	63 012	12 840	35.1	40.7	8.43	8.99	295.89	365.89
June	94 461	78 334	23 497	17 967	70 964	63 296	12 871	35.1	40.6	8.47	9.03	297.30	366.62
July	94 773	78 601	23 571	18 013	71 202	63 517	12 901	35.1	40.6	8.51	9.05	298.70	367.43
August	95 014	78 790	23 608	18 034	71 406	63 654	12 906	35.0	40.5	8.51	9.09	297.85	368.15
September	95 325	79 070	23 617	18 019	71 708	63 874	12 880	35.1	40.5	8.55	9.12	300.11	369.36
October	95 611	79 337	23 626	18 024	71 985	64 083	12 868	34.9	40.5	8.54	9.15	298.05	370.58
November	95 960	79 649	23 639	18 016	72 321	64 325	12 846	35.0	40.4	8.56	9.19	299.60	371.28
December	96 087	79 805	23 673	18 023	72 414	64 441	12 848	35.1	40.5	8.60	9.22	301.86	373.41
1985													
January	96 353	80 017	23 672	18 009	72 681	64 657	12 833	34.9	40.3	8.60	9.27	300.14	373.58
February	96 477	80 128	23 621	17 966	72 856	64 758	12 784	34.8	40.1	8.63	9.29	300.32	372.53
March	96 823	80 428	23 661	17 939	73 162	65 007	12 758	34.9	40.4	8.66	9.32	302.23	376.53
April	97 018	80 588	23 644	17 886	73 374	65 113	12 701	34.9	40.5	8.68	9.35	302.93	378.68
May	97 292	80 818	23 632	17 855	73 660	65 307	12 673	34.9	40.4	8.69	9.37	303.28	378.55
June	97 437	80 939	23 592	17 819	73 845	65 382	12 635	34.9	40.5	8.73	9.39	304.68	380.30
July	97 626	81 006	23 549	17 776	74 077	65 432	12 596	34.8	40.4	8.73	9.42	303.80	380.57
August	97 819	81 200	23 546	17 756	74 273	65 615	12 593	34.8	40.6	8.76	9.43	304.85	382.86
September	98 023	81 385	23 528	17 718	74 495	65 750	12 556	34.8	40.6	8.79	9.44	305.89	383.26
October	98 210	81 556	23 529	17 708	74 681	65 917	12 556	34.8	40.7	8.78	9.46	305.54	385.02
November	98 419	81 745	23 520	17 697	74 899	66 069	12 545	34.8	40.7	8.81	9.49	306.59	386.24
December	98 587	81 893	23 518	17 693	75 069	66 197	12 550	34.9	40.9	8.86	9.55	309.21	390.60
1986													
January	98 710	81 995	23 530	17 686	75 180	66 293	12 546	35.0	40.7	8.84	9.53	309.40	387.87
February	98 817	82 058	23 485	17 663	75 332	66 365	12 530	34.8	40.7	8.87	9.56	308.68	389.09
March	98 910	82 155	23 428	17 624	75 482	66 403	12 498	34.8	40.7	8.88	9.58	309.02	389.91
April	99 098	82 333	23 427	17 616	75 671	66 531	12 495	34.7	40.5	8.88	9.56	308.14	387.18
May	99 223	82 433	23 349	17 593	75 874	66 606	12 474	34.8	40.7	8.89	9.59	309.37	390.31
June	99 130	82 351	23 263	17 530	75 867	66 533	12 424	34.7	40.7	8.90	9.58	308.83	389.91
July	99 448	82 669	23 235	17 497	76 213	66 810	12 389	34.6	40.6	8.91	9.60	308.29	389.76
August	99 561	82 761	23 225	17 489	76 336	66 909	12 399	34.7	40.7	8.93	9.61	309.87	391.13
September	99 907	82 997	23 216	17 498	76 691	67 108	12 411	34.6	40.7	8.93	9.60	308.98	390.72
October	100 094	83 125	23 208	17 477	76 886	67 206	12 396	34.6	40.6	8.95	9.62	309.67	390.57
November	100 280	83 275	23 204	17 472	77 076	67 344	12 407	34.7	40.7	8.99	9.64	311.95	392.35
December	100 484	83 463	23 237	17 478	77 247	67 493	12 425	34.6	40.8	9.00	9.66	311.40	394.13
1987													
January	100 655	83 610	23 232	17 465	77 423	67 614	12 405	34.7	40.8	9.01	9.67	312.65	394.54
February	100 887	83 851	23 296	17 499	77 591	67 845	12 438	34.9	41.2	9.04	9.69	315.50	399.23
March	101 136	84 072	23 307	17 507	77 829	67 991	12 446	34.7	41.0	9.06	9.71	314.38	398.11
April	101 474	84 365	23 342	17 525	78 132	68 237	12 465	34.7	40.8	9.07	9.71	314.73	396.17
May	101 701	84 589	23 390	17 542	78 311	68 426	12 481	34.8	41.0	9.10	9.73	316.68	398.93
June	101 872	84 748	23 390	17 537	78 482	68 552	12 482	34.7	40.9	9.10	9.74	315.77	398.37
July	102 218	85 058	23 455	17 593	78 763	68 798	12 521	34.7	41.0	9.11	9.74	316.12	399.34
August	102 388	85 216	23 506	17 630	78 882	68 926	12 560	34.9	40.9	9.17	9.80	320.03	400.82
September	102 617	85 482	23 566	17 691	79 051	69 139	12 614	34.7	40.8	9.18	9.85	318.55	401.88
October	103 109	85 840	23 655	17 729	79 454	69 416	12 637	34.8	41.1	9.21	9.84	320.51	404.42
November	103 340	86 041	23 711	17 775	79 629	69 594	12 678	34.8	41.0	9.26	9.87	322.25	404.67
December	103 634	86 287	23 772	17 809	79 862	69 826	12 707	34.6	41.0	9.27	9.89	320.74	405.49

Table 20-4. Nonfarm Payroll Employment, Hours, and Earnings—*Continued*

(Wage and salary workers on nonfarm payrolls, seasonally adjusted.)

Year and month	All wage and salary workers, (thousands)					Production or nonsupervisory workers on private payrolls							
		Private				Number (thousands)		Average hours per week		Average hourly earnings, dollars		Average weekly earnings, dollars	
	Total	Total	Goods–producing		Service–providing	Total private	Manufac-turing	Total private	Manufac-turing	Total private	Manufac-turing	Total private	Manufac-turing
			Total	Manufac-turing									
1988													
January	103 728	86 363	23 668	17 790	80 060	69 833	12 684	34.6	41.1	9.28	9.91	321.09	407.30
February	104 180	86 791	23 769	17 823	80 411	70 228	12 706	34.7	41.1	9.28	9.92	322.02	407.71
March	104 456	87 009	23 824	17 844	80 632	70 371	12 712	34.5	40.9	9.30	9.94	320.85	406.55
April	104 701	87 249	23 880	17 874	80 821	70 578	12 733	34.6	41.0	9.35	9.99	323.51	409.59
May	104 928	87 447	23 896	17 892	81 032	70 693	12 747	34.6	41.0	9.40	10.02	325.24	410.82
June	105 291	87 776	23 951	17 916	81 340	71 000	12 767	34.6	41.1	9.41	10.04	325.59	412.64
July	105 514	88 020	23 966	17 926	81 548	71 210	12 774	34.7	41.1	9.44	10.05	327.57	413.06
August	105 635	88 091	23 926	17 891	81 709	71 273	12 752	34.5	40.9	9.45	10.07	326.03	411.86
September	105 975	88 341	23 942	17 914	82 033	71 456	12 764	34.5	41.0	9.50	10.12	327.75	414.92
October	106 243	88 573	23 987	17 966	82 256	71 649	12 812	34.7	41.1	9.55	10.16	331.39	417.58
November	106 582	88 836	24 030	18 003	82 552	71 872	12 851	34.5	41.1	9.57	10.19	330.17	418.81
December	106 871	89 135	24 054	18 025	82 817	72 144	12 864	34.6	40.9	9.59	10.20	331.81	417.18
1989													
January	107 133	89 359	24 097	18 057	83 036	72 361	12 882	34.7	41.1	9.64	10.23	334.51	420.45
February	107 391	89 579	24 080	18 055	83 311	72 545	12 880	34.5	41.2	9.67	10.26	333.62	422.71
March	107 583	89 761	24 069	18 060	83 514	72 663	12 878	34.5	41.1	9.69	10.29	334.31	422.92
April	107 756	89 916	24 100	18 055	83 656	72 788	12 867	34.6	41.1	9.74	10.28	337.00	422.51
May	107 874	89 998	24 089	18 040	83 785	72 826	12 852	34.4	41.0	9.72	10.30	334.37	422.30
June	107 991	90 079	24 052	18 013	83 939	72 906	12 822	34.4	40.9	9.76	10.33	335.74	422.50
July	108 030	90 125	24 027	17 980	84 003	72 943	12 790	34.5	40.9	9.81	10.36	338.45	423.72
August	108 077	90 088	24 048	17 964	84 029	72 931	12 790	34.5	40.9	9.82	10.39	338.79	424.95
September	108 326	90 299	24 000	17 922	84 326	73 080	12 745	34.4	40.8	9.86	10.41	339.18	424.73
October	108 437	90 404	23 997	17 895	84 440	73 176	12 723	34.6	40.8	9.92	10.43	343.23	425.54
November	108 714	90 657	24 009	17 886	84 705	73 392	12 713	34.4	40.7	9.92	10.44	341.25	424.91
December	108 809	90 734	23 949	17 881	84 860	73 468	12 705	34.3	40.5	9.97	10.49	341.97	424.85
1990													
January	109 144	90 993	23 981	17 796	85 163	73 701	12 739	34.4	40.5	10.00	10.51	344.00	425.66
February	109 397	91 220	24 074	17 896	85 323	73 901	12 848	34.3	40.6	10.06	10.64	345.06	431.98
March	109 618	91 324	24 025	17 870	85 593	73 963	12 823	34.4	40.7	10.10	10.70	347.44	435.49
April	109 652	91 275	23 966	17 845	85 686	73 928	12 806	34.3	40.6	10.12	10.68	347.12	433.61
May	109 801	91 202	23 887	17 796	85 914	73 839	12 755	34.3	40.6	10.14	10.74	347.80	436.04
June	109 820	91 264	23 847	17 774	85 973	73 824	12 736	34.4	40.7	10.19	10.77	350.54	438.34
July	109 773	91 213	23 746	17 704	86 027	73 773	12 675	34.3	40.6	10.21	10.81	350.20	438.89
August	109 569	91 112	23 646	17 647	85 923	73 705	12 622	34.2	40.5	10.23	10.80	349.87	437.40
September	109 485	91 048	23 572	17 610	85 913	73 606	12 601	34.2	40.5	10.27	10.87	351.23	440.24
October	109 321	90 878	23 470	17 574	85 851	73 466	12 576	34.1	40.4	10.29	10.92	350.89	441.17
November	109 175	90 725	23 283	17 428	85 892	73 316	12 439	34.2	40.2	10.31	10.89	352.60	437.78
December	109 118	90 650	23 203	17 395	85 915	73 250	12 413	34.2	40.3	10.33	10.93	353.29	440.48
1991													
January	108 998	90 524	23 060	17 329	85 938	73 103	12 351	34.1	40.2	10.36	10.97	353.28	440.99
February	108 698	90 216	22 903	17 214	85 795	72 815	12 243	34.1	40.1	10.38	10.98	353.96	440.30
March	108 542	90 054	22 780	17 141	85 762	72 666	12 191	34.0	40.0	10.40	11.00	353.60	440.00
April	108 325	89 840	22 687	17 093	85 638	72 496	12 158	34.0	40.1	10.44	11.03	354.96	442.30
May	108 203	89 705	22 617	17 069	85 586	72 395	12 142	34.0	40.1	10.47	11.08	355.98	444.31
June	108 283	89 722	22 569	17 042	85 714	72 417	12 134	34.1	40.5	10.51	11.13	358.39	450.77
July	108 233	89 635	22 508	17 016	85 725	72 383	12 132	34.1	40.5	10.53	11.17	359.07	452.39
August	108 252	89 685	22 493	17 025	85 759	72 435	12 151	34.1	40.6	10.54	11.18	359.41	453.91
September	108 285	89 742	22 467	17 011	85 818	72 453	12 143	34.1	40.6	10.57	11.22	360.44	455.53
October	108 293	89 700	22 416	16 997	85 877	72 421	12 138	34.2	40.6	10.58	11.25	361.84	456.75
November	108 235	89 608	22 315	16 960	85 920	72 350	12 103	34.1	40.6	10.60	11.26	361.46	457.16
December	108 261	89 620	22 274	16 916	85 987	72 394	12 074	34.1	40.7	10.63	11.26	362.48	458.28
1992													
January	108 313	89 625	22 213	16 839	86 100	72 422	12 009	34.1	40.6	10.63	11.24	362.48	456.34
February	108 242	89 553	22 144	16 831	86 098	72 406	12 018	34.1	40.7	10.66	11.30	363.51	459.91
March	108 301	89 586	22 127	16 805	86 174	72 421	12 006	34.1	40.7	10.69	11.33	364.53	461.13
April	108 457	89 718	22 131	16 830	86 326	72 570	12 029	34.3	40.9	10.71	11.36	367.35	464.62
May	108 584	89 831	22 134	16 834	86 450	72 684	12 045	34.2	40.9	10.73	11.39	366.97	465.85
June	108 640	89 878	22 096	16 825	86 544	72 725	12 041	34.1	40.8	10.75	11.41	366.58	465.53
July	108 714	89 897	22 077	16 822	86 637	72 731	12 047	34.2	40.8	10.77	11.43	368.33	466.34
August	108 851	89 968	22 044	16 782	86 807	72 815	12 020	34.2	40.8	10.81	11.47	369.70	467.98
September	108 888	90 059	22 021	16 762	86 867	72 921	12 005	34.3	40.8	10.81	11.46	370.78	467.57
October	109 061	90 233	22 028	16 750	87 033	73 076	12 001	34.2	40.8	10.84	11.47	370.73	467.98
November	109 205	90 364	22 042	16 758	87 163	73 219	12 008	34.2	40.9	10.86	11.49	371.41	469.94
December	109 418	90 540	22 075	16 768	87 343	73 411	12 029	34.2	40.9	10.88	11.51	372.10	470.76
1993													
January	109 725	90 824	22 132	16 790	87 593	73 678	12 056	34.3	41.1	10.92	11.55	374.56	474.71
February	109 962	91 060	22 189	16 806	87 773	73 940	12 075	34.3	41.1	10.93	11.58	374.90	475.94
March	109 916	91 009	22 142	16 795	87 774	73 855	12 074	34.1	40.8	10.98	11.58	374.42	472.46
April	110 223	91 285	22 130	16 771	88 093	74 077	12 055	34.4	41.5	10.98	11.63	377.71	482.65
May	110 496	91 545	22 189	16 766	88 307	74 332	12 056	34.3	41.1	11.01	11.66	377.64	479.23
June	110 660	91 691	22 165	16 742	88 495	74 438	12 038	34.3	41.0	11.02	11.67	377.99	478.47
July	110 960	91 900	22 186	16 742	88 774	74 615	12 041	34.4	41.1	11.04	11.69	379.78	480.46
August	111 119	92 091	22 203	16 741	88 916	74 793	12 049	34.3	41.2	11.07	11.72	379.70	482.86
September	111 359	92 318	22 251	16 768	89 108	74 981	12 081	34.4	41.3	11.09	11.77	381.50	486.10
October	111 638	92 596	22 306	16 778	89 332	75 229	12 093	34.4	41.3	11.11	11.79	382.18	486.93
November	111 901	92 833	22 347	16 800	89 554	75 443	12 116	34.4	41.3	11.14	11.83	383.22	488.58
December	112 203	93 094	22 413	16 815	89 790	75 662	12 142	34.4	41.4	11.17	11.88	384.25	491.83

Table 20-4. Nonfarm Payroll Employment, Hours, and Earnings—*Continued*

(Wage and salary workers on nonfarm payrolls, seasonally adjusted.)

Year and month	All wage and salary workers, (thousands)					Number (thousands)		Average hours per week		Average hourly earnings, dollars		Average weekly earnings, dollars	
	Total	Private				Total private	Manufac-turing	Total private	Manufac-turing	Total private	Manufac-turing	Total private	Manufac-turing
		Total	Goods–producing		Service–providing								
			Total	Manufac-turing									
1994													
January	112 473	93 326	22 463	16 853	90 010	75 875	12 181	34.4	41.4	11.19	11.89	384.94	492.25
February	112 665	93 515	22 451	16 862	90 214	76 075	12 199	34.2	40.9	11.23	11.98	384.07	489.98
March	113 133	93 943	22 549	16 896	90 584	76 436	12 234	34.5	41.7	11.23	11.95	387.44	498.32
April	113 490	94 267	22 640	16 932	90 850	76 734	12 275	34.5	41.7	11.26	11.96	388.47	498.73
May	113 829	94 565	22 704	16 962	91 125	77 013	12 305	34.5	41.8	11.28	11.98	389.16	500.76
June	114 139	94 865	22 765	17 011	91 374	77 265	12 353	34.5	41.8	11.30	12.00	389.85	501.60
July	114 498	95 197	22 808	17 027	91 690	77 566	12 369	34.6	41.8	11.33	12.02	392.02	502.44
August	114 801	95 495	22 877	17 082	91 924	77 802	12 429	34.5	41.7	11.34	12.05	391.23	502.49
September	115 155	95 818	22 947	17 114	92 208	78 069	12 460	34.4	41.6	11.37	12.09	391.13	502.94
October	115 361	96 017	22 974	17 144	92 387	78 253	12 490	34.5	41.8	11.42	12.12	393.99	506.62
November	115 786	96 419	23 051	17 187	92 735	78 600	12 527	34.5	41.8	11.43	12.15	394.34	507.87
December	116 056	96 668	23 096	17 218	92 960	78 839	12 559	34.5	41.8	11.46	12.16	395.37	508.29
1995													
January	116 377	96 980	23 144	17 259	93 233	79 086	12 593	34.5	41.8	11.47	12.19	395.72	509.54
February	116 588	97 181	23 102	17 264	93 486	79 240	12 601	34.4	41.7	11.52	12.25	396.29	510.83
March	116 808	97 381	23 151	17 263	93 657	79 423	12 600	34.4	41.5	11.54	12.25	396.98	508.38
April	116 971	97 537	23 174	17 278	93 797	79 560	12 609	34.3	41.2	11.56	12.25	396.51	504.70
May	116 962	97 544	23 121	17 260	93 841	79 577	12 592	34.2	41.2	11.58	12.28	396.04	505.94
June	117 189	97 744	23 140	17 250	94 049	79 740	12 575	34.3	41.2	11.62	12.31	398.57	507.17
July	117 260	97 823	23 119	17 218	94 141	79 811	12 538	34.3	41.1	11.66	12.38	399.94	508.82
August	117 538	98 109	23 165	17 241	94 373	80 059	12 568	34.3	41.2	11.68	12.39	400.62	510.47
September	117 777	98 347	23 207	17 246	94 570	80 253	12 566	34.3	41.2	11.71	12.41	401.65	511.29
October	117 926	98 462	23 205	17 215	94 721	80 373	12 535	34.3	41.2	11.75	12.44	403.03	512.53
November	118 070	98 607	23 198	17 207	94 872	80 451	12 517	34.3	41.3	11.77	12.45	403.71	514.19
December	118 210	98 744	23 208	17 230	95 002	80 604	12 548	34.2	40.9	11.79	12.49	403.22	510.84
1996													
January	118 192	98 742	23 194	17 206	94 998	80 529	12 520	33.8	39.7	11.84	12.60	400.19	500.22
February	118 627	99 142	23 280	17 229	95 347	80 914	12 531	34.3	41.3	11.86	12.56	406.80	518.73
March	118 882	99 350	23 275	17 192	95 607	81 092	12 489	34.3	41.1	11.88	12.50	407.48	513.75
April	119 047	99 532	23 316	17 204	95 731	81 259	12 505	34.2	41.2	11.94	12.69	408.35	522.83
May	119 376	99 847	23 357	17 221	96 019	81 515	12 514	34.3	41.3	11.96	12.70	410.23	524.51
June	119 647	100 119	23 399	17 226	96 248	81 733	12 526	34.4	41.5	12.02	12.76	413.49	529.54
July	119 875	100 328	23 417	17 222	96 458	81 921	12 516	34.3	41.4	12.04	12.79	412.97	529.51
August	120 078	100 574	23 479	17 255	96 599	82 118	12 543	34.3	41.5	12.08	12.82	414.34	532.03
September	120 296	100 729	23 498	17 253	96 798	82 243	12 544	34.4	41.6	12.12	12.85	416.93	534.56
October	120 534	100 980	23 546	17 268	96 988	82 476	12 558	34.4	41.4	12.14	12.84	417.62	531.58
November	120 826	101 261	23 583	17 276	97 243	82 664	12 561	34.4	41.5	12.19	12.88	419.34	534.52
December	121 003	101 432	23 599	17 285	97 404	82 831	12 569	34.4	41.7	12.23	12.95	420.71	540.02
1997													
January	121 232	101 639	23 619	17 298	97 613	82 973	12 579	34.3	41.4	12.27	12.99	420.86	537.79
February	121 526	101 928	23 686	17 316	97 840	83 252	12 592	34.5	41.6	12.30	13.00	424.35	540.80
March	121 843	102 235	23 738	17 339	98 105	83 478	12 613	34.5	41.8	12.35	13.04	426.08	545.07
April	122 134	102 531	23 767	17 351	98 367	83 727	12 618	34.6	41.8	12.37	13.04	428.00	545.07
May	122 396	102 795	23 809	17 362	98 587	83 943	12 630	34.5	41.7	12.42	13.06	428.49	544.60
June	122 642	102 982	23 834	17 387	98 808	84 080	12 649	34.4	41.6	12.45	13.09	428.28	544.54
July	122 918	103 232	23 860	17 387	99 058	84 320	12 645	34.5	41.6	12.48	13.09	430.56	544.54
August	122 911	103 294	23 951	17 451	98 960	84 264	12 697	34.6	41.6	12.55	13.17	434.23	547.87
September	123 417	103 738	23 997	17 466	99 420	84 659	12 710	34.6	41.7	12.58	13.17	435.27	549.19
October	123 756	104 018	24 053	17 513	99 703	84 869	12 746	34.5	41.8	12.65	13.28	436.43	555.10
November	124 063	104 302	24 111	17 555	99 952	85 053	12 774	34.6	41.8	12.70	13.32	439.42	556.78
December	124 361	104 595	24 183	17 587	100 178	85 288	12 798	34.6	42.0	12.73	13.35	440.46	560.70
1998													
January	124 629	104 859	24 264	17 621	100 365	85 438	12 819	34.6	41.9	12.77	13.34	441.84	558.95
February	124 814	105 028	24 283	17 627	100 531	85 605	12 828	34.6	41.7	12.82	13.39	443.57	558.36
March	124 962	105 170	24 264	17 637	100 698	85 629	12 822	34.5	41.5	12.87	13.43	444.02	557.35
April	125 240	105 424	24 339	17 636	100 901	85 845	12 813	34.5	41.3	12.91	13.41	445.40	553.83
May	125 641	105 766	24 361	17 624	101 280	86 124	12 790	34.5	41.5	12.95	13.45	446.78	558.18
June	125 846	105 967	24 386	17 607	101 460	86 274	12 772	34.4	41.4	12.97	13.43	446.17	556.00
July	125 967	106 037	24 237	17 421	101 730	86 271	12 553	34.5	41.4	12.99	13.34	448.16	552.28
August	126 322	106 363	24 421	17 564	101 901	86 572	12 705	34.5	41.4	13.07	13.46	450.92	557.24
September	126 543	106 558	24 420	17 558	102 123	86 735	12 713	34.4	41.3	13.10	13.53	450.64	558.79
October	126 735	106 734	24 406	17 512	102 329	86 885	12 676	34.5	41.4	13.13	13.52	452.99	559.73
November	127 020	106 976	24 395	17 466	102 625	87 039	12 631	34.5	41.5	13.16	13.54	454.02	561.91
December	127 364	107 285	24 454	17 449	102 910	87 307	12 622	34.5	41.5	13.19	13.56	455.06	562.74
1999													
January	127 471	107 386	24 390	17 429	103 081	87 332	12 604	34.4	41.3	13.26	13.60	456.14	561.68
February	127 872	107 727	24 426	17 395	103 446	87 681	12 574	34.5	41.3	13.28	13.63	458.16	562.92
March	128 004	107 833	24 379	17 369	103 625	87 710	12 563	34.3	41.3	13.31	13.69	456.53	565.40
April	128 381	108 142	24 428	17 342	103 953	87 974	12 538	34.3	41.2	13.37	13.75	458.59	566.50
May	128 593	108 359	24 442	17 334	104 151	88 156	12 531	34.4	41.4	13.41	13.80	461.30	571.32
June	128 845	108 573	24 440	17 296	104 405	88 335	12 505	34.4	41.3	13.45	13.86	462.68	572.42
July	129 166	108 831	24 481	17 307	104 685	88 528	12 523	34.4	41.5	13.50	13.91	464.40	575.87
August	129 336	108 970	24 473	17 289	104 863	88 645	12 504	34.4	41.5	13.53	13.93	465.43	578.10
September	129 548	109 147	24 492	17 281	105 056	88 796	12 495	34.3	41.5	13.59	13.99	466.14	580.59
October	129 952	109 496	24 523	17 273	105 443	89 120	12 483	34.4	41.4	13.62	14.00	468.53	579.60
November	130 251	109 754	24 560	17 282	105 691	89 305	12 485	34.4	41.4	13.63	14.00	468.87	579.60
December	130 509	109 972	24 579	17 280	105 930	89 511	12 494	34.4	41.4	13.68	14.06	470.59	582.08

Table 20-4. Nonfarm Payroll Employment, Hours, and Earnings—*Continued*

(Wage and salary workers on nonfarm payrolls, seasonally adjusted.)

Year and month	All wage and salary workers, (thousands)					Production or nonsupervisory workers on private payrolls							
	Total	Private				Number (thousands)		Average hours per week		Average hourly earnings, dollars		Average weekly earnings, dollars	
		Total	Goods–producing		Service–providing	Total private	Manufac-turing	Total private	Manufac-turing	Total private	Manufac-turing	Total private	Manufac-turing
			Total	Manufac-turing									
2000													
January	130 760	110 188	24 630	17 285	106 130	89 684	12 495	34.4	41.5	13.74	14.13	472.66	586.40
February	130 885	110 283	24 604	17 283	106 281	89 762	12 482	34.4	41.6	13.79	14.15	474.38	588.64
March	131 380	110 646	24 706	17 305	106 674	90 028	12 491	34.4	41.4	13.83	14.18	475.75	587.05
April	131 674	110 865	24 685	17 300	106 989	90 272	12 479	34.4	41.6	13.89	14.24	477.82	592.38
May	131 905	110 753	24 645	17 280	107 260	90 172	12 463	34.3	41.3	13.92	14.23	477.46	587.70
June	131 871	110 979	24 680	17 302	107 191	90 340	12 471	34.3	41.3	13.96	14.29	478.83	590.18
July	131 953	111 094	24 709	17 318	107 244	90 464	12 475	34.3	41.4	14.02	14.32	480.89	592.85
August	132 001	111 167	24 682	17 287	107 319	90 493	12 435	34.2	41.0	14.05	14.37	480.51	589.17
September	132 129	111 382	24 637	17 227	107 492	90 656	12 381	34.2	41.1	14.10	14.40	482.22	591.84
October	132 137	111 391	24 644	17 213	107 493	90 663	12 357	34.3	41.1	14.17	14.48	486.03	595.13
November	132 345	111 583	24 628	17 203	107 717	90 777	12 339	34.2	41.0	14.22	14.52	486.32	595.32
December	132 445	111 639	24 573	17 177	107 872	90 789	12 301	34.0	40.4	14.26	14.51	484.84	586.20
2001													
January	132 436	111 600	24 521	17 101	107 915	90 749	12 230	34.2	40.7	14.28	14.49	488.38	589.74
February	132 560	111 646	24 478	17 032	108 082	90 709	12 157	34.1	40.5	14.35	14.56	489.34	589.68
March	132 527	111 577	24 413	16 944	108 114	90 629	12 085	34.1	40.5	14.40	14.58	491.04	590.49
April	132 247	111 242	24 249	16 803	107 998	90 429	11 981	34.0	40.5	14.44	14.64	490.96	592.92
May	132 230	111 193	24 130	16 666	108 100	90 376	11 859	34.0	40.4	14.48	14.69	492.32	593.48
June	132 064	110 953	23 974	16 513	108 090	90 149	11 733	34.0	40.3	14.52	14.74	493.68	594.02
July	131 867	110 709	23 837	16 382	108 030	90 042	11 638	34.0	40.6	14.55	14.80	494.70	600.88
August	131 719	110 548	23 670	16 230	108 049	89 890	11 446	33.9	40.3	14.58	14.86	494.26	598.86
September	131 550	110 292	23 544	16 118	108 006	89 647	11 399	33.8	40.2	14.62	14.90	494.16	598.98
October	131 198	109 915	23 380	15 969	107 818	89 356	11 285	33.7	40.1	14.64	14.89	493.37	597.09
November	130 900	109 563	23 211	15 825	107 689	89 013	11 175	33.8	40.1	14.70	14.96	496.86	599.90
December	130 661	109 302	23 086	15 706	107 575	88 883	11 078	33.9	40.2	14.73	15.03	499.35	604.21
2002													
January	130 578	109 193	22 960	15 585	107 618	88 839	11 001	33.8	40.2	14.74	15.05	498.21	605.01
February	130 510	109 089	22 887	15 517	107 623	88 795	10 952	33.9	40.3	14.77	15.12	500.70	609.34
March	130 481	109 034	22 792	15 450	107 689	88 724	10 901	33.9	40.6	14.80	15.15	501.72	615.09
April	130 415	108 957	22 713	15 406	107 702	88 624	10 866	33.9	40.5	14.81	15.17	502.06	614.39
May	130 411	108 907	22 667	15 367	107 744	88 521	10 836	33.9	40.6	14.86	15.23	503.75	618.34
June	130 383	108 891	22 639	15 334	107 744	88 430	10 818	34.0	40.7	14.93	15.27	507.62	621.49
July	130 204	108 756	22 588	15 309	107 616	88 279	10 804	33.8	40.4	14.97	15.27	505.99	616.91
August	130 224	108 745	22 527	15 233	107 697	88 208	10 740	33.9	40.5	15.02	15.34	509.18	621.27
September	130 289	108 763	22 497	15 196	107 792	88 204	10 715	33.9	40.5	15.05	15.38	510.20	622.89
October	130 408	108 864	22 435	15 143	107 973	88 278	10 685	33.8	40.3	15.10	15.45	510.38	622.64
November	130 409	108 869	22 409	15 091	108 000	88 204	10 648	33.8	40.4	15.14	15.48	511.73	625.39
December	130 198	108 642	22 323	15 020	107 875	88 017	10 595	33.8	40.5	15.20	15.55	513.76	629.78

Table 20-5. Money Stock, Reserves, and Monetary Base

(Averages of daily figures; billions of dollars, seasonally adjusted.)

Year and month	Money stock measures			Reserves, adjusted for change in reserve requirements				Monetary base
	M1	M2	M3	Total	Nonborrowed	Nonborrowed plus extended credit	Required	Monetary base
1959								
January	138.9	286.6	288.8	11 112	10 560	10 560	10 614	40 425
February	139.4	287.7	289.9	11 129	10 624	10 624	10 675	40 605
March	139.7	289.2	291.4	11 081	10 482	10 482	10 621	40 615
April	139.7	290.1	292.3	11 116	10 424	10 424	10 684	40 694
May	140.7	292.2	294.4	11 058	10 317	10 317	10 637	40 731
June	141.2	294.1	296.3	10 972	10 043	10 043	10 566	40 750
July	141.7	295.2	297.4	11 109	10 148	10 148	10 693	40 896
August	141.9	296.4	298.5	11 168	10 177	10 177	10 720	40 992
September	141.0	296.7	298.8	11 128	10 202	10 202	10 686	41 034
October	140.5	296.5	298.5	11 057	10 150	10 150	10 616	40 903
November	140.4	297.1	299.1	11 052	10 194	10 194	10 609	40 822
December	140.0	297.8	299.7	11 109	10 168	10 168	10 603	40 880
1960								
January	140.0	298.2	300.1	11 081	10 194	10 194	10 567	40 794
February	139.9	298.5	300.4	10 884	10 074	10 074	10 430	40 666
March	139.8	299.4	301.4	10 796	10 155	10 155	10 373	40 616
April	139.6	300.1	302.2	10 767	10 161	10 161	10 341	40 621
May	139.6	300.9	303.0	10 840	10 344	10 344	10 396	40 639
June	139.6	302.3	304.5	10 885	10 451	10 451	10 406	40 689
July	140.2	304.1	306.4	10 994	10 615	10 615	10 493	40 794
August	141.3	306.9	309.3	11 078	10 782	10 782	10 536	40 895
September	141.2	308.4	311.0	11 147	10 932	10 932	10 520	41 040
October	140.9	309.5	312.2	11 216	11 049	11 049	10 554	41 097
November	140.9	310.9	313.6	11 299	11 166	11 166	10 556	41 130
December	140.7	312.4	315.2	11 247	11 172	11 172	10 503	40 977
1961								
January	141.1	314.1	317.1	11 324	11 259	11 259	10 553	40 960
February	141.6	316.5	319.9	11 229	11 096	11 096	10 580	40 945
March	141.9	318.3	321.9	11 108	11 038	11 038	10 563	40 851
April	142.1	319.9	323.8	11 123	11 066	11 066	10 507	40 823
May	142.7	322.2	326.5	11 035	10 940	10 940	10 480	40 791
June	142.9	324.3	328.9	11 087	11 024	11 024	10 497	40 902
July	142.9	325.6	330.5	11 124	11 070	11 070	10 508	40 980
August	143.5	327.6	332.7	11 234	11 169	11 169	10 655	41 227
September	143.8	329.5	334.8	11 289	11 251	11 251	10 709	41 417
October	144.1	331.1	336.5	11 413	11 342	11 342	10 881	41 651
November	144.8	333.4	338.8	11 482	11 384	11 384	10 891	41 782
December	145.2	335.5	340.8	11 499	11 366	11 366	10 915	41 853
1962								
January	145.2	337.5	343.0	11 490	11 403	11 403	10 867	41 864
February	145.7	340.1	346.1	11 301	11 233	11 233	10 799	41 810
March	146.0	343.1	349.4	11 259	11 170	11 170	10 788	41 923
April	146.4	345.5	352.1	11 330	11 258	11 258	10 838	42 096
May	146.8	347.5	354.2	11 384	11 323	11 323	10 867	42 194
June	146.6	349.3	356.3	11 328	11 226	11 226	10 855	42 259
July	146.5	350.8	358.0	11 394	11 302	11 302	10 860	42 398
August	146.6	352.8	360.1	11 355	11 231	11 231	10 826	42 491
September	146.3	354.9	362.5	11 383	11 303	11 303	10 893	42 537
October	146.7	357.2	365.1	11 450	11 387	11 387	10 972	42 700
November	147.3	359.8	368.0	11 492	11 372	11 372	10 936	42 861
December	147.8	362.7	371.3	11 604	11 344	11 344	11 033	42 957
1963								
January	148.3	365.2	374.2	11 567	11 421	11 421	11 062	43 008
February	148.9	367.9	377.2	11 456	11 290	11 290	10 995	43 155
March	149.2	370.7	380.2	11 404	11 255	11 255	10 970	43 289
April	149.7	373.3	383.1	11 449	11 319	11 319	10 992	43 444
May	150.4	376.1	386.2	11 426	11 216	11 216	10 996	43 586
June	150.4	378.4	388.8	11 398	11 139	11 139	10 981	43 780
July	151.3	381.1	391.5	11 530	11 232	11 232	11 075	44 058
August	151.8	383.6	394.5	11 484	11 155	11 155	11 039	44 149
September	152.0	386.0	397.3	11 503	11 184	11 184	11 075	44 339
October	152.6	388.3	400.0	11 457	11 137	11 137	11 060	44 444
November	153.7	391.5	403.8	11 547	11 198	11 198	11 106	44 744
December	153.3	393.2	405.9	11 730	11 397	11 397	11 239	45 003
1964								
January	153.7	395.2	408.5	11 643	11 369	11 369	11 204	45 042
February	154.3	397.6	411.3	11 547	11 261	11 261	11 150	45 112
March	154.5	399.8	413.6	11 563	11 285	11 285	11 177	45 371
April	154.8	401.7	415.8	11 537	11 326	11 326	11 185	45 470
May	155.3	404.2	418.9	11 523	11 263	11 263	11 169	45 651
June	155.6	407.1	422.1	11 595	11 326	11 326	11 220	45 959
July	156.8	410.1	425.5	11 651	11 387	11 387	11 275	46 143
August	157.8	413.4	429.2	11 795	11 480	11 480	11 374	46 410
September	158.7	416.9	433.0	11 863	11 518	11 518	11 432	46 714
October	159.2	419.1	435.9	11 888	11 567	11 567	11 490	46 823
November	160.0	422.1	439.3	11 998	11 598	11 598	11 591	47 106
December	160.3	424.7	442.4	12 011	11 747	11 747	11 605	47 161

Table 20-5. Money Stock, Reserves, and Monetary Base—*Continued*

(Averages of daily figures; billions of dollars, seasonally adjusted.)

Year and month	Money stock measures			Reserves, adjusted for change in reserve requirements				
	M1	M2	M3	Total	Nonborrowed	Nonborrowed plus extended credit	Required	Monetary base
1965								
January	160.7	427.5	445.8	11 952	11 653	11 653	11 537	47 281
February	160.9	430.4	449.1	11 883	11 479	11 479	11 472	47 500
March	161.5	433.2	452.0	11 884	11 472	11 472	11 518	47 584
April	162.0	435.4	454.5	12 043	11 571	11 571	11 701	47 721
May	161.7	437.1	456.4	11 912	11 417	11 417	11 578	47 799
June	162.2	440.1	459.9	12 005	11 467	11 467	11 643	48 061
July	163.1	442.9	463.3	12 073	11 544	11 544	11 720	48 281
August	163.7	445.8	466.8	12 079	11 531	11 531	11 682	48 453
September	164.9	449.5	471.1	12 071	11 517	11 517	11 662	48 712
October	166.0	452.6	474.9	12 118	11 630	11 630	11 759	49 029
November	166.7	455.7	478.3	12 087	11 655	11 655	11 735	49 234
December	167.8	459.2	482.1	12 316	11 872	11 872	11 892	49 620
1966								
January	169.1	462.0	485.1	12 295	11 875	11 875	11 916	49 850
February	169.6	464.6	487.8	12 193	11 711	11 711	11 846	50 054
March	170.5	467.2	490.8	12 164	11 604	11 604	11 822	50 171
April	171.8	469.3	494.0	12 258	11 621	11 621	11 903	50 439
May	171.3	470.1	495.4	12 263	11 575	11 575	11 922	50 591
June	171.6	471.2	497.1	12 256	11 549	11 549	11 901	50 754
July	170.3	470.9	497.8	12 371	11 629	11 629	11 993	51 019
August	170.8	472.6	499.6	12 165	11 430	11 430	11 798	50 989
September	172.0	475.4	502.3	12 229	11 460	11 460	11 858	51 154
October	171.2	475.7	501.4	12 199	11 465	11 465	11 867	51 200
November	171.4	477.3	502.0	12 205	11 598	11 598	11 820	51 422
December	172.0	480.2	505.4	12 223	11 690	11 690	11 884	51 565
1967								
January	171.9	481.6	509.1	12 334	11 924	11 924	11 931	51 876
February	173.0	485.1	514.5	12 280	11 916	11 916	11 911	52 173
March	174.8	489.7	519.9	12 438	12 237	12 237	12 024	52 494
April	174.2	492.1	522.6	12 488	12 342	12 342	12 138	52 517
May	175.7	497.2	527.7	12 418	12 329	12 329	12 053	52 682
June	177.0	502.0	533.1	12 457	12 351	12 351	12 104	52 867
July	178.1	506.3	537.7	12 722	12 607	12 607	12 304	53 165
August	179.7	510.8	542.5	12 678	12 598	12 598	12 313	53 347
September	180.7	514.7	546.8	12 846	12 758	12 758	12 504	53 670
October	181.6	518.2	550.2	13 088	12 959	12 959	12 752	54 044
November	182.4	521.2	553.9	13 131	12 999	12 999	12 773	54 241
December	183.3	524.8	557.9	13 180	12 952	12 952	12 805	54 579
1968								
January	184.3	527.4	560.4	13 239	12 993	12 993	12 852	54 892
February	184.7	530.4	563.6	13 188	12 815	12 815	12 801	55 171
March	185.5	533.2	567.0	13 186	12 527	12 527	12 849	55 436
April	186.6	535.7	569.2	13 117	12 432	12 432	12 782	55 692
May	188.0	538.9	572.3	13 130	12 389	12 389	12 771	55 872
June	189.4	542.6	575.9	13 251	12 557	12 557	12 923	56 323
July	190.5	545.6	580.6	13 455	12 928	12 928	13 105	56 626
August	191.8	549.4	585.6	13 440	12 875	12 875	13 110	56 976
September	192.7	553.6	590.6	13 435	12 931	12 931	13 074	57 160
October	194.0	557.6	595.8	13 529	13 086	13 086	13 283	57 477
November	196.0	562.4	601.7	13 649	13 104	13 104	13 340	57 887
December	197.4	566.8	607.2	13 767	13 021	13 021	13 341	58 357
1969								
January	198.7	569.3	607.9	13 629	12 893	12 893	13 383	58 597
February	199.3	571.9	609.1	13 714	12 879	12 879	13 460	58 917
March	200.0	574.4	610.8	13 653	12 751	12 751	13 434	58 999
April	200.7	575.7	611.5	13 471	12 468	12 468	13 304	59 062
May	200.8	576.5	611.6	13 844	12 470	12 470	13 589	59 552
June	201.3	578.5	612.1	13 795	12 410	12 410	13 491	59 794
July	201.7	579.5	610.1	13 491	12 239	12 239	13 266	59 713
August	201.7	580.1	607.7	13 784	12 565	12 565	13 547	60 137
September	202.1	582.1	608.5	13 822	12 743	12 743	13 549	60 357
October	202.9	583.4	608.9	13 904	12 754	12 754	13 741	60 633
November	203.6	585.4	613.5	14 172	12 969	12 969	13 943	61 229
December	203.9	587.9	615.9	14 168	13 049	13 049	13 882	61 569
1970								
January	206.2	589.6	616.1	14 087	13 128	13 128	13 914	61 792
February	204.9	586.2	613.2	14 099	13 019	13 019	13 891	61 931
March	205.7	587.2	615.6	14 071	13 173	13 173	13 908	62 205
April	206.6	588.3	619.5	14 209	13 364	13 364	14 057	62 653
May	207.2	591.4	624.2	14 007	13 040	13 040	13 850	62 977
June	207.6	595.3	627.1	14 078	13 197	13 197	13 888	63 189
July	208.2	599.3	635.9	14 159	12 799	12 799	13 993	63 444
August	210.1	605.1	645.1	14 282	13 445	13 445	14 108	63 725
September	211.9	611.3	654.5	14 447	13 847	13 847	14 203	64 087
October	212.9	616.4	662.3	14 480	14 017	14 017	14 274	64 303
November	213.6	621.0	669.2	14 470	14 055	14 055	14 236	64 574
December	214.3	626.4	677.0	14 558	14 225	14 225	14 309	65 013

Table 20-5. Money Stock, Reserves, and Monetary Base—*Continued*
(Averages of daily figures; billions of dollars, seasonally adjusted.)

Year and month	Money stock measures			Reserves, adjusted for change in reserve requirements				
	M1	M2	M3	Total	Nonborrowed	Nonborrowed plus extended credit	Required	Monetary base
1971								
January	215.4	632.8	685.4	14 604	14 240	14 240	14 371	65 545
February	217.3	640.9	695.7	14 819	14 488	14 488	14 565	66 037
March	218.7	649.8	706.4	14 798	14 479	14 479	14 603	66 378
April	219.9	658.3	713.6	14 759	14 606	14 606	14 591	66 731
May	221.9	666.7	723.3	14 982	14 698	14 698	14 763	67 315
June	223.6	673.1	730.2	15 057	14 564	14 564	14 855	67 678
July	225.2	679.9	738.6	15 125	14 302	14 302	14 941	68 155
August	225.8	685.8	744.3	15 190	14 380	14 380	14 994	68 413
September	226.6	692.6	751.9	15 423	14 928	14 928	15 234	68 751
October	227.2	698.4	760.2	15 211	14 854	14 854	15 049	68 603
November	227.7	704.5	768.2	15 247	14 864	14 864	15 010	68 894
December	228.2	710.1	775.9	15 230	15 104	15 104	15 049	69 108
1972								
January	230.0	717.6	783.7	15 369	15 347	15 347	15 163	69 853
February	232.2	725.6	792.8	15 363	15 331	15 331	15 211	70 368
March	234.2	733.4	800.5	15 480	15 382	15 382	15 291	70 820
April	235.4	738.3	807.7	15 651	15 534	15 534	15 495	71 031
May	235.8	743.3	816.0	15 739	15 628	15 628	15 600	71 525
June	236.8	749.8	824.7	15 909	15 809	15 809	15 706	71 817
July	239.1	759.8	835.9	15 835	15 597	15 597	15 642	72 173
August	241.2	769.0	846.9	16 010	15 623	15 623	15 822	72 623
September	243.3	778.5	856.6	16 000	15 459	15 459	15 788	72 984
October	245.0	786.9	865.8	16 193	15 637	15 637	15 981	73 644
November	246.3	793.8	875.7	16 441	15 833	15 833	16 088	74 370
December	249.1	802.1	885.8	16 645	15 595	15 595	16 361	75 167
1973								
January	251.3	810.2	896.2	16 708	15 548	15 548	16 450	75 925
February	252.0	814.0	906.0	16 714	15 120	15 120	16 516	76 160
March	251.5	815.2	914.8	16 923	15 099	15 099	16 714	76 663
April	252.6	819.6	922.3	16 731	15 020	15 020	16 508	76 962
May	254.8	826.7	932.2	16 672	14 829	14 830	16 533	77 393
June	256.9	833.4	940.9	16 746	14 895	14 903	16 528	77 842
July	257.9	836.9	950.6	16 988	15 035	15 067	16 705	78 531
August	258.1	839.1	959.4	16 796	14 631	14 657	16 624	78 781
September	258.0	839.4	966.0	16 735	14 883	14 909	16 505	79 316
October	259.1	842.7	972.0	16 924	15 448	15 464	16 672	80 173
November	260.9	848.7	977.2	16 978	15 585	15 585	16 753	80 479
December	262.7	855.3	984.9	17 021	15 723	15 723	16 717	81 073
1974								
January	263.6	859.5	993.8	17 222	16 171	16 174	17 060	81 850
February	265.1	864.1	1 002.3	17 125	15 933	15 933	16 941	82 341
March	266.5	870.0	1 010.5	17 131	15 817	15 817	16 997	82 835
April	267.0	872.8	1 020.7	17 298	15 561	15 561	17 116	83 621
May	267.4	874.5	1 029.1	17 423	14 833	15 491	17 263	84 432
June	268.6	878.0	1 038.0	17 367	14 361	15 587	17 169	84 895
July	269.7	881.8	1 044.4	17 486	14 185	15 615	17 323	85 439
August	270.5	884.5	1 049.0	17 391	14 055	15 592	17 203	85 974
September	271.3	888.1	1 053.1	17 385	14 102	15 731	17 204	86 377
October	272.4	893.3	1 058.6	17 349	15 536	16 021	17 228	86 513
November	273.6	898.4	1 063.6	17 453	16 201	16 361	17 248	87 043
December	274.0	901.9	1 069.7	17 550	16 823	16 970	17 292	87 535
1975								
January	273.7	906.1	1 075.3	17 273	16 874	17 010	17 126	87 756
February	274.8	913.9	1 082.5	17 271	17 123	17 176	17 077	88 192
March	276.2	924.8	1 089.8	17 439	17 333	17 370	17 239	88 916
April	275.9	934.9	1 095.6	17 498	17 387	17 398	17 340	89 116
May	279.1	947.8	1 105.8	17 353	17 288	17 291	17 198	89 610
June	282.7	963.3	1 119.0	17 715	17 488	17 504	17 513	90 817
July	284.3	975.7	1 129.3	17 632	17 331	17 351	17 445	91 373
August	284.7	983.6	1 135.6	17 660	17 449	17 461	17 465	91 700
September	286.0	991.7	1 146.1	17 834	17 438	17 452	17 643	92 119
October	285.4	997.9	1 153.9	17 587	17 397	17 408	17 380	92 448
November	286.6	1 006.8	1 163.6	17 849	17 789	17 794	17 566	93 373
December	286.8	1 016.0	1 169.9	17 822	17 692	17 704	17 556	93 887
1976								
January	288.2	1 026.4	1 181.4	17 616	17 537	17 549	17 376	94 281
February	290.5	1 040.1	1 193.2	17 806	17 725	17 734	17 587	95 039
March	292.4	1 049.7	1 204.3	17 875	17 821	17 824	17 651	95 786
April	294.4	1 060.5	1 216.4	17 719	17 675	17 675	17 564	96 479
May	295.8	1 071.9	1 227.5	17 940	17 826	17 826	17 731	97 251
June	296.4	1 077.8	1 236.3	17 946	17 820	17 820	17 732	97 732
July	297.9	1 087.0	1 246.6	17 846	17 714	17 714	17 612	98 234
August	299.7	1 099.3	1 259.9	18 053	17 953	17 953	17 846	98 888
September	300.0	1 111.2	1 268.5	18 009	17 948	17 948	17 808	99 446
October	302.1	1 125.1	1 280.9	18 077	17 983	17 983	17 858	100 066
November	303.4	1 138.0	1 294.3	18 340	18 268	18 268	18 083	100 892
December	305.9	1 151.7	1 309.7	18 388	18 335	18 335	18 115	101 515

Table 20-5. Money Stock, Reserves, and Monetary Base—*Continued*

(Averages of daily figures; billions of dollars, seasonally adjusted.)

Year and month	Money stock measures			Reserves, adjusted for change in reserve requirements				
	M1	M2	M3	Total	Nonborrowed	Nonborrowed plus extended credit	Required	Monetary base
1977								
January	307.9	1 164.9	1 322.2	18 421	18 353	18 353	18 156	102 237
February	311.2	1 177.3	1 335.2	18 299	18 227	18 227	18 100	102 654
March	313.6	1 188.2	1 348.1	18 405	18 301	18 301	18 190	103 337
April	315.7	1 199.3	1 360.3	18 479	18 406	18 406	18 287	104 076
May	317.0	1 208.8	1 373.8	18 585	18 379	18 379	18 377	104 630
June	319.0	1 218.0	1 387.8	18 471	18 208	18 208	18 324	105 186
July	321.0	1 227.5	1 401.2	18 748	18 425	18 425	18 473	106 394
August	323.0	1 237.8	1 415.9	18 919	17 858	17 858	18 719	107 185
September	324.9	1 246.6	1 428.4	18 873	18 247	18 247	18 664	107 923
October	326.4	1 254.0	1 441.8	18 963	17 658	17 658	18 753	108 750
November	328.4	1 262.1	1 456.9	19 012	18 150	18 150	18 761	109 560
December	330.5	1 269.9	1 470.1	18 990	18 420	18 420	18 800	110 324
1978								
January	334.1	1 279.3	1 485.9	19 290	18 806	18 806	19 023	111 449
February	335.0	1 285.2	1 497.7	19 561	19 155	19 155	19 319	112 450
March	336.6	1 291.9	1 512.7	19 286	18 958	18 958	19 087	112 778
April	339.6	1 300.0	1 528.2	19 408	18 851	18 851	19 260	113 377
May	344.7	1 310.3	1 544.1	19 655	18 443	18 443	19 436	114 418
June	347.1	1 318.7	1 555.6	19 868	18 774	18 774	19 691	115 376
July	348.5	1 325.0	1 567.9	20 118	18 801	18 801	19 921	116 273
August	350.4	1 334.3	1 583.9	19 912	18 772	18 772	19 744	116 904
September	352.7	1 345.4	1 597.5	19 994	18 934	18 934	19 801	118 112
October	353.4	1 352.4	1 611.2	20 109	18 832	18 832	19 947	119 044
November	355.2	1 358.9	1 630.0	19 872	19 169	19 169	19 650	119 733
December	356.9	1 365.6	1 644.2	19 753	18 885	18 885	19 521	120 445
1979								
January	358.2	1 371.2	1 656.4	19 821	18 818	18 818	19 606	121 272
February	359.6	1 377.5	1 668.8	19 396	18 423	18 423	19 187	121 504
March	362.1	1 387.5	1 682.9	19 429	18 439	18 439	19 271	122 065
April	367.7	1 401.8	1 700.5	19 504	18 587	18 587	19 328	122 819
May	369.4	1 410.0	1 710.9	19 553	17 788	17 788	19 412	123 487
June	373.6	1 423.3	1 728.3	19 808	18 390	18 390	19 587	124 635
July	378.1	1 435.6	1 744.1	19 992	18 822	18 822	19 782	125 810
August	379.7	1 447.4	1 762.4	20 008	18 923	18 923	19 786	127 079
September	379.7	1 454.6	1 783.4	20 007	18 667	18 667	19 816	128 309
October	380.9	1 460.5	1 796.7	20 375	18 353	18 353	20 103	129 458
November	380.5	1 465.6	1 798.7	20 398	18 492	18 492	20 153	130 369
December	381.4	1 473.3	1 808.3	20 720	19 248	19 248	20 279	131 143
1980								
January	385.4	1 482.3	1 822.7	20 693	19 452	19 452	20 442	131 998
February	389.7	1 494.2	1 841.4	20 682	19 027	19 027	20 471	132 785
March	388.1	1 499.5	1 849.8	20 703	17 879	17 978	20 517	133 607
April	383.4	1 501.8	1 853.9	20 629	18 174	18 726	20 432	134 740
May	384.6	1 512.1	1 866.8	20 440	19 421	20 164	20 262	134 998
June	389.4	1 529.5	1 884.7	20 575	20 196	20 503	20 372	135 679
July	394.9	1 546.4	1 904.1	20 796	20 401	20 654	20 511	136 637
August	400.1	1 562.4	1 921.7	21 011	20 352	20 594	20 709	137 977
September	405.4	1 574.5	1 935.7	21 232	19 921	20 011	20 977	139 220
October	409.1	1 584.9	1 953.7	21 147	19 837	19 837	20 941	140 150
November	410.4	1 595.4	1 974.9	22 150	20 091	20 091	21 629	141 566
December	408.1	1 599.4	1 995.1	22 015	20 325	20 328	21 501	142 004
1981								
January	410.9	1 606.5	2 020.1	21 673	20 278	20 348	21 298	141 462
February	414.4	1 618.3	2 039.1	21 840	20 536	20 557	21 489	142 270
March	418.7	1 636.2	2 057.7	22 072	21 072	21 086	21 791	143 029
April	427.0	1 658.9	2 086.0	22 187	20 849	20 857	22 018	143 917
May	424.4	1 664.0	2 102.5	22 442	20 219	20 224	22 184	144 587
June	425.5	1 670.6	2 118.7	22 326	20 289	20 295	21 988	145 001
July	427.9	1 682.8	2 138.8	22 329	20 650	20 653	21 989	145 839
August	427.8	1 695.2	2 158.0	22 356	20 936	21 017	22 064	146 467
September	427.5	1 706.5	2 179.8	22 487	21 031	21 332	22 073	146 941
October	428.5	1 721.9	2 204.7	22 296	21 115	21 553	22 018	147 062
November	430.9	1 735.7	2 226.4	22 338	21 675	21 840	21 993	147 749
December	436.2	1 754.9	2 254.0	22 443	21 807	21 956	22 124	149 021
1982								
January	442.2	1 769.9	2 275.3	22 669	21 152	21 349	22 251	149 991
February	441.5	1 774.1	2 284.0	22 551	20 762	20 994	22 248	150 459
March	442.4	1 786.1	2 302.6	22 452	20 898	21 206	22 091	150 660
April	446.8	1 803.6	2 328.1	22 337	20 769	21 014	22 064	151 606
May	446.5	1 815.2	2 343.0	22 402	21 285	21 461	22 043	152 868
June	447.9	1 826.4	2 360.1	22 368	21 164	21 268	22 060	153 861
July	449.1	1 835.4	2 373.2	22 182	21 490	21 541	21 868	154 385
August	452.5	1 850.4	2 397.6	22 348	21 833	21 926	22 036	155 470
September	457.5	1 863.9	2 413.6	22 686	21 752	21 871	22 302	156 629
October	464.6	1 874.7	2 435.0	22 889	22 412	22 553	22 485	157 716
November	471.1	1 888.0	2 447.0	23 354	22 733	22 921	22 952	158 667
December	474.3	1 909.8	2 460.2	23 600	22 966	23 152	23 100	160 127

Table 20-5. Money Stock, Reserves, and Monetary Base—*Continued*

(Averages of daily figures; billions of dollars, seasonally adjusted.)

Year and month	Money stock measures			Reserves, adjusted for change in reserve requirements				
	M1	M2	M3	Total	Nonborrowed	Nonborrowed plus extended credit	Required	Monetary base
1983								
January	476.7	1 962.8	2 488.4	23 226	22 697	22 854	22 678	161 136
February	483.8	2 000.0	2 517.4	23 901	23 319	23 597	23 466	163 170
March	490.2	2 018.2	2 533.7	24 414	23 621	23 939	23 981	165 052
April	492.8	2 031.5	2 553.5	24 900	23 890	24 295	24 424	166 549
May	499.8	2 046.2	2 569.3	24 860	23 907	24 420	24 411	167 842
June	504.3	2 057.0	2 585.4	25 277	23 641	24 599	24 797	169 393
July	509.0	2 069.0	2 597.1	25 356	23 903	24 480	24 848	170 129
August	511.6	2 078.0	2 610.9	25 376	23 830	24 320	24 929	171 208
September	513.4	2 086.7	2 626.9	25 435	23 994	24 509	24 937	172 411
October	517.2	2 102.2	2 646.1	25 454	24 610	24 866	24 949	173 584
November	518.5	2 114.9	2 673.4	25 396	24 491	24 497	24 867	174 605
December	520.8	2 125.9	2 697.0	25 367	24 593	24 595	24 806	175 467
1984								
January	524.4	2 140.5	2 714.2	25 451	24 736	24 740	24 838	176 896
February	527.0	2 160.9	2 742.0	25 874	25 307	25 312	24 968	177 930
March	530.8	2 177.8	2 771.4	25 821	24 869	24 896	25 153	178 964
April	534.0	2 194.0	2 800.3	25 749	24 516	24 560	25 276	179 962
May	536.6	2 207.4	2 828.3	25 935	22 946	22 983	25 365	180 859
June	540.6	2 218.8	2 850.5	26 138	22 837	24 710	25 379	182 034
July	542.1	2 228.1	2 873.0	26 023	20 099	25 107	25 394	183 053
August	542.4	2 235.0	2 887.4	26 080	18 063	25 106	25 400	183 830
September	543.9	2 248.3	2 905.4	26 125	18 883	25 341	25 475	184 684
October	543.9	2 262.3	2 930.3	26 281	20 264	25 322	25 664	185 271
November	547.3	2 284.6	2 957.0	26 518	21 901	25 738	25 820	186 106
December	551.2	2 309.6	2 990.5	26 896	23 710	26 314	26 061	187 241
1985								
January	555.7	2 334.8	3 016.7	27 064	25 669	26 719	26 321	188 095
February	562.5	2 356.5	3 039.7	27 604	26 315	27 119	26 755	189 666
March	565.7	2 368.7	3 055.8	27 616	26 023	27 082	26 941	190 337
April	569.4	2 377.9	3 061.5	27 899	26 577	27 445	27 163	191 377
May	575.2	2 393.2	3 078.8	28 180	26 846	27 380	27 427	192 783
June	582.9	2 416.9	3 104.3	28 867	27 662	28 328	27 945	194 738
July	590.7	2 434.7	3 114.3	29 162	28 055	28 562	28 322	195 984
August	598.0	2 449.3	3 133.2	29 676	28 604	29 173	28 842	198 024
September	604.4	2 461.0	3 150.8	30 054	28 765	29 421	29 357	199 372
October	607.9	2 471.7	3 167.1	30 502	29 315	29 944	29 758	200 763
November	611.9	2 480.9	3 182.0	30 904	29 164	29 694	29 986	202 151
December	619.1	2 494.9	3 207.6	31 541	30 223	30 722	30 478	203 540
1986								
January	620.4	2 504.6	3 231.6	31 548	30 778	31 275	30 466	204 233
February	624.1	2 515.1	3 249.7	31 675	30 791	31 283	30 661	205 343
March	632.6	2 535.3	3 276.4	32 132	31 372	31 890	31 250	206 964
April	640.1	2 560.1	3 306.8	32 567	31 674	32 308	31 794	208 173
May	652.0	2 588.4	3 331.0	33 313	32 437	33 021	32 435	210 224
June	661.2	2 609.2	3 353.6	33 991	33 188	33 719	33 072	211 823
July	672.0	2 632.2	3 383.7	34 707	33 966	34 344	33 834	213 464
August	680.6	2 652.3	3 409.7	35 249	34 376	34 841	34 508	215 258
September	688.4	2 672.9	3 436.3	35 681	34 672	35 243	34 991	216 855
October	695.2	2 692.1	3 455.8	36 308	35 467	35 964	35 591	218 694
November	705.0	2 705.2	3 466.7	37 288	36 537	36 955	36 387	220 764
December	724.0	2 731.6	3 498.7	38 841	38 015	38 317	37 668	223 430
1987								
January	729.2	2 747.0	3 523.7	39 260	38 681	38 905	38 190	225 359
February	729.8	2 750.9	3 533.3	39 062	38 505	38 788	37 869	226 621
March	732.8	2 756.8	3 541.7	38 914	38 386	38 650	37 993	227 156
April	743.1	2 771.1	3 561.8	39 628	38 635	38 906	38 772	229 098
May	745.8	2 777.3	3 578.2	39 904	38 868	39 156	38 836	230 587
June	743.5	2 779.1	3 593.7	39 546	38 770	39 043	38 313	231 383
July	744.9	2 785.1	3 601.3	39 167	38 494	38 689	38 308	232 070
August	746.7	2 794.1	3 621.9	39 298	38 651	38 783	38 247	233 643
September	748.5	2 804.6	3 643.5	39 204	38 264	38 673	38 420	234 743
October	756.4	2 819.4	3 668.0	39 893	38 950	39 399	38 804	237 165
November	752.7	2 823.4	3 680.9	39 364	38 739	39 133	38 424	238 941
December	749.4	2 830.6	3 685.9	38 918	38 141	38 624	37 899	239 846
1988								
January	755.4	2 851.6	3 708.2	39 480	38 398	38 770	38 228	241 812
February	757.0	2 874.7	3 736.4	39 456	39 059	39 264	38 318	242 829
March	761.1	2 895.0	3 761.4	39 340	37 588	39 066	38 395	243 850
April	767.3	2 915.0	3 787.6	39 698	36 705	39 329	38 814	245 807
May	771.4	2 930.9	3 814.2	40 031	37 453	39 560	38 984	247 495
June	778.8	2 943.9	3 834.6	40 343	37 261	39 814	39 448	249 241
July	783.1	2 954.9	3 852.4	40 579	37 139	39 678	39 688	251 010
August	784.9	2 959.5	3 866.1	40 534	37 293	39 946	39 564	252 127
September	784.6	2 964.0	3 877.1	40 400	37 561	39 620	39 384	253 445
October	783.4	2 971.6	3 890.2	40 458	38 158	39 940	39 405	254 626
November	784.3	2 985.9	3 908.4	40 546	37 684	40 007	39 372	255 773
December	786.0	2 993.8	3 928.3	40 428	38 712	39 956	39 366	256 866

Table 20-5. Money Stock, Reserves, and Monetary Base—Continued

(Averages of daily figures; billions of dollars, seasonally adjusted.)

Year and month	Money stock measures			Reserves, adjusted for change in reserve requirements				
	M1	M2	M3	Total	Nonborrowed	Nonborrowed plus extended credit	Required	Monetary base
1989								
January	784.8	2 996.7	3 936.0	40 409	38 760	39 798	39 265	257 889
February	783.2	2 997.5	3 940.1	40 359	38 872	39 922	39 204	258 286
March	782.6	3 005.3	3 961.1	39 889	38 076	39 411	38 970	259 215
April	778.7	3 011.3	3 970.1	39 580	37 291	38 998	38 767	259 550
May	774.6	3 017.1	3 974.5	39 346	37 626	38 823	38 304	260 305
June	773.9	3 033.9	3 995.5	39 125	37 635	38 551	38 216	261 154
July	779.3	3 059.8	4 019.4	39 477	38 783	38 889	38 494	262 283
August	780.7	3 081.8	4 028.8	39 436	38 761	38 802	38 544	262 872
September	781.9	3 099.7	4 036.1	39 705	39 012	39 034	38 760	263 757
October	786.6	3 120.6	4 047.5	40 170	39 615	39 636	39 130	264 875
November	787.7	3 138.9	4 062.7	40 137	39 788	39 809	39 188	265 756
December	792.1	3 157.4	4 076.0	40 430	40 164	40 184	39 489	267 669
1990								
January	794.4	3 171.7	4 088.0	40 687	40 247	40 272	39 644	269 508
February	797.3	3 184.6	4 094.5	40 732	39 284	39 819	39 732	271 112
March	800.7	3 195.4	4 096.8	40 664	38 540	40 491	39 783	273 058
April	805.5	3 207.3	4 104.4	40 865	39 257	40 641	39 994	275 235
May	804.0	3 205.5	4 106.3	40 773	39 441	40 313	39 819	276 787
June	809.4	3 218.8	4 114.2	40 687	39 806	40 152	39 900	278 955
July	811.4	3 230.4	4 128.0	40 600	39 842	40 122	39 732	281 010
August	817.5	3 248.9	4 144.6	40 900	39 973	40 101	40 025	284 126
September	821.2	3 260.9	4 151.4	41 112	40 487	40 494	40 199	287 270
October	819.9	3 264.4	4 154.3	40 804	40 394	40 412	39 964	289 196
November	821.7	3 268.4	4 149.4	40 925	40 695	40 720	39 998	291 198
December	824.1	3 277.2	4 152.1	41 699	41 374	41 397	40 035	293 267
1991								
January	826.4	3 292.9	4 174.4	42 243	41 709	41 736	40 102	297 712
February	832.0	3 310.0	4 190.8	42 055	41 803	41 837	40 250	300 894
March	837.9	3 327.2	4 198.1	41 818	41 577	41 629	40 633	302 660
April	841.9	3 337.4	4 204.6	41 877	41 646	41 732	40 851	303 025
May	848.6	3 349.2	4 205.5	42 433	42 130	42 218	41 399	304 239
June	857.5	3 359.1	4 207.5	42 734	42 394	42 402	41 741	305 520
July	862.6	3 362.7	4 201.0	43 016	42 409	42 455	42 112	307 240
August	868.1	3 361.9	4 195.4	43 433	42 669	42 969	42 346	309 369
September	871.3	3 361.8	4 189.0	43 587	42 942	43 244	42 657	310 759
October	878.3	3 366.0	4 192.4	44 006	43 746	43 757	42 951	312 742
November	887.1	3 370.2	4 197.1	44 571	44 463	44 464	43 679	314 930
December	896.3	3 376.7	4 204.8	45 451	45 258	45 259	44 461	317 507
1992								
January	910.0	3 386.5	4 211.5	46 325	46 091	46 092	45 333	319 617
February	924.7	3 405.5	4 231.4	47 600	47 522	47 524	46 546	322 587
March	935.9	3 408.9	4 232.5	48 292	48 201	48 203	47 267	324 332
April	943.0	3 405.5	4 221.2	49 061	48 971	48 973	47 934	326 733
May	950.2	3 403.2	4 215.6	49 366	49 212	49 212	48 363	328 812
June	954.6	3 399.5	4 214.1	49 303	49 074	49 074	48 380	330 150
July	964.5	3 402.1	4 216.1	49 799	49 515	49 515	48 824	333 317
August	975.3	3 406.8	4 224.3	50 525	50 275	50 275	49 587	336 999
September	988.6	3 416.6	4 231.2	51 425	51 138	51 138	50 413	340 785
October	1 004.1	3 430.6	4 230.2	52 753	52 610	52 610	51 692	344 608
November	1 015.8	3 433.4	4 225.5	53 685	53 581	53 581	52 643	347 687
December	1 024.3	3 430.8	4 215.8	54 332	54 208	54 209	53 178	350 754
1993								
January	1 029.8	3 425.4	4 198.0	54 901	54 736	54 737	53 639	353 556
February	1 033.0	3 421.8	4 200.5	54 657	54 612	54 612	53 565	355 395
March	1 037.8	3 418.5	4 203.5	54 971	54 879	54 879	53 739	357 852
April	1 046.5	3 418.4	4 204.7	55 367	55 294	55 294	54 263	360 901
May	1 065.9	3 444.0	4 236.0	56 664	56 543	56 543	55 668	364 909
June	1 075.3	3 449.9	4 236.5	57 100	56 919	56 919	56 209	367 901
July	1 085.5	3 451.0	4 234.0	57 760	57 516	57 516	56 693	371 462
August	1 095.3	3 455.1	4 234.6	58 216	57 864	57 864	57 265	374 621
September	1 105.3	3 462.4	4 244.4	58 883	58 455	58 455	57 800	378 338
October	1 113.2	3 465.2	4 249.8	59 563	59 277	59 277	58 485	381 503
November	1 123.7	3 477.8	4 267.0	60 217	60 128	60 128	59 100	384 023
December	1 129.3	3 483.3	4 277.6	60 460	60 378	60 378	59 390	386 462
1994								
January	1 131.3	3 484.6	4 274.6	60 811	60 738	60 738	59 354	390 125
February	1 135.9	3 485.3	4 259.5	60 478	60 407	60 407	59 331	393 276
March	1 139.7	3 491.1	4 270.7	60 296	60 240	60 240	59 315	396 064
April	1 139.5	3 494.6	4 280.7	60 511	60 387	60 387	59 373	398 863
May	1 143.0	3 503.5	4 291.9	59 989	59 789	59 789	59 123	401 453
June	1 145.7	3 493.0	4 291.1	60 076	59 743	59 743	58 962	404 506
July	1 150.9	3 498.6	4 311.7	60 362	59 904	59 904	59 251	407 740
August	1 151.2	3 496.0	4 312.5	60 000	59 531	59 531	58 997	409 686
September	1 152.3	3 496.5	4 320.9	59 825	59 338	59 338	58 780	411 813
October	1 150.6	3 495.2	4 331.7	59 352	58 972	58 972	58 561	413 998
November	1 150.3	3 496.8	4 345.8	59 339	59 090	59 090	58 352	416 699
December	1 149.9	3 496.2	4 360.0	59 369	59 160	59 160	58 209	418 194

Table 20-5. Money Stock, Reserves, and Monetary Base—*Continued*

(Averages of daily figures; billions of dollars, seasonally adjusted.)

Year and month	Money stock measures			Reserves, adjusted for change in reserve requirements				
	M1	M2	M3	Total	Nonborrowed	Nonborrowed plus extended credit	Required	Monetary base
1995								
January	1 150.4	3 501.2	4 383.1	59 349	59 213	59 217	58 010	420 913
February	1 146.4	3 499.0	4 384.8	58 630	58 571	58 571	57 668	421 684
March	1 145.8	3 500.6	4 405.4	58 220	58 151	58 151	57 405	424 748
April	1 147.7	3 508.6	4 426.2	58 001	57 891	57 891	57 249	427 943
May	1 144.2	3 531.8	4 465.6	57 686	57 537	57 537	56 812	430 618
June	1 143.9	3 558.8	4 505.5	57 432	57 159	57 159	56 449	430 260
July	1 146.1	3 579.0	4 532.5	57 886	57 514	57 514	56 781	430 743
August	1 146.2	3 600.3	4 566.6	57 608	57 326	57 326	56 604	431 396
September	1 142.1	3 611.1	4 585.7	57 363	57 085	57 085	56 394	431 864
October	1 137.7	3 622.3	4 602.7	56 741	56 495	56 495	55 656	432 625
November	1 134.3	3 631.0	4 614.2	56 284	56 079	56 079	55 330	433 003
December	1 126.7	3 640.0	4 625.2	56 430	56 173	56 173	55 140	434 400
1996								
January	1 122.2	3 657.6	4 658.4	55 844	55 806	55 806	54 380	434 698
February	1 117.1	3 673.1	4 687.6	54 616	54 582	54 582	53 760	432 734
March	1 120.5	3 697.9	4 722.0	55 313	55 292	55 292	54 174	435 887
April	1 122.0	3 708.1	4 739.3	55 210	55 120	55 120	54 087	437 021
May	1 115.0	3 719.8	4 776.4	54 083	53 956	53 956	53 177	437 687
June	1 114.4	3 734.3	4 800.7	54 196	53 810	53 810	53 088	440 040
July	1 112.4	3 749.4	4 826.9	53 439	53 071	53 071	52 421	442 556
August	1 102.3	3 757.7	4 846.4	52 221	51 888	51 888	51 263	444 689
September	1 097.4	3 767.8	4 873.1	51 358	50 990	50 990	50 311	446 130
October	1 087.0	3 780.7	4 913.4	50 056	49 768	49 768	49 049	446 828
November	1 082.0	3 795.0	4 933.0	49 761	49 547	49 547	48 709	448 697
December	1 078.4	3 815.3	4 972.0	50 149	49 994	49 994	48 733	451 921
1997								
January	1 080.3	3 829.9	5 000.1	49 653	49 608	49 608	48 429	453 422
February	1 077.2	3 841.1	5 029.7	48 705	48 663	48 663	47 673	454 594
March	1 069.7	3 854.9	5 065.1	47 858	47 701	47 701	46 692	456 350
April	1 061.7	3 870.2	5 104.3	47 310	47 109	47 109	46 361	457 971
May	1 063.2	3 884.1	5 132.0	46 668	46 425	46 425	45 405	459 693
June	1 064.7	3 903.2	5 163.3	46 946	46 579	46 579	45 632	462 176
July	1 067.4	3 923.7	5 222.5	46 780	46 370	46 370	45 563	464 641
August	1 072.7	3 952.6	5 277.8	46 952	46 354	46 354	45 697	466 855
September	1 067.8	3 970.7	5 317.5	46 285	45 848	45 848	44 984	469 297
October	1 066.8	3 989.5	5 362.5	45 972	45 702	45 702	44 557	471 862
November	1 068.8	4 011.1	5 403.1	46 399	46 246	46 246	44 730	475 823
December	1 071.4	4 031.5	5 446.5	46 848	46 523	46 523	45 163	479 838
1998								
January	1 073.8	4 056.1	5 493.9	46 665	46 455	46 455	44 872	482 027
February	1 077.5	4 089.2	5 528.0	45 733	45 675	45 675	44 200	483 367
March	1 076.1	4 112.9	5 593.3	45 863	45 822	45 822	44 512	485 197
April	1 075.0	4 134.9	5 629.0	46 150	46 078	46 078	44 762	487 269
May	1 076.1	4 158.2	5 670.8	45 548	45 395	45 395	44 275	489 041
June	1 076.8	4 184.2	5 711.6	45 454	45 203	45 203	43 838	491 791
July	1 076.0	4 205.9	5 736.1	44 928	44 670	44 670	43 558	494 422
August	1 073.4	4 230.7	5 800.1	45 110	44 839	44 839	43 579	497 869
September	1 079.7	4 271.9	5 866.5	44 872	44 621	44 621	43 177	502 201
October	1 086.6	4 313.1	5 937.8	44 934	44 760	44 760	43 362	506 521
November	1 092.7	4 352.4	5 994.7	44 882	44 799	44 799	43 263	509 955
December	1 094.8	4 384.4	6 036.6	45 141	45 024	45 024	43 627	513 708
1999								
January	1 094.7	4 407.8	6 063.8	44 588	44 382	44 382	43 102	516 500
February	1 096.5	4 435.9	6 114.2	44 274	44 159	44 159	43 079	521 001
March	1 097.1	4 442.5	6 114.7	43 929	43 864	43 864	42 660	525 012
April	1 099.2	4 466.0	6 147.7	43 657	43 491	43 491	42 497	528 848
May	1 100.3	4 492.9	6 183.9	43 991	43 864	43 864	42 769	533 495
June	1 099.7	4 515.4	6 221.3	43 354	43 210	43 210	42 059	536 946
July	1 099.7	4 542.7	6 253.2	42 298	41 989	41 989	41 174	540 464
August	1 098.0	4 562.2	6 282.6	42 160	41 816	41 816	41 000	544 424
September	1 097.5	4 578.7	6 307.1	42 063	41 724	41 724	40 853	549 841
October	1 102.6	4 596.6	6 361.3	41 609	41 327	41 327	40 458	557 010
November	1 111.1	4 621.0	6 446.5	41 788	41 552	41 552	40 458	570 637
December	1 121.5	4 650.2	6 535.4	41 809	41 488	41 488	40 512	593 155
2000								
January	1 118.7	4 677.5	6 583.5	42 215	41 842	41 842	40 196	590 750
February	1 109.2	4 694.5	6 617.0	40 961	40 854	40 854	39 849	573 522
March	1 108.2	4 720.1	6 683.7	40 346	40 167	40 167	39 137	571 987
April	1 108.2	4 758.9	6 735.4	40 527	40 223	40 223	39 369	572 675
May	1 105.2	4 765.9	6 759.8	40 630	40 268	40 268	39 658	574 036
June	1 106.0	4 786.7	6 810.1	40 412	39 932	39 932	39 295	575 580
July	1 104.7	4 804.3	6 860.9	40 317	39 747	39 747	39 173	576 412
August	1 103.0	4 837.0	6 931.9	39 762	39 183	39 183	38 743	577 337
September	1 100.2	4 868.8	6 989.7	39 722	39 244	39 244	38 603	578 037
October	1 100.7	4 883.1	7 008.6	39 413	38 995	38 995	38 264	580 271
November	1 092.8	4 894.0	7 023.1	39 440	39 157	39 157	38 132	582 281
December	1 084.7	4 932.1	7 100.5	38 537	38 327	38 327	37 110	584 765

Table 20-5. Money Stock, Reserves, and Monetary Base—*Continued*

(Averages of daily figures; billions of dollars, seasonally adjusted.)

Year and month	Money stock measures			Reserves, adjusted for change in reserve requirements				
	M1	M2	M3	Total	Nonborrowed	Nonborrowed plus extended credit	Required	Monetary base
2001								
January	1 093.2	4 986.3	7 207.0	37 836	37 763	37 763	36 452	588 195
February	1 099.8	5 030.9	7 279.2	38 285	38 234	38 234	36 778	590 140
March	1 107.5	5 083.3	7 345.6	38 247	38 189	38 189	36 847	592 670
April	1 105.9	5 129.2	7 462.3	38 467	38 416	38 416	37 190	595 877
May	1 116.7	5 154.4	7 541.9	38 551	38 338	38 338	37 532	599 003
June	1 125.8	5 199.0	7 629.6	39 233	39 003	39 003	37 871	601 580
July	1 138.0	5 233.4	7 668.0	39 791	39 508	39 508	38 383	606 823
August	1 149.2	5 266.5	7 678.3	40 019	39 836	39 836	38 811	615 202
September	1 201.2	5 377.0	7 836.5	58 186	54 801	54 801	39 169	639 481
October	1 163.9	5 362.9	7 871.6	45 489	45 362	45 362	44 163	630 484
November	1 165.3	5 403.3	7 945.5	40 965	40 881	40 881	39 513	630 301
December	1 172.9	5 445.1	8 006.2	41 243	41 177	41 177	39 595	635 617
2002								
January	1 179.0	5 469.1	8 017.9	41 576	41 526	41 526	40 181	641 597
February	1 185.2	5 507.4	8 069.6	41 335	41 305	41 305	39 964	646 583
March	1 187.1	5 508.3	8 082.8	40 768	40 689	40 689	39 347	649 991
April	1 172.6	5 494.8	8 085.0	40 635	40 565	40 565	39 424	654 077
May	1 183.3	5 557.5	8 152.4	39 406	39 294	39 294	38 145	657 784
June	1 188.9	5 587.7	8 180.9	39 469	39 327	39 327	38 231	662 317
July	1 195.7	5 635.5	8 227.1	39 679	39 487	39 487	38 301	666 838
August	1 184.5	5 673.4	8 293.7	39 961	39 628	39 628	38 353	669 833
September	1 191.3	5 699.1	8 335.3	39 209	38 980	38 980	37 722	671 399
October	1 202.6	5 737.0	8 346.9	39 171	39 028	39 028	37 636	674 250
November	1 202.2	5 777.3	8 470.0	39 760	39 489	39 489	38 122	677 611
December	1 210.4	5 792.9	8 525.8	40 217	40 138	40 138	38 208	681 899

Table 20-6. Interest Rates, Bond Yields, and Stock Price Indexes

(Not seasonally adjusted.)

| Year and month | Short-term rates | | | | | U.S. Treasury securities | | Bond yields | | | | Stock price indexes | | |
| | Federal funds | Federal reserve discount rate [1] | U.S. Treasury bills, 3-month | U.S. Treasury bills, 6-month | Bank prime rate | 1-year | 10-year | Domestic corporate (Moody's) | | State and local bonds (Bond Buyer) | Fixed-rate first mortgages | Dow Jones industrials (30 stocks) | Standard and Poor's composite (500 stocks) [2] | Nasdaq composite |
								Aaa	Baa					
1945														
January	...	...	0.38	...	...	...	...	2.69	3.46	...	...	153.95	13.49	...
February	...	...	0.38	...	...	...	...	2.65	3.41	...	...	157.24	13.94	...
March	...	...	0.38	...	...	...	...	2.62	3.38	...	...	157.31	13.93	...
April	...	...	0.38	...	...	...	...	2.61	3.36	...	...	160.34	14.28	...
May	...	...	0.38	...	...	...	...	2.62	3.32	...	...	165.52	14.82	...
June	...	...	0.38	...	...	...	...	2.61	3.29	...	...	167.37	15.09	...
July	...	...	0.38	...	...	...	...	2.60	3.26	...	...	163.92	14.78	...
August	...	...	0.38	...	...	...	...	2.61	3.26	...	...	166.17	14.83	...
September	...	...	0.38	...	...	...	...	2.62	3.24	...	...	177.85	15.84	...
October	...	...	0.38	...	...	...	...	2.62	3.20	...	...	185.06	16.50	...
November	...	...	0.38	...	...	...	...	2.62	3.15	...	...	190.34	17.04	...
December	...	...	0.38	...	...	...	...	2.61	3.10	...	...	192.68	17.33	...
1946														
January	...	...	0.38	...	...	...	...	2.54	3.01	...	...	199.23	18.02	...
February	...	...	0.38	...	...	...	...	2.48	2.95	...	...	198.56	18.07	...
March	...	...	0.38	...	...	...	...	2.47	2.94	...	...	194.23	17.53	...
April	...	...	0.38	...	...	...	...	2.46	2.96	...	...	205.71	18.66	...
May	...	...	0.38	...	...	...	...	2.51	3.02	...	...	206.80	18.70	...
June	...	...	0.38	...	...	...	...	2.49	3.03	...	...	207.33	18.58	...
July	...	...	0.38	...	...	...	...	2.48	3.03	...	...	202.28	18.05	...
August	...	...	0.38	...	...	...	...	2.51	3.03	...	...	199.45	17.70	...
September	...	...	0.38	...	...	...	...	2.58	3.10	...	...	172.74	15.09	...
October	...	...	0.38	...	...	...	...	2.60	3.15	...	...	169.47	14.75	...
November	...	...	0.38	...	...	...	...	2.59	3.17	...	...	168.74	14.69	...
December	...	...	0.38	...	...	...	...	2.61	3.17	...	...	174.29	15.13	...
1947														
January	...	...	0.38	...	...	...	...	2.57	3.13	...	...	176.15	15.21	...
February	...	...	0.38	...	...	...	...	2.55	3.12	...	...	181.43	15.80	...
March	...	...	0.38	...	...	...	...	2.55	3.15	...	...	176.69	15.16	...
April	...	...	0.38	...	...	...	...	2.53	3.16	...	...	171.23	14.60	...
May	...	...	0.38	...	...	...	...	2.53	3.17	...	...	168.63	14.34	...
June	...	...	0.38	...	...	...	...	2.55	3.21	...	...	173.76	14.84	...
July	...	...	0.66	...	...	...	...	2.55	3.18	...	...	183.53	15.77	...
August	...	...	0.75	...	...	...	...	2.56	3.17	...	...	180.08	15.46	...
September	...	...	0.80	...	...	...	...	2.61	3.23	...	...	176.81	15.06	...
October	...	...	0.85	...	...	...	...	2.70	3.35	...	...	181.95	15.45	...
November	...	...	0.92	...	...	...	...	2.77	3.44	...	...	181.52	15.27	...
December	...	...	0.95	...	...	...	...	2.86	3.52	...	...	179.24	15.03	...
1948														
January	...	...	0.97	...	...	...	...	2.86	3.52	...	...	176.30	14.83	...
February	...	...	1.00	...	...	...	...	2.85	3.53	...	...	168.64	14.10	...
March	...	...	1.00	...	...	...	...	2.83	3.53	...	...	169.77	14.30	...
April	...	...	1.00	...	...	...	...	2.78	3.47	...	...	180.05	15.40	...
May	...	...	1.00	...	...	...	...	2.76	3.38	...	...	186.51	16.15	...
June	...	...	1.00	...	...	...	...	2.76	3.34	...	...	191.06	16.82	...
July	...	...	1.00	...	...	...	...	2.81	3.37	...	...	187.07	16.42	...
August	...	...	1.06	...	...	...	...	2.84	3.44	...	...	181.77	15.94	...
September	...	...	1.09	...	...	...	...	2.84	3.45	...	...	180.34	15.76	...
October	...	...	1.12	...	...	...	...	2.84	3.50	...	...	185.16	16.19	...
November	...	...	1.14	...	...	...	...	2.84	3.53	...	...	176.76	15.29	...
December	...	...	1.16	...	...	...	...	2.79	3.53	...	...	176.30	15.19	...
1949														
January	...	...	1.17	...	2.00	...	...	2.71	3.46	...	...	179.63	15.36	...
February	...	...	1.17	...	2.00	...	...	2.71	3.45	...	...	174.54	14.77	...
March	...	...	1.17	...	2.00	...	...	2.70	3.47	...	...	175.87	14.91	...
April	...	...	1.17	...	2.00	...	...	2.70	3.45	...	...	175.63	14.89	...
May	...	...	1.17	...	2.00	...	...	2.71	3.45	...	...	173.93	14.78	...
June	...	...	1.17	...	2.00	...	...	2.71	3.47	...	...	165.60	13.97	...
July	...	...	1.02	...	2.00	...	...	2.67	3.46	...	...	173.34	14.76	...
August	...	...	1.04	...	2.00	...	...	2.62	3.40	...	...	179.25	15.29	...
September	...	...	1.07	...	2.00	...	...	2.60	3.37	...	...	180.92	15.49	...
October	...	...	1.05	...	2.00	...	...	2.61	3.36	...	...	186.57	15.89	...
November	...	...	1.08	...	2.00	...	...	2.60	3.35	...	...	191.49	16.11	...
December	...	...	1.10	...	2.00	...	...	2.58	3.31	...	...	196.78	16.54	...
1950														
January	...	1.50	1.07	...	2.00	...	...	2.57	3.24	...	...	199.75	16.88	...
February	...	1.50	1.12	...	2.00	...	...	2.58	3.24	...	...	203.31	17.21	...
March	...	1.50	1.12	...	2.00	...	...	2.58	3.24	...	...	206.25	17.35	...
April	...	1.50	1.15	...	2.00	...	...	2.60	3.23	...	...	212.76	17.84	...
May	...	1.50	1.16	...	2.00	...	...	2.61	3.25	...	...	219.30	18.44	...
June	...	1.50	1.15	...	2.00	...	...	2.62	3.28	...	...	221.02	18.74	...
July	...	1.50	1.16	...	2.00	...	...	2.65	3.32	...	...	205.31	17.38	...
August	...	1.59	1.20	...	2.00	...	...	2.61	3.23	...	...	216.61	18.43	...
September	...	1.75	1.30	...	2.08	...	...	2.64	3.21	...	...	223.20	19.08	...
October	...	1.75	1.31	...	2.25	...	...	2.67	3.22	...	...	229.24	19.87	...
November	...	1.75	1.36	...	2.25	...	...	2.67	3.22	...	...	229.08	19.83	...
December	...	1.75	1.34	...	2.25	...	...	2.67	3.20	...	...	229.18	19.75	...

[1] Discount window borrowing, Federal Reserve Bank of New York.
[2] 1941–1943 = 10.
. . . = Not available.

Table 20-6. Interest Rates, Bond Yields, and Stock Price Indexes—*Continued*

(Not seasonally adjusted.)

| Year and month | Short-term rates | | | | | U.S. Treasury securities | | Bond yields | | | Fixed-rate first mortgages | Stock price indexes | | |
| | Federal funds | Federal reserve discount rate[1] | U.S. Treasury bills, 3-month | U.S. Treasury bills, 6-month | Bank prime rate | 1-year | 10-year | Domestic corporate (Moody's) | | State and local bonds (Bond Buyer) | | Dow Jones industrials (30 stocks) | Standard and Poor's composite (500 stocks)[2] | Nasdaq composite |
								Aaa	Baa					
1951														
January	...	1.75	1.34	...	2.44	...	...	2.66	3.17	...	...	244.41	21.21	...
February	...	1.75	1.36	...	2.50	...	...	2.66	3.16	...	...	253.16	22.00	...
March	...	1.75	1.40	...	2.50	...	...	2.78	3.23	...	...	249.36	21.63	...
April	...	1.75	1.47	...	2.50	...	...	2.87	3.35	...	...	253.02	21.92	...
May	...	1.75	1.55	...	2.50	...	...	2.89	3.40	...	...	254.45	21.93	...
June	...	1.75	1.45	...	2.50	...	...	2.94	3.49	...	...	249.32	21.55	...
July	...	1.75	1.56	...	2.50	...	...	2.94	3.53	...	...	253.61	21.93	...
August	...	1.75	1.62	...	2.50	...	...	2.88	3.50	...	...	264.93	22.89	...
September	...	1.75	1.63	...	2.50	...	...	2.84	3.46	...	...	273.37	23.48	...
October	...	1.75	1.54	...	2.62	...	...	2.89	3.50	...	...	269.85	23.36	...
November	...	1.75	1.56	...	2.75	...	...	2.96	3.56	...	...	259.65	22.71	...
December	...	1.75	1.73	...	2.85	...	...	3.01	3.61	...	...	266.15	23.41	...
1952														
January	...	1.75	1.57	...	3.00	...	...	2.98	3.59	...	...	271.64	24.19	...
February	...	1.75	1.54	...	3.00	...	...	2.93	3.53	...	...	264.72	23.75	...
March	...	1.75	1.59	...	3.00	...	...	2.96	3.51	...	...	264.45	23.81	...
April	...	1.75	1.57	...	3.00	...	...	2.93	3.50	...	...	262.46	23.74	...
May	...	1.75	1.67	...	3.00	...	...	2.93	3.49	...	...	261.63	23.73	...
June	...	1.75	1.70	...	3.00	...	...	2.94	3.50	...	...	268.39	24.38	...
July	...	1.75	1.81	...	3.00	...	...	2.95	3.50	...	...	276.05	25.08	...
August	...	1.75	1.83	...	3.00	...	...	2.94	3.51	...	...	276.70	25.18	...
September	...	1.75	1.71	...	3.00	...	...	2.95	3.52	...	...	272.41	24.78	...
October	...	1.75	1.74	...	3.00	...	...	3.01	3.54	...	...	267.78	24.26	...
November	...	1.75	1.85	...	3.00	...	...	2.98	3.53	...	...	276.38	25.03	...
December	...	1.75	2.09	...	3.00	...	...	2.97	3.51	...	...	285.96	26.04	...
1953														
January	...	1.88	1.96	...	3.00	...	...	3.02	3.51	2.44	...	288.45	26.18	...
February	...	2.00	1.97	...	3.00	...	...	3.07	3.53	2.59	...	283.96	25.86	...
March	...	2.00	2.01	...	3.00	...	...	3.12	3.57	2.65	...	286.79	25.99	...
April	...	2.00	2.19	...	3.03	2.36	2.83	3.23	3.65	2.67	...	275.29	24.71	...
May	...	2.00	2.16	...	3.25	2.48	3.05	3.34	3.78	2.82	...	276.84	24.84	...
June	...	2.00	2.11	...	3.25	2.45	3.11	3.40	3.86	3.03	...	266.89	23.95	...
July	...	2.00	2.04	...	3.25	2.38	2.93	3.28	3.86	2.95	...	270.33	24.29	...
August	...	2.00	2.04	...	3.25	2.28	2.95	3.24	3.85	2.90	...	272.20	24.39	...
September	...	2.00	1.79	...	3.25	2.20	2.87	3.29	3.88	2.87	...	261.90	23.27	...
October	...	2.00	1.38	...	3.25	1.79	2.66	3.16	3.82	2.71	...	270.72	23.97	...
November	...	2.00	1.44	...	3.25	1.67	2.68	3.11	3.75	2.60	...	277.09	24.50	...
December	...	2.00	1.60	...	3.25	1.66	2.59	3.13	3.74	2.59	...	281.15	24.83	...
1954														
January	...	2.00	1.18	...	3.25	1.41	2.48	3.06	3.71	2.50	...	286.64	25.46	...
February	...	1.79	0.97	...	3.25	1.14	2.47	2.95	3.61	2.42	...	292.13	26.02	...
March	...	1.75	1.03	...	3.13	1.13	2.37	2.86	3.51	2.39	...	299.16	26.57	...
April	...	1.63	0.97	...	3.00	0.96	2.29	2.85	3.47	2.47	...	310.93	27.63	...
May	...	1.50	0.76	...	3.00	0.85	2.37	2.88	3.47	2.49	...	322.85	28.73	...
June	...	1.50	0.64	...	3.00	0.82	2.38	2.90	3.49	2.47	...	327.91	28.96	...
July	0.80	1.50	0.72	...	3.00	0.84	2.30	2.89	3.50	2.32	...	341.27	30.13	...
August	1.22	1.50	0.92	...	3.00	0.88	2.36	2.87	3.49	2.26	...	346.06	30.73	...
September	1.06	1.50	1.01	...	3.00	1.03	2.38	2.89	3.47	2.31	...	352.71	31.45	...
October	0.85	1.50	0.98	...	3.00	1.17	2.43	2.87	3.46	2.34	...	358.29	32.18	...
November	0.83	1.50	0.93	...	3.00	1.14	2.48	2.89	3.45	2.32	...	375.71	33.44	...
December	1.28	1.50	1.15	...	3.00	1.21	2.51	2.90	3.45	2.36	...	393.84	34.97	...
1955														
January	1.39	1.50	1.22	...	3.00	1.39	2.61	2.93	3.45	2.40	...	398.43	35.60	...
February	1.29	1.50	1.17	...	3.00	1.57	2.65	2.93	3.47	2.43	...	410.26	36.79	...
March	1.35	1.50	1.28	...	3.00	1.59	2.68	3.02	3.48	2.44	...	408.91	36.50	...
April	1.43	1.63	1.59	...	3.00	1.75	2.75	3.01	3.49	2.41	...	423.00	37.76	...
May	1.43	1.75	1.45	...	3.00	1.90	2.76	3.04	3.50	2.38	...	421.55	37.60	...
June	1.64	1.75	1.41	...	3.00	1.91	2.78	3.05	3.51	2.41	...	440.83	39.78	...
July	1.68	1.75	1.60	...	3.00	2.02	2.90	3.06	3.52	2.54	...	462.17	42.69	...
August	1.96	1.97	1.90	...	3.23	2.37	2.97	3.11	3.56	2.60	...	457.31	42.43	...
September	2.18	2.18	2.07	...	3.25	2.36	2.97	3.13	3.59	2.58	...	476.44	44.34	...
October	2.24	2.25	2.23	...	3.40	2.39	2.88	3.10	3.59	2.51	...	452.65	42.11	...
November	2.35	2.36	2.24	...	3.50	2.48	2.89	3.10	3.58	2.45	...	476.60	44.95	...
December	2.48	2.50	2.54	...	3.50	2.73	2.96	3.15	3.62	2.57	...	484.58	45.37	...
1956														
January	2.45	2.50	2.41	...	3.50	2.58	2.90	3.11	3.60	2.50	...	474.75	44.15	...
February	2.50	2.50	2.32	...	3.50	2.49	2.84	3.08	3.58	2.44	...	475.53	44.43	...
March	2.50	2.50	2.25	...	3.50	2.61	2.96	3.10	3.60	2.57	...	502.67	47.49	...
April	2.62	2.65	2.60	...	3.65	2.92	3.18	3.24	3.68	2.70	...	511.05	48.05	...
May	2.75	2.75	2.61	...	3.75	2.94	3.07	3.28	3.73	2.68	...	495.21	46.54	...
June	2.71	2.75	2.49	...	3.75	2.74	3.00	3.26	3.76	2.54	...	485.33	46.27	...
July	2.75	2.75	2.31	...	3.75	2.76	3.11	3.28	3.80	2.65	...	509.75	48.78	...
August	2.73	2.81	2.60	...	3.84	3.10	3.33	3.43	3.93	2.80	...	511.69	48.49	...
September	2.95	3.00	2.84	...	4.00	3.35	3.38	3.56	4.07	2.93	...	495.03	46.84	...
October	2.96	3.00	2.90	...	4.00	3.28	3.34	3.59	4.17	2.95	...	483.81	46.24	...
November	2.88	3.00	2.99	...	4.00	3.44	3.49	3.69	4.24	3.16	...	479.36	45.76	...
December	2.94	3.00	3.21	...	4.00	3.68	3.59	3.75	4.37	3.22	...	492.02	46.44	...

[1]Discount window borrowing, Federal Reserve Bank of New York.
[2]1941–1943 = 10.
. . . = Not available.

Table 20-6. Interest Rates, Bond Yields, and Stock Price Indexes—*Continued*

(Not seasonally adjusted.)

Year and month	Federal funds	Federal reserve discount rate [1]	U.S. Treasury bills, 3-month	U.S. Treasury bills, 6-month	Bank prime rate	1-year	10-year	Aaa	Baa	State and local bonds (Bond Buyer)	Fixed-rate first mortgages	Dow Jones industrials (30 stocks)	Standard and Poor's composite (500 stocks) [2]	Nasdaq composite
1957														
January	2.84	3.00	3.11	...	4.00	3.37	3.46	3.77	4.49	3.18	...	485.90	45.43	...
February	3.00	3.00	3.10	...	4.00	3.38	3.34	3.67	4.47	3.00	...	466.83	43.47	...
March	2.96	3.00	3.08	...	4.00	3.42	3.41	3.66	4.43	3.09	...	472.77	44.03	...
April	3.00	3.00	3.07	...	4.00	3.49	3.48	3.67	4.44	3.13	...	485.42	45.05	...
May	3.00	3.00	3.06	...	4.00	3.48	3.60	3.74	4.52	3.27	...	500.83	46.78	...
June	3.00	3.00	3.29	...	4.00	3.65	3.80	3.91	4.63	3.41	...	505.29	47.55	...
July	2.99	3.00	3.16	...	4.00	3.81	3.93	3.99	4.73	3.39	...	514.65	48.51	...
August	3.24	3.15	3.37	...	4.42	4.01	3.93	4.10	4.82	3.54	...	487.97	45.84	...
September	3.47	3.50	3.53	...	4.50	4.07	3.92	4.12	4.93	3.53	...	471.80	43.98	...
October	3.50	3.50	3.58	...	4.50	4.01	3.97	4.10	4.99	3.42	...	443.38	41.24	...
November	3.28	3.23	3.31	...	4.50	3.57	3.72	4.08	5.09	3.37	...	436.73	40.35	...
December	2.98	3.00	3.04	...	4.50	3.18	3.21	3.81	5.03	3.04	...	436.96	40.33	...
1958														
January	2.72	2.94	2.44	...	4.34	2.65	3.09	3.60	4.83	2.91	...	445.69	41.12	...
February	1.67	2.75	1.53	...	4.00	1.99	3.05	3.59	4.66	3.02	...	444.16	41.26	...
March	1.20	2.35	1.30	...	4.00	1.84	2.98	3.63	4.68	3.06	...	450.15	42.11	...
April	1.26	2.03	1.13	...	3.83	1.45	2.88	3.60	4.67	2.96	...	446.91	42.34	...
May	0.63	1.75	0.91	...	3.50	1.37	2.92	3.57	4.62	2.92	...	460.04	43.70	...
June	0.93	1.75	0.83	...	3.50	1.23	2.97	3.57	4.55	2.97	...	471.98	44.75	...
July	0.68	1.75	0.91	...	3.50	1.61	3.20	3.67	4.53	3.09	...	488.30	45.98	...
August	1.53	1.75	1.09	...	3.50	2.50	3.54	3.85	4.67	3.35	...	507.55	47.70	...
September	1.76	1.91	2.44	...	3.83	3.05	3.76	4.09	4.87	3.54	...	521.81	48.96	...
October	1.80	2.00	2.63	...	4.00	3.19	3.80	4.11	4.92	3.45	...	539.85	50.95	...
November	2.27	2.40	2.67	...	4.00	3.10	3.74	4.09	4.87	3.32	...	557.11	52.50	...
December	2.42	2.50	2.77	3.01	4.00	3.29	3.86	4.08	4.85	3.33	...	566.44	53.49	...
1959														
January	2.48	2.50	2.82	3.09	4.00	3.36	4.02	4.12	4.87	3.42	...	592.30	55.62	...
February	2.43	2.50	2.70	3.13	4.00	3.54	3.96	4.14	4.89	3.36	...	590.72	54.77	...
March	2.80	2.92	2.80	3.13	4.00	3.61	3.99	4.13	4.85	3.30	...	609.13	56.15	...
April	2.96	3.00	2.95	3.27	4.00	3.72	4.12	4.23	4.86	3.39	...	617.00	57.10	...
May	2.90	3.05	2.84	3.33	4.23	3.96	4.31	4.37	4.96	3.57	...	630.80	57.96	...
June	3.39	3.50	3.21	3.52	4.50	4.07	4.34	4.46	5.04	3.71	...	631.52	57.46	...
July	3.47	3.50	3.20	3.82	4.50	4.39	4.40	4.47	5.08	3.71	...	662.81	59.74	...
August	3.50	3.50	3.38	3.87	4.50	4.42	4.43	4.43	5.09	3.58	...	660.58	59.40	...
September	3.76	3.83	4.04	4.70	5.00	5.00	4.68	4.52	5.18	3.78	...	635.49	57.05	...
October	3.98	4.00	4.05	4.53	5.00	4.80	4.53	4.57	5.28	3.62	...	637.35	57.00	...
November	4.00	4.00	4.15	4.54	5.00	4.81	4.53	4.56	5.26	3.55	...	646.43	57.23	...
December	3.99	4.00	4.49	4.85	5.00	5.14	4.69	4.58	5.28	3.70	...	671.36	59.06	...
1960														
January	3.99	4.00	4.35	4.74	5.00	5.03	4.72	4.61	5.34	3.72	...	655.39	58.03	...
February	3.97	4.00	3.96	4.30	5.00	4.66	4.49	4.56	5.34	3.60	...	624.89	55.78	...
March	3.84	4.00	3.31	3.61	5.00	4.02	4.25	4.49	5.25	3.57	...	614.70	55.02	...
April	3.92	4.00	3.23	3.55	5.00	4.04	4.28	4.45	5.20	3.56	...	619.98	55.73	...
May	3.85	4.00	3.29	3.58	5.00	4.21	4.35	4.46	5.28	3.60	...	615.63	55.22	...
June	3.32	3.65	2.46	2.74	5.00	3.36	4.15	4.45	5.26	3.55	...	644.39	57.26	...
July	3.23	3.50	2.30	2.71	5.00	3.20	3.90	4.41	5.22	3.50	...	625.83	55.84	...
August	2.98	3.18	2.30	2.59	4.85	2.95	3.80	4.28	5.08	3.33	...	624.47	56.51	...
September	2.60	3.00	2.48	2.83	4.50	3.07	3.80	4.25	5.01	3.42	...	598.10	54.81	...
October	2.47	3.00	2.30	2.73	4.50	3.04	3.89	4.30	5.11	3.53	...	582.47	53.73	...
November	2.44	3.00	2.37	2.66	4.50	3.08	3.93	4.31	5.08	3.40	...	601.14	55.47	...
December	1.98	3.00	2.25	2.50	4.50	2.86	3.84	4.35	5.10	3.40	...	609.54	56.80	...
1961														
January	1.45	3.00	2.24	2.47	4.50	2.81	3.84	4.32	5.10	3.39	...	632.20	59.72	...
February	2.54	3.00	2.42	2.60	4.50	2.93	3.78	4.27	5.07	3.31	...	650.02	62.17	...
March	2.02	3.00	2.39	2.54	4.50	2.88	3.74	4.22	5.02	3.45	...	670.57	64.12	...
April	1.49	3.00	2.29	2.47	4.50	2.88	3.78	4.25	5.01	3.48	...	684.90	65.83	...
May	1.98	3.00	2.29	2.45	4.50	2.87	3.71	4.27	5.01	3.43	...	693.03	66.50	...
June	1.73	3.00	2.33	2.54	4.50	3.06	3.88	4.33	5.03	3.52	...	691.46	65.62	...
July	1.17	3.00	2.24	2.45	4.50	2.92	3.92	4.41	5.09	3.51	...	690.67	65.44	...
August	2.00	3.00	2.39	2.66	4.50	3.06	4.04	4.45	5.11	3.52	...	718.64	67.79	...
September	1.88	3.00	2.28	2.68	4.50	3.06	3.98	4.45	5.12	3.53	...	711.02	67.26	...
October	2.26	3.00	2.30	2.66	4.50	3.05	3.92	4.42	5.13	3.42	...	703.01	68.00	...
November	2.61	3.00	2.48	2.70	4.50	3.07	3.94	4.39	5.11	3.41	...	724.74	71.08	...
December	2.33	3.00	2.60	2.88	4.50	3.18	4.06	4.42	5.10	3.47	...	728.44	71.74	...
1962														
January	2.15	3.00	2.72	2.94	4.50	3.28	4.08	4.42	5.08	3.34	...	705.15	69.07	...
February	2.37	3.00	2.73	2.93	4.50	3.28	4.04	4.42	5.07	3.21	...	711.95	70.22	...
March	2.85	3.00	2.72	2.87	4.50	3.06	3.93	4.39	5.04	3.14	...	714.20	70.29	...
April	2.78	3.00	2.73	2.83	4.50	2.99	3.84	4.33	5.02	3.06	...	690.29	68.05	...
May	2.36	3.00	2.69	2.78	4.50	3.03	3.87	4.28	5.00	3.11	...	643.71	62.99	...
June	2.68	3.00	2.73	2.80	4.50	3.03	3.91	4.28	5.02	3.25	...	572.65	55.63	...
July	2.71	3.00	2.92	3.08	4.50	3.29	4.01	4.34	5.05	3.27	...	581.79	56.97	...
August	2.93	3.00	2.82	2.99	4.50	3.20	3.98	4.35	5.06	3.23	...	602.50	58.52	...
September	2.90	3.00	2.78	2.93	4.50	3.06	3.98	4.32	5.03	3.11	...	597.02	58.00	...
October	2.90	3.00	2.74	2.84	4.50	2.98	3.93	4.28	4.99	3.02	...	580.67	56.17	...
November	2.94	3.00	2.83	2.89	4.50	3.00	3.92	4.25	4.96	3.04	...	628.83	60.04	...
December	2.93	3.00	2.87	2.91	4.50	3.01	3.86	4.24	4.92	3.07	...	648.38	62.64	...

[1] Discount window borrowing, Federal Reserve Bank of New York.
[2] 1941–1943 = 10.
. . . = Not available.

Table 20-6. Interest Rates, Bond Yields, and Stock Price Indexes—*Continued*

(Not seasonally adjusted.)

Year and month	Short-term rates					U.S. Treasury securities		Bond yields			Fixed-rate first mortgages	Stock price indexes		
	Federal funds	Federal reserve discount rate [1]	U.S. Treasury bills, 3-month	U.S. Treasury bills, 6-month	Bank prime rate	1-year	10-year	Domestic corporate (Moody's)		State and local bonds (Bond Buyer)		Dow Jones industrials (30 stocks)	Standard and Poor's composite (500 stocks) [2]	Nasdaq composite
								Aaa	Baa					
1963														
January	2.92	3.00	2.91	2.96	4.50	3.04	3.83	4.21	4.91	3.10	...	672.10	65.06	...
February	3.00	3.00	2.92	2.98	4.50	3.01	3.92	4.19	4.89	3.15	...	679.74	65.92	...
March	2.98	3.00	2.89	2.95	4.50	3.03	3.93	4.19	4.88	3.05	...	674.63	65.67	...
April	2.90	3.00	2.90	2.98	4.50	3.11	3.97	4.21	4.87	3.10	...	707.12	68.76	...
May	3.00	3.00	2.93	3.01	4.50	3.12	3.93	4.22	4.85	3.11	...	720.84	70.14	...
June	2.99	3.00	2.99	3.08	4.50	3.20	3.99	4.23	4.84	3.21	...	719.15	70.11	...
July	3.02	3.24	3.18	3.31	4.50	3.48	4.02	4.26	4.84	3.22	...	700.75	69.07	...
August	3.49	3.50	3.32	3.44	4.50	3.53	4.00	4.29	4.83	3.13	...	714.16	70.98	...
September	3.48	3.50	3.38	3.50	4.50	3.57	4.08	4.31	4.84	3.20	...	738.53	72.85	...
October	3.50	3.50	3.45	3.58	4.50	3.64	4.11	4.32	4.83	3.20	...	747.53	73.03	...
November	3.48	3.50	3.52	3.65	4.50	3.74	4.12	4.33	4.84	3.30	...	743.24	72.62	...
December	3.38	3.50	3.52	3.66	4.50	3.81	4.13	4.35	4.85	3.27	...	759.96	74.17	...
1964														
January	3.48	3.50	3.52	3.64	4.50	3.79	4.17	4.39	4.83	3.22	...	777.07	76.45	...
February	3.48	3.50	3.53	3.67	4.50	3.78	4.15	4.36	4.83	3.14	...	793.02	77.39	...
March	3.43	3.50	3.54	3.72	4.50	3.91	4.22	4.38	4.83	3.28	...	812.19	78.80	...
April	3.47	3.50	3.47	3.66	4.50	3.91	4.23	4.40	4.85	3.28	...	820.96	79.94	...
May	3.50	3.50	3.48	3.60	4.50	3.84	4.20	4.41	4.85	3.20	...	823.13	80.72	...
June	3.50	3.50	3.48	3.56	4.50	3.83	4.17	4.41	4.85	3.20	...	817.65	80.24	...
July	3.42	3.50	3.46	3.56	4.50	3.72	4.19	4.40	4.83	3.18	...	844.25	83.22	...
August	3.50	3.50	3.50	3.61	4.50	3.74	4.19	4.41	4.82	3.19	...	835.31	82.00	...
September	3.45	3.50	3.53	3.68	4.50	3.84	4.20	4.42	4.82	3.23	...	863.55	83.41	...
October	3.36	3.50	3.57	3.72	4.50	3.86	4.19	4.42	4.81	3.25	...	875.27	84.85	...
November	3.52	3.62	3.64	3.81	4.50	3.91	4.15	4.43	4.81	3.18	...	880.03	85.44	...
December	3.85	4.00	3.84	3.95	4.50	4.02	4.18	4.44	4.81	3.13	...	866.73	83.96	...
1965														
January	3.90	4.00	3.81	3.94	4.50	3.94	4.19	4.43	4.80	3.06	...	889.91	86.12	...
February	3.98	4.00	3.93	4.00	4.50	4.03	4.21	4.41	4.78	3.09	...	894.42	86.75	...
March	4.04	4.00	3.93	4.00	4.50	4.06	4.21	4.42	4.78	3.17	...	896.45	86.83	...
April	4.09	4.00	3.93	3.99	4.50	4.04	4.20	4.43	4.80	3.15	...	907.72	87.97	...
May	4.10	4.00	3.89	3.95	4.50	4.03	4.21	4.44	4.81	3.17	...	927.50	89.28	...
June	4.04	4.00	3.80	3.86	4.50	3.99	4.21	4.46	4.85	3.24	...	878.07	85.04	...
July	4.09	4.00	3.84	3.90	4.50	3.98	4.20	4.48	4.88	3.27	...	873.44	84.91	...
August	4.12	4.00	3.84	3.95	4.50	4.07	4.25	4.49	4.88	3.24	...	887.71	86.49	...
September	4.01	4.00	3.92	4.07	4.50	4.20	4.29	4.52	4.91	3.35	...	922.20	89.38	...
October	4.08	4.00	4.03	4.19	4.50	4.30	4.35	4.56	4.93	3.40	...	944.78	91.39	...
November	4.10	4.00	4.09	4.24	4.50	4.37	4.45	4.60	4.95	3.45	...	953.31	92.15	...
December	4.32	4.42	4.38	4.55	4.92	4.72	4.62	4.68	5.02	3.54	...	955.20	91.73	...
1966														
January	4.42	4.50	4.59	4.71	5.00	4.88	4.61	4.74	5.06	3.52	...	985.93	93.32	...
February	4.60	4.50	4.65	4.82	5.00	4.94	4.83	4.78	5.12	3.64	...	977.15	92.69	...
March	4.65	4.50	4.59	4.78	5.35	4.97	4.87	4.92	5.32	3.72	...	926.43	88.88	...
April	4.67	4.50	4.62	4.74	5.50	4.90	4.75	4.96	5.41	3.56	...	943.46	91.60	...
May	4.90	4.50	4.64	4.81	5.50	4.93	4.78	4.98	5.48	3.65	...	890.71	86.78	...
June	5.17	4.50	4.50	4.65	5.52	4.97	4.81	5.07	5.58	3.77	...	888.83	86.06	...
July	5.30	4.50	4.80	4.93	5.75	5.17	5.02	5.16	5.68	3.95	...	875.89	85.84	...
August	5.53	4.50	4.96	5.27	5.88	5.54	5.22	5.31	5.83	4.12	...	817.55	80.65	...
September	5.40	4.50	5.37	5.79	6.00	5.82	5.18	5.49	6.09	4.12	...	791.66	77.81	...
October	5.53	4.50	5.35	5.62	6.00	5.58	5.01	5.41	6.10	3.93	...	778.11	77.13	...
November	5.76	4.50	5.32	5.54	6.00	5.54	5.16	5.35	6.13	3.86	...	806.56	80.99	...
December	5.40	4.50	4.96	5.07	6.00	5.20	4.84	5.39	6.18	3.86	...	800.88	81.33	...
1967														
January	4.94	4.50	4.72	4.74	5.96	4.75	4.58	5.20	5.97	3.54	...	830.55	84.45	...
February	5.00	4.50	4.56	4.59	5.75	4.71	4.63	5.03	5.82	3.52	...	851.12	87.36	...
March	4.53	4.50	4.26	4.22	5.71	4.35	4.54	5.13	5.85	3.55	...	858.12	89.42	...
April	4.05	4.10	3.84	3.89	5.50	4.11	4.59	5.11	5.83	3.60	...	868.66	90.96	...
May	3.94	4.00	3.60	3.80	5.50	4.15	4.85	5.24	5.96	3.89	...	883.74	92.59	...
June	3.98	4.00	3.54	3.89	5.50	4.48	5.02	5.44	6.15	3.96	...	872.66	91.43	...
July	3.79	4.00	4.21	4.72	5.50	5.01	5.16	5.58	6.26	4.02	...	888.51	93.01	...
August	3.90	4.00	4.27	4.83	5.50	5.13	5.28	5.62	6.33	3.99	...	912.48	94.49	...
September	3.99	4.00	4.42	4.96	5.50	5.24	5.30	5.65	6.40	4.12	...	923.46	95.81	...
October	3.88	4.00	4.56	5.07	5.50	5.37	5.48	5.82	6.52	4.29	...	907.55	95.66	...
November	4.13	4.18	4.73	5.25	5.68	5.61	5.75	6.07	6.72	4.34	...	865.44	92.66	...
December	4.51	4.50	4.97	5.49	6.00	5.71	5.70	6.19	6.93	4.43	...	887.20	95.30	...
1968														
January	4.60	4.50	5.00	5.24	6.00	5.43	5.53	6.17	6.84	4.29	...	884.78	95.04	...
February	4.71	4.50	4.98	5.17	6.00	5.41	5.56	6.10	6.80	4.31	...	847.20	90.75	...
March	5.05	4.66	5.17	5.33	6.00	5.58	5.74	6.11	6.85	4.54	...	834.76	89.09	...
April	5.76	5.20	5.38	5.49	6.20	5.71	5.64	6.21	6.97	4.34	...	893.38	95.67	...
May	6.11	5.50	5.66	5.83	6.50	6.14	5.87	6.27	7.03	4.54	...	905.23	97.87	...
June	6.07	5.50	5.52	5.64	6.50	5.98	5.72	6.28	7.07	4.49	...	906.82	100.53	...
July	6.02	5.50	5.31	5.41	6.50	5.65	5.50	6.24	6.98	4.33	...	905.33	100.30	...
August	6.03	5.48	5.09	5.23	6.50	5.43	5.42	6.02	6.82	4.21	...	883.73	98.11	...
September	5.78	5.25	5.19	5.25	6.45	5.45	5.46	5.97	6.79	4.38	...	922.82	101.34	...
October	5.91	5.25	5.35	5.41	6.25	5.57	5.58	6.09	6.84	4.49	...	955.48	103.76	...
November	5.82	5.25	5.45	5.60	6.25	5.75	5.70	6.19	7.01	4.60	...	964.13	105.40	...
December	6.02	5.36	5.96	6.06	6.60	6.19	6.03	6.45	7.23	4.82	...	968.39	106.48	...

[1] Discount window borrowing, Federal Reserve Bank of New York.
[2] 1941–1943 = 10.
... = Not available.

Table 20-6. Interest Rates, Bond Yields, and Stock Price Indexes—Continued

(Not seasonally adjusted.)

| Year and month | Short-term rates | | | | | U.S. Treasury securities | | Bond yields | | | Fixed-rate first mortgages | Stock price indexes | | |
| | Federal funds | Federal reserve discount rate [1] | U.S. Treasury bills, 3-month | U.S. Treasury bills, 6-month | Bank prime rate | 1-year | 10-year | Domestic corporate (Moody's) | | State and local bonds (Bond Buyer) | | Dow Jones industrials (30 stocks) | Standard and Poor's composite (500 stocks) [2] | Nasdaq composite |
								Aaa	Baa					
1969														
January	6.30	5.50	6.14	6.28	6.95	6.34	6.04	6.59	7.32	4.85	. . .	935.00	102.04	. . .
February	6.61	5.50	6.12	6.30	7.00	6.41	6.19	6.66	7.30	4.98	. . .	931.31	101.46	. . .
March	6.79	5.50	6.02	6.16	7.24	6.34	6.30	6.85	7.51	5.26	. . .	916.52	99.30	. . .
April	7.41	5.95	6.11	6.13	7.50	6.26	6.17	6.89	7.54	5.19	. . .	927.38	101.26	. . .
May	8.67	6.00	6.04	6.15	7.50	6.42	6.32	6.79	7.52	5.33	. . .	954.88	104.62	. . .
June	8.90	6.00	6.44	6.75	8.23	7.04	6.57	6.98	7.70	5.75	. . .	896.62	99.14	. . .
July	8.61	6.00	7.00	7.24	8.50	7.60	6.72	7.08	7.84	5.75	. . .	844.02	94.71	. . .
August	9.19	6.00	6.98	7.19	8.50	7.54	6.69	6.97	7.86	6.00	. . .	825.46	94.18	. . .
September	9.15	6.00	7.09	7.32	8.50	7.82	7.16	7.14	8.05	6.26	. . .	826.72	94.51	. . .
October	9.00	6.00	7.00	7.29	8.50	7.64	7.10	7.33	8.22	6.09	. . .	832.52	95.52	. . .
November	8.85	6.00	7.24	7.62	8.50	7.89	7.14	7.35	8.25	6.30	. . .	841.10	96.21	. . .
December	8.97	6.00	7.82	7.90	8.50	8.17	7.65	7.72	8.65	6.82	. . .	789.23	91.11	. . .
1970														
January	8.98	6.00	7.87	7.78	8.50	8.10	7.79	7.91	8.86	6.63	. . .	782.93	90.31	. . .
February	8.98	6.00	7.13	7.22	8.50	7.59	7.24	7.93	8.78	6.22	. . .	756.22	87.16	. . .
March	7.76	6.00	6.63	6.58	8.39	6.97	7.07	7.84	8.63	6.05	. . .	777.63	88.65	. . .
April	8.10	6.00	6.51	6.60	8.00	7.06	7.39	7.83	8.70	6.65	. . .	771.65	85.95	. . .
May	7.94	6.00	6.84	7.02	8.00	7.75	7.91	8.11	8.98	7.00	. . .	691.97	76.06	. . .
June	7.60	6.00	6.68	6.86	8.00	7.55	7.84	8.48	9.25	6.93	. . .	699.30	75.59	. . .
July	7.21	6.00	6.45	6.51	0.00	7.10	7.46	8.44	9.40	6.42	. . .	712.81	75.72	. . .
August	6.61	6.00	6.41	6.55	8.00	6.98	7.53	8.13	9.44	6.17	. . .	731.98	77.92	. . .
September	6.29	6.00	6.12	6.46	7.83	6.73	7.39	8.09	9.39	6.31	. . .	759.39	82.58	. . .
October	6.20	6.00	5.91	6.21	7.50	6.43	7.33	8.03	9.33	6.37	. . .	763.74	84.37	. . .
November	5.60	5.85	5.28	5.42	7.28	5.51	6.84	8.05	9.38	5.71	. . .	769.28	84.28	. . .
December	4.90	5.52	4.87	4.89	6.92	5.00	6.39	7.64	9.12	5.47	. . .	821.51	90.05	. . .
1971														
January	4.14	5.23	4.44	4.47	6.29	4.57	6.24	7.36	8.74	5.35	. . .	849.04	93.49	. . .
February	3.72	4.91	3.70	3.78	5.88	3.89	6.11	7.08	8.39	5.23	. . .	879.69	97.11	. . .
March	3.71	4.75	3.38	3.50	5.44	3.69	5.70	7.21	8.46	5.17	. . .	901.29	99.60	. . .
April	4.15	4.75	3.86	4.03	5.28	4.30	5.83	7.25	8.45	5.37	7.31	932.54	103.04	. . .
May	4.63	4.75	4.14	4.36	5.46	5.04	6.39	7.53	8.62	5.90	7.43	925.51	101.64	. . .
June	4.91	4.75	4.75	4.97	5.50	5.64	6.52	7.64	8.75	5.95	7.53	900.45	99.72	. . .
July	5.31	4.88	5.40	5.63	5.91	6.04	6.73	7.64	8.76	6.06	7.60	887.81	99.00	. . .
August	5.56	5.00	4.94	5.22	6.00	5.80	6.58	7.59	8.76	5.82	7.70	875.41	97.24	. . .
September	5.55	5.00	4.69	4.97	6.00	5.41	6.14	7.44	8.59	5.37	7.69	901.22	99.40	. . .
October	5.20	5.00	4.46	4.60	5.90	4.91	5.93	7.39	8.48	5.06	7.63	872.15	97.29	. . .
November	4.91	4.90	4.22	4.38	5.53	4.67	5.81	7.26	8.38	5.20	7.55	822.11	92.78	. . .
December	4.14	4.63	4.01	4.23	5.49	4.60	5.93	7.25	8.38	5.21	7.48	869.92	99.17	. . .
1972														
January	3.50	4.50	3.38	3.66	5.18	4.28	5.95	7.19	8.23	5.12	7.44	904.65	103.30	. . .
February	3.29	4.50	3.20	3.63	4.75	4.27	6.08	7.27	8.23	5.28	7.33	914.37	105.24	. . .
March	3.83	4.50	3.73	4.12	4.75	4.67	6.07	7.24	8.24	5.31	7.30	939.23	107.69	. . .
April	4.17	4.50	3.71	4.23	4.97	4.96	6.19	7.30	8.24	5.43	7.29	958.17	108.81	. . .
May	4.27	4.50	3.69	4.12	5.00	4.64	6.13	7.30	8.23	5.30	7.37	948.22	107.65	. . .
June	4.46	4.50	3.91	4.35	5.04	4.93	6.11	7.23	8.20	5.33	7.37	943.44	108.01	. . .
July	4.55	4.50	3.98	4.50	5.25	4.96	6.11	7.21	8.23	5.41	7.40	925.94	107.21	. . .
August	4.80	4.50	4.02	4.55	5.27	4.98	6.21	7.19	8.19	5.30	7.40	958.36	111.01	. . .
September	4.87	4.50	4.66	5.13	5.50	5.52	6.55	7.22	8.09	5.36	7.42	950.60	109.39	. . .
October	5.04	4.50	4.74	5.13	5.73	5.52	6.48	7.21	8.06	5.18	7.42	944.10	109.56	. . .
November	5.06	4.50	4.78	5.09	5.75	5.27	6.28	7.12	7.99	5.02	7.43	1 001.20	115.05	. . .
December	5.33	4.50	5.07	5.30	5.79	5.52	6.36	7.08	7.93	5.05	7.44	1 020.32	117.50	. . .
1973														
January	5.94	4.77	5.41	5.62	6.00	5.89	6.46	7.15	7.90	5.05	7.44	1 026.82	118.42	. . .
February	6.58	5.05	5.60	5.83	6.02	6.19	6.64	7.22	7.97	5.13	7.44	974.05	114.16	. . .
March	7.09	5.50	6.09	6.51	6.30	6.85	6.71	7.29	8.03	5.29	7.46	957.36	112.42	. . .
April	7.12	5.50	6.26	6.52	6.61	6.85	6.67	7.26	8.09	5.15	7.54	944.12	110.27	. . .
May	7.84	5.90	6.36	6.62	7.01	6.89	6.85	7.29	8.06	5.15	7.65	922.41	107.22	. . .
June	8.49	6.33	7.19	7.23	7.49	7.31	6.90	7.37	8.13	5.17	7.73	893.90	104.75	. . .
July	10.40	6.98	8.01	8.12	8.30	8.39	7.13	7.45	8.24	5.40	8.05	903.61	105.83	. . .
August	10.50	7.29	8.67	8.65	9.23	8.82	7.40	7.68	8.53	5.48	8.50	883.73	103.80	. . .
September	10.78	7.50	8.29	8.45	9.86	8.31	7.09	7.63	8.63	5.10	8.82	909.99	105.61	. . .
October	10.01	7.50	7.22	7.32	9.94	7.40	6.79	7.60	8.41	5.05	8.77	967.63	109.84	. . .
November	10.03	7.50	7.83	7.96	9.75	7.57	6.73	7.67	8.42	5.18	8.58	878.99	102.03	. . .
December	9.95	7.50	7.45	7.56	9.75	7.27	6.74	7.68	8.48	5.12	8.54	824.08	94.78	. . .
1974														
January	9.65	7.50	7.77	7.65	9.73	7.42	6.99	7.83	8.48	5.22	8.54	857.25	96.11	. . .
February	8.97	7.50	7.12	6.96	9.21	6.88	6.96	7.85	8.53	5.20	8.46	831.33	93.45	. . .
March	9.35	7.50	7.96	7.83	8.85	7.76	7.21	8.01	8.62	5.40	8.41	874.01	97.44	. . .
April	10.51	7.60	8.33	8.32	10.02	8.62	7.51	8.25	8.87	5.73	8.58	847.79	92.46	. . .
May	11.31	8.00	8.23	8.40	11.25	8.78	7.58	8.37	9.05	6.02	8.97	830.26	89.67	. . .
June	11.93	8.00	7.90	8.12	11.54	8.67	7.54	8.47	9.27	6.13	9.09	831.45	89.79	. . .
July	12.92	8.00	7.55	7.94	11.97	8.80	7.81	8.72	9.48	6.68	9.28	783.01	82.82	. . .
August	12.01	8.00	8.96	9.11	12.00	9.36	8.04	9.00	9.77	6.71	9.59	729.30	76.03	. . .
September	11.34	8.00	8.06	8.53	12.00	8.87	8.04	9.24	10.18	6.76	9.96	651.29	68.12	. . .
October	10.06	8.00	7.46	7.74	11.68	8.05	7.90	9.27	10.48	6.57	9.98	638.62	69.44	. . .
November	9.45	8.00	7.47	7.52	10.83	7.66	7.68	8.89	10.60	6.61	9.79	642.11	71.74	. . .
December	8.53	7.81	7.15	7.11	10.50	7.31	7.43	8.89	10.63	7.05	9.62	596.50	67.07	. . .

[1]Discount window borrowing, Federal Reserve Bank of New York.
[2]1941–1943 = 10.
. . . = Not available.

Table 20-6. Interest Rates, Bond Yields, and Stock Price Indexes—*Continued*

(Not seasonally adjusted.)

Year and month	Short-term rates					U.S. Treasury securities		Bond yields				Stock price indexes		
	Federal funds	Federal reserve discount rate [1]	U.S. Treasury bills, 3-month	U.S. Treasury bills, 6-month	Bank prime rate	1-year	10-year	Domestic corporate (Moody's)		State and local bonds (Bond Buyer)	Fixed-rate first mortgages	Dow Jones industrials (30 stocks)	Standard and Poor's composite (500 stocks) [2]	Nasdaq composite
								Aaa	Baa					
1975														
January	7.13	7.40	6.26	6.36	10.05	6.83	7.50	8.83	10.81	6.82	9.43	659.09	72.56	. . .
February	6.24	6.82	5.50	5.62	8.96	5.98	7.39	8.62	10.65	6.39	9.11	724.89	80.10	. . .
March	5.54	6.40	5.49	5.62	7.93	6.11	7.73	8.67	10.48	6.73	8.90	765.06	83.78	. . .
April	5.49	6.25	5.61	6.00	7.50	6.90	8.23	8.95	10.58	6.95	8.82	790.94	84.72	. . .
May	5.22	6.12	5.23	5.59	7.40	6.39	8.06	8.90	10.69	6.97	8.91	836.55	90.10	. . .
June	5.55	6.00	5.34	5.61	7.07	6.29	7.86	8.77	10.62	6.94	8.89	845.70	92.40	. . .
July	6.10	6.00	6.13	6.50	7.15	7.11	8.06	8.84	10.55	7.07	8.89	856.29	92.49	. . .
August	6.14	6.00	6.44	6.94	7.66	7.70	8.40	8.95	10.59	7.17	8.94	815.52	85.71	. . .
September	6.24	6.00	6.42	6.92	7.88	7.75	8.43	8.95	10.61	7.44	9.13	818.29	84.67	. . .
October	5.82	6.00	5.96	6.25	7.96	6.95	8.14	8.86	10.62	7.39	9.22	831.27	88.57	. . .
November	5.22	6.00	5.48	5.80	7.53	6.49	8.05	8.78	10.56	7.43	9.15	845.52	90.07	. . .
December	5.20	6.00	5.44	5.85	7.26	6.60	8.00	8.79	10.56	7.31	9.10	840.80	88.70	. . .
1976														
January	4.87	5.79	4.87	5.14	7.00	5.81	7.74	8.60	10.41	7.07	9.02	929.34	96.86	. . .
February	4.77	5.50	4.88	5.20	6.75	5.91	7.79	8.55	10.24	6.94	8.81	971.72	100.64	. . .
March	4.84	5.50	5.00	5.44	6.75	6.21	7.73	8.52	10.12	6.91	8.76	988.55	101.08	. . .
April	4.82	5.50	4.86	5.18	6.75	5.92	7.56	8.40	9.94	6.60	8.73	992.52	101.93	. . .
May	5.29	5.50	5.20	5.62	6.75	6.40	7.90	8.58	9.86	6.87	8.77	988.82	101.16	. . .
June	5.48	5.50	5.41	5.77	7.20	6.52	7.86	8.62	9.89	6.87	8.85	985.60	101.77	. . .
July	5.31	5.50	5.23	5.53	7.25	6.20	7.83	8.56	9.82	6.79	8.93	993.20	104.20	. . .
August	5.29	5.50	5.14	5.40	7.01	6.00	7.77	8.45	9.64	6.61	9.00	981.63	103.29	. . .
September	5.25	5.50	5.08	5.30	7.00	5.84	7.59	8.38	9.40	6.51	8.98	994.38	105.45	. . .
October	5.02	5.50	4.92	5.06	6.77	5.50	7.41	8.32	9.29	6.30	8.93	951.96	101.89	. . .
November	4.95	5.43	4.75	4.88	6.50	5.29	7.29	8.25	9.23	6.29	8.81	944.58	101.19	. . .
December	4.65	5.25	4.35	4.51	6.35	4.89	6.87	7.98	9.12	5.94	8.79	976.87	104.66	. . .
1977														
January	4.61	5.25	4.62	4.83	6.25	5.29	7.21	7.96	9.08	5.87	8.72	970.63	103.81	. . .
February	4.68	5.25	4.67	4.90	6.25	5.47	7.39	8.04	9.12	5.88	8.67	941.75	100.96	. . .
March	4.69	5.25	4.60	4.88	6.25	5.50	7.46	8.10	9.12	5.89	8.69	946.10	100.57	. . .
April	4.73	5.25	4.54	4.80	6.25	5.44	7.37	8.04	9.07	5.72	8.75	929.12	99.05	. . .
May	5.35	5.25	4.96	5.20	6.41	5.84	7.46	8.05	9.01	5.75	8.82	926.30	98.76	. . .
June	5.39	5.25	5.02	5.21	6.75	5.80	7.28	7.95	8.91	5.62	8.86	916.57	99.29	. . .
July	5.42	5.25	5.19	5.40	6.75	5.94	7.33	7.94	8.87	5.63	8.94	908.21	100.18	. . .
August	5.90	5.27	5.49	5.83	6.83	6.37	7.40	7.98	8.82	5.62	8.94	872.27	97.75	. . .
September	6.14	5.75	5.81	6.04	7.13	6.53	7.34	7.92	8.80	5.51	8.90	853.37	96.23	. . .
October	6.47	5.80	6.16	6.43	7.52	6.97	7.52	8.04	8.89	5.64	8.92	823.96	93.74	. . .
November	6.51	6.00	6.10	6.41	7.75	6.95	7.58	8.08	8.95	5.49	8.92	828.52	94.28	. . .
December	6.56	6.00	6.07	6.40	7.75	6.96	7.69	8.19	8.99	5.57	8.96	818.80	93.82	. . .
1978														
January	6.70	6.37	6.44	6.70	7.93	7.28	7.96	8.41	9.17	5.71	9.02	781.08	90.25	. . .
February	6.78	6.50	6.45	6.74	8.00	7.34	8.03	8.47	9.20	5.62	9.16	763.58	88.98	. . .
March	6.79	6.50	6.29	6.63	8.00	7.31	8.04	8.47	9.22	5.61	9.20	756.37	88.82	. . .
April	6.89	6.50	6.29	6.73	8.00	7.45	8.15	8.56	9.32	5.79	9.36	794.66	92.71	. . .
May	7.36	6.84	6.41	7.02	8.27	7.82	8.35	8.69	9.49	6.03	9.58	838.56	97.41	. . .
June	7.60	7.00	6.73	7.23	8.63	8.09	8.46	8.76	9.60	6.22	9.71	840.25	97.66	. . .
July	7.81	7.23	7.01	7.44	9.00	8.39	8.64	8.88	9.60	6.28	9.74	831.72	97.19	. . .
August	8.04	7.43	7.08	7.37	9.01	8.31	8.41	8.69	9.48	6.12	9.79	887.93	103.92	. . .
September	8.45	7.83	7.85	7.99	9.41	8.64	8.42	8.69	9.42	6.09	9.76	878.64	103.86	. . .
October	8.96	8.26	7.99	8.55	9.94	9.14	8.64	8.89	9.59	6.13	9.86	857.70	100.58	. . .
November	9.76	9.50	8.64	9.24	10.94	10.01	8.81	9.03	9.83	6.19	10.11	804.30	94.71	. . .
December	10.03	9.50	9.08	9.36	11.55	10.30	9.01	9.16	9.94	6.50	10.35	807.96	96.11	. . .
1979														
January	10.07	9.50	9.35	9.47	11.75	10.41	9.10	9.25	10.13	6.46	10.39	837.39	99.71	. . .
February	10.06	9.50	9.32	9.41	11.75	10.24	9.10	9.26	10.08	6.31	10.41	825.18	98.23	. . .
March	10.09	9.50	9.48	9.47	11.75	10.25	9.12	9.37	10.26	6.33	10.43	847.85	100.11	. . .
April	10.01	9.50	9.46	9.49	11.75	10.12	9.18	9.38	10.33	6.28	10.50	864.97	102.07	. . .
May	10.24	9.50	9.61	9.54	11.75	10.12	9.25	9.50	10.47	6.25	10.69	837.41	99.73	. . .
June	10.29	9.50	9.06	9.06	11.65	9.57	8.91	9.29	10.38	6.12	11.04	838.65	101.73	. . .
July	10.47	9.69	9.24	9.24	11.54	9.64	8.95	9.20	10.29	6.13	11.09	836.96	102.71	. . .
August	10.94	10.24	9.52	9.49	11.91	9.98	9.03	9.23	10.35	6.20	11.09	873.55	107.36	. . .
September	11.43	10.70	10.26	10.20	12.90	10.84	9.33	9.44	10.54	6.52	11.30	878.51	108.60	. . .
October	13.77	11.77	11.70	11.66	14.39	12.44	10.30	10.13	11.40	7.08	11.64	840.52	104.47	. . .
November	13.18	12.00	11.79	11.82	15.55	12.39	10.65	10.76	11.99	7.30	12.83	815.79	103.66	. . .
December	13.78	12.00	12.04	11.84	15.30	11.98	10.39	10.74	12.06	7.22	12.90	836.14	107.78	. . .
1980														
January	13.82	12.00	12.00	11.84	15.25	12.06	10.80	11.09	12.42	7.35	12.88	860.75	110.87	. . .
February	14.13	12.52	12.86	12.86	15.63	13.92	12.41	12.38	13.57	8.16	13.04	878.22	115.34	. . .
March	17.19	13.00	15.20	15.03	18.31	15.82	12.75	12.96	14.45	9.16	15.28	803.57	104.69	. . .
April	17.61	13.00	13.20	12.88	19.77	13.30	11.47	12.04	14.19	8.63	16.33	786.35	102.97	. . .
May	10.98	12.94	8.58	8.65	16.57	9.39	10.18	10.99	13.17	7.59	14.26	828.20	107.69	. . .
June	9.47	11.40	7.07	7.30	12.63	8.16	9.78	10.58	12.71	7.63	12.71	869.86	114.55	. . .
July	9.03	10.87	8.06	8.06	11.48	8.65	10.25	11.07	12.65	8.13	12.19	909.79	119.83	. . .
August	9.61	10.00	9.13	9.41	11.12	10.24	11.10	11.64	13.15	8.67	12.56	947.33	123.50	. . .
September	10.87	10.17	10.27	10.57	12.23	11.52	11.51	12.02	13.70	8.94	13.20	946.68	126.51	. . .
October	12.81	11.00	11.62	11.63	13.79	12.49	11.75	12.31	14.23	9.11	13.79	949.17	130.22	. . .
November	15.85	11.47	13.73	13.50	16.06	14.15	12.68	12.97	14.64	9.56	14.21	971.09	135.65	. . .
December	18.90	12.87	15.49	14.64	20.35	14.88	12.84	13.21	15.14	10.20	14.79	945.97	133.48	. . .

[1]Discount window borrowing, Federal Reserve Bank of New York.
[2]1941–1943 = 10.
. . . = Not available.

Table 20-6. Interest Rates, Bond Yields, and Stock Price Indexes—*Continued*

(Not seasonally adjusted.)

Year and month	Short-term rates					U.S. Treasury securities		Bond yields			Fixed-rate first mortgages	Stock price indexes		
	Federal funds	Federal reserve discount rate [1]	U.S. Treasury bills, 3-month	U.S. Treasury bills, 6-month	Bank prime rate	1-year	10-year	Domestic corporate (Moody's)		State and local bonds (Bond Buyer)		Dow Jones industrials (30 stocks)	Standard and Poor's composite (500 stocks) [2]	Nasdaq composite
								Aaa	Baa					
1981														
January	19.08	13.00	15.02	14.08	20.16	14.08	12.57	12.81	15.03	9.66	14.90	962.14	132.97	. . .
February	15.93	13.00	14.79	14.05	19.43	14.57	13.19	13.35	15.37	10.09	15.13	945.51	128.40	. . .
March	14.70	13.00	13.36	12.81	18.05	13.71	13.12	13.33	15.34	10.16	15.40	987.18	133.19	. . .
April	15.72	13.00	13.69	13.45	17.15	14.32	13.68	13.88	15.56	10.62	15.58	1 004.86	134.43	. . .
May	18.52	13.87	16.30	15.29	19.61	16.20	14.10	14.32	15.95	10.77	16.40	979.53	131.73	. . .
June	19.10	14.00	14.73	14.09	20.03	14.86	13.47	13.75	15.80	10.67	16.70	996.27	132.28	. . .
July	19.04	14.00	14.95	14.74	20.39	15.72	14.28	14.38	16.17	11.14	16.83	947.95	129.13	. . .
August	17.82	14.00	15.51	15.52	20.50	16.72	14.94	14.89	16.34	12.26	17.29	926.26	129.63	. . .
September	15.87	14.00	14.70	14.92	20.08	16.52	15.32	15.49	16.92	12.92	18.16	853.39	118.27	. . .
October	15.08	14.00	13.54	13.82	18.45	15.38	15.15	15.40	17.11	12.83	18.45	853.26	119.80	. . .
November	13.31	13.03	10.86	11.30	16.84	12.41	13.39	14.22	16.39	11.89	17.83	860.43	122.92	. . .
December	12.37	12.10	10.85	11.52	15.75	12.85	13.72	14.23	16.55	12.91	16.92	878.29	123.79	. . .
1982														
January	13.22	12.00	12.28	12.83	15.75	14.32	14.59	15.18	17.10	13.28	17.40	853.42	117.28	. . .
February	14.78	12.00	13.48	13.61	16.56	14.73	14.43	15.27	17.18	12.97	17.60	833.16	114.50	. . .
March	14.68	12.00	12.68	12.77	16.50	13.95	13.86	14.58	16.82	12.82	17.16	812.34	110.84	. . .
April	14.94	12.00	12.70	12.80	16.50	13.98	13.87	14.46	16.78	12.58	16.89	844.93	116.31	. . .
May	14.45	12.00	12.09	12.16	16.50	13.34	13.62	14.26	16.64	11.95	16.68	846.74	116.35	. . .
June	14.15	12.00	12.47	12.70	16.50	14.07	14.30	14.81	16.92	12.44	16.70	804.37	109.70	. . .
July	12.59	11.81	11.35	11.88	16.26	13.24	13.95	14.61	16.80	12.20	16.82	818.41	109.38	. . .
August	10.12	10.68	8.68	9.88	14.39	11.43	13.06	13.71	16.32	11.23	16.27	832.11	109.65	. . .
September	10.31	10.00	7.92	9.37	13.50	10.05	12.34	12.94	15.63	10.66	15.43	917.27	122.43	. . .
October	9.71	9.68	7.71	8.29	12.52	9.32	10.91	12.12	14.73	9.68	14.61	988.73	132.66	. . .
November	9.20	9.35	8.07	8.34	11.85	9.16	10.55	11.68	14.30	10.06	13.83	1 027.76	138.10	. . .
December	8.95	8.73	7.94	8.16	11.50	8.91	10.54	11.83	14.14	9.96	13.62	1 033.10	139.37	. . .
1983														
January	8.68	8.50	7.86	7.93	11.16	8.62	10.46	11.79	13.94	9.50	13.25	1 064.31	144.27	. . .
February	8.51	8.50	8.11	8.23	10.98	8.92	10.72	12.01	13.95	9.58	13.04	1 087.40	146.80	. . .
March	8.77	8.50	8.35	8.37	10.50	9.04	10.51	11.73	13.61	9.20	12.80	1 129.58	151.88	. . .
April	8.80	8.50	8.21	8.30	10.50	8.98	10.40	11.51	13.29	9.04	12.78	1 168.43	157.71	. . .
May	8.63	8.50	8.19	8.22	10.50	8.90	10.38	11.46	13.09	9.11	12.63	1 212.86	164.10	. . .
June	8.98	8.50	8.79	8.89	10.50	9.66	10.85	11.74	13.37	9.52	12.87	1 221.47	166.39	. . .
July	9.37	8.50	9.08	9.26	10.50	10.20	11.38	12.15	13.39	9.53	13.42	1 213.94	166.96	. . .
August	9.56	8.50	9.34	9.51	10.89	10.53	11.85	12.51	13.64	9.72	13.81	1 189.22	162.42	. . .
September	9.45	8.50	9.00	9.15	11.00	10.16	11.65	12.37	13.55	9.58	13.73	1 237.04	167.16	. . .
October	9.48	8.50	8.64	8.83	11.00	9.81	11.54	12.25	13.46	9.66	13.54	1 252.20	167.65	. . .
November	9.34	8.50	8.76	8.93	11.00	9.94	11.69	12.41	13.61	9.74	13.44	1 250.00	165.23	. . .
December	9.47	8.50	9.00	9.17	11.00	10.11	11.83	12.57	13.75	9.89	13.42	1 257.65	164.36	. . .
1984														
January	9.56	8.50	8.90	9.01	11.00	9.90	11.67	12.20	13.65	9.63	13.37	1 258.89	166.39	. . .
February	9.59	8.50	9.09	9.18	11.00	10.04	11.84	12.08	13.59	9.64	13.23	1 164.45	157.25	. . .
March	9.91	8.50	9.52	9.66	11.21	10.59	12.32	12.57	13.99	9.94	13.39	1 161.98	157.44	. . .
April	10.29	8.87	9.69	9.84	11.93	10.90	12.63	12.81	14.31	9.96	13.65	1 152.72	157.60	. . .
May	10.32	9.00	9.83	10.31	12.39	11.66	13.41	13.28	14.74	10.49	13.94	1 143.42	156.55	. . .
June	11.06	9.00	9.87	10.51	12.60	12.08	13.56	13.55	15.05	10.67	14.42	1 121.14	153.12	. . .
July	11.23	9.00	10.12	10.52	13.00	12.03	13.36	13.44	15.15	10.42	14.67	1 113.29	151.08	. . .
August	11.64	9.00	10.47	10.61	13.00	11.82	12.72	12.87	14.63	9.99	14.47	1 212.82	164.42	. . .
September	11.30	9.00	10.37	10.47	12.97	11.58	12.52	12.66	14.35	10.10	14.35	1 213.52	166.11	. . .
October	9.99	9.00	9.74	9.87	12.58	10.90	12.16	12.63	13.94	10.25	14.13	1 199.30	164.82	. . .
November	9.43	8.83	8.61	8.81	11.77	9.82	11.57	12.29	13.48	10.17	13.64	1 211.31	166.27	247.00
December	8.38	8.37	8.06	8.28	11.06	9.33	11.50	12.13	13.40	9.95	13.18	1 188.96	164.48	242.53
1985														
January	8.35	8.00	7.76	8.00	10.61	9.02	11.38	12.08	13.26	9.51	13.08	1 238.16	171.61	260.85
February	8.50	8.00	8.27	8.39	10.50	9.29	11.51	12.13	13.23	9.65	12.92	1 283.23	180.88	285.52
March	8.58	8.00	8.52	8.90	10.50	9.86	11.86	12.56	13.69	9.77	13.17	1 268.84	179.42	280.43
April	8.27	8.00	7.95	8.23	10.50	9.14	11.43	12.23	13.51	9.42	13.20	1 266.38	180.62	280.90
May	7.97	7.81	7.48	7.65	10.31	8.46	10.85	11.72	13.15	9.01	12.91	1 279.41	184.90	287.51
June	7.53	7.50	6.95	7.09	9.78	7.80	10.16	10.94	12.40	8.69	12.22	1 314.00	188.89	290.45
July	7.88	7.50	7.08	7.20	9.50	7.86	10.31	10.97	12.43	8.81	12.03	1 343.17	192.54	302.04
August	7.90	7.50	7.14	7.32	9.50	8.05	10.33	11.05	12.50	9.08	12.19	1 326.19	188.31	298.25
September	7.92	7.50	7.10	7.27	9.50	8.07	10.37	11.07	12.48	9.27	12.19	1 317.95	184.06	287.94
October	7.99	7.50	7.16	7.33	9.50	8.01	10.24	11.02	12.36	9.08	12.14	1 351.58	186.18	285.37
November	8.05	7.50	7.24	7.30	9.50	7.88	9.78	10.55	11.99	8.54	11.78	1 432.89	197.45	304.36
December	8.27	7.50	7.10	7.14	9.50	7.67	9.26	10.16	11.58	8.42	11.26	1 517.02	207.26	320.24
1986														
January	8.14	7.50	7.07	7.16	9.50	7.73	9.19	10.05	11.44	8.08	10.88	1 534.85	208.19	328.54
February	7.86	7.50	7.06	7.11	9.50	7.61	8.70	9.67	11.11	7.44	10.71	1 652.74	219.37	348.79
March	7.48	7.10	6.56	6.57	9.10	7.03	7.78	9.00	10.50	7.08	10.08	1 757.36	232.33	368.28
April	6.99	6.83	6.06	6.08	8.83	6.44	7.30	8.79	10.19	7.19	9.94	1 807.06	237.98	382.54
May	6.85	6.50	6.15	6.19	8.50	6.65	7.71	9.09	10.29	7.54	10.14	1 801.81	238.46	388.49
June	6.92	6.50	6.21	6.27	8.50	6.73	7.80	9.13	10.34	7.87	10.68	1 867.71	245.30	398.60
July	6.56	6.16	5.83	5.86	8.16	6.27	7.30	8.88	10.16	7.51	10.51	1 809.92	240.18	385.90
August	6.17	5.82	5.53	5.55	7.90	5.93	7.17	8.72	10.18	7.21	10.20	1 843.45	245.00	375.62
September	5.89	5.50	5.21	5.35	7.50	5.77	7.45	8.89	10.20	7.11	10.01	1 813.48	238.27	358.26
October	5.85	5.50	5.18	5.26	7.50	5.72	7.43	8.86	10.24	7.08	9.97	1 817.06	237.36	355.05
November	6.04	5.50	5.35	5.41	7.50	5.80	7.25	8.68	10.07	6.84	9.70	1 883.65	245.09	358.08
December	6.91	5.50	5.53	5.55	7.50	5.87	7.11	8.49	9.97	6.87	9.31	1 924.09	248.61	354.90

[1] Discount window borrowing, Federal Reserve Bank of New York.
[2] 1941–1943 = 10.
. . . = Not available.

Table 20-6. Interest Rates, Bond Yields, and Stock Price Indexes—*Continued*

(Not seasonally adjusted.)

| Year and month | Short-term rates | | | | | U.S. Treasury securities | | Bond yields | | | | Stock price indexes | | |
	Federal funds	Federal reserve discount rate[1]	U.S. Treasury bills, 3-month	U.S. Treasury bills, 6-month	Bank prime rate	1-year	10-year	Domestic corporate (Moody's) Aaa	Baa	State and local bonds (Bond Buyer)	Fixed-rate first mortgages	Dow Jones industrials (30 stocks)	Standard and Poor's composite (500 stocks)[2]	Nasdaq composite
1987														
January	6.43	5.50	5.43	5.44	7.50	5.78	7.08	8.36	9.72	6.66	9.20	2 065.13	264.51	384.24
February	6.10	5.50	5.59	5.59	7.50	5.96	7.25	8.38	9.65	6.61	9.08	2 202.34	280.93	411.71
March	6.13	5.50	5.59	5.60	7.50	6.03	7.25	8.36	9.61	6.65	9.04	2 292.61	292.47	432.19
April	6.37	5.50	5.64	5.90	7.75	6.50	8.02	8.85	10.04	7.55	9.83	2 302.66	289.32	422.75
May	6.85	5.50	5.66	6.05	8.14	7.00	8.61	9.33	10.51	8.00	10.60	2 291.12	289.12	416.64
June	6.73	5.50	5.67	5.99	8.25	6.80	8.40	9.32	10.52	7.79	10.54	2 384.02	301.38	423.70
July	6.58	5.50	5.69	5.76	8.25	6.68	8.45	9.42	10.61	7.72	10.28	2 481.73	310.09	429.01
August	6.73	5.50	6.04	6.15	8.25	7.03	8.76	9.67	10.80	7.82	10.33	2 655.02	329.36	448.45
September	7.22	5.95	6.40	6.64	8.70	7.67	9.42	10.18	11.31	8.26	10.89	2 570.81	318.66	442.82
October	7.29	6.00	6.13	6.69	9.07	7.59	9.52	10.52	11.62	8.70	11.26	2 224.58	280.16	385.05
November	6.69	6.00	5.69	6.19	8.78	6.96	8.86	10.01	11.23	7.95	10.65	1 931.88	245.01	318.76
December	6.77	6.00	5.77	6.36	8.75	7.17	8.99	10.11	11.29	7.96	10.65	1 910.07	240.96	314.55
1988														
January	6.83	6.00	5.81	6.25	8.75	6.99	8.67	9.88	11.07	7.69	10.43	1 947.35	250.48	339.29
February	6.58	6.00	5.66	5.93	8.51	6.64	8.21	9.40	10.62	7.49	9.89	1 980.65	258.13	353.58
March	6.58	6.00	5.70	5.91	8.50	6.71	8.37	9.39	10.57	7.74	9.93	2 044.32	265.74	375.55
April	6.87	6.00	5.91	6.21	8.50	7.01	8.72	9.67	10.90	7.81	10.20	2 036.14	262.61	377.23
May	7.09	6.00	6.26	6.56	8.84	7.40	9.09	9.90	11.04	7.91	10.46	1 988.91	256.12	371.88
June	7.51	6.00	6.46	6.71	9.00	7.49	8.92	9.86	11.00	7.78	10.46	2 104.95	270.68	385.99
July	7.75	6.00	6.73	6.99	9.29	7.75	9.06	9.96	11.11	7.76	10.43	2 104.23	269.05	391.43
August	8.01	6.37	7.06	7.39	9.84	8.17	9.26	10.11	11.21	7.79	10.60	2 051.28	263.73	379.60
September	8.19	6.50	7.24	7.43	10.00	8.09	8.98	9.82	10.90	7.66	10.48	2 080.07	267.97	382.17
October	8.30	6.50	7.35	7.50	10.00	8.11	8.80	9.51	10.41	7.46	10.30	2 144.33	277.40	385.02
November	8.35	6.50	7.76	7.86	10.05	8.48	8.96	9.45	10.48	7.46	10.27	2 099.04	271.02	372.90
December	8.76	6.50	8.07	8.22	10.50	8.99	9.11	9.57	10.65	7.61	10.61	2 148.59	276.51	375.80
1989														
January	9.12	6.50	8.27	8.36	10.50	9.05	9.09	9.62	10.65	7.35	10.73	2 234.68	285.41	389.33
February	9.36	6.59	8.53	8.55	10.93	9.25	9.17	9.64	10.61	7.44	10.65	2 304.31	294.01	404.09
March	9.85	7.00	8.82	8.85	11.50	9.57	9.36	9.80	10.67	7.59	11.03	2 283.10	292.71	404.00
April	9.84	7.00	8.65	8.65	11.50	9.36	9.18	9.79	10.61	7.49	11.05	2 348.92	302.25	417.14
May	9.81	7.00	8.43	8.41	11.50	8.98	8.86	9.57	10.46	7.25	10.77	2 439.57	313.93	435.99
June	9.53	7.00	8.15	7.93	11.07	8.44	8.28	9.10	10.03	7.02	10.20	2 494.89	323.73	447.63
July	9.24	7.00	7.88	7.61	10.98	7.89	8.02	8.93	9.87	6.96	9.88	2 554.04	331.93	446.70
August	8.99	7.00	7.90	7.74	10.50	8.18	8.11	8.96	9.88	7.06	9.99	2 691.12	346.61	461.83
September	9.02	7.00	7.75	7.74	10.50	8.22	8.19	9.01	9.91	7.26	10.13	2 693.41	347.33	469.28
October	8.84	7.00	7.64	7.62	10.50	7.99	8.01	8.92	9.81	7.22	9.95	2 692.01	347.40	469.69
November	8.55	7.00	7.69	7.49	10.50	7.77	7.87	8.89	9.81	7.14	9.77	2 642.50	340.22	454.69
December	8.45	7.00	7.63	7.42	10.50	7.72	7.84	8.86	9.82	6.98	9.74	2 728.47	348.57	449.02
1990														
January	8.23	7.00	7.64	7.55	10.11	7.92	8.21	8.99	9.94	7.10	9.90	2 679.24	339.97	439.35
February	8.24	7.00	7.74	7.70	10.00	8.11	8.47	9.22	10.14	7.22	10.20	2 614.19	330.45	424.53
March	8.28	7.00	7.90	7.85	10.00	8.35	8.59	9.37	10.21	7.29	10.27	2 700.13	338.47	436.10
April	8.26	7.00	7.77	7.84	10.00	8.40	8.79	9.46	10.30	7.39	10.37	2 708.27	338.18	429.00
May	8.18	7.00	7.74	7.76	10.00	8.32	8.76	9.47	10.41	7.35	10.48	2 793.82	350.25	442.60
June	8.29	7.00	7.73	7.63	10.00	8.10	8.48	9.26	10.22	7.24	10.16	2 894.84	360.39	462.31
July	8.15	7.00	7.62	7.52	10.00	7.94	8.47	9.24	10.20	7.19	10.04	2 934.23	360.03	455.83
August	8.13	7.00	7.45	7.38	10.00	7.78	8.75	9.41	10.41	7.32	10.10	2 681.89	330.75	396.33
September	8.20	7.00	7.36	7.32	10.00	7.76	8.89	9.56	10.64	7.43	10.18	2 550.69	315.41	368.57
October	8.11	7.00	7.17	7.16	10.00	7.55	8.72	9.53	10.74	7.49	10.18	2 460.54	307.12	338.02
November	7.81	7.00	7.06	7.03	10.00	7.31	8.39	9.30	10.62	7.18	10.01	2 518.58	315.29	347.72
December	7.31	6.79	6.74	6.70	10.00	7.05	8.08	9.05	10.43	7.09	9.67	2 610.92	328.75	370.21
1991														
January	6.91	6.50	6.22	6.28	9.52	6.64	8.09	9.04	10.45	7.08	9.64	2 587.60	325.49	376.67
February	6.25	6.00	5.94	5.93	9.05	6.27	7.85	8.83	10.07	6.91	9.37	2 863.05	362.26	442.59
March	6.12	6.00	5.91	5.92	9.00	6.40	8.11	8.93	10.09	7.10	9.50	2 920.12	372.28	469.10
April	5.91	5.98	5.65	5.71	9.00	6.24	8.04	8.86	9.94	7.02	9.49	2 925.55	379.68	496.32
May	5.78	5.50	5.46	5.61	8.50	6.13	8.07	8.86	9.86	6.95	9.47	2 928.43	377.99	490.93
June	5.90	5.50	5.57	5.75	8.50	6.36	8.28	9.01	9.96	7.13	9.62	2 968.14	378.29	490.38
July	5.82	5.50	5.58	5.70	8.50	6.31	8.27	9.00	9.89	7.05	9.58	2 978.19	380.23	489.37
August	5.66	5.50	5.33	5.39	8.50	5.78	7.90	8.75	9.65	6.90	9.24	3 006.09	389.40	513.25
September	5.45	5.20	5.22	5.25	8.20	5.57	7.65	8.61	9.51	6.80	9.01	3 010.36	387.20	520.56
October	5.21	5.00	4.99	5.04	8.00	5.33	7.53	8.55	9.49	6.68	8.86	3 019.74	386.88	528.92
November	4.81	4.58	4.56	4.61	7.58	4.89	7.42	8.48	9.45	6.73	8.71	2 986.13	385.92	536.58
December	4.43	4.11	4.07	4.10	7.21	4.38	7.09	8.31	9.26	6.69	8.50	2 958.66	388.51	544.10
1992														
January	4.03	3.50	3.80	3.87	6.50	4.15	7.03	8.20	9.13	6.54	8.43	3 227.06	416.08	615.73
February	4.06	3.50	3.84	3.93	6.50	4.29	7.34	8.29	9.23	6.74	8.76	3 257.27	412.56	632.05
March	3.98	3.50	4.04	4.18	6.50	4.63	7.54	8.35	9.25	6.76	8.94	3 247.42	407.36	619.60
April	3.73	3.50	3.75	3.87	6.50	4.30	7.48	8.33	9.21	6.67	8.85	3 294.10	407.41	582.79
May	3.82	3.50	3.63	3.75	6.50	4.19	7.39	8.28	9.13	6.57	8.67	3 376.79	414.81	581.47
June	3.76	3.50	3.66	3.77	6.50	4.17	7.26	8.22	9.05	6.49	8.51	3 337.79	408.27	566.66
July	3.25	3.02	3.21	3.28	6.02	3.60	6.84	8.07	8.84	6.13	8.13	3 329.41	415.05	568.72
August	3.30	3.00	3.13	3.21	6.00	3.47	6.59	7.95	8.65	6.16	7.98	3 307.46	417.93	569.00
September	3.22	3.00	2.91	2.96	6.00	3.18	6.42	7.92	8.62	6.25	7.92	3 293.93	418.48	580.68
October	3.10	3.00	2.86	3.04	6.00	3.30	6.59	7.99	8.84	6.41	8.09	3 198.70	412.50	585.01
November	3.09	3.00	3.13	3.34	6.00	3.68	6.87	8.10	8.96	6.36	8.31	3 238.49	422.84	630.86
December	2.92	3.00	3.22	3.36	6.00	3.71	6.77	7.98	8.81	6.22	8.22	3 303.15	435.64	661.28

[1]Discount window borrowing, Federal Reserve Bank of New York.
[2]1941–1943 = 10.

Table 20-6. Interest Rates, Bond Yields, and Stock Price Indexes—*Continued*

(Not seasonally adjusted.)

Year and month	Short-term rates					U.S. Treasury securities		Bond yields			Fixed-rate first mortgages	Stock price indexes		
	Federal funds	Federal reserve discount rate [1]	U.S. Treasury bills, 3-month	U.S. Treasury bills, 6-month	Bank prime rate	1-year	10-year	Domestic corporate (Moody's)		State and local bonds (Bond Buyer)		Dow Jones industrials (30 stocks)	Standard and Poor's composite (500 stocks) [2]	Nasdaq composite
								Aaa	Baa					
1993														
January	3.02	3.00	3.00	3.14	6.00	3.50	6.60	7.91	8.67	6.16	8.02	3 277.73	435.23	691.13
February	3.03	3.00	2.93	3.07	6.00	3.39	6.26	7.71	8.39	5.87	7.68	3 367.26	441.70	681.71
March	3.07	3.00	2.95	3.05	6.00	3.33	5.98	7.58	8.15	5.64	7.50	3 440.73	450.16	684.49
April	2.96	3.00	2.87	2.97	6.00	3.24	5.97	7.46	8.14	5.76	7.47	3 423.62	443.08	665.33
May	3.00	3.00	2.96	3.07	6.00	3.36	6.04	7.43	8.21	5.73	7.47	3 478.18	445.25	686.45
June	3.04	3.00	3.07	3.20	6.00	3.54	5.96	7.33	8.07	5.63	7.42	3 513.81	448.06	695.38
July	3.06	3.00	3.04	3.16	6.00	3.47	5.81	7.17	7.93	5.57	7.21	3 529.44	447.29	703.40
August	3.03	3.00	3.02	3.14	6.00	3.44	5.68	6.85	7.60	5.45	7.11	3 597.03	454.13	725.15
September	3.09	3.00	2.95	3.06	6.00	3.36	5.36	6.66	7.34	5.29	6.92	3 592.29	459.24	745.94
October	2.99	3.00	3.02	3.12	6.00	3.39	5.33	6.67	7.31	5.25	6.83	3 625.81	463.90	771.31
November	3.02	3.00	3.10	3.26	6.00	3.58	5.72	6.93	7.66	5.47	7.16	3 674.71	462.89	764.04
December	2.96	3.00	3.06	3.23	6.00	3.61	5.77	6.93	7.69	5.35	7.17	3 744.10	465.95	762.94
1994														
January	3.05	3.00	2.98	3.15	6.00	3.54	5.75	6.92	7.65	5.31	7.06	3 868.37	472.99	787.77
February	3.25	3.00	3.25	3.43	6.00	3.87	5.97	7.08	7.76	5.40	7.15	3 905.62	471.58	787.81
March	3.34	3.00	3.50	3.78	6.06	4.32	6.48	7.48	8.13	5.91	7.68	3 816.99	463.81	785.93
April	3.56	3.00	3.68	4.09	6.45	4.82	6.97	7.88	8.52	6.23	8.32	3 661.49	447.23	732.30
May	4.01	3.24	4.14	4.60	6.99	5.31	7.18	7.99	8.62	6.19	8.60	3 708.00	450.90	727.76
June	4.25	3.50	4.14	4.55	7.25	5.27	7.10	7.97	8.65	6.11	8.40	3 737.58	454.83	723.21
July	4.26	3.50	4.33	4.75	7.25	5.48	7.30	8.11	8.80	6.23	8.61	3 718.31	451.40	713.49
August	4.47	3.76	4.48	4.88	7.51	5.56	7.24	8.07	8.74	6.21	8.51	3 797.48	464.24	738.87
September	4.73	4.00	4.62	5.04	7.75	5.76	7.46	8.34	8.98	6.28	8.64	3 880.60	466.96	763.94
October	4.76	4.00	4.95	5.39	7.75	6.11	7.74	8.57	9.20	6.52	8.93	3 868.10	463.81	762.46
November	5.29	4.40	5.29	5.72	8.15	6.54	7.96	8.68	9.32	6.97	9.17	3 792.44	461.01	760.42
December	5.45	4.75	5.60	6.21	8.50	7.14	7.81	8.46	9.10	6.80	9.20	3 770.30	455.19	734.96
1995														
January	5.53	4.75	5.71	6.21	8.50	7.05	7.78	8.46	9.08	6.53	9.15	3 872.46	465.25	758.01
February	5.92	5.25	5.77	6.03	9.00	6.70	7.47	8.26	8.85	6.22	8.83	3 953.73	481.92	784.24
March	5.98	5.25	5.73	5.89	9.00	6.43	7.20	8.12	8.70	6.10	8.46	4 062.78	493.15	807.16
April	6.05	5.25	5.65	5.77	9.00	6.27	7.06	8.03	8.60	6.02	8.32	4 230.67	507.91	825.34
May	6.01	5.25	5.67	5.67	9.00	6.00	6.63	7.65	8.20	5.95	7.96	4 391.58	523.81	859.77
June	6.00	5.25	5.47	5.42	9.00	5.64	6.17	7.30	7.90	5.84	7.57	4 510.77	539.35	906.04
July	5.85	5.25	5.42	5.37	8.80	5.59	6.28	7.41	8.04	5.92	7.61	4 684.78	557.37	979.36
August	5.74	5.25	5.40	5.41	8.75	5.75	6.49	7.57	8.19	6.06	7.86	4 639.27	559.11	1 009.59
September	5.80	5.25	5.28	5.30	8.75	5.62	6.20	7.32	7.93	5.91	7.64	4 746.76	578.77	1 051.00
October	5.76	5.25	5.28	5.32	8.75	5.59	6.04	7.12	7.75	5.80	7.48	4 760.48	582.92	1 022.15
November	5.80	5.25	5.36	5.27	8.75	5.43	5.93	7.02	7.68	5.64	7.38	4 935.82	595.53	1 046.64
December	5.60	5.25	5.14	5.13	8.65	5.31	5.71	6.82	7.49	5.45	7.20	5 136.11	614.57	1 047.04
1996														
January	5.56	5.24	5.00	4.92	8.50	5.09	5.65	6.81	7.47	5.43	7.03	5 179.38	614.42	1 024.95
February	5.22	5.00	4.83	4.77	8.25	4.94	5.81	6.99	7.63	5.43	7.08	5 518.74	649.54	1 094.02
March	5.31	5.00	4.96	4.96	8.25	5.34	6.27	7.35	8.03	5.79	7.62	5 612.25	647.07	1 092.65
April	5.22	5.00	4.95	5.06	8.25	5.54	6.51	7.50	8.19	5.94	7.93	5 579.86	647.17	1 135.63
May	5.24	5.00	5.02	5.12	8.25	5.64	6.74	7.62	8.30	5.98	8.07	5 616.71	661.23	1 220.54
June	5.27	5.00	5.09	5.25	8.25	5.81	6.91	7.71	8.40	6.02	8.32	5 671.52	668.50	1 205.00
July	5.40	5.00	5.15	5.30	8.25	5.85	6.87	7.65	8.35	5.92	8.25	5 496.27	644.07	1 105.61
August	5.22	5.00	5.05	5.13	8.25	5.67	6.64	7.46	8.18	5.76	8.00	5 685.51	662.68	1 134.25
September	5.30	5.00	5.09	5.24	8.25	5.83	6.83	7.66	8.35	5.87	8.23	5 804.01	674.88	1 186.44
October	5.24	5.00	4.99	5.11	8.25	5.55	6.53	7.39	8.07	5.72	7.92	5 996.22	701.45	1 234.04
November	5.31	5.00	5.03	5.07	8.25	5.42	6.20	7.10	7.79	5.59	7.62	6 318.36	735.67	1 259.83
December	5.29	5.00	4.91	5.04	8.25	5.47	6.30	7.20	7.89	5.64	7.60	6 435.87	743.25	1 292.15
1997														
January	5.25	5.00	5.03	5.10	8.25	5.61	6.58	7.42	8.09	5.72	7.82	6 707.05	766.22	1 345.41
February	5.19	5.00	5.01	5.06	8.25	5.53	6.42	7.31	7.94	5.63	7.65	6 917.46	798.39	1 349.17
March	5.39	5.00	5.14	5.26	8.30	5.80	6.69	7.55	8.18	5.76	7.90	6 901.14	792.16	1 282.86
April	5.51	5.00	5.16	5.37	8.50	5.99	6.89	7.73	8.34	5.88	8.14	6 657.51	763.93	1 225.00
May	5.50	5.00	5.05	5.30	8.50	5.87	6.71	7.58	8.20	5.70	7.94	7 242.33	833.09	1 352.56
June	5.56	5.00	4.93	5.13	8.50	5.69	6.49	7.41	8.02	5.53	7.69	7 599.61	876.29	1 422.45
July	5.52	5.00	5.05	5.12	8.50	5.54	6.22	7.14	7.75	5.35	7.50	7 990.65	925.29	1 531.14
August	5.54	5.00	5.14	5.19	8.50	5.56	6.30	7.22	7.82	5.41	7.48	7 948.42	927.74	1 596.74
September	5.54	5.00	4.95	5.09	8.50	5.52	6.21	7.15	7.70	5.39	7.43	7 866.59	937.02	1 660.15
October	5.50	5.00	4.97	5.09	8.50	5.46	6.03	7.00	7.57	5.38	7.29	7 875.82	951.16	1 682.17
November	5.52	5.00	5.14	5.17	8.50	5.46	5.88	6.87	7.42	5.33	7.21	7 677.35	938.92	1 600.97
December	5.50	5.00	5.16	5.24	8.50	5.53	5.81	6.76	7.32	5.19	7.10	7 909.82	962.37	1 567.00
1998														
January	5.56	5.00	5.04	5.03	8.50	5.24	5.54	6.61	7.19	5.06	6.99	7 808.36	963.36	1 570.23
February	5.51	5.00	5.09	5.07	8.50	5.31	5.57	6.67	7.25	5.10	7.04	8 323.62	1 023.74	1 714.87
March	5.49	5.00	5.03	5.04	8.50	5.39	5.65	6.72	7.32	5.21	7.13	8 709.48	1 076.83	1 781.27
April	5.45	5.00	4.95	5.06	8.50	5.38	5.64	6.69	7.33	5.23	7.14	9 037.43	1 112.20	1 852.30
May	5.49	5.00	5.00	5.14	8.50	5.44	5.65	6.69	7.30	5.20	7.14	9 080.09	1 108.42	1 836.39
June	5.56	5.00	4.98	5.12	8.50	5.41	5.50	6.53	7.13	5.12	7.00	8 872.96	1 108.39	1 795.74
July	5.54	5.00	4.96	5.03	8.50	5.36	5.46	6.55	7.15	5.14	6.95	9 097.15	1 156.58	1 941.58
August	5.55	5.00	4.90	4.95	8.50	5.21	5.34	6.52	7.14	5.10	6.92	8 478.54	1 074.63	1 784.75
September	5.51	5.00	4.61	4.63	8.49	4.71	4.81	6.40	7.09	4.99	6.72	7 909.80	1 020.64	1 663.43
October	5.07	4.86	3.96	4.05	8.12	4.12	4.53	6.37	7.18	4.93	6.71	8 164.47	1 032.47	1 615.69
November	4.83	4.63	4.41	4.42	7.89	4.53	4.83	6.41	7.34	5.03	6.87	9 005.78	1 144.43	1 888.72
December	4.68	4.50	4.39	4.40	7.75	4.52	4.65	6.22	7.23	4.98	6.72	9 018.68	1 190.05	2 071.03

[1] Discount window borrowing, Federal Reserve Bank of New York.
[2] 1941–1943 = 10.

Table 20-6. Interest Rates, Bond Yields, and Stock Price Indexes—*Continued*

(Not seasonally adjusted.)

Year and month	Short-term rates					U.S. Treasury securities		Bond yields			Fixed-rate first mortgages	Stock price indexes		
	Federal funds	Federal reserve discount rate [1]	U.S. Treasury bills, 3-month	U.S. Treasury bills, 6-month	Bank prime rate	1-year	10-year	Domestic corporate (Moody's)		State and local bonds (Bond Buyer)		Dow Jones industrials (30 stocks)	Standard and Poor's composite (500 stocks) [2]	Nasdaq composite
								Aaa	Baa					
1999														
January	4.63	4.50	4.34	4.33	7.75	4.51	4.72	6.24	7.29	5.01	6.79	9 345.86	1 248.77	2 357.80
February	4.76	4.50	4.44	4.44	7.75	4.70	5.00	6.40	7.39	5.03	6.81	9 322.94	1 246.58	2 356.99
March	4.81	4.50	4.44	4.47	7.75	4.78	5.23	6.62	7.53	5.10	7.04	9 753.64	1 281.66	2 391.14
April	4.74	4.50	4.29	4.37	7.75	4.69	5.18	6.64	7.48	5.08	6.92	10 443.50	1 334.76	2 537.89
May	4.74	4.50	4.50	4.56	7.75	4.85	5.54	6.93	7.72	5.18	7.15	10 853.88	1 332.07	2 512.60
June	4.76	4.50	4.57	4.82	7.75	5.10	5.90	7.23	8.02	5.37	7.55	10 704.03	1 322.55	2 520.96
July	4.99	4.50	4.55	4.58	8.00	5.03	5.79	7.19	7.95	5.36	7.63	11 052.22	1 380.99	2 741.26
August	5.07	4.56	4.72	4.87	8.06	5.20	5.94	7.40	8.15	5.58	7.94	10 935.48	1 327.49	2 642.45
September	5.22	4.75	4.68	4.88	8.25	5.25	5.92	7.39	8.20	5.69	7.82	10 714.03	1 318.17	2 807.95
October	5.20	4.75	4.86	4.98	8.25	5.43	6.11	7.55	8.38	5.92	7.85	10 396.89	1 300.01	2 815.28
November	5.42	4.86	5.07	5.20	8.37	5.55	6.03	7.36	8.15	5.86	7.74	10 809.80	1 391.00	3 230.55
December	5.30	5.00	5.20	5.44	8.50	5.84	6.28	7.55	8.19	5.95	7.91	11 246.37	1 428.68	3 739.88
2000														
January	5.45	5.00	5.32	5.50	8.50	6.12	6.66	7.78	8.33	6.08	8.21	11 281.27	1 425.59	4 013.49
February	5.73	5.24	5.55	5.72	8.73	6.22	6.52	7.68	8.29	6.00	8.33	10 541.93	1 388.87	4 410.87
March	5.85	5.34	5.69	5.85	8.83	6.22	6.26	7.68	8.37	5.83	8.24	10 483.38	1 442.21	4 802.99
April	6.02	5.50	5.66	5.81	9.00	6.15	5.99	7.64	8.40	5.75	8.15	10 944.32	1 461.36	3 863.64
May	6.27	5.71	5.79	6.10	9.24	6.33	6.44	7.99	8.90	6.00	8.52	10 580.28	1 418.48	3 528.42
June	6.53	6.00	5.69	5.97	9.50	6.17	6.10	7.67	8.48	5.80	8.29	10 582.93	1 461.96	3 865.48
July	6.54	6.00	5.96	6.00	9.50	6.08	6.05	7.65	8.35	5.63	8.15	10 662.98	1 473.00	4 017.69
August	6.50	6.00	6.09	6.07	9.50	6.18	5.83	7.55	8.26	5.51	8.03	11 014.51	1 485.46	3 909.60
September	6.52	6.00	6.00	5.98	9.50	6.13	5.80	7.62	8.35	5.56	7.91	10 967.88	1 468.05	3 875.82
October	6.51	6.00	6.11	6.04	9.50	6.01	5.74	7.55	8.34	5.59	7.80	10 440.96	1 390.14	3 333.82
November	6.51	6.00	6.17	6.06	9.50	6.09	5.72	7.45	8.28	5.54	7.75	10 666.08	1 375.04	3 055.42
December	6.40	6.00	5.77	5.68	9.50	5.60	5.24	7.21	8.02	5.22	7.38	10 652.52	1 330.93	2 657.81
2001														
January	5.98	5.52	5.15	4.95	9.05	4.81	5.16	7.15	7.93	5.10	7.03	10 682.76	1 335.63	2 656.86
February	5.49	5.00	4.88	4.71	8.50	4.68	5.10	7.10	7.87	5.18	7.05	10 774.58	1 305.75	2 449.57
March	5.31	4.81	4.42	4.28	8.32	4.30	4.89	6.98	7.84	5.13	6.95	10 081.33	1 185.85	1 986.66
April	4.80	4.28	3.87	3.85	7.80	3.98	5.14	7.20	8.07	5.27	7.08	10 234.52	1 189.84	1 933.93
May	4.21	3.73	3.62	3.62	7.24	3.78	5.39	7.29	8.07	5.29	7.15	11 004.95	1 270.37	2 181.13
June	3.97	3.47	3.49	3.45	6.98	3.58	5.28	7.18	7.97	5.20	7.16	10 767.19	1 238.71	2 112.05
July	3.77	3.25	3.51	3.45	6.75	3.62	5.24	7.13	7.97	5.20	7.13	10 444.50	1 204.45	2 033.98
August	3.65	3.16	3.36	3.29	6.67	3.47	4.97	7.02	7.85	5.03	6.95	10 314.70	1 178.50	1 929.71
September	3.07	2.77	2.64	2.63	6.28	2.82	4.73	7.17	8.03	5.09	6.82	9 042.57	1 044.64	1 573.31
October	2.49	2.02	2.16	2.12	5.53	2.33	4.57	7.03	7.91	5.05	6.62	9 220.75	1 076.59	1 656.43
November	2.09	1.58	1.87	1.88	5.10	2.18	4.65	6.97	7.81	5.04	6.66	9 721.83	1 129.68	1 870.06
December	1.82	1.33	1.69	1.78	4.84	2.22	5.09	6.77	8.05	5.25	7.07	9 979.89	1 144.93	1 977.71
2002														
January	1.73	1.25	1.65	1.73	4.75	2.16	5.04	6.55	7.87	5.16	7.00	9 923.81	1 140.21	1 976.77
February	1.74	1.25	1.73	1.82	4.75	2.23	4.91	6.51	7.89	5.11	6.89	9 891.05	1 100.67	1 799.72
March	1.73	1.25	1.79	2.01	4.75	2.57	5.28	6.81	8.11	5.29	7.01	10 500.96	1 153.79	1 863.05
April	1.75	1.25	1.72	1.93	4.75	2.48	5.21	6.76	8.03	5.22	6.99	10 165.18	1 112.03	1 758.80
May	1.75	1.25	1.73	1.86	4.75	2.35	5.16	6.75	8.09	5.19	6.81	10 080.49	1 079.27	1 660.31
June	1.75	1.25	1.70	1.79	4.75	2.20	4.93	6.63	7.95	5.09	6.65	9 492.44	1 014.05	1 505.49
July	1.73	1.25	1.68	1.70	4.75	1.96	4.65	6.53	7.90	5.02	6.49	8 616.53	903.59	1 346.09
August	1.74	1.25	1.62	1.60	4.75	1.76	4.26	6.37	7.58	4.95	6.29	8 685.48	912.55	1 327.36
September	1.75	1.25	1.63	1.60	4.75	1.72	3.87	6.15	7.40	4.74	6.09	8 160.79	867.81	1 251.07
October	1.75	1.25	1.58	1.56	4.75	1.65	3.94	6.32	7.73	4.88	6.11	8 048.12	854.63	1 241.91
November	1.34	0.83	1.23	1.27	4.35	1.49	4.05	6.31	7.62	4.95	6.07	8 625.73	909.93	1 409.15
December	1.24	0.75	1.19	1.24	4.25	1.45	4.03	6.21	7.45	4.85	6.05	8 526.67	899.18	1 387.15

[1]Discount window borrowing, Federal Reserve Bank of New York.
[2]1941–1943 = 10.

Table 20-7. Composite Indexes of Economic Activity and Selected Index Components

Year and month	Cyclical composite indexes, 1996 = 100				Selected components of leading index			Selected component of coincident index	Selected components of lagging index	
	Leading	Coincident	Lagging	Ratio, coincident to lagging	Vendor performance (slower deliveries diffusion index, percent)	Interest rate spread, 10-year Treasury bonds less federal funds [1]	Index of consumer expecta-tions [1,2]	Personal income less transfer payments (billions of 1996 dollars)	Change in manufac-turing labor cost per unit of output [3]	Consumer installment credit outstanding (percent of personal income)
1959										
January	57.1	36.3	77.6	46.8	61.8	1.54	95.2	1 669.0	. . .	12.8
February	57.7	36.5	77.9	46.9	67.3	1.53	95.8	1 677.9	. . .	12.9
March	58.3	36.9	77.9	47.4	66.3	1.19	96.4	1 692.5	. . .	12.9
April	58.2	37.2	78.2	47.6	64.8	1.16	96.9	1 704.6	. . .	12.9
May	58.4	37.5	78.6	47.7	63.0	1.41	97.5	1 718.1	. . .	13.0
June	58.3	37.6	78.9	47.7	63.7	0.95	97.2	1 724.0	. . .	13.0
July	58.1	37.4	79.3	47.2	59.1	0.93	96.9	1 720.8	2.4	13.2
August	57.8	36.9	80.3	46.0	57.4	0.93	96.7	1 711.6	5.8	13.4
September	57.7	36.9	80.8	45.7	57.5	0.92	96.4	1 711.4	6.8	13.6
October	57.3	36.9	81.3	45.4	58.5	0.55	96.1	1 713.8	9.4	13.7
November	56.8	37.1	81.2	45.7	54.6	0.53	95.8	1 725.7	9.9	13.7
December	57.9	37.8	80.9	46.7	53.7	0.70	98.7	1 744.6	1.4	13.8
1960										
January	57.6	38.1	80.4	47.4	46.2	0.73	101.7	1 753.6	-3.7	13.8
February	57.1	38.1	80.8	47.2	31.7	0.52	104.6	1 754.3	-4.1	13.8
March	56.5	38.0	81.3	46.7	28.8	0.41	102.6	1 755.3	-2.8	13.9
April	56.6	38.1	81.3	46.9	28.9	0.36	100.6	1 761.0	-2.7	14.0
May	56.7	38.0	82.0	46.3	32.3	0.50	98.6	1 765.1	-1.8	14.0
June	56.8	37.9	82.5	45.9	34.8	0.83	98.2	1 763.6	6.8	14.1
July	56.8	37.8	82.7	45.7	35.8	0.67	97.9	1 764.5	7.8	14.2
August	57.0	37.8	82.4	45.9	38.0	0.82	97.5	1 761.8	4.8	14.2
September	56.9	37.7	82.1	45.9	37.3	1.20	96.1	1 762.7	2.8	14.3
October	56.7	37.7	82.0	46.0	36.2	1.42	94.8	1 768.6	2.8	14.3
November	56.6	37.5	82.1	45.7	37.6	1.49	93.4	1 757.7	3.3	14.4
December	56.7	37.2	82.4	45.1	40.4	1.86	93.9	1 745.7	1.9	14.5
1961										
January	57.0	37.2	82.4	45.1	39.2	2.39	94.4	1 760.4	3.7	14.5
February	57.0	37.1	82.2	45.1	41.1	1.24	94.9	1 760.3	5.6	14.4
March	57.8	37.3	81.7	45.7	42.1	1.72	96.0	1 768.3	3.3	14.3
April	58.4	37.4	81.3	46.0	47.5	2.29	97.0	1 774.2	0.0	14.2
May	58.7	37.7	80.8	46.7	47.9	1.73	98.1	1 783.9	-2.7	14.1
June	59.2	38.0	80.3	47.3	49.3	2.15	98.2	1 799.6	-3.6	14.0
July	59.3	38.1	79.8	47.7	49.4	2.75	98.4	1 804.1	-6.2	14.0
August	59.9	38.3	79.8	48.0	50.6	2.04	98.5	1 812.1	-8.4	14.0
September	59.6	38.4	80.0	48.0	50.7	2.10	97.9	1 816.6	-7.6	14.0
October	60.1	38.7	80.1	48.3	52.4	1.66	97.4	1 836.4	-5.0	14.0
November	60.5	39.0	79.8	48.9	51.1	1.33	96.8	1 854.3	-4.1	14.0
December	60.9	39.2	80.2	48.9	55.8	1.73	99.0	1 863.2	-4.6	14.0
1962										
January	60.9	39.1	80.7	48.5	57.1	1.93	101.2	1 857.0	-0.5	14.0
February	61.2	39.3	80.5	48.8	56.2	1.67	103.4	1 866.7	-0.5	14.0
March	61.2	39.5	80.8	48.9	57.0	1.08	101.1	1 879.4	0.9	14.0
April	61.2	39.7	81.0	49.0	47.4	1.06	98.8	1 891.5	2.9	14.1
May	60.8	39.8	81.2	49.0	45.2	1.51	96.5	1 894.9	3.3	14.2
June	60.4	39.8	81.5	48.8	43.3	1.23	95.5	1 900.8	5.8	14.2
July	60.7	39.9	81.6	48.9	45.1	1.30	94.4	1 909.9	1.4	14.3
August	60.8	40.0	81.8	48.9	43.7	1.05	93.4	1 911.8	1.9	14.3
September	61.0	40.1	81.8	49.0	45.1	1.08	95.3	1 914.2	0.9	14.3
October	61.1	40.2	81.9	49.1	46.7	1.03	97.3	1 917.9	-0.9	14.4
November	61.7	40.3	82.0	49.1	48.7	0.98	99.2	1 928.8	-1.9	14.5
December	61.8	40.3	82.2	49.0	50.1	0.93	99.4	1 937.9	-2.8	14.5
1963										
January	62.1	40.3	82.2	49.0	50.4	0.91	99.7	1 931.2	-1.9	14.5
February	62.4	40.5	82.2	49.3	51.0	0.92	99.9	1 935.8	-2.3	14.8
March	62.9	40.7	82.2	49.5	54.9	0.95	98.0	1 944.5	-2.8	14.9
April	63.3	40.9	82.3	49.7	58.2	1.07	96.0	1 951.2	-5.1	15.0
May	63.5	41.0	82.4	49.8	56.4	0.93	94.1	1 959.4	-4.6	15.0
June	63.6	41.2	82.5	49.9	56.3	1.00	95.1	1 971.7	-4.2	15.0
July	63.5	41.3	82.6	50.0	43.6	1.00	96.0	1 972.6	-2.3	15.1
August	63.5	41.3	83.1	49.7	48.5	0.51	97.0	1 980.8	-1.9	15.2
September	64.1	41.5	83.2	49.9	49.7	0.60	97.0	1 994.2	-0.9	15.3
October	64.3	41.7	83.3	50.1	47.4	0.61	97.0	2 006.5	0.5	15.3
November	64.3	41.7	84.0	49.6	48.7	0.64	97.0	2 010.0	1.0	15.4
December	64.5	41.9	84.0	49.9	47.6	0.75	97.8	2 025.0	2.4	15.4
1964										
January	64.9	42.0	83.8	50.1	55.3	0.69	98.6	2 025.6	-1.4	15.5
February	65.1	42.3	84.0	50.4	51.9	0.67	99.4	2 043.0	0.0	15.6
March	65.4	42.3	84.2	50.2	60.3	0.79	98.7	2 052.1	1.0	15.7
April	65.7	42.6	84.5	50.4	57.7	0.76	97.9	2 064.2	0.5	15.7
May	66.0	42.8	84.2	50.8	61.4	0.70	97.2	2 077.4	0.0	15.8
June	66.1	42.9	84.3	50.9	57.6	0.67	97.8	2 086.8	-1.4	15.9
July	66.5	43.1	84.2	51.2	61.8	0.77	98.5	2 096.8	0.5	15.9
August	66.8	43.3	84.8	51.1	66.2	0.69	99.1	2 113.3	0.5	15.9
September	67.1	43.6	85.0	51.3	71.9	0.75	99.8	2 122.6	0.5	16.0
October	67.1	43.3	85.4	50.7	71.2	0.83	100.4	2 125.5	1.0	16.1
November	67.3	43.8	85.0	51.5	70.3	0.63	101.1	2 139.2	-1.4	16.1
December	67.6	44.2	85.1	51.9	67.8	0.33	101.7	2 159.3	-1.9	16.1

[1] Not seasonally adjusted.
[2] Copyright, University of Michigan, Survey Research Center, first quarter 1966 = 100.
[3] Monthly data are 6-month percent change at annual rate; annual data are for the 6-month period ending in September.
. . . = Not available.

Table 20-7. Composite Indexes of Economic Activity and Selected Index Components—*Continued*

Year and month	Cyclical composite indexes, 1996 = 100				Selected components of leading index			Selected component of coincident index	Selected components of lagging index	
	Leading	Coincident	Lagging	Ratio, coincident to lagging	Vendor performance (slower deliveries diffusion index, percent)	Interest rate spread, 10-year Treasury bonds less federal funds [1]	Index of consumer expectations [1,2]	Personal income less transfer payments (billions of 1996 dollars)	Change in manufacturing labor cost per unit of output [3]	Consumer installment credit outstanding (percent of personal income)
1965										
January	68.0	44.3	85.7	51.7	68.5	0.29	102.4	2 160.3	-2.9	16.2
February	68.1	44.5	86.2	51.6	68.1	0.23	103.0	2 170.9	-3.3	16.4
March	68.5	44.8	86.3	51.9	65.9	0.17	103.2	2 180.9	-6.1	16.4
April	68.5	45.0	86.7	51.9	69.4	0.11	103.4	2 190.8	-6.1	16.5
May	68.7	45.2	87.1	51.9	68.9	0.11	103.7	2 204.9	-3.8	16.5
June	68.8	45.4	87.2	52.1	69.3	0.17	103.9	2 211.7	-3.8	16.6
July	68.9	45.7	87.3	52.3	65.1	0.11	104.1	2 225.9	-3.8	16.6
August	68.9	45.8	87.4	52.4	65.4	0.13	104.3	2 237.7	-3.4	16.7
September	69.1	46.0	87.7	52.5	61.2	0.28	105.3	2 255.9	-1.0	16.4
October	69.8	46.4	87.9	52.8	59.1	0.27	106.3	2 280.0	0.5	16.6
November	70.3	46.7	88.2	52.9	65.1	0.35	107.3	2 297.0	1.5	16.5
December	70.8	47.0	88.3	53.2	73.5	0.30	104.9	2 308.8	0.5	16.5
1966										
January	70.7	47.2	88.6	53.3	74.9	0.19	102.4	2 312.8	2.0	16.6
February	70.8	47.4	89.2	53.1	80.1	0.23	100.0	2 322.6	4.0	16.6
March	71.3	47.8	89.3	53.5	86.4	0.22	98.7	2 333.2	2.5	16.6
April	71.2	47.9	89.8	53.3	79.3	0.08	97.3	2 333.9	3.5	16.6
May	70.6	48.0	90.2	53.2	74.6	-0.12	96.0	2 341.8	2.0	16.6
June	70.2	48.4	90.8	53.3	71.6	-0.36	94.2	2 356.6	4.5	16.6
July	70.0	48.5	91.3	53.1	73.1	-0.28	92.5	2 368.3	4.5	16.5
August	69.6	48.6	91.4	53.2	74.3	-0.31	90.7	2 375.5	3.9	16.4
September	69.5	48.7	91.4	53.3	72.4	-0.22	90.5	2 381.4	3.9	16.3
October	69.1	49.0	91.1	53.8	68.7	-0.52	90.4	2 392.9	1.9	16.2
November	69.0	49.0	91.9	53.3	62.6	-0.60	90.2	2 401.7	5.4	16.2
December	68.8	49.1	91.8	53.5	57.9	-0.56	92.3	2 397.8	2.4	16.2
1967										
January	69.2	49.3	91.9	53.6	48.2	-0.36	94.3	2 419.0	3.4	16.1
February	68.9	49.2	92.1	53.4	49.9	-0.37	96.4	2 417.5	1.9	16.1
March	69.0	49.3	92.2	53.5	38.0	0.01	95.7	2 426.6	4.3	16.1
April	69.2	49.4	92.3	53.5	36.9	0.54	95.0	2 427.1	3.4	16.1
May	69.8	49.4	92.0	53.7	34.4	0.91	94.3	2 430.8	1.4	16.1
June	70.3	49.5	92.6	53.5	36.5	1.04	94.7	2 440.3	4.3	16.1
July	70.6	49.6	92.5	53.6	40.9	1.37	95.1	2 452.1	4.8	16.0
August	71.4	49.9	92.1	54.2	44.8	1.38	95.5	2 462.1	3.8	15.9
September	71.5	50.0	92.1	54.3	46.5	1.31	94.0	2 464.4	1.4	16.0
October	71.6	50.0	92.2	54.2	51.1	1.60	92.6	2 461.0	0.9	16.0
November	71.8	50.5	91.9	55.0	51.4	1.62	91.1	2 475.3	0.0	15.9
December	72.3	50.9	91.9	55.4	49.9	1.19	92.2	2 499.7	-1.4	15.9
1968										
January	72.1	50.8	91.8	55.3	50.6	0.93	93.2	2 502.4	-0.5	15.7
February	72.6	51.0	92.2	55.3	53.9	0.85	94.3	2 522.5	1.9	15.7
March	72.8	51.2	92.4	55.4	54.0	0.69	92.8	2 535.2	2.8	15.6
April	72.1	51.3	92.6	55.4	49.0	-0.12	91.4	2 544.9	6.2	15.6
May	72.3	51.6	93.0	55.5	49.4	-0.24	89.9	2 560.1	5.7	15.6
June	72.5	51.8	93.2	55.6	49.9	-0.35	89.8	2 572.0	7.1	15.6
July	73.0	52.0	93.0	55.9	55.9	-0.52	89.7	2 588.6	6.1	15.6
August	72.5	52.1	93.4	55.8	47.8	-0.61	89.6	2 597.5	3.7	15.6
September	73.2	52.3	93.4	56.0	48.4	-0.32	90.3	2 609.3	5.1	15.6
October	73.9	52.5	93.5	56.1	53.3	-0.33	90.9	2 613.3	4.6	15.7
November	74.1	52.8	93.7	56.4	61.0	-0.12	91.6	2 624.1	3.7	15.7
December	74.1	52.9	94.0	56.3	58.3	0.01	93.7	2 633.4	3.6	15.8
1969										
January	74.3	53.0	94.4	56.1	63.6	-0.26	95.9	2 634.2	2.3	15.8
February	74.4	53.2	94.5	56.3	60.1	-0.42	98.0	2 643.9	1.8	15.9
March	74.2	53.5	94.9	56.4	60.5	-0.49	95.7	2 656.2	1.3	15.9
April	74.4	53.6	95.2	56.3	63.9	-1.24	93.4	2 665.3	2.2	15.9
May	73.8	53.7	95.8	56.1	64.9	-2.35	91.1	2 674.8	5.4	15.9
June	73.5	53.9	96.0	56.1	67.0	-2.33	89.6	2 683.9	4.5	15.9
July	73.1	54.1	96.0	56.4	65.7	-1.89	88.1	2 698.0	4.5	15.8
August	73.1	54.3	96.3	56.4	70.3	-2.50	86.6	2 715.7	7.3	15.7
September	73.3	54.3	96.3	56.4	68.9	-1.99	84.3	2 720.7	6.7	15.7
October	72.8	54.5	96.3	56.6	66.8	-1.90	81.9	2 726.6	5.8	15.7
November	72.4	54.3	96.3	56.4	64.1	-1.71	79.6	2 726.8	5.3	15.7
December	72.1	54.4	96.7	56.3	66.8	-1.32	78.3	2 729.9	7.1	15.7
1970										
January	71.4	54.1	97.1	55.7	57.9	-1.19	77.1	2 725.6	11.1	15.7
February	70.7	54.2	97.0	55.9	57.7	-1.74	75.8	2 727.1	8.3	15.7
March	70.5	54.2	97.2	55.8	49.3	-0.69	74.3	2 733.9	8.7	15.6
April	69.8	54.1	96.8	55.9	48.7	-0.71	72.7	2 739.1	7.4	15.3
May	70.3	54.1	96.5	56.1	67.2	-0.03	71.2	2 741.0	5.6	15.4
June	70.5	54.0	96.5	56.0	66.1	0.24	72.7	2 735.5	4.7	15.4
July	70.4	54.1	96.0	56.4	49.8	0.25	74.2	2 749.5	0.8	15.4
August	70.7	54.1	96.1	56.3	46.1	0.92	75.7	2 756.1	2.1	15.3
September	70.6	54.0	95.6	56.5	46.5	1.10	74.2	2 755.3	0.4	15.3
October	70.4	53.5	95.6	56.0	39.0	1.13	72.8	2 732.4	1.7	15.3
November	70.4	53.3	95.3	55.9	37.8	1.24	71.3	2 729.0	2.1	15.3
December	71.7	53.8	94.5	56.9	37.5	1.49	72.8	2 733.7	0.0	15.2

[1] Not seasonally adjusted.
[2] Copyright, University of Michigan, Survey Research Center, first quarter 1966 = 100.
[3] Monthly data are 6-month percent change at annual rate; annual data are for the 6-month period ending in September.

Table 20-7. Composite Indexes of Economic Activity and Selected Index Components—*Continued*

Year and month	Cyclical composite indexes, 1996 = 100				Selected components of leading index			Selected component of coincident index	Selected components of lagging index	
	Leading	Coincident	Lagging	Ratio, coincident to lagging	Vendor performance (slower deliveries diffusion index, percent)	Interest rate spread, 10-year Treasury bonds less federal funds [1]	Index of consumer expectations [1,2]	Personal income less transfer payments (billions of 1996 dollars)	Change in manufacturing labor cost per unit of output [3]	Consumer installment credit outstanding (percent of personal income)
1971										
January	72.4	54.1	94.2	57.4	39.8	2.10	74.4	2 762.4	0.8	15.4
February	73.0	54.1	94.0	57.6	44.2	2.39	75.9	2 762.2	0.8	15.4
March	73.4	54.2	93.7	57.8	45.0	1.99	75.9	2 771.8	2.1	15.4
April	73.7	54.4	93.3	58.3	48.9	1.68	75.9	2 779.5	0.4	15.4
May	74.1	54.6	93.1	58.6	49.4	1.76	75.9	2 789.8	1.2	15.4
June	74.3	54.7	92.6	59.1	47.9	1.61	76.7	2 788.2	1.6	15.2
July	74.2	54.6	92.9	58.8	47.4	1.42	77.6	2 789.9	0.4	15.4
August	74.4	54.7	93.4	58.6	49.7	1.02	78.4	2 805.4	2.5	15.5
September	74.6	55.0	93.3	58.9	48.9	0.59	78.0	2 808.1	-2.0	15.6
October	74.9	55.1	92.9	59.3	50.9	0.73	77.6	2 817.5	-2.8	15.6
November	75.3	55.4	92.8	59.7	50.9	0.90	77.2	2 832.2	-3.6	15.7
December	76.4	55.8	92.6	60.3	53.3	1.79	81.8	2 855.4	-1.6	15.6
1972										
January	77.0	56.2	91.2	61.6	55.2	2.45	86.3	2 873.2	-4.4	15.6
February	77.6	56.4	91.0	62.0	52.6	2.79	90.9	2 887.7	-4.8	15.5
March	77.9	56.7	91.4	62.0	57.1	2.24	88.0	2 903.1	0.0	15.6
April	78.0	57.1	91.7	62.3	55.0	2.02	85.1	2 924.4	1.2	15.7
May	78.0	57.3	91.9	62.4	56.1	1.86	82.2	2 936.4	2.1	15.8
June	78.1	57.3	92.1	62.2	57.7	1.65	85.2	2 910.4	1.2	16.1
July	78.7	57.5	92.3	62.3	61.7	1.56	88.3	2 957.5	3.8	15.9
August	79.6	58.0	92.0	63.0	62.9	1.41	91.3	2 988.4	2.1	15.9
September	80.2	58.3	91.7	63.6	65.5	1.68	90.1	3 001.9	1.6	15.9
October	80.6	58.9	91.9	64.1	73.0	1.44	89.0	3 044.5	1.6	15.7
November	81.0	59.3	91.8	64.6	74.5	1.22	87.8	3 068.5	1.2	15.7
December	81.4	59.8	91.7	65.2	80.7	1.03	83.0	3 088.9	-0.4	15.8
1973										
January	81.5	60.0	92.4	64.9	83.7	0.52	78.1	3 083.2	1.2	16.0
February	81.6	60.4	93.2	64.8	85.2	0.06	73.3	3 100.6	1.6	16.1
March	81.1	60.5	93.7	64.6	87.5	-0.38	71.3	3 103.1	2.5	16.2
April	80.5	60.5	94.4	64.1	86.7	-0.45	69.3	3 106.0	5.4	16.2
May	80.3	60.7	94.6	64.2	86.6	-0.99	67.3	3 127.3	4.9	16.2
June	80.1	60.9	95.5	63.8	85.6	-1.59	65.9	3 139.2	7.1	16.3
July	79.7	61.1	95.8	63.8	85.2	-3.27	64.4	3 153.2	7.0	16.4
August	79.1	60.9	96.5	63.1	86.7	-3.10	63.0	3 142.0	7.8	16.4
September	79.1	61.2	96.7	63.3	90.1	-3.69	64.4	3 163.8	6.1	16.3
October	79.1	61.7	96.4	64.0	88.7	-3.22	65.7	3 194.2	4.4	16.3
November	79.0	62.0	96.7	64.1	96.8	-3.30	67.1	3 204.9	5.6	16.2
December	77.8	62.0	97.0	63.9	92.8	-3.21	61.2	3 198.2	5.2	16.2
1974										
January	77.6	61.8	97.5	63.4	91.8	-2.66	55.3	3 164.7	6.4	16.3
February	77.0	61.7	97.4	63.3	88.8	-2.01	49.4	3 143.3	6.3	16.3
March	77.3	61.6	97.5	63.2	88.9	-2.14	54.2	3 120.9	7.9	16.3
April	76.4	61.5	98.1	62.7	82.1	-3.00	59.1	3 102.4	8.3	16.3
May	76.3	61.7	98.7	62.5	74.5	-3.73	63.9	3 110.8	9.5	16.2
June	75.6	61.7	99.1	62.3	73.1	-4.39	61.8	3 114.7	10.7	16.1
July	75.0	61.8	99.6	62.0	69.2	-5.11	59.7	3 125.5	10.6	16.0
August	74.1	61.5	100.2	61.4	66.3	-3.97	57.6	3 109.8	12.5	16.0
September	72.7	61.4	100.6	61.0	51.8	-3.30	55.5	3 103.6	12.0	15.9
October	72.1	61.3	100.8	60.8	45.3	-2.16	53.3	3 108.1	13.9	15.8
November	71.1	60.7	100.8	60.2	34.0	-1.77	51.2	3 080.1	15.3	15.7
December	69.9	59.8	101.2	59.1	23.2	-1.10	50.8	3 063.1	21.1	15.6
1975										
January	69.6	59.5	100.5	59.2	19.5	0.37	50.4	3 045.8	19.3	15.6
February	69.7	59.0	99.5	59.3	15.9	1.15	50.0	3 027.1	18.6	15.6
March	70.1	58.5	98.9	59.2	17.3	2.19	56.6	3 024.9	20.1	15.5
April	71.8	58.5	97.8	59.8	21.7	2.74	63.2	3 022.3	18.2	15.4
May	72.6	58.6	96.8	60.5	22.7	2.84	69.8	3 038.4	15.7	15.2
June	73.1	58.8	94.5	62.2	24.9	2.31	70.1	3 044.6	7.8	14.7
July	74.1	59.0	94.3	62.6	28.7	1.96	70.4	3 047.6	6.7	14.8
August	74.4	59.4	93.7	63.4	35.1	2.26	70.7	3 075.7	6.0	14.7
September	74.9	59.7	93.5	63.9	43.8	2.19	70.4	3 088.0	2.9	14.7
October	75.3	59.9	93.4	64.1	44.8	2.32	70.2	3 103.3	3.2	14.6
November	75.7	60.0	93.1	64.4	46.8	2.83	69.9	3 114.3	3.2	14.5
December	75.8	60.3	93.0	64.8	41.2	2.80	73.7	3 117.4	3.9	14.6
1976										
January	77.3	60.9	92.9	65.6	54.0	2.87	77.4	3 143.8	5.9	14.5
February	78.2	61.2	92.7	66.0	56.1	3.02	81.2	3 168.1	2.9	14.5
March	78.3	61.4	92.5	66.4	56.7	2.89	80.6	3 185.2	5.5	14.5
April	78.2	61.7	92.2	66.9	57.3	2.74	80.1	3 205.5	3.8	14.6
May	78.6	61.8	92.0	67.2	58.3	2.61	79.5	3 218.3	3.5	14.5
June	78.6	62.0	91.8	67.5	58.6	2.38	81.5	3 218.8	4.1	14.6
July	79.2	62.2	91.7	67.8	54.0	2.52	83.5	3 234.2	3.5	14.5
August	79.3	62.4	91.6	68.1	55.2	2.48	85.5	3 246.7	5.1	14.5
September	79.5	62.5	91.7	68.2	52.6	2.34	85.6	3 252.9	4.1	14.5
October	79.4	62.5	92.1	67.9	49.0	2.39	85.8	3 255.0	4.4	14.6
November	79.8	63.0	91.9	68.6	47.2	2.34	85.9	3 284.6	4.4	14.5
December	80.6	63.4	91.7	69.1	53.3	2.22	85.3	3 295.7	2.8	14.6

[1]Not seasonally adjusted.
[2]Copyright, University of Michigan, Survey Research Center, first quarter 1966 = 100.
[3]Monthly data are 6-month percent change at annual rate; annual data are for the 6-month period ending in September.

Table 20-7. Composite Indexes of Economic Activity and Selected Index Components—*Continued*

	Cyclical composite indexes, 1996 = 100				Selected components of leading index			Selected component of coincident index	Selected components of lagging index	
Year and month	Leading	Coincident	Lagging	Ratio, coincident to lagging	Vendor performance (slower deliveries diffusion index, percent)	Interest rate spread, 10-year Treasury bonds less federal funds [1]	Index of consumer expectations [1,2]	Personal income less transfer payments (billions of 1996 dollars)	Change in manufacturing labor cost per unit of output [3]	Consumer installment credit outstanding (percent of personal income)
1977										
January	80.4	63.3	91.7	69.0	55.3	2.60	84.8	3 294.9	3.7	14.5
February	80.8	63.7	91.7	69.5	65.1	2.71	84.2	3 307.1	3.4	14.5
March	81.3	64.2	91.6	70.1	49.6	2.77	84.0	3 322.2	2.1	14.6
April	81.3	64.4	91.9	70.1	54.6	2.64	83.8	3 328.6	2.1	14.7
May	81.3	64.7	92.0	70.3	55.4	2.11	83.6	3 347.0	3.0	14.8
June	81.7	65.1	92.5	70.4	53.3	1.89	82.9	3 355.8	4.9	14.9
July	81.6	65.4	92.5	70.7	58.3	1.91	82.2	3 372.1	4.6	14.9
August	81.6	65.5	92.8	70.6	53.5	1.50	81.5	3 382.2	4.9	15.0
September	81.7	65.9	93.0	70.9	56.7	1.20	79.6	3 408.5	7.0	15.0
October	81.6	66.2	93.2	71.0	53.6	1.05	77.8	3 441.6	8.0	15.1
November	81.6	66.5	93.4	71.2	56.3	1.07	75.9	3 462.9	7.3	15.1
December	81.8	66.8	93.1	71.8	57.1	1.13	75.8	3 479.6	6.0	15.0
1978										
January	81.0	66.4	93.9	70.7	55.6	1.26	75.7	3 470.4	7.5	15.1
February	81.3	66.9	94.0	71.2	63.4	1.25	77.2	3 491.0	9.6	15.1
March	81.5	67.5	94.1	71.7	58.9	1.25	69.5	3 518.7	7.4	15.2
April	82.2	68.3	94.0	72.7	57.1	1.26	71.1	3 551.0	5.6	15.2
May	82.1	68.5	94.4	72.6	57.4	0.99	73.0	3 555.3	5.0	15.3
June	82.1	68.9	95.0	72.5	61.1	0.86	68.1	3 576.3	5.5	15.5
July	81.8	69.0	95.2	72.5	59.4	0.83	72.0	3 588.7	4.9	15.5
August	81.9	69.3	95.3	72.7	60.6	0.37	67.0	3 606.5	2.5	15.5
September	82.2	69.4	95.8	72.4	60.0	-0.03	69.8	3 621.6	4.3	15.6
October	82.3	69.8	95.9	72.8	64.7	-0.32	71.7	3 640.2	6.3	15.5
November	81.5	70.1	96.6	72.6	64.5	-0.95	62.8	3 652.5	6.9	15.6
December	81.1	70.5	96.8	72.8	63.5	-1.02	53.8	3 675.5	7.4	15.6
1979										
January	80.9	70.4	97.1	72.5	66.4	-0.97	58.4	3 680.1	8.5	15.6
February	81.0	70.6	97.4	72.5	64.0	-0.96	62.2	3 694.9	9.4	15.7
March	81.3	71.1	96.9	73.4	66.7	-0.97	53.7	3 711.6	9.6	15.7
April	80.1	70.6	98.1	72.0	75.6	-0.83	53.3	3 681.8	10.7	15.8
May	80.7	71.0	98.1	72.4	63.7	-0.99	54.9	3 686.3	10.0	15.9
June	80.4	71.1	98.9	71.9	61.4	-1.38	51.4	3 697.0	10.5	15.9
July	79.5	71.1	99.2	71.7	57.4	-1.52	44.2	3 699.2	9.0	15.8
August	79.7	71.1	99.6	71.4	52.9	-1.91	49.3	3 705.8	10.9	15.9
September	79.9	71.1	100.3	70.9	50.7	-2.10	53.6	3 703.9	10.8	15.9
October	78.8	71.3	100.7	70.8	46.9	-3.47	49.5	3 724.0	9.0	15.9
November	78.4	71.4	101.0	70.7	46.8	-2.53	52.0	3 739.1	9.5	15.8
December	78.0	71.5	101.0	70.8	42.2	-3.39	51.5	3 752.4	10.0	15.7
1980										
January	78.3	71.6	101.2	70.8	42.1	-3.02	54.1	3 751.6	8.1	15.6
February	78.5	71.6	101.5	70.5	46.0	-1.72	54.9	3 737.8	6.6	15.6
March	75.8	71.3	102.8	69.4	39.1	-4.44	44.3	3 719.6	8.4	15.5
April	74.1	70.7	103.6	68.2	36.9	-6.14	44.4	3 688.2	10.7	15.5
May	74.3	70.1	102.8	68.2	29.8	-0.80	45.3	3 664.5	15.1	15.3
June	75.9	69.8	101.8	68.6	32.4	0.31	53.0	3 665.9	16.0	15.1
July	77.0	69.6	100.0	69.6	36.3	1.22	53.4	3 648.8	19.0	14.9
August	78.0	69.8	98.8	70.6	40.1	1.49	59.6	3 657.1	19.1	14.8
September	78.9	70.3	97.7	72.0	41.2	0.64	67.2	3 668.1	14.1	14.6
October	79.3	70.9	97.1	73.0	46.5	-1.06	68.9	3 720.9	11.2	14.4
November	79.3	71.3	97.2	73.4	46.8	-3.17	76.2	3 749.3	5.6	14.2
December	78.3	71.5	97.9	73.0	50.1	-6.06	59.7	3 772.2	5.1	14.1
1981										
January	78.1	71.6	98.2	72.9	49.7	-6.51	67.2	3 774.3	4.6	14.1
February	78.1	71.5	98.3	72.7	48.5	-2.74	61.4	3 761.0	3.4	14.0
March	78.8	71.6	98.1	73.0	48.7	-1.58	61.4	3 766.4	6.2	14.0
April	79.5	71.5	98.2	72.8	51.2	-2.04	68.1	3 751.1	7.5	14.1
May	79.0	71.5	99.3	72.0	50.2	-4.42	72.9	3 759.2	8.5	14.0
June	78.2	71.7	99.5	72.1	47.9	-5.63	70.5	3 781.5	8.4	14.0
July	77.9	72.0	99.5	72.4	44.9	-4.76	66.4	3 825.0	6.7	13.7
August	78.2	72.0	99.6	72.3	49.6	-2.88	70.1	3 844.2	7.6	13.6
September	77.7	71.8	100.3	71.6	45.9	-0.55	68.3	3 840.0	7.1	13.7
October	77.0	71.6	100.0	71.6	37.7	0.07	61.5	3 830.3	8.4	13.7
November	76.7	71.3	99.8	71.4	40.5	0.08	55.6	3 826.9	9.3	13.7
December	77.0	70.9	99.4	71.3	41.2	1.35	56.8	3 817.3	9.6	13.6
1982										
January	76.7	70.5	99.6	70.8	40.1	1.37	62.9	3 801.4	14.6	13.7
February	76.8	70.9	98.8	71.8	40.8	-0.35	58.7	3 810.3	8.4	13.7
March	76.4	70.7	98.3	71.9	36.4	-0.82	53.1	3 811.9	8.2	13.7
April	76.9	70.6	98.3	71.8	38.2	-1.07	61.1	3 830.9	5.5	13.6
May	77.2	70.6	98.1	72.0	42.1	-0.83	62.0	3 835.5	5.2	13.6
June	77.0	70.2	98.2	71.5	45.2	0.15	60.1	3 812.8	3.1	13.6
July	77.6	70.0	97.7	71.6	45.8	1.36	57.6	3 797.0	-2.2	13.6
August	77.4	69.7	97.5	71.5	45.3	2.94	60.9	3 795.8	3.3	13.5
September	78.2	69.6	97.1	71.7	45.9	2.03	66.9	3 786.1	2.0	13.6
October	78.6	69.3	96.5	71.8	46.5	1.20	70.4	3 781.0	3.1	13.5
November	79.1	69.2	95.5	72.5	46.9	1.35	71.0	3 781.9	2.4	13.5
December	79.9	69.2	94.4	73.3	48.6	1.59	67.9	3 794.6	3.2	13.5

[1] Not seasonally adjusted.
[2] Copyright, University of Michigan, Survey Research Center, first quarter 1966 = 100.
[3] Monthly data are 6-month percent change at annual rate; annual data are for the 6-month period ending in September.

Table 20-7. Composite Indexes of Economic Activity and Selected Index Components—*Continued*

Year and month	Cyclical composite indexes, 1996 = 100				Selected components of leading index			Selected component of coincident index	Selected components of lagging index	
	Leading	Coincident	Lagging	Ratio, coincident to lagging	Vendor performance (slower deliveries diffusion index, percent)	Interest rate spread, 10-year Treasury bonds less federal funds [1]	Index of consumer expecta-tions [1,2]	Personal income less transfer payments (billions of 1996 dollars)	Change in manufac-turing labor cost per unit of output [3]	Consumer installment credit outstanding (percent of personal income)
1983										
January	81.2	69.6	93.8	74.2	46.7	1.78	65.2	3 792.9	0.0	13.6
February	82.0	69.5	93.7	74.2	49.9	2.21	71.2	3 792.5	-0.2	13.6
March	83.0	69.8	93.4	74.7	50.8	1.74	80.9	3 806.6	-0.6	13.6
April	83.6	70.1	93.2	75.2	52.7	1.60	86.9	3 809.5	-2.6	13.6
May	84.5	70.5	92.6	76.1	51.9	1.75	93.4	3 833.7	-3.7	13.5
June	85.2	70.9	92.7	76.5	56.8	1.87	89.2	3 845.3	-4.9	13.6
July	85.7	71.4	92.8	76.9	58.9	2.01	91.1	3 879.1	-2.0	13.7
August	85.5	71.3	93.2	76.5	60.2	2.29	88.2	3 872.3	-3.4	13.8
September	85.8	72.3	93.1	77.7	60.7	2.20	85.8	3 912.6	-3.2	13.8
October	86.5	72.7	93.0	78.2	62.8	2.06	86.1	3 953.6	-2.4	13.8
November	86.7	73.1	93.5	78.2	67.5	2.35	87.9	3 974.8	-0.4	13.9
December	86.8	73.6	93.8	78.5	62.1	2.36	91.0	4 013.9	0.6	14.0
1984										
January	87.8	74.2	93.8	79.1	64.4	2.11	97.0	4 040.9	-0.2	14.0
February	88.0	74.5	94.7	78.7	61.5	2.25	93.2	4 079.7	0.4	14.2
March	87.8	74.9	95.2	78.7	65.5	2.41	97.7	4 109.1	0.8	14.2
April	87.7	75.2	95.7	78.6	64.6	2.34	91.4	4 143.5	1.6	14.2
May	87.9	75.6	96.3	78.5	62.5	3.09	90.6	4 157.2	0.2	14.5
June	87.5	76.0	96.9	78.4	56.2	2.50	89.8	4 195.3	-0.4	14.6
July	87.5	76.2	97.6	78.1	59.1	2.13	91.9	4 224.2	1.4	14.6
August	87.1	76.4	98.1	77.9	55.2	1.08	93.7	4 256.2	2.2	14.7
September	87.1	76.7	98.4	77.9	52.8	1.22	96.4	4 295.7	3.7	14.7
October	87.1	76.7	98.7	77.7	49.3	2.17	91.6	4 262.9	2.9	14.9
November	87.6	77.1	98.6	78.2	48.1	2.14	91.5	4 292.2	3.3	14.9
December	88.0	77.3	98.6	78.4	48.8	3.12	87.9	4 318.0	3.3	15.0
1985										
January	88.7	77.3	98.7	78.3	50.4	3.03	90.3	4 320.4	4.9	15.1
February	88.7	77.5	98.9	78.4	48.6	3.01	86.5	4 322.9	3.4	15.3
March	88.9	77.8	99.1	78.5	46.7	3.28	87.3	4 337.5	5.1	15.5
April	88.6	77.8	99.0	78.6	46.1	3.16	87.0	4 335.0	2.4	15.6
May	88.9	78.0	99.4	78.5	48.0	2.88	84.2	4 338.1	2.4	15.8
June	89.5	78.0	99.5	78.4	47.1	2.63	91.1	4 351.4	2.6	15.8
July	89.5	78.0	99.7	78.2	45.7	2.43	87.4	4 348.0	2.0	16.0
August	89.7	78.4	99.7	78.6	46.6	2.43	86.3	4 361.0	2.2	16.1
September	89.9	78.5	99.5	78.9	49.5	2.45	84.2	4 364.8	-0.6	16.3
October	89.7	78.6	100.2	78.4	50.0	2.25	80.8	4 397.7	5.2	16.3
November	89.7	78.8	100.1	78.7	48.5	1.73	84.5	4 391.0	3.4	16.4
December	90.6	79.1	100.4	78.8	49.3	0.99	88.1	4 427.5	3.2	16.4
1986										
January	90.6	79.2	100.2	79.0	50.1	1.05	85.3	4 410.8	-0.4	16.5
February	90.8	79.3	100.3	79.1	49.8	0.84	87.8	4 435.6	0.4	16.6
March	91.0	79.4	100.7	78.8	50.5	0.30	86.9	4 478.2	3.7	16.5
April	91.6	79.7	100.0	79.7	50.7	0.31	88.5	4 481.2	-2.1	16.7
May	91.8	79.6	100.1	79.5	50.2	0.86	87.5	4 482.4	-0.6	16.8
June	92.3	79.6	100.1	79.5	49.9	0.88	90.3	4 483.5	-0.6	16.8
July	92.3	79.9	100.1	79.8	49.9	0.74	88.5	4 492.8	2.0	16.9
August	92.4	80.0	100.0	80.0	50.8	1.00	85.9	4 508.1	1.2	16.9
September	92.5	80.4	99.4	80.9	49.6	1.56	81.3	4 512.8	-2.5	17.0
October	93.0	80.4	100.1	80.3	51.3	1.58	87.1	4 509.1	1.6	17.2
November	92.9	80.5	100.0	80.5	52.0	1.21	81.6	4 515.7	-0.8	17.1
December	93.6	81.0	99.5	81.4	52.8	0.20	78.3	4 538.3	-2.3	17.0
1987										
January	93.5	80.7	100.1	80.6	51.5	0.65	80.9	4 540.2	-0.2	16.9
February	94.2	81.4	99.4	81.9	51.2	1.15	81.6	4 557.5	-2.3	16.7
March	94.4	81.6	99.2	82.3	51.9	1.12	83.3	4 575.4	-0.2	16.6
April	94.5	81.7	99.3	82.3	52.8	1.65	84.7	4 567.8	-4.0	16.7
May	94.4	82.0	99.4	82.5	54.0	1.76	80.6	4 593.6	-2.1	16.6
June	94.7	82.2	99.5	82.6	56.8	1.67	80.8	4 600.5	-1.6	16.6
July	95.2	82.6	99.3	83.2	58.9	1.87	83.3	4 621.6	-4.4	16.6
August	95.2	82.8	99.3	83.4	60.3	2.03	85.8	4 651.3	-1.6	16.6
September	95.3	83.0	99.5	83.4	61.5	2.20	84.2	4 657.1	-2.9	16.6
October	94.9	83.5	99.7	83.8	62.2	2.23	80.4	4 689.9	-2.4	16.6
November	94.0	83.7	99.7	84.0	64.9	2.17	72.7	4 711.1	-2.4	16.5
December	93.9	84.2	99.5	84.6	62.7	2.22	76.7	4 762.9	-2.0	16.4
1988										
January	94.0	84.1	99.9	84.2	62.0	1.84	80.9	4 735.4	0.6	16.5
February	94.8	84.6	99.8	84.8	61.2	1.63	81.9	4 759.1	0.6	16.5
March	95.2	84.9	100.0	84.9	57.3	1.79	85.2	4 767.5	2.8	16.5
April	95.0	85.0	100.3	84.7	58.6	1.85	82.4	4 778.3	2.6	16.5
May	95.2	85.2	100.3	84.9	56.9	2.00	87.3	4 784.1	4.0	16.6
June	95.8	85.5	100.7	84.9	65.6	1.41	85.7	4 800.1	5.7	16.5
July	95.2	85.7	100.5	85.3	58.4	1.31	82.3	4 820.1	4.0	16.4
August	95.4	85.9	100.7	85.3	57.4	1.25	88.8	4 825.9	3.0	16.5
September	95.2	86.0	100.4	85.7	55.2	0.79	89.5	4 835.2	1.4	16.4
October	95.4	86.3	100.7	85.7	54.8	0.50	87.0	4 863.7	6.0	16.3
November	95.4	86.6	100.9	85.8	52.1	0.61	86.3	4 870.1	3.6	16.3
December	95.7	87.0	100.7	86.4	53.0	0.35	85.5	4 910.0	1.6	16.2

[1] Not seasonally adjusted.
[2] Copyright, University of Michigan, Survey Research Center, first quarter 1966 = 100.
[3] Monthly data are 6-month percent change at annual rate; annual data are for the 6-month period ending in September.

Table 20-7. Composite Indexes of Economic Activity and Selected Index Components—*Continued*

Year and month	Cyclical composite indexes, 1996 = 100				Selected components of leading index			Selected component of coincident index	Selected components of lagging index	
	Leading	Coincident	Lagging	Ratio, coincident to lagging	Vendor performance (slower deliveries diffusion index, percent)	Interest rate spread, 10-year Treasury bonds less federal funds [1]	Index of consumer expectations [1,2]	Personal income less transfer payments (billions of 1996 dollars)	Change in manufacturing labor cost per unit of output [3]	Consumer installment credit outstanding (percent of personal income)
1989										
January	95.8	87.3	101.0	86.4	53.9	-0.03	89.9	4 944.6	0.8	16.4
February	95.3	87.3	101.8	85.8	54.0	-0.19	88.8	4 949.4	3.5	16.4
March	94.5	87.4	102.2	85.5	52.5	-0.49	87.6	4 963.1	5.1	16.4
April	94.9	87.6	101.8	86.1	52.2	-0.66	83.2	4 955.6	0.4	16.4
May	94.2	87.4	102.6	85.2	49.1	-0.95	80.1	4 934.4	2.7	16.5
June	94.3	87.4	102.9	84.9	46.5	-1.25	82.0	4 947.6	3.3	16.5
July	94.5	87.3	103.1	84.7	46.1	-1.22	85.5	4 954.1	6.3	16.5
August	94.8	87.7	102.7	85.4	44.0	-0.88	80.3	4 959.1	2.3	16.6
September	95.1	87.6	102.4	85.5	43.9	-0.83	88.6	4 952.8	0.4	16.6
October	94.8	87.6	102.8	85.2	43.3	-0.83	87.2	4 962.2	5.4	16.5
November	95.2	87.9	102.6	85.7	42.5	-0.68	84.3	4 986.8	2.9	16.5
December	95.6	88.1	102.7	85.8	43.5	-0.61	85.5	4 995.9	2.5	16.5
1990										
January	95.7	88.1	102.1	86.3	48.2	-0.02	83.4	5 004.8	-0.2	16.4
February	95.0	88.6	102.0	86.9	44.4	0.23	81.3	5 029.6	1.1	16.3
March	95.5	88.8	102.1	87.0	47.2	0.31	81.3	5 031.3	0.9	16.2
April	95.0	88.8	102.0	87.1	47.2	0.53	83.9	5 055.9	0.0	16.1
May	94.9	89.0	102.0	87.3	48.2	0.58	79.3	5 045.7	0.7	16.1
June	94.9	89.1	102.0	87.4	49.8	0.19	76.6	5 054.1	1.5	16.0
July	94.9	89.1	102.1	87.3	46.4	0.32	77.3	5 075.2	2.3	16.0
August	93.7	89.0	102.0	87.3	50.1	0.62	62.9	5 050.0	2.1	16.0
September	93.0	88.8	102.0	87.1	48.9	0.69	58.8	5 044.6	2.3	15.9
October	92.1	88.4	102.0	86.7	48.1	0.61	50.9	4 997.6	1.7	16.0
November	91.5	88.0	102.1	86.2	48.6	0.58	52.8	4 995.3	2.8	16.0
December	91.8	87.8	101.8	86.2	47.2	0.77	53.7	5 001.2	4.5	15.8
1991										
January	91.4	87.4	101.9	85.8	44.4	1.18	55.2	4 946.3	4.7	15.8
February	92.4	87.3	101.3	86.2	44.7	1.60	62.0	4 945.2	5.3	15.8
March	93.4	87.1	101.2	86.1	43.9	1.99	84.5	4 950.4	5.8	15.7
April	93.5	87.3	100.3	87.0	45.0	2.13	74.7	4 960.8	4.7	15.6
May	93.8	87.5	99.8	87.7	46.0	2.29	71.5	4 958.2	3.7	15.6
June	94.1	87.7	99.2	88.4	47.1	2.38	75.9	4 986.7	0.7	15.4
July	95.0	87.7	98.7	88.9	49.6	2.45	74.4	4 971.1	0.4	15.4
August	94.5	87.7	98.3	89.2	48.3	2.24	75.3	4 971.5	1.1	15.3
September	94.5	87.9	97.9	89.8	48.8	2.20	76.4	4 981.3	-1.3	15.2
October	94.3	87.8	97.6	90.0	50.2	2.32	70.5	4 958.9	-0.7	15.2
November	94.1	87.7	97.4	90.0	50.1	2.61	61.9	4 969.6	0.7	15.1
December	93.5	87.7	97.2	90.2	49.4	2.66	61.5	4 993.9	2.6	14.9
1992										
January	94.1	87.8	96.3	91.2	48.7	3.00	59.1	4 991.6	2.7	14.8
February	94.7	88.0	95.8	91.9	49.3	3.28	61.8	5 018.8	1.3	14.7
March	95.1	88.2	95.6	92.3	50.3	3.56	70.3	5 019.4	1.6	14.7
April	95.0	88.4	95.2	92.9	47.4	3.75	70.5	5 028.1	1.3	14.6
May	95.1	88.5	95.0	93.2	50.0	3.57	71.2	5 044.3	0.2	14.5
June	95.0	88.6	94.5	93.8	50.8	3.50	70.7	5 048.2	-0.4	14.4
July	94.7	88.9	94.1	94.5	52.5	3.59	67.6	5 039.0	-1.8	14.4
August	94.9	88.7	94.5	93.9	50.3	3.29	69.5	5 035.6	-0.5	14.5
September	94.9	89.0	94.1	94.6	51.2	3.20	67.4	5 049.6	0.9	14.3
October	95.2	89.3	93.9	95.1	48.6	3.49	67.5	5 079.8	-0.2	14.2
November	95.7	89.5	94.2	95.0	51.3	3.78	78.2	5 100.2	-0.2	14.2
December	97.1	90.5	93.3	97.0	51.5	3.85	89.5	5 292.3	0.4	13.8
1993										
January	96.3	89.7	94.1	95.3	52.3	3.58	83.4	5 036.8	0.2	14.4
February	96.4	89.8	94.2	95.3	51.7	3.23	80.6	5 036.4	0.0	14.4
March	95.5	89.7	94.3	95.1	52.7	2.91	75.8	5 013.3	-1.1	14.4
April	95.8	90.3	94.2	95.9	52.8	3.01	76.4	5 115.6	1.1	14.3
May	95.4	90.5	94.2	96.1	51.5	3.04	68.5	5 135.8	0.9	14.2
June	95.8	90.6	94.2	96.2	50.4	2.92	70.4	5 125.8	0.5	14.3
July	95.2	90.7	94.4	96.1	51.0	2.75	64.7	5 124.5	1.8	14.3
August	95.7	90.9	94.3	96.4	51.8	2.65	65.8	5 145.3	2.3	14.3
September	95.9	91.2	94.4	96.6	51.3	2.27	66.8	5 140.5	2.9	14.4
October	96.2	91.5	94.1	97.2	50.7	2.34	72.5	5 149.6	0.7	14.5
November	96.6	91.7	94.1	97.4	50.9	2.70	70.3	5 164.6	1.1	14.6
December	97.4	92.7	93.7	98.9	51.5	2.81	78.8	5 355.9	0.7	14.3
1994										
January	97.6	92.0	94.6	97.3	54.4	2.70	86.4	5 110.9	0.7	14.9
February	97.1	92.4	94.2	98.1	57.0	2.72	83.5	5 168.8	-0.5	14.9
March	98.0	93.0	94.2	98.7	55.4	3.14	85.1	5 191.8	-0.9	15.0
April	97.6	93.4	94.2	99.2	57.2	3.41	82.6	5 260.0	-1.4	15.0
May	97.8	93.8	94.5	99.3	60.2	3.17	84.2	5 292.6	-1.9	15.1
June	97.7	94.1	94.9	99.2	60.3	2.85	82.7	5 286.0	-2.1	15.2
July	97.2	94.2	95.1	99.1	58.1	3.04	78.5	5 288.3	-2.3	15.3
August	97.7	94.7	95.2	99.5	61.6	2.77	80.8	5 298.4	-2.8	15.4
September	97.8	94.9	95.6	99.3	62.5	2.73	83.5	5 328.0	-2.1	15.5
October	97.9	95.4	95.8	99.6	64.9	2.98	85.1	5 373.8	-1.6	15.6
November	98.0	95.8	96.4	99.4	64.7	2.67	84.8	5 373.4	-2.0	15.8
December	98.0	96.2	96.7	99.5	64.8	2.36	88.8	5 394.6	-3.2	15.8

[1] Not seasonally adjusted.
[2] Copyright, University of Michigan, Survey Research Center, first quarter 1966 = 100.
[3] Monthly data are 6-month percent change at annual rate; annual data are for the 6-month period bending in September.

Table 20-7. Composite Indexes of Economic Activity and Selected Index Components—*Continued*

Year and month	Cyclical composite indexes, 1996 = 100				Selected components of leading index			Selected component of coincident index	Selected components of lagging index	
	Leading	Coincident	Lagging	Ratio, coincident to lagging	Vendor performance (slower deliveries diffusion index, percent)	Interest rate spread, 10-year Treasury bonds less federal funds [1]	Index of consumer expecta-tions [1,2]	Personal income less transfer payments (billions of 1996 dollars)	Change in manufac-turing labor cost per unit of output [3]	Consumer installment credit outstanding (percent of personal income)
1995										
January	98.0	96.5	97.2	99.3	62.7	2.25	88.4	5 393.6	-4.1	16.0
February	97.5	96.5	97.7	98.8	60.7	1.55	85.9	5 391.8	-3.2	16.1
March	97.0	96.6	98.1	98.5	56.9	1.22	79.8	5 393.3	-3.7	16.2
April	96.8	96.6	98.7	97.9	56.3	1.01	83.8	5 402.0	-2.0	16.3
May	96.8	96.7	99.0	97.7	53.3	0.62	80.1	5 396.0	-2.2	16.5
June	97.2	97.0	99.5	97.5	51.8	0.17	84.1	5 416.7	-1.6	16.7
July	97.4	96.9	99.7	97.2	51.3	0.43	87.4	5 424.0	1.3	16.7
August	98.0	97.5	99.5	98.0	49.1	0.75	86.1	5 429.8	-1.5	16.9
September	98.0	97.7	99.7	98.0	50.0	0.40	78.8	5 450.5	-2.7	17.1
October	97.9	97.8	99.8	98.0	48.4	0.28	80.8	5 461.8	-3.3	17.1
November	98.0	98.1	99.8	98.3	45.3	0.13	79.7	5 487.5	-2.7	17.3
December	98.5	98.3	99.9	98.4	47.5	0.11	83.7	5 499.9	-3.5	17.3
1996										
January	97.6	98.1	100.0	98.1	47.8	0.09	78.7	5 496.9	-6.1	17.4
February	98.8	98.7	99.9	98.8	49.5	0.59	77.8	5 542.8	-3.8	17.4
March	99.1	98.9	99.8	99.1	49.6	0.96	86.2	5 559.5	-2.8	17.4
April	99.4	99.2	99.8	99.4	49.4	1.29	83.0	5 564.9	-3.3	17.5
May	99.9	99.6	99.9	99.7	49.9	1.50	79.2	5 590.7	-3.7	17.6
June	100.3	100.0	99.9	100.1	52.8	1.64	84.0	5 630.0	-3.5	17.6
July	100.4	100.2	100.2	100.0	50.8	1.47	86.5	5 629.8	-3.2	17.7
August	100.4	100.5	100.0	100.5	51.9	1.42	87.3	5 656.1	-3.5	17.7
September	100.8	100.8	100.1	100.7	50.0	1.53	90.1	5 678.6	-4.1	17.7
October	100.9	101.0	100.1	100.9	50.9	1.29	89.9	5 670.0	-4.1	17.7
November	101.2	101.4	100.1	101.3	51.2	0.89	93.9	5 687.4	-4.3	17.7
December	101.1	101.6	100.3	101.3	52.0	1.01	91.8	5 712.1	-3.2	17.7
1997										
January	101.4	101.8	100.3	101.5	49.7	1.33	91.3	5 726.0	-2.9	17.7
February	102.1	102.4	100.1	102.3	52.1	1.23	94.9	5 750.6	-4.4	17.7
March	102.2	102.7	100.1	102.6	53.1	1.30	93.6	5 776.4	-5.3	17.6
April	102.2	103.0	100.2	102.8	53.4	1.38	92.5	5 789.3	-5.5	17.7
May	102.6	103.2	100.4	102.8	55.0	1.21	96.6	5 816.7	-5.5	17.7
June	102.9	103.6	100.4	103.2	54.6	0.93	98.9	5 839.2	-6.3	17.6
July	103.5	104.1	100.1	104.0	54.7	0.70	102.6	5 859.4	-6.3	17.6
August	103.4	104.3	100.4	103.9	55.2	0.76	100.3	5 896.3	-5.6	17.6
September	103.8	104.8	100.5	104.3	54.8	0.67	100.7	5 915.7	-4.7	17.5
October	104.1	105.2	100.7	104.5	54.9	0.53	102.8	5 948.3	-3.5	17.5
November	104.3	105.7	101.0	104.7	55.2	0.36	102.3	5 990.5	-2.6	17.4
December	104.1	106.0	101.0	105.0	53.9	0.31	96.1	6 018.5	-1.2	17.4
1998										
January	104.2	106.5	101.1	105.3	53.0	-0.02	102.2	6 070.7	-1.8	17.3
February	104.8	106.9	101.4	105.4	52.8	0.06	104.2	6 117.9	0.0	17.2
March	105.0	107.3	101.8	105.4	53.0	0.16	101.9	6 161.6	1.6	17.2
April	105.2	107.6	101.6	105.9	52.4	0.19	104.3	6 187.4	-0.4	17.3
May	105.2	107.9	101.8	106.0	51.5	0.16	101.7	6 224.8	-0.2	17.2
June	104.8	108.1	102.4	105.6	50.9	-0.06	99.3	6 257.9	0.4	17.2
July	105.1	108.1	102.4	105.6	50.2	-0.08	100.0	6 278.3	-0.2	17.2
August	105.4	108.8	102.7	105.9	50.3	-0.21	98.3	6 309.9	-2.4	17.2
September	105.2	109.1	102.8	106.1	50.8	-0.70	93.9	6 327.9	-1.4	17.3
October	105.5	109.4	102.8	106.4	49.8	-0.54	87.5	6 339.9	-2.2	17.4
November	106.5	109.7	102.8	106.7	50.4	0.00	94.3	6 369.0	-2.0	17.3
December	106.7	110.0	102.6	107.2	48.5	-0.03	91.9	6 375.5	-3.0	17.3
1999										
January	107.1	110.2	103.1	106.9	51.0	0.09	95.7	6 385.1	-1.4	17.4
February	107.7	110.7	103.2	107.3	50.8	0.24	103.6	6 404.7	-0.2	17.5
March	107.8	110.9	103.3	107.4	52.3	0.42	99.0	6 415.3	-1.8	17.5
April	107.6	111.0	103.5	107.2	49.5	0.44	97.4	6 399.6	-1.2	17.5
May	108.2	111.4	103.4	107.7	52.1	0.80	97.6	6 421.3	-2.0	17.6
June	108.8	111.6	103.1	108.2	52.6	1.14	99.8	6 445.7	-1.8	17.6
July	109.0	111.9	103.8	107.8	54.0	0.80	99.2	6 451.3	-1.6	17.7
August	109.0	112.3	104.0	108.0	51.4	0.87	98.4	6 474.9	-1.8	17.7
September	109.0	112.3	104.3	107.7	55.8	0.70	101.5	6 461.3	-0.8	17.7
October	109.2	112.8	104.2	108.3	56.2	0.91	97.1	6 511.4	-1.8	17.6
November	109.8	113.4	104.5	108.5	56.8	0.61	101.0	6 561.4	-1.6	17.6
December	110.3	113.9	105.0	108.5	56.7	0.98	101.1	6 611.9	-0.6	17.6
2000										
January	110.6	114.5	105.3	108.7	55.0	1.21	108.6	6 699.7	5.4	17.5
February	110.0	114.6	106.0	108.1	54.7	0.79	107.8	6 726.6	7.4	17.5
March	110.2	115.2	105.8	108.9	54.3	0.41	101.7	6 758.4	5.0	17.5
April	110.3	115.5	106.0	109.0	55.4	-0.03	103.7	6 775.9	2.9	17.5
May	109.9	115.7	106.1	109.0	55.2	0.17	104.8	6 796.8	0.2	17.6
June	109.9	116.0	106.7	108.7	54.4	-0.43	100.8	6 830.0	-0.4	17.7
July	109.8	116.0	106.5	108.9	53.8	-0.49	104.5	6 865.9	-3.4	17.7
August	109.5	116.0	106.9	108.5	53.5	-0.67	104.0	6 891.0	-3.9	17.8
September	109.5	116.3	107.0	108.7	49.3	-0.72	103.4	6 893.7	-4.2	17.9
October	109.2	116.2	107.6	108.0	51.1	-0.77	100.7	6 906.9	-0.2	18.0
November	108.9	116.2	108.1	107.5	50.3	-0.79	101.6	6 913.8	2.3	18.1
December	108.2	116.3	107.7	108.0	52.8	-1.16	90.7	6 913.7	0.4	18.1

[1] Not seasonally adjusted.
[2] Copyright, University of Michigan, Survey Research Center, first quarter 1966 = 100.
[3] Monthly data are 6-month percent change at annual rate; annual data are for the 6-month period ending in September.

NOTES AND DEFINITIONS

TABLE 20-1
INDUSTRIAL PRODUCTION AND
CAPACITY UTILIZATION

See the Notes and Definitions for Tables 2-1 through 2-3.

TABLE 20-2
SUMMARY CONSUMER AND
PRODUCER PRICE INDEXES

See the Notes and Definitions for Tables 8-1 through 8-3.

TABLE 20-3
SUMMARY LABOR FORCE, EMPLOYMENT,
AND UNEMPLOYMENT

See the Notes and Definitions for Tables 10-1 through 10-3.

TABLES 20-4
NONFARM PAYROLL EMPLOYMENT,
HOURS, AND EARNINGS

See the Notes and Definitions for Tables 10-5 through 10-10.

TABLE 20-5
MONEY STOCK, RESERVES, AND MONETARY BASE

See the Notes and Definitions for Tables 12-1 through 12-3.

TABLE 20-6
INTEREST RATES, BOND YIELDS, AND
STOCK PRICE INDEXES

See the Notes and Definitions for Tables 12-9 and 12-10.

TABLE 20-7
COMPOSITE INDEXES OF ECONOMIC ACTIVITY
AND SELECTED INDEX COMPONENTS

See the Notes and Definitions for Table 1-11.

PART D

STATE AND REGIONAL DATA

Table 21-1. Gross Domestic Product by State and Region

(Billions of dollars; index numbers, 1996 = 100.)

Year	United States	Alabama	Alaska	Arizona	Arkansas	California	Colorado	Connect-icut	Delaware	District of Columbia	Florida	Georgia	Hawaii
VALUE													
1977	1 985.7	26.5	7.5	19.2	14.9	229.5	25.2	29.5	6.0	15.2	66.4	41.2	9.4
1978	2 249.0	30.4	9.1	22.8	17.3	263.6	29.4	33.0	6.6	16.6	77.5	46.8	10.5
1979	2 503.9	33.6	10.8	27.2	19.0	295.1	34.0	36.7	7.2	18.1	88.8	52.2	12.0
1980	2 731.6	36.1	15.0	30.3	20.1	328.2	38.4	40.6	7.8	19.6	101.4	56.9	13.4
1981	3 069.8	40.1	21.5	33.4	22.6	368.5	44.1	45.1	8.7	21.4	116.0	64.3	14.5
1982	3 217.6	41.4	23.1	34.3	23.2	393.2	47.7	49.0	9.3	22.6	125.6	69.1	15.5
1983	3 446.6	45.1	22.3	38.3	25.0	426.0	50.5	53.9	10.4	24.3	139.8	77.4	16.9
1984	3 866.3	49.8	23.6	44.5	28.3	484.5	56.0	61.2	11.7	26.4	158.8	89.5	18.6
1985	4 151.4	53.6	25.9	49.3	29.1	529.4	59.1	66.6	13.0	28.4	173.5	99.3	20.0
1986	4 355.9	56.1	18.6	54.6	30.4	567.4	59.9	72.8	14.1	30.0	188.1	108.9	21.5
1987	4 683.2	60.8	22.0	59.1	32.3	624.6	63.4	81.4	15.8	32.4	207.3	117.9	23.4
1988	5 092.2	65.8	21.4	63.4	34.6	685.1	66.7	89.7	17.1	35.6	227.2	127.7	26.0
1989	5 411.4	68.3	22.9	66.0	36.8	743.5	70.0	95.0	19.2	38.2	244.6	135.0	28.8
1990	5 706.7	71.6	24.8	68.9	38.4	798.9	74.7	98.9	20.3	40.4	258.3	141.4	32.3
1991	5 895.4	76.0	22.0	71.9	41.3	814.7	79.4	100.4	22.2	42.2	269.8	148.7	34.0
1992	6 209.1	81.1	22.4	79.0	44.6	831.6	85.8	103.8	23.1	44.5	285.5	160.8	35.5
1993	6 513.0	84.5	23.0	85.5	47.2	847.9	93.6	107.9	23.8	46.6	305.0	172.2	36.3
1994	6 930.8	89.7	23.1	95.7	50.9	879.0	101.5	112.4	25.1	47.5	325.6	187.6	36.8
1995	7 300.5	95.5	24.8	104.6	53.8	925.9	109.0	118.6	27.6	48.4	344.8	203.5	37.2
1996	7 715.9	99.3	25.8	112.9	56.8	973.4	117.1	124.2	29.0	48.5	366.3	219.5	37.5
1997	8 225.0	104.2	26.6	122.3	59.1	1 045.3	129.6	135.0	31.3	50.5	389.5	235.7	38.5
1998	8 750.2	109.7	24.7	132.9	61.3	1 125.3	139.9	142.7	32.7	52.1	415.6	254.9	39.4
1999	9 251.5	115.1	25.6	144.6	65.0	1 213.4	152.3	149.0	34.7	55.4	442.6	276.5	40.7
2000	9 801.2	119.3	28.1	153.5	66.8	1 330.0	169.3	161.9	37.2	60.0	471.6	295.5	42.5
2001	10 137.2	121.5	28.6	160.7	67.9	1 359.3	173.8	166.2	40.5	64.5	491.5	299.9	43.7
QUANTITY INDEX													
1977	58.6	59.5	64.6	38.8	56.7	53.9	50.0	56.0	51.4	88.3	43.0	42.2	62.7
1978	61.8	63.5	70.5	42.7	60.8	57.7	54.1	58.8	53.3	90.8	46.8	44.8	65.5
1979	63.7	65.0	74.0	46.9	61.6	59.9	57.7	61.1	53.8	91.9	49.9	46.9	69.2
1980	63.6	64.7	84.9	48.1	60.5	61.4	59.6	62.2	52.8	91.1	52.6	47.3	71.0
1981	65.2	65.6	97.9	49.1	62.6	63.3	62.2	63.2	53.7	89.4	55.0	49.1	69.6
1982	64.1	63.8	100.5	47.1	60.7	63.1	63.3	63.9	54.1	86.8	55.8	49.8	69.6
1983	66.0	66.8	97.6	50.1	62.9	65.5	64.0	67.0	58.3	88.0	59.0	53.1	72.1
1984	71.0	70.7	102.2	55.8	68.3	71.3	67.9	72.6	62.6	90.2	63.8	58.6	74.3
1985	73.9	73.9	113.2	59.7	69.0	75.3	69.1	76.1	67.2	91.6	67.0	62.8	76.2
1986	75.4	75.0	92.7	63.7	70.2	78.0	68.3	80.3	69.6	92.7	69.9	66.4	78.6
1987	78.7	79.0	108.4	66.4	72.6	83.2	70.0	87.1	75.3	95.9	74.2	69.6	82.5
1988	82.8	82.5	107.0	69.0	75.2	88.2	71.5	92.9	78.1	100.3	78.6	72.7	88.1
1989	84.7	82.6	108.7	69.4	77.1	92.4	72.4	94.5	84.2	103.2	81.6	74.2	94.2
1990	85.9	83.8	107.8	70.0	77.7	95.3	74.3	94.5	86.1	104.9	82.9	75.1	101.7
1991	85.7	86.1	97.3	70.6	81.3	93.8	76.4	92.3	88.9	103.0	83.5	76.1	102.7
1992	87.8	89.5	97.5	75.6	85.7	93.1	80.3	92.5	88.4	104.4	85.8	80.0	104.3
1993	89.7	90.9	98.7	79.6	88.3	92.3	85.2	93.2	89.6	105.6	88.9	83.4	103.5
1994	93.4	94.2	98.0	87.1	93.2	93.6	90.4	94.6	91.9	104.4	92.6	89.0	102.2
1995	96.3	97.3	102.3	93.4	96.3	96.8	95.0	97.3	97.4	102.5	95.7	94.0	101.2
1996	100.0	100.0	100.0	100.0	100.0	100.0	100.0	100.0	100.0	100.0	100.0	100.0	100.0
1997	104.9	103.4	101.1	107.0	103.2	105.7	108.7	106.8	103.9	101.6	104.3	105.6	100.5
1998	110.2	107.1	96.7	115.8	105.6	112.6	115.8	111.3	105.5	102.3	109.4	112.0	100.4
1999	115.1	111.2	97.2	125.2	111.3	120.2	124.3	114.9	110.2	105.7	114.7	119.1	101.5
2000	120.5	113.1	95.9	131.8	112.8	129.3	135.1	122.4	115.1	111.5	119.7	125.2	103.7
2001	121.0	112.8	95.0	136.1	112.2	129.4	136.0	123.2	123.3	115.6	121.9	124.8	103.6

Table 21-1. Gross Domestic Product by State and Region—*Continued*

(Billions of dollars; index numbers, 1996 = 100.)

Year	Idaho	Illinois	Indiana	Iowa	Kansas	Kentucky	Louisiana	Maine	Maryland	Massachu- setts	Michigan	Minnesota	Mississippi
VALUE													
1977	7.1	115.4	47.4	26.3	20.3	28.5	39.4	7.6	35.5	49.7	88.1	36.3	16.0
1978	8.3	128.7	53.3	30.1	22.6	32.0	45.3	8.4	39.4	55.6	98.1	41.1	17.9
1979	9.2	140.3	57.7	32.8	26.2	35.3	52.1	9.3	43.5	61.6	104.2	46.4	20.2
1980	9.8	146.5	58.4	34.0	28.0	36.7	64.0	10.2	47.3	68.2	102.9	49.7	21.5
1981	10.5	160.0	63.8	37.7	31.6	40.6	77.7	11.2	52.8	76.0	113.3	54.6	24.2
1982	10.5	163.6	63.5	36.6	33.0	41.6	79.1	12.1	56.0	81.7	113.2	56.4	24.9
1983	11.6	172.1	67.9	36.7	34.8	43.3	77.8	13.1	61.9	90.9	125.0	60.6	26.2
1984	12.5	192.7	77.4	41.0	38.1	49.0	83.8	14.9	69.8	104.0	141.0	69.9	29.2
1985	13.0	205.7	81.1	42.4	40.5	51.7	85.1	16.1	77.0	115.1	151.3	74.4	30.7
1986	13.1	217.9	85.7	43.1	41.3	53.5	76.2	17.5	84.2	126.1	161.1	77.9	31.4
1987	13.8	231.8	92.0	45.2	44.0	56.8	77.0	19.4	92.5	139.6	167.6	84.0	33.8
1988	15.0	250.3	99.2	48.8	46.3	61.2	83.7	21.7	102.7	152.3	178.2	90.1	36.0
1989	16.7	263.5	106.7	52.7	48.3	65.1	86.6	23.1	109.6	159.2	186.9	96.2	37.7
1990	17.7	275.8	110.8	55.8	51.5	67.9	94.9	23.5	115.0	160.0	190.8	100.4	39.2
1991	18.7	285.7	114.2	57.7	53.6	70.8	95.9	23.6	117.6	161.5	194.2	103.9	41.3
1992	20.4	303.2	123.6	61.1	56.3	76.7	91.2	24.4	120.7	167.3	206.7	111.9	44.2
1993	22.8	317.2	131.5	62.8	58.4	80.9	95.6	25.4	126.4	175.7	222.9	115.4	47.4
1994	24.9	342.3	141.7	69.2	62.2	86.9	104.1	26.5	134.0	188.0	246.8	125.0	51.4
1995	27.2	359.5	148.4	71.7	64.1	91.5	112.2	28.0	139.5	197.5	254.2	131.8	54.6
1996	28.1	375.9	155.1	77.0	68.2	95.5	116.9	28.9	145.1	210.1	265.1	141.5	56.6
1997	29.4	400.3	163.0	81.7	73.0	101.5	123.5	30.4	154.6	223.6	279.5	152.3	58.7
1998	31.0	423.2	176.1	83.1	76.6	107.6	122.6	32.2	164.1	241.4	293.2	163.0	61.7
1999	34.6	440.9	181.3	85.5	80.2	112.4	133.9	34.1	173.8	257.8	312.1	171.5	64.2
2000	36.8	466.3	189.8	89.7	84.5	117.2	145.0	36.3	185.0	283.1	323.7	186.1	66.2
2001	36.9	475.5	189.9	90.9	87.2	120.3	148.7	37.4	195.0	287.8	320.5	188.1	67.1
QUANTITY INDEX													
1977	52.1	67.5	65.2	68.8	67.2	62.5	78.8	61.4	59.2	54.1	75.3	55.4	61.0
1978	56.6	70.2	68.1	72.9	68.8	65.3	83.1	63.2	61.5	56.8	78.2	58.3	63.0
1979	57.7	71.3	68.6	74.2	73.2	67.0	83.0	64.8	63.1	58.9	77.4	61.0	65.3
1980	58.0	68.7	64.7	72.5	71.9	65.1	86.0	65.9	63.2	59.9	70.4	60.6	64.0
1981	58.1	69.3	65.3	74.8	73.9	66.8	89.8	66.6	64.6	61.4	70.5	62.2	66.2
1982	55.5	66.4	61.1	69.6	72.9	64.3	86.5	67.4	63.8	61.5	65.7	60.9	64.2
1983	58.0	67.2	62.8	66.8	73.5	64.2	84.9	70.2	67.0	65.3	70.0	62.9	65.5
1984	60.1	72.1	68.8	71.8	77.4	70.1	89.9	75.7	72.0	71.6	76.2	69.8	70.7
1985	61.6	74.4	70.5	73.4	80.6	72.4	90.4	79.2	76.4	76.4	79.6	72.6	72.5
1986	60.2	76.1	71.9	72.4	80.5	72.3	86.8	83.0	80.3	80.6	81.1	73.2	72.5
1987	61.5	78.8	75.3	73.9	83.7	75.1	86.3	88.6	85.0	86.5	82.3	76.8	76.7
1988	64.5	82.3	78.5	77.2	85.3	78.4	91.4	95.5	91.0	91.5	85.1	79.5	78.8
1989	69.0	83.7	81.4	80.3	85.9	80.4	89.9	97.8	93.6	92.2	86.1	81.9	79.4
1990	71.1	84.5	81.9	82.4	87.8	81.1	92.4	96.1	94.5	89.1	84.9	82.4	79.4
1991	73.0	84.5	81.6	83.0	88.8	81.5	92.1	93.4	92.7	86.6	82.9	82.6	81.2
1992	77.5	87.4	86.2	85.9	90.8	85.7	86.2	93.5	92.3	87.0	85.4	86.7	84.8
1993	84.2	89.0	89.3	86.2	91.5	88.5	88.0	94.3	93.8	88.8	89.5	87.0	88.2
1994	90.1	94.0	94.1	93.0	95.4	93.8	94.6	96.0	96.7	92.9	96.5	92.0	93.7
1995	97.5	96.8	96.7	95.0	96.3	97.1	99.7	97.7	98.0	95.4	97.4	94.5	98.0
1996	100.0	100.0	100.0	100.0	100.0	100.0	100.0	100.0	100.0	100.0	100.0	100.0	100.0
1997	104.3	104.9	103.8	105.9	105.8	104.9	103.3	103.6	104.4	104.6	104.1	106.3	102.2
1998	110.4	109.4	110.7	107.0	109.8	109.2	103.4	107.6	108.7	111.4	107.7	112.3	105.9
1999	123.4	113.0	113.1	109.6	113.7	111.6	110.8	112.1	113.1	117.7	113.0	117.0	109.2
2000	132.0	117.5	117.1	113.6	117.3	114.7	107.6	116.7	117.7	127.0	115.6	124.9	110.1
2001	131.1	117.5	114.9	113.0	118.4	115.2	107.2	117.6	120.8	126.5	112.2	123.9	108.8

Table 21-1. Gross Domestic Product by State and Region—*Continued*

(Billions of dollars; index numbers, 1996 = 100.)

Year	Missouri	Montana	Nebraska	Nevada	New Hampshire	New Jersey	New Mexico	New York	North Carolina	North Dakota	Ohio	Oklahoma	Oregon
VALUE													
1977	41.8	6.4	13.5	7.5	6.4	66.8	10.4	178.0	44.1	5.3	98.1	23.9	22.3
1978	47.1	7.5	15.5	9.1	7.5	74.2	11.9	197.4	50.4	6.5	109.1	27.1	25.9
1979	51.8	8.2	17.1	10.6	8.5	82.7	13.6	215.4	55.3	7.3	119.2	31.6	29.1
1980	53.7	9.0	17.9	12.1	9.4	90.5	16.2	234.3	59.8	7.6	123.7	37.7	30.7
1981	58.8	10.3	20.4	13.6	10.6	100.6	19.1	259.4	66.7	9.9	134.9	45.5	32.1
1982	61.6	10.3	20.6	14.2	11.4	107.3	19.9	280.3	69.7	10.0	136.3	49.5	31.9
1983	66.4	10.6	21.2	15.3	12.7	119.1	20.6	303.5	78.4	10.0	145.9	48.0	33.9
1984	76.0	11.2	24.1	16.9	14.9	134.6	22.3	339.2	89.8	10.8	165.0	51.9	37.9
1985	79.5	11.2	25.4	18.4	16.8	147.0	23.5	366.7	98.2	10.8	175.9	53.4	40.0
1986	85.0	11.2	25.8	20.0	18.7	159.7	22.5	393.6	106.3	9.8	184.0	49.0	42.1
1987	90.4	11.6	26.8	22.2	21.5	176.2	23.2	425.6	114.7	10.2	193.7	48.9	45.0
1988	97.1	11.9	29.0	25.4	23.3	197.6	24.0	462.5	126.2	9.7	207.4	52.8	49.7
1989	102.7	12.8	31.2	28.5	24.1	208.4	25.5	479.6	135.9	10.6	219.3	54.7	53.5
1990	104.8	13.4	33.5	31.6	23.9	217.0	27.2	502.2	141.1	11.5	230.0	57.8	57.8
1991	110.4	14.1	35.5	33.7	24.9	224.3	30.9	504.7	147.5	11.6	235.9	59.7	60.6
1992	116.0	15.1	37.6	36.5	26.4	235.5	32.9	535.3	160.0	12.7	250.4	62.0	64.1
1993	119.7	16.2	38.7	39.9	27.5	246.7	37.1	551.2	168.8	12.9	260.9	65.0	69.8
1994	130.0	17.0	42.0	45.0	29.4	258.1	41.8	575.6	182.2	13.9	280.9	67.0	75.1
1995	139.5	17.5	44.1	49.4	32.4	271.4	42.2	597.6	194.6	14.5	295.7	70.0	81.1
1996	146.5	18.1	47.8	54.6	35.1	285.7	44.1	633.8	204.3	15.9	306.3	74.9	91.7
1997	155.8	18.9	49.3	59.2	37.5	300.0	47.8	663.4	221.6	15.9	326.5	79.4	97.5
1998	163.4	20.0	51.3	63.8	40.5	316.9	48.5	718.7	241.2	17.1	346.6	82.2	102.9
1999	168.9	20.6	53.5	69.5	43.4	332.2	49.2	743.9	260.6	17.1	357.4	85.4	110.4
2000	177.1	21.7	55.6	75.5	47.4	357.5	52.6	798.4	272.9	18.6	370.6	90.9	121.4
2001	181.5	22.6	57.0	79.2	47.2	365.4	55.4	826.5	275.6	19.0	373.7	93.9	120.1
QUANTITY INDEX													
1977	64.3	77.6	59.5	33.7	39.2	54.0	53.1	67.4	49.5	71.0	69.6	71.9	54.5
1978	67.5	83.3	63.0	37.9	43.2	56.3	56.1	69.9	52.8	79.6	72.1	75.2	58.1
1979	69.2	83.5	64.8	40.7	45.8	58.5	56.7	71.3	54.3	81.6	73.3	78.7	60.5
1980	66.5	83.6	63.7	41.9	47.1	58.7	58.4	71.1	54.6	77.8	70.3	82.4	59.9
1981	66.9	87.0	67.3	43.5	48.7	59.9	59.5	72.3	56.2	89.6	70.8	87.3	57.9
1982	65.9	83.2	65.2	42.7	49.3	59.7	58.5	72.8	54.9	86.3	66.9	89.8	54.4
1983	68.0	82.7	63.8	43.7	52.5	63.6	59.3	74.6	57.9	84.5	69.4	85.6	54.9
1984	74.4	84.4	69.4	46.1	59.3	68.7	62.6	79.5	63.5	87.9	75.6	90.3	58.7
1985	75.4	82.4	72.2	48.1	64.9	72.2	64.8	81.9	67.4	87.7	78.4	91.5	60.2
1986	77.6	81.7	71.3	50.3	69.6	75.6	63.4	84.4	69.9	81.5	79.0	85.6	61.1
1987	80.2	81.9	71.8	53.2	77.8	80.8	63.4	88.5	72.9	82.0	81.3	83.6	63.1
1988	83.3	80.9	75.1	58.3	81.8	87.1	64.1	92.9	77.2	76.3	84.1	88.1	67.2
1989	85.0	84.2	77.7	63.1	81.6	88.6	65.4	93.0	79.7	80.3	85.7	87.6	69.4
1990	83.8	85.5	80.9	68.0	77.8	88.7	66.7	93.6	79.6	83.1	86.8	88.3	72.5
1991	85.0	87.7	83.7	69.9	78.5	88.4	74.1	90.3	79.6	82.7	85.9	89.0	73.7
1992	86.8	91.7	86.5	73.8	80.9	90.3	77.3	92.6	83.3	88.4	88.7	90.4	75.7
1993	87.1	95.4	86.6	78.8	82.1	91.9	85.7	92.8	86.2	87.0	90.1	92.4	79.6
1994	92.2	97.8	92.1	86.2	85.0	93.8	95.6	94.8	92.3	92.3	94.7	93.6	83.6
1995	96.9	98.8	94.7	91.7	93.0	96.2	96.8	96.1	96.7	94.5	97.7	95.9	88.7
1996	100.0	100.0	100.0	100.0	100.0	100.0	100.0	100.0	100.0	100.0	100.0	100.0	100.0
1997	104.7	103.0	102.4	105.4	105.9	102.9	108.0	102.7	106.7	99.8	105.1	104.4	105.9
1998	107.9	107.5	105.3	110.9	114.0	106.7	112.3	109.7	113.6	106.5	110.2	107.9	112.5
1999	110.1	110.1	108.9	118.0	121.3	110.6	114.0	113.2	118.9	106.1	112.6	110.9	121.5
2000	113.7	113.2	112.0	125.0	131.4	116.5	118.7	119.4	122.2	112.2	115.1	113.7	136.1
2001	114.2	114.6	112.1	127.4	129.1	116.5	124.5	120.9	120.5	112.0	114.0	114.8	136.1

Table 21-1. Gross Domestic Product by State and Region—*Continued*

(Billions of dollars; index numbers, 1996 = 100.)

Year	Pennsyl-vania	Rhode Island	South Carolina	South Dakota	Tennessee	Texas	Utah	Vermont	Virginia	Washing-ton	West Virginia	Wisconsin	Wyoming
VALUE													
1977	100.6	7.3	20.3	5.1	33.6	131.6	10.4	3.4	44.1	36.0	14.7	40.9	5.7
1978	112.3	8.0	23.3	6.0	38.3	151.1	12.1	4.0	49.5	42.0	16.3	45.7	6.9
1979	123.2	8.9	26.0	6.7	42.4	174.5	13.9	4.5	54.9	48.2	17.8	50.6	8.3
1980	130.6	9.7	28.2	6.8	45.4	207.5	15.5	4.9	60.5	52.0	19.1	53.4	10.8
1981	142.0	10.8	31.6	7.7	50.5	250.6	17.6	5.5	68.0	57.7	20.5	57.7	13.3
1982	145.7	11.4	32.9	7.7	52.3	265.8	18.6	5.8	73.4	60.8	21.2	59.5	13.1
1983	155.3	12.3	36.4	8.1	57.3	270.9	19.9	6.3	81.3	65.4	20.8	63.0	12.2
1984	171.0	13.8	42.0	9.3	64.7	296.8	22.3	7.0	92.2	71.1	22.8	70.1	12.9
1985	180.8	15.2	44.7	9.8	69.3	315.8	24.1	7.7	100.7	74.5	23.5	74.2	13.0
1986	190.9	16.5	48.4	10.2	74.2	299.6	24.5	8.3	110.3	80.5	23.9	78.1	11.2
1987	206.7	17.9	53.3	10.8	81.5	304.7	25.2	9.3	121.1	86.9	24.5	82.4	11.1
1988	224.7	19.7	58.2	11.3	87.8	334.8	27.2	10.5	131.8	95.6	26.4	90.0	11.7
1989	238.2	21.1	62.3	12.1	92.4	357.0	28.7	11.3	141.8	104.7	27.3	95.4	12.0
1990	249.9	21.6	66.1	13.0	95.0	388.1	31.4	11.8	148.2	115.5	28.3	100.4	13.4
1991	260.6	21.8	68.8	14.1	102.0	403.3	33.7	11.8	154.0	122.5	29.3	104.9	13.6
1992	275.3	22.7	71.9	15.1	111.8	424.7	35.7	12.6	161.8	130.6	30.9	112.3	13.6
1993	288.2	23.6	76.0	16.3	119.8	452.6	38.4	13.2	170.8	138.2	32.2	119.5	14.1
1994	301.1	24.4	81.5	17.2	129.7	482.7	42.2	13.7	179.7	146.3	34.8	127.2	14.4
1995	318.8	25.7	86.9	18.3	136.8	513.9	46.3	14.0	189.0	151.3	36.3	133.7	14.9
1996	329.7	26.7	89.9	19.4	142.1	553.2	51.5	14.7	200.0	161.8	37.2	141.0	15.9
1997	347.3	29.4	95.4	19.8	151.7	608.6	55.1	15.5	212.1	175.2	38.3	148.2	16.2
1998	365.0	30.8	101.4	20.6	162.2	641.4	59.1	16.3	228.0	192.0	39.0	157.7	16.4
1999	380.2	31.9	106.8	21.7	170.8	678.8	62.6	17.2	241.5	208.5	40.5	164.9	17.0
2000	399.5	36.1	112.2	23.5	177.4	738.3	68.4	18.1	260.8	218.1	40.9	173.0	19.1
2001	408.4	36.9	115.2	24.3	182.5	763.9	70.4	19.1	273.1	223.0	42.4	177.4	20.4
QUANTITY INDEX													
1977	69.3	64.5	48.9	57.3	52.2	55.0	45.6	49.9	53.4	52.5	78.7	61.2	72.0
1978	72.0	66.3	52.4	61.1	55.8	58.1	49.1	55.0	56.1	56.8	80.5	64.0	78.8
1979	73.4	68.4	54.8	63.8	57.5	60.0	51.5	57.4	57.9	60.4	81.3	66.1	81.9
1980	71.9	68.3	55.1	60.8	56.9	62.3	52.6	59.1	58.9	60.5	81.0	65.0	89.7
1981	72.0	69.7	57.0	64.2	58.2	65.9	54.7	60.9	60.5	62.0	79.7	64.9	94.0
1982	69.1	69.0	55.8	62.4	57.0	66.1	54.2	60.3	60.7	61.3	77.4	63.3	88.2
1983	70.8	71.1	59.3	61.8	60.1	66.0	55.8	62.8	63.4	62.4	74.2	64.5	83.3
1984	74.8	76.3	65.4	67.7	65.0	70.4	60.2	66.4	68.2	64.7	78.7	68.9	87.8
1985	76.4	80.7	67.5	70.3	67.4	73.3	63.3	70.6	71.5	65.4	79.4	71.3	88.8
1986	77.8	84.6	70.7	71.5	69.7	70.7	62.9	73.8	75.3	68.1	79.7	72.4	83.6
1987	81.9	88.4	75.4	72.1	74.2	70.4	62.9	79.8	79.8	71.1	80.4	74.4	81.8
1988	85.7	94.4	79.5	72.7	77.2	75.2	65.8	86.9	83.7	75.4	84.0	78.7	86.4
1989	87.5	97.1	82.2	74.7	78.3	76.9	66.9	91.0	86.8	79.5	84.3	80.3	85.4
1990	88.4	95.8	84.6	78.0	77.8	79.5	70.5	91.4	87.3	84.4	85.3	81.7	90.1
1991	88.9	92.6	85.1	82.2	80.5	80.8	73.3	88.5	86.7	86.3	86.0	82.7	91.7
1992	91.2	93.3	86.8	85.7	85.9	83.4	75.7	92.2	88.0	89.3	88.8	86.4	91.2
1993	92.9	94.6	89.5	90.0	89.5	86.8	79.4	94.1	90.6	91.6	90.8	89.9	94.4
1994	94.7	95.2	94.1	93.4	94.6	91.2	85.3	96.3	93.8	94.5	96.0	93.4	96.1
1995	98.0	98.2	97.7	96.8	97.6	95.4	91.2	96.4	96.3	95.2	98.3	95.8	98.3
1996	100.0	100.0	100.0	100.0	100.0	100.0	100.0	100.0	100.0	100.0	100.0	100.0	100.0
1997	103.4	107.9	104.9	101.6	105.1	108.1	104.8	104.4	104.0	106.5	101.2	104.2	100.7
1998	106.8	110.8	109.5	104.9	110.4	114.2	110.7	108.6	109.2	114.6	101.5	109.5	103.7
1999	110.0	112.8	113.9	110.8	114.5	119.4	115.8	113.3	112.3	122.6	105.1	113.6	106.1
2000	113.5	125.1	118.1	118.4	117.3	124.5	123.4	118.6	118.5	125.4	103.9	117.7	110.4
2001	113.6	125.5	118.5	119.6	118.6	126.3	124.1	123.1	120.8	125.2	104.8	118.6	115.0

Table 21-1. Gross Domestic Product by State and Region—*Continued*

(Billions of dollars; index numbers, 1996 = 100.)

Year	New England	Mideast	Great Lakes	Plains	Southeast	Southwest	Rocky Mountain	Far West
VALUE								
1977	103.7	402.1	389.8	148.6	389.5	185.1	54.8	312.1
1978	116.5	446.5	434.9	168.8	444.9	213.0	64.3	360.2
1979	129.5	490.1	472.0	188.3	497.6	246.9	73.6	405.9
1980	143.0	530.0	484.8	197.7	549.5	291.6	83.5	451.4
1981	159.1	585.0	529.7	220.7	622.9	348.7	95.7	508.0
1982	171.4	621.3	536.1	225.9	654.5	369.5	100.1	538.8
1983	189.3	674.5	574.0	237.7	708.7	377.7	104.8	579.8
1984	215.7	752.6	646.2	269.2	799.8	415.5	114.9	652.5
1985	237.5	812.9	688.3	282.8	859.5	442.0	120.4	708.2
1986	259.9	872.5	726.7	293.2	907.7	425.8	119.9	750.2
1987	289.1	949.2	767.5	311.4	981.1	435.7	125.1	824.1
1988	317.2	1 040.3	825.0	332.4	1 066.6	475.0	132.6	903.2
1989	333.8	1 093.1	871.7	353.8	1 133.7	503.2	140.3	981.8
1990	339.7	1 144.8	908.0	370.5	1 190.3	541.9	150.6	1 060.8
1991	344.0	1 171.6	934.9	386.8	1 245.5	565.7	159.4	1 087.5
1992	357.1	1 234.4	996.2	410.8	1 320.7	598.6	170.5	1 120.7
1993	373.3	1 282.9	1 052.0	424.0	1 400.3	640.3	185.0	1 155.2
1994	394.4	1 341.3	1 138.9	459.5	1 504.1	687.2	200.0	1 205.3
1995	416.2	1 403.3	1 191.4	484.0	1 599.4	730.6	214.9	1 269.7
1996	439.6	1 471.8	1 243.6	516.2	1 684.3	785.0	230.7	1 344.7
1997	471.3	1 547.1	1 317.4	547.8	1 791.6	858.1	249.2	1 442.4
1998	503.9	1 649.5	1 396.8	575.1	1 905.3	905.0	266.4	1 548.1
1999	533.3	1 720.2	1 456.6	598.4	2 030.0	958.0	287.1	1 667.9
2000	582.9	1 837.6	1 523.4	635.0	2 145.9	1 035.3	315.3	1 815.7
2001	594.7	1 900.2	1 537.0	647.9	2 205.6	1 073.8	324.1	1 853.8
QUANTITY INDEX								
1977	54.4	64.8	68.6	62.5	52.8	54.2	53.2	53.4
1978	57.2	67.2	71.4	65.7	56.1	57.4	57.6	57.2
1979	59.3	68.8	72.1	68.0	58.0	59.8	60.3	59.7
1980	60.3	68.4	68.5	66.4	58.7	62.0	62.2	61.1
1981	61.7	69.2	68.9	68.5	60.6	65.2	64.6	62.8
1982	62.0	68.6	65.4	66.5	59.8	65.3	63.8	62.4
1983	65.3	70.9	67.5	67.1	62.1	65.3	64.3	64.4
1984	71.3	75.6	73.0	72.8	67.2	69.8	67.9	69.3
1985	75.6	78.3	75.6	74.9	70.0	72.6	69.3	72.8
1986	79.8	80.8	76.9	75.3	72.0	70.7	68.2	74.9
1987	86.0	85.1	79.2	77.7	75.5	70.7	69.1	79.6
1988	91.4	89.9	82.5	80.2	79.3	74.9	71.1	84.4
1989	92.6	91.1	84.0	82.3	81.2	76.2	72.6	88.4
1990	90.6	91.8	84.5	83.2	82.0	78.2	75.0	91.8
1991	88.4	90.2	84.0	84.2	82.8	79.7	77.2	90.8
1992	89.0	92.1	87.0	87.1	85.3	82.6	80.6	91.1
1993	90.4	93.1	89.5	87.6	88.2	86.2	85.2	91.3
1994	93.3	95.0	94.6	92.7	92.9	91.1	90.2	93.1
1995	96.1	97.0	97.0	95.6	96.5	95.2	95.0	96.0
1996	100.0	100.0	100.0	100.0	100.0	100.0	100.0	100.0
1997	105.4	103.1	104.6	105.0	104.6	107.6	106.3	105.6
1998	111.2	108.0	109.4	108.8	109.4	113.7	112.5	112.1
1999	116.4	111.7	113.0	112.2	114.3	119.1	119.9	119.5
2000	125.0	117.0	116.5	117.2	117.9	124.2	128.7	127.7
2001	125.0	118.3	115.3	117.2	118.4	126.5	129.6	127.9

Table 21-2. Personal Income and Employment by State and Region

(Millions of dollars, except as noted.)

Year	Total	Nonfarm	Farm	Derivation of personal income						Per capita (dollars)		Population (thousands)	Total employment (thousands)
				Earnings by place of work	Less: Personal contributions for social insurance	Plus: Adjustment for residence	Equals: Net earnings by place of residence	Dividends, interest, and rent	Transfer payments	Personal income	Disposable personal income		
UNITED STATES													
1972	988 362	965 175	23 187	785 638	27 892	-229	757 517	132 683	98 162	4 723	4 125	209 275	94 317
1973	1 107 992	1 072 094	35 898	881 106	35 555	-244	845 307	150 538	112 147	5 242	4 609	211 349	98 433
1974	1 220 181	1 189 050	31 131	955 807	40 331	-264	915 212	172 277	132 692	5 720	5 003	213 334	100 118
1975	1 326 214	1 296 261	29 953	1 018 049	42 417	-313	975 319	182 921	167 974	6 155	5 460	215 457	98 907
1976	1 469 752	1 443 832	25 920	1 133 101	46 761	-339	1 086 001	200 924	182 827	6 756	5 951	217 554	101 597
1977	1 630 901	1 605 707	25 194	1 260 972	51 791	-377	1 208 804	226 977	195 120	7 421	6 508	219 761	105 049
1978	1 841 340	1 812 135	29 205	1 426 887	59 514	-410	1 366 963	264 398	209 979	8 291	7 242	222 098	109 689
1979	2 072 839	2 041 891	30 948	1 592 777	69 923	-398	1 522 456	315 322	235 061	9 230	8 017	224 569	113 289
1980	2 313 921	2 292 617	21 304	1 729 911	76 988	-454	1 652 469	381 662	279 790	10 183	8 848	227 225	114 231
1981	2 588 335	2 560 348	27 987	1 896 642	91 773	-443	1 804 426	465 884	318 025	11 280	9 752	229 466	115 304
1982	2 756 954	2 732 508	24 446	1 984 358	98 765	-520	1 885 073	517 181	354 700	11 901	10 344	231 664	114 557
1983	2 935 040	2 918 117	16 923	2 106 552	105 667	-508	2 000 377	551 913	382 750	12 554	11 014	233 792	116 057
1984	3 260 064	3 228 886	31 178	2 349 155	117 982	-579	2 230 594	635 439	394 031	13 824	12 186	235 825	121 091
1985	3 498 662	3 467 624	31 038	2 528 400	133 141	-603	2 394 656	682 691	421 315	14 705	12 908	237 924	124 512
1986	3 697 359	3 665 380	31 979	2 676 617	145 041	-575	2 531 001	717 155	449 203	15 397	13 528	240 133	126 981
1987	3 945 515	3 907 792	37 723	2 876 817	156 295	-608	2 719 914	757 070	468 531	16 284	14 213	242 289	130 416
1988	4 255 000	4 218 399	36 601	3 111 553	176 235	-651	2 934 667	823 435	496 898	17 403	15 282	244 499	134 518
1989	4 582 429	4 539 071	43 358	3 302 615	190 911	-664	3 111 040	931 066	540 323	18 566	16 207	246 819	137 241
1990	4 885 525	4 841 640	43 885	3 508 380	202 934	-737	3 304 709	986 055	594 761	19 572	17 135	249 623	139 427
1991	5 065 416	5 026 507	38 909	3 605 195	214 239	-788	3 390 168	1 005 433	669 815	20 023	17 615	252 981	138 664
1992	5 376 622	5 331 348	45 274	3 853 906	225 952	-797	3 627 157	997 830	751 635	20 960	18 486	256 514	139 305
1993	5 598 446	5 554 845	43 601	4 019 490	237 265	-798	3 781 427	1 018 460	798 559	21 539	18 947	259 919	141 996
1994	5 878 362	5 832 931	45 431	4 212 378	253 544	-860	3 957 974	1 086 612	833 776	22 340	19 598	263 126	145 572
1995	6 192 235	6 155 539	36 696	4 412 022	268 271	-893	4 142 858	1 163 537	885 840	23 255	20 335	266 278	149 359
1996	6 538 103	6 488 613	49 490	4 653 407	279 891	-914	4 372 602	1 236 804	928 697	24 270	21 045	269 394	152 607
1997	6 928 545	6 881 936	46 609	4 938 494	297 384	-969	4 640 141	1 326 244	962 160	25 412	21 863	272 647	156 230
1998	7 418 497	7 374 402	44 095	5 300 751	315 807	-1 022	4 983 922	1 450 391	984 184	26 893	23 016	275 854	160 256
1999	7 779 521	7 732 905	46 616	5 653 630	336 901	-1 030	5 315 699	1 445 370	1 018 452	27 880	23 730	279 040	163 348
2000	8 398 871	8 358 242	40 629	6 088 880	357 843	-1 060	5 729 977	1 598 302	1 070 592	29 760	25 206	282 224	167 284
2001	8 677 490	8 637 420	40 070	6 241 977	371 690	-1 093	5 869 194	1 637 213	1 171 083	30 413	25 889	285 318	167 536
2002	8 891 093	8 853 730	37 363	6 333 541	383 415	-1 368	5 948 758	1 653 541	1 288 794	30 832	26 974	288 369	. . .
ALABAMA													
1972	12 544	12 162	382	10 076	378	171	9 869	1 243	1 432	3 544	3 163	3 540	1 471
1973	14 181	13 616	565	11 378	484	188	11 081	1 429	1 671	3 960	3 538	3 581	1 526
1974	15 786	15 416	370	12 477	559	198	12 115	1 676	1 995	4 351	3 880	3 628	1 552
1975	17 537	17 101	436	13 519	603	203	13 119	1 860	2 558	4 765	4 292	3 681	1 543
1976	19 893	19 397	496	15 474	693	217	14 998	2 083	2 812	5 323	4 769	3 737	1 594
1977	22 005	21 607	397	17 191	777	246	16 661	2 341	3 003	5 817	5 207	3 783	1 651
1978	24 923	24 399	524	19 564	888	269	18 945	2 720	3 258	6 500	5 803	3 834	1 714
1979	27 855	27 314	541	21 559	1 020	296	20 835	3 235	3 784	7 199	6 395	3 869	1 739
1980	30 781	30 549	232	23 068	1 117	327	22 278	4 048	4 455	7 892	6 996	3 900	1 736
1981	34 137	33 630	507	25 036	1 307	425	24 155	4 996	4 987	8 712	7 702	3 919	1 724
1982	36 052	35 637	414	25 782	1 384	446	24 844	5 688	5 520	9 185	8 197	3 925	1 692
1983	38 487	38 198	290	27 539	1 523	440	26 456	6 063	5 968	9 783	8 728	3 934	1 722
1984	42 681	42 202	479	30 601	1 681	492	29 412	7 042	6 227	10 800	9 689	3 952	1 787
1985	46 015	45 550	465	33 056	1 890	503	31 670	7 735	6 611	11 583	10 329	3 973	1 831
1986	48 704	48 256	448	34 948	1 956	526	33 518	8 253	6 933	12 202	10 884	3 992	1 868
1987	51 846	51 334	513	37 380	2 083	535	35 832	8 856	7 159	12 912	11 457	4 015	1 923
1988	55 699	54 911	788	40 252	2 345	531	38 437	9 779	7 482	13 842	12 380	4 024	1 982
1989	60 044	59 119	926	42 638	2 554	550	40 634	11 187	8 224	14 899	13 241	4 030	2 019
1990	64 095	63 267	828	45 311	2 719	529	43 121	11 722	9 252	15 826	14 091	4 050	2 062
1991	67 650	66 526	1 123	47 736	2 915	536	45 356	12 094	10 199	16 503	14 728	4 099	2 074
1992	72 282	71 304	978	51 127	3 098	574	48 602	12 105	11 575	17 400	15 562	4 154	2 113
1993	75 439	74 441	999	53 380	3 287	600	50 693	12 370	12 376	17 901	15 983	4 214	2 176
1994	79 832	78 775	1 057	56 165	3 534	647	53 279	13 511	13 042	18 739	16 672	4 260	2 200
1995	83 903	83 131	772	58 317	3 755	680	55 242	14 575	14 087	19 527	17 335	4 297	2 263
1996	87 221	86 375	846	60 577	3 870	674	57 381	14 935	14 906	20 138	17 797	4 331	2 298
1997	91 284	90 353	931	63 185	4 055	719	59 849	15 761	15 673	20 899	18 394	4 368	2 346
1998	96 481	95 431	1 050	66 696	4 226	800	63 271	17 143	16 067	21 904	19 265	4 405	2 397
1999	100 422	99 127	1 295	70 020	4 445	833	66 408	17 421	16 593	22 668	19 924	4 430	2 415
2000	105 485	104 627	858	72 252	4 547	905	68 611	19 301	17 573	23 694	20 833	4 452	2 428
2001	109 388	108 109	1 279	74 545	4 735	928	70 738	19 686	18 964	24 477	21 547	4 469	2 410
2002	112 592	111 837	756	76 177	4 961	1 049	72 266	19 775	20 552	25 096	22 504	4 487	. . .

. . . = Not available.

Table 21-2. Personal Income and Employment by State and Region—*Continued*

(Millions of dollars, except as noted.)

Year	Total	Nonfarm	Farm	Earnings by place of work	Less: Personal contributions for social insurance	Plus: Adjustment for residence	Equals: Net earnings by place of residence	Dividends, interest, and rent	Transfer payments	Personal income	Disposable personal income	Population (thousands)	Total employment (thousands)
ALASKA													
1972	1 939	1 937	2	1 822	52	-76	1 694	142	103	5 939	5 103	326	158
1973	2 266	2 264	2	2 011	65	-94	1 852	169	246	6 801	5 931	333	167
1974	2 795	2 793	2	2 689	97	-210	2 383	205	207	8 108	6 891	345	189
1975	3 932	3 928	4	4 223	162	-613	3 448	252	233	10 600	8 932	371	227
1976	4 736	4 732	4	5 294	203	-884	4 206	299	231	12 048	10 151	393	243
1977	4 906	4 901	5	4 918	180	-454	4 285	342	279	12 346	10 437	397	237
1978	5 013	5 008	5	4 803	171	-325	4 307	407	299	12 464	10 695	402	237
1979	5 328	5 325	4	5 021	186	-290	4 545	492	291	13 204	11 162	404	241
1980	6 002	5 998	4	5 621	212	-329	5 080	578	343	14 807	12 738	405	244
1981	6 902	6 900	2	6 542	270	-471	5 802	695	405	16 492	13 862	418	253
1982	8 263	8 261	2	7 567	312	-562	6 693	847	723	18 379	15 699	450	278
1983	9 302	9 299	2	8 458	354	-620	7 483	1 030	789	19 045	16 569	488	298
1984	9 958	9 956	2	9 084	373	-638	8 074	1 214	671	19 385	17 091	514	310
1985	10 756	10 754	2	9 541	401	-631	8 509	1 371	876	20 200	17 903	532	318
1986	10 721	10 714	7	9 290	399	-570	8 321	1 410	991	19 699	17 673	544	311
1987	10 427	10 417	10	8 795	374	-533	7 888	1 499	1 039	19 334	17 206	539	312
1988	10 776	10 765	11	9 030	412	-557	8 061	1 598	1 117	19 882	17 827	542	318
1989	11 778	11 772	6	9 856	474	-619	8 763	1 786	1 230	21 526	19 003	547	331
1990	12 566	12 559	8	10 445	504	-654	9 287	1 923	1 356	22 712	19 931	553	341
1991	13 243	13 235	8	11 006	538	-696	9 772	2 008	1 463	23 226	20 616	570	349
1992	14 039	14 031	8	11 598	555	-726	10 317	2 092	1 629	23 846	21 174	589	353
1993	14 789	14 776	12	12 054	586	-738	10 730	2 244	1 815	24 671	21 948	599	361
1994	15 168	15 152	15	12 219	615	-755	10 849	2 454	1 865	25 141	22 282	603	367
1995	15 513	15 497	17	12 333	632	-758	10 943	2 623	1 948	25 667	22 758	604	368
1996	15 762	15 745	17	12 389	639	-772	10 979	2 695	2 088	25 901	22 872	609	372
1997	16 488	16 468	20	12 699	659	-766	11 273	2 952	2 262	26 898	23 650	613	378
1998	17 138	17 116	22	13 164	686	-812	11 667	3 026	2 445	27 645	24 201	620	385
1999	17 600	17 574	26	13 445	695	-805	11 945	2 975	2 680	28 170	24 697	625	385
2000	18 806	18 792	14	14 182	728	-858	12 596	3 192	3 018	29 960	26 197	628	396
2001	19 660	19 648	12	14 953	778	-939	13 236	3 271	3 152	31 027	27 128	634	405
2002	20 467	20 457	10	15 763	834	-1 180	13 749	3 291	3 428	31 792	28 381	644	. . .
ARIZONA													
1972	9 013	8 793	220	7 002	254	-32	6 716	1 479	817	4 487	3 958	2 009	850
1973	10 476	10 223	253	8 134	338	-31	7 765	1 733	977	4 929	4 400	2 125	925
1974	11 854	11 450	404	9 086	387	-41	8 659	2 016	1 179	5 329	4 729	2 224	955
1975	12 640	12 410	229	9 294	398	-47	8 849	2 155	1 636	5 528	5 016	2 286	935
1976	14 262	13 914	348	10 544	439	-47	10 059	2 396	1 807	6 074	5 474	2 348	976
1977	16 122	15 840	282	12 008	508	-56	11 443	2 750	1 929	6 642	5 944	2 427	1 048
1978	19 100	18 764	336	14 240	613	-69	13 558	3 374	2 168	7 586	6 734	2 518	1 149
1979	22 702	22 291	412	16 892	767	-71	16 054	4 189	2 459	8 604	7 591	2 639	1 241
1980	26 255	25 761	494	19 034	875	-80	18 078	5 205	2 972	9 590	8 493	2 738	1 285
1981	29 950	29 516	434	21 113	1 063	-16	20 034	6 440	3 476	10 658	9 348	2 810	1 317
1982	31 629	31 217	412	21 840	1 132	-9	20 699	7 047	3 883	10 945	9 634	2 890	1 320
1983	34 601	34 271	330	23 778	1 249	2	22 531	7 825	4 245	11 654	10 346	2 969	1 383
1984	39 521	38 965	556	27 374	1 434	7	25 946	9 088	4 487	12 885	11 471	3 067	1 511
1985	43 957	43 436	521	30 519	1 677	20	28 862	10 068	5 027	13 808	12 232	3 184	1 632
1986	47 848	47 349	499	33 232	1 869	40	31 403	10 934	5 512	14 463	12 826	3 308	1 712
1987	52 003	51 368	635	36 052	2 010	68	34 109	11 867	6 027	15 130	13 404	3 437	1 778
1988	55 837	55 066	771	38 781	2 258	110	36 633	12 648	6 556	15 795	14 073	3 535	1 848
1989	60 011	59 326	685	40 496	2 431	169	38 234	14 254	7 523	16 568	14 677	3 622	1 881
1990	63 319	62 678	641	42 618	2 558	231	40 291	14 694	8 335	17 187	15 226	3 684	1 910
1991	66 077	65 349	729	44 521	2 734	221	42 007	14 699	9 371	17 441	15 458	3 789	1 918
1992	70 120	69 479	641	47 612	2 909	239	44 942	14 339	10 839	17 907	15 927	3 916	1 942
1993	74 900	74 105	795	51 170	3 151	252	48 272	14 954	11 674	18 424	16 345	4 065	2 029
1994	82 014	81 497	517	55 942	3 508	259	52 693	16 779	12 542	19 320	17 096	4 245	2 163
1995	88 870	88 116	754	61 136	3 850	273	57 559	17 958	13 353	20 050	17 701	4 432	2 282
1996	95 787	95 145	642	66 330	4 146	299	62 482	19 232	14 073	20 883	18 253	4 587	2 414
1997	103 702	103 083	618	71 851	4 474	320	67 696	21 192	14 814	21 892	19 045	4 737	2 526
1998	112 895	112 119	776	79 105	4 869	361	74 597	23 057	15 240	23 118	19 989	4 883	2 643
1999	120 264	119 456	808	85 537	5 253	412	80 695	23 455	16 114	23 939	20 658	5 024	2 728
2000	131 046	130 473	573	93 527	5 678	438	88 287	25 982	16 778	25 361	21 871	5 167	2 826
2001	137 331	136 619	712	97 001	5 969	449	91 481	26 859	18 991	25 878	22 428	5 307	2 859
2002	142 725	141 767	957	99 953	6 246	592	94 299	27 233	21 192	26 157	23 240	5 456	. . .

. . . = Not available.

Table 21-2. Personal Income and Employment by State and Region—*Continued*

(Millions of dollars, except as noted.)

Year	Total	Nonfarm	Farm	Derivation of personal income						Per capita (dollars)		Population (thousands)	Total employment (thousands)
				Earnings by place of work	Less: Personal contributions for social insurance	Plus: Adjustment for residence	Equals: Net earnings by place of residence	Dividends, interest, and rent	Transfer payments	Personal income	Disposable personal income		
ARKANSAS													
1972	6 893	6 388	505	5 393	198	18	5 214	786	893	3 415	3 076	2 018	867
1973	8 203	7 270	934	6 435	254	15	6 196	931	1 077	3 985	3 581	2 058	902
1974	9 191	8 339	851	7 037	294	8	6 751	1 134	1 306	4 376	3 904	2 100	927
1975	10 047	9 240	807	7 432	310	8	7 130	1 273	1 644	4 655	4 227	2 158	905
1976	11 179	10 531	648	8 311	349	-2	7 959	1 413	1 807	5 155	4 620	2 169	941
1977	12 514	11 786	729	9 348	395	-6	8 947	1 628	1 939	5 670	5 100	2 207	981
1978	14 587	13 392	1 196	11 017	458	-12	10 548	1 915	2 125	6 509	5 858	2 241	1 022
1979	16 084	15 073	1 011	11 906	528	-12	11 366	2 289	2 429	7 088	6 333	2 269	1 033
1980	17 363	16 978	385	12 231	577	-1	11 653	2 824	2 885	7 586	6 741	2 289	1 035
1981	19 638	18 767	871	13 577	677	-18	12 882	3 491	3 265	8 564	7 616	2 293	1 030
1982	20 539	19 897	642	13 776	722	-14	13 040	3 947	3 551	8 952	7 905	2 294	1 014
1983	21 848	21 455	393	14 661	779	-42	13 840	4 172	3 836	9 476	8 466	2 306	1 043
1984	24 496	23 638	858	16 761	865	-63	15 833	4 692	3 971	10 560	9 512	2 320	1 084
1985	26 211	25 373	838	17 804	965	-66	16 773	5 181	4 257	11 264	10 121	2 327	1 104
1986	27 364	26 593	770	18 601	1 046	-88	17 467	5 390	4 507	11 734	10 567	2 332	1 116
1987	28 540	27 608	932	19 708	1 113	-106	18 489	5 387	4 664	12 184	10 925	2 342	1 143
1988	30 493	29 221	1 272	21 207	1 252	-140	19 816	5 788	4 889	13 016	11 696	2 343	1 177
1989	32 410	31 243	1 167	22 240	1 372	-141	20 727	6 366	5 317	13 813	12 372	2 346	1 197
1990	34 159	33 276	883	23 372	1 458	-207	21 707	6 696	5 756	14 495	12 975	2 357	1 212
1991	36 164	35 181	983	24 879	1 567	-221	23 091	6 746	6 327	15 175	13 611	2 383	1 238
1992	39 322	38 052	1 270	27 311	1 703	-259	25 350	6 889	7 084	16 276	14 620	2 416	1 264
1993	41 190	39 979	1 212	28 582	1 806	-270	26 506	7 101	7 584	16 769	15 052	2 456	1 311
1994	43 498	42 165	1 333	30 335	1 964	-292	28 079	7 530	7 889	17 441	15 566	2 494	1 340
1995	45 995	44 576	1 419	31 917	2 064	-270	29 583	7 934	8 478	18 141	16 149	2 535	1 394
1996	48 700	46 885	1 815	33 579	2 137	-263	31 179	8 586	8 935	18 934	16 807	2 572	1 418
1997	51 055	49 349	1 706	34 934	2 259	-260	32 415	9 254	9 386	19 628	17 325	2 601	1 441
1998	53 784	52 283	1 500	36 736	2 370	-267	34 100	10 065	9 619	20 479	18 011	2 626	1 468
1999	55 919	54 217	1 701	38 931	2 503	-293	36 136	9 881	9 902	21 087	18 545	2 652	1 486
2000	58 930	57 663	1 267	40 566	2 591	-335	37 640	10 880	10 410	22 000	19 295	2 679	1 509
2001	61 304	60 211	1 092	41 727	2 718	-327	38 682	11 148	11 473	22 750	19 996	2 695	1 508
2002	63 463	62 524	939	43 040	2 860	-502	39 677	11 225	12 560	23 417	20 970	2 710	. . .
CALIFORNIA													
1972	112 211	109 995	2 216	87 368	3 109	-113	84 146	16 546	11 518	5 451	4 801	20 585	9 369
1973	124 102	121 139	2 963	96 657	3 897	-97	92 663	18 761	12 678	5 947	5 291	20 868	9 844
1974	138 734	135 063	3 672	106 884	4 423	-109	102 351	21 364	15 019	6 553	5 809	21 173	10 163
1975	152 721	149 424	3 297	115 984	4 718	2	111 268	22 707	18 746	7 091	6 360	21 537	10 287
1976	171 412	167 924	3 488	130 732	5 242	103	125 593	25 007	20 813	7 815	6 945	21 935	10 633
1977	191 536	187 973	3 563	146 803	5 963	-50	140 790	28 438	22 308	8 570	7 571	22 350	11 120
1978	219 674	216 166	3 508	168 168	6 911	-61	161 196	34 436	24 042	9 618	8 450	22 839	11 803
1979	252 213	247 568	4 645	191 708	8 314	-35	183 359	42 511	26 343	10 846	9 479	23 255	12 462
1980	286 289	280 549	5 739	213 877	8 969	-84	204 824	50 770	30 695	12 029	10 497	23 801	12 777
1981	320 691	316 238	4 453	233 668	10 981	256	222 943	61 712	36 035	13 205	11 541	24 286	12 970
1982	341 872	337 183	4 689	247 494	12 026	260	235 727	66 588	39 557	13 774	12 119	24 820	12 899
1983	367 505	363 219	4 286	267 409	13 203	267	254 472	70 854	42 178	14 491	12 769	25 360	13 219
1984	411 616	406 613	5 002	300 918	15 056	240	286 102	82 098	43 416	15 927	14 032	25 844	13 852
1985	447 103	442 074	5 029	327 930	16 947	186	311 169	88 236	47 698	16 909	14 815	26 441	14 360
1986	477 762	472 269	5 494	352 886	19 008	126	334 005	92 316	51 441	17 628	15 442	27 102	14 789
1987	517 348	510 718	6 631	385 758	21 248	43	364 552	98 827	53 969	18 625	16 142	27 777	15 396
1988	561 121	554 136	6 985	419 509	24 067	1	395 443	108 090	57 588	19 713	17 239	28 464	16 134
1989	606 701	599 896	6 806	449 232	25 825	-19	423 388	120 813	62 501	20 765	17 985	29 218	16 556
1990	655 567	648 561	7 006	482 926	27 681	-76	455 169	130 572	69 826	21 882	19 021	29 960	16 970
1991	669 842	663 950	5 893	490 699	29 099	-40	461 560	130 471	77 811	21 983	19 268	30 471	16 878
1992	701 572	694 997	6 574	512 714	30 163	8	482 560	128 721	90 291	22 650	20 005	30 975	16 527
1993	714 107	706 788	7 319	520 223	30 828	78	489 473	129 798	94 836	22 833	20 144	31 275	16 506
1994	735 104	727 891	7 214	533 114	32 081	119	501 152	136 049	97 903	23 348	20 536	31 484	16 692
1995	771 470	764 482	6 988	553 877	33 346	144	520 675	148 704	102 091	24 339	21 294	31 697	17 093
1996	812 404	804 819	7 586	584 012	34 494	161	549 679	156 465	106 260	25 373	21 921	32 019	17 505
1997	861 557	853 311	8 247	625 540	36 392	119	589 267	165 594	106 696	26 521	22 630	32 486	17 842
1998	931 564	923 847	7 718	677 677	38 952	154	638 879	181 128	111 557	28 240	23 935	32 988	18 560
1999	995 326	986 825	8 501	734 146	42 664	165	691 647	187 256	116 423	29 712	24 709	33 499	19 050
2000	1 100 679	1 093 393	7 286	818 771	47 157	144	771 757	208 498	120 424	32 363	26 422	34 010	19 658
2001	1 129 868	1 123 382	6 486	830 829	48 353	200	782 675	213 091	134 103	32 655	27 007	34 600	19 834
2002	1 155 247	1 147 594	7 653	837 419	49 354	347	788 412	216 024	150 811	32 898	28 286	35 116	. . .

. . . = Not available.

Table 21-2. Personal Income and Employment by State and Region—*Continued*

(Millions of dollars, except as noted.)

Year	Total	Nonfarm	Farm	Earnings by place of work	Less: Personal contributions for social insurance	Plus: Adjustment for residence	Equals: Net earnings by place of residence	Dividends, interest, and rent	Transfer payments	Personal income	Disposable personal income	Population (thousands)	Total employment (thousands)
COLORADO													
1972	11 520	11 167	352	9 268	292	4	8 979	1 597	944	4 791	4 170	2 405	1 149
1973	13 252	12 794	458	10 671	386	3	10 287	1 864	1 101	5 310	4 643	2 496	1 243
1974	14 901	14 344	558	11 903	441	4	11 467	2 162	1 273	5 864	5 103	2 541	1 276
1975	16 347	15 860	486	12 914	469	8	12 454	2 311	1 582	6 321	5 573	2 586	1 285
1976	18 148	17 794	354	14 362	518	9	13 853	2 556	1 740	6 895	6 050	2 632	1 340
1977	20 400	20 119	281	16 206	592	12	15 626	2 903	1 871	7 567	6 597	2 696	1 411
1978	23 625	23 407	218	18 821	701	20	18 140	3 456	2 029	8 539	7 423	2 767	1 505
1979	27 342	27 124	217	21 722	866	20	20 877	4 195	2 270	9 596	8 295	2 849	1 594
1980	31 442	31 153	289	24 624	1 003	28	23 648	5 152	2 642	10 809	9 347	2 909	1 654
1981	36 154	35 883	271	27 965	1 250	5	26 720	6 345	3 089	12 141	10 430	2 978	1 722
1982	39 632	39 467	164	30 407	1 402	1	29 006	7 120	3 506	12 945	11 098	3 062	1 765
1983	42 523	42 180	343	32 436	1 487	-2	30 948	7 706	3 868	13 570	11 928	3 134	1 794
1984	46 762	46 335	427	35 686	1 648	7	34 045	8 705	4 012	14 751	13 028	3 170	1 892
1985	49 467	49 075	391	37 727	1 841	16	35 901	9 350	4 215	15 416	13 575	3 209	1 926
1986	51 062	50 670	393	38 719	1 951	22	36 790	9 705	4 668	15 772	13 922	3 237	1 925
1987	53 528	53 044	484	40 364	2 005	34	38 394	10 153	4 980	16 417	14 452	3 260	1 915
1988	56 387	55 814	573	42 425	2 196	49	40 278	10 858	5 251	17 285	15 250	3 262	1 981
1989	60 760	60 146	614	44 900	2 380	66	42 586	12 435	5 739	18 548	16 261	3 276	2 017
1990	65 095	64 182	912	48 307	2 565	91	45 833	13 046	6 216	19 680	17 232	3 308	2 055
1991	68 992	68 343	649	51 230	2 818	91	48 503	13 482	7 007	20 369	17 839	3 387	2 102
1992	74 207	73 582	625	55 690	3 037	93	52 747	13 590	7 870	21 227	18 560	3 496	2 152
1993	80 212	79 370	842	60 643	3 318	93	57 417	14 281	8 515	22 196	19 349	3 614	2 253
1994	85 860	85 378	482	64 425	3 617	97	60 906	16 028	8 926	23 055	20 013	3 724	2 368
1995	92 947	92 434	512	69 305	3 904	104	65 505	17 572	9 870	24 289	21 095	3 827	2 448
1996	100 012	99 402	610	74 738	4 181	106	70 664	18 976	10 373	25 514	21 967	3 920	2 545
1997	108 765	108 148	617	81 591	4 524	107	77 174	20 805	10 786	27 067	23 126	4 018	2 657
1998	118 413	117 649	764	89 653	4 937	108	84 824	22 850	10 739	28 764	24 410	4 117	2 762
1999	128 386	127 447	940	99 503	5 416	112	94 199	22 944	11 243	30 380	25 647	4 226	2 847
2000	143 043	142 516	527	111 211	5 993	95	105 312	25 896	11 835	33 060	27 736	4 327	2 959
2001	148 239	147 529	709	114 685	6 232	113	108 566	26 718	12 954	33 455	28 284	4 431	2 989
2002	149 481	148 816	665	114 201	6 278	113	108 036	27 085	14 360	33 170	28 773	4 507	. . .
CONNECTICUT													
1972	17 488	17 412	76	12 790	455	781	13 115	2 869	1 505	5 697	4 941	3 070	1 416
1973	19 154	19 067	87	14 154	579	803	14 378	3 158	1 618	6 241	5 450	3 069	1 480
1974	20 955	20 865	90	15 360	660	836	15 536	3 516	1 904	6 813	5 949	3 076	1 511
1975	22 329	22 248	81	15 987	679	911	16 219	3 600	2 510	7 239	6 409	3 085	1 468
1976	24 334	24 246	88	17 464	730	1 006	17 740	3 910	2 684	7 885	6 895	3 086	1 493
1977	26 909	26 821	88	19 401	807	1 115	19 709	4 364	2 836	8 712	7 622	3 089	1 546
1978	30 081	29 996	85	21 819	923	1 267	22 163	5 003	2 915	9 720	8 428	3 095	1 616
1979	34 008	33 927	81	24 550	1 098	1 441	24 894	5 880	3 234	10 971	9 448	3 100	1 675
1980	38 726	38 641	85	27 432	1 245	1 685	27 872	7 122	3 731	12 439	10 655	3 113	1 709
1981	43 380	43 296	84	29 972	1 484	1 868	30 356	8 719	4 305	13 865	11 817	3 129	1 732
1982	46 782	46 672	110	31 979	1 626	2 024	32 376	9 604	4 801	14 903	12 678	3 139	1 731
1983	49 963	49 852	111	34 508	1 751	2 146	34 903	9 893	5 166	15 799	13 776	3 162	1 749
1984	55 906	55 774	132	38 654	1 966	2 295	38 984	11 582	5 340	17 580	15 411	3 180	1 831
1985	60 063	59 931	132	42 235	2 238	2 431	42 427	11 932	5 704	18 763	16 298	3 201	1 890
1986	64 598	64 453	145	45 769	2 482	2 588	45 875	12 664	6 059	20 038	17 305	3 224	1 949
1987	71 099	70 955	144	51 011	2 763	2 719	50 967	13 822	6 309	21 895	18 742	3 247	1 997
1988	78 551	78 393	158	56 521	3 130	2 902	56 293	15 454	6 804	24 007	20 815	3 272	2 054
1989	84 703	84 558	145	59 621	3 335	2 797	59 083	18 050	7 569	25 797	22 364	3 283	2 048
1990	87 935	87 751	185	61 622	3 465	2 768	60 925	18 466	8 543	26 712	23 259	3 292	2 019
1991	88 344	88 181	164	61 792	3 591	2 820	61 021	17 734	9 588	26 747	23 275	3 303	1 937
1992	93 779	93 588	191	64 965	3 704	3 461	64 722	17 795	11 263	28 412	24 412	3 301	1 918
1993	96 866	96 652	215	67 239	3 839	3 466	66 866	18 279	11 721	29 272	25 035	3 309	1 939
1994	99 788	99 598	190	69 332	4 031	3 505	68 806	18 865	12 117	30 092	25 763	3 316	1 923
1995	104 315	104 139	176	72 132	4 269	4 119	71 983	19 333	12 999	31 381	26 603	3 324	1 961
1996	109 354	109 174	180	75 317	4 448	4 892	75 761	20 248	13 344	32 773	27 433	3 337	1 992
1997	116 421	116 248	173	80 953	4 808	4 887	81 033	21 442	13 946	34 759	28 580	3 349	2 020
1998	124 880	124 674	206	86 358	5 066	6 020	87 313	23 515	14 052	37 108	30 219	3 365	2 047
1999	130 579	130 342	237	91 906	5 383	5 966	92 489	23 800	14 289	38 560	31 198	3 386	2 076
2000	141 413	141 211	202	98 863	5 702	6 467	99 628	26 830	14 955	41 446	33 142	3 412	2 115
2001	145 548	145 358	190	101 700	5 913	6 389	102 176	27 525	15 847	42 377	34 195	3 435	2 112
2002	148 211	148 052	159	101 855	6 005	7 498	103 347	27 712	17 152	42 829	35 982	3 461	. . .

. . . = Not available.

Table 21-2. Personal Income and Employment by State and Region—*Continued*

(Millions of dollars, except as noted.)

Year	Total	Nonfarm	Farm	Derivation of personal income						Per capita (dollars)		Population (thousands)	Total employment (thousands)
				Earnings by place of work	Less: Personal contributions for social insurance	Plus: Adjustment for residence	Equals: Net earnings by place of residence	Dividends, interest, and rent	Transfer payments	Personal income	Disposable personal income		
DELAWARE													
1972	3 043	2 992	51	2 553	92	-65	2 395	432	215	5 303	4 425	574	293
1973	3 400	3 302	98	2 891	119	-93	2 679	475	247	5 871	4 895	579	305
1974	3 701	3 617	85	3 107	134	-104	2 869	531	301	6 347	5 315	583	302
1975	3 962	3 867	95	3 280	139	-105	3 035	525	401	6 729	5 709	589	292
1976	4 356	4 270	87	3 603	151	-116	3 337	586	434	7 349	6 147	593	296
1977	4 707	4 649	58	3 860	163	-127	3 570	660	478	7 913	6 632	595	296
1978	5 179	5 116	63	4 278	184	-156	3 939	741	499	8 658	7 266	598	304
1979	5 718	5 663	56	4 686	213	-176	4 297	851	570	9 549	7 950	599	312
1980	6 427	6 413	14	5 155	239	-222	4 694	1 040	693	10 803	8 984	595	312
1981	7 076	7 034	42	5 547	281	-240	5 026	1 261	789	11 873	9 799	596	314
1982	7 626	7 559	66	5 962	309	-260	5 392	1 394	839	12 727	10 657	599	317
1983	8 191	8 111	80	6 433	332	-305	5 796	1 506	889	13 529	11 487	605	326
1984	9 061	8 964	97	7 082	363	-342	6 377	1 750	934	14 816	12 668	612	341
1985	9 927	9 823	105	7 754	413	-381	6 961	1 961	1 006	16 056	13 749	618	359
1986	10 531	10 384	147	8 196	446	-382	7 368	2 072	1 090	16 781	14 330	628	372
1987	11 423	11 308	114	8 973	488	-436	8 049	2 231	1 142	17 933	15 391	637	389
1988	12 507	12 322	184	9 880	558	-492	8 830	2 418	1 259	19 312	16 675	648	405
1989	13 778	13 584	194	10 750	621	-586	9 543	2 874	1 360	20 930	18 015	658	418
1990	14 476	14 338	138	11 368	658	-682	10 027	2 986	1 462	21 620	18 598	670	423
1991	15 204	15 075	129	11 781	696	-679	10 406	3 157	1 640	22 257	19 288	683	417
1992	15 939	15 827	112	12 319	713	-668	10 938	3 155	1 845	22 936	19 940	695	416
1993	16 663	16 553	110	13 027	743	-831	11 454	3 250	1 959	23 590	20 468	706	424
1994	17 378	17 257	121	13 587	795	-862	11 930	3 327	2 121	24 218	20 886	718	428
1995	18 237	18 145	92	14 140	850	-888	12 402	3 555	2 280	24 992	21 496	730	447
1996	19 369	19 259	110	14 703	903	-788	13 012	3 873	2 485	26 140	22 332	741	458
1997	20 145	20 065	80	15 571	956	-992	13 623	4 033	2 489	26 807	22 605	751	470
1998	21 879	21 751	128	16 836	1 030	-1 119	14 687	4 582	2 610	28 662	24 196	763	487
1999	22 716	22 590	127	18 049	1 098	-1 342	15 608	4 414	2 694	29 312	24 734	775	499
2000	24 455	24 353	102	19 088	1 147	-1 406	16 535	5 019	2 901	31 092	26 222	787	510
2001	25 624	25 457	167	19 959	1 209	-1 412	17 338	5 133	3 152	32 166	27 288	797	510
2002	26 084	26 027	57	20 323	1 262	-1 610	17 451	5 165	3 468	32 307	28 021	807	. . .
DISTRICT OF COLUMBIA													
1972	4 517	4 517	0	7 724	155	-4 150	3 419	651	447	6 073	5 254	744	671
1973	4 785	4 785	0	8 208	189	-4 435	3 585	691	510	6 522	5 628	734	664
1974	5 266	5 266	0	9 022	213	-4 894	3 915	760	592	7 306	6 332	721	676
1975	5 731	5 731	0	9 974	228	-5 505	4 240	758	732	8 068	7 026	710	680
1976	6 110	6 110	0	10 850	242	-6 075	4 532	815	762	8 775	7 523	696	677
1977	6 615	6 615	0	11 916	259	-6 720	4 937	890	788	9 702	8 411	682	683
1978	7 001	7 001	0	12 987	287	-7 503	5 197	996	808	10 448	8 963	670	696
1979	7 432	7 432	0	14 188	335	-8 458	5 394	1 138	900	11 336	9 591	656	709
1980	7 881	7 881	0	15 624	377	-9 696	5 550	1 310	1 021	12 347	10 480	638	707
1981	8 617	8 617	0	16 955	452	-10 637	5 866	1 620	1 131	13 530	11 328	637	696
1982	9 389	9 389	0	18 048	496	-11 296	6 257	1 871	1 261	14 805	12 471	634	681
1983	9 823	9 823	0	18 875	606	-11 669	6 600	1 906	1 317	15 532	13 202	632	677
1984	10 847	10 847	0	20 516	677	-12 593	7 246	2 213	1 389	17 126	14 571	633	700
1985	11 534	11 534	0	21 899	801	-13 385	7 712	2 438	1 385	18 177	15 443	635	714
1986	12 146	12 146	0	23 300	903	-14 218	8 179	2 513	1 455	19 030	16 192	638	734
1987	12 898	12 898	0	25 090	993	-15 286	8 811	2 581	1 506	20 251	17 100	637	747
1988	14 147	14 147	0	27 631	1 156	-16 805	9 670	2 863	1 614	22 440	19 196	630	770
1989	15 174	15 174	0	29 369	1 285	-17 925	10 159	3 405	1 610	24 311	20 769	624	778
1990	16 078	16 078	0	31 517	1 422	-19 101	10 993	3 341	1 743	26 561	22 864	605	789
1991	16 651	16 651	0	33 118	1 511	-20 262	11 345	3 349	1 957	27 711	24 086	601	775
1992	17 533	17 533	0	35 000	1 587	-21 503	11 910	3 388	2 236	29 341	25 716	598	768
1993	18 251	18 251	0	36 395	1 675	-22 372	12 348	3 467	2 435	30 658	26 912	595	768
1994	18 499	18 499	0	37 252	1 767	-23 050	12 435	3 591	2 474	31 395	27 337	589	747
1995	18 217	18 217	0	37 588	1 826	-23 401	12 362	3 462	2 393	31 380	27 286	581	740
1996	18 517	18 517	0	37 872	1 866	-23 489	12 517	3 402	2 599	32 352	27 712	572	722
1997	19 135	19 135	0	39 034	1 908	-24 325	12 802	3 765	2 568	33 704	28 393	568	718
1998	20 255	20 255	0	40 678	1 990	-25 352	13 336	4 231	2 689	35 836	29 937	565	722
1999	20 785	20 785	0	43 876	2 194	-27 763	13 920	4 185	2 681	36 452	29 953	570	736
2000	22 849	22 849	0	46 950	2 349	-29 131	15 471	4 619	2 759	39 970	32 739	572	766
2001	23 262	23 262	0	49 161	2 536	-30 843	15 782	4 619	2 860	40 539	33 260	574	762
2002	24 760	24 760	0	51 511	2 703	-31 737	17 071	4 609	3 080	43 371	36 888	571	. . .

. . . = Not available.

Table 21-2. Personal Income and Employment by State and Region—*Continued*

(Millions of dollars, except as noted.)

Year	Total	Nonfarm	Farm	Derivation of personal income						Per capita (dollars)		Population (thousands)	Total employment (thousands)
				Earnings by place of work	Less: Personal contributions for social insurance	Plus: Adjustment for residence	Equals: Net earnings by place of residence	Dividends, interest, and rent	Transfer payments	Personal income	Disposable personal income		
FLORIDA													
1972	35 365	34 591	774	25 182	914	-11	24 257	7 357	3 750	4 703	4 136	7 520	3 338
1973	41 495	40 628	866	29 519	1 229	-10	28 280	8 690	4 525	5 235	4 633	7 927	3 666
1974	46 712	45 773	939	32 589	1 422	-1	31 166	10 091	5 456	5 616	4 989	8 317	3 766
1975	50 353	49 315	1 038	34 046	1 456	-10	32 580	10 691	7 082	5 895	5 334	8 542	3 676
1976	55 438	54 365	1 073	37 241	1 574	10	35 677	11 877	7 884	6 376	5 732	8 695	3 730
1977	62 309	61 234	1 075	41 674	1 774	21	39 921	13 673	8 715	7 010	6 285	8 889	3 929
1978	72 332	71 047	1 285	48 257	2 100	25	46 182	16 497	9 653	7 921	7 058	9 132	4 235
1979	84 094	82 728	1 366	55 147	2 537	21	52 631	20 305	11 158	8 879	7 864	9 471	4 457
1980	98 882	97 127	1 755	63 416	2 967	15	60 464	25 110	13 308	10 049	8 857	9 840	4 695
1981	114 110	112 640	1 469	70 995	3 638	114	67 471	31 114	15 525	11 195	9 839	10 193	4 881
1982	123 450	121 545	1 905	76 007	4 033	136	72 110	33 740	17 600	11 789	10 278	10 471	4 970
1983	135 842	133 174	2 668	84 369	4 445	161	80 085	36 551	19 206	12 637	11 276	10 750	5 185
1984	151 952	150 010	1 941	94 549	5 054	212	89 707	42 053	20 191	13 764	12 395	11 040	5 529
1985	166 919	164 967	1 952	103 855	5 841	257	98 271	46 596	22 052	14 705	13 085	11 351	5 809
1986	179 952	177 853	2 098	112 331	6 498	313	106 146	49 921	23 885	15 423	13 666	11 668	6 056
1987	196 939	194 689	2 251	124 217	7 086	374	117 505	53 936	25 498	16 415	14 540	11 997	6 141
1988	216 505	213 633	2 871	136 719	8 092	451	129 079	59 530	27 895	17 593	15 650	12 306	6 444
1989	240 687	238 064	2 623	145 630	8 922	531	137 239	72 268	31 180	19 045	16 919	12 638	6 657
1990	258 479	256 251	2 228	155 631	9 462	639	146 809	76 991	34 679	19 832	17 711	13 033	6 802
1991	268 304	265 582	2 722	160 515	9 988	660	151 188	77 963	39 155	20 068	18 039	13 370	6 778
1992	279 028	276 490	2 538	171 411	10 610	697	161 498	73 012	44 518	20 441	18 319	13 651	6 829
1993	296 927	294 321	2 606	182 048	11 346	723	171 425	77 661	47 841	21 320	19 082	13 927	7 073
1994	311 909	309 683	2 225	190 871	12 200	754	179 426	81 453	51 030	21 905	19 550	14 239	7 314
1995	333 525	331 269	2 256	202 726	13 021	782	190 487	88 225	54 813	22 942	20 428	14 538	7 576
1996	355 136	353 157	1 979	215 167	13 646	807	202 328	94 832	57 976	23 909	21 060	14 853	7 831
1997	377 673	375 452	2 221	227 679	14 412	840	214 107	102 604	60 962	24 869	21 709	15 186	8 103
1998	405 146	402 569	2 577	245 877	15 404	899	231 371	111 407	62 368	26 161	22 724	15 487	8 403
1999	425 157	422 150	3 007	264 503	16 385	957	249 076	112 219	63 862	26 978	23 390	15 759	8 676
2000	455 313	453 551	1 762	284 163	17 440	1 029	267 751	120 070	67 491	28 366	24 455	16 051	8 959
2001	475 607	473 783	1 824	296 484	18 526	1 024	278 983	123 220	73 404	29 048	25 109	16 373	9 083
2002	494 027	491 982	2 045	307 535	19 554	1 063	289 045	125 033	79 949	29 559	26 207	16 713	. . .
GEORGIA													
1972	19 411	18 906	505	16 298	571	-58	15 669	2 000	1 742	4 038	3 556	4 807	2 253
1973	22 064	21 245	819	18 513	736	-56	17 722	2 345	1 998	4 497	3 992	4 907	2 356
1974	24 312	23 608	704	19 954	832	-56	19 066	2 757	2 490	4 867	4 319	4 995	2 374
1975	26 061	25 403	658	20 806	855	-47	19 905	2 887	3 269	5 152	4 657	5 059	2 313
1976	29 189	28 545	644	23 597	961	-78	22 558	3 120	3 511	5 694	5 101	5 126	2 399
1977	32 423	32 052	371	26 394	1 074	-98	25 222	3 510	3 691	6 221	5 541	5 212	2 503
1978	36 945	36 367	578	30 154	1 246	-81	28 827	4 119	4 000	6 989	6 186	5 286	2 622
1979	41 633	41 017	617	33 755	1 462	-99	32 194	4 900	4 539	7 722	6 756	5 391	2 705
1980	46 489	46 430	59	36 736	1 644	-117	34 975	6 066	5 448	8 474	7 442	5 486	2 747
1981	52 536	52 018	518	40 868	1 973	-29	38 866	7 487	6 183	9 435	8 247	5 568	2 785
1982	56 801	56 121	680	43 789	2 170	-71	41 548	8 488	6 766	10 054	8 838	5 650	2 802
1983	62 145	61 682	463	47 908	2 411	-114	45 383	9 427	7 335	10 849	9 514	5 728	2 886
1984	71 100	70 149	951	55 221	2 766	-180	52 275	11 100	7 725	12 185	10 748	5 835	3 081
1985	78 364	77 592	772	60 998	3 215	-199	57 585	12 373	8 407	13 143	11 518	5 963	3 224
1986	85 126	84 315	811	66 557	3 611	-243	62 703	13 402	9 021	13 990	12 269	6 085	3 354
1987	92 007	91 141	867	72 059	3 896	-244	67 919	14 535	9 554	14 820	12 930	6 208	3 455
1988	100 277	99 141	1 136	78 216	4 361	-237	73 617	16 358	10 302	15 876	13 931	6 316	3 568
1989	107 725	106 392	1 334	82 675	4 685	-202	77 788	18 612	11 326	16 803	14 687	6 411	3 634
1990	115 414	114 223	1 191	87 892	5 001	-117	82 775	20 009	12 630	17 722	15 523	6 513	3 691
1991	121 094	119 580	1 515	91 213	5 269	-123	85 821	20 706	14 567	18 201	16 032	6 653	3 647
1992	130 684	129 116	1 568	99 152	5 637	-158	93 356	21 098	16 230	19 170	16 920	6 817	3 727
1993	138 771	137 343	1 427	105 345	6 058	-155	99 132	22 002	17 637	19 886	17 475	6 978	3 899
1994	149 165	147 275	1 890	112 808	6 585	-195	106 028	24 272	18 866	20 841	18 285	7 157	4 058
1995	159 800	158 103	1 697	120 919	7 118	-240	113 561	26 066	20 174	21 806	19 059	7 328	4 229
1996	172 935	171 133	1 802	130 414	7 594	-293	122 527	28 749	21 660	23 055	20 021	7 501	4 379
1997	183 757	181 947	1 810	139 471	8 142	-330	130 999	30 623	22 135	23 911	20 605	7 685	4 499
1998	200 104	198 238	1 866	151 678	8 781	-409	142 487	34 930	22 687	25 447	21 836	7 864	4 664
1999	213 508	211 421	2 088	165 065	9 504	-385	155 175	34 680	23 653	26 536	22 720	8 046	4 797
2000	231 412	229 814	1 598	177 875	10 110	-476	167 288	38 757	25 366	28 103	24 015	8 234	4 918
2001	239 754	237 837	1 917	183 091	10 515	-494	172 081	39 748	27 924	28 523	24 463	8 406	4 921
2002	245 707	244 411	1 296	185 814	10 878	-313	174 623	40 336	30 748	28 703	25 221	8 560	. . .

. . . = Not available.

Table 21-2. Personal Income and Employment by State and Region—*Continued*

(Millions of dollars, except as noted.)

Year	Total	Nonfarm	Farm	Earnings by place of work	Less: Personal contributions for social insurance	Plus: Adjustment for residence	Equals: Net earnings by place of residence	Dividends, interest, and rent	Transfer payments	Personal income	Disposable personal income	Population (thousands)	Total employment (thousands)
HAWAII													
1972	4 660	4 527	134	3 831	115	0	3 715	623	323	5 697	4 918	818	453
1973	5 178	5 040	138	4 246	151	0	4 095	716	368	6 151	5 325	842	473
1974	5 965	5 608	357	4 881	175	0	4 706	819	441	6 952	6 052	858	485
1975	6 465	6 255	210	5 213	190	0	5 022	875	568	7 388	6 578	875	499
1976	7 032	6 857	175	5 632	204	0	5 427	936	668	7 880	6 964	892	505
1977	7 652	7 465	187	6 133	224	0	5 908	1 034	709	8 356	7 351	916	509
1978	8 497	8 328	169	6 770	259	0	6 512	1 226	759	9 148	7 993	929	527
1979	9 679	9 482	197	7 647	304	0	7 343	1 501	835	10 188	8 881	950	556
1980	11 140	10 750	390	8 744	342	0	8 401	1 776	962	11 512	10 054	968	575
1981	12 041	11 835	206	9 204	402	0	8 802	2 113	1 126	12 309	10 748	978	569
1982	12 846	12 604	242	9 847	434	0	9 413	2 212	1 221	12 927	11 514	994	568
1983	14 056	13 712	344	10 654	470	0	10 184	2 531	1 341	13 880	12 354	1 013	579
1984	15 328	15 095	234	11 524	506	0	11 018	2 914	1 397	14 912	13 322	1 028	585
1985	16 316	16 101	214	12 325	571	0	11 754	3 070	1 491	15 693	13 959	1 040	602
1986	17 259	16 998	260	13 113	626	0	12 487	3 208	1 564	16 409	14 560	1 052	616
1987	18 574	18 343	231	14 228	692	0	13 536	3 407	1 631	17 392	15 242	1 068	647
1988	20 399	20 145	254	15 704	805	0	14 899	3 754	1 746	18 891	16 536	1 080	674
1989	22 483	22 246	237	17 216	912	0	16 303	4 273	1 907	20 540	17 758	1 095	702
1990	24 915	24 670	245	19 154	1 017	0	18 137	4 514	2 263	22 375	19 415	1 113	731
1991	26 198	25 995	203	20 264	1 100	0	19 164	4 705	2 328	23 046	20 085	1 137	752
1992	27 859	27 671	188	21 785	1 157	0	20 628	4 518	2 713	24 045	21 112	1 159	754
1993	29 068	28 887	181	22 184	1 181	0	21 003	5 072	2 992	24 784	21 811	1 173	750
1994	29 740	29 563	177	22 300	1 211	0	21 088	5 406	3 245	25 044	22 094	1 188	745
1995	30 202	30 040	161	22 244	1 223	0	21 020	5 539	3 643	25 234	22 287	1 197	742
1996	30 393	30 233	160	22 303	1 216	0	21 087	5 584	3 723	25 249	22 206	1 204	741
1997	31 218	31 055	164	22 699	1 235	0	21 463	5 990	3 765	25 765	22 590	1 212	742
1998	31 841	31 661	180	23 067	1 271	0	21 796	6 240	3 804	26 201	22 914	1 215	744
1999	32 626	32 428	198	23 694	1 317	0	22 377	6 320	3 929	26 957	23 491	1 210	742
2000	34 384	34 201	184	24 837	1 369	0	23 468	6 827	4 089	28 354	24 625	1 213	764
2001	35 625	35 440	186	25 698	1 438	0	24 260	6 993	4 372	29 034	25 302	1 227	772
2002	37 397	37 195	202	27 166	1 547	. . .	25 619	7 072	4 705	30 040	26 716	1 245	. . .
IDAHO													
1972	3 168	2 829	339	2 521	83	16	2 454	407	307	4 150	3 750	763	347
1973	3 683	3 215	467	2 931	110	19	2 840	494	348	4 709	4 222	782	365
1974	4 349	3 702	647	3 466	129	22	3 360	571	418	5 382	4 788	808	381
1975	4 635	4 233	402	3 609	145	28	3 492	629	514	5 571	4 996	832	393
1976	5 241	4 884	357	4 078	163	35	3 950	706	585	6 116	5 476	857	419
1977	5 751	5 500	251	4 446	181	36	4 300	823	629	6 510	5 814	883	435
1978	6 668	6 343	325	5 189	208	43	5 024	975	669	7 319	6 522	911	460
1979	7 363	7 128	235	5 603	246	48	5 405	1 180	778	7 894	7 023	933	470
1980	8 280	7 873	407	6 133	267	62	5 928	1 419	933	8 735	7 779	948	466
1981	9 050	8 655	395	6 517	312	54	6 260	1 718	1 072	9 405	8 286	962	463
1982	9 368	8 982	386	6 495	325	63	6 234	1 904	1 231	9 621	8 557	974	453
1983	10 128	9 541	586	7 174	346	65	6 893	1 935	1 300	10 315	9 240	982	464
1984	10 968	10 466	501	7 741	377	78	7 443	2 193	1 332	11 069	9 956	991	474
1985	11 577	11 119	458	8 131	417	86	7 799	2 338	1 440	11 647	10 452	994	476
1986	11 851	11 377	474	8 269	434	101	7 936	2 393	1 522	11 968	10 799	990	476
1987	12 422	11 838	584	8 750	454	110	8 406	2 444	1 572	12 611	11 356	985	490
1988	13 354	12 721	633	9 485	525	127	9 087	2 587	1 680	13 548	12 175	986	512
1989	14 721	13 863	857	10 442	587	142	9 997	2 912	1 812	14 803	13 152	994	529
1990	16 054	15 081	974	11 448	641	154	10 961	3 122	1 971	15 858	14 064	1 012	553
1991	16 825	16 026	799	11 914	704	168	11 379	3 254	2 192	16 158	14 323	1 041	570
1992	18 382	17 581	801	13 157	756	173	12 574	3 367	2 441	17 153	15 115	1 072	590
1993	20 105	19 040	1 065	14 560	817	182	13 926	3 554	2 626	18 133	16 007	1 109	617
1994	21 399	20 706	694	15 393	900	204	14 697	3 925	2 777	18 687	16 469	1 145	653
1995	22 869	22 073	796	16 199	949	230	15 480	4 377	3 012	19 425	17 103	1 177	673
1996	24 173	23 298	876	16 966	987	260	16 238	4 650	3 285	20 093	17 628	1 203	695
1997	25 226	24 557	669	17 541	1 044	292	16 789	5 044	3 394	20 534	17 944	1 229	715
1998	27 066	26 149	917	18 879	1 102	321	18 098	5 469	3 499	21 612	18 876	1 252	742
1999	28 901	27 872	1 030	20 579	1 182	356	19 753	5 468	3 680	22 656	19 691	1 276	759
2000	31 177	30 382	794	22 191	1 275	432	21 348	5 891	3 938	23 987	20 684	1 300	788
2001	32 363	31 400	963	22 773	1 320	425	21 878	6 102	4 383	24 506	21 262	1 321	798
2002	33 585	32 572	1 013	23 396	1 375	476	22 497	6 198	4 890	25 042	22 325	1 341	. . .

. . . = Not available.

Table 21-2. Personal Income and Employment by State and Region—*Continued*

(Millions of dollars, except as noted.)

Year	Total	Nonfarm	Farm	Derivation of personal income — Earnings by place of work	Less: Personal contributions for social insurance	Plus: Adjustment for residence	Equals: Net earnings by place of residence	Dividends, interest, and rent	Transfer payments	Per capita (dollars) — Personal income	Per capita (dollars) — Disposable personal income	Population (thousands)	Total employment (thousands)
ILLINOIS													
1972	59 280	58 241	1 040	47 978	1 668	-46	46 264	7 846	5 170	5 266	4 534	11 258	5 156
1973	66 471	64 615	1 856	53 558	2 113	-65	51 379	8 981	6 111	5 903	5 122	11 260	5 351
1974	72 877	71 179	1 698	58 155	2 398	-79	55 678	10 239	6 960	6 464	5 584	11 274	5 442
1975	78 990	76 534	2 456	61 955	2 477	-105	59 373	10 761	8 856	6 986	6 113	11 306	5 342
1976	86 598	84 877	1 721	67 915	2 716	-86	65 113	11 658	9 828	7 623	6 609	11 360	5 458
1977	95 637	93 882	1 755	75 188	2 974	-20	72 194	13 053	10 391	8 385	7 256	11 406	5 587
1978	106 079	104 523	1 556	83 415	3 366	65	80 115	14 947	11 018	9 277	8 008	11 434	5 748
1979	117 000	115 189	1 811	91 249	3 871	148	87 526	17 508	11 966	10 243	8 784	11 423	5 811
1980	126 662	126 335	327	95 059	4 152	247	91 154	20 940	14 567	11 077	9 519	11 435	5 688
1981	140 177	138 494	1 683	102 778	4 823	184	98 138	25 315	16 724	12 250	10 502	11 443	5 684
1982	145 889	145 067	822	104 636	5 067	111	99 679	27 807	18 403	12 771	11 108	11 423	5 583
1983	151 615	152 144	-529	107 666	5 272	74	102 468	29 465	19 681	13 289	11 630	11 409	5 542
1984	167 548	166 503	1 045	120 277	5 841	-31	114 405	33 365	19 779	14 682	12 925	11 412	5 746
1985	176 786	175 288	1 499	127 583	6 496	-102	120 986	34 770	21 030	15 508	13 610	11 400	5 815
1986	185 432	184 229	1 203	134 620	7 041	-162	127 417	36 080	21 925	16 204	14 304	11 387	5 928
1987	196 947	195 728	1 218	144 350	7 550	-251	136 549	37 849	22 549	17 289	15 038	11 391	6 073
1988	210 272	209 751	521	155 127	8 492	-346	146 288	40 682	23 302	18 461	16 141	11 390	6 233
1989	224 024	222 205	1 819	163 526	9 194	-381	153 951	45 225	24 848	19 634	17 054	11 410	6 344
1990	237 593	236 206	1 387	173 203	9 786	-287	163 131	47 603	26 859	20 744	18 032	11 453	6 442
1991	245 952	245 383	569	178 159	10 350	-315	167 494	49 229	29 229	21 260	18 595	11 569	6 418
1992	264 869	263 399	1 470	192 446	10 867	-386	181 194	50 349	33 326	22 650	19 915	11 694	6 403
1993	274 221	272 937	1 284	200 606	11 473	-396	188 736	50 813	34 672	23 220	20 327	11 810	6 496
1994	288 509	286 768	1 741	210 738	12 281	-449	198 008	54 744	35 758	24 219	21 099	11 913	6 672
1995	304 767	304 404	364	220 715	13 029	-548	207 139	59 424	38 205	25 379	22 053	12 008	6 838
1996	322 790	320 789	2 001	233 061	13 566	-652	218 843	63 968	39 978	26 672	23 008	12 102	6 944
1997	340 594	338 811	1 783	246 656	14 427	-722	231 507	67 940	41 147	27 950	23 922	12 186	7 055
1998	362 081	360 921	1 161	262 004	15 197	-722	246 085	74 532	41 464	29 505	25 097	12 272	7 211
1999	373 813	373 038	775	276 454	16 024	-839	259 591	72 453	41 769	30 246	25 625	12 359	7 296
2000	401 803	400 641	1 161	294 113	16 736	-975	276 402	81 264	44 138	32 297	27 338	12 441	7 436
2001	413 044	411 953	1 091	300 146	17 267	-1 271	281 609	84 051	47 384	32 990	27 981	12 520	7 404
2002	419 858	419 090	768	301 858	17 629	-899	283 330	85 048	51 479	33 320	29 052	12 601	. . .
INDIANA													
1972	23 593	23 010	583	19 385	721	149	18 812	2 808	1 972	4 455	3 896	5 296	2 367
1973	27 177	25 887	1 290	22 332	925	193	21 599	3 258	2 320	5 100	4 504	5 329	2 483
1974	29 103	28 307	796	23 396	1 043	254	22 607	3 762	2 734	5 440	4 729	5 350	2 493
1975	31 197	30 040	1 157	24 423	1 062	299	23 660	4 086	3 451	5 830	5 159	5 351	2 405
1976	35 002	33 863	1 139	27 710	1 189	350	26 870	4 506	3 626	6 516	5 710	5 372	2 489
1977	38 910	38 104	805	30 859	1 326	412	29 945	5 105	3 860	7 199	6 286	5 405	2 578
1978	43 602	42 794	808	34 604	1 521	466	33 549	5 822	4 231	8 006	6 964	5 446	2 671
1979	48 256	47 564	691	37 817	1 749	544	36 612	6 801	4 843	8 814	7 637	5 475	2 713
1980	51 881	51 495	386	38 730	1 823	667	37 574	8 230	6 077	9 449	8 246	5 491	2 632
1981	56 752	56 422	330	41 401	2 127	713	39 987	9 991	6 774	10 355	8 990	5 480	2 611
1982	58 494	58 215	279	41 325	2 184	778	39 918	11 018	7 558	10 698	9 362	5 468	2 530
1983	61 063	61 323	-261	42 944	2 290	826	41 479	11 464	8 119	11 203	9 865	5 450	2 550
1984	67 928	67 255	674	48 187	2 529	985	46 643	12 883	8 403	12 445	11 006	5 458	2 653
1985	71 752	71 177	575	50 987	2 813	1 070	49 243	13 655	8 854	13 143	11 578	5 459	2 709
1986	75 382	74 925	457	53 530	3 031	1 167	51 666	14 284	9 432	13 821	12 199	5 454	2 770
1987	80 258	79 620	638	57 682	3 244	1 241	55 679	14 867	9 712	14 664	12 896	5 473	2 866
1988	85 759	85 606	153	61 852	3 651	1 332	59 533	15 921	10 305	15 616	13 742	5 492	2 954
1989	92 630	91 798	832	66 313	3 969	1 415	63 760	17 763	11 106	16 770	14 625	5 524	3 031
1990	97 907	97 196	712	69 646	4 195	1 486	66 936	18 836	12 135	17 616	15 390	5 558	3 091
1991	101 147	101 033	114	71 741	4 464	1 510	68 787	18 852	13 508	18 009	15 791	5 616	3 093
1992	108 845	108 264	581	77 566	4 746	1 646	74 466	19 052	15 327	19 181	16 840	5 675	3 143
1993	114 675	113 978	697	82 092	5 064	1 725	78 752	19 579	16 344	19 982	17 475	5 739	3 221
1994	121 537	120 927	610	87 089	5 494	1 870	83 465	21 125	16 947	20 978	18 250	5 794	3 315
1995	126 525	126 305	220	90 449	5 774	2 056	86 730	22 590	17 204	21 623	18 775	5 851	3 409
1996	132 890	131 910	980	94 568	5 967	2 210	90 810	23 985	18 094	22 501	19 443	5 906	3 450
1997	139 459	138 470	990	99 129	6 313	2 437	95 254	25 484	18 722	23 418	20 121	5 955	3 511
1998	149 318	148 739	580	105 921	6 668	2 471	101 724	28 329	19 265	24 891	21 417	5 999	3 583
1999	154 405	154 175	230	111 222	7 000	2 729	106 951	27 392	20 062	25 543	21 979	6 045	3 638
2000	164 543	164 042	501	116 581	7 197	3 015	112 400	30 609	21 534	27 010	23 340	6 092	3 688
2001	168 622	167 960	661	117 623	7 345	3 357	113 636	31 374	23 612	27 522	23 839	6 127	3 632
2002	173 889	173 677	212	119 990	7 642	4 011	116 359	31 677	25 852	28 233	24 983	6 159	. . .

. . . = Not available.

Table 21-2. Personal Income and Employment by State and Region—*Continued*

(Millions of dollars, except as noted.)

| Year | Total | Nonfarm | Farm | Derivation of personal income | | | | | | Per capita (dollars) | | Population (thousands) | Total employment (thousands) |
				Earnings by place of work	Less: Personal contributions for social insurance	Plus: Adjustment for residence	Equals: Net earnings by place of residence	Dividends, interest, and rent	Transfer payments	Personal income	Disposable personal income		
IOWA													
1972	12 796	11 323	1 473	9 870	370	94	9 594	1 986	1 216	4 473	3 937	2 861	1 316
1973	15 460	12 747	2 712	12 115	472	88	11 731	2 335	1 394	5 398	4 796	2 864	1 374
1974	16 050	14 349	1 701	12 244	554	84	11 774	2 662	1 613	5 596	4 840	2 868	1 407
1975	17 841	15 892	1 949	13 440	597	100	12 944	2 913	1 984	6 192	5 438	2 881	1 407
1976	19 106	17 905	1 201	14 263	650	92	13 704	3 209	2 193	6 580	5 729	2 904	1 455
1977	21 225	19 999	1 226	15 815	700	66	15 181	3 698	2 346	7 283	6 351	2 914	1 488
1978	24 630	22 199	2 431	18 538	792	62	17 808	4 246	2 576	8 438	7 389	2 919	1 514
1979	26 584	25 036	1 548	19 579	941	72	18 710	4 996	2 878	9 114	7 906	2 917	1 557
1980	28 181	27 560	621	19 787	1 003	93	18 877	5 905	3 400	9 671	8 366	2 914	1 541
1981	31 894	30 174	1 720	21 928	1 131	120	20 917	7 118	3 860	10 968	9 496	2 908	1 513
1982	32 425	31 691	734	20 916	1 159	193	19 951	8 067	4 407	11 227	9 797	2 888	1 476
1983	32 967	33 037	-70	20 931	1 181	209	19 959	8 295	4 713	11 485	10 105	2 871	1 479
1984	36 586	35 320	1 266	23 906	1 281	242	22 867	8 954	4 766	12 798	11 431	2 859	1 506
1985	37 903	36 387	1 516	24 890	1 396	283	23 778	9 055	5 070	13 395	11 974	2 830	1 503
1986	39 144	37 240	1 905	25 880	1 479	275	24 677	9 180	5 288	14 020	12 568	2 792	1 501
1987	41 225	38 911	2 313	27 961	1 616	272	26 617	9 173	5 435	14 899	13 238	2 767	1 523
1988	42 399	41 067	1 333	28 871	1 816	310	27 365	9 373	5 661	15 315	13 574	2 768	1 567
1989	45 888	43 793	2 094	31 333	1 981	319	29 671	10 197	6 019	16 562	14 601	2 771	1 611
1990	48 313	46 343	1 970	32 907	2 100	325	31 132	10 712	6 469	17 372	15 288	2 781	1 646
1991	49 849	48 443	1 405	33 730	2 214	351	31 868	10 941	7 040	17 818	15 708	2 798	1 666
1992	53 161	51 000	2 161	36 675	2 314	376	34 737	10 810	7 614	18 862	16 698	2 818	1 681
1993	53 391	52 849	542	36 683	2 422	345	34 606	10 702	8 084	18 820	16 582	2 837	1 705
1994	57 999	55 627	2 371	40 724	2 608	342	38 458	11 218	8 323	20 345	17 961	2 851	1 740
1995	60 171	58 582	1 589	41 682	2 760	385	39 308	12 111	8 752	20 985	18 491	2 867	1 800
1996	64 696	61 383	3 313	45 155	2 856	413	42 712	12 858	9 127	22 464	19 756	2 880	1 832
1997	67 938	64 806	3 131	47 129	3 017	459	44 572	13 900	9 466	23 499	20 509	2 891	1 859
1998	71 280	69 471	1 810	49 099	3 181	506	46 424	15 246	9 610	24 555	21 421	2 903	1 903
1999	72 908	71 630	1 278	51 257	3 303	527	48 481	14 561	9 866	24 989	21 746	2 918	1 920
2000	77 730	75 933	1 797	54 046	3 397	567	51 215	16 044	10 471	26 540	23 175	2 929	1 942
2001	79 822	78 401	1 421	54 994	3 530	543	52 008	16 585	11 230	27 225	23 769	2 932	1 931
2002	82 642	80 448	2 194	57 079	3 680	395	53 794	16 750	12 098	28 141	25 083	2 937	. . .
KANSAS													
1972	10 405	9 428	977	7 886	293	453	8 046	1 375	984	4 613	4 085	2 256	1 048
1973	11 943	10 553	1 390	9 114	373	468	9 209	1 591	1 143	5 274	4 662	2 264	1 090
1974	12 965	11 898	1 068	9 722	430	483	9 775	1 877	1 313	5 717	4 996	2 268	1 122
1975	14 097	13 281	816	10 419	471	497	10 444	2 065	1 587	6 186	5 470	2 279	1 133
1976	15 448	14 853	595	11 448	521	514	11 441	2 245	1 763	6 721	5 935	2 299	1 169
1977	16 937	16 426	511	12 463	556	560	12 467	2 540	1 930	7 307	6 410	2 318	1 208
1978	18 853	18 556	297	13 853	648	605	13 811	2 945	2 097	8 082	7 065	2 333	1 252
1979	21 690	20 960	730	16 018	765	654	15 907	3 476	2 307	9 240	8 003	2 347	1 298
1980	23 781	23 677	104	16 887	847	731	16 771	4 266	2 744	10 038	8 674	2 369	1 312
1981	26 824	26 546	278	18 601	997	759	18 362	5 299	3 163	11 248	9 614	2 385	1 326
1982	28 789	28 231	558	19 519	1 065	782	19 236	5 986	3 566	11 989	10 273	2 401	1 310
1983	29 888	29 580	308	20 275	1 102	760	19 933	6 163	3 792	12 373	10 825	2 416	1 327
1984	32 971	32 266	706	22 699	1 208	804	22 294	6 824	3 853	13 602	12 035	2 424	1 370
1985	34 784	34 022	763	23 891	1 329	850	23 413	7 303	4 069	14 330	12 635	2 427	1 375
1986	36 256	35 372	885	25 027	1 419	835	24 443	7 497	4 316	14 904	13 244	2 433	1 375
1987	38 107	36 964	1 143	26 475	1 495	911	25 892	7 721	4 494	15 583	13 749	2 445	1 428
1988	40 207	39 133	1 074	27 941	1 662	925	27 204	8 264	4 740	16 331	14 427	2 462	1 440
1989	42 267	41 525	742	29 050	1 784	972	28 238	8 868	5 161	17 093	14 973	2 473	1 463
1990	45 104	43 749	1 354	31 089	1 882	982	30 189	9 346	5 569	18 177	16 005	2 481	1 484
1991	46 990	46 011	979	32 040	2 005	961	30 996	9 866	6 128	18 806	16 628	2 499	1 499
1992	50 407	49 037	1 370	34 840	2 112	994	33 722	9 877	6 808	19 905	17 671	2 532	1 512
1993	52 250	50 950	1 301	36 352	2 211	1 010	35 151	9 974	7 126	20 438	18 066	2 557	1 536
1994	54 857	53 528	1 329	38 116	2 359	960	36 718	10 663	7 475	21 258	18 751	2 581	1 564
1995	56 627	55 898	729	39 310	2 472	974	37 811	11 097	7 718	21 771	19 080	2 601	1 613
1996	60 074	58 650	1 423	41 726	2 585	1 131	40 273	11 873	7 928	22 977	20 029	2 615	1 646
1997	63 728	62 351	1 377	44 419	2 765	1 057	42 711	12 679	8 338	24 182	20 913	2 635	1 692
1998	67 896	66 676	1 221	47 398	2 945	1 049	45 502	13 981	8 414	25 519	22 045	2 661	1 741
1999	69 997	68 615	1 382	50 081	3 085	612	47 608	13 670	8 719	26 134	22 518	2 678	1 756
2000	73 882	73 252	629	52 102	3 204	660	49 557	15 009	9 315	27 439	23 596	2 693	1 776
2001	76 828	76 164	664	53 852	3 354	775	51 273	15 473	10 082	28 432	24 485	2 702	1 784
2002	78 322	77 891	430	54 522	3 475	581	51 628	15 652	11 042	28 838	25 393	2 716	. . .

. . . = Not available.

Table 21-2. Personal Income and Employment by State and Region—*Continued*

(Millions of dollars, except as noted.)

Year	Total	Nonfarm	Farm	Earnings by place of work	Less: Personal contributions for social insurance	Plus: Adjustment for residence	Equals: Net earnings by place of residence	Dividends, interest, and rent	Transfer payments	Personal income	Disposable personal income	Population (thousands)	Total employment (thousands)
KENTUCKY													
1972	12 394	11 837	557	9 859	349	103	9 613	1 340	1 442	3 715	3 265	3 336	1 392
1973	13 974	13 349	625	11 127	445	61	10 744	1 520	1 710	4 145	3 686	3 372	1 461
1974	15 741	15 037	704	12 434	513	29	11 950	1 754	2 036	4 607	4 018	3 417	1 496
1975	17 113	16 600	513	13 171	546	15	12 640	1 929	2 544	4 933	4 397	3 469	1 465
1976	19 283	18 700	583	14 964	610	-19	14 335	2 151	2 797	5 462	4 848	3 530	1 523
1977	21 788	21 076	712	17 018	682	5	16 341	2 480	2 966	6 095	5 365	3 575	1 579
1978	24 501	23 863	638	19 103	783	18	18 338	2 994	3 169	6 784	5 957	3 611	1 645
1979	27 838	27 134	705	21 332	909	10	20 432	3 723	3 683	7 640	6 714	3 644	1 668
1980	30 159	29 588	572	22 455	976	34	21 513	4 197	4 449	8 231	7 267	3 664	1 646
1981	33 439	32 460	978	24 479	1 144	-2	23 333	5 102	5 004	9 110	7 996	3 670	1 639
1982	35 319	34 429	890	25 240	1 214	-11	24 015	5 832	5 471	9 589	8 429	3 683	1 621
1983	36 423	36 201	222	25 589	1 260	19	24 348	6 159	5 916	9 859	8 708	3 694	1 629
1984	40 877	39 793	1 084	29 180	1 399	-56	27 725	7 035	6 117	11 062	9 869	3 695	1 683
1985	42 703	41 878	825	30 391	1 550	-66	28 775	7 542	6 386	11 558	10 266	3 695	1 706
1986	44 234	43 651	582	31 334	1 658	-38	29 639	7 890	6 705	11 995	10 665	3 688	1 742
1987	47 081	46 092	089	33 776	I 787	-66	31 923	8 196	6 962	12 782	11 317	3 683	1 775
1988	49 939	49 278	661	35 791	2 001	-75	33 715	8 865	7 358	13 570	12 033	3 680	1 827
1989	53 696	52 661	1 034	38 146	2 190	-116	35 840	9 823	8 033	14 602	12 852	3 677	1 877
1990	57 175	56 213	963	40 269	2 338	-66	37 866	10 486	8 823	15 478	13 617	3 694	1 919
1991	60 329	59 336	992	41 806	2 490	-97	39 220	10 990	10 119	16 207	14 330	3 722	1 916
1992	65 060	63 842	1 218	45 748	2 675	-326	42 748	11 139	11 173	17 278	15 272	3 765	1 964
1993	67 559	66 521	1 038	47 690	2 822	-352	44 516	11 286	11 757	17 722	15 636	3 812	2 009
1994	70 781	69 719	1 063	50 078	3 045	-440	46 593	11 947	12 242	18 389	16 166	3 849	2 053
1995	74 080	73 428	652	51 781	3 222	-491	48 068	12 870	13 141	19 056	16 679	3 887	2 129
1996	78 221	77 215	1 006	54 446	3 352	-596	50 499	13 816	13 906	19 957	17 390	3 920	2 162
1997	82 927	81 838	1 089	57 595	3 564	-641	53 390	14 772	14 764	20 979	18 194	3 953	2 212
1998	88 148	87 191	957	60 997	3 743	-614	56 640	16 458	15 050	22 118	19 124	3 985	2 254
1999	91 218	90 487	730	64 662	3 971	-839	59 851	15 832	15 535	22 702	19 582	4 018	2 298
2000	98 215	96 853	1 362	68 852	4 123	-802	63 927	17 704	16 583	24 258	20 987	4 049	2 341
2001	101 223	100 249	973	70 491	4 304	-1 032	65 154	18 185	17 883	24 878	21 525	4 069	2 319
2002	105 013	104 144	869	72 376	4 499	-662	67 216	18 342	19 455	25 657	22 650	4 093	. . .
LOUISIANA													
1972	13 515	13 149	366	10 951	370	-22	10 559	1 505	1 452	3 593	3 214	3 762	1 488
1973	15 132	14 539	593	12 255	469	-38	11 748	1 709	1 676	3 994	3 587	3 789	1 550
1974	17 233	16 611	622	13 817	550	-56	13 212	2 063	1 958	4 510	4 015	3 821	1 598
1975	19 263	18 838	425	15 341	610	-04	14 647	2 221	2 396	4 956	4 458	3 887	1 641
1976	21 960	21 505	455	17 655	696	-115	16 844	2 454	2 662	5 557	4 950	3 952	1 702
1977	24 636	24 184	453	19 872	768	-141	18 962	2 771	2 903	6 135	5 449	4 016	1 756
1978	28 314	27 941	373	22 952	902	-189	21 862	3 305	3 148	6 951	6 131	4 073	1 848
1979	32 342	31 831	511	26 118	1 072	-235	24 811	3 961	3 570	7 813	6 842	4 139	1 899
1980	37 301	37 119	182	29 591	1 239	-340	28 013	5 017	4 272	8 833	7 709	4 223	1 968
1981	42 990	42 742	248	33 816	1 533	-367	31 917	6 318	4 756	10 037	8 686	4 283	2 036
1982	45 955	45 702	253	35 324	1 631	-345	33 348	7 110	5 497	10 558	9 269	4 353	2 029
1983	47 754	47 537	216	35 710	1 617	-326	33 767	7 741	6 246	10 865	9 647	4 395	1 990
1984	51 171	50 861	309	38 028	1 714	-319	35 995	8 759	6 417	11 628	10 388	4 400	2 032
1985	53 432	53 211	221	38 906	1 828	-288	36 790	9 538	7 104	12 121	10 820	4 408	2 020
1986	53 005	52 793	212	37 660	1 805	-233	35 622	9 592	7 792	12 028	10 867	4 407	1 939
1987	53 287	52 919	368	37 872	1 806	-197	35 869	9 515	7 903	12 266	11 061	4 344	1 915
1988	56 239	55 678	561	40 179	2 002	-178	37 999	10 019	8 222	13 113	11 876	4 289	1 947
1989	59 528	59 132	396	41 883	2 163	-142	39 578	11 014	8 936	13 997	12 586	4 253	1 966
1990	64 229	63 884	345	45 303	2 337	-120	42 845	11 575	9 809	15 215	13 673	4 222	2 020
1991	68 179	67 760	419	47 823	2 528	-128	45 167	11 743	11 269	16 030	14 441	4 253	2 045
1992	72 466	72 000	466	50 650	2 633	-116	47 900	11 606	12 960	16 880	15 258	4 293	2 055
1993	75 911	75 434	478	52 497	2 779	-109	49 609	11 991	14 311	17 587	15 875	4 316	2 104
1994	80 872	80 324	547	55 472	3 019	-120	52 333	12 797	15 741	18 602	16 762	4 347	2 147
1995	84 573	83 997	576	58 116	3 184	-137	54 795	13 832	15 946	19 314	17 355	4 379	2 217
1996	87 879	87 131	747	60 434	3 302	-143	56 989	14 595	16 294	19 978	17 750	4 399	2 265
1997	92 286	91 720	566	63 623	3 512	-145	59 966	15 559	16 761	20 874	18 419	4 421	2 319
1998	97 458	97 108	350	67 518	3 704	-143	63 670	16 812	16 975	21 948	19 399	4 440	2 369
1999	99 052	98 529	522	68 976	3 772	-104	65 100	16 547	17 404	22 205	19 671	4 461	2 387
2000	103 630	103 218	412	71 551	3 848	-88	67 615	18 169	17 846	23 185	20 496	4 470	2 420
2001	109 317	108 988	330	74 527	4 064	-115	70 348	18 515	20 455	24 454	21 643	4 470	2 426
2002	113 725	113 247	478	77 010	4 263	-195	72 552	18 665	22 508	25 370	22 866	4 483	. . .

. . . = Not available.

Table 21-2. Personal Income and Employment by State and Region—*Continued*

(Millions of dollars, except as noted.)

Year	Total	Nonfarm	Farm	Derivation of personal income						Per capita (dollars)		Population (thousands)	Total employment (thousands)
				Earnings by place of work	Less: Personal contributions for social insurance	Plus: Adjustment for residence	Equals: Net earnings by place of residence	Dividends, interest, and rent	Transfer payments	Personal income	Disposable personal income		
MAINE													
1972	3 999	3 930	69	3 088	105	-20	2 963	546	490	3 864	3 500	1 035	453
1973	4 520	4 368	151	3 476	132	-11	3 334	606	580	4 319	3 876	1 046	470
1974	5 050	4 850	200	3 813	149	-6	3 658	694	698	4 764	4 281	1 060	478
1975	5 386	5 304	82	3 948	157	-19	3 772	728	887	5 019	4 553	1 073	475
1976	6 222	6 056	166	4 649	179	-22	4 447	808	966	5 708	5 159	1 090	498
1977	6 789	6 658	131	5 050	196	-25	4 829	920	1 040	6 142	5 557	1 105	513
1978	7 531	7 440	90	5 613	225	-23	5 366	1 052	1 113	6 751	6 075	1 115	532
1979	8 434	8 357	76	6 218	258	-16	5 943	1 235	1 255	7 497	6 711	1 125	546
1980	9 474	9 428	46	6 815	289	-14	6 512	1 493	1 469	8 408	7 502	1 127	555
1981	10 459	10 341	118	7 359	338	-51	6 970	1 817	1 672	9 231	8 166	1 133	554
1982	11 223	11 119	104	7 792	370	-50	7 372	2 015	1 836	9 873	8 657	1 137	556
1983	12 078	12 007	71	8 415	400	-41	7 974	2 125	1 980	10 551	9 373	1 145	568
1984	13 480	13 364	117	9 376	445	-31	8 900	2 517	2 063	11 665	10 423	1 156	591
1985	14 575	14 473	102	10 232	505	-11	9 717	2 686	2 173	12 533	11 143	1 163	610
1986	15 754	15 662	92	11 093	565	28	10 557	2 930	2 267	13 463	11 895	1 170	635
1987	17 289	17 156	133	12 273	626	47	11 695	3 260	2 335	14 595	12 779	1 185	658
1988	19 036	18 922	114	13 628	722	61	12 967	3 594	2 475	15 813	13 887	1 204	692
1989	20 600	20 472	128	14 616	797	60	13 879	4 053	2 667	16 886	14 827	1 220	708
1990	21 521	21 365	156	15 101	824	59	14 337	4 204	2 981	17 473	15 408	1 232	707
1991	21 820	21 716	104	14 940	846	50	14 145	4 218	3 458	17 638	15 640	1 237	683
1992	22 676	22 506	169	15 581	894	66	14 753	4 102	3 820	18 309	16 310	1 239	686
1993	23 292	23 137	155	15 984	944	103	15 143	4 125	4 024	18 749	16 705	1 242	698
1994	24 174	24 028	145	16 496	1 000	140	15 637	4 347	4 191	19 453	17 254	1 243	709
1995	25 046	24 932	114	16 821	1 051	183	15 954	4 691	4 402	20 142	17 832	1 243	711
1996	26 434	26 289	145	17 586	1 085	209	16 710	5 037	4 687	21 163	18 620	1 249	721
1997	27 773	27 681	92	18 413	1 145	240	17 508	5 362	4 903	22 134	19 286	1 255	735
1998	29 469	29 343	125	19 570	1 210	274	18 634	5 825	5 010	23 404	20 236	1 259	755
1999	30 680	30 537	143	20 837	1 289	291	19 839	5 704	5 136	24 218	20 871	1 267	771
2000	32 867	32 736	131	22 012	1 340	332	21 005	6 445	5 416	25 732	22 065	1 277	793
2001	34 491	34 379	112	22 967	1 420	345	21 892	6 724	5 875	26 853	23 122	1 284	799
2002	35 991	35 893	98	23 810	1 501	482	22 791	6 812	6 387	27 804	24 503	1 294	. . .
MARYLAND													
1972	21 593	21 438	154	15 115	503	2 991	17 603	2 415	1 575	5 291	4 457	4 081	1 781
1973	23 923	23 690	233	16 830	647	3 192	19 375	2 743	1 805	5 822	4 933	4 109	1 846
1974	26 378	26 190	188	18 386	734	3 466	21 118	3 173	2 087	6 382	5 368	4 133	1 868
1975	28 592	28 364	228	19 538	775	3 851	22 614	3 378	2 601	6 878	5 887	4 157	1 846
1976	31 442	31 244	197	21 562	842	4 166	24 887	3 734	2 820	7 536	6 455	4 172	1 866
1977	34 360	34 213	147	23 487	914	4 574	27 146	4 169	3 045	8 191	6 960	4 195	1 919
1978	38 168	37 964	204	26 127	1 040	4 939	30 026	4 798	3 345	9 062	7 688	4 212	2 003
1979	42 381	42 209	172	28 775	1 216	5 372	32 931	5 668	3 782	10 035	8 467	4 223	2 061
1980	47 475	47 411	64	31 444	1 351	5 945	36 038	6 916	4 521	11 230	9 530	4 228	2 075
1981	52 861	52 720	140	34 546	1 615	6 405	39 337	8 353	5 171	12 403	10 405	4 262	2 102
1982	56 730	56 584	146	36 339	1 742	6 983	41 581	9 381	5 768	13 246	11 167	4 283	2 090
1983	61 372	61 285	87	39 535	1 944	7 358	44 948	10 151	6 273	14 228	12 173	4 313	2 158
1984	68 506	68 236	270	44 271	2 187	8 048	50 132	11 855	6 519	15 693	13 413	4 365	2 253
1985	74 852	74 570	282	48 590	2 551	8 693	54 731	13 207	6 913	16 961	14 573	4 413	2 357
1986	80 612	80 320	291	52 655	2 845	9 315	59 125	14 075	7 411	17 966	15 447	4 487	2 444
1987	87 731	87 435	297	57 800	3 085	10 102	64 817	15 170	7 745	19 216	16 337	4 566	2 572
1988	96 072	95 717	355	63 397	3 572	11 175	71 000	16 840	8 232	20 626	17 767	4 658	2 669
1989	104 005	103 653	352	67 886	3 909	12 033	76 009	19 065	8 931	22 001	18 767	4 727	2 727
1990	110 450	110 114	336	72 024	4 182	12 522	80 364	20 265	9 821	23 012	19 702	4 800	2 761
1991	114 466	114 177	290	73 219	4 354	13 210	82 074	21 309	11 083	23 516	20 257	4 868	2 684
1992	119 417	119 092	326	76 257	4 484	14 051	85 824	21 185	12 409	24 255	20 991	4 923	2 659
1993	124 076	123 767	309	79 204	4 677	14 522	89 049	22 086	12 941	24 956	21 547	4 972	2 683
1994	129 849	129 561	287	82 622	4 977	14 950	92 595	23 545	13 709	25 850	22 240	5 023	2 733
1995	135 115	134 897	219	86 111	5 215	15 013	95 909	24 835	14 371	26 650	22 893	5 070	2 796
1996	140 809	140 442	367	89 354	5 416	15 291	99 228	26 301	15 280	27 545	23 426	5 112	2 837
1997	148 826	148 590	235	94 776	5 738	15 430	104 468	28 433	15 924	28 857	24 353	5 157	2 904
1998	158 501	158 204	297	100 840	6 087	16 507	111 260	30 994	16 247	30 455	25 566	5 204	2 960
1999	167 360	167 025	335	107 926	6 514	17 581	118 993	31 441	16 926	31 851	26 690	5 255	3 025
2000	180 941	180 574	367	116 064	6 915	19 571	128 721	34 481	17 740	34 060	28 393	5 312	3 101
2001	190 015	189 589	426	122 248	7 402	20 534	135 381	35 377	19 257	35 279	29 551	5 386	3 128
2002	197 156	196 771	385	127 108	7 836	20 931	140 203	35 900	21 053	36 121	30 990	5 458	. . .

. . . = Not available.

Table 21-2. Personal Income and Employment by State and Region—*Continued*

(Millions of dollars, except as noted.)

Year	Total	Nonfarm	Farm	Derivation of personal income Earnings by place of work	Less: Personal contributions for social insurance	Plus: Adjustment for residence	Equals: Net earnings by place of residence	Dividends, interest, and rent	Transfer payments	Per capita (dollars) Personal income	Disposable personal income	Population (thousands)	Total employment (thousands)
MASSACHUSETTS													
1972	29 420	29 350	70	22 826	753	-110	21 963	4 146	3 311	5 106	4 385	5 762	2 697
1973	32 108	32 031	77	24 958	946	-134	23 879	4 540	3 689	5 551	4 804	5 784	2 787
1974	34 802	34 726	76	26 564	1 048	-149	25 366	5 059	4 376	6 024	5 202	5 777	2 811
1975	37 100	37 025	75	27 529	1 063	-154	26 313	5 124	5 663	6 439	5 645	5 762	2 728
1976	40 208	40 125	83	30 118	1 147	-181	28 790	5 530	5 887	6 994	6 101	5 749	2 756
1977	43 863	43 778	85	33 113	1 254	-222	31 637	6 122	6 104	7 636	6 633	5 744	2 833
1978	48 698	48 588	110	37 087	1 424	-285	35 378	6 866	6 454	8 480	7 343	5 743	2 959
1979	54 427	54 333	94	41 410	1 684	-357	39 369	7 931	7 127	9 472	8 134	5 746	3 079
1980	61 329	61 219	110	46 010	1 905	-479	43 626	9 546	8 157	10 673	9 121	5 746	3 142
1981	68 242	68 124	118	50 252	2 283	-598	47 371	11 622	9 249	11 830	10 013	5 769	3 155
1982	73 889	73 756	133	54 043	2 536	-728	50 778	13 096	10 015	12 803	10 935	5 771	3 157
1983	80 376	80 207	170	59 610	2 804	-904	55 901	13 878	10 597	13 859	11 896	5 799	3 230
1984	90 815	90 626	189	67 780	3 224	-1 176	63 381	16 436	10 999	15 549	13 415	5 841	3 422
1985	98 329	98 160	169	74 427	3 719	-1 360	69 348	17 576	11 405	16 720	14 336	5 881	3 533
1986	105 976	105 792	184	80 751	4 133	-1 497	75 121	18 727	12 128	17 954	15 316	5 903	3 630
1987	115 761	115 605	156	88 921	4 555	-1 679	82 687	20 447	12 627	19 504	16 557	5 935	3 661
1988	127 580	127 401	178	98 108	5 133	-1 923	91 053	22 846	13 681	21 334	18 370	5 980	3 771
1989	135 096	134 931	165	101 884	5 442	-2 047	94 396	25 182	15 518	22 458	19 248	6 015	3 744
1990	139 772	139 621	151	103 656	5 568	-2 099	95 988	26 457	17 327	23 208	19 902	6 023	3 647
1991	142 464	142 291	173	103 382	5 709	-2 152	95 520	26 942	20 002	23 671	20 415	6 018	3 480
1992	149 096	148 921	174	109 642	5 965	-2 263	101 414	26 774	20 907	24 731	21 399	6 029	3 512
1993	154 262	154 092	170	114 052	6 258	-2 413	105 381	27 380	21 501	25 453	21 945	6 061	3 579
1994	161 886	161 731	155	119 718	6 684	-2 598	110 437	28 656	22 793	26 559	22 808	6 095	3 651
1995	170 052	169 901	151	125 641	7 148	-2 703	115 789	30 199	24 063	27 689	23 593	6 141	3 686
1996	180 237	180 070	167	133 668	7 522	-2 936	123 209	32 300	24 727	29 166	24 580	6 180	3 752
1997	191 596	191 425	171	141 985	8 099	-3 180	130 707	34 990	25 898	30 773	25 646	6 226	3 845
1998	205 176	205 077	100	152 694	8 644	-3 358	140 692	38 469	26 016	32 714	27 041	6 272	3 929
1999	217 066	216 970	95	164 987	9 390	-3 811	151 785	38 555	26 725	34 360	28 099	6 317	3 993
2000	241 963	241 859	104	184 521	10 397	-4 544	169 580	44 224	28 158	38 034	30 485	6 362	4 104
2001	248 778	248 680	98	187 754	10 686	-4 773	172 295	45 705	30 778	38 864	31 709	6 401	4 118
2002	250 966	250 865	100	186 014	10 722	-4 818	170 474	46 225	34 267	39 044	33 179	6 428	. . .
MICHIGAN													
1972	44 815	44 335	480	36 545	1 299	111	35 356	5 139	4 319	4 966	4 272	9 025	3 687
1973	50 370	49 761	609	41 310	1 700	137	39 747	5 727	4 896	5 552	4 815	9 072	3 858
1974	53 984	53 288	696	43 078	1 841	139	41 376	6 496	6 112	5 926	5 165	9 109	3 854
1975	57 191	56 576	615	43 988	1 852	152	42 288	6 932	7 972	6 279	5 554	9 108	3 695
1976	64 588	64 079	509	50 635	2 112	195	48 718	7 629	8 241	7 084	6 175	9 117	3 844
1977	72 863	72 269	594	57 945	2 396	221	55 770	8 544	8 549	7 957	6 874	9 157	4 016
1978	81 287	80 739	548	65 130	2 745	268	62 652	9 575	9 060	8 834	7 562	9 202	4 188
1979	89 727	89 151	576	71 023	3 132	308	68 199	11 109	10 419	9 701	8 310	9 249	4 234
1980	95 967	95 415	553	71 910	3 183	353	69 080	13 095	13 792	10 369	9 009	9 256	4 039
1981	102 455	101 940	515	75 458	3 671	381	72 168	15 679	14 609	11 125	9 621	9 209	3 992
1982	104 477	104 058	419	74 572	3 714	390	71 248	16 912	16 317	11 462	10 027	9 115	3 837
1983	110 771	110 571	200	78 959	3 977	424	75 406	18 120	17 245	12 243	10 675	9 048	3 881
1984	122 857	122 340	517	88 148	4 480	487	84 155	21 424	17 279	13 576	11 876	9 049	4 059
1985	133 728	133 106	622	96 939	5 185	507	92 261	23 417	18 051	14 734	12 804	9 076	4 257
1986	142 146	141 705	441	103 186	5 667	490	98 009	25 128	19 009	15 573	13 550	9 128	4 373
1987	148 191	147 616	575	107 467	5 937	509	102 039	26 466	19 685	16 130	13 998	9 187	4 511
1988	158 529	158 023	506	115 954	6 646	517	109 825	28 202	20 502	17 198	15 010	9 218	4 612
1989	169 113	168 217	896	122 567	7 200	513	115 880	31 387	21 846	18 276	15 850	9 253	4 744
1990	177 103	176 436	667	127 387	7 498	458	120 347	33 089	23 668	19 020	16 587	9 311	4 826
1991	181 495	180 944	552	128 886	7 805	475	121 556	33 227	26 712	19 307	16 885	9 400	4 755
1992	192 038	191 471	566	138 147	8 225	532	130 454	33 413	28 171	20 259	17 856	9 479	4 787
1993	203 828	203 211	617	147 527	8 735	639	139 431	34 288	30 109	21 365	18 681	9 540	4 850
1994	219 121	218 658	463	159 335	9 614	697	150 418	38 485	30 217	22 830	19 926	9 598	5 027
1995	231 594	230 890	705	169 934	10 226	702	160 410	39 496	31 688	23 934	20 785	9 676	5 188
1996	238 095	237 575	520	172 677	10 629	741	162 789	42 298	33 008	24 398	21 002	9 759	5 298
1997	250 216	249 687	529	179 943	11 226	801	169 519	45 131	35 567	25 509	21 868	9 809	5 385
1998	264 520	264 000	519	191 718	11 782	839	180 775	48 694	35 051	26 860	22 866	9 848	5 438
1999	276 187	275 375	812	203 047	12 491	834	191 390	47 549	37 248	27 906	23 758	9 897	5 535
2000	292 786	292 315	471	213 701	12 940	857	201 618	52 925	38 242	29 408	25 119	9 956	5 649
2001	296 480	296 092	389	211 955	13 010	939	199 884	54 116	42 481	29 629	25 346	10 006	5 550
2002	303 745	303 287	458	214 561	13 378	1 148	202 331	54 384	47 031	30 222	26 541	10 050	. . .

. . . = Not available.

Table 21-2. Personal Income and Employment by State and Region—*Continued*

(Millions of dollars, except as noted.)

Year	Total	Nonfarm	Farm	Derivation of personal income						Per capita (dollars)		Population (thousands)	Total employment (thousands)
				Earnings by place of work	Less: Personal contributions for social insurance	Plus: Adjustment for residence	Equals: Net earnings by place of residence	Dividends, interest, and rent	Transfer payments	Personal income	Disposable personal income		
MINNESOTA													
1972	17 898	16 887	1 010	14 289	517	-30	13 742	2 393	1 762	4 628	4 038	3 867	1 780
1973	21 099	18 882	2 218	16 995	662	-37	16 296	2 752	2 051	5 431	4 807	3 885	1 878
1974	22 757	21 073	1 684	17 972	761	-33	17 179	3 174	2 405	5 838	5 065	3 898	1 921
1975	24 404	23 102	1 302	18 919	806	-33	18 080	3 445	2 879	6 216	5 429	3 926	1 920
1976	26 623	25 807	816	20 578	896	-42	19 640	3 804	3 179	6 729	5 841	3 957	1 977
1977	30 085	28 550	1 535	23 406	977	-54	22 375	4 327	3 382	7 559	6 552	3 980	2 034
1978	33 924	32 271	1 653	26 574	1 141	-69	25 364	4 942	3 618	8 471	7 311	4 005	2 123
1979	37 996	36 721	1 276	29 589	1 358	-87	28 144	5 819	4 034	9 409	8 050	4 038	2 222
1980	42 157	41 236	921	31 830	1 497	-90	30 242	7 062	4 853	10 320	8 867	4 085	2 254
1981	46 546	45 568	978	34 293	1 753	-130	32 411	8 581	5 554	11 320	9 685	4 112	2 241
1982	49 546	48 750	796	35 550	1 877	-153	33 520	9 780	6 247	11 992	10 309	4 131	2 201
1983	52 158	52 090	68	37 185	2 010	-182	34 992	10 435	6 731	12 594	10 866	4 141	2 228
1984	59 267	57 904	1 363	43 055	2 269	-237	40 550	11 718	6 999	14 255	12 431	4 158	2 336
1985	63 152	61 924	1 228	46 020	2 558	-286	43 176	12 444	7 532	15 093	13 168	4 184	2 399
1986	66 784	65 264	1 520	48 815	2 774	-327	45 713	13 169	7 902	15 881	13 899	4 205	2 432
1987	71 570	69 588	1 982	52 882	3 002	-379	49 501	13 837	8 232	16 899	14 671	4 235	2 526
1988	75 578	74 437	1 141	56 093	3 394	-460	52 239	14 638	8 702	17 592	15 308	4 296	2 599
1989	82 277	80 306	1 971	60 566	3 700	-444	56 422	16 535	9 321	18 966	16 459	4 338	2 654
1990	87 795	85 928	1 867	64 363	3 954	-476	59 933	17 764	10 099	20 000	17 318	4 390	2 712
1991	90 714	89 643	1 071	66 220	4 212	-484	61 524	18 219	10 971	20 427	17 755	4 441	2 737
1992	97 025	95 867	1 158	71 956	4 511	-519	66 927	18 099	11 999	21 582	18 707	4 496	2 783
1993	99 787	99 716	72	73 757	4 746	-523	68 488	18 559	12 740	21 903	18 890	4 556	2 840
1994	107 152	105 988	1 163	79 052	5 118	-564	73 369	20 417	13 365	23 241	20 047	4 610	2 930
1995	113 217	112 607	610	82 439	5 413	-603	76 423	22 676	14 118	24 295	20 859	4 660	3 022
1996	122 080	120 228	1 852	89 159	5 736	-681	82 742	24 689	14 648	25 904	21 980	4 713	3 086
1997	129 020	128 156	864	93 598	6 096	-775	86 726	27 287	15 007	27 086	22 921	4 763	3 141
1998	140 031	138 688	1 343	101 880	6 507	-832	94 541	30 162	15 327	29 092	24 516	4 813	3 214
1999	147 151	145 838	1 313	109 068	6 963	-930	101 175	30 072	15 904	30 194	25 643	4 873	3 283
2000	159 037	157 776	1 261	117 378	7 383	-1 050	108 946	33 248	16 843	32 231	27 147	4 934	3 354
2001	164 784	164 037	748	120 934	7 739	-1 135	112 061	33 974	18 749	33 059	27 969	4 985	3 364
2002	170 142	168 931	1 211	124 118	8 060	-1 150	114 908	34 509	20 726	33 895	29 297	5 020	. . .
MISSISSIPPI													
1972	7 403	6 886	516	5 918	208	73	5 784	700	919	3 208	2 900	2 307	979
1973	8 489	7 779	711	6 779	264	94	6 608	822	1 059	3 613	3 287	2 350	1 019
1974	9 362	8 830	532	7 261	303	123	7 081	978	1 302	3 936	3 544	2 379	1 031
1975	10 093	9 706	387	7 595	322	150	7 422	1 066	1 604	4 205	3 846	2 400	1 001
1976	11 562	10 980	582	8 807	363	182	8 627	1 174	1 761	4 757	4 315	2 430	1 039
1977	12 937	12 322	615	9 884	403	223	9 704	1 325	1 908	5 259	4 785	2 460	1 071
1978	14 445	13 985	459	10 972	461	279	10 790	1 562	2 093	5 806	5 226	2 488	1 102
1979	16 425	15 707	719	12 383	535	337	12 186	1 858	2 382	6 549	5 877	2 508	1 117
1980	17 868	17 660	209	12 808	584	426	12 649	2 357	2 862	7 076	6 347	2 525	1 114
1981	20 061	19 703	358	14 109	692	456	13 873	2 951	3 236	7 901	7 034	2 539	1 110
1982	21 223	20 803	420	14 525	740	475	14 259	3 399	3 566	8 301	7 524	2 557	1 082
1983	22 120	22 031	90	14 894	780	531	14 645	3 554	3 921	8 615	7 772	2 568	1 091
1984	24 397	23 927	470	16 616	852	595	16 359	4 034	4 003	9 463	8 589	2 578	1 121
1985	25 679	25 248	431	17 551	947	625	17 229	4 191	4 259	9 922	8 998	2 588	1 129
1986	26 695	26 515	180	18 016	1 022	611	17 605	4 565	4 525	10 293	9 376	2 594	1 136
1987	28 249	27 718	531	19 217	1 076	650	18 791	4 723	4 735	10 913	9 906	2 589	1 147
1988	30 177	29 517	660	20 588	1 214	690	20 064	5 086	5 026	11 695	10 657	2 580	1 176
1989	32 281	31 780	501	21 652	1 330	733	21 054	5 762	5 464	12 540	11 364	2 574	1 196
1990	33 928	33 599	329	22 750	1 397	757	22 109	5 856	5 963	13 156	11 920	2 579	1 210
1991	35 775	35 323	452	23 900	1 494	787	23 193	5 965	6 618	13 766	12 518	2 599	1 218
1992	38 398	37 865	533	25 778	1 586	806	24 999	6 011	7 388	14 635	13 319	2 624	1 242
1993	40 768	40 304	464	27 622	1 717	830	26 735	6 178	7 855	15 355	13 925	2 655	1 297
1994	44 077	43 381	697	30 065	1 897	863	29 031	6 714	8 332	16 392	14 811	2 689	1 347
1995	46 242	45 669	573	31 167	2 012	939	30 094	7 062	9 086	16 984	15 316	2 723	1 379
1996	48 898	47 973	925	32 752	2 076	987	31 663	7 538	9 696	17 793	15 990	2 748	1 404
1997	51 598	50 756	842	34 371	2 186	1 106	33 291	8 155	10 151	18 580	16 653	2 777	1 432
1998	55 072	54 212	859	36 770	2 307	1 167	35 629	9 118	10 324	19 635	17 561	2 805	1 471
1999	56 799	55 934	865	38 424	2 420	1 239	37 243	8 913	10 644	20 082	17 941	2 828	1 496
2000	59 597	59 037	559	39 429	2 468	1 423	38 384	9 852	11 361	20 920	18 712	2 849	1 503
2001	61 922	61 062	860	40 188	2 537	1 625	39 276	9 999	12 647	21 653	19 421	2 860	1 478
2002	64 242	63 865	377	41 048	2 663	1 886	40 271	10 086	13 884	22 370	20 408	2 872	. . .

. . . = Not available.

Table 21-2. Personal Income and Employment by State and Region—*Continued*

(Millions of dollars, except as noted.)

Year	Total	Nonfarm	Farm	Derivation of personal income						Per capita (dollars)		Population (thousands)	Total employment (thousands)
				Earnings by place of work	Less: Personal contributions for social insurance	Plus: Adjustment for residence	Equals: Net earnings by place of residence	Dividends, interest, and rent	Transfer payments	Personal income	Disposable personal income		
MISSOURI													
1972	21 120	20 376	745	17 519	632	-702	16 185	2 824	2 111	4 443	3 877	4 753	2 242
1973	23 574	22 331	1 242	19 505	794	-734	17 977	3 165	2 432	4 937	4 358	4 775	2 325
1974	25 277	24 609	668	20 411	886	-760	18 766	3 642	2 869	5 282	4 626	4 785	2 341
1975	27 494	26 777	717	21 685	925	-769	19 991	3 904	3 599	5 733	5 090	4 795	2 291
1976	30 416	29 933	483	24 132	1 021	-846	22 265	4 295	3 856	6 306	5 556	4 824	2 365
1977	33 874	33 153	721	27 040	1 120	-986	24 933	4 869	4 071	6 991	6 162	4 845	2 424
1978	37 933	36 996	937	30 338	1 290	-1 139	27 909	5 612	4 411	7 787	6 818	4 871	2 513
1979	42 601	41 394	1 208	33 794	1 487	-1 302	31 005	6 621	4 976	8 713	7 598	4 889	2 580
1980	46 217	45 979	238	35 187	1 606	-1 516	32 064	8 086	6 067	9 390	8 195	4 922	2 554
1981	51 576	50 751	825	38 403	1 872	-1 661	34 869	9 895	6 812	10 457	9 082	4 932	2 549
1982	54 396	54 078	318	39 615	2 011	-1 728	35 875	11 081	7 439	11 035	9 515	4 929	2 525
1983	57 919	58 058	-138	42 105	2 152	-1 757	38 197	11 748	7 975	11 716	10 321	4 944	2 571
1984	64 479	64 125	354	47 164	2 397	-1 884	42 883	13 385	8 212	12 960	11 479	4 975	2 679
1985	69 342	68 641	701	50 941	2 702	-2 002	46 237	14 212	8 893	13 868	12 240	5 000	2 753
1986	72 859	72 401	457	53 526	2 931	-2 050	48 545	14 903	9 411	14 505	12 814	5 023	2 817
1987	77 115	76 472	643	57 059	3 124	-2 180	51 755	15 597	9 762	15 250	13 440	5 057	2 855
1988	81 744	81 171	573	60 653	3 463	-2 263	54 927	16 533	10 284	16 086	14 221	5 082	2 905
1989	87 050	86 215	835	63 872	3 753	-2 397	57 722	18 260	11 068	17 083	15 026	5 096	2 960
1990	91 000	90 420	579	66 331	3 937	-2 637	59 756	19 325	11 919	17 743	15 603	5 129	2 994
1991	95 730	95 270	460	68 084	4 130	-2 623	61 331	20 308	14 091	18 514	16 390	5 171	2 963
1992	101 493	100 839	655	72 577	4 334	-2 697	65 545	20 998	14 950	19 454	17 265	5 217	2 980
1993	106 298	105 925	373	75 875	4 555	-2 781	68 539	21 593	16 166	20 166	17 882	5 271	3 066
1994	112 314	111 746	568	80 497	4 915	-2 795	72 787	22 828	16 699	21 094	18 628	5 324	3 142
1995	117 640	117 475	165	84 421	5 236	-2 893	76 292	23 471	17 877	21 873	19 237	5 378	3 227
1996	123 992	123 065	926	89 105	5 445	-3 070	80 590	24 671	18 730	22 828	19 951	5 432	3 288
1997	131 144	130 160	984	94 275	5 766	-3 227	85 282	26 115	19 747	23 926	20 799	5 481	3 364
1998	138 987	138 525	462	99 454	6 012	-3 335	90 107	28 700	20 180	25 171	21 796	5 522	3 420
1999	143 814	143 611	203	104 408	6 338	-3 037	95 033	27 779	21 001	25 857	22 372	5 562	3 461
2000	154 099	153 481	618	110 984	6 596	-3 279	101 108	30 720	22 270	27 493	23 786	5 605	3 511
2001	159 093	158 525	568	113 595	6 848	-3 369	103 379	31 318	24 396	28 221	24 448	5 637	3 493
2002	163 603	163 294	309	116 184	7 127	-3 587	105 470	31 410	26 722	28 841	25 552	5 673	. . .
MONTANA													
1972	3 132	2 716	416	2 451	84	0	2 367	455	310	4 355	3 874	719	319
1973	3 646	3 059	587	2 854	108	0	2 746	542	358	5 012	4 444	727	333
1974	3 966	3 491	475	3 035	123	1	2 914	633	420	5 380	4 755	737	344
1975	4 341	3 933	408	3 268	132	2	3 138	697	506	5 794	5 166	749	344
1976	4 703	4 473	230	3 499	145	3	3 357	783	563	6 200	5 485	759	359
1977	5 119	5 049	70	3 755	165	4	3 595	909	615	6 636	5 833	771	372
1978	6 053	5 742	312	4 507	194	3	4 317	1 063	673	7 721	6 837	784	390
1979	6 549	6 435	115	4 734	222	6	4 518	1 275	756	8 299	7 248	789	397
1980	7 211	7 095	116	5 036	242	14	4 808	1 512	892	9 143	8 009	789	394
1981	8 147	7 943	204	5 535	284	26	5 277	1 840	1 030	10 244	8 999	795	396
1982	8 580	8 418	162	5 629	300	18	5 346	2 077	1 157	10 672	9 473	804	392
1983	8 991	8 876	115	5 879	312	10	5 577	2 149	1 265	11 045	9 842	814	400
1984	9 609	9 565	44	6 204	332	6	5 878	2 397	1 334	11 705	10 478	821	410
1985	9 785	9 857	-72	6 258	358	4	5 904	2 482	1 399	11 900	10 657	822	409
1986	10 143	9 905	238	6 516	369	-1	6 146	2 496	1 501	12 465	11 269	814	404
1987	10 463	10 189	274	6 743	380	-3	6 361	2 521	1 581	12 996	11 652	805	409
1988	10 693	10 609	83	6 866	430	-1	6 435	2 596	1 662	13 362	11 916	800	419
1989	11 693	11 293	400	7 523	467	-2	7 054	2 843	1 796	14 623	12 946	800	427
1990	12 416	12 049	367	7 939	499	-4	7 435	2 983	1 998	15 516	13 778	800	437
1991	13 337	12 797	540	8 684	547	-14	8 123	3 090	2 124	16 471	14 700	810	447
1992	14 076	13 649	426	9 233	597	-6	8 631	3 128	2 317	17 045	15 191	826	459
1993	15 178	14 411	767	10 189	641	-5	9 543	3 147	2 488	17 968	16 031	845	474
1994	15 499	15 149	350	10 269	684	-1	9 584	3 334	2 581	17 995	15 963	861	499
1995	16 297	15 938	359	10 600	717	1	9 885	3 628	2 784	18 592	16 533	877	508
1996	16 992	16 714	279	10 984	748	3	10 240	3 857	2 895	19 173	16 967	886	524
1997	17 726	17 521	206	11 340	776	-7	10 557	4 233	2 936	19 920	17 554	890	531
1998	18 942	18 640	302	12 125	804	-4	11 317	4 594	3 031	21 225	18 679	892	543
1999	19 405	19 010	396	12 805	832	-1	11 971	4 455	2 980	21 621	18 967	898	550
2000	20 744	20 538	205	13 401	868	4	12 537	4 911	3 296	22 961	20 090	903	561
2001	21 769	21 526	243	14 070	926	4	13 147	5 095	3 526	24 044	21 092	905	567
2002	22 650	22 395	256	14 749	990	-18	13 741	5 147	3 762	24 906	22 251	909	. . .

. . . = Not available.

Table 21-2. Personal Income and Employment by State and Region—*Continued*

(Millions of dollars, except as noted.)

Year	Total	Nonfarm	Farm	Derivation of personal income						Per capita (dollars)		Population (thousands)	Total employment (thousands)
				Earnings by place of work	Less: Personal contributions for social insurance	Plus: Adjustment for residence	Equals: Net earnings by place of residence	Dividends, interest, and rent	Transfer payments	Personal income	Disposable personal income		
NEBRASKA													
1972	6 873	6 059	814	5 530	198	-118	5 214	1 040	619	4 527	4 001	1 518	748
1973	8 054	6 825	1 229	6 486	255	-121	6 110	1 208	735	5 269	4 674	1 529	775
1974	8 404	7 634	770	6 611	292	-130	6 189	1 376	840	5 465	4 787	1 538	793
1975	9 507	8 395	1 112	7 441	311	-137	6 992	1 496	1 018	6 168	5 508	1 541	790
1976	9 996	9 404	592	7 770	342	-145	7 283	1 622	1 091	6 453	5 740	1 549	811
1977	10 870	10 337	533	8 353	367	-143	7 843	1 850	1 177	6 993	6 140	1 554	831
1978	12 674	11 566	1 108	9 859	423	-166	9 269	2 104	1 301	8 120	7 178	1 561	855
1979	13 742	12 985	756	10 529	495	-195	9 839	2 459	1 444	8 784	7 668	1 564	877
1980	14 578	14 482	96	10 689	542	-211	9 936	2 951	1 691	9 272	8 099	1 572	879
1981	16 866	16 016	851	12 207	625	-251	11 332	3 592	1 942	10 685	9 410	1 579	874
1982	17 761	17 034	727	12 512	670	-258	11 584	4 033	2 143	11 228	9 709	1 582	864
1983	18 379	17 910	470	12 831	698	-272	11 861	4 205	2 313	11 601	10 299	1 584	870
1984	20 601	19 505	1 095	14 720	773	-322	13 625	4 584	2 392	12 968	11 662	1 589	889
1985	21 778	20 385	1 393	15 754	861	-347	14 546	4 696	2 537	13 743	12 356	1 585	902
1986	22 379	21 029	1 350	16 167	915	-345	14 907	4 798	2 674	14 215	12 776	1 574	902
1987	23 553	21 911	1 642	17 241	983	-342	15 916	4 872	2 765	15 035	13 473	1 567	930
1988	25 119	23 161	1 958	18 527	1 098	-374	17 055	5 168	2 896	15 984	14 314	1 571	953
1989	26 581	24 806	1 776	19 316	1 186	-383	17 747	5 742	3 092	16 878	15 011	1 575	971
1990	28 591	26 438	2 154	20 855	1 264	-382	19 210	6 039	3 342	18 077	16 061	1 582	995
1991	29 853	27 872	1 982	21 589	1 337	-400	19 851	6 383	3 618	18 706	16 663	1 596	999
1992	31 548	29 484	2 064	22 972	1 396	-436	21 139	6 462	3 947	19 575	17 456	1 612	1 006
1993	32 513	30 832	1 681	23 644	1 472	-444	21 728	6 535	4 249	20 001	17 803	1 626	1 029
1994	34 325	32 664	1 662	25 035	1 580	-457	22 998	6 917	4 411	20 942	18 598	1 639	1 070
1995	36 293	35 024	1 270	26 163	1 646	-484	24 033	7 576	4 684	21 903	19 326	1 657	1 081
1996	39 618	37 097	2 521	28 900	1 726	-518	26 657	7 988	4 973	23 670	20 871	1 674	1 107
1997	40 724	39 058	1 665	29 527	1 824	-565	27 139	8 399	5 186	24 148	21 069	1 686	1 122
1998	43 313	41 740	1 573	31 117	1 930	-583	28 604	9 242	5 467	25 541	22 184	1 696	1 149
1999	45 293	43 694	1 599	32 922	2 026	-627	30 270	9 333	5 691	26 569	23 033	1 705	1 169
2000	47 599	46 643	956	34 102	2 102	-654	31 346	10 363	5 889	27 781	24 007	1 713	1 188
2001	49 642	48 478	1 165	35 240	2 185	-639	32 416	10 803	6 423	28 861	25 012	1 720	1 191
2002	51 086	50 069	1 018	36 194	2 303	-817	33 073	10 979	7 034	29 544	26 137	1 729	. . .
NEVADA													
1972	3 038	2 993	46	2 520	79	-45	2 397	423	219	5 557	4 924	547	280
1973	3 478	3 419	59	2 891	105	-54	2 731	495	252	6 114	5 425	569	304
1974	3 873	3 836	37	3 153	119	-57	2 977	582	313	6 490	5 735	597	317
1975	4 345	4 310	35	3 483	129	-58	3 296	618	431	7 009	6 353	620	326
1976	4 993	4 955	38	4 011	147	-67	3 796	712	484	7 719	6 893	647	349
1977	5 798	5 769	29	4 703	175	-83	4 446	817	535	8 550	7 588	678	384
1978	7 035	7 012	24	5 742	217	-116	5 408	1 024	603	9 780	8 595	719	432
1979	8 237	8 226	11	6 634	270	-131	6 234	1 295	708	10 765	9 389	765	468
1980	9 544	9 485	60	7 587	313	-158	7 116	1 566	862	11 780	10 348	810	490
1981	10 833	10 807	26	8 430	382	-167	7 881	1 901	1 050	12 780	11 187	848	502
1982	11 448	11 408	40	8 733	401	-168	8 165	2 112	1 171	12 986	11 449	882	497
1983	12 145	12 114	31	9 197	428	-176	8 594	2 274	1 278	13 465	11 959	902	502
1984	13 351	13 310	41	10 064	475	-188	9 402	2 598	1 352	14 435	12 848	925	528
1985	14 581	14 546	35	10 911	541	-196	10 174	2 907	1 501	15 332	13 573	951	551
1986	15 716	15 684	32	11 739	602	-214	10 923	3 111	1 682	16 027	14 141	981	577
1987	17 281	17 236	44	12 995	673	-239	12 083	3 387	1 810	16 886	14 833	1 023	623
1988	19 544	19 483	62	14 827	791	-278	13 758	3 803	1 984	18 180	15 905	1 075	670
1989	22 256	22 179	77	16 675	910	-325	15 440	4 538	2 278	19 568	17 144	1 137	720
1990	25 194	25 114	80	18 852	1 023	-384	17 445	5 127	2 622	20 639	18 081	1 221	767
1991	27 349	27 276	73	19 895	1 094	-391	18 410	5 692	3 248	21 100	18 636	1 296	780
1992	30 199	30 146	53	21 868	1 173	-412	20 283	6 195	3 722	22 347	19 683	1 351	788
1993	32 386	32 291	94	23 655	1 285	-465	21 905	6 534	3 947	22 949	20 111	1 411	831
1994	35 878	35 812	65	26 160	1 451	-513	24 196	7 568	4 114	23 930	21 050	1 499	913
1995	39 377	39 325	52	28 742	1 617	-561	26 563	8 374	4 440	24 897	21 891	1 582	968
1996	43 331	43 282	49	31 671	1 779	-631	29 261	9 318	4 752	26 004	22 585	1 666	1 041
1997	47 258	47 210	48	34 297	1 906	-630	31 762	10 443	5 054	26 789	23 313	1 764	1 108
1998	52 017	51 945	72	37 657	2 050	-707	34 900	11 768	5 348	28 069	24 230	1 853	1 151
1999	55 439	55 379	60	41 070	2 233	-800	38 038	11 904	5 497	28 655	24 651	1 935	1 217
2000	60 149	60 066	83	44 300	2 370	-835	41 095	13 255	5 798	29 794	25 526	2 019	1 273
2001	63 200	63 105	96	46 555	2 526	-863	43 166	13 458	6 577	30 128	25 887	2 098	1 306
2002	65 571	65 453	118	48 286	2 665	-996	44 626	13 525	7 421	30 169	26 636	2 173	. . .

. . . = Not available.

Table 21-2. Personal Income and Employment by State and Region—*Continued*

(Millions of dollars, except as noted.)

| Year | Total | Nonfarm | Farm | Derivation of personal income | | | | | | Per capita (dollars) | | Population (thousands) | Total employment (thousands) |
				Earnings by place of work	Less: Personal contributions for social insurance	Plus: Adjustment for residence	Equals: Net earnings by place of residence	Dividends, interest, and rent	Transfer payments	Personal income	Disposable personal income		
NEW HAMPSHIRE													
1972	3 457	3 438	20	2 459	90	252	2 621	514	322	4 423	3 893	782	350
1973	3 913	3 889	24	2 793	116	283	2 960	575	378	4 880	4 350	802	374
1974	4 313	4 297	16	3 012	132	329	3 209	653	452	5 279	4 685	817	381
1975	4 642	4 622	19	3 158	137	359	3 379	686	576	5 592	5 030	830	370
1976	5 301	5 280	21	3 656	154	410	3 911	772	618	6 258	5 584	847	394
1977	6 009	5 989	20	4 153	176	480	4 457	891	661	6 892	6 118	872	418
1978	6 960	6 939	21	4 845	205	572	5 212	1 026	722	7 786	6 852	894	446
1979	8 007	7 984	23	5 538	248	680	5 970	1 214	823	8 781	7 727	912	469
1980	9 164	9 150	14	6 136	280	849	6 705	1 492	968	9 915	8 757	924	483
1981	10 377	10 353	24	6 760	337	958	7 381	1 841	1 155	11 079	9 753	937	494
1982	11 284	11 266	18	7 287	376	1 048	7 959	2 063	1 261	11 906	10 583	948	500
1983	12 495	12 480	15	8 169	422	1 173	8 920	2 234	1 342	13 041	11 596	958	520
1984	14 198	14 177	21	9 237	480	1 387	10 145	2 658	1 396	14 534	12 969	977	556
1985	15 767	15 742	25	10 430	570	1 510	11 370	2 938	1 459	15 819	13 999	997	590
1986	17 300	17 073	26	11 669	651	1 594	12 611	3 243	1 544	16 974	14 916	1 025	622
1987	19 369	19 325	44	13 208	738	1 721	14 191	3 507	1 591	18 371	16 144	1 054	640
1988	21 390	21 343	48	14 589	841	1 882	15 630	4 032	1 729	19 759	17 493	1 083	665
1989	22 792	22 744	48	15 208	889	1 974	16 293	4 585	1 914	20 635	18 279	1 105	665
1990	23 029	22 987	42	15 115	899	2 013	16 228	4 642	2 159	20 703	18 441	1 112	648
1991	23 609	23 566	43	14 961	920	2 055	16 096	4 627	2 885	21 270	19 057	1 110	621
1992	24 652	24 596	56	16 010	978	2 123	17 155	4 411	3 086	22 055	19 774	1 118	634
1993	25 273	25 233	40	16 682	1 021	2 181	17 841	4 449	2 982	22 376	19 949	1 129	647
1994	26 990	26 949	40	17 663	1 106	2 262	18 819	4 762	3 410	23 622	21 083	1 143	672
1995	28 650	28 618	32	18 650	1 188	2 297	19 758	5 235	3 656	24 750	22 021	1 158	686
1996	30 228	30 192	36	19 838	1 248	2 446	21 036	5 606	3 587	25 733	22 652	1 175	703
1997	32 397	32 362	35	21 358	1 343	2 641	22 656	5 999	3 743	27 238	23 709	1 189	724
1998	35 198	35 162	36	23 259	1 453	2 723	24 529	6 829	3 840	29 187	25 356	1 206	747
1999	37 121	37 082	39	24 944	1 552	3 082	26 474	6 738	3 909	30 377	26 174	1 222	764
2000	41 265	41 230	35	27 488	1 688	3 651	29 451	7 664	4 150	33 266	28 337	1 240	786
2001	42 779	42 743	36	28 315	1 761	3 864	30 418	7 048	4 513	33 969	29 218	1 259	793
2002	43 703	43 664	39	28 843	1 826	3 917	30 934	7 877	4 892	34 276	30 285	1 275	. . .
NEW JERSEY													
1972	40 507	40 404	103	29 132	1 104	3 335	31 364	5 479	3 665	5 521	4 828	7 337	3 184
1973	44 327	44 188	139	32 020	1 379	3 489	34 130	6 089	4 108	6 043	5 331	7 335	3 288
1974	48 236	48 084	152	34 450	1 537	3 678	36 592	6 829	4 815	6 576	5 779	7 335	3 301
1975	51 658	51 546	112	35 924	1 599	3 960	38 284	7 120	6 254	7 037	6 269	7 341	3 191
1976	56 572	56 455	118	39 500	1 715	4 303	42 088	7 700	6 784	7 703	6 797	7 344	3 248
1977	62 130	62 004	126	43 504	1 881	4 695	46 318	8 584	7 228	8 462	7 386	7 342	3 325
1978	69 206	69 063	143	48 695	2 163	5 273	51 805	9 732	7 669	9 408	8 193	7 356	3 464
1979	77 188	77 053	134	53 850	2 511	6 019	57 357	11 323	8 508	10 469	9 030	7 373	3 555
1980	86 877	86 753	125	59 123	2 806	7 111	63 428	13 698	9 751	11 778	10 137	7 376	3 608
1981	96 717	96 559	158	64 451	3 297	7 747	68 901	16 891	10 924	13 057	11 198	7 407	3 643
1982	104 023	103 853	171	68 896	3 610	8 281	73 566	18 449	12 008	13 999	12 004	7 431	3 651
1983	112 284	112 082	202	75 020	3 978	8 515	79 556	19 793	12 935	15 036	13 036	7 468	3 752
1984	124 377	124 176	201	83 243	4 507	8 900	87 636	23 420	13 321	16 549	14 414	7 515	3 933
1985	133 549	133 317	232	90 530	5 112	9 260	94 678	24 940	13 932	17 652	15 227	7 566	4 049
1986	142 617	142 382	235	97 739	5 729	9 838	101 847	26 084	14 686	18 711	16 105	7 622	4 146
1987	155 179	154 916	263	107 638	6 380	10 384	111 641	28 234	15 304	20 230	17 272	7 671	4 249
1988	170 764	170 506	257	119 472	7 262	10 658	122 868	31 570	16 326	22 142	19 129	7 712	4 349
1989	182 298	182 047	250	125 672	7 749	10 192	128 115	36 521	17 661	23 595	20 391	7 726	4 388
1990	192 117	191 892	226	132 044	8 106	10 515	134 453	38 211	19 453	24 748	21 487	7 763	4 346
1991	195 796	195 579	216	133 440	8 486	10 328	135 283	38 159	22 353	25 055	21 785	7 815	4 206
1992	208 197	207 983	214	142 158	8 944	11 632	144 847	37 714	25 637	26 419	23 008	7 881	4 205
1993	213 419	213 172	247	147 545	9 128	11 557	149 973	36 673	26 773	26 849	23 271	7 949	4 233
1994	220 817	220 554	263	153 208	9 689	11 424	154 943	38 561	27 314	27 553	23 816	8 014	4 272
1995	233 209	232 941	268	160 833	10 188	12 103	162 748	41 463	28 997	28 851	24 887	8 083	4 339
1996	246 659	246 377	282	169 602	10 590	13 116	172 128	44 525	30 005	30 266	25 932	8 150	4 397
1997	260 705	260 492	213	178 204	11 093	15 027	182 137	47 627	30 940	31 720	26 885	8 219	4 461
1998	278 788	278 562	226	190 132	11 740	16 674	195 067	52 454	31 267	33 640	28 245	8 287	4 540
1999	288 796	288 596	200	200 109	12 375	17 689	205 423	51 247	32 126	34 547	28 718	8 360	4 602
2000	318 222	317 954	268	218 793	13 312	20 190	225 672	58 578	33 972	37 734	31 192	8 433	4 767
2001	328 743	328 503	240	222 368	13 700	22 009	230 677	60 933	37 133	38 625	32 237	8 511	4 783
2002	339 889	339 629	260	227 919	14 298	23 095	236 717	61 680	41 493	39 567	34 109	8 590	. . .

. . . = Not available.

Table 21-2. Personal Income and Employment by State and Region—*Continued*

(Millions of dollars, except as noted.)

Year	Total	Nonfarm	Farm	Derivation of personal income — Earnings by place of work	Less: Personal contributions for social insurance	Plus: Adjustment for residence	Equals: Net earnings by place of residence	Dividends, interest, and rent	Transfer payments	Per capita (dollars) — Personal income	Disposable personal income	Population (thousands)	Total employment (thousands)
NEW MEXICO													
1972	4 054	3 904	150	3 259	106	-20	3 133	498	423	3 761	3 381	1 078	440
1973	4 568	4 376	193	3 656	137	-17	3 502	569	497	4 137	3 722	1 104	461
1974	5 160	4 999	161	4 071	159	-16	3 897	668	596	4 568	4 091	1 130	478
1975	5 866	5 675	191	4 597	176	-13	4 408	733	725	5 045	4 597	1 163	491
1976	6 606	6 471	135	5 175	197	-13	4 965	824	817	5 527	4 991	1 195	512
1977	7 459	7 311	147	5 881	226	-11	5 644	943	872	6 087	5 494	1 225	539
1978	8 571	8 389	182	6 761	265	-11	6 486	1 132	954	6 847	6 121	1 252	568
1979	9 756	9 538	218	7 618	314	-10	7 294	1 365	1 096	7 619	6 805	1 281	593
1980	11 002	10 811	190	8 367	353	-4	8 011	1 683	1 308	8 402	7 520	1 309	598
1981	12 440	12 315	126	9 297	429	-12	8 857	2 090	1 494	9 334	8 253	1 333	613
1982	13 493	13 372	122	9 899	468	-15	9 416	2 434	1 643	9 894	8 716	1 364	621
1983	14 455	14 326	130	10 512	496	-11	10 004	2 661	1 790	10 367	9 346	1 394	633
1984	15 889	15 739	149	11 565	546	-4	11 015	2 991	1 882	11 215	10 151	1 417	658
1985	17 259	17 045	214	12 496	616	3	11 883	3 340	2 036	11 999	10 827	1 438	678
1986	17 883	17 686	197	12 787	652	10	12 145	3 541	2 197	12 226	11 083	1 463	684
1987	18 756	18 525	231	13 356	681	24	12 699	3 723	2 334	12 686	11 382	1 479	703
1988	19 854	19 540	314	14 147	761	35	13 420	3 945	2 489	13 322	11 959	1 490	739
1989	21 183	20 804	378	14 942	827	42	14 156	4 304	2 722	14 085	12 585	1 504	755
1990	22 739	22 325	413	16 008	884	48	15 172	4 579	2 988	14 944	13 381	1 522	767
1991	24 358	23 944	413	17 099	968	51	16 181	4 822	3 355	15 661	14 052	1 555	790
1992	25 964	25 496	468	18 334	1 022	55	17 368	4 841	3 755	16 274	14 587	1 595	803
1993	27 819	27 286	533	19 792	1 109	61	18 744	5 005	4 069	16 999	15 178	1 636	832
1994	29 670	29 213	457	20 955	1 211	72	19 816	5 464	4 390	17 636	15 706	1 682	865
1995	31 716	31 333	383	22 146	1 311	74	20 909	5 936	4 870	18 435	16 444	1 720	907
1996	33 232	32 846	386	22 809	1 349	82	21 541	6 426	5 264	18 964	16 836	1 752	918
1997	34 860	34 337	523	23 934	1 405	88	22 617	6 827	5 416	19 641	17 330	1 775	933
1998	36 857	36 251	607	25 285	1 470	92	23 907	7 311	5 639	20 551	18 119	1 793	949
1999	37 725	37 010	715	26 207	1 537	104	24 774	7 035	5 916	20 865	18 345	1 808	953
2000	39 692	39 209	484	27 627	1 615	116	26 127	7 284	6 281	21 788	19 048	1 822	975
2001	42 260	41 577	683	29 405	1 730	114	27 788	7 506	6 966	23 081	20 252	1 831	990
2002	44 352	43 675	677	30 822	1 850	61	29 033	7 612	7 707	23 908	21 429	1 855	. . .
NEW YORK													
1972	101 636	101 237	399	81 551	3 107	-3 672	74 772	14 871	11 993	5 538	4 757	18 352	8 350
1973	108 803	108 294	508	87 114	3 843	-3 892	79 379	16 209	13 215	5 980	5 164	18 195	8 468
1974	117 323	116 839	484	92 307	4 238	-4 118	83 951	18 035	15 337	6 492	5 586	18 073	8 395
1975	125 420	125 009	410	96 585	4 399	-4 467	87 718	18 398	19 304	6 955	6 068	18 032	8 175
1976	134 395	133 969	426	103 472	4 637	-4 913	93 923	19 842	20 631	7 477	6 499	17 975	8 128
1977	145 544	145 195	349	112 044	4 958	-5 468	101 618	22 162	21 764	8 153	7 063	17 852	8 202
1978	159 114	158 663	451	123 050	5 506	-6 120	111 424	24 948	22 742	8 979	7 750	17 720	8 381
1979	175 040	174 490	550	135 126	6 321	-6 972	121 833	28 965	24 242	9 927	8 514	17 634	8 591
1980	194 906	194 372	534	148 641	6 983	-8 186	133 472	33 508	27 926	11 095	9 480	17 567	8 622
1981	217 203	216 659	544	162 990	8 295	-8 947	145 748	40 024	31 430	12 364	10 459	17 568	8 700
1982	234 717	234 201	516	175 264	9 074	-9 815	156 375	43 898	34 444	13 344	11 252	17 590	8 710
1983	250 945	250 588	357	186 818	9 736	-10 286	166 796	46 892	37 257	14 188	12 154	17 687	8 772
1984	279 294	278 840	454	206 812	10 774	-10 937	185 101	55 149	39 044	15 739	13 531	17 746	9 058
1985	297 729	297 215	513	222 806	12 253	-11 573	198 979	57 863	40 886	16 734	14 278	17 792	9 293
1986	317 914	317 295	619	239 999	13 482	-12 467	214 050	60 372	43 492	17 827	15 191	17 833	9 495
1987	340 068	339 380	688	259 231	14 497	-13 287	231 446	63 852	44 770	19 031	16 060	17 869	9 553
1988	369 668	369 086	582	281 706	16 384	-14 012	251 310	70 792	47 566	20 604	17 583	17 941	9 769
1989	395 022	394 312	710	293 378	17 492	-13 654	262 232	81 365	51 425	21 966	18 582	17 983	9 844
1990	419 743	419 033	710	309 976	18 476	-14 036	277 464	85 320	56 959	23 292	19 879	18 021	9 819
1991	431 672	431 072	599	312 257	19 011	-13 895	279 350	87 391	64 930	23 820	20 479	18 123	9 570
1992	455 657	455 017	641	334 208	19 944	-15 964	298 301	84 547	72 809	24 972	21 539	18 247	9 501
1993	464 201	463 489	712	340 317	20 474	-15 887	303 955	82 924	77 322	25 263	21 668	18 375	9 527
1994	478 586	478 028	559	347 730	21 321	-15 864	310 544	86 970	81 072	25 926	22 185	18 459	9 570
1995	503 163	502 686	477	363 361	22 461	-17 340	323 559	93 271	86 333	27 163	23 225	18 524	9 621
1996	530 990	530 356	634	386 538	23 353	-19 443	343 742	97 209	90 039	28 566	24 211	18 588	9 711
1997	553 543	553 207	337	405 509	24 657	-21 387	359 465	103 133	90 945	29 670	24 896	18 657	9 857
1998	590 406	589 859	547	435 454	26 002	-23 921	385 531	111 002	93 873	31 478	26 220	18 756	10 054
1999	616 292	615 571	720	460 679	27 625	-24 892	408 162	111 739	96 391	32 638	26 909	18 883	10 244
2000	665 762	665 141	621	501 699	29 675	-28 115	443 909	121 831	100 022	35 041	28 801	19 000	10 494
2001	684 704	683 908	796	514 033	30 786	-29 960	453 286	124 783	106 635	35 878	29 614	19 084	10 475
2002	684 070	683 440	630	506 089	30 682	-32 151	443 256	125 868	114 946	35 708	30 443	19 158	. . .

. . . = Not available.

Table 21-2. Personal Income and Employment by State and Region—*Continued*

(Millions of dollars, except as noted.)

Year	Total	Nonfarm	Farm	Derivation of personal income						Per capita (dollars)		Population (thousands)	Total employment (thousands)
				Earnings by place of work	Less: Personal contributions for social insurance	Plus: Adjustment for residence	Equals: Net earnings by place of residence	Dividends, interest, and rent	Transfer payments	Personal income	Disposable personal income		
NORTH CAROLINA													
1972	20 647	19 826	821	17 422	633	4	16 793	2 096	1 759	3 899	3 417	5 296	2 602
1973	23 492	22 264	1 229	19 856	818	2	19 039	2 428	2 025	4 365	3 853	5 382	2 720
1974	25 904	24 732	1 172	21 504	931	9	20 582	2 812	2 510	4 743	4 162	5 461	2 743
1975	27 889	26 779	1 110	22 339	968	14	21 386	3 043	3 460	5 039	4 524	5 535	2 647
1976	31 233	30 047	1 186	25 129	1 081	15	24 063	3 427	3 743	5 584	4 960	5 593	2 754
1977	34 339	33 452	888	27 583	1 188	22	26 417	3 918	4 004	6 058	5 358	5 668	2 851
1978	38 921	37 749	1 172	31 414	1 377	21	30 058	4 563	4 300	6 780	5 972	5 740	2 948
1979	43 288	42 511	777	34 558	1 607	18	32 969	5 419	4 899	7 461	6 519	5 802	3 051
1980	48 648	47 989	659	37 700	1 783	23	35 941	6 846	5 862	8 247	7 208	5 899	3 060
1981	54 704	53 642	1 061	41 662	2 124	-27	39 511	8 461	6 732	9 184	8 007	5 957	3 082
1982	58 324	57 269	1 055	43 641	2 286	-36	41 320	9 502	7 503	9 690	8 562	6 019	3 051
1983	63 685	63 064	621	47 674	2 514	-54	45 106	10 514	8 065	10 480	9 231	6 077	3 138
1984	72 659	71 370	1 289	54 757	2 847	-90	51 820	12 450	8 390	11 788	10 432	6 164	3 305
1985	79 105	77 949	1 156	59 636	3 249	-153	56 234	13 875	8 995	12 649	11 159	6 254	3 410
1986	84 988	83 855	1 132	64 056	3 585	-214	60 257	15 102	9 628	13 444	11 847	6 322	3 512
1987	91 734	90 651	1 083	69 718	3 900	-295	65 522	16 116	10 095	14 325	12 518	6 404	3 631
1988	100 196	98 791	1 405	76 054	4 420	-350	71 284	18 007	10 905	15 461	13 596	6 481	3 774
1989	108 585	106 935	1 650	81 331	4 827	-401	76 104	20 399	12 082	16 539	14 435	6 565	3 864
1990	115 609	113 504	2 104	85 831	5 110	-446	80 275	21 855	13 478	17 348	15 241	6 664	3 929
1991	120 648	118 262	2 386	88 399	5 390	-450	82 560	22 573	15 515	17 784	15 665	6 784	3 891
1992	130 627	128 321	2 307	96 804	5 806	-499	90 500	22 885	17 242	18 939	16 738	6 897	3 993
1993	139 239	136 622	2 617	102 719	6 205	-539	95 975	24 049	19 215	19 770	17 441	7 043	4 119
1994	147 793	144 946	2 847	108 925	6 708	-601	101 616	26 288	19 888	20 563	18 043	7 187	4 238
1995	157 634	154 951	2 683	115 043	7 181	-678	107 184	28 250	22 199	21 462	18 790	7 345	4 392
1996	167 638	164 684	2 953	121 409	7 524	-742	113 143	30 570	23 925	22 350	19 456	7 501	4 501
1997	179 691	176 708	2 983	129 677	8 075	-815	120 787	33 575	25 329	23 468	20 284	7 657	4 650
1998	192 577	190 336	2 242	138 439	8 610	-846	128 983	37 591	26 003	24 661	21 226	7 809	4 766
1999	202 455	200 362	2 093	148 028	9 183	-936	137 909	37 315	27 232	25 468	21 879	7 949	4 864
2000	217 727	215 211	2 517	158 316	9 663	-1 063	147 590	41 228	28 910	26 939	23 122	8 082	4 943
2001	224 094	221 487	2 607	161 595	9 981	-1 061	150 553	41 356	32 185	27 308	23 531	8 206	4 902
2002	229 356	227 405	1 951	163 725	10 324	-1 453	151 948	41 544	35 864	27 566	24 250	8 320	. . .
NORTH DAKOTA													
1972	2 761	2 100	661	2 263	75	-61	2 128	357	276	4 377	4 002	631	288
1973	3 903	2 392	1 511	3 321	99	-64	3 158	438	308	6 172	5 659	632	300
1974	3 881	2 733	1 148	3 205	117	-77	3 011	518	353	6 120	5 438	634	308
1975	4 044	3 118	926	3 258	133	-83	3 042	590	413	6 334	5 650	638	314
1976	3 990	3 527	463	3 125	147	-98	2 880	651	459	6 184	5 513	645	326
1977	4 172	3 914	258	3 151	143	-105	2 903	762	507	6 427	5 762	649	331
1978	5 294	4 447	847	4 147	166	-117	3 864	878	552	8 136	7 278	651	346
1979	5 477	4 982	495	4 187	195	-135	3 857	1 011	610	8 398	7 491	652	354
1980	5 297	5 644	-347	3 675	213	-152	3 309	1 266	722	8 095	7 085	654	356
1981	6 820	6 513	308	4 791	252	-174	4 365	1 628	828	10 342	9 056	660	360
1982	7 352	7 080	272	5 000	272	-177	4 551	1 870	930	10 990	9 831	669	361
1983	7 704	7 384	320	5 267	284	-180	4 803	1 869	1 032	11 386	10 263	677	367
1984	8 375	7 831	544	5 776	301	-186	5 290	1 993	1 092	12 307	11 149	680	368
1985	8 673	8 044	629	5 990	326	-185	5 479	2 029	1 165	12 811	11 623	677	366
1986	8 788	8 155	634	6 001	342	-181	5 478	2 030	1 280	13 126	11 965	670	360
1987	8 968	8 331	638	6 195	358	-182	5 655	1 963	1 351	13 565	12 297	661	365
1988	8 352	8 508	-156	5 597	392	-187	5 018	1 977	1 357	12 745	11 438	655	369
1989	9 280	8 962	318	6 271	422	-192	5 657	2 154	1 468	14 357	12 916	646	373
1990	10 121	9 509	612	6 896	448	-190	6 257	2 270	1 595	15 872	14 313	638	376
1991	10 318	9 893	426	7 054	482	-202	6 370	2 296	1 653	16 230	14 603	636	385
1992	11 242	10 423	819	7 896	507	-223	7 166	2 276	1 800	17 614	15 931	638	390
1993	11 362	10 962	400	7 913	539	-241	7 133	2 300	1 928	17 719	15 915	641	400
1994	12 177	11 465	712	8 638	574	-255	7 809	2 401	1 967	18 885	17 008	645	415
1995	12 243	12 016	227	8 497	588	-274	7 635	2 563	2 045	18 899	16 919	648	421
1996	13 607	12 705	902	9 640	613	-301	8 726	2 727	2 154	20 921	18 798	650	430
1997	13 332	13 365	-33	9 099	642	-323	8 134	2 941	2 257	20 520	18 244	650	434
1998	14 709	14 060	649	10 301	662	-345	9 294	3 138	2 278	22 716	20 297	648	441
1999	14 848	14 482	366	10 494	688	-369	9 436	3 063	2 348	23 046	20 561	644	444
2000	16 022	15 413	609	11 227	710	-388	10 129	3 358	2 535	24 990	22 299	641	449
2001	16 422	16 134	288	11 426	757	-405	10 264	3 503	2 654	25 798	22 973	637	452
2002	16 846	16 578	268	11 853	804	-579	10 471	3 546	2 830	26 567	24 048	634	. . .

. . . = Not available.

Table 21-2. Personal Income and Employment by State and Region—*Continued*

(Millions of dollars, except as noted.)

Year	Total	Nonfarm	Farm	Derivation of personal income						Per capita (dollars)		Population (thousands)	Total employment (thousands)
				Earnings by place of work	Less: Personal contributions for social insurance	Plus: Adjustment for residence	Equals: Net earnings by place of residence	Dividends, interest, and rent	Transfer payments	Personal income	Disposable personal income		
OHIO													
1972	50 410	49 829	580	41 040	1 379	-126	39 534	6 437	4 439	4 691	4 106	10 747	4 710
1973	56 188	55 456	732	45 785	1 776	-154	43 855	7 202	5 131	5 218	4 576	10 767	4 902
1974	61 722	60 864	858	49 524	1 988	-131	47 406	8 163	6 153	5 733	5 015	10 766	4 964
1975	65 556	64 692	864	51 232	2 019	-77	49 136	8 614	7 807	6 087	5 368	10 770	4 809
1976	72 611	71 779	833	57 104	2 231	-87	54 785	9 422	8 403	6 753	5 926	10 753	4 889
1977	80 906	80 179	727	63 948	2 477	-100	61 370	10 605	8 931	7 511	6 555	10 771	5 034
1978	89 887	89 209	677	71 092	2 816	-119	68 158	12 162	9 567	8 326	7 251	10 795	5 207
1979	99 899	99 097	802	78 144	3 263	-141	74 740	14 271	10 889	9 251	8 008	10 799	5 298
1980	109 120	108 528	592	81 735	3 448	-156	78 130	17 261	13 728	10 103	8 797	10 801	5 215
1981	118 479	118 335	144	86 828	3 996	-467	82 365	20 842	15 272	10 982	9 502	10 788	5 151
1982	123 547	123 292	255	87 662	4 106	-588	82 969	22 812	17 766	11 485	10 048	10 757	4 983
1983	130 647	130 741	-94	91 901	4 317	-709	86 875	24 782	18 991	12 167	10 658	10 738	4 978
1984	144 407	143 600	807	102 544	4 835	-841	96 868	28 179	19 360	13 449	11 856	10 738	5 183
1985	153 456	152 669	787	109 303	5 410	-929	102 964	29 738	20 754	14 295	12 566	10 735	5 316
1986	160 236	159 646	590	113 930	5 793	-964	107 174	31 034	22 029	14 933	13 152	10 730	5 431
1987	168 668	168 019	648	120 556	6 158	-1 005	113 393	32 318	22 957	15 675	13 701	10 760	5 583
1988	180 757	180 093	664	130 177	6 819	-1 060	122 297	34 509	23 950	16 739	14 707	10 799	5 721
1989	193 035	191 992	1 042	136 988	7 360	-1 101	128 526	38 654	25 854	17 825	15 565	10 829	5 845
1990	204 114	203 062	1 052	144 263	7 740	-1 091	135 432	40 762	27 920	18 788	16 439	10 864	5 911
1991	210 117	209 586	531	147 150	8 103	-1 127	137 920	41 264	30 933	19 196	16 835	10 946	5 888
1992	222 812	221 863	948	157 194	8 502	-1 181	147 511	41 223	34 078	20 202	17 774	11 029	5 903
1993	232 463	231 702	761	164 589	8 965	-1 261	154 363	42 645	35 455	20 940	18 337	11 101	6 011
1994	245 156	244 172	984	173 959	9 711	-1 313	162 935	45 286	36 936	21 982	19 206	11 152	6 195
1995	255 313	254 546	767	180 582	10 228	-1 299	169 055	47 440	38 818	22 790	19 808	11 203	6 363
1996	264 162	263 110	1 052	186 222	10 548	-1 301	174 373	49 601	40 187	23 496	20 257	11 243	6 462
1997	279 367	277 824	1 543	196 810	11 180	-1 376	184 254	53 412	41 701	24 772	21 273	11 277	6 573
1998	293 208	292 135	1 073	207 789	11 730	-1 484	194 575	56 682	41 951	25 921	22 175	11 312	6 688
1999	304 342	303 717	625	218 176	12 328	-1 353	204 495	56 996	42 850	26 849	22 972	11 335	6 765
2000	319 653	318 902	752	227 800	12 639	-1 303	213 857	60 460	45 336	28 130	24 040	11 364	6 860
2001	326 876	326 142	734	230 607	12 923	-1 285	216 399	61 331	49 147	28 699	24 562	11 390	6 796
2002	334 832	334 532	300	234 847	13 393	-1 397	220 057	61 657	53 118	29 317	25 600	11 421	. . .
OKLAHOMA													
1972	10 682	10 243	440	8 316	289	72	8 100	1 343	1 240	4 020	3 567	2 657	1 183
1973	12 188	11 435	754	9 495	375	82	9 202	1 590	1 397	4 524	4 055	2 694	1 221
1974	13 623	13 154	469	10 451	440	106	10 116	1 855	1 651	4 986	4 399	2 732	1 256
1975	15 176	14 759	417	11 492	481	140	11 151	2 005	2 020	5 475	4 904	2 772	1 269
1976	16 867	16 519	347	12 777	528	175	12 425	2 218	2 224	5 974	5 322	2 823	1 305
1977	18 874	18 689	185	14 394	601	151	13 944	2 538	2 393	6 586	5 835	2 866	1 359
1978	21 518	21 336	182	16 500	709	147	15 938	3 012	2 567	7 387	6 477	2 913	1 428
1979	25 200	24 534	666	19 334	847	161	18 648	3 614	2 938	8 485	7 425	2 970	1 483
1980	29 131	28 819	312	22 003	994	169	21 178	4 548	3 405	9 580	8 329	3 041	1 551
1981	34 067	33 707	360	25 509	1 245	192	24 456	5 753	3 857	11 003	9 422	3 096	1 630
1982	37 887	37 406	481	28 027	1 391	197	26 833	6 696	4 358	11 817	10 036	3 206	1 678
1983	38 579	38 398	181	27 824	1 373	235	26 686	7 120	4 774	11 725	10 285	3 290	1 642
1984	41 683	41 309	374	30 004	1 472	285	28 817	7 981	4 885	12 687	11 244	3 286	1 672
1985	43 396	43 012	384	30 943	1 590	326	29 678	8 558	5 160	13 265	11 767	3 271	1 655
1986	43 222	42 580	642	30 500	1 601	374	29 273	8 426	5 523	13 288	12 038	3 253	1 595
1987	43 221	42 651	569	30 384	1 612	422	29 193	8 236	5 791	13 464	12 034	3 210	1 607
1988	45 153	44 379	774	31 703	1 779	469	30 393	8 634	6 126	14 257	12 748	3 167	1 617
1989	48 090	47 264	826	33 509	1 927	493	32 076	9 494	6 520	15 265	13 576	3 150	1 632
1990	51 027	50 205	822	35 596	2 047	560	34 109	9 900	7 017	16 205	14 256	3 149	1 665
1991	52 947	52 300	648	36 833	2 190	590	35 233	10 020	7 695	16 674	14 797	3 175	1 678
1992	56 155	55 347	808	39 214	2 302	627	37 540	9 997	8 619	17 437	15 538	3 221	1 692
1993	58 395	57 507	888	41 071	2 390	650	39 331	9 993	9 070	17 955	16 001	3 252	1 729
1994	60 800	59 937	862	42 403	2 526	699	40 575	10 624	9 600	18 531	16 470	3 281	1 763
1995	63 333	62 999	334	43 409	2 632	727	41 505	11 364	10 464	19 144	17 011	3 308	1 815
1996	66 289	65 893	395	45 321	2 736	745	43 330	11 992	10 967	19 846	17 506	3 340	1 866
1997	69 951	69 201	750	48 248	2 896	799	46 151	12 548	11 252	20 739	18 151	3 373	1 915
1998	74 677	74 063	613	51 463	3 063	834	49 234	13 923	11 519	21 930	19 179	3 405	1 965
1999	77 512	76 513	1 000	54 094	3 192	882	51 784	13 748	11 980	22 551	19 721	3 437	1 981
2000	82 931	82 172	759	57 598	3 337	946	55 206	15 102	12 623	24 007	20 947	3 454	2 023
2001	86 550	85 846	704	59 937	3 542	934	57 330	15 351	13 869	24 945	21 803	3 470	2 041
2002	87 818	87 189	629	59 778	3 658	1 083	57 204	15 471	15 143	25 136	22 376	3 494	. . .

. . . = Not available.

Table 21-2. Personal Income and Employment by State and Region—*Continued*

(Millions of dollars, except as noted.)

| Year | Total | Nonfarm | Farm | Derivation of personal income | | | | | | Per capita (dollars) | | Population (thousands) | Total employment (thousands) |
				Earnings by place of work	Less: Personal contributions for social insurance	Plus: Adjustment for residence	Equals: Net earnings by place of residence	Dividends, interest, and rent	Transfer payments	Personal income	Disposable personal income		
OREGON													
1972	10 153	9 862	291	7 975	295	-50	7 631	1 499	1 023	4 625	4 023	2 195	1 001
1973	11 497	11 099	397	9 018	381	-55	8 582	1 710	1 205	5 135	4 487	2 239	1 058
1974	13 062	12 558	504	10 088	439	-61	9 588	1 988	1 486	5 726	4 969	2 281	1 089
1975	14 367	13 954	414	10 810	467	-29	10 313	2 180	1 874	6 181	5 446	2 325	1 105
1976	16 398	16 010	388	12 427	526	-13	11 888	2 461	2 049	6 913	6 039	2 372	1 156
1977	18 431	18 096	335	14 021	602	-70	13 348	2 843	2 239	7 556	6 511	2 439	1 223
1978	21 272	20 935	336	16 248	708	-128	15 412	3 421	2 438	8 476	7 285	2 510	1 297
1979	24 275	23 875	399	18 380	835	-199	17 346	4 203	2 726	9 415	8 068	2 578	1 352
1980	26 930	26 449	481	19 738	906	-246	18 587	5 099	3 244	10 196	8 788	2 641	1 353
1981	28 981	28 592	389	20 365	1 024	-259	19 082	3 746	3 746	10 862	9 395	2 668	1 324
1982	29 654	29 377	277	20 127	1 054	-245	18 827	6 597	4 230	11 128	9 644	2 665	1 274
1983	31 392	31 112	280	21 150	1 108	-229	19 813	7 040	4 539	11 832	10 352	2 653	1 300
1984	34 309	33 903	406	23 277	1 216	-276	21 785	7 893	4 631	12 866	11 320	2 667	1 348
1985	36 205	35 777	428	24 730	1 348	-311	23 071	8 259	4 876	13 547	11 876	2 673	1 379
1986	38 003	37 450	554	26 084	1 456	-355	24 273	8 730	5 000	14 162	12 345	2 684	1 414
1987	40 274	39 783	491	27 861	1 567	-416	25 878	9 169	5 227	14 911	13 004	2 701	1 464
1988	44 030	43 363	667	30 788	1 813	-487	28 488	9 840	5 702	16 062	14 190	2 741	1 532
1989	48 060	47 447	613	33 243	2 021	-540	30 683	11 212	6 165	17 222	14 933	2 791	1 587
1990	52 178	51 530	648	36 333	2 179	-609	33 544	11 890	6 743	18 242	15 992	2 860	1 639
1991	54 891	54 243	648	38 030	2 354	-649	35 027	12 390	7 474	18 744	16 332	2 929	1 648
1992	58 163	57 534	629	40 655	2 495	-705	37 455	12 389	8 319	19 441	16 922	2 992	1 666
1993	61 916	61 151	766	43 357	2 658	-772	39 927	13 072	8 917	20 232	17 557	3 060	1 711
1994	66 130	65 475	654	46 291	2 890	-847	42 554	14 297	9 279	21 187	18 304	3 121	1 796
1995	71 209	70 628	581	49 033	3 121	-1 010	44 902	16 268	10 039	22 362	19 339	3 184	1 861
1996	75 561	74 844	717	52 841	3 333	-1 219	48 290	16 858	10 413	23 270	19 957	3 247	1 937
1997	80 575	79 755	820	56 626	3 573	-1 426	51 627	18 178	10 770	24 385	20 742	3 304	2 004
1998	85 305	84 582	723	59 928	3 757	-1 508	54 663	19 254	11 388	25 446	21 674	3 352	2 041
1999	89 080	88 429	651	63 887	3 962	-1 794	58 131	18 801	12 148	26 247	22 214	3 394	2 065
2000	95 508	94 855	653	68 401	4 205	-2 087	62 109	20 659	12 739	27 836	23 416	3 431	2 110
2001	98 026	97 384	642	69 035	4 309	-1 948	62 778	21 010	14 238	28 222	23 933	3 473	2 108
2002	100 481	99 783	698	69 847	4 419	-2 291	63 137	21 051	16 292	28 533	24 782	3 522	. . .
PENNSYLVANIA													
1972	55 755	55 358	397	44 238	1 621	-370	42 248	6 968	6 539	4 683	4 058	11 905	5 247
1973	61 420	60 892	528	48 715	2 035	-333	46 347	7 799	7 274	5 168	4 509	11 885	5 402
1974	67 674	67 162	512	52 997	2 300	-339	50 359	8 819	8 496	5 704	4 952	11 864	5 419
1975	73 412	72 940	472	56 156	2 396	-371	53 388	9 320	10 703	6 170	5 438	11 898	5 302
1976	80 837	80 278	558	61 571	2 588	-359	58 624	10 279	11 934	6 800	5 975	11 887	5 353
1977	89 035	88 527	508	67 852	2 820	-357	64 675	11 563	12 796	7 493	6 549	11 882	5 429
1978	98 539	97 988	551	75 271	3 169	-367	71 735	13 104	13 701	8 305	7 234	11 865	5 564
1979	109 533	108 843	690	82 906	3 657	-390	78 859	15 287	15 387	9 225	7 996	11 874	5 672
1980	120 478	120 013	465	88 494	3 982	-424	84 088	18 720	17 670	10 151	8 817	11 868	5 638
1981	132 632	131 960	672	94 889	4 644	-411	89 835	22 928	19 870	11 184	9 642	11 859	5 605
1982	140 802	140 231	571	97 006	4 876	-243	91 887	26 118	22 797	11 887	10 323	11 845	5 495
1983	147 437	147 064	372	100 501	5 088	-82	95 332	27 592	24 513	12 455	10 944	11 838	5 455
1984	159 652	158 819	833	109 375	5 639	109	103 844	31 434	24 375	13 512	11 880	11 815	5 606
1985	170 034	169 204	830	115 971	6 305	258	109 924	34 150	25 960	14 445	12 689	11 771	5 714
1986	178 938	178 064	874	122 132	6 828	371	115 675	35 844	27 419	15 186	13 360	11 783	5 809
1987	190 657	189 805	852	132 000	7 405	472	125 067	37 481	28 109	16 142	14 123	11 811	5 999
1988	205 200	204 507	693	142 998	8 353	704	135 349	40 391	29 460	17 323	15 203	11 846	6 166
1989	222 195	221 260	935	152 870	9 002	893	144 761	45 753	31 681	18 725	16 401	11 866	6 267
1990	235 802	234 903	900	162 095	9 527	957	153 525	48 112	34 166	19 810	17 422	11 903	6 344
1991	244 892	244 290	603	165 912	10 024	947	156 835	49 204	38 853	20 438	18 037	11 982	6 261
1992	258 186	257 138	1 048	176 607	10 606	1 075	167 076	48 214	42 897	21 427	18 876	12 049	6 268
1993	267 020	266 065	956	182 992	11 207	1 266	173 051	48 759	45 211	22 032	19 421	12 120	6 311
1994	275 337	274 547	790	189 064	11 862	1 414	178 616	50 650	46 071	22 632	19 886	12 166	6 384
1995	285 923	285 347	576	195 616	12 388	1 654	184 883	53 053	47 988	23 439	20 511	12 198	6 487
1996	299 001	298 006	995	203 510	12 679	1 828	192 659	55 587	50 755	24 467	21 246	12 220	6 545
1997	313 457	312 826	631	213 061	13 333	2 053	201 782	59 088	52 587	25 635	22 111	12 228	6 659
1998	330 733	330 002	731	226 378	13 957	1 922	214 342	63 417	52 974	27 008	23 186	12 246	6 751
1999	342 357	341 610	748	237 595	14 701	2 148	225 043	62 026	55 288	27 916	23 922	12 264	6 854
2000	365 626	364 676	950	251 750	15 286	2 415	238 878	68 819	57 929	29 759	25 453	12 286	6 997
2001	378 350	377 510	840	258 915	15 959	2 475	245 430	70 783	62 137	30 752	26 370	12 303	7 008
2002	390 560	390 004	557	265 071	16 626	2 979	251 424	71 191	67 945	31 663	27 804	12 335	. . .

. . . = Not available.

Table 21-2. Personal Income and Employment by State and Region—*Continued*

(Millions of dollars, except as noted.)

Year	Total	Nonfarm	Farm	Derivation of personal income — Earnings by place of work	Less: Personal contributions for social insurance	Plus: Adjustment for residence	Equals: Net earnings by place of residence	Dividends, interest, and rent	Transfer payments	Per capita (dollars) — Personal income	Disposable personal income	Population (thousands)	Total employment (thousands)
RHODE ISLAND													
1972	4 515	4 507	9	3 454	136	55	3 374	596	546	4 625	4 067	976	447
1973	4 863	4 856	7	3 674	172	70	3 573	669	621	4 972	4 379	978	452
1974	5 154	5 144	10	3 765	187	88	3 665	759	729	5 405	4 753	954	439
1975	5 531	5 521	10	3 902	191	81	3 793	777	961	5 844	5 240	946	424
1976	6 093	6 083	10	4 382	209	89	4 261	847	985	6 411	5 697	950	442
1977	6 690	6 681	9	4 821	229	103	4 696	953	1 041	7 004	6 238	955	459
1978	7 364	7 354	10	5 342	258	102	5 186	1 069	1 109	7 693	6 753	957	475
1979	8 222	8 214	8	5 938	299	110	5 750	1 243	1 229	8 595	7 468	957	484
1980	9 243	9 235	8	6 483	330	124	6 276	1 546	1 421	9 742	8 520	949	486
1981	10 306	10 298	9	6 976	376	154	6 754	1 918	1 634	10 815	9 465	953	486
1982	11 073	11 045	29	7 349	407	208	7 149	2 129	1 795	11 605	10 207	954	477
1983	11 896	11 857	39	7 926	443	264	7 747	2 240	1 909	12 439	10 977	956	482
1984	13 194	13 160	34	8 793	497	333	8 630	2 628	1 936	13 717	12 171	962	507
1985	14 229	14 184	45	9 553	547	393	9 398	2 734	2 098	14 685	13 011	969	522
1986	15 233	15 186	47	10 322	609	418	10 131	2 912	2 190	15 587	13 724	977	541
1987	16 478	16 434	44	11 219	667	488	11 040	3 171	2 266	16 651	14 524	990	550
1988	18 205	18 157	48	12 404	756	564	12 211	3 577	2 417	18 271	16 052	996	564
1989	19 670	19 635	35	13 076	808	627	12 895	4 153	2 622	19 657	17 249	1 001	566
1990	20 287	20 255	33	13 361	842	669	13 188	4 185	2 915	20 167	17 771	1 006	555
1991	20 444	20 409	35	13 063	867	701	12 897	4 009	3 537	20 228	17 862	1 011	528
1992	21 269	21 232	38	13 859	927	727	13 659	3 925	3 685	21 005	18 625	1 013	534
1993	22 090	22 057	32	14 323	969	771	14 125	3 972	3 992	21 761	19 249	1 015	538
1994	22 612	22 584	28	14 729	1 017	848	14 561	4 079	3 972	22 257	19 629	1 016	538
1995	23 787	23 759	27	15 408	1 058	869	15 219	4 371	4 196	23 389	20 639	1 017	541
1996	24 818	24 793	26	15 934	1 080	929	15 783	4 768	4 267	24 310	21 334	1 021	545
1997	26 293	26 276	17	16 765	1 141	977	16 601	5 091	4 601	25 643	22 286	1 025	552
1998	27 673	27 656	17	17 712	1 203	1 051	17 560	5 458	4 655	26 837	23 176	1 031	560
1999	28 762	28 744	17	18 633	1 275	1 138	18 496	5 430	4 836	27 645	23 836	1 040	571
2000	30 741	30 725	16	19 899	1 344	1 275	19 830	5 899	5 011	29 257	24 983	1 051	584
2001	32 061	32 046	15	20 567	1 409	1 289	20 447	6 046	5 567	30 256	26 016	1 060	587
2002	33 276	33 260	16	21 381	1 493	1 127	21 016	6 103	6 158	31 107	27 384	1 070	. . .
SOUTH CAROLINA													
1972	9 795	9 563	232	8 127	283	145	7 990	927	878	3 603	3 172	2 718	1 262
1973	11 181	10 864	317	9 268	369	159	9 058	1 085	1 038	4 029	3 567	2 775	1 328
1974	12 678	12 322	356	10 383	429	174	10 128	1 244	1 307	4 459	3 940	2 843	1 365
1975	13 689	13 404	286	10 795	442	185	10 538	1 370	1 782	4 720	4 277	2 900	1 326
1976	15 462	15 223	239	12 309	505	221	12 025	1 538	1 899	5 257	4 702	2 941	1 376
1977	16 990	16 800	190	13 557	555	244	13 225	1 753	2 013	5 684	5 070	2 989	1 411
1978	19 264	19 014	249	15 395	643	261	15 014	2 046	2 204	6 334	5 635	3 041	1 467
1979	21 744	21 476	268	17 246	749	286	16 784	2 427	2 533	7 044	6 198	3 087	1 510
1980	24 429	24 386	43	18 809	835	320	18 294	3 051	3 084	7 794	6 880	3 135	1 527
1981	27 504	27 321	182	20 818	997	352	20 173	3 778	3 553	8 651	7 597	3 179	1 541
1982	29 096	28 905	190	21 565	1 064	385	20 886	4 298	3 911	9 071	8 041	3 208	1 518
1983	31 614	31 569	45	23 392	1 180	399	22 611	4 838	4 165	9 775	8 661	3 234	1 552
1984	35 696	35 433	264	26 592	1 339	448	25 700	5 666	4 331	10 910	9 727	3 272	1 631
1985	38 536	38 349	187	28 387	1 506	505	27 386	6 347	4 803	11 666	10 376	3 303	1 663
1986	40 974	40 899	76	30 108	1 664	569	29 012	6 860	5 102	12 258	10 901	3 343	1 706
1987	44 136	43 896	240	32 656	1 785	614	31 485	7 359	5 293	13 056	11 563	3 381	1 748
1988	47 923	47 593	330	35 605	2 029	633	34 209	8 076	5 638	14 045	12 512	3 412	1 820
1989	51 276	50 933	343	38 081	2 236	588	36 434	8 487	6 356	14 834	13 082	3 457	1 871
1990	56 158	55 890	269	40 906	2 396	508	39 019	9 971	7 168	16 040	14 190	3 501	1 926
1991	58 406	58 038	368	41 931	2 511	509	39 929	10 339	8 138	16 358	14 565	3 570	1 899
1992	61 803	61 455	348	44 333	2 631	548	42 251	10 437	9 115	17 071	15 229	3 620	1 912
1993	64 711	64 387	325	46 361	2 783	570	44 149	10 816	9 746	17 665	15 731	3 663	1 948
1994	68 511	68 048	463	48 526	2 974	654	46 206	11 811	10 494	18 489	16 404	3 705	1 998
1995	72 050	71 692	358	50 842	3 171	753	48 423	12 431	11 196	19 221	16 968	3 749	2 057
1996	76 287	75 865	422	53 331	3 281	862	50 912	13 375	12 000	20 096	17 646	3 796	2 102
1997	81 045	80 595	451	56 327	3 485	987	53 830	14 516	12 700	20 998	18 364	3 860	2 165
1998	86 672	86 363	309	59 973	3 700	1 059	57 332	16 165	13 175	22 115	19 259	3 919	2 220
1999	91 075	90 669	406	64 193	3 915	1 110	61 387	15 849	13 838	22 914	19 947	3 975	2 267
2000	97 410	96 957	453	67 737	4 065	1 307	64 978	17 809	14 623	24 209	21 135	4 024	2 302
2001	100 902	100 337	564	69 306	4 206	1 373	66 472	18 225	16 204	24 840	21 724	4 062	2 271
2002	104 302	103 869	433	70 783	4 380	1 581	67 983	18 382	17 936	25 395	22 704	4 107	. . .

. . . = Not available.

Table 21-2. Personal Income and Employment by State and Region—*Continued*

(Millions of dollars, except as noted.)

Year	Total	Nonfarm	Farm	Derivation of personal income				Dividends, interest, and rent	Transfer payments	Per capita (dollars)		Population (thousands)	Total employment (thousands)
				Earnings by place of work	Less: Personal contributions for social insurance	Plus: Adjustment for residence	Equals: Net earnings by place of residence			Personal income	Disposable personal income		

SOUTH DAKOTA

Year	Total	Nonfarm	Farm	Earnings	Less	Plus	Equals	Div	Transfer	PI	DPI	Pop	Emp
1972	2 754	2 188	566	2 167	69	7	2 105	366	282	4 065	3 776	677	309
1973	3 505	2 479	1 027	2 835	92	7	2 750	430	325	5 163	4 767	679	323
1974	3 520	2 834	687	2 716	106	8	2 618	523	379	5 178	4 711	680	326
1975	3 862	3 156	706	2 925	115	10	2 820	593	448	5 667	5 232	681	326
1976	3 840	3 562	279	2 804	124	12	2 692	652	496	5 591	5 093	687	336
1977	4 376	3 936	440	3 204	127	13	3 090	756	530	6 351	5 867	689	342
1978	5 064	4 446	618	3 762	146	15	3 631	860	573	7 347	6 747	689	355
1979	5 621	4 965	656	4 117	175	16	3 959	1 017	645	8 158	7 476	689	360
1980	5 625	5 510	115	3 808	187	18	3 639	1 230	756	8 142	7 362	691	354
1981	6 517	6 116	401	4 308	211	15	4 111	1 534	872	9 451	8 570	690	349
1982	6 847	6 539	308	4 331	224	12	4 119	1 757	970	9 915	8 936	691	346
1983	7 066	6 889	176	4 483	239	6	4 250	1 776	1 040	10 195	9 346	693	354
1984	8 101	7 483	618	5 369	264	-1	5 104	1 913	1 084	11 619	10 772	697	364
1985	8 340	7 798	542	5 518	293	-4	5 221	1 969	1 150	11 942	11 047	698	367
1986	8 691	8 107	583	5 764	316	-11	5 428	2 057	1 207	12 486	11 560	696	368
1987	9 199	8 442	757	6 232	347	-18	5 866	2 073	1 260	13 217	12 174	696	383
1988	9 639	8 963	676	6 558	389	-25	6 144	2 176	1 319	13 807	12 711	698	390
1989	10 288	9 617	672	6 916	429	-35	6 452	2 405	1 431	14 767	13 531	697	398
1990	11 312	10 354	958	7 742	464	-54	7 224	2 557	1 531	16 227	14 837	697	412
1991	11 897	11 052	845	8 143	501	-65	7 577	2 661	1 659	16 907	15 475	704	423
1992	12 732	11 793	939	8 853	533	-81	8 239	2 687	1 806	17 862	16 325	713	434
1993	13 297	12 453	845	9 279	564	-96	8 619	2 755	1 924	18 413	16 736	722	445
1994	14 177	13 194	983	9 972	612	-120	9 240	2 921	2 016	19 399	17 704	731	467
1995	14 454	13 931	523	9 902	638	-143	9 121	3 162	2 171	19 588	17 780	738	475
1996	15 883	14 676	1 207	10 993	661	-171	10 160	3 430	2 292	21 399	19 477	742	483
1997	16 288	15 457	831	11 089	696	-171	10 222	3 695	2 370	21 885	19 684	744	488
1998	17 497	16 474	1 023	11 936	747	-211	10 978	4 105	2 415	23 453	21 109	746	498
1999	18 442	17 363	1 079	12 782	795	-216	11 770	4 192	2 480	24 576	21 996	750	511
2000	19 511	18 475	1 035	13 486	832	-232	12 422	4 466	2 623	25 815	23 124	756	521
2001	20 146	19 305	841	13 750	879	-220	12 650	4 675	2 820	26 566	23 764	758	523
2002	20 316	19 975	342	13 720	928	-289	12 504	4 784	3 028	26 694	24 263	761	. . .

TENNESSEE

Year	Total	Nonfarm	Farm	Earnings	Less	Plus	Equals	Div	Transfer	PI	DPI	Pop	Emp
1972	15 569	15 203	366	13 044	464	-191	12 389	1 640	1 540	3 808	3 413	4 088	1 924
1973	17 786	17 256	530	14 842	596	-181	14 065	1 916	1 806	4 298	3 853	4 138	2 025
1974	19 732	19 376	356	16 147	684	-191	15 273	2 256	2 202	4 696	4 210	4 202	2 055
1975	21 378	21 099	279	16 917	708	-189	16 020	2 473	2 885	5 017	4 542	4 261	1 983
1976	24 132	23 734	398	19 217	788	-184	18 245	2 724	3 162	5 574	5 027	4 329	2 052
1977	26 887	26 562	325	21 566	887	-240	20 440	3 084	3 363	6 108	5 513	4 402	2 135
1978	30 761	30 414	347	24 824	1 017	-307	23 499	3 602	3 660	6 895	6 189	4 462	2 228
1979	34 535	34 152	383	27 527	1 183	-358	25 986	4 301	4 247	7 618	6 829	4 533	2 282
1980	38 268	38 028	240	29 537	1 292	-424	27 822	5 315	5 130	8 319	7 449	4 600	2 264
1981	42 556	42 149	406	32 241	1 532	-460	30 249	6 507	5 799	9 196	8 227	4 628	2 263
1982	45 043	44 751	292	33 338	1 644	-417	31 278	7 392	6 373	9 695	8 709	4 646	2 224
1983	47 884	47 921	-37	35 497	1 780	-430	33 287	7 767	6 830	10 276	9 251	4 660	2 247
1984	53 675	53 291	384	40 043	2 002	-431	37 610	9 011	7 054	11 453	10 376	4 687	2 354
1985	57 750	57 442	307	43 169	2 268	-447	40 454	9 766	7 530	12 247	11 055	4 715	2 411
1986	61 581	61 392	189	46 071	2 497	-488	43 086	10 346	8 149	12 995	11 742	4 739	2 490
1987	66 524	66 279	245	50 161	2 731	-523	46 908	10 949	8 667	13 909	12 512	4 783	2 593
1988	71 901	71 603	297	54 086	3 066	-536	50 484	12 093	9 324	14 910	13 470	4 822	2 680
1989	77 105	76 751	354	57 355	3 358	-564	53 433	13 492	10 180	15 883	14 295	4 854	2 754
1990	82 267	81 926	342	60 668	3 568	-602	56 497	14 364	11 405	16 808	15 181	4 894	2 797
1991	86 583	86 181	402	63 348	3 822	-579	58 947	14 632	13 004	17 433	15 779	4 967	2 796
1992	94 465	93 931	534	69 564	4 104	-441	65 019	14 750	14 696	18 707	16 931	5 050	2 858
1993	100 394	99 886	508	74 342	4 415	-563	69 365	15 105	15 925	19 541	17 676	5 138	2 965
1994	106 855	106 302	553	79 588	4 826	-636	74 127	16 158	16 570	20 426	18 414	5 231	3 087
1995	114 260	113 895	365	84 702	5 181	-715	78 806	17 316	18 138	21 449	19 297	5 327	3 172
1996	119 287	119 028	259	87 890	5 366	-662	81 862	18 395	19 030	22 022	19 674	5 417	3 225
1997	125 457	125 169	288	92 609	5 693	-799	86 116	19 449	19 891	22 814	20 300	5 499	3 302
1998	134 241	134 105	136	98 554	6 022	-919	91 613	21 776	20 853	24 101	21 426	5 570	3 387
1999	141 046	141 008	38	105 017	6 374	-1 000	97 643	21 855	21 549	25 014	22 265	5 639	3 444
2000	149 936	149 658	278	110 655	6 603	-1 170	102 881	23 785	23 270	26 290	23 448	5 703	3 509
2001	154 130	153 838	292	112 771	6 826	-1 321	104 624	24 156	25 349	26 808	23 909	5 749	3 478
2002	158 717	158 385	332	116 266	7 159	-2 311	106 797	24 206	27 714	27 378	24 891	5 797	. . .

. . . = Not available.

Table 21-2. Personal Income and Employment by State and Region—*Continued*

(Millions of dollars, except as noted.)

Year	Total	Nonfarm	Farm	Derivation of personal income						Per capita (dollars)		Population (thousands)	Total employment (thousands)
				Earnings by place of work	Less: Personal contributions for social insurance	Plus: Adjustment for residence	Equals: Net earnings by place of residence	Dividends, interest, and rent	Transfer payments	Personal income	Disposable personal income		
TEXAS													
1972	49 287	47 966	1 321	40 358	1 366	-128	38 864	6 307	4 117	4 192	3 711	11 759	5 334
1973	56 283	54 077	2 206	45 985	1 782	-155	44 048	7 324	4 911	4 683	4 158	12 019	5 608
1974	63 719	62 513	1 207	51 454	2 101	-132	49 221	8 650	5 849	5 194	4 570	12 268	5 822
1975	72 117	70 770	1 347	58 057	2 326	-130	55 600	9 281	7 236	5 738	5 112	12 568	5 938
1976	82 087	80 778	1 309	66 672	2 635	-95	63 942	10 191	7 954	6 362	5 632	12 903	6 207
1977	92 059	90 768	1 291	75 298	2 996	-308	71 994	11 479	8 587	6 979	6 128	13 192	6 521
1978	106 800	105 762	1 038	87 307	3 537	-429	83 341	13 931	9 528	7 912	6 960	13 498	6 898
1979	124 003	122 220	1 784	100 905	4 302	-436	96 167	17 010	10 826	8 929	7 763	13 887	7 222
1980	142 772	142 089	683	114 532	5 048	-544	108 940	21 130	12 703	9 957	8 616	14 338	7 511
1981	167 976	165 913	2 063	133 967	6 366	-352	127 248	26 357	14 371	11 391	9 753	14 746	7 925
1982	183 378	182 082	1 296	143 994	7 058	-425	136 511	30 477	16 390	11 961	10 344	15 331	8 098
1983	193 793	192 133	1 660	150 691	7 267	-408	143 016	32 320	18 457	12 303	10 832	15 752	8 087
1984	214 431	212 822	1 609	165 744	7 981	-470	157 293	37 843	19 295	13 396	11 871	16 007	8 468
1985	231 003	229 498	1 505	177 720	8 932	-499	168 289	42 035	20 679	14 196	12 584	16 273	8 720
1986	234 594	233 379	1 215	178 130	9 151	-459	168 520	43 191	22 883	14 165	12 681	16 561	8 561
1987	240 782	238 844	1 938	182 466	9 263	-458	172 744	43 724	24 315	14 486	12 926	16 622	8 773
1988	255 402	253 543	1 859	193 727	10 268	-461	182 997	46 831	25 573	15 324	13 751	16 667	8 935
1989	274 343	272 454	1 889	206 201	11 207	-470	194 525	51 701	28 117	16 323	14 579	16 807	9 066
1990	297 569	294 850	2 719	224 620	12 235	-504	211 881	54 357	31 332	17 446	15 589	17 057	9 307
1991	314 726	312 044	2 681	237 542	13 319	-577	223 647	55 688	35 390	18 090	16 253	17 398	9 469
1992	337 934	334 869	3 065	255 454	14 225	-589	240 640	55 616	41 678	19 028	17 133	17 760	9 557
1993	356 784	353 022	3 762	271 857	15 198	-597	256 061	55 945	44 778	19 645	17 662	18 162	9 863
1994	377 583	374 448	3 135	286 929	16 402	-648	269 878	59 840	47 864	20 339	18 270	18 564	10 192
1995	402 097	399 618	2 479	304 128	17 656	-714	285 758	64 296	52 043	21 209	19 005	18 959	10 539
1996	428 726	426 754	1 972	324 926	18 805	-771	305 349	68 149	55 228	22 167	19 708	19 340	10 847
1997	468 950	466 209	2 741	357 328	20 476	-886	335 966	74 629	58 355	23 756	20 990	19 740	11 288
1998	511 964	509 364	2 600	393 136	22 184	-943	370 009	82 360	59 594	25 398	22 340	20 158	11 702
1999	539 527	535 174	4 354	422 007	23 643	-972	397 392	80 766	61 369	26 244	23 082	20 558	11 938
2000	586 587	583 766	2 821	458 488	25 362	-1 048	432 078	89 890	64 619	27 992	24 475	20 955	12 297
2001	608 466	605 742	2 724	474 958	26 692	-1 086	447 181	90 523	70 763	28 472	24 987	21 371	12 412
2002	618 560	615 891	2 669	477 903	27 314	-1 152	449 436	90 985	78 139	28 401	25 527	21 780	. . .
UTAH													
1972	4 514	4 417	97	3 649	127	5	3 528	584	403	3 979	3 558	1 135	494
1973	5 057	4 919	138	4 103	165	8	3 946	642	469	4 326	3 865	1 169	523
1974	5 686	5 582	104	4 589	192	11	4 408	745	533	4 743	4 228	1 199	545
1975	6 355	6 282	73	5 062	209	14	4 867	828	659	5 150	4 647	1 234	553
1976	7 302	7 222	80	5 834	237	17	5 614	966	722	5 739	5 118	1 272	580
1977	8 331	8 261	69	6 675	270	22	6 426	1 115	790	6 328	5 629	1 316	613
1978	9 606	9 528	78	7 681	313	27	7 394	1 335	876	7 041	6 254	1 364	651
1979	11 026	10 935	92	8 705	380	35	8 361	1 673	993	7 786	6 891	1 416	679
1980	12 464	12 400	64	9 600	426	52	9 226	2 064	1 174	8 464	7 515	1 473	689
1981	14 078	14 038	40	10 702	519	54	10 237	2 474	1 368	9 290	8 204	1 515	699
1982	15 282	15 237	45	11 358	565	54	10 847	2 859	1 576	9 807	8 640	1 558	709
1983	16 481	16 445	36	12 064	602	43	11 505	3 264	1 712	10 333	9 218	1 595	721
1984	18 223	18 163	61	13 444	674	38	12 807	3 681	1 735	11 233	10 075	1 622	764
1985	19 462	19 401	62	14 364	756	40	13 648	3 950	1 865	11 846	10 594	1 643	793
1986	20 367	20 276	91	14 956	804	35	14 187	4 142	2 039	12 248	10 943	1 663	805
1987	21 208	21 085	123	15 615	842	25	14 799	4 198	2 211	12 638	11 245	1 678	835
1988	22 225	22 017	208	16 601	939	24	15 687	4 238	2 300	13 156	11 706	1 689	870
1989	23 843	23 641	202	17 723	1 021	21	16 723	4 604	2 515	13 977	12 448	1 706	903
1990	25 939	25 693	246	19 394	1 105	17	18 306	4 821	2 812	14 983	13 207	1 731	945
1991	27 750	27 526	224	20 823	1 207	10	19 626	4 978	3 146	15 592	13 792	1 780	967
1992	29 788	29 526	262	22 590	1 294	6	21 302	4 979	3 508	16 217	14 331	1 837	986
1993	31 950	31 641	309	24 338	1 396	8	22 951	5 180	3 819	16 830	14 823	1 898	1 034
1994	34 579	34 366	212	26 394	1 532	7	24 869	5 802	3 908	17 638	15 445	1 960	1 112
1995	37 278	37 116	162	28 445	1 673	6	26 778	6 293	4 206	18 508	16 149	2 014	1 160
1996	40 354	40 192	162	30 777	1 793	17	29 000	6 909	4 445	19 514	16 926	2 068	1 228
1997	43 696	43 511	185	33 342	1 938	19	31 422	7 579	4 695	20 613	17 792	2 120	1 282
1998	46 772	46 537	235	35 819	2 040	23	33 802	8 112	4 857	21 594	18 680	2 166	1 321
1999	48 923	48 672	251	38 071	2 170	24	35 925	7 940	5 058	22 203	19 112	2 203	1 351
2000	52 518	52 328	189	40 701	2 293	22	38 430	8 754	5 334	23 410	20 127	2 243	1 391
2001	54 764	54 467	297	42 234	2 406	27	39 856	9 062	5 845	24 033	20 706	2 279	1 403
2002	55 953	55 715	238	42 772	2 483	2	40 291	9 172	6 490	24 157	21 289	2 316	. . .

. . . = Not available.

Table 21-2. Personal Income and Employment by State and Region—*Continued*

(Millions of dollars, except as noted.)

Year	Total	Nonfarm	Farm	Earnings by place of work	Less: Personal contributions for social insurance	Plus: Adjustment for residence	Equals: Net earnings by place of residence	Dividends, interest, and rent	Transfer payments	Personal income	Disposable personal income	Population (thousands)	Total employment (thousands)
VERMONT													
1972	1 934	1 859	75	1 486	54	-21	1 411	293	230	4 176	3 667	463	211
1973	2 131	2 053	78	1 633	68	-20	1 545	325	261	4 548	4 041	469	220
1974	2 304	2 240	64	1 721	76	-17	1 629	362	313	4 869	4 325	473	222
1975	2 492	2 426	65	1 809	79	-11	1 719	377	396	5 192	4 631	480	220
1976	2 791	2 710	81	2 042	87	-5	1 949	414	428	5 753	5 164	485	228
1977	3 041	2 972	69	2 224	96	-2	2 127	472	442	6 179	5 500	492	236
1978	3 506	3 408	98	2 611	114	-1	2 496	544	466	7 036	6 257	498	252
1979	3 972	3 863	108	2 926	133	6	2 798	646	528	7 853	6 939	506	261
1980	4 460	4 349	111	3 181	147	14	3 048	786	626	8 702	7 663	513	266
1981	5 010	4 885	125	3 481	175	18	3 324	965	720	9 717	8 520	516	271
1982	5 340	5 218	122	3 643	190	24	3 477	1 060	803	10 287	9 091	519	272
1983	5 740	5 656	83	3 937	206	23	3 754	1 126	859	10 968	9 717	523	279
1984	6 345	6 265	80	4 345	229	29	4 145	1 327	873	12 048	10 706	527	290
1985	6 887	6 789	98	4 809	265	30	4 574	1 410	903	12 994	11 484	530	302
1986	7 392	7 296	96	5 219	296	34	4 058	1 495	939	13 842	12 168	534	313
1987	8 100	7 982	118	5 805	327	42	5 519	1 616	964	14 992	13 084	540	323
1988	8 905	8 783	121	6 392	376	49	6 065	1 817	1 023	16 197	14 218	550	337
1989	9 769	9 642	127	6 877	415	52	6 514	2 137	1 118	17 517	15 315	558	344
1990	10 193	10 087	106	7 102	430	52	6 723	2 213	1 257	18 047	15 831	565	344
1991	10 332	10 238	95	7 126	446	52	6 732	2 224	1 376	18 171	16 021	569	337
1992	10 999	10 834	165	7 653	468	53	7 239	2 201	1 560	19 204	17 005	573	344
1993	11 357	11 238	119	7 963	488	55	7 530	2 195	1 632	19 657	17 383	578	352
1994	11 898	11 779	119	8 270	517	62	7 815	2 359	1 724	20 379	18 038	584	362
1995	12 449	12 349	100	8 520	555	69	8 034	2 553	1 862	21 135	18 708	589	365
1996	13 073	12 939	133	8 959	575	76	8 459	2 704	1 909	22 019	19 308	594	371
1997	13 752	13 657	95	9 348	606	86	8 828	2 911	2 013	23 026	20 018	597	376
1998	14 738	14 617	121	9 969	635	98	9 432	3 231	2 075	24 547	21 258	600	386
1999	15 575	15 434	141	10 688	678	108	10 118	3 262	2 195	25 757	22 272	605	394
2000	16 752	16 610	142	11 468	717	122	10 873	3 549	2 331	27 465	23 603	610	405
2001	17 627	17 493	133	12 019	762	139	11 396	3 687	2 544	28 756	24 853	613	408
2002	18 167	18 085	83	12 255	794	130	11 591	3 754	2 822	29 464	26 066	617	. . .
VIRGINIA													
1972	21 657	21 362	294	17 175	571	928	17 532	2 501	1 624	4 486	3 842	4 828	2 263
1973	24 396	24 007	390	19 325	736	1 000	19 589	2 882	1 926	4 972	4 293	4 907	2 384
1974	27 300	26 946	354	21 373	843	1 129	21 658	3 361	2 281	5 484	4 701	4 978	2 451
1975	30 005	29 706	299	22 937	801	1 388	23 434	3 680	2 891	5 934	5 209	5 056	2 425
1976	33 538	33 273	266	25 591	991	1 611	26 211	4 143	3 184	6 534	5 704	5 133	2 501
1977	37 439	37 246	193	28 534	1 099	1 851	29 285	4 689	3 464	7 192	6 242	5 206	2 585
1978	42 483	42 167	317	32 271	1 254	2 185	33 202	5 468	3 813	8 040	6 940	5 284	2 697
1979	47 894	47 715	179	35 863	1 475	2 583	36 971	6 563	4 360	8 995	7 760	5 325	2 769
1980	54 627	54 538	89	39 767	1 655	3 159	41 271	8 153	5 202	10 176	8 784	5 368	2 802
1981	61 470	61 166	303	44 179	1 987	3 385	45 576	9 910	5 984	11 291	9 681	5 444	2 820
1982	66 326	66 211	115	47 319	2 187	3 460	48 592	11 178	6 556	12 075	10 419	5 493	2 832
1983	71 985	71 941	44	51 501	2 449	3 440	52 492	12 421	7 072	12 936	11 284	5 565	2 905
1984	80 697	80 385	312	58 462	2 787	3 553	59 228	14 101	7 367	14 298	12 562	5 644	3 054
1985	87 362	87 149	212	63 953	3 238	3 674	64 389	15 210	7 762	15 286	13 348	5 715	3 198
1986	94 364	94 107	257	69 424	3 632	3 825	69 617	16 479	8 268	16 237	14 184	5 812	3 335
1987	102 817	102 457	360	76 261	4 008	4 043	76 296	17 878	8 643	17 332	15 028	5 932	3 502
1988	112 022	111 526	496	82 813	4 552	4 445	82 706	20 110	9 207	18 556	16 181	6 037	3 582
1989	121 058	120 441	616	88 602	4 992	4 682	88 292	22 769	9 996	19 780	17 162	6 120	3 683
1990	127 614	126 978	636	92 362	5 273	5 405	92 493	24 147	10 974	20 527	17 890	6 217	3 727
1991	132 536	131 954	582	94 729	5 537	5 866	95 059	25 284	12 193	21 033	18 396	6 301	3 667
1992	140 207	139 570	636	100 526	5 804	6 203	100 925	25 514	13 768	21 858	19 161	6 414	3 689
1993	147 223	146 708	515	105 252	6 130	6 565	105 687	26 832	14 704	22 616	19 777	6 510	3 765
1994	154 982	154 363	618	110 255	6 552	6 702	110 404	28 996	15 582	23 507	20 457	6 593	3 852
1995	161 442	160 895	546	114 656	6 876	6 929	114 708	30 092	16 642	24 202	20 996	6 671	3 943
1996	169 938	169 415	524	120 820	7 211	6 675	120 283	31 843	17 813	25 173	21 699	6 751	4 026
1997	180 190	179 785	405	128 887	7 720	7 226	128 394	33 321	18 476	26 385	22 554	6 829	4 129
1998	193 007	192 598	409	138 108	8 242	7 096	136 963	37 096	18 948	27 968	23 694	6 901	4 205
1999	204 727	204 397	331	148 654	8 937	8 346	148 064	36 949	19 715	29 246	24 534	7 000	4 296
2000	221 778	221 296	482	161 907	9 602	7 575	159 880	41 128	20 770	31 210	26 199	7 106	4 425
2001	232 730	232 278	452	169 233	10 189	8 218	167 262	42 325	23 144	32 338	27 196	7 197	4 445
2002	238 325	238 015	311	172 214	10 521	8 065	169 758	42 776	25 791	32 676	28 336	7 294	. . .

. . . = Not available.

Table 21-2. Personal Income and Employment by State and Region—*Continued*

(Millions of dollars, except as noted.)

Year	Total	Nonfarm	Farm	Derivation of personal income						Per capita (dollars)		Population (thousands)	Total employment (thousands)
				Earnings by place of work	Less: Personal contributions for social insurance	Plus: Adjustment for residence	Equals: Net earnings by place of residence	Dividends, interest, and rent	Transfer payments	Personal income	Disposable personal income		
WASHINGTON													
1972	16 307	15 775	531	12 565	456	72	12 180	2 342	1 785	4 731	4 217	3 447	1 481
1973	18 473	17 693	780	14 287	590	88	13 785	2 688	2 000	5 312	4 723	3 477	1 558
1974	20 999	20 087	912	16 132	687	131	15 576	3 087	2 336	5 919	5 268	3 548	1 622
1975	23 641	22 714	927	18 007	764	197	17 439	3 335	2 866	6 533	5 834	3 619	1 659
1976	26 502	25 734	769	20 283	858	244	19 668	3 704	3 130	7 181	6 398	3 691	1 739
1977	29 544	28 928	616	22 750	963	223	22 011	4 222	3 312	7 832	6 961	3 772	1 815
1978	34 536	33 762	774	26 788	1 150	266	25 904	5 052	3 580	8 887	7 823	3 886	1 939
1979	39 987	39 233	755	30 887	1 384	318	29 821	6 171	3 995	9 965	8 699	4 013	2 061
1980	45 338	44 447	891	34 127	1 539	383	32 971	7 478	4 889	10 913	9 544	4 155	2 110
1981	50 418	49 573	845	37 022	1 835	428	35 615	9 127	5 676	11 903	10 378	4 236	2 126
1982	53 161	52 395	766	38 301	1 950	460	36 811	9 951	6 399	12 431	11 038	4 277	2 101
1983	56 435	55 346	1 089	40 392	2 052	480	38 820	10 628	6 987	13 124	11 769	4 300	2 148
1984	60 901	59 863	1 038	43 166	2 206	538	41 498	12 142	7 261	14 021	12 630	4 344	2 224
1985	64 847	64 100	746	45 836	2 482	581	43 934	12 954	7 958	14 738	13 241	4 400	2 290
1986	69 114	68 049	1 065	49 204	2 741	601	47 064	13 607	8 443	15 522	13 969	4 453	2 365
1987	73 872	72 816	1 055	52 794	2 948	653	50 499	14 458	8 915	16 300	14 572	4 532	2 486
1988	80 130	79 188	943	57 527	3 369	740	54 899	15 630	9 601	17 270	15 494	4 640	2 618
1989	88 616	87 562	1 054	63 039	3 772	824	60 090	18 068	10 458	18 670	16 583	4 746	2 738
1990	98 143	97 071	1 072	70 240	4 157	926	67 009	19 550	11 584	20 017	17 753	4 903	2 864
1991	104 786	103 651	1 135	74 962	4 554	970	71 377	20 273	13 136	20 850	18 573	5 026	2 898
1992	112 634	111 258	1 375	81 775	4 926	1 036	77 884	20 225	14 525	21 825	19 459	5 161	2 930
1993	117 621	116 046	1 575	85 122	5 085	1 099	81 136	20 790	15 694	22 282	19 905	5 279	2 975
1994	123 337	122 138	1 199	88 442	5 409	1 162	84 195	22 742	16 400	22 946	20 412	5 375	3 087
1995	129 681	128 420	1 260	92 096	5 721	1 294	87 670	24 409	17 603	23 660	20 999	5 481	3 128
1996	139 328	137 642	1 686	98 912	6 070	1 474	94 316	26 618	18 393	25 015	22 001	5 570	3 220
1997	150 203	148 844	1 358	107 271	6 638	1 644	102 278	28 888	19 037	26 469	23 092	5 675	3 328
1998	163 192	161 753	1 439	117 375	7 214	1 723	111 884	31 713	19 595	28 285	24 354	5 770	3 409
1999	174 148	173 028	1 120	128 136	7 896	1 980	122 219	31 372	20 557	29 807	25 217	5 843	3 471
2000	186 843	185 572	1 271	135 901	8 245	2 237	129 894	35 299	21 650	31 605	26 939	5 912	3 553
2001	191 645	190 535	1 109	137 200	8 446	2 148	130 901	36 503	24 240	31 976	27 255	5 993	3 553
2002	198 221	196 851	1 370	139 603	8 701	2 692	133 594	36 921	27 706	32 661	28 703	6 069	. . .
WEST VIRGINIA													
1972	6 617	6 576	41	5 250	202	-113	4 935	684	998	3 682	3 259	1 797	684
1973	7 268	7 214	54	5 669	248	-116	5 305	782	1 181	4 026	3 590	1 805	700
1974	8 085	8 046	40	6 249	281	-130	5 838	912	1 336	4 457	3 929	1 814	711
1975	9 154	9 131	23	7 036	311	-157	6 568	1 008	1 579	4 974	4 399	1 841	717
1976	10 287	10 275	11	7 966	351	-193	7 422	1 125	1 740	5 479	4 823	1 877	739
1977	11 535	11 530	5	8 994	387	-225	8 382	1 278	1 875	6 053	5 339	1 906	758
1978	12 872	12 853	19	10 038	437	-262	9 339	1 455	2 078	6 703	5 930	1 920	781
1979	14 411	14 384	27	11 061	509	-272	10 281	1 705	2 426	7 432	6 532	1 939	791
1980	15 947	15 931	15	11 866	552	-299	11 015	2 106	2 826	8 172	7 162	1 951	784
1981	17 325	17 341	-16	12 462	633	-277	11 552	2 577	3 196	8 866	7 779	1 954	764
1982	18 403	18 430	-27	12 812	672	-232	11 909	2 979	3 515	9 439	8 328	1 950	743
1983	18 723	18 741	-19	12 548	664	-189	11 694	3 148	3 881	9 626	8 534	1 945	724
1984	20 081	20 062	19	13 445	719	-137	12 589	3 575	3 918	10 417	9 279	1 928	735
1985	20 853	20 837	16	13 885	782	-115	12 987	3 694	4 172	10 936	9 736	1 907	735
1986	21 578	21 542	36	14 135	817	-89	13 229	3 921	4 428	11 464	10 258	1 882	735
1987	22 198	22 195	2	14 522	852	-23	13 647	3 998	4 553	11 950	10 688	1 858	742
1988	23 259	23 231	28	15 194	940	8	14 262	4 233	4 764	12 708	11 429	1 830	755
1989	24 440	24 386	55	15 694	1 005	87	14 776	4 628	5 037	13 529	12 059	1 807	762
1990	26 133	26 096	37	16 897	1 060	68	15 905	4 878	5 350	14 579	12 997	1 793	783
1991	27 367	27 346	21	17 463	1 125	68	16 407	4 938	6 022	15 214	13 602	1 799	784
1992	29 101	29 049	52	18 493	1 182	80	17 392	4 940	6 770	16 109	14 451	1 806	795
1993	30 375	30 317	58	19 145	1 235	91	18 000	4 945	7 430	16 712	14 995	1 818	807
1994	31 666	31 611	55	20 210	1 322	132	19 020	5 144	7 502	17 395	15 549	1 820	829
1995	32 611	32 596	15	20 710	1 385	165	19 489	5 408	7 714	17 882	15 940	1 824	846
1996	33 771	33 773	-2	21 201	1 409	190	19 981	5 788	8 001	18 527	16 459	1 823	855
1997	35 202	35 206	-5	21 918	1 447	307	20 779	6 077	8 346	19 351	17 141	1 819	867
1998	36 738	36 741	-3	22 771	1 483	375	21 662	6 538	8 537	20 234	17 895	1 816	881
1999	37 472	37 483	-11	23 598	1 539	423	22 482	6 374	8 616	20 682	18 285	1 812	881
2000	39 438	39 430	8	24 648	1 577	423	23 494	6 942	9 002	21 821	19 274	1 807	889
2001	41 174	41 162	12	25 619	1 664	485	24 440	7 122	9 612	22 862	20 220	1 801	890
2002	42 575	42 557	17	26 329	1 739	524	25 114	7 160	10 300	23 628	21 223	1 802	. . .

. . . = Not available.

Table 21-2. Personal Income and Employment by State and Region—*Continued*

(Millions of dollars, except as noted.)

Year	Total	Nonfarm	Farm	Derivation of personal income						Per capita (dollars)		Population (thousands)	Total employment (thousands)
				Earnings by place of work	Less: Personal contributions for social insurance	Plus: Adjustment for residence	Equals: Net earnings by place of residence	Dividends, interest, and rent	Transfer payments	Personal income	Disposable personal income		
WISCONSIN													
1972	20 670	19 885	785	15 843	599	286	15 530	3 060	2 080	4 595	3 996	4 498	2 014
1973	23 182	22 215	966	17 847	767	312	17 392	3 440	2 349	5 130	4 472	4 518	2 116
1974	25 512	24 655	857	19 344	880	338	18 803	3 919	2 791	5 622	4 876	4 538	2 159
1975	27 697	26 787	910	20 578	930	343	19 992	4 230	3 475	6 061	5 315	4 570	2 148
1976	30 578	29 777	801	22 871	1 022	388	22 237	4 558	3 783	6 670	5 824	4 585	2 211
1977	34 218	33 028	1 189	25 864	1 128	429	25 166	4 995	4 057	7 417	6 438	4 613	2 293
1978	38 408	37 223	1 185	29 049	1 296	484	28 237	5 707	4 465	8 292	7 142	4 632	2 382
1979	43 302	41 847	1 455	32 460	1 519	523	31 463	6 730	5 109	9 281	8 028	4 666	2 465
1980	47 881	46 402	1 479	34 536	1 633	547	33 449	8 191	6 241	10 161	8 811	4 712	2 449
1981	52 018	50 848	1 170	36 317	1 886	597	35 028	9 909	7 081	11 006	9 482	4 726	2 424
1982	54 819	53 794	1 025	37 141	1 972	618	35 787	11 123	7 909	11 592	10 073	4 729	2 382
1983	56 873	56 441	432	38 462	2 039	673	37 096	11 298	8 479	12 046	10 562	4 721	2 385
1984	62 423	61 485	938	42 670	2 234	789	41 225	12 596	8 603	13 182	11 589	4 736	2 478
1985	65 733	64 805	928	44 997	2 455	877	43 420	13 140	9 173	13 845	12 170	4 748	2 510
1986	69 101	67 894	1 207	47 577	2 633	959	45 903	13 685	9 513	14 530	12 761	4 756	2 552
1987	73 378	72 141	1 237	50 971	2 815	1 067	49 224	14 362	9 792	15 358	13 456	4 778	2 621
1988	78 126	77 395	730	54 667	3 189	1 228	52 706	15 281	10 138	16 201	14 180	4 822	2 702
1989	84 013	82 466	1 548	58 482	3 486	1 265	56 261	16 953	10 799	17 299	15 074	4 857	2 760
1990	89 025	87 887	1 139	61 930	3 713	1 361	59 577	17 815	11 632	18 152	15 809	4 905	2 835
1991	92 669	91 966	703	64 143	3 951	1 398	61 590	18 322	12 758	18 667	16 272	4 964	2 861
1992	99 454	98 620	834	69 647	4 234	1 491	66 904	18 730	13 819	19 790	17 260	5 025	2 916
1993	104 337	103 772	565	73 544	4 469	1 584	70 659	19 207	14 471	20 519	17 855	5 085	2 974
1994	110 570	109 902	668	78 106	4 827	1 691	74 971	20 716	14 883	21 538	18 662	5 134	3 067
1995	115 960	115 505	455	81 482	5 105	1 751	78 127	22 104	15 728	22 365	19 336	5 185	3 148
1996	121 864	121 023	841	85 206	5 304	1 927	81 828	23 838	16 198	23 301	19 979	5 230	3 201
1997	128 920	128 481	440	89 685	5 656	2 125	86 155	25 923	16 842	24 481	20 837	5 266	3 258
1998	137 759	136 896	863	95 895	5 942	2 282	92 235	28 407	17 117	26 004	22 041	5 298	3 316
1999	143 589	142 698	891	101 772	6 336	2 456	97 891	28 015	17 683	26 926	22 806	5 333	3 382
2000	152 572	152 164	407	106 673	6 565	2 597	102 706	31 042	18 824	28 389	24 213	5 374	3 441
2001	157 832	157 286	546	109 312	6 799	2 721	105 233	31 743	20 855	29 196	25 026	5 406	3 430
2002	163 216	162 758	458	112 427	7 110	2 956	108 273	31 970	22 973	29 996	26 336	5 441	. . .
WYOMING													
1972	1 633	1 500	134	1 304	47	-3	1 253	251	130	4 709	4 251	347	172
1973	1 912	1 752	159	1 533	63	-7	1 463	298	151	5 410	4 814	353	182
1974	2 250	2 133	117	1 813	76	-13	1 723	356	171	6 172	5 393	365	194
1975	2 550	2 479	71	2 053	87	-16	1 950	396	204	6 701	5 945	380	203
1976	2 852	2 802	50	2 299	100	-23	2 176	448	229	7 212	6 342	395	214
1977	3 355	3 309	46	2 728	116	-30	2 582	518	255	8 152	7 169	412	231
1978	4 044	3 974	69	3 313	144	-39	3 130	628	286	9 384	8 225	431	250
1979	4 777	4 678	99	3 916	178	-56	3 682	766	329	10 572	9 122	452	267
1980	5 573	5 487	86	4 537	208	-77	4 253	929	392	11 753	10 166	474	280
1981	6 333	6 282	51	5 075	257	-87	4 731	1 132	470	12 879	11 051	492	290
1982	6 710	6 678	33	5 138	268	-83	4 787	1 383	541	13 251	11 545	506	288
1983	6 493	6 450	43	4 897	247	-61	4 589	1 265	638	12 723	11 229	510	275
1984	6 812	6 795	18	5 103	257	-55	4 791	1 400	621	13 493	12 020	505	277
1985	7 117	7 096	21	5 331	282	-54	4 995	1 463	659	14 242	12 704	500	278
1986	6 941	6 900	41	5 094	278	-42	4 774	1 439	727	14 004	12 616	496	265
1987	6 770	6 712	57	4 868	270	-27	4 570	1 460	740	14 194	12 757	477	260
1988	6 962	6 914	48	4 989	296	-22	4 670	1 526	765	14 968	13 467	465	265
1989	7 510	7 429	81	5 286	313	-16	4 957	1 733	820	16 383	14 612	458	267
1990	8 159	8 014	145	5 716	337	-12	5 367	1 907	885	17 985	16 067	454	272
1991	8 636	8 421	215	6 021	362	-4	5 655	1 995	986	18 805	16 873	459	279
1992	9 061	8 861	200	6 301	381	-13	5 907	2 062	1 092	19 434	17 412	466	282
1993	9 515	9 271	244	6 708	398	-17	6 293	2 047	1 176	20 113	17 948	473	287
1994	9 954	9 856	98	6 911	423	-20	6 468	2 245	1 241	20 726	18 457	480	300
1995	10 293	10 204	90	7 034	437	-20	6 577	2 404	1 312	21 216	18 881	485	303
1996	10 609	10 545	64	7 116	447	-19	6 650	2 567	1 393	21 732	18 861	488	306
1997	11 433	11 258	175	7 574	464	-17	7 093	2 898	1 442	23 360	20 199	489	310
1998	12 129	12 065	65	7 905	493	-19	7 393	3 264	1 472	24 714	21 324	491	316
1999	12 931	12 782	149	8 468	513	-23	7 932	3 479	1 520	26 294	22 619	492	319
2000	13 805	13 710	96	9 006	538	-33	8 434	3 771	1 600	27 941	23 796	494	329
2001	14 609	14 475	134	9 625	582	-40	9 004	3 876	1 729	29 587	25 283	494	336
2002	15 208	15 160	48	10 034	624	-46	9 364	3 957	1 887	30 494	26 734	499	. . .

. . . = Not available.

Table 21-2. Personal Income and Employment by State and Region—Continued

(Millions of dollars, except as noted.)

Year	Total	Nonfarm	Farm	Earnings by place of work	Less: Personal contributions for social insurance	Plus: Adjustment for residence	Equals: Net earnings by place of residence	Dividends, interest, and rent	Transfer payments	Per capita Personal income	Per capita Disposable personal income	Population (thousands)	Total employment (thousands)
NEW ENGLAND													
1972	60 814	60 496	318	46 102	1 593	936	45 446	8 964	6 404	5 031	4 366	12 088	5 573
1973	66 688	66 264	423	50 689	2 013	993	49 668	9 874	7 145	5 490	4 794	12 148	5 783
1974	72 577	72 122	455	54 235	2 251	1 079	53 063	11 043	8 472	5 970	5 206	12 157	5 843
1975	77 479	77 146	333	56 334	2 307	1 166	55 194	11 291	10 994	6 363	5 629	12 176	5 685
1976	84 948	84 498	449	62 310	2 507	1 296	61 099	12 280	11 568	6 959	6 113	12 207	5 811
1977	93 301	92 899	402	68 762	2 757	1 449	67 454	13 723	12 124	7 612	6 672	12 257	6 007
1978	104 140	103 725	415	77 318	3 149	1 632	75 802	15 560	12 778	8 465	7 376	12 303	6 280
1979	117 069	116 679	390	86 580	3 720	1 864	84 724	18 147	14 197	9 483	8 204	12 345	6 515
1980	132 395	132 022	373	96 056	4 196	2 179	94 039	21 984	16 372	10 701	9 226	12 372	6 641
1981	147 774	147 297	477	104 799	4 992	2 350	102 156	26 883	18 735	11 883	10 175	12 436	6 692
1982	159 591	159 075	515	112 092	5 507	2 527	109 112	29 967	20 512	12 800	11 007	12 468	6 694
1983	172 548	172 059	489	122 565	6 026	2 660	119 199	31 496	21 853	13 755	11 956	12 544	6 828
1984	193 939	193 366	573	138 186	6 840	2 838	134 184	37 148	22 607	15 341	13 402	12 642	7 198
1985	209 851	209 280	571	151 686	7 844	2 993	146 834	39 276	23 741	16 471	14 292	12 741	7 447
1986	226 352	225 762	590	164 823	8 737	3 166	159 253	41 972	25 127	17 638	15 220	12 833	7 688
1987	248 095	247 457	638	182 438	9 677	3 338	176 099	45 903	26 093	19 156	16 426	12 951	7 829
1988	273 667	273 000	667	201 642	10 957	3 535	194 219	51 318	28 129	20 915	18 145	13 085	8 082
1989	292 630	291 981	648	211 282	11 686	3 463	203 059	58 162	31 408	22 200	19 216	13 182	8 075
1990	302 739	302 066	673	215 956	12 028	3 461	207 390	60 167	35 182	22 884	19 860	13 230	7 920
1991	307 013	306 401	612	215 264	12 379	3 526	206 412	59 755	40 846	23 175	20 185	13 248	7 586
1992	322 471	321 678	793	227 711	12 935	4 167	218 942	59 208	44 320	24 299	21 135	13 271	7 628
1993	333 140	332 409	731	236 243	13 519	4 163	226 887	60 401	45 852	24 984	21 651	13 334	7 754
1994	347 347	346 670	677	246 210	14 355	4 219	236 073	63 068	48 206	25 928	22 428	13 396	7 854
1995	364 297	363 698	599	257 171	15 269	4 835	246 737	66 382	51 178	27 040	23 232	13 473	7 950
1996	384 144	383 456	687	271 302	15 958	5 615	260 959	70 663	52 522	28 340	24 091	13 555	8 085
1997	408 231	407 648	583	288 822	17 141	5 651	277 332	75 796	55 103	29 924	25 114	13 642	8 252
1998	437 134	436 529	606	309 563	18 220	6 809	298 160	83 326	55 648	31 829	26 505	13 734	8 424
1999	459 782	459 109	672	331 994	19 566	6 774	319 201	83 490	57 090	33 227	27 450	13 838	8 568
2000	505 001	504 371	629	364 251	21 187	7 303	350 368	94 611	60 022	36 195	29 458	13 952	8 788
2001	521 283	520 699	584	373 322	21 950	7 253	358 625	97 534	65 124	37 096	30 580	14 052	8 817
2002	530 315	529 819	496	374 158	22 341	8 336	360 153	98 483	71 679	37 494	32 062	14 144	. . .
MIDEAST													
1972	227 051	225 946	1 105	180 314	6 582	-1 931	171 800	30 816	24 435	5 281	4 551	42 992	19 526
1973	246 658	245 151	1 507	195 779	8 212	-2 072	185 495	34 005	27 157	5 758	4 993	42 837	19 973
1974	268 578	267 157	1 421	210 268	9 155	-2 310	198 803	38 148	31 628	6 289	5 431	42 709	19 960
1975	288 774	287 457	1 317	221 455	9 538	-2 638	209 279	39 499	39 996	6 758	5 921	42 728	19 485
1976	313 712	312 326	1 385	240 559	10 174	-2 994	227 391	42 956	43 365	7 352	6 412	42 667	19 568
1977	342 391	341 203	1 189	262 663	10 995	-3 404	248 265	48 027	46 099	8 047	6 981	42 547	19 855
1978	377 206	375 794	1 412	290 408	12 349	-3 934	274 125	54 318	48 763	8 892	7 689	42 421	20 411
1979	417 293	415 690	1 603	319 530	14 253	-4 605	300 672	63 233	53 388	9 852	8 462	42 358	20 900
1980	464 044	462 844	1 201	348 481	15 739	-5 473	327 269	75 193	61 582	10 978	9 421	42 272	20 962
1981	515 105	513 548	1 557	379 378	18 582	-6 082	354 713	91 078	69 314	12 169	10 357	42 329	21 061
1982	553 286	551 817	1 470	401 514	20 106	-6 350	375 058	101 111	77 117	13 055	11 125	42 382	20 946
1983	590 053	588 954	1 099	427 182	21 683	-6 470	399 029	107 841	83 183	13 869	11 980	42 544	21 141
1984	651 738	649 883	1 855	471 299	24 147	-6 816	440 336	125 820	85 582	15 268	13 221	42 687	21 891
1985	697 625	695 663	1 962	507 549	27 436	-7 129	472 985	134 559	90 081	16 302	14 049	42 794	22 486
1986	742 758	740 592	2 166	544 020	30 233	-7 543	506 244	140 960	95 554	17 277	14 880	42 991	22 999
1987	797 956	795 743	2 213	590 732	32 850	-8 052	549 830	149 549	98 576	18 476	15 780	43 190	23 509
1988	868 357	866 285	2 073	645 084	37 286	-8 772	599 026	164 872	104 459	19 992	17 238	43 435	24 127
1989	932 472	930 030	2 442	679 925	40 057	-9 048	630 820	188 984	112 669	21 394	18 352	43 585	24 421
1990	988 666	986 357	2 309	719 024	42 372	-9 826	666 827	198 234	123 605	22 592	19 498	43 762	24 482
1991	1 018 680	1 016 844	1 836	729 727	44 083	-10 351	675 293	202 569	140 818	23 115	20 053	44 071	23 912
1992	1 074 930	1 072 589	2 341	776 549	46 277	-11 377	718 895	198 203	157 832	24 214	21 047	44 392	23 816
1993	1 103 630	1 101 296	2 334	799 480	47 904	-11 746	739 830	197 158	166 642	24 680	21 381	44 717	23 946
1994	1 140 466	1 138 446	2 020	823 463	50 412	-11 988	761 064	206 642	172 760	25 361	21 907	44 970	24 134
1995	1 193 865	1 192 233	1 632	857 650	52 928	-12 858	791 864	219 638	182 363	26 421	22 777	45 186	24 430
1996	1 255 345	1 252 958	2 388	901 579	54 807	-13 486	833 286	230 897	191 162	27 661	23 647	45 384	24 670
1997	1 315 810	1 314 315	1 495	946 156	57 684	-14 195	874 277	246 079	195 454	28 868	24 452	45 580	25 069
1998	1 400 562	1 398 633	1 929	1 010 318	60 805	-15 290	934 223	266 678	199 661	30 565	25 714	45 822	25 514
1999	1 458 307	1 456 176	2 130	1 068 235	64 507	-16 578	987 149	265 052	206 106	31 630	26 419	46 106	25 960
2000	1 577 854	1 575 546	2 308	1 154 345	68 684	-16 476	1 069 185	293 347	215 323	34 013	28 307	46 390	26 636
2001	1 630 698	1 628 230	2 468	1 186 684	71 592	-17 198	1 097 894	301 629	231 175	34 952	29 235	46 655	26 667
2002	1 662 520	1 660 631	1 890	1 198 021	73 407	-18 493	1 106 122	304 413	251 985	35 434	30 521	46 919	. . .

. . . = Not available.

Table 21-2. Personal Income and Employment by State and Region—*Continued*

(Millions of dollars, except as noted.)

Year	Total	Nonfarm	Farm	Earnings by place of work	Less: Personal contributions for social insurance	Plus: Adjustment for residence	Equals: Net earnings by place of residence	Dividends, interest, and rent	Transfer payments	Personal income	Disposable personal income	Population (thousands)	Total employment (thousands)
GREAT LAKES													
1972	198 768	195 300	3 468	160 791	5 667	373	155 497	25 290	17 981	4 869	4 221	40 824	17 933
1973	223 387	217 934	5 453	180 831	7 281	422	173 973	28 608	20 807	5 456	4 758	40 947	18 710
1974	243 198	238 293	4 904	193 498	8 150	521	185 869	32 579	24 750	5 926	5 152	41 037	18 911
1975	260 632	254 629	6 002	202 175	8 340	613	194 448	34 623	31 561	6 341	5 581	41 105	18 399
1976	289 377	284 375	5 002	226 235	9 271	760	217 724	37 773	33 881	7 026	6 130	41 187	18 891
1977	322 534	317 463	5 071	253 804	10 301	942	244 445	42 300	35 788	7 799	6 771	41 353	19 508
1978	359 263	354 489	4 774	283 289	11 744	1 165	272 710	48 213	38 340	8 655	7 479	41 510	20 196
1979	398 184	392 849	5 335	310 693	13 535	1 381	298 539	56 419	43 226	9 569	8 241	41 611	20 521
1980	431 511	428 174	3 337	321 969	14 239	1 657	309 387	67 718	54 405	10 350	8 971	41 694	20 024
1981	469 882	466 040	3 842	342 782	16 503	1 409	327 688	81 737	60 458	11 282	9 733	41 648	19 862
1982	487 227	484 426	2 801	345 336	17 044	1 309	329 601	89 672	67 953	11 743	10 248	41 492	19 316
1983	510 969	511 221	-252	359 931	17 895	1 288	343 323	95 130	72 516	12 352	10 814	41 366	19 336
1984	565 164	561 183	3 981	401 826	19 920	1 390	383 295	108 446	73 423	13 654	12 012	41 393	20 120
1985	601 455	597 045	4 410	429 809	22 359	1 424	408 873	114 720	77 861	14 522	12 730	41 418	20 607
1986	632 297	628 399	3 898	452 844	24 165	1 490	430 168	120 220	81 909	15 253	13 386	41 455	21 053
1987	667 441	663 124	4 317	481 026	25 703	1 561	456 884	125 863	84 694	16 048	13 999	41 590	21 654
1988	713 443	710 869	2 574	517 776	28 797	1 671	490 650	134 595	88 197	17 100	14 978	41 721	22 222
1989	762 815	756 678	6 137	547 876	31 208	1 711	518 378	149 984	94 454	18 218	15 853	41 873	22 724
1990	805 743	800 787	4 956	576 428	32 932	1 928	545 424	158 105	102 214	19 143	16 693	42 091	23 105
1991	831 381	828 912	2 469	590 079	34 673	1 942	557 347	160 894	113 140	19 564	17 122	42 496	23 016
1992	888 017	883 617	4 400	635 000	36 574	2 103	600 529	162 767	124 721	20 698	18 192	42 903	23 152
1993	929 524	925 601	3 923	668 357	38 706	2 291	631 942	166 532	131 050	21 480	18 785	43 275	23 552
1994	984 893	980 427	4 466	709 226	41 925	2 496	669 797	180 355	134 741	22 594	19 691	43 590	24 277
1995	1 034 159	1 031 650	2 510	743 162	44 362	2 662	701 462	191 054	141 643	23 544	20 444	43 924	24 945
1996	1 079 799	1 074 406	5 393	771 735	46 015	2 924	728 644	203 690	147 465	24 408	21 032	44 239	25 355
1997	1 138 557	1 133 273	5 284	812 223	48 801	3 267	766 688	217 889	153 980	25 589	21 924	44 494	25 783
1998	1 206 886	1 202 690	4 196	863 328	51 319	3 386	815 395	236 643	154 848	26 983	23 011	44 728	26 237
1999	1 252 336	1 249 004	3 332	910 672	54 179	3 826	860 319	232 405	159 612	27 849	23 721	44 969	26 616
2000	1 331 356	1 328 063	3 293	958 868	56 076	4 191	906 983	256 300	168 073	29 437	25 111	45 227	27 074
2001	1 362 854	1 359 433	3 421	969 643	57 344	4 461	916 760	262 615	183 479	29 986	25 634	45 449	26 811
2002	1 395 541	1 393 345	2 196	983 682	59 152	5 820	930 350	264 737	200 454	30 555	26 764	45 673	. . .
PLAINS													
1972	74 607	68 361	6 246	59 525	2 154	-357	57 014	10 342	7 252	4 505	3 965	16 563	7 731
1973	87 538	76 209	11 329	70 369	2 746	-393	67 230	11 919	8 389	5 264	4 675	16 628	8 065
1974	92 855	85 130	7 725	72 882	3 145	-425	69 312	13 770	9 772	5 570	4 865	16 672	8 219
1975	101 249	93 722	7 527	78 086	3 358	-415	74 313	15 007	11 929	6 047	5 347	16 743	8 181
1976	109 419	104 990	4 429	84 120	3 703	-512	79 905	16 478	13 036	6 488	5 701	16 864	8 439
1977	121 538	116 314	5 223	93 431	3 989	-650	88 792	18 803	13 942	7 171	6 291	16 950	8 657
1978	138 372	130 481	7 891	107 071	4 607	-808	101 656	21 588	15 129	8 126	7 114	17 028	8 958
1979	153 711	147 042	6 669	117 812	5 416	-975	111 420	25 398	16 893	8 990	7 810	17 097	9 248
1980	165 837	164 088	1 749	121 862	5 896	-1 128	114 838	30 767	20 232	9 637	8 365	17 208	9 251
1981	187 045	181 684	5 361	134 531	6 841	-1 323	126 367	37 647	23 031	10 834	9 377	17 264	9 212
1982	197 115	193 403	3 713	137 443	7 277	-1 329	128 837	42 575	25 703	11 399	9 864	17 292	9 083
1983	206 081	204 948	1 133	143 077	7 666	-1 417	133 995	44 490	27 596	11 895	10 442	17 325	9 196
1984	230 380	224 434	5 946	162 690	8 494	-1 585	152 612	49 370	28 398	13 254	11 752	17 382	9 513
1985	243 973	237 200	6 773	173 003	9 463	-1 691	161 849	51 708	30 415	14 020	12 414	17 402	9 664
1986	254 901	247 568	7 333	181 170	10 175	-1 804	169 191	53 633	32 078	14 656	13 011	17 393	9 755
1987	269 737	260 619	9 118	194 045	10 924	-1 919	181 202	55 235	33 300	15 477	13 660	17 428	10 011
1988	283 039	276 440	6 599	204 239	12 213	-2 075	189 951	58 129	34 959	16 143	14 258	17 533	10 223
1989	303 631	295 224	8 407	217 324	13 254	-2 160	201 910	64 162	37 560	17 256	15 167	17 595	10 430
1990	322 236	312 741	9 494	230 182	14 050	-2 432	213 700	68 011	40 524	18 208	15 999	17 698	10 619
1991	335 351	328 184	7 167	236 861	14 880	-2 464	219 517	70 675	45 159	18 794	16 581	17 843	10 670
1992	357 609	348 443	9 166	255 768	15 707	-2 586	237 475	71 208	48 925	19 838	17 526	18 026	10 787
1993	368 899	363 685	5 213	263 503	16 510	-2 730	244 264	72 417	52 217	20 258	17 836	18 210	11 021
1994	393 000	384 212	8 788	282 034	17 766	-2 889	261 378	77 366	54 256	21 381	18 802	18 381	11 328
1995	410 645	405 532	5 113	292 414	18 754	-3 037	270 623	82 657	57 364	22 138	19 376	18 550	11 640
1996	439 948	427 804	12 144	314 677	19 621	-3 196	291 860	88 237	59 852	23 520	20 466	18 705	11 871
1997	462 173	453 353	8 819	329 136	20 806	-3 545	304 786	95 014	62 373	24 517	21 199	18 851	12 102
1998	493 714	485 634	8 080	351 186	21 984	-3 751	325 451	104 573	63 691	26 001	22 420	18 988	12 365
1999	512 453	505 233	7 220	371 012	23 198	-4 040	343 774	102 670	66 009	26 787	23 113	19 131	12 542
2000	547 878	540 974	6 904	393 325	24 225	-4 376	364 725	113 208	69 946	28 430	24 472	19 271	12 740
2001	566 738	561 043	5 695	403 792	25 291	-4 449	374 051	116 332	76 354	29 257	25 231	19 371	12 738
2002	582 958	577 185	5 772	413 669	26 376	-5 446	381 847	117 631	83 480	29 942	26 377	19 469	. . .

. . . = Not available.

Table 21-2. Personal Income and Employment by State and Region—*Continued*

(Millions of dollars, except as noted.)

Year	Total	Nonfarm	Farm	Derivation of personal income						Per capita (dollars)		Population (thousands)	Total employment (thousands)
				Earnings by place of work	Less: Personal contributions for social insurance	Plus: Adjustment for residence	Equals: Net earnings by place of residence	Dividends, interest, and rent	Transfer payments	Personal income	Disposable personal income		
SOUTHEAST													
1972	181 809	176 449	5 360	144 697	5 141	1 046	140 602	22 778	18 429	3 951	3 484	46 019	20 523
1973	207 663	200 031	7 632	164 967	6 650	1 117	159 434	26 539	21 690	4 419	3 920	46 992	21 636
1974	232 035	225 036	6 999	181 226	7 642	1 235	174 819	31 037	26 179	4 839	4 275	47 955	22 069
1975	252 583	246 321	6 262	191 935	8 023	1 476	185 387	33 500	33 695	5 177	4 654	48 788	21 642
1976	283 155	276 573	6 582	216 260	8 963	1 666	208 963	37 231	36 961	5 719	5 103	49 514	22 351
1977	315 802	309 850	5 952	241 594	9 988	1 901	233 507	42 451	39 844	6 277	5 585	50 312	23 208
1978	360 348	353 191	7 157	275 962	11 567	2 208	266 603	50 246	43 499	7 050	6 243	51 113	24 309
1979	408 144	401 042	7 102	308 456	13 586	2 576	297 446	60 687	50 012	7 852	6 915	51 977	25 020
1980	460 761	456 322	4 439	337 984	15 221	3 125	325 888	75 091	59 782	8 713	7 666	52 881	25 378
1981	520 469	513 582	6 887	374 242	18 237	3 553	359 558	92 690	68 221	9 705	8 505	53 627	25 676
1982	556 531	549 701	6 829	393 118	19 745	3 777	377 149	103 552	75 829	10 259	9 028	54 249	25 577
1983	598 511	593 514	4 996	421 282	21 401	3 835	403 716	112 354	82 441	10 911	9 674	54 856	26 111
1984	669 482	661 122	8 361	474 255	24 026	4 025	454 254	129 517	85 711	12 060	10 768	55 515	27 394
1985	722 928	715 546	7 382	511 589	27 278	4 230	488 541	142 049	92 338	12 864	11 419	56 199	28 241
1986	768 564	761 773	6 791	543 241	29 790	4 450	517 901	151 720	98 943	13 517	12 002	56 861	28 986
1987	825 358	817 279	8 079	587 548	32 122	4 761	560 187	161 446	103 725	14 345	12 684	57 536	29 715
1988	894 629	884 124	10 505	636 703	36 272	5 241	605 672	177 944	111 013	15 393	13 676	58 120	30 733
1989	968 835	957 836	10 999	675 927	39 632	5 603	641 898	204 806	122 131	16 495	14 585	58 733	31 480
1990	1 035 261	1 025 106	10 155	717 193	42 120	6 348	681 421	218 552	135 288	17 395	15 431	59 516	32 078
1991	1 083 034	1 071 067	11 967	743 742	44 635	6 828	705 935	223 972	153 127	17 901	15 950	60 501	31 954
1992	1 153 443	1 140 995	12 448	800 898	47 467	7 109	760 539	220 385	172 519	18 753	16 720	61 508	32 440
1993	1 218 508	1 206 260	12 248	844 983	50 584	7 393	801 792	230 336	186 380	19 487	17 342	62 531	33 474
1994	1 289 941	1 276 593	13 347	893 298	54 626	7 469	846 141	246 622	197 178	20 290	17 995	63 574	34 464
1995	1 366 116	1 354 202	11 913	940 896	58 170	7 715	890 441	264 061	211 614	21 147	18 702	64 602	35 597
1996	1 445 912	1 432 636	13 276	992 020	60 767	7 494	938 747	283 021	224 144	22 038	19 348	65 611	36 465
1997	1 532 165	1 518 878	13 287	1 050 277	64 550	8 196	993 923	303 667	234 576	22 986	20 044	66 655	37 465
1998	1 639 428	1 627 176	12 252	1 124 117	68 593	8 198	1 063 722	335 100	240 607	24 242	21 056	67 627	38 485
1999	1 718 850	1 705 786	13 065	1 200 070	72 947	9 351	1 136 473	333 834	248 543	25 067	21 725	68 569	39 306
2000	1 838 870	1 827 314	11 556	1 277 950	76 637	8 727	1 210 040	365 624	263 206	26 456	22 894	69 506	40 144
2001	1 911 543	1 899 341	12 202	1 319 578	80 265	9 302	1 248 615	373 684	289 244	27 169	23 562	70 357	40 130
2002	1 972 043	1 962 240	9 804	1 352 318	83 801	8 733	1 277 250	377 532	317 262	27 683	24 562	71 237	. . .
SOUTHWEST													
1972	73 036	70 905	2 131	58 935	2 015	-108	56 813	9 626	6 597	4 173	3 697	17 503	7 807
1973	83 516	80 110	3 406	67 270	2 633	-121	64 517	11 217	7 782	4 655	4 145	17 943	8 215
1974	94 357	92 116	2 241	75 063	3 087	-82	71 893	13 188	9 275	5 141	4 535	18 354	8 511
1975	105 799	103 614	2 185	83 439	3 381	-50	80 009	14 174	11 616	5 631	5 037	18 789	8 633
1976	119 822	117 682	2 140	95 168	3 993	21	91 391	15 629	12 803	6 218	5 528	19 270	9 001
1977	134 513	132 608	1 905	107 580	4 331	-225	103 024	17 709	13 781	6 825	6 023	19 710	9 467
1978	155 988	154 250	1 738	124 809	5 123	-363	119 323	21 449	15 216	7 730	6 810	20 180	10 043
1979	181 662	178 582	3 080	144 749	6 229	-356	138 164	26 178	17 320	8 744	7 634	20 777	10 539
1980	209 160	207 480	1 680	163 935	7 270	-459	156 206	32 565	20 388	9 762	8 493	21 426	10 944
1981	244 433	241 451	2 982	189 886	9 102	-188	180 596	40 640	23 198	11 118	9 564	21 985	11 485
1982	266 387	264 076	2 311	203 760	10 049	-252	193 459	46 654	26 274	11 688	10 113	22 791	11 717
1983	281 428	279 127	2 301	212 804	10 386	-182	202 237	49 925	29 266	12 024	10 605	23 405	11 746
1984	311 524	308 835	2 688	234 687	11 433	-183	223 071	57 903	30 549	13 102	11 631	23 776	12 309
1985	335 615	332 990	2 625	251 678	12 815	-150	238 713	64 000	32 902	13 888	12 322	24 166	12 685
1986	343 547	340 994	2 553	254 649	13 272	-36	241 341	66 092	36 114	13 974	12 520	24 585	12 552
1987	354 762	351 389	3 373	262 257	13 566	55	248 746	67 550	38 467	14 335	12 785	24 748	12 861
1988	376 245	372 527	3 717	278 357	15 066	153	263 443	72 058	40 744	15 135	13 562	24 860	13 138
1989	403 626	399 848	3 778	295 149	16 392	234	278 991	79 753	44 882	16 092	14 348	25 083	13 334
1990	434 654	430 059	4 595	318 842	17 725	336	301 453	83 530	49 671	17 105	15 239	25 411	13 650
1991	458 108	453 637	4 471	335 995	19 211	284	317 068	85 228	55 811	17 676	15 826	25 917	13 856
1992	490 173	485 190	4 983	360 614	20 457	332	340 489	84 793	64 891	18 503	16 607	26 491	13 994
1993	517 898	511 920	5 978	383 890	21 849	367	362 408	85 897	69 592	19 099	17 116	27 116	14 453
1994	550 067	545 095	4 971	406 229	23 648	381	382 963	92 708	74 396	19 806	17 723	27 772	14 984
1995	586 017	582 066	3 950	430 820	25 449	360	405 731	99 555	80 731	20 620	18 414	28 420	15 543
1996	624 034	620 638	3 396	459 386	27 037	354	432 703	105 799	85 532	21 504	19 051	29 020	16 046
1997	677 462	672 830	4 632	501 361	29 251	321	472 430	115 195	89 837	22 868	20 137	29 625	16 663
1998	736 392	731 797	4 595	548 989	31 586	345	517 748	126 652	91 992	24 352	21 354	30 240	17 259
1999	775 029	768 153	6 876	587 845	33 625	425	554 646	125 005	95 378	25 141	22 034	30 827	17 599
2000	840 256	835 620	4 637	637 239	35 992	451	601 698	138 258	100 301	26 761	23 343	31 399	18 121
2001	874 607	869 784	4 823	661 301	37 932	411	623 780	140 239	110 588	27 350	23 946	31 978	18 302
2002	893 454	888 522	4 932	668 456	39 068	583	629 971	141 302	122 181	27 419	24 573	32 585	. . .

. . . = Not available.

Table 21-2. Personal Income and Employment by State and Region—*Continued*

(Millions of dollars, except as noted.)

Year	Total	Nonfarm	Farm	Earnings by place of work	Less: Personal contributions for social insurance	Plus: Adjustment for residence	Equals: Net earnings by place of residence	Dividends, interest, and rent	Transfer payments	Per capita (dollars) Personal income	Per capita (dollars) Disposable personal income	Population (thousands)	Total employment (thousands)
ROCKY MOUNTAIN													
1972	23 967	22 629	1 338	19 193	634	22	18 582	3 293	2 093	4 464	3 946	5 368	2 482
1973	27 549	25 739	1 810	22 092	831	22	21 283	3 839	2 427	4 984	4 404	5 527	2 646
1974	31 152	29 252	1 900	24 807	961	25	23 872	4 466	2 814	5 514	4 846	5 650	2 740
1975	34 227	32 787	1 441	26 906	1 041	36	25 901	4 861	3 465	5 920	5 264	5 782	2 778
1976	38 246	37 175	1 072	30 072	1 164	42	28 950	5 458	3 838	6 465	5 714	5 916	2 912
1977	42 955	42 237	718	33 809	1 324	44	32 529	6 267	4 159	7 066	6 215	6 079	3 060
1978	49 995	48 994	1 001	39 511	1 560	54	38 005	7 458	4 533	7 990	7 019	6 257	3 257
1979	57 057	56 299	758	44 681	1 892	55	42 843	9 088	5 126	8 861	7 732	6 439	3 406
1980	64 971	64 009	962	49 930	2 146	78	47 862	11 076	6 033	9 856	8 611	6 592	3 482
1981	73 763	72 801	961	55 794	2 620	51	53 225	13 509	7 029	10 940	9 500	6 743	3 571
1982	79 572	78 782	790	59 026	2 859	53	56 220	15 342	8 010	11 526	10 028	6 904	3 608
1983	84 615	83 493	1 122	62 451	2 994	55	59 513	16 319	8 784	12 028	10 646	7 035	3 654
1984	92 374	91 323	1 051	68 178	3 288	74	64 964	18 376	9 034	12 994	11 560	7 109	3 817
1985	97 408	96 548	860	71 811	3 654	91	68 248	19 583	9 577	13 590	12 063	7 168	3 882
1986	100 304	99 128	1 236	73 554	3 836	114	69 832	20 175	10 358	13 940	12 415	7 200	3 876
1987	104 390	102 868	1 523	76 341	3 950	139	72 530	20 776	11 084	14 487	12 857	7 206	3 909
1988	109 620	108 076	1 544	80 366	4 386	177	76 157	21 805	11 659	15 220	13 512	7 203	4 047
1989	118 525	116 372	2 153	85 873	4 768	211	81 317	24 527	12 682	16 384	14 463	7 234	4 143
1990	127 663	125 019	2 645	92 804	5 148	246	87 903	25 878	13 882	17 476	15 388	7 305	4 261
1991	135 540	133 113	2 427	98 671	5 637	252	93 285	26 800	15 455	18 127	15 987	7 477	4 365
1992	145 514	143 199	2 315	106 971	6 065	254	101 160	27 126	17 228	18 907	16 640	7 696	4 469
1993	156 962	153 734	3 227	116 438	6 570	262	110 130	28 208	18 623	19 772	17 363	7 939	4 664
1994	167 291	165 456	1 835	123 392	7 155	287	116 524	31 334	19 433	20 473	17 902	8 171	4 931
1995	179 684	177 765	1 919	131 583	7 680	322	124 225	34 274	21 184	21 442	18 740	8 380	5 093
1996	192 141	190 151	1 990	140 581	8 156	367	132 791	36 959	22 391	22 432	19 446	8 565	5 299
1997	206 847	204 996	1 851	151 388	8 747	393	143 035	40 559	23 253	23 651	20 375	8 746	5 495
1998	223 322	221 039	2 283	164 381	9 376	430	155 434	44 289	23 598	25 041	21 498	8 918	5 683
1999	238 547	235 782	2 765	179 426	10 112	467	169 781	44 286	24 480	26 230	22 405	9 094	5 826
2000	261 286	259 475	1 812	196 509	10 968	520	186 061	49 223	26 002	28 194	23 950	9 267	6 027
2001	271 743	269 396	2 347	203 388	11 465	530	192 452	50 853	28 438	28 819	24 621	9 429	6 092
2002	276 877	274 657	2 220	205 152	11 750	526	193 928	51 559	31 390	28 926	25 333	9 572	. . .
FAR WEST													
1972	148 309	145 089	3 220	116 081	4 106	-212	111 763	21 575	14 971	5 312	4 677	27 918	12 742
1973	164 994	160 655	4 339	129 109	5 190	-212	123 707	24 538	16 749	5 824	5 169	28 328	13 405
1974	185 428	179 944	5 484	143 828	5 940	-307	137 581	28 045	19 802	6 438	5 694	28 801	13 865
1975	205 471	200 585	4 887	157 719	6 431	-501	150 787	29 966	24 718	7 002	6 262	29 346	14 103
1976	231 073	226 212	4 861	178 378	7 181	-618	170 579	33 119	27 375	7 721	6 847	29 929	14 625
1977	257 866	253 132	4 734	199 327	8 106	-434	190 788	37 697	29 382	8 440	7 442	30 553	15 287
1978	296 027	291 211	4 816	228 519	9 415	-365	218 739	45 567	31 721	9 462	8 297	31 285	16 235
1979	339 719	333 708	6 011	260 277	11 292	-338	248 648	56 173	34 898	10 628	9 268	31 965	17 141
1980	385 242	377 678	7 564	289 693	12 281	-434	276 979	67 268	40 995	11 752	10 250	32 780	17 549
1981	429 865	423 945	5 920	315 231	14 894	-212	300 124	81 702	48 039	12 857	11 219	33 434	17 744
1982	457 245	451 227	6 017	332 069	16 178	-255	315 636	88 307	53 301	13 414	11 802	34 086	17 618
1983	490 834	484 801	6 033	357 260	17 616	-278	339 366	94 357	57 112	14 138	12 481	34 716	18 045
1984	545 463	538 740	6 723	398 033	19 832	-323	377 878	108 858	58 727	15 443	13 648	35 321	18 848
1985	589 808	583 353	6 456	431 274	22 292	-370	408 613	116 796	64 399	16 367	14 393	36 037	19 499
1986	628 576	621 164	7 412	462 317	24 832	-412	437 073	122 383	69 120	17 074	15 011	36 815	20 072
1987	677 776	669 314	8 462	502 431	27 502	-492	474 436	130 748	72 591	18 006	15 682	37 641	20 929
1988	736 000	727 078	8 922	547 385	31 257	-580	515 548	142 715	77 738	19 096	16 763	38 542	21 946
1989	799 895	791 101	8 793	589 259	33 914	-678	554 667	160 690	84 538	20 233	17 585	39 534	22 634
1990	868 563	859 505	9 058	637 951	36 562	-797	600 592	173 577	94 394	21 388	18 649	40 610	23 312
1991	896 310	888 350	7 960	654 856	38 740	-806	615 310	175 539	105 460	21 635	18 997	41 428	23 305
1992	944 465	935 637	8 828	690 395	40 469	-799	649 127	174 139	121 199	22 367	19 756	42 226	23 019
1993	969 886	959 940	9 947	706 595	41 623	-798	664 174	177 510	128 202	22 662	19 999	42 798	23 134
1994	1 005 357	996 031	9 326	728 526	43 657	-834	684 034	188 517	132 805	23 234	20 445	43 271	23 600
1995	1 057 453	1 048 393	9 060	758 325	45 660	-891	711 774	205 915	139 763	24 173	21 184	43 745	24 161
1996	1 116 779	1 106 564	10 215	802 129	47 530	-986	753 613	217 538	145 629	25 201	21 833	44 314	24 817
1997	1 187 299	1 176 642	10 657	859 131	50 403	-1 058	807 670	232 045	147 584	26 353	22 590	45 054	25 402
1998	1 281 057	1 270 904	10 153	928 869	53 930	-1 150	873 789	253 129	154 139	27 972	23 811	45 798	26 289
1999	1 364 218	1 353 663	10 556	1 004 377	58 766	-1 255	944 356	258 628	161 234	29 335	24 556	46 506	26 930
2000	1 496 369	1 486 878	9 491	1 106 392	64 074	-1 400	1 040 918	287 732	167 719	31 694	26 181	47 213	27 754
2001	1 538 024	1 529 494	8 531	1 124 270	65 851	-1 403	1 057 017	294 326	186 681	32 025	26 725	48 026	27 978
2002	1 577 384	1 567 333	10 052	1 138 085	67 521	-1 428	1 069 136	297 885	210 363	32 344	27 973	48 769	. . .

. . . = Not available.

NOTES AND DEFINITIONS

TABLE 21-1
GROSS DOMESTIC PRODUCT BY STATE AND REGION

SOURCE: U.S. DEPARTMENT OF COMMERCE, BUREAU OF ECONOMIC ANALYSIS

Gross state product (GSP) is the sum of the gross products originating (GPOs) in all industries in the state. In concept, each industry's gross product originating in the state is equal to its gross output (sales or receipts and other operating income, commodity taxes, and inventory change) in that state minus its intermediate inputs (consumption of goods and services purchased from other U.S. industries or imported) in that state, and the sum of all states would therefore equal U.S. gross domestic product (GDP). For explanation of GDP, see the Notes and Definitions to Tables 1-1 through 1-10. GPO is equivalent to the economists' concept of "value added," but the latter term is not often used in the context of U.S. economic statistics, to avoid confusion with a somewhat different concept known as "Census value added" that is used in censuses and surveys of manufactures. GSP and GPO are calculated only on an annual basis.

Definitions and notes on the data

The value of an industry's GPO is equal to the market value of its gross output (which consists of sales or receipts and other operating income, commodity taxes, and inventory change) minus the value of its intermediate inputs (which consist of energy, raw materials, semifinished goods, and services that are purchased from domestic industries or from foreign sources). In concept, this is equal to the sum of labor and property-type incomes earned in that industry in the production of GDP plus commodity (indirect business) taxes. Property-type income is the sum of corporate profits, proprietors' income, rental income of persons, net interest, capital consumption allowances, business transfer payments, and the current surplus of government enterprises less subsidies.

In practice, gross state product, like national GDP by industry, is measured using the incomes data rather than data on gross output and intermediate inputs, which are not available on a sufficiently detailed and timely basis. See the Notes and Definitions to Chapter 15.

Therefore, the value of gross domestic product by state is defined as the sum of labor and property-type incomes originating in each of 63 industries in that state plus indirect business taxes. Because of insufficient information, the statistical discrepancy is not allocated to individual industries or states.

The quantity indexes of gross state product are aggregates of the real output of each industry in the state, net of intermediate inputs, based on chained constant-dollar estimates, and expressed as index numbers, 1996 = 100. They are derived by applying national implicit deflators calculated for each industry group to the current-dollar GSP estimates for that industry group and applying the chain-type index formula used in the national accounts to aggregate the industry groups to the state total. See the Notes and Definitions to Chapter 15 for an explanation of the methods for deflating national gross product by industry, which are the source of these implicit deflators used for gross product by state.

To the extent that a state's output is produced and sold in national markets at relatively uniform prices, or sold locally at national prices, GSP captures the differences across states that reflect the relative differences in the mix of goods and services that the states produce. However, real GSP does not capture geographic differences in the prices of goods and services produced and sold locally.

Data availability and references

Recent values for GSP by state and industry are published in "Gross State Product by Industry, 1999–2001," Survey of Current Business, June 2003. This article contains a description of the methodology and references to other relevant materials. Further detail and historical values back to 1977 can be found on the BEA Web site <http://www.bea.gov>.

TABLE 21-2
PERSONAL INCOME AND EMPLOYMENT BY STATE AND REGION

SOURCE: U.S. DEPARTMENT OF COMMERCE, BUREAU OF ECONOMIC ANALYSIS (BEA).

This table contains annual time-series data on personal income and employment for the United States, each state, the District of Columbia, and eight geographic regions. All revisions available through October 2003 are included. Population and per capita income use Census Bureau population figures incorporating the results of Census 2000.

With one significant exception concerning U.S. residents working abroad and foreign residents working in the United States, which will be discussed below, these data utilize the same income concepts and definitions as the personal income estimates contained in the national income and product accounts (NIPAs). Summaries of these definitions can be found in the Notes and Definitions for Tables 4-1 and 4-2.

Additional Notes on the State and Regional Data

The U.S. data that accompany the state data represent the total of the state data. They differ from those in the

NIPAs mainly in that the state data consist of only the income earned by persons who live within the United States, but include in that total all foreign residents working in the United States. NIPA totals include the labor earnings and retirement fund revenues of federal civilian and military personnel abroad and U.S. residents on foreign assignment for less than a year. However, earnings of foreign residents are included in the NIPA totals only if they live and work in the United States for a year or more.

The dividends, interest, and rent total include the capital consumption adjustment for rental income of persons. Total employment is the total number of jobs, full-time plus part-time; each job that any person holds is counted at full weight. The employment estimates are on a place-of-work basis. Both wage and salary employment and self-employment are included. The main source for the wage and salary employment estimates is Bureau of Labor Statistics estimates from unemployment insurance data (the ES-202 data). Self-employment is estimated mainly from individual and partnership federal income tax returns.

This concept of employment differs from that in the Current Population Survey (CPS), which is derived from a monthly count of persons employed; any individual appears only once in the CPS in a given month no matter how many different jobs he or she might hold. (See the Notes and Definitions to Tables 10-1 through 10-3.) In addition, a self-employed individual who files more than one Schedule C income-tax filing will be counted more than once in the state figures. Finally, the state figures include members of the Armed Forces, who are not covered in the CPS. Because of these differences and other possible reporting inconsistencies, the BEA estimates are different from, and usually larger than, state employment estimates from the CPS.

The employment estimates correspond closely in coverage to the earnings estimates. However, the earnings estimates include the income of limited partnerships and of tax-exempt cooperatives, for which there are no corresponding employment estimates.

The state-level earnings estimates are adjusted to a place-of-residence basis by BEA to adjust for interstate and international commuting. The difference between earnings by place of residence and earnings by place of work is shown in the "Adjustment for residence" column. This adjustment is a net figure: income received by state (or area) residents from employment outside the state, minus income paid to persons residing outside the state but working in the state. There is a negative adjustment for the United States as a whole reflecting net payments

to foreign residents working in the United States. The effect of interstate commuting can be seen in its most extreme form by comparing the District of Columbia, with its $32 billion in net payments to persons living outside D.C. in 2002, to Maryland, which received $21 billion net from employment sources outside the state in that year.

The states are divided into regions as follows:

- **New England:** Connecticut, Maine, Massachusetts, New Hampshire, Rhode Island, Vermont
- **Mideast:** Delaware, District of Columbia, Maryland, New Jersey, New York, Pennsylvania
- **Great Lakes:** Illinois, Indiana, Michigan, Ohio, Wisconsin
- **Plains:** Iowa, Kansas, Minnesota, Missouri, Nebraska, North Dakota, South Dakota
- **Southeast:** Alabama, Arkansas, Florida, Georgia, Kentucky, Louisiana, Mississippi, North Carolina, South Carolina, Tennessee, Virginia, West Virginia
- **Southwest:** Arizona, New Mexico, Oklahoma, Texas
- **Rocky Mountain:** Colorado, Idaho, Montana, Utah, Wyoming
- **Far West:** Alaska, California, Hawaii, Nevada, Oregon, Washington

These regional groupings are the ones used by the Bureau of Economic Analysis. They differ from the region and division definitions used by the U.S. Bureau of the Census.

Data availability and references

The data provided here are from a larger data set maintained by the Bureau of Economic Analysis. The latest data, along with revisions for previous years, are published each year in an article in the *Survey of Current Business*. The most recent revisions are presented in two articles, "State Personal Income and Per Capita Personal Income, 2002," *Survey of Current Business*, May 2003, and "State Personal Income, Revised Estimates for 1999–2001," *Survey of Current Business*, October 2002. The 2002 estimates were updated on the BEA Internet site on July 23, 2003.

The comprehensive revision made in 2000 is described in "Comprehensive Revision of State Personal Income: Revised Estimates for 1969–1998, Preliminary Estimates for 1999," *Survey of Current Business*, June 2000.

These articles along with all the current and historical data are on the BEA Internet site at <http://www.bea.gov>.

INDEX

INDEX